Works by Judson Jer

Time's Fool: A Story in Sonnets
Based on Those of Shakespeare
John Daniel & Co., 1992

The Youthful Look: A Memoir
University of Arkansas Press, 1992

Jonah & Job
John Daniel & Co., 1991

Nude
Applezaba Press, 1991

Myrtle Whimple Selected Poems
Sticks Press, 1990

Flight from Innocence
University of Arkansas Press, 1990

The Village: New & Selected Poems
Dolphin-Moon Press, 1987

On Being a Poet
Writer's Digest Books, 1984

Partita in Nothing Flat
Barnwood Press, 1983

The Poet's Handbook
Writer's Digest Books, 1980, 1986

Thirty Years of Poetry:
Poems 1949-1979
Cedar Rock Press, 1979

Publishing Poetry
Cedar Rock Press, 1979

Public Domain
Trunk Press, 1977

The Village and Other Poems
Trunk Press, 1976

Families of Eden: Communes and
the New Anarchism
Seabury Press, 1974

I Never Saw . . .
Albert Whitman, 1974

Culture Out of Anarchy:
The Reconstruction of American
Higher Learning
Herder & Herder, 1971

Plays for an Imaginary Theater
University of Illinois Press, 1970

Poetry: Premeditated Art
Houghton Mifflin, 1968

The Fell of the Dark
Houghton Mifflin, 1966

The Poet and the Poem
Writer's Digest Books,
1963, 1974, 1979

Light in the West
Golden Quill Press, 1962

p. 44, 54, 80, 84, 107, 123,
123, 124, 127, 137, 144, 172, 191, 192
197, (219), 223, 226, 235, 242, 250, 257
281, 294, 316, 329, 337, 354, 367, 373,
379, 384,

✳

336, 337, 348

p. 44
✳ p. 54
✳ p. 80

1993 Poet's Market

1993
Poet's Market

*Where & How to Publish
Your Poetry*

Edited by

*Michael J. Bugeja
and
Christine Martin*

*Assisted by
J. Lynne Bloss*

Writer's
Digest
Books

Cincinnati, Ohio

If you are a poetry publisher and would like to be considered for a listing in the next edition of Poet's Market, *please request a questionnaire from* Poet's Market, *1507 Dana Ave., Cincinnati, Ohio 45207.*

Distributed in Canada by McGraw-Hill,
300 Water Street
Whitby Ontario L1N 9B6.
Also distributed in Australia by Kirby Books, Private Bag No. 19, P.O. Alexandria NSW2015.

Managing Editor, Market Books Department:
Constance J. Achabal
Assistant Managing Editor: Glenda Tennant Neff

This 1993 hardcover edition of Poet's Market *features a "self-jacket" that eliminates the need for a separate dust jacket. It provides sturdy protection for your book while it saves paper, trees and energy.*

International Standard Serial Number
0883-5470
International Standard Book Number
0-89879-582-6

Contents

Resources

Indexes

From the Editors

From Michael J. Bugeja

As many readers know, I am a journalist and teacher as well as a poet and poetry columnist for *Writer's Digest*. I began reading that magazine when I was 13 and published my first poem that year in a California anthology (that didn't charge fees and gave me a free copy). Eventually I went into the news business, though, because I had a keen desire to write and publish and journalism seemed the best way to sate the need. Now, as a journalism prof, I advise new students who tell me that they want to be a network anchor or managing editor for *The New York Times*.

And they tell me this before they have written their first news story or taped their first segment.

What would *you* say to them? Would you dampen their dreams, explaining that in all likelihood they will never make it to the Big Leagues? Or cite statistics that show almost all journalism majors lucky enough to find jobs start at local radio or TV stations or at weekly or small daily newspapers? Would you jolt them by adding that most journalists will never even see a network or New York newsroom?

Knowing students want encouragement so they can keep their dreams alive, I ask my aspiring anchors and editors, "Who are your role models?"

Typically they have none. They don't know what values Peter Jennings may have embraced to anchor the evening news. They just want his job.

That's not the way to go about making dreams come true, I explain. If, say, you want to be network anchor for ABC News, then you have to be willing to work hard, make sacrifices, know the competition, be patient, excel and persist . . . just like Peter Jennings did when he was climbing *his* career ladder.

Instead of killing dreams, I provide ways to achieve them. That puts the burden on students. If the dream is intact, the rest is up to them.

I want to do the same in **Poet's Market**.

It's perfectly all right to dream about becoming the next Emily Dickinson or Robert Frost. But both of these poets persisted in the wake of failure. Indeed, Dickinson was never honored as a poet in her lifetime and Frost got his start in England because American editors weren't interested in his work.

Some of you are accomplished poets who already have scaled down the scope of your dreams. All you want is to publish a book so that you can feel good about the time and effort you've invested in verse. Or just one poem in a respected magazine.

Or one signed rejection from *The New Yorker*.

Or one encouraging critique.

Or one . . .

As you can see, the process of scaling down dreams is slow and painful. You needn't put yourself through that. Instead, make this the year to revive your dreams, whatever they may be — publication to Pulitzers — and go about the business of understanding how to achieve them.

Ask yourself:

- Who are my role models in verse?
- What values got them where I want to be?
- What are my values and where are they taking me?

Perhaps **Poet's Market** will be a vehicle to shape your values and verse so that you can achieve your goals or ambitions. My role, then, is to give you tips about market trends, manuscripts, editors and the business of being a poet.

You have to do the rest.

Maybe you will work harder this year, make more sacrifices, know the competition better, be more patient, excel finally or persist. Or maybe you will just read or write more poems.

Even if you do all of the above, your dream may not come true. But if you aim high and have values and work habits, you'll end up accomplishing more than anyone with any other attitude would ever have imagined.

And that, in itself, is a dream.

Michael J. Bugeja

Michael J. Bugeja

Michael J. Bugeja *is an internationally published writer and poet with more than 450 credits in literary magazines, including* **The Georgia Review, Indiana Review, Quarterly West, Graham House Review** *and* **Antioch Review.** *His writing has been anthologized in* **Contemporary Literary Criticism, Anthology of Magazine Verse & Yearbook of American Poetry** *and* **American Signatures: 9 New Writers** *(Kaleido-scope, 1986). He has three book-length collections of poetry:* **What We Do For Music** *(Amelia Press, 1990);* **The Visionary** *(Taxus Press, 1990); and* **Platonic Love** *(Orchises Press, 1991). In addition, he has written a book of social criticism titled* **Culture's Sleeping Beauty: Essays on Poetry, Prejudice, and Belief** *(Whitston, 1992). He writes a monthly poetry column for* **Writer's Digest** *and frequently keynotes writing conferences and workshops across the country. He is also a full professor at the E.W. Scripps School of Journalism, Ohio University, Athens, Ohio, where he teaches ethics and writing.*

From Christine Martin

Since our very first edition of **Poet's Market** in 1986, this edition—probably more than any other—has experienced the most changes. And yet, like its predecessors, many elements remain the same.

Sadly Judson Jerome, who not only developed the first edition, but also edited every succeeding one, passed away in August of 1991, just months before the 1992 book hit the shelves. This edition not only pays tribute to Jud, but also serves to introduce readers to Michael Bugeja, who has helped carry on the personal touch that Jud initiated and readers have grown to love. If you have just read Michael's introductory comments, then you have a sense of his commitment to help aspiring writers.

As you read through the Publishers of Poetry section, you will discover approximately 300 new listings. In these listings and others, you will at times find comments from Michael about editors, response times, the type of poetry generally found in a magazine and/or the magazine's appearance. Such comments not only provide a personal touch, but they also provide a clearer picture of the market you may be considering.

For example, the listing for *The Chattahoochee Review* says: "This is a nice market for those with good work having trouble finding a home. The editorial staff here is professional and courteous—it even sends out acknowledgment postcards letting you know that it has received your manuscript—and is open to good poems, regardless of style."

Responding to readers

Some of the other changes in the Publishers of Poetry listings were prompted by the results of a random survey of **Poet's Market** readers. While we have always believed readers found a publisher's sample lines of poetry helpful, survey results indicated that not only do 68% of respondents want poetry samples, but 46% buy **Poet's Market** specifically to read them!

Consequently, we encouraged publishers to update their lines of poetry so readers can better determine the most current editorial tastes. With very few exceptions, all poetry samples over two years old have been deleted and, if possible, replaced with new lines chosen by the publication's editor or myself.

Also as a result of the survey, we asked publishers to specify their reading periods, that is, whether they only read manuscripts during a certain time of the year, certain months or even certain dates. We also added information to listings about what rights a publisher either buys or acquires when accepting work from a poet. And, finally, we have indicated whether or not a publication reviews books of poetry and the length and type of such reviews. You'll find each of these areas, as well as current trends in poetry publishing, covered in the introduction to the Publishers of Poetry section.

Other comments and questions raised by the readers survey—as well as information about our respondents themselves—are addressed in A Dialogue: **Poet's Market** and Its Readers, beginning on page 7.

Providing advice

In this edition, you'll also find The Business of Poetry completely updated. This article provides information on how to submit your manuscript—from what supplies you will need to how your manuscript should be typed and whether or not you should include a cover letter. It also explains how to go about mailing your material and keeping records as to where it's sent. Other topics include simultaneous and/or multiple submissions, anthologies, poetry readings and book publishing options.

As in years past, we have included 12 Close-up interviews with both poets and editors who provide advice to those wanting to join their field. This year's "Close-up" subjects are a diverse group. Many of them are influenced by the other arts. Ruth Daigon, for instance, a poet and editor of *Poets On:*, is also a former concert soprano who finds sound essential in her poetry. Fred Chappell has patterned one of his poems as a prologue to Aaron Copland's **Appalachian Spring**. Havana-born poet Ricardo Pau-Llosa, also an art critic and curator, pays attention to visual associations. And children's poet Arnold Adoff says his major influences are jazz and the work of the Russian constructivist painters of the early 1900s.

Other poets and editors have found themselves influenced by their environment. Sharon Martin inherited the love of poetry from her grandmother. Living in the Pacific Northwest influenced Art Homer, poet and coeditor of *The Nebraska Review*. Poet and former countryman R.T. Smith writes about birds because they are features of his old landscape. And Elton Glaser, who grew up in Louisiana, acknowledges a sense of place in his work.

On somewhat different levels, poet Minnie Bruce Pratt found strength in the community of women's liberation. Richard Jackson, editor of *The Poetry Miscellany*, and Lucia Cordell Getsi, editor of *The Spoon River Poetry Review*, have both found themselves interested in a larger community. He's seeking chapbook manuscripts by poets from Central and Eastern Europe. She welcomes translations. Terri Lee Grell's publication, *Lynx*, also has an international connection. It publishes renga, traditional linked-verse poetry with roots in ancient Japan.

Though their interests and influences are varied, these 12 individuals offer advice and/or provide examples for aspiring poets to follow.

Continuing traditions

Besides continuing to provide new markets and more detailed information in the Publishers of Poetry section and continuing to feature helpful articles and Close-up interviews, this edition of **Poet's Market** includes listings of arts agencies (where poets may inquire about grants) in the United States and Canada as well as detailed listings of contests and awards. There are also sections on writing colonies, organizations and publications useful to poets. The last thing you'll find are indexes to help make it easier for you to narrow down the best markets for your work.

As has been our tradition for the past seven years, we continue to welcome comments from our readers—not just when we conduct a special survey. Please don't hesitate to let us know how you feel about the changes in this edition or what your experience has been with a particular publisher—good or bad.

Finally, we hope the hundreds of new poetry samples and the dozen Close-up interviews in this edition of **Poet's Market** provide you with hours of enjoyable reading. That's the way Jud would have wanted it.

Christine Martin

Christine Martin

Christine Martin *is an editor for Writer's Digest Books who has previously worked on* Humor and Cartoon Markets, Novel and Short Story Writer's Market *and the 1992 edition of* Poet's Market. *She shares with Michael J. Bugeja the editorship of the* 1993 Poet's Market.

How to Use Your Poet's Market

Seeing page after page of poetry publishers may be daunting, especially if you're just beginning to consider sending out work. Yet, **Poet's Market** doesn't only provide listings of poetry publishers, it is also specifically designed to help you determine which ones are the best markets for your work. All you need to know is how to use it.

The first step, however, is to consider your poetry itself. Do you write poetry that makes a political statement? Poetry about wildlife? religious symbols? other poets? Do you write haiku? prose poems? About a certain area? In a language other than English?

Maybe you don't write any specific type of poetry at all. Maybe the answer depends on which one of your works we're talking about. No matter. If you've put craft into your poems, you'll find a place for them.

Start with the indexes

All Publishers of Poetry listings are coded as to what category of poetry they are seeking. Publishers that desire poetry within certain realms—that is, on certain subjects, in certain forms or from certain areas—may be quickly identified by a **IV** and word(s) denoting the specialization(s). For example, *Iowa Woman* is coded **IV-Women** because the publication seeks material "by women, about women and for women."

Once you've considered your own poetry, you don't have to comb each page for compatible listings. The next step is to turn to the Subject Index, beginning on page 471. Here you will find all publishers with **IV** codes divided for you according to their specialization.

Glance through the boldface headings to locate the specialization that matches your work. If you write lyric poetry, for instance, check under **Form/Style**. If you don't immediately find a matching specialization, look under **Themes**. If you're an older adult who writes about the animals and the lake near your home, check under both **Senior Citizen** and **Nature/Rural/Ecology** and write down those publishers that sound interesting.

Publishers may classify themselves as **Regional** in the Subject Index, but checking the Geographical Index is also helpful. Here you'll find a list of the publishers located in your state or country. While some publishers don't consider themselves explicitly "regional" in terms of the poetry they accept, they are often more open to writers from their own area.

Another index that will be useful to you, particularly if you're trying to publish a small collection of poems, is the Chapbook Publishers Index. This lists those publishers who consider chapbook manuscripts, typically 20-25 pages of poetry linked by a theme. You'll also find more information about chapbook and book publishing in The Business of Poetry.

Finally, if you've heard about a particular publisher, but can't seem to locate its listing, check the General Index. All imprints and/or publications located at the same address are grouped together. The General Index lists all titles in the book, however, and includes cross references where necessary.

Check market codes

Once you have a list of possible markets for your work—because of specialization or location or an interest in chapbooks—look up their listings and check the market category codes following their titles to discover how open they are to submissions.

Besides the **IV** code already discussed, publishers may also have **I**, **II**, **III** or **V**. Those with I are open to beginners' submissions, so if you're just starting out, try submitting to them. Publishers with II codes are general markets which expect poets to be familiar with literary journals and magazines. Those coded III are limited as to the number of submissions they accept, so chances of publishing with these folks are limited too. Finally, those with V are not accepting unsolicited manuscripts. Although you may have picked such a publisher out of the Geographical Index, you can't submit your poetry to it at this time. That's okay. Cross it off your list and move on to the next one.

When you discover publishers with more than one code, read their listings carefully to determine if they're still possible markets for your work. For instance, a publisher may be I, IV-Humor, which means either it wants humorous material as well as poetry from beginners or humorous material only, including poetry from beginners. For more information about market category codes, see the introduction to the Publishers of Poetry section.

Also, as you read the listings based on the indexes, others will attract your eye. Don't feel limited by those on your list. Many publications don't want to be noted for a specialization and are open to ALL types of work.

Read carefully

When you've narrowed your list of possible markets by using the indexes and checking market categories, read each listing *carefully*. Look for the general purpose of the publisher and statements about its interests in poetry. For example, *The Single Scene* is a magazine for Ohio singles that wants poetry with a "positive, upbeat approach to single living." They also say, "but we're neither Yuppies or Pollyannas. Humorous treatments get top priority."

Also, the list of poets recently published and the sample lines of poetry will give you insight into what level of writing an editor is looking for as well as editorial preferences.

Consider the date a publisher was founded as well. Older publishers have more stability, and sometimes more prestige, than younger ones. However, newer publishers, especially those new to this edition (designated by a ‡), are often more receptive to submissions.

Carefully reading the description of a publication's format will help you visualize how your poetry will appear in its pages. Better yet, review sample copies. This is the best way for you to determine whether your poetry is right for a publication. Sample copies can be ordered from publishers or often found on the shelves of your library or local bookstore.

However, don't just locate a sample copy, decide your work is appropriate and submit to that market without knowing submission procedures. Inappropriate submissions will not only leave a bad impression of your work, they can also affect a publisher's willingness to accept unsolicited manuscripts from others as well.

If you haven't already done so, read The Business of Poetry. It explains how you should submit your work, including what a manuscript should look like, how it should be mailed and how to keep records of where it was sent. Most publishers also include specific submission procedures in their listings. Finally, many publishers offer guidelines, usually for a self-addressed, stamped envelope (SASE). Send for them. The goal, after all, is to increase — not decrease — your chances of acceptance.

Other resources

As you begin submitting your poetry, you may want to consider other resources open to poets. For support services and feedback from others, consider joining one of the groups listed in Organizations Useful to Poets. If you're looking for a place to get away and write, check Writing Colonies. And if you're concerned about changes that occur with publishers, consult the magazines listed in Publications Useful to Poets.

Finally, if you don't recognize a symbol or an abbreviation being used, refer to the Key to Symbols on page 20 or the Glossary. And, for easy reference, you will find a list of U.S. and Canadian Postal Codes on page 451.

A Dialogue: Poet's Market and Its Readers

by Michael J. Bugeja

The 17-page fax was sent from F&W Publications in Cincinnati to my office in Athens, Ohio, in preparation for our annual editorial planning session. It was the longest such transmission that our small machine had ever received and probably the most informative, too—page upon page of single-spaced data drawn from a random readership survey of writers who use **Poet's Market.**

So I was introduced to you before you met me in the current edition. But you may be interested in a few facts (from the fax) about yourself.

Did you know that 40% of you have published up to 10 poems? Or that 27% are regularly publishing more than 11 poems each year? In other words, two thirds of our readership experience success on a regular basis in the poetry world. Congratulations! About a quarter of our readers are just starting to send out poems and the rest are editors or newcomers (perfecting their wares).

In general, the typical **Poet's Market** reader is apt to write free or formal verse (mostly lyric and sonnet) with topics and themes drawn from religion, politics and nature (quite a combo!).

The best part of the survey, however, was a section titled Additional Comments in which you asked questions or made statements that you considered important or wanted us to address. So during our planning session, we decided to establish a dialogue. After all, we asked and you answered. Now it's our turn.

Here are a few of your questions and comments and my answers, short and long:

"Making it" as a poet

One reader writes: *I would like to read about a poet who knew nobody but made it on the quality of his poetry.*

Short answer: You're looking at him (or reading him).

Long answer: I studied poetry in the English department while I was working as a teacher in the journalism department. I'm still teaching journalism and composing poems. Over the years my world would have been kinder if a few more colleagues in journalism saw me as a journalist (I worked for United Press International) and a few in English saw me as a poet. Instead, journalism-types tended to see me as a poet and poet-types as a journalist.

When it came to poetry, the only friend I could count on was my muse.

So when I see a statement like the one above, I want to say, yes, a few editors do publish people who "network" or somehow befriend them. Some editors publish poets who happen to share the same tastes—free or formal verse—without regard to merit of the manuscript. But the majority of editors publish poets simply because they want to please the audience and gain subscriptions.

The bottom line is this: If you want to make it as a poet, then you have to make good poems. Editors will publish them. Your work may not appear in **The New Yorker** or **The American Poetry Review**, but that's okay. Keep racking up small credits and write articles for poetry magazines to help beginners publish, too. You'll be noticed. Aim higher. Prestigious publishers will take your work. Write about that so other poets can follow your lead. Share your knowledge, reap the rewards and one day you, too, will "make it."

Researching markets

Another reader writes: *Sometimes the editor will say "I like your poems but we only want political poems." I'd like more subjective information from editors. Most of them have specific prejudices and preferences which they let you know after you send your poems. I'd like to know before.*

Short answer: Wouldn't we all!

Long answer: We encourage editors to make comments that will help you place your work, and we wish more would take the opportunity to do so. But poets also have a responsibility to read magazines *before* they send to them.

This costs money and time. Of course, I know that most poets (including me) can't take out subscriptions or buy sample copies of every magazine in which they would like their poems to appear. But you can peruse periodicals in the library, visit the English department at your local college (many teachers will share shelves of literary journals) or join a writers' group and trade magazines.

Occasionally I rely solely on a listing in **Poet's Market** because an entry intrigues me. But I realize that I am unfamiliar with the publication and am taking a chance, so I don't anticipate an acceptance but hope for a comment or an encouraging rejection.

To increase your chances, you might want to keep a file of your rejections for marketing purposes. Separate them into three piles:

● *Rejections with comments.* You may be close to publishing if editors are taking time to comment, so take advantage of the opportunity and order a sample copy. That should impress them. Study poems and select some of yours that may suit editorial tastes. That should make an even better impression!

● *Rejections with encouraging copy.* Some rejections lack a personal comment but contain printed copy saying that editors found merit in your poems and would like to see more. Consider this an invitation. The rejection may look standard, but editors wouldn't have sent it if your work didn't come close.

● *Standard rejections.* These are blunt and cold: "Thank you for sending your work but it doesn't suit our editorial needs." If you have received one of these, you might want to check out the magazine anyway to determine what, if anything, has gone wrong. (Usually nothing has—the staff probably is too busy to reply—but check in case you are sending religious poems to editors who publish political ones, or vice versa.)

By the way, if editors are writing "I like your poems but we only want political poems," you must be quite accomplished. If so, you especially should be studying magazines before you send to them. A little research goes a long way when your poems are coming close.

You just might double your acceptance rate.

Poor audience for poetry

A reader complains: *There are thousands of poets and hundreds of readers. Why? Because of the kind and type of poetry being published. Who would want to read it?*

Short answer: Many more than are reading now if poets subscribed to magazines or bought sample copies.

Long answer: It's too easy to blame editors for killing the audience. The myth is that verse no longer rhymes or scans and that is why people aren't reading it. Maybe. More likely, if there was a market for a certain type of poem, publishers would exploit it for profit if nothing else.

But the mass market just isn't there.

Having previously researched this, I discovered something startling: I asked non-English majors why they had stopped reading poetry and two thirds of respondents replied that sometime, somewhere, some teacher told them they didn't understand what a poem meant. And they got a poor grade. So instead of memorizing poems, as students used to do when verse was mostly rhymed and metered, they started memorizing meanings of poems and spitting them back on tests. Poetry was killed in the process.

This is what I believe: If teachers concentrate on poetry "appreciation" in the classroom, instead of "explication"—dissecting poems and quizzing students on what poems mean—the audience in time would increase.

For the record, a poem should mean what we want it to. The more meanings the better.

Reading poetry books

An enthusiastic reader writes: *Print a short list of your favorite books of poetry [read] in the previous year—it will help sales of poetry!*

Short answer: To praise books by some poets is to slight dozens of others not mentioned and to put my taste on the line.

Long answer: But I'll tell you anyway. Keep in mind that I'm not recommending these particular books nor promoting certain poetic styles. I'm sharing them to let you know why a poet reads books to sharpen his or her own writing. Here goes:

Ararat by Louise Gluck. (Ecco, 1990). Her clarity reminds me that simple words always work best.

The Creole Mephistopheles by Laurence Lieberman. (Scribner's, 1989). His stanza patterns remind me that poems should appeal to the eye *and* the ear.

The House of Memory by David Citino. (Ohio State, 1990). His verse fills my spirit and reminds me that poems also should ennoble.

The Jaguar of Sweet Laughter by Diane Ackerman. (Random, 1991). Her free and formal poems remind me that verse should enlighten as well as please.

New and Collected Poems by Ishmael Reed. (Atheneum, 1988). The fire of Reed's early poems stokes my muse.

Sweet Home, Saturday Night by David Baker. (Arkansas University Press, 1991). His free verse is so structured he sets new standards for me.

Finally, all the books by Sharon Olds, Raymond Carver, Bruce Weigl, Colette Inez and Carolyn Forche remind me that poems should take risks. And, of course, those masters to whom we always return for inspiration: Shakespeare, Donne, Walt Whitman, Emily Dickinson, Robert Frost, William Carlos Williams, Robert Lowell, Elizabeth Bishop, Robert Hayden, James Wright and Sylvia Plath.

The best advice is to read good, bad and excellent books so that you can develop your own standards. Never judge a book by its cover or other poets by the books that they read.

Parting poetic shots

Reader: *Why list publications at all that are not interested in submissions?*

Answer: So you won't send there when your submissions aren't wanted.

Reader: *As I lack the time and expertise, I would like to see an article on guiding the poet to find an agent.*

Answer: Reputable agents don't handle poetry (except as a courtesy for best-selling prose authors).

Reader: *I'm not interested in pays-in-copies publishers. How about more publishers that pay in bucks?*

Answer: Poems are composed to enrich the reader, not the poet. Moreover, we seek to list as wide a range of poetry publishers as possible to provide outlets for an equally wide range of poets. Also, many of the publishers who pay only in copies produce fine publications.

The Business of Poetry

by Michael J. Bugeja

Too often poets forget that art is a business, too. The fact is, to share poetry, you have to get your verse to market, and at first the process may seem unpleasant, complex or just plain inconvenient.

We agree. We feel you should be spending more time composing manuscripts than figuring out how to market them, so we have tried to simplify the business aspects of poetry in one comprehensive article, from equipment and supplies to book publishing options and all the phases in between.

No matter if you are just starting out as a poet, or publishing regularly as one, you can refer to topics covered in this article for answers, updates or advice.

Supplies and equipment

Several options exist, but in any case, you'll have to spend money to market your poems. If you plan to market poems abroad, you'll need to invest in International Reply Coupons (IRCs). These work in lieu of an individual country's stamps and can be used by the editor to return your work. (One IRC equals one ounce of surface mail.) Some post offices don't carry IRCs, but that shouldn't sway you. If you still want to send work abroad, send the editor a letter, noting that you're sending a disposable manuscript and if you don't hear back in six months, you will assume that your manuscript has been rejected. Never send cash in lieu of stamps. (Editors have to wait until they get several dollars from U.S. writers to meet foreign exchange minimums.)

In any case, you'll need to purchase stamps to send your poems to magazines (international and domestic) and to have them returned from U.S. markets in self-addressed, stamped envelopes (SASEs).

As for supplies, you will need a ream of bond paper (no onionskin), a box of #10 ($4\frac{1}{2} \times 9\frac{1}{2}$) business envelopes in which to send poems, a box of #9 (4×9) business envelopes (or #10 envelopes folded into thirds) in which poems will be returned, a few pads of scratch paper for early drafts of poems, pens and pencils for signing letters and copyediting and file folders to keep poems and records. You should anticipate total costs of about $50-75 every four months depending on how much you write or how often you submit, of course.

For poets without access to typewriters

Invest in pads and pens or pencils. You cannot send handwritten work to editors because most will reject it outright. Instead, work diligently on poems until you have about a dozen that are in final form, then take the poems to a photocopying center or library and ask to rent a typewriter. Type the poems in standard format (see The Standard Manuscript), then photocopy them on white bond paper (25% cotton rag), making about 10 copies of each poem so you have extras to spare. Send out copies of those extras when your poems are returned soiled; this way, you won't have to retype them.

If you cannot rent a typewriter, hire a typist. Talk the typist out of the usual per page rate (why pay $2 for a 14-line poem?) and into an hourly one.

Though the process without a typewriter is complicated, if you don't have access to one, this may be the way that gets you into the business of being a poet.

Equipment costs: $0.

Extra supplies and/or services: $15-50 for copies and typing.

For those with access to typewriters

Invest in ribbons. Use cloth or film, but be sure in any case that the type is dark and clear. You'll also want to buy correction paper, tape or fluid to type final drafts without mistakes. (Some electric units have built-in correction tape.) Unless your typewriter has a built-in memory, you may want to take your final drafts to a copying center to make extras of poems (on 25% white cotton bond) that you intend to submit. This saves you from having to retype when you receive soiled poems back from magazines.

Equipment costs: $20-500 (from secondhand manuals to memory electronic units).

Extra supplies and/or services: $15-50 for ribbons and correction materials, $10 for photocopying, $25 and up for service/repairs.

For those with word processors or computers with select software

Invest in memory disks and ribbons designed for your unit. If you have a typical word processor, the type should be crisp. If you have a computer, you'll need a printer. Spring for letter-quality instead of dot-matrix (even "near letter quality" is too faint to read on some models). Using dot-matrix with a modern computer system is like mounting used tires on a Mercedes Benz.

You might as well go the extra mile and purchase a letter-quality unit and, while you're at it, an extra font in the same style as the one in your printer.

Equipment costs: $150-several thousand dollars (for secondhand units to the state-of-the-art computer models with appropriate software).

Extra supplies and/or services: $15-75 for ribbons and disks, $50 and up for computer repair.

Reference materials

Obviously, you have found this directory. If you haven't done so already, read How to Use **Poet's Market**, on page 5. The several categories of markets (coded **I, II, III, IV, V**) will help you determine which magazines publish poems similar to yours.

Serious poets seldom rely solely on directories for tips about markets. They either subscribe to several magazines, study them at the local library or send away for sample copies (always a good investment). Some publications—*ACM (Another Chicago Magazine)* and *The Ohio Review*, to name two—are open, generally, to all forms of poetry; nonetheless, anyone who reads these magazines knows that the respective editors have different tastes. In fact, what might work for *ACM* probably won't for *The Ohio Review*. So consult sample copies before sending in your work. Otherwise you will be wasting paper, stamps and both your time and the editor's.

In addition to consulting directories or studying sample copies, consult magazines like *Writer's Digest* or *Poets & Writers* to keep abreast of new markets or to record changes with old ones. If you cannot afford subscriptions to writing magazines, again, go to the library and read them.

In your study, den or work area at home, you'll also want some reference books. A good home library might consist of a dictionary (I use the 2,500-page Random House second edition unabridged, but Webster's New World editions are also excellent), a thesaurus (nothing beats the Penguin Roget's), a rhyming dictionary (again, I use Random's), **Princeton Encyclopedia of Poetry & Poetics** (to look up forms and categories of poems and/or poetic techniques and terms), a poetry text (I recommend Judson Jerome's **The Poet's Handbook** and also admire John Drury's **Creating Poetry**, both from Writer's Digest Books) and access to encyclopedias (I use the Britannica). You can buy the above (sans the Britannica) for about $125. Encyclopedias can cost up to $1,000 or more. Again, however, there is absolutely nothing wrong with checking out or consulting such books in the library. A personal library, though, is a great convenience if you find yourself using these books often.

The standard manuscript

Once you have studied the markets and perfected your poems, it's time to prepare a manuscript. You should send three to five poems, with or without a cover letter (see Cover Letters). Your #10 envelope should be addressed to the person specified in the publication's listing (or Poetry Editor if no name appears) and your #9 envelope (or folded #10 envelope) should be addressed to yourself.

As for the poems, here are some typing rules:

• Use good bond paper (20-25% cotton) and dark cloth or film ribbons on typewriters and printers.

• Leave at least 1″ margins on all sides of the page.

• Type your name and address in the upper right-hand corner.

• Type the title of your poem flush left or centered in all caps or initial caps. (I use all caps to distinguish my title from my first line and flush left to create an attractive white space.) After you type the title, drop down two lines.

• Type or print poems single-spaced, one poem to a page. (Single-spacing saves paper, eliminates irregular spacing between stanzas and helps the editor visualize the shape of the poem.)

• Drop down two lines to indicate stanzas.

• Indicate if your poem is longer than a page. Type your name (address is optional) at the top left margin of each additional page and underneath that, in parentheses, a key word from the title of the poem along with the page number and stanza information. This is how it should appear:

Michael J. Bugeja
(The Professional, page 2, begin new stanza)
or
Michael J. Bugeja
(The Professional, page 2, no new stanza)

Putting such information on additional pages helps editors assemble poems if they get shuffled during handling. Stanza information helps editors visualize poems on the page. After providing the information, drop down six spaces and continue typing the poem.

• Proofread your poem, especially if you are going to make photocopies of the original. Nothing turns off editors more than misspellings, typos and grammatical and punctuation errors.

Finally, arrange the poems in an order that you think will entice an editor to continue reading. Some editors like several poems on a theme. Others like to see the range of your work, formal to free verse. Some editors want your best poem first and perhaps a light one at the end to leave an upbeat impression. In the end, the choice is yours.

Fold the entire manuscript in thirds. Do not fold each poem individually because editors hate to expend the extra energy to unravel each work. (Multiply that energy times thousands of submissions in a month and you will sympathize with the editor.) Also, save the cost of paper clips. You don't need them, even though some editorial assistants prefer them. Using paper clips soils poems quicker, and then you'll have to retype them.

Before you put the #9 (or folded #10) self-addressed, stamped envelope (SASE) inside the #10 with your folded manuscript, we should discuss whether poets need copyrights and/or cover letters.

The question of copyrights

Copyright notices on poems, even on book-length manuscripts, are unnecessary. Some editors I know are put off by the mark because it implies that you are an amateur or overly concerned about someone stealing your work. Other editors know that you own the copyright and don't mind if you put "Copyright 1993 by John Doe" on your poems, if this makes you feel better. Keep in mind that most magazines are copyrighted, and book publishers usually take out copyrights in your name.

If you want to bone up on origins of copyright law, you might want to order **The Nature of Copyright** by L. Ray Patterson and Stanley W. Lindberg (University of Georgia Press, 1991).

If you want to take out copyrights on your work, you can solicit forms by writing the Copyright Office, Library of Congress, Washington DC 20559.

Cover letters

This is a judgment call. Check individual listings to see if specific editors encourage or discourage cover letters. Many will not say and, typically, never end up seeing your cover letters anyway because editorial assistants remove them from incoming manuscripts and route only poems to readers on the staff.

On the other hand, some small press editors may feel slighted when poets submit without a word or two about themselves.

If you decide to use a cover letter, make it brief (no longer than 100 words).

Here are some typing rules:

● Use plain white paper (no letterhead saying you are a poet).

● Type the date in the upper left corner. Drop down two lines.

● Type your address *only* (no name), single spaced, flush left. Drop down two lines.

● Type the name and title of the editor (consult the listings and if you can't locate a specific name, use "Poetry Editor") and then the address of the magazine, all flush left. Drop down two more lines.

● Type the salutation and the editor's full name. Don't guess at courtesy titles—Mr., Mrs. or Ms.—or appear informal by using first names: "Dear John" or "Jane." Drop down two lines.

● In the first paragraph, tell the editor that you are sending a manuscript for consideration. List titles of poems.

● In the second paragraph, share your publishing credits or writing interests. If you have read the particular magazine, mention that.

● In the third paragraph, you might want to add some personal data about your job or hobbies.

● In the last paragraph, thank the editor for his or her time. Drop down two lines.

● Type "Sincerely" as the closing salutation or "Best Wishes" if you have had contact before with the editor.

The decision to send cover letters is up to you. Personally I never do unless I have read the publication. Poets who send letters to unknown editors often create opportunities to embarrass themselves, such as telling an editor with no interest in politics why you love protest poems (or an activist one why you hate them).

It's a vicious circle. The more general you make a letter, the less need for it. At least if you have read the publication you'll have something interesting to say.

After you have composed your cover letter, or decided against using one, you are ready to send your work to market.

Mailing the manuscript

If you are using a cover letter, fold it in thirds and put it on top of your folded manuscript. Make sure the outer envelope and the inner self-addressed one are stamped. Typically, one first class stamp on a #10 envelope will pay for three pages of poetry, a cover letter and SASE. If you are not using a letter, you can send four pages of poetry.

Don't overstuff the envelope. You don't want to risk delaying the mail or paying additional postage on your returned work, especially since many editors will include subscrip-

SAMPLE COVER LETTER

February 17, 1993
246 S. Campus Dr.
Collegeville OK 13579

Jane Doe, Poetry Editor
Lighthouse Quarterly
866 Erie Ave.
Shoreline MI 81790

Dear Jane Doe,

Please consider the enclosed poems: "Thaw," "Heresy"
and "The Converts."

I enjoyed the sonnet sequence you published in the Fall
1992 issue and thought you might like to see my poems.
My work has appeared before in *Amelia* and *Poets On:*.

Although I work as a teacher in Oklahoma, I grew up
in New Jersey about one mile from Giants Stadium and
two miles from William Carlos Williams' house in
Rutherford.

Thanks for your time and consideration.

Sincerely,

Martha Jones

Martha Jones

tion material in your SASE. If you want to be safe, invest in a postal scale (available at most supply shops for about $8-15 for a one-pound maximum unit).

Once your manuscript is in the mail, don't worry about it for another three to four months. Instead, concentrate on composing more poems and keeping records of ones making the rounds.

Business folders

You want to keep two types: one containing originals of poems so that if your manuscript is lost in the mail or at the magazine, you will have a backup and another folder to indicate where and when a manuscript has been sent. (Note: If you use a computer, as I do, you still want to keep a set of printed originals and business logs. While it's easy to keep business files on disk, and even to make backups of those disks, you never know when the next power outage is going to strike or when your computer will go down, requiring a service call.)

A business log is a record of when, where and what happened to a manuscript. It contains the title of each poem, the name of the targeted magazine and the date sent. You may have to refer to the date if tracking down a lost or late manuscript. You also should record the date of the magazine's response. Finally, you may want to make some comments about the submission, especially if you have written the editor to check the status of a late manuscript.

You can use file cards to keep these records. I prefer keeping them on sheets of paper kept in a file folder of poems so that I have records and originals in the same place.

This is how a sample entry looks:

THAW:
> *New England Review*, sent 9-1-89, rejected 1-12-90;
> *The Kenyon Review*, sent 1-15-90, rejected 5-19-90;
> *Missouri Review*, sent 5-21-90, rejected 10-6-90;
> *Hawai'i Review*, sent 10-8-90, no response as of 4-15-91,
> query sent 4-15-91, accepted 5-2-91.

As you can see, such records not only help poets keep track of manuscripts but also provide marketing information—response times, reading cycles—about specific publications.

Response times

As poets, we want the best of both worlds. We would like our poems read closely—no scanning one or two lines and then rejecting the entire batch, please—and then we would like to know, preferably within a month, the status of our manuscript. Some magazines with adequate staff fulfill these goals. Most do not. Typically, virtuous editors who read every poem closely also are the slowest to respond because, well, they are reading manuscripts! Many small press publishers operate at a loss and many editors at literary magazines donate their time. Both labor out of love, and love's complaint is usually tardiness.

That said, editors have an obligation to process your work in a timely manner. If you haven't heard back within three or four months, send a letter (with SASE) inquiring about the status of your work. Consult your logs and name the poems sent and the date of submission. Ask when editors anticipate making a decision. Don't press the staff to act quickly or vent your frustrations in a personal letter. Simply send an inquiry, wait another month and if the magazine still has not contacted you, cut your losses. Send a postcard withdrawing the poems.

There are plenty of listings in **Poet's Market**. Eventually your work will find a home.

Simultaneous/multiple submissions

Editors assume that all submitted work is original and not previously published elsewhere. They also assume that it is not being considered at another magazine. If it is, you are engaging in the practice of simultaneous submissions.

Some editors have no qualms about considering poems that also are being considered by other editors. Others consider this an insult. The jury is still out on the issue, but many more poets these days are sending manuscripts to more than one editor at a time. They believe, rightly so, that many editors are too slow to respond and that the market for poems is limited at best. So a manuscript of three to five poems sent to two or more editors stands a better chance of acceptance.

But there are risks, too. When an editor accepts a poem that is out at two or more places, the poet has to telephone or write the other editors immediately, withdrawing his or her work. Don't tell the editors that one particular poem has been accepted and others rejected at a rival's magazine, so they should consider the remaining "rejected" ones. Withdraw *all* poems at once. If asked to explain, tell the truth and suffer the consequences, usually four-letter words like "okay," "fine" or "?$&!".

Personally I don't practice or promote simultaneous submissions. First, recordkeeping becomes more complicated. Second, if you are not publishing regularly as a poet, you'll only collect rejections quicker while still perfecting your craft. That can be discouraging. Third, if you are publishing regularly as a poet, you're more likely to end up with poems being accepted at several places at once. Why taint your good name?

All poets share one virtue: patience.

If you are unsure, but leaning toward simultaneous submissions, pick one listing from category II (general) and several from category III (limited). The latter usually will reject you anyway, eliminating the worry about being accepted simultaneously. And if you are accepted, say, at *Amelia* and *The New Yorker*, I'm sure that *Amelia* Editor Fred Raborg will understand and release any claim on your poem.

For the record, the term "multiple" submissions is often used interchangeably with "simultaneous." Some editors define "multiple" as more than one poem in a submission (send three to five) and others as more than one manuscript by the same poet sent to the same publication. In other words, you send five poems to *Nahant Bay* and then compose five more and send those before the editor has responded to your first submission. Unless you are submitting to different contests sponsored by a magazine, this also is considered a taboo.

Rights

If your work is accepted for publication, you'll receive a formal or an informal contract. An informal agreement is a letter from the editor telling you that he or she has accepted your poem(s). The editor is buying or, more commonly, acquiring first rights. (Most magazines do not pay for poetry beyond copies of the issue containing your work.)

Acquiring first rights in North America means that the editor will publish your work before anyone else does in a U.S. or Canadian periodical. Technically, copyright reverts back to you and does not further obligate you in this situation. In practice, if you use the poem in a subsequent book, you should mention that the work appeared originally in a certain magazine.

If you receive a formal contract, terms will be spelled out. Many formal contracts are for first rights with the additional right to reprint the work in any future edition or anthology of the magazine or in any form or medium ordained by the publisher.

Some formal contracts, however, are for all rights. Now you ought to be wary. Selling all rights essentially means that you no longer own the poem. You will need the publisher's permission to reprint your own work in a future collection.

You don't have to sign contracts relinquishing all rights. Write the editor and offer first rights, and if the editor refuses, ask how you can go about regaining the right to reprint your work. Typically a formal contract will contain a clause explaining just that. Some agreements grant reprint rights only in books in which you are the sole author. In general, however, only a few publishers purchase all rights. Usually they will let you reprint work or will reassign copyright to you upon written request.

Anthologies

Some anthologies are legitimate, published by respected houses such as Morrow and featuring the best contemporary poets writing today. To be included in such a work is a high honor. The poets receive free copies of the anthology and are often paid handsomely for their contributions.

Then there are those other "anthologies." These are produced by companies who advertise contests in writing magazines, promise big prizes, deliver many certificates and charge $35-45 (or more) for a copy of the anthology containing the poet's work.

In the business, this is known as "vanity" publishing because someone is banking on a beginner's desire to have poems printed no matter what the cost. Typically these companies will also try to sell you space in the anthology for your picture and biography, charging even higher fees. Some will offer to print up your poem in a fine font and put it in a frame. A few will sell you deluxe versions of your "award" certificate or even T-shirts.

There is nothing wrong with this as long as you know that these contests and anthologies have no literary value. In fact, if you list them as credits in a cover letter to an editor, you may *decrease* your chances of placing poems. (Some editors will stereotype you as vain, more concerned with *being* a poet than with *writing* poems for readers.)

The truth is, anyone who invests enough time and energy (as opposed to money) is capable of composing publishable verse.

If your desire to publish is strong, check out the magazines in the I category (for beginners). Some of these are annuals requiring you to buy anthologies or subscriptions, but our questionnaires, as well as letters from readers, help us screen out listings that exploit poets. Ones included here should be harmless, but if you have had a problem with any, please write to us.

Contests

Many poets like to submit to poetry contests. Some contests, however, are not geared to celebrate poets or their work but to generate start-up funds for new publications and to increase readership or revenue for others. Nonetheless, a few contests do pay substantial sums for poems and that is enough to tempt many writers, including me.

Here are some tips:

- Identify and avoid vanity presses (see Anthologies).
- Study the market. If a magazine sponsors a contest you want to enter, order a sample copy—preferably the "awards" issue—or scan it in the library. You want to get a feel for the type of poems that the editor (or the editor's judges) like.
- Consider club contests. Many states have poetry societies or writers' federations. These sponsor several contests each year. Prizes are small because dues are limited, but winning a contest is always a thrill.

If you intend to enter a contest, request guidelines and follow all rules. (You don't want to be disqualified on a technicality.) Almost all contests have reading fees associated with them, so use common sense when deciding how many to enter.

If you decide to enter poetry contests, you should also know the caliber of the competition and the value of your work. If you don't, don't enter.

Poetry readings

The quickest way to sate the need to publish or win contests is to read your poems before an audience. When you do, you share your love of verse and meet other writers, teachers and librarians. Moreover, reaction to your poems—good, bad or indifferent—is part of the learning experience.

You can schedule readings through local groups, clubs or churches. Or ask your librarian. If you write children's poems, in particular, the library is a great resource and children a greater audience. If you write science fiction poems, contact nearby SF organizations or ask the adviser of the Science Club at the high school. Some cafés sponsor poetry readings. Some bookstores do, too. Read the Arts and Entertainment section of your newspaper to get a feel for the type of events in your neighborhood. If you schedule a reading, contact your cable company to see if a camera operator from the local access channel will cover the event.

There is no end to the possibilities, but it takes initiative and drive. After you have found a place to read, design and photocopy some fliers announcing the event and post them in strategic places. Local shopper tabloids usually offer free space in the classifieds where you can list readings. Church and/or club bulletins and library newsletters also provide space. Write a news release in the concise style of your community newspaper and send it to the managing editor. Get out the word.

After you have promoted the event, you should concentrate on perfecting your performance. Assemble a selection of poems that are related thematically or that tell a story when read in sequence. Tape-record yourself so that you can hear your voice and make adjustments. (Most beginning readers recite poems too quickly, so make a conscious effort to slow down the cadence to allow listeners to appreciate each word and line of your verse.)

When you read, share a few details about your poems with the audience. Some might want to know, for instance, what caused you to write about a certain topic. Make these comments brief. Above all, do not read more than 30 or 40 minutes (the shorter the better) and don't take questions from the audience (too pretentious) but mingle with guests afterward and answer questions then.

A good time will be had by all (especially if there are free cookies and cider).

Book manuscripts

After you have done several readings and published extensively, it's time to start thinking about assembling a chapbook or book. A chapbook is a slim volume of about 20-25 pages (although some editors want no more than a dozen and others as many as 40). Research listings (see Chapbook Publishers Index, page 453) to familiarize yourself with length and submission requirements. A book-length collection consists of 48-80 pages.

Here are some tips for assembling a collection:

• Type poems according to the style mentioned earlier for individual poems (without the address in the upper right corner).

• Pick a title from one of the poems to represent your entire collection. (If no title works, then pick a line or image from a particular poem or invent a new title.)

• Group your poems according to a theme or plot so that each individual poem plays off another work in the collection. The complete work should read like a novel in verse. (Volumes of so-called "selected" or "collected" poems are for famous poets a la Emily Dickinson and Dylan Thomas.)

• Type a cover sheet with the title of the collection centered on the page and your name, address and telephone number in the lower right-hand corner.

• Include a contents page and an acknowledgements page listing magazines in which poems originally appeared.

As for mailing, poetry collections require manila envelopes (9 × 12) for the manuscript and the SASE. Because weights vary, take your manuscript to the post office or purchase a standard postal scale. Weigh the two envelopes, manuscript and any other contents (checks, entry forms, cover letters) to determine what it will cost to mail the collection. Take away the outer envelope and any checks, forms or letters to determine the cost of the SASE.

You should simultaneously submit chapbook or book manuscripts because they are so very difficult to place. Almost every publisher allows this as long as you inform the press when your manuscript is accepted elsewhere. The process is expensive, including stamps for envelopes, extra supplies and fees (avoid any over $15).

Don't despair when you receive rejections. Poets often wait years before publishing that first book. I waited a decade and had more than 200 poems accepted by category II and III magazines before my first collection appeared.

The surest route to book publication is to write excellent poems and to collect so many magazine acceptances that editors, sooner or later, take note.

Book publishing options

Books are more difficult to place than chapbooks, chiefly because production costs are higher and because the market for poetry is not good. Thus, many houses (especially university-affiliated ones) will require reading fees to recover costs. Many small press and chapbook publishers also require fees.

Here are your options:

Standard publishing. A commercial, literary or small press publisher considers submissions or conducts competitions. If your work is chosen — and again, competition is extraordinarily keen (with one or two books chosen out of hundreds each year) — the publisher pays all production costs and you usually get a 10% royalty on the wholesale price. Sometimes you get no royalties but 10% of the press run.

Cooperative publishing. You work with the publisher in some capacity and share the burdens. Arrangements vary, so be wary. Make sure you can fulfill your end of the bargain before signing agreements. Some will require you to pay certain costs of production. Others will require that you participate in the printing or marketing phases of production. In any case, cooperative publishing is respected in the literary and small press world, and you should look into it if you cannot place your collections with publishers offering standard contracts.

Self-publishing. True, many good poets have self-published. (Also many impatient ones.) The practice really isn't respected as it is overlooked, especially by reviewers. Do it only if you are not interested in making a name for yourself in poetry but simply want to share your work with friends, colleagues and loved ones. Typically you'll work with printers, invent a name for your "press," publish your book, own all copies, advertise to sell them and collect all proceeds. But mostly you will foot the bill, so schedule modest press runs of 100 to 300 copies.

Also look into cheaper ways to make books, especially if you own or have access to a computer with design programs. Design pages on the screen, print out typeset galleys, assemble the book and take it to a photocopying center. Representatives there will help you choose a cover and explain ways to bind your book. You can save hundreds of dollars.

Before you decide to self-publish, check out **The Complete Guide To Self-Publishing** by Tom and Marilyn Ross ($16.95 from Writer's Digest Books).

Vanity/subsidy presses. Avoid these. Nobody respects them. Under these arrangements you pay a "press" to manufacture and advertise your book. Ads are usually collective — 20 books getting one blurb line apiece — and placed in the general media (as opposed to specific markets). Sometimes you own all the copies, sometimes you don't. Some agreements are less offensive than others but all bank on your general ignorance of publishing.

Consider this: It costs about the same amount of money to produce a book under the typical vanity contract as it does to buy a used printing press or high-tech computer equipment.

Do the latter, become a reputable poetry publisher yourself and we'll list you in **Poet's Market**.

Key to Symbols and Abbreviations

‡ *New listing*
ms — *manuscript;* mss — *manuscripts*
b&w — *black-and-white (photo or illustration)*
SASE — *self-addressed, stamped envelope*
SAE — *self-addressed envelope*
IRC — *International Reply Coupon, for reply mail from countries outside your own.*

Important Market Listing Information

● *Listings are based on questionnaires and verified copy. They are not advertisements nor are markets reported here necessarily endorsed by the editors of this book.*
● *Information in the listings comes directly from the publishers and is as accurate as possible, but publications and editors come and go, and poetry needs fluctuate between the publication date of this directory and the time you use it.*
● **Poet's Market** reserves the right to exclude any listing that does not meet its requirements.

The Markets

Publishers of Poetry

In leading off this largest and most useful section of **Poet's Market,** we should focus on trends, that is, what types of poems editors of magazines seem to be buying these days. To do so, we have to assess the impact of the New Formalist movement (an outcry by editors and poets for a more traditional verse emphasizing form, rhyme and meter).

The movement began in the late 1980s and has not so much run its course as accomplished its mission: reinstating the good name of rhyme and meter within the poetry publishing world.

What it has not done, to the embitterment of some, is replaced free verse as the most popular form of poetry. As you will discover in the listings that follow, editors overwhelmingly still prefer free verse. But, as you will also see if you read sample copies of these magazines, the selections aren't as free as they used to be. This has become known as "structured free verse," a fancy way of saying that the poetry has form and shows a high degree of craft.

So thanks to the New Formalist movement, we have ended up with a new democracy of poetry in which a well-penned sonnet is as apt to appear in a prestigious journal as an obscure freestyle lyric focusing on a moment or image. And, in general, free verse poets are paying more attention to such concerns as the line (to convey meaning or insight) and the stanza (to give a uniform shape to the work).

Another legacy of the New Formalist movement has been the establishment of more markets for traditional verse. Some, like *The Formalist* ("dedicated to metrical poetry written in the great tradition of English-language verse") and *Hellas* ("meter is especially welcome, as well as rhymed and stanzaic verse"), are looking for sound *and* sense, a difficult task for any poet.

The rigors of rhyme and meter often make bad formal poems easy to reject because such poems typically fail to enlighten readers, focusing instead on singsong and leading to the unfortunate label of "greeting card verse." But the New Formalist magazines, mostly founded between 1988 and 1990, are setting standards again for traditionalists and thus will continue to balance poetry so that free verse alone does not dictate what's taught in the academy or practiced in your den.

Market trends

After reading dozens upon dozens of literary and small press magazines and sending more than 60 of my own poems to market last year, this is what I can tell you about market trends:

Best shot: For formalists, the old mainstay of the sonnet. (Villanelles, curiously enough, are not popular in formalist magazines but increasingly so in publications that typically feature free verse.) Rhymed, metered and (occasionally) interlocking patterns of three- and four-line stanzas seem welcome, too.

For free verse practitioners, the most popular poem seems again to be the lyric, usually under 30 lines. The drift continues away from confessional poetry—seemingly personal details of the poet's life shared too readily with the audience—with new interest in work composed in the third person.

Good bets: For formalists, narrative poems (which tell a story) and dramatic poems (which depict a character sharing thoughts) of about two pages in blank verse or rhymed stanzas. All topics, it seems, except intensely political ones. Some interest in repeating-line patterns, namely triolet and pantoum.

For free versers, the narrative poem—100 lines or less on any topic—with renewed interest in sociopolitical topics. Some interest in longer lyric poems (50 lines or so) that have strong themes (environment, religion).

Risky poems: For formalists, the sestina, a form which uses end words in a repeating pattern of six six-line stanzas with a three-line envoy. Some editors dislike the complexity of the form and believe it works well in Romance languages (such as Italian, French and Spanish) but not in English.

For free versers, as usual, the riskiest remains the long poem (more than 100 lines). Also, poems in pretty shapes (which word-processing bards seem to be generating in increasing numbers). Finally, any poem using obscene, racial or lewd language whose intent solely is to shock.

Reading periods

Now that we have covered what's new in poetry, let's see what's new in this section of **Poet's Market**—namely, information in listings about reading periods, book reviews and rights.

In our survey of **Poet's Market** readers, some of you noted that certain magazines do not read in the summer or have odd reading cycles (only a few months during the year). Others wanted to know if publications accepted reviews of poetry books and some inquired about rights (which ones editors buy/acquire when accepting poems).

So we sent questionnaires to editors about their reading cycles and, whenever possible, have included specific dates. Consider the listing for *Trestle Creek Review*, which lists a reading period of January 1 through March 15. If you would have sent a manuscript here before January 1 or after March 15, it would have been held until the next year's reading cycle. (Editors of most magazines would have returned your manuscripts unread.)

Book reviews

Several editors let us know that they publish reviews of poetry books. Some receive books in the mail from publishing houses and then assign critics to review them. Others consider unsolicited reviews. (Before sending a review to a specific publication, read a sample copy or query the editor with a self-addressed, stamped envelope.)

Basically, there are three types of reviews:

1. *The Essay Review* (or "omnibus" review) is about 10 manuscript pages in length and features several books by the same author or by several authors. If the latter, the collections should have something in common—a review of ecology books, say, or ones with musical themes. The review should carry a title, just like an essay, and the introduction should be about a page or so. (See the Glossary for multi-book review.)

2. *The Standard Review* is about four or five manuscript pages and concentrates on a single book (perhaps briefly mentioning other books by the same author).

3. *The Book Brief* is similar to the standard review, except it is shorter: about two manuscript pages.

By far, the book brief is the easiest type of review to place. It takes up little space in the magazine, increasing its chance of acceptance. If you never have composed a review, begin by mastering this type and then, when you have published a few, work your way up the critical ladder.

Rights

Now for the question of rights. We asked editors what rights they buy/acquire when accepting poems as it's important that you know what you are selling to a publication when you send poems to an editor. In general, most editors buy "first rights" and assume that your poems haven't been published elsewhere. After your poems appear in the magazine, rights revert back to you. (For more detailed discussion about "rights," look under that heading in The Business of Poetry beginning on page 10.)

Publications

We should also include a word about the three main types of publications listed here: small press, literary and commercial magazines.

Typically a small press publication is founded by a person who loves poetry so much that he or she invests time and money putting out a magazine. Although some small press publishers receive grants from arts councils or agencies, most receive no funding whatsoever and rely on subscriptions. The small press is noted for lively poetry about a wide range of topics—some traditional, some taboo—and in a vast variety of styles (haiku to experimental).

Literary magazines, on the other hand, most often are associated with colleges and universities. Because they are funded (at least in part) by state governments or by grants, they usually are well-edited and professionally printed and designed. Unlike many small press publications, topics and/or styles of poems tend to be open because excellence is the sole criterion. (In practice, many literary editors rely on personal taste or aesthetics, again requiring freelancers to check out sample copies before sending manuscripts.) Nonetheless, literary magazines are responsible for publishing the work of many master poets in this century, from Ezra Pound to Lucille Clifton. Publishing poems in them carries lots of clout in building a poetic career.

And then there are commercial magazines such as *The New Yorker*, *The Atlantic* and *Cosmopolitan* whose editors receive thousands of poems each month. These are national publications which are available at most newsstands and typically publish only a handful of poems in each issue. Payment is exceptional, the prestige factor is high and competition (as you can imagine) unbelievably fierce. That doesn't mean you shouldn't send to these magazines, of course. It *does* mean that you should be publishing regularly in the small press and literary worlds first.

Market categories

Finally, all of the listings in this section include one or more Roman numerals in their heading. These "codes," selected by editors and/or publishers, may help you determine the most appropriate markets for your poetry. The market category codes and their explanation are as follows:

I. **Publishers very open to beginners' submissions.** For acceptance, some require fees, purchase of the publication or membership in an organization, but they are not, so far as we can determine, exploitative of poets, and they often encourage new writers. They publish much of the material they receive and frequently respond with criticism and suggestions.

II. **The general market to which most poets familiar with literary journals and magazines should submit.** Typically they accept 10% or less of poems received and usually reject others without comment. They pay at least one copy. A poet developing a list of publication credits will find many of these to be respected names in the literary world.

III. **Limited markets,** typically overstocked. This code is used by many prestigious magazines and publishers to discourage widespread submissions from poets who have not published elsewhere—although many do on occasion publish relatively new and/or little-known poets.

IV. **Specialized publications** which encourage contributors from a specific geographical area, age-group, sex, sexual orientation or ethnic background or which accept poems in specific forms (such as haiku) or on specific themes. In most **IV** listings we also state the specialty (e.g. **IV-Nature/rural/ecology**). Often a listing emphasizes more than one subject area; these listings are marked with two codes.

V. **Listings which do not accept unsolicited manuscripts.** You cannot submit to these without specific permission to do so. If the press or magazine for some reason seems especially appropriate for you, you might query with SASE. But, in general, these folks prefer to locate poets themselves. Sometimes though, they are just temporarily overstocked or have projects lined up for the next few years.

We have included these listings because it is important to know not only where to send your poetry but also where NOT to submit it. Also, many are interesting publishers to know about, and this book is widely used as a reference by librarians, researchers, publishers, suppliers and others who need to have as complete a listing of poetry publishers as possible.

ABBEY; ABBEY CHEAPOCHAPBOOKS (II), Dept. PM, 5360 Fallriver Row Court, Columbia MD 21044, phone (301)730-4272, founded 1970, editor David Greisman. They want "**poetry that does for the mind what that first sip of Molson Ale does for the palate. No pornography & politics.**" They have published poetry by Richard Peabody, Vera Bergstrom, Margot Treitel, Harry Calhoun, Wayne Hogan and Tom Bilicke. *Abbey*, a quarterly, aims "to be a journal but to do it so informally that one wonders about my intent." It is magazine-sized, 20-26 pgs., photocopied. They publish about 150 of 1,000 poems received/year. Press run is 200. Subscription: $2. Sample: 50¢ postpaid. **Guidelines available for SASE. Pays 1-2 copies. Reports in 1 month.** *Abbey Cheapochapbooks* come out 1-2 times a year averaging 10-15 pgs. **For chapbook consideration query with 4-6 samples, bio and list of publications. Reports in 2 months. Pays 25-50 copies.** The editor says he is "definitely seeing poetry from 2 schools—the nit'n'grit school and the textured/reflective school. I much prefer the latter."

ABIKO QUARTERLY LITTER-ARY RAG (I, IV-Translations), 8-1-8 Namiki, Abiko, Chiba Japan 270-11, phone 011-81-471-84-7904, founded 1988, poetry editor Vincent Broderick, is a literary-style quarterly journal "**heavily influenced by James Joyce's** Finnegan's Wake. **We publish all kinds, even religious poems, including original and translations.**" They have recently published poetry by Kenji Miyazawa, Murray Thompson, Yonah Wollach and Fumiaki Den. It is magazine-sized, desktop published with Macintosh laser printer. Press run 350 for 150 subscribers of which 10 are libraries, 100 shelf sales. **Sample postpaid: 900 yen. Pays 1 copy. Editors always comment on rejections.**

ABORIGINAL SF (IV-Science fiction), Box 2449, Woburn MA 01888-0849, founded 1986, editor Charles C. Ryan, is a full-color, slick magazine appearing quarterly. "**Poetry should be 1-2 pp., double-spaced. Subject matter must be science fiction, science or space-related. No long poems, no fantasy.**" The magazine is 116 pgs., with 8 illustrations. Circulation: 23,000, mostly subscriptions. Subscriptions for "special" writer's rate: $15/4 issues." **Sample: $3.50 postpaid. Pays $20/poem and 2 copies. Buys first North American serial rights. Reports in 2-3 months, has no backlog. No simultaneous submissions. Good photocopies, dot-matrix OK. Send SASE for guidelines.** Reviews related books of poetry in 100-300 words.

ABRAXAS MAGAZINE (V); GHOST PONY PRESS (III), 2518 Gregory St., Madison WI 53711, phone (608)238-0175, *Abraxas* founded 1968, Ghost Pony Press in 1980, by editor/publisher Ingrid Swanberg, who says "Ghost Pony Press is a small press publisher of poetry books; *Abraxas* is a literary journal (irregular) publishing contemporary poetry, criticism, translations and reviews of small press books. *Do not confuse these separate presses!*" *Abraxas* **no longer considers unsolicited material, except as announced as projects arise.** She is interested by "**contemporary lyric, concrete experimental.**" **Does not want to see** "**political posing; academic regurgitations.**" They have recently published poetry by William Stafford, Ivan Argüelles, Denise Levertov, César Vallejo and Andrea Moorhead. As a sample the editor selected the final lines of an untitled poem by próspero saíz:

the beautiful grief of the moon is my beam of silence
Dawn
the splendor of the moon dies
my lips open to a gentle breeze

> *she rides a silken yellow scarf into the vanishing clouds*
> *i am still here.*

The magazine is 80 pgs. (160 pgs., double issues) flat-spined, 6×9, litho offset, with original art on its matte card cover, using "unusual graphics in text, original art and collages, concrete poetry, exchange ads only, letters from contributors, essays." It appears "irregularly, 4-9 month intervals." Press run 600, 550 circulation, 300 subscriptions of which 150 are libraries. Subscription: $16/4 issues, $20/4 issues, overseas. **Sample: $4 postpaid ($6 double issues). Pays 1 copy plus 40% discount on additional copies.** *Abraxas* **will announce submission guidelines as projects arise. To submit to Ghost Pony Press, inquire with SASE plus 5-10 poems and cover letter. Photocopy, dot-matrix, previously published material OK for book publication by Ghost Pony Press, which reports on queries in 1-3 months, mss in 3 months. Payment varies per project. Send SASE for catalog to buy samples. Editor sometimes comments briefly on rejections.** They have recently published **Zen Concrete & Etc.**, a selection of poetry by d.a. levy.

ACM (ANOTHER CHICAGO MAGAZINE) (II); LEFT FIELD PRESS (V), 3709 N. Kenmore, Chicago IL 60613, founded 1976, poetry editor Barry Silesky. *ACM* is a literary biannual, **emphasis on quality, experimental, politically aware** prose, fiction, poetry, reviews, cross-genre work and essays. The editor wants **"no religious verse."** They have published prose and poetry by Michael McClure, Jack Anderson, Jerome Sala, Nance VanWinkel, Nadja Tesich, Wanda Coleman, Thomas McGrath and Marilyn Krysl. As a sample, the editor selected these lines (poet unidentified):

> *The black trunk of the ancient tree splits*
> *into two branches at eye level.*
> *Thus Lopo Gonclaveo crossed*
> *the equator. No boiling waters. No harm*

The editor says *ACM* is digest-sized, 196 pp., offset with b&w art and ads. Circulation 1,500, 500 subscriptions of which 100 are libraries. **Sample: $7 postpaid. Pays $5/page and 1 copy. Buys first serial rights. Reports in 2-3 months, has 3-6 month backlog. Submit 3-8 pgs. typed. Simultaneous submissions, clear photocopy OK.** Reviews books of poetry in 250-500 words. This is a well-edited, surprising magazine that appreciates good writing, traditional to experimental, with an emphasis on message. So if you have good poems that pertain to social or political concerns, this may be the market for you. **They do not accept freelance submissions for chapbook publication.**

ACUMEN MAGAZINE; EMBER PRESS (I, II), 6 The Mount, Higher Furzeham, Brixham, S. Devon TQ5 8QY England, phone (0803)851098, press founded 1971, *Acumen* founded 1984, poetry editor Patricia Oxley, is a "small press publisher of a general literary magazine with emphasis on good poetry." They want **"well-crafted, high quality, imaginative poems showing a sense of form. No experimental verse of an obscene type."** They have recently published poetry by Elizabeth Jennings, William Oxley, Gavin Ewart, D.J. Enright, Peter Porter, Kathleen Raine and R.S. Thomas. As a sample Mrs. Oxley selected these lines from "The Green Field" by Dannie Abse:

> *As soft-eyed lovers for the very first time,*
> *turning out the light for the first time,*
> *blot out all detail, all colours,*
> *and whisper the old code-words, 'Love you'.*

Acumen appears in April and October of each year, digest-sized, 100 pgs. flat-spined, professionally printed with illustrations and ads. Of about 12,000 poems received they accept about 90. Press run is 650 for 400 subscriptions (15 libraries). $10 per issue, $25 subscription. **Sample: $10 postpaid. Pays "by negotiation" and one copy. No previously published poems; simultaneous submissions OK, if not to UK magazines. Reports in one month.** Reviews books of poetry in up to 300 words, single format or 600 words, multi-book. Patricia Oxley advises, "Read *Acumen* carefully to see what kind of poetry we publish. Also read widely in many poetry magazines, and don't forget the poets of the past—they can still teach us a great deal."

ADASTRA PRESS (II), Dept. PM, 101 Strong St., Easthampton MA 01027, phone (413)527-3324, founded 1980 by Gary Metras, who says, "I publish poetry because I love poetry. I produce the books on antique equipment using antique methods because I own the equipment and because it's cheaper— I don't pay myself a salary—it's a hobby—it's **a love affair with poetry and printing of fine editions.** I literally sweat making these books and I want the manuscript to show me the author also sweated." All his books and chapbooks are **limited editions, handset, letterpress,** printed with handsewn signatures. "Chances of acceptance are slim. About 1 in 200 submissions is accepted, which means I only take 1 or 2 unsolicited mss a year." The chapbooks are in square-spine paper wrappers, cloth editions also handcrafted. He wants **"no rhyme, no religious. Poetry is communication first, although it is art. Long poems and thematic groups are nice for chapbooks. No subjects are tabu, but topics should be drawn from real life experiences. I include accurate dreams as real life."** Poets published include Judith Neeld, W.D. Ehrhart, Joseph Langland and David Chorlton. 1-4 such chapbooks are brought out each year. Author is paid in copies, usually 10% of the print run. "I only read chapbook manuscripts in the month of February, picking one or two for the following year. Queries, with a sample of 3-5 poems from a chapbook manuscript, are read throughout the year and if I like what I see in the sample, I'll ask you to submit the ms in February. Do not submit or query about full-length collections. I will only be accepting chapbook manuscripts of 12-18 double-spaced pages. Any longer collections would be a special invitation to a poet. If you want to see a typical handcrafted Adastra chapbook, send $5 and I'll mail a current title. If you'd like a fuller look at what, how and why I do what I do, send check for $11.50 ($10 plus $1.50 postage and handling) and I'll mail a copy of **The Adastra Reader: Being the Collected Chapbooks in Facsimile with Author Notes, Bibliography and Comments on Hand Bookmaking,** published in 1987. This is a 247-page anthology covering Adastra publishing from 1979-1986."

ADRIFT (II, IV-Ethnic), 4D, 239 East 5th St., New York NY 10003, founded 1980, editor Thomas McGonigle, who says, "The **orientation of magazine is Irish, Irish-American. I expect reader-writer knows and goes beyond Yeats, Kavanagh, Joyce, O'Brien." The literary magazine is open to all kinds of submissions, but does not want to see "junk." Simultaneous submissions OK.** They have published poetry by James Liddy, Thomas McCarthy, Francis Stuart and Gilbert Sorrentino. *Adrift* appears twice a year and has a circulation of 1,000 with 200 subscriptions, 50 of which go to libraries. Price per issue is $4, subscription $8. **Sample: $5 postpaid. Magazine pays, rate varies; contributors receive 1 copy.** Magazine-sized, 32 pgs., offset on heavy stock, cover matte card, saddle-stapled. Reviews books of poetry.

THE ADVOCATE (I), 301A Rolling Hills Park, Prattsville NY 12468, phone (518)299-3103, editor Remington Wright, founded 1987, is an advertiser-supported tabloid appearing bimonthly, 12,000 copies distributed free, **using original, previously unpublished works,** such as feature stories, essays, 'think' pieces, letters to the editor, profiles, humor, fiction, poetry, puzzles, cartoons or line drawings. They want **"nearly any kind of poetry, any length, but not religious or pornographic. Poetry ought to speak to people and not be so oblique as to have meaning only to the poet. If I had to be there to understand the poem, don't send it."** As a sample here are the opening lines from "The Kerry Eileen" by Joyce A. Story:

> *It was June the thirteenth when the ship was first seen*
> *By the captain and crew of the* Kerry Eileen
> *She then seemed to dissolve in the darkening greys*
> *Of the sky and the sea and the leaden-like haze.*

Sample: $2 postpaid. Pays 2 copies. Acquires first rights only. Reports in 6-8 weeks; publishes accepted material an average of 4-6 months after acceptance. No simultaneous submissions. Editor "occasionally" comments on rejections. Accepts about 25% of poems received. Reviews books of poetry. Offers occasional contests. The editor says, "All submissions and correspondence must be accompanied by a self-addressed, stamped envelope with sufficient postage."

AEGINA PRESS, INC.; UNIVERSITY EDITIONS (I, II), 59 Oak Lane, Spring Valley, Huntington WV 25704, founded 1983, publisher Ira Herman, is **primarily subsidy for poetry,** strongly committed to publishing new or established poets. Publishes subsidy titles under the University Editions imprint. Aegina has published non-subsidized poetry as well. **Authors of books accepted on a non-subsidized basis receive a 15% royalty.** "We try to provide a way for talented poets to have their collections published, which otherwise might go unpublished because of commercial, bottom-line considerations. Aegina Press will publish quality poetry that the large publishers will not handle because it is not commercially viable. We believe it is unfair that a poet has to have a 'name' or a following in order to have a book of poems accepted by a publisher. Poetry is the purest form of literary art, and it should be made available to those who appreciate it." Poets published include Barbara Everest. The editor selected these sample lines from **Malignant Moons** by Spencer Balanon:

> *Perhaps we too are lost*
> *Like a child feeling the dark*
> *Stroking the cornered shadows*

"**Most poetry books we accept are subsidized by the author (or an institution).** In return, the author receives all sales proceeds from the book, and any unsold copies left from the print run

---

Market conditions are constantly changing! If you're still using this book and it is 1994 or later, buy the newest edition of Poet's Market at your favorite bookstore or order directly from Writer's Digest Books.

belong to the author. Minimum print run is 500 copies. We can do larger runs as well. Our marketing program includes submission to distributors, agents, other publishers, and bookstores and libraries." **Manuscripts should be typed and no shorter than 40 pages. There is no upper length limit. Simultaneous and photocopied submissions OK. Reporting time is 1 month for full manuscripts, 7-10 days for queries.** They publish perfect-bound (flat-spined) paperbacks with glossy covers. **Sample books are available for $5 each plus $1.50 postage and handling.**

AERIAL (V), P.O. Box 25642, Washington DC 20007, phone (202)333-1544, founded 1984, editor Rod Smith, editorial assistants Gretchen Johnson and Wayne Kline, a yearly publication. Issue #6/7 was the John Cage issue. They have recently published work by Jackson MacLow, Melanie Neilson, Steve Benson, Phyllis Rosenzweig and Charles Bernstein. Two special issues are in the works, on Barrett Watten and Bruce Andrews, therefore **they're not looking for new work at this time.** As a sample the editor selected these lines from "subtracted words" by P. Inman:

> *still dollar in its pale*
> *mice sight. Parts of knock*
> *in a river of propellor blade.*
> *Wage sand gist. Keyhole*
> *college, its brink on. An*
> *ash stelm of mind ball*

The magazine is 6×9, offset, varies 60-180 pgs. Circulation is 1,000. **Sample postpaid: $7.50. Poets should submit 1-10 pages. Reporting time is 1 week-2 months and time to publication is 3-12 months.** Also looking for critical/political/philosophical writing.

AETHLON: THE JOURNAL OF SPORT LITERATURE (IV-Sports), East Tennessee State University, Johnson City TN 37614-0002, founded 1983, general editor Don Johnson, Professor of English, ETSU, poetry editor Robert W. Hamblin, Professor of English, Southeast Missouri State University, Cape Girardeau MO 63701. (Submit poetry to this address.) *Aethlon* publishes a variety of sport-related literature, including scholarly articles, fiction, poetry, personal essays and reviews; 6-10 poems/issue; two issues annually, fall and spring. **Subject matter must be sports-related; no restrictions regarding form, length, style or purpose. They do not want to see "doggerel, cliché-ridden or oversentimental" poems.** Some poets published are Neal Bowers, Joseph Duemer, Robert Fink, Jan Mordenski, H.R. Stonebeck, Jim Thomas, Stephen Tudor and Don Welch. The magazine is digest-sized, offset printed, flat-spined, with illustrations and some ads, 200 pgs./issue. Circulation is 1,000 of which 750 are sub-scriptions, 250 to libraries. Subscription is included with membership ($30) in the Sport Literature Association. **Sample: $12.50 postpaid. Contributors receive 5 offprints and a copy of the issue in which their poem appears. Submissions are reported on in 6-8 weeks and the backlog time is 6-12 months; "only typed mss with SASE considered."** Will accept simultaneous submissions.

AFRICA WORLD PRESS (IV-Ethnic), Box 1892, Trenton NJ 08607, founded 1979, editor Kassahun Checole, publishes poetry by Africans, African-Americans, Caribbean and Latin Americans. Two poetry publications by Africa World Press are: **Under A Soprano Sky** by Sonia Sanchez and **From the Pyramid to the Projects** by Askia Muhammad Toure, winner of an American Book Award for 1989. **Authors receive 7½% royalty; number of copies negotiable. Considers simultaneous submissions. Send SASE for catalog.**

AFRO-HISPANIC REVIEW (IV-Ethnic), Romance Languages, #143 Arts & Sciences, University of Missouri, Columbia MO 65211, founded 1982, editors Marvin A. Lewis and Edward J. Mullen, uses some **poetry related to Afro-Hispanic life and issues.** Appears 3 times a year. They have published poetry by Manuel Zapata Olivella, Melvin E. Lewis and Antar Al Basir. **Pays 5 copies. Sample copy $5. Reports in 6 weeks.** Reviews books of poetry in "about 500 words."

AGNI (II), Boston University, 236 Bay State Rd., Boston MA 02215, phone (617)353-5389, founded 1972, editor Askold Melnyczuk. "*Agni* is a biannual journal of poetry, fiction and essays by both emerging and established writers. Poets whose work we have published include Derek Walcott, Patricia Traxler, Tom Sleigh, Maxine Scates, Mark Halliday, Marjorie Agosin and Ha Jin." As a sample the editor offers these lines from Rafael Campo's poem, "Grandfather's Will":

> *I leave you the plantation, and the pain*
> *Of sugar. I leave you even the scattered sins*
> *Of island life: thirst in spite of water*
> *Everywhere, to not escape, and to think*
> *You rose above the sea on purpose. Tanks*
> *Are crushing my body now — the traitors*
> *In our house have come for me. A word of caution:*
> *Remember me. Bury me in the ocean.*

> *Burn me to brown sugar—drink me, a potion*
> *In your coffee. It grows on your plantation.*

Agni is typeset, printed offset and perfect-bound. Circulation is 1,500 by subscription, mail order and bookstore sales. Subscription: $12. **Sample: $7. Pays $10/page, $150 maximum, plus 2 copies and one-year subscription. Buys first serial rights. They will consider simultaneous submissions but not previously published poems. Reads submissions October 1 through June 1 only. Mss received at other times will be returned unread. Reports in 1-4 months.** The editor says, "We are not reading until January 1993 because of overstock."

AG-PILOT INTERNATIONAL MAGAZINE (IV-Specialized), 405 Main St., Mt. Vernon WA 98273, phone (206)336-9737, editor Tom Wood, "is intended to be a fun-to-read, technical, as well as humorous and serious publication for the ag pilot and operator." It appears monthly, 48-64 pgs., circulation 8,400. "Interested in **agri-aviation (crop dusting) related poetry ONLY.**" **Buys 1/issue, pays $10-50.**

THE AGUILAR EXPRESSION (I, II), (formerly *The Adroit Expression*), P.O. Box 304, Webster PA 15087, phone (412)379-8019, founded 1986, editor/publisher Xavier F. Aguilar, appears 2 times/year, and is **"open to all types of poetry, including erotica that is well written."** They have recently published poetry by Jonathan M. Berkowitz and Diane U. Lewis. As a sample the editor selected the poem "Moon Magic" by Ellen S. Sandry:

> *The old and simpler nature*
> *that you unleash in me*
> *jars my restless spirit*
> *to creativity.*

The editor describes it as magazine-sized, 5-7 pgs., circulation 100. **Sample postpaid: $5. Reports in 1 month. Pays 1 copy. "We are also now seeking poetry manuscripts as we wish to publish 1 or 2 chapbooks in 1993-1994. Send SASE for details."** The editor says, "In publishing poetry, I try to exhibit the unique reality that we too often take for granted and acquaint as mediocre. We encourage poetics that deal with *now*, which our readers can relate to."

AHSAHTA PRESS; COLD DRILL; COLD-DRILL BOOKS; POETRY IN PUBLIC PLACES (IV-Regional), English Dept., Boise State University, Boise ID 83725, phone (208)385-1246. Ahsahta Press is a project to publish **contemporary poetry of the American West.** But, say editors Tom Trusky, Orv Burmaster and Dale Boyer, "**Spare us paens to the pommel, Jesus in the sagebrush, haiku about the Eiffel Tower, 'nice' or 'sweet' poems.**" The work should "**draw on the cultures, history, ecologies of the American West.**" They publish collections (45 + pgs.) of individual poets in handsome flat-spined paperbacks with plain matte covers, with an appreciative introduction, at most 3/year. Occasionally they bring out an anthology on cassette of their authors. And they have published an anthology (94 pgs.) **Women Poets of the West**, with an introduction by Ann Stanford. Some of their poets are Susan Deal, Leo Romero, David Baker, Linda Bierds, Philip St. Clair and Gretel Ehrlich. Here are some lines from Gerrye Payne's "Machines," in the collection **The Year-God:**

> *Machines sit to hand, vortices of possibility.*
> *Under their blank gaze biological life*
> *Flares and dies, is ashamed.*
> *The neighbor's tractor hums, clearing brush,*
> *inventing geometry in random chaparral.*

You may submit only during their January 1 through March 31 reading period each year—a sample of 15 of your poems with SASE. They will report in about 2 months. Multiple and simultaneous submissions, photocopy, dot-matrix OK. If they like the sample, they'll ask for a book ms. If it is accepted, **you get 25 copies of the 1st and 2nd printings and a 25% royalty commencing with the 3rd.** They seldom comment on the samples, frequently on the mss. Send SASE for their catalog and order a few books, if you don't find them in your library. "Old advice but true: read what we publish before submitting. **75% of the submissions we receive should never have been sent to us. Save stamps, spirit and sweat.**" *Cold Drill* publishes "primarily Boise State University students, faculty and staff, but will consider writings by Idahoans—or writing about Idaho by 'furriners.' " They do some of the most creative publishing in this country today, and it is worth buying a **sample of** *cold-drill* **for $9** just to see what they're up to. This annual "has been selected as top undergraduate literary magazine in the U.S. by such important acronyms as CSPA, CCLM and UCDA." It comes in a box stuffed with various pamphlets, postcards, posters, a newspaper, even 3-D comics with glasses to read them by. **No restrictions on types of poetry.** As yet they have published no poets of national note, but Tom Trusky offers these lines as a sample, from Patrick Flanagan, "Postcard From a Freshman":

> *The girls here are gorgeous, studying hard,*
> *many new friends, roommate*
> *never showers, tried to*

> *kill myself, doctor says*
> *i'm getting better*

Circulation is 400, including 100 subscribers, of which 20 are libraries. **"We read material throughout the year, notifying only those whose work we've accepted December 15-January 1st. Manuscripts should be photocopies with author's name and address on separate sheet, simultaneous submissions OK. Payment: 1 copy."** They also publish two 24-page chapbooks and one 75-page flat-spined paperback/year. **Query about book publication.** "We want to publish a literary magazine that is exciting to read. We want more readers than just our contributors and their mothers. Our format and our content have allowed us to achieve those goals, so far." Poetry in Public Places is a series of 8 monthly posters/year "presenting the poets in Boise State University's creative students series and poets in BSU's Ahsahta Press poetry series." These, like all publications emanating from BSU, are elegantly done, with striking art. The posters are on coated stock.

AIM MAGAZINE (IV-Social issues, ethnic), 7308 S. Eberhart Ave., Chicago IL 60619, phone (312)874-6184, founded 1974, poetry editor Henry Blakely, is a magazine-sized quarterly, circulation 10,000, glossy cover, **"dedicated to racial harmony and peace."** They use 3-4 poems ("poetry with social significance mainly") in each issue. **They ask for 32 lines average length.** They have published poems by J. Douglas Studer, Wayne Dowdy and Maria DeGuzman. They have 3,000 subscriptions of which 15 are libraries. Single copy: $2.50; subscription $10. **Sample postpaid: $4. Pays $3/poem. You will not receive an acceptance slip: "We simply send payment and magazine copy."** They receive only about 30 submissions/year of which they use half. Photocopy, simultaneous submissions OK, no dot-matrix. **Reports in 3-6 weeks.** The editor's advice: "Read the work of published poets."

‡AIREINGS (II, IV-Women), #24, Brudenell Rd., Leeds, West Yorkshire LS6 1BD, United Kingdom, phone 0532-785893, founded 1980, editor Jean Barker. "Poems acceptable from all over the world. **Primarily like women's work** as we are a Women's Co-op running the mag and like to redress the balance a bit, but we are **happy to receive work by men also. Poetry on all subjects. We do draw a line on sexist/racist stuff, but we like a broad spectrum of work as long as it is not too long, as we only run to 40 pgs."** They have recently published poetry by Geoffrey Holloway, Janet Faraday, Pauline Kirk, Jean Barker, Jane Legge and Mary Sheepshanks. As a sample the editor selected these lines (poet unidentified):

> *No one seeks my opinion*
> *Though they may well require my son.*
> *So, folding currants into yellow paste,*
> *I watch them sink, like soldiers into sand.*

The magazine appears twice a year, "illustrated by our own artist. No ads yet, but we may have to later, if we are under extreme financial pressure." They publish about 5% of the poetry received. *Aireings* is digest-sized, 40 pgs., saddle-stapled, photocopied from typescript with matte b&w card cover. They print 300-350 copies for 100 subscriptions (10 libraries) and shelf sales. It costs £1.25/copy, which includes UK postage (overseas: Payment in sterling £4.50. Other currencies: (by check) equivalent of £10 or in notes equivalent of £6.50.). **Pays 2 copies. "Work should be typed if possible—just legible if not." Simultaneous submissions and previously published (if not in the North of England) OK. Reports "after our editorial deadlines, which are the 1st of January and July."** Reviews books of poetry in 500 words.

ALABAMA LITERARY REVIEW (II), English Dept., Troy State University, Troy AL 36082, phone (205)670-3000, ext. 3286, poetry editor Ed Hicks, a biannual, **wants poetry that is "imagistic—*but* in motion. Will look at anything."** They have recently published poetry by R.T. Smith, Ed Peaco, Joanne M. Riley and Martha Payne. As a sample the editor selected these lines from "Late Fall" by Diane Swan:

> *It's hard to tell birds*
> *from wind-rushed leaves*
> *as they skirl up in the funnels*
> *of blinking October light*

The beautifully printed 100-page, 6×9 magazine, matte cover with art, b&w art and some colored pages inside, receives 300 submissions/year, uses 30, has a 2-month backlog. **Reads submissions September 1 through July 31 only. Will consider simultaneous submissions. Sample: $4.50 postpaid. Query not necessary. Reports in 1-2 months. Pays copies. Acquires first rights. Sometimes comments on rejections.**

ALASKA QUARTERLY REVIEW (II), College of Arts and Sciences, University of Alaska Anchorage, 3221 Providence Dr., Anchorage AK 99508, phone (907)786-4775. Started in 1981, Ronald Spatz and James Jakob Liszka, executive editors; Thomas Sexton, poetry editor. "A journal devoted to contemporary literary art. We publish both traditional and experimental fiction, poetry, essays and criticism on contemporary writing, literature and philosophy of literature." They publish two double-issues a year, **each using about 18 pgs. of poetry.** They have a circulation of 1,000; 200 subscribers, of which 25 are libraries, $4 an issue, $8 per subscription, **$4 for a sample** (postpaid). They receive up to 2,000 submissions each year, of which they take about 40. **Pay depends on funding. Acquires first North American serial rights. They take up to 4 months to report, and there is usually no comment on mss. No query. Manuscripts are** *not* **read from May 15 through August 15.**

‡ALBATROSS; THE ANABIOSIS PRESS (II, IV-Nature), 125 Horton Ave., Englewood FL 34223, founded 1985, editors Richard Smyth and Richard Brobst. *Albatross* appears in the spring and fall. **"We consider the albatross to be a metaphor for an environment that must survive. This is not to say that we publish only environmental or nature poetry, but that we are biased toward such subject matters. We publish mostly free verse 200 lines/poem maximum, and we prefer a narrative style, but again, this is not necessary. We do not want trite rhyming poetry which doesn't convey a deeply felt experience in a mature expression with words."** They have recently published poetry by Simon Perchik, Michael Jennings, Karen Volkman and Elizabeth Rees. As a sample, the editors selected these lines by Polly Buckingham:

> *Many white birds scatter like*
> *doves in a sand dollar,*
> *and I receive you, my body*
> *a murex, whelk, moonshell.*

The magazine is 32-36 pgs., 5½ × 8½, laser typeset with linen cover, some b&w drawings, and, in addition to the poetry, has an interview with a poet in each issue. Circulation 200, 75 subscribers of which 10 are libraries. Many complimentary copies are sent out to bookstores, poets and libraries. **Subscription: $5/2 issues. Sample: $3 postpaid. Send SASE for guidelines. Pays 2 copies. Acquires all rights. Returns rights. "Previous publication in** *Albatross* **must be mentioned in all subsequent reprintings." Reports in 4-6 months, has 6-12 month backlog. "Poems should be typed single-spaced, with name and address in left corner and length in lines in right corner. Photocopies are accepted, but we do not appreciate simultaneous submissions." Also holds a chapbook contest. Submit 16-20 pgs. poetry, any theme, any style. Deadline is February 15 of each year. Include name, address and phone number on the title page. Charges $5 reading fee (check payable to** *Albatross***). Winner receives $50 and 25 copies of his/her published chapbook. All entering receive a free copy of the winning chapbook.** "The Anabiosis Press is now a nonprofit organization. Membership fee is $20 plus $20/year for membership dues." Comments? "We expect a poet to read as much contemporary poetry as possible."

THE ALCHEMIST (II), Box 123, Lasalle, Quebec H8R 3T7 Canada, founded 1974, poetry editor Marco Fraticelli, is a 100 pgs., small, digest-sized, flat-spined, handsomely printed and illustrated with b&w drawings. It is an irregularly-issued literary journal using mostly poetry. **No restrictions on form, style or content. Considers simultaneous submissions.** They have a print run of 500, 200 subscriptions, of which 30 are libraries, and they send out some 200 complimentary copies. Subscription $12 for 4 issues, $3/issue. They have a 6-month backlog. **Sample: $2 postpaid. Reports in 1 month. Pays 2 copies.**

ALDEBARAN (II), Roger Williams College, 1 Old Ferry Rd., Bristol RI 02809, editor Debra L. Malewieki, publishes a spring and a fall issue. *"Aldebaran* publishes both poetry and fiction in traditional, contemporary and experimental forms; we are receptive to nearly all styles and topics. We would like to see more diversity in our magazine and encourage submissions from writers of all genres, from fantasy to dark fiction, science fiction, comedy, horror and drama, as well as classical and contemporary poetry and fiction." The magazine is 50-100 pgs., side-stapled or perfect-bound, digest-sized. Press run is 300. **Sample postpaid: $5. Subscription: $10 for 2 issues. Send SASE for guidelines. Submit no more than 5 poems at a time. Reads submissions February 1 through April 1 and September 1 through November 1. Reports in 6-12 weeks.** Student-run publication. Seldom comments on rejections.

ALGILMORE (I), Dept PM, 125 N. Main St., Galena IL 61036, phone (815)777-9688, founded 1968 as Studio Five, thought-merchant Jay Son, conducts New Age sessions and publishes videotapes, cassettes and flyers, for "higher thoughts—New Age—**no restriction on style, length, subject, good teaching thoughts. Longhand acceptable, spelling mistakes OK. Clarity important. No jokes, militant, smut. We are interested in the message. We would like a cover page with bio of the poet and a snapshot if possible. SASE. We prefer to retain copies** (due to the high cost of postage) and each poet has a personal file in our office. Allow 30 days for report. We are currently working with Larian, An-Dabney Faulkner, Lloyd A. Jackson, Jim Wheeler, Edward Ainsworth, Ruff Reiter and Lyn Hampel." As a sample the editor selected these lines:

> *Do you know—your writing on the*
> *pages of my heart—.*

"We will be having 8-12 contests a year and newsletters—open to all poet[...] for contest poems only. All poets submitting poems are put on our contest[...] create a subject to be written about. Reward with cash rewards. Winners ar[...] newsletter."

ALICEJAMESBOOKS; BEATRICE HAWLEY AWARD (IV-Regional, women, e[...] Ave., Cambridge MA 02140, phone (617)354-1408, founded 1973. "An author's collective, w[...] lishes exclusively **poetry, with an emphasis on poetry by women; authors are exclusively from the New England Area.** We strongly encourage submissions by poets of color." Offers Beatrice Hawley Award for poets who cannot meet the work commitment due to geographical or financial restraints. They publish flat-spined paperbacks of high quality, both in production and contents, no children's poetry, and their books have won numerous awards and been very respectably reviewed. "Each poet becomes a working member of the co-op with a two-year work commitment." That is, you have to live close enough to **attend meetings and participate in the editorial and publishing process.** They publish about 4 books, 72 pgs., each year in editions of 1,000, paperbacks—no hardbacks. **Query first, but no need for samples: simply ask for dates of reading periods, which are in early spring and early fall. Simultaneous submissions OK, but "we would like to know when a manuscript is being submitted elsewhere." Reports in 2-3 months. Send two copies of the ms. Payment: authors receive 100 paperback copies.**

ALIVE NOW!; POCKETS; WEAVINGS (IV-Religious, children); THE UPPER ROOM (V), 1908 Grand Ave., P.O. Box 189, Nashville TN 37202, phone (615)340-7200. This publishing company brings out about 20 books a year and four magazines: *The Upper Room, alive now!, Pockets* and *Weavings.* Of these, two use freelance poetry. *Pockets, Devotional Magazine for Children,* which comes out 11 times a year, circulation 68,000-70,000, is for children 6-12, "offers stories, activities, prayers, poems—all **geared to giving children a better understanding of themselves as children of God. Some of the material is not overtly religious but deals with situations, special seasons and holidays, ecological concerns from a Christian perspective."** It uses 3-4 pgs. of poetry per issue. **Sample: free with 7×9 SAE and 4 first class stamps. Ordinarily 24-line limit on poetry. Pays $25-50.** Send SASE for themes and guidelines. The other magazine which uses poetry is *alive now!,* a bimonthly, circulation 75,000, for a general Christian audience interested in reflection and meditation. **Guidelines and themes list free (with SASE). They buy 30 poems a year, avant-garde and free verse. Submit 5 poems, 10-45 lines. Pays $10-25.** *The Upper Room* magazine does not accept poetry.

ALLEGHENY REVIEW (I, IV-Students), Box 32, Allegheny College, Meadville PA 16335, founded 1983, editors Lauren Dyer and Joe Misch. "Each year *Allegheny Review* compiles and publishes a review of the nation's best **undergraduate literature.** It is entirely composed of and by college under-graduates and is nationally distributed both as a review and as a classroom text, particularly suited to creative writing courses. We will print **poetry of appreciable literary merit on any topic, submitted by college undergraduates. No limitations except excessive length (2-3 pgs.)** as we wish to represent as many authors as possible, although exceptions are made in areas of great quality and interest." They have published poetry by Eric Sanborn, Cheryl Connor, Rick Alley and Kristi Coulter. The *Review* appears in a 6×9, flat-spined, professionally-printed format, b&w photo on glossy card cover. **Submissions should be accompanied by a letter "telling the college poet is attending, year of graduation, any background, goals and philosophies that the author feels are pertinent to the work submitted." Reports 1-2 months following deadline. Submit 3 to 5 poems, typed, photocopy, dot-matrix OK. Sample: $3.50 and 11×18 SASE. Poem judged best in the collection earns $50-75 honorarium.** "Ezra Pound gave the best advice: 'Make it new.' We're seeing far too much imitation; there's already been a Sylvia Plath, a Galway Kinnell. Don't be afraid to try new things. Be innovative. Also, traditional forms are coming 'back in style,' or so we hear. Experiment with them; write a villanelle, a sestina or a sonnet. And when you submit, please take enough pride in your work to do so professionally. Handwritten or poorly-typed and proofed submissions definitely convey an impression, a negative one."

ALLY PRESS CENTER (V), Dept. PM, 524 Orleans St., St. Paul MN 55107, founded 1973, owner Paul Feroe, **publishes and distributes work by Robert Bly, Michael Meade, James Hillman and Robert Moore, including books, cassette tapes and videotapes.** Two to three times a year a complete catalog is mailed out along with information about Bly's reading and workshop schedule. **The press is not accepting unsolicited mss at this time.** Book catalog is free on request.

ALMS HOUSE PRESS (I), P.O. Box 668, Stony Point NY 10980, founded 1985, poetry editors Lorraine De Gennaro and Alana Sherman, holds an **annual poetry competition with $7 entry fee (contestants receive a copy of a chapbook). "We have no preferences with regard to style as long as the poetry is high caliber. We like to see previous publication in the small press, but we are open to new writers. We look for variety and excellence and are open to experimental forms as well as traditional forms. Any topics as long as the poems are not whiny or too depressing, pornographic or religious."** They

recently published chapbooks by Martin Anderson and Sandra Marshburn. As a sample they
selected these lines by Steven Lautermilch:

> *Fisher, fishwife, hold each to each.*
> *Your children, small fry, grow only to feed*
> *the sighing grave. And your roofs,*
> *like these keels,*
> *are the bed and birth of shells.*

**Submit 16- to 24-page chapbook including all front matter, title page and table of contents,
between March 1 and May 31. Name, address and phone number should appear on title page
only. Winner receives 15 copies. Send SASE for current rules. Sample copy: $4 postpaid. They
offer a critical and editorial service for $25.**

ALOHA, THE MAGAZINE OF HAWAII AND THE PACIFIC (IV-Regional), Suite 309, 49 S. Hotel St.,
Honolulu HI 96813, editor Cheryl Chee Tsutsumi, is a bimonthly (every 2 months) "consumer magazine with Hawaii and Pacific focus." Circulation 65,000. **"Not interested in lengthy poetry. Poems
should be limited to 100 words or less. Subject should be focused on Hawaii."** Poems are matched to
color photos, so it is "difficult to say" how long it will be between acceptance and publication. As a
sample we selected these lines by William Beyer:

> *Elusive gulls*
> *ascend,*
> *descend*
> *with perfect grace,*
> *in celebration*
> *above the constant rhythm*
> *of a rising tide.*

Aloha is magazine-sized, 80 pgs., flat-spined, elegantly printed on glossy stock with many full-
color pages, glossy card cover in color. They publish 6 of more than 50 poems received/year.
**Sample postpaid: $2.95. Send SASE for guidelines. Pays $30 plus 1 copy (and up to 10 at dis-
count). Ms should be double-spaced, typed, name, address and phone number on all mss. Reports within 2 months.**

ALPHA BEAT SOUP; ALPHA BEAT PRESS (I, IV-Form/style), 31 A Waterloo St., New Hope PA 18938,
founded 1987, poetry editor David Christy, appears twice a year **emulating the Beat literary tradition.**
Alpha Beat Soup is "an international poetry and arts journal featuring Beat, 'post-Beat independent'
and modern writing." Christy says that **25% of each issue is devoted to little known or previously
unpublished poets.** They have recently published works by Pradip Choudhuri, Joan Reid, Erling Friis-
Baastad, Janine Pommy Vega, Ana Pine, George Dowden and Charles Bukowski. *ABS* is 7 × 8½, 50-
75 pgs., photocopied from IBM laser printer, card cover offset, graphics included. They will use 50%
of most poetry received. Press run is 600 for 400 paid subscriptions (11 of them libraries). Subscription:
$15. Single copy: $8. **Sample: $10 (includes first-class postage). Pays 1 copy. Simultaneous submissions
and previously published poems OK. Editor comments on rejections "only on request."** Reviews books
of poetry in approximately 700 words, multi-book format. **Alpha Beat Press publishes chapbooks and
supplements.**

**ALTA NAPA PRESS (IV-Bilingual/foreign language, translations); GONDWANA BOOKS (IV-
Form)**, 1969 Mora Ave., Calistoga CA 94515, founded 1976, FAX (707)226-7708, publishes various
kinds of books, but the imprint **Gondwana Books is for epic poetry only.** A number of the books in
their catalog (available for 9 × 12 SASE and $1) are by the editor, Carl T. Endemann. He **publishes
other authors on a "co-operative basis," which means partial or full subsidy** but gives no details of
how that works. Write directly for information, and when you do **send 3 poems, and your cover letter
should include biographical background, personal or aesthetic philosophy, poetic goals and principles,
and the hour, date and place of your birth.** He says, "No, I am not a fortune teller!" but he is apparently
interested in **astrology and reincarnation.** He says he wants poetry which is **"clear, clean, concise/
rhythm, reason and 'rammar/rare rational rhymes"** on any subject of universal appeal; **"spiritual
OK, but effusions of personal frustrations no. No trite drivel. Sex yes, porno no. No spectator sports."**
He has published Erme Burton Hand (2 books of poetry for children and juniors) and Carl Heinz
Kurz (2 poetry books of translations from German). Here are some lines from the editor's poem
"Xenia at 94":

> *Yet in your eyes*
> *Glittering still*
> *The blueish diamonds*
> *That I remember*
> *Through the centuries*

He publishes 3-4 chapbooks (30-148 pgs.) and 3-4 flat-spined paperbacks (50-240 pgs.)/year.

Advice: "Join a *good* creative writing class now for three years and read *Writer's Digest* in depth. Poetry is not a commercial endeavor, but it can eventually pay for itself — mainly give you the feeling of having done something *worthwhile* which *no* money can buy." He offers **criticism for $1.30/page of ms.**

ALTERNATIVE PRESS MAGAZINE (I, II), P.O. Box 205, Hatboro PA 19040, founded 1989, poetry editor Bob Lennon, coeditor Lynne Budnick-Lennon, appears quarterly using **"experimental, philosophical poetry; open to many subjects and styles. Nothing pornographic, traditional, religious, no worn-out love poems."** They have published poetry by Dave Brock. As a sample the editor selected these lines from "WELcome 2 my bRAIN" by Lori Steinberg:

> *WATER on the bRAIN*
> *DUGH!!*
> *BoinK/BoinK!!*
> *where am i??*
> > *KANSAS!?*
> *RUFF! RUFF!*

"Alternative Press **will attempt to print many poems submitted unlike some magazines that print trash and reject most poems. Submit up to 5 poems — remember that we publish a digest-sized mag and longer pieces have a harder time finding a place." Reports within 2 weeks-2 months. Simultaneous submissions and previously published poems OK. Guidelines available for SASE.** It is photocopied from typescript, digest-sized, 36 pgs. with matte card cover, saddle-stapled. Press run is 200 for about 50 subscribers, and growing. Some shelf sales. Subscription: $10 for 4 issues. **Sample postpaid: $3. Inquire about reduced rates for back issues. "Poets from Canada and overseas should include $1 extra for each issue ordered." Pays 1-3 copies and "occasionally small sums." Editor comments on submissions "sometimes."** He says, "We like to publish new poets, but they should read at least one copy to see what the magazine is about. Send poetry that comes from inside, not works that conform to outdated modes of writing. Response to this listing has been outstanding, but everyone who submits stands a fair chance at being published. This includes our friends in Europe, Australia and Canada too. We are trying to lose our sanity at *APM.* The amount of poetry that we receive adds to this but a lot of normal, bland and unfeeling poetry is no help. Creative people should avoid creative writing courses."

THE AMARANTH REVIEW; WINDOW PUBLICATIONS (II), P.O. Box 56235, Phoenix AZ 85079, founded 1989, editor Dana L. Yost. "Window Publications is a small press publisher of poetry, fiction and nonfiction. *The Amaranth Review* is a literary journal (twice a year) that exists as a forum for contemporary thought. All questions have answers, and we believe that literature provides a sound vehicle for the exploration of alternatives. **In poetry, quality, while subjective, is our main concern — no preferred form, length, subject matter or style. We publish what we like and prefer to place few if any restrictions on those who contribute — I would rather wade through dozens of poems that I don't like rather than take the chance of discouraging someone and possibly missing that 'one' poem every editor is waiting for."** They have recently published poetry by Diana Chang, Scott Owens, Sapphire, and Anne McKay. As a sample the editor selected these lines from "Eating My Words" by Mali:

> *At the So Real Cafe, I come to the end of my mind.*
> *On this crimson edge I grow new eyes, tiny like*
> *those antenna eyes on deep sea fish, wide open*
> *without lids and slow, searching for other life*

Amaranth is magazine-sized, 60+ pgs., offset professional printing in small type, 80# matte cover stock. "We average around 300 submissions per month; in our last issue we published 32 poems." Press run: 1,500 for 280 subscriptions of which 2 are libraries, 230 shelf sales. Subscription: $11. **Sample postpaid: $5.50, back issue; $6.50, current issue. Send SASE for guidelines. Pays 2 copies plus 40% discount on extras, "additionally, we now offer a small cash award. Inquire for current rate." Buys first North American serial rights. Simultaneous submissions OK. Reads submissions from October 1 through March 31 for the spring; from April 1 through September 30 for the fall. Reports in 1 month.** "We publish 250-1,000 word reviews of books of poetry, both freelance and staff written." **For books or chapbook publication query with 5-10 sample poems, bio and publications. Pays 10-15% royalties. Editor comments on submissions "usually only when requested to do so."** Sponsors Fall and Spring Edition contests offering cash prizes and publication. Send SASE for guidelines. "We also publish *Grand Prize,* a contest newsletter for writers (6 issues for $10.95)." The editor says, "The advice I would give a beginning poet would be to write from the heart, to write honest poetry that means something to you — find out what you really care about and then tap into the power of those feelings. And never quit — I don't care how many times you are rejected or how many people laugh when you tell them you're a poet — if you are a poet you have no choice but to write, and quitting is never an option. There are hundreds of small magazines publishing poetry today, and with enough perseverance and some careful market analysis (treat your **Poet's Market** like a bible) you will see your work in print."

‡**AMATEUR WRITERS JOURNAL/FOUR SEASONS POETRY CLUB MAGAZINE (I)**, 3653 Harrison St., Bellaire OH 43906, founded 1967, editor/publisher Rosalind Gill. Though **you have to buy a copy to see your work in print,** *AWJ* "accepts all types of articles, essays, short stories and **poetry of any theme. No avant-garde or pornographic material accepted. Prefer material of seasonal nature to be submitted in the season prevalent at the time. Length up to 40 regular lines (no longer than 10 words per line). Rhymed or unrhymed. Also accept haiku, limericks and all types of short poems. Do not want to see pornographic—pertaining to raw sex."** Considers simultaneous submissions. They have recently published poetry by Robert Lowery, Eleanore M. Barker, Elsie Watkins and Remelda Gibson. As a sample the editor selected the first stanza of "Inspiration" by Donna Dietrich:

> In the darkness, words come
> prancing across my pillow,
> clogging my veins and synapses
> tap-dancing across my brain.
> I quickly reach for the light switch
> blinding my bleary eyes.

AWJ is a quarterly, with 38 pgs., magazine-sized, photocopied from typescript, side-stapled with colored paper cover, circulation 500+, subscription $7.50/year. **Sample postpaid: $1.85. Send SASE for guidelines. Reports "upon publication." Backlog varies, but seasonal poetry is published immediately. "More than one per page. Single-spaced, camera-ready if writer has a typewriter available. "Photocopy OK."** Certificates of merit are given for "best of issue." The editor advises: "Always adhere to editor's guidelines; send seasonal poems in correct season; write or print legibly if you can't send typed material."

‡**AMBER (III)**, #404, 40 Rose St., Dartmouth, Nova Scotia B3A 2T6 Canada, phone (902)461-4934, founded 1967, editor Hazel F. Goddard, appears 4 times/year (in January, April, July and October). "*Amber* and its one-page supplement, *Marsh & Maple*, promote and distribute current work." They want **"free verse, half page, regular line lengths (not over 56 characters preferred), also haiku and occasional sonnet. Any subject, but must be in good taste, *not vulgar*. Original, bright content. No religious verse."** They have recently published poetry by John D. Engle, Jr., Diana K. Rubin and Tony Cosier. As a sample the editor selected these lines (poet unidentified):

> i am a symphony
> blazing syllables of light
> across each phrase
> lengthening like eighth notes
> from a phantom violin
> to touch the inner ear

The editor says *Amber* is 28 pgs., stapled. They receive about 500 poems a year, use roughly 70%. Press run is 100 for 90 subscribers of which 3 are libraries. Single copy $2.50; subscription: $10. **Sample postpaid: $1. Previously published poems OK; no simultaneous submissions. "Prefer poems to be seasonal, if on nature."** Time between acceptance and publication is 1-6 months. **Seldom comments on rejections. Pays 1 copy.** The editor says, "I receive many books of poets' poems. If up to an average standard I select from them for publication in my magazine. Most poems are from well-crafted poets, a few new writers. Need not be professional but *must* be good work. When space allows, I list contests poets may like to enter, comment on books poets send and devote centrefold to personal chatting, poets' successes, etc."

AMBIT (III), 17 Priory Gardens, Highgate, London N6 5QY, England, phone 340-3566, editor Martin Bax; poetry editors Edwin Brock, Carol Ann Duffy and Henry Graham; prose editor J.G. Ballard; and art editor Mike Foreman. A 96 pgs. quarterly, **pay "variable plus 2 free copies," sample £5,** subscription £20. As a sample the editor selected these excerpts from "Two Poems For Two Suicides" by Henry Graham:

> 1
>
> All right then
> who would fardels bare?
> Or the world away out of earshot
> careless of your one foot in too many graves
> every waking hour.
>
> 2
>
> It got to seem like a war,
> casualties

I used to say,
though no one was shooting at us.
Or were they?

AMELIA; CICADA; SPSM&H; THE AMELIA AWARDS (II, IV-Form), 329 "E" St., Bakersfield CA 93304 or P.O. Box 2385, Bakersfield CA 93303, phone (805)323-4064. *Amelia*, founded 1983, Frederick A. Raborg, Jr., poetry editor, is a quarterly magazine that publishes chapbooks as well. Central to its operations is a series of contests, most with entry fees, spaced evenly throughout the year, awarding more than $3,500 annually, but they publish many poets who have not entered the contests as well. Among poets published are Pattiann Rogers, Stuart Freibert, John Millett, David Ray, Larry Rubin, Charles Bukowski, Maxine Kumin, Charles Edward Eaton and Shuntaro Tanikawa. These sample lines are by Rhina P. Espaillat:

> *Cousins from home are practicing their English*
> *picking out what they can, slippery vowels*
> *queasy in their ears, stiff consonants*
> *bristling like Saxon spears too tightly massed*
> *for the leisurely tongues of my home town . . .*

AMELIA *eighteen*

Matt Mulhern
Jack Curtis ♦ Michael Lassell
Phyllis K. Collier

"We believe humor is a vital part of the presentation of literature," says Amelia Editor Frederick A. Raborg, Jr. "We have been experimenting with using cartoons on our cover, and this one was chosen not only for its delightful humor, but also because we were featuring a story by Matt Mulhern, who stars as the lieutenant on the television series 'Major Dad.'" Raborg adds that poetry is an important feature as well, "making up at least 50% of every issue." The cartoonist here is Rick Stromoski, who has, Raborg says, "an almost old-fashioned style that appeals to all ages."

They are "**receptive to all forms to 100 lines. We do not want to see the patently-religious or overtly-political. Erotica is fine; pornography, no.**" The digest-sized, flat-spined magazine is offset on high-quality paper and usually features an original four-color cover; its circulation is about 1,250, with 522 subscriptions, of which 28 are libraries. **Sample postpaid: $7.95. Submit 3-5 poems, photocopies OK, dot-matrix acceptable but discouraged, no simultaneous submissions except for entries to the annual Amelia Chapbook Award. Reports in 2-12 weeks, the latter if under serious consideration. Pays $2-25/poem plus 2 copies.** "Almost always I try to comment." The editor comments, "*Amelia* is not afraid of strong themes, but we do look for professional, polished work even in handwritten submissions. Poets should have something to say about matters other than the moon. We like to see strong **traditional pieces as well as the contemporary and experimental. And neatness *does* count.**" Subscriptions to *Amelia* are $25/year. Fred Raborg edits this publication out of love and sometimes suffers delays at the printer's, complaints about delays, etc. On the plus side, he responds to submissions in a timely manner and pays promptly (how many editors can claim that?), but the process of publication—from time of acceptance to appearance—can be slow. Nonetheless, *Amelia* is highly recommended because it includes so many voices and styles. Its editor reads all work closely and often encourages writers. *Cicada* is a quarterly magazine that publishes **haiku, senryu and other Japanese forms**, plus essays on the form—techniques and history—as well as fiction which in some way incorporates haiku or Japanese poetry in its plot, and reviews of books pertaining to Japan and its poetry or collections of haiku. Among poets published are Roger Ishii, H.F. Noyes, Knute Skinner, Katherine Machan

Aal, Ryah Tumarkin Goodman and Ryokufu Ishizaki. These sample lines are by Hugh Finn of Zimbabwe:

> *Its green enquiry*
> *Welcomed, the bean lifts luggage*
> *Into warm summer.*

They are receptive to experimental forms as well as the traditional. "Try to avoid still-life as haiku; strive for the *whole* of an emotion, whether minuscule or panoramic. Erotica is fine; the Japanese are great lovers of the erotic." The magazine is offset on high quality paper, with a circulation of 600, with 432 subscriptions of which 26 are libraries. Subscription: $14/year. Sample: $4.50 postpaid. Submit 3-10 haiku or poems, photocopies OK, dot-matrix acceptable but discouraged, no simultaneous submissions. Reports in 2 weeks. No payment, except three "best of issue" poets each receive $10 on publication plus copy. "I try to make some comment on returned poems always." *SPSM&H* is a quarterly magazine that publishes only sonnets, sonnet sequences, essays on the form—both technique and history—as well as romantic or Gothic fiction which, in some way, incorporates the form, and reviews of sonnet collections or collections containing a substantial number of sonnets. Among poets published are Margaret Ryan, Harold Witt, Sharon E. Martin, Rhina P. Espaillat and Robert Wolfkill. They are "receptive to experimental forms as well as the traditional, and appreciate wit when very good." Perhaps it may help to know the editor's favorite Shakespearean sonnet is #29, and he feels John Updike clarified the limits of experimentation with the form in his "Love Sonnet" from **Midpoint**. The magazine is offset on high quality paper, with a circulation of 600, for 432 subscribers and 26 libraries. Subscription: $14/year. Sample: $4 postpaid. Submit 3-5 poems, photocopies OK, dot-matrix acceptable but discouraged, no simultaneous submissions. Reports in 2 weeks. No payment, except two "best of issue" poets each receive $14 on publication plus copy. "I always try to comment on returns." The following annual contests have various entry fees: The Amelia Awards (six prizes of $200, $100, $50 plus three honorable mentions of $10 each); The Anna B. Janzen Prize for Romantic Poetry ($100, annual deadline January 2); The Bernice Jennings Traditional Poetry Award ($100, annual deadline January 2); The Georgie Starbuck Galbraith Light/Humorous Verse Prizes (six awards of $100, $50, $25 plus three honorable mentions of $5 each, annual deadline March 1); The Charles William Duke Longpoem Award ($100, annual deadline April 1); The Lucille Sandberg Haiku Awards (six awards of $100, $50, $25 plus three honorable mentions of $5 each, annual deadline April 1); The Grace Hines Narrative Poetry Award ($100, annual deadline May 1); The Amelia Chapbook Award ($250, book publication, 50 copies and 7½% royalty, annual deadline July 1); The Johanna B. Bourgoyne Poetry Prizes (six awards of $100, $50, $25, plus three honorable mentions of $5 each), The Douglas Manning Smith Epic/Heroic Poetry Prize ($100, annual deadline August 1); The Hildegarde Janzen Prize for Oriental Forms of Poetry (six awards of $50, $30, $20 and three honorable mentions of $5 each, annual deadline September 1); The Eugene Smith Prize For Sonnets (six awards of $140, $50, $25 and three honorable mentions of $5 each); The A&C Limerick Prizes (six awards of $50, $30, $20 and three honorable mentions of $5 each); The Montegue Wade Lyric Poetry Prize ($100, annual deadline November 1).

AMERICA; FOLEY POETRY CONTEST (II), 106 W. 56th St., New York NY 10019, phone (212)581-4640, founded 1909, poetry editor Patrick Samway, S. J., is a weekly journal of opinion published by the Jesuits of North America. They primarily publish articles on religious, social, political and cultural themes. They are "looking for imaginative poetry of all kinds. We have no restrictions on form or subject matter, though we prefer to receive poems of 35 lines or less." They have published poetry by Howard Nemerov, Fred Chappell, William Heyen and Eve Shelnutt. *America* is magazine-sized, 24 pgs., professionally printed on thin stock with thin paper cover, circulation 35,000. Subscription: $33. Sample: $1.25 postpaid. Pays $1.40/line plus 2 copies. Send SASE for excellent guidelines. Reports in 2 weeks. The annual Foley Poetry Contest offers a prize of $500, usually in late winter. Send SASE for rules. The editor says, "*America* is committed to publishing quality poetry as it has done for the past 80 years. We would encourage beginning and established poets to submit their poems to us."

AMERICAN ASSOCIATION OF HAIKUISTS NEWSLETTER (V); RED PAGODA (IV-Form); WALPURGIS NIGHT (IV-Horror), Dept. PM, 125 Taylor St., Jackson TN 38301, phone (901)427-7714. *RP* was founded in 1982, *AAH* and its newsletter in 1983, and *WN* in 1988, editor Lewis Sanders. *AAHN* and *RP* are both haiku publications. You may join the American Association of Haikuists for $10 and receive the newsletter, 10 or fewer pages on white paper of photocopied typescript stapled at the corner (1-2 a year). The editor says, "*American Association of Haikuists Newsletter* is not accepting *any* submissions this year. You may continue sending material for our other publications, however." *RP* is a journal that will consider "haiku, modern and traditional. Renga, tanka, heibun, senyru, linked poems, articles and book reviews on books and subjects dealing with haiku." The editor says, "I try to publish 4 times a year, but sometimes run late." They have published haiku by Alexis Rotella, John

J. Soldo and Elizabeth Lamb. *Red Pagoda* is digest-sized, 52 pgs., saddle-stapled, photocopied from various typescripts on bond paper with red paper cover. Subscription (4 issues) is $16 in the U.S. mailed first class; $24 outside the U.S. mailed airmail. Libraries receive a 10% discount on subscriptions. Checks should be made out to Henry L. Sanders. **You must buy a copy to see your work in print (price is $4/copy), but poets do not have to subscribe or purchase a copy to be published. Editor sometimes comments on rejections.** *WN*, a horror magazine, appears intermittently using: "gothic horror/modern horror/erotic vampire poetry not more than 2 pgs. in length (1-page poems preferred). Nothing obscene or pornographic." *WN* is newsletter format on colored paper. Sample: $4. Pays 1 copy. "Poets who are accepted do not have to purchase a copy to be published, but if they do I will give an extra copy. If this proves too costly, I will have to revert to simply charging per copy." Reports in 3 weeks. Editor comments on rejections "often."

AMERICAN ATHEIST PRESS; GUSTAV BROUKAL PRESS; AMERICAN ATHEIST (IV-Theme), P.O. Box 2117, Austin TX 78768-2117, phone (512)458-1244, founded 1958, editor R. Murray-O'Hair, publishes the monthly magazine with 30,000 circulation, *American Atheist*, and under various imprints some dozen books a year reflecting "concerns of Atheists, such as separation of state and church, civil liberties and atheist news." **Poetry is used primarily in the poetry section of the magazine. It must have "a particular slant to atheism, dealing with subjects such as the atheist lifestyle. Anticlerical poems and puns are more than liable to be rejected. Any form or style is acceptable. Preferred length is under 40 lines."** Poets they have published include Julia Rhodes Pozonzycki, Allan Case and Thomas A. Easton. Of their 17,000 subscriptions, 1,000 are libraries. The magazine-sized format is professionally printed, with art and photos, glossy, color cover; subscription, $25, single copy price $2.95, **sample: free.** They receive over 20-30 poetry submissions/week, use about 36/year. **Submit typed, double-spaced (photocopy, dot-matrix, simultaneous submissions OK). Time-dependent poems (such as winter) should be submitted 4 months in advance. Reports within 3-4 months. Pays "first-timers"** 10 copies or 6-month subscription or $12 credit voucher for AAP products. Thereafter, $15/poem plus 10 copies. **Buys one-time rights. Guidelines available for SASE, but a label is preferred to an envelope. Sometimes comments on rejected mss.** Reviews related books of poetry in 500-1,000 words. They do not normally publish poetry in book form but will consider it.

AMERICAN COLLEGIATE POETS (I, IV-Students/alumni, foreign languages), P.O. Box 44044-L, Los Angeles CA 90044, founded 1975, editor and manager Dr. Val. M. Churillo, offers 2 contests/year for poems up to 14-16 lines by anyone who is or has ever been a college student (whether graduate or not) desiring to have their work anthologized. Winners and entrants are published in $15 perfect-bound anthologies. There is an entry fee of $3 for the first, and $1 for each additional poem; cash prizes of $100, $50, $30, and 2 of $20. You may purchase copies at $15 each (none are given free to contestants). Foreign language poems welcome. Send SASE for rules.

THE AMERICAN COWBOY POET MAGAZINE (IV-Themes), Dept. PM, P.O. Box 326, Eagle ID 83616, phone (208)888-9838, founded 1988 as *The American Cowboy Poet Newspaper*, magazine format in January 1991, publisher/editor Rudy Gonzales. *ACPM* is a quarterly "about real cowboys" using **"authentic cowboy poetry. Must be clean—entertaining."** It publishes articles including "Featured Poet," stories of cowboy poetry gatherings and news of coming events. Subscription: $12/year, $15 Canada, $20 overseas. **Sample postpaid: $3. Send SASE for guidelines. Editor often comments on rejections.**

AMERICAN DANE (IV-Ethnic), 3717 Harney St., Omaha NE 68131-3844, phone (402)341-5049, founded 1916, editor Jennifer Denning-Kock, is the monthly magazine of the Danish Brotherhood in America, circulation 10,000, which uses **poetry with a Danish ethnic flavor. Sample: $1.50 postpaid. Send SASE for guidelines. Buys 1-3 poems/year. Pays $35 maximum plus 2 copies. Buys first rights only. Reports in 2 weeks, up to 1-year backlog. Simultaneous submissions OK. Reads submissions June 1 through September 1 only.** The magazine is 20-28 pgs., magazine-sized. Subscription: $12.

AMERICAN KNIGHT; PAISLEY VOICES POETRY COMPETITION (I), Rt. 1, Box 274, South Haven MN 55382-9727, founded 1989, editor Nancy Morín, is a quarterly publishing **poetry by those who contribute poetry or subscribe. "Open-minded acceptance; we prefer poetry with reflective insight and that which encourages the reader to release the limitations of physical and emotional perception. Nothing trite, no 'mushy-love' rhymes."** They have recently published poetry by Andy Roman, T.N. Turner and Clebo Rainey. These sample lines are the editor's:

> *In some rites*
> *you can find*
> *the sweat of 'flow'*
> *and the sweat of vanity.*
> *Yes, I'd rather be the initiate;*
> *never, never the mystic slave.*

The editor says, "To make a living in America today is quite a rare thing. *AK* has been developed for poets and poetry. It is here to give those who love the excitement of seeing their work in print and knowing that their poetry is being read by others, a chance to reach and enhance a broader audience. **Never hold back for rhyming reasons. This can be a great blockade when trying to get a point across to readers. This is a nonprofit quarterly written by the writers who contribute poetry or prose. Cost per issue: $2 plus 85¢ loose stamps. Donations are greatly appreciated however, and can be made to** *American Knight.*" The editor describes it as 11×17 folded at center, printed on 20 lb. or heavier paper, typed, with art on cover, more than 8 pgs. **Sample postpaid: $2.50. Send SASE for guidelines. Pays "at least 1" copy but requests 95¢ postage to receive "pay" copy. Deadlines February 20, May 23, August 23, November 20 (yearly). Send up to 5 poems. Do not staple. Reports in 3-4 weeks.** The Paisley Voices Poetry Competition, held annually, is open to all poets, all forms and themes. Cash awards of $75, $50, $25, $15, $10 and 5 awards of $5 plus 15 honorable mentions. $5 entry fee for up to 5 poems, original, unpublished, 60-line limit. Deadline February 1 yearly, entries received after that date will be entered in the following year's competition. Send SASE for guidelines.

AMERICAN LITERARY REVIEW, A National Journal of Poems and Stories, University of North Texas Press, P.O. Box 13856, Denton TX 76203. Declined listing.

THE AMERICAN LITERARY REVIEW, 45 Thurston Rd., Newton MA 02164. Declined listing.

AMERICAN POETRY REVIEW (III), 1704 Walnut St., Philadelphia PA 19103, founded 1972, is probably the **most widely circulated (24,000 copies bimonthly) and best-known periodical devoted to poetry in the world.** Poetry editors are Stephen Berg, David Bonanno and Arthur Vogelsang, and they have **published most of the leading poets writing in English and many translations.** The poets include Gerald Stern, Brenda Hillman, John Ashbery, Norman Dubie, Marvin Bell, Galway Kinnell, James Dickey, Lucille Clifton and Tess Gallagher. *APR* is a newsprint tabloid with 15,000 subscriptions, of which 1,000 are libraries. **Sample and price per issue: $2.75.** They receive about 4,000 submissions/year, use 200. **Pays $1.25/line. Reports in 3 months, has 1-3 year backlog. No simultaneous submissions.** The magazine is also a major resource for opinion, reviews, theory, news and ads pertaining to poetry. Each year the editors award the Jerome J. Shestack Prizes of $1,000, $500 and $250 for the best poems, in their judgment, published in *APR*. This is a high-prestige tabloid that is also apt to take material, however occasionally, from a relative unknown. On the other hand, there are excellent poets who place regularly in top markets (*The New Yorker* et. al.) who cannot place here, which means that its editors have distinct tastes.

THE AMERICAN SCHOLAR (III), 1811 Q St. NW, Washington DC 20009, phone (202)265-3808, founded 1932, associate editor Sandra Costich, is an academic quarterly which **uses about 5 poems/ issue, pays $50 each. Buys first rights only.** Two-month response time. They have published poets such as Robert Pack, Alan Shapiro and Gregory Djanikian. As a sample we selected these lines from "Art and Worship" by Bruce Bawer:

> *If a sculpture, story, symphony,*
> *or some plain strain played on a violin*
> *seems to articulate a verity*
> *resoundingly, it is because it springs*
> *out of a kindred sensibility,*
> *soaring above the universal din*
> *to remind us all that we are kin*
> *with anyone whom song inspires to sing.*

"We would like to see poetry that develops an image, a thought or event, without the use of a single cliché or contrived archaism. The most hackneyed subject matter is self-conscious love; the most tired verse is iambic pentameter with rhyming endings. The usual length of our poems is 30 lines. From 1-4 poems may be submitted at one time; *no more* **for a careful reading."** Study before submitting (sample: $5.75, guidelines available for SASE).

AMERICAN TOLKIEN SOCIETY; MINAS TIRITH EVENING STAR; W.W. PUBLICATIONS (IV-Themes), P.O. Box 373, Highland MI 48357-0373, phone (313)887-4703, founded 1967, editor Philip W. Helms. There are special poetry issues. Membership in the ATS is open to all, regardless of country of residence, and entitles one to receive the journal. Dues are $5 per annum to addresses in US and $10 elsewhere. Their magazines and chapbooks use **poetry of fantasy about Middle-Earth and Tolkien.** They have published poetry by Thomas M. Egan, Anne Etkin, Nancy Pope and Martha Benedict. *Minas Tirith Evening Star* is magazine-sized, offset from typescript with cartoon-like b&w graphics. **Pays contributor's copies.** They have a press run of 400 for 350 subscribers of which 10% are libraries. Single copy: $3.50; subscription: $5. **Sample postpaid: $1.50. Send SASE for guidelines. Prefer photo-**

copies. No simultaneous submissions; previously published poems "maybe." Reports in 2 weeks. Editor sometimes comments on rejections. Reviews related books of poetry; length depends on the volume, "a sentence to several pages." Under imprint of W.W. Publications they publish collections of poetry 50-100 pgs. **For book or chapbook consideration, submit sample poems. Publishes 2 chapbooks/year.** They sometimes sponsor contests.

‡**THE AMERICAN VOICE (II)**, 332 W. Broadway, Louisville KY 40202, phone (502)562-0045, founded 1985, editor Frederick Smock, is a literary quarterly publishing North and South American writers. They prefer **free verse, avant-garde.** They have recently published poetry by Olga Broumas, Odysseus Elytis, Cheryl Clarke, Marge Piercy and Ernesto Cardenal. As a sample here is one stanza of a long poem, "Mother's Day at the Air Force Museum," by George Ella Lyon:

> *My son loves the machine guns.*
> *He looks through a sight,*
> *he strafes the still air.*
> *At home, his Lego men*
> *die smiling.*

TAV is elegantly printed, flat-spined, 140+ pgs. of high-quality stock with matte card cover printed in silver, circulation 2,000 with 800 subscriptions of which 100 are libraries. Subscription: $12/year. Sample postpaid: $5. Pays $150/poem and 2 copies. (They pay $75 to translator of a poem.) Reports in 6 weeks, has a 3-month backlog. No simultaneous submissions; photocopy and dot-matrix OK. Occasionally comments on rejections.

AMERICAN WRITING: A MAGAZINE; NIERIKA EDITIONS (II), 4343 Manayunk Ave., Philadelphia PA 19128, phone (215)483-7051, founded 1990, editor Alexandra Grilikhes, appears twice a year using "**innovative work, strong imagery; interested in the voice of the loner. No cerebral, academic poetry.**" They have published poetry by Ivan Argüelles, Nico Vassilakis, Charles Fishman, John M. Bennett and Portia Wright. As a sample the editor selected these lines from "The Snake" by Ruth L. Schwartz:

> *I want both of you*
> *to rub my skin to fire,*
> *the gray sparked into orange, stroked*
> *like magic back to blue,*
> *the bark as it sheds*
> *its burning strips, peels*
> *itself like fingers arms and legs*
> *hissing in every flaming limb*

AW is digest-sized, flat-spined, 70+ pgs., professionally printed, with matte card cover. Press run 1,000 for 100 subscriptions in their first year. Subscription: $8. **Sample postpaid: $5. Guidelines on subscription form. Reporting time varies. "If it's a 'possible,' we may keep it 3 months."** Pays 2 copies/accepted submission group. The editor says, "Many magazines print the work of the same authors [the big names] who often publish 'lesser' works that way. *AW* is interested in the work itself, its particular strength and energy, rather than in the long lists of credits. We like to know *something* about the authors, however."

THE AMICUS JOURNAL (V), Dept. PM, 40 W. 20th St., New York NY 10011, phone (212)727-2700, poetry editor Francesca Lyman, is the **journal of the Natural Resources Defense Council, a quarterly with a circulation of about 60,000, which pays $25/poem.** The poetry is "nature based, but *not* 'nature poetry.' " They are not currently accepting submissions "because our cup runneth over with poetry." They have used poems by some of the best known poets in the country, including David Wagoner, Gary Snyder, David Ignatow, Marvin Bell and William Stafford. *The Amicus Journal* is finely-printed, saddle-stapled, on high quality paper with glossy cover, using much art, photography and cartoons. **Free sample for SASE.**

ANACONDA PRESS (II), Submit to the editor closest to you: editor-in-chief Andy Lowry, P.O. Box 146227, Chicago IL 60614; West Coast associate editor Bayla Winters, 2700 Scott Rd., Burbank CA 91504; Midwest associate editor Beij Beltrisi, P.O. Box 445, Richmond IN 47375-0445. They publish 2-6 poetry chapbooks and 1 annual anthology. "**We're looking for daring, vibrant, eccentric works. Please no academia.**" Reports in 4-6 weeks. Submit maximum of 5 poems. Pays 1-2 copies. Rights revert to authors. Write for most recent announcement of upcoming anthologies. They also publish *fuel*, a mini-magazine of poetry and art. **Submissions open.**

ANALECTA (IV-Students), Liberal Arts Council, FAC 19, University of Texas, Austin TX 78712, phone (512)471-6563, founded 1974, editor Isabel Ramírez, is an annual of literary works and photography by **college/university students and graduate students chosen in an annual contest**, a 150-page magazine, glossy plates for interior artwork in b&w, 7×10, flat-spined, soft cover. **No restrictions on**

type; limited to 5 poems/submission. Deadline is in mid-October; write for specifics. Submissions cannot be returned. "Our purpose is to provide a forum for excellent student writing. Works must be previously unpublished." Of about 800 submissions received, they publish about 40. Press run 800 for 700 subscribers, 100 shelf sales. **Sample postpaid: $7.50. Send SASE for guidelines. Prizes in each category. Pays 1 copy and monetary prizes vary. Entries must be typed; name should appear on cover sheet only.** As a sample, the editor selected this excerpt from "A Car" by Eric Rasmussen:

> *This car is mine.*
>
> *I drive it naked, drive it fat;*
> *Drive it crooked with my shoes off,*
> *Baking my feet on the hot pedals.*

THE AND REVIEW; MID-OHIO CHAPBOOK PRIZE (II), 10485 Iams Rd., Plain City OH 43064, founded 1987, publishes one double-issue a year. **They are "open to all forms and styles, but prefer shorter, imagistic poems. No self-indulgent first attempts."** They have recently published poetry by J.B. Goodenough, Diane Glancy and William Matthews. As a sample the editors selected these lines from "Inside the Trackhoe" by Peter Blair:

> *Calling it* hillside *can't convey the soil*
> *with twisted roots and bark, and dead*
> *mud snakes mashed in dozer treads.*

Their press run is 500 with 200 subscriptions of which 10 are libraries. The magazine consists of "all poetry with one or two reviews of new books of poetry. We also feature in each issue an author reviewing his/her own book." It is digest-sized, professionally printed with a matte card cover, using b&w photos and ink drawings. No ads. **They receive 4,000 poems annually and publish 50-55.** Subscription: $5. **Sample: $5 postpaid. Pays 1 copy. Acquires first rights. Reports in 1 month. Guidelines available for SASE.** Reviews books of poetry in 500 words, single format. The Mid-Ohio Chapbook Prize is awarded annually to the best 2 chapbooks of 15-20 pages received between April and June and between October and December. A $10 reading fee is required for entry. Winning manuscripts are published in a special supplement within the magazine. Each author receives 25 copies of the magazine. **Editor sometimes comments on rejections.** The editors pass on Marvin Bell's advice, "Making the simple complicated is commonplace; making the complicated simple, awesomely simple, that's creativity."

‡ANHINGA PRESS; ANHINGA PRIZE; CYNTHIA CAHN MEMORIAL PRIZE (II), P.O. Box 10595, Tallahassee FL 32302-0595, phone (904)575-5592, founded 1972, poetry editors Rick Campbell and Van Brock, publishes **"books, chapbooks and anthologies of poetry. We also offer the Anhinga Prize for poetry—$500 and publication—for a book-length manuscript each year. We want to see contemporary poetry which respects language. We're inclined toward poetry that is not obscure, that can be understood by any literate audience." Considers simultaneous submissions.** They have recently published poetry by Sherry Rind, Yvonne Sapia, Judith Kitchen, Ricardo Pau-Llosa, Robert J. Levy, Michael Mott, Rick Lott, Will Wells, Gary Corseri, Julianne Seeman, Nick Bozanic, Jean Monahan and P.V. LeForge. As a sample the editors selected these lines from **The Secret Life of Moles:**

> *The sun migrates across whatever scenes*
> *death can spare:*
> *and we have many of these small reprieves*
> *living within us.*
> *When we die, will life stop again?*
> *And for whom?*

Send SASE for rules (submissions accepted in January) of the Anhinga Prize for poetry, which requires an entry fee, for which all contestants receive a copy of the winning book. The contest has been judged by such distinguished poets as William Stafford, Louis Simpson, Henry Taylor, Hayden Carruth and Denise Levertov. A sample chapbook will be mailed for $3. Send a "business size" SASE for catalog and contest information. **"We do not read manuscripts except those entered in our competition."** The Cynthia Cahn Memorial Prize is for the best single poem previously unpublished and submitted during September. Entry fee $3/poem, $5 for 2 poems, $10 for 5 poems (5 poem limit). Send SASE for further guidelines, responses, name of winner.

ANIMA: THE JOURNAL OF HUMAN EXPERIENCE (II, IV-Women/Feminism), 1053 Wilson Ave., Chambersburg PA 17201, founded 1974, editor Barbara Rotz. *Anima* "celebrates the wholistic vision that emerges from thoughtful and imaginative encounters with the differences between woman and man, East and West, yin and yang—*anima* and *animus*. **Written largely by and about women** who are pondering new experiences of themselves and our world, this equinoctial journal welcomes contributions, verbal and visual, from the known and unknown. We publish very few poems, but they are carefully selected. **We are not interested in simply private experiences. Poetry must communicate.**

Advise all would-be poets to study the kinds of things we do publish. No restrictions on length, form, or such matters." There are 5-10 pages of poetry in each semiannual issue of the elegantly-printed and illustrated 8½" square, glossy-covered magazine, 1,000 subscriptions of which 150 are libraries. Price per issue: $5.95. **Sample: $3.95. Slow reporting—sometimes 3-6 months. Payment is offprints with covers.**

ANIMAL TALES; HOLIDAY WRITING CONTEST (I, IV-Themes), P.O. Box 2220, Payson AZ 85547, founded 1989, editor Berta I. Pickett, appears every other month, using **"light verse and traditional poems about animals and the people who love them."** It is 32 pgs., saddle-stapled, magazine-sized. Press run 400 for 350 subscribers. Subscription: $19.95. **Sample postpaid: $4.95. Send SASE for guidelines. Pays $5-20 and 1 copy. Buys first rights. Reports in 6-8 weeks.** Holiday Writing Contests are offered occasionally for animal stories with Thanksgiving or Christmas themes, with a prize of $25, entry fee $5/poem.

ANJOU (V), P.O. Box 322 Station P., Toronto, Ontario M5S 2S8 Canada, founded 1980, edited by Richard Lush and Roger Greenwald, publishes broadsides of poetry. **"We do not wish to receive submissions because we publish only by solicitation."**

ANSUDA PUBLICATIONS; THE PUB (II), P.O. Box 158JA, Harris IA 51345, founded 1978, "is a small press operation, publishing independently of outside influences, such as grants, donations, awards, etc. Our operating capital comes from magazine and book sales only." Their magazine *The Pub* "uses some poetry, and we also publish separate chapbooks of individual poets. We **prefer poems with a social slant and originality—we do *not* want love poems, personal poems that can only be understood by the poet, or anything from the haiku family of poem styles. No limits on length, though very short poems lack the depth we seek—no limits on form or style, but rhyme and meter must make sense. Too many poets write senseless rhymes using the first words to pop into their heads. As a result, we prefer blank and free verse."** They have recently published Michael Estabrook, Meeta Bharat Gajjar and Terry Everton. They offer no sample because "most of our poems are at least 25-30 lines long and every line complements all other lines, so it is hard to pick out only four lines to illustrate." *The Pub*, which appears irregularly (1-3 times a year) is a low-budget publication, digest-sized, mimeographed on inexpensive paper, making it possible to print 80 or more pages and sell copies for $3 (the price of a sample). Its minimum print-run is 300 for 130 subscriptions, of which 7 are libraries. Each issue has 3-12 pages of poetry, but **"we would publish more if we had it; our readers would like more poetry."** Everything accepted goes into the next issue, so there is no backlog. **Reports immediately to 1 month. Pays 2 copies. Acquires first rights. Guidelines available for SASE.** They also publish 1-2 chapbooks (24-28 pgs.)/year. For these, query with 3-6 sample poems. "We are *not* interested in past credits, who you studied under, etc. Names mean nothing to us and we have found that small press is so large that big names in one circle are unknown in another circle. In fact, **we get better material from the unknowns who have nothing to brag about (usually)."** Replies to queries immediately, reports in 1-2 months on submissions, no dot-matrix, simultaneous submissions only if clearly indicated. Pays royalties plus 5 copies for chapbooks. Daniel Betz adds, "About all I have left to say is to tell the novice to keep sending his work out. It won't get published in a desk drawer. There are so many little mags out there that eventually you'll find homes for your poems. Yes, some poets get published on their first few tries, but I've made first acceptances to some who have been submitting for 5 to 10 years with no luck, until their poem and my mag just seemed to click. It just takes time and lots of patience."

ANT FARM (V-Form), P.O. Box 15513, Santa Fe NM 87506-5513, founded 1990, editor Kate Bremer, appears twice a year publishing **poems of 4 lines or less, "immediate, impactful, available," not "ungrounded spiritual, philosophical stuff, poems about relationships that have ended, limericks or clever, cute poems. She is currently not accepting submissions "due to the overwhelming and unmanageable volume of mail."** They have published poetry by Joan Logghe, Diane Randolph and Miriam Sagan. As a sample the editor selected this complete poem, "Connections," by Mary McGinnis:

> the dead bird from your dream
> leaves feathers for our fence.

It is 4×5 professionally printed with matte card cover, press run 300. **Sample: $3. Reports in up to 6 months. Editor comments "sometimes." Pays 1 copy.**

ANTAEUS; THE ECCO PRESS (II), 100 W. Broad St., Hopewell NJ 08525, phone (609)466-4748, editor-in-chief Daniel Halpern. *Antaeus* is a semiannual that has published poetry by many of our major poets, such as Czeslaw Milosz, Paul Bowles, Robert Hass, Louise Gluck, Robert Pinsky, Seamus Heaney, Joyce Carol Oates, W.S. Merwin, James Merrill, Carolyn Forché, Mark Strand and Charles Simic. It is 275 pp., 6×9, offset, flat-spined, with 4-color cover. They have 7,000 subscribers. Subscription: $30. **Sample postpaid: $10. Send SASE for guidelines. Reports in 6-8 weeks. Pays $10/page.** The Ecco Press reports on mss in 2-3 months.

ANTHOLOGY OF MAGAZINE VERSE & YEARBOOK OF AMERICAN POETRY (III, IV-Anthology), % Monitor Book Company, P.O. Box 9078, Palm Springs CA 92263, phone (619)323-2270, founded 1950, editor Alan F. Pater. The annual **Anthology** is a selection of the **best poems published in American magazines during the year and is also a basic reference work for poets.** Alan F. Pater says, "We want poetry that is 'readable' and in any poetic form; we also want translations. **All material must first have appeared in magazines.** Any subject matter will be considered; we also would like to see some rhyme and meter, preferably sonnets." They have published poetry by Margaret Atwood, Stanley Kunitz, Robert Penn Warren, Richard Wilbur, Maxine Kumin and John Updike. Indeed, the anthology is a good annual guide to the best poets actively publishing in any given year. For the most part selections are made by the editor from magazines, but some poets are solicited for their work which has been in magazines in a given year.

ANTIETAM REVIEW (IV-Regional), Washington County Arts Council, Bryan Center, 3rd Floor, 82 W. Washington St., Hagerstown MD 21740, an annual founded 1981, poetry editors Crystal Brown and Ann Knox, looks for **"well-crafted literary quality poems. We discourage inspirational verse, haiku, doggerel." Uses poets only from the states of Maryland, Pennsylvania, Virginia, West Virginia, Delaware and District of Columbia. Needs 18 poems/issue, up to 30 lines each.** Poets they have recently published include Sharon Negri, Naomi Thiers and Eleanor Ross Taylor. The editor chose this sample from "Granite Wings Over Harper's Ferry" by Beth George:

> *Montana Eleanor, beloved only child,*
> *died at age four, the epitaph says —*
> *over one hundred years ago.*
> *Her angel holds fresh lilies,*
> *the orange petal shocking streaks*
> *on granite fingers and dark grey sky.*

AR is 48 pgs., 8½×11, saddle-stapled, glossy paper with glossy card cover and b&w photos throughout. Press run is 1,000. **Sample: $3 back issue, $5 current postpaid. Do not submit mss from April through September. "We read from October 1 through March 1 annually." Pays $20/ poem, depending on funding, plus 2 copies. Buys first North American serial rights.** The editors seem open to all styles of poetry, free and formal, as long as the author is from the designated region. Overall, a good read; but poems have to compete with prose. Ones used, however, are featured in attractive boxes on the page.

THE ANTIGONISH REVIEW (II), St. Francis Xavier University, Antigonish, Nova Scotia B2G 1C0 Canada, phone (902)867-3962, FAX (902)867-5153, founded 1970, editor George Sanderson, poetry editor Peter Sanger. This high-quality quarterly "tries to produce the kind of literary and visual mosaic that the modern sensibility requires or would respond to." They want poetry **not over "80 lines, i.e., 2 pgs.; subject matter can be anything, the style is traditional, modern or post-modern limited by typographic resources. Purpose is not an issue."** No "erotica, scatalogical verse, excessive propaganda toward a certain subject." They have published poetry by Milton Acorn, Andy Wainwright, Janice Kulyk-Keefer, M. Travis Lane and Douglas Lochhead. *TAR* is flat-spined, 6×9, 150 pgs. with glossy card cover, offset printing, using "in-house graphics and cover art, no ads." They accept about 10% of some 2,500 submissions/year. Press run is 1,100 for 800 subscriptions. Subscription: $18. **Sample postpaid: $3. Pays 2 copies. No simultaneous submissions or previously published poems.** Editor "sometimes" comments on rejections. The poetry editor advises, "The time for free verse form is exhausting itself as a technical possibility. **We are sympathetic to poets working with strong rhythmic patterns.** Poets will have to return to the traditional devices of rhythm, rhyme and manipulation of line length. Many more poets would and could be published if more of them were also readers of the full range of poetry in English, old and new. We are *not* responsible for return of submissions sent with improper postage. **Must include self-addressed stamped envelope (SASE) or International Reply Coupons (IRC) if outside Canada."**

THE ANTIOCH REVIEW (III), Box 148, Yellow Springs OH 45387, founded 1941, "is an independent quarterly of critical and creative thought . . . **For 45 years, now, creative authors, poets and thinkers have found a friendly reception . . . regardless of formal reputation."** Poetry editor: David St. John. "We get far more poetry than we can possibly accept, and the competition is keen. Here, where form and content are so inseparable and reaction is so personal, it is difficult to state requirements or limitations. Studying recent issues of *The Review* should be helpful. No 'light' or inspirational verse." Recently published poets: Ralph Angel, Jorie Graham, Mark Strand, Karen Fish, Michael Collier and Andrew Hudgins. Circulation is primarily to their 4,000 subscribers, of which half are libraries. They receive about 3,000 submissions/year, publish 20 pages of poetry in each issue, have about a 6-month backlog. Subscription: $25. **Sample: $5.50. Reads submissions September 1 through May 15 only. Pays $15/published page plus 2 copies. General guidelines for contributors available for SASE. Reports in 6-8 weeks.** Reviews books of poetry in 300 words, single format. In sum, a tough market to crack, and when you crack it, you get no special treatment thereafter. As David St. John says, "I have a policy of publishing a poet only once during my tenure as poetry editor. It may be a dumb policy, but it's one way to help keep the magazine open to new folks. I'd like to think that there's at least one place where new poets feel they have a shot."

‡ANTIPODES (IV-Regional), 8 Big Island, Warwick NY 10990, founded 1987, poetry editor Paul Kane, is a biannual of Australian poetry and fiction and criticism and reviews of Australian writing. They want **work from Australian poets only. No restrictions as to form, length, subject matter or style.** They have recently published poetry by A.D. Hope, Judith Wright and John Tranter. As a sample the editor selected these lines from "Poetry and Religion" by Les Murray:

> *Religions are poems. They concert*
> *our daylight and dreaming mind, our*
> *emotions, instinct, breath and native gesture*
> *into the only whole thinking: poetry*

The editor says *Antipodes* is 180 pgs., 8½×11, perfect-bound, with graphics, ads and photos. They receive about 500 submissions a year, accept approximately 10%. Press run is 500 for 200 subscribers. Subscription: $20. **Sample postpaid: $17. No previously published poems or simultaneous submissions. Cover letter required. They editor says they "prefer photocopies which do not have to be returned." Seldom comments on rejections. Reports in 2 months. Pays 1 copy. Acquires first North American serial rights.** Reviews books of poetry in 500-1,500 words.

‡ANTIPOETRY AND THE CORRUPTION OF MUSE (II), P.O. Box 2043, Montgomery AL 36102-2043, founded 1992, editor Jake Stohlm, is a biannual mini literary magazine. They want, **"poetry that many would feel is a perverted form of creative writing and poetry that escapes the realm of the physical. We don't want to see poetry about pretty flowers blooming or about people falling in love."** They have recently published poetry by Blacky Hix and Bill Shields. As a sample the editor selected these lines from "Eyes Pulled Down Part 2" by Kevin Redlake:

> *Have you said your prayers today?*
> *Have you wiped your tears away?*
> *Your dad has seen them falling down*
> *On an angel's time streaked gown*
> *While hurt in hell the bluebirds fell;*
> *As death slept and black flames wept.*

It is digest-sized, saddle-stapled, with card cover, number of pages varies. Press run is 500. Subscription: $5. **Sample postpaid: $4. No previously published poems or simultaneous submissions. Reads submissions November through March only. Time between acceptance and publication is 2 months. Often comments on rejections. Reports in 2-3 weeks. Pays 1-2 copies. Acquires first North American serial rights.**

ANYTHING THAT MOVES: BEYOND THE MYTHS OF BISEXUALITY (IV-Specialized, themes), #24, 2404 California St., San Francisco CA 94115, phone (415)564-2226 (BABN), founded 1991, attention fiction/poetry editor, managing editor Karla Rossi. This quarterly uses **"material only considered from those who consider themselves bisexual, whether they identify as such or not. Pen names are permissible with written notification, however author's real name and address must accompany submission (not to be published). Submissions need not address bisexuality specifically, but may be on topics/ themes/subjects of interest to bisexuals. Special consideration given to people of color, those differently abled, those living with HIV disease or AIDS, and those whose work has been denied/censored/erased in mainstream literary communities and publications."** As a sample here are these lines from a poem appearing in *ATM*:

> *No longer coward, traitor to the cause,*
> *I walked Fifth Avenue with them today.*
> *Unpunished by the prejudicial laws,*
> *I wanted, still, to count as proud and gay.*

It is professionally printed, magazine-sized with glossy paper cover, 64 pgs. saddle-stapled. Press run 5,000 for 1,000 subscribers of which 100 are libraries, 3,000 shelf sales. Subscription: $25. **Sample postpaid: $10. Reports in 6-8 weeks. Pays 2 copies. No comments on rejections. "Accepted material cannot be returned. Do not send original copy. Shorter poems are more likely to be accepted. Notification of use will be in the form of 2-copy payment, although notification of acceptance will be given 6-8 weeks upon receipt of submission.** *ATM* is published by the Bay Area Bisexual Network (BABN), a nonprofit institution and is distributed nationally, with a small international distribution."

‡APPALACHIA (II, IV-Nature), 5 Joy St., Boston MA 02108, phone (617)523-0636, founded 1876, poetry editor Parkman Howe, editor-in-chief Sandy Stott, is a "semiannual journal of mountaineering and conservation which describes activities outdoors and asks questions of an ecological nature." They

want poetry relating to the outdoors and nature—specifically weather, mountains, rivers, lakes, woods and animals. "No conquerors' odes." They have recently published poetry by Reg Saner, Macklin Smith, Glenda Cassutt, Mary Oliver and Justin Askins. The editor says it is 160 pgs., 6×9, professionally printed with color cover, using photos, graphics and a few ads. They receive about 200 poems a year, use 10-15. Press run is 10,000. Subscription: $10/year. **Sample postpaid: $5. No previously published poems or simultaneous submissions. Cover letter required. Submit maximum of 6 poems. "We favor shorter poems—maximum of 36 lines usually."** Time between acceptance and publication is 1 year. Seldom comments on rejections. **Send SASE for guidelines. Reports in 4-6 weeks. Pays 1 copy. Acquires first rights.** Reviews "some" books of poetry in 200-400 words, usually single format. Offers an annual award, The Appalachia Poetry Prize, given since 1972. The editor says, "Our readership is very well versed in the outdoors—mountains, rivers, lakes, animals. We look for poetry that helps readers see the natural world in fresh ways."

APPALACHIAN HERITAGE (IV-Regional), Hutchins Library, Berea College, Berea KY 40404, phone (606)986-9341, ext. 5260, FAX (606)986-9494, founded 1973, editor Sidney Saylor Farr, a literary quarterly with Southern Appalachian emphasis. The journal publishes several poems in each issue, and the editor wants to see **"poems about people, places, the human condition, etc., with Southern Appalachian settings. No style restrictions but poems should have a maximum of 25 lines, prefer 10-15 lines."** She does not want "blood and gore, hell-fire and damnation, or biased poetry about race or religion." She has published poetry by Jim Wayne Miller, Louise McNeill and Bettie Sellers. The flat-spined magazine is 6×9, professionally printed on white stock with b&w line drawings and photos, glossy white card cover with four-color illustration. **Sample copy: $5. Contributors should type poems one to a page, simultaneous submissions are OK, and mss are reported on in 2-4 weeks. Pays 3 copies. Acquires first rights.** Reviews books of poetry.

APPLEZABA PRESS (II), P.O. Box 4134, Long Beach CA 90804, founded 1977, poetry editor D. H. Lloyd, is "dedicated to publishing modern poetry and distributing to the national market." They publish both chapbooks and flat-spined collections of individual poets and occasional anthologies, about 3 titles/year. **"As a rule we like 'accessible' poetry, some experimental. We do not want to see traditional."** They have published poetry by Leo Mailman, Gerald Locklin, John Yamrus, Toby Lurie and Nichola Manning. These sample lines are from Lyn Lifshin's "Kent State 1970":

> The ROTC building
> still smoking
> the Guard moved in, feet on the
> grass. By
> Monday just
> after noon sirens Blood sinking into warm
> ground. Parents picking up phones
> that burned
> their hands

No query. Submit book ms with brief cover letter mentioning other publications and bio. Reports in 3 months. Simultaneous submissions, photocopy OK, dot-matrix accepted but not preferred. Pays 8-12% royalties and 10 author's copies. Buys all rights, does not return them. Send SASE for catalog to order samples. The books are digest-sized, flat-spined paperbacks with glossy covers, sometimes with cartoon art, attractively printed.

APROPOS (I, IV-Subscribers), RD 4, Ashley Manor, Easton PA 18042, founded 1989, editor Ashley C. Anders, appears 6 times/year, and **publishes all poetry submitted by subscribers (subscription: $25/year)** except that judged by the editor to be pornographic or in poor taste. Each issue awards prizes of $50, $25 and $10. All poems are judged by subscribers. **Maximum length 46 lines. Sample: $3 postpaid. Simultaneous submissions and previously published poems OK. Send SASE for guidelines.** It is digest-sized, 57 pgs., plastic ring bound, with heavy stock cover, desktop published. As a sample, the editor selected her own "Simple Poem":

> If I can write a simple poem
> that makes somebody smile,
> or wipes away a teardrop,
> then my poem will be worthwhile.
>
> It need not win a trophy,
> for that would not mean as much,
> as knowing that my simple poem
> and someone's heart will touch.

Special contests for subscribers are offered throughout the year at no additional fee. Prizes of $25, $10 and $5.

AQUARIUS (II), Flat 10, Room A, 116 Sutherland Ave., Maida-Vale, London, W9, England, poetry editor Eddie Linden, is a literary biannual publishing quality poetry. **Payment is by arrangement. Sample: £3 or $10 US.** Subscription in US $50. The latest issue (19/20), guest edited by Hilary Davies, contains poetry, fictional prose, essays, interviews and reviews.

ARARAT (IV-Ethnic), 585 Saddle River Rd., Saddle Brook NJ 07662, phone (201)797-7600. Editor-in-Chief: Leo Hamalian. 80% freelance written. **Emphasizes Armenian life and culture for Americans of Armenian descent and Armenian immigrants. They do not want to see traditional, sentimental love poetry.** "Most are well-educated; some are Old World." Quarterly magazine. Circ. 2,400. Pays on publication. Publishes ms an average of 1 year after acceptance. Buys first North American serial rights and second (reprint) rights to material originally published elsewhere. Submit seasonal/holiday material at least 3 months in advance. Photocopied and previously published submissions OK. Computer printout submissions acceptable. Reports in 6 weeks. Sample copy $3 plus 4 first class stamps. Any verse that is Armenian in theme. Buys 6/issue. Pays $10.

‡ARC; CONFEDERATION POETS PRIZE (II), P.O. Box 7368, Ottawa, Ontario K1L 8E4 Canada, founded 1978, coeditors Nadine McInnis and John Barton, is a biannual of poetry, poetry-related articles, interviews and book reviews. **"Our tastes are eclectic. Our focus is Canadian, but we also publish writers from elsewhere."** They have recently published poetry by Anne Szumigalski, Heather Spears, Robert Preist and Erin Moure. The editors say *Arc* is 84-96 pgs., perfect-bound, with laminated 2-color cover, artwork and ads. They receive about 400 submissions a year, accept 40-50 poems. Press run is 580 for 200 subscribers of which 30 are libraries, 100 shelf sales. Single copy: $5 Canadian/US; subscription: $18 Canadian/US. **Cost of sample varies. No previously published poems or simultaneous submissions. Cover letter required. Submit 5-8 poems, single spaced, with name and address on each page. Send SASE for guidelines. Reports in 3-6 months. Pays $15 Canadian/page plus 2 copies. Buys first North American serial rights.** "We do not accept unsolicited book reviews." The Confederation Poets Prize is an annual award of $100 for the best poem published in *Arc*.

ARGONAUT (IV-Science fiction/fantasy), P.O. Box 4201, Austin TX 78765, founded 1972, editor/publisher Michael Ambrose, is an **"annual magazine anthology of science fiction and weird fantasy, illustrated." They want "speculative, weird, fantastic poetry with vivid imagery or theme, up to 30 lines. Prefer traditional forms. Nothing ultramodernistic, non-fantastic."** They have published poetry by Sardonyx, J.R. Ericson, Robert R. Medcalf, Jr. and Joey Froehlich. The editor describes it as 60 pgs., digest-sized, typeset. They accept 5-8 of 100-200 poems received. Press run: 300 for 50 subscriptions of which 3 are libraries. Subscription: $5. **Sample postpaid: $5. Send SASE for guidelines. Pays 2 copies. Submit no more than 5 poems at a time. Reports in 4-8 weeks. Editor comments on submissions "occasionally."** He says, "Too much of what I see is trite, limited in scope or language, and inappropriate for the themes of *Argonaut*. Poets should know what the particular market to which they submit is looking for and not simply shotgun their submissions."

‡ARIEL, A REVIEW OF INTERNATIONAL ENGLISH LITERATURE (III), English Dept., University of Calgary, Calgary, Alberta T2N 1N4 Canada, phone (403)220-4657, founded 1970, is a "critical, scholarly quarterly with about 5-8 pgs. of poetry in each issue," circulation 825, subscriptions of which 650 are libraries. As a sample here are lines from "Ecstasy!" by Fritz Hamilton:

> being the
> Jackson Pollock of
> poetry I

> dance over the paper in
> the street with
> my pen poised to

> pour my words of
> poetry onto
> the world &

Ariel is professionally printed, flat-spined, 100+ pp., digest-sized, with glossy card cover. Subscription: $22 institutions; $14 individuals. They receive about 300 freelance submissions of poetry per year, use 20-30. **Sample: $6 postpaid. Prefer 4-8 poems. No long poems. No simultaneous submissions. Reports in 4-6 weeks. Pays 10 offprints plus 1 copy. Editor comments on rejections, "only occasionally and not by request."**

‡ARIZONA LITERARY REVIEW (I, II), P.O. Box 2426, Prescott AZ 86302, phone (602)776-2848, founded 1991, publisher/editor Stephen Bruno, is a monthly literary publication "containing fiction, nonfiction, satire, interviews, short stories, essays, columns, departments, poetry photography and art (all aspects)." They want poems **3-30 lines in length. They do not want "subject matter that has violent and/or derogatory interpretations as applied to any specific group of people."** They have recently published poetry by Gabrielle Riddle, Laura Beeler Dodds and Anna Braga. As a sample they selected these lines from "Posthumous accolades":

> *Posthumous accolades; an enlightened path*
> *memories of possibilities*
> *remembrances of truths*
> *probable causes and definite results*
> *A heart attached with failing grip*
> *surrendering to inevitable retreat.*

It is 44 pgs., 11 × 14 on high quality recyclable newsprint, not bound. Press run is 25,000 for 5,000 subscribers, 20,000 shelf sales. Single copy: $1; subscription: $24. **Sample postpaid: $1.50. No previously published poems or simultaneous submissions. Often comments on rejections. Send SASE for guidelines. Reports in 4-10 weeks. Pays $5/poem plus 2-5 copies.**

‡**THE ARIZONA UNCONSERVATIVE (I)**, P.O. Box 23683, Tempe AZ 85285, founded 1991, poetry editor Christopher Ehren Hay, is "a monthly collection of poems, short fiction (less than 500 words), essays and articles relating to contemporary life." They want **"contemporary poetry — try to say something." They do not want "poetry that looks like it was written before this century."** The editor prefers not to include sample lines of poetry because "we'd really rather not limit anyone's idea of the range we are interested in." *AzUn* is 2 double-sided 8½ × 11 pages of recycled paper, photocopied and tri-folded, including one photo or cartoon. Press run is 250 for 200+ subscribers. Subscription: $1/month. **Sample postpaid: $1. "We would request that out-of-state submitters purchase a sample copy and all are strongly encouraged to subscribe because of untraditional format." Previously published poems and simultaneous submissions OK. Cover letter required.** Time between acceptance and publication is 2 months maximum. **Seldom comments on rejections. However "criticism will be provided with the purchase of a sample copy or subscription." Send SASE for guidelines. Reports in 1 month. Pays 7¢/ line. Buys one-time rights.** The editor says, "Say something that is important to you! Don't just write poetry the way you are told it should be. Write honestly and cut out all the triteness and clichés."

ARJUNA LIBRARY PRESS; JOURNAL OF REGIONAL CRITICISM (I, II), 1025 Garner St., Space 18, Colorado Springs CO 80905, library founded 1963, press founded 1979, editor Joseph A. Uphoff, Jr. "The Arjuna Library Press is avant garde, designed to endure the transient quarters and marginal funding of the literary phenomenon (as a tradition) while presenting a context for the development of current mathematical ideas in regard to theories of art and literature; photocopy printing allows for very limited editions and irregular format. Quality is maintained as an artistic materialist practice." He wants to see **"surrealist prose poetry, dreamlike, short and long works, not obscene, profane (will criticize but not publish), unpolished work."** He is currently publishing work by Simon Perchik, Brian Groth and Ron Ellis. As an example the editor has selected these lines from "The Ninth" by William Passera:

> *Inside earth heaven*
> *no one leaves . . .*
> *save the few*
> > *who jump*
> *clear fences*
> *never heard from again,*
> *except in night dreams*

JRC is published on loose photocopied pages of collage, writing and criticism, appearing frequently in a varied format. Press run: 1 copy each. **Pays "notification." Previously published poems and simultaneous submissions OK.** "I like ingenuity, legibility, convenience, polish. I expect some sympathy for mathematical, logical and philosophical exposition and criticism. These arguments remain our central ambition." Arjuna Library Press publishes 6-12 chapbooks/ year, averaging 50 pgs. **To submit to the press, send complete ms, cover letter including bio, publications, "any information the author feels is of value." The press pays royalties "by agreement, if we ever make a profit" and copies. Send 50¢ for sample.** Reviews books of poetry "occasionally." The editor says, "English is a representation that conveys its image or preconception by convention. Its idioms and metaphors may be subjunctive (fantasy) or code (governed by the ethics of irony), and we can only have foreknowledge by example. Teaching and learning English can involve ignorance or contempt, but a poverty of the intellect will result from such a philosophical refusal. Though we conceive of a writer's intent we can only agree with facts perceived, by whatever poetic means, as being legitimate."

THE ARK (V), Dept. PM, 35 Highland Ave., Cambridge MA 02139, phone (617)547-0852, founded 1970 (as BLEB), poetry editor Geoffrey Gardner, publishes books of poetry. **"We are unable to take on new projects at this time."** They have published poetry by David Budbill, John Haines, Joseph Bruchac, Elsa Gidlow, W.S. Merwin, Eliot Weinberger, Kathy Acker, George Woodcock, Kathleen Raine, Marge Piercy and Linda Hogan. The editor selected these lines by Kenneth Rexroth (a translation from the Sanskrit) as a sample:

> *You think this is a time of Shiva's waking*
> *You are wrong*
> *You are Shiva*
> *But you dream*

THE UNIVERSITY OF ARKANSAS PRESS; ARKANSAS POETRY AWARD (III), Fayetteville AR 72701, founded 1980, acquisitions editor Scot Danforth, publishes flat-spined paperbacks and hardback collections of individual poets. Miller Williams, director of the press, says, **"We are not interested in poetry that says, 'Guess what I mean' or 'Look what I know.' "** They have published poetry by Frank Stanford, Henri Coulette, Enid Shomer and John Ciardi. As a sample, here is the opening stanza of "The Good Sheriff" by Eric Nelson:

> *Just as we run out*
> *of hope and firewood*
> *spring suddenly shoots*
> *green bullets through.*

That's from his book **The Interpretation of Waking Life**, digest-sized, 81 pgs., flat-spined, elegantly printed on eggshell stock with matte 3-color card cover. **Query with 5-10 sample poems. Replies to query in 2 weeks, to submissions in 2-4 weeks. No replies without SASE. Ms should be double-spaced with 1½" margins. Clean photocopy OK. No dot-matrix unless letter quality. Discs compatible with IBM welcome. Pays: 10% royalty contract plus 10 author's copies. Send SASE for catalog to buy samples.** The Arkansas Poetry Award competition is open to any original ms by a living American poet whose work has not been previously published or accepted for publication in book form. Chapbooks, self-published books, and books produced with the author's subsidy are not considered previously published books. No translations. Submit 50-80 pgs., not more than one poem/page, counting title page in page count. An acknowledgments page listing poems previously published should accompany ms. Author's name should appear on the title page only. $10 reading fee. Postmark no later than May 1. Publication the following spring. A $500 cash advance is part of the award.

‡ARNAZELLA (II), Bellevue Community College, 3000 Landerholm Circle SE, Bellevue WA 98007-6484, phone (206)641-2341, established 1979, advisor Laura Burns, is a literary annual, published in spring, using **well-crafted poetry, no "jingles, greeting card" poetry.** They have published poetry by William Stafford, Judith Skillman and Coleen McElroy. The editor describes this student publication (which uses work from off campus) as 75 pgs., 6×8, offset, using photos and drawings. Of 150-200 poems received/year they use about 30. Press run 500 for 3 subscriptions, one of which is a library. **Sample: $5 postpaid. Send SASE for guidelines. Pays 1 copy. Submit up to 3 poems. Deadline is usually at beginning of February. Reports in 1-4 months.**

ARROWOOD BOOKS, INC. (II), P.O. Box 2100, Corvallis OR 97339, phone (503)753-9539, founded 1985, editor Lex Runciman, is a "small press publisher of quality literary works." He publishes sewn paperbacks and hardcover books, always on acid-free papers, 1-2/year, 60-80 pgs. Poets published include Anne Pitkin, Lisa Steinman and Madeline DeFrees. **Query first. Simultaneous submissions, photocopies, poems previously published in magazines all OK. Reports to queries in 3 weeks, on mss in 2 months. Pays royalties and advance.** He offers a 10% writer's discount (limit 1 copy) on samples. He advises, "Write well, and work hard to separate the act of writing from the fear of publishing (or not)."

‡ARS POETICA PRESS; PHOENIX (II), 1200 E. Ocean Blvd. #64, Long Beach CA 90802, phone (213)495-0925 (founded 1987). Publishers John Brander and Pia Ganguly publish "poetry anthologies and a poetry quarterly. The operation would also assist self-publishers to produce quality books. This part of the operation would be commercial but would not operate as a vanity press." At the time of responding John Brander had not fully determined the policies of Ars Poetica Press and the forthcoming literary journals. Send SASE for details.

 The double dagger before a listing indicates that the listing is new in this edition. New markets are often the most receptive to submissions.

ART TIMES: CULTURAL AND CREATIVE JOURNAL (II), P.O. Box 730, Mount Marion NY 12456-0730, phone (914)246-6944, editor Raymond J. Steiner, a monthly tabloid newspaper devoted to the arts that publishes some poetry and fiction. The editor wants to see **"traditional and contemporary poetry with high literary quality."** He does not want to see "poorly written, pointless prose in stanza format." He has published poetry by Helen Wolfert and Anne Mins. *Art Times* focuses on cultural and creative articles and essays. The paper is 16-20 pgs., on newsprint, with reproductions of artwork, some photos, advertisement-supported. Circulation is 15,000, of which 5,000 are by request and subscriptions; most distribution is free through galleries, theatres, etc. They receive 700-1,000 poems/month, use only 40-50 a year. Subscription is $15/year. **Sample: $1 postage cost. Guidelines available for SASE. They have a 2-year backlog. Pay is 6 free copies plus one year complimentary subscription. Submissions are reported on in 6 months. There is a 20-line limit for poetry. Simultaneous submissions OK. Typed mss should be submitted to the editor. Criticism of mss is provided "at times but rarely."**

ART-CORE! (I), P.O. Box 49324, Austin TX 78765, founded 1988, publisher/editor Patty Morales, is a quarterly **using poems of "one page or less, alternative, underground, off-beat, avant-garde, uncensored—typed or visual layout. Occasional theme or special subject issues. No mainstream or lengthy poems."** The editor describes it as 24 pgs., magazine-sized, offset. Press run 2,000 for 150 subscribers, 1,000 copies distributed free locally. They accept about 50 of 300 poems submitted/year. Subscription: $6. **Sample postpaid: $2.50. Send SASE for guidelines. Pays 1 copy. Responds within 3 months.** Patty Morales adds, "We are happy to announce *APEX*, a new poetry publication sponsored by Art-Core and Electric Lord Productions. Our premier issue will be a book of erotic poetry. Publication is planned annually. We are searching for a select group of poets and artists to participate. Interested parties should submit a short sample of their work and SASE."

ARTE PUBLICO PRESS; THE AMERICAS REVIEW (IV-Ethnic), University of Houston, Houston TX 77204-2090, founded 1972, editor Julian Olivares, publisher Nicolas Kanellos. (Note: *The Americas Review* is also the name of another magazine with a political focus published in Berkeley CA.) Each year the press publishes 20 books of fiction and 2 of poetry by **US Hispanic writers.** They have recently published books by Gary Soto, Ed Vega and Sandra Cisneros. *The Americas Review* is a triquarterly of fiction and poetry. The publisher says it is digest-sized, 120-200 pgs., flat-spined, circulation 3,000; 2,100 subscribers (of which 40% are libraries). **Pays a varying amount plus 5 copies. Reports in 4 months. No simultaneous submissions. Reads submissions September 1 through June 30 only.** Reviews books of poetry in 750-1,000 words, single format; in up to 2,000 words, multi-book. **For book publication, publish first in the magazine. They pay a $500 advance and 25 copies for book publication. Contract stipulates 40% reprint fee to press.**

ARTFUL DODGE (II, IV-Translations), Dept. of English, College of Wooster, Wooster OH 44691, founded 1979, poetry editor Daniel Bourne, is an annual literary magazine that "takes a strong interest in poets who are continually testing what they can get away with successfully in regard to subject, perspective, language, etc., but who also show mastery of current American poetic techniques—its varied textures and its achievement in the illumination of the particular. What all this boils down to is that we require high craftsmanship as well as a vision that goes beyond *one's own* storm windows, grandmothers or sexual fantasies—to paraphrase Hayden Carruth. **Poems can be on any subject, of any length, from any perspective, in any voice, but we don't want anything that does not connect with both the human and the aesthetic. Thus, we don't want cute, rococo surrealism, someone's warmed-up, left-over notion of an avant-garde that existed 10-100 years ago, or any last bastions of rhymed verse in the civilized world.** On the other hand, we are interested in poems that utilize stylistic persuasions both old and new to good effect. We are not afraid of poems which try to deal with large social, political, historical, and even philosophical questions—especially if the poem emerges from one's own life experience and is not the result of armchair pontificating. We often offer encouragement to writers whose work we find promising, but *Artful Dodge* **is more a journal for the already emerging writer than for the beginner looking for an easy place to publish. We also have a sustained commitment to translation, especially from Polish and other East European literatures,** and we feel the interchange between the American and foreign works on our pages is of great interest to our readers. We also feature interviews with such outstanding literary figures as Jorge Luis Borges, W.S. Merwin, Nathalie Sarraute, Stanislaw Baranczak, Omar Pound, Gwendolyn Brooks, John Giorno, William Least Heat-Moon, Cynthia Macdonald, Tim O'Brien, Lee Smith and William Matthews. Recent and forthcoming poets include Naomi Shihab Nye, Walter McDonald, Alberta Turner, David Ignatow, Jim Daniels, Peter Wild, William Stafford, Karl Krolow (German), Tomasz Jastrun (Polish), Mahmud Darwish (Palestinian) and Tibor Zalan (Hungarian)." There are about 60-80 pgs. of poetry in each issue, circulation 1,000 for 100 subscriptions of which 30 are libraries. They receive at least 2,000 poems/year, use 60, and the backlog is 1-12 months between acceptance and publication. **Sample: $5 for recent issues, $3 for others. "No simultaneous submissions but typed photocopies of any technological persuasion are OK. Please limit submissions to 6 poems. Long poems may be of any length, but send only one at a**

time. We encourage translations, but we ask as well for original text and statement from translator that he/she has copyright clearance and permission of author." Reports in up to 5 months. Pays 2 copies, plus, currently, at least $5 honorarium because of grants from Ohio Arts Council. The digest-sized, perfect-bound format is professionally printed, glossy cover, with art, ads.

ARTS END BOOKS; NOSTOC MAGAZINE (II), P.O. Box 162, Newton MA 02168, founded 1978, poetry editor Marshall Brooks. "We publish good contemporary writing. Our interests are broad and so are our tastes. People considering sending work to us should examine a copy of our magazine and/or our catalog; check your library for the former, send us a SASE for the latter." Their publications are distinguished by excellent presswork and art in a variety of formats: postcard series, posters, pamphlets, flat-spined paperbacks and hardbacks. The magazine appears irregularly in printruns of 300-500, about 30 pgs. of poetry in each, 100 subscriptions of which half are libraries. **Sample: $2.50 postpaid.** They receive a few hundred submissions per year, use 25-30; "**modest payment plus contributor's copies. A cover letter is a very good idea for any kind of submission;** we receive *very* few good, intelligent cover letters; what to include? That's up to the writer, whatever he/she feels important in terms of the work, in terms of establishing a meeting." **Tries to report within a few weeks, discourages simultaneous submissions, frequently comments on rejected mss.** Reviews books of poetry "on occasion, length varies." Brooks says, "We try to respond warmly to writers interested in making genuine contact with us and our audience."

ARTS INDIANA LITERARY SUPPLEMENT; POETRY ON THE BUSES (IV-Regional), Suite 701, 47 S. Pennsylvania St., Indianapolis IN 46204-3622. *Arts Indiana Literary Supplement* is an annual publication, 33 pgs., using poems and short stories **by residents of Indiana.** "Writers should send no more than 3 poems and/or one short story." Poems up to 40 lines. "New work will be given first consideration, but previously published work will be considered if the author has maintained copyright or can arrange written permission for re-publication." Simultaneous submissions OK if so noted. Payment $20 for each accepted poem (unpublished). One poem will receive a cash award of $500 in addition. Send SASE for guidelines. Deadline early March. *Poetry on the Buses* selects 12 poems to be printed on 11×28 placards and displayed inside METRO buses, a new poem each month. Open to poets 18 or older living within Marion and contiguous counties. Submit 4 copies of no more than 3 poems no longer than 17 lines, 81 spaces/line. Deadline late June. Send SASE for entry form.

ASCENT (II), P.O. Box 967, Urbana IL 61801, founded 1975, editor Audrey Curley, appears 3 times/year, using **poetry that is "eclectic, shorter rather than longer."** They have recently published poetry by E.M. Schorb and William Hathaway. As a sample the editor selected these lines from "A Blue Iris" by David Ray:

> Such profligate prosperity—a blue iris
> with pin tossed away, asprawl
> > in a wastebasket.
> The corpse lies waxen and the speech
> drones along with easy affection,
> > no loss of control.

The editor describes it as 6×9, 64 pgs., professionally printed with matte card cover. They accept about 5% of 750 poems received/year. Print run 900 copies for 250 subscribers of which 90 are libraries. Subscription $3/year. **Sample $2. Pays 3 copies.** Best buy in the lit world, and Audrey Curley is a fine editor with a good eye for detail. She says, "I am usually the sole reader. Poems are rejected or accepted from 2-8 weeks, usually closer to 2 weeks. Acceptances are usually published within the year."

THE ASHLAND POETRY PRESS (V, II, IV-Anthologies, themes), Ashland University, Ashland OH 44805, founded 1969, editor Robert McGovern, publishes anthologies on specific themes and occasional collections. He has published collections by Harold Witt, Alberta Turner and Richard Snyder. As a sample he selected lines from "Jacqueline Du Pré" by Leonard Trawick:

> Jacqueline du Pré, when your muscles came untuned,
> wasn't the music still there, all those silent years— —
> just as, after the last note, when players poise their bows
> triumphant for one still moment before the applause,
> the whole quartet hangs perfect in the air?

That poem appears in **80 on the 80's: A Decade's History in Verse** edited by Robert McGovern and Joan Baranow. "Watch publications such as *Poets & Writers* for calls for mss, but don't submit otherwise." On collections, poet gets 10% royalty; anthologies, poets are paid stipulated price when sufficient copies are sold. Write for book and price list. "We do not read unsolicited mss; anthology readings take quite a bit of time." Considers simultaneous submissions.

ASYLUM (II, IV-Form, translations), P.O. Box 6203, Santa Maria CA 93456, founded 1985, editor Greg Boyd, is "an annual literary anthology with emphasis on short fiction, **the prose poem and poetry. No restrictions on form, subject matter, style or purpose, though we are especially receptive to prose poems, absurdist writing and contemporary modes of surrealism and dada.**" They have recently published poetry by Thomas Wiloch, Russell Edson, Edouard Roditi and Robert Peters. As a sample, the editor selected these lines from "Twenty Shores" by Cynthia Hendershot:

> *I dream of a tree with razors*
> *instead of fruit. Every word*
> *that falls from your orange tongue*
> *falls on my palm like a drop of blood.*

Asylum is 128-160 pgs., 8½×11, perfect-bound, professionally printed with varnished coated stock cover. They accept about 1% of submissions. Print run 1,000 for 200 subscriptions of which 20 are libraries. Subscription: $10. **Sample postpaid: $7.95. Pays 3 copies. Acquires first North American serial rights. Put name and address on each page. No simultaneous submissions. Reports in 2 weeks-3 months.** Regarding reviews of books of poetry, "authors should query before submitting material."

ATALANTIK (IV-Ethnic, foreign language), 7630 Deercreek Dr., Worthington OH 43085, phone (614)885-0550, founded 1979, editor Prabhat K. Dutta, is a "literary quarterly **mainly in Bengali** and containing short stories, poems, essays, sketches, book reviews, interviews, cultural information, science articles, cinema/theater news, children's pages, serialized novels, etc., **with occasional English writings (non-religious, non-political.)**" They have published "all major poets of West Bengal, India (Sunil Gangopadhyay, Manas Roychoudhury, Santosh Chakrabarty, Surajit Ghosh, Dibyendu Palit, Krishna Dhar, Tanushree Bhattacharya, etc.) as well as of Bangladesh (Shamsur Rahaman, Begum Sufia Kamal, Abu Jafar Obeyadullah, Ashraf Siddique, Al Mahmood, Alam Khorshed, etc.)." As a sample the editor selected these lines from "Riddle" by Bijay Kumar Dutta:

> *It is like the medieval Search of alchemy*
> *To transmute base metals*
> *Into gold*
> *Is it not life's riddle, — of*
> *The Search for the means*
> *For transmutation of base emotions*
> *Into eternal love?*

"*Atalantik,* the first Bengali literary magazine in USA, was started to keep Bengali language alive to Bengalees in USA. Number of pages differ widely and average out to 60. Original printing by electric press in Calcutta, India; USA printing is by offset or photocopy and the number varies according to order; artwork both on the cover and inside the magazine." It is magazine-sized, flat-spined, with b&w matte card cover. The annual subscription is $20. Some copies are distributed free. **Sample: $6 postpaid. Send SASE for guidelines. Pays 1-2 copies. Simultaneous submissions and previously published poems OK. Reports in 1 month.** Reviews books of poetry in 200-2,000 words, single or multi-book format. "We are actively and seriously considering publishing books under 'Atalantik Publications.' " **For book consideration submit sample poems, cover letter with bio and publications. Simultaneous submissions, photocopies, dot-matrix OK. Pays "25 copies usually, may vary."** Editor sometimes comments on rejections. The operations of a smaller version of *Atalantik* are managed by Keshab Dutta, from 36B, Bakul Bagan Road, Calcutta-700025, India (phone 75-1620) for distribution in India.

THE ATLANTEAN PRESS REVIEW; THE ATLANTEAN PRESS (II, IV-Themes, translations), (formerly *The Romanticist*), 354 Tramway, Milpitas CA 95035, founded 1990, publisher Patricia LeChevalier. Atlantean Press was founded to publish Romantic fiction, drama and poetry, beginning with republication of work by Victor Hugo that is out-of-print. *The Atlantean Press Review*, published annually, includes a small amount of poetry as well as fiction, drama and essays. "**We are looking for intelligent, thoughtful poems that address human values and aspirations.**" *The Review* is approximately 200 pgs., 7½×7½, perfect-bound. **Sample: $10. Pays up to $2/line plus copies. Buys North American serial rights. Reads submissions August 15 through February 1 only. Send SASE for guidelines. Reports in 1 month. Often comments on rejections.** "We'd be very interested in competent translations of Victor Hugo's poetry."

THE ATLANTIC (II), 745 Boylston St., Boston MA 02116, phone (617)536-9500, founded 1857, poetry editor Peter Davison, publishes 1-5 poems monthly in the magazine. **Some of the most distinguished poetry in American literature** has been published by this magazine, including work by William Matthews, Mary Oliver, Stanley Kunitz, Rodney Jones, May Swenson, Galway Kinnell, Philip Levine, Red Hawk, Tess Gallagher, Donald Hall and W.S. Merwin. The magazine has a circulation of 500,000, of which 5,800 are libraries (**sample postpaid: $3**). They receive some 75,000 poems/year, of which they use 35-40 and have a backlog of 6-12 months. **Submit 3-5 poems with SASE, no dot-matrix, no simultaneous submissions. Pays about $3/line. Buys first North American serial rights only.** Peter Davison says he wants "to see poetry of the highest order; we do *not* want to see workshop rejects. Watch out for workshop uniformity. Beware of the present indicative. Be yourself."

THE ATLANTIC MONTHLY PRESS, 19 Union Square W., New York NY 10003. Declined listing.

ATLANTIS: A WOMEN'S STUDIES JOURNAL (IV-Feminist), Mount Saint Vincent University, Halifax, Nova Scotia B3M 2J6 Canada, phone (902)443-4450, ext. 319, founded 1975, editor Deborah Poff, managing editor Maurice Michaud or literary editor Margaret Harry, appears twice a year using **poetry "certainly no longer than 5 ms pgs.; should have a feminist perspective, preferably academic. No cutsie greeting-card poems about marshmallow women or by men without a hint of feminist consciousness."** They have recently published poetry by Liliane Welch. The editor describes it as magazine-sized, 150 pgs., flat-spined with card cover. They accept about 5-10% of submissions. Press run 1,000 with 600 subscribers of which 55% are libraries. Subscription: Canada $20; US $30 (Canadian). **Sample postpaid: $7.50 Canadian. Pays 1 copy. Reports in 6-12 weeks.**

ATTICUS REVIEW/PRESS (II, IV-Form), P.O. Box 927428, San Diego CA 92192, founded 1981, poetry editor H. Polkinhorn, is a "small press publisher of cut-up and experimental and visual/verbal work," publishing the magazine *Atticus Review*, chapbooks and flat-spined editions, wanting **"open form, open subject matter, experimental." They do not want to see traditional forms.** *Atticus Review* is magazine-sized, clipped on one side, glossy card cover, $4 a copy (plus $1 "transportation"). *AR* appears 2 times a year. They receive about 500 poems/year, 25-50 accepted. **Sample postpaid: $4. Pays 2 copies. Simultaneous submissions, previously published OK. Reports in 4-6 weeks. They publish 1 chapbook a year. Submit samples. Chapbook publication pays 10% of run.**

AUGURIES (IV-Science fiction/fantasy), 48 Anglesey Rd., Alverstoke, Gosport, Hants, PO122EQ England, founded 1983, editor Nik Morton, uses **science fiction and fantasy poetry, "any length, any style, good imagery."** They have published poetry by Garry Legg, J.V. Stewart, Steve Sneyd, Dave W. Hughes and John Light. As a sample the editor selected these lines from "Chill Factor" by John Francis Haines:

> *Beneath our feet: the ice;*
> *Beneath the ice: the city,*
> *Its locked, distorted face*
> *Held static, without pity . . .*

The digest-sized periodical is lithographed from photoreduced typeset on bond paper, thin glossy card cover with b&w art, 76 or more pgs., saddle-stapled. They take about 40% of 50 poems received/year. Press run 250 for 150 subscriptions, about 50 shelf sales. Price per issue: $5 (cash); subscription: $20. **Sample back issue: $5 postpaid. Pays 1 copy. Acquires first British and American serial rights. No simultaneous submissions. Previously published poems "not usually"** used. **Reports in 2 months. Editor comments on rejections "if possible."** Reviews books of poetry, "albeit briefly (150-200 words)." He says, "My choice of poetry is very subjective, may even appear arbitrary: if it appeals to me, I will accept (perhaps offering advice where necessary before acceptance). Be patient, I have material for issues up to #24 and #15 is just out!"

AURA LITERARY/ARTS MAGAZINE (II), Box 76, University of Alabama at Birmingham, Birmingham AL 35294, phone (205)934-3216, founded 1974, editor Nan Smith, a semiannual magazine that publishes "fiction and art though majority of acceptances are poetry—90-100 per year. **Length—open, style open, subject matter open. We are looking for quality poetry. Both first-time and often published poets are published here."** *Aura* has published work by Lyn Lifshin, Adrian C. Louis and William Miller. The 6×9 magazine is 100-140 pgs., perfect-bound, printed on white matte with b&w photos, lithography and line art. Circulation is 500, of which 40-50 are subscriptions; other sales are to students and Birmingham residents. Price per issue is $2.50, subscription $6. **Sample available for $2.50 postpaid, guidelines for SASE. Pay is 2 copies. Writers should submit "3-5 poems, with SASE, no simultaneous submissions, will take photocopies or even neatly hand written."** Reporting time is 2-3 months. The editor says, "Quality is our quantity. If it's good we will find a place for it, if not this issue, the next."

AWEDE PRESS (II), Dept. PM, Box 376, Windsor VT 05089, phone (802)484-5169, founded 1975, editor Brita Bergland. Awede is a small press that publishes letterpress books, sewn with drawn-on covers, graphically produced. The editor wants **"contemporary, 'language' poetry with a strong visual interest."** They have published poetry by Charles Bernstein, James Sherry, Rosemarie Waldrop and Hannah Weiner. Awede publishes 2 poetry chapbooks/year, 32 pgs., 6×9, flat-spined. **Freelance submissions are accepted, but author should query first. Queries are answered in 2 weeks, mss reported**

on in 4-5 months. Simultaneous submissions are acceptable, as are photocopied mss. Pay is in author's copies, 10% of run. No subsidy publishing, book catalog free on request, with SASE a must. Sample books available at list price of $8-10.

THE BABY CONNECTION NEWS JOURNAL (V), Drawer 13320, San Antonio TX 78213-0320, phone Tues.-Sat. 12:30-5:30 CST (512)493-6278, founded 1986, Ms. Gina G. Morris, C.I.D.I./editor, is "a monthly news journal **to support, educate, move and inspire new and expectant parents** in their role of rearing babies and preschoolers 0-5 years of age. Parenting is such a tough job—our publication strives to reward and motivate positive and nurturing parenting skills." They publish **"poetry only on the subjects of mothering, fathering, birthing, pregnancy, child rearing, the power, the love, the passion and momentum, fertility." They are currently not accepting poetry submissions. "We have received over 6,000 pieces and are overwhelmed."** They have published poetry by Alex Grayton, Barbara Kane, E.K. Alasky, Jim McConnell and Laura Rodley. As a sample the editor selected these lines from "Night Music" by Marc Swan:

> The moon casts a mosaic of light and dark
> against her bedroom wall. I lean low to
> tuck her in & kiss her goodnight. Dad,
> she whispers, look at Peter Pan's shadow. I hug
> her tightly, close to my chest. If it gets lost
> you can sew it back on. Yes, she says,
>   I will.

The tabloid-sized newsprint publication is 8 pgs. Press run: 30,000 for 1,700 subscriptions of which 10% are libraries. Subscription: $9/year. **Sample postpaid: $3 for 2 different issues. Pays 5 copies. "We offer a reduced rate subscription of $4.75 for 6 months so we can be assured the poet knows our context and cares enough to follow us for a term."** Reviews books of poetry. They also publish 5-8 chapbooks and flat-spined paperbacks/year averaging 16-72 pgs. **Pays 6 copies and honorarium averaging $25.**

‡BACKYARD PRESS (V), 8306-B Pitter Pat, Austin TX 78736-7955, founded 1988, publisher Phillip T. Stephens, focuses on poetry in performance projects: books (2 paperbacks/year) and videos. He publishes "poetry developed for a listening audience and poetry reflecting diverse cultural consciousness." He has recently published poetry by Albert Huffstickler. **Publication is by invitation only. "I do not accept any solicitations. I become familiar with poets through personal encounters with their work in performance. Come to Austin and read."** He pays 10% royalties and/or 10% of press run. For samples, send SASE and check for $10 (1 book) or $15 (2). He suggests poets "Get a live audience. You get more immediate feedback. I don't mean 'pat on the back' writer's groups, but open mikes and open readings following paid readings. Start traveling to open mikes in other towns. Listen to what the other poets are doing, but pay more attention to audience response. Avoid college creative writing classes, or at least take no more than one."

‡BAD ATTITUDE (IV-Lesbian, erotica), P.O. Box 390110, Cambridge MA 02139, founded 1984, contact Jasmine Sterling, is a lesbian sex magazine appearing 4-6 times/year. They want **"lesbian erotic poetry."** Press run is 3,000. Subscription: $24/year. **Sample postpaid: $5. No previously published poems; simultaneous submissions OK. Seldom comments on rejections. Reports "immediately." Pays 2 copies.** Reviews books of poetry.

BAD HAIRCUT (II, IV-Social issues), 1055 Adams SE #4, Olympia WA 98501, founded 1987, poetry editors Kimberlea and Ray Goforth, is a "small press magazine with world-wide distribution, publication schedule varies. **Progressive politics, human rights and environmental themes. Free verse is preferred. Don't want to see anything by bad poets in** *love*." They recently published poetry by Lyn Lifshin, Edward Mycue, Henry Mason, B.Z. Niditch and Ivan Argüelles. As a sample the editors selected these lines by Richard Curtis:

> on a dark road my friend and I
> spoke thoughts and things,
> He felt that life is a balancing. . . .
> That the universal leger balances.
> And I thought of ghettos and death camps
> . . . of plague and cribdeath.
> And I voiced not a word of my views of the world—
> There being disillusion enough, as it is.

Their object is "to bring together thoughts of peace from around the world." *Bad Haircut* is digest-sized, using some art and ads. Of thousands of poems received each year, they say, they use 25. Press run is 1,000 for 300 subscriptions (3 libraries), and it is carried by 4 stores. $4 per issue, $14 for a subscription. **Sample postpaid: $4. Send SASE for guidelines. Pay is "a tearsheet,** maybe one copy." Acquires first North American serial rights. No simultaneous submissions. Previously published poetry OK. Rejections in 1 day; acceptances can take up to 2 months. Editors comment on rejections "always — as poets ourselves, we learned to hate form rejections." They also publish a line of poetry postcards.

THE BAD HENRY REVIEW; 44 Press (II), Box 150045, Van Brunt Station, Brooklyn NY 11215-0001, founded 1981, poetry editors Evelyn Horowitz, Michael Malinowitz and Mary du Passage. They have published poetry by John Ashbery, Gilbert Sorrentino, Stephen Sandy and William Matthews. Press run is 500-1,000 for 200 subscriptions of which 15 are for libraries; 200-300 for shelf sales. *The Bad Henry Review* is an annual publishing quality poetry, 64 pgs., digest-sized. Per issue $6; subscription $12/2 issues. **Sample: $4. Pays 1 copy with half price discount for contributors. Submit no more than 5 poems, include SASE. No simultaneous submissions. No previously published poems unless advised.** Rarely comments on rejected mss. The editor comments, "We've done one issue of long poems and we are doing an issue on photography in 1993." 44 Press publishes about 1 book of poetry/year.

‡**BAKUNIN (II)**, P.O. Box 1853, Simi Valley CA 93062-1853, founded 1990, editor Jordan Jones, is a semiannual. **"We are looking for poems that challenge accepted pieties and norms. We are also interested in powerful personal poems."** They want **"avant-garde and mainstream poetry of humor, pathos and social comment. No trite or hackneyed verse; no poem that uses but does not earn the word love."** They have recently published poetry by Sandra McPherson, Dennis Schmitz and Benjamin Saltman. As a sample the editor selected the opening lines of "The Aqueduct" by Dorianne Laux:

> *We played there on hot L.A. summers, kids poking through*
> *the slick algae and bloated tires, the delicate rafts*
> *of mosquito eggs. Open boxcars pulled gray squares*
> *of sky overhead as we took apples and crackers*
> *from our pockets and ate, watched the cursing workers*
> *from the can factory gathering at the silver lunch truck*

Bakunin is 96 pgs., digest-sized, offset on acid-free recycled paper, perfect-bound, with laminated cover, b&w artwork and some ads. They receive about 500 submissions a year, publish approximately 5%. The free verse is mostly lyric, and the poems tend to be one-page. Press run is 750 for 50 subscribers, 275 shelf sales. **Sample postpaid: $5. No previously published poems; simultaneous submissions OK, "if the author indicates they are such." Cover letter required.** Time between acceptance and publication is 6-12 months. **Seldom comments on rejections. Send SASE for guidelines. Reports in 2 weeks-3 months. Pays 2 copies. Acquires first North American serial rights.** "We publish 250- to 750-word reviews of single books, magazines or whole presses." The editor says, "*Bakunin* is a magazine for the dead Russian anarchist in all of us."

BANGTAIL (II), 3137 W. Paradise Ln., Phoenix AZ 85023, founded 1989, editor William Dudley, appears twice a year. **They want "contemporary poetry of any form and subject, quality in language & imagery, unique presentation & style — Experimental High Energy/Beat Culture/Avant-Garde Poetry."** As a sample the editor selected these lines by Patricia Gentner:

> *New York walkers*
> *move slyly,*
> *corner-eyed glances*
> *catch marauding*
> *yellow drones.*

The editor describes it as 30 pgs., saddle-stapled, digest-sized, offset printed from large type. Press run 250. Subscription: $7. **Sample: $3.50. Pays 1 copy.** The editor says, "We would like to see some humorous poetry and also any b&w artwork."

THE BANK STREET PRESS; THE PORT AUTHORITY POETRY REVIEW (V), 24 Bank St., New York NY 10014, phone (212)255-0692, founded 1985, poetry editor Mary Bertschmann. A small group of poets meet at the Bank Street home of Mary Bertschmann and publish their poetry annually in a series of flat-spined paperbacks called *The Port Authority Poetry Review*. Review books of poetry. **Sample $7 including postage and handling.** The Bank Street Press also publishes solo collections of poetry. They have published **Goslings on the Tundra** ($20 including postage and handling) and, more recently, **52 Sonnets** ($12 including postage and handling), both limited, fine print volumes by Mary York Sampson. As a sample the editor selected this sonnet:

> *The progress of this day is worth remark,*
> *The air is full of starch and the blue sky*
> *Is like the rare occurrence of an honest eye*
> *That says in the long hours before dark*
> *There'll be a fair deal, a new life spark;*

And well before the sky begins to die,
Before the blood spills in the West nearby,
And the city turns into tombstones stark,
This fine spring day will flaunt its lion heart,
Truth will be allowed, and growth, in this free
Symbiotic mix of justice and light;
Morning, noon, afternoon all counterpart,
A universal purr exclaims as we
Scout this isthmus between the shores of night.

BANTAM DOUBLEDAY DELL PUBLISHING GROUP (V), 666 Fifth Ave., New York NY 10103, phone (212)765-6500, **accepts mss only from agents.**

BAPTIST SUNDAY SCHOOL BOARD; LIVING WITH PRESCHOOLERS; LIVING WITH CHILDREN; LIVING WITH TEENAGERS; HOME LIFE (IV-Religious); MATURE LIVING (IV-Religious, senior citizen), 127 Ninth Ave. N., Nashville TN 37234, the publishing agency for Southern Baptists. "We publish magazines, monthlies, quarterlies, books, filmstrips, films, church supplies, etc., for Southern Baptist churches." **Query with samples.** For most of their publications they want **"inspirational and/ or religious poetry. No 'word pictures'. We want poetry with a message to inspire, uplift, motivate, amuse. No longer than 24 lines,"** typed, double-spaced, no simultaneous submissions. Reports within 2 months, rate of pay figured on number of lines submitted. The biggest of the monthlies is *Home Life*, which began in 1947. Circulation 750,000; 20,000 subscriptions — a magazine-sized, saddle-stapled, slick magazine, 60+ pgs., illustrated (no ads). Its poetry editors, Charlie Warren and Mary Paschall Darby, say they want **"religious poetry; treating marriage, family life and life in general from a Christian perspective. We rarely publish anything of more than 25 lines."** Sample: $1 to authors with SASE! **Submit no more than 6 poems at a time. "Prefer original, but photocopy and dot-matrix acceptable. Query unnecessary."** Send SASE for guidelines. Reports in 6-8 weeks. **Pays $15-24.** *Mature Living: A Christian Magazine for Senior Adults*, founded in 1977, is a monthly mass circulation (330,000) magazine providing **"leisure reading for senior adults. All material used is compatible with a Christian lifestyle."** The poetry they use is of Christian content, inspirational, about "nature/God," rhymed, 8-24 lines. Assistant editor Judy Pregel says, **"We dislike free verse or poems where a word is dragged in just to piece out a meter."** Apparently you do not have to be a senior citizen to submit. *Mature Living* is magazine-sized, 52 pgs., saddle-stapled, using large print on pulp stock, glossy paper cover, with color and b&w art. They "receive hundreds" of poems/year, use about 125-150. Most of their distribution is through churches who buy the magazine in bulk for their senior adult members. **For sample, send 9 × 12 self-addressed envelope and 85¢ postage. Pays $5-25. Reports in 6-8 weeks, but there might be a 3-year delay before publication.**

‡BARNWOOD PRESS; BARNWOOD; BARNWOOD PRESS COOPERATIVE (III), P.O. Box 146, Selma IN 47383, phone (317)288-0145, founded 1978, editors Tom Koontz, Haven Koontz and Thom Tammaro, publishes *Barnwood* 3 times/year and 1 paperback collection of poetry every 2 or 3 years. **"We have no conscious preconception."** However, they do not want poetry that is **"visionless, bigotted, poorly crafted or stereotypical."** They have recently published poetry by Bly, Friman, Goedicke and Stafford. As a sample the editors selected these lines from "Light Casualties" by Robert Francis:

Did the guns whisper when they spoke
That day? Did death tiptoe his business?
And afterwards in another world
Did mourners put on light mourning,
Casual as rain, as snow, as leaves?
Did a few tears fall?

The editors say *Barnwood* is 16 pgs., photo offset and saddle-stitched. They receive about 1000 poems a year, publish 36. Press run is 500 for 200 subscribers of which 50 are libraries. Subscription: $6/year, "includes membership in Barnwood Press Cooperative which provides discount on Barnwood books." **Sample postpaid: $2. Previously published poems ("please tell us where and when") and simultaneous submissions OK, if noted. Reads submissions September 1 through May 31 only.** Time between acceptance and publication is 1 year. **Seldom comments on rejections. Reports in 1 month. Pays $25/poem plus 5 copies. Buys first North American serial rights only.** Reviews chapbooks of poetry in 500-1,000 words. **Query first for book publication. Replies to queries in 1 month, to mss (if invited) in 1-6 months. Pays 100 author's copies (10% of press run).** The editors add, "While our magazine is chef's choice or taste of the house, we try to recognize a wide variety of effective poems and we look to the poets to show us what can make effective poetry."

‡WILLIAM L. BAUHAN, PUBLISHER (V, IV-Regional), P.O. Box 443, Old County Road, Dublin NH 03444, phone (603)563-8020, founded 1959, editor William L. Bauhan, publishes poetry and art, especially New England regional books. **They currently accept no unsolicited poetry.** They have recently published books of poetry by Henry Chapin, Dorothy Richardson, May Sarton and Ruth Feldman.

BAY AREA POETS COALITION (BAPC); POETALK (I), P.O. Box 11435, Berkeley CA 94701-2435, phone (510)845-8409, founded 1974. Coalition sends monthly poetry letter, *Poetalk*, to over 400 people. They publish annual anthology (13th — 140 pgs., out in February 1992), giving one page to each member of BAPC who has had work published in *Poetalk* during the prior year. *Poetalk* publishes approximately 50 poets in each issue. BAPC has 160 members, 70 subscribers, but *Poetalk* is open to all. **Predictable rhyme only if clever vocabulary. Each poem 3 × 4″ maximum. One poem from each new submitter will usually be printed. Typewritten, single-spaced OK. Simultaneous and previously published work OK. All subject matter should be in good taste. Poems appear on 3 legal-size pages. Send 4 poems (on 1 page) and a self-addressed, stamped postcard for acknowledgment every 6 months. Response time: 2 weeks-4 months.** You'll get copy of *Poetalk* in which your work appears. Write (with SASE) for 2 months' free copies. Membership: $12 for 12 months' *Poetalk*, copy of anthology and other privileges; extra outside US. The editor chose these sample lines by Maggi H. Meyer:

> *Raindrops bud the trees.*
> *Sharp sun glares on grass.*
> *I squint, acknowledge*
> *Nature's ying/yang.*

BAPC holds monthly readings, contests, etc.; has mailing list open to local members; a PA system members may use for a small fee. People from 26 states other than California and 8 countries have contributed to *Poetalk* or entered their 12th annual contest.

BAY WINDOWS (IV-Gay/lesbian), 1523 Washington St., Boston MA 02118, FAX (617)266-5973, founded 1983, poetry editors Rudy Kikel and Patricia A. Roth. *Bay Windows* **is a weekly gay and lesbian newspaper** published for the New England community, regularly using **"short poems of interest to lesbians and gay men. Poetry that is 'experiential' seems to have a good chance with us, but we don't want poetry that just 'tells it like it is.' Our readership doesn't read poetry all the time. A primary consideration is giving** *pleasure.* **We'll overlook the poem's (and the poet's) tendency not to be informed by the latest poetic theory, if it** *does* **this: pleases. Pleases, in particular, by articulating common gay or lesbian experience, and by doing that with some attention to form. I've found that a lot of our choices were made because of a strong image strand. Humor is** *always* **welcome—and hard to provide with craft. Obliquity, obscurity? Probably not for us. We won't presume on our audience."** They have recently published poetry by Robert Friend, Cynthia de Geus, James Broughton, Judith Saunders and Walta Borawski. As a sample Rudy Kikel and Pat Schwartz picked Emma Morgan's complete poem "Untitled":

> *I went walking down the street*
> *straight into the lack of you*
> *It left your impression*
> *in gooseflesh on my skin*
> *Now I shudder when the wind blows*

"We try to run four poems (two by lesbians, two by gay men) each month," print run 13,000, 700 subscriptions of which 15 are libraries. Subscription: $40; per issue: 50¢. They receive about 300 submissions/year, use 1 in 6, have a 3-month backlog. **Sample postpaid: $1. Submit 3-5 poems, "5-25 lines are ideal; include short biographical blurb."** Poems by men should be sent care of Rudy Kikel, *Bay Windows,* at the address above; by women, care of Patricia Roth Schwartz, Weeping Willow Farm, 1212 Birdsey Rd., Waterloo NY 13165. **Reports in 1 month. Pays copies. Acquires first rights.** Editors "often" comment on rejections. They review books of poetry in about 750 words—"Both single and omnibus reviews (the latter are longer)."

BEAR TRIBE PUBLISHING; WILDFIRE MAGAZINE (IV-Nature, themes, ethnic), P.O. Box 9167, Spokane WA 99209, phone (509)258-7275, founded 1965 (the magazine's former name, *Many Smokes Earth Awareness Magazine*), poetry editor Elisabeth Robinson. The magazine uses **short poetry on topics appropriate to the magazine, such as earth awareness, self-sufficiency, sacred places, native people,** etc. Press run is 10,000 for 6,000 subscriptions of which 5% are libraries, 3,500 shelf sales. Subscription: $15. **Sample postpaid: $4. Send SASE for guidelines. Reports in "6 months or more."** They have published poetry by Gary Snyder, W. D. Ehrhart, P. J. Brown and Evelyn Eaton. The quarterly devotes 1-2 pgs. to poetry each issue. They want a **"positive and constructive viewpoint, no hip or offensive language."** Poets published receive 4-issue subscription. The press publishes books that incorporate Native American poems and songs, but no collections by individuals.

‡**THE BELLADONNA REVIEW (I)**, 745 N. Hendricks St., Montebello CA 90640, founded 1992, editor Paul Quintero, is a monthly literary magazine which **"accepts all poetry; open to length, subject matter and style."** The editor says it is about 15 pgs., photocopied, using a clear plastic cover and ads. Subscription: $22. **Sample postpaid: $2. Previously published poems OK; no simultaneous submissions. Submit complete ms with $1/poem reading fee. Make checks or money orders payable to the editor. Reports in 1 month on rejections, 2-6 months on accepted mss. Pays 25¢/line plus 1 copy. Buys all rights. Rights revert to authors upon publication.** The editor says, "I don't send acceptance slips. I just send payment and one free copy of the issue in which the author's work appears. I encourage beginning poets to submit here, as they have a very good chance of getting published."

BELLFLOWER PRESS (III, IV-Humor, social issues, women/feminism), Box 87 Dept. WD, Chagrin Falls OH 44022-0087, founded 1974, poetry editor/owner Louise Wazbinski, **publishes poetry** *books* **50% of the time on a subsidized basis.** She wants **"poetry that crystallizes the attitudes held by our society."** They have published poetry by Judy Kronenfeld. As a sample here are lines from "Lente, Lente" in her book **Shadow of Wings:**

> *Slowly my father wades into his ripe age.*
> *His great barrel chest, split and healed again,*
> *cleaves the pool . . .*
> *I remember when he took the cold air in,*
> *and threw his coat wide.*

Reports in 2-4 weeks on queries, 6-8 weeks on mss. "Contract depends upon subvention by author, usually 50%. Often the author will subsidize a small percentage and receive books as payment. In other cases, there is no subsidy and the author receives a royalty based on the specific arrangements made at the time of agreement."

BELLOWING ARK PRESS; BELLOWING ARK (II), P.O. Box 45637, Seattle WA 98145, phone (206)545-8302, founded 1984, editor Robert R. Ward. *Bellowing Ark* is a bimonthly literary tabloid that **"publishes only poetry which demonstrates in some way the proposition that existence has meaning or, to put it another way, that life is worth living. We have no strictures as to length, form or style; only that the work we publish is to our judgment life-affirming."** They do not want **"academic poetry, in any of its manifold forms."** Poets recently published include Natalie Reciputi, Harold Witt, Katherine Lewis, Susan McCaslin, Muriel Karr and Mark Allan Johnson. As a sample the editor selected these lines from "Ancient Poets" by Paula Milligan:

> *Ancient truth must be the same, then as now.*
> *It endures, for it has no shades*
>
> *Angels in Hesiod's pastures, luminous;*
> *Sight behind Homer's dark eyes*
>
> *Light is bright in any age.*

The paper is tabloid-sized, 28 pgs., printed on electrobright stock with b&w photos and line drawings. Circulation is 1,000, of which 200+ are subscriptions and 600+ are sold on newsstands. Price is $2/issue, subscription is $15/year. **Sample postpaid: $3. Pay is 2 copies. The editors say, "absolutely** *no* **simultaneous submissions, prefer not to see dot-matrix or photocopy."** They reply to submissions in 2-6 weeks and publish within the next 1 or 2 issues. Occasionally they will criticize a ms if it seems to "display potential to become the kind of work we want." Reviews books of poetry. Bellowing Ark Press publishes collections of poetry by invitation only.

BELL'S LETTERS POET (I), P.O. Box 2187, Gulfport MS 39505, founded 1956 as *Writer's Almanac*, 1958 as *Thunderhead for Writers*, 1966 as *Bell's Letters* (a play on words), publisher and editor Jim Bell, is a quarterly which **you must buy ($4/issue, $16 subscription) to be included.** The editor says "many say they stay up with it all night the day it arrives," and judging by the many letters from readers, that seems to be the case. **Though there is no payment for poetry accepted, many patrons send awards of $5-20 to the poets whose work they especially like. Subscription "guarantees them a byline each issue." Poems are "12-20 lines in good taste."** They have recently published poetry by Phyllis Owen, Dr. C. David Hay, Gloria Gebhardt and Kay White. As a sample of the spirit of *BL* poetry the editor chose these lines by Lucile Valois:

> *Lost in apple blossom yesterday*
> *Forgotten crickets chirp for me,*
> *Again the dappled pony neighs.*

It is digest-sized, 72 pgs., offset from typescript on plain bond paper (including cover). **Sample: $1, to cover postage. Send SASE for guidelines. Ms may be typed or even hand-written. No simultaneous submissions. Previously published poems OK "if cleared with prior publisher." Reports in 10 days. Acceptance of poems by subscribers go immediately into the next issue.** "Our publication dates fall quarterly on the spring and autumn equinox and winter and summer solstice. Deadline for poetry submissions is 45 days prior to publication." Reviews books of poetry in "one abbreviated paragraph." "50 BL Classics" is a competition in each issue. Readers are asked to vote on their favorite poems, and the winners are announced in the next issue, along with awards sent them by patrons.

THE BELOIT POETRY JOURNAL (II), Box 154, RFD 2, Ellsworth ME 04605, phone (207)667-5598, founded 1950, editor Marion K. Stocking, a well-known, long-standing quarterly of quality poetry and reviews. "**We publish the best poems we receive, without bias as to length, school, subject or form.** It is our hope to discover the growing tip of poetry and to introduce new poets alongside established writers. We publish occasional chapbooks on special themes to diversify our offerings." They want "**fresh, imaginative poetry, with a distinctive voice. We tend to prefer poems that make the reader share an experience rather than just read about it, and these we keep for up to 3 months,** circulating them among our readers, and continuing to winnow out the best. At the quarterly meetings of the Editorial Board we read aloud all the surviving poems and put together an issue of the best we have." They have recently published poetry by Sherman Alexie, Hillel Schwartz, Lola Haskins, William Carpenter and Susan Tichy. The editor chose this sample from "12,000 Bones of Frogs and Toads" by Albert Goldbarth:

> *Real whales, real worms, are words*
> *defining an abstraction. Any oblong*
> *of the world an open door defines, is open*
> *encyclopediacally — and a man will exit,*
> *labor, and return*
> *to sleep at the end of a day of each*
> *least sliver of cedarwood, each cattle louse,*
> *instructing him.*

It's an attractively printed, digest-sized, saddle-stapled, 40-page format, with tasteful art on the card covers. All styles of verse — providing they articulate ideas or emotions intelligently and concisely — are featured. The editor is also keen on providing as much space as possible for poems and so does not include contributors' notes. **Sample copy: $4, includes guidelines, or SASE for guidelines alone.** They have a circulation of 1,400, 575 subscriptions, of which 325 are libraries. **Submit any time, without query, any legible form.** *"No simultaneous submissions.* **Any length of ms, but most poets send what will go in a business envelope for one stamp. Don't send your life's work." Payment: 3 copies. Acquires first serial rights.** No backlog: "We clear the desk at each issue." Reviews books of poetry in an average of 500 words, usually single format.

"Poetry is essential to our publication and makes up approximately 70% of each issue," says Robert J. Nesbitt, assistant editor of Beneath the Surface, a creation of Canada's McMaster University Society for English (M.U.S.E). "Fiction and literary essays are also utilized," he says, adding that the title of the publication arose from the idea that "you often have to go beneath the surface of works to find greater meaning." Nesbitt concedes that such a task is not always easy, as this cover by Tor Foss illustrates.

‡BENEATH THE SURFACE (II), % The Dept. of English, Chester New Hall, McMaster University, Hamilton, Ontario L8S 4S8 Canada, founded 1911, editor changes yearly, is a biannual using "**top quality poetry/prose that achieves universality through individual expression.**" They want "**quality**

poetry; any form; no restrictions." They have recently published poetry by Dorothy Livesky and John Barlow. As a sample the editor selected these lines from "War Monument" by tristanne j. connolly:

> a soldier's soul
> ascending, but concrete
> is heavy to lift
> war monument, the cross on top
> forgotten til the very last minute

It is 30-50 pages, professionally printed, saddle-stapled, with cover art, drawings and b&w photographs. They receive about 250 submissions a year, use approximately 10%. Press run is 150 for 8 subscribers of which 3 are libraries, 92 shelf sales. Subscription: $8/year. **Sample postpaid: $4. No previously published poems or simultaneous submissions. Submit 4-6 poems with cover letter, including short bio. Reads submissions September through April only. Often comments on rejections. Reports in 4-6 weeks. Pays nothing—not even copies. Acquires first North American serial rights.** Rarely reviews books of poetry, "though we do include literary essays when submitted." The editor says, "Do not get discouraged. Getting work in respectable literary journals takes much love and even more hard work. Be patient and allow your work to evolve and mature."

BENNETT & KITCHEL (IV-Form), P.O. Box 4422, East Lansing MI 48826, phone (517)355-1707, founded 1989, editor William Whallon, publishes 2-3 hardbacks/year of **"poetry of form and meaning. No free verse, blank verse, off rhyme, sestinas or haiku. Shakespearean sonnets should be as good as those of the Immortal Bard, but lyrics cannot be expected to come close."** As an example of what he likes the editor chose these lines about Gettysburg by L.R. Lind:

> . . . there in a cannon's mouth
> A bird had built her frail, capricious nest
> And filled it with young to fly both north and south.

Bennett & Kitchel recently published **Part Comanche**, 52 poems of rhythm and rhyme, by Troxey Kemper. **Sample postpaid: $6. Reports in 2 weeks. Terms "variable, negotiable." Simultaneous submissions and previously published poems OK if copyright is clear. Minimum volume for a book "might be 750 lines." If a book is accepted, publication within 9 months. Editor comments on submissions "seldom."** He suggests, "Heed the advice of Goethe to Hugo: Work more, write less."

BERKELEY POETRY REVIEW (II), 700 Eshleman Hall, University of California, Berkeley CA 94720, founded 1973, editor Cynthia Pierce, is an annual review "which publishes poems and translations of local as well as national and international interest. **We are open to any form or length which knows how to express itself through that form."** They have published poetry by Federico Garcia Lorca, Thom Gunn, August Kleinzahler, Robert Hass and John Tranter. The editors describe it as a flat-spined paperback, averaging 150 pgs., circulation 500. Subscription: $10/year. **Simultaneous submissions, photocopies, dot-matrix, previously published poems (if not copyrighted) all OK. Reads submissions September through June only. Pays 1 copy.** They also publish books. For book publication **submit 5 sample poems with bio. Include SASE; allow 2-6 months for reply.**

BERKELEY POETS COOPERATIVE (WORKSHOP & PRESS) (II), Box 459, Berkeley CA 94701, founded 1969, poetry editor Charles Entrekin (plus rotating staff), is "a nonprofit organization which offers writers the opportunity to explore, develop and publish their works. Our primary goals are to maintain a free workshop open to writers and to publish outstanding collections of poetry and fiction by individual writers." The *New York Times* has called it **"the oldest and most successful poetry co-operative in the country."** Chapbooks have been published by Linda Watanabe McFerrin and Chitra Divakaruni. Charles Entrekin says he prefers **"modern imagist—open to all kinds, but we publish very little rhyme."** They publish two 64-page chapbooks by individuals each year, for which the **poets receive 50% of the profit and 20 copies. You can order a sample book for $3.** Criticism sometimes provided on rejected mss. Poets elsewhere might consider BPWP as a model for forming similar organizations.

BEYOND (IV-Science fiction/fantasy), Dept. PM, P.O. Box 136, New York NY 10024, phone (212)874-5914, founded 1985, editor Shirley Winston, is a quarterly magazine of **science fiction and fantasy.** For poetry, the editor wants **"anything short of a major epic"** on those themes. She does not often use anything longer than 120 lines. *Beyond* does not print material in the horror genre. She has published poetry by Dan Crawford and Genevieve Stephens. The magazine-sized *Beyond* is 54 pgs., saddle-stapled, offset from letter-quality word processor printout, with b&w drawings to illustrate the pieces and a b&w drawing on the cover. Circulation is 200. Subscription: $17/year. **Sample: $5 postpaid. Pay is 3¢/line plus 1 copy. Submissions "must be legible (dot-matrix is OK if dark enough)." Reports in 3 months.** The editor **"always" provides criticism on rejected mss.**

‡THE BIG NOW; BIG NOW PUBLICATIONS (I, II), 6716 Clayton Ave., #3N, St. Louis MO 63139, founded 1990, submissions editor Theresa M. Mozelewski, is a semiannual which publishes "good poetry and art, specifically work which displays the artist's consciousness of his/her place in the tradition to which he/she belongs. **We would like to see work by authors who are conscious of form and tradition, though not necessarily formal or traditional. We do not publish poems with predictable, uninspired themes and/or structure.**" They have recently published poetry by Jason Sommer. As a sample the editor selected these lines from "The Dark Family of My First Ever Girlfriend" by Ben Vance:

> *You made me dial the phone, a Dallas number, your boyfriend.*
> *You told him about your grandparents' hiss-whispered shouting*
> *match over a receipt for a dozen roses your grandmother never received.*
> *He hung up on you when he realized you were drunk and*
> *that I was a boy.*

It is 30-40 pgs., digest-sized, saddle-stapled, b&w, with possible spot color in the future. They accept approximately 30% of poetry received. Press run is 1,000-1,500. "All are distributed free to various points in St. Louis." **Sample: $1 for postage. Previously published poems and simultaneous submissions OK.** "However, please let us know if works are under consideration elsewhere and, if published, where and when." Time between acceptance and publication is 4-6 months. **Seldom comments on rejections. May charge criticism fees. Reports within 2 weeks. Pays 2 copies. Acquires first or reprint rights.** The editor advises poets to "read; experience; live."

BILINGUAL REVIEW PRESS; BILINGUAL REVIEW/REVISTA BILINGÜE (IV-Ethnic, bilingual), Hispanic Research Center, Arizona State University, Tempe AZ 85287, phone (602)965-3867, journal founded 1974, press in 1976. Managing editor Karen Van Hooft says they are "a small-press publisher of U.S. Hispanic creative literature and of a journal containing poetry and short fiction in addition to scholarship." The journal contains some poetry in each issue; they also publish flat-spined paperback collections of poetry. **"We publish poetry by and/or about U.S. Hispanics and U.S. Hispanic themes. We do not publish translations in our journal or literature about the experiences of Anglo Americans in Latin America. We have published a couple of poetry volumes in bilingual format (Spanish/English) of important Mexican poets."** They have recently published poetry by Alberto Ríos, Demetria Martínez, Pablo Medina, Carolina Hospital and Ricardo Pau-Llosa. The editor says the journal, which appears 3 times a year, is 7×10, 96 pgs., flat-spined, offset, with 2-color cover. They use less than 10% of hundreds of submissions received each year. Press run is 1,000 for 850+ subscriptions. Subscriptions are $16 for individuals, $28 for institutions. **Sample: $6 individuals/$10 institutions postpaid. Pays 2 copies. Acquires all rights. Submit "2 copies, including ribbon original if possible, with loose stamps for return postage. For book submissions, inquire first with 4-5 sample poems, bio, publications." Pays $100 advance, 10% royalties and 10 copies.** Reviews books of US Hispanic poetry only.

BIRD WATCHER'S DIGEST (IV-Nature), P.O. Box 110, Marietta OH 45750, founded 1978, editor Mary Beacom Bowers, is a specialized but promising market for poems of **"true literary merit"** in which birds figure in some way, at least by allusion. **2-3 poems are used in each bimonthly issue and earn $10/poem.** Some poets who have appeared there recently include Susan Rea, Nancy G. Westerfield, Suzanne Freemans and William D. Barney. **"Preferred: no more than 20 lines, 40 spaces, no more than 3 poems at a time, no queries." Sample postpaid: $3.50. Reports in 2 months.** They have up to a year's backlog and use 12-20 of the approximately 500 poems received each year.

BIRMINGHAM POETRY REVIEW (II, IV-Translations), English Department, University of Alabama at Birmingham, Birmingham AL 35294, phone (205)934-8573, founded 1988, editor Robert Collins, associate editor Randy Blythe. Appears twice a year using poetry of **"any style, form, length or subject. We are biased toward exploring the cutting edge of contemporary poetry. Style is secondary to the energy, the *fire* the poem possesses. We don't want poetry with cliché-bound, worn-out language."** They have published poetry by Blumenthal, Carlson, Frost, Linda, Glaser, Harrod, Mueller, Horne and Jaeger. They describe their magazine as 50 pgs., 6×9, offset, with b&w cover. Their press run is 600 for Fall Issue, 500 for Spring Issue, 275 subscriptions. Subscription: $3. **Sample: $2 postpaid.** Guidelines available for SASE. **Pays 2 copies and one-year subscription. Submit 3-5 poems, "no more. No cover letters. We are impressed by good writing; we are unimpressed by publication credits. It should go without saying, but we receive more and more manuscripts with insufficient return postage. If it costs you forty-five cents to mail your manuscript, it will cost us that much to return it if it is rejected. Hereafter, manuscripts with insufficient return postage will be discarded." No simultaneous submissions, and previously published poems only if they are translations. Reports in 1-3 months. Editor sometimes comments on rejections.** He says, "Advice to beginners: Read as much good contemporary poetry, national and international, as you can get your hands on. Then be persistent in finding your own voice."

BISHOP PUBLISHING CO. (IV-Themes), 2131 Trimble Way, Sacramento CA 95825, professor Roland Dickison, is a "small press publisher of **folklore in paperbacks, including contemporary** and out-of-print." They want to see **"American folk poetry, either current or historical. No modern free verse.** Folk poetry is usually anonymous."

BITS PRESS (III, IV-Humor), English Dept., Case Western Reserve University, Cleveland OH 44106, phone (216)795-2810, founded 1974, poetry editor Robert Wallace. **"Bits Press is devoted to poetry. We publish chapbooks (and sometimes limited editions) by young as well as well-known poets. Our main attention at present is given to light verse and funny poems."** The chapbooks are distinguished by elegant but inexpensive format. They have published chapbooks by David R. Slavitt, John Updike and Margaret Lally. These sample lines are from Richard Wilbur's **Some Atrocities**:

> If a sheepdog ate a cantaloupe,
> Would it make him frisk like an antelope?
> Would he feel all pleased and jolly?
> Or would he be a Melon Collie?

The few chapbooks they publish are mostly solicited. Send $2 for a sample chapbook; payment to poet in copies (10%+ of run). Acquires one-time rights.

BLACK AMERICAN LITERATURE FORUM (IV-Ethnic), Dept. of English, Indiana State University, Terre Haute IN 47809, founded 1967 (as *Negro American Literature Forum*), poetry editors Sterling Plumpp, Thadious M. Davis, Pinkie Gordon Lane and E. Ethelbert Miller, is a "magazine primarily devoted to the analysis of African American literature, **although one issue per year focuses on poetry by African Americans."** No specifications as to form, length, style, subject matter or purpose. They have published poems by Amiri Baraka, Gwendolyn Brooks, Dudley Randall and Owen Dodson. *Forum* is 6×9, 200 pgs. with photo on the cover. Individual subscriptions: $20 USA, $27 foreign. They receive about 500 submissions per year, use 50. **Sample postpaid: $10. Submit maximum of 6 poems to editor Joe Weixlmann. Pays in copies. Reports in 3-4 months. Send SASE for guidelines. The editors sometimes comment on rejections.**

BLACK BEAR PUBLICATIONS; BLACK BEAR REVIEW; POETS ELEVEN . . . AUDIBLE (II, IV-Social), 1916 Lincoln St., Croydon PA 19021-8026, founded 1984, poetry and art editor Ave Jeanne, review and audio editor Ron Zettlemoyer. *Black Bear Review* is a semiannual international literary and fine arts magazine that also publishes chapbooks and holds an annual poetry competition. Recent poets published in *BBR* include Sherman Alexie, Jose Garcia, Alan Akmakjian, Joe Salerno and Andrew Gettler. *Poets Eleven . . . Audible* has released poetry on tape by A.D. Winans, Tony Moffeit, Kevin Zepper and Mike Maggio. As a sample from *BBR*, the editor has selected the poem "o" by Ann Yarmal:

> I am a cupped hand
> I am womb, stomach, intestine
> I am ears and eyes and mouth
> I am the hollow of arms and legs
> I am the sound of one hand clapping

Circulation of *BBR* is 500, of which 300 are subscriptions; 15 libraries. Price: $5/issue; subscription $10, $15 overseas. Catalog is available for SASE. The magazine is perfect-bound, digest-sized, 64 pgs., offset from typed copy on white stock, with line drawings, collages and woodcuts. The editors explain that *Poets Eleven . . . Audible* was started for accommodation of longer poems for the reader to take part in poetry as a listener; **the author may submit up to 10 minutes of original poetry. SASE for return of your tape; sample copies available for $4.50 postpaid.** Contributor receives 25% royalties. "We like well crafted poetry that mirrors real life – void of camouflage, energetic poetry, avant-garde, free verse and haiku which relate to the world today. We seldom publish the beginner, but will assist when time allows. No traditional poetry is used. The underlying theme of *BBR* is social and political, but the review is interested also in environmental, war/peace, ecological and minorities themes." Submissions are reported on in 2 weeks, **publication is in 6-12 months, any number of poems may be submitted, one to a page, photocopies are OK but they prefer not to read dot-matrix. They publish two chapbooks/year.** Most recently published **A Destiny Going Sour** by Steve Levi. Chapbook series requires a **reading fee of $5, complete ms and cover letter.** For book publication, they would prefer that *"BBR* has published the poet and is familiar with his/her work, but we will read anyone who thinks they have something to say." **Queries are answered in 2 weeks, mss in 2; simultaneous submissions are not considered. "Submissions without SASE will be trashed."** A sample of *BBR*: $5 postpaid; back copies when available are $4 postpaid. **Guidelines available for SASE. Pays contributor's copy.** Considers reviews of recent issues of literary magazines, maximum 250 words. **Acquires first North American serial rights.** "We appreciate a friendly, brief cover letter. Tell us about the poet; omit degrees or any other pretentious dribble. All submissions are handled with objectivity and quite often rejected material is directed to another market. If you've not been published before—mention it. We are always interested in aiding those who support small press. We frequently suggest poets keep up with **Poet's Market** and read the listings and reviews in issues of *Black Bear*. Most recent issues of *BBR* include extensive reviews on small press markets—current releases of chapbooks and the latest literary magazines. We make an effort to keep our readers informed and on top of the small press scene. Camera-ready ads are printed free of charge as a support to small press publishers. We do suggest reading issues before submitting to absorb the flavor and save on wasted postage. Send your best! Our yearly poetry competition offers cash awards to poets." Annual deadline is November 1. Guidelines are available for a SASE.

BLACK BOOKS BULLETIN; BBB: WORDSWORK; THIRD WORLD PRESS (IV-Ethnic), 7524 S. Cottage Grove Ave., Chicago IL 60619, phone (312)651-0700. *BBB* is an annual about **"Black literature and current issues facing the African-American community using Afrocentric poetry, style open."** They have published poetry by Gwendolyn Brooks, Kalamu ya Salaam and Estella Conwill Majozo. Focus is on book reviews. *bbb: wordswork* is a bimonthly journal also focusing on issues facing the African-American community and including Afrocentric poetry. Write for further information.

‡BLACK BOUGH (II, IV-Form), P.O. Box 465, Somerville NJ 08876, founded 1991, editors Kevin Walker and Charles Easter, is a biannual that publishes "haiku and related forms which demonstrate the distinctiveness of haiku as well as its connection to western traditions in poetry." They want **"haiku, senryu, tanka, haibun and sequences. No renga, articles, academic essays or long poems."** They have recently published work by Jean Jorgensen, Francine Porad and Penny Harter. As a sample the editor selected this haiku by Jim Kacian:

> *children*
> *running naked*
> *Easter morning*

The editor says *bb* is 30 pgs., digest-sized, professionally printed, saddle-stitched, with cover art, no ads. They receive about 5,200 poems a year, use 5-10%. Press run is 200 for 100 subscribers. Subscription: $7.50. **Sample postpaid: $4. No previously published poems or simultaneous submissions.** "Submit no more than 20 haiku; prefer several haiku/page." Time between acceptance and publication is 3-6 months. **Comments on rejections "if requested." Reports in 3-4 weeks. Pays nothing—not even contributor's copies. Acquires first rights.** They are also mail order sellers of poetry and poetry on tape. Write for free catalog.

BLACK BUZZARD PRESS; BLACK BUZZARD REVIEW; VISIONS—INTERNATIONAL, THE WORLD JOURNAL; THE BLACK BUZZARD ILLUSTRATED POETRY CHAPBOOK SERIES (II, IV-Translations), 1110 Seaton Lane, Falls Church VA 22046, founded 1979, poetry editor Bradley R. Strahan, associate editor Shirley G. Sullivan. "We are an independent nonsubsidized press dedicated to publishing fine accessible poetry and translation (particularly from lesser known languages such as Armenian, Gaelic, Urdu, Vietnamese, etc.) accompanied by original illustrations of high quality in an attractive format. **We want to see work that is carefully crafted and exciting work that transfigures everyday experience or gives us a taste of something totally new; in all styles except concrete and typographical 'poems.' Nothing purely sentimental. No self-indulgent breast beating. No sadism, sexism or bigotry. No unemotional pap. No copies of Robert Service or the like. Usually under 100 lines but will consider longer."** They have published poetry by Ted Hughes, Marilyn Hacker, James Dickey, Allen Ginsberg and Marge Piercy; and Bradley Strahan says that "no 4 lines can possibly do even minimal justice to our taste or interest!" *Visions*, a digest-sized, saddle-stapled magazine finely printed on high-quality paper, appears 3 times a year, uses 56 pages of poetry in each issue. Circulation 750 with 300 subscriptions of which 50 are libraries, **sample: $3.50 postpaid. Current issue: $4.50.** They receive *well* over a thousand submissions each year and use 140, have a 3-18 month backlog. "*Visions* is international in both scope and content, publishing poets from all over the world and having readers in 48+ U.S. states, Canada and 24 other foreign countries." *Black Buzzard Review* is a "more or less annual informal journal, dedicated mostly to North American poets and entirely to original English-language poems. We are *letting it all hang out* here, unlike the approach of our prestigious international journal *Visions*, and taking a more wide-open stance on what we accept (including the slightly outrageous)." **Sample of BBR: $2.50 plus $1 postage. Current issue: $3.50 plus $1 postage.** It is magazine-sized, 36 pp., side-stapled, with matte card cover. **"Poems must be readable (not faded, light photocopy or smudged) and not handwritten. We resent having to pay postage due, so use adequate postage! No more than 8 pages, please." Reports in 3 days-3 weeks, pays in copies or $5-10 "if we get a grant." Buys first North American serial rights.** Reviews books of poetry in "up to 2 paragraphs." To submit for the chapbook series, send samples (5-10 poems) and a *brief* cover letter **"pertinent to artistic accomplishments." Reports in 3 days-3 weeks, pays in copies, usually provides criticism. Send $4 for sample chapbook.** Bradley Strahan adds that in *Visions* "We sometimes publish helpful advice about 'getting published' and the art and craft of poetry, and often discuss poets and the world of poetry on our editorial page."

BLACK FLY REVIEW (II), University of Maine, Fort Kent ME 04743, phone (207)834-3162, ext. 118, founded 1980, editors Roland Burns and Wendy Kindred. **"We want poetry with strong, sensory images that evoke a sense of experience, place, person; poetry that generates ideas; no overtly philosophical poetry, bad poetry."** They have recently published poetry by Walter McDonald, Terry Plunkett, Michael Cadnum and Connie Voisine. The annual is digest-sized, 56 pp., using woodcuts and prints by Wendy Kindred, professionally printed in small type on tinted, heavy stock with matte card cover with art. They accept 40-50 of 500-600 submissions per year. Press run of 700-1,000 for 50 subscriptions of which 30 are libraries, and 500 shelf sales. **Sample postpaid: $3. Send SASE for guidelines. Pays 5 copies. Acquires first North American rights. No simultaneous submissions or previously published poems. Reports in 6 months.** Roland Burns advises, "The publishing situation for poets is good and getting better. There are more good poets writing in America than at any other time. The essence of poetry is the image that provides sensory focus and that generates a sense of experience, place, persons, emotions, ideas."

BLACK MOUNTAIN REVIEW; LORIEN HOUSE (IV-Themes), P.O. Box 1112, Black Mountain NC 28711-1112, phone (704)669-6211, founded 1969, editor David A. Wilson, is a small press publishing many books under the Lorien House imprint (poetry on a subsidy basis) and the annual *Black Mountain Review*. They want **poetry with "quality form/construction—a full thought, specifically fitting the theme, 16-80 lines. No blatant sex, violence, horror."** As a sample, the editor selected these lines from "Border Crossing" by Judson Jerome in *BMR #7* "On Thomas Wolfe":

> *Many return world-wiser, holy,*
> *tender to busy travelers of here.*
> *Their eyes are objective as glass.*
> *The present cannot betray them.*
> *Their knowledge cannot be uttered or believed.*

BMR is digest-sized, saddle-stapled, 44 pgs. with matte card cover, photocopied from typescript. Press run "about 300" of which they sell about 200. They accept 1-5 poems of about 200 received per year. **Sample postpaid: $4. Send SASE for guidelines. Pays 2 copies plus $5 for poems. Buys first or reprint rights. Previously published poetry OK. Reports in a few days.** Reviews books of poetry when an issue has room—usually 3-6 books. **Query regarding subsidized book publication. Editor comments on submissions "occasionally," and he offers "full analysis and marketing help" for $1/typed page of poetry.** He says, *"Please* send for the current theme. Do *not* send general poetry. Since the current themes are American writers, the poetry must be *on* the writer for the issue. This makes the project more demanding, but some research and original new work will give you a good chance for publication."

BLACK RIVER REVIEW; STONE ROLLER PRESS (II, IV-Translations), 855 Mildred Ave., Lorain OH 44052-1213, phone (216)244-9654, founded 1985, poetry editor Michael Waldecki, editorial contact Kaye Coller, is a literary annual using **"contemporary poetry, any style, form and subject matter, 50 line maximum (usually), poetry with innovation, craftsmanship and a sense of excitement and/or depth of emotion. Do *not* want Helen Steiner Rice, greeting card verse, poetry that mistakes stilted, false or formulaic diction for intense expression of feeling."** They have published poetry by James Margorian, Adrian Louis, Christopher Franke, Catherine Hammond, Sylvia Foley and Leslie Leyland Fields. As a sample the editor selected these lines from "Drought" by Stephen R. Roberts:

> *The reptilian trunk of a pine crawls up*
> *to needles as loose as an old man's teeth.*
> *There is a fear of frictions.*
> *Poison ivy slumbers in green smiles,*
> *and the crow's harsh voice*
> *could spark the woodpile.*
> *Everything is burned and older.*
> *Children are telling children,*
> *four more weeks and we all die.*

The magazine-sized annual is photocopied from typescript on quality stock, saddle-stapled with matte card cover with art, about 60 pgs., using ads, circulation 400 (sold in college bookstore). **Sample: $3 (backcopy); $3.50 (current issue); $6 (two copies of any issue) postpaid. Pays 1 copy. Submit between January and May 1, limit of 10, photocopy OK, no simultaneous submissions. Will consider previously published poems if acknowledged. Send SASE for guidelines. Editor may comment on submissions.** Reviews books of poetry. Kaye Coller comments, "We want strong poems that show a depth of vision beyond the commonplace. We don't care if a poet is well-known or not, but we don't publish amateurs. An amateur is not necessarily a new poet, but one who doesn't believe in revision, tends to be preachy, writes sentimental slush, tells the reader what to think and/or concludes the poem with an explanation in case the reader didn't get the point. If we think we can use one or more of a poet's poems, we keep them until the final choices are made in June; otherwise, we send them back as soon as possible. Follow the ms mechanics in **Poet's Market. We are also looking for poems written in Spanish. If selected, they will be published with English translation by either the poet or one of our staff."**

THE BLACK SCHOLAR; THE BLACK SCHOLAR PRESS (IV-Ethnic), P.O. Box 2869, Oakland CA 94609, founded 1969, publisher Robert Chrisman, uses **poetry "relating to/from/of the black American and other 'Third World' experience."** The bimonthly magazine is basically scholarly and research-oriented. They have published poetry by Ntozake Shange, Jayne Cortez, Andrew Salkey and D.L. Smith. The editor says it is 64 pgs., 7×10, with 10,000 subscribers of which 60% are libraries, 15% shelf sales. Single copy $5; subscription $30. **Sample back issue: $6 prepaid. Send SASE for guidelines. Pays 10 copies and subscription. Enclose "letter & bio or curriculum vita, SASE, phone number, no originals."** Reviews books of poetry. They also publish 1-2 books a year, average 100 pgs., flat-spined. **Send query letter.** For sample books, send 8½×11 SASE for catalog, average cost $10.95 including postage and handling. "We only publish one issue every year containing poetry. Please be advised—it is against our policy to discuss submissions via telephone. Also, we get a lot of mss, but read *every single one*, thus patience is appreciated."

BLACK SPARROW PRESS (III), 24 Tenth St., Santa Rosa CA 95401, phone (707)579-4011, founded 1966, assistant to the publisher Michele Filshie, publishes poetry, fiction, literary criticism and bibliography in flat-spined paperbacks, hardcovers and deluxe/limited editions (hardback). "We do not publish chapbooks. Our books are 150 pgs. or longer." They have published poetry by Tom Clark, Wanda Coleman, Robert Kelly, Diane Wakoski, John Weiners and Edward Dorn. **Reports in 2 months. Pays 10% minimum royalties plus author's copies.**

BLACK TIE PRESS (III), P.O. Box 440004, Houston TX 77244-0004, phone (713)789-5119, founded 1986, publisher and editor Peter Gravis. "Black Tie Press is committed to publishing innovative, distinctive and engaging writing. We publish books; we are not a magazine or literary journal. We are not like the major Eastern presses, university presses or other small presses in poetic disposition. To get a feel for our publishing attitude, we urge you to buy one or more of our publications before submitting." **Sample postpaid: $7.** He is **"only interested in imaginative, provocative, at risk writing. No rhyme."** Published poets include Harry Burrus, Guy Beining, Sekou Karanja, Craig Cotter, Donald Rawley, Dieter Weslowski, Laura Ryder and Toni Ortner. **"We have work we want to publish, hence, unsolicited material is not encouraged. However, we will read and consider material from committed, serious writers as time permits. Write, do not call about material. No reply without SASE."** Reports in 2-6 weeks. Author receives 10% of press run. Peter Gravis says, "Too many writers are only interested in getting published and not interested in reading or supporting good writing. Black Tie hesitates to endorse a writer who does not, in turn, promote and patronize (by actual purchases) small press publications. Once Black Tie publishes a writer, we intend to remain with that artist."

THE BLACK WARRIOR REVIEW (II), P.O. Box 2936, Tuscaloosa AL 35486-2936, phone (205)348-4518, founded 1974. Poets whose work has recently appeared in *Black Warrior Review* include Jorie Graham, Sherod Santos, Linda Gregg, Laura Moriarty, Lyn Hejinian and Gerald Stern. As a sample the editor selected these lines from "A Grace It Had, Devouring" by H.L. Hix:

> . . . I know from what we have for dinner
> What our farts will smell like in bed. We always kiss
> When we leave the house. We do the dishes together.
> *He paused. Snow fell.* Thirteen years is a lot of dishes.
>
> *She pushed a bran flake back and forth, back and forth*
> *On the rim of her bowl. Her nose always turned red*
> *When she tried not to cry.*

It is a 6×9 semiannual of 144 pages. Circulation 2,000. **Sample postpaid: $5. Send SASE for guidelines. Address submissions to the Poetry Editor. Submit 3-6 poems, simultaneous (say so) and photocopied submissions OK. Awards one $500 prize annually. Pays $5-10/printed page plus two copies. Buys first rights. Reports in 1-3 months.** Reviews books of poetry in single or multi-book format. "We solicit a nationally-known poet for the chapbook. For the remainder of the issue, we solicit a few poets, but the bulk of the material is chosen from unsolicited submissions. Many of our poets have substantial publication credits, but our decision is based simply on the quality of the work submitted."

BLIND ALLEYS (II); SEVENTH SON PRESS (V), % Michael S. Weaver, Rutgers University, Box 29, Camden NJ 08102, founded 1981, *Blind Alleys* founded 1982 by Michael S. Weaver, editors Michael S. Weaver and Aissatou Mijiza. They have published poetry by Lucille Clifton, Arthur Winfield Knight,

Kimiko Hahn, Peter Harris and Ethelbert Miller. *BA* appears twice a year, digest-sized, 78 pgs., saddle-stapled, professionally printed on thin stock, matte card cover, circulation 500. **Sample: $5 postpaid. All submissions must be addressed to Michael S. Weaver. Submit about 5 poems in a batch, none longer than 100 lines. Pays 2 copies.** Reviews book of poetry. **The press publishes broadsides but is not presently accepting unsolicited book mss.**

‡BLIND BEGGAR PRESS; LAMPLIGHT EDITIONS; NEW RAIN (IV-Ethnic, anthology, children), P.O. Box 437, Williamsbridge Station, Bronx NY 10467, phone and FAX (914)683-6792, founded 1976, literary editor Gary Johnston, business manager C.D. Grant, publishes work **"relevant to Black and Third World people, especially women."** New Rain is an annual anthology of such work. Lamplight Editions is a subsidiary which publishes "educational materials such as children's books, manuals, greeting cards with educational material in them, etc." They want to see **"quality work that shows a concern for the human condition and the condition of the world—arts for people sake."** They have published work by Judy D. Simmons, A.H. Reynolds, Mariah Britton, Kurt Lampkins, Rashidah Ismaili, Jose L. Garza and Carletta Wilson. As a sample the editor selected the first five lines of Brenda Connor-Bey's "Crossroad of the Serpent":

> *Like a serpent*
> *splitting open fields*
> *this road always brings me back*
> *to this magical place of healing*
> *to this place of hidden waters*

New Rain is a digest-sized, saddle-stapled or perfect-bound, 60-200 page chapbook, finely printed, with simple art, card covers. **Sample: $5 postpaid.** They also publish about 3 collections of poetry by individuals per year, 60-100 pgs., flat-spined paperback, glossy, color cover, good printing on good paper. **Sample: $5.95. For either the anthology or book publication, first send sample of 5-10 poems with cover letter including your biographical background, philosophy and poetic principles. Considers simultaneous submissions. Reads submissions January 15 through September 1 only.** They reply to queries in 3-4 weeks, submissions in 2-3 months, pay in copies (the number depending on the print run). Acquires all rights. Returns them "unconditionally." Willing to work out individual terms for subsidy publication. Catalog available for SASE.

BLUE LIGHT PRESS (V), P.O. Box 642, Fairfield IA 52556, phone (515)472-7882, founded 1988, partner Diane Frank, publishes 3 paperbacks, 3 chapbooks/year. **"We like poems that are emotionally honest and uplifting. Women, Visionary Poets, Iowa Poets, San Francisco Poets. No rhymed poetry or dark poetry." They are currently accepting work by invitation only.** They have recently published poetry by Thomas Centolella, Nancy Berg, Louise Nayer and Meg Fitz-Randolph. As a sample the editor selected these lines from **The Houses Are Covered in Sound** by Louise Nayer:

> *There was something*
> *moving in a garbage can,*
> *a white light glowing in a spiral.*
> *I thought it was a child,*
> *no the wind, no the part*
> *of myself that glowed.*

That book is flat-spined, digest-sized, professionally printed, 60 pgs., with elegant matte card cover: $10. They have also published two anthologies of Iowa poets. They have an editorial board and provide criticism for $20-30/hour. "We also work in person with local poets. We have an ongoing poetry workshop and give classes periodically."

‡BLUE LIGHT REVIEW (II), P.O. Box 1621, Pueblo CO 81002, founded 1983 (magazine), poetry editor Paul Dilsaver. The *Review* is a semiannual literary magazine, circulation 200, which uses about 30 pgs. of poetry in each issue: inexpensively printed (offset from various varieties of typescript) in a digest-sized saddle-stapled format. **Sample: $4. Reports in 6 months. Pays 1 copy. Acquires first North American serial rights.** Here is the opening stanza of "November Morning" by Victoria McCabe:

> *Someone is walking behind,*
> *walking very deliberately behind,*
> *as if he had a mission*
> *he walks, whoever he is, behind.*

Reviews books of poetry in 100-400 words.

BLUE RYDER (III), (formerly *Heathenzine* and *Temm Poetry Magazine*, now combined), P.O. Box 587, Olean NY 14760, founded 1989, editor Ken Wagner, is subtitled "America's Underbelly At Its Best," publishes choice reprints from underground, alternative, special interest, small and micropress publications, appears every other month. **Submit 2-5 previously published poems; crisp, dark photocopies as they originally appeared, along with name, address and ordering information for the publication—**

you must still have the rights to the piece. "Beat generation and Modernist do best, through there is no objection to more academic or classical pieces as long as it's not stupid, contrite rhyme." They have published poetry by Lyn Lifshin, Thomas Krampf, John Bennett, Patrick McKinnon, Dan Sicoli, Todd Moore and Cheryl Townsend. As a sample the editor selected these lines by Laura Albrecht:

> *You looked into the face of America and saw its stars and stripes teeth*
> *ripping children apart.*

BR reviews other magazines and reprints excerpts only, but **considers previously published work submitted by writers.** It is magazine-sized, 40-44 pgs., saddle-stapled, with 60 lb. color cover. They use up to 18 poets per year. Press run 700 for 250 subscribers of which 4 are libraries, 350 shelf sales. Subscription: $10. **Sample postpaid: $3. Send SASE for guidelines. Pays 1 copy. Reports in 3 months.** The editor says, "Your very best bet is to send a published chap as I'm always looking for good chaps to excerpt from."

BLUE UNICORN, A TRIQUARTERLY OF POETRY; BLUE UNICORN POETRY CONTEST (II, IV-Translations), 22 Avon Rd., Kensington CA 94707, phone (415)526-8439, founded 1977, poetry editors Ruth G. Iodice, Harold Witt and Daniel J. Langton, wants **"well-crafted poetry of all kinds, in form or free verse, as well as expert translations on any subject matter. We shun the trite or inane, the soft-centered, the contrived poem. Shorter poems have more chance with us because of limited space."** They have published poetry by James Applewhite, Kim Cushman, Charles Edward Eaton, Patrick Worth Gray, Joan LaBombard, James Schevill, John Tagliabue and Gail White. These sample lines are from "Melville" by Laurence Snydal:

> *Here he comes now, slow, down along the docks*
> *He visits daily. See his old slouch hat,*
> *His greasy overcoat. He gives a pat*
> *To pockets, fishes out a key, unlocks*
> *His dusty office. What he does inside*
> *Is just what every customsman would do*
> *In New York City, 1882.*
> *And nothing shows he's nothing left to hide.*

The magazine is **"distinguished by its fastidious editing, both with regard to contents and format."** The editorial team puts a lot of work into a little space, and the product is usually a great read. It is 56 pgs., narrow digest-sized, saddle-stapled, finely printed, with some art. **Sample postpaid: $5.** They receive over 35,000 submissions a year, use about 200, have a year's backlog. **Submit 3-5 poems on normal typing pages, original or clear photocopy or clear, readable dot-matrix, no simultaneous submissions or previously published poems. Reports in 1-3 months, payment one copy, guidelines available for SASE.** They sponsor an annual contest with small entry fee to help support the magazine, with prizes of $100, $75 and $50, distinguished poets as judges, publication of 3 top poems and 6 honorable mentions in the magazine. Entry fee: $4 for first poem, $3 for others to a maximum of 5. Write for current guidelines. **Criticism occasionally offered.** "We would advise beginning poets to read and study poetry—both poets of the past and of the present; concentrate on technique; and **discipline yourself by learning forms before trying to do without them.** When your poem is crafted and ready for publication, study your markets and then send whatever of your work seems to be compatible with the magazine you are submitting to."

BLUELINE (IV-Regional), English Dept., Potsdam College, Potsdam NY 13676, founded 1979, editor-in-chief Anthony Tyler, and an editorial board, "is an annual literary magazine dedicated to prose and poetry about the Adirondacks and other regions similar in geography and spirit." They want **"clear, concrete poetry pertinent to the countryside and its people. It must go beyond mere description, however. We prefer a realistic to a romantic view. We do not want to see sentimental or extremely experimental poetry."** Usually 44 lines or fewer, though "occasionally we publish longer poems" on "nature in general, Adirondack Mountains in particular. Form may vary, can be traditional or contemporary." They have published poetry by Phillip Booth, George Drew, Eric Ormsby, L.M. Rosenberg, John Unterecker, Lloyd Van Brunt, Laurence Josephs, Maurice Kenny and Nancy L. Nielsen. It's a handsomely printed, 112-page, 6×9 magazine with 40-45 pgs. of poetry in each issue, circulation 600. Sample copies: $6 on request. They have a 3- to 11-month backlog. **Submit September 1 through November 30, no more than 5 poems with short bio. No simultaneous submissions. Photocopy, dot-matrix OK if neat and legible. Reports in 2-10 weeks. Pays copies. Acquires first North American serial rights. Guidelines available for SASE. Occasionally comments on rejections.** Reviews books of poetry in 500-750 words, single and multi-book format. "We are interested in both beginning and established poets whose poems evoke universal themes in nature and show human interaction with the natural world. We look for **thoughtful craftsmanship rather than stylistic trickery.**"

BOA EDITIONS, LTD. (III). 92 Park Ave., Brockport NY 14420, phone (716)637-3844, founded 1976, poetry editor A. Poulin, Jr., **generally does not accept unsolicited mss.** They have published some of the major American poets, such as W. D. Snodgrass, John Logan, Isabella Gardner and Richard Wilbur, and they publish introductions by major poets of those less well-known. For example, Gerald Stern wrote the foreword for Li-Young Lee's *Rose.* **Query with samples. Pays royalties.**

BOGG PUBLICATIONS; BOGG (II), 422 N. Cleveland St., Arlington VA 22201, founded 1968, poetry editors John Elsberg (USA), George Cairncross (UK: 31 Belle Vue St., Filey, N. Yorkshire YO 14 9HU, England) and Sheila Martindale (Canada: P.O. Box 23148, 380 Wellington St., London, Ontario NGA 5N9). ISSN: 0882-648X. "We publish *Bogg* magazine and occasional free-for-postage pamphlets." The magazine uses a great deal of poetry in each issue (with several featured poets) — **"poetry in all styles, with a healthy leavening of shorts (under 10 lines). Our emphasis on good work per se and Anglo-American cross-fertilization."** This is one of the liveliest small press magazines published today. It started in England and in 1975 began including a supplement of American work; it now is published in the US and mixes US, Canadian and UK work with reviews of small press publications on both sides of the Atlantic. It's thick (64 pgs.), typeset, saddle-stitched, in a 6×9 format that leaves enough white space to let each poem stand and breathe alone. They have recently published work by Ann Menebroker, Steve Richmond, Joyce Odam and Charles Bukowski. As a sample we selected this complete poem, "New Age Rebel," by Paul Dilsaver:

> she thought Woodstock
> was a subdivision

They accept all styles, all subject matter. "Some have even found the magazine's sense of play offensive. Overt religious and political poems have to have strong poetical merits — statement alone is not sufficient. Prefer typewritten manuscripts, with author's name and address on each sheet. Photocopy OK. We will reprint previously published material, but with a credit line to a previous publisher." No simultaneous submissions. Prefers to see 6 poems. About 40 pgs. of poetry per issue, print run of 750, 400 subscriptions of which 20 are libraries. **Sample $3.50 postpaid.** Subscription: $12 for 3 issues. They receive over 10,000 American poems/year and use 100-150. "We try to accept only for next 2 issues. SASE required or material discarded (no exceptions)." **Reports in 1 week. Pays 2 copies. Guidelines available for SASE. Acquires one-time rights.** Reviews books and chapbooks of poetry in 250 words, single format. Their occasional pamphlets and chapbooks are by invitation only, the author receiving 25% of the print run, and you can get **chapbook samples free for SASE.** Better make it at least 2 ounces worth of postage. John Elsberg advises, "Become familiar with a magazine before submitting to it. Always enclose SASE. Long lists of previous credits irritate me. Short notes about how the writer has heard about or what he finds interesting or annoying in *Bogg,* I read with some interest."

‡BOLD PRINT (I), 2602 W. Main, Richmond VA 23220, phone (804)355-8584, founded 1982, editor Kyle Hogg, is a "small press publisher of everything and anything. Writers, **do what you want to do. Make your own styles. Follow your own rules.** Get your head out of the poetry books and into your own notebooks. Shake all that big time stuff off and get sweaty, loud, cool down, be yourself and act yourself. You won't be by yourself." He has recently published poetry by Joel Poudrier, Michael Dombrowski, Barbara Goldman and many others. As a sample he selected these lines from Kris Lemoines "Cridersville Dragstrip":

> Henry would order four 20 oz. cups of "Pabst"
> Walk to the stall in the restroom
> Sit and take off his hat
> Pull a tube of Brel Cream
> From his sports coat pocket
> And carefully apply a half
> Dozen handfuls to his hair

Bold Print is 20 pgs., photocopied front and back, stapled at the corner. It appears every 12-18 months, "whenever I can afford to put it out to all the folks who want it." Press run is about 1,200. It is distributed through the mail. **"Samples are available for $4 or $5 if you're a new person to the *Bold Print* scene. Much cheaper — donations — later." Pays 1 copy. Submit in any readable form. Simultaneous and previously published poems OK.** "I write every person a letter with the issue I send." The editor says, "Don't follow any paths your mind's feet don't fit on. Just 'cuz you see some poetry in some book doesn't mean it's any better than your own. Don't write above yourself. Follow your true feelings, rhymes, words and beats. Beat up on the poetry rules — poetry is a free for all and you got as good a shot as the next guy. You may not hit the mark, but at least you threw it out there. The greatest poets of today are rap music lyricists. They knock established poetry loop, loop, loopy. Listen to rap and wear your poetry with pride. Send letters with submissions, so I know a bit about you."

‡BOMB MAGAZINE (III), Suite 1002 A, 594 Broadway, New York NY 10012, founded 1981, managing editor Ameena Meer, is a quarterly magazine that "encourages a dialogue among artists of various media. **We encourage poetry by people of color and serious poetry by experienced poets; shorter is better. Experiments with form and language are also encouraged. No limericks, inspirational verse, clever or greeting card styles.**" They have recently published poetry by David Mamet, Harold Pinter and A.C. Purcell. As a sample the editor selected these lines by Agha Shahid Ali:

> *Cries Majnoon:*
> *Those in tatters*
> *May now demand love:*
> *I've declared a fashion*
> *of ripped collars.*
> *The breezes are lost*
> *travellers today,*
> *knocking, asking*
> *for a place to stay.*
> *I tell them*
> *to go away.*

BOMB is 96 pages, saddle-stiched with 4-color cover. "We receive about 100 manuscripts a month; we accept 2 or 3 every 4 months." Press run is 12,000 for 2,000 subscriptions of which 600 are libraries. Single copy: $4; subscription: $16/year. **Sample postpaid: $5. No previously published poems; simultaneous submissions OK. "Poetry should be legibly typed." Reads submissions May 1 through July 1 only.** Time between acceptance and publication is 4-6 months. **Reports in 4 months. Pays $50. Buys first North American serial rights.** The editor says, "Writers should be current with literary scene and be well-educated in classical and contemporary poetry."

BONE & FLESH PUBLICATIONS (II), P.O. Box 349, Concord NH 03302-0349, founded 1988, coeditors Lester Hirsh and Frederick Moe, *Bone & Flesh* literary journal now appears annually. "**We are looking for quality calibre work from seasoned writers with a literary slant. All forms: prose poems, short fiction, haiku, essays and artwork are welcome. Themes may vary but should focus on the substance of our lives or the link with other lives and times. We do not want to see anything that is overtly fundamentalist, banal, trite or conventional. Submissions are accepted February through May only.**" *Always* **query before submitting.** They have recently published works by Don Skiles, Jack Veasey, Beret Strong, David Chorlton, R. Nikolas Macioci, Sheila Murphy, Lisa Yeager and Michael Wurster. As a sample the editors selected these lines by B.Z. Niditch:

> *The European wakes up*
> *from his daily nightmare,*
> *"We are one flesh and spirit*
> *from the Atlantic to the Urals"*
> *and when he sleepwalks*
> *snoring over Nietzche*
> *I am dismissed*
> *for pre-war morals.*

Bone & Flesh is 50-55 pgs., 7 × 8, with occasional supplements. Subscription: $7. **Sample postpaid: $5. Editors attempt to comment on rejections and provide encouragement "when appropriate." Reports in 1-3 months. Pays copies. Acquires first North American serial rights.** Reviews chapbooks of poetry in 100-200 words, single-book format. In addition to the magazine, Bone & Flesh Publications has also recently published **Next Stop Coney Island** by Bayla Winters and **Old Bones,** a compilation chapbook.

‡BOOTS: FOR FOLKS WITH THEIR BOOTS ON! (I, IV-Themes), P.O. Box 766, Challis ID 83226, phone (208)879-4475, founded 1990, editor Ethie Corrigan, is a biannual magazine using "**well-crafted cowboy poetry and historical pieces (Western Americana). No modernistic mumbo-jumbo.**" They have recently published poetry by Wallace McRae, Gwen Peterson, Sandy Seaton and Mike Logan. As a sample we selected the first two stanzas of "The Bullrider's Mother" by Terry Fuhriman:

> *If you've never been to a Junior Rodeo*
> *Let me tell you the contestants aren't very old*
> *But what they lack in experience*
> *They make up for by being daring and bold*
>
> *Every event involves some kind of danger*
> *In one form or another*
> *But I think the most dangerous place in the house*
> *Is sittin' next to a bullrider's mother*

"The theme of this issue was women in Western development," says Ethie Corrigan, editor and publisher of the biannual magazine Boots: For Folks With Their Boots On! "We particularly wantted to pay tribute to pioneer women," she says. The publication generally features articles of Western Americana and poetry makes up 50 to 65% of their offerings. They look for cowboy poetry and historical and/or character pieces. The illustration here was created by Cary Schwarz, a fulltime saddle maker who also owns a few cattle and has done every Boots cover to date, Corrigan says.

Boots is 56 pgs., web press printed, saddle-stitched, with glossy cover, photos and ads. Press run is 3,000 for 700 subscribers of which 2 are libraries. Single copy: $4.50; subscription: $8. **Sample postpaid: $2.50. Previously published poems OK; no simultaneous submissions. Submit typed poems January through March for fall issue; April through September for spring. Always comments on rejections. Reports "immediately." Pays copies "exact number depends on length."** Reviews related books of poetry "now and then."

BOREALIS PRESS; TECUMSEH PRESS LTD.; JOURNAL OF CANADIAN POETRY (V), Dept. PM, 9 Ashburn Dr., Ottawa, Ontario K2E 6N4 Canada, founded 1972. Borealis and Tecumseh are imprints for books, including **collections of poetry, by Canadian writers only, and they are presently not considering unsolicited submissions. Send SASE (or SAE with IRCs) for catalog to buy samples.** Poets published include John Ferns and Russell Thornton. These sample lines are by Fred Cogswell:

> *Often in dreams, when powerless to wake*
> *Or move and thereby ease my pounding heart,*
> *I have felt like a mouse that cannot squeal*
> *When the sprung trap pins its broken spine or*
> *Like a rabbit mesmerized by a snake's*
> *Unchanging otherness of lidless eyes.*

The annual *Journal* publishes reviews and criticism, not poetry. **Sample postpaid: $6.95.**

BOSTON LITERARY REVIEW (BLUR) (II), P.O. Box 357, W. Somerville MA 02144, phone (617)625-6087, founded 1984, editor Gloria Mindock, appears twice a year using **"work with a strong voice and individual style; experimental work welcome. Submit 5-10 poems."** They have published poetry by Stuart Friebert, David Ray, Eric Pankey and Richard Kostelanetz. The editor describes it as "24 pgs., 4×12, offset, no ads." They publish about 60 of 4,800 poems received per year. Press run: 500 for 55 subscriptions of which 5 are libraries. Subscription: $6/year. **Sample postpaid: $4. Pays 2 copies. All rights revert to author. Reports in 2-4 weeks. Editor comments on submissions "sometimes."**

‡THE BOSTON PHOENIX: PHOENIX LITERARY SECTION (PLS) (III), 126 Brookline Ave., Boston MA 02215, phone (617)536-5390, founded 1966, poetry editor Lloyd Schwartz is a monthly book review with one poem in almost every issue. As **"most poetry is solicited,"** no submission information was provided. Press run is 150,000. Single copy $1.50. **Reports in 1 month. Pays $50.**

BOSTON REVIEW (II), 33 Harrison Ave., Boston MA 02111, editor Josh Cohen, founded 1975, a bimonthly arts, culture and politics magazine, uses about a **page and a half of poetry per issue, or 12 poems a year,** for which they receive about 700 submissions. Circulation 20,000 nationally including subscriptions and newsstand sales. **Sample: $4 postpaid.** They have a 4-6 month backlog. **Submit any time to Sean Broderick, poetry editor, no more than 6 poems, photocopy OK, simultaneous submis-**

sions discouraged; reports in 2 months "if you include SASE," pay varies. Buys first serial rights. Reviews books of poetry. The editor advises, "To save the time of all those involved, poets should be sure to send only *appropriate* poems to particular magazines. This means that a poet should not submit to a magazine that he/she has not read. Poets should also avoid lengthy cover letters and allow the poems to speak for themselves."

BOTTOMFISH (II), De Anza College, Creative Writing Program, 21250 Stevens Creek Blvd., Cupertino CA 95014, editor Robert Scott. This college-produced magazine appears annually. They have published poetry by Chitra Divakaruni, Janice Dabney and Charles Safford. This poetry sample is from "Blowout" by Walter Griffin:

> Suddenly you are there, out by the highway, arm
> wrestling the dark with the wheel in your hands
> gauging the distance between odometers and stars
> that shimmer like ghosts in the falling air
> as the wheel comes loose from the column and
> your brakeless car rolls toward the cliff

Bottomfish is 7 × 8¼, well-printed on heavy stock with tasteful b&w graphics, 60 pgs. perfect-bound. Circulation is 500, free to libraries, schools, etc., but $4/copy to individual requests. "Before submitting, writers are strongly urged to purchase a sample copy; subject matter is at the writer's discretion, as long as the poem is skillfully and professionally crafted." Best submission times: September through February 1. Deadline: February 1 each year. Reporting time is 2-6 months, depending on backlog. Pay is 2 copies. The editor says, "Spare us the pat, generic greeting-card phrases. We want sharp, sensory images that carry a strong theme."

‡BOUILLABAISSE (I, IV-Form/style), % Alpha Beat Press, 31 A Waterloo St., New Hope PA 18938, phone (215)862-0299, founded 1991, editors Dave Christy and Ana Pine, is a biannual using "poetry that reflects life and its ups and downs." They want **modern, beat poetry; poetry from the streets of life — no limit. No rhythm, Christian or sweet poetry."** They have recently published poetry by Charles Bukowski, Joy Walsh and Erling Friis-Baastad. As a sample the editors selected these lines by Janine Pommy Vega:

> Archangel Mary falls into the water
> killing the bridges, the Tappanzee and
> railroad tresks. Her backside against the pier, they promenade
> across her, River Edge to Harlem
> and time runs out

The editors say it is 160 pgs., 8½ × 11, offset, saddle-stitched, with graphics. They receive 200 + submissions a year, accept 30%. Press run is 500 for 250 subscribers of which 5 are libraries. Subscription: $15. **Sample postpaid: $10. Previously published poems and simultaneous submissions OK.** Cover letter required. Always comments on rejections. Send SASE for guidelines. Reports "immediately." Pays 1 copy. Reviews books of poetry in 250-500 words. They also publish 2 paperbacks and 2 chapbooks/year. "We work with each individual on their project." **Replies to queries "immediately," to mss within 3 weeks. Pays author's copies.** The editors say, "Keep writing and reading."

BOULEVARD (II), % editor Richard Burgin, P.O. Box 30386, Philadelphia PA 19103, phone (215)561-1723, founded 1985, appears 3 times a year. **"We've published everything from John Ashbery to Howard Moss to a wide variety of styles from new or lesser known poets. We're eclectic. Do not want to see poetry that is uninspired, formulaic, self-conscious, unoriginal, insipid."** They have published poetry by Amy Clampitt, John Ashbery, Molly Peacock, Jorie Graham and Mark Strand. As a sample editor Richard Burgin selected these lines from "Three Soundings of January Snow" by Stuart Lishan:

> Snow arias the ground tonight. It quilts
> the house; it sounds like a samba of whispers,
> Muffled, like a mitten slipped over love, like guilt.

Boulevard is 175 + pgs., flat-spined, digest-sized, professionally printed, with glossy card cover. Their press run is 2,800 with 700 subscriptions of which 200 are libraries. Subscription: $12. **Sample: $6 postpaid. Pays $25-250/poem, depending on length, plus 2 copies. Buys first North American serial rights. "Prefer name and number on each page with SASE. Encourage cover letters but don't require them. Will consider simultaneous submissions but not previously published poems." Reads submissions September 1 through May 30 only.** Editor sometimes comments on rejections. Richard Burgin says, "We believe the grants we have won from the National Endowment for the Arts etc., as well as the anthologies which continue to recognize us, have rewarded our commitment. My advice to poets: 'Write from your heart as well as your head.' "

BOX DOG PRESS; HEY MAGAZINE (I), P.O. Box 9609, Seattle WA 98109, founded 1983, editor Craig Joyce, publishes chapbooks and a quarterly magazine. He wants **poetry that is "experimental, innovative, good work in any genre/style"** but not **"metaphysical, racist, sexist, ultra-pretentious."** They have published poetry by Cholah Ciccone. The editor says *HEY* **"covers the range of styles and tastes, but please no pretentions. Simplicity and truth are preferable."** He says it's 40 pgs., magazine-sized, and it uses about 20 submissions/year. Press run is 400. Single copy $2.50; subscription: $8.50. Sample: $2 postpaid. **Pays 2 copies. Acquires one-time rights. Simultaneous submissions, previously published poems OK. For chapbook consideration send sample poems and $10 reading fee.**

BRANCH REDD BOOKS; BRANCH REDD REVIEW; BRANCH REDD POETRY BROADSHEETS; BRANCH REDD POETRY CHAPBOOKS (III), 4805 B St., Philadelphia PA 19120, phone (215)324-1462, editor Bill Sherman, is a "small press publisher of poetry" that **discourages unsolicited mss.** He has published poetry by Allen Fisher, Pierre Joris, Asa Benveniste, Eric Mottram, Kate Ruse-Glason and Shreela Ray. As a sample the editor selected these lines (poet unidentified):

> *Her hair, her blue nightslip, more*
> *Frustration. Earlier*
> *news of Bunting's death.*

The *Branch Redd Review* appears irregularly in varied formats with a press run of 500, **pays at least 5 copies.**

GEORGE BRAZILLER, INC. (II), 60 Madison Ave., New York NY 10010, phone (212)889-0909, founded 1955, editor Adrienne Baxter, is a major literary publisher. In 1980 they published **Classic Ballroom Dances** by Charles Simic, from which this sample poem, "Bedtime Story, " was selected:

> *When a tree falls in a forest*
> *And there's no one around*
> *To hear the sound, the poor owls*
> *Have to do all the thinking.*
>
> *They think so hard they fall off*
> *Their perch and are eaten by ants,*
> *Who, as you already know, all look like*
> *Little Black Riding Hoods.*

It is digest-sized, professionally printed, flat-spined, 64 pgs. with glossy card cover, $3.95. **"We consider reprints of books of poetry as well as new poems. If submitting a book for reprint,** *all* **reviews of the book should be submitted as well. Submit sample of work, never** *entire* **original pgs." Reports in 1 month or less. Payment varies in each case. Buys all rights.** The editor says, "We are a small publishing house that publishes few books (in general) each year. Still, we have published many well-known authors and are always open and receptive to new writers of every kind--and from all parts of the world."

BREAKTHROUGH!; AARDVARK ENTERPRISES (I, IV-Membership/subscription), 204 Millbank Dr. SW, Calgary, Alberta T2Y 2H9 Canada, phone (403)256-4639, founded 1982, poetry editor J. Alvin Speers. *Breakthrough!* is a general interest quarterly with 13-page "Poetry Corner." Aardvark publishes chapbooks on subsidy arrangements. *Breakthrough!*'s editor says, **"Prefer rhyme—no porn. Any length."** They have published poetry by Ellen Sandry, Edna·Janes Kayser, Muriel Kovinow and W. Ray Lundy. As a sample the editor selected these lines from his poem "Writers Role":

> *I have been there, with the author,*
> *As he told me of his trip*
> *In the schooner on the high sea,*
> *Where strong winds the sails did rip.*
>
> *On the mountain, or the highway,*
> *While adventure did enthrall,*
> *I have felt excited heartbeat*
> *Through the story's telling all.*

The editor says *Breakthrough!* is "dedicated to life improvement, starting with primary re-

---

ALWAYS submit a ms or query with a self-addressed, stamped envelope (SASE) within your country or a self-addressed envelope and International Reply Coupons (IRCs) purchased from the post office for other countries.

source — the individual" and describes it as "52 pgs., digest-sized, plus ad inserts periodically. Good quality photocopy, color heavy paper cover, using b&w illustrations." They receive about 100 poems a month, use approximately 20%. Press run is "over 200 and growing nicely." Subscription: $15. **Sample postpaid: $5. Send SASE for guidelines. Pays "small cash award to best 3 items per issue, chosen by readers' votes. Subscribers only submissions." Acquires one-time rights. Simultaneous submissions, previously published poems OK. Submit seasonal items "well in advance." Replies "prompt! Usually by return mail."** Reviews books of poetry in up to 1 page, for subscribers only. **For subsidized chapbook publication query with 3-5 samples, bio, previous publications.** "We publish for hire — quoting price with full particulars. We do not market these except by special arrangement. Prefer poet does that. We strongly recommend seeing our books first. Same goes for submitting to *Breakthrough!*; best to see magazine first." Send SASE for catalog to buy book samples. Periodic poetry contests close March 17th — small entry fee. Contest anthology published if sufficient interest. Details for SASE. Please note US stamps cannot be used in Canada. The editor advises, "Be professional and considerate. Support periodicals that 'showcase' work, by subscription. Need for this is accentuated by numbers unable to continue."

BREITENBUSH BOOKS, INC. (V), %Far Corner Books, P.O. Box 82157, Portland OR 97282, founded 1977, managing editor Tom Booth, publishes 2-3 flat-spined paperbacks/cloth editions each year, 64-150 pgs., 6×9. They have published books by Mary Barnard, Naomi Shihab Nye, Ingrid Wendt, William Greenway and Peter Sears. **"We have temporarily suspended the publication of new poetry volumes and are not currently accepting submissions."**

THE BRIDGE: A JOURNAL OF FICTION AND POETRY (II), 14050 Vernon St., Oak Park MI 48237, founded 1990, editor Jack Zucker, appears twice a year using **"exciting, realistic poetry."** It has recently published poetry by Ruth Whitman and Daniel Hughes. It is digest-sized, 160 pgs., perfect-bound, press run 700. Subscription: $8. **Sample postpaid: $5. Pays 2 copies. Acquires first rights. Editor comments on submissions "occasionally."** An editorial board of 3 considers mss; decision made by editor and 1 special editor. Reviews books of poetry and prose in 1-10 pgs.

BRILLIANT STAR (IV-Children), % Hill, Baha'i National Center, Wilmette IL 60091, is a Baha'i bimonthly for children, appearing in a magazine-sized format. **"Poems are always illustrated, so think about how your poem will look. Our readers are ages 5-14. Write for *them* not for yourself. We do not want to see Christmas themes in any form. If you are not familliar with the Baha'i Faith, research is encouraged."** As a sample the editor selected these lines from "Hooray for Skin" by Susan Eugle:

> *Suppose, when God created skin,*
> *He turned the skinside outside in*
> *So when you talk to Mrs. Jones,*
> *Your eyes meet over fat and bones*
> *And tissues, blue and white and red,*
> *That stretch from toe to hand to head.*
> *It makes me glad to have a skin*
> *To keep the outside boneside in.*

Considers simultaneous submissions. Sample: free with 9×12 SASE (sufficient postage for 5 oz.); objectives are printed in the masthead. "Contributors receive two copies."

BROKEN STREETS (I, IV-Religious, children), 57 Morningside Dr. E., Bristol CT 06010, founded 1979, poetry editor Ron Grossman, is a **"Christian-centered outreach ministry to poets. Chapbooks are sent free to encourage poets."** The digest-sized magazine, photocopied typescript, 40-50 pp., card covers, appears 4-5 times a year — 250 copies, **$3.50 for a sample.** The editor wants **"Christian-centered, city poetry, feelings, etc., usually 5-15 lines, haiku, no more than 5 poems at a time, not necessary to query, but helpful." Reports in 1 week.** Uses about 150 of the 200 poems submitted/year — by children, old people, etc. No pay but copies. Reviews books of poetry. He has published Bettye K. Wray and Naomi Rhoads.

BRUNSWICK PUBLISHING COMPANY (I), Rt. 1, Box 1A1, Lawrenceville VA 23868, founded 1978, poetry editor Walter J. Raymond, is a **partial subsidy publisher. Query with 3-5 samples. Response in 2 weeks with SASE. If invited, submit double-spaced, typed ms** (photocopy, dot-matrix OK). **Reports in 3-4 weeks, reading fee only if you request written evaluation. Poet pays 80% of cost, gets same percentage of profits for market-tester edition of 500,** advertised by leaflets mailed to reviewers, libraries, book buyers and bookstores. Samples are flat-spined, matte-covered, 54 pgs. paperbacks. **Send SASE for "Statement of Philosophy and Purpose," which explains terms, and catalog to order samples.** That Statement says: "We publish books because that is what we like to do. Every new book published is like a new baby, an object of joy! We do not attempt to unduly influence the reading public as to the value of our publications, but we simply let the readers decide that themselves. We refrain from the artificial beefing up of values that are not there. . . . We are not competitors in the publishing world, but offer what we believe is a needed service. We strongly believe that in an open society every person who has something of value to say and wants to say it should have the chance and opportunity to do so."

BRUSSELS SPROUT (IV-Form), P.O. Box 1551, Mercer Island WA 98040, phone (206)232-3239, Francine Porad, art and poetry editor since 1988. This magazine of **haiku, senryu and art** appears each January, May and September. **They want "any format (1-4 lines); subject matter open; seeking work that captures the haiku moment in a fresh way."** It has recently published poetry by Elizabeth St. Jacques, Anne McKay, George Swede, Michael Dylan Welch and Elizabeth S. Lamb. As a sample the editor selected these haiku by H.F. Noyes and Christopher Herold respectively:

spring miracle—	*willow shadows*
each seed knowing	*in and out of my cup . . .*
what to become	*tea leaves settling*

The magazine is digest-sized, professionally printed, 44-48 pgs. saddle-stapled with matte b&w card cover featuring an artist each issue. **Sample postpaid: $5.50. Guidelines available for SASE. No payment, other than 3 $10 Editor's Choice Awards each issue. Submit only original work, 4-12 poems (can be on one sheet), name and address on each sheet. Do not submit mss from May 25 to June 15. No simultaneous submissions or previously published poems. Reports in 3 weeks. Editor sometimes comments on rejections.** Reviews books of haiku "sometimes, but list those received with a brief comment or sample of work." *Brussels Sprout* sponsors Haiku Northwest, an informal group of writers meeting 5-6 times yearly to share work. The editor advises, "For the record, no editor enjoys saying 'no.' Keep writing, rewriting and sending out your manuscripts. If you value your work, you will find an editor who feels the same."

BUFFALO SPREE MAGAZINE (II), 4511 Harlem Rd., Buffalo NY 14226, founded 1967, poetry editor Janet Goldenberg, is the quarterly regional magazine of western New York. It has a controlled circulation (21,000) in the Buffalo area, mostly distributed free (with 3,000 subscriptions, of which 25 are libraries). Its glossy pages feature general interest articles about local culture, plus book reviews, fiction and poetry contributed nationally. It receives about 300 poetry submissions/year and uses about 25, which have ranged from work by Robert Hass and Carl Dennis to first publications by younger poets. As an example, the editor chose 5 lines of Martha Bosworth's "Alien in Spring":

> *I am a tall pale animal in boots*
> *trampling forget-me-nots and scaring birds*
> *from the lemon tree: with my long-handled claw*
> *I pull down lemons—tear-shaped, dimpled, round,*
> *bouncing they vanish into vines and weeds.*

They use 5-7 poems/issue, **paying $20 for each; these are selected 3-6 months prior to publication. Sample postpaid: $3.75. Considers simultaneous submissions, "but we must be advised that poems have been or are being submitted elsewhere."**

BYLINE MAGAZINE (IV-Themes), P.O. Box 130596, Edmond OK 73013, founded 1981, editor Marcia Preston, is a **magazine for the encouragement of writers and poets, using 9-12 poems/issue about writers or writing, paying $5-10/poem.** They have about 3,000 subscriptions, receive about 2,500 submissions per year, of which they use 144. *Byline* is professionally printed, magazine-sized, with illustrations, cartoons and ads. **Sample: $3 postpaid. No more than 4 poems per submission, photocopies OK, no reprints, reports within a month, rates $5-10, guidelines available for SASE. Buys first North American serial rights.** Marcia Preston advises "We are happy to work with new writers, but please read a few samples to get an idea of our style."

‡C.L.A.S.S. MAGAZINE (IV-Regional), 900 Broadway, New York NY 10003, editor Constance M. Weaver, is a monthly magazine, circulation 250,000, covering **Caribbean/American/African Third World news and views. Publishes 10-20 poems a year, 22-30 lines, on appropriate themes. Submit maximum of 10 poems. Pays $10 maximum.** It has a slick full-sized format with full-color glossy paper cover. **Subscription: $15, $20 overseas. Sample: $2.50.**

‡CAERMAEN BOOKS; AKLO: A JOURNAL OF THE FANTASTIC (IV-Form/style), 10-12 Castle Gate, Clitheroe, Lancashire BB7 1A2 England, founded 1985, coeditor Mark Valentine, publishes *Aklo* twice yearly. They want **"any prose poetry and verse in the tradition of the 1890s decadent poets."** They have recently published poetry by Alexis Lykiard, Sylvia Bruce, John Gale and John Adlard. The editor says *Aklo* is 80 pgs., A5, saddle-stapled, with card cover and art, no ads. They receive about 30 submissions a year, use approximately one third. Press run is 300 for 100 subscribers. Single copy: £3. **Sample postpaid: £4.50 by overseas mail. Previously published poems and simultaneous submissions OK. Cover letter required.** Time between acceptance and publication is 1 year. **Always comments on**

rejections. Reports in 2 weeks. Pays "negotiable" amount plus 2 copies. Mark Valentine says, "We find it very difficult to acquire quality prose poetry—it seems to be a neglected art."

CALAPOOYA COLLAGE; CAROLYN KIZER POETRY AWARDS (II), P.O. Box 309, Monmouth OR 97361, phone (503)838-6292, founded 1981, editor Thomas L. Ferte. *CC* is a literary annual using **"all kinds" of poetry.** They have published poetry by Robert Bly, Joseph Bruchac, Octavio Paz, Marge Piercy, William Stafford, Ursula K. LeGuin, Patricia Goedicke, David Wagoner and David Ray. It is tabloid-sized, 48 pgs. Press run 1,500 for 250 subscribers of which 16 are libraries. They accept about 6% of 6,000 poems received annually. **Sample postpaid: $4. Reads submissions September 1 through June 1 only. Pays 2 copies. Reports in 4-8 weeks.** Reviews books of poetry in 600-1,000 words. All poems accepted for publication are eligible for annual $700 Carolyn Kizer Poetry Awards.

CALDER PUBLICATIONS LTD.; RIVERRUN PRESS INC (V), 9-15 Neal St., London WC2H 9TU England, phone (071)497-1741, publisher John Calder, a literary book publisher. On their list are Samuel Beckett, Breyten Breytenbach, Erich Fried, Paul Eluard, Pier Paolo Passolini and Howard Barker. **"We do not read for the public,"** says John Calder, and he wants **no unsolicited mss.**

THE CALIFORNIA QUARTERLY (II), 100 Sproul Hall, University of California, Davis CA 95616, founded 1971, appears 2-4 times/year, using **poetry of "literary quality, no specs."** They have published poetry by Laura Jensen, Alan Williamson, Colette Inez and Sal Cetrano. As a sample here are the concluding lines from "Waiting for the Bus" by Lee Bartlet:

> *Slowly thick snakes rouse themselves from under the vines.*
> *Fear-Ball begins to sweat, holding his rifle tight to his chest. He wants his mamma*
> *Do-da*

It is digest-sized, flat-spined, 80+ pgs., professionally printed, offset, with glossy card cover. They accept about 25 of 2,500 poems received/year. Press run 600. Subscription: $14/4 issues. **Sample postpaid: $4. Reports in 6-8 weeks. Pays $4/page plus 1 copy. Do not submit June through September.**

CALLALOO (IV-Ethnic), Johns Hopkins University Press, #275, 701 W. 40th St., Baltimore MD 21211, phone (301)516-6987, founded 1976, editor Charles H. Rowell. Devoted to **poetry dealing with North America, Europe, Africa, Latin and Central America, South America and the Caribbean.** They have published poetry by Rita Dove, Jay Wright, Alice Walker, Yusef Komunyakaa, Aimé Césaire, Nicolás Guillén and Michael Harper. The magazine is a thick quarterly with a varying amount of poetry in its nearly 200 pgs., circulation 1,400, with 1,400 subscriptions of which half are libraries. Subscription: $21, $45 for institutions. **"We have no specifications for submitting poetry except authors should include SASE." Reports in 6 months. Pays copies.** The *Callaloo* Poetry Series is published by the University of Virginia Press.

‡CALLALOO POETRY SERIES (IV-Ethnic), Department of English, Wilson Hall, University of Virginia, Charlottesville VA 22903, Attn: Charles Rowell. The *Callaloo* Poetry Series is published by the University of Virginia Press, and **all inquiries and submissions should be directed to Charles Rowell at the above address.** The University of Virginia also sponsors the journal *Callaloo* published by John Hopkins University Press; see separate listing for *Callaloo*. The University of Virginia publishes 2-5 flat-spined paperbacks a year, 40-60 pages. **"Please inquire before submitting to chapbook series."**

CALYX, A JOURNAL OF ART & LITERATURE BY WOMEN (IV-Women, lesbian), P.O. Box B, Corvallis OR 97339, phone (503)753-9384, founded 1976, managing editor M. Donnelly, is a journal edited by a collective editorial board, **publishes poetry, prose, art, reviews and interviews by and about women.** They want **"excellently crafted poetry that also has excellent content."** They have published poetry by Diane Glancy, Robin Morgan, Rebecca Seiferle, Lin Max and Carol Ann Russell. As a sample the editor selected these lines from "Watching My Mother Dress" by Cornelia Hoogland:

> *She, who loudhosannahed every chore,*
> *cleaned and cared for us while she peeled potatoes,*
> *in one deft spiral paring, who spun rooms*
> *and bottles through her dusting cloth, lingered.*

Each issue is 7×8, handsomely printed on heavy paper, flat-spined, glossy color cover, 125-200 pgs., of which 50-60 are poetry. **Sample for the single copy price: $8 plus $1.50 postage.** *Calyx* is open to submissions twice annually: March 1 through April 15 and October 1 through November 15. Mss received when not open to reading will be returned unread. Send up to 6 poems with SASE and short biographical statement. **"We accept copies in good condition and clearly readable. We report in 2-6 months." Pays copies. Guidelines available for SASE.** They say, "Read the publication and be familiar with what we have published."

CAMELLIA (II), P.O. Box 4092, Ithaca NY 14852, editor Tomer Inbar, "is a quarterly poetry magazine currently available for free in the San Francisco/Oakland Bay area, Madison, Seattle, Ithaca and D.C., or by sending a 52¢ SASE. **We publish poetry in the W.C. Williams tradition. The poetry of things, moment and sharpness. We encourage young writers and like to work with the writers who publish with us (i.e., publishing them again to widen the forum or exposure of their work). Our main goal is to get the poetry out. We do not want to see poetry where the poem is subordinate to the poet or poetry where the noise of the poetic overshadows the voice. We look for poetry that is honest and sharp and unburdened.**" As a sample the editor selected these lines from "Pausing At A Still Life" by T.N. Turner:

> What more can be said
> About things?
>
> A blackbird
> On the wing;
>
> A brown monk
> Reading a brown Bible
> In a brown room

The editor describes *Camellia* as digest-sized, 20-24 pgs., desktop published. The first thing that catches your eye is the design. The editors make up for this modest-looking, stapled publication with creative typesetting inside, featuring lively free avant-garde verse with titles in large points and varied fonts. The look is old *New York Quarterly*, and all the poems aim to take a risk with image or freestyle form. "We receive approximately 300-350 poems/issue and publish about 20." Press run 500-900. Subscription: $5/year. $7 overseas. **Sample: 52¢ SASE. Pays 2 copies. Simultaneous submissions and previously published poems OK. Reports "ASAP." Editor comments on submissions "if asked for or if I want to see more but am not satisfied with the poems sent. We currently publish two regular issues per year and are instituting a series of special project issues (an additional two per year). One will be poetry in translation: the other a mini chapbook (by invitation only)."**

CANADIAN DIMENSION: A SOCIALIST NEWS MAGAZINE (IV-Political), 707-228 Notre Dame Ave., Winnipeg, Manitoba R3B 1N7 Canada, phone (204)957-1519, founded 1964, editorial contact Tanya Lester, appears 8 times/year, using "**short poems on labour, women, native and other issues. Nothing more than one page.**" They have published poetry by Tom Wayman and Milton Acorn. It is 48-56 pgs., magazine-sized, slick, professionally printed, with glossy paper cover. Press run: 4,500-5,000 for 3,000 subscriptions of which 800 are libraries, 1,000 shelf sales. Subscription: $30.50 US ($24.50 Canadian). **Sample postpaid: $1.50. Pays 5 copies. Simultaneous submissions OK. Reports in 1 month. Editor comments on submissions "rarely."** Reviews books of poetry in 750-1,200 words, single or multi-book format.

CANADIAN LITERATURE (IV-Regional), 2029 West Mall, University of British Columbia, Vancouver, British Columbia V6T 1Z2 Canada, phone (604)822-2780, founded 1959, poetry editor L.R. Ricou, is a quarterly review which publishes **poetry by Canadian poets. "No limits on form. Less room for long poems."** They have published poems by Atwood, Ondaatje, Layton and Bringhurst. The following sample lines are from "Birds" by John Pass:

> And a snowy owl
>
> is an exception. Once
> I stood by goalposts at the local school
> and watched one watch the hard white field
> from the crossbar, utterly unruffled, at home
>
> and extraordinary there, a genius
> of moonlight and the small hot shadows, of quickness
> subtleties, exquisite contrasts.

Each issue is professionally printed, large digest-sized, flat-spined, with 190+ pgs., of which about 10 are poetry. It has 2,000 circulation, two-thirds of which are libraries. **Sample for the cover price: $15 Canadian.** They receive 100-300 submissions per year, of which they use 10-12. **No photocopy, round-dot-matrix, simultaneous submissions or reprints. Reports within the month, pays $10/poem plus 1 copy. Buys first rights.** Reviews books of poetry in 500-1,000 words, depending on the number of books.

CANADIAN WRITER'S JOURNAL (IV-Themes), Gordon M. Smart Publications, P.O. Box 6618, Depot 1, Victoria, British Columbia V8P 5N7 Canada, is a very **limited market for poetry using only "short poems or portions thereof as part of 'how-to' articles relating to the writing of poetry and occasional**

short poems with tie-in to the writing theme." But it is a publication of interest to poets. "Every issue has a variety of how-to and motivational articles for writers, many by accomplished and well-published authors" and "several regular columns with interesting and useful information ranging from writing tips to the viewpoint from behind the editor's desk." It appears quarterly, subscription $15.

CANAL LINES (I, IV-Regional), 55 Main St. #3, Brockport NY 14420-1903, phone (716)637-0584, founded 1987, editor Joseph Hoffman, appears 3-4 times a year. **"Subject matter and style are open, although material connected to New England/Upstate New York is preferred. Length is limited to 100 lines."** They have recently published poetry by William Heyen, Paul Root, John Sweet and David Michael Nixon. As a sample the editor selected these lines by Skip Harris:

> *I'm just a poor poet workin' hard*
> *on the tenth draft of a sixteen bar blues.*
> *I've been drinkin' all over town.*
> *I always let the barmaids choose*

Canal Lines is digest-sized, 16 pgs., saddle-stapled with matte card cover, photocopied from typescript. The verse inside is varied (free to formal). Press run 100. They accept about 40-50% of 60-70 submissions per year. **Sample postpaid: $1.25. Pays 3 copies. "A report on any submission takes 6-7 weeks or longer."** The editor says, "Patience and determination are a must. A well-written/thought-out poem may be rejected numerous times before finally finding a 'home.' A rejection slip is *not* a statement of failure, but an ongoing process to bring a poem into the proper light."

‡**CANDLESTONES (I)**, P.O. Box 49001, St. Petersburg FL 33743, founded 1990, editor Ann Blain, is a quarterly literary arts magazine. "The purpose is to encourage artists and poets who have not been published and share creativity with people who usually do not buy poetry." Uses poetry, b&w art and photos, and short stories. **"I want poetry that the poet is proud of. Some long poems are accepted and I always need short poems. No poems containing profanity and no pornographic poetry."** They have recently published poetry by Helen A. Hardy. As a sample the editor selected these lines by Holly Blain:

> *Sun-dappled kisses*
> *Echo off my skin to you*
> *Caught in the web of our love.*
> *We stare*
> *and understand.*

"We accept simultaneous submissions and previously published works. We like cover letters just because they are interesting reading." Seldom comments on rejections. Reports in 3 months. Pays 3 copies. The editor says, "*Candlestones* is an outgrowth of a monthly coffee house held in my home. Most contributors are under 30. Its twofold purpose is to give people a chance to have their creative efforts viewed by others and show the general populace (people who would never buy a book of poetry) the artistic achievement around them. It has been distributed in gas stations, factories, bookstores, record stores and beauty parlors. My advice is to submit. If one place rejects it, submit somewhere else. One poet I know wrote a poem in 1922. When it was submitted in 1990, it was printed. Don't wait so long. But be patient with the small press."

CANOE PRESS (II), 1587 Lake Dr., Traverse City MI 49684, phone (616)946-7680, founded 1988, publisher Brian Browning, poetry editor Joe Dionne. "We publish books of poetry, also chapbooks, broadsheets in quality letterpress on a hand-fed Chandler and Price. We do our own sewing and binding and in every way try to produce a *work of art*." They have published poetry by Lee Upton, Jack Driscoll, Al Drake, Barbara Drake and F. Richard Thomas. They publish 1 chapbook a year averaging 25 pgs.

THE CAPE ROCK (II), Department of English, Southeast Missouri State University, Cape Girardeau MO 63701, founded 1964, appears twice yearly and consists of **64 pgs. of poetry and photography, with a $200 prize for the best poem in each issue and $100 for featured photography.** It's a handsomely printed, flat-spined, digest-sized magazine, **sample: $3, guidelines available for SASE. "No restrictions on subjects or forms. Our criterion for selection is the quality of the work. We prefer poems under 70 lines; no long poems or books, no sentimental, didactic or cute poems."** They have published such poets as Stephen Dunning, Joyce Odam, Judith Phillips Neeld, Lyn Lifshin, Virginia Brady Young, Gary Pacernik and Laurel Speer. Their circulation is about 500, with 200 subscribers, of whom half are libraries. They have a 2 to 8-month backlog and **report in 1-3 months. Do not submit mss in May, June or July. Pays 2 copies.** A good publication that, in recent years, has become more difficult to break into, probably because the magazine is improving and appealing to more writers.

‡CAPERS AWEIGH MAGAZINE (I, IV-Regional), P.O. Box 96, Sydney, Nova Scotia B1P 6G9 Canada, phone (902)564-1924, founded 1992, publisher John MacNeil, is a quarterly of **poetry and short fiction** "of, by and for Cape Bretoners at home and away." They want work by Cape Bretoners only. Nothing profane. The publisher says it is 50-60 pgs., 5×8, desktop published, stapled, including computer graphics and trade ads. Press run is 500. Subscription: $20. **Sample postpaid: $5. Previously published poems OK; no simultaneous submissions. Cover letter required. Seldom comments on rejections. Pays 1 copy.**

CAPPER'S (I, IV-Nature, inspirational, humor), 616 Jefferson St., Topeka KS 66607, founded 1879, poetry editor Nancy Peavler, is a biweekly tabloid (newsprint) going to **370,000 mail subscribers,** mostly small-town and farm people. Uses 6-8 poems in each issue—payment **$3-6 per poem.** They want short poems (**4-10 lines preferred, lines of one-column width**) "relating to everyday situations, nature, inspirational, humorous." They have published Helen Harrington, Emma Walker, Sheryl Nelms, Alice Mackenzie Swaim, Ralph W. Seager and Ida Fasel. "**Most poems used in** *Capper's* **are upbeat in tone and offer the reader a bit of humor, joy, enthusiasm or encouragement. Short poems of this type fit our format best.**" **Submit 4-6 poems at a time.** Does not return mss. **No simultaneous submissions. Reports within 4-5 months. Buys one-time rights. Send 85¢ for sample.** Not available on newsstand. The editor says "Poems chosen are upbeat, sometimes humorous, always easily understood."

CARAVAN PRESS; EDGAR LEE MASTERS AWARD (III), Suite 279, 15445 Ventura Blvd., Sherman Oaks CA 91403, founded 1980, poetry editor Olivia Sinclair-Lewis, is "a small press presently publishing approximately 6-7 works per year including poetry, photojournals, calendars, novels, etc. We look for quality, freshness and that touch of genius." In poetry, "**we want to see verve, natural rhythms, discipline, impact,** etc. We are flexible but **verbosity, triteness and saccharine make us cringe.**" They have published books by Scott Sonders, Bebe Oberon, Walter Calder, Exene Vida, Carlos Castenada, Claire Bloome and G. G. Henke. Their tastes are for poets such as Charles Bukowski, Sylvia Plath, Erica Jong and Bob Dylan. "**We have strong liaisons with the entertainment industry and like to see material that is media-oriented and au courant.**" **Sample postpaid: $8. Query first, with 2-3 poems and résumé. If invited to submit, send double-spaced, typed ms (photocopy, dot-matrix OK).** "No manuscripts will be read without SASE." **Simultaneous submissions OK.** They reply "ASAP." They offer 20% royalty contract, 10-50 copies, advance or honorarium depending on grants or award money. "Please study what we publish before submitting." **Criticism offered on rejected mss. (Note: Fee charged if criticism requested.)** "We sponsor the Edgar Lee Masters Awards, established in 1981, including a poetry award with a $2,500 grand prize annually plus each winner (and the five runners up in poetry) will be published in a clothbound edition and distributed to selected university and public libraries, news mediums, etc. There is a one-time only $10 administration and reading fee per entrant. Further application and details available with a #10 SASE."

THE CARIBBEAN WRITER (IV-Regional), University of the Virgin Islands, RR 02, P.O. Box 10,000, Kingshill, St. Croix, USVI 00850, phone (809)778-0246, founded 1987, editor Dr. Erika Waters, is an annual literary magazine **with a Caribbean focus. The Caribbean must be central to the literary work or the work must reflect a Caribbean heritage, experience or perspective. Blind submissions only: name, address and title of ms should appear on a separate sheet. Title only on ms. Payment is 2 copies. Acquires first North American serial rights.** They have recently published poetry by Audre Lorde, O.R. Dathorne, Julia Alvarez and Ian McDonald. As a sample the editor selected the opening lines of "A Cultural Trip" by Opal Palmer Adisa:

> *Press me to your bread-fruit chest;*
> *enfold me in your mango arms;*
> *kiss me with those shoe-black lips;*
> *let me taste your guava sip.*

The magazine is handsomely printed on heavy pebbled stock, flat-spined, 110 pp., 6×9, with glossy card cover, using advertising and b&w art by Caribbean artists. Press run is 1,500. Single copy: $9 plus $1.50 postage; subscription: $14 for 2 years. **Sample: $5 plus $1.50 postage. Send SASE for guidelines.** (Note: postage to and from the Virgin Islands is the same as within the United States.) **Simultaneous submissions OK.** "Best to avoid submitting mss in the summer." **Deadline is September 30 of each year.** The annual appears in the spring. Reviews books of poetry and fiction in 500 words.

‡CARLETON ARTS REVIEW (II), Box 41, 18th Floor, Davidson Douton Tower, Carleton University, Ottawa, Ontario K1S 5B6 Canada, phone (613)567-3525, founded 1982, is a 60-page biannual publishing poetry, prose, graphics, reviews and criticism. "**All kinds of poetry accepted and encouraged.**" They have recently published poetry by Stan Regal, Brian Burke, Calvin White and Alan Packwood. They receive 200-300 poems a year, publish about 10%. Press run is 400 for 50 subscribers most of which

Close-up

Ricardo Pau-Llosa
Poet

For what seemed to be the whole night
he burned, an effigy on the coast
commemorating the day of St. John. It stood

above a pyramid of trash, itself made of trash,
his jewels falling to the pyre at its feet,
the glow eclipsing night and Havana.

The flames increased the giant and all around
people stood at a safe distance and gazed,
a human halo watching a flame the shape of a man,

a man turning into a constellation.

(from "Ostiones Y Cangrejos Moros," published in *New
England Review* and included in **Cuba**, Carnegie Mellon
University Press, 1993)

Born in Havana, Cuba, Ricardo Pau-Llosa has lived in the United States since the age of six, began writing poetry as a freshman at Miami-Dade Community College and began publishing his work in literary magazines in the late 1970s. Currently he is also an associate professor in the English department at Miami-Dade's South Campus. "My work as a college professor is highly enriching," he says. "I teach creative writing and advanced composition, and teaching has impelled me to write more succinctly."

Pau-Llosa says ideas for poetry can come from numerous sources, including literature one has read, the recollections of others, hopes, dreams, experiences. He says that from the late 1970s to 1989 he was less concerned with the expression of personal feeling than with philosophy, history, history of ideas and aesthetics. "Inevitably, personal feelings came out in those poems gathered in my first book, **Sorting Metaphors** (Anhinga Press, 1983), and my second one, **Bread of the Imagined** (Bilingual Press/Editorial Bilingüe, 1992). But my focus was on producing a poetry of ideas and philosophical reflection."

He says all of this began to change markedly with **Cuba** (to be published this year by Carnegie Mellon University Press). "While writing the poems in **Cuba**, emotions and personal childhood memories combined (at times collided) with reflections on Cuban history, literature and art. These poems were written far more intuitively than anything I had ever done before. **Cuba** turned out to be a very liberating experience for me. I experimented with narrative and far more conversational tones than I had worked with before." He says the collection just "happened," it was not planned. The poems just started coming one after the other, unlike the slow, methodical writing he had done previously.

Pau-Llosa says his poetry is not specifically political, but an ethical and moral challenge. "I don't belong to any group; I have been no one's protégé. In ethnic and political terms and the expectations attached to them in the contemporary scene in the United States, I am the quintessential alien: a Cuban exile writing in English and a liberal who is also an anti-communist. I am interested in philosophy, art and history and not at all interested in gratuitously parading feelings, flashing neuroses or poeticizing on the banalities of everyday life. Among other subjects, I am concerned with the desperate history of my native country, Cuba, but I am not at all interested in catchy, simplistic and marketable ethnic themes. I don't mambo."

In addition to his poetry and teaching, Pau-Llosa is an art critic and curator specializing in 20th century Latin American art. "There is no question that my activities as an art critic and curator have had a profound influence on my poetry. Even when the influence is not direct or thematically noticeable, constant exposure to the products of the visual imaginations of others has, I think, trained me to pay attention to visual associations.

"The visual arts have also played a major role in my reconstruction of my Cuban heritage. I was six when I left Cuba and 14 when I first moved to Miami. In the early 1970s in Miami there was far more activity in the Cuban exile community in the visual arts than in any other high cultural expression. Comparatively, there was little good Cuban literature being written in Miami, and very few of the established Cuban writers in exile settled here (preferring New York, Europe or Latin America). The opposite was true for the visual artists—some of the artists who came into exile with established reputations in Cuba held regular 'tertulias' (get-togethers of artists and writers) at their Miami studios. The Latin American art galleries became important centers of cultural activity.

"Other Latin American artists began exhibiting in Miami from the early 1970s on, so the city became a hub for the visual arts from Latin America. In contrast, the Spanish-language literary scene never really took off. In the 1970s there was not much high cultural activity in any of the non-Cuban sectors of the city, either. A handful of excellent North American writers and painters were active in Miami, of course, but for a sense of cultural community—a large population interested in the life of a particular art form—one had to look to the Cubans and other Latin Americans and their interest in the works of their visual artists. As a result, unconsciously at first but with time consciously, I linked the visual arts to cultural continuity, and I forged my links with my Cuban origins through painting and sculpture. It seemed natural for me to write about these artists' works and, with time, I did that more and more, eventually writing books and essays, curating exhibitions, basing a number of my poems on paintings, sculptures and photographs."

Pau-Llosa says his publishing experiences have been excellent. He sends his work out cold to editors. He does not have a specific marketing plan in mind when looking for a publisher. Some of the poems he would least expect an editor to want are often those accepted. "When one considers how beleaguered editors are with work and shrinking budgets and how buried they are in submissions, I must say that, on the whole, they are an admirable group of individuals. I have relied on their professionalism and objectivity and have not been disappointed. My experience has been that it is not who you know but what you write that counts."

Pau-Llosa's advice to students, unpublished writers or those just breaking into print is: "Read constantly in other fields (not just what you enjoy or identify with, and not just works in the genre you are pursuing); learn other languages and read their literatures; write with passion and intelligence. Reject all stereotypes, especially anti-intellectual biases (very common in this culture, even among writers). Embrace the critical process as an integral part of creativity and don't accept facile boundaries between literary, poetic, analytical critical and philosophical discourse. Originality is in ideas not feelings."

—Deborah Cinnamon

are libraries, 150 shelf sales. Subscription: $7. **Sample postpaid: $3.50. No previously published poems or simultaneous submissions. "Please include a short biography and list of publications." Submit in September or December. Often comments on rejections. Reports in 1-2 months. Pays 2 copies.**

‡CARNEGIE MELLON MAGAZINE (II, IV-Specialized/alumni), Carnegie Mellon University, Pittsburgh PA 15213, phone (412)268-2132, editor Ann Curran, is the **alumni magazine for the university and limits selections to writers connected with the university, no payment. Direct submissions to Gerald Costanzo, poetry editor.** As a sample here is the opening stanza of "A Daughter" by Lee Upton:

> *Water on the white blossoms,*
> *warm, almost like the touch of oil.*
> *To be ridiculous and beautiful was*
> *one task for a daughter.*

CAROLINA QUARTERLY (III), Greenlaw Hall CB# 3520, University of North Carolina, Chapel Hill NC 27599-3520, founded 1948, editor Will Phillips, is a small literary magazine that appears three times a year using poetry of **"all kinds, though we seek excellence always."** They have recently published poets such as David St. John, Lois Marie Harrod, David James Smith and Emily Hiestard. As a sample the editor selected these lines from a poem by Cathy Eisenhower:

> *You'll know by its odor, sour, almost pale green*
> *in the Basra air, stirring a little,*
> *the red corolla darkening as petals*
> *drop away, as winter-thin pods sway*
> *like sickles. Sometimes I wake to hear*
> *seeds fall into darkness, into wind, the earth open*
> *suddenly, nothing like a flower.*

It's a professionally printed, 6 × 9, flat-spined magazine, glossy color card cover, with 90 pgs. of which about 30 are poetry, circulation 1,000, with 400 subscriptions, of which about half are libraries. They receive thousands of submissions per year, use 40-60. **Sample: $5 postpaid. Submit no more than 2-6 poems. Use of poems over 300 lines is impractical. No simultaneous submissions. Submissions read *very slowly* May — September; reporting time somewhat longer. Pays $15/author plus 2 copies. Buys first North American serial rights. Guidelines available for SASE. Sometimes comments on rejections.** Reviews books of poetry. This handsome publication has an elegant, understated design. It commands much respect in the literary world and publishes mostly lyric free verse with an emphasis on image and metaphor.

CAROLINA WREN PRESS (IV-Women, ethnic, gay/lesbian, social issues), P.O. Box 277, Carrboro NC 27510, phone (919)560-2738, founded 1976, editor-in-chief Elaine Goolsby, poetry editor Marilyn Bulman, publishes **"primarily women and minorities, though men and majorities also welcome."** They have recently published poetry by T.J. Reddy, Jaki Shelton Green, Mary Kratt and Judy Hogan. As a sample the editor selected these lines from **This Road Since Freedom** by C. Eric Lincoln:

> *Come Back*
> *Martin Luther King*
> *Play with me*
> *and hold my hand*
> *and help me still the turbulence*
> *the agitation that shakes me*
> *when I walk the streets of Boston*
> *where once you drew your strength.*

Send query letter. No more than 12 pages of poetry. Reports in 3 months. Pays 10% of print run in copies. Publishes 3 books/year. Send (9½ × 12 SASE for catalog and guidelines (include postage for 3 ounces). They say, "Write about the things most difficult to touch. Find you own voice and don't lose it!"

CAROUSEL MAGAZINE (II), Rm. 217 University Center, University of Guelph, Guelph, Ontario N1G 2W1 Canada, founded 1983, editor Michael Carbert, is an annual using **"any type of well-written, typed poetry, as well as short stories, graphics or short plays. We do not usually publish rhyming poetry. Mss should be well-edited before they are sent. Original, minimalist, off-beat material is encouraged."** They have published poetry by John B. Lee, Anne Burke, James Harrison, Mary Melfi and W.P. Kinsella. It is flat-spined, 89 pgs. Their press run is 500. They accept about 30-40 of 150 pieces received. **Sample: $4 postpaid. Send SASE for guidelines. Pays 1 copy. They will consider simultaneous submissions. Reports in 3-4 months. Type name and address on each page.**

CARPENTER PRESS (V), P.O. Box 14387, Columbus OH 43214, founded 1973, primarily to publish fiction, editor Bob Fox, publishes **an occasional full-length collection of poems, flat-spined. No unsolicited mss. Query, no samples.** They have published poetry by Steve Kowit and David Shevin. **Pays 10% royalties, 10% of press run in copies. Send $1 p&h for illustrated catalog to purchase samples.**

CAT FANCY (IV-Themes, children), P.O. Box 6050, Mission Viejo CA 92690, phone (714)855-8822, founded 1965, editor K.E. Segnar. *Cat Fancy* is a magazine-sized monthly that uses **poems on the subject of cats. "No more than 30 short lines; open on style and form, but a conservative approach is recommended.** In our children's department we occasionally use longer, rhyming verse that tells a story about cats. No eulogies for pets that have passed away."** They have published poetry by Lola Sneyd and Edythe G. Tornow. It has a press run of 332,713 for 242,804 subscribers, 32,764 shelf sales. Subscription: $23.97. **Sample postpaid: $4.50. Pays $20/poem plus 2 copies. Name and address "in upper left-hand corner." Reports in 6 weeks. Editor sometimes comments on submissions, "especially if the ms is appealing but just misses the mark for our audience."** She says, "We have an audience that very much appreciates sensitive and touching work about cats. As for advice — get input from knowledgeable sources as to the marketability of your work, and be open to learning how your work might be improved. Then send it out, and hang on. Rejection may not mean your work is bad. We are able to accept very few submissions, and the competition is fierce. Timing and luck have a lot to do with acceptance, so keep trying!"

THE CATHARTIC (II), P.O. Box 1391, Ft. Lauderdale FL 33302, phone (305)967-9378, founded 1974, edited by Patrick M. Ellingham, "**is a small poetry magazine devoted to the unknown poet** with the understanding that most poets are unknown in America." He says, "While there is no specific type of poem I look for, **rhyme for the sake of rhyme is discouraged. Any subject matter except where material is racist or sexist in nature. Overly-long poems, over 80 lines, are not right for a small magazine normally. I would like to see some poems that take chances with both form and language.** I would like to see poems that get out of and forget about self ['I'] and look at the larger world and the people in it with an intensity that causes a reader to react or want to react to it. I am gravitating toward work that looks at the darker side of life, is intense and uses words sparingly." **Considers sexually explicit material.** Recently published poets include Joy Walsh, Harry E. Knickerbocker, Laurel Speer and Paul Weinman. It's a modest, 28-page pamphlet, offset printed from typescript, consisting mostly of poems and appearing twice a year. **Sample postpaid: $3.** He receives over 1,000 submissions per year, of which he uses about 60. No backlog. **Photocopy, dot-matrix, simultaneous submissions OK, submit 5-10 poems. Reports in 1 month. Uses reviews of small press books as well as some artwork and photography. Guidelines available for SASE. Contributors receive 1 copy.** He advises, "The only way for poets to know whether their work will get published or not is to submit. It is also essential to read as much poetry as possible — both old and new. Spend time with the classics as well as the new poets. Support the presses that support you — the survival of both is essential to the life of poetry."

CATS MAGAZINE (IV-Themes), P.O. Box 290037, Port Orange FL 32029, editor Linda J. Walton, is a monthly magazine **about cats, including light verse about cats. Pays 50¢ a line. Free sample copy is available when accompanied by a 9 × 12 envelope with $1.21 postage. All submissions or requests must have SASE. Payment on publication.**

WM CAXTON LTD. (I, II), 12037 Hwy. 42, Ellison Bay WI 54210, phone (414)854-2955, founded 1986, publisher K. Luchterhand. **"About 50% of our books involve an author's subvention of production costs with enhanced royalties and/or free copies in return." Acquires all rights.** They want "any serious **poetry, not children's or doggerel."** They have published poetry by David Koenig and Caroline Sibr. Write or call to purchase sample copies.

CCR PUBLICATIONS (II), 2745 Monterey Hwy #76, San Jose CA 95111-3129, founded as Realities Library in 1975, as CCR Publications in 1987, editor and publisher Ric Soos. "I am going to take one book, and follow it through all stages with the author. I will not even consider a new book until the current project is finished. Please keep in mind when you contact me for projects, that I believe in Jesus Christ, and that anything I publish will be to help further the Gospel if it is for that purpose. In **poetry, I look for items that will not hinder the spread of the Gospel. In other words, the poet need not be Christian, does not need to mention Christ by name. But I will no longer be publishing for Shock Value."** He publishes those **"who support me in some respect . . . Support is not always financial." Query with sample poems.** He has published books of poetry by Ruth Daigon and Ella Blanche Salmi.

‡CEILIDH: AN INFORMAL GATHERING FOR STORY & SONG (II, IV-Translations), Box 6367, San Mateo CA 94403, phone (415)591-9902, founded 1981, poetry editors Patrick S. Sullivan and Perry Oei, is interested in **"experimental poetry, translations, long poems and language poetry. Not interested in**

satire, word play or other less than literary poetry." They have published Patrick Smith, John Moffitt, Sarah Bliumis and translations by Joseph Salemi. These sample lines selected by the editors are from "Crotched Mountain" by William Doreski:

> *how cities design themselves*
> *around the fluid architecture*
> *of the random gesture, defying*
> *closure, disdaining nature,*
> *forever about to begin.*

There are 32-64 pgs. per issue. Winter and summer issues are devoted to fiction; spring and fall issues each use about 36 pages of poetry. Circulation to 400 subscribers, of which 100 are libraries. Subscription: $15 for 4 issues. **Sample: $5 postpaid.** They have a 2-3 month backlog. **The best time to submit is January through March and July through September 1. Photocopy, dot-matrix OK, but no simultaneous submissions. Reports in 6-8 weeks. Pays 2 copies. Guidelines available for SASE. Occasionally offers criticism of rejected mss.** Usually a contest with each issue with prizes from cash to gift certificates to poetry books. Some of their contest judges: Gerald Frassetti, James K. Bell, Michael Thornton. The editor says, "We recommend that poets send for our guidelines and a sample copy. The best way to determine what we will publish is to see what we have published."

CENCRASTUS (IV-Ethnic), One Abbeymount Techbase, Edinburgh EH8 8EJ Scotland, phone (031)661-5687, founded 1979, editor Raymond Ross, is a quarterly magazine **"to create the intellectual and imaginative conditions for a new Scottish nation"** which uses **"no light verse; long poem a specialty; all poetry to be relevant to Scotland or peripheral living."** They have published poetry by Edwin Morgan, Kenneth White, Sorley Maclean, Gael Turnbull, Douglas Dunn and international poets. As a sample we selected these lines from "A Legacy" by Irene Evans:

> *Because I believe she is*
> *there still listening. From within*
> *the cellar of herself*
> *she hands me something*
> *to take away from here.*
> *To keep.*

There are 3-8 pages of poetry in each issue. Circulation to 1,000 subscriptions of which a fourth are libraries. **Sample: £1.85 postpaid from USA.** They receive over 400 submissions/year and use 30 with a 1-2 issue backlog. **Submit 4-8 poems, typed, no query. Reports in 1-2 months. Pays £7.50/poem or £30/page.** Reviews books of poetry. You have to become familiar with this magazine before sending to it because it is an international journal of literature, arts and affairs. Poems are few, but powerful (with focus on image and idea rather than on feelings and personal experience).

THE CENTENNIAL REVIEW (III), 312 Linton Hall, Michigan State University, East Lansing MI 48824-1044, phone (517)355-1905, founded 1957, managing editor Cheryllee Finney, appears 3 times/year. They want **"that sort of poem which, however personal, bears implications for communal experience."** They have recently published poetry by David Citino and Dimitris Tsaloumas. As a sample the editor selected these lines from "Those Who Claimed We Hated Them" by Sherri Szeman:

> *. . . We clicked tongues in sympathy*
> *at the blue-black scratchings on their forearms.*
>
> *But we had all suffered during the war.*
> *We suffered, as they did. We had only*
>
> *feigned gaiety at their misfortunes, to*
> *convince our oppressors to spare our homes.*

It is 240 pgs., 6 × 9, desktop published, perfect-bound, with 3-color cover, art, graphics and ads. They receive about 500 poems a year, accept about 2%. Press run is 1,000 for 800 subscribers. Subscription: $10/year. **Sample postpaid: $5. No previously published poems or simultaneous submissions. Seldom comments on rejections. Send SASE for guidelines. Reports in about 2 months. Pays 2 copies plus 1-year subscription. Acquires all rights. Returns them "when asked by authors for reprinting."**

UNIVERSITY OF CENTRAL FLORIDA CONTEMPORARY POETRY SERIES (II), % English Department, University of Central Florida, Orlando FL 32816, founded 1970, poetry editors Judith Hemschemeyer and Don Stap, publishes **two 50- to 80-page hardback or paperback collections each year**. They have recently published poetry by Rebecca McClanahan Devet and William Hathaway. As a sample the editors selected the last nine lines of the poem "You Ask" by Jean Burden:

> *I walk toward a dark cabin*
> *carrying two flames in my mind,*
> *pressing the weeds down,*
> *What lasts?*
> *The turning day, falling water*
> *over stones, the sweet disorder*
> *of leaves,*
> *moons that come and go,*
> *wings.*

"Please send a reading fee of $7, a SASE for return of ms and a self-addressed postcard for acknowledgment of receipt of ms." Reads submissions September through April. Reports in 2 months.

CHALK TALK (IV-Children), 1550 Mills Rd., RR 2, Sidney, British Columbia V8L 3S1 Canada, phone (604)656-1858, founded 1987, editor Virginia Lee, is a "non-glossy magazine **written by children for children** (with parents' pages), stories, poems, drawings, published 10 months/year. **Any form or subject matter.**" It is magazine-sized, 24 pgs., newsprint. No July or August issues. Approximately 3 pgs. each month are poems. Press run 3,000 for 1,500 subscribers of which 15% are libraries. Subscription: $14 (incl. GST) CDN, $17 US and foreign. **Sample postpaid: $2. Send SASE for guidelines. Pays "as many copies as requested." Simultaneous submissions OK.** Reviews books of poetry.

CHAMINADE LITERARY REVIEW; THE UNTERECKER PRIZES (II, IV-Regional), 3140 Waialae Ave., Honolulu HI 96816, founded 1986, editor Loretta Petrie, appears twice yearly. **"No jingles, pop"** poetry. They have recently published poetry by Lyn Lifshin, Mel Takahara, Naomi Shihab Nye and Gene Frumkin. As a sample the editor selected the first stanza of "Ancient Hawaiian Village" by Meridith Carson:

> *You must believe that things gone are still there,*
> *just as they were,*
> *or the crabs in their holes would not listen so intently*
> *under the new black sand that has*
> *partly buried Kamoamoa.*

CLR features the work of many well-known creative writers and thus, at first blush, seems like a mainstream literary magazine. But poems, prose and artwork play off each other for added effect and unify such themes as ecology, love, nature, etc. The handsomely printed magazine averages 175 pgs., flat-spined, 6×9 with glossy card cover. They accept about 25% of 500 poems received/year. Press run 500 for 350 subscribers of which 6 are libraries. Subscription: $10/year, $18/2 years. **Sample postpaid: $4. Pays year's subscription. Previously published poems OK.** The Unterecker Prizes (cash awards) are awarded yearly to Hawaiian poets published in the magazine, and they give **special consideration to Hawaii's writers or Hawaii subject matter.**

CHANGING MEN: ISSUES IN GENDER, SEX AND POLITICS (IV-Feminist), 306 N. Brooks, Madison WI 53715, founded 1979, poetry editor Bob Vance, is described as **"a pro-feminist journal for men — politics, poetry, graphics, news."** He wants work which **"expresses the emotional, intellectual and sensual complexity of living in America in an age enlightened by but not yet freed by feminism, gay liberation, socialism and ethnic beauty. A concern for form and invention is appreciated."** They have published poetry by Sidney Miller, Louie Crew, T. Obatala, Sesshu Foster, Assotto Saint and Denis O'Donovan. Though the poetry is "so varied" the editor felt he could not select 4 representative lines, here are the opening lines of James Broughton's "Afternoon in Ceylon" to illustrate the quality, if not variety, of poetry in the magazine:

> *Luncheon had made us hungry for one another*
> *After the curry and fried bananas*
> *we added our own heat to the hot afternoon*
> *simmering in sweat and coconut oil*

Uses about 6 pgs. of poetry in each magazine-sized issue, circulation 6,000, 2,000 subscriptions of which 10% are libraries. They have a backlog for 2-4 issues. **Sample postpaid: $6. Submit up to 5 poems, photocopy, simultaneous submissions OK. Reports in 2-6 months. Pays copies. Send SASE for guidelines.** Editor sometimes comments on rejections.

‡CHANTS (II), RR1 Box 1738, Dexter ME 04930, founded 1989, editor Terrell Hunter, appears twice a year. The editor says their goal is "to publish the best poetry we can find." They want **"strong, serious, good poetry: any style. No greeting card, clichéd, sappy or trendy poetry."** They have recently published poetry by Lyn Lifshin, Michael Kreps and Desmond Egan. As a sample the editor selected these lines from "The Father" by Muriel Karr:

> *Who chops the tail of the worm? When he wakes*

> *the father will wash his face, strangle the worm,*
> *eat it for breakfast. The worm has no chance*
> *against the pale freckled hands of the father.*
> *The coiled worm will die and the father knows it.*
> *This his inner truth—source of his strength.*

Chants is 64 pgs., digest-sized, professionally printed, flat-spined, with photo or graphic on cover but no inside art. It features narrative, lyric, dramatic (and even erotic) free verse. They accept about 10% of poems received. Press run is 500. Single copy: $3. **Sample: $3 plus $1 postage. No previously published poems or simultaneous submissions.** Time between acceptance and publication is up to 6 months—occasionally longer." **"Sometimes comments on rejections. Reports in 1-3 months. Pays 2 copies.** The editor says, "Send for a back issue. Proofread. In most cases, avoid academic language or situations—they're usually boring!"

CHAPMAN (IV-Ethnic); CHAPMAN PRESS (V), 4 Broughton Place, Edinburgh EH1 3RX Scotland, phone (031)557-2207, founded 1970, editor Joy Hendry, "provides an outlet for new work by **established Scottish writers and for new, up-and-coming writers also,** for the discussion and criticism of this work and for reflection on current trends in Scottish life and literature. But *Chapman* is not content to follow old, well-worn paths; it throws open its pages to new writers, new ideas and new approaches. In the international tradition revived by MacDiarmid, *Chapman* **also features the work of foreign writers and broadens the range of Scottish cultural life."** They have published poetry and fiction by Alasdair Gray, Liz Lochhead, Sorley MacLean, T.S. Law, Tom Scott and Una Flett. As a sample the editor selected these lines from Judy Steel's poem "For Nicole Boulanger" who, Steel says, "was born in the same year as my daughter and died in the Lockerbie air disaster of 1988":

> *You died amongst these rolling Border hills:*
> *The same our daughters played and rode and walked in -*
> *They make a nursery fit to shape and mould*
> *A spirit swift as water, free as air.*
>
> *But you, west-winging through the Christmas dark*
> *Found them no playground but a mortuary -*
> *Your young life poised for flight to woman's years*
> *Destroyed as wantonly as moorland game.*

Chapman appears 4 times a year in a 6×9 perfect-bound format, 104 pgs., professionally printed in small type on matte stock with glossy card cover, art in 2 colors, circulation 2,000 for 900 subscriptions of which 200 are libraries. They receive "thousands" of freelance submissions of poetry/year, use about 200, **have a 4- to 6-month backlog. No simultaneous submissions. Sample: £2.50 (overseas). Pays £8/page. Reports "as soon as possible."** Reviews books of poetry. **Chapman Press is not interested in unsolicited mss.**

THE CHARITON REVIEW PRESS; THE CHARITON REVIEW (II), Northeast Missouri State University, Kirksville MO 63501, phone (816)785-4499, founded 1975, editor Jim Barnes. *The Chariton Review* began in 1975 as a twice yearly literary magazine and in 1978 added the activities of the Press, producing "limited editions (not chapbooks!) of **full-length collections . . . for the purpose of introducing solid, contemporary poetry to readers.** The books go free to the regular subscribers of *The Chariton Review*; others are sold to help meet printing costs." The poetry published in both books and the magazine is, according to the editor, **"open and closed forms—traditional, experimental, mainstream. We do not consider verse, only poetry in its highest sense, whatever that may be. The sentimental and the inspirational are not poetry for us."** They have recently published poets such as Michael Spence, Neil Myers, Sam Maio, Andrea Budy, Charles Edward Eaton, Wayne Dodd and Harold Witt. There are 40-50 pages of poetry in each issue of the *Review*, a 6×9 flat-spined magazine of over a hundred pages, professionally printed, glossy cover with photographs, circulation about 600 with 400 subscribers of which 100 are libraries. **Sample: $2.50 postpaid. Do *not* write for guidelines.** They receive 7,000-8,000 submissions/year, of which they use 35-50, with never more than a 6-month backlog. **Submit 5-7 poems, typescript single-spaced, no carbons, dot-matrix or simultaneous submissions. Payment: $5/ printed page. Buys first North American serial rights. Contributors are expected to subscribe or buy copies.** No question, Jim Barnes is a tough sell because he has high standards. But he also is a fine poet who loves the music of verse and has a keen editorial eye. No need to plug your work with a cover letter here. If you meet his standards, you'll be alongside some of our most respected contemporary writers. **To be considered for book publication, query first—samples of books $3 and $5. Payment for book publication: $500 with 20 or more copies. Usually no criticism is supplied.**

CHARNEL HOUSE (V), 1712 Avenue Rd., P.O. Box 54541, North York, Ontario M5M 4N5 Canada, phone (416)924-5670, founded 1979, editor Crad Kilodney, is **"only interested in very bad poetry, but overstocked for the time being. No submissions until further notice."**

CHASTITY & HOLINESS MAGAZINE; CHRISTIANIC POETIC MINISTRY; C.J.L. PRESS/ART CO.; THE POLYGLOT ARMY (IV-Religious), 22006 Thorncliffe P.O., Toronto, Ontario M4H 1N9 Canada, phone (416)423-6781, founded 1988, editor-in-chief Cecil Justin Lam, publishes "Christianic works, Christianic long poems and books by new inspirational writers. Old writers also accepted. Poetry should be **religious, Christianic, inspirational. All styles, all forms. No restriction as to poetic expressions. No limit to length. The longer is usually the more welcome; Christ and inspired poetry related, to spread the Gospel of love and truth. No secular poetry with no fixed aim of life view. No garbage talker and poets who do not know what is happening and what they are doing with their words.**" They have published poetry by Thomas Kretz, David Castleman and Hugh Alexander. As a sample the editor selected these lines by Joanna M. Weston:

> Explode into joy,
> oh my soul
> Explode into
> movement
> into
> dance
> Swirl with
> the cymbals

The magazine appears twice a year and is 8½ × 7, 28 pgs., photocopied from typescript with paper cover. They accept about 30% of 100 poems received a year. Press run: 200 for 50 subscriptions of which all are libraries. Subscription: $10. **Sample postpaid: $5. Send SASE for guidelines. Pays "prayers and rewards plus 1 copy."** Simultaneous submissions and previously published poems OK. Reports immediately. **For book publication by C.J.L. Press submit 3 samples, bio, publications. Reports in 1 month. Pays 1 copy plus 20% royalties. "Awards will be granted on the basis of Christianic literary performance."** The editor says, "All living creatures, men or aliens may submit to us. The central goal of our publishing firm is to present the World and the Universe with the Holy Sacrifice and Resurrected life of Christ. Intensive Research must be carried out in ensuring all co-ordinative aspects of publishing and economics may match." He provides criticism for $100/100 pgs. Reviews books of poetry. "Constructive comments will be used to encourage the on-going of writing ventures. The publication of any work may imply success at a premature timing; therefore considerable on-the-line efforts must be constantly attended."

THE CHATTAHOOCHEE REVIEW (II), DeKalb College, 2101 Womack Rd., Dunwoody GA 30338, phone (404)551-3166, founded 1980, editor-in-chief Lamar York, a quarterly of poetry, short fiction, essays, reviews and interviews, published by DeKalb College. **"We like to publish beginners alongside professional writers. We are open to poetry from traditional forms to avant-garde and any subject matter or length or style."** They have published poetry by Fred Chappell, Rosemary Daniell, Ed Minus, Bettie Sellers and Jessie Hill Ford. *The Review* is 6 × 9, professionally printed on white stock with b&w reproductions of artwork, 90 pgs., flat-spined, with one-color card cover. Circulation is 1,000, of which 500 are complimentary copies sent to editors and "miscellaneous VIP's." Subscription: $15/year. **Sample: $4 postpaid. Guidelines for SASE. Pays 2 copies. Acquires first rights. Writers should send 1 copy of each poem and a cover letter with bio material. Reports in 2 months and time to publication is 3-4 months. Queries will be answered in 1-2 weeks. No simultaneous submissions. Photocopied or dot-matrix mss are OK but disks are not.** Reviews books of poetry and short fiction in 1,500 words, single or multi-book format. This is a nice market for those with good work having trouble finding a home. The editorial staff here is professional and courteous—it even sends out acknowledgment postcards letting you know that it has received your manuscript—and is open to good poems, regardless of style.

CHELSEA; CHELSEA AWARD COMPETITION (III, IV-Translations), P.O. Box 5880, Grand Central Station, New York NY 10163, founded 1958, editor Sonia Raiziss, associate editors Richard Foerster, Alfred de Palchi and Caila Rossi, is a long-established, high-quality literary annual aiming to promote intercultural communication. **"We look for intelligence and sophisticated technique in both experimental and traditional forms. Always interested in translations of contemporary poets. Length: 5-7 pgs. per submission. Although our tastes are eclectic, we lean toward the cosmopolitan avant-garde. Do not want to see 'inspirational' verse, pornography or poems that rhyme merely for the sake of rhyme."** They have recently published poetry by Edward Hirsch, Karl Shapiro, Laura (Riding) Jackson, Richard Howard and James Laughlin. The editors say *Chelsea* is "160-240 pgs., flat-spined, 6 × 9, offset, cover art varies, occasional use of photographs, ads." Circulation: 1,300, 600 subscriptions of which 200 are libraries. Subscription: $11. **Sample: $4 or more depending on issue. Send SASE for a brochure describing all past issues. Pays $5/page and 2 copies. Buys first North American serial rights. Reports immediately to 3 months. 5-7 pgs. of poetry are ideal; long poems should not exceed 10 pgs.; must be typed; clean photocopy OK; include brief bio; no simultaneous submissions.** "We try to comment favorably on above-average mss; otherwise, we do not have time to provide critiques." Guidelines for their annual

Chelsea Award Competition, $500 for poetry, available for SASE to P.O. Box 1040, York Beach ME 03910. Richard Foerster, associate editor, comments: "Beginners should realize that a rejection often has more to do with the magazine's production schedule and special editorial plans than with the quality of the submission. They should also realize that editors of little magazines are always over-worked (and almost invariably unpaid) and that it is necessary haste and not a lack of concern or compassion that makes rejections seem coldly impersonal."

CHICAGO REVIEW (III), 5801 S. Kenwood, Chicago IL 60637, founded 1946, poetry editor Anne Myles. **"A sure hand, showing originality and precision of language, form and tone — while avoiding the clichés of critical consensus — is the sole requirement for inclusion in** *CR*, overriding formal affiliation, regional bias or previous history of publication. We have recently published poets as diverse as Kathleen Spivack, J.B. Goodenough, Kathleen Norris, Turner Cassity, Michael Donaghy, Meena Alexander and Adrian C. Lewis; out of the 1,500 submissions we receive each year, we accept around 50." **New submissions read October through June. Payment in copies. Sample: $5.50 postpaid. Response time: 3-4 months, longer in some cases.** Circulation: 2,000. Does not currently review books of poetry, "but we will begin listing books received." Annual contest; write for details.

CHICKADEE MAGAZINE; THE YOUNG NATURALIST FOUNDATION (IV-Children, nature), Suite 306, 56 The Esplanade, Toronto, Ontario M5E 1A7 Canada, founded 1979, senior editor Lizann Flatt, is a magazine **for children 3-9 about nature** appearing 10 times/year. They want **"evocative poetry; poems that play with words; humorous poetry; no longer than 50 lines. Nothing religious, anthropo-morphic; no formal language; no poetry that is difficult to understand."** As a sample they selected these lines from "The Lunch Bunch" by Gwen Molnar:

> *The dining room wall to wall*
> *With birds and beasts and fish,*
> *The whole menagerie looked on*
> *As I downed every dish.*

It is magazine-sized, professionally published, 32 pgs. printed in full-color, with paper cover. They accept 1-2% of 500 poems received. Circulation: 25,800 within US and 100,000 within Canada. Subscription: $14.95 US. **Sample postpaid: $3.75. Send SASE for writers' guidelines. Pays $10-75/poem plus 2 copies. Buys all rights. Simultaneous submissions considered but not encouraged.** "*Chickadee* is a 'hands-on' science and nature publication designed to entertain and educate 3-9 year olds. Each issue contains photos, illustrations, an easy-to-read animal story, a craft project, puzzles, a science experiment and a pullout poster."

CHICORY BLUE PRESS (V, IV-Women, senior citizens), 795 East St. N., Goshen CT 06756, phone (203)491-2271, founded 1988, publisher Sondra Zeidenstein, publishes **2-3 chapbooks/year. Though she accepts no unsolicited mss, she is currently accepting queries for chapbooks by women past 60. Replies to queries and mss (if invited) in 3 months. Pays royalties, honorarium or 10 author's copies.** She has published poetry by Honor Moore and Pattiann Rogers. **Samples can be ordered from the press. Seldom comments on rejections.**

CHILDREN'S ALBUM (IV-Children), P.O. Box 6086, Concord CA 94524, phone (510)671-9852, founded 1984, editor Margo M. Lemas. *Children's Album* is a bimonthly literary magazine featuring **fiction and poetry written** *only* **by children 8-14.** Crafts, written by adults for children in that age group, are also included. Adult input is needed in the areas of crafts, science projects, covers, fillers, jokes, word puzzles and cartoons. The magazine uses original artwork, graphics, no ads. Subscription: $15. **Sample: $3 postpaid. Guidelines available with SASE. Pays children 1 year free subscription. Reports in 2-8 weeks, backlog up to a year.**

CHILDREN'S BETTER HEALTH INSTITUTE; BENJAMIN FRANKLIN LITERARY AND MEDICAL SOCI-ETY, INC.; HUMPTY DUMPTY'S MAGAZINE; TURTLE MAGAZINE FOR PRESCHOOL KIDS; CHIL-DREN'S DIGEST; CHILDREN'S PLAYMATE; JACK AND JILL; CHILD LIFE (IV-Children), 1100 Water-way Blvd., Box 567, Indianapolis IN 46206. This publisher of magazines stressing health for children has a **variety of needs for mostly short, simple poems, for which they pay $15 minimum. Send SASE for guidelines.** For example, *Humpty Dumpty* is for ages 4-6; *Turtle* is for preschoolers, similar empha-sis, uses many stories in rhyme — and action rhymes, etc.; *Children's Digest* is for preteens (10-13); *Jack and Jill* is for ages 7-10. *Child Life* is for ages 9-11. *Children's Playmate* is for ages 6-8. All appear 8 times a year in a 6½ × 9, 48-page format, slick paper with cartoon art, very colorful. The editors suggest that writers who wish to appear regularly in their publications **study current issues carefully. Sample postpaid: 75¢.**

CHIMERA POETRY MAGAZINE FOR CHILDREN; CHIMERA SUMMER POETRY CONTEST (I, IV-Children), P.O. Box 1007, Merchantville NJ 08109, founded 1990, editor Michael Northen, appears quarterly using **"primarily poetry by children (ages 18 and under), poetry written by adults for children**

and articles on poetry or teaching poetry written by young writers or teachers. For young writers any form or subject is fine (though I am not crazy about love poetry). I use a limited amount of adult poetry for children. It should be under 30 lines and honest (not cute, saccharine or condescending). No adult poetry for adults." The editor chose 2 sample poems, the first, "The Snow Mountains Are Still" by Hamilton Young Ward, age 7:

> Snowy mountains, snowy mountains
> in the distance, how fragile and
> real and still you are.

And the second, "Eyes of Dawn" by Lara Narcisi, age 16:

> Copper coins reflect back
> Reminders of a once-golden world
> Now gone but still revealed through
> Cat's eyes of amber dawn.

The magazine is "to provide a publication where young writers can have poetry accepted and printed; to give writers for children a forum for writing." It is 52-64 pgs., photocopied from typescript with printed card cover, digest-sized. Press run 200 copies for 100 subscribers, including 10 schools and libraries. It is distributed free to contributing teachers, schools and adults. Subscription: $8/year. **Sample: $2.50. Pays adults 1 copy. "Young writers other than Featured Poets do not receive payment. The magazine is kept inexpensive so that young writers, if they wish, can afford copies of issues with their poems in print. I work closely with schools and encourage class submissions by teachers. Schools with several students submitting receive a free copy. Since I encourage beginning poets I have no strict guidelines other than name, address, school and grade should be included on each poem. No SASE is necessary for young writers, though it is appreciated. I like comments from writers about their writing. Acceptance in about one month. I try to comment on serious poetry submitted by individuals. I encourage classroom submissions but cannot respond to each poem."** Reviews books of poetry if written for children or by young writer (under 18). Summer poetry contest runs from June 1 through July 20. Prizes awarded in 2 age groups (5-12, 13-18). No entry fee. Winners printed in summer issue of *Chimera*. He adds, "I also try to assist school districts or towns that are running poetry contests for children. Once a year I publish a chapbook with representative poetry from four talented young writers who have been printed in *Chimera*. This year it was called **The Girl in the Glass**. Basically, I try to do whatever it takes to encourage young poets."

‡CHIPS OFF THE WRITER'S BLOCK (IV-Themes); CATHARSIS (I), P.O. Box 83371, Los Angeles CA 90083, founded 1986, editor Wanda Windham. *Chips* is a bimonthly 16-page, magazine-sized newsletter offering "motivation and preparation for the published and soon-to-be-published writer" and using "occasional poetry related to writing, that is, the writing world of your personal muse, ups and downs of writing life, etc." *Catharsis* is a 40-page, digest-sized quarterly poetry journal using **"poetry of all genres with lengths from 1-40 lines. Poems should be meaningful, expressing your deepest emotions."** As a sample we selected this poem, "Seizing the Moment," by Barbara Grant Richardson:

> You come to me in the darkness
> of the night.
> Seizing the moment of fulfillment
> and reaching the extremity of my soul.
> Where no other has gone
> in the darkness of the night.

Sample postpaid: $2 for *Chips*, $3 for *Catharsis*. Previously published poems and simultaneous submissions OK. Always comments on rejections. Send SASE for guidelines. Reports in 3-6 weeks. Pays 1 copy.

CHIRON REVIEW; CHIRON BOOKS; CHIRON REVIEW POETRY CONTEST (I, II), Rt. 2 Box 111, St. John KS 67576-2212, founded 1982 as *Kindred Spirit*, editor Michael Hathaway, assistant editor Jane Hathaway, contributing editor (poetry) Gerald Locklin, is a tabloid quarterly using photographs of featured writers. They have recently published poetry by John Gilgun, Antler, Steve Mason, Adrian C. Louis and Miriam Sagan. Their press run is about 1,000. Each issue is 24-32 pgs. and "contains dozens of poems." **Sample: $2 postpaid ($4 overseas or institutions). Send SASE for guidelines. Send 5 poems "typed or printed legibly." They will consider simultaneous submissions but not previously published poems. Pays 1 copy. Buys first-time rights. Reports in 2-4 weeks.** Reviews books of poetry in 500-900 words. For book publication submit complete ms. They publish 1-3 books/year, flat-spined, professionally printed, **paying 25% of press run of 100-200 copies.** Their annual poetry contest offers awards of $100 plus 1-page feature in Winter issue, $50, and 5 free subscriptions and a Chiron Press book; entry fee $4 for up to 6 poems.

THE CHRISTIAN CENTURY (II, IV-Religious, social issues), Dept. PM, 407 S. Dearborn St., Chicago IL 60605, founded 1884, named *The Christian Century* 1900, founded again 1908, joined by *New Christian* 1970, poetry editor Dean Peerman. This "ecumenical weekly" is a liberal, sophisticated journal of news, articles of opinion and reviews from a generally Christian point-of-view, **using approximately one poem/issue, not necessarily on religious themes but in keeping with the literate tone of the magazine.** "No pietistic or sentimental doggerel, please." They have recently published poems by Robert Beum, Joan Rohr Myers, Ida Fasel, Jill Baumgaertner, David Abrams, Catherine Shaw and J. Barrie Shepherd. As a sample the editor selected this poem "Grain Silos," by James Worley:

> *Cathedrals of the oldest preached religion,*
> *towers erected to the oldest useful god*
> *(the one now worshiped three times every day*
> *by those who can, invoked by those who can't)*
> *these cylinders of homage (oblong praise)*
> *project a plenty that is its own reward,*
> *a yearning that has grown its own response:*
> *the deity whom these raised prayers rise to laud*
> *resides (when crops are good) in grateful guts.*

The journal is magazine-sized, printed on quality newsprint, using b&w art, cartoons and ads, about 30 pgs., saddle-stapled. **Payment: usually $20/poem plus 1 copy and discount on additional copies. Acquires all rights. Inquire about reprint permission. Sample: $1.50 postpaid. No simultaneous submissions. Submissions without SASE or SAE and IRCs will not be returned.** Reviews books of poetry in 300-400 words, single format; 400-500 words, multi-book.

THE CHRISTIAN SCIENCE MONITOR (II), 1 Norway St., Boston MA 02115, phone (617)450-2000, founded 1908, a national daily newspaper with a weekly international edition. **Poetry used regularly in The Home Forum, editor Alice Hummer. Pays $25 and up.**

THE CHRISTOPHER PUBLISHING HOUSE (II), 24 Rockland St., Commerce Green, Hanover MA 02339, phone (617)826-7474, FAX (617)826-5556, managing editor Nancy Lucas, says **"We will review all forms of poetry." Submit complete ms.**

THE CHRONICLE OF THE HORSE (IV-Themes), P.O. Box 46, Middleburg VA 22117, phone (703)687-6341, founded 1937, assistant editor Cynthia Foley, is a weekly magazine using **short poetry related to horses "the shorter the better. No free verse."** The magazine is devoted to English horse sports, such as horse shows and steeplechasing. It averages 68 pgs., magazine-sized. Subscription: $42. **Sample postpaid: $2. Pays $15/poem.** "We review books submitted to us but do not accept reviews for publication." **No simultaneous submissions. Buys first North American rights. Reports in 2-4 weeks. Summer "is not a good time"** to submit. 1-3 editors read poems.

CIMARRON REVIEW (II), 205 Morrill Hall, Oklahoma State University, Stillwater OK 74078-0135, founded 1967, poetry editors Thomas Reiter, Randy Phillis and Sally Shigley, is a quarterly literary journal. **"We emphasize quality and style. We like clear, evocative poetry (lyric or narrative) controlled by a strong voice. No obscure poetry. No sing-song verse. No quaint prairie verse. No restrictions as to subject matter, although we tend to publish more structured poetry (attention to line and stanza).** Also, we are conscious of our academic readership (mostly other writers) and attempt to accept poems that everyone will admire." Among poets they have recently published are Robert Cooperman, James McKean, David Citino, Tess Gallagher and Albert Goldbarth. This magazine, 6×9, 100 or 150 pgs., perfect-bound, boasts a handsome design, including a color cover and attractive printing. It has changed focus recently since Gordon Weaver took over the editorship so check a sample copy to get a feel for content. There are 15-25 pages of poetry in each issue, circulation of 500, mostly libraries. **Submit to Deborah Bransford, managing editor, any time, 3-5 poems, name and address on each poem, typed, single- or double-spaced. Clear photocopies acceptable. No simultaneous submissions. Replies within 4-6 weeks. They pay $15 for each poem published. Buys all rights. "Permission for a reprinting is granted upon request."** Reviews books of poetry in 500-900 words, single-book format, occasionally multi-book. All reviews are assigned. Subscription rates: $3/issue, $12/year ($15, Canada), $30 for 3 years ($40, Canada), plus $2.50 for all international subscriptions.

CITY LIGHTS BOOKS (III), 261 Columbus Ave., San Francisco CA 94133, phone (415)362-1901, founded 1955, edited by Lawrence Ferlinghetti and Nancy J. Peters, achieved prominence with the publication of Allen Ginsberg's **Howl** and other **poetry of the "Beat" school.** They publish **"poetry and advance-guard writing in the libertarian tradition."** Paper and cloth. **Simultaneous submissions OK, payment varies, reporting time 4-6 weeks.**

CITY SCRIPTUM (I), City College of San Francisco, 50 Phelan Ave., San Francisco CA 94112, phone (415)239-3000, founded 1988, editor-in-chief Brown Miller, appears twice a year using "any form from closed (traditional) to open (so-called 'free verse') but must be inventive, resonant, memorable, worth reading, nothing trite, wordy, sentimental, or any kind that reveals lack of knowledge about 20th Century verse." They have published poetry by Lyn Lifshin, A.D. Winans and Seaborn Jones. As a sample the editor selected these lines from "Winter in Auschwitz" by Gayle Leyton:

> a small boy
> has lost his birthday
> his mother
> keeper of his secrets
> wanders under the earth
> calling his name

It is handsomely printed, magazine-sized, 58 pgs. with matte card cover. Press run 1,000 for 10 subscribers of which 5 are libraries, 20 shelf sales. Subscription: $8. **Sample postpaid: $4 (when available). Send SASE for guidelines. Reports in 2-6 months. Pays 2 copies. Do not submit July through August.** The editor advises, "Read widely. Know the important poetry and poetic theories/criticism of this century. Then strive for a voice and vision of your own. Avoid too much of the discursive. Create surprise/magic that rings true."

THE CLASSICAL OUTLOOK (IV-Themes, translations), Classics Dept., Park Hall, University of Georgia, Athens GA 30602, founded 1924, poetry editors Prof. David Middleton (original English verse) and Prof. Jane Phillips (translations and original Latin verse), "is an internationally circulated quarterly journal (4,000 subscriptions, of which 250 are libraries) for high school and college Latin and Classics teachers, published by the American Classical League." They invite submissions of "original poems in English on classical themes, verse translations from Greek and Roman authors, and original Latin poems. Submissions should, as a rule, be written in traditional poetic forms and should demonstrate skill in the use of meter, diction and rhyme if rhyme is employed. Original poems should be more than mere exercise pieces or the poetry of nostalgia. Translations should be accompanied by a photocopy of the original Greek or Latin text. Latin originals should be accompanied by a literal English rendering of the text. Submissions should not exceed 50 lines." They have published work by Francis Fike and Roy Fuller. There are 2-3 magazine-sized pages of poetry in each issue, and they use 55% of the approximately 150 submissions they receive each year. They have a 6- to 12-month backlog, 4-month lead time. **Submit 2 copies, double-spaced. Receipt is acknowledged by letter. Poetry is refereed by poetry editors. Reports in 3-6 months. Pays 5 complimentary copies. Sample copies available from the American Classical League, Miami University, Oxford OH 45056 for $7.50. Guidelines available for SASE.** Reviews books of poetry "if the poetry is sufficiently classical in nature."

CLEANING BUSINESS MAGAZINE; WRITERS PUBLISHING SERVICE CO. (IV-Themes), 1512 Western Ave., P.O. Box 1273, Seattle WA 98111, phone (206)622-4241, FAX (206)622-6876, founded 1976, poetry editor William R. Griffin. *CBM* (formerly Service Business Magazine) is "a quarterly magazine for cleaning and maintenance professionals" and uses some poetry relating to their interests. "To be considered for publication in *Cleaning Business*, submit poetry that relates to our specific audience—cleaning and self-employment." He has published poetry by Don Wilson, Phoebe Bosche, Trudie Mercer and Joe Keppler. The editor says it is 8½ × 11, 100 pgs., offset litho, using ads, art and graphics. Of 50 poems received, he uses about 10. Press run is 5,000 for 3,000 subscriptions (100 of them libraries), 500 shelf sales. Subscription: $20. Per issue $5. **Sample: $3 postpaid. Send SASE and $3 for guidelines. Pays $5-10 plus 1 copy. Simultaneous submissions OK; no previously published poems.** Writers Publishing Service Co. is an imprint for subsidized publication of poetry (author's expense) and other services to writers. William Griffin suggests that "poets identify a specific market and work to build a readership that can be tapped again and again over a period of years with new books."

CLEVELAND STATE UNIVERSITY POETRY CENTER; CSU POETRY SERIES (II); CLEVELAND POETS SERIES (IV-Regional), Cleveland State University, Cleveland OH 44115, director Nuala Archer, editors Leonard Trawick and David Evett. The Poetry Center was founded in 1962, first publications in 1971. **The Poetry Center publishes the CSU Poetry Series for poets in general and the Cleveland Poets Series for Ohio poets. "Open to many kinds of form, length, subject matter, style and purpose. Should be well-crafted, clearly of professional quality, ultimately serious (even when humorous). No light verse, devotional verse or verse in which rhyme and meter seem to be of major importance."** They have published poetry by Martha Collins, Eric Trethewey, Naomi Clark and Stephen Tapscott. As a sample Leonard Trawick selected these lines from **Inland, Thinking of Waves** by Sarah Provost (CSU Poetry Center, 1991):

> It seems to be spring, sweetie,
> here in the heart of the green
> proprieties. The thirsty wind is a rascal,

> *makes quick work of our splendid*
> *coifs . . . .*

Books are chosen for publication from the entries to the CSU Poetry Center Prize contest. (Write for free catalog and sampler of some 65 Poetry Center books.) Deadline March 1. Entry fee: $10. The winner receives $1,000 and publication. They publish some other entrants in the Poetry Series, providing 50 copies (of press run of 1,000) and 10% royalty contract. The Cleveland Poets Series (for Ohio poets) offers 100 copies of a press run of 600. To submit for all series, send ms between December 1 and March 1. Reports on all submissions for the year by the end of July. Mss should be for books of 50-100 pgs., pages numbered, poet's name and address on cover sheet, clearly typed. Photocopies OK, and poems may have been previously published (listed on an acknowledgement page). Send SASE for guidelines. The Center also publishes other volumes of poetry, including chapbooks (20-30 pgs.), with a **$5 reading fee for each submission** (except for Ohio residents).

THE CLIMBING ART (IV-Themes), Fairfield Communications, 5620 S. 49th, Lincoln NE 68516, phone (402)421-2591, founded 1986, editor Pat Ament, is a quarterly magazine "read mainly by mountain enthusiasts who appreciate good writing about mountains and mountaineering. We are open to all forms and lengths. The only requirement is that the work be fresh, well-written and in some way of interest to those who love the mountains. If in doubt, submit it." As a sample we selected "Our Mission" by John Grey:

> *The mountain has size on its side,*
> *the sense that things that big*
> *need not have opinions*
> *or make peace with the world.*
> *We, on the other hand,*
> *are at the bottom,*
> *suburbs, impossible affairs,*
> *promotions missed.*

It is 32 pgs., magazine-sized, professionally printed on heavy stock with glossy card cover. Press run: 3,000 for 1,800 subscriptions of which 5 are libraries, 1,200 shelf sales. They use 1-4 poems/ issue of 100-200 submissions received/year. Subscription: $12. **Sample postpaid: $2.75. Pays 3 copies and subscription. Acquires one-time rights. Simultaneous submissions and previously published poems OK. Reports in 2 months.** Reviews books of poetry only if they concern mountains.

CLOCKWATCH REVIEW (II, III), James Plath, Dept. of English, Illinois Wesleyan University, Bloomington IL 61702, phone (309)556-3352, founded 1983, James Plath is editor, and Lynn Devore, James McGowan and Pamela Muirhead are associate editors. "We publish a variety of styles, leaning toward poetry which goes beyond the experience of self in an attempt to SAY something, without sounding pedantic or strained. We like a **strong, natural voice**, and lively, unusual combinations in language. Something *fresh, and that includes subject matter as well. It has been our experience that extremely short/long poems are hard to pull off.* Though we'll publish exceptions, we prefer to see poems that can fit on one published page (digest-sized) which runs **about 32 lines or less**." They have published Peter Wild, Martha Vertreace, John Knoepfle, Rita Dove and Peter Meinke. Asked for a sample, the editors say "trying to pick only four lines seems like telling people what detail we'd like to see in a brick, when what we're more interested in is the design of the *house*." The 80-page, semiannual *CR* is printed on glossy paper with colored, glossy cover. They use 7-10 unsolicited poems in each issue, with 1 featured poet. Circulation is 1,400, with 120 subscribers, of which 25 are libraries. They send out 300 complimentary copies and "The balance is wholesale distribution and single-copy sales." Sample: $4 postpaid. They receive 7,800 submissions per year, use 20-30. No backlog. **Prefer batches of 5-6 poems.** "We are not bowled over by large lists of previous publications, but brief letters of introduction or sparse mini-vitas are read out of curiosity. One poem per page, typed, single-spacing OK, photocopy OK if indicated that it is not a simultaneous submission (which we do NOT accept). Reports in 2 weeks; 2 months if under serious consideration. Payment is 3 copies, and, when possible, small cash awards—currently $10/poem." They will comment "if asked, and if time permits."

CLOUD RIDGE PRESS (V), Dept. PM, 2135 Stony Hill Rd., Boulder CO 80303, founded 1985, editor Elaine Kohler, a "literary small press for unique works in poetry and prose." They publish letterpress and offset books in both paperback and hardcover editions. In poetry, they want **"strong images of the numinous qualities in authentic experience grounded in a landscape and its people."** The first book, published in 1985, was **Ondina: A Narrative Poem** by John Roberts. The book is 6×9¼, handsomely printed on buff stock, cloth bound in black with silver decoration and spine lettering, 131 pages. Eight hundred copies were bound in Curtis Flannel and 200 copies bound in cloth over boards, numbered and signed by the poet and artist. This letterpress edition, priced at $18/cloth and $12/

paper, is not available in bookstores but only by mail from the press. The trade edition was photo-offset from the original, in both cloth and paper bindings, and is sold in bookstores. The press plans to publish 1-2 books/year. **Since they are not accepting unsolicited mss, writers should query first. Queries will be answered in 2 weeks and mss reported on in 1 month. Simultaneous submissions are acceptable, as are photocopied or dot-matrix mss. Royalties are 10% plus a negotiable number of author's copies.** A brochure is free on request; send #10 SASE.

CLUBHOUSE; YOUR STORY HOUR (I, IV-Children, teens), P.O. Box 15, Berrien Springs MI 49103, poetry editor Elaine Trumbo, **pays about $12 for poems under 24 lines plus 2 contributor's copies. Buys first or second rights.** The publication is printed in conjunction with the **Your Story Hour** radio program, founded 1949, which is designed to teach the Bible and moral life to children. The magazine, *Clubhouse*, started with that title in 1982, but as *Good Deeder*, its original name, it has been published since 1951. Elaine Trumbo says, **"We do like humor or mood pieces. Don't like mushy-sweet 'Christian' poetry. We don't have space for long poems. Best—16 lines or under."** They have published poetry by Lillian M. Fisher, Audrey Osofsky, Sharon K. Motzko, Bruce Bash and Craig Peters. As a sample the editor selected these lines from "Nurses Office" by Eileen Spinelli:

> *And it hurts behind my ear,*
> *And I've got a cut right here,*
> *And a rash between my toes,*
> *And a pimple on my nose.*
> *Ouch, my knee feels sore and tender-*
> *Bumped it on my bike's back fender.*
> *I can't tell you all I've got.*
> *Where's the aspirin?*
> *Bring the cot!*
> *I need T.L.C. and rest.*

Too bad I'll miss that spelling test!
The magazine has a circulation of 10,000, with 10,000 subscriptions of which maybe 5 are librar-ies. Subscription: $5 for 6 issues/year. **Sample: 3 oz. postage. Writer's guidelines are available for SASE. Submit mss in March and April. Simultaneous submissions OK. The "evaluation sheet" for returned mss gives reasons for acceptance or rejection.** The editor advises, "Give us poetry with freshness and imagination. We most often use mood pieces and humorous poems that appeal to children."

COCHRAN'S CORNER (I, IV-Subscribers), P.O.Box 2036, Waldorf MD 20604, phone (301)843-0485, founded 1985, poetry editor Billye Keene, is a **"family type" quarterly open to beginners, preferring poems of 20 lines or less. You have to be a subscriber to submit.** "Any subject or style (except porn)." She has published poetry by J. Alvin Speers, Becky Knight and Francesco BiVone. *CC* is 58 pgs. saddle-stapled, desktop published, with matte card cover, press run of 500. Subscription: $15. **Send SASE for guidelines. Sample: $5 plus SASE. Pays 2 copies. Acquires first rights. Simultaneous submissions and previously published poems OK. Reports in average of 3 months.** Reviews books of poetry. Contests in March and July; $3 entry fee for 2 poems. "We provide criticism if requested at the rate of $1 per page. Write from the heart, but don't forget your readers. You must work to find the exact words that mirror your feelings, so the reader can share your feelings."

THE COE REVIEW (II), Coe College, 1220 1st Ave. NE, Cedar Rapids IA 52402, phone (319)399-8660, founded 1972, poetry editor James Nulick, is "an annual little literary magazine with **emphasis on the innovative and unselfconscious** poetry and fiction. We are **open to virtually any and all subject matter.**" They have published poetry by James Galvin and Jan Weissmiller. The annual is 100-150 pgs., flat-spined, digest-sized with matte card cover. "Each issue includes 4-8 reproductions of works of art, usually photographs, lithography and etched prints." Circulation is about 500. **Sample: $4 postpaid. Send SASE for guidelines. Pays 1 copy. Reports in 6-8 weeks.** Accepted work appears in the next issue, published in Spring. **No simultaneous submissions. Photocopy OK. Include "brief cover letter."** The editor says, "We are supportive in the endeavors of poets whose material is original and tasteful. We are eclectic in our publication choices in that variety of subject matter and style make the *Coe Review* exciting."

‡COFFEE HOUSE PRESS (III), Suite 400, 27 North 4th St., Minneapolis MN 55401, phone (612)338-0125, founded 1984, editorial assistant Michael Wiegers, publishes 10 paperbacks/year. They want poetry that is **"challenging and lively; influenced by the Beats, the NY School or Black Mountain. No traditional or formalistic; nothing that relies on conventional assumptions like rhyme and meter."** They have recently published poetry collections by Victor Hernandez Cruz, Anne Waldman, Andrei

Codrescu and Linda Hogan. As a sample the editor selected these lines fr⊘
Steve Levine:

> The family that eats together
> eats together and eats together, rides a
> tiny Honda together, two of them, huge
> matching bellies heading north

Previously published poems OK; no simultaneous submissions. Cover let
include a SASE if you want your manuscript returned." Seldom comments ⊘
to queries in 1 month, to mss in 6 months. Pays 8% royalties, $500 honorar ... author's
copies. Write for catalog to order sample.

COFFEEHOUSE POETS' QUARTERLY (I, II), 3412 Erving, Berthoud CO 80513, founded 1990, editors Ray Foreman and Barbara Shukle. **They want "free verse that is fresh, imaginative and clear, that brings the reader into the poet's experience."** They have recently published poetry by Albert Huffstickler, David Castleman, T. Kilgore Splake and Terry Everton. As a sample the editors selected the first 6 lines of "The San Francisco Pit Band Blues" by Ray Clark Dickson:

> back when six-a-day vaudeville was alive
> & frisky & the drummer's rim shot tagged
> the dancer's body at the apex of her thrust
> the albino piano player smoked the ivories
> with both hands, keys all nicotined with
> yellow & stained with gin

It is 40 pgs. Press run 300 for 170 subscribers, balance sample copies and shelf sales. They accept about 10% of 2,000 poems submitted/year. "We showcase well-crafted quality poetry from known and unknown poets and promote contact between poets and audience through the Poets' Dialogue Network." Subscription: $8. **Sample, with guidelines, postpaid: $3. Submit up to 5 poems. Reports in about 2 weeks. Pays "with discount on copies."** The editors say, "Good poems convey experience in language, image and psychological clarity. What few poetry readers there are, are intelligent, sophisticated and discerning. Submit only your best work."

COKEFISH (I), 31 Waterloo St, New Hope PA 18938, founded 1990, editor Ana Pine, is a monthly journal **with an entry fee of $1/3 poems. "I want to see work that has passion behind it. From the traditional to the avant-garde, provocative to discreet, trivial to the significant. Am interested in social issues, alternative, avant-garde, erotica and humor for people with nothing to hide."** They have recently published poetry by Charles Bukowski, Herschell Silverman, Elliot, A.D. Winans and Arlene Mandell. As a sample the editor selected these lines from "Contortionist" by Albert Huffstickler:

> The hardest parts the recovery
> Unkinking limbs locked into place
> Till distortions become the truer way
> There's pain and exposure in realignment . . .
> And a blood-deep sorrow you can't account for

The format is 60 pgs., side-stapled on heavy paper with a cover printed on both sides on colored photocopy paper. Press run 300 for 150 subscribers. Subscription: $15. **Sample postpaid: $4. Send SASE for guidelines. Pays 1 copy. Accepts 30% of mss received. Note entry fee: $1/3 poems, additional $1 for additional poems. Simultaneous submissions and previously published poems OK. Reports in 1 week.** Reviews books of poetry in ½ page. The editor advises, "Spread the word; don't let your poems sit and vegetate in a drawer. Send me stuff that will make my hair stand up on end."

CO-LABORER; WOMAN'S NATIONAL AUXILIARY CONVENTION (IV-Religious), P.O. Box 5002, Antioch TN 37011-5002, phone (615)731-6812, founded 1935, editor Lorene Miley, is "a bimonthly publication **to give women a missionary vision and challenge. We'll consider any length or style as long as the subject is missions."** They do not want to see poetry which is not religious or not related to missions. The editor selected these lines from "Grownups" by Debbie Payne Anderson:

> "Debbie — —ee!"
> The cry swells as I climb from the
> Car and slam the door behind me.
> They press as close as they dare.
>
> Sweet urchins
> With their little bloated tummies
> And grimy hands extending in welcome.
> An inquisitive girl reaches out
> To stroke the soft material of my

)ress and pat my pale skin.

-page magazine uses at least one poem/issue, circulation 15,000. **Sample postpaid: $1.** copies.

COLLAGES & BRICOLAGES, THE JOURNAL OF INTERNATIONAL WRITING (II, IV-Translations, feminist, political, social issues, humor), P.O. Box 86, Clarion PA 16214, founded in 1986, editor Marie-José Fortis. *C&B* is a "small literary magazine with **a strong penchant for literary, feminist, avant-garde work.** Strongly encourages poets and fiction writers, as well as essayists, whether English-speaking or foreign. **(Note: Writers sending their work in a foreign language must have their ms accompanied with an English translation.)** We are presently looking for **poetry that is socially aware — politically engaged. No sexism, racism or glorification of war. We are going towards focus-oriented issues."** As a sample the editor selected these lines by Diane Hamill Metzger:

> *We adapt to the sanction of walls,*
> *Speak brashly the language of impostors*
> *Are shrouded in trappings of brown.*

The annual is magazine-sized, 100 + pgs., flat-spined, with card cover. They accept 5% of 150 poetry submissions/year. Press run 400. **Sample postpaid: $6, or $3 for back issue. Reads submissions August 15 through November 30 only. Reports in 1-3 months. Pays 2 copies. Acquires first rights.** "It is recommended that potential contributors order a copy, so as to know what kind of work is desirable. **Enclose a personalized letter.** Be considerate to editors, as many of them work on a voluntary basis and sacrifice much time and energy to encourage writers." Marie-José Fortis says, "It is time to stop being too plastic and too polite and too careful. The Berlin Wall is down. Eastern Europe will bring to us powerful, daring literary voices, with much to tell. The American writer should follow a similar path. With what was revealed as the temptation of war and the neglect of an effort for peace, too many things are left unsaid."

‡COLLEGE & CAREER PUBLISHING; CALIFORNIA WORK WORLD (IV-Children/teen/young adult), P.O. Box 900, Ontario CA 91761-8900, founded 1989. *California Work World* is a "monthly newsletter/workbook to help junior high and high school students learn about college and jobs as well as how to be a good citizen in our world and cope with problems encountered along the way." They want **"rhyming poems with messages for teenagers; 5-40 lines. No non-rhyming, free-form verse."** As a sample the editor selected these lines by Beverly Bassler:

> *Success with life's struggles begins with one's self,*
> *Jump in, get your feet wet, get off the shelf!*
>
> *We're all in this world on a stage, in a play;*
> *Each person's unique in his style and his way.*
>
> *Find something of value . . . stay focused . . . begin,*
> *To reach for your goals by the power from within!*

CWW is 16 pages, glue bound, with puzzles and illustrations. Press run is 6,000. **Sample postpaid: $1. Previously published poems and simultaneous submissions OK.** Time between acceptance and publication is 3-4 months. "Poems are tested with groups of teenagers, and they choose favorites." **Often comments on rejections. "If comments are desired, poet must include SASE." Send SASE for guidelines. Reports in 2-3 months. Pays $15 and 35 copies.**

COLLEGE ENGLISH; NATIONAL COUNCIL OF TEACHERS OF ENGLISH (II), % James C. Raymond, Drawer AL, University of Alabama, Tuscaloosa AL 35487, phone (205)348-6488, editor Louise Smith, assistant editor Anita Angor, University of Massachusetts, Amherst, MA. This journal, which goes 8 times/year to members of the National Council of Teachers of English (membership: $30, includes subscription to *CE*), is a scholarly journal for the English discipline, but includes poetry by such poets as James Tate, Michael Pettit and Norman Stock. It is 100 pgs., saddle-stapled, with matte card cover, 7½ × 9½, circulation 16,000. **Sample postpaid: $4.50. Pays 6 copies. Reports in 4 months maximum.**

‡COLOR WHEEL; 700 ELVES PRESS (IV-Nature, spiritual), RR 2, Box 806, Warner NH 03278, founded 1990, editor Frederick Moe, appears approximately 3 times/year. *"Color Wheel* uses high quality prose and **poetry related to spiritual, ecological and mythological themes. All forms of poetry are welcome, including longer poems (2-4 pages). No rhymed verse."** They have recently published poetry by Walt Franklin, Will Inman, Nina Silver and Carol Edson. The editor says it is 32-40 pgs., 8 × 11, saddle-stapled, with heavy cover stock, cover art, graphics and line drawings. They receive about 300 submissions a year, use an average of 10%. Press run is 300 for 25 subscribers of which 4 are libraries, 100 + shelf sales. Single copy: $5; subscription: $8 (2 issues). **Sample postpaid: $4.50. Make checks payable to Frederick Moe. No simultaneous submissions. Reads submissions January 1 through August 15 only. Seldom comments on rejections. Send SASE for guidelines. Reports in up to**

1 month. Pays 2 copies. **700 Elves Press publishes 2 chapbooks/year.** "Some 700 Elves Press chapbooks are thematic anthologies including various writers. I have published chapbooks on elemental poems and plan other thematic chapbooks and occasional individual collections." **Poets should first be published in** *Color Wheel*. **Replies to queries and mss in 1 month. Pays "negotiable" number of author's copies. For sample chapbooks "send SASE for our small, homespun catalog."** Frederick Moe says, "*Color Wheel* is esoteric yet focused in content. Poets should be familiar with the evolution of the magazine and type of material we publish before sending work. I encourage 'new' voices and appreciate creative approaches to the material."

COLORADO NORTH REVIEW (III), UC 208, University Center, University of Northern Colorado, Greeley CO 80639, founded 1963 as *Nova*, editor L. Christopher Baxter, appears twice a year (December and May). **"We consider all mss without bias, regardless of style, form, genre or so-called 'schools.' I open all the mail myself and look primarily for poetic integrity, that is a synthesis between original vision and a unique and organic means of expressing it. Overly poetic language (i.e. artificial) and clichéd sentiments are frowned upon."** They have published poetry by Florence Elon, Anselm Hollo, Robert Long, Phyllis Koestenbaum and Eileen Myles. As a sample the editor selected these lines from "Les L'armes Sanglant DEnfer" by William Hathaway:

> Go ahead! Rename candy tears,
> red as bloody beads we pricked
> on fingertips for holy love
> as kids. The ones stinging spit-
> fire cinnamon we called "red hots."

It is 100-120 pgs., flat-spined (with occasional double issues of up to 220 pgs.), printed on 70 lb. vellum paper. They received over 900 mss for a recent issue, accepted 74 poems from 39 poets (and 12 pieces of fiction). Press run is 2,500 for 65 subscriptions of which 40 are libraries. Subscription: $8. **Sample postpaid: $4.50. Do not submit mss during June or July. Send SASE for guidelines. Pays 2 copies plus** *CNR* **T-shirts when available. No simultaneous submissions please! Reports in 1-2 months. Editor comments "when time allows or in exceptional cases."** Reviews books of poetry.

COLORADO REVIEW (II, IV-Translations, themes), Dept. of English, 359 Eddy Bldg., Colorado State University, Ft. Collins CO 80523, phone (303)491-6428, founded 1955 as *Colorado State Review*, resurrected 1977 under "New Series" rubric, renamed *Colorado Review* 1985. General and poetry editor Bill Tremblay. *Colorado Review* is a journal of contemporary literature which appears twice annually; it combines short fiction, poetry, interviews with or articles about significant contemporary poets and writers, articles on literature, culture, and the arts, translations of poetry from around the world and reviews of recent works of the literary imagination. **"We're interested in poetry that explores experience in deeply felt new ways; merely descriptive or observational language doesn't move us. Poetry that enters into and focuses on the full range of experience, weaving sharp imagery, original figures and surprising though apt insight together in compressed precise language and compelling rhythm is what triggers an acceptance here."** They have recently published poetry by Tess Gallagher, James Galvin, Jorie Graham and Brendan Galvin. They have a circulation of 1,500, 300 subscriptions of which 100 are libraries. They use about 10% of the 500-1,000 submissions they receive per year. **Sample: $5 postpaid. Submit about 5 poems, typewritten or clear photocopy. Reads submissions September 1 through April 1 only. Reports in 3-6 months. Pays $20/printed page. Buys first North American serial rights. Reviews books of poetry, both single and multi-book format. "When work is a near-miss, we will provide brief comment and encouragement,"** Bill Tremblay says. "Our attitude is that we will publish the best work that comes across the editorial desk. We see poetry as a vehicle for exploring states of feeling, but we aren't interested in sentimentality (especially metaphysical)."

COLUMBIA: A MAGAZINE OF POETRY & PROSE; EDITORS' AWARDS (II), 404 Dodge Hall, Columbia University, New York NY 10027, phone (212)280-4391, founded 1977, is a literary semiannual using "quality short stories, novel excerpts, translations, interviews, nonfiction and **poetry, usually no longer than 2 pgs. Nothing juvenile, sentimental, simply descriptive."** They have published poetry by Henri Cole, Theresa Svoboda, Eamon Grennan and Jimmy Santiago-Baca. It is digest-sized, approximately 180 pgs., with coated cover stock. They publish about 12 poets each issue from 400 submissions. Press run 1,250 for 1,000 subscriptions of which 100 are libraries, 400 shelf sales. **Sample postpaid: $6. Send SASE for guidelines. Pays up to 4 copies. Submit double spaced mss. Reports in 1-3 months. "Very brief comments at editor's discretion."** They offer annual honorarium Editors' Awards for the best poems published annually.

‡COLUMBIA UNIVERSITY TRANSLATION CENTER; TRANSLATION; TRANSLATION CENTER AWARDS (V), 412 Dodge, Columbia University, New York NY 10027, phone (212)854-2305, founded 1972, director Frank MacShane. "Translation Center publishes only foreign contemporary literature in English language translations and also gives annual awards and grants to translators. *Translation* magazine publishes **contemporary foreign poetry/literature in English language translations.** (Note: we do not review and do not accept translated plays.)" They have recently published translations of poetry by Anne Hébert, Sandor Csoori, Fernando Pessoa, Thomas Günther and Richard Pietrass. As a sample we selected these lines from "Body" by Eugénio de Andrade, translated from the Portugese by Alexis Levitin:

> *The sea — whenever I touch*
> *a body the sea is what I feel*
> *wave after wave*
> *against the palm of my hand.*

Translation is a biannual, circulation 2,000. Subscription: $18. **Sample postpaid: $9. Not currently accepting unsolicited manuscripts. Please write for further information. Send SASE for guidelines and descriptions of the various award programs they administer.** Columbia University Translation Center Awards are grants to a translator for an outstanding translation of a substantial part of a book-length literary work. Awards range from $1,000-2,000 and are designed mainly to recognize excellence. Translations from any language into English are eligible, and specific awards exist for translations from the French Canadian, Dutch, Portuguese and Italian. All applications will automatically be considered for all awards for which they are eligible. The Center generally discourages applicants who are retranslating a work unless a special reason exists.

COMMONWEAL (III, IV-Religious), 15 Dutch St., New York NY 10038, phone (212)732-0800, poetry editor Rosemary Deen, appears every 2 weeks, circulation 20,000, is a general-interest magazine for college-educated readers **by Catholics.** The editor selected this sample from "One is One," a sonnet by Marie Ponsot:

> *Heart, you bully, you punk, I'm wrecked, I'm shocked*
> *stiff. You? you still try to rule the world — though*
> *I've got you: identified, starving, locked*
> *in a cage you will not leave alive . . .*

Sample: $3. Prefers serious, witty, well-written poems of up to 75 lines. Does not publish inspirational poems. Considers simultaneous submissions. Reads submissions September 1 through June 30 only. Pays 50¢ a line. Buys all rights. Returns rights when requested by the author. Reviews books of poetry in 750-1,000 words, single or multi-book format.

COMMUNICATIONS PUBLISHING GROUP; COLLEGE PREVIEW, A GUIDE FOR COLLEGE-BOUND STUDENTS; DIRECTIONS, A GUIDE TO CAREER ALTERNATIVES; JOURNEY, A SUCCESS GUIDE FOR COLLEGE AND CAREER-BOUND STUDENTS; VISIONS, A SUCCESS GUIDE FOR NATIVE AMERICAN STUDENTS; FIRST OPPORTUNITY, A GUIDE FOR VOCATIONAL TECHNICAL STUDENTS (IV-Youth, themes, ethnic), Dept. PM, 225 PennTower, 3100 Broadway, Kansas City MO 64111, phone (816)221-4404, editor Georgia Clark. These five publications are 40% freelance written. All are designed to inform and motivate their readers in regard to college preparation, career planning and life survival skills. All except *First Opportunity*, which is quarterly, appear in spring and fall. *College Preview* is for Black and Hispanic young adults, ages 16-21. Circ. 600,000. *Directions* is for Black and Hispanic young adults, ages 18-25. Circ. 500,000. *Journey* is for Asian-American high school and college students, ages 16-25. Circ. 200,000. *Visions* is for Native American students and young adults, ages 16-25. Circ. 100,000. *First Opportunity* is for Black and Hispanic young adults, ages 16-21. Circ. 500,000. **All these magazines pay on acceptance. Submit seasonal/holiday material 6 months in advance. Simultaneous, photocopied and previously published submissions OK. Computer printout submissions OK; prefers letter-quality. "Include on manuscript your name, address, phone and Social Security numbers." Reports in 2 months. Sample copy of any for 9 × 12 SAE with 4 first class stamps. Writer's guidelines for #10 SASE. They use free verse. Each magazine buys 5 poems/year. Submit up to 5 poems at one time. Length: 10-25 lines. Pays $10-50/poem.**

COMMUNITIES: JOURNAL OF COOPERATION (IV-Social issues), Rt. 1, Box 155, Rutledge MO 63563, phone (816)883-5543, founded 1972, managing editor Laird Schaub, is a "quarterly publication on **intentional communities, cooperatives, social and global transformation,**" using poetry relevant to those themes. It is magazine-sized, professionally printed on newsprint stock with 2-color glossy paper cover, 56 pgs., saddle-stapled. **Pays 3 copies. Previously published poems and simultaneous submissions OK. No comment on rejections.**

A COMPANION IN ZEOR (IV-Science fiction/fantasy), 307 Ashland Ave., McKee City NJ 08232, phone (609)645-6938, founded 1978, editor Karen Litman, is a **SF, fantasy fanzine appearing irregularly (last published issue December 1990; hopes to publish again this year). "Material used is now limited to creations based solely on works (universes) of Jacqueline Lichtenberg. No other submission**

types considered. **Prefer nothing obscene. Homosexuality not acceptable unless very relevant to the piece. Prefer a 'clean' publication image."** As a sample, we selected these lines from "Fire Also Purifies" by Lisa Calhoun:

> *A death is a birth, and the reverse is true,*
> *out of the turmoil emerges something new.*

It is magazine-sized, photocopied from typescript, press run 100. **Send SASE for guidelines. Pays copies. Acquires first rights. "Always willing to work with authors or poets to help in improving their work."** Reviews books of poetry.

CONCHO RIVER REVIEW; FORT CONCHO MUSEUM PRESS (IV-Regional), 213 E. Ave. D, San Angelo TX 76903, phone (915)657-4441, founded 1984, poetry editor Gerald M. Lacy. "The Fort Concho Museum Press is entering its sixth year of publishing *Concho River Review*, a literary journal published twice a year. **Work by Texas writers, writers with a Texas connection and writers living in the Southwest preferred. Prefer shorter poems, few long poems accepted; particularly looking for poems with distinctive imagery and imaginative forms and rhythms. The first test of a poem will be its imagery."** Short reviews of new volumes of poetry are also published. *CRR* is 120-138 pgs., flat-spined, digest-sized, with matte card cover, professionally printed. They use 35-40 of 600-800 poems received/year. Press run: 300 for about 200 subscriptions of which 10 are libraries. Subscription: $12. Sample postpaid: $4. Pays 1 copy. Acquires first rights. **"Please submit 3-5 poems at a time. Use regular legal-sized envelopes—no big brown envelopes; no replies without SASE. Type must be letter-perfect, sharp enough to be computer scanned."** Reports in 2-8 weeks. The editor says, "We're always looking for good, strong work—from both well-known poets and those who have never been published before."

CONDITIONED RESPONSE PRESS; CONDITIONED RESPONSE; CONDITIONED RESPONSE AN-NUAL CHAPBOOK SEARCH (V), P.O. Box 3816, Ventura CA 93006, founded 1982, poetry editor John McKinley, is a small press publisher of poetry only—magazine and occasional chapbooks. **They are not accepting unsolicited material at this time.** *Conditioned Response* appears biannually and has a circulation of 200. Subscription: $4 for 2 issues. The digest-sized publication contains poetry only, no illustrations except a cover photograph. It is professionally printed on lightweight stock, 24 pgs., matte card cover, saddle-stapled. Reviews books of poetry. The editor says, "Poets may receive $10 worth of chaps and mags for only $4 postpaid."

CONFLUENCE PRESS (II, IV-Regional), Lewis Clark State College, Lewiston ID 83501, phone (208)799-2336, founded 1975, poetry editor James R. Hepworth, is an "independent publisher of fiction, poetry, creative nonfiction and literary scholarship. **We are open to formal poetry as well as free verse. No rhymed doggerel, 'light verse,' 'performance poetry,' 'street poetry,' etc. We prefer to publish work by poets who live and work in the northwestern United States."** They have published poetry by John Daniel, Greg Keeler, Nancy Mairs and Robert Wrigley. They print about 3 books and 2 chapbooks a year. **Query with 6 sample poems, bio, list of publications. No simultaneous submissions. Reports in 3 weeks to queries, 2 months to mss. Pays $100 advance and 10% royalties plus copies. Buys all rights. Returns rights when book goes out of print.** Editor sometimes comments on rejections. Send SASE for catalog to order samples.

CONFRONTATION MAGAZINE (II), English Dept., C. W. Post of Long Island University, Greenvale NY 11548, founded 1968, editor-in-chief Martin Tucker, is "a semiannual literary journal with **interest in all forms.** Our only criterion is high literary merit. We think of our audience as an educated, lay group of intelligent readers. **We prefer lyric poems. Length generally should be kept to 2 pages. No sentimental verse."** They have published poetry by Karl Shapiro, T. Alan Broughton, David Ignatow, Philip Appleman, Jane Mayhall and Joseph Brodsky. Basically a magazine, they do on occasion publish "book" issues or "anthologies." It's a digest-sized professionally-printed, flat-spined, journal of 190 + pgs. with a circulation of about 2,000. **Sample:** $3 postpaid. They receive about 1,200 submissions per year, publish 150, have a 6- to 12-month backlog. **Submit no more than 10 pgs., clear copy (photocopy OK). Do not submit mss June-August. "Prefer single submissions." Reports in 6-8 weeks. Pays: $5-50 and copy of magazine.** Reviews books of poetry.

CONJUNCTIONS (III), Bard College, Box 115, Annandale-on-Hudson NY 12504, founded 1981, managing editor Bradford Morrow, is an elegant, fat journal appearing twice/year. **"Potential contributor should be familiar with the poetry published in the journal."** They have published poetry by John Ashbery, Robert Kelly, Charles Stein and Michael Palmer. As a sample here are these lines from "Paulownia" by Barbara Guest:

> *ravenous the still dark a fishnet—*
> *robber walk near formidable plaits*
> *a glaze—the domino overcast—*

> *violet. shoulder.*

Like *The Quarterly*, this publication is distributed by Random House. It is 400+ pgs., 6×9, flat-spined, professionally printed. Press run 7,500 for 600 subscribers of which 200 are libraries. Subscription: $18. **Sample postpaid: $12. Pays copies.**

THE CONNECTICUT POETRY REVIEW (II), P.O. Box 3783, New Haven CT 06525, founded 1981, poetry editors J. Claire White and James William Chichetto, is a "small press that puts out an annual magazine. **We look for poetry of quality which is both genuine and original in content. No specifications except length: 10-40 lines.**" The magazine has won high praise from the literary world; they have recently published such poets as Gary Metras, Robert Peters, Peter Wild and Linda Pastan. Each issue seems to feature a poet. As a sample they selected these lines by Odysseus Elytis (translated by Jeffrey Carson):

> *Maybe I'm still in the state of a medicinal*
> *herb or of a cold Friday's snake*
> *Or perhaps of one of those sacred beasts*
> *with its big ear full of heavy sounds*
> *and metallic noise from censers.*

The flat-spined, 60-page, large digest-sized journal is "printed letterpress by hand on a Hacker Hand Press from Monotype Bembo." Most of the 60 pgs. are poetry, but they also have reviews. Circulation is 400, with 80 subscriptions of which 35 are libraries. **Sample: $3.50 postpaid.** They receive over 900 submissions a year, use about 20, have a 3-month backlog, **report in 3 months, pay $5/poem plus 1 copy.** The editors advise, "Study traditional and modern styles. Study poets of the past. Attend poetry readings. And write. Practice on your own."

CONNECTICUT RIVER REVIEW; NATIONAL FALL POETRY CONTEST; BRODINE CONTEST; CONNECTICUT POETRY SOCIETY (II), P.O. Box 2171, Bridgeport CT 06608, founded 1978, appears twice yearly. Editor Robert Isaacs. They want poetry that has **"depth of emotion, the truly seen (imaginary or actual), in which sound and sense are one. All forms are welcome, except haiku. We look for high quality, well-crafted poems."** They have published poetry by Joseph Bruchac, Donald Jenkins, Simon Perchik, Viola Shipley and Paul Zimmer. Each of the plain but attractively printed, digest-sized issues contains about 40 pgs. of poetry, has a circulation of about 500, with 175 subscriptions of which 5% are libraries. They receive about 2,000 submissions per year, use about 70. Subscription: $10. **Sample: $5 postpaid. Deadlines: February 15 and August 15. Submit no more than 3-5 poems. No simultaneous submissions. Poems over 40 lines have little chance of acceptance, unless exceptional. Rejections within 2 weeks, acceptances could take 2 months. Pays 1 copy. Guidelines available with SASE.** The National Fall Poetry Contest, deadline August 1, has a $2 entry fee per poem and prizes of $100, $50, and $25. Send SASE for rules. The Brodine Contest, Box 112, Stratford, CT 06497, guidelines available in February; send SASE. Deadline is July 15, $2 fee per poem. Three cash awards plus publication in the *Connecticut River Review*.

CONTEXT SOUTH (II), 2100 Memorial Blvd. #4504, Kerrville TX 78028, founded 1988, editor/publisher David Breeden, appears twice a year using **"any form, length, subject matter. Looking for strong rhythms, clear vision. Nothing sentimental."** They have recently published poetry by Andrea Hollander Budy and Wayne Dodd. As a sample the editor selected these lines by David Keith:

> *They are sadly miserably left in*
> *Their miserable world where they*
> *Do all they can do, repeating faithfully*
> *The same lines, driving down St.*
> *Charles eternally in the same direction.*

It is 65 pgs. digest-sized, saddle-stapled, using fiction, criticism and book reviews as well as poetry. They accept less than 1% of poems received. Press run 500 for 60 subscribers of which 6 are libraries. **Sample: $5. Pays 1 copy. Acquires first serial rights. Simultaneous submissions OK. Reads submissions January 1 through March 31 only.** Reviews books of poetry in 500 words maximum. The editor advises, "Read every poem you can find from the beginning of time. Every poem encapsulates the entire tradition."

CONVERGING PATHS (IV-Spiritual, themes), P.O. Box 63, Mt. Horeb WI 53572, founded 1986, editor Kyril Oakwind, is a quarterly **"Pagan/Wiccan magazine focusing on traditional Wicca, using a few poems: short, fits in one column or occasionally one page, inspirational, Pagan poetry. Suggested**

Market categories: (I) Beginning; (II) General; (III) Limited; (IV) Specialized; (V) Closed.

subjects: earth, mother, God of the hunt, death and rebirth, initiation, Celtic or British myths and gods. Our prime consideration is whether it is overtly Pagan/Wiccan in symbolism and emotionally moving to our staff. If so, it doesn't *have* to be technically perfect or have traditional form. No long, long poems or those unrelated to the Pagan theme of our magazine or bad poetry. If you are not sure what the Pagan/Wiccan religion is, please read a sample copy before submitting." The editor describes it as magazine-sized, 32 pgs., stapled. Press run 200 for 100+ subscriptions of which 1 is a library, 20-30 shelf sales. Subscription: $14. **Sample postpaid: $4. Pays 1 copy. Acquires first rights. Reports in 2-3 months.** Reviews books of Pagan poetry.

‡**CONVICTIONS (IV-Specialized)**, Box 1749, Corvallis OR 97339-1749, phone (503)754-1564, founded 1990, is a quarterly "by and for prisoners and their people." They want **"poetry only from prisoners or ex-prisoners. Nothing religious."** They have recently published poetry by Raymond Ringo Fernandez and Elmo Chattman, Jr. As a sample the editor selected these lines by Michael La Bruno:

> *Misguided*
> *mangled tangled*
> *souls*
> *Conveyor-belted*
> *to justice's*
> *revolving doors*
> *Tormented*
> *they whirl*
> *frisbee footed*
> *weaving*
> *grotesques.*

"We consider simultaneous submissions and previously published poems." Seldom comments on rejections. **Reports in 3 months. Pays $5-50 plus 1-year subscription.** Offers an annual contest for prisoners including a poetry category. 1st prize: $50; 2nd: $25. These and honorable mentions also receive a 1-year subscription. The editor says, "We get far more poems than we can use, so only top quality material should be submitted."

THE COOL TRAVELER (I, IV-Themes), P.O. Box 11975, Philadelphia PA 19145, phone (215)440-0592, founded 1988, editor Bob Moore, appears 4 times/year, using **"poetry that contains references about places, especially different countries, but I'll look at it all."** They have recently published poetry by Brandel France, John J. Koller and Anne Louise Huffman. Its format is long and slender, about 64 pages, saddle-stapled. Press run: 1,000 copies printed. "We are in over 100 bookstores nationally and some in Canada and England. Our publication continues to grow in popularity. We only accept about 15 poems/year now. This is an important change." Subscription: $10. **Sample: $3. Pays in copies.** Submitting poets should, in a cover letter, "say something about themselves—a short one or two lines to be printed with their work." **Reports in 1 month, sometimes asks for rewrites. Editor comments on submissions "often."** Reviews books of poetry in 1,000 words or so, single or multi-book format. He says, "There are many local papers and publications that want poetry."

COOP. ANTIGRUPPO SICILIANO; TERZA PAGINA (II, IV-Translations), Via Argenteria, Km 4, Trapani, Sicily, Italy, 91100, phone 0923-38681, founded 1968, poetry editor Nat Scammacca, is a group of over 100 poets involved in international activities pertaining to poetry including readings, sponsored visits, and publication in the weekly (except in August) cultural newspaper, or in collections or anthologies. **Free samples.** Scammacca says, "**We translate and publish short poems almost every week in** *Terza Pagina* **and, on occasion, in our anthologies.** We have published several thousand American poems and have included 20 American poets including Simpson, Stafford, Bly, Ferlinghetti, Corso, Ignatow, etc. We like **ironical poetry, committed poetry (anti-atomic), intelligent poetry;** we do not want poetry that makes no sense, rhetorical stuff, sentimental, or poets who think each word or line is God-sent. The poem must *communicate.* We prefer short poems, but if the poem is exceptional, we want it. Short poems we can translate into Sicilian and Italian and use in our weekly in a week's time." The editor selected a sample from *Dawn Patrol* "Balla con me" by Donald Everett Axinn:

> *. . . Pilots need to test*
> *the exact moment*
> *when gravity leans on*
> *the plane's nose*
> *pushes it down into a fall*
> *and us with it . . .*

Send poems of 4-15 lines to Nat Scammacca. Considers simultaneous submissions. "The poet must send his best poetry. If it is difficult but makes sense he can explain why he wants us to publish the poem, why he wants us to suffer. We want, otherwise, enjoyable, witty, intelligent and if possible great poetry." Apparently one gets acquainted by submitting to the weekly. If you want to send a book ms, query first, with cover letter giving biographical background, personal or aesthetic philosophy. Payment in copies of the published book. "They are lucky when we publish them," says the editor. The nonprofit cooperative is supported by government funds; it organizes poetry tours, radio and TV appearances and readings for some of the authors they have published. "We want other poets to be sufficiently confident in themselves so as not to ask for our opinion concerning their poetry. We prefer having the poet himself explain why he writes, for whom and why he writes as he does. We do not want to substitute our methods for his methods." (See listing for Cross-Cultural Communications.)

COPPER BEECH PRESS (III), P.O. Box 1852, English Dept., Brown University, Providence RI 02912, phone (401)863-2393, founded 1973, poetry editor Randy Blasing, publishes **books of all kinds of poetry**, about three 48-page, flat-spined paperbacks a year. Recently published Christopher Buckley, Margaret Holley, Charles O. Hartman and Robert Cording. **Free catalog. Query with 5 poems, biographical information and publications. Do not submit mss from Memorial Day to Labor Day. Considers simultaneous submissions. Replies to queries in 1 month, to submissions in 3 months; payment: 10% of press run.**

CORNERSTONE: THE VOICE OF THIS GENERATION (IV-Religious), Jesus People USA, 939 W. Wilson, Chicago IL 60640, phone (312)989-2080, editor Dawn Herrin, is a mass-circulation (50,000), low-cost ($2 per copy), bimonthly **directed at youth, covering "contemporary issues in the light of Evangelical Christianity." They use avant-garde, free verse, haiku, light verse, traditional — "no limits except for epic poetry. (We've not got the room.)" Buys 10-50 poems per year, uses 1-2 pgs. per issue, has a 2- to 3-month backlog. Submit maximum of 5 poems. Pays $10 for poems having 1-15 lines, $25 for poems having 16 lines or more. Buys first or one-time rights. Sample: $2. Send SASE for guidelines.**

CORNFIELD REVIEW (II), Ohio State University, 1465 Mt. Vernon Ave., Marion OH 43302-5695, phone (614)389-2361, FAX (614)389-6786, founded 1974, is an annual of poetry, artwork, short fiction and personal narrative. **"We are open to all forms of high quality poetry, and we are interested in new talent."** It is 6×9, flat-spined, printed on heavy slick stock with b&w graphics, glossy cover with art, approximately 40-48 pgs. Their press run is about 500. **Sample: $4.50 postpaid. Pays 3 copies. Send no more than 5 poems with brief cover letter. No simultaneous submissions or previously published poems. Reports within 2-3 months. "Submissions should be typed or letter-quality dot-matrix, copyright reverts to contributor."**

CORONA (II), Dept. of History and Philosophy, Montana State University, Bozeman MT 59717, phone (406)994-5200, founded 1979, poetry editors Lynda and Michael Sexson, "is an interdisciplinary annual bringing together reflections from those who stand on the edges of their disciplines; those who sense that insight is located not in things but in relationships; those who have deep sense of playfulness; and those who believe that the imagination is involved in what we know." In regard to poetry they want **"no sentimental greeting cards; no slap-dash."** They have published poems by Wendy Battin, William Irwin Thompson, Frederick Turner and James Dickey. Asked for a sample, they said, "See journal for examples. We are not interested in cloned poems or homogenized poets." Journal is perfect-bound, 125-140 pgs., professionally printed, using about 20-25 pgs. of poetry per issue, circulation 2,000. **Sample postpaid: $7. Submit any number of pages, photocopy and dot-matrix OK, no simultaneous submissions. Reports in 1 week to 9 months. Payment is "nominal" plus 2 contributor's copies.** The editors advise, "Today's poet survives only by the generous spirits of small press publishers. Read and support the publishers of contemporary artists by subscribing to the journals and magazines you admire."

‡CORONA PUBLISHING CO.; CORONA POETS (IV-Regional), 1037 S. Alamo, San Antonio TX 78210, founded 1977, editor David Bowen, is a general trade book publisher that publishes **Texas poets only. "Shorter forms. All books in our series are 64 pgs. No religious, inspirational."** They have published poetry by Wendy Barker and Robert Fink. They have published 8 books in the Corona Poets series and publish 1-2/year. **Sample postpaid: $5. Pays 10% royalties on net sales plus 25 author's copies. Acquires all rights and returns them.**

COSMIC TREND; PARA*phrase (I, IV-Themes, love/romance/erotica), P.O. Box 323, Clarkson Rd., Mississauga, Ontario L5J 3Y2 Canada, founded 1984, *Cosmic Trend* poetry editor George Le Grand, *PARA*phrase* editor Tedy Asponsen. *Cosmic Trend* publishes 3 chapbook anthologies and narrated music cassettes a year of **"New Age mind-expanding material of any style, short or medium length; also: humorous, unusual or zany entries (incl. graphics) with deeper meaning. We ignore epics, run-of-a-mill romantic and political material."** They have recently published poetry by Jim Allen, Iris Litt, Kathleen Lee Mendel and Charles David Rice. As a sample the editor selected these lines by Jiri Jirasek:

> *There are times when love moves*
> *distant galaxies*
> *and sings like music*
> *of the newborn dawn*
> *when everyone is real in the timeless now*
> *and a storm is making love to calm.*
> *There are times within the now.*

PARA*phrase — Newsletter of Cosmic Trend (irregular: 2-3 times a year). Publishes "condensed life-stories and/or visions with insight, beyond the normal and related poetry." **They will consider simultaneous submissions and previously published poems "with accompanied disclosure and references." Pays 1 copy/published project. Rights revert to authors upon publication. Send $1 for guidelines or $5 for sample publication and guidelines.** Brief guidelines: $1 for each two poems submitted, plus $1 for postage. Minimum fee $2 plus postage (No US postal stamps, please.) **Response time is usually less than 3 weeks. Editor "often" comments on submissions.** Reviews books of poetry only by special arrangement. Cosmic Trend publishes electronic music cassette tapes in addition to their poetry/music anthology accompaniments. He says, "Share your adventure of poetry beyond the usual presentation! Cosmic Trend can choose your poems for narration with music and inclusion into our cassette accompaniments to our illustrated anthologies."

COSMOPOLITAN (IV-Women), 224 W. 57th St., New York NY 10019, founded 1886, is a monthly magazine "aimed at a female audience 18-34," part of the Hearst conglomerate, though it functions independently editorially. They want **freshly-written free verse, not more than 25 lines, either light or serious, which addresses the concerns of young women. Prefer shorter poems, use 1-4 poems each issue. "We cannot return submissions without SASE."** They have a circulation of 2,987,970. **Buy sample at newsstand. Reports in 3-5 weeks. Pays $25.** "Please do not phone; query by letter if at all, though queries are unnecessary before submitting. **Poems shouldn't be too abstract. The poem should convey an image, feeling or emotion that our reader could perhaps identify with. We do publish mostly free verse, although we're also open to well-crafted rhyme poems."**

COTEAU BOOKS; THUNDER CREEK PUBLISHING CO-OP; WOOD MOUNTAIN SERIES (III, IV-Regional, children), 401-2206 Dewdney Ave., Regina, Saskatchewan S4R 1H3 Canada, phone (306)777-0170, founded 1975, managing editor Shelley Sopher, a "small literary press that publishes poetry, fiction, drama, anthologies, criticism, children's books — **only by Canadian writers." Poetry should be "of general interest to Canadian or American audience."** They have published poetry by Nancy Mattson, Kim Morrissey and Dennis Cooley and 2 anthologies of Saskatchewan poetry. Writers should submit 30-50 poems "and indication of whole ms," typed; simultaneous and American submissions not accepted. Letter should include publishing credits and bio and SAE with IRC if necessary. Queries will be answered in 2-3 weeks and mss reported on in 2-4 months. Authors receive 10% royalty; 10 copies. Their attractive catalog is free for 9×12 SASE or SAE with IRC and sample copies can be ordered from it. The editor says: "Membership has changed through the years in the Thunder Creek Publishing Co-op, but now stands at ten. Each member has a strong interest in Canadian writing and culture. Generally, poets would have published a number of poems and series of poems in literary magazines and anthologies before submitting a manuscript." However, the imprint Wood Mountain Series is for first collections, reflecting their commitment to publishing new writers.

COTTONWOOD; COTTONWOOD PRESS (II, IV-Regional), Box 20, 400 Kansas Union, University of Kansas, Lawrence KS 66045, founded 1965, poetry editor Philip Wedge. **The press "is auxiliary to** *Cottonwood Magazine* **and publishes material by authors in the region. Material is usually solicited."** For the magazine they are looking for "strong narrative or sensory impact, non-derivative, not 'literary,' not 'academic.' Emphasis on Midwest, but publishes the best poetry received regardless of region. Poems should be 60 lines or less, on daily experience, *perception.*" They have published poetry by Rita Dove, Allen Ginsberg, Walter McDonald, Patricia Traxler and Ron Schreiber. The 6×9, flat-spined (112 + pgs.) magazine is published 3 times/year, printed from computer offset, with photos, using 20-30 pages of poetry in each issue. They have a circulation of 500-600, with 150 subscriptions of which 75 are libraries. They receive about 2,000 submissions/year, use about 30, have a maximum of 1-year backlog. Price per issue: $5. **Sample: $3 postpaid. Submit up to 5 pgs., dot-matrix, photocopy OK. No simultaneous submissions. Reports in 2-5 months. They sometimes provide criticism on rejected mss. Pays 1 copy.** The editors advise, "Read the little magazines and send to ones you like."

COUNCIL FOR INDIAN EDUCATION (IV-Ethnic, themes), 517 Rimrock Rd., Billings MT 59102, phone (406)252-7451, founded 1963, poetry editor Sally Old Coyote, is a non-profit corporation publishing material (small paper-bound books) to use in schools with Indian students. "We publish one poetry book per year. All content is approved by an intertribal editorial board." They want **"poetry**

on Native American themes or cowboy poetry. No vulgarity, sex, prejudice or complaining." They have recently published poetry by Jess Schwiddi. As a sample the editor selected these lines:

> Eyes on the sunrise: nature's way
> Rhythm of the Indian's great new day
> Dance to the rhythm
> Chant and hum
> Never loose the rhythm of the rawhide drum.

Previously published poems and simultaneous submissions OK. Often comments on rejections. **Replies to mss in 2-4 months. Pays author's copies. Write for catalog to obtain samples.**

COUNTRY JOURNAL (II), P.O. Box 8200, Harrisburg PA 17105, phone (717)657-9555, poetry editor Donald Hall, editor Peter V. Fossel, is a bimonthly magazine featuring country living **for people who live in rural areas or who are thinking about moving there. They use free verse and traditional.** Circ. 200,000. Average issue includes 6-8 feature articles and 10 departments. They have recently published poems by Mary Oliver, Kate Barnes and Wendell Berry. As a sample, here are lines from Maxine Kumin's "The Confidantes":

> Whoa, Ebony!—and I put my palms
> flat on the twitching satin skin
> that smells like old fruit, and memory begins.

Of 4,000-5,000 poems received each year they accept 10-12. Subscription: $24. **Sample postpaid: $4. Reports in 1-2 months. Editor comments on submissions "seldom." Pays $50/poem on acceptance. Buys first North American serial rights. Submit seasonal material 1 year in advance. Photocopied submissions OK. Computer printout submissions acceptable, prefers letter-quality; "dot-matrix submissions are acceptable if double spaced."**

COUNTRY WOMAN; REIMAN PUBLICATIONS (IV-Women, humor), P.O. Box 643, Milwaukee WI 53201, founded 1970, managing editor Kathy Pohl. *Country Woman* "is a bimonthly magazine dedicated to the lives and interests of country women. Those who are both involved in farming and ranching and those who love country life. In some ways, it is very similar to many women's general interest magazines, and yet its subject matter is closely tied in with rural living and the very unique lives of country women. **We like short (4-5 stanzas, 16-20 lines) traditional rhyming poems that reflect on a season or comment humorously or seriously on a particular rural experience. Also limericks and humorous 4- to 8-line filler rhymes. No experimental poetry. Poetry will not be considered unless it rhymes. Always looking for poems that focus on the seasons. We don't want rural putdowns, poems that stereotype country women, etc. All poetry must be positive and upbeat. Our poems are fairly simple, yet elegant. They often accompany a high-quality photograph."** *CW* has published poems by Hilda Sanderson, Edith E. Cutting and Ericka Northrop. *CW,* appearing 6 times a year, is magazine-sized, 68 pgs., glossy paper with much color photography. Circulation to 1 million. Subscriptions, $16.98/year, $2/copy. They receive about 1,200 submissions of poetry per year, use 40-50 (unless they publish an anthology). Their backlog is 1 month to 3 years. "We're always welcoming submissions." **Sample postpaid: $2. Submit maximum of 6 poems. Photocopy OK if stated not a simultaneous submission. Reports in 2-3 months. Pays $10-40 per poem plus copy. Buys first rights (generally) or reprint rights (sometimes).** They hold various contests for subscribers only. One of their anthologies, *Cattails and Meadowlarks: Poems from the Country,* is 90+ pgs., saddle-stapled with high-quality color photography on the glossy card cover, poems in large, professional type with many b&w photo illustrations.

THE COUNTRYMAN (IV-Rural), Sheep St., Burford, Oxon OX18 4LH England, phone 0993 (Burford) 822258, founded 1927, editor Christopher Hall, a bimonthly magazine "on rural matters." The editor wants **poetry on rural themes, "accessible to general readership but not jingles."** It is a handsome, flat-spined, digest-sized magazine, 200+ pgs., using popular articles and ads. As a sample the editor selected this complete poem, "January omen," by Jane A. Mares:

> At the cold birth of the year
> I saw what was better unseen:
> The Raven or Grimcrag, the grief-bringer,
> With his tone of ill-tidings,
> A-top the tall stone,
> Wiping his bill clean.

They pay a maximum of £20/poem. Submissions should be short. Reporting time is "within a week usually," and time to publication is "3 months-3 years." Buys all rights "but we stipulate never to refuse permission to reprint at author's wish." Reviews books of poetry in "25 words upwards." The editor says, "Not all our poems are *about* birds or flowers or animals. Personal reaction to rural experience is valued if it comes in a form to which our readers (high-income, quiet not violently green British for the most part) can relate. We get quite a few American submissions which I always read with much interest, not least because of my own love of the few

American landscapes I know. Too often these submissions are too obviously American (because of tell-tale species or phrases) and I generally rule these out because 95% of my readers expect a British mag."

‡COVER MAGAZINE (II), P.O. Box 1215, Cooper Station, New York NY 10276, founded 1986, contact editor/publisher Jeffrey C. Wright, is a "broad-based arts monthly covering all the arts in every issue, a 40-page tabloid sold on newsstands and in select bookstores nationwide." They want **"shorter poems—2-24 lines generally, favoring new romantic work. Nothing stodgy or simplistic."** They have published poetry by Robert Creeley and Molly Peacock. As a sample the editor chose one line:
    Let all but love be now our foe.
Cover tries "to reach a cutting edge/front-line audience in touch with the creative fields." Entirely supported by subscriptions, sales and ads. Press run is 9,000 for 900 subscriptions (11 of them libraries), 1,200 shelf sales. Out of 250 submissions of poetry they accept 25. Single copy: $1; 2-year subscription: $15. **Sample: $3 postpaid. Pays nothing, not even a copy. Submit 4-5 poems with cover letter. Reports in 2 months. Editor often comments on rejections.**

CRAB CREEK REVIEW (II), 4462 Whitman Ave. N., Seattle WA 98103, phone (206)633-1090, founded 1983, editor Linda J. Clifton, appears 2 times/year, 32 pgs., attractively printed on newsprint. They publish **poetry which is "free or formal, with clear imagery, wit, voice that is interesting and energetic, accessible to the general reader rather than full of very private imagery and obscure literary allusion; also translations."** They have published poetry by Elizabeth Murawski, Maxine Kumin, William Stafford and Eastern European, Japanese, Chinese and Latin American writers. They have about 20 pgs. of poetry in each issue, circulation 350, 200 subscriptions of which 20 are libraries, receive 400-500 submissions/year from which they choose 50-60 poems. **Acquires first North American serial rights. Rights revert to author upon publication.** "No unsolicited mss until 1993." Sample postpaid: $3, subscription $8/volume of 3 issues. Listed in *Index of American Periodical Verse.*

CRAMPED AND WET (I), 1012 29th, Sioux City IA 51104, founded 1986, editor Kidd Smiley, is a quarterly. **"I like real stuff but I want to see fun too. There's room for hard tough stuff yet I like to end up with a real warm feeling. No real conceptual self-indulgent s***."** They have published poetry by John McKinley, Rob Treinen, Charles Luden, A.Q. Passmore and Jason Murphy. As a sample the editor selected this untitled poem by D. Castleman:
    Mercy?
    Do you ask for mercy?
    You will be given a toad
    and a bucket of salt,
    and nothing more.
    Do not ask for more.
    There is none.
C and W's size varies. It is 20-30 pgs., offset printed. They accept about 1-2% of 1,000 poems/year. Press run: 150. **Sample postpaid: $2;** checks or money orders must be made out to Rob Treinen. **Pays 1 copy. Editor comments on submissions "once in a while. I return the submission or inform of acceptance within a couple of months—that is if the writer includes a SASE."** He advises. "Do what you want, feel good about yourself. The most radical attitude is the positive one. Practice self-parody like some practice self-discipline." **The magazine supports the right for anyone to say anything derogatory at anytime or anyplace.**

CRAZYHORSE (II), Dept. of English, University of Arkansas, Little Rock AR 72204, founded 1960, managing editor Zabelle Stodola, poetry editor Ralph Burns, fiction editor Judy Troy, is a highly respected literary magazine appearing twice a year. They have published poetry by Alberto Rios, Mark Jarman, Bill Matthews and Yusef Komunyakaa. As a sample, here are the closing lines from "For Victor Jara: Mutilated and Murdered, the Soccer Stadium, Santiago, Chile" by Miller Williams (see listing for University of Arkansas Press):
    Would we have stayed to an end or would we have folded our faces?
    Awful and awful. Good friend. You have embarrassed our hearts.
It is 145 pgs., 6 × 9 offset. Press run 900. Subscription: $10. **Sample postpaid: $5. Pays $10/printed page plus 2 copies. Reports in 1-2 months. Offers two $500 awards for best poem and best story. No submissions May-August.** Reviews books of poetry. To get a sense of the quality of the magazine, see the anthology, **The Best of Crazyhorse** (University of Arkansas Press, 1990).

‡CRAZYQUILT QUARTERLY (II), P.O. Box 632729, San Diego CA 92163-2729, founded 1986, editor Jackie Ball, is a literary quarterly which has published poetry by Bertha Rogers, Larry D. Griffin, Virginia R. Terris and June Owens. As a sample the editor selected these lines by Charles B. Dickson from "The Clown":

> Their fragile bodies bent like ampersands,
> They hunch in nursing homes. Their eyes alight,
> To chuckle at his gibes, watch antic hands
> Pluck roses from the air for their delight.

The magazine is digest-sized, saddle-stapled, 90+ pgs., professionally printed on good stock with matte card cover, circulation 200, subscription $14.95. **Sample: $4.50 plus $1 postage; back issue $2.50. Pays 2 copies. Acquires first rights. One poem to a page. Dot-matrix, previously published poems and simultaneous submissions all OK. Reports in 10-12 weeks, time to publication 12-15 months.**

CREAM CITY REVIEW (II), P.O. Box 413, Dept. of English, University of Wisconsin at Milwaukee, Milwaukee WI 53201, phone (414)229-4708, editor-in-chief Sandra Nelson, poetry editors Aedan Hanley and Amy Minett, is a nationally distributed literary magazine published twice a year by the Creative Writing Program. The editors will consider **any poem that is well-crafted and especially those poems that "have a voice, have place or play with the conventions of what poetry is. We get very little humor or parody, and would enjoy getting more."** They have recently published poetry by May Sarton, Philip Dacey, Amiri Baraka, Tess Gallagher, Cathy Song, Mary Oliver and Philip Levine. *CCR* is 5½ × 8½, perfect-bound, with full-color cover on 70 lb. paper. Circulation 2,000, 300+ subscriptions of which 15 are libraries. **Sample: $5 postpaid. Send SASE for guidelines. "Include SASE when submitting and please submit no more than 5 poems at a time." Payment varies with funding and includes 2 copies. Buys first rights. Reports in 2 months, longer in summer. Simultaneous submissions OK. Editors sometimes comment on rejections. Reviews books of poetry in 1-2 pgs. "We give an award of $100 to the best poem published in** *Cream City Review* **each year."** They add, "We are always looking for strong poems on any subject."

CREATIVE WITH WORDS PUBLICATIONS (C.W.W.); SPOOFING; WE ARE POETS AND AUTHORS, TOO (I, IV-Children, seniors), Box 223226, Carmel CA 93922, phone (408)649-1682, founded 1975, poetry editor Brigitta Geltrich, **offers criticism for a fee.** It focuses "on furthering **folkloristic tall tales** and such; creative writing abilities in **children** (poetry, prose, language-art); creative writing in **senior citizens** (poetry and prose)." The editors organize and sponsor an **annual poetry contest, offer feedback on mss submitted to this contest** and publish on a wide range of themes relating to human studies and the environment that influence human behaviors. **$5 reading fee/poem, includes a critical analysis.** The publications are anthologies of children's poetry, prose and language art; anthologies of senior citizen poetry and prose; and *Spoofing: an Anthology of Folkloristic Yarns and Such*, which has an announced theme for each issue. **"Want to see: folkloristic themes, poetry for and by children; poetry by senior citizens; topic (inquire). Do not want to see: too mushy; too religious; too didactic; expressing dislike for fellowmen; political; pornographic; death and murder poetry."** Latest themes are "A CWW Christmas"; "It's a Matter of Love"; "A CWW Easter" and "A Time for Seasons and Holidays." **Guidelines available for SASE.** *Spoofing!* and *We are Poets and Authors, Too!*, an anthology of poems by children, are low-budget publications, photocopied from typescript, saddle-stapled, card covers with cartoon-like art. **Submit 20-line, 40 spaces wide maximum, poems geared to specific audience and subject matter.** They have published poetry by Sarah Hammond, Mark Eaton and Hilary Hersom. As a sample the editor selected these lines by Tara Thatcher:

> Peaceful serene
> The waves lap against the sand.
> Slowly night descends.
> Stars light the dark like candles.
> The water beckons . . . Trust me.

"Query with sample poems, short personal biography, other publications, poetic goals, where you read about us, for what publication and/or event you are submitting." Their contests have prizes of $15, $10, $5 and $1, but they hope to increase them. "No conditions for publication, but CWW is dependent on author/poet support by purchase of a copy or copies of publication." They offer a 20% reduction on any copy purchased. The editor advises, "Trend is proficiency. Poets should research topic; know audience for whom they write; check topic for appeal to specific audience; should not write for the sake of rhyme, rather for the sake of imagery and being creative with the language. Feeling should be expressed (but no mushiness). Topic and words should be chosen carefully; brevity should be employed."

THE CREATIVE WOMAN (IV-Women, feminist, themes), 413 N. Douglas Ave., Arlington Hts. IL 60004-6122, phone (708)255-1232, founded 1977, editor Margaret Choudhury, "is published four times a year. **We focus on a special topic in each issue, presented from a feminist perspective."** They want poetry **"recognizing, validating, celebrating women's experience, especially fresh and original style."** They have published poetry by Marge Piercy and Larissa Vasilyeva. As a sample here are lines from "The Fishwife's Declaration of Independence" by Olivia Diamond:

> *This fishwife cries to ply her cutter*
> *in deeper more crystal schools of marlin*
> *and never peddle her fry in any market;*
> *her coach is kinetic, her compass private,*
> *her steerage personal, her passage free,*
> *and no husband stands at the helm.*

The Creative Woman is magazine-sized, 40 pgs., professionally printed with b&w graphics, ads. They use about 5% of several hundred unsolicited poems received each year. Press run of 2,000 for 600 subscriptions (65 libraries). Subscription: $14, $20 institutions. **Sample postpaid: $5. Pays 4 copies and opportunity to purchase more at half price. Mss should be double-spaced, name and address on each page. No simultaneous submissions or previously published poetry. Reports within up to 1 year.**

‡**CREATIVITY UNLIMITED PRESS; ANNUAL CREATIVITY UNLIMITED PRESS POETRY COMPETI-TION (I)**, 30819 Casilina, Rancho Palos Verdes, CA 90274, phone (213)541-4844, founded 1989, editor Shelley Stockwell, publishes annually a collection of poetry submitted to their **contest, $4 fee for 1-5 poems; prizes of $300, $150 and $75 in addition to publication. Deadline December 31. "Clever sponta-neous overflows of rich emotion, humor and delightful language encouraged. No inaccessible, verbose, esoteric, obscure poetry. Limit 3 pgs. per poem double spaced, one side of page."** As a sample the editor selected her own "Freeway Dilemma":

> *Of all enduring questions*
> *A big one I can't answer;*
> *How come, whenever I change lanes,*
> *The other lane goes faster?*

They also accept freelance submissions for book publication. "Poems previously published will be accepted provided writer has maintained copyright and notifies us." Editor comments on submissions "always. Keep it simple and accessible." Sample copies of their anthologies avail-able for 40% off list.

CREEPING BENT (III), 433 W. Market St., Bethlehem PA 18018, phone (215)866-5613, founded 1984, editor Joseph Lucia, a literary magazine that focuses on serious poetry, fiction, book reviews and essays, with very occasional chapbooks published under the same imprint. **"Please note that during much of 1993 we will be accepting very little (possibly no) unsolicited material. We publish only work that evidences a clear awareness of the current situation of poetry. We take a special interest in poems that articulate a vision of the continuities and discontinuities in the human relationship to the natural world."** The editor does not want **"any attempt at verse that clearly indicates the writer hasn't taken a serious look at a recent collection of poetry during his or her adult life."** They have recently published work by Turner Cassity, Charles Edward Eaton, Renée Ashley, Brigit Kelly, Walter McDonald, Don-ald Revell, Harry Humes and Patricia Wilcox. As a sample, he chose these lines from Mark Stevick's "Idiom":

> *The language of objects is not*
> *unknown to us. What they mean*
> *they articulate to our eyes and*
> *our hands; we listen and learn*
> *from them as we can, make them*
> *our ambassadors. You, listening*
> *in your room, will recognize*
> *your debt to their reliable idiom,*
> *though they are not yours, nor you.*

Creeping Bent is digest-sized, nicely printed on heavy stock with some b&w artwork, 48-64 pgs., saddle-stapled with glossy white card cover printed in black and one other color. It appears at least once a year, sometimes more often. Circulation is 250, of which 175 are subscriptions, 25 go to libraries, and 25 are sold on newsstands. Subscription: $6/year. Sample: $3 postpaid. **Guide-lines for SASE. Pay is 2 copies plus a 1-year subscription. "Absolutely no simultaneous submis-sions!" Photocopied and dot-matrix mss are OK. Reporting time is usually 2-3 weeks and time to publication is 6 months at most.** The editor says, "Before submitting to any magazine pub-lished by anyone with a serious interest in contemporary writing, make certain you understand something about the kind of work the magazine publishes. Be familiar with current styles and approaches to poetry, even if you eschew them."

CRESCENT MOON (II, IV-Love/romance/erotica, occult, religious, spirituality, women/femi-nism), 18 Chaddesley Rd., Kidderminster, England DY10 3AD, founded 1988, editor Jeremy Robin-son, publishes about 10 books and chapbooks/year **on arrangements subsidized by the poet.** He wants **"poetry that is passionate and authentic. Any form or length."** Not **"the trivial, insincere or derivative."**

They have published studies of Robert Graves, D.H. Lawrence, Thomas Hardy, J.M.W. Turner, John Cowper Powys, Lawrence Durrell and Renaissance painting, including poetry by the editor. As a sample the editor selected the first of five stanzas from his "Aphrodite's Mirror":

> *Shaving one day in Aphrodite's mirror,*
> *Using her sea-foam as ointment and the shell*
> *For a basin, I caught sight of myself*
> *In that speckled glass and wondered if*
> *This love of ours was going to last beyond*
> *A mere Rising-From-The-Sea-Attended-By-Nymphs.*

The chapbook **Black Angel** is 45 pgs., flat-spined, photocopied from typescript, digest-sized, with matte card cover. **Sample, postpaid, in response to "written requests." Inquiries welcome. Reports on queries in 4 weeks, on mss in 8. "I am putting together some anthologies of new American poetry, particularly poetry about love (any aspect) and poetry by women. I would like to hear from interested poets."**

CRICKET, THE MAGAZINE FOR CHILDREN; LADYBUG, THE MAGAZINE FOR YOUNG CHILDREN (IV-Children), P.O. Box 300, Peru IL 61354, *Cricket* founded 1973, *Ladybug* founded 1990, publisher and editor-in-chief Marianne Carus. *Cricket* is a monthly, circulation 120,000, **using "serious, humorous, nonsense rhymes, limericks" for children. They sometimes use previously published work.** The attractive 7×9 magazine, 64 pgs., saddle-stapled, color cover and b&w illustrations inside, receives over 1,000 submissions/month, uses 10-12, and has up to a 2-year backlog. **No query. Submit poems—up to 25 lines, no restrictions on form. Sample: $2. Guidelines available for SASE. Reports in 3-4 months.** They hold poetry contests for children ages 5-9 and 10-14. Current contest themes and rules appear in each issue. *Ladybug*, also monthly, circulation 120,000, is similar in format (same price for sample copy) and requirements but is aimed at younger children (ages 2-7). **Payment for both is up to $3/line and 2 copies. "All submissions are automatically considered for both magazines."**

CROSS-CULTURAL COMMUNICATIONS; CROSS-CULTURAL REVIEW OF WORLD LITERATURE AND ART IN SOUND, PRINT, AND MOTION; CROSS-CULTURAL MONTHLY; CROSS-CULTURAL REVIEW CHAPBOOK ANTHOLOGY; INTERNATIONAL WRITERS SERIES (II, IV-Translations, bilingual), 239 Wynsum Ave., Merrick NY 11566-4725, phone (516)868-5635, FAX (516)379-1901, founded 1971, Stanley H. and Bebe Barkan. Stanley Barkan began CCC as an educational venture, a program in 27 languages at Long Island University, but soon began publishing collections of poetry translated into English from various languages—some of them (such as Estonian) quite "neglected"—in bilingual editions. During the 70s he became aware of Antigruppo (a group against groups), a movement with similar international focus in Sicily, and the two joined forces. (See Coop. Antigruppo listing; CCC is the American representative of Coop. Antigruppo.) CCR began as a series of chapbooks (6-12 a year) of collections of poetry translated from various languages and continues as the **Holocaust, Women Writers, Latin American Writers, Asian-American Writers, International Artists, Art & Poetry, Jewish, Israeli, Dutch, Turkish,** and **Long Island** and **Brooklyn Writers Chapbook Series** (with a number of other permutations in the offing)—issued simultaneously in palm-sized and regular paperback and cloth-binding editions and boxed and canned, as well as audiocassette and videocassette. **All submissions should be preceded by a query letter with SASE; the Holocaust series is for survivors. Send SASE for guidelines. Pays 10% of print run.** In addition to publications in these series, CCC has published anthologies, translations and collections by dozens of poets from many countries. As a sample the editor selected the beginning of a poem by Pablo Neruda, as translated from the Spanish by Maria Jacketti:

> *Quartz opens its eyes in the snow*
> *and covers itself with thorns,*
> *slides into whiteness,*
> *becomes its own whiteness:*

That's from the bilingual collection **Heaven Stones**, the second in the **Cross-Cultural Review International Writers Series** published in 1992. It is 80 pgs., digest-sized, smythe-sewn paper and cloth, professionally printed with photo of the Chilean poet on the back—$15 (paperback), $25 (cloth). **Sample chapbook: $7 postpaid.** *Cross-Cultural Monthly* focuses on bilingual poetry and prose. **Subscription: $36. Sample: $3 postpaid. Pays 1 copy.** CCC co-produced (with David Curzon, Vice-President of the UN Society of Writers) the 1990-1991 Reading Series at the United Nations, and, in its third decade, continues to produce the International Festival of Poetry, Writing and Translation with the International Poets and Writers Literary Arts Week in New York.

CRUCIBLE; SAM RAGAN PRIZE (II), Barton College, College Station, Wilson NC 27893, phone (919)399-6456, founded 1964, editor Terrence L. Grimes, is an annual using **"poetry that demonstrates originality and integrity of craftsmanship as well as thought. Traditional metrical and rhyming poems**

are difficult to bring off in modern poetry. The best poetry is written out of deeply felt experience which has been crafted into pleasing form. No very long narratives." They have recently published poetry by Robert Grey, R.T. Smith and Anthony S. Abbott. As a sample the editor selected these lines from "Toward Short Off Mountain" by Mary C. Snotherly:

> So dense the fog, each man trudged alone,
> accompanied only by a stumble of boots,
> slap of laurel, by his own separate breathing,
> and like thunder roll, the barks resounding.

It is 100 pgs., 6×9, professionally printed on high-quality paper with matte card cover. Press run 500 for 200 subscribers of which 50 are libraries, 100 shelf sales. **Sample postpaid: $5. Send SASE for guidelines for contests (prizes of $150 and $100), and the Sam Ragan Prize ($150) in honor of the Poet Laureate of North Carolina. Submit between Christmas and mid-March. Reports in 3 months or less. "We require a short biography including a list of publications, in case we decide to publish the work."** No comments on rejections. Editor leans toward free verse with attention paid particularly to image, line, stanza and voice. The magazine itself is professionally designed with good type selection and point sizes highlighting bylines and titles of poems—all in all, a nice product.

CRYSTAL RAINBOW (V), 340 Granada Drive, Winter Park FL 32789, editor Louise M. Turmenne, is a quarterly inspirational newsletter using **"seasonal, traditional rhyme or free verse, 24 lines maximum. Purpose to comfort, encourage, inspire and challenge our readers to improve themselves and reach out to help others. No sexual situations. We are still over-stocked with acceptances for this year."** Recently published poets include Danny A. Witten, J. Alvin Speers, Laurie Kay Olson and Bryan K. Bullock. As a sample the editor selected these lines from "Lost Time" by Tina West:

> Each second we let go by,
> Will turn into lost days.
> Precious moments we can never recapture,
> Memories we can never regain.

The newsletter is 28 pgs., 7×8½, photocopy from typescript, with illustrations and classified ads—$3.50 per issue, $11.75 per year. **Sample $3.50 plus SASE (75¢ postage). Send SASE for guidelines.** They sponsor one yearly potpourri contest (2 categories) with entry fee of $2.50 per poem + SASE, prizes divided from receipts. Louise Turmenne says, "Touch the heart of the reader. Feel the joy and pain they feel. Embrace them with your words. Emphasize relationships. Keep it brief."

CUMBERLAND POETRY REVIEW; THE ROBERT PENN WARREN POETRY PRIZE (II, IV-Translations), P.O. Box 120128, Acklen Station, Nashville TN 37212, phone (615)373-8948, founded 1981, is a biannual, 100+ pgs., 6×9, flat-spined. *CPR* presents poets of diverse origins to a widespread audience. "Our aim is to support the poet's effort to keep up the language. We accept special responsibility for reminding American readers that not all excellent poems in English are being written by U.S. citizens. We have published such poets as Laurence Lerner, Donald Davie, Emily Grosholz and Rachel Hadas." Circulation: 500. As a sample the editorial board selected these lines by Seamus Heaney:

> When Dante snapped a twig in the bleeding wood
> a voice sighed out of blood that bubbled up
> like sap at the end of green sticks on a fire.

Sample: $7 postpaid. Back issues: $7. Submit poetry, translations or poetry criticism with SASE or SAE with IRC. Reports in 3 months. Acquires first rights. Returns rights "on request of author providing he acknowledges original publication in our magazine." They award The Robert Penn Warren Poetry Prize annually. Winners receive $500, $300 and $200. For contest guidelines, send SASE.

CUTBANK; THE RICHARD HUGO MEMORIAL POETRY AWARD (II), English Dept., University of Montana, Missoula MT 59812, phone (406)243-5231, founded 1973, coeditors Dennis Held and Peter Fong, an annual publishing "the best poetry, fiction, reviews, interviews and artwork available to us." Offers 2 annual awards for best poem and piece of fiction each year, The Richard Hugo Memorial Poetry Award and The A.B. Guthrie, Jr., Short Fiction Award. Winners announced in spring issue. They have recently published poetry by James Crumley, Stephen Dobyns, Kim Barnes and Dara Wier. As a sample the editor selected these lines by Robert Wrigley:

> Perhaps some tatter of cloud passed
> before the moon just then
> and in that moment her hands ceased
> imploring and began simply to accept.
> Whoever we would be for the next twenty years
> took residence behind our eyes.

There are about 80 pgs. of poetry in each issue, which has a circulation of about 400, 250+ subscriptions of which 10-20% are libraries. Price per issue: $6.95. Subscription: $12/two issues. **Sample: $4 postpaid. Submission guidelines for SASE. Submit 3-5 poems, single-spaced. Photocopies OK, dot-matrix discouraged, simultaneous submissions OK if informed. Reads submissions August 15 through February 28 only. Reports in 2 months. Pays in copies. "All rights return to author upon publication."** Reviews books of poetry in 500 words, single or multi-book format.

CWM (II,IV-Themes), % Geof Huth, 317 Princetown Rd., Schenectady NY 12306, (or % David Kopaska-Merkel, 1300 Kicker Rd., Tuscaloosa AL 35414, phone (205)553-2284), founded 1990, co-geologians Ge(of Huth) and David Kopaska-Merkel. (These "geologians" also edit dbqp and *Dreams and Nightmares*, but *CWM* has no relation to their other imprints.) This magazine, published annually on set themes, is **"not tied down by ideas of proper style, form or substance, and presents work for the person of divergent tastes. The only considerations will be length and quality (as we see it). Extremely long poems will be at a disadvantage."** Poems must be on the theme of the issue. Theme for the 1993 issue will be "What lies beneath the surface." "Unusual pieces of any kind are welcome, and should be submitted in whatever form the author deems most suitable." Press run: 100. **Send SASE for guidelines. Pays "at least one copy."** Reviews books of poetry.

‡CYANOSIS (II), Suite 30, 318 Mendocino Ave., Santa Rosa CA 95404, founded 1989, editor Darin DeStefano, is a biannual forum for artists and writers of various disciplines to present controversial, experimental or provocative work. They want **"poetry with thematic experimentation, a sense of craft and unusual form or language use. 1-10 pages. Lean toward disturbing or provocative topics. No flowery prose or rhyme without careful execution."** They have recently published poetry by Daniel Davidson, George Albon, David Bromige and Gwendolyn Albert. As a sample the editor selected these lines from "Malleable" by John McNally:

> *Skin riddle comic modesty. Clifftop guillotine hands. Beneath his lid a razor, a*
> *lurking wreck, the stunned soldier dry as the prow of a cactus flower.*

The editor says it is 150 pgs., perfect-bound, offset, with coated cover. They receive about 500 poems a year, accept approximately 12%. Press run is 1,000 for 300 subscribers of which 25 are libraries, 500 shelf sales. Single copy: $6.95; subscription: $14 (2 issues). **Sample postpaid: $7. Simultaneous submissions OK. Informative cover letter requested. "Would like to know as much as possible about the writer." Often comments on rejections. Send SASE for guidelines — "prefer you send work with request." Reports in 2-6 weeks. Pays 1-3 copies.** Offers $25 honorarium "for outstanding submission" to 1 contributor/issue. The editor says, "Forget the market, forget selling and fame. Allow the words in your blood to make the paper. Allow the marrow of your dreams to speak. If money is involved, sew the lips shut and be done with it."

‡CYPHERS (III), 3 Selskar Terrace, Dublin 6 Ireland, founded 1975, appears 2-3 times yearly. They have recently published poetry by Pearse Hutchinson, Paul Durcan, Medbh McGuckian and P.J. Kavanagh. The editor says it is 52 pgs., A5. Press run is 650 for 250 subscribers of which 20 are libraries. **Sample postpaid: $5. No previously published poems or simultaneous submissions. Seldom comments on rejections. Reports in 3-4 months. Pays £7/page.**

DAGGER OF THE MIND; K'YI-LIH PRODUCTIONS; BREACH ENTERPRISES (IV-Science Fiction/ Fantasy/Horror), 1317 Hookridge Dr., El Paso TX 79925, phone (915)591-0541, founded 1989, executive editor Arthur William Lloyd Breach, assistant editor Sam Lopez, wants **"poetry that stirs the senses and emotions. Make the words dance and sing, bring out the fire in the human soul. Show flair and fashion. No four-letter words, nothing pornographic, vulgar, blasphemous, obscene and nothing generally in bad taste."** They have published poetry by Jessica Amanda Salmonson. The quarterly *DOTM* is magazine-sized, saddle-stapled, with high glossy covers. They use about 50 of 100-150 poems received per year. Press run 4,000-5,000 with 100 subscribers. Subscription: $8/half year, $16/year. **Sample postpaid: $3.50. Pays $1-5/poem plus 1 copy. Buys first North American serial rights and reprint rights. "Send in batches of 10. I will consider simultaneous submissions only if told in advance that they are such. Length is open as is style. Be creative and try to reflect something about the human condition. Show me something that reflects what is going on in the world. Be sensitive but not mushy. Be intelligent not sophomoric. Don't try to carbon copy any famous poet. You lead the way—don't follow. I don't like the trend toward blood and gore and obscenity. Report back in 4 weeks tops.** *DOTM* is devoted to *quality* horror. The key word is quality. *DOTM* is a publication under the division of K'yi-Lih Productions whose main heading is Breach Enterprises. All publications to appear in the market will come under K'yi-Lih Productions." The editor will evaluate work and review books of poetry for a fee, depending on length and quantity. He says, "I'm planning an anthology of Lovecraftian related material. The paperback will be predominantly Cthulhu Mythos fiction, but I do intend to publish some poetry."

DAILY MEDITATION (IV-Religious), Box 2710, San Antonio TX 78299, editor Ruth S. Paterson, is a **nonsectarian** religious quarterly that uses **inspirational poems up to 14 lines. Pays 14¢ a line. Sample postpaid: $1.**

THE DALHOUSIE REVIEW (II), Suite 314, Sir James Dunn Bldg., Halifax, Nova Scotia B3H 3J5 Canada, founded 1921, phone (902)494-2541, is **a prestige literary quarterly** with 136 pgs. per issue in a 6×9 format, professionally printed on heavy stock with matte card cover. They prefer poems of 40 lines or less. As a sample the editor selected these lines from "Weather" by Alan R. Wilson:

> *The rain that plummets*
> *to the roofs of houses,*
>
> *the wind that pitches*
> *like a heavy object*
> *into trees,*
>
> *the sleet that drops*
> *the faces of the men*
> *and women hurrying by—*
>
> *the freefall of turbulence.*

Individual copies range in cost from $6.50-25. Subscription: $19/year within Canada, $28/year outside Canada (both in Canadian dollars). **Contributors receive $3 for a first poem. For each poem after (in the same issue) he or she will receive $2 per poem, 2 complimentary copies of issue and 15 offprints.**

DANCE CONNECTION (IV-Themes), #604, 815 1st St. SW, Calgary, Alberta T2P 1N3 Canada, phone (403)237-7327, founded 1983, editor Heather Elton, uses **poems about dance—"any length, format, subject except bad poetry talking about the extended graceful lines of ballet."** It is magazine-sized, 52 pgs., desktop published, saddle-stapled. Press run 3,000 for 675 subscribers of which 35 are libraries. 400 shelf sales. Subscription: $17 individuals, $28 institution. **Sample postpaid: $4. Reports in 3 months. Pays 3 copies and "occasional honorarium." Acquires all rights. Returns rights. Deadline for their literary issue is May 1.** The editor says they "very occasionally publish poetry. When we get larger we will publish more, but now space is a precious commodity for review/calendars/news/columns and feature departments."

DANDELION (II), The Alexandra Centre, 922-9th Ave. SE, Calgary, Alberta T2G 0S4 Canada, phone (403)265-0524, founded 1975, poetry editors Deborah Miller and Allan Serafina, managing editor Chris Horgan, appears twice a year. They want **"quality--We are open to any form, style, length. No greeting card verse."** They have published poetry by Claire Harris, Susan Ioannoce and Robert Hilles. As a sample the editor selected these lines by Roger Nash:

> *On Sabbath evenings, a slow hand*
> *tuned the guitar. A fast hand*
> *moved the shifting stars. And, somewhere,*
> *while we were growing up, there was a street still*
> *made of gold of tin of slush*

It is 6×9, 102 pgs., with full-color cover, professionally printed and bound. They accept about 10% of 600 mss received. Press run 750. **Sample postpaid: $6. Send SASE for a short statement of their needs. Reports in 4-6 weeks. Pays honorarium plus 1 copy. Acquires one-time rights. Submit in January through March and July through September for issues in June and December.** Reviews books of poetry in 500-1,200 words; preference is for books by Alberta writers. Query Alexandra Pett, reviews editor, first. *blue buffalo* is a magazine which falls under the Dandelion Magazine Society umbrella. *blue buffalo* is also published twice yearly, but submissions are accepted *only* from Alberta writers.

JOHN DANIEL AND COMPANY, PUBLISHER; FITHIAN PRESS (II), P.O. Box 21922, Santa Barbara CA 93121, phone (805)962-1780, founded 1980, reestablished 1985. John Daniel, a general small press publisher, specializes in literature, both prose and poetry. Fithian Press is a subsidy imprint open to all subjects. **"Book-length mss of any form or subject matter will be considered, but we do not want to see pornographic, libelous, illegal or sloppily written poetry."** He has recently published books by Thomas Claire, Jack Swanson and Judson Jerome. As a sample John Daniel selected "Promises" from the book **These Fringes of Time** by Thelma Shaw:

> *One poet said*
> *his sky is scrawled*
> *with flying birds*

> *and here on my desk*
> *is the plumage*
> *of nesting words.*

> *It's quite all right,*
> *I say to them,*
> *You flew once,*
> *you will again.*

He publishes 10 flat-spined paperbacks, averaging 64 pgs., per year. **For free catalog of either imprint, send 10 sample poems and bio. Reports on queries in 2 weeks, on mss in 8 weeks. Simultaneous submissions, photocopy, dot-matrix OK, or disks compatible with Macintosh. Pays 10-50% of net receipts royalties. Buys English-language book rights. Returns them upon termination of contract. Fithian Press books (50% of his publishing) are subsidized, the author paying production costs and receiving royalties of 50% of net receipts. Books and rights are the property of the author, but publisher agrees to warehouse and distribute for one year if desired.** John Daniel advises, "Poetry does not make money, alas. It is a labor of love for both publisher and writer. But if the love is there, the rewards are great."

DAUGHTERS OF SARAH (IV-Feminist, religious, social issues, themes), 3801 N. Keeler, Box 411179, Chicago IL 60618, phone (312)736-3399, founded 1974, editor Reta Finger, a quarterly magazine "integrating feminist philosophy with biblical-Christian theology and making connections with social issues." The magazine includes only "occasional" poetry. The editor says, **"Do not prefer rhyming poetry; must be short enough for one 5½×8½ page, but prefer less than 20 lines. Topics must relate to Christian feminist issues, but prefer specifics to abstract terminology." She does not want** "greeting-card type verse or modern poetry so obscure one can't figure out what it means." As a sample she chose the following lines by Ann Bailey:

> *Who would lay her head on stone,*
> *Would crush the dark to dust?*
> *What dreamstruck one will hurl herself toward holiness*
> *and fight for her own blessings?*
> *Who here would risk her life to wrestle with the Lord?*

The magazine is digest-sized, 64 pgs., with photos and graphics, web offset. Its circulation is 4,500, of which 4,400 are subscriptions, including about 250 libraries; bookstore sales are 50. Price per issue, $4.50; subscription $18/year. **Free sample; guidelines are available for SASE.** *Daughters of Sarah* **pays $15-30/poem plus 2-3 copies. Buys one-time rights. Poets should submit two copies of each poem (prefers shorter poems) to the editor, who reports in 1-2 months; time to publication is 3-18 months. Considers simultaneous submissions.** "Write first for list of upcoming themes, since we mostly choose our poetry to fit with a particular theme."

THE DAYSPRING PRESS: THE NEW ANGLICAN REVIEW; THE NEW CATHOLIC REVIEW; POET'S FORUM (I, IV-Religious), 18600 W. 58th Ave., Golden CO 80403-1070, phone (303)279-2462, founded 1983, editor John C. Brainerd, who describes his operation as a **"little-literary and religious forum. We publish almost everything received (or find its natural market)."** They want **"short lyrics, up to 5-page narrative poems, trading in the deeper human sensibilities. No prurient, scandalous or malicious material will be published."** They have published poetry by Michael Davidson and Heland James. All magazines are in the same format: digest-sized (large print available), photocopied from Courier pica, elite and condensed, about 40 pgs., with paper cover. All are monthly, with an annual "best of" edition. Press run: 1,000 for 250 subscriptions. Each sells for $2.57/issue. Subscription: $18 (12 issues). **Sample postpaid: $2.57. Send SASE and $2.57 for 20-page catalog (includes "writer's guidelines"). Pays 50% net over expenses (accounted). Reports in 1-4 weeks.** Reviews books of poetry. The editor says, "Discover—by intuition—where your heart is. Orbit (and write) very nearby."

DBQP; ALABAMA DOGSHOE MOUSTACHE; A VOICE WITHOUT SIDES; &; HIT BROADSIDES; THE SUBTLE JOURNAL OF RAW COINAGE; DBQPRESCARDS (IV-Form), 317 Princetown Rd., Schenectady NY 12306, founded 1987, poetry editor Ge(of Huth). "dbqp is the name of the overall press. *Alabama Dogshoe Moustache* publishes **language poetry (usually very short) & visual poetry.** *A Voice Without Sides* is an occasional magazine in very small runs (about 24 copies) and in strange formats (in jars, as earrings, etc.); it uses the same type of poetry as *ADM*. *&* is a series of leaflets each featuring a single poem. *Hit Broadsides* is a broadside series. *The Subtle Journal of Raw Coinage* is a monthly that publishes coined words but occasionally will publish an issue of *pwoermds* (one-word poems—that is, a word coined to be a poem, as Aram Saroyan's 'eyeye') or poems written *completely* with neologisms. *dbqprescards* is a postcard series publishing mostly poetry. These publications are generally handmade magazines, leaflets, broadsides and objects of very small size. **I am interested only in short language poetry and visual poetry. No traditional verse or mainstream poetry."** They have recently published poetry by John M. Bennett, Bob Grumman and Jonathan Branner. As a sample the editor selected this complete poem by rbarnes:

> *covered,*
> *tinsel yard,*
> *organic seized*
> *filed and under.*

Their major poetry magazine is *Alabama Dogshoe Moustache*, which appears in various formats up to 15 pgs., magazine-sized, held together with thread, staples, fasteners, or packaged inside containers. Its press run is 50-100 with 10 subscriptions. Price per issue 40¢-$2.50. **Sample: $1 or $2 postpaid. Catalog available for SASE. Pays "at least 2 copies." Reports within 2 weeks. Editor "always" comments on rejections.** Occasionally reviews books of poetry. The editor says, "Most of the poetry I reject is from people who know little about the kind of poetry I publish. I don't mind reading these submissions, but it's usually a waste of time for the submitters. If you are familiar with the work of the poets I publish, you'll have a much better idea about whether or not I'll be interested in your work."

DEATHREALM (IV-Horror, fantasy), 3223-F Regents Park, Greensboro NC 27405, founded 1987, editor Mark Rainey, is a quarterly using **"mostly tales of horror/dark fantasy. Small amount of poetry in each issue. No poetry reviews. Use your imagination. I do not place restrictions on theme, style or length, though epic-scale pieces are not recommended. I like rhyming poetry (if it's not too elementary) as well as free-style."** They have recently published poetry by Ardath Mayhar, Jessica Amanda Salmonson and Mary Elizabeth Counselman. It is magazine-sized, 56 pgs., saddle-stapled. They accept 10-12 of 200-300 poems received/year. Press run 1,000 for 200 subscribers, 700-800 shelf sales. Subscription: $15. **Sample postpaid: $4. Reads submissions January 1 through June 1 only. Send SASE for guidelines. Pays $2-5 plus 1 copy. Buys first North American serial rights. Editor often comments on rejections. Reports in 2-6 weeks.**

DELAWARE VALLEY POETS, INC. (IV-Membership, anthology), P.O. Box 6203, Lawrenceville NJ 08648, phone (609)737-0222, publications director L.M. Harrod. "We publish contemporary anthologies and broadsides of **poetry by invitation to submit and books or chapbooks by members who are ready to publish."** They have published poetry by Maxine Kumin, Theodore Weiss, Lois Marie Harrod and Jana Harris. As a sample, they selected these lines from "Mr. Kurtz, I Presume" by John Falk:

> *and a blue mantle of water unclasps,*
> *Slides down from the clouds and reclothes*
> *The worn and broken armature of stones.*

They publish 1-3 books per year averaging 90 pages. **Members submit 6 samples, bio, publications. Reports in 6 months. "For anthologies, poets must have some connection with the basic organization.** Anthologies are paid for by DPV, Inc., and all sales go to the organization. Individual authors pay printing costs; individual editorial services and distribution are provided by DVP. All sales go to the author." Patricia Groth advises, "Poets serious about their work need to read all the poetry they can find, write poetry, attend poetry readings and find someone to trade poetry and criticism with. If there is no workshop available, start one."

‡DELHI-LONDON POETRY QUARTERLY (II, IV-Nature, political, occult, religious, spirituality), 50 Penywern Rd., London SW5 9SX England, phone (370)2255, founded 1977, poetry editor G. Warrier, is a literary quarterly with "emphasis on international writing, on spiritual, mystical, philosophical, occult themes." **They want "1-2 pgs. maximum, contemporary style"** and do not want "traditional, experimental." They have recently published poetry by Elizabeth Bartlett and Richard Bodien. As a sample the editor selected these lines (poet unidentified):

> *I tied my sword to a tree*
> *I watched it fall.*
> *I saw a silent wall shed*
> > *its edgelessness*

The magazine is beautifully printed with full-color covers, 7½×9½, 60 pgs., flat-spined. There are b&w drawings throughout. It appears twice a year, press run of 5,000 for 2,000 subscriptions and 1,500 shelf sales. They accept about 10% of 500-1,000 submissions received/year. **Sample: £5. Pays £5/poem. Previously published poems and simultaneous submissions OK. Their reports are "very late."** They sometimes sponsor contests.

DENVER QUARTERLY (II), Dept. of English, University of Denver, Denver CO 80208, phone (303)871-2892, founded 1965, editor Donald Revell, a quarterly literary journal that publishes fiction, poems, book reviews and essays. **There are no restrictions on the type of poetry wanted.** They have published poetry by James Merrill, Linda Pastan and William Matthews. *Denver Quarterly* is 6×9, handsomely printed on buff stock, average 160 pgs., flat-spined with two-color matte card cover. Circulation is

1,000, of which 600 are subscriptions (300 to libraries) and approximately 300 are sold on newsstands. Price per issue $5, subscription $15/year to individuals and $18 to institutions. **Samples of all issues after Spring 1985 are available for $5 postpaid, guidelines for SASE. Pay is 2 copies and $5/page. No submissions read between May 15 and September 15 each year. Reporting time is 2-3 months.** Reviews books of poetry.

DESCANT (III, IV-Regional), Box 314, Station P, Toronto, Ontario M5S 2S8 Canada, founded 1970, editor-in-chief Karen Mulhallen, is "a quarterly journal of the arts committed to being the finest in Canada. **While our focus is primarily on Canadian writing we have published writers from around the world.**" Some of the poets they have recently published are Lorna Crozier, Stephen Pender and Libby Scheier. They selected this sample from "Isla Grande" by Lake Sagaris:

> *I had caught children in my womb like clams*
> *watched them pried open and consumed and tossed away*
> *and still I was young.*

It is an elegantly printed and illustrated flat-spined publication with colored, glossy cover, oversized digest format, 140+ pgs., heavy paper, with a circulation of 1,200 (800 subscriptions, of which 20% are libraries). **Sample: $8 postpaid.** They receive 1,200 freelance submissions/year, of which they use less than 10, with a 2-year backlog. **Guidelines available for SASE. Submit typed ms, unpublished work not in submission elsewhere, photocopy OK, name and address on first page and last name on each subsequent page. SASE with Canadian stamps or coupons. Reports within 4 months. Pays "approximately $100." Buys first-time rights.** Karen Mulhallen says, "Best advice is to know the magazine you are submitting to. Choose your markets carefully."

DESCANT: TEXAS CHRISTIAN UNIVERSITY LITERARY JOURNAL (II), English Dept., Texas Christian University, Fort Worth TX 76129, phone (817)921-7240, founded 1956, editors Betsy Colquitt, Stan Trachtenberg and Harry Opperman, appears twice a year. They want **"well-crafted poems of interest. No restrictions as to subject matter or forms. We usually accept poems 40 lines or fewer but sometimes longer poems."** They have published poems by Walter McDonald and Lyn Lifshin. It is 6×9, 92 pgs., saddle-stapled, professionally printed, with matte card cover. Their press run is 500, going to 350 subscribers. "We publish 30-40 pgs. of poetry per year. We receive probably 4,000-5,000 poems annually." Single copy: $6; volume: $12, 18 foreign. **Sample: $4 postpaid. Pays 2 copies. No simultaneous submissions. Reports in 6-8 weeks,** usually no more than 8 months until publication.

THE DEVIL'S MILLHOPPER PRESS; THE DEVIL'S MILLHOPPER; KUDZU POETRY CONTEST (II), College of Humanities, University of South Carolina at Aiken, 171 University Parkway, Aiken SC 29801, founded 1976, editor Stephen Gardner, assistant editor Carol Jennings, publishes one magazine issue of *The Devil's Millhopper* each year and one chapbook, winner of an annual competition. **They want to see any kind of poetry, except pornography or political propaganda, up to 100 lines.** Some of the poets they have published are Susan Ludvigson, Ann Darr, Lynne H. de Courcy, Ricardo Pau-Llosa, Katherine Soniat, Walt McDonald, R.T. Smith and Dorothy Barresi. The print run of *Devil's Millhopper* is 500. The annual chapbook has a print run of 600, going to 375 subscribers of which 20 are libraries. The magazine is digest-sized, 32-40 pgs., saddle-stapled, printed on good stock with card cover and using beautiful b&w original drawings inside and on the cover. **Sample: $2.50 postpaid. Send regular, non-contest submissions September and October only. They want name and address on every page of submissions; simultaneous submissions acceptable. Photocopy and dot-matrix OK if it is dark, readable type. Pays copies. Acquires first North American serial and reprint rights. Rights automatically revert to author upon publication. Reports usually in 2 months.** Sometimes the editor comments on rejected mss. Send SASE for their annual Kudzu Poetry Contest rules (prizes of $50, $100 and $150, $3/poem entry fee), annual Sand River Contest for poetry in traditional fixed forms (prizes of $300, $150 and $50, $3/poem entry fee), chapbook competition rules and guidelines for magazine submissions. Send Kudzu contest submissions September 1-October 15; Sand River Contest submissions June 1-July 1; chapbook contest submissions January 1-February 1. Chapbook competition requires either $5 reading fee or $9 subscription for 2 years. Pays $50 plus 50 copies. The editor advises, "There is no substitute for reading a lot and writing a lot or for seeking out tough criticism from others who are doing the same."

‡DIALOGUE: A JOURNAL OF MORMON THOUGHT; MARGARET RAMPTON MUNK POETRY AWARD (IV-Religious), University Station UMC 7805, Logan UT 84322-7805, founded 1966, poetry editor Linda Sillitoe, "is an independent quarterly established to express Mormon culture and to examine the relevance of religion to secular life. It is edited by Latter-Day Saints who wish to bring their faith into dialogue with the larger stream of Judeo-Christian thought and with human experience as a whole and to foster artistic and scholarly achievement based on their cultural heritage. The views expressed are those of the individual authors and are not necessarily those of the Mormon Church or of the editors." **They publish 3-5 poems in each issue, "humorous and serious treatments of Mormon**

topics or universal themes from a Mormon perspective. **Under 40 lines preferred. Must communicate with a well-educated audience but not necessarily sophisticated in poetic criticism. Free verse OK but only if carefully crafted.**" They have recently published poetry by Michael Collins, R.A. Christmas, May Swenson and Linda Sillitoe. The editor selected these sample lines from "You Heal" by Emma Lou Thayne:

> After things happen, under the scarring
> you heal. It takes its jagged course
> upward and then . . .

They have a circulation of 4,000-4,500 subscriptions of which 150 are libraries. The journal has an elegant 6×9 format, 170+ pgs., with color, artistically decorated cover and tasteful b&w drawings within. They receive about 70 submissions/year, use 12-16. **Sample: $7 postpaid. Submit typed ms in triplicate, 1 poem/page. Acknowledges in 10 days, reports in 2 months. Payment is 10 offprints plus one contributor's copy. Acquires first publication rights.** Sponsors the Margaret Rampton Munk Poetry Award annually; three prizes: first, $100; second, $75; third, $50.

JAMES DICKEY NEWSLETTER (II), DeKalb College, 2101 Womack Rd., Dunwoody GA 30338, founded 1984, editor Joyce M. Pair, a biannual newsletter devoted to critical articles/studies of James Dickey's works/biography and bibliography. They **"publish a few poems of *high* quality."** It is 30+ pgs. of ordinary paper, neatly offset (back and front), with a card back-cover, stapled top left corner. As a sample here are the opening lines from "Haft Blossom" by R.T. Smith:

> Long-sleeping, I rose in the morning
> and opened the door to sunlight.
> Trough water woke me with sunlight,
> dark and the other stars having
> yielded their power . . .

The newsletter is published in the fall and spring. Single copy price is $3.50, subscription to individuals $5/year; $10 to institutions. **Sample available for $3.50 postage. Contributors should follow MLA style and standard ms form, sending 1 copy, double-spaced. Pays 5 copies. Acquires first rights.** Reviews "only works on Dickey or that include Dickey." The editor's advice is: "Acquire more knowledge of literary history, metaphor, symbolism and grammar, and, to be safe, the poet should read a couple of our issues."

DICKINSON STUDIES; HIGGINSON JOURNAL (V); DICKINSON-HIGGINSON PRESS (I), 1330 Massachusetts Ave. NW, Apt. 503, Washington DC 20005-4150, phone (202)638-1671, founded 1968, poetry editor F. L. Morey. *Dickinson Studies* and *Higginson Journal* are publications of Dickinson-Higginson Press (membership $50 individuals, $100 for libraries for 3 years). **Both magazines are overstocked through 1993.** They are semiannuals, sometimes with bonus issues, all distributed free to about 250 subscribers of which 125 are libraries. *Dickinson Studies* is principally for scholarship on Emily Dickinson, but uses poems about her. *Higginson Journal* **has a special poetry issue about every two years and uses a few poems in each issue.** The journals are both digest-sized, about 30 pgs., saddle-stapled, typeset with card covers and b&w art. **Sample postpaid: $4.** The Dickinson-Higginson Press also has subsidy-published several collections of poems, the poet putting up all printing costs, plus 10% for editing and handling; 25 copies free to poet. "All payments in advance, before scheduling definitely."

DIE YOUNG (V), P.O. Box 11066, Milwaukee WI 53211, founded 1990, editors Jesse Glass, Jr., and Skip Fox, is a journal appearing irregularly, **accepting no unsolicited poetry,** that has published poetry by Robert Creeley, Karl Shapiro, Richard Eberhart, Kathleen Raine, Burton Raffel and Tom Clark. **Sample postpaid: $3. Those who wish to submit may query with SASE.**

‡DIONYSOS: THE LITERATURE AND ADDICTION TRIQUARTERLY (IV-Theme), University of Wisconsin, 1800 Grand Ave., Superior WI 54880, phone (715)394-8465, founded 1989, editor Roger Forseth. *Dionysos* publishes "work and information on any aspect of the relation between addiction and the cultural/aesthetic scene, including articles, book and article reviews, film and theater commentary, occasional poems and short stories, interviews, research and critical notes." They want **"short poems, primarily, on alcohol/drugs/addiction only. No sentimental or *purely* confessional poetry."** They have recently published poetry by Hayden Carruth and William Wyatt. As a sample the editor selected the last lines of "Alcoholic" by Judson Jerome:

> The sonofabitch (God bless him) drank and died
> because we understood away his pride.

They receive about 10 poems a year, use 2. Press run is 350 for 200 subscribers of which 30 are libraries, 10 shelf sales. Single copy: $3 ($4 overseas); subscription: $8. **Previously published poems and simultaneous submissions OK. Submit 2 copies with SASE. Deadlines: 1st of September, January and May for issues appearing October, February and June.** Time between acceptance and publication is 3-6 months. **Always comments on rejections. Reports by "return mail." Pays 5 copies.**

‡DISABILITY ARTS MAGAZINE (IV-Theme), 10 Woad Lane, Great Coates, Grimsby DN37 9NH Great Britain, phone 0472-280031, founded 1991, editor Roland Humphrey, is a quarterly that "has two primary concerns: access to the arts and the promotion of disability arts—disability as subject for art rather than merely metaphor." They want **any poetry where disability is the theme. "Nothing thoughtless."** As a sample we selected the last lines of "Look Again" by Elaine Bennett:

> So when people look
> And don't like what they see,
> They don't really 'look'
> Because they are frightened of me.
>
> Afraid that this person,
> Disabled and lame,
> Could be their reflection,
> Because deep down we're the same.

DAM is 52 pgs., 6⅞×9¹³⁄₁₆, perfect-bound, with full-color laminated card cover and photos, "designed to be kept." Press run is 1,000 for 1,000 subscribers of which 100 are libraries. Single copy: £4 (£6 international); subscription: £12 (£18 outside E.E.C.). **No previously published poems or simultaneous submissions. Seldom comments on rejections. Reports in 3 months maximum. Pays disabled people only—£5 a poem (variable).**

DOC(K)S; EDITIONS NEPE; ZERROSCOPIZ; ANTHOLOGIES DE L 'AN 2.000; LES ANARTISTES (II, IV-Bilingual/foreign language), Le Moulin de Ventabren, 13122 Ventabren, France 13122, uses **"concrete, visual, sound poetry; performance; mail-art; metaphysical poetry,"** not "poesie à la queue-leu-leu" ... whatever that means. They have published work by J.F. Bory, Nani Balestrini, Bernard Heidsieck, James Koller and Franco Beltrametti. The magazine *Doc(k)s* is published 4 times a year and has a circulation of 1,100, of which 150 are subscriptions. **Pay for poetry is 5 copies. There are no specifications for submissions.** *Doc(k)s* is an elegantly produced volume, 7×10, over 300 pgs., flat-spined, using heavy paper and glossy full-color card covers. Most of it is in French. We cannot quote a sample, because concrete poetry, a cross between poetry and graphic art, requires the visual image to be reproduced. Nepe Editions publishes collections of poetry, mostly in French.

DOLPHIN LOG (IV-Children, themes), 8440 Santa Monica Blvd., Los Angeles, CA 90069, phone (213)656-4422, founded 1981, editor Beth Kneeland, is a bimonthly educational publication for children offered by The Cousteau Society. "Encompasses all areas of science, ecology and the environment as they relate to our global water system. Philosophy of magazine is to delight, instruct and instill an environmental ethic and understanding of the interconnectedness of living organisms, including people." They want to see **"poetry related to the marine environment, marine ecology or any water-related subject matter to suit the readership of 7 to 15-year-olds and which will fit the concept of our magazine. Short, witty poems, thought-provoking poems encouraged. No dark or lengthy ones (more than 20 lines). No talking animals."** The editor excerpted these sample lines from "Garbage Pirates" by Marianne Dyson:

> Their treasure bags ready
> The garbage pirates three,
> Set sail in a wagon boat
> Upon the Sidewalk Sea.
>
> They steer around bottle fish
> With broken, jagged teeth,
> And pinch their noses at the smell
> Of trash on Driveway Beach.

It is magazine-sized, 20 pgs., saddle-stapled, offset, using full-color photographs widely throughout, sometimes art, no advertising. It circulates to 100,000 members, approximately 860 library subscriptions. **Membership: $28/year for a Cousteau Society family membership, $10/year for** *Dolphin Log* **only. Sample: $2 plus 9×12 SAE with 75¢ postage. Pays $25 on publication and 3 copies. Reports within 2 months. Dot-matrix, photocopies OK. Double-spaced. Rights include one-time use in** *Dolphin Log,* **the right to grant reprints for use in other publications, and worldwide translation rights for use in other Cousteau Society publications.** The editor advises, "Become familiar with our magazine by requesting a sample copy and our guidelines. We are committed to a particular style and concept to which we strictly adhere and review submissions consistently. We publish only a very limited amount of poetry each year."

DOLPHIN-MOON PRESS; SIGNATURES (II, IV-Regional), P.O. Box 22262, Baltimore MD 21203, founded 1973, president James Taylor, is **"a limited edition (500-1,000 copies) press which emphasizes quality work (regardless of style), often published in unusual/'radical' format."** The writer is usually allowed a strong voice in the look/feel of the final piece. "We've published magazines, anthologies, chapbooks, pamphlets, perfect-bound paperbacks, records, audio cassettes and comic books. **All styles are read and considered, but the work should show a strong spirit and voice. Although we like the feel of 'well-crafted' work, craft for its own sake won't meet our standards either."** They have recently published work by Gian Lombardo, John Strausbaugh, Josephine Jacobsen and William Burroughs. They have also previously published a collection by the late Judson Jerome, **The Village: New and Selected Poems, $10.95 paperback, $15.95 hardcover. Send SASE for catalog and purchase samples or send $10 for their 'sampler' (which they guarantee to be up to $20 worth of their publications). To submit, first send sample of 6-10 pgs. of poetry and a brief cover letter. Replies to query in 2-4 weeks, to submission of whole work (if invited) in 2-4 weeks. Payment in author's copies. Acquires first edition rights.** "Our future plans are to continue as we have since 1973, publishing the best work we can by local, up-and-coming and nationally recognized writers—in a quality package."

THE DOMINION REVIEW (II), Old Dominion University, Bal 200, English Dept., Norfolk VA 23529-0078, phone (804)683-3000, founded 1982, faculty advisor Wayne Ude, Creative Writing, says, **"There are no specifications as to subject matter or style, but we are dedicated to the free verse tradition and will continue to support it.** They have published poetry by Bob Perlongo, Paul Genega and Grace P. Simpson. *TDR* is flat-spined, 80 pgs., digest-sized, professionally printed, and appears each spring. They have 300 subscriptions. **Submissions read from September 1 through December 7; allow to March 15 for replies. Guidelines available for SASE. No pay. Acquires first North American serial rights. They will not consider previously published poems.** Cover letter and brief bio requested.

‡DRAGON'S TEETH PRESS; LIVING POETS SERIES (II), El Dorado National Forest, 7700 Wentworth Springs Rd., Georgetown CA 95634, founded 1970, poetry editor Cornel Lengyel. Published poets include Francis Weaver, Marcia Lee Masters and Stanley Mason. As a sample, the editor selected the beginning lines of "Not Just By Word of Mouth Alone" from **The Thirteenth Labor** by Ronald Belluomini:

> My sole being elliptic
> I have now and anciently dreamt in
> the treasuries of hope about
> a scheme to elude delusion's wrath,
> but I have broken
> my egg-shaped dream with collusion's fact.

Dragon's Teeth Press "subsidy publishes 25% of books if book has high literary merit, but very limited market"—which no doubt applies to books of poetry. They publish other books on 10% royalty contract. **Simultaneous and photocopied submissions OK, computer printout acceptable. Reports in 2 weeks on queries, 1 month on mss.**

‡DREAM INTERNATIONAL QUARTERLY (I, IV-Theme), % Tim Scott, Apt. 2B, 4147 N. Kedvale Ave., Chicago IL 60641, phone (312)794-0697, founded 1981, associate editor Tim Scott. **"Poetry must be dream-inspired and/or dream-related. This can be interpreted loosely, even to the extent of dealing with the transitory as a theme. No radically feminist or conservative poetry. Nothing written expressly or primarily to advance a political or religious ideology."** They have recently published poetry by Stephen Eppley and Carmen Pursifull. As a sample the editor selected these lines from "The Sovereignty of Grass" by Richard Scott:

> And above this divorce of matter and mind,
> course rivers,
> April's wars proving in the aftermath
> the poverty of flesh. The Sovereignty of Grass.

DIQ is 64-84 pgs., 8½×11, with vellum cover and drawings. "Also offer a deluxe edition with protective plastic overlay and toothcomb binding." They receive about 100 poems a year, accept about one fifth. Press run is 200 for 150 subscribers of which 2 are libraries. Single copy: $5.50; subscription $25 for 2 years. **Sample postpaid: $5. Previously published poems and simultaneous submissions OK. Cover letter required.** "As poetry submissions go through the hands of two readers, poets should enclose one additional first class stamp, along with the standard SASE." **Do not submit mss between Thanksgiving and Christmas. Time between acceptance and publication is 6 months. Often comments on rejections. Send $1 for guidelines. Reports in 1-4 weeks. Pays 1 copy. Acquires first North American serial or reprint rights.** Considers reviewing books of poetry "if the poet is a former contributor to *DIQ*. Such reviews usually run to about five hundred words." Tim Scott says, "Don't get discouraged. Discouragement is the beginning writer's biggest enemy. If you are good at your craft, you will eventually find an outlet for it.

Know your literary predecessors and the tradition in which you are working. Read everything from Shakespeare and Donne to Baudelaire and Rimbaud, from Crane and Hopkins to Plath and Sexton."

‡THE DREAM SHOP; VERSE WRITERS GUILD OF OHIO; OHIO HIGH SCHOOL POETRY CONTESTS (IV-Membership, students), poetry editor Beth Leslie, 1434 West Milltown Rd., Wooster OH 44691, founded 1928. The Verse Writers Guild of Ohio is a state poetry society open to members from outside the state, an affiliate of the National Federation of State Poetry Societies. *The Dream Shop* is their poetry magazine, appearing three times a year. Only members of VWG may submit poems. They do not want to see poetry which is highly sentimental, overly morbid or porn — and nothing over 40 lines. "We use beginners' poetry, but would like it to be good, tight, revised. In short, not first drafts." They have recently published poetry by Yvonne Hardenbrook, Frankie Paino, Bonnie Jacobson and J.A. Totts. The editor selected these sample lines from "Portrait of Daruma (Hakuin Ekaku, 1685-1768)" by Jim Brooks:

> How is it the word "tango"
> follows me into this corner
> of shaped light, follows me
> among sacred statues — wooden,
> bronze and sandstone eyes
> closed or half-closed on faces
> full of quiet, full of almost
> too remote tranquility? . . .

"Ours is a forum for our members, and we do use reprints, so new members can get a look at what is going well in more general magazines." Annual dues including *The Dream Shop*: $12. Senior (over 65): $8. Single copies: $2. The magazine is photocopied from typescript (typeset title page), digest-sized, 48 pgs., with matte card cover. "All rights revert to poet after publication." The Verse Writer's Guild sponsors an annual contest for unpublished poems written by high school students in Ohio with categories of traditional, modern, and several other categories. March deadline, with 3 money awards in each category. For contest information write Verse Writer's Guild of Ohio, 1798 Sawgrass Dr., Reynoldsburg OH 43068.

Dry Crik Review *is "dedicated to the well-crafted and artful insights of a disappearing breed of men and women," says Editor John C. Dofflemyer, speaking of contemporary cowboy poetry, which constitutes more than 75% of his publication. This cover illustration, he says, is "representative of the cowboy and/or rural culture. It is an example of both the intricacies of the lifestyle and those of poetry." The artist is Lesley A. Fry, whose subjects are most generally wildlife.*

DREAMS AND NIGHTMARES (IV-Science fiction/fantasy), 1300 Kicker Rd., Tuscaloosa AL 35404, phone (205)553-2284, founded 1986, editor David C. Kopaska-Merkel, is published quarterly. The editor says, "I want to see intriguing poems in any form or style which are under about 60 lines (but will consider longer poems). All submissions must be either science fiction, fantasy or horror (I prefer supernatural horror to gory horror). Nothing trite or sappy, very long poems, poems without fantastic content, excessive violence or pointless erotica. Sex and/or violence is OK if there is a good reason." He has recently used poetry by Lisa Kucharski, Robert Frazier, Donna Zelzer, Ed Mycue, D.F. Lewis,

Wendy Rathbone and Thomas Wiloch. As a sample he selected these lines from "Bodies of Light" by Wendy Rathbone:

> *Theirs are bodies of light*
> *and voices so kind you must*
> *curl your toes to keep your balance*
> *These men have gone to the moon*
> *more often than astronauts*

It has 24 pgs., digest-sized, photocopied from typescript, saddle-stapled, with a colored card stock cover and b&w illustrations. They accept about 80 of 1,000-1,500 poems received. Press run is 200 for 70 subscriptions. **Samples: $1.25 in stamps.** Subscription: $5/4 issues. **Send SASE for guidelines. Pays $3/poem plus 2 copies. Buys first North American serial rights. No simultaneous submissions. "Rarely" uses previously published poems. Reports in 2-10 weeks.** The editor says "There are more magazines publishing fantastic poetry than ever before, and more good fantastic poetry is being written, sold for good money and published. The field is doing very well."

DRUID PRESS (II), Dept. PM, 2724 Shades Crest Rd., Birmingham AL 35216, phone (205)967-6580, founded 1981, president Anne George. **"We do individual chapbooks. We want to see concrete images, free verse, any subject matter. No June-moon rhymes."** They have published poetry by R.T. Smith, Sue Walker, Sue Scalf, John Brugaletta and many others. **For chapbook or book consideration query with 5 samples, bio, publications. Simultaneous submissions, photocopies, dot-matrix OK, but no previously published material. Reports in 3 weeks. Pays "negotiable" number of author's copies. Sample books: $4 postpaid.**

DRY CRIK REVIEW (IV-Themes), P.O. Box 51, Lemon Cove CA 93244-0051, founded 1991, editor John C. Dofflemyer, is a quarterly **of cowboy poetry.** "The function of *Dry Crik Review* is to inspire and communicate not only within the range livestock culture but to enhance an understanding of the people and dilemmas facing this livelihood with the urban majority, honestly. **Well-crafted expression must demonstrate insight gained from experience within this rural culture. Topics range from pastoral to political, humorous to serious. No slapstick doggerel or barnyard-pet poetry, please! Prefer shorter unpublished works."** They have recently published poetry by Paul Zarzyski, Kell Robertson, Charles Potts, Rod McQueary, Greg Keeler and Jon Forrest Glade. As a sample the editor selected these lines from "By Any Other Name" by Vess Quinlan:

> *Just short of 65*
> *Eating nitro like peppermints*
> *Cranky and cynical*
> *He knew firsthand*
> *What poverty*
> *Can do to a man*
> *Cowboying for rich folks*
> *Taught him what money does.*

It is digest-sized, 48 pgs., photocopied from typescript on quality textured paper, matte card cover. It features free and formal verse with a distinct Western flavor. Press run 500 for 300 subscribers of which 25 are libraries, 20% shelf sales. Subscription: $20. **Sample postpaid: $7, some back issues more. No simultaneous submissions. Submission quantity 1-5. Cover letter preferred with first submission. Send SASE for guidelines. Pays 2 copies, more compensation for special Fall issue. Acquires one-time rights. Reports within 3 months.** Reviews books of poetry in 350-400 words, single format. This magazine is lively and engaging with a sense of humor and social commitment to the land and environment—a rare combination.

‡DUENDE PRESS (V), P.O. Box 571, Placitas NM 87043, founded 1964, editor Larry Goodell, **is currently not accepting unsolicited poetry. "Submissions will be burned."** As a sample he offers these lines of his own:

> *Language is a barrier to intellect*
> *Which is a barrier to the Garbage Heart*
> *Of America.*

Interested writers can send $2 for duende rare books list.

DUST (FROM THE EGO TRIP); CAMEL PRESS (IV-Themes), HC 80, Box 160, Big Cove Tannery PA 17212, phone (717)573-4526, founded 1981, poetry consultant Katharyn Howd Machan, publisher James Hedges, who describes himself as "editor/printer of scholarly and scientific journals, does occasional poetry chapbooks for fun." *Dust (From the Ego Trip)* is "an intermittent journal of personal reminiscences." For it he wants **"autobiographical material (can address any subject, but written from the viewpoint of an active participant in the events described). Mss should average about 2,500 words**

and can be one long poem or a collection of related shorter poems. Any style OK, and any language using the roman alphabet. No religious (evangelizing) material or other material written primarily to advance a point of view. Any topic is OK, and coarse language is OK, but only if used artistically." As a sample James Hedges selected these lines by recent author Renée Smith:

> *The golden child,*
> *so wise,*
> *uncomplaining*
> *Beautiful liquid eyes*

He publishes 1-2 chapbooks a year under the Camel Press imprint, average 20 pgs. **Query with "a few sample poems." No bio, publications needed because, "we judge on material only, status of poet is irrelevant." Simultaneous submissions, photocopies, previously published material OK, but he prefers not to have dot-matrix. Reports in 10 days. Pays 50 copies plus half of net after production costs are recovered.** He is open to subsidy publishing of poetry of "artistic merit," though he has never done any. To buy samples, request catalog. "I always write a cover letter, but I'm not a poetry critic, just a considerate publisher. I do a bit of poetry because I want to encourage the art and broaden my catalog. Everything I publish is handset in metal type and letterpress printed on fine paper. The authors are expected to do most of the promotion. Press run normally 500, and I give away about 400 copies to friends, plus 50 for the author. The author can order more copies in advance if he expects to sell a large number. Financial arrangements are negotiable."

DUSTY DOG; DUSTY DOG REVIEWS (II), P.O. Box 1103, Zuni NM 87327, phone (505)782-4958, founded 1990, editor/publisher John Pierce, appears three times a year using **"high caliber, well-crafted poetry, any style. No restrictions on length. No rhyming poetry, nothing *overtly* pornographic or religious. No light verse. No haiku."** They have recently published poetry by Belinda Subraman, Sue Saniel Elkind, Joanne Lowery, Hugh Fox, Errol Miller, R. Nikolas Macioci, Janet McCann and James Weil. As a sample the editor selected these lines by Simon Perchik:

> *I work a ceremony: my shadow in front*
> *guarding the Earth from the sun. I draw*
> *this makeshift sled: a fence*
> *carrying off a season: a scraping*
> *as if the sun was afraid to come*

With #6, *Dusty Dog* has become a nonsubscription publication. It is professionally printed on tinted paper. Press run is 150-200. **Samples available for SASE. "Currently publishing 4-page pamphlets of poetry; some pamphlets by a single author in which case payment is 25 copies, some pamphlets contain four poems all by different authors in which case payment is 5 copies/ author. All rights return to authors and artists upon publication. Submit 6-10 high caliber, well-crafted poems and SASE with proper return postage." Simultaneous submissions OK. Reports in 2-4 weeks.** *Dusty Dog Reviews* is a review magazine appearing irregularly, reviewing small press poetry magazines and chapbooks, 30-50/issue, average length 200 words. Subscription: $4.50. Sample: $2. The editor advises, "Become very familiar with **Poet's Market** and what is said at the beginning of the book. The small press magazines are often 1 person staff and work very hard for you, the poet. Be patient with them, and support the magazines you like. If poets don't subscribe to the magazines that publish them, it is very hard for the magazine to continue publishing."

THE EAGLE (IV-Ethnic), Eagle Wing Press, Inc., P.O. Box 579MO, Naugatuck CT 06770, phone (203)729-0035, founded 1981, poetry editor Terry Roaix, is an **American Indian newspaper** appearing every other month. **Poems must be on American Indian themes or written by American Indians. "Try to avoid 'typical' pieces that try to sound 'Indian'. We are looking for clear, concise, strong poetry."** They have recently published poetry by Marcella Taylor and John Fox. As a sample the editor selected lines from the poem "We the Criminals" by Sean Lawrence:

> *selling white lies*
> *in a blind man's trade*
> *sorting through beads*
> *in a timeless charade*
> *of meaningless treaties*
> *and the money we made.*

The newspaper is tabloid-sized, about 28 pgs., unstapled, with graphics and ads, circulation 4,000 with 1,500 subscriptions of which 120 are libraries, about 600 shelf sales. Subscription: $10/year. **Sample postpaid: $2.50. Pays 2 copies, up to 5 more on request. "Rights revert to author after publication, with *Eagle* reserving right to reprint."** Reviews books of poetry by Native Americans.

EARTH'S DAUGHTERS: A FEMINIST ARTS PERIODICAL (IV-Women/Feminist, themes), Box 622, Station C, Buffalo NY 14209, phone (716)837-7778, founded 1971. The "literary periodical with strong feminist emphasis" appears 3 times a year, irregularly spaced. Its "format varies. Most issues are flat-spined, digest-sized issues of approximately 60 pgs. We also publish chapbooks, magazine-sized and tabloid-sized issues. Past issues have included broadsheets, calendars, scrolls and one which could be assembled into a box." Poetry can be "up to 40 lines (rare exceptions for exceptional work), free form, experimental—we like unusual work. All must be strong, supportive of women in all their diversity. We like work by new writers, but expect it to be well-crafted. We want to see work of technical skill and artistic intensity. We rarely publish work in classical form, and we never publish rhyme or greeting card verse." They have published poetry by Christine Cassidy, Rose Romano, Lyn Lifshin, Helen Ruggieri, Joan Murray, Susan Fantl Spivack, "and many fine 'unknown' poets, writers and artists." They publish poetry by men if it is supportive of women. As a sample the editor selected *#36 Over the Transom* "A Shape Soft Enough to Wear" by Lynn Martin:

> ... *Two women can talk the night*
> *into a shape soft enough to wear*
> *one more time. It's almost as if*
> *The same onion planted over & over,*
> *never decays, grows like a prayer* ...

"Our purpose is to publish primarily work that otherwise might never be printed, either because it is unusual, or because the writer is not well known." Subscription: $14/3 issues for individuals; $22 for institutions. **Sample: $4 postpaid. Send SASE for guidelines. Some issues have themes, which are available for SASE after April of each year. Pays 2 copies and reduced prices on further copies. Length of reporting time is atrociously long if mss is being seriously considered for publication, otherwise within 3 weeks. Simultaneous submissions, photocopies, dot-matrix OK. "Per each issue, authors are limited to a total of 150 lines of poetry, prose or a combination of the two. Submissions in excess of these limits will be returned unread. Business-size envelope is preferred, and use sufficient postage—we do not accept mail with postage due." Editor comments "whenever we have time to do so—we want to encourage new writers."** The collective says: "Once you have submitted work, please be patient. We only hold work we are seriously considering for publications, and it can be up to a year between acceptance and publication. If you must contact us (change of address, notification that a simultaneous submission has been accepted elsewhere), be sure to state the issue theme, the title(s) of your work and enclose SASE."

EASTERN CARIBBEAN INSTITUTE (I, IV-Regional), P.O. Box 1338, Frederiksted, U.S. Virgin Islands 00841, phone (809)772-1011, founded 1982, editor S.B. Jones-Hendrickson, editorial contact Sandra Thomas, is a "small press publisher with plans to expand," especially interested in poetry of the Caribbean and Eastern Caribbean "but open to all subjects, styles and forms." As a sample the editor selected these lines from **On The Wings of Love and Time** by Eldon X. Williams:

> *How often I wondered about your promises,*
> *And how long you'll be true. Now I know*
> *your promises were only to make me blue.*

Their books are softcover, averaging 60 pgs. Sample copies available for purchase. **Submit 5 sample poems, cover letter with bio and previous publications. Simultaneous submissions and previously published poems OK. Reads submissions January to May only. Reports in 1 month. Pays 50 copies.** The editor says, "In our part of the world, poetry is moving on a new level. People who are interested in regional poetry should keep an eye on the Caribbean region. There is a new focus in the Virgin Islands."

EDICIONES UNIVERSAL (IV-Ethnic, foreign language, regional), 3090 SW 8th St., Miami FL 33135, phone (305)642-3234, founded 1964, general manager Marta Salvat-Golik, is a small press subsidy publisher of Spanish language books. "We specialize in Cuban authors and themes." They have recently published books of poetry by Olga Rosalo and Amelia del Castillo. Poets "must be able to purchase in advance 75% of the copies, due to the fact that poetry does not sell well." Poets receive the copies they paid for. **Submit sample, bio, publications. Reports in 4 weeks.**

EIDOS MAGAZINE: SEXUAL FREEDOM AND EROTIC ENTERTAINMENT FOR WOMEN, MEN & COUPLES (IV-Erotica/Women), P.O. Box 96, Boston MA 02137, founded 1982, poetry editor Brenda Loew Tatelbaum. "Our press publishes erotic literature, photography and artwork. Our purpose is to provide an alternative to women's images and male images and sexuality depicted in mainstream publications like *Playboy, Penthouse, Playgirl,* etc. We provide a forum for the discussion and examination of two highly personalized dimensions of human sexuality: desire and satisfaction. We do not want to see angry poetry or poetry that is demeaning to either men or women. We like experimental, avant-garde material that makes a personal, political, cultural statement about sensu-sexuality."

Poets they have recently published include D. Heather Ballew, Sgt. Cheryl McElroy, Jennifer G. Bradley, Taja Backus and Cheryl Townsend. *Eidos* is professionally printed, tabloid-format, with fine photography and art, **number of poems per issue varies**, print run 10,000, over 7,000 subscriptions. **Sample: $10 postpaid.** They receive hundreds of poems per year, use about 50. No backlog right now. **1 page limit on length, format flexible, photocopy, dot-matrix, simultaneous submissions OK. Reports in 1-2 months. Pays 1 copy. Acquires first North American serial rights. Guidelines available for SASE. Only accepts sexually explicit material. Comment or criticism provided as often as possible.** Brenda Loew Tatelbaum advises, "There is so much poetry submitted for consideration that a rejection can sometimes mean a poet's timing was poor. We let poets know if the submission was appropriate for our publication and suggest they resubmit at a later date. Keep writing, keep submitting, keep a positive attitude."

THE EIGHTH MOUNTAIN PRESS; EIGHTH MOUNTAIN POETRY PRIZE (IV-Women, feminist), 624 SE 29th Ave., Portland OR 97214, founded 1985, editor Ruth Gundle, is a "small press publisher of **feminist literary works by women.**" They have recently published poetry by Karen Mitchell, Irena Klepfisz, Maureen Seaton and Lori Anderson. They publish 1 book of poetry per year, averaging 115 pgs. **"We now publish poetry *only* through the Eighth Mountain Poetry Prize." Pays 8-10% royalties. Buys all rights. Returns rights if book goes out of print.** The Eighth Mountain Poetry Prize is an annual award of a $1,000 advance and publication for a book of 50-120 pgs. written by a woman, no restrictions as to subject matter. Send SASE for rules. **Submit during January; postmark deadline February 1.** Entry fee: $10. "The selection will be made anonymously. Therefore, the ms must have a cover sheet giving all pertinent information (title, name, address, phone number). No identifying information except the title should appear on any other ms page. The contest will be judged by a different feminist poet each year, whose name will be announced after the winning ms has been chosen." The 1992 contest was judged by Linda Hogan. Previous judges have included Andre Lorde, Marilyn Hacker and Judy Grahn.

EL BARRIO; CASA DE UNIDAD (V, IV-Ethnic, regional), 1920 Scotten, Detroit MI 48209, phone (313)843-9598, founded 1981, poetry editor Marta Lagos. They publish **poetry from Latino residents of the SW Detroit area concerning life, family, politics, repression, etc., but do not normally accept unsolicited material. Query first.** They have recently published poetry by Lolita Hernandez, Gloria House and Jose Garza. As a sample the editor selected these lines from "Let Us Stop This Madness" by Trinidad Sanchez, Jr.:

> *Let us destroy the factories*
> *that make the guns*
> *that shoot the bullets*
> *that kill our children.*
> *Let us take a stand*
> *to share life,*
> *to break bread*
> *with each other.*

El Barrio is published "to keep the Latino people of the SW Detroit area informed, to give them an opportunity to speak to the community." It appears 3-4 times a year, is magazine-sized, about 28 pgs., professionally printed with commissioned art on the matte card cover, using up to 3 poems/issue. Their press run is 5,000, $3/issue, $12 for a subscription. **"Please call for a sample copy." They sometimes use previously published poems.** The press has published 2 anthologies: **Detroit: La Onda Latina en Poesía—Latin Sounds in Poetry**, Vols. I and II ($6 each).

‡EL TECOLOTE (IV-Ethnic), Box 40037, San Francisco, CA 94140, phone (415)252-5957, founded 1970, is a "community newspaper with **subject matter primarily about Latin America.** Much cultural coverage in general, but not a lot of poetry." Monthly. They want **"short (1 page or less) poems inspired by life in U.S. Latino communities or in Latin America. Would like to see poetry that acknowledges the struggle of Latino/as who must live in a culture different from their own.** The struggle both uncovers our history and creates a positive role model for the future. Open to poetry by either sex, sexual preference, and all ages." They have published poetry by Manilio Argueta from El Salvador. *El Tecolote* (The Owl) is a tabloid, 16 pgs., using art, graphics, and ads, press run 10,000. They accept about 1 out of 10 pages of poetry submitted. **Submit double-spaced, with name and address on each sheet. Simultaneous submissions and previously published poems OK.**

Use the General Index to find the page number of a specific publication or publisher.

THE ELEVENTH MUSE; POETRY WEST; POETRY WEST CONTEST (II, IV-Regional), P.O. Box 2413, Colorado Springs CO 80901, coordinating editor Sandra McNew. Poetry West is a nonprofit organization of poets and supporters of poetry in the Pikes Peak region. It publishes work from all parts of the country in its literary journal, *the eleventh MUSE*, and **"is especially interested in well-crafted and striking visions that are rich in detail."** They have recently published poetry by Lois Hayna, Janice Hays and Tony Moffeit. As an example "of the richness of detail preferred (many styles are acceptable)," the editor selected these lines from "The Best Hamburgers" by Holly Hildebrand:

> *The best hamburgers*
> *are made in 1962*
> *in mock turtle's old cottage*
> *on redman road*
> *and eaten while we watch*
> *errol flynn die with his boots on*

The editor says *the eleventh MUSE* is printed with matte card cover and saddle-stapled. It's solid small press product, featuring a wide selection of verse, from lyric and narrative to beat. Subscription (2 issues): $7/year. **Sample postpaid: $4. No previously published poems or simultaneous submissions. Submit up to 5 poems. Reports within 6-8 weeks. Pays 1 copy. Acquires first North American serial rights.** A Poetry West Contest is held annually with a May 1 deadline for poems up to 40 lines. Prizes of $100, $50 and $25 are offered, along with publication. Entry fee is $3 for non-members; members may enter 3 poems free. Submit poems in duplicate with name and address on one copy only. Poems cannot be returned. Recent judges include Jack Meyers and Reg Saner. Poetry West is also committed to developing regional artists. Each month it sponsors readings and workshops in local galleries, coffeehouses and colleges. Membership is $20/year and includes 2-3 newsletters and 2 issues of *the eleventh MUSE*. Poets may also apply to read by sending 10 poems and a brief bio. Payment varies.

11TH ST. RUSE; BIG FISH (I), 322 E. 11th St. #23, New York NY 10003, phone (212)475-5312, founded 1987, editor Lucid. *11th St. Ruse* appears every 2 months, 4 pgs. mimeo, wants **poems "short, without subterfuge, preferably written very quickly."** They have recently published poetry by Teres d' Compagnie and Richard Kostelanetz. As a sample the editor selected these lines (poet unidentified):

> *But for thirty minutes, every two*
> *hours? That makes six hours a day.*
> *How*
> *did I fail to do this arithmetic*

Press run is 190. Price per issue: 33¢. **Sample postpaid: $1. Make checks payable to Ellen Carter. Pays 1 copy. Reports in 1 day-3 months.** "I have another magazine, *Big Fish*, and I am currently seeking poems in foreign languages without translations."

ELF: ECLECTIC LITERARY FORUM (Elf Magazine) (II), P.O. Box 392, Tonawanda NY 14150, founded 1990, editor C.K. Erbes, is a quarterly. **"Subject matter and form are open, but we are looking for well-crafted poetry. We prefer poems of 30 lines or less, but will consider longer poems. No trite, hackneyed, ill-crafted effluvia."** They have recently published poetry by Gwendolyn Brooks, John Dickson, Martha Vertreace, David Romtvedt, John Tagliague and Ann Fox Chandonnet. As a sample the editor selected these lines from "The Poet" by S.J. DiChristina:

> *The poet turns a perfect drop of water and*
> *rolls it round the yellow bowls of tulips*
> *—he combs the sable silks of Iowa corn as*
> *it tips and elbows in the flatland heat*
> *—he illusions in a speck of sand, and*
> *—nacres himself an orient pearl, . . .*

Elf is magazine-sized, 52-56 pgs. with semi-gloss cover, professionally printed, saddle-stapled. They use approximately 140 poems/year. Circulation 4,000. Subscription: $12. **Sample postpaid: $4.50. Send SASE for guidelines. Pays 2 copies. Acquires first North American serial rights. Editor comments when possible. "Accepted writers are asked to submit a byline of 25 words or less."** Poems are circulated to an editorial board of professional poets and writers; responses in 4-6 weeks.

‡ELK RIVER REVIEW; LIMESTONE LITERARY LEAGUE (I, II), 606 Coleman Ave., Athens AL 35611-3216, founded 1991, poetry editor Tom McDougle, founder and editor John Chambers, is a semiannual review of poetry and short fiction published by the Limestone Literary League. **"Open to all types of poetry, no line limit. We want poems that are well-crafted, musical, provocative."** They have recently published poetry by Charles Ghigna, Andrew Hudgins, R.T. Smith, Sue Scalf, Sue Walker and Anne George. As a sample we selected these lines from "Snowflakes and Satellites" by Bettye Cannizzo:

> *One delights the eye like a baby's smile,*

> *tickles the tongue like a Margarita.*
> *The other jolts the imagination like poetry,*
> *stimulates the mind like philosophy.*

ERR is 62-84 pgs., 7×9, offset, saddle-stitched, with 80 lb. glossy cover with b&w photo and b&w line drawings inside. Press run is 1,000 for 500 subscribers of which 10 are libraries, 200 shelf sales. Subscription: $10. **Sample postpaid: $5. No previously published poems. Often comments on rejections. Criticism fee: $5. Send SASE for guidelines. Reports in 2-4 months. Pays 3 copies.** Reviews novels and poetry collections (including chapbooks) of regional interest.

‡**ELLIPSE (V, IV-Translations, bilingual),** C.P. 10, FLSH Université de Sherbrooke, Sherbrooke, Quebec J1K 2R1 Canada, phone (819)821-7277, founded 1969, editors P. Godbout/C. Bouchara, **publishes French-English poetry in translation.** That is, on facing pages appear either poems in English and a French translation or poems in French and an English translation. **Currently they are not accepting unsolicited mss.** They have recently published poetry by D.G. Jones, Lorna Crozier, R. Choquette and M. Beaulieu. As a sample, these are the opening lines of "Winter Uplands" by Archibald Lampman:

> *The frost that sings like fire upon my cheek,*
> *The loneliness of this forsaken ground,*
> *The long white drift upon whose powdered peak*
> *I sit in the great silence as one bound;*

translated as "Des hauts plateaux d'hiver" by Joseph Bonenfant:

> *Le feu de la froidure aux joues cingle et me pique,*
> *Dans l'abandonnement de ce sol delaissé,*
> *Sur le long banc de neige à la cime poudreuse*
> *Je suis une frontière au centre du silence;*

The magazine appears twice yearly in an elegant flat-spined, 6×9 format, professionally printed, 90+ pgs. Subscription: $10. **Sample postpaid: $5.**

ELLIPSIS MAGAZINE (II), Westminster College of Salt Lake City, 1840 S. 1300 East, Salt Lake City UT 84105, founded 1967, appears twice a year using **"all kinds of good poetry. Limited on space."** They have published work by William Stafford, William Kloefkorn, Lyn Lifshin and Ron Carlson. The editor describes it as 80-112 pgs., digest-sized, flat-spined. Subscription: $12/year. **Sample: $8 postpaid. Pays $15/page plus 1 copy. Responds within 3 months.**

EMBERS (II), P.O. Box 404, Guilford CT 06437, phone (203)453-2328, founded 1979, poetry editors Katrina Van Tassel, Charlotte Garrett and Mark Johnson, a "poetry journal of talented new and occasional well-known poets." The editors say, **"no specifications as to length, form or content. Interested in new poets with talent; not interested in lighter way-out verse, porn or poetry that is non-comprehensible."** They have published poetry by Brendan Galvin, Marilyn Waniek and Sue Ellen Thompson. *Embers* is digest-sized, nicely printed on white stock with an occasional b&w photograph or drawing, 52 pgs. flat-spined with one-color matte card cover handsomely printed in black; it appears twice a year—spring/summer and fall/winter. Price per issue is $6, subscription $11/year. **Sample available for $3 postpaid. Pay for acceptance is 2 copies. Rights revert to author after publication. Submissions must be typed, previously unpublished, with name, address and brief bio of poet. Deadlines: "basically March 15 and October 15, but we read continuously."** They sponsor a chapbook contest, deadline January 1. Winner is reported by March 1. Write for details. Editors' advice is "Send for sample copies of any publication you are interested in. Be patient. Most editors read as quickly as they can and report likewise. If a poet sends in work at the beginning of a reading time, or long before a deadline, he/she will have to wait longer for answers. *Embers* editors are interested in the poet's voice and would like to read up to five submissions showing variety of subject, form, etc."

‡**EMERALD CITY COMIX & STORIES (II),** P.O. Box 95402, Seattle WA 98145, phone (206)784-0162, founded 1985, editor Nils Osmar, is a tabloid appearing twice a year, circulation 12,000, using "fantasy, SF, fiction, poetry, comics, reviews." They want **"any and all well-written poetry on any theme, no racist, misogynist."** They have recently published poetry by Laurel Speer and Robert Bowie. As a sample the editor selected these lines by Judith Skillman:

> *We walk until the path*
> *is a swath cut in the back*
> *of the first animal: snow.*
> *Its marble skin recedes like a claw.*

The paper is 8-12 pgs., newsprint. They print 15-20 of 50-60 poems received/year. The paper is distributed free, supported by ads. **Send SASE for guidelines. Pays 2 copies. They will consider simultaneous submissions and previously published poems** "but we like to know where previously published." **Reports in 2-3 months. Editor comments on rejections "sometimes."** They sometimes sponsor contests.

EMERALD COAST REVIEW; WEST FLORIDA LITERARY FEDERATION; FRANCIS P. CASSIDY LITER-ARY CENTER; THE LEGEND; BACK DOOR POETS; WISE (WRITERS IN SERVICE TO EDUCATION) (IV-Regional), P.O. Box 1644, Pensacola FL 32597, located at WFLF/Cassidy Literary Center, Pensacola Cultural Center, 402 S. Jefferson St., Pensacola FL 32501. The WFLF was founded in 1987 and began the Cassidy Literary Center, a regional writers' resource and special collection library. One of their programs is WISE, which provides over 50 area writers who volunteer their time to share their writing and writing experiences with local students. They sponsor a Student Writers Network for students in grades 9-12 and scholarships for area college student writers. They publish *The Legend*, a newsletter bringing literary arts news to 800-1,000 area writers and their supporters. Back Door Poets, one of their subgroups, conducts open microphone poetry readings the third Saturday of each month and sponsors "Poetry & Patriotism," a non-stop, 24-hour vigil reading of American poetry in Seville Square to commemorate American Independence Day. Membership in WFLF ranges from $5/year for students to $350 and up for life-time memberships. The *Emerald Coast Review* is an **annual limited to Gulf Coast regional writers. Send SASE for guidelines. Submit with required form (included in guidelines) May 1 to July 31. Pays copies. Sample postpaid: $12.**

EMRYS JOURNAL (II), P.O. Box 8813, Greenville SC 29604, founded 1982, managing editor Linda Julian, an annual, wants **"all kinds of poetry, though we don't publish poems of more than 2-3 pgs."** They have published poetry by Linda Pasten, Maxine Kumin, R.T. Smith, Neal Bowers, Jim Peterson and Carl Dennis. As a sample, here are lines from "Gargoyles" by Gail Regier:

> *Gray nights they vomit rain*
> *Out into the wind's skirl.*
> *They curse us*
> *And their curses come to pass.*

It is handsomely printed, 6 × 9 flat-spined, up to 120 pgs. "For our last issue we received about 650 poems from 40 states. We printed 350." Press run 350 for 250 subscribers of which 10 are libraries. **Sample postpaid: $10. Pays 5 copies. Send SASE for guidelines. Editor never comments on rejections.** They say, "We try to report within 6 weeks of the end of our reading period," but don't indicate when the reading period is.

THE EMSHOCK LETTER (IV-Subscribers), P.O. Box 411,Troy ID 83871-0411, phone (208)835-4902, founded 1977, editor Steve Erickson, appears 3-12 times a year, occasionally with **poetry and other writings by subscribers. It is "a philosophical, metaphysical, sometimes poetic expression of ideas and events.** It covers a wide range of subjects and represents a free-style form of expressive relation. It is a newsletter quite unlike any other." The editor describes it as magazine-sized, 5-7 pgs., photocopied from typescript on colored paper, subscription: $25. **Pays 2 copies following publication. "Poets [who are subscribers] should submit poetry which contains some meaning, preferably centering on a philosophic theme and preferably 50 lines or less. Any good poetry (submitted by a subscriber) will be considered for inclusion and will receive a personal reply by the editor, whether or not submitted material is published in** *The Emshock Letter.*" Reviews books of poetry only if written by subscribers.

EN PASSANT POETRY (II), 4612 Sylvanus Dr., Wilmington DE 19803, founded 1975, poetry editor James A. Costello, a poetry review, irregular, **uses about 34 pgs. of poetry/issue, pays 2 copies.** They have published poetry by Léon-Paul Fargue, Judith Goodenough, Robert King, Mark Nepo and Celia Strome. It is a flat-spined, digest-sized format with matte cover, tasteful b&w art, professional printing, circulation 300. **Sample copies $2.50.**

‡ENITHARMON PRESS (V), 36 St. George's Ave., London N7 0HD England, phone (071)607-7194, FAX (071)607-8694, founded 1969, poetry editor Stephen Stuart-Smith, is a publisher of fine editions of poetry and literary criticism in paperback and some hardback editions, about 12 volumes per year averaging 80 pages. **"Substantial backlog of titles to produce, so no submissions possible before 1995."** They have published books of poetry by John Heath-Stubbs, Phoebe Hesketh, David Gascoyne, Jeremy Hooker, Frances Horovitz, Ruth Pitter, Edwin Brock and Jeremy Reed.

‡EPIPHANY: A JOURNAL OF LITERATURE (I), P.O. Box 2699, University of Arkansas, Fayetteville AR 72701, founded 1990, editor Dora Rainey is a quarterly of poetry, short fiction, reviews, interviews and translations. **"We like free verse with strong images. We like to see poetry with content and meaning not just description."** As a sample the editor selected these lines by Maggie Aldridge Smith:

> *from earliest dawn*
> *through night shadows*
> *on top of hot noons*

> *under cool evenings*
> *bare feet wade the stream*

Epiphany is digest-sized, saddle-stapled, with card cover. They receive over 3,000 submissions a year, use about 5%. Press run is 300. Subscription: $12; send to 408 E. Tulsa, Siloam Springs AR 72761. Sample postpaid: $4. No previously published poems or simultaneous submissions. Always comments on rejections. Send SASE for guidelines. Reports in 1-2 months. Pays 1 copy.

EPOCH; BAXTER HATHAWAY PRIZE (III), 251 Goldwin Smith, Cornell, Ithaca NY 14853, founded 1947, has a distinguished and long record of publishing **exceptionally fine poetry** and fiction. They have published work by such poets as Ashbery, Ammons, Eshleman, Wanda Coleman, Molly Peacock, Robert Vander Molen and Alvin Aubert. The magazine appears 3 times a year in a professionally printed, 6×9 flat-spined format with glossy color cover, 100+ pgs., which goes to 1,000 subscribers. They use less than 1% of the many submissions they receive each year, have a 2- to 12-month backlog. Sample postpaid: $5. Reports in 2 months. "We *don't read* unsolicited mss between May 15 and September 15." Pays 50¢/line. Buys first serial rights. Occasionally provides criticism on mss. The annual Baxter Hathaway prize of $1,000 is awarded for a long poem or, in alternate years, a novella. Write for details. The editor advises, "I think it's extremely important for poets to read other poets. I think it's also very important for poets to read the magazines that they want to publish in. Directories are not enough."

‡EQUILIBRIUM [10]; EAGLE PUBLISHING PRODUCTIONS (I, IV-Themes), Box 162, Golden CO 80402, founded 1982. "We are not responsible for any mail being received without our $3 processing fee for all submissions. We publish everything and I mean everything dealing with equilibrium: balance, opposites, pairs, equality, opposite and equal reactions, etc." They are open to "all types, lengths and styles. Very lenient!" on themes given above. The quarterly is striking in appearance, photocopied on pocket-edition 4¼×8½ sheets of various colors, about 70 pgs., saddle-stapled with glossy b&w paper cover, using many photos, drawings and cartoons throughout. One page is devoted to "Poems," each with an illustration. The following sample is from "The Supposition of Opposition" by Caral Davis:

> *The sun rises, just to fall.*
> *It's all for one and one for all.*
> *It rains on the rich and on the poor,*
> *The rich get richer and the poor get poorer.*
> *Winter withers summer away, only to revive*
> *another day.*

Circulation 10,000, price per issue $4. Sample: $4 plus 5 (regular) stamps. Pays $15 and up plus 1 copy. Reports in 6 months. "We prefer to hold in files until needed!" Backlog 1-12 months. Editor sometimes comments on rejections. He says, "We prefer for poets to keep a photocopy and send us the original for our files. They may be handwritten if you wish for your poem printed as such. It is best for the poet (even youngsters) to include art, pictures, etc., too. Letter and queries arriving at our office will become the property of our company and material may and will be published 'as-is.' "

‡EQUINOX (II), P.O. Box 9984, Oakland CA 94613, founded 1991 (first issue 1992), editors Karen Fiser and Alice Connelly Nagle, is a biannual literary journal appearing "on or about the vernal and autumnal equinoxes. We especially welcome submissions from members of groups whose lives and work have historically been marginalized, whether by race, class, gender, age, disability, sexuality or culture." They have recently published work by Diana O'Hehir and, in their series on Writers in Community, an interview with poet Alberto Rios. The editors describe *Equinox* as 180 pgs., perfect-bound, using photos and graphics. Single copy: $8; subscription: $13, $25 institutions. No previously published poems or simultaneous submissions. Cover letter, with short bio, preferred. Often comments on rejections.

EQUINOX PRESS (V); BRITISH HAIKU SOCIETY; BLITHE SPIRIT (IV-Form/style, membership), Sinodun, Shalford, Braintree Essex CM7 5HN England, phone 0371-851097, founded 1990, c/o Mr. David Cobb. Equinox publishes poetry (mainly haiku and senryu), 1-2 volumes/year. They have a waiting list at present and are unable to consider submissions. BHS publishes a quarterly journal, *Blithe Spirit*, a quarterly newsletter and other occasional publications (pamphlets, folios). *Blithe Spirit* publishes only haiku, senryu and tanka sent in by society members. As a sample the Equinox editor selected this haiku (poet unidentified):

> • *a cloudless sky*
> *painters stretch ladders*
> *to their farthest rungs*

EUROPEAN JUDAISM (IV-Religious, ethnic), Kent House, Rutland Gardens, London, England SW7 1BX, phone (071)584-2754, founded 1966, poetry editor Edouard Roditi, is a "twice-yearly magazine with emphasis on European Jewish theology/philosophy/literature/history, with **some poetry in every issue. It should preferably be short, as it is often used as filler, and should have Jewish content or reference. We do not want hackneyed, overblown rubbish.**" They have published poetry by Alan Sillito, Erich Fried and Ruth Fainlight. As a sample the editor selected these lines by Moris Farhi:

> *why does a man have to die*
> *leaving remains*
>
> *if die he must*
> *why not*
> *incorporeal*
> *like memory*

It is a glossy, elegant 7×10 flat-spined magazine, rarely art or graphics, 68 pgs. They have a print run of 950, about 50% of which goes to subscribers (few libraries). Single copy: $9; subscription: $18. **Sample can be obtained gratis from Pergamon Press, Headington Hill Hall, Oxford, England 0X3 OBW. Pays 1 copy.**

EVANGEL (IV-Religious), P.O. Box 535002, Indianapolis IN 46253-5002, weekly since 1897, poetry editor Vera Bethel, **publishes an 8-page paper for adults. Nature and devotional poetry, 8-16 lines, "free verse or with rhyme scheme."** The circulation is 35,000; it is sold in bulk to Sunday schools. **Sample for 6×9 SASE. Pays: $10. Photocopy, simultaneous submissions OK. Reports in 1 month.** The editor advises, "Do not write abstractions. Use concrete words to picture concept for reader."

EVENT (II, IV-Themes), Douglas College, P.O. Box 2503, New Westminster, British Columba V3L 5B2 Canada, founded 1971, editor Dale Zieroth, is "a literary magazine publishing **high-quality contemporary poetry,** short stories and reviews. **All good-quality work is considered.**" They have recently published Tom Wayman, Elisabeth Harvor and Richard Lemm. These sample lines are from "Poetry" by Don Domanski:

> *is it a side street or a cat's jaw?*
> *cerecloth or the body's flesh?*
> *I've named it the heart's pillow*
> *wind in a mirror   cloud-rope*
> *lighthouse on the edge of a wound*
> *beadwork   the mote's halo   wolf-ladder*

It appears three times a year as a 6×9 flat-spined, 128+ pgs., glossy-covered, finely printed paperback with a circulation of 1,000 for 700 subscriptions, of which 50 are libraries. **Sample postpaid: $5. Reports in 2-3 months. Pays honorarium. Sometimes they have special thematic issues, such as: work, feminism, peace and war, coming of age. They comment on some rejections.**

THE EVERGREEN CHRONICLES (IV-Gay, lesbian), P.O. Box 8939, Minneapolis MN 55408, is "a semiannual literary journal dedicated to presenting the best of lesbian and gay literary and visual artists. **The artistry presented is not limited to 'gay' or 'lesbian' themes, but extends to life, in all its dimensions.**" Subscription: $15. Sample postpaid: $7.95. "**Send 4 copies of your work, up to 10 pgs. of poetry. Pays 1 copy. Acquires first-time rights. Deadlines: July 1 and January 1. Please include a short biographical paragraph describing yourself and your work.**" Reviews books of poetry in 500 words, single format.

EXIT 13 (II), % Tom Plante, 22 Oakwood Ct., Fanwood NJ 07023, phone (908)889-5298, founded 1987, poetry editor Tom Plante, is a "contemporary poetry annual" using **poetry that is "short, to the point, with a sense of geography."** They have recently published poetry by Joel Lewis, Dawn Zapletal, Miriam Sagan, Errol Miller and Alexis Rotella. As a sample the editor selected the following lines by John Grey:

> *Somewhere, in an acetylene desert*
> *dry as babies' dreams,*
> *between tall, prickly green*
> *shafts of cactus,*
> *lizards communicate, invent, understand.*

Their press run is 300. *Exit 13*, #4, was 56 pgs. **Sample postpaid: $5,** *payable to T. Plante.* **Guidelines available for SASE. Pays 1 copy. Acquires first-time and possible anthology rights. They accept simultaneous submissions and previously published poems. Reads submissions March 1 through November 30 only. Reports in 3 months.** Reviews books of poetry and magazines in a "Publications Received" column, using 25-30 words/listing. The editor advises, "Write about what you know. Study geography. *Exit 13* looks for adventure. Every state and region is welcome.

Send a snapshot of an 'Exit 13' road sign and receive a free copy of the issue in which it appears."

EXPEDITION PRESS (II, IV-Love, religious), #2306, 105 E. Walnut St., Kalamazoo MI 49007-5253, publisher Bruce W. White, who publishes chapbooks of **love poems and religious poems. "I dislike violence."** He likes to see **"fresh new approaches, interesting spatial relationships, as well as quality artwork. We dislike political diatribes."** Some poets he has published are J. Kline Hobbs, Jim DeWitt, Martin Cohen and C. VanAllsburg. **Submit ms of 20-30 pgs. and brief bio. Photocopy, dot-matrix, simultaneous submissions OK. Ms on cassette OK. Reports in 1 month. Pays 100 copies.** Bruce White provides **"much"** criticism on rejected mss.

EXPERIMENT IN WORDS; WRITER, POET AND ARTIST OF THE YEAR AWARDS (II), P.O. Box 470186, Ft. Worth TX 76147, founded 1990, editor/publisher Robert W. Howington. *EIW* appears annually. The editor says, **"I want stuff that is so far out there they don't even have a map to tell you where it is ... create unique thoughts, images, dialogue and narrative ... go outside the ordinary. Use a different structure, content, style or voice."** They have recently published poetry by Lyn Lifshin, Dan Nielsen, Richard Kostelanetz, Robert Nagler, Daniel Quinn, John Grey, Kenward Bradley and Anne Detroit. *EIW* is magazine-sized, stapled at the corners, photocopied from typescript on mimeo paper, 50-60 pgs. Press run 500 for 250 subscribers. Subscription: $5. **Sample: $5 check, cash or stamps. Make check payable to Robert W. Howington. Please send SASE for guidelines before submitting. Pays 1 copy. Acquires one-time rights. Reports in 1-3 months.** The editor comments, " 'It's Alive! It's Alive!' describes my magazine. I want the words to walk off of the page and jump onto my readers and show them something they've never seen before in the written word. Create new categories. Be bold. Be real. Be honest. No phonies allowed here!"

‡EXPERIMENTAL BASEMENT PRESS (IV-Form/style), 3740 N. Romero Rd., #A-191, Tucson AZ 85705, phone (602)293-3287, founded 1990, editor C.L. Champion, publishes *Experimental Basement* 3 times/year and 2-4 chapbooks/year as well as "poems written on mediums such as toilet paper, golf balls, matchbook covers—everything really, as long as it's readable." He wants **the oddest and most bizarre stuff possible, visual, conceptual or language poetry** that breaks an egg and expands the beauty of language/poetry. **No mainstream poetry; no rhyme, unless experimenting with it."** He has recently published poetry by John Bennett and Paul Weinman. As a sample here is the first stanza of "Meet Jack" by Pauline Brick, C.L. Champion and Tim O. Pratt:

> bAlD mArK anD
> waIt Lin
> e. acRosS buiLdinG to LefT mEeT mY NeIghBoR.
> JacK.

He says every issue of *Experimental Basement* is printed differently. Press run is 250 for 25 subscribers. Subscription: $8 for 3 issues. **Sample, including guidelines, postpaid: $3. No previously published poems. Always comments on rejections. Reports "same day." Pays 1 copy. For chapbook consideration, query with 5-10 poems.** "If the poet is shy as an umbrella, then there is no need for a bio or letter; however, I enjoy reading the things." **Replies to queries and mss "same day." Pays 10 author's copies.** The editor says, "Write what comes from the gut, what pleases your own self. I like anything experimental. I often enjoy inserting 'insertabus experimentus' into the magazines—poetry printed on weird objects. I also love to review books and chapbooks."

EXPLORATIONS (II), 11120 Glacier Highway, Juneau AK 99801, editor Professor Art Petersen, phone (907)789-4418, founded 1980. The annual literary magazine of the University of Alaska, Southeast. **"The editors respond favorably to 'language really spoken by men and women.' Standard form as well as innovation is encouraged as well as appropriate and fresh aspects of imagery (allusion, metaphor, simile, symbol...)."** The editor selected this sample from "Seven come eleven" by Charles Bukowski:

> I've never ever quite met
> anybody
> like myself—
> living with deadly calm
> inside this hurricane of hell.

It is digest-sized, nicely printed, with front and back cover illustration in one color, saddle-stapled. The editors tend to go for smaller-length poems (with small line breaks for tension) and often print two on a page—mostly lyric free verse with a focus on voice. They offer a $100 prize for poetry and publish the best of the submissions received. **An entry/reading fee is required: $2/ poem (up to 10, 60 lines maximum); those paying reader/contest entry fees of $4 or more will receive a copy of the publication. Submit entries with 3- or 4-line biography January through March. Pay is 2 contributor copies. Submissions are reported on in May, publication is annual, out in May. Mss should be typed with name and address on the back. Photocopies and simultane-**

ous submissions OK. "Replies for unselected manuscripts made only to SASE."

EXPLORER MAGAZINE; EXPLORER PUBLISHING CO. (I, IV-Inspirational, nature, love), P.O. Box 210, Notre Dame IN 46556, phone (219)277-3465, founded 1960, editor and publisher Raymond Flory, a semiannual magazine that contains **short inspirational, nature and love poetry** as well as prose. The editor wants **"poetry of all styles and types; should have an inspirational slant but not necessary. Short poems preferred—up to 16 lines. Good 'family' type poetry always needed. No real long poetry or long lines; no sexually explicit poetry or porno."** He has published poems by Marion Schoeberlein, Edna James Kayser and Carrie Quick. *Explorer* is digest-sized, photocopied from typed copy (some of it not too clear) on thin paper, 31 pgs., cover of the same paper with title superimposed on a water-color painting, folded and saddle-stapled. Circulation is 200, subscription price $6/year. **Sample available for $3, guidelines for SASE. Pay is 1 copy. Subscribers vote for the poems or stories they like best and prizes are awarded; four prizes each issue: $25, $20, $15 and $10; first-prize winner in each issue receives a plaque along with the cash prize. Writers should submit 3-4 poems, typed or photocopied; dot-matrix OK. Material must be previously unpublished; no simultaneous submissions. Reporting time is 1 week and time to publication 1-2 years.** Explorer Publishing Company does not presently publish books except for an anthology about every 4 years; it is a paperback, digest-sized book with an average page count of 20. The editor says, "Over 90% of the poets submitting poetry to *Explorer* have not seen a copy of the magazine. Order a copy first—then submit. This will save poets stamps, frustration, etc. This should hold true for whatever market a writer is aiming for!"

‡EXPRESSIONS FORUM REVIEW (I), 2837 Blue Spruce Lane, Wheaton MD 20906, founded 1991, is a quarterly of poetry, **"any kind, any form, 20 lines maximum. No sex-related matters, no obscenity."** Single copy: $3; subscription: $12. **Previously published poems and simultaneous submissions OK. Submit 1-4 poems with $2 reading fee. Typewritten poems preferred; do not send original copies. Seldom comments on rejections. Send SASE for guidelines. Reports in 1 month. Pays 1 copy.** Reading fee includes entry into spring and fall poetry contests. 1st prize: $100; 2nd: $50; 3rd: $25 (and 25 honorable mentions). The editor says, "Speak from the heart and soul."

EXQUISITE CORPSE (II), P.O. Box 25051, Baton Rouge LA 70894, founded 1983, editor Andrei Codrescu (whom you can often hear in commentary segments of "All Things Considered," The National Public Radio news program). This curious and delightful monthly ($20/year), when you unfold it, is 6″ wide and 16″ long, 20 pgs., saddle-stapled, professionally printed in 2 columns on quality stock. The flavor of Codrescu's comments (and some clues about your prospects in submitting here) may be judged by this note: "A while ago, alarmed by the number of poems aimed at the office—a number only the currency inflation and Big Macs can hold candles to—we issued an edict against them. Still they came, and some even came live. They came in the mail and under the door. We have no poetry insurance. If we are found one day smothered under Xerox paper, who will pay for the burial? The *Corpse* wants a jazz funeral. Rejections make poets happy. Having, in many cases, made their poems out of original, primal, momentary rejections, the rejection of these rejections affirms the beings forced to such deviousness." Has published poems by Carol Bergé, Charles Plymell, Lawrence Ferlinghetti, Alice Notley, and many others. **Payment: "Zilch/Nada." You take your chances inserting work into this wit machine. As of 1990 this is their policy: ". . . we are abolishing the SASE-based privacy system . . . Your submissions will be answered directly in the pages of our publication. Look for your name and for our response to your work in the next *Corpse*. We will continue returning your submissions by SASE if you wish, but as to what we think of your *écriture*, please check 'Body Bag,' our new editorial column. Please rest assured that your work will receive the same malevolently passionate attention as before. Only now we are going to do it in public."**

FABER AND FABER, INC. (V), 50 Cross St., Winchester MA 01890, phone (617)721-1427, editor Betsy Uhrig, has a distinguished list of poetry publications but is accepting **no unsolicited mss.**

FAMILY EARTH (I, IV-Ecology), 129 W. Lincoln Ave., Gettysburg PA 17325, managing editor Denise Weldon-Siviy, founded 1990, is a family-oriented annual focusing on the environment, using poetry that **"must deal in some way with the environment. Shorter poems, 10-30 lines are preferred. Cannot consider material over 40 lines due to page layout. All forms and styles are acceptable. No laments abusive to working mothers. I am still receiving a high percentage of negative—world is awful will end any minute—poetry. Anything with a positive attitude has a good chance."** As a sample here are lines from "Swan Song—USA" by Charlotte Partin:

> Redwood, cypress, maples,
> cotton fields—celebrate me
> from freeway to Main Street.

It is 24 pgs., photocopied, digest-sized with colored paper cover. Press run is 200 for 100 subscriptions, 100 shelf sales. They accept about 25% of 100 submissions received/year. Subscription:

$3/year. **Sample: $2 postpaid. Pays $1-3/poem plus 1 copy. Buys one-time rights. Send SASE for guidelines. Reports in 2 weeks. Editor always comments on rejections.** Reviews books of poetry if they deal with the environment, conservation, etc.

FARMER'S MARKET; MIDWEST FARMER'S MARKET, INC. (IV-Regional), P.O. Box 1272, Galesburg IL 61402, founded 1981, editors Jean C. Lee, John Hughes, Jim McCurry and Lisa Ress, is a biannual seeking **"to provide a forum for the best of regional poetry and fiction."** They want poems that are **"tightly structured, with concrete imagery, specific to Midwestern themes and values, reflective of the clarity, depth and strength of Midwestern life. Not interested in highly abstract or experimental work, or light verse."** They have recently published poetry by Jared Carter, Jim Elledge, Tony Cosier, Elaine Pankowski, Susan Firer and Christine Swanberg. As a sample, they offer these lines from "Hollyhocks on the Alley" by Joseph Gastiger:

> . . . *These are*
> *your dog-sniffed roses of the dirty poor,*
> *trash bouquets a boy brings to his mother.*
>
> *They bleed a harsh and frowsy, not a lovely*
> *scent, as if you smell the fuel*
> *they burn, a rubbish fire.*

FM is digest-sized, 100-140 pgs., perfect-bound with card cover, handsomely printed with graphics and photos. The poems are almost always accessible . . . clear, crafted lyric free verse. All in all, this is an enjoyable read. Circulation 500 for 150 subscriptions, of which 15 are libraries. **Sample: $4.50 plus $1 postage and handling.** They receive about 1,500 submissions/year, of which they use 50-60, have a 6-month backlog. **Submit up to 10 pages, typed or letter-quality printout, photocopies OK, would rather not have simultaneous submissions. Reports in 6-8 weeks (summer replies take longer). Pays 1 copy. Acquires one-time rights. They comment on rejections, "only if we think the work is good."**

FAT TUESDAY (II), RD2 Box 4220, Manada Gap Rd., Grantville PA 17028, founded 1981, poetry editors F.M. Cotolo, Kristen von Oehrke, B. Lyle Tabor and Lionel Stevroid, is an annual which calls itself **"a Mardi Gras of literary and visual treats featuring many voices, singing, shouting, sighing and shining, expressing the relevant to irreverent.** On Fat Tuesday (the Tuesday before Ash Wednesday, when Lent begins) the editors hold The Fat Tuesday Symposium. In ten years no one has shown up." They want **"prose poems, poems of irreverence, gems from the gut. Usually shorter, hit-the-mark, personal stuff inseparable from the voice of the artist. Form doesn't matter."** Poets they have published include Mark Cramer, Mary Lee Gowland, Chuck Taylor, Patrick Kelly Charles Bukowski, Gerald Locklin and Randy Klutts. As a sample they offer these lines by John Quinnett:

> *It is enough to be alive,*
> *To be here drinking this cheap red wine*
> *While the chili simmers on the stove*
> *& the refrigerator hums deep into the night.*

The digest-sized magazine is typeset (large type, heavy paper), 36-50 pgs., saddle-stapled, card covers, (sometimes magazine-sized, unbound) with cartoons, art and ads. Circulation 200 with 20-25 pgs. of poetry in each issue. **Sample: $5 postpaid.** They receive hundreds of submissions each year, use 3-5%, have a 3-5 month backlog. **No previously published material. "Photocopy, dot-matrix, handwritten OK; we'll read anything." Reads submissions August 1 through November 22. Reports in 1-2 weeks. Pays 1 copy. Rights revert to author after publication.** The editors say, "Our tip for authors is simply to be themselves. Poets should use their own voice to be heard. Publishing poetry is as lonely as writing it. We have no idea about current trends, and care less. We encourage all to buy a sample issue to see what they have which best fits our style and format, and also to help support the continuation of our publication. We rely on no other means but sales to subsidize our magazine, and writers should be sensitive to this hard fact which burdens many small presses."

FEELINGS: AMERICA'S BEAUTIFUL POETRY MAGAZINE; ANDERIE POETRY PRESS; QUARTERLY EDITOR'S CHOICE AWARDS (I, II), P.O. Box 390, Whitehall PA 18052, founded 1989, editors Carl and Carole Heffley, a quarterly magazine, uses **"high-quality (free, blank or rhymed), understandable poems on any aspect of life, no more than 20 lines, no pornography. Likes traditional as well as hardbiting prose and poetry."** They have recently published poetry by Peter Layton, T. Kilgore Splake, Bettye K.Wray, Michelle Beers and Katherine VonAhnen. As a sample here are the opening lines from coeditor Carl Heffley's "It Would Have Been Great":

> *Sometimes I think about how great*
> *it would have been to live in Paris back*
> *when it really was The City Of Lights,*

> *and Hemingway could be found sitting*
> *in an out of the way little bistro,*
> *writing his tight little stories.*
> *How wonderful it would have been*
> *to stroll down the rue di Lodeon,*
> *stop in Sylvia Beach's Shakespeare and*
> > *Company*
>
> *book store for a chat and a capachino . . . .*

Feelings is magazine-sized, saddle-stapled with heavy paper cover, professionally printed on lightweight paper, using "photography appropriate to the season or subject." Subscription: $20. **Sample postpaid: $5.50. Send SASE for guidelines. Reports in 6 weeks. Pays $10 for 3 Editor's Choice Awards in each issue. Acquires first rights.** Also runs several contests throughout the year with prizes ranging from $10 to $50. **"We publish chapbooks, info/price list upon request with SASE."** Mss on "how-to" write, publish poetry welcome. Payment for articles varies.

FEH! A JOURNAL OF ODIOUS POETRY (IV-Themes, humor), P.O. Box 5806, Station B, Montreal, Quebec H3B 4T1 Canada, founded 1986, editors Simeon Stylites and Morgana Malatesta, appears 3 times a year, using **"silliness and nonsense, but *good* silliness and nonsense; nasty stuff, but *good* nasty stuff; insanity; truth."** They have recently published poetry by Morticia and Andrew Savage. As a sample the editor selected these lines by Ferdinand Giaclepousse:

> *I believe in God and Bigfoot*
> *and the right to worship as I please.*
> *I've seen angels, demons and the Virgin Mama*
> *in the midst of my D.T.'s*

It is 24 pgs., $7 \times 8\frac{1}{2}$ with photocopied paper cover. Their press run is 200 with about 40 subscriptions, and sales through bookstores. **Sample: $1.50 postpaid. Guidelines available for SASE. Pays 2 copies. Acquires one-time rights. Considers simultaneous submissions and previously published poems. Reports within 6 weeks. Editors sometime comment on rejections, if asked.** Simeon Stylites says "The purpose and function of *Feh!* is, simply, to pour out clouds of righteous fire onto the sense-fleeing writers of poems that no one can understand. We see the high places that are given to fools, enunchs and 'academic' poets, and the chalice-cup of Sense overflows with tears! We hear the lamentations of the ten thousand cacographer-martyrs, and their cry that a grand Rectification is due! And we're trying to help bring it about."

FELLOWSHIP IN PRAYER (IV-Religious), 291 Witherspoon St., Princeton NJ 08542, phone (609)924-6863, founded 1950, editor M. Ford-Grabowsky, is an interfaith bimonthly **"concerned with prayer, meditation and spiritual life"** using poetry **"pertaining to spirituality; brief."** It is digest-sized, professionally printed, 48 pgs., saddle-stapled with glossy card cover. Press run: 20,000. They accept about 2% of submissions received. Subscription: $16. **Sample postpaid: free. Pays 5 copies. Double-spaced submissions. Simultaneous submissions and "sometimes" previously published poems OK. Reports in 1 month.** Reviews books of poetry in 75 words, single format.

FEMINIST STUDIES (IV-Women), %Women's Studies Program, College Park MD 20742, founded 1969, poetry editor Alicia Ostriker, **"welcomes a variety of work that focuses on women's experience, on gender as a category of analysis, and that furthers feminist theory and consciousness."** They have published poetry by Janice Mirikitani, Paula Gunn Allen, Cherrie Moraga, Audre Lorde, Judith Small, Milana Marsenich, Lynda Schraufnagel, Valerie Fox, Diane Glancy. The elegantly-printed, flat-spined, 360+ pgs., paperback appears 3 times a year in an edition of 7,000, goes to 8,000 subscribers, of which 1,500 are libraries. There are **4-10 pgs. of poetry in each issue. Sample: $10 postpaid. Manuscripts are reviewed twice a year, in May and December. Deadlines are May 1 and December 1. Authors will receive notice of the board's decision by June 30 and January 30. No pay.**

FENNEL STALK (II), 2448 W. Freeway Lane, Phoenix AZ 85021, phone (602)995-5338, FAX (602)864-9351, founded 1986, poetry editors Karen Bowden, Peter Bailey, Ron Dickson, Douglas May and August Shaefer. **"All forms, lengths, subject matter and styles except inspirational or sing-song rhyme or poems straining to be traditional. We select based on our response measured in spine tingles, shivers, skin temperature and neuro activity, as much as on how our lives are going when we read your work. Writers should not take rejection too seriously, although taking acceptance too seriously is probably deadlier."** They have recently published poetry by Peter Bakowski, Jared Carter and Clarissa Pinkola Estés. As a sample they selected these lines from "Unique" by Errol Miller:

> *beneath the white-oaks a Greek goddess*
> *takes a bomb from her purse*
> *polishes her fingernails*
> *and shreds cabbages and magnolia blossoms*

Their magazine appears twice a year, digest-sized, typeset (desktop publisher) and printed on quality stock, saddle-stapled, with a b&w card cover using b&w art, photos, graphics. Their press run is 200-300 with 35 subscriptions (3 libraries). Subscription: $10. **Sample postpaid: $4. Make checks payable to Ron Dickson. Please put name and address on each page. Reports in 2-4 months. Pays contributor's copy. Editors sometimes comment on rejections "if asked." Send SASE for information.** Reviews books of poetry "sometimes."

THE FIDDLEHEAD (II, IV-Regional, students), Campus House, University of New Brunswick, Box 4400, Fredericton, New Brunswick E3B 5A3 Canada, founded 1945, poetry editors Robert Gibbs, Robert Hawkes and Don MacKay. From its beginning in 1945 as a local little magazine **devoted mainly to student writers, the magazine retains an interest in poets of the Atlantic region and in young poets** but prints poetry from everywhere. It is **open to good work of every kind, looking always for vitality, freshness and surprise.** Among the poets whose work they have published are Joe Blades, Cory Brown, rienzi crusz and Daniel Sundahl. As a sample, the editor chose a stanza by Karen Connelly:

> We are not in the forest
> and there are no guns under the bed now,
> no wolf-threats, no axe-bladed animal nights.
> This is the gleaming city
> where the gravel is thing and false
> and salty over ice.

The Fiddlehead is a handsomely printed, 6×9 flat-spined paperback (140+ pgs.) with b&w graphics, colored cover, usually paintings by New Brunswick artists. Circulation is 1,000. Subscription price is $18/year (US). **Sample available for $6 (US). Pay is $10-12/printed page. They use less than 10% of submissions. Reporting time 2-6 months, backlog 6-18 months.** Reviews books by Canadian authors only.

FIELD; FIELD TRANSLATION SERIES (II, IV-Translations), Rice Hall, Oberlin College, Oberlin OH 44074, phone (216)775-8408, founded 1969, editors Stuart Friebert and David Young, is a literary journal appearing twice a year with "emphasis on poetry, translations and essays by poets." They want the **"best possible" poetry.** They have recently published poetry by Thylias Moss, Seamus Heaney, Charles Simic and Sharon Olds. The handsomely printed digest-sized journal is flat-spined, has 100 pgs., rag stock with glossy card color cover, circulation 2,500. Subscription: $12 a year, $20 for 2 years. **Sample: $6 postpaid. Pays $20-40/page plus 2 copies. Reports in 2 weeks, has a 3-6 month backlog.** They also publish books of translations in the Field Translation Series, averaging 150 pgs., flat-spined and hardcover editions. **Query regarding translations. Pays 10-15% royalties with $400 advance and 10 author's copies.** Write for catalog to buy samples.

‡FIGHTING WOMAN NEWS (IV-Themes), 6741 Tung Ave., W., Theodore AL 36582, founded 1975, poetry editor Debra Pettis, provides "a communications medium for **women in martial arts, self-defense, combative sports.**" They want **poetry "relevant to our subject matter and nothing else."** They have recently published poetry by Dana Ridgeway. As a sample the editor selected these lines from "Practice" by Cathy Drinkwater Better:

> become
> the moment
> concentrate
> be one
> with the impact
> timing
> is all

Fighting Woman News appears quarterly in a magazine-sized, saddle-stapled format, 24 pgs. or more, finely printed, with graphics and b&w photos, circulation 3,500. **Sample postpaid: $3.50, "and if you say you're a poet, we'll be sure to send a sample with poetry in it."** Uses only 1 or 2 poems in each issue. **"If your poem *really* requires an audience of martial artists to be appreciated, then send it." Simultaneous submissions, photocopy OK. Replies "ASAP." Pays copies. Acquires one-time rights.** "Because our field is so specialized, most interested women subscribe. It is not a requirement for publication, but **we seldom publish a nonsubscriber.**" The editor advises, "Read first; write later. To guarantee publication of your poem(s), submit a hard-core martial arts nonfiction article. Those are what we really need! Fighters who are also writers can have **priority access to our very limited poetry space by doing articles.** Please do not send any poems if you have not read any issues of *FWN*."

FIGMENT: TALES FROM THE IMAGINATION (IV-Science fiction/fantasy, form), P.O. Box 3128, Moscow ID 83843-0477, founded 1989, editors Barb and J.C. Hendee, *Figment* is a quarterly using **sci-fi and fantasy poems. Send SASE for guidelines.** They have published poetry by Steve Sneyd, Thomas

Close-up

Minnie Bruce Pratt
Poet

© 1990 JEB (Joan E. Biren)

One night before I left I sat halfway down,
halfway up the stairs, as he reeled at the bottom,
shouting Choose, choose. Man or woman, her or him,
me or the children. There was no place to be
simultaneous, or between. Above, the boys slept
with nightlights as tiny consolations in the dark,
like the flowers of starry campion, edge of the water.

"If you're from a so-called minority culture — and so-called I emphasize — that means you're going to come into your life as a poet in a very different way," says Minnie Bruce Pratt. "Certainly that's been true for me.

"I was of the generation of women that married the men who were doing the things we really wanted to do, and I married a poet," she says. "So I didn't really start writing poetry until I began to leave that marriage. It was at a time that I was becoming involved in women's liberation, and also I was beginning to live as a lesbian.

"It wasn't the falling in love so much as the fact of my really coming back to myself and coming back to my body also. It's really impossible to be a poet if you aren't living in your own body, if you're alienated from your sensual self," Pratt adds.

The lines above are from "No Place," one of the poems in her second full-length collection, **Crime Against Nature** (Firebrand Books, 1990), which is about being a lesbian and being a mother. The book was not only honored as the 1989 Lamont Poetry Selection by the Academy of American Poets, but it was also nominated for the Pulitzer Prize.

Pratt is quick to credit the social change communities of women's liberation, gay and lesbian liberation and the civil rights movement. "I feel like they gave me a life," she says. "My being able to write poetry really came out of a cultural context where women were saying to each other 'We have stories to tell. We have things to say that nobody has heard and we haven't had the courage to tell. And we have things to say that people have wanted us not to talk about.' "

For Pratt, courage grew out of working with a group of other women on *Feminary*, a literary journal based out of Durham, North Carolina. "It was a lesbian collective, and all the women were artists or writers. We showed each other work, commented on work, did writing sessions together and really taught each other how to be writers in a way that we had no role models for," she says, noting that in her entire undergraduate and graduate education she only read one woman poet (Emily Dickinson).

Being part of a women's community also gave Pratt the confidence to do readings. "I really recommend, from my own experience, doing readings — before you've published — because you learn a lot from people in how they respond to your work. You learn what interests them, what they remember, what moves them. It tells you something about how effective your images are being, and it keeps you within the ancient tradition of poetry, which was an oral medium.

"I would go to women's studies conferences, mostly, and lesbian conferences, and if they had an open mike or some kind of reading series, I would sign up and read," she says.

"I was able to do this because I was getting affirmation from my writing peers that I had something worth reading. It was part of having a home group to fall back on."

Pratt points out, however, that young poets from various subcultures should choose workshops, conferences and writing classes carefully. One's writing can suffer tremendously when people do not understand the content, the language and/or the tradition you're writing out of, she says. "The criticism can be destructively hard and unhelpful."

Involvement in the collective also helped Pratt produce **The Sound of One Fork**, a chapbook she carried to conferences and sold after readings. "I loved doing my own chapbook," she says, adding that she didn't have a full-length collection and didn't want to wait to have her work published.

"I wasn't doing the work within a literary circuit. I was doing it very much within my women's community, and one of the things we were doing was learning how to do everything ourselves," says Pratt. "I bartered with someone to do the printing for me, but all the other work, except the typesetting and artwork, I did myself. I laid it out, pasted it up, burned the plates for the printer, hand collated it, stapled it, trimmed it and distributed it."

There was a gap, however, between the chapbook and Pratt's first full-length collection, **We Say We Love Each Other** (first published by Spinsters Book Company in 1985 and reprinted by Firebrand Books in 1992). "I think it was directly related to how I thought of myself as a writer," she says. "The chapbook I did in the context of the journal collective. Then I moved and left the collective, and I think that made it more difficult for me to do my second book. I was more on my own as a writer than I had been, and I lost some of my confidence."

As a result of her experience, Pratt encourages each poet to build a community base. "To have one or two people or a group in your life on a pretty regular basis to just provide a reality, the reality of taking your work seriously, is something that's very important," she says, adding that the people involved need not necessarily be other poets.

Surprisingly, few of the poems in Pratt's second book were published previously. "When people say you have to have your work published in periodicals before it can come out as a book, that is an argument for people who publish acceptably mainstream material where there are many periodicals available to them," she says. "There are many different communities, African-American, Asian-American, Latino, lesbian and gay, and we have our own ways of doing things. We're not necessarily going to follow this particular pattern.

"I think that something that is very, very hopeful in this country right now for a young poet is that the monolithic presentation of poetry that I was given, the Anglo-European male tradition, is cracking and crumbling and in between the cracks are sprouting wonderful and amazing poets from all kinds of traditions," Pratt says. "There are poems being written about experiences people have had for thousands of years that nobody has ever written about in poetry until now. **Crime Against Nature** is a whole book about something that people couldn't even talk about until a few years ago."

She adds, "My encouragement to young poets is be true to your own life and your own experience in your poetry and the lives you have seen around you. Write about the things you know that nobody else knows. And build support for that work in your community."

— Christine Martin

A. Easton and John Grey. As a sample, here are lines from "Advice from an Old Hand, to a Young Man Shipping Out" by Lori Ann White:

> *Poor boy. I hear you weep for Mother Earth.*
> *Tell me, does your mother love you well?*
> *Does she cradle you on acid clouds? Swaddle you in muck?*
> *You should mourn a woman, not a heartless shell.*
> *Why praise a hunk of rock for giving birth?*

Figment is digest-sized, 60 pgs., saddle-stapled, printed in Palantino 8.5-9.0, with glossy bond cover. Press run 500 for 200+ subscribers, 50-100 shelf sales. Subscription: $14.50. **Sample postpaid: $4. Pays $2-10 plus 1 copy. Buys first North American serial rights. Rights revert on publication. Reports in 2 months.** "We expect our genre poetry to be written for 'readers,' not other poets."

THE FIGURES (V), 5 Castle Hill Ave., Great Barrington MA 01230-1552, phone (413)528-2552, founded 1975, publisher/editor Geoffrey Young, is a small press publishing poetry and fiction. They have recently published poetry by Lyn Hejinian, Clark Coolidge, Ron Padgett and Christopher Dewdney. **They pay 10% of press run. However, they currently accept no unsolicited poetry.**

FINE MADNESS (II), P.O. Box 31138, Seattle WA 98103-1138, founded 1982, president Louis Bergsagel. *Fine Madness* is a twice-yearly magazine. **They want "contemporary poetry of any form and subject. We look for highest quality of thought, language and imagery. We look for the mark of the individual: unique ideas and presentation; careful, humorous, sympathetic. No careless poetry, sexist poetry, greeting-card poetry, poetry that 10,000 other people could have written."** No previously published poems or simultaneous submissions. They have published poetry by Tess Gallagher, David Young and David Ignatow. *Fine Madness* is digest-sized, 64 pgs., perfect-bound, flat-spined, offset printing, 2-3 color card cover. Their press run is 800 for 100 subscriptions of which 10 are libraries. They accept about 40 of 1,000 poems received. Subscription: **$9. Sample postpaid: $4. Guidelines available for SASE. Pays 1 copy plus subscription. Submit 3-10 poems, preferably originals, not photocopy, 1 poem/ page. Reports in 2-3 months.** They give 2 annual awards to editors' choice of $50 each. Coeditor Sean Bentley says, "If you don't read poetry, don't send us any."

‡FIREBRAND BOOKS (IV-Feminist, lesbian, ethnic), 141 The Commons, Ithaca NY 14850, phone (607)272-0000, founded 1984, editor and publisher Nancy K. Bereano, "is a **feminist and lesbian** publishing company committed to producing quality work in multiple genres by ethnically diverse women." They publish both quality trade paperbacks and hardbacks. **Simultaneous submissions acceptable with notification. Replies to queries within 2 weeks, to mss within one month. Pays royalties.** As a sample, here is a stanza of a sestina, "great expectations," from the book **Living As A Lesbian** by Cheryl Clarke:

> *dreaming the encounter intense as engines*
> *first me then you oh what a night*
> *of rapture and risk and dolphin*
> *acrobatics after years of intend-*
> *ing to find my lesbian sources in the window*
> *of longing wide open in me*

The book is 94 pgs., flat-spined, elegantly printed on heavy stock with a glossy color card cover, a photo of the author on the back, $7.95. Send for catalog to buy samples.

‡FIREWEED: A FEMINIST QUARTERLY (IV-Women), P.O. Box 279, Station B, Toronto, Ontario M5T 2W2 Canada, phone (416)323-9512, founded 1978, edited by the Fireweed Collective, is a feminist arts and political journal that **"especially welcomes contributions by women of color, working-class women, native women, lesbians and women with disabilities."** As a sample we selected the opening lines of "These Military Men" by Joy Hewitt Mann:

> *My husband was*
> *a military man.*
> *Dinner*
> *5:30*
> *sharp.*
> *No give.   No take.*

It is digest-sized, 100-120 pgs., flat-spined, with 3- or 4-color cover. Press run: 2,000. Subscription: $14 in Canada, $17 in US. **Sample postpaid: $4 in Canada, $5 in US. Pays $20/contributor/issue plus 2 copies. Simultaneous submissions OK. Editor comments on submissions "occasionally."**

‡FIREWEED: POETRY OF WESTERN OREGON (IV-Regional), 1330 E. 25th Ave., Eugene OR 97403, founded 1989, is a quarterly publishing the work of **poets living in Western Oregon or having close connections to the region. However, poems need not be regional in subject; any theme, subject, length**

or form is acceptable. They have recently published poetry by Vern Rutsala, Barbara Drake, Lisa Steinmann and Lex Runciman. As a sample the editors selected these lines from "Fault" by Barbara La Morticella:

> *Quick hold me;*
> *for once, let me hold you.*
>
> *Our children's suitcases are packed,*
> *and even the hills move in waves.*

Fireweed is 44 pgs., digest-sized, laser printed and saddle-stapled with card cover. "We receive several hundred poems and publish about ¼ or ⅓ of them." Press run is 200 for 125 subscribers of which 10 are libraries, 25 shelf sales. Subscription: $10. **Sample postpaid: $2.50. No previously published poems; simultaneous submissions OK. Cover letter with brief bio required. Often comments on rejections.** They do not publish guidelines for poets but will answer inquiries with SASE. **Reports in 2-4 months. Pays 1 copy. Acquires first North American serial rights.** Reviews books of poetry by Oregon poets in 500-750 words, single format. They add, "We occasionally have special issues organized by theme, compiled by a guest editor or focused on newcomers to *Fireweed*. Support your local magazines by sending work and buying subscriptions! Submit to the smaller little publications *first!*"

FIRST HAND (IV-Gay, subscribers), Box 1314, Teaneck NJ 07666, phone (201)836-9177, founded 1980, poetry editor Bob Harris, is a **"gay erotic publication written mostly by its readers."** The digest-sized monthly has a circulation of 70,000 with 3,000 subscribers of which 3 are libraries, and uses 1-2 pgs. of poetry in each issue, for which they **pay $25/poem.** They have published poems by Michael Swift and Robert Patrick. The editor selected these sample lines from "To a Model" by Karl Tierney:

> *I assure you, I mean no*
> *disrespect when I discover,*
> *beyond sex and half asleep,*
> *you deflate to only half the monster*
> *and will be that much easier*
> *to battle out the door at dawn.*

Submit poems no longer than 1 typed page. No queries. Reports in 6 weeks. Editor Bob Harris sometimes comments on rejected mss. They have an 18-month backlog. The editor advises, "Make sure what you're writing about is obvious to future readers. **Poems need not be explicitly sexual, but must deal overtly with gay situations and subject matter.**" Reviews books of poetry.

‡FIRST TIME; NATIONAL HASTINGS POETRY COMPETITION (I, II), Burdett Cottage, 4 Burdett Place, George Street, Old Town, Hastings, East Sussex TN34 3ED England, phone 0424-428855, founded 1981, editor Josephine Austin, who says the magazine is **open to "all kinds of poetry—our magazine goes right across the board—which is why it is one of the most popular in Great Britain."** The magazine appears twice a year. The following lines are from "Why a Poet?" by R.M. Griffiths:

> *Of all types of people*
> *and all their differences in depth,*
> *the poet is the deepest,*
> *Or is it just the most vacuous?*

The digest-sized magazine, 24 pgs. saddle-stapled, contains several poems on each page, in a variety of small type styles, on lightweight stock, b&w photographs of editor and 1 author, glossy one-color card cover. **Sample: 50p. plus postage. "Please send dollars." Pay is 1 copy. Poems submitted must not exceed 30 lines, must not have been published elsewhere, and must have name and address of poet on each. Maximum time to publication is 2 months. Poets should send 10 sample poems.** The annual National Hastings Poetry Competition for poets 18 and older offers awards of £100, 50, and 25, £1/poem entry fee. The editor advises, "Keep on 'pushing your poetry.' If one editor rejects you then study the market and decide which is the correct one for you. Try to type your own manuscripts as longhand is difficult to read and doesn't give a professional impression. Always date your poetry — ©1993 and sign it. Follow your way of writing, don't be a pale imitation of someone else—sooner or later styles change and you will either catch up or be ahead."

FISHDRUM (II, IV-Regional, religious), 626 Kathryn Ave., Santa Fe NM 87501, founded 1988, editor Robert Winson, is a literary magazine appearing 2-4 times a year. **"I love West Coast poetry, the exuberant, talky, often elliptical and abstract 'continuous nerve movie' that follows the working of the mind and has a relationship to the world and the reader. Philip Whalen's work, for example, and much of Calafia, The California Poetry, edited by Ishmael Reed. Also magical-tribal-incantatory poems, exemplified by the future/primitive Technicians of the Sacred, ed. Rothenberg. FishDrum has a soft spot for schmoozy, emotional, imagistic stuff. Literate, personal material that sings and surprises,**

OK?" They have published poetry by Philip Whalen, Joy Harjo, Arthur Sze, Nathaniel Tarn, Alice Notley, John Brandi, Steve Richmond, Jessica Hagedorn, Leo Romero and Leslie Scalapino. As a sample the editor selected these lines from "Advice to the Unborn Baby" by Miriam Sagan:

> *Angel, I felt you greedy at my neck*
> *Months before you were conceived*
> *You said I'm back, open the door*
> *I'm UPS with a package especially for you.*

FD is digest-sized, 40 pgs., saddle-stapled, professionally printed, with glossy card cover. "Of 300 or so unsolicited submissions last year, accepted fewer than twenty." Press run 500 for 100 subscriptions of which 10 are libraries, 400 shelf sales. Subscription: $10 for 4 issues. **Sample postpaid: $3. Pays 2 or more copies. Acquires first serial rights. Contributors may purchase advance copies at $1.50 each in addition to contributor's copies. Reports quickly. "We're looking for New Mexico authors, also prose: fiction, essays, what-have-you, and artwork, scores, cartoons, etc. — just send it along. We are also interested in poetry, prose and translations concerning the practice of Zen. We publish chapbooks, but solicit these from our authors."** Reviews books of poetry. Reviews books or chapbooks of poetry in long essays and/or capsule reviews.

FLEETING MONOLITH ENTERPRISES (II); VERTICAL IMAGES (IV-Regional), 62 Langdon Park Rd., London N6 5QG England, phone (081)340-5807, founded 1986, editor Mike Diss. Fleeting Monolith publishes about 3 chapbooks/year. *Vertical Images* is an annual using primarily poets connected with the Vertical Images poetry group: "All those submitting work are given equal representation in the magazine, which grows largely out of consistent workshop practice every 2 weeks. We suggest moving to London, joining the group and taking it from there." For their chapbooks, Fleeting Monolith wants **"inspired/delirious/challenging/manic work—who cares about form! Nothing dead/academic/po-faced/sensitive stuff."** They have published poetry by Slaughter District, Chris Brown, Jondi Keane and the editor, who chose the following complete poem (poet unidentified) as a sample:

> *nurses cheer the birth of a 3 oz. child*
> *crushing 67 aphids*

Their chapbooks are in a variety of formats and **payment depends "entirely on the format and scope of each work." All rights remain with author. Sample postpaid: £2.** "Series of free poetry broadsheets available on request — IRC preferred." The editor says, "*L'art, c'est un connerie*-. Artaud said that, but we wish we had. Poetry can be a garden shed: Michaux said that (who cares about form! count this, count that!) and he wasn't English either — in fact, not many poets are, now that Keats and Lewis Carroll are dead. Buster Keaton was a poet and Jean Tinguely is a poet. At Fleeting Monolith, only a small part of the living process of poetry gets crystallized into books. Write us a letter, send us something, join the network of creative discontent."

FLIPSIDE (II), Dixon Hall, California University of Pennsylvania, California PA 15419, founded 1987, poetry editor L.A. Smith, is a literary tabloid appearing twice a year **using poetry. "Sentimentality is forbidden."** They have published poetry by Charles Bukowski and Arthur Winfield Knight. As a sample the editor selected the poem "Mother Lover" by Michael Bagamery:

> *Make-up on that face*
> *Like rubble.*
> *Ivy won't run up a building*
> *Unless it stands.*

The tabloid is 64 pgs., professionally printed. Press run 5,000, distributed free to the public, libraries, writing schools, colleges, advertisers, poets, etc. They accept less than 5% of hundreds of poems submitted. **Sample postpaid: $2. Send SASE for guidelines. Reports in 2 months. Pays as many copies as you want.**

THE FLORIDA REVIEW (II), Dept. of English, University of Central Florida, Orlando FL 32816, phone (407)823-2038, founded 1972, editor Russ Kesler, is a "literary biannual with emphasis on short fiction and poetry." They want **"poems filled with real things, real people and emotions, poems that might conceivably advance our knowledge of the human heart."** They have published poetry by Knute Skinner, Elton Glaser and Walter McDonald. It is 128 pgs., flat-spined, professionally printed, with glossy card cover. Press run 1,000 for 400 subscriptions of which 50 are libraries. Shelf sales: 50. **Sample postpaid: $4.50. Send SASE for guidelines. Pays 3 copies, small honorarium occasionally available. Acquires all rights. Returns them "upon publication, when requested." Submit no more than 6 poems. Simultaneous submissions OK. Reports in 1-3 months. Editor comments on submissions "occasionally."** Reviews books of poetry in 1,500 words, single format; 2,500-3,000 words, multi-book.

FLUME PRESS (II), 4 Casita, Chico CA 95926, phone (916)342-1583, founded 1984, poetry editors Casey Huff and Elizabeth Renfro, publishes poetry chapbooks. **"We have few biases about form, although we appreciate control and crafting, and we tend to favor a concise, understated style, with**

emphasis on metaphor rather than editorial commentary." **Considers simultaneous submissions.** They have recently published chapbooks by Tina Barr, Randall Freisinger, Leonard Kress, Carol Gordon, Gayle Kaune and Luis Omar Salinas. As a sample, the editor selected these lines from "Touch Pool" by Pamela Uschuk:

> *Around and around*
> *the holding pool, rays soar*
> *like squadrons of angels, now and then lifting*
> *a wing to test the edge*
> *as if they would swim through the glass to the sea*

Chapbooks are chosen from an annual competition, March 1 through June 30. $6 entry fee. Submit 20-28 pgs., including title, contents, and acknowledgments. Name and address on a separate sheet. "Flume Press editors read and respond to every entry." **Winner receives $100 and 25 copies. Sample: $5 plus $1.50 postage and handling.**

FOLIO: A LITERARY JOURNAL (II), Dept. of Literature, Gray Hall, The American University, Washington DC 20016, phone (202)885-2973, founded 1984, editors change annually, is a biannual. They have recently published poetry by Jean Valentine, Henry Taylor and William Stafford. There are 12-20 poems published in each 64- to 72-page issue. It is 6×9, perfect-bound, neatly printed from typeset. **Sample postpaid: $5. Submit from August to November 1 or January to March 1, up to 6 pgs., include a brief bio/contributor's note, photocopy, dot-matrix OK. Considers simultaneous submissions. Reads submissions September 1 through March 1 only. Pays 2 copies. Acquires first rights. Comments on rejections** "when possible." They also sponsor a contest open to all contributors with a $75 prize for the best poem of the fall and spring issue.

FOOLSCAP (I, II), 78 Friars Road, East Ham, London E6 1LL England, phone 081-470-7680, founded 1987, editor Judi Benson, appears in January/February, May and September. **"We are looking for poetry which surprises as well as informs. We look for confidence and a sense of humor, though veer away from flippancy and trite over-used rhyme. We like our poetry to reflect today's world and the issues that concern us all without laborious political banner waving. In other words, we are looking for craft as much as statement."** They have recently published poetry by Ian Duhig, Frances Wilson and Myra Schneider. As a sample the editor selected a short poem, "Filmclip: Leningrad, October, 1935," by Ken Smith:

> *Dark comes early, and wet snow.*
> *The citizens hurry from work,*
> *scarfed, buttoned, thinking of supper,*
> *the tram clanking and squealing*
> *in whose glass an arm has wiped*
> *a V of lit space wherein smoke,*
> *old and young wrapped for winter,*
> *eyes focussed somewhere ahead,*
> *dreaming perhaps of a sausage,*
> *of bread, coffee, a warm bed,*
> *a bullet in the back of the brain.*
> *Then they're gone. Next comes*
> *the future. It looks like the past.*

The editor describes *Foolscap* as approximately 52 pgs., A4, camera-ready photocopying, with b&w illustrations. "No ads, no reviews, no frills, though we do include short prose pieces and welcome good translations." They accept about 120 of 1,200 poems received per year. Press run is between 160-200 for 100+ subscribers. "Copies also sold at poetry readings, bookshops, libraries and to universities." **Subscription: $16/£6. Pays 1 copy. Submit** "no more than 6/time. Best if overseas not to have to return mss. Allow ample IRCs and 1-2 months for response. Publication could take as long as a year due to backlog of accepted material." The editor says, "We accept a wide range of styles from both unpublished poets as well as well-known poets from all geographical locations. We advise people to get a copy of *Foolscap* before submitting and suggest 'new' poets share their work with others before submitting."

FOOTWORK: THE PATERSON LITERARY REVIEW; HORIZONTES; ALLEN GINSBERG POETRY AWARDS; THE PATERSON POETRY PRIZE; PASSAIC COUNTY COMMUNITY COLLEGE POETRY CENTER LIBRARY (II, IV-Regional, bilingual/foreign language), Passaic County Community College, Cultural Affairs Dept., College Blvd., Paterson NJ 07509. A wide range of activities pertaining to poetry are conducted by the Passaic County Community College Poetry Center, including the annual literary magazine *Footwork*, founded 1979, editor and director Maria Mazziotti Gillan, using **poetry of "high quality" under 100 lines.** They have published poetry by David Ray, Diane Wakoski, William Stafford, Sonia Sanchez, Laura Boss and Marge Piercy. *Footwork: The Paterson Literary Review* is magazine-sized, 160 pgs., saddle-stapled, professionally printed with glossy card 2-color cover, using b&w art and photos, circulation 1,000 with 100 subscriptions of which 50 are libraries. **Sample postpaid: $5. Pays 1 copy. Acquires first rights. Reports in 1 year. Simultaneous submissions OK. Send no more than 5 poems/submission. Reads submissions September through January only.** *Horizontes*, founded in 1983, editor, José Villalongo, is an annual Spanish language literary magazine using **poetry of high quality no longer than 20 lines. Will accept English translations, but Spanish version must be included.** They have published poetry by Nelson Calderon, Jose Kozer and Julio Cesar Mosches. *Horizontes* is magazine-sized, 120 pgs., saddle-stapled, professionally printed with full color matte cover, using b&w graphics and photos, circulation 800 with 100 subscriptions of which 20 are libraries. **Sample postpaid: $4. Reads submissions September through January only. Pays 2 copies. Acquires first rights. Reports in 3-4 months. Accepts simultaneous submissions. "On occasion we do consider published works but prefer unpublished works."** The Poetry Center of the college conducts The Allen Ginsberg Poetry Awards Competition each year. Entry fee $5. Prizes of $150, $25 and $10, deadline March 1. Send SASE for rules. They also publish a **New Jersey Poetry Resources** book, the **PCC Poetry Contest Anthology** and the **New Jersey Poetry Calendar.** The Paterson Poetry Prize of $1,000 is awarded each year (split between poet and publisher) to a book of poems published in the previous year. Publishers should write with SASE for application form to be submitted by Feb. 1. Passaic County Community College Poetry Center Library has an extensive collection of contemporary poetry and seeks small press contributions to help keep it abreast. The Distinguished Poetry Series offers readings by poets of international, national and regional reputation. Poetryworks/USA is a series of programs produced for UA Columbia-Cablevision.

FOR POETS ONLY (I), P.O. Box 4855, Schenectady NY 12304, founded 1985, poetry editor L.M. Walsh, **requires a $3 entry fee for each poem submitted, which may win a $10 prize (at least five promised for each issue). Others accepted are paid for with one copy of the magazine. Acquires one-time rights.** In an issue of 35 pgs. of poems—some with more than one to a page—16 were awarded prizes. They have published poems by J. Bernier, C. Weirich and Alice Mackenzie Swaim. *FPO* is digest-sized, 36 pgs., saddle-stapled, photocopied from typescript with glossy card cover. It appears quarterly. The editor rejects about 10% of poetry received. Press run is 200. Per copy: $3. **Sample postpaid: $3.50. Any subject. No pornography. No comments on rejections.** The editor advises, "For beginning poets: a quote from Horst Bienek in his **The Cell:** 'We are distressed but *not in despair,* distressed but *not destroyed,* persecuted but *not forsaken,* cast down but *not destroyed.*'"

‡FORBIDDEN LINES MAGAZINE (II, IV-Science fiction/fantasy/horror), P.O. Box 23, Chapel Hill NC 27514, founded 1990, is a bimonthly "devoted to publishing science fiction, fantasy and horror fiction and poetry, as well as experimental fiction, interviews and book reviews." They want **"contemporary and traditional poetry, in any form, length or style. Science fiction/fantasy/horror related only, please." They do not want "strained rhymes, clichéd language, first drafts or anything non-genre, no matter how good."** As a sample the editor selected the first lines of "Echo" by Jon Carson:

> He planted the old sound to fall in the rain,
> Amidst the thunder of a nameless age
> That he thought glorious.
> Asleep with a slumber in the deep of the stars.
> The sound had stilled two billion years
> Before awakening to warmer breath.

FL is 62 pgs., magazine-sized, saddle-stapled, newsprint usually photographic art on paper cover. "Amount of poetry we receive varies; we accept 1-4 poems per issue." Press run is 500 for 20 subscribers, 75-85% shelf sales. Subscription: **$14/year. Sample postpaid: $1.95 and 9 × 12 SASE. No previously published poems or simultaneous submissions. "Photocopies and computer print-outs are OK if readable. Mss cannot be returned, so please send a disposable copy."** Seldom **comments on rejections. Reports within 1 month. Pays 1 copy.** The editor says, "We recommend that poets purchase a copy of the magazine before submitting to get a better idea of what we publish. We like poetry that engages the mind *and* the emotions, uses vivid imagery and shows a command of rhythm (not necessarily meter); we tend to print what we like. Beginning poets shouldn't be afraid to submit. We judge all the poetry we receive on its own merits, not on the list of credentials attached."

FOREST BOOKS (III, IV-Translations), 20 Forest View, Chingford, London E4 7AY United Kingdom, phone 081-529-8470, founded 1984, director Brenda Walker, publishes 15-20 paperbacks/year. They have published **Enchanting Beasts: An Anthology of Modern Women Poets in Finland**, a handsomely printed flat-spined book of 126 pgs. **Pays 10% royalties plus 20 copies.** Samples may be purchased through Dufour Editions, P.O. Box 449, Chester Springs PA 19425.

THE FORMALIST (II, IV-Form, translations), 525 S. Rotherwood, Evansville IN 47714, founded 1990, editor William Baer, appears twice a year, **"dedicated to *metrical* poetry written in the great tradition of English-language verse."** They have recently published poetry by Donald Justice, Mona Van Duyn, John Updike, Karl Shapiro, X.J. Kennedy, May Swenson, John Frederick Nims and Donald Hall. As a sample the editor chose the opening stanza from "The Amateurs of Heaven" by Howard Nemerov:

> *Two lovers to a midnight meadow came*
> *High in the hills, to lie there hand in hand*
> *Like effigies and look up at the stars,*
> *The never-setting ones set in the North*
> *To circle the Pole in idiot majesty,*
> *And wonder what was given them to wonder.*

"We are interested in metrical poetry written in the traditional forms, including ballads, sonnets, couplets, the Greek forms, the French forms, etc. We will also consider metrical translations of major formalist non-English poets—from the Ancient Greeks to the present. We are not, however, interested in haiku (or syllabic verse of any kind) or sestinas. Although we do publish poetry which skillfully employs enjambment, we have a marked prejudice against excessive enjambment. Only rarely do we accept a poem over 2 pages, and we have no interest in any type of erotica, blasphemy, vulgarity or racism. Finally, like all editors, we suggest that those wishing to submit to *The Formalist* become thoroughly familiar with the journal beforehand." *The Formalist* considers submissions throughout the year, 3-5 poems at one time. We do *not* consider simultaneous submissions, previously published work, or disk submissions. A brief cover letter is recommended and a SASE is necessary for the return of the mss. Subscription: $12. Sample postpaid: $6.50. Payment 2 copies. Acquires first North American serial rights. Reports within 8 weeks. See also the contest listing the World Order of Narrative and Formalist Poets. Contestants must subscribe to *The Formalist* to enter.

FOX CRY (I), University of Wisconsin Fox Valley, Midway Road, Menasha WI 54952, phone (414)832-2600, founded 1973, editor Professor Don Hrubesky, is a literary annual using **poems up to 50 lines long, deadline February 1.** They have published poetry by Shirley Anders, David Graham, Clifford Wood, Laurel Mills and Don Hrubesky. As a sample, the editor selected these lines (poet unidentified):

> *She was out there with the leaves*
> *the old woman bent but broad of back*
> *In long even pulls, she collected*
> *the detritus of the sun's decline.*

Their press run is 400. **Sample postpaid: $5. Send SASE for guidelines. Submit mss from September 1 through February 1. Submit maximum of 3 poems. They will consider simultaneous submissions. Pays 1 copy.**

FRANK: AN INTERNATIONAL JOURNAL OF CONTEMPORARY WRITING AND ART (II, IV-Form, translations), Frank Brooks, B.P. 29, 94301 Vincennes Cedex France, founded 1983, editor, David Applefield. *Frank* is a literary semiannual that "encourages work of seriousness and high quality which falls often between existing genres. Looks favorably at true internationalism and stands firm against ethnocentric values. Likes translations. Publishes foreign dossier in each issue. Very eclectic." There are no subject specifications, but the magazine "discourages sentimentalism and easy, false surrealism. Although we're in Paris, most Paris-poems are too thin for us. Length is open." They have published poetry by Rita Dove, Derek Walcott, Duo Duo, Raymond Carver, Tomas Tranströmer, James Laughlin, Breytenbach, Michaux, Gennadi Aigi, W.S. Merwin, Edmond Jabes, John Berger, and many lesser known poets. The journal is digest-sized, flat-spined 224 pgs., offset in b&w with color cover and photos, drawings and ads. Circulation is 4,000, of which 2,000 are bookstore sales and subscriptions. Subscription $30 (individuals), $60 (institutional) for 4 issues. Sample: $8 postpaid airmail from Paris. Pay is $5/printed page and 2 copies. Guidelines available for SASE. Poems must be previously unpublished. Submissions are reported on in 3 months, publication is in 1-4 months. "Send only what you feel is fresh, original, and provocative in either theme or form. Work of craft that also has political and social impact is encouraged." The editor often provides some criticism on rejected mss. Editor organizes readings in US and Europe for *Frank* contributors.

FREDRICKSON-KLOEPFEL PUBLISHING CO. (F-K BOOKS) (I, IV-Themes), 7748 17th SW, Seattle WA 98106, phone (206)767-4915, "established 1983 as an outlet for J. Fred Blair's poetry and pamphlets, went public 1990," editor John F. Blair, publishes **anthologies on specific themes.** He "tries to publish at least one selection from each contributor; 1,000 words max, likes strong viewpoint, vibrant poetics, earthy style. A collection of poems and short prose on one subject from a myriad of sources establishes a panoramic discourse or Antho-logue. Wants mss from male and female poets on maleness for 'Hold the Macho.' Also wants positive items about the work-a-day life for 'Our Daily Bread.' Have a glut of negative things (are poets afraid of work?) already and nothing for counterpoint. Ergo: No dialogue." He has recently published poetry by Ralph La Charity, Judith Skillman, John Grey and Jeffrey Zable. As a sample the editor selected these lines from "Beyond Games" by Joanne Seltzer:

> You tell me to be grateful
> for the things I do have.
> Two eyes. Twenty eight teeth.
> What about my losses?
> Hope. Unanswered Valentines.
> Snowflakes that melt in my hand.

Reports in 3 months. "After book is completed, contributors may purchase copies at print cost for promotion in their locales. They should make a small profit wholesaling them and get full mark-up on the ones they retail. Any profit I make will be shared across the board with contributors."

FREE FOCUS (I, IV-Women/feminist); OSTENTATIOUS MIND (I, IV-Form/style), 224 82nd St., Brooklyn NY 11209, *Free Focus* founded 1985, *Ostentatious Mind* founded 1987, poetry editor Patricia D. Coscia. *Free Focus* "is a literary magazine only for creatiave women, who reflect their ideas of love, nature, beauty and men and also express the pain, sorrow, joy andenchantment that their lives generate. *Free Focus* needs poems of all types on the subject matters above. Nothing x-rated, please. The poems can be as short as 2 lines or as long as 2 pages. The objective of this magazine is to give women poets a chance to be fullfilled in the art of poetry, for freedom of expression for women is seldom described in society." They have recently published poetry by Helen Tzagoloff, Elizabeth Hahn Ph.D., Patricia A. Pierkowski, D.R. Middleton, Crystal Beckner, Elaine F. Powell, Kris Anderson, Carol L. Clark and Mary Anderson. As a sample the editor selected these lines from "A Woman I Once Knew" by Maura Schroeder:

> She sleeps in the desert alone,
> Carving ancestral bone,
> from waking mountains.
> She sleeps in the desert alone,
> Wading in salt-soaked rivers,
> with wounds unfolded.

Ostentatious Mind "is a co-ed literary magazine for material of stream of consciousness and experimental poems. The poets deal with the political, social and psychological." They have recently published poetry by Paul Weinman, Rod Farmer, L. Mason, Dr. John J. Soldo, Carl A. Winderl, James W. Penha, Max M. Katze and Joe Lackey. As a sample the editor selected this poem, "Poetic Wax," by Sheryl L. Nelms:

> comes in 1.5 liter
>
> bottles
>
> at Majestic
> Liquors

Both magazines are printed on 8×14 paper, folded in the middle and stapled to make a 10-page (including cover) format, with simple b&w drawings on the cover and inside. The two magazines appear every 6-8 months. Sample of either is $3.50 postpaid. Send SASE for guidelines. Pays 1-2 copies. Poems should be typed neatly and clearly on white typing paper. Submit only 3 poems at one time. Simultaneous submissions and previously published poems OK. Reports "as soon as possible." The editor says, "I think that anyone can write a poem who can freely express intense feelings about their experiences. A dominant thought should be ruled and expressed in writing, not by the spoken word, but the written word."

FREE LUNCH (II), P.O. Box 7647, Laguna Niguel CA 92607-7647, founded 1988, editor Ron Offen, is a "poetry journal interested in publishing whole spectrum of what is currently being produced by American poets. Also features a 'Mentor Series,' in which an established poet introduces a new, unpublished poet. Mentors have included Maxine Kumin, James Dickey and Lucille Clifton. Always try to comment on submissions. Especially interested in experimental work and work by unestablished poets. Hope to provide all serious American poets with free subscription. For details on free subscription send SASE. Prefer no more than 3 poems per submission. No restriction on form, length, subject matter, style, purpose. Don't want cutsie, syrupy, sentimental, preachy religious or aggressively 'uplifting' verse. No aversion to form, rhyme." Poets recently published include Neal Bowers, Billy Collins, Kendra Kopelke, Paul Violi, Paul Zavatsky and Leila Zeiger. As a sample we selected these lines from "The Domestication of Language" by Joe Irwin:

> the open mouth kiss
> not language

is the reason the jaw is hinged

FL is published 3 times a year. It is 32-40 pgs., saddle-stapled, digest-sized, attractively printed and designed, featuring free verse that shows attention to craft with well-knowns and newcomers alongside each other. Press run is 1,000 with 75 subscriptions of which 10 are libraries. Subscription $10 ($13 foreign). **Sample postpaid: $5 ($6 foreign). Pays 1 copy plus subscription. Send SASE for guidelines. They will consider simultaneous submissions. Editor usually comments on rejections and tries to return submissions in 2 months.** He quotes Archibald MacLeish, " 'A poem should not mean/ But be.' Poetry is concerned primarily with language, rhythm and sound; fashions and trends are transitory and to be eschewed; perfecting one's work is often more important than publishing it."

FRENCH BROAD PRESS (III), The Asheville School, Asheville NC 28806, phone (704)255-7909, founded 1989, publishers Jessica Bayer and J.W. Bonner, publishes 20- to 40- page chapbooks. **"Any style or form welcome. Considers sexually explicit material."** They have published poetry by Thomas Meyer, Jeffrey Beam and Jonathan Williams. "We're slow. May take 6 months to respond to a ms and up to 2 years before publication. Many of our poets have paid 'in kind': typesetting mss and covers on disks or pasting up the book for printing." **Pays 10% of press run.** Write to buy samples or order from The Captain's Bookshelf, 26½ Battery Park Ave., Asheville NC 28801.

FRIENDS JOURNAL (II, IV-Themes), 1501 Cherry St., Philadelphia PA 19102, phone (215)241-7277, founded 1827 as *The Friend* and 1844 as *Friends Intelligencer,* 1955 as *Friends Journal,* appears monthly, magazine-sized, circulation 9,000+. **"The *Journal* seeks poetry that resonates with Quakerism and Quaker concerns, such as peace and nonviolence, spiritual seeking, the sanctuary movement, the nuclear freeze." No multiple or simultaneous submissions. Pays 2 copies/poem.** Subscription: $18/ year.

FROGMORE PAPERS; FROGMORE POETRY PRIZE (II), 42 Morehall Ave., Folkestone, Kent, England, founded 1983, poetry editor Jeremy Page, is a literary quarterly with emphasis on new poetry and short stories. **"Quality is generally the only criterion, although pressure of space means very long work (over 100 lines) is unlikely to be published."** They have recently published poetry by B.C. Leale, Geoffrey Holloway, Myra Schneider, Frances Wilson, Linda France, Pauline Stainer and John Latham. As a sample the editor selected these lines by Elizabeth Garrett:

> *I rock on my heels and test*
> *My breath's spillage on the air.*
> *I shall fold it with the weather*
> *For safe keeping, in a camphor chest.*

The magazine is 26 pgs. saddle-stapled with matte card cover, photocopied in photoreduced typescript. Their press run is 250 with 80 subscriptions. They accept a tenth of poetry received. Subscription: £7 ($12). **Sample postpaid: £2.50 ($4). Pays 1 copy. Reports in 3-6 months. Considers simultaneous submissions. Editor sometimes comments on rejections.** Reviews books of poetry in 2-3 sentences, single format. Write for information about the annual Frogmore Poetry Prize. The editor says, "My advice to people starting to write poetry would be: Read as many recognized modern poets as you can and don't be afraid to experiment."

FROGPOND: QUARTERLY HAIKU JOURNAL; HAIKU SOCIETY OF AMERICA; HAIKU SOCIETY OF AMERICA AWARDS/CONTESTS (IV-Form, translation), % Japan Society, 333 E. 47th St., New York NY 10017, has been publishing *Frogpond* since 1978, now edited by Sylvia Forges-Ryan, and **submissions should go directly to her** at 87 Bayard Ave., North Haven CT 06473. *Frogpond* is a stapled spine quarterly of 48 pgs., 5½×8½, of haiku, senryu, haiku sequences, renga, more rarely tanka, and translations of haiku. It also contains book reviews, some news of the Society, contests, awards, publications and other editorial matter—a dignified, handsome little magazine. Poets should be familiar with modern developments in English-language haiku as well as the tradition. **Haiku should be brief, fresh, using clear images and non-poetic language. Focus should be on a moment keenly perceived.** Ms. Forges-Ryan hopes contributors will be familiar with contemporary haiku and senryu as presented in *The Haiku Handbook* (Wm. J. Higginson) and *The Haiku Anthology* (Cor van den Heuvel, Ed.). Recent contributors include William J. Higginson, Geraldine C. Little, Elizabeth St. Jacques, Anita Virgil, Hiroaki Sato, Christopher Herold and Alexis Rotella. Considerable variety is possible, as these two examples from the magazine illustrate:

> *on shore alone*
> *as the ebbing tide*
> *takes the moon with it*
> — L. A. Davidson

> *Late late autumn*
> *the last pumpkin*
> *caves into itself*
> — Garry Gay

Each issue has between 25 and 35 pages of poetry. The magazine goes to 600 subscribers, of which 15 are libraries, as well as to over a dozen foreign countries. **Sample postpaid: $5.** Make check payable to Haiku Society of America. They receive about 8,000 submissions/year and use about 400-450. Accepted poems usually published within 6-12 months, reporting within 6 weeks. They are flexible on submission format: haiku on 3 × 5 cards or several to a page or one to a page or half-page. Ms. Forges-Ryan prefers 5-20 at one submission, no photocopy or dot-matrix. No simultaneous submissions. They hope contributors will become HSA members, but it is not necessary, and all contributors receive a copy of the magazine in payment. Send SASE for Information Sheet on the HSA and submission guidelines. Reviews books of poetry usually in 1,000 words or less. The Society also sponsors the Harold G. Henderson Haiku Award Contest, The Gerald Brady Senryu Award Contest, The Haiku Society of America Renku Contest, The Nicholas A. Virgilio Memorial Haiku Competition for High School Students and gives Merit Book Awards for books in the haiku field. Two "best-of-issue" prizes are given "through a gift from the Museum of Haiku Literature, Tokyo."

FRONTIERS: A JOURNAL OF WOMEN STUDIES (IV-Feminist), Mesa Vista Hall, Rm 2142, University of New Mexico, Albuquerque NM 87131-1586, founded 1975, is published 3 times a year, circulation 1,000, 6 × 9, flat-spined, 200-208 pgs. **Sample: $8. Uses poetry on feminist themes.** They have published work by Audré Lorde, Janice Mirikitani, Carol Wolfe Konek and Opal Palmer Adisa. **Pays 2 copies. Reports in 3-5 months. No simultaneous submissions.** "We are not currently publishing reviews of any books, poetry or otherwise. However, we might consider extensive review essays, if from a clear theoretical perspective."

FURRY CHICLETS: A LAWPOETS CREATION (I, IV-Themes), 914 5th St., Santa Monica CA 90403, founded 1990, editors Charles Carreon and Tom Brill, an annual, wants **"impact poetry, stories and anything else that fits. Test your freedom here. Poems: 1 page."** As a sample the editor selected these lines from "The Picnic" by Corrine De Winter:

> It was not that I starved
> or craved
> or harbored the desire to be saved.
> It was the hourglass,
> the shaken mixture
> that my heart is,
> that my brain is,
> which leaks continually
> to form a new landscape . . .

It consists of photocopied pages stapled at the top to a blue matte backing, 30-40 pgs. **Back issues available for $4. Make checks payable to Charles Carreon.** "Each issue receives a thematic subtitle (e.g., 1991 issue: *'Demi Monde,'* 1992 issue: *'Non Grata'*), and works are selected to fit the theme. Most important to us is the spirit of rebellion. We promote the poet as troublemaker, provocateur, high-wire artist and dirt-cheap entertainer of the twisted and the blest." Editors often comment on rejections. They try to respond in 6 weeks.

FUTURIFIC MAGAZINE (IV-Themes), Foundation for Optimism, 280 Madison Ave., New York NY 10016, phone (212)684-4913, founded 1976, publisher Balint Szent-Miklosy, is a monthly newsmagazine dealing with **current affairs and their probable outcomes. "We pride ourselves on the accuracy of our forecasting. No other limits than that the poet try to be accurate in predicting the future."** They want to see "positive upbeat poetry glorifying humanity and human achievements." *Futurific* is magazine-sized, 32 pgs., saddle-stapled, on glossy stock, with b&w photos, art and ads, circulation 10,000. Subscription: $120; for students and individuals: $60. **Sample postpaid: $10. Pays 5 copies.** The editor says, "*Futurific* is made up of the words Future-Terrific. Poets should seek out and enjoy the future if they want to see their work in *Futurific*."

G.W. REVIEW (II, IV-Translations), Marvin Center Box 20, George Washington University, Washington DC 20052, phone (202)994-7288, founded 1980, editor Sarah Aitken, appears 2 times a year. "The magazine is published for distribution to the university community, the Washington, D.C. metropolitan area and an increasing number of national subscribers." They have published poetry by William Stafford, Robin Becker, Gary Fincke and Julia Alvarez. It is 64 pgs., perfect-bound with cover photograph. They receive about 3,300 poems a year and accept 50-60. Their annual press run averages 4,000 copies. Subscriptions: $5/year, $8/2 years. **Sample postpaid: $3. Pays 5 copies.** They consider simultaneous submissions but not previously published poems. **Reports in 1-3 months.** The staff does not read manuscripts from May 15 through August 15. Editor sometimes comments on rejections when the staff likes the work but thinks it needs to be revised.

‡GAIN PUBLICATIONS (V), P.O. Box 2204, Van Nuys CA 91404, (818)786-1981, founded 1982. **Currently accepts no unsolicited poetry.**

GAIRM; GAIRM PUBLICATIONS (IV-Ethnic, foreign language), 29 Waterloo St., Glasgow, G2 6BZ Scotland, editor Derick Thomson, founded 1952. *Gairm* is a quarterly, circulation 2,000, which uses **poetry in Scottish Gaelic only**. It has published the work of all significant Scottish Gaelic poets, and much poetry translated from European languages. An anthology of such translations, **European Poetry in Gaelic**, appeared in August 1990 (price £7.50 or $15). **All of the publications of the press are in Scottish Gaelic. Sample of *Gairm*: $3. Reads submissions October 1 through July 31 only.** Reviews books of poetry in 500-700 words, single format; 100 words, multi-book format.

GALAXY PRESS (III), 71 Recreation St., Tweed Heads, N.S.W. 2485 Australia, phone 075-361997, founded 1979, editor Lance Banbury, is a small press publisher of short modernist to semi-traditional poems in chapbooks. He wants **"post-modernist short to medium-length verse, or didactic blank verse. No poetry of an anecdotal type."** As a sample he chose these lines from "Autumn to Summer Sequence" by Dorian Cooke:

> *Let me remember, while the nights escape*
> *Towards October, every old shortcoming*
> *Of the hairy summer; for I cannot sleep*
> *In the unwiving cold and keep this swarming*
> *Pageantry at bay. December is deep*
> *Way off and out of earshot when I'm dreaming.*

Query with 5 samples. Reports in 1 month. Pays 2 copies. Lance Banbury says, "Will consider any new, original ideas."

THE GAMUT (II), English Dept., Cleveland State University, 1218 Fenn Tower, 1983 E. 24th St., Cleveland OH 44115, editors Leonard Trawick and Louis T. Milic, first published in 1980. *The Gamut, a Journal of Ideas and Information,* is "a general interest magazine with literary and art emphasis." Prints an average of 2 pages of poetry each issue. **Send SASE for guidelines.** Leonard Trawick says they want **"poems that are more or less accessible to the educated reader, but not too simple; no trivial, greeting card, 'inspirational' poetry."** They have recently published poetry by David Citino, Roy Bently, Richard Jackson and Jeff Gundy. The magazine has a press run of 1,500 going to 900+ subscribers of which 50 are libraries. Price per issue: $6. Subscription: $15. **Pays an average of $15/ page plus 2 copies. Buys first serial rights. Reports within 2 months.** On rejection, editor comments "on the good ones." As a sample Prof. Trawick selected these lines from "Primary Colors" by Barbara Moore (*The Gamut #35* Spring 1992):

> *We think back with amazement*
> *on the sharp, blue notebooks of childhood —*
> *page after page of passionate color,*
> *pure colors of the north . . . .*

Professor Trawick says, "In selecting a poem perhaps the first thing we require is that the language be right. It may be complex and challenging, or it may be ostensibly simple, but if the poem doesn't work on the level of diction and syntax, it doesn't work at all for us."

GÁVEA-BROWN PUBLICATIONS; GÁVEA-BROWN: A BI-LINGUAL JOURNAL OF PORTUGUESE-AMERICAN LETTERS AND STUDIES (IV-Ethnic, bilingual), Box O, Brown University, Providence RI 02912, phone (401)863-3042, founded 1980, editors Onésimo T. Almeida and George Monteiro, is a small press publisher of books and a journal **relating to the Portuguese-American experience**. They publish flat-spined collections of poetry in their journal. They have published poetry by Jorge de Sena, João Teixeira de Medeiros and Thomas Braga. *Gávea-Brown* is handsomely printed, 100+ pgs., digest-sized, flat-spined, with a glossy colored card cover. Its "purpose is to provide a vehicle for the **creative expression of the Portuguese immigrant experience**." It has a circulation of 450. $15 for a subscription (double issue). **Sample postpaid: $15 for a double issue, $7.50 for a pre-1982 single issue. Pays 3 copies. Reports in 3 months.** Has a 1-year backlog. Reviews books of poetry "related to the area covered by our journal." **Submit sample poems and query regarding book publication. Photocopy, dot-matrix OK. Pays copies.** The books resemble the journal in format.

THE GAY MEN'S PRESS; GAY VERSE (IV-Gay), P.O. Box 247, London N17 9QR, England, phone (081)365-1545, founded 1979, poetry editor Martin Humphries. "We are the major British publishers of books of gay interest, aiming to reflect and record the extent and variety of our gay culture." **Gay Verse** is a series of poetry publications by various writers. They publish flat-spined paperbacks and want **"poetry that has something to say about the experiences of being gay in the context of wider society. No form, style, length restrictions. No egocentric coming out reflections or self-indulgent pornography."** They have published poetry by John Gambril Nicholson and Steve Cranfield. **"Prefer introductory letter in advance."** Send 4-8 sample poems, bio and statement of aesthetic or poetic aims. **"We actively seek new and unpublished poets with something of pertinence to say." Pays advance** ("varies").

GAZELLE PUBLICATIONS (V), 5580 Stanley Dr., Auburn CA 95603, founded 1976, editor Ted Wade, is a publisher for home schools and compatible markets including **books of verse for children. He is not currently considering unsolicited manuscripts and is inactive in the area of poetry.**

GENERATOR; GENERATOR PRESS (V), 8139 Midland Rd., Mentor OH 44060, founded 1987, poetry editor John Byrum, is a yearly magazine "devoted to the presentation of **language poetry and 'concrete' or visual poetic modes.**" They have published poetry by Susan Bee, Charles Bernstein, Bruce Andrews, Sheila E. Murphy, Stephen Ratcliffe and Ron Silliman. As a sample the editor selected these lines by Tom Beckett:

> *Sex and thought are identical — only reversed*
> *Insulated between witness and wetness*
> *one never knows what one needs*
> *Things get done in a major miniseries*
> *The world is all that takes the place*
> *of allegorical invasions*

Generator is magazine-sized, side-stapled, using b&w graphics, photocopied, with matte card cover. Press run is 200 copies for 25 subscriptions of which 10 are libraries. **Sample: $5 postpaid.** Generator Press also publishes the **Generator Press chapbook series. Approximately 4 new titles/ year. They are not currently accepting unsolicited manuscripts for either the magazine or chapbook publication.** The editor adds, "Worthwhile writers do not need advice and should not heed any but their own."

GEORGIA JOURNAL (IV-Regional), P.O. Box 27, Athens GA 30603-0027, phone (404)354-0463, poetry editor Janice Moore. The *Georgia Journal* is a quarterly magazine, circulation 15,000, covering the state of Georgia. Send SASE for guidelines. **Sample: $3.** They use poetry "mostly from **Southern writers but not entirely. It should be suitable for the general reader.**" Publishes 20-30 poems per year. **Submit maximum of 3-4 poems, maximum length 30 lines. Pays in copies. Acquires first rights. Reports in 2-3 months.**

UNIVERSITY OF GEORGIA PRESS; CONTEMPORARY POETRY SERIES (II), Terrell Hall, University of Georgia, Athens GA 30602, phone (404)542-2830, press founded 1938, series founded 1980. Series editor Bin Ramke, publishes four collections of poetry/year, **two of which are by poets who have not had a book published,** in simultaneous hardcover and paperback edition. "**Writers should query first for guidelines and submission periods. Please enclose SASE.**" There are no **restrictions on the type of poetry submitted,** but "familiarity with our previously published books in the series may be helpful." **$10 submission fee.** Manuscripts are *not* returned after the judging is completed.

THE GEORGIA REVIEW (III), The University of Georgia, Athens GA 30602-9009, phone (706)542-3481, founded 1947, editor Stanley W. Lindberg, associate editor Stephen Corey. This is a distinguished, professionally printed, flat-spined quarterly, 200+ pgs., 7×10, glossy card cover. They have published poetry by Galway Kinnell, Yusef Komunyakaa, Pattiann Rogers, Gerald Stern, Lisel Mueller, Seamus Heaney, Linda Pastan, Albert Goldbarth, Rita Dove and Charles Simic. "Also have featured first-ever publications by many new voices over the years, but encourage all potential contributors to become familiar with past offerings before submitting." As a sample, Stephen Corey selected these lines from "Not the Occult" by Stephen Dunn:

> *. . . I love the local and crude*
> *somehow made beautiful, all the traces*
> *of how it got that way erased.*
> *And I love the corporeal body itself,*
> *designed to fail,*
> *and the mind, the helpless mind,*
> *regularly impelled to think about it.*

They use 60-70 poems a year, less than one-half percent of those received. Circulation: 5,700. Subscription: $18/year. **Sample: $6 postpaid. No submissions accepted during June, July and August. Rarely uses translations. Submit 3-5 poems. Pays $2/line. Buys first North American serial rights. Reports in 1-3 months. No simultaneous submissions.** Reviews books of poetry. "Our poetry reviews range from 500-word 'Book Briefs' on single volumes to 5,000-word essay reviews on multiple volumes." *The Georgia Review* is one of the best publications in America today. It respects its audience, edits intelligently and has won or been nominated for awards in competition with such slicks as *The Atlantic, The New Yorker* and *Esquire*. Needless to say, competition is extremely tough, always fair, but, because of the volume of manuscripts and the editors' work ethic, response time can be slow. This is a market, however, that is worth the wait — and the money for a sample issue.

THE GETTYSBURG REVIEW (II), Gettysburg College, Gettysburg PA 17325, phone (717)337-6770, founded 1988, editor Peter Stitt, is a multidisciplinary literary quarterly using **any poetry except that which is "badly written."** They accept 2-3% of submissions received. Press run 3,000 for 1,500 subscriptions. **Sample postpaid: $6. Pays $2/line.** In five years, Editor Peter Stitt has created a well-respected and -edited journal that features fine writing in all genres. Stitt is one of the country's leading critics, so his eye is particularly sharp. Send only your best work, hope for the best and know you are competing with the best. Response time can be slow during peak cycles, especially in the late fall.

GIANTS PLAY WELL IN THE DRIZZLE (I), 326-A 4th St., Brooklyn NY 11215, founded 1983, editor Martha King, is a poetry newsletter appearing 2-6 times/year. The editor wants **"energy in breath, sound, intellect, passion in wit, in irreverence, in high seriousness, and oh those dirty dogs."** They have published poetry by Robert Creeley, Sheila Murphy, Laurie Price and Tom Clark. As a sample the editor selected these lines from "Found in a Finch Egg" by Brent MacKay:

> *All the misspent loose change of youth*
> *hard raining down the skull's softest rut*
> *seems but a blue folded fin*
> *tucked in a pocket*
> *lost in the wash.*

It is 6-10 pgs., stapled at the corner. Press run 600 for 550 on a free mailing list. **Sample free for a first class stamp. Pays 3-5 copies. Editor "sometimes" comments on rejections.** "This is a free publication. Friends send stamps and money to keep it going. Please ask for a sample before submitting! The very small format imposes some limits as to length."

GINGER HILL (II), c/o English Dept., Room 314, Spotts World Cultures Building, Slippery Rock University, Slippery Rock PA 16057, phone (412)738-2043, founded 1963, is an annual literary magazine using **"academic poetry, with preference for excellent free verse, but all forms considered. 27-line limit. No greeting card verse, no sentimentality, no self-serving or didactic verse."** They have recently published poetry by Elizabeth R. Curry and William Greenway. As a sample we selected the beginning lines of "Verboten" by Lee Wonsettler:

> *poems and psychiatrists and love affairs*
> *begin with I*
> *only to risk failure from a flawed beginning*
> *leading to obliquity*

It is digest-sized, "varies in format and layout every year," perfect-bound, with 2,000 distributed free, mostly to the State System of Higher Education in Pennsylvania. **Send SASE for guidelines. Pays 2 copies. Submissions must be postmarked on or before December 1 of each year.** They say, "We choose about 5-10% of all submissions. Excellence is stressed."

‡GIORNO POETRY SYSTEMS RECORDS; DIAL-A-POEM POETS (V), 222 Bowery, New York NY 10012, phone (212)925-6372, founded 1965, poetry editor John Giorno, "star of Andy Warhol's movie, *Sleep* (1963), who publishes a poetry magazine in three formats: LP record, Compact Disc and cassette; and a videopak series. He originated Dial-A-Poem in 1968, installing it in many cities in the United States and Europe. He says he has published poetry on the surface of ordinary objects: Matchbook Poems, T-Shirt Poems, Cigarette Package Poems, Window Curtain Poems, Flag Poems, Chocolate Bar Poems, and Silk-Screen and Lithograph Poem Prints. **No submission information provided.**

‡GLOBAL TAPESTRY JOURNAL; BB BOOKS (II), Spring Bank, Longsight, Copster Green, Blackburn, Lancs. BB1 9EU United Kingdom, founded 1963, poetry editor Dave Cunliffe. **"Experimental, avant-garde — specializing in exciting high-energy new writing. Mainly for a bohemian and counter-culture audience. Poetry in the Beat tradition. Don't want contrived, traditional, pompous and academic or pretentious mainstream."** Also considers sexually explicit material. In addition to the magazine, *Global Tapestry Journal*, BB Books publishes chapbooks. "We want honest, uncontrived writing, strong in form and content. We don't want 'weekend hobby verse' and poetry without energy." They have recently published poetry by Robert Peters, Chris Torrance, Patricia Pogson, Tina Morris and Jay Findlay. As a sample the editor selected these lines by Paul Donnelly:

> *i say we're more like clouds that*
> *print themselves on water*
> *but can't stay anywhere long*

GTJ is 9 × 6, 72 pgs., saddle-stapled, typeset in a variety of mostly small sizes of type, rather crowded format, casual pasteup, with b&w drawings, photos, collages, display and classified ads, with a 2-color matte card cover, circulation 1,150 with 450 subscriptions of which 50 are libraries. Subscription (4 issues): $20. **Sample postpaid: $3. Send SASE for guidelines. Considers previously published poems. Responds "soon,"** has an 18-month backlog. **Pays 1 copy.** BB Books publishes about 4 chapbooks of poetry/year. To submit for chapbook publication send 6 samples, cover letter giving publication credits. **Pays 10% of press run in copies. Send SASE (wit...** **if foreign) for catalog to buy samples.** David Cunliffe comments, "The United Kingdom ... limited number of magazines and small press ventures publishing poetry from unknowns. Ma... little mags are self-publishing cliques or small-time vanity operations. Simultaneous submission and simultaneous publication are often resented. There is much readership crossover among the non-poet subscribers and they resent seeing the same work in many magazines over a short period. We typeset for a few United Kingdom mags and publishers and we see this in the setting jobs we do every week. Many of the editors circulate poet blacklists to help prevent this tendency from spreading."

DAVID R. GODINE, PUBLISHER, Horticultural Hall, 300 Massachusetts Ave., Boston MA 02115. Declined listing. "One result of being listed in reference guides like *Poet's Market* is the submission of massive amounts of unsolicited manuscripts. Godine is a small company, and we simply do not have the staff to handle all of the unsolicited writing we receive. We have never accepted any work from the piles of unsolicited material we receive, so we have decided that it is not worth our while to be listed in directories."

GOLDEN ISIS MAGAZINE; GOLDEN ISIS PRESS; POEM OF THE YEAR CONTEST (IV-Mystical/ Occult), 23233 Saticoy St., Bldg. 105, Box 137, West Hills CA 91304, founded 1980, editor Gerina Dunwich. "**Golden Isis** is a mystical literary magazine of poetry, magick, pagan/Egyptian artwork, Wiccan news, occult fiction, letters, book reviews and classified ads. **Occult, Egyptian, cosmic, euphonic and Goddess-inspired poems, mystical haiku and magickal chants are published. We are also interested in New Age spiritual poetry, astrological verses and poems dealing with peace, love and ecology. All styles considered; under 60 lines preferred. We do not want to see pornographic, Satanic, sexist or racist material.**" Recently published poets include Robert Louis Sullivan, Stan Proper, Sandra Tatum and T. Kretz. The magazine is digest-sized, 25-30 pgs., desktop publishing, saddle-stapled with paper cover. International circulation is 5,000. Single copy $3 postpaid, subscription $10/year. "**No postal money orders, please.**" **Pays 1 copy. Reports within 2-3 weeks. Occasionally comments on rejected material. Submit 1 poem/page, typed single-spaced, name and address on upper left corner and the number of lines on upper right corner; photocopied, previously published and simultaneous submissions OK. All rights revert back to author upon publication.** Reviews books of poetry, "length varies." Age of Aquarius is a digest-sized "psychedelic journal of 60's counter-culture in the 90's." Sample $3. Circulation: 3,600. Pays 1 copy. Golden Isis Press **is now accepting mss for chapbook publication. Send complete ms and $5 reading fee. "Please make checks payable to Golden Isis." "We offer a small advance, 10 free copies of the published work, and 10% royalty on every copy sold for as long as the book remains in print."** Sample chapbook (Circle of Shadows by Gerina Dunwich): $4.95. The magazine sponsors an annual "Poem of the Year" contest that offers cash prizes. Entry fee: $1/ poem, deadline December 1, no limit on number of poems entered. Poems should be up to 60 lines, any form, with author's name and address on upper left corner of each page. Free guidelines and contest rules for SASE.

GOLDEN QUILL PRESS (I), RFD #1, Avery Rd., Francestown NH 03043, publishes a great deal of poetry on a subsidy basis. **Pays maximum 10% royalties. Submit complete ms. Photocopy, dot-matrix OK. Reports in 2 weeks on queries, 1 month on submissions.**

GOOD HOUSEKEEPING (II, IV-Humor, women), Hearst Corp., 959 8th Ave., New York NY 10019, poetry editor Andrea Krantz, circulation 5,000,000, women's magazine, uses up to 3 poems/issue for which they pay $10/line. Light verse and traditional. Submit up to 10 poems; maximum length: 25 lines. They no longer return or critique manuscripts. "We look for poems of emotional interest to American women. Must be wholesome, clever, upbeat or poignant. Poets whose work interests us will hear from us within 4-5 weeks of receipt of a manuscript. We ask that poets send inexpensive copies of their work, and do *not* enclose SASEs or postage. We do accept multiple submissions." Send seasonal material 6-12 months before publication date. Submit short humorous verses, anecdotes and 'daffinition' to "Light Housekeeping" editor, Rosemary Leonard. Enclose SASE because they do return these mss. Pays $25 for 2-4 lines; $50, 5-8 lines. Buys first North American serial rights. Usually overstocked.

Market conditions are constantly changing! If you're still using this book and it is 1994 or later, buy the newest edition of Poet's Market *at your favorite bookstore or order directly from Writer's Digest Books.*

ONS (III, IV-Regional), 469 Queen St., Fredericton, New Brunswick E3B 1E5
450-4251, FAX (506)459-4991, managing editor S. Alexander, founded 1956, a
Canadian fiction, poetry and literary history. **Writers should be advised that
anuscripts by Canadian poets only.** They receive approximately 400 mss/year,
arly, 3-4 of these being poetry collections. Writers recently published include
B. Lee and W.J. Keith. As a sample the editor selected these lines from "Elegy:
David Anderson, 1970-1987" published in **Clarity Between Clouds** (1991) by Susan
...ou:

> *This wilderness under a road,*
> *moment by moment changing,*
> *constantly gathers into itself and absorbs*
> *time, shape, a thousand minuscule deaths,*
> *and sings back a fluid permanence*
>
> *where nothing, ever, is lost*
> *but, passing at dawn, remembered.*

Unsolicited Canadian mss considered if individual poems have been previously published in literary journals. SASE essential (IRCs or Canadian postage stamps only). Reports in 10-12 weeks. Authors receive royalty of 10% of retail sale price on all copies sold. Copies available to author at 40% discount.

THE GOPHERWOOD REVIEW (II), Box 58784, Houston TX 77258, founded 1990, editors Sandra Reiff and Sharron Crowson, appears twice a year, "plus summer Texas issue." They solicit most material, but "accept *some* unsolicited poetry. Experimental, surreal and imagistic, only very high quality; it must leave us speechless, breathless and/or changed. Nothing cliched, sentimental, bland, overwritten, underdone or voiceless." They have recently published poetry by B.Z. Niditch, Philip Dacey, Marge Piercy, Guy Beining and Sheila E. Murphy. As a sample the editor selected these lines from "Death" by Patrick Lawler:

> *One of my deaths is my dinner.*
> *One of my deaths sends me a map*
> *Showing me how to get to where*
> *He is waiting. Another has*
> *forgotten what I look like*

It is magazine-sized, 44 pgs., desktop and laser printed, with matte card cover. Press run 200 for 100 subscribers. Subscription: $9. **Sample: $4.50 postpaid. Pays 1 copy. Acquires first rights. Send SASE for guidelines. "We like interesting cover letters and bio, try to respond within 3 weeks, have 6-month backlog, often comment on rejections."** Reviews books of poetry in 1,000 words maximum, single format. The editors advise, "Good poetry does not come easily; revise and rewrite. Compare your work with those you admire. If it lacks something — power, impact, a voice — don't submit it until it's your best effort. There is a great deal of lukewarm poetry out there. Don't settle for that. Make it catch fire." They sponsor an annual poetry and short fiction contest. Send SASE for rules.

GOSPEL PUBLISHING HOUSE; PENTECOSTAL EVANGEL; LIVE; HI-CALL; JUNIOR TRAILS (IV-Religious, children/teens), The General Council of the Assemblies of God, 1445 Boonville, Springfield MO 65802, phone (417)862-2781, FAX (417)862-8558, editor Richard G. Champion. *Pentecostal Evangel* is a weekly magazine containing **inspirational articles and news of the Assemblies of God for members of the Assemblies and other Pentecostal and charismatic Christians**, circulation 280,000. **Religious and inspirational poetry.** "All poems submitted to us should be related to religious life. We are Protestant, evangelical, Pentecostal, and any doctrines or practices portrayed should be in harmony with the official position of our denomination (Assemblies of God)." **Free sample copy and writer's guidelines. Submit maximum 3 poems. Submit seasonal/holiday material 6 months in advance. Computer printout submissions acceptable, prefers letter-quality. Reports in 3 months. Pays 50-75¢/line on acceptance. Buys first and/or second rights.** *Live* is a weekly for adults in Assemblies of God Sunday schools, circulation 200,000. **Traditional free and blank verse, 12-20 lines.** "Please do not send large numbers of poems at one time." Submit seasonal material 1 year in advance; do not mention Santa Claus, Halloween or Easter bunnies. Computer printout submissions acceptable. Free sample copy and writer's guidelines for 7 × 10 SASE and 40¢ postage. **Letters without SASE will not be answered. Pays 25¢/line on acceptance. Buys first and/or second rights.** *Hi-Call* is a weekly magazine of **Christian fiction and articles for teenagers, 12-17**, circulation 78,000. **Free verse, light verse and traditional, 10-40 lines. Buys 50 poems/year.** Submit seasonal/holiday material 18 months in advance. Simultaneous, photocopied and previously published submissions OK if typed, double-spaced, on 8 × 11 paper. Computer printout submissions acceptable; prefers letter-quality. Reports in 6 weeks. Sample copy for 8 × 11 SAE and 2 first class stamps; writer's guidelines for SAE. **Pays 25¢/line for first rights, 15¢/line**

for second rights; minimum of $2.50. *Junior Trails* is a weekly tabloid covering **religious fiction and biographical, historical and scientific articles with a spiritual emphasis for boys and girls ages 10-11,** circulation 75,000. **Free verse and light verse. Buys 6-8 poems/year. Submit seasonal/holiday material 15 months in advance. Simultaneous and previously published submissions OK. Computer printout submissions acceptable, prefers letter-quality. Reports in 3-6 weeks. Sample copy and writer's guidelines for 9 × 12 SAE and 2 first class stamps. Pays 20¢/line on acceptance. Buys first and/or second rights.** "We like poems showing contemporary children positively facing today's world."

GOTTA WRITE NETWORK LITMAG; MAREN PUBLICATIONS (I, IV-Science fiction/Fantasy, subscription), 612 Cobblestone Circle, Glenview IL 60025, founded 1988, editor/publisher Denise Fleischer, is a desktop published quarterly saddle-stapled, 48-page magazine featuring "general poetry, articles, short stories and market listings. *GWN* now spans 39 states, Canada and England. Half of the magazine is devoted to science fiction and fantasy in a section called 'Sci-Fi Fan Galleria.' **I'm open to well-crafted, clear poetry that doesn't have to be dissected to understand its message. Poetry that leaves the reader with a special feeling. Can be of any genre. No sexually graphic material, obscenities or lengthy poetry."** She has published poetry by H.R. Felgenhauer, John Grey, C.R. Riehle, Anne Simon and C. David Hay. As a sample, the editor selected these lines from "i saw isolde once" by Charles Rampp:

> *hidden more fully than warblers*
> *in forest's morning woods, quiet*
> *as mushroom fairy dance ring*
> *in the churchyard, this love of ours.*

"*Gotta Write Network* subscribers receive more than a quarterly magazine. In subscribing, they become part of a support group of both beginners and established poets. I offer critiques at request, will even retype a poem to point out spelling errors and suggest other appropriate markets. Members are from all walks of life: housewives, religious persons, seniors, nursing home residents. Five reside in prisons." Press run: 200 for 70 subscribers. "I'm striving to give beginners a positive starting point and to encourage them to venture beyond rejection slips and writer's block. Publication can be a reality if you have determination and talent. There are over a thousand U.S. litmags waiting for submissions. So what are you waiting for?" Subscription: $15. **Sample postpaid: $3.75.** The editor says, **"I encourage poets to purchase a sample copy before subscribing. This way they can see just how varied the information is." Pays 1 copy. Acquires first North American serial rights. Reports in 1-2 months. Include a cover letter and SASE.** Reviews books of poetry in 1-2 typewritten pages, single format. "Prefer that a b&w photo of book accompany the submission." Maren Publications has published 1 chapbook, **Poetry Cafe,** and a short story anthology, **Life In General.** She adds, "Write the way you feel the words. Don't let others mold you into an established poet's style. Poetry is about personal imagery. Write clearly or ask your family for a typewriter for Christmas. Most of all, love what you do."

‡GRAFFITI OFF THE ASYLUM WALLS (IV-Humor, erotica), P.O. Box 515, Fayetteville AR 72702-0515, founded 1991, "curator" BrYan Westbrook, is an "illiterary journal published whenever I receive enough suitable material." He wants **"stuff you would be afraid to show your mother, priest and/or shrink; also anything that can make me laugh. No sonnets; no pro-religious or animal rights poetry; nothing boring."** They have recently published poetry by Cheryl Townsend, Belinda Subraman, harland ristan and Scott C. Holstad. As a sample he selected these lines from "Cheap Date" by Richard Cody:

> *His hands played over her fine young body,*
> *seeking to unleash forbidden pleasures.*
> *"You better enjoy this . . ." he whispered.*
> *"You're going back to the graveyard tomorrow."*

GOTAW is 8½ × 11, laser printed, stapled with colored paper cover, drawings, photos and cartoons. Press run is 200. "Due to the irregular publishing schedule, I do not offer subscriptions; but, if requested, will notify interested parties whenever an issue is due." **Sample postpaid: $2.50. Previously published poems and simultaneous submissions OK. Cover letter required. "A personal bio is preferred over a publication list. I want to know who you are more than where you've been." Often comments on rejections. Send SASE for guidelines. Reports "usually next day, never more than 2 weeks." Pays 1 copy. Acquires one-time rights.** Reviews "*anything* someone wants to send me. Length varies with how much I think needs to be said." BrYan Westbrook says, "Throughout history the preserved literature of any period has mainly been what the people of that time actually enjoyed. Scholars have placed these works upon lofty pedestals and declared them the only true art. It's time we stop trying to imitate what others have considered entertainment and get on with creating the art we really want for ourselves. *GOTAW* is my contribution to this endeavor."

GRAHAM HOUSE REVIEW (II, IV-Translations), Box 5000, Colgate University, Hamilton NY 13346, phone (315)824-1000, ext. 262, founded 1976, poetry editors Peter Balakian and Bruce Smith, appears yearly. "We publish contemporary poetry, poetry in translation, essays and interviews. **No preferences for styles or schools, just good poetry.**" They have published poems by Seamus Heaney, Marilyn Hacker, Maxine Kumin, Michael Harper and Carolyn Forché. *GHR* is digest-sized, flat-spined, 120 pgs., professionally printed on heavy stock, matte color card cover with logo, using 100 pgs. of poetry in each issue, circulation 500, with 300 subscriptions of which 50 are libraries. They receive about 2,000 freelance submissions of poetry/year, use 20-50. **Sample postpaid: $7.50. No photocopies. Reports in 2 months or less. Pays 2 copies.** Editors play fair and are efficient, usually returning work within stated response times. The magazine has a lot of respect in the poetry world and can be difficult to crack.

GRAIN; SHORT GRAIN CONTEST (II), Box 1154, Regina, Saskatchewan S4P 3B4 Canada phone (306)757-6310, is a literary quarterly. "*Grain* strives for artistic excellence, seeks material that is accessible as well as challenging to our readers. Ideally, a *Grain* poem should be **well-crafted, imaginatively stimulating, distinctly original.**" They have recently published poems by Elizabeth Brewster and James Gurley. The editor selected as a sample the opening of "The Children" by Patrick Lane:

> The children are singing.
> Hear them as they rise out of the deep hollows,
> the tangles of wildwood and wandering vines.
> They are lifting from the shadows
> where the black creek water flows
> over mud and stones. They have left behind
> the green whip of a snake
> thrown like a thin necklace into the trees . . .

It is digest-sized, professionally printed with chrome-coated cover, 144 pgs., circulation 1,200+, with 850 subscriptions of which 100 are libraries. Subscription: $15 (Canadian), $19 for US, $21 for other foreign destinations. They receive about 700 freelance submissions of poetry/year, use 80-140 poems. **Sample: $5 plus IRC (or 80¢ Canadian postage). They want "no poetry that has no substance." Submit maximum of 8 poems. Photocopies OK. Prefers letter-quality to dot-matrix. Send SASE for guidelines. Reports in 3-4 months. Pays $30+/poem. Buys first North American serial rights.** The editor comments, "Only work of the highest literary quality is accepted. Read several back issues." *Grain* holds an annual Short Grain Contest. Entries are either prose poems (a lyric poem written as a prose paragraph or paragraphs in 500 words or less) or postcard stories (also 500 words or less). Prizes in each category, $250 first, $150 second, $100 third and honorable mentions. All winners and honorable mentions receive regular payment for publication in *Grain*. Entry fee of $15 (Canadian) includes a one-year subscription. Additional entries are $5 each. Entries are normally accepted between January 1 and April 30.

GRAND STREET, Room 906, 131 Varick St., New York NY 10013. Declined listing. "We'd prefer not to be listed. We already receive enough poetry submissions to keep us very busy."

GRASSLANDS REVIEW (I, II), NT Box 13706, Denton TX 76203, phone (817)565-2050, founded 1989, editor Laura B. Kennelly, is a magazine "**to encourage beginning writers and to give creative writing class experience in editing essays, fiction, poetry; using any type of poetry; shorter poems stand best chance.**" They have recently published poetry by Michael Denney, Mike Ballard, Steve Sneyd, Laurel Speer, Kathleen Gunton Dear, Gerald Locklin and Santiago Espel. As a sample the editor selected these lines by Jendi Reiter:

> I would not try to capture the leaves' gifts,
> Like yellow paper they fall to the floor
> by the cold chapel steps, embrace the columns
> in their blown showers, until the air seems to bear
> a cloud of something lighter than rain,
> a final burden descending in grace from the tree

GR is 94 pgs., professionally printed, digest-sized, photocopied, saddle-stapled with card cover. They accept 20-40 of 400 submissions received. Press run 300. Subscription (2 issues): $4 for individuals, $10 institutions. **Sample postpaid: $1. Pays 2 copies. Submit only during October and March. Reports in 8-10 weeks.** Editor comments on submissions "sometimes."

‡**GRAVEN IMAGES (I)**, P.O. Box 2412, Bellingham WA 98227, founded 1991, editor Clayton Walter, is a quarterly of "**free verse poetry—up to 30 lines; subject: life, imagination, fact, fiction, feelings.**" **They do not want "x-tremely pornographic or rhyming poetry."** They have recently published poetry by Jeff Flugel and Larry L. Randall. As a sample the editor selected these lines (poet unidentified):

> I have the feeling that my life

"This cover symbolizes the area which gives our magazine its name," says *Laura B. Kennelly, editor of* Grasslands Review. *"The stalks of grass suggest that beauty may be found in all sorts of places—academic or nonacademic. Poets we publish may be postal workers or university professors, Ivy League students or museum shipping clerks."* Poetry makes up one half to two thirds of the publication. The cover illustration is a photocopy of a black-and-white photo that arrived unsolicited from Sue Cazaly, a freelance photographer from San Francisco, California.*

is the abridged adaptation
of an unpublished novel
written with a shaking hand
in a foreign language
By an illiterate
Blind man

GI is 32 pgs., digest-sized, photocopied, stapled with card stock cover. Press run is 150 for 78 subscribers. Single copy: $2.50; subscription $10 plus $2.40 postage. **Sample postpaid: $3.10. No simultaneous submissions. Often comments on rejections. Reports within a month. Pays 1 copy.** Reviews chapbooks. The editor says, "Poets should try to send poetry which strikes some sort of nerve, puts pressure on the reader to think or feel about the subject at hand. We prefer to veer away from love poems, and a bit of violent visceral imagery never hurts."

GRAYWOLF PRESS (V), Suite 203, 2402 University Ave., Saint Paul MN 55114, phone (612)641-0077, founded 1975, poetry editor Scott Walker, **does not read unsolicited mss.** They have published poetry by Tess Gallagher, Linda Gregg, Jack Gilbert, Chris Gilbert and William Stafford. **Pays 7½-10% royalties, 10 author's copies, advance negotiated.**

GREAT LAKES POETRY PRESS (I, IV-Anthology), Box 56703, Harwood Heights IL 60656, phone (312)478-1761, founded 1987, poetry editor Chuck Kramer, publishes the annual **American Anthology of Contemporary Poetry.** "This book provides new poets with the opportunity to publish their work and is **open to poetry that deals with almost any topic. We do not, however, publish poems that are obscene, violent, sexist or racist."** The anthology is published each December and **submissions may be sent during May and June.** The anthology sells for $19.99 plus $3.50 postage and handling. It is digest-sized, professionally printed, 2 poems to a page, 40 pgs., flat-spined with varnished card cover. **"You do not have to purchase a copy to be included."** Sample anthology: $4. Great Lakes also publishes books that are organized around specific themes or topics. For instance, in 1992 they published **Step into the Light: Poems from Recovery.** As a sample the editor selected these lines from "Words" by C.J. Laity:

> *The woman descends the stairs*
> *there is her son in the cellar*
> *the handsome one with the brains*
> *sniffing liquid paper from a towel*
> *Her son is talking to the freezer*
> *his eyes do not see her*
> *they are wide open in R.E.M.*
> *following things which she can't fathom*

"Manuscripts for these books are solicited through newspaper advertising and personal contact.

To learn the topic of our current project, send us a SASE and request that information. To be placed on our mailing list, send your name and address." They also publish single author collections of poetry on both a commercial and subsidy basis. "For more information, let us know what you have in mind (include a SASE) and we'll get back to you."

GREAT PLAINS CANAL AND AVALON DISPATCH (I, IV-Nature/rural/ecology), Dept. PM, 212 W. First St., San Angelo TX 76903, phone (915)655-3792, founded 1963 as *Cyclotron*; name change to *Cyclo*Flame* in 1966; to annual in 1970; hiatus from 1976-1986. *Avalon Dispatch* was a newsletter *CF* from 1967; added *Great Plains Canal* in 1985. Editor Vernon Payne describes the publication as a "literary newsletter, emphasis on conservation of resources by poetry and letters; nonfiction." He wants **poetry of "timely significance . . . does not want light verse, trite on trivial preachments, work lacking in an elementary knowledge of poetry."** He has published poetry by Lilith Lorraine, Archibald Henderson, Walter Kidd, Alice Makenzie Swaim, Ed Falkowski, Sandra Fowler, Goldie L. Morales, Jack Murphy and Stella Tremble. As a sample he selected these lines by Lucia Clark Markham:

> *Oh, far away on some enchanted shore*
> *The natal music of our souls was born,*
> *And we shall wake some philharmonic morn*
> *To capture once again its ringing score,*
> *And mingle all of Life's untuned arrears*
> *Into the Grand Finale of the Spheres.*

The editor advocates a canal to carry excess water from the Yukon to the Rio Grande, or Antarctic icebergs drawn to Australia for its Outback, or great bladders of water drawn from the Amazon River to Mediterranean coasts. The newsletter is 10 pgs., magazine-sized, photocopied from typescript on bond paper, corner-stapled. Press run is 500. Subscription: $10 a year. **Sample postpaid: $1. Pays $1 "token" plus 2 (or more) copies. Reports in "matter of weeks." Published poems OK if credit line included.** Reviews books of poetry in 1 paragraph to 3 pages. The editor says, "Cuss or dirty words should be abandoned for more accurate and factual adjectives, etc. It would be very helpful to the poet to write for a copy of *GPC* before submitting work to it."

GREEN FUSE (III, IV-Political, ecology, social issues), 3365 Holland Dr., Santa Rosa CA 95404, phone (707)544-8303, founded 1984, editor Brian Boldt, is published in April and October. **"We are looking for accessible free verse—with strong concrete details and images—that celebrates earth's beauty, the harmony in diversity and poetic sanity and truth in an age of prosaic lies and madness. We no longer accept simultaneous submissions and previously published work (unless, of course, you've written the perfect Green Fuse poem). Sentimental and religious work, poems submitted without a SASE and work stinking of nicotine will be folded into origami."** They have recently published poetry by Antler, John Brandi, Elizabeth Herron and Elliot Richman. As a sample the editor selected the following lines by Lynn Trombetta:

> *Cover me in yellow leaves, in duff,*
> *and the gossamer tracings of spiders;*
> *blanket me in the damp breath of mushrooms,*
> *surround me with darkness, below and above,*
> *turn me like a sky.*
> *I want to die and rise again.*

Green Fuse is 48 pgs., digest-sized, offset, perfect-bound, with b&w illustrations on the cover and throughout. Press run is 500 for subscriptions, shelf and reading sales. Subscriptions: $13 for 3 issues, $16 for 4. Sample postpaid: $4. **"Please submit no more than three poems—or 60 lines or less."** Do not submit mss February-March and August-September. Send SASE for guidelines. Pays 1 copy, more to featured poets. Acquires first rights. Editor "sometimes" comments on rejections and reports within 3 months. Of 1,700 poems received a year, he accepts about 70.

‡GREEN MOUNTAINS REVIEW (II), Johnson State College, Johnson VT 05656, phone (802)635-2356, founded 1975, poetry editor Neil Shepard, appears twice a year and includes poetry (and other writing) by well-known authors and promising newcomers. They have published poetry by Denise Levertov, William Stafford, Hayden Carruth, Theodore Weiss, Roger Weingarten and Amy Clampitt. *GMR* is digest-sized, flat-spined, 90-120 pgs. Of 300 submissions they publish 30 authors. Press run is 1,000 for 200 subscriptions of which 20 are libraries. Subscription is $8.50/year. **Sample: $4.75 postpaid. Send SASE for guidelines. Pays 1 copy. Acquires first North American serial rights. Submit no more than 5 poems. No simultaneous submissions. Reads submissions September 1 through May 15 only. Reports in 2-3 months.** Editor sometimes comments on rejection slip.

‡GREEN WORLD PRESS; THE INSTITUTE FOR ECOSOPHICAL STUDIES (V, IV-Animals, nature, ethnic), P.O. Box 417, Bethlehem PA 18016, phone (215)867-6447, founded 1987, editor/publisher Jean Pearson, is a "small press publisher of poemcards and poetry notecards, **began publishing poetry**

chapbooks in 1992, by invitation only." She publishes "poems on animals and nature and by primal peoples. Very well-crafted, showing empathy for animals and deep regard for the natural world. No cynical, sentimental, human-centered poems." She has published poetry by Sarah Kirsch and Tommy Olofsson. As a sample the editor selected these lines by Paulus Utsi:

> *The fire doesn't burn*
> *if you lack love*
> *The reindeer cannot live*
> *if you lose faith in him.*

"At present I produce poetry postcards and notecards for non-profit organizations such as The Wildlife Information Center (Allentown, PA) and PAWS (Philadelphia). I also published **The Reindeer's Land** a chapbook of poems, by Paulus Utsi in 1992. Poets should understand the nature and behavior of live animals and plants before writing about them." **Sample poemcards: 50¢ postpaid.** The Institute for Ecosophical Studies sponsors an annual "evening of eco-poetry."

THE GREENFIELD REVIEW PRESS (V); THE GREENFIELD REVIEW LITERARY CENTER; ITHACA HOUSE (V), Dept. PM, P.O. Box 308, Greenfield Center NY 12833, phone (518)584-1728, founded 1971, poetry editor Joseph Bruchac III, all from a nest of literary activity, The Greenfield Review Literary Center, which publishes a regular newsletter, has a poetry library and offers workshops and lectures in a former gas station. **Send large SASE with 2 oz. postage for a handout on "marketing tips" and sample copy of the newsletter.** Joe Bruchac advises, "Buy books of poetry and literary magazines. The community you support is your own. Don't be in too much of a hurry to be published." Ithaca House, an imprint acquired in 1986, has been one of the longest-going and highly respected small press publishers in the country since 1970, and continues under Greenfield Review Press. **Neither is accepting unsolicited mss until at least 1994 because of their involvement in several large projects.**

GREENHOUSE REVIEW PRESS (V), 3965 Bonny Doon Rd., Santa Cruz CA 95060, founded 1975, publishes a series of poetry chapbooks and broadsides. **"Unsolicited mss are not accepted."** Send SASE for catalog to buy samples. **Pays copies.**

GREEN'S MAGAZINE (I, II); CLOVER PRESS (V), P.O. Box 3236, Regina, Saskatchewan S4P 3H1 Canada, founded 1972, editor David Green. *Green's Magazine* is a literary quarterly with a balanced diet of short fiction and poetry; Clover Press publishes chapbooks. They publish **"free/blank verse examining emotions or situations."** They do not want greeting card jingles or pale imitations of the masters. Some poets published are Sheila Murphy, Mary Balazs, Robert L. Tener, B.Z. Niditch, Joyce Carbone and Arthur Winfield Knight. As a sample the following lines are from "First Church of Christ Itinerant" by Joan Ritty:

> *Weekdays he figures*
> *our income tax returns,*
> *but Sundays in March*
> *he preaches as if wrong*
> *is the only way*
> *this congregation does things.*
> *His sermons are palettes*
> *of muddy blue and grey,*
> *temptation is bright red*
> *sin*
> *alizarin crimson.*

The magazine is digest-sized, 100 pgs., with line drawings. A sample chapbook is also digest-sized, 60 pgs., typeset on buff stock with line drawings, matte card cover, saddle-stapled. Circulation is 400, subscriptions $12. **Sample: $4 postpaid.** Guidelines available for SASE. (International Reply Coupons for U.S. queries and/or mss). Payment is 2 free copies. Acquires first North American serial rights. Submissions are reported on in 8 weeks, publication is usually in 3 months. The editor prefers typescript, complete originals. Occasionally reviews books of poetry "up to 150-200 words." Freelance submissions are accepted for the magazine but not for books; query first on latter. Comments are usually provided on rejected mss. "Would-be contributors are urged to study the magazine first."

THE GREENSBORO REVIEW; GREENSBORO REVIEW LITERARY AWARD; AMON LINER POETRY AWARD (II), English Dept., University of North Carolina, Greensboro NC 27412, phone (919)334-5459, founded 1966, editor Jim Clark. *TGR* appears twice yearly and has published poetry by Donald Junkins, Naomi Clark, Paul Rice and Elizabeth Kirschner. As a sample the editor selected these lines from "Back in Oregon" by Robert P. Cooke:

> *Out west*
> *the old river brewed darkness.*

> *So much unlike*
> *twenty years ago —*
> *bright suns, young firm body,*
>   *my ex-wife fly-*
> *fishing in a bluish cascade*
>   *of cutthroat and crayfish.*

The digest-sized, 120+ pgs., flat-spined magazine, colored matte cover, professional printing, uses about 25 pgs. of poetry in each issue. Circulation 500 for 300 subscriptions of which 100 are libraries. Uses about 2.5% of the 2,000 submissions received each year. **Sample postpaid: $4. "Submissions must arrive by September 15 to be considered for the Winter issue (acceptances in December) and February 15 to be considered for the Summer issue (acceptances in May). Manuscripts arriving after those dates will be held for consideration with the next issue." No simultaneous submissions. Reports in 2-4 months. Pays 3 copies. Acquires first North American serial rights.** *TGR* has a fine reputation in the literary world as a publisher of powerful verse. Editors like free verse with structure and content that enlightens readers, with emphasis on voice. They offer the Amon Liner Poetry Award and a $250 Greensboro Review Literary Award in poetry and in fiction each year.

‡**GREYRAVEN PRESS; FICTION DEBUT MAGAZINE (I, II)**, P.O. Box 1005, Marysville WA 98270-1005, founded 1990, senior editor Todd A. Phillips. *Fiction Debut Magazine*, a bimonthly, publishes "new works of short fiction and poetry by new authors—occasionally work by established writers." They want **"poetry no longer than one printed page, any type as long as it has a good sense of flow. I dislike poems which carry rhyming to an extreme or poems which would be offensive to readers."** As a sample we selected the lines from "The Poet Sews" by Barbara J. Petoskey:

> *As the needle's thum-a, thum-a*
>   *Hums her foot's even rhythm,*
> *She scans the woven line—*
> *Two threads entwined*
>   *In a sonnet of Stitches,*
>   *Precise, perfectable,*
> *Where an armhole pairs its couplet sleeve,*
>   *And a button rhymes each hole.*

FD is 48 pgs., digest-sized, printed and photocopied, saddle-stapled with card cover. They receive about 800 poems a year, use approximately 50. Press run is 300 for 50 subscribers, 150 shelf sales. Subscription $14/year. **Sample postpaid: $3.50. No previously published poems or simultaneous submissions.** Time between acceptance and publication is 6 months. **Often comments on rejections. Send SASE for guidelines. Reports "generally within 2 months." Pays $5 for all poems used plus 1 copy. Buys first rights only.** The editor says, "I encourage new contributors to purchase samples. I originally intended for poetry to be filler in *FD*, but I have received so much quality work that I am considering a special poetry edition and possibly a separate magazine for poems."

GROVE WEIDENFELD, Division of Grove Press Inc., 4th Floor, 841 Broadway, New York NY 10003-4793.

GRUE MAGAZINE (IV-Horror), Box 370, New York NY 10108, founded 1985, editor Peggy Nadramia, a horror fiction magazine "with emphasis on the experimental, offbeat, rude." The editor wants **"Poems of any length including prose-poems, with macabre imagery and themes. Not interested in Poe rip-offs, (although we'll look at rhyming poems if subject is weird enough), 'straight' vampire, ghost or werewolf poems."** She has published poems by t. Winter-Damon, W. Gregory Stewart, Steve Sneyd, Robert Frazier, G. Sutton Breiding and Bruce Boston. As a sample she selected these lines from "Angels of Anarchy" by Andrew Darlington:

> *in the red light from the dashboard*
> *my mistress hands me the knife,*
> *she wears a carnelian in her fly,*
> *her needle extracts the moth from my tongue,*
> *where its eggs are laid beneath my skin.*
> *The moon sheds blood over the Headrow*
> *where I dissolve in double shadows.*

The magazine is digest-sized, 96 pgs., offset, with a glossy b&w cover, "sharp" graphics, and "a centerfold that is unique." It appears 3 times a year and has a circulation of 3,000, of which 500 are subscriptions and 1,000 are newsstand sales. Price per issue is $4.50, subscription $13/year. **Sample: $4.50 postpaid; guidelines are available for SASE. Poets receive 2 copies plus $5 per poem upon publication to a maximum of $5 per issue. They should submit up to 5 poems at a** time, photocopied or dot-matrix mss are OK. Submissions are reported on in 3 to 6 months and time to publication is 12 to 18 months. The editor usually provides criticism of rejected mss. Her advice is: "We like poems that go for the throat, with strong, visceral controlling images. We're also interested in poems that comment upon, or challenge the conventions of, the horror genre itself."

GUERNICA EDITIONS INC.; ESSENTIAL POET SERIES, PROSE SERIES, DRAMA SERIES; INTERNA-TIONAL WRITERS (IV-Regional, translations, ethnic/nationality), Box 633 Station NDG, Montreal, Quebec H4A 3R1 Canada, founded 1978, poetry editor Antonio D'Alfonso. "We wish to bring together the **different and often divergent voices that exist in Canada. We are interested in translations. We are mostly interested right now in prose poetry and essays.**" They have recently published poetry by Nicole Brossard (Quebec), Jean-Paul Daoust (Quebec), Antonio Barolini (Italy/USA) and Pier Georgio Di Cicco (Canada). **Query with 1-2 pgs. of samples. Send SASE (Canadian stamps only) or SAE and IRCs for catalog.** The editor comments, "We are interested in promoting a polycultural view of literature by bridging languages and cultures. Besides our specialization in international translation, we also focus on the work of Italian, Italian/Canadian and Italian/American writers."

GUILD PRESS; FULL CIRCLE SERIES (I, IV-Ethnic), P.O. Box 22583, Robbinsdale MN 55422, founded 1978, senior editor Leon Knight, **"The Leading Publisher of Minority Authors in Minnesota," wants poems to 40 line max., nothing sexually graphic.** They have published poetry by Gary Smith, Bernard U. Finney, Jr. and Nancy Ellen Williams (Big Mama). As a sample the editor selected these lines (poet unidentified):

> I thought poetry
>> made a difference
>> . . .
> But photography
>> doesn't alter sunsets:
> poetry does not
>> restrain the wind

The Full Circle Series are **annual anthologies of 35-50 poets. Individual collections are published "by invitation only" to poets who have appeared in the "open-invitation" anthologies. Send SASE for guidelines. Pays copies.**

GULF STREAM MAGAZINE (II), English Dept., Florida International University North Miami Campus, N. Miami FL 33181, phone (305)940-5599, founded 1989, editor Lynne Barrett, associate editors Chris Gleason and Kitty Oliver, is the biannual literary magazine associated with the creative writing program at FIU. They want **"poetry of any style and subject matter as long as it is of high literary quality."** They have published poetry by Gerald Costanzo, Judith Berke and Mike Carson. The handsome magazine is digest-sized, flat-spined, 90+ pgs. on quality stock with glossy card cover. They accept less than 10% of poetry received. Press run: 750. Subscription: $7.50. **Sample postpaid: $4. Send SASE for guidelines. Pays 2 free subscriptions. Acquires first North American serial rights. Submit no more than 5 poems. Reads submissions September 15 through April 30 only. Reports in 6-8 weeks. No simultaneous submissions. Editor comments on submissions "if we feel we can be helpful."**

‡GUT PUNCH PRESS (III), P.O. Box 105, Cabin John MD 20818, founded 1987, editor Derrick Hsu, publishes 1-2 paperbacks/year. They want **"free verse with an innovative edge and possibly a sense of humor. No language school or formal narrative style."** They have recently published poetry collections by Richard Peabody and Reuben Jackson. **Replies to queries in 1 month, to mss (if invited) in 3 months. No poems previously published in book form or simultaneous submissions. Cover letter required.** Time between acceptance and publication is 1 year. Often comments on rejections. **Pays royalties ("determined on an individual basis") and 50 author's copies. For sample books, send SASE for list and order form.** Books are $7.95 postpaid.

GUYASUTA PUBLISHER (I), The Sterling Building, 440 Friday Rd., Pittsburgh PA 15209, phone (412)821-6211, FAX (412)821-6099, founded 1988, owner Cynthia Shore-Sterling. **"Guyasuta offers both straight and co-op publishing. We publish approximately 25 collections of poetry each year.** Our line has recently been expanded to trade paperback, self-help and quality short fiction." They accept mss throughout the year. They own a 67-acre farm in New York which is presently being developed into Guyasuta Writers and Artists Colony. As a sample the owner selected these lines from Diana Rubin's poem "Let Them Eat Cake" from her book **Spirits In Exile**:

> Yet, the homeless woman interjected and still persisted.
> "Cake, please, cake."
> As an unending saga unfolded before
> my eyes in gruesome repetition:

> *Those who haven't bread are often forced to eat cake.*

They will consider simultaneous submissions and unsolicited manuscripts of 25-60 poems. For further information send SASE for catalog and guidelines. Sample: $5.95 (includes shipping).

GYPSY (II); VERGIN' PRESS (V), % Belinda Subraman and S. Ramnath, 10708 Gay Brewer, El Paso TX 79935, founded 1984 (in Germany), general editor Belinda Subraman, publishes poetry, fiction, interviews, articles, artwork and reviews. She wants **poetry that is "striking, moving, but not sentimental, any style, any subject matter.** They have recently published poetry by Peter Wild, Jay Griswold, Antler and Katharyn Howd Machan. As a sample, she selected these lines by Lou Hertz:

> *Oh yes I look.*
> *I know better, but I can't resist.*
> *I know she's having fun at my expense*
> *And yet I'm flattered.*
> *She could be teasing someone else.*
> *Not me.*

Gypsy appears twice a year, with subscribers and contributors from the U.S., Canada, England, Europe, and other foreign countries. It is magazine-sized, offset, usually a hard spine, around 56-90 pages. Circulation is 1,000 for 300 subscriptions of which 40 are libraries, about 20 shelf sales. Subscription: $14 a year; per issue: $8. **Sample: $7 postpaid. Pays 1-3 copies or $5-15. Reports in 1-3 months.** She publishes **2-3 books/year under the Vergin' Press imprint but at present is not accepting unsolicited submissions for these.** New writers establish themselves with her by acceptance in *Gypsy*. She **sometimes comments on rejections.** Belinda Subraman says, "This is not a place for beginners. I'm looking for the best in all genres. Although I don't have anything against work of total self-absorption (guess I write some of that myself), I am just about fed up with it. I'd like to see work with a more universal appeal, a searching to connect, an understanding or a trying to understand other peoples in the universe. Please do not submit blindly. **We are planning a series of paperback anthologies on important issues. Send SASE for details.** Also please be advised that poetry is only about ⅓ (or less) of our focus these days. We value other forms of expression equally (if not more)."

HAIGHT ASHBURY LITERARY JOURNAL (II, IV-Social issues), Dept. PM, 558 Joost Ave., San Francisco CA 94127, phone (415)221-2017, founded 1979-1980, editors Lena Diethelm, Joanne Hotchkiss, Alice Rogoff and Will Walker, is a newsprint tabloid that appears 1-3 times a year. They use **"all forms and lengths, subject matter sometimes political, but open to all subjects. Poems of background — prison, minority experience — often published, as well as poems of protest and of Central America. Few rhymes."** They have published poetry by Leslie Simon, Jack Micheline, Gary David, Bill Shields and Eugene Ruggles. The tabloid has photos of featured poets on the cover, uses graphics, ads, 16 pgs., circulation 2,000. $25 for a lifetime subscription, which includes all back issues. **Sample postpaid: $2.50. Make checks payable to Alice Rogoff. Send SASE for guidelines. Pays 3 copies. Reports in 2 months. Submit up to 6 poems or 8 pgs.** Photocopy OK, simultaneous OK "if we are informed. Each issue changes its theme and emphasis. Don't be discouraged if rejected, and please submit again."

HAIKU HEADLINES: A MONTHLY NEWSLETTER OF HAIKU AND SENRYU (IV-Form), 1347 W. 71st, Los Angeles CA 90044, founded 1988, editor/publisher David Priebe, uses **haiku and senryu** only. They have recently published haiku by Matthew Louviere, Dorothy McLaughlin, Mark Arvid White and Yvonne Hardenbrook. As a sample the editor selected these haiku by Rengé:

> *whatever language*   *carnival balloon*
> *random objects speak: the rain*   *rising up . . . and up . . . fading*
>   *speaks it fluently*   *into the darkness*

The newsletter is 8 pgs., 8½ × 11, stapled and punched for a three-ring notebook, desktop publishing. They accept about 10% of submissions. Their press run is 275 with 160 subscriptions of which 3 are libraries. Subscription: $18. **Sample postpaid: $1.50. Pays 1 copy with SASE, or free extra copy to subscribers. Haiku may be submitted with up to 10 per single page. Submissions are "answered with proof sheets of acceptances, suggested revisions sheets, with occasional notes on originals — within 4-6 weeks."** Monthly contest Readers' Choice Awards: The Awards Kitty (average $20 — contributions of postage stamps by the voters) is divided half for the 1st place winner; two runners-up share the other half. *HH* also sponsored a Rhyming Haiku Contest (prizes $100, $50, $25) and published **Ecopoems**, an anthology of the 100 winners.

HAIKU JOURNAL; GEPPO HAIKU JOURNAL; HAIKU JOURNAL MEMBERS' ANTHOLOGY (I, IV-Form, membership), P.O. Box 1250, Gualala CA 95445, phone (707)882-2226, *HJ* founded 1977 and first published by the Yuki Teipei Haiku Society, editor Jane Reichhold. *HJ* is devoted to haiku and haiku criticism; contest winners and **"members' haiku only are published here."** *Geppo* is a mimeographed newsletter for members using **haiku, especially traditional haiku: 17 syllables with a KIGO."**

The editor describes these as "around 60 pgs., 6×9, nicely printed on heavy paper, card stock cover." Press run 300 for 100 subscriptions of which 10 are libraries. **Sample postpaid: $4.50. Send SASE for guidelines. Simultaneous submissions and previously published poems OK. Editor comments on submissions "especially if response is requested."** They have an annual contest in the spring. Send SASE for rules.

HALF TONES TO JUBILEE (II), English Department, Pensacola Junior College, 1000 College Blvd., Pensacola FL 32504, phone (904)484-1400, founded 1986, faculty editors Walter Spara and Allan Peterson, is an annual literary journal featuring poetry and short fiction. They have published poetry by R.T. Smith, Sue Walker, Larry Rubin and Simon Perchik. As a sample we selected these lines from "Penpal Who Has Not Written" by Andrea Hollander Budy:

> You are the one I've never met who
> wrote so splendidly when I needed you
> and I am the one who, after awhile, let
> years grow like a row of taverns
> between receiving and giving
> back. . .

HTTJ is digest-sized, 100+ pgs., perfect-bound with matte card cover, professionally printed. Press run is 500. They receive 1,000 submissions/year, use 50-60. Subscriptions: $4. **Sample: $4. No previously published work, no simultaneous submissions, SASE mandatory. Reads submissions August 1 through May 15 only. Reports in 2-3 months, faster when possible. Pays 2 copies. Acquires first rights.** *HTTJ* sponsors an annual poetry competition, $300 first prize, $200 second, two $50 third prizes. Entry fee $2/poem. Send SASE for rules, deadlines.

HAMMERS; DOUBLESTAR PRESS (II), 1718 Sherman #205, Evanston IL 60201, founded 1989, editor Nat David. *Hammers*, "an end of millennium irregular poetry magazine," appears at least twice a year. Many of the poets they have published are from the Chicago area, although each issue also includes the work of poets from a variety of other geographical regions. In 1999, the editor intends to publish in book form **The Best of Hammers**. They want **"honest, well-written poetry from the depths of the poet's universe and experience, which is cognizant of our interconnectedness."** They have recently published poetry by Antler, Victor di Suvero, Morgan Gibson, Effie Mihopoulos, Luis Rodriguez, Cindy Salach and Michael Warr. As a sample the editor selected these lines from "Molly in The Kitchen" by John Dickson:

> . . . read as Frank O'Hara read,
> the way he'd read his poems to Jane and Larry,
> Grace, and all his hundred thousand friends,
> each poem a celebration of knowing them—
> marking their lives, welding them all together.

Price per issue: $5. **Sample postpaid: $6. Editor seldom comments on submissions. Reports ASAP. Pays 1 copy.**

THE HAMPDEN-SYDNEY POETRY REVIEW (III, IV-Translations), P.O. Box 126, Hampden-Sydney VA 23943, poetry editor Tom O'Grady, has published such poets as A.R. Ammons, Dick Allen, James Dickey, X.J. Kennedy, William Stafford and James Schevill. He features traditional and free verse alongside each other. The free verse is structured, with attention paid to line length, break and stanza, and you'll find the work of well-known and relative unknown poets side-by-side. **"We also publish translations."** As a sample here is the first stanza of Michael Egan's "The Hex":

> There are hexes here in our country.
> The farmers touch-up hexsigns; the Brethren
> sidestep crones, arointing
> the evil eye.

The quarterly is 6×9, handsomely printed on heavy stock paper and perfect-bound with 2-color, glossy covers. In general, the writing is accessible, clear, with emphasis on idea and sound. **Sample: $5 postpaid.** 1975-90 Anthology, 140 poets, 330 pgs., $12.95 postpaid.

HANGING LOOSE PRESS (V); HANGING LOOSE (I, II, IV-Teens/students), 231 Wyckoff St., Brooklyn NY 11217, founded 1966, poetry editors Robert Hershon, Dick Lourie, Mark Pawlak and Ron Schreiber. The press accepts no unsolicited book mss, but welcomes work for the magazine. The magazine has published poets such as Paul Violi, Donna Brook, Kimiko Hahn, Ron Overton, Jack Anderson and Frances Phillips. *Hanging Loose* is flat-spined, 96 pgs., offset, now in its 25th year, on heavy stock with a 2-color glossy card cover. One section contains **poems by high-school-age poets. The editor says it "concentrates on the work of new writers."** It appears 3 times a year. **Sample postpaid: $6.50. Submit 4-6 "excellent, energetic" poems, no simultaneous submissions. "Would-be contributors should read the magazine first." Reports in 1-12 weeks. Pays.**

Close-up

Arnold Adoff
Poet

It Is Late

When We Walk   Back From Our Healthy Walk Tonight
The
Moon Is So Full   It Is Almost   Bursting   O p e n
Like That Over
ripe   Pumpkin In   Our
G a r d e n

The
Moon Is Hanging Like That   Pumpkin
Without   A F a c e
Over
Our
H e d g e

We Want To   Carve   A Face
Into
This Harvest Moon Tonight And Have It   Grin An
Autumn   Greeting
In The   Fall Air

Seeds Of   Starlight
S c a t t e r   Everywhere

"To do anything for young people is an extraordinary experience," Arnold Adoff asserts. He has devoted his entire career to children, first as a teacher, counselor and reading specialist, and eventually, fulltime poet and lecturer. "I take a world view," he says, explaining that he tries to address children "as if they were first-class citizens of the world." He is obviously reaching them, as he was awarded the National Council of Teachers of English Award for Excellence in Poetry for Children in 1988. In addition, The American Library Association has designated six of his books as Notable Books for Children.

"I really always only wanted to be a poet—always a poet," he says, adding, "Poetry and puberty happened at the same time." Adoff began his career as a teacher and counselor in the public schools of Harlem, where he spent 12 years. That experience gave him exposure to and insight into African-American culture. His first book, **I Am the Darker Brother** (1968), is an anthology born of his involvement with black Americans. Today, nine anthologies and 15 poetry books carry his byline.

Adoff's ideas germinate in the commonplace and in small things so usual they're often overlooked. **Greens** (Lothrop, Lee & Shepard Books), a collection of poems about a garden hose, money, evergreen trees and grasshoppers, among other green things, exemplifies this approach. He presents such common things as "freshly seen or freshly visualized.

"Impressions are my first concern. I attempt to frame what I see," he explains. He jots notes on legal pads and carries with him Post-it note pads and green file cards for noteworthy impressions. Using only one side of the paper or cards enables him to create long scrolls, each pertaining to a single idea. At the revision stage, he tacks the scrolls onto his bookcases. "I'm a slow writer when I want to write well. I've been known to do 75 drafts of a single poem," he reveals.

Sometimes a Post-it bearing only a title serves to spur him to work at the beginning of the day. Once an idea has captured his interest, he expands it on sheets of paper, then progresses to his electronic typewriter.

"I feel a rhythm and a beat that is inevitable. Inevitability is my goal," Adoff says. In his predominant form, shaped colloquial speech, he takes a semantic line of force and adds a rhythmic line of force. "I sing as well as say," he explains. He says that in all his work, he aims for "more inference and implication, less bald, flat-out statement.

"I'm never far from working. Work and life are very closely, organically, synthesized in our lives," the poet says of life in Yellow Springs, Ohio, with his wife, children's author Virginia Hamilton. Regarding rural living, the New York native comments, "I've never become a farmer. I've never been comfortable in the quiet. You live inside your head a lot." He has found an escape from the intensity of creating, however, in pruning trees, painting fences and chopping wood.

Photo by J. Lynne Bloss

Adoff and Hamilton spend time every other month in New York City, where their two grown children live. There, Adoff meets with his major influences, jazz and paintings, especially the work of the Russian constructivist painters of the early 1900s. The latter feature skyscrapers, which have prompted the vertical format Adoff frequently uses. "I don't believe writing is for self-expression. I write to create art," he says.

Adoff regards his most exciting work as "a synthesis of reality and fantasy." **Flamboyan** (Harcourt Brace Jovanovich), for example, is based on a tropical tree and a young girl who enables herself to fly through self-empowerment when she creates magic. **The Cabbages Are Chasing the Rabbits** (Harcourt Brace Jovanovich) is another fantasy in which a garden of vegetables rebels against the rabbits who eat them. A chain reaction ensues until, finally, hunters abandon their guns.

"I welcome people because not nearly as many people are writing poetry as should be," Adoff says of newcomers to the children's poetry field. He advises, "Get *Writer's Digest*, get query letters out, agonize over rejections, approach the field as you would approach any of the arts. Read the way a surgeon reads—to keep up. Try to do something fresh and see if you can come in that way. Have a lifelong commitment; you'll be a better person for it even if you're never published."

Arnold Adoff's commitment to his art is evident. As he describes himself, "I'm still trying to become a poet. As good as I get, I can always get better."

—J. Lynne Bloss

HANGMAN BOOKS (II), 2 May Rd., Rochester, Kent ME1 2HY England, founded 1982, editor Jack Ketch, publishes selected books of poetry on a cooperative basis. Jack Ketch says, "We receive no grant, **therefore we expect the writers to put their money where their mouth is. We don't advertise this fact as we are not a vanity press, we only approach a writer with this proposal if we are sufficiently impressed with their work and want to help them (this is very rare)."** They want "personal" poetry, **"none rhyming, none political, bla bla bla." 60% of press run belongs to poet.** They have recently published poetry by Criss Broderick, N. Sparkes and B. Childish. As a sample the editor selected these lines from **May My Piss Be Gentle** by Mark Lowe:

> all those tears
> all that madness and grief
> in that big old house of ours
> and i think back
> and it's like i'm drowning
> in a whole fucking river
> of unnecessary sadness

That is from a handsomely printed flat-spined book, 110 pgs.

HANSON'S: A SYMPOSIUM OF LITERARY AND SOCIAL INTEREST (II), 113 Merryman Court, Annapolis MD 21401, phone (410)626-0744, founded 1988, is a semiannual using **"all forms, styles, subjects and points of view reflective of intelligence and a sense of beauty."** As a sample the editor selected these lines from "Voices" by Robert Johnson:

> Will the Spirits of the Age forgive a man,
> If he speaks of small concerns?
> Or the Spirits of All Time,
> If he speaks of himself?
> Poetry is lost upon those who question it,
> And dead to those who take up pen
> To write a perfect line.

It is magazine-sized, 75-100 pgs., saddle-stapled with matte card cover. Press run 3,000 for 1,500 subscriptions including 2 library systems. "We receive thousands of poems per year, publish about 30-40 per year." **Sample postpaid: $5. Send SASE for guidelines with 2 first class stamps. Reads submissions October 1 through August 31 only. Pays $10-20 plus 1 copy. Buys first North American serial rights. "Previous publication is not a prerequisite. We'd rather see honest, careful art, than a resume." Reports in 2-3 weeks. Editor seldom comments on submissions.** The editor says, "As *Hanson's* is in no way a standard literary magazine, the review of a sample copy is the best method for determining the suitability of your work for submission."

HARCOURT BRACE JOVANOVICH, PUBLISHERS; HBJ CHILDREN'S BOOKS; GULLIVER BOOKS (IV-Children), 1250 Sixth Ave., San Diego CA 92101, phone (619)699-6810, HBJ Children's Books and Gulliver Books publish hardback and trade paperback books for children. They have recently published books of children's poetry by Jane Yolen, Arnold Adoff, James Dickey, e.e. cummings, Lee Bennett Hopkins and Carl Sandburg. **Submit complete ms. No dot-matrix. Pays favorable advance, royalty contract and copies. Send SASE for guidelines and book catalog.**

HARD ROW TO HOE; MISTY HILL PRESS (I, IV-Nature, rural, ecology), P.O. Box 541-I, Healdsburg CA 95448, phone (707)433-9786. *Hard Row to Hoe,* taken over from Seven Buffaloes Press in 1987, editor Joe E. Armstrong, is a "book review newsletter of literature from rural America with a section reserved for short stories (about 2,000 words) and **poetry featuring unpublished authors. The subject matter must apply to rural America including nature and environmental subjects. Poems of 30 lines or less given preference, but no arbitrary limit. No style limits. Do not want any subject matter not related to rural subjects."** As a sample the editor selected "How It Happened" by Kathleen M. McCann:

> Put me three miles
> into my run,
> Cutting through
> a darkened cemetery
> past ponds & headstones.
>
> Once more let me hear
> a whole sky open
> with their coming:
>
> Geese!
> Pumping through this night

in glory,
absolute glory.

HRTH is magazine-sized, 12 pgs., side-stapled, appearing 3 times a year, 3 pgs. reserved for short stories and poetry. Press run 300. Subscription: $7/year. **Sample postpaid: $2. Send SASE for guidelines. Pays 3 copies. Acquires one-time rights. Editor comments on rejections "if I think the quality warrants."** Reviews books of poetry in 600-700 words.

HARP-STRINGS; EDNA ST. VINCENT MILLAY AWARD; ELIZABETH B. BROWNING SONNETS AWARD; DYLAN THOMAS VILLANELLE AWARD (I), 310 S. Adams St., Beverly Hills FL 32665, founded 1989, editor Madelyn Eastlund, appears 3 times/year. **They want poems of "14-70 lines, narratives, lyrics, ballads, sestinas, rondeau, redouble, blank verse. Nothing 'dashed off,' trite, broken prose masquerading as poetry."** They have recently published poetry by Barbara Nightingale, Dorothy Winslow Wright, Taylor Graham and Ralph Hammond. As a sample the editor selected a stanza from "The Last Holdout" by Ruth Rodgers:

They'll be back today with all their charts and briefs,
their honey-coated voices. They'll tell her once again
how these new miles of highway will affect the traffic flow;
they'll cite statistics, flatter her with bribes,
press her to sign away her past with their silver pen.

It is 36 pgs., digest-sized, saddle-stapled, professionally printed in colored ink on quality colored matte stock with matte card cover. She accepts 5-10% of poems received **in February, June and October only. Press run 100 for 75 subscribers. Subscription: $20. Sample postpaid: $5.50 for previous year, $6.50 for current year. Pays 1 copy. Acquires one-time rights. "I am interested in seeing poems that have won awards but have not been published."** Sponsors 3 contests each year: Elizabeth B. Browning Sonnets Award (Shakespearean or Petrarchan Sonnet, deadline March 15); Edna St. Vincent Millay Award (narrative from 32 to 75 lines, deadline July 15); Dylan Thomas Villanelle Award (deadline November 15). Entry fee: $2/poem, $5/3 poems. Cash awards of $10-40 and publication. "Stanley Kunitz once said, 'Poetry today has become easier to write but harder to remember.' *Harp-Strings* wants poetry to remember, poetry that haunts, poetry the reader wants to read again and again."

THE HARTLAND POETRY QUARTERLY; HARTLAND PRESS (I, II, IV-Children, themes), Dept. PM, 168 Fremont, Romeo MI 48065, phone (313)752-5507, founded 1989, contact David Bock. **"Prefer 24 lines or less; no style restrictions; no pornography—none—nada—nil! Looking for serious poems by Viet Nam veterans and I mean serious—don't send the one-and-only angry poem—I got that stuff coming out of my ears. Very, very open to good children's poems written only by children under 15 for a special 'coming out' part of the magazine."** They have published poetry by Loriann Zimmer, T. Kilgore Splake and Laurence W. Thomas. Their quarterly is digest-sized, spine-stapled, 25-30 pgs. They accept about 15% of 300-500 poems received/year. Press run 500, with 70 subscribers of which 15 are libraries, 300 shelf sales. Subscription: $8. **Sample postpaid: $1. Pays 2 copies. Reports in 8-10 weeks. Include bio with submission.** Reviews books of poetry. **They publish 2 chapbooks/year of poets already published in the quarterly. Pays 20 copies.** The editor says, "Write about what you have lived. Read, read, write, write—repeat cycle 'till death. Support as many small publications as you can afford."

‡THE HARVARD ADVOCATE (IV-Specialized/university affiliation), 21 South St., Cambridge MA 02138, founded 1866, is a quarterly literary magazine, circulation 4,000, publishes poetry, fiction and art only by those affiliated with Harvard University. Sample: $5. **Reads submissions September through May 1 only. In submitting state your exact relationship to Harvard. Does not pay. Reads submissions September 1 through May 31 only.** Reviews books of poetry in 1,000 words, single or multi-book format.

‡HAWAI'I PACIFIC REVIEW (II), 1060 Bishop St., Honolulu HI 96813, founded 1986, editor Elizabeth Fischel, is an annual literary journal "publishing quality poetry, short fiction and personal essays from writers worldwide. **Although we publish poems of all styles and themes, our journal does exhibit an international flavor and we wish to encourage this. Quality of poetic technique and expression is our greatest criterion. Although we do publish beginning poets on occasion, we do not publish amateurish poetry. We look for *fresh* topics, themes and styles."** They have recently published poetry by Sibyl James and Michael L. Johnson. As a sample the editor selected this poem, "April Night when the Full Moon is Brighter than the Northern Lights" by Sheila Nickerson:

A small button moon moves up the sky
searching for a hole,
but seamless night does not oblige.
What is lost and mismatched must travel loose.

> *See, Mother Wind opens her button box*
> *and we tumble out, rolling across the dark:*
> *some bright, some not, all made of bone.*

HPR is 80-120 pgs., 6×9, professionally printed on quality paper, perfect-bound, with coated card cover; each issue features original artwork. They receive 800-1,000 poems, accept 30-40. Press run is approximately 1,000 for 200 shelf sales. Single copy: $5-6. **Sample postpaid: $3. No previously published poems; simultaneous submissions OK. Cover letter with 5-line bio required. Seldom comments on rejections. Send SASE for guidelines. Reports within 3 months. Pays 2 copies. Acquires first North American serial rights.** A beautifully designed publication, *HPR* features mostly free verse that speaks to America's past and present with a focus on cultural diversity. The poems are insightful, informative and (in many cases) well-made.

HAWAI'I REVIEW (I, II), % Department of English, 1733 Donaghho Rd., University of Hawai'i, Honolulu HI 96822, phone (808)956-8548, poetry editors Kathy Banggo and Jacqueline Chun. "We are interested in **all sorts of poetry, from free verse to formal lyricism, rhyme and meter; heroic narrative, haiku, light verse, satire and experimentation; we're also interested in poems translated from other languages; and while** *Hawai'i Review* **has published poets with established reputations like Eric Chock and W.S. Merwin, the beginner is also welcome.**" They have recently published poetry by lyn lifshin, Lois-Ann Yamanaka and Tony Quagliano, among others, and translations by Carolyn Tipton and Alexis Levitin. As a sample the editors selected the poem "The Pearl" by Cai Qi-Jiao, translated by Edward Morin and Dennis Ding:

> *The wound inside*
> *The oyster's tender body*
> *Expands into a hard, rough obstruction.*
> *Month by month, year after year,*
> *Wrapped in layer upon adhesive layer,*
> *It becomes mellow and smooth.*
> *Here you see crystaline grief and sea tears,*
> *Yet all humankind treasures it!*
> *I sense that it still wears the salt smell of the ocean,*
> *That its glistening teardrops bear*
> *The laments of sun, moon, stars, and clouds.*

HR appears 3 times yearly, 160 pgs., flat-spined, 6½×9½, professionally printed on heavy stock with b&w or color cover, 150 subscriptions of which 40 are libraries. Up to 1,800 are used by University of Hawai'i students. Subscription: $15/one year; $25/two years. **Sample: $5. Send SASE for guidelines.** "Artwork to accompany poetry is welcomed." **Pays $10-60 plus 2 copies. Buys first North American serial rights. Editors rarely comment on rejections. Reporting time: 3-4 months.** Publication 9-12 months thereafter. Does not normally review books, but "authors can query." The staff rotates regularly. Sometimes one staff rejects work that has "come close" and suggests sending the same manuscript in the next year to see what the new editors think. The editors say, "Good poetry shows more than psuedo-literary erudition; it will, as Anthony Wallace says, *sing* and *mean.*"

HAYDEN'S FERRY REVIEW (II), Matthews Center, Arizona State University, Tempe AZ 85287-1502, phone (602)965-1243, founded 1986, managing editor Salima Keegan, is a handsome literary magazine appearing twice a year. They have published poetry by Dennis Schmitz, Maura Stanton, Ai, and David St. John. *HFR* is 6×9, 120+ pgs., flat-spined with glossy card cover. Press run 1,000 for 100 subscribers of which 30 are libraries, 500 shelf sales. They accept about 3% of 800 submissions annually. Subscription: $10. **Sample postpaid: $6. Send SASE for guidelines.** "**No specifications other than limit in number (6) and no simultaneous submissions. We would like a brief bio for contributor's note included.**" **Reports in 8-10 weeks of deadlines. Deadlines: February 28 for Spring/Summer issue; September 30 for Fall/Winter. Submissions circulated to two poetry editors. Contributors receive galley proofs. Editor comments on submissions** "often." **Pays 2 copies.**

HEAVEN BONE PRESS; HEAVEN BONE MAGAZINE (II, IV-Spiritual, nature/ecology), P.O. Box 486, Chester NY 10918, phone (914)469-9018, founded 1986, poetry editor Steve Hirsch, publishes poetry, fiction, essays and reviews with "**an emphasis on spiritual, metaphysical, esoteric and ecological concerns.**" Issue #9 includes poetry and fiction by Charles Bukowski, Marge Piercy, Kirpal Gordon and Hart Sprager. As a sample the editor chose "Five-Petaled Regular Corolla Rose" by Edward Mycue:

> *has surrounding fingers that play*
> *with your nose from the inner en-*
> *velope. This is not the Rose of*
> *Sharon. That spindling hollyhock*

is as near to a rose as a hemlock.
The rosary has five sacred mysteries
and five decades of Ave Marias, &
each begins with a paternoster, ends
with a Gloria, repeated in formula
like a prayer or/and magic-mystic
charm: more of a path than pastime.
Rose, you single step, pilgrimage,
you Rose, of colored hope, chafe.
You are window, compass, pleasantly
rote: I know you now, know you not.

Heaven Bone is magazine-sized, saddle-stapled, 64 pgs., using b&w art, photos and ads, on recycled bond stock with glossy 4-color recycled card cover. They have a press run of 1,000. Of 250-350 poems received they accept 18-30. Subscription: $14.95. **Sample postpaid: $5. Pays 2 copies. Acquires first North American serial rights. Submit 3-10 poems. Simultaneous submissions and previously published poems OK "if notified." Reports in 2 weeks to 6 months, up to 6 months until publication.** Reviews books of poetry. Editor advises, "Please be familiar with the magazine before sending mss. Break free of common 'poetic' limitations and speak freely with no contrivances. No forced end-line rhyming please. Channel the muse and music without being an obstacle to the poem." Annual chapbook contest; send SASE for guidelines.

HELICON NINE EDITIONS; MARIANNE MOORE POETRY PRIZE (III), P.O. Box 22412, Kansas City MO 64113, phone (913)722-2999, founded 1977, editor Gloria Vando Hickok. Helicon Nine, formerly a literary magazine, now is a publisher of books of poetry as well as fiction, creative nonfiction and anthologies. **"Our one requirement is excellence; nothing pedestrian."** They have published poetry by Joyce Carol Oates, Grace Paley, Ellen Gilchrist and James Dickey. As a sample the editor selected these lines from "A Physics of Postwar Music" by Biff Russ from her first book, **Black Method**, winner of the 1991 Marianne Moore Poetry Prize:

The first lesson was science:
you held your violin towards the light,
cupping your hand behind its waist,
showing me that (except for a small piece of wood
propped between front and back) I would see
nothing inside.

Afterwards you started to play: the sound came out
of its emptiness, shaped like the human body.

They are not encouraging submissions at this time. Please query. "Payment varies, but we're in the publishing business to *help* poets and authors, not to hinder them or take advantage. We **publish *beautiful* books and try to get them into the hands of readers.** We have national distributors making sure our books are made available throughout the States. We also aggressively pursue new markets and book reviews and advertise in many trade publications as well as exhibit at the ABA, etc." The Marianne Moore Poetry Prize is given annually, $1,000 for an unpublished poetry ms of at least 50 pgs. The award includes publication by Helicon Nine Editions. Deadline: January 31.

HELLAS: A JOURNAL OF POETRY AND THE HUMANITIES; THE LOUIS NIGRONI HELLAS AWARD (II, IV-Form), 304 S. Tyson Ave., Glenside PA 19038, phone (215)884-1086, founded 1988, editor Gerald Harnett. *Hellas* is a semiannual that wants poetry of **"any kind but especially poems in meter. We prize elegance and formality in verse, but specifically encourage poetry of the utmost boldness and innovation, so long as it is not willfully obscurantist; no ignorant, illiterate, meaningless free verse or political poems."** They have published poetry by Marcus, Moore, Butler, Kessler and many others. As a sample we selected these lines from "Seed" by Charley Custer:

Within the hard damp dark, marooned
in rot between dead root and weed
through every bitter winter wound
and solstice, is the seed.

It is 172 pgs., 6×9, flat-spined, offset, using b&w art. Press run is 750. Subscription: $12. **Sample postpaid: $7.75. Send SASE for guidelines. Pays 1 copy. Acquires first North American serial rights.** They will consider simultaneous submissions and previously published poems "if they let us know, but please don't bother unless it's specifically suited to *Hellas*." Reports in 2-3 months. Editor comments on rejections "happily if requested. If I don't understand it, I don't print it. On the other hand, we don't want obvious, easy, clichéd or sentimental verse." The best poem or group of poems annually is awarded The Louis Nigroni Hellas Award ($200). Their flyer says, *"Hellas* is a lively and provocative assault on a century of modernist barbarism in the arts. A unique, Miltonic wedding of *paideia* and *poesis*, engaging scholarship and original poetry, *Hellas* has become the forum of a remarkable new generation of poets, critics and theorists committed to the renovation of the art of our time . . . **Meter is especially welcome, as well as rhymed and stanzaic verse. We judge a poem by its verbal artifice, its formal harmony and its truth. Lines should not end arbitrarily, diction should be precise: we suggest that such principles can appear 'limiting' only to an impoverished imagination. To the contrary: we encourage any conceivable boldness and innovation, so long as it is executed with discipline and is not a masquerade for self-indulgent obscurantism. . . . We do not print poems about Nicaragua, whales or an author's body parts. We do specifically welcome submissions from newer authors."**

HEN'S TEETH (V), P.O. Box 689, Brookings SD 57006, founded 1988, editor Janice H. Mikesell. She expects to publish a book every 2 years but **will not be open for submissions. "I publish material that I have either written or co-edited only. Unsolicited material, unless accompanied by a SASE, will not even be returned."** She has published **Women Houses & Homes: an anthology of prose, poetry and photography,** $8 (plus $1 postage), a 52-page, saddle-stapled book, cut with a roof-line top, professionally printed with a cover photograph of a "painted lady" Victorian house. Most recent publication is **A Survivor's Manual: a book of poems,** $6 (plus $1 postage), a 52-page, perfect-bound quality paperback with an arresting cover photo.

HERESIES (IV-Women/feminism, lesbian, themes), P.O. Box 1306, Canal St. Station, New York NY 10013, founded 1977, editorial collective, is a "feminist publication on art and politics." **Poetry "must be by women and fit into the specific issue theme."** They have published poetry by Adrienne Rich, Alice Walker and Margaret Randall. *Heresies,* one of the oldest and best-known feminist publications, appears 1-2 times a year in a 96-page, flat-spined, magazine-sized format, offset with half-tones, 2-color glossy card cover, using nonprofit, book related exchange ads. They accept about 10 out of 100 submissions. Press runs 5,000 for 1,500 subscriptions of which a fourth are libraries, 1,500 shelf sales. Per issue: $6.75; subscription: $23/4 issues. **Sample, back issues postpaid: $6. Send SASE for guidelines. Pays small honorarium plus 3 copies. Simultaneous submissions OK. Reports in 8-12 months.**

‡HERSPECTIVES (IV-Women, feminism), Box 2047, Squamish, British Columbia V0N 3G0 Canada, phone (604)892-5723, founded 1989, editor Mary Billy, uses **"poetry that expresses women's lives in a positive experiential way — open to almost anything by, for or about women. Nothing obscure, intellectual, wheel-spinners."** As a sample the editor selected these lines by Gert Beadle:

> When they have closed
>   The windows where I fled
> And gave the empty house
>   to fire
>   Will they remember how
>   I loved a mystery

It appears quarterly in a 40-50 page stapled format. Uses 4-6 poems/issue. Press run 250 for 85 subscribers of which 1 is a library. Subscription: $22-35 ($35-45 US); $40-50 for businesses and organizations. **Sample postpaid: $6. Pays 1 copy. Simultaneous submissions and previously published poetry OK. Editor often comments on rejections.** Reviews books of poetry in 500-750 words. They also use fiction and other writing. **"We are mainly interested in giving new writers exposure. I don't like poetry that is so obscure only the mentally defective can understand it. We are about openness and ideas, about women's creative expression, wherever that may lead them."**

HIGH PLAINS LITERARY REVIEW (III), Suite 250, 180 Adams St., Denver CO 80206, phone (303)320-6828, founded 1986, editor Robert O. Greer, associate poetry editor Ray Gonzalez, appears 3 times/year using **"high quality poetry, fiction, essays, book reviews and interviews."** The format is 135 pgs., 70 lb. paper, heavy cover stock. Subscription: $20. **Sample postpaid: $7. Pays $10/published page for poetry.**

HIGH PLAINS PRESS (IV-Regional), P.O. Box 123, Glendo WY 82213, phone (307)735-4370, founded 1985, poetry editor Nancy Curtis, considers poetry **"specifically relating to Wyoming and the West, particularly those poems based on historical people/events. We're mainly a publisher of historical nonfiction, but do publish a book of poetry about every other year."** They have published poetry by Peggy Simson Curry, Robert Roripaugh and Mary Alice Gunderson. As a sample she quoted these lines from the book **No Roof But Sky** by Jane Candia Coleman. The poem is "Geronimo photographed at Ft. Sill (1905)":

> Bring me the elusive images
> of my life, and I will smile for you —
> over and over — an exchange of illusions

like the dying change into light.

Reports in 2 months, publication in 18-24 months. Pays 10% of sales. Buys first rights. Catalog available on request; sample chapbooks $5.

HIGH/COO PRESS; MAYFLY (IV-Subscriber, form), 4634 Hale Dr., Decatur IL 62526, phone (217)877-2966, founded 1976, editor Randy Brooks. High/Coo is a small press publishing nothing but **haiku in English.** "We publish haiku poemcards, minichapbooks and a bibliography of haiku publications in addition to flat-spined paperbacks and hardbound cloth editions and the magazine *Mayfly*, evoking emotions from contemporary experience. We are not interested in orientalism nor Japanese imitations." They publish no poetry except haiku. They have published haiku by Elizabeth S. Lamb, Virgil Hutton and Lee Gurga. As a sample we selected this haiku by Helen J. Sherry:

> bag lady
>   moving her everything
>   out of the sun

Mayfly is 16 pgs., saddle-stapled, 3×5, professionally printed on high-quality stock, one haiku/page. It appears in February, May and September. They publish "about 50" of an estimated 3,000 submissions. Subscription: $10. **Sample postpaid: $3.50. A Macintosh computer disk of samples and haiku-related stacks is available for $1 postage and handling. Guidelines available for SASE. Pays $5/poem and no copies. "Contributors are required to be subscribers." Submit no more than 5 haiku/issue. No simultaneous submissions or previously published poems. High/ Coo Press considers mss "by invitation only."** Randy Brooks says, "Publishing poetry is a joyous work of love. We publish to share those moments of insight contained in evocative haiku. We aren't in it for fame, gain or name. We publish to serve an enthusiastic readership of haiku writers."

HIGHLIGHTS FOR CHILDREN (IV-Children), 803 Church St., Honesdale PA 18431, phone (717)253-1080, founded 1946, appears every month except July-August is a combined issue. Using **poetry for children aged 2-12.** "Meaningful and/or fun poems accessible to children of all ages. Rarely publish a poem longer than 16 lines, most are shorter. **No poetry that is unintelligible to children, poems containing sex, violence or unmitigated pessimism.**" They have published poetry by Nikki Giovanni, Aileen Fisher, John Ciardi, A.A. Milne, Myra Cohn Livingston, Langston Hughes and William Jay Smith. It is generally 44 pgs., magazine-sized, full-color throughout. They purchase 6-10 of 300 submissions/year. Press run 3.3 million for approximately 3 million subscribers. Subscription: $19.95 (one year; reduced rates for multiple years). **Sample postpaid: free. Payment "money varies" plus 2 copies. Buys all rights. Submit ms typed with very brief cover letter. Please indicate if simultaneous submission. Reports "generally within 1 month." Editor comments on submissions "occasionally, if ms has merit or author seems to have potential for our market."** He says, "We are always open to submissions of poetry not previously published. However, we purchase a very limited amount of such material. We may use the verse as 'filler,' or illustrate the verse with a full-page piece of art. Please note that we do not buy material from anyone under 16 years old."

HIPPOPOTAMUS PRESS; OUTPOSTS POETRY QUARTERLY; OUTPOSTS ANNUAL POETRY COMPETITION (II, IV-Form), 22 Whitewell Rd., Frome, Somerset BA11 4EL England, *Outposts* founded 1943, Hippopotamus Press founded 1974, poetry editor Roland John, who explains, "*Outposts* is a general poetry magazine that welcomes all work either from the recognized or the unknown poet. **The Hippopotamus Press is specialized, with an affinity with Modernism. No Typewriter, Concrete, Surrealism.** The press publishes 6 full collections per year." They have published in *OPQ* poetry by John Heath-Stubbs, Peter Dale and Elizabeth Jennings. *Outposts* is digest-sized, 70-100 pgs., flat-spined, litho, in professionally set small type, using ads. Of 120,000 poems received he uses about 300. Press run is 3,000 for 2,800 subscriptions of which 10% are libraries, 2% of circulation through shelf sales. Subscription: $24. **Sample postpaid: $8. Pays $8/poem plus 1 copy. Copyright remains with author. Simultaneous submissions, previously published poems OK. Reports in 2 weeks plus post time.** Reviews books of poetry in 200 words for "Books Received" page. Uses full essays up to 4,000 words. The magazine also holds an annual poetry competition. Hippopotamus Press publishes 6 books a year, averaging 80 pgs. **For book publication query with sample poems. Simultaneous, previously published, dot-matrix, photocopies all OK. Reports in 6 weeks. Pays 10% minimum royalties plus 20 paper copies, 6 cloth. Send for book catalog to buy samples.**

HIRAM POETRY REVIEW (II), P.O. Box 162, Hiram OH 44234, founded 1967, poetry editors Hale Chatfield and Carol Donley, is a semiannual with occasional special supplements. "We favor new **talent—and except for one issue in two years, read *only* unsolicited mss.**" They are interested in "**all kinds of high quality poetry**" and have published poetry by Grace Butcher, David Citino, Michael Finley, Jim Daniels, Peter Klappert and Harold Witt. As a sample they offer these lines from "Three Musics" by William Johnson:

Grief has a sound
the way snow ticks
and falls away
from the metal light pole.

There are 30 + pgs. of poetry in the professionally printed, digest-sized, saddle-stapled magazine (glossy cover with b&w photo). It has a circulation of 400, 250 subscriptions of which 150 are libraries. They receive about 7,500 submissions/year, use 50, have up to a 6-month backlog. Single copy: $2; subscription: $4. **Sample: free! No carbons, photocopies or simultaneous submissions. "Send 4-5 fresh, neat copies of your best poems." Reports in 2-5 months. Pays 2 copies plus year's subscription. Acquires first North American serial rights.** Reviews books of poetry in single or multi-book format, no set length. Along with *Ascent* this well-designed, -illustrated and -edited publication is one of the best buys in the literary world . . . and a good read, too. Editors feature mostly free verse. Some of which takes too much risk but pays off, nonetheless in excitement.

HOLIDAY HOUSE, INC. (IV-Children), Dept. PM, 425 Madison Ave., New York NY 10017, phone (212)688-0085, founded 1936, editor-in-chief Margery Cuyler, is a trade children's book house. They have published hardcover books for children by Myra Cohn Livingston. They publish 3 books a year averaging 32 pages but are interested in publishing more poetry books for ages 8-12. **Submit 5 sample poems. No simultaneous submissions or previously published poems. Photocopy and dot-matrix OK. They offer an advance and royalties. Editor rarely comments on rejections.**

THE HOLLINS CRITIC (II), P.O. Box 9538, Hollins College VA 24020, phone (703)362-6317, founded 1964, editor John Rees Moore, publishes critical essays, poetry and book reviews, appears 5 times yearly in a 20-page magazine-sized format, circulation 500, **uses a few short poems in each issue, interesting in form, content or both.** They have recently published poetry by David Galler, Jane Varley, B.Z. Niditch and Dixie Partridge. As a sample, here are a few lines from "Shifting Night" by Mattie F. Quesenberry:

I slip out of my bone-bordered enclave,
wave my hands in the air.

The night shifts, shorn from the sky.
The stars fall away from their center.
This tilting, timed for now,
lifts my feet from the ground.
I fix my eyes to the network of lights
tacked to night's blanket of curved space.

Sample: $1.50. Submit up to 5 poems, none over 35 lines, must be typewritten. No photocopies. Reports in 6 weeks (slower in the summer). Pays $25/poem plus 5 copies. When John Rees Moore is accepting poems (sometimes the magazine is overstocked), he publishes verse that excites the mind, eye and sense. This is the place where some of the most "underrated" poets can find a home, and readers typically discover poets whose work they will follow over the course of several years.

HOLMGANGERS PRESS; KESTREL CHAPBOOK SERIES (V), 95 Carson Ct., Shelter Cove, Whitethorn CA 95489, phone (707)986-7700, founded 1974, editor Gary Elder, was "founded primarily to bring out **young or unjustly ignored 'older' poets.** We have since published collections of fiction, novels, history, graphic art and experimental works as well." **Holmgangers Press is currently not accepting unsolicited mss. Replies to queries in 3-4 days, to mss (if invited) in 1 month. Pays 10% royalties. For sample books or chapbooks, query with SASE.**

HENRY HOLT & COMPANY (V), 115 W. 18th St., New York NY 10011, **accepts no unsolicited poetry.**

HOME PLANET NEWS (II), Dept. PM, P.O. Box 415, Stuyvesant Station, New York NY 10009, phone (718)769-2854, founded 1979, editors Enid Dame and Donald Lev, is a tabloid (newsprint) journal, appearing 3-4 times a year presenting a "lively, eclectic and comprehensive view of contemporary literature." They want **"honest, well-crafted poems, open or closed form, on any subject, but we will not publish any work which seems to us to be racist, sexist, ageist, anti-semitic or has undue emphasis on violence. Poems under 30 lines stand a better chance. We lean somewhat toward poetry with urban sensibility but are not rigid about this."** They have published poetry by Hayden Carruth, Cornelius Eady, Norman Rosten, Daniel Berrigan, Will Inman, Toi Derricotte, Fritz Hamilton, Leo Connellan, Lyn Lifshin, Antler, William Packard and Denise Duhamel. As a sample the editors selected these lines from "Clotheslines" by Robbie Casey:

Clothes on a rope

> *gallop in the wind*
> *freer than the bodies they cover*
> *will ever be*

They use approximately 13 full 11 × 16 pgs. of poetry in each 24-page issue. Circulation 1,000 with 400 subscriptions of which 8 are libraries. Of 1,200 submissions/year, they use about 50-60. Publication could take one year from acceptance. Subscription: $8/year. **Sample: $3 postpaid. Submit 3-6 poems typed double-spaced, with SASE. Reports within 3 months. Payment: 4 copies and year's subscription.** Reviews books of poetry. "We cosponsor 'Day of the Poet,' a poetry festival and contest which takes place each October in Ulster County, New York."

HONEST ULSTERMAN (II, IV-Regional), 102 Elm Park Mansions, Park Walk, London SW10 0AP United Kingdom, founded 1968, editors Robert Johnstone and Tom Clyde, is a literary magazine appearing 3-4 times a year using "**technically competent poetry and prose, book reviews. Special reference to Northern Irish and Irish literature. Lively, humorous, adventurous, outspoken.**" They have published poetry by Seamus Heaney, Paul Muldoon, Gavin Ewart, Craig Raine, Fleur Adcock, and Medbh McGuckian. The editor describes it as "75-100 pgs., A-5 (digest-sized), photolithographic, phototypeset, photographs and line drawings. Occasionally color covers." Press run: 1,000 for 300+ subscriptions. Subscription: $28. **Sample postpaid: $7. Pays "a nominal fee" plus 2 copies.** "Potential contributors are strongly advised to read the magazine before submitting two copies of their work." **Editor comments on submissions "occasionally."** Reviews books of poetry in 500-1,000 words, single or multi-book format.

HONEYBROOK PRESS (V), P.O. Box 883, Rexburg ID 83440, phone (208)356-1456, founded 1984, proprietor Donnell Hunter, specializes in fine printing, letterpress, handset type, of chapbooks of poetry. Donnell Hunter says, "This is more of a hobby press. I have asked some 'name' poets for mss, and I have done some subsidized work." He has published books by himself, William Stafford, Marvin Bell and Nina Wicker.

HOPSCOTCH: THE MAGAZINE FOR GIRLS (IV-Children), P.O. Box 164, Bluffton OH 45817-0164, phone (419)358-4610, founded 1989, editor Marilyn B. Edwards, is a bimonthly magazine for **girls 6-12. "No length restrictions. In need of short poems for various holidays. Nothing abstract, experimental."** They have published poetry by Bette Killion, Sue Carloni and Cathy Drinkwater Better. As a sample we selected the last lines of "Grandma Was A Dancer?" by Barbara Early-Fezzey:

> *Grandma was really a dancer?*
> *It should come to me as no surprise.*
> *When she holds me and kisses me sweetly*
> *I see her love dance in her eyes.*

The editor describes *Hopscotch* as "full-color cover, 50 pgs. of 2-color inside, 7 × 9, saddle-stapled." They use about 30-35 of some 2,000 poems received/year. Press run 8,500 for 7,800 subscribers of which 6,500 are libraries, 200 to inquiring schools and libraries. Subscription: $15. **Sample postpaid: $3. Reports in 2-3 weeks. Pays $10-40. Buys first American serial rights. Submit no more than 6 poems/submission.** The few poems in this children's magazine address the audience, challenging young girls to pursue their dreams. To see how, order a sample copy (or check one out at the library) because it is too easy for poets who write children's verse to forget that each magazine targets a specific audience . . . in a specific way.

‡HORSES WEST (IV-Animals), 3824 Smith St., Everett WA 98201, editor Dale Swant, is a monthly tabloid covering regional and national news and current information on the training, showing, feeding and care of horses, circulation 12,000, which only uses **horse-related poetry, including light verse.** "No greeting-card-level poetry." **Sample for #5 SAE plus 3 first class stamps. Submit maximum of 5 poems up to 28 lines. Pays $10.**

HOUGHTON MIFFLIN CO. (V), 2 Park St., Boston MA 02108, founded 1850, poetry editor Peter Davison. Houghton Mifflin is a high-prestige trade publisher that puts out both hardcover and paperback books, but **poetry submission is by invitation only.** They have issued poetry books by Donald Hall, May Swenson, Ai, William Matthews, Margaret Atwood and Andrew Hudgins. **Authors are paid 10% royalties on hardcover books, 6% royalties on paperbacks (minimum), $1,000 advance and 12 author's copies.**

HOUSE OF MOONLIGHT (I), 15 Oakwood Rd., Bracknell, Berkshire RG12 2SP United Kingdom, founded 1981, editor John Howard, publishes 4-page leaflets of poems by individual poets at irregular intervals. "**Poems on love, death and the universe — common themes expressed in an uncommon way. Long poems up to 100 lines preferred.**" They have published poetry by Steve Sneyd and John Francis Haines. **Pays 5 copies. Acquires all rights. Returns rights if** "acknowledgment that I published first."

Reports in a month. "I am happy to receive submissions/inquiries from the United States—but only ones enclosing International Reply Coupons can be responded to. Checks payable to 'House of Moonlight' and/or in US currency are not acceptable. Also if poetry is to be regarded as a 'disposable ms' then they should be marked as such."

HOUSEWIFE-WRITER'S FORUM (IV-Women, humor), P.O. Box 780, Lyman WY 82937, phone (307)786-4513, founded 1988, editor/publisher Diane Wolverton, is a magazine of "prose, poetry, information and open forum communication for and by housewives or any woman who writes while juggling a busy schedule. **We have no specifications as to form, subject, style or purpose. Length maximum 30 lines. We publish both serious poetry and humorous. Nothing pornographic, but erudite expression is fine."** As a sample she selected these lines from "Off Limits" by Katherine H. Brooks:

> *I used to save a lot of stuff.*
> *Till Mother hollered "That's enough!"*
> *And made me have, all day, a fear*
> *That something nice would disappear.*
> *I hurried home from school, to see*
> *What damage had been done to me,*
> *And when I went to find the rocks*
> *I'd hidden underneath my socks,*
> *I saw it—almost in a flash—*
> *That all my things were in the trash.*

Diane Wolverton describes the magazine as "a small market for women who aspire to write for larger women's markets or support each other in the quest for finding time and energy to write." It is 40 pgs., desktop published, using some art, graphics and ads, appearing bimonthly. Press run is 1,200. **Sample postpaid: $4. Send SASE for guidelines. Pays 1 copy plus $1-2/poem. Buys first-time rights. "Simultaneous submissions are OK." Reports in 2 months.** She holds contests in several categories, humorous and serious, with $2/poem fee, April 15 deadline."

HOWLING DOG (II), 8419 Rhode, Utica MI 48317, founded 1985, editor Mark Donovan, is a literary journal of "letters, words and lines." The editor likes **"found poetry, graphically interesting pieces, humorous work, avant-garde, experimental, fun and crazy. All forms. All subjects, but we tend to have a light satirical attitude towards sex and politics."** He has published poems by Arthur Winfield Knight, Keith Wilson, John Sinclair, Carlos Cumpian and M.L. Liebler. As a sample the editor selected these lines by Kurt Olsson:

> *The children made such a fuss about seeing*
> *the Indian graveyard that, of course, the stand*
> *of silver birch disappointed them—so we didn't stop,*
> *continued on instead up the remains of a logger's road*

Howling Dog appears 2 times a year. It is 64 pgs., digest-sized, flat-spined offset. Press run 500 for 100 subscriptions of which 3 are libraries. They receive some 4,000 submissions/year, use maybe 150. Subscription: $20/4 issues. **Sample postpaid: $4. Send SASE for guidelines. Pays with copies and discount. Acquires first-time rights. Submit 3-4 poems with name and address on each page. "We don't use much rhyme or poems under 10 lines."** Simultaneous submissions OK. **Previously published poems OK "but let us know." Reporting time 2-3 months, longer if we like it.** Reviews books of poetry in 200 words, single format. **They are not presently considering book mss.** Mark Donovan says, "We produce an effect similar to the howl of a dog with its foot caught in the fence. Something that may not be pleasant or permanent, yet still heard by everyone in the neighborhood. We only accept the highest quality contemporary artistic expressions."

HRAFNHOH; LANGUAGE INFORMATION CENTRE (IV-Religious, political, spirituality, ethnic, themes), 32 Stryd Ebeneser, Pontypridd, Wales via GB, phone 0443 492243, founded 1987, editor Joseph Biddulph, is a "small press publishing linguistic and literary works, with historical, heraldic and genealogical subjects added, in the irregular magazine *Hrafnhoh*." They use **"poetry in traditional verse forms with a spiritual, Christian inspiration and purpose, with an active concern for technique and conveying a serious message in an evocative and entertaining style. Admirers of Baroque and Welsh or Irish Bardie verse are invited to attempt submissions. Verse and very short prose on African or Afro-American themes are also welcome, as are submissions in Latin, Esperanto and other languages.** They have published poetry by John Waddington-Feather. The editor describes *Hrafnehoh* as digest-sized, 12-24 pgs., photocopied from typescript, illustrated with sketches and old prints. He accepts about 2 of 6-10 poems received. Press run: 100-500. **Sample postpaid: £3 outside Europe. Pays "as many copies as required." Simultaneous submissions and previously published poems OK. Reports as soon as possible. Editor comments on submissions "not at any length and only if specifically requested."** He says, "Almost all unsolicited submissions are in one form—free verse—and without substance, i.e., without a definite purpose, message or conclusion. I am anxious to obtain verse with a strong technique and understanding of meter, with some real and substantial message."

THE HUDSON REVIEW; THE BENNETT AWARD (III), 684 Park Ave., New York NY 10021. *The Hudson Review* is a high-quality flat-spined quarterly, which **pays 50¢ a line for poetry. Reports in 6-8 weeks. Poetry is read from April 1 through September 30.** Many people consider this a closed market that publishes only the literary elite. This is an unfair stereotype for one of this country's most influential magazines. Work by new writers appears in every issue. They also sponsor the Bennett Award, established in memory of Joseph Bennett, a founding editor of *HR*. Every other year $15,000 is given to honor a writer "of significant achievement, in any literary genre or genres, whose work has not received the full recognition it deserves, or who is at a critical stage in his or her career—a stage at which a substantial grant might be particularly beneficial in furthering creative development. There are no restrictions as to language or nationality. **The Bennett Award is not open to nominations, and *The Hudson Review* will not accept nominations or applications in any form.**"

HUDSON VALLEY ECHOES (II), (formerly *Echoes*), P.O. Box 7, La Grangeville NY 12540, founded 1985, editor Marcia W. Grant, "is a national literary quarterly that features quality prose and poetry from well-established as well as emerging writers. *Hudson Valley Echoes* **has no rigid specifications as to form, length, subject matter or style. Excellence is the determining factor. Usual length of accepted poems is 20-40 lines, longer if exceptional. Editors want to see poems whose ideas and imagery are clearly focused, well-crafted and unusual. No sing-song rhyme, erotica or effusive amateur efforts.**" They have published poetry by Robert Cooperman, Fr. Benedict Auer, Johy Grey, Ruth Daigon and Gayle Elen Harvey. As a sample the editor selected these lines from "The Nights Before You Left" by John M. Davis:

> *Late summer night breathes,*
> *worn with old weather.*
> *Stale winds weave through branches,*
> *stir winged things:*
> *crickets and June bugs shape a night*
> *slow as the stars.*

HVE is 5½ × 8½, 44 pgs., saddle-stapled, offset with matte cover and interior pages printed on recycled paper. It is a lively little magazine. First, the poems are top-rate (mostly free verse). Second, the magazine is well-edited and attractively produced. Third, it contains small features that indicate editorial love: a letters section, quotes from poets like Frost and Jong, illustrations and contributor's notes! Press run averages 250 for about 100 subscriptions, of which 12 are libraries. Distributors provide some shelf sales. Subscription: $15 (libraries, $12.) **Sample postpaid: $4.50 current issue; $3 back issue. Send SASE for guidelines. Reports in generally 6-12 weeks. Pays 1 copy. Acquires one-time rights. "Five poems should be the maximum submitted at one time. Include name and address on every submission. Contributor's notes requested." Previously published submissions considered if poet owns rights. Editor "rarely" comments on submissions.** The editor advises poets to read good poetry in order to know good poetry. "Familiarize yourself with our magazine before you submit."

THE HUMAN QUEST (IV-Political), 1074 23rd Ave. N., St. Petersburg FL 33704, editor Edna Ruth Johnson, is a "humanistic monthly dealing with society's problems, especially peace. We use practically no poetry." It is magazine-sized, appears 9 times a year, circulation 10,000, of which 1,000 go for library subscriptions. **Send for free sample. Pays copies.**

HUTTON PUBLICATIONS; RHYME TIME; MYSTERY TIME; WRITERS' INFO (I, IV-Themes), P.O. Box 1870, Hayden ID 83835, poetry editor Linda Hutton. *Rhyme Time*, founded 1981, and published bimonthly beginning in 1987, consists of 3-5 sheets of typing paper, stapled at the corner, offset both sides from typescript, "**featuring rhymed poetry with some free verse and blank verse. We sponsor several contests each year, both with and without entry fees. 16 lines maximum, no avant-garde, haiku or sugary work.**" As a sample the editor selected "Inspiration" by Jonathan P. Rose:

> *Poet Sir Phillip Sidney*
> *Relished pies of kidney,*
> *Penned verse with a classical bent,*
> *Prototypical Elizabethan gent.*

Sample and guidelines free for SASE (two stamps), price regularly $1.50, subscription $10, circulation 200, 75 subscriptions (2 libraries). She uses about half of the 300 submissions received annually. **Pays 1 copy.** *Mystery Time*, founded 1983, is an annual digest-sized chapbook, 44-52 pgs., stapled-spine, containing 1-2 pages in each issue of **humorous poems about mysteries and mystery writers.** As a sample the editor selected these lines from "My Desire" by Helen Mitchell:

> *I'd like to write a mystery*

> *That leads my readers on and on,*
> *And right at the end of my book,*
> *Just who done it on them would dawn.*

Circulation: 100, sample $3.50, uses 4-6 of the 12-15 submissions received. **Guidelines available. Pays 25¢/line.** *Writers' Info*, founded 1984, is a monthly consisting of 3 sheets of typing paper, stapled at the corner, offset both sides from typescript. Tipsheet for the beginning freelancer. As a sample the editor selected "SASE" by Katherine A. Paulsen:

> *When mail-time comes and leaves me*
> *Feeling pretty glum,*
> *It merely means another*
> *Dejection slip has come.*

Writers' Info **"needs short poems about freelancing (fewer than 16 lines)" and pays up to $10 for first rights. Payment in copies for reprint rights. A sample copy is free for a #10 SASE with 2 oz. postage.**

‡HYACINTH HOUSE PUBLICATIONS; BROWNBAG PRESS; PSYCHOTRAIN (II, IV-Translations), P.O. Box 120, Fayetteville AR 72702-0120, founded 1989, contact Shannon Frach. *Brownbag Press* and *PsychoTrain* are both semiannual magazines. *Brownbag Press* seeks "forceful writing full of spark and vigor for a widely diverse, intelligent, fairly left-of-center audience." *PsychoTrain* uses "bizarre, avant-garde material with a delightfully psychotic edge. Heady and chaotic." The editors want **poetry that is "avant-garde, confessional, contemporary, erotic, experimental, gay/lesbian, pagan/occult or punk. Also dada, surrealism and decadent writing at its best. Be bold. Morbid humor is always a plus here. No religious poetry, inept rhyming, overly-academic poetics or saccharine writing of any description. We prefer two-fisted, dynamic, very intense poetry. We are always interested in good translations — especially translations of lively (if not outright brazen) material from countries which tend to favor tame, non-confrontational, bland poetry for the bulk of their literary exports. House interests are especially high in Romanian and Chinese literatures. Don't be afraid to show us street language from any culture."** They have recently published poetry by Tom Caufield, Albert Huffstickler, F.M. Cotolo and Michael Brownstein. As a sample the editors selected these lines from "Jesus on a pogo stick" by Randal Seyler:

> *Wrapped in the stars and stripes*
> *sleeping behind a McDonald's —*
> *bloody palms and a pawn ticket*
> *won't buy a McDLT when*
> *the rapture comes.*

Brownbag is 24 pgs., digest-sized; *PsychoTrain* is 45 pgs., magazine-sized. Both are photocopied and stapled with card covers. Press run for each is 300 for 100+ subscribers, 125+ shelf sales. **Sample postpaid: $3 for** *Brownbag*, **$3 for** *PsychoTrain*. **Previously published poems and simultaneous submissions OK.** Time between acceptance and publication is 1 year. **Often comments on rejections. Send SASE for guidelines. Reports in "2 weeks to 6 months — depends on the backlog." Pays 1 copy.** Acquires one-time rights. Hyacinth House has also just started **a chapbook series. "Presently we're using solicited material only,** although we plan to open this to the general writing public in the future — please don't send us unsolicited chapbook mss at this time." The editors say, "Hyacinth House is a very friendly place to send submissions. We may end up having to reject your submissions, but we'll still respect you in the morning. We encourage both new and established 'name' writers to submit here. Anyone sending us material should be aware that we don't like pretentious, windy, overly-serious poetry; we also dislike smarmy, trite rhymes about God and family. Send those to your hometown newspaper, not us. Don't send us poems that only took you five minutes to write. Also, please be aware that when you submit to one Hyacinth House publication, you're submitting to them all. If you submit to *Brownbag*, but the piece would work better in *PsychoTrain*, that's where it's going. Hyacinth House exists as a tribute to financially disadvantaged persons who still have the nerve to aspire to active participation within the humanities despite their lack of cash and yuppie credentials. We are attempting to establish a forum in which professors will read material written in trailer courts, homeless shelters and housing projects while those authors can simultaneously read down-to-earth, yet well-crafted poetry from distinguished writers respected in the overall scope of contemporary letters. We invite the participation of both well-established writers and talented new voices."

ICON; HART CRANE AWARD (II), English Dept., Kent State University, Trumbull Campus, 4314 Mahoning Ave. NW, Warren OH 44483, phone (216)847-0571, founded 1966, faculty advisor Dr. Robert Brown, appears twice a year. **"We prefer experimental poetry, poetry that takes risks in terms of form and subject matter, but will consider anything well-written. No religious, sentimental, formulaic or prosaic poetry."** They have published poetry by Gay Brewer and William Greenway. As a sample the editor selected these lines from "To Bartleby..." by Margaret Pinkerton:

> *Bartleby, you bother me.*
> *I find the words that brought you fame*
> *more distinctive than your name....*

It is digest-sized, 40-80 pgs., saddle-stapled, with matte card cover, printed in black. Poems and a few illustrations/photos grace the pages of this professionally printed and designed magazine. Artwork is especially attractive, not so much illustrating poems as lending a mood to the entire issue. They accept 5% of 1,000 poems submitted. Press run 1,000 for 50 subscribers of which 10 are libraries. Distributed free to students and faculty. Subscription: $5. **Sample postpaid: $2. Pays 2 copies. Submit September 1 through March 1 only. Reports in 1-3 months.** The Hart Crane Award of $100 for poetry and a Kenneth Patchen Award of $100 for prose are given annually.

IHCUT (I), P.O. Box 612, Napavine WA 98565, founded 1989, contact Larry L. Randall, is an inexpensively produced newsletter appearing every other month. **"I am open to anything so long as it is exciting and original. Length does not matter, and the purpose should be to birth a new type of animal or way of thinking. I would rather not see rhyming poetry."** They have recently published poetry by Karen Tom, Julie Brinson Yopp, Alysio K. Harpootian and Laura Powell. As a sample the editor selected these lines from an untitled poem by Njuzu:

> *it seems people have*
> *forgotten to feel*
> *to just be*
> *hurry scurry worry*
> *what a mess*
> *if only they could see.*

It is 15-20 pgs., photocopied, side-stapled on ordinary paper. Press run 20. **Sample postpaid: $2. Send SASE for guidelines. Pays 1 copy. Reports in 1 week. Previously published poems and simultaneous submissions OK.**

UNIVERSITY OF ILLINOIS PRESS (III), 54 E. Gregory Dr., Champaign IL 61820, phone (217)333-0950, founded 1918, poetry editor Laurence Lieberman, publishes **collections of individual poets, 65-105 pgs.** Poets they have published include Brendan Galvin, S.J. Marks, Laura Mullen, Robert Wrigley and Lynn Emanuel. **Open for poetry submissions one month a year—usually February. There is a $10 handling fee. Query with "brief resume of publications, awards, etc." Samples optional. Typescript preferred. Royalty contract and 10 copies. Editor comments on many submissions. Send SASE for poetry list.** Laurence Lieberman comments: "Poets would do well to acquaint themselves with at least a few books from our list before deciding whether to submit their work to Illinois."

‡ILLUMINATIONS (II), Ryde School, Queens Rd., Ryde, Isle of Wight PO33 3BE England, founded 1982, editor Simon Lewis, is an annual "international magazine of contemporary writing, mainly poetry, some prose, some in translation." They want **"poetry with something to say and a sense of nerve as well as style."** They do not want to see "anything twee or bland." They have recently published poetry by Glyn Maxwell, Jack Mapanje and Diane Wakoski. As a sample we selected the first stanza of "When Your Time Has Gone" by Thomas Kretz:

> *Thin grey hair*
> *a skirt around a bald dome*
> *which can no longer hula*
> *to the drum of exotic ideas . . .*

Illuminations is 40 pgs., approximately $5\frac{7}{8} \times 8\frac{1}{4}$, professionally printed, saddle-stitched, with heavy paper cover. They accept 5-10% of the poetry received. Press run is 500 for 300 subscribers of which 10 are libraries, 50 shelf sales. Single copy: £3 ($5); subscription: £10 ($20) for 3 issues. **Sample postpaid: "variable (£3 upwards)." Previously published poems OK; no simultaneous submissions. Cover letter required. Seldom comments on rejections. Reports within 2 months. Pays 3 copies, "2 of same issue, 1 of next."** The editor says, "I look for good *poems* rather than at poets' resumes. My judgment is unashamedly subjective."

IMAGO LITERARY MAGAZINE; CITY OF BRISBANE POETRY AWARD (II, IV-Regional), School of Communication and Organisational Studies, Q.U.T., GPO Box 2434, Brisbane 4001 Queensland, Australia, phone (07)864-2976, founded 1988, appears three times a year, publishing "the best **Australian writing, placing particular emphasis on Queensland writing and culture, but also welcomes submissions from overseas. Poems preferably short—up to about 50 lines, most from 12-25 lines. Our main criterion is good writing."** They have recently published poetry by Tom Shapcott, Bruce Dawe, Graeme Wilson and Nancy Cato. As a sample we selected these lines from "Falling Away" by Rosemary Allan-Coleman:

> *How discomfited we are by beauty*

> *that has had its day*
> *rose gone blowsy*
> *fungus leaking fluids*
> *flesh falling in folds.*

It is digest-sized, 90 pgs., with glossy card cover. They accept about 10% of 500 poems from about 150 writers. Press run 800 for 350 subscribers of which 36 are libraries. Subscription: $A15 in Australia. **Sample postpaid: $A7.50. Comments if requested. Reports in 1-6 months. Pays $A30-40 plus 1 copy. Buys first Australian serial rights. They publish the winning poems of the City of Brisbane Poetry Award (annual).** Reviews books of poetry in 600 words—"usually commissioned. Unsolicited reviews would have to be of books relevant to *Imago* (Queensland or writing)."

IMPLOSION PRESS; IMPETUS (I, II, IV-Erotica, women), 4975 Comanche Trail, Stow OH 44224, phone (216)688-5210, founded 1984, poetry editor Cheryl Townsend, publishes *Impetus*, a quarterly literary magazine, chapbooks, special issues. The editor would like to see "**strong social protest with raw emotion. No topic is taboo. Material should be straight from the gut, uncensored and real. Absolutely no nature poetry or rhyme for the sake of rhyme, oriental, or 'Kissy, kissy I love you' poems. Any length as long as it works. All subjects okay, providing it isn't too rank.** *Impetus* is now publishing an annual erotica and all female issue. Material should reflect that theme." They have published poetry by Charles Bukowski, Ron Androla, Kurt Nimmo and Lonnie Sherman. As a sample the editor selected these lines from "Gun-shy" by B. Arcus Shoenborn:

> *Instead,*
> *I hid in my bedroom.*
> *Soaked between blooded sheets,*
> *I explored immaculate concepts.*
> *Then my white heart severed;*
> *It gushed rivers of angry rapists.*
> *One flagged a revolver;*
> *he held it to my head and said,*
> *I'd live, but couldn't tell.*

The 7½ × 9 magazine is photocopied from typescript, saddle-stapled. Circulation about 500, with 300 subscriptions. Generally a 3-month backlog. **Sample postpaid: $3; make check payable to Cheryl Townsend.** The editor says, "I prefer shorter, to-the-point work." Previously published work OK if it is noted when and where. **Usually reports within 1 month. Pays 1 copy. Acquires first rights. Send SASE for guidelines.** In her comments on rejection, the editor usually refers poets to other magazines she feels would appreciate the work more. Reviews books of poetry. She says, "Bear with the small press. We're working as best as we can and usually harder. We can only do so much at a time. Support the small presses!"

‡INDIA CURRENTS (IV-Ethnic, regional), P.O. Box 21285, San Jose CA 95151, phone (408)274-6966, founded 1987, is a monthly magazine about Indian culture in the U.S. They want "**poetry that offers an insight into India, Indians, Indian Americans; very brief works stand a better chance of acceptance.**" They do not want "**poetry that exploits mystery or exoticism about India or long poems (over 300 words). Readership is 70% Indian, 30% non-Indian.**" They have recently published poetry by Chitra Divakaruni. It is 72 pgs, 8½ × 11, offset, newsprint, saddle-stitched. They receive 50-75 submissions a year, "accept fewer than 12." Press run is 27,000 for 9,000 subscribers. Rest distributed free at stores, restaurants and libraries. Single copy: $2; subscription: $20. **Sample postpaid: $3. Previously published poems and simultaneous submissions OK.** Time between acceptance and publication is 6-12 months. **Send SASE for guidelines. Reports in 3 months. Pays $5-10. Buys one-time North American serial rights.** Reviews books of poetry in 300 words maximum. The editor says, "*India Currents* has a heavy tilt in favor of arts. We feel that arts can contribute to global understanding and peace by bringing it about at a personal level. America needs to learn about India just as India needs to learn about America."

INDIANA REVIEW (II), 316 N. Jordan Ave., Indiana University, Bloomington IN 47405, founded 1982, is a biannual of new fiction and poetry. "In general the *Review* looks for fresh, original poems of insight, poems that are challenging without being obtuse. We'll consider all types of poems—free verse,

---

 The double dagger before a listing indicates that the listing is new in this edition. New markets are often the most receptive to submissions.

traditional, experimental. Reading a sample issue is the best way to determine if *IR* is a potential home for your work. Any subject matter is acceptable if it is written well. No poetry that is cliché, amateurish or fake." They have published poetry by David Mura, Silivia Curbelo, Naomi Shihab Nye, Pattiann Rogers and Stephen Dobyns. The magazine uses about 40-60 pgs. of poetry in each issue (6×9, flat-spined, 200 pages, color matte cover, professional printing). The magazine has 600 subscriptions of which 120 are libraries. They receive about 8,000 submissions/year of which they use about 60. **Sample postpaid: $5. Submit no more than 4-5 pgs. of poetry. Photocopy, dot-matrix OK if readable. Please indicate stanza breaks on poems over 1 page. "Simultaneous submissions very strongly discouraged." Pays $5/page when available ($10 minimum/poem), plus 2 copies and remainder of year's subscription. Buys first North American serial rights only. "We try to respond to manuscripts in two to three months. Reading time is often slower during summer months."** This is an increasingly difficult market, especially for long poems. Its elegant design and literary reputation are making it a top place to submit, so send only your best. Despite a high volume, however, it usually honors its stated response time.

INDIGO MAGAZINE: THE SPANISH-CANADIAN PRESENCE IN THE ARTS (IV-Foreign languages, translations, themes), Rm 252, Atkinson College, York University, North York, Ontario M3T 1P3 Canada, phone (416)736-2100, ext. 6632, founded 1989, editor-in-chief Prof. Margarita Feliciano, appears twice a year using **"poetry to be thematically of Hispanic contents if written in French or English (not the case if written in Spanish)."** They have published poetry by Rafael Barreto-Rivera and Rosemary Sullivan. As a sample the editor selected these lines (poet unidentified):

> *I was born on this lip of stone*
> *Jutting out over the jungle*
> *I've never wanted to go down.*
> *As a child I would run to the edge to catch the birds*
> *or follow the lizards with my hand along the ledges.*

It is professionally printed, flat-spined, 150+ pgs., with glossy card cover. "I accept 50% of submissions (about 40). Press run 300 for 50 subscribers. Subscription: $25. **Price of sample, payment, reporting time not given. The editor says she always comments on rejections.**

INFINITY LIMITED: A JOURNAL FOR THE SOMEWHAT ECCENTRIC (II), P.O. Box 2713, Castro Valley CA 94546, phone (510)581-8172, founded 1988, editor-in-chief Genie Lester, is a "literary quarterly dedicated to presenting emerging talent attractively illustrated. Staff artists illustrate most work, but we encourage writer-artists to submit their own illustrations." They want poetry that is **"clever, amusing, interesting, thoughtful, original, moving."** They have published poetry by Thomas Kretz, Errol Miller and Thomas Chase. As a sample we selected the first stanza of "Family Album" by Paul Grant:

> *When cars had running boards*
> *and could be parked for free, keys*
> *left in the ignition so as not to make*
> *an unsightly, uncomfortable bulge*
> *in pants pockets, windows down*
> *to whatever breeze strolled by*

It is magazine-sized, "printed on 60 lb. bond with parchment cover (2-3 color)" and appears "more or less quarterly, 4 times a year. We receive about 25 submissions per week, use about 25 poems per issue." Press run 1,000 for 250+ subscriptions. Subscription: $10. **Sample postpaid: $3.95. Send SASE for guidelines. Pays 2 copies. Acquires one-time or first reprint rights. Simultaneous submissions and occasionally previously published poems OK. Reads submissions January 1 through June 1 and September 1 through November 15. Reports within 3 months. Editor comments on submissions "if writing or art shows promise."** The editor says, "We are small but growing rapidly, probably because we are willing to work with our writers and artists. We make an effort to present material attractively. The poetry we publish usually deals in an original way with concerns common to all of us."

INKSHED—POETRY AND FICTION (II); INKSHED PRESS (V), 387 Beverley Rd., Hull, N. Humberside HU5 ILS England, founded 1985, editorial director Anthony Smith, poetry editor Lesli Markham, is biannual using **"any good quality poetry, traditional or contemporary, not sexist or racist."** They have recently published poetry by Gerald Locklin, Richard Paul Schmonsees and Roshan Kagda. As a sample the editors selected this poem, "Glass Vase," by Mary Maher:

> *A blower's alter-lung*
> *it swung against the hour from the fire.*
>
> *The roundness swells*
> *and thins with each restraining breath.*

The song is silent but seen:
only the membrane sings phrased in steam.

timed in old alder spoons
worn smooth by wind's sublimated tongue.

Air, glazed and cool
keys the eye.

Inkshed is digest-sized, perfect-bound, 80 pgs., printed on gloss paper from typeset. Their press run is 500 with 100 subscriptions. Subscription: $12 for 2 issues. **Sample postpaid: $5. "Please send cash only & U.S. dollars or Sterling—dollar cheques are too expensive to exchange." Pays 1 copy. They consider simultaneous submissions and previously published poems. Reports in 1 month.** Reviews books of poetry in 150-200 words/book. **Inkshed Press publishes 1 chapbook/ year averaging 30 pgs., but only by invitation.** Anthony Smith advises, "Please study what is being written today—note trends but don't copy—be an individual, that's what poetry is about."

INKSTONE: A MAGAZINE OF HAIKU (IV-Form), P.O. Box 75009, Hudson Bay P.O., Toronto, Ontario M4W 3T3 Canada, founded 1982, poetry editors Keith Southward, Marshall Hryciuk and J. Louise Fletcher, "is a publication dedicated to the development of a distinctive English language haiku and to the craft of writing as it relates to haiku. Submissions reflecting these concerns are welcomed. We publish haiku and related forms, plus reviews, articles related to haiku. **Poems must be haiku or related but we use a very liberal definition of haiku."** They have published haiku by Carol Montgomery, Alexis Rotella, Akira Kowano and Guy Beining. There are roughly 20 pgs. of poetry and reviews/articles in the digest-sized format, 40 pgs., offset from typescript, matte card cover, circulation 100, accepting "perhaps 10%" of the poems submitted each year, poems appear as space permits, usually in the next issue after acceptance. **Sample postpaid: $5.50. Submit any number of poems, preferably 1 per 5½ ×8½ sheet, typewritten. Reports within 6 weeks.** Editor "occasionally" comments on rejections. **Pays 1 copy. Acquires first serial rights.** Reviews books of poetry in 1 to 3 pgs., single or multi-book format.

INKY BLUE (I), (formerly *Celery/Inky Blue*), P.O. Box 385, Comptche CA 95427, founded 1989, editor Cat Spydell, appears quarterly (or thereabouts). *IB* wants **"thought-provoking poetry, with a tendency to avoid the mundane. No sexist, red-necked-beer-bellied-middle-American-women-are-only-good-if-they-have-flat-heads poetry."** She has recently published poetry by Gerald Locklin, Lyn Lifshin, Andrew Demcak, Patti Sirens and Glenn Bach. As a sample the editor chose these lines:

Bing cherries color lips, when bitten:
while the red is still glistening
match your lips against mine,
mark my mouth still sweet potency

I want this stain
to last.

The magazine averages 45 pgs. and is digest-sized with matte card cover. Press run is 85-300 depending on funding. The editor accepts 75% or more of submissions, usually at least one poem, if possible. Subscription: $22/year. **Sample: $5 plus $1 postage and handling. Pays 1 copy. Rights revert to poet after publication. Previously published poems and simultaneous submissions OK. Poems without a SASE or without the poet's name and address on each page will not be considered. "I read poetry every three months, so it may take that long for a response." Publication time from time of acceptance can be as long as one year.** The editor says, "I prefer poetry about country living to city life. I like poetry that celebrates woman as Goddess and also enjoy poetry that is upbeat and life-affirming, believe it or not, but will consider anything interesting, except for rhyming poetry. I tend not to accept rhyming poetry (unless it's extremely well-written) or poetry with the words neon, groin or O'r (as in the old English over) or any English that you would not feel comfortable speaking in a public place. Create your own reality! Don't be a shrinking violet. Submit."

INNISFREE MAGAZINE (II), P.O. Box 277, Manhattan Beach CA 90266, phone (310)545-2607, FAX (310)546-5862, founded 1981, editor Rex Winn, appears every other month with many short stories and poetry. **"Items of merit: Entertainment value—humor, fright, emotional experience; Something for the reader to take away—inspiration, enlightenment, interesting information; Writing craft— structure, style and technique."** They have recently published poetry by William Doreski and Josephine C. Radai. As a sample, the editor selected these lines by Arlene Joffee Pollack:

My impulses ride herd on me
And I, astonished,
Powerless, stare

> At the world around me
> Through a beggar's eyes,
> Rattling the empty beggar cup
> And yet ashamed to own the cup
> At all.

It is 56 pgs., magazine-sized, saddle-stapled, professionally printed with matte card cover. They accept about 15% of poetry received. Press run 350-500 for 200 subscribers of which 3 are libraries. Subscription: $25. **Sample postpaid: $5. Reads submissions January 1 through October 31. Send SASE for guidelines. Pays "splattered awards" but no copies. Acquires first rights. "If a person asks, I will comment. Sometimes I can't resist anyway!"** Previously published poems and simultaneous submissions OK. Verse seems to play second fiddle to fiction here, but the editor tries to make space for all types, haiku to formal (including verse by children).

‡INSECTS ARE PEOPLE TOO; PUFF 'N' STUFF PRODUCTIONS (IV-Theme), P.O. Box 146486, Chicago IL 60614, phone (312)772-8686, founded 1989, publisher H.R. Felgenhauer, an infrequent publication focusing solely on **"poems about insects doing people things and people doing insect things."** The first issue was a collection of the publisher's own poems. As a sample he selected these lines from "The Law and Order Buffoons":

> wanted to conquer Central America
> brutally massacre the entire population
> so we could all have fabulous plantations
> down there with mountain gorillas in bondage
> cultivating cocaine and marijuana for fun and profit.

Insects is 8½×11, stapled down the side, with card cover, b&w art and graphics. Press run is 400. Single copy: $3. **Sample postpaid: $4. Previously published poems and simultaneous submissions OK. Often comments on rejections. Reports "immediately." Pay varies. Puff 'N' Stuff Productions publishes 1 chapbook/year. Replies to queries and mss in 10 days. Pay is negotiable.** H.R. Felgenhauer says, "Hit me with your best shot. Never give up—editors have tunnel-vision. The *BEST* mags you almost *NEVER* even hear about. Don't believe reviews. Write for yourself. Prepare for failure, not success."

INSIGHT PRESS (V), P.O. Box 25, Drawer 249, Ocotillo CA 92259, founded 1983, publishers John and Merry Harris. The Harrises publish short poetry chapbook anthologies containing the work of **"pre-selected writers (no submissions without invitation, please"). The work published must be "short, non-academic poetry for the layman—clarity and lucidity a must. Prefer humorous, inspirational poetry."** They have published poems by L.C. Dancer, Elizabeth Lee, Jack Adler, Falling Blossom (Cherokee) and Merry Harris. The chapbooks are paperback, flat-spined, 40-50 pgs. "We sell our chapbooks at cost and send out at least 50 of first run for promotion of our poets, who are then widely reprinted." Sample: $3 for "Laughter: a Revelry." Merry Harris advises, "1) one tip for beginners: Join an amateur press association, as I did 40 years ago, to learn basics while being published. Amateur does NOT mean 'Amateurish.' AMAT = LOVE! 2) Join a local writers' co-op. 3) *Avoid those who exploit writers.* 4) As for technique, keep it simple, avoid erudite phrasing and pseudo-intellectualism. We do not publish other people's books. We publish *Merry-Go-Round, Contest Carousel* and *Roadrunner,* literary newsletters containing essays or writing (by Merry)." **Not open to submission.**

‡INTERIM (II), Department of English, University of Nevada, Las Vegas, Las Vegas NV 89154, phone (702)739-3172, magazine, founded in Seattle, 1944-55, revived 1986. Editor A. Wilber Stevens, associate editors James Hazen and Joseph B. McCullough, English editor John Heath-Stubbs. Member CLMP, New York. Indexed in **Index of American Periodical Verse.** Appears twice a year, 48 pgs. each issue. Professionally printed. Circulation 600. **Publishes the best poetry and short fiction it can find, no specific demands in form, new and established writers.** They have published poems by John Heath-Stubbs, William Stafford, Richard Eberhart, Diane Wakoski, Stephen Stepanchev, Jim Barnes and Anca Vlasopolos. As a sample we selected these lines from "Winter's Tale" by Charlotte F. Otten:

> Her voice is silent now,
> sunk deep into the tap root of her brain.
> A stroke that struck her throat
> blizzarded all sound.
> Words swirl around her like an early snow
> clinging to unfallen leaves.

Pays two contributor's copies and a two-year subscription. *Interim* **acquires copyright.** Poems may be reprinted elsewhere with a permission line noting publication in *Interim*. **Submit 4-6 poems, SASE and brief biographical note. No simultaneous submissions. Decision in 2 months.**

Sample copy $5. Individual subscriptions $8 one year, $13 two years, $16 three years; libraries $14/year.

Volume Ten   Number Two   Fall/Winter 1991-92   Five Dollars

"We try constantly to have some tie-in between cover and content," says A. Wilber Stevens, founder and editor of Interim. "In this case, a chair Art Editor Loucinda Wilder Stevens did for the Fall 1986 cover intrigued the distinguished Scots poet George Bruce. Bruce's subsequent poem on a chair (with references to Van Gogh) leads off this issue." Although they have revived short fiction, poetry plays the major role in the publication, Wilber Stevens says. The artist of this illustration is Gina M. Cinque.

INTERNATIONAL BLACK WRITERS; BLACK WRITER MAGAZINE (I, IV-Ethnic), P.O. Box 1030, Chicago IL 60690, founded 1970, contact Mable Terrell, executive director. *BWM* is a "quarterly literary magazine to showcase new writers and poets and provide educational information for writers. **Open to all types of poetry.**" The editor describes it as magazine-sized, 30 pgs., offset printing, with a glossy cover, circulation 1,000, 200 subscriptions. Subscription: $19/year. Sample: $1.50 postpaid. **Pays 10 copies. Reports in 10 days, has 1 quarter backlog. For chapbook publication (40 pgs.), submit 2 sample poems and cover letter with short bio. Simultaneous submissions OK. Pays copies. For sample chapbook send SASE with bookrate postage.** They offer awards of $100, $50 and $25 for the best poems published in the magazine and present them to winners at annual awards banquet. *IBW* is open to all writers.

‡INTERNATIONAL OLYMPIC LIFTER (IOL) (IV-Themes), P.O. 65855, Los Angeles CA 90065, founded 1973, poetry editor Dale Rhoades, is a bimonthly "for the serious weight lifter, coach, administrator and enthusiast." They want **poetry about olympic-style weight lifting—occasionally use poetry about nature, the environment or health. "We prefer balanced meter, rhyming 10-16 lines."** Press run is 3,000 for 2,700 subscribers of which approximately 5% are libraries. Subscription: $25. **Sample postpaid: $4.50. No previously published poems; simultaneous submissions OK. Reports "immediately." Pays $10-25.** The editor says, "Know your market. Often we get poems on body building, power lifting, running or aerobics which are all foreign to olympic lifting. Purchase a copy to understand our requirements."

INTERNATIONAL POETS OF THE HEART; THE LAY POET (IV-Membership), P.O. Box 463, Midvale UT 84047-0463, founded 1988, poetry editor Bob Curtis. International Poets of the Heart is an organization (membership $10/year and $12/year outside US) "for the mutual interaction of the ideas and ideals as concepts from the heart. Our purpose is the meaningful communication of these concepts, 'heart to heart.'" They publish a newsletter, *The Lay Poet*, of "how-to and general commentary on poetry submissions on a quarterly basis. **We solicit poetry for the newsletter, and ask comments from the membership. We recognize that 'feelings' are not only 'mushy love songs,' but emotions that may range from anger to euphoria. However, for the purposes of this organization, we seek those feelings from the positive side of life's experience."** They have recently published poetry by Joy Bischof, Martha Knight Foster, Henry W. Gurley and Jean Cameron. As a sample the editor selected these lines from his poem "Whispers of a Tender Heart":

> *The lines of middle age have*
> *Slowly crept upon her*
> *But they have been*

> *Gentle in their approach*
> *Enhancing the attractiveness*
> *Of youth*
> *Now blossomed into the*
> *Beauty of womanhood*

The editor says, "We want to have **poetry submissions by members, and then we will print what we can and ask comments on those pieces.**" Submissions accepted only from members. No payment. Reviews books of "up to about 100 poems" in single format. The editor says, "Beauty is in the eye of the beholder, and judgment of any art is always subjective. When we ask the question 'Is it any good?', What we are really saying is, 'Do you experience the wonder of this concept in the same way that I do?' The answer to the question? It might need polishing and refinement, but you wrote it. Therefore, it is good."

INTERSTATE RELIGIOUS WRITERS ASSOCIATION (IRWA) NEWSLETTER AND WORKSHOPS (IV-Membership, religious), 300 Cherry Hill Rd. NW, Cedar Rapids IA 52405, phone (319)396-2732, founded 1981, coeditors Marvin Ceynar and Barbara Ceynar, publishes a newsletter that "gives information mostly about religious writing but also information about secular publications that religious people feel comfortable publishing in." It uses **poetry by members suitable for an ecumenical Christian readership.** As a sample Barbara Ceynar selected these lines by Carole Johnston:

> *Just below and hidden*
> *in separate beds*
> *in hopes of many colors*
> *lies this year's spring*
> *already stirring with swellings*
> *and tremors of radiant promises*
> *awaiting some silent earthy signal*
> *to burst triumphantly through*
> *winter's*
> *cold hold on beauty.*

IRWA Newsletter appears 6 times a year, magazine-sized, 11 pgs., 200 subscribers. They receive about 24 poems a year and "accept many of them." Subscription: $12. **Sample postpaid: $2.15. Pays 2-5 copies. Simultaneous submissions and previously published poems OK. Reports immediately. Editor sometimes comments on rejections.**

INTERTEXT (V, IV-Translations), 2633 East 17th Ave., Anchorage AK 99508-3207, founded 1982, poetry editor Sharon Ann Jaeger, is "devoted to producing lasting works in every sense. We specialize in poetry, translations and short works in the fine arts and literary criticism. **We publish work that is truly excellent—no restrictions on form, length or style. Cannot use religious verse.** Like both surrealist and realist poetry, poetry with intensity, striking insight, vivid imagery, fresh metaphor, musical use of language in both word sounds and rhythm. Must make the world—in all its dimensions—come alive." To give a sense of her taste she says, "I admire the work of Louise Glück, William Stafford, Jim Wayne Miller, Eleanor Wilner, Antonio Ramos Rosa and Rainer Maria Rilke." As a sample the editor chose these lines (poet unidentified):

> *From this room with its coarse bed*
> *we see the path of fire,*
> *Suddenly the vertebra cracks,*
> *it pushes toward us*
> *the wheel of human matter.*
> *All the gods are men*
> *with a fissure of darkness.*

She says, "Given the projects we have in train, Intertext will not be looking at any unsolicited mss until 1995." Query first with 3 samples only and SASE. "Cover letter optional—the sample poems are always read first—but no form letters, please. If sample poems are promising, then the complete ms will be requested." Photocopy OK. Simultaneous queries OK. Payment: 10% royalty after costs of production, promotion and distribution have been recovered. No longer publishes chapbooks but only "full-length collections by poets of demonstrated achievement."

INTRO (IV-Students), AWP, Old Dominion University, Norfolk VA 23529-0079, phone (804)683-3839, founded 1970, publications manager D.W. Fenza. See Associated Writing Programs under Organizations Useful to Poets. **Students in college writing programs belonging to AWP may submit to this consortium of magazines publishing student poetry, fiction and plays.** They are open as to the type of poetry submitted except they do not want "non-literary, haiku, etc." As to poets they have published, they say, "In our history, we've introduced Dara Wier, Carolyn Forché, Greg Pope, Norman Dubie and others." Circulation 9,500. **Programs nominate *Intro* works in the fall. Ask the director of your writing program for more information.**

‡INVERTED OSTRICH (I, IV-Social issues), 246 Nollyn Dr., Dallastown PA 17313, founded 1991, editor Tammy Winand, is a bimonthly newsletter "for promotion of free expression and social commentary using poetry, short fiction and essays/opinion items." They want **any style/form; up to 25 lines. "Prefer pieces with some comment on social issues/state of the world. No mushy love poetry or meaningless rambling."** They have recently published poetry by Dawn Zapletal and Serena Fusek. As a sample the editor selected these lines from "She Didn't Want to Wait Till Her Mother Died" by Lyn Lifshin:

> she can't let go
> she says like
> a siamese twin
> she doesn't
> know how to

It is 5 pgs., 8½ × 11, photocopied, stapled down the side, with paper cover and b&w art. Press run is 25 for 5 subscribers. Subscription: $9. **Sample postpaid: $1. No previously published poems or simultaneous submissions. Include cover letter which "introduces poet as a person" and mentions recent publications. "Writers' addresses appear with their works unless they request otherwise . . . sort of a 'pen pal' network for lonely and misunderstood artists." Always comments on rejections. Reports in 2-6 weeks. Pays 1 copy.** The editor says, "I do all the work for *Inverted Ostrich* myself. In the future I hope to expand number of pages per issue, but need more submissions. As I pay from my pocket to print/mail the newsletter, I appreciate purchase of sample copies, subscriptions and of course friendly donations!"

IOTA (II), 67 Hady Crescent, Chesterfield, Derbyshire S41 0EB Great Britain, phone +44246-276532 (UK: 0246-276532), founded 1988, editor David Holliday, is a quarterly wanting **"any style and subject; no specific limitations as to length, though, obviously, the shorter a poem is, the easier it is to get it in, which means that poems over 40 lines can still get in if they seem good enough. No concrete poetry (no facilities), or self-indulgent logorrhea."** They have recently published poetry by Michael Hatwell, Martin Sullivan, John Gonzalez, James Kirkup, Alun Rees and Thomas Land. As a sample the editor selected these lines by Kevin Goldstein-Jackson:

> Pangolin — a name
> that sounds romantic, royal:
> a present for love. . .
>
> Pangolin — a rogue:
> a lovely name disguising
> scaly ant-eater.

Iota is printed from typescript, saddle-stapled, 32 pgs., with colored paper cover. Their press run is 400 with 250 subscriptions of which 6 are libraries. They publish about 200 of 4,000 poems received. Subscription: $8 (£4). **Sample: $2 (£1) postpaid "but sometimes sent free." Pays 2 copies. Acquires first British serial rights only.** The editor prefers name and address on each poem, typed, "but provided it's legible, am happy to accept anything." He considers simultaneous submissions, but previously published poems "only if outstanding." **Reports in 1-3 weeks (unless production of the next issue takes precedence). Editor usually comments on rejections, "but detailed comment only when time allows and the poem warrants it."** Reviews books of poetry in about 200 words, single or multi-book format. He says, "I am after crafted verse that says something; self-indulgent word-spinning is out. All editors have their blind spots; the only advice I can offer a beginning poet is to find a sympathetic editor (and you will only do that by seeing their magazines) and not to be discouraged by initial lack of success. Keep plugging!"

UNIVERSITY OF IOWA PRESS; EDWIN FORD PIPER POETRY AWARDS (III), Iowa City IA 52242. The University of Iowa Press offers annually the Edwin Ford Piper Poetry Awards **for book-length (50-120 pgs.) mss by poets who have already published at least one full-length book in edition of at least 750 copies. Two awards are given each year of $1,000 plus publication with standard royalty contract. (This competition is the only way in which this press accepts poetry). Manuscripts are received annually in February and March only.** Judges are nationally prominent poets. All writers of English are eligible, whether citizens of the United States or not. Poems from previously published books may be included only in manuscripts of selected or collected poems, submissions of which are encouraged. **Simultaneous submissions OK if press is immediately notified if the book is accepted by another publisher. No reading fee is charged, but stamped, self-addressed packaging is required or mss will not be returned.** "These awards have been initiated to encourage poets who are beyond the first-book stage to submit their very best work."

IOWA REVIEW (II), 308 EPB, University of Iowa, Iowa City IA 52242, phone (319)335-0462, founded 1970, editor David Hamilton (first readers for poetry and occasional guest editors vary), appears 3 times a year in a flat-spined, 200 page professionally printed format. The editor says, "We simply look for poems that at the time we read and choose, we admire. **No specifications as to form, length, style, subject matter or purpose.** There are around 30-40 pgs. of poetry in each issue and currently we like to give several pages to a single poet." Circulation 1,200-1,300 with 1,000 subscriptions of which about half are libraries. They receive about 5,000 submissions/year, use about 100. **Sample postpaid: $5. Reads submissions September 1 through May 1 only. Their backlog is "around a year. Sometimes people hit at the right time and come out in a few months."** They report in 1-4 months. Pays $1 a line, 2-3 copies and a year's subscription. Buys first North American serial rights. Occasional comments on rejections or suggestions on accepted poems. This is one of the top markets in poetry. Responds relatively quickly and, despite its high number of submissions, manages every so often to encourage promising work with a word or two on a rejection slip, evidence that the staff reads closely. Chances, however, are slim because this is a major "credit" for many top poets publishing today. The editor advises, "That old advice of putting poems in a drawer for 9 years was rather nice; I'd at least like to believe the poems had endured with their author for 9 months."

IOWA WOMAN (IV-Women), P.O. Box 680, Iowa City IA 52244, phone (319)338-9858, founded 1976, poetry editor Sandra Witt. "We are a literary quarterly with interest in women's issues. It is a literary magazine that has received national recognition for editorial excellence. We are publishing work **by women, about women, and for women. Prefer contemporary poetry that is clear and concise. Prefer narrative and lyric. No greeting-card verse."** They have recently published poetry by Lyn Lifshin, Alice Friman, Rochelle Nameroff and Jeane Emmons. As a sample the editor selected these lines by Maria S. Wickwire:

> She forgot and forgot, releasing
> small things with infinite patience and love
> gently pulling threads from the tapestry she had kept so long in place.
>
> As she forgot the foxes, they came out from the trees
> and leaned their soft noses into her palms.
> All the forgotten birds came down in a flock, returning their wordless songs.

Iowa Woman is elegantly printed, 48 pgs., magazine-sized, 4-color cover with "original cover art and illustrations." Of 2,000 poems received "I accept about 30." Press run is 4,000 for 2,000 subscriptions. **Sample postpaid: $4. Guidelines available for SASE. Pays subscription and extra copies. Acquires first-time rights. No simultaneous submissions.** Reviews books of poetry in 500-1,000 words. "No guarantee that books sent will be reviewed; this is at the discretion of our reviewers." They hold an annual poetry contest with first place prize of $150. $6 entry fee, 3 poems, for non-subscribers. Last year's judge was Leslie Ullman. All entrants receive a copy of the issue with the winners. Deadline December 15.

‡IRIS: A JOURNAL ABOUT WOMEN (II, IV-Translations, women), Women's Studies, Box 323, HSC, University of Virginia, Charlottesville VA 22903, founded 1980, poetry editor Judy Longley, is a semiannual magazine that **"focuses on issues concerning women worldwide. We also feature quality poetry, prose and artwork—mainly by women, but will also accept work by men if it illuminates some aspect of a woman's reality. We also welcome translations. Form and length are unspecified.** The poetry staff consists of experienced poets with a diversity of tastes who are looking for new and original language in well-crafted poems." Poets who have appeared in *Iris* include Sharon Olds, Gary Snyder, Mary Oliver, Linda Hogan, Lisel Mueller, Linda Pastan, Shirley Anders and Michael McFee. As a sample of poetry recently published, Ms. Longley selected these lines by Pamela Uschuk:

> Woman, you compose poems
> steal fire from the sun
> held hostage by some invisible coast
> until the flame blue pony of imagination
> hauls grief from your bones.

Iris is magazine-sized, professionally printed on heavy, glossy stock with a full-color glossy card cover, 72 pgs., saddle-stapled, using graphics, photos and cartoons. It has a circulation of 3,000, with 50 library subscriptions, 1,000 shelf sales. Single copy: $4; subscription: $15 for 2 years. **Sample: $5 postpaid. Pays 1 copy. Acquires first rights. Reports in 6-8 months. "Name, address, phone number should be listed on every poem. Cover letter should include list of poems submitted.** Because we are a feminist magazine, we receive a lot of poetry that tends to focus on the political experience of coming to consciousness. We are interested in *all* aspects of the reality of women's lives and because we see many poems on the same topics, freshness of imagery and style becomes even more important. Don't limit yourself to the political or to any single topic of women's reality."

IRON PRESS; IRON (II), 5 Marden Terrace, Cullercoats, North Shields, Tyne & Wear, NE30 4PD England, phone (091)2531901, founded 1973, poetry editors Peter Mortimer and David Stephenson, "publishes contemporary writing both in magazine form (*Iron*) and in individual books. Magazine concentrates on poetry, the books on prose and drama." They are "**open to many influences, but no 19th century derivatives please, or work from people who seem unaware anything has happened poetically since Wordsworth.**" Peter Mortimer says, "Writing is accepted and published because when I read it I feel the world should see it—if I don't feel that, it's no good. What's the point of poetry nobody understands except the poet?" The poets they have recently published include John Whitworth, Richard Kostelanitz and William Oxley. *Iron* is 8¼×7¾, flat-spined, professionally printed in small type, 1-3 columns, using b&w photos and graphics, three-color glossy card cover, about 50 pgs. of poetry in each issue, circulation 850, 500 subscriptions of which 30 are libraries. **Sample: $8 (bills only, no checks) postpaid, or £2.50p.** Submit a maximum of 5 poems. "**Just the poems—no need for long-winded backgrounds. The poems must stand by themselves.**" He reports in "**2 weeks maximum,**" **pays £10/page.** He always comments on rejections "**provided poets keep to our maximum of 5 poems per submission.**" They do not invite poetry submissions for books, which they commission themselves. The editor advises, "don't start submitting work too soon. It will only waste your own and editors' time. Many writers turn out a few dozen poems, then rush them off before they've learnt much of the craft, never mind the art." And about his occupation as editor, this journalist, poet, playwright and humorist says, "Small magazines and presses contain some awful writing, which is inevitable. They also contain a kind of truth which the large commercial organizations (over-burdened with marketing men, accountants and financial advisors) have long forgotten. And the good writing in small presses more than compensates for the awful."

ISRAEL HORIZONS (IV-Ethnic), #403, 224 W. 35th St., New York NY 10001, founded 1952, editor Ralph Seliger, poetry consultants Jon Shevin and Rochelle Ratner. A quarterly Socialist-Zionist periodical, circulation 5,000, 8½×11, 32 pgs., **uses poetry reflecting Israeli and Jewish culture and concerns.** *Israel Horizons* deals with the Israeli left and the peace camp in Israel, including but not exclusively *Mapam* and the Kibbutz Artzi Federation; Israeli culture and life and current challenges to Israeli Society; the world Jewish community and its achievements and current problems, from a Socialist-Zionist world view; and general examinations of questions confronting socialism in our day. It also contains editorial comments, regular columns on various topics and book and film reviews. "We also print letters to the editor on occasion." They have an international readership with readers in the U.S., Israel, Canada and 22 other countries. Subscription: $10/year. **Sample: $3 and SASE.**

ISSUES (IV-Religious), P.O. Box 424885, San Francisco CA 94142, founded 1973, is an 8-12 pg. newsletter of Messianic Judaism distributed free, circulation 50,000, which uses some **poetry relevant to that cause. Considers simultaneous submissions. Send SASE for free sample. Pays.**

ITALIAN AMERICANA (IV-Ethnic), URI/CCE, 199 Promenade St., Providence RI 02908-5090, founded 1974, editor Carol Bonomo Ahearn, appears twice a year using **2-4 poems "on Italian-American subjects, no more than 3 pgs. No trite nostalgia or food poems; no poems about grandparents."** As a sample the editor selected these lines from "Inside the Inside of the Moon" by Brian McCormick:

> *Armstrong's hop from module videos*
> *To earth: Mom Vecchio lays down a heart.*
> *She asks, "When is he going to go in?"*
> *This puts a stop to the conversation.*

It is 150-200 pgs., 6×9 professionally printed, flat-spined. Press run is 2,000 for 1,500 subscribers of which 200 are libraries. 200 go free to college students, the rest to individual adult subscribers. Subscription: $25. **Sample postpaid: $12.50. Reports in 4-6 weeks. Pays year's subscription. Acquires all rights. Do not submit in December or January. Name on first page only. Editor occasionally comments on rejections.** They have 2 readers, anonymous peer review of mss. Reviews books of poetry in 1,000 words, multi-book format.

ITALICA PRESS (IV-Translations), #605, 595 Main St., New York NY 10044, phone (212)935-4230, founded 1985, publishers Eileen Gardiner and Ronald G. Musto, is a small press publisher of **English translations of Italian works** in Smyth-sewn paperbacks, averaging 175 pgs. **Query with 10 sample translations of important 20th Century or medieval and Renaissance Italian poets. Include bio and list of publications. Simultaneous submissions, photocopies, dot-matrix OK, but material should not be "totally" previously published. Reports on queries in 3 weeks, on mss in 3 months. Pays 7-15% royalties plus 10 author's copies. Buys English language rights. Editor sometimes comments on rejections.**

JACARANDA REVIEW (II, IV-Translations), Dept. of English, University of California at Los Angeles, Los Angeles CA 90024-1530, phone (310)825-3429, founded 1984, poetry editor Katherine Swiggart, is a literary journal appearing twice a year. "**We publish all kinds, from poems by poets who publish**

in the *New Yorker* to L.A. Beat poets, to translations from the Japanese. Subject matter and style are open. As to length, we'd be interested in a good long poem, but they seem hard to come by. No inspirational verse, etc." They have published poetry by Carolyn Forché, Barry Spacks, Alfred Corn and Phyllis Janowitz. The editor describes it as digest-sized, 100-124 pgs., with 2- or 4-color covers, no art inside the magazine, 4-6 ads/issue. They accept 40-50 of 750-1,000 poems received a year. Press run is 1,000 for 100 subscriptions (25 of them libraries), about 400 shelf sales. Subscription: $8. **Sample: $4 postpaid. Pays 3 copies plus 20% discount on additional copies. Simultaneous submissions OK. Reports in 4-6 weeks. Editor often comments on promising rejections.** The editor says, "We'd like to see more emotionally adventurous poetry, poetry which could but chooses not to hide behind its technical proficiency. We want poetry that matters, that changes the way people think and feel by the necessity of their vision. That's a lot to ask, but good poets deserve demanding readers."

JACKSON'S ARM (III), % Sunk Island Publishing, Box 74, Lincoln LN1 1QG England, founded 1985, editor Michael Blackburn, is a small press publisher of poetry chapbooks and translations. **"No specifications as to subject or style. The poetry I want to publish should be vigorous and imaginative, with a firm grasp of everyday realities. Nothing bland, safe or pretentious."** The press publishes occasional chapbooks, books, cards and cassettes. However, the editor says **he does not usually accept freelance submissions. Payment is in copies: 10% of print run.** Mr. Blackburn advises, "Read everything you can, in particular *contemporary* poets and writers. Get hold of all the 'small' poetry magazines you can, as well as the more commercial and prestigious."

JAPANOPHILE (IV-Ethnic), P.O. Box 223, Okemos MI 48864, phone (517)349-1795, founded 1974, poetry editor Earl R. Snodgrass, is a literary quarterly about Japanese culture (not just in Japan). Issues include articles, art, a short story and **poetry (haiku or other Japanese forms or any form if it deals with Japanese culture). Note: karate and ikebana in the US are examples of Japanese culture.** They have recently published poetry by Linda McFerrin, Dan Weinrich, Alexis Rotella, David Swirnoff, Lenard D. Moore, Mimi Hinman and reprints of Basho. There are 10-15 pgs. of poetry in each issue (digest-sized, about 50 pgs., saddle-stapled). They have a circulation of 400 with 100 subscriptions of which 30 are libraries. They receive about 500 submissions a year, use 70, have a 1-month backlog. **Sample postpaid: $4. Summer is the best time to submit. Photocopy OK. Reports in 2 months. Pays $1 for haiku to $15 for longer poems. Send SASE for guidelines.** They also publish books under the Japanophile imprint, but so far none have been of poetry. Query with samples and cover letter (about 1 pg.) giving publishing credits, bio.

JEOPARDY (II), College Hall 132, Western Washington University, Bellingham WA 98225, phone (206)676-3118, founded 1964, is an annual. **"We are willing to look at anything, but space limitations make publishing overlong stories, poems, essays difficult."** They have recently published poetry by William Stafford, James Bertolino, Chris Jacox-Kyle, David Lee, Sam Hamill and Naomi Clark. The editor describes it as 108 pgs., size varies, offset. They occasionally review poetry. They use about 50 of 500 submissions received. Press run 4,000. **Sample postpaid: $4. Send SASE for guidelines. Reads submissions September 1 through January 15, reports in February. Pays 2 copies.** When funds are available they offer competition for cash prizes. Recent judges include Madeline DeFrees, Ingrid Hill and Irene McKinney. **"Prefer poetry of no more than 3 single-spaced, legal paper in length."** Their editorial staff usually consists of 3-5 people.

JEWISH CURRENTS (V), Suite 601, 22 E. 17th St., New York NY 10003, phone (212)924-5740, founded 1946, editor Morris U. Schappes, is a magazine appearing 11 times a year that publishes **poetry on Jewish themes. "We have been forced to declare a temporary moratorium on all poetry acceptances owing to the size of our backlog of material already accepted and awaiting publication in this category."** The editor says it is 48 pgs., 5 × 8, offset, saddle-stapled. Press run is 2,900 for 2,800 subscribers of which about 10% are libraries. Subscription: $20/year. **Sample postpaid: $2. Pays 6 copies.** Reviews books of poetry.

JEWISH SPECTATOR (IV-Religious), 4391 Park Milano, Calabasas CA 91302, phone (818)883-5141, founded 1935, poetry editor Robert Bleiweiss. A 64-page Judaic scholarly quarterly that uses **Judaically oriented poetry.** Subscribers: 1,200. **Pays "nothing." No simultaneous submissions or previously published poems.**

JOE SOAP'S CANOE (II), 30 Quilter Rd., Felixstowe, Suffolk, IP11 7JJ England, phone 0394-275569, founded 1978, poetry editor Martin Stannard, is engaged in "magazine and occasional booklet/chapbook publication; for a new poetry of optimism and despair, **caters especially to poets who are awake. I really only ever want to see good poetry, but life isn't like that. I'll promise to read whatever I'm sent. No limits, as long as it's in English."** He has recently published work by Tom Raworth, Lydia Tomkiw,

Kenneth Koch, Paul Violi and Geoff Hattersley. As a sample the editor selected these lines from "Al and Clare" by Peter Sansom:

> *Dusk is falling, you're afraid of heights,*
> *and night rung by rung decants last moments*
> *into our brimming glasses, into a blue*
> *earthenware jug, into our hands.*

Joe Soap's Canoe appears annually, 100 pgs. perfect-bound format—"it's really a paperback book." The editor describes the magazine as "quite brilliant—in fact, of all the poetry magazines published in the U.K. it's one of the 2 or 3 always worth reading. It's certainly never boring. Some people hate it. I can relate to that . . ." Circulation 400-500, 200 subscriptions of which 32 are libraries. Subscription: £6 or $12 overseas; per copy: £4 or $8. He receives "thousands" of submissions each year, uses 60-70. **Sample $2 or £1.25. Reports within 2 months. Pays in copies. Photocopy, dot-matrix OK. No simultaneous submissions. Reads submissions April through September only.** Send 9×5 envelope with return postage for catalog to buy samples. **The editor comments on rejections "only when I'm provoked."** Any advice for poets? "No—the world is too large and poetry too various. I'm no advice agency and no tipster. Beginners should simply begin. And know when to stop. Reading the magazine before submitting may save them and me time, as well as doing some small thing for the world of trees."

THE JOHNS HOPKINS UNIVERSITY PRESS (V), Suite 725, 701 W. 40th St., Baltimore MD 21211, founded 1878, editor-in-chief, Eric Halpern. "One of the largest American university presses, Johns Hopkins is a publisher mainly of scholarly books and journals. We do, however, publish short fiction and poetry in the series Johns Hopkins: Poetry and Fiction, edited by John Irwin on 10% royalty contracts. **Unsolicited submissions are not considered.**"

THE JOURNAL (III), Ohio State University, Department of English, 164 W. 17th Ave., Columbus OH 43210, founded 1972, coeditors Kathy Fagan and Michelle Herman, appears twice yearly with reviews, essays, quality fiction and poetry. **"We're open to all forms; we tend to favor work that gives evidence of a mature and sophisticated sense of the language."** They have published poetry by David Baker, T.R. Hummer, Cynthia Ozick and Carol Frost. The following sample is from the poem "The Helmet of Mambrino" by Linda Bierds:

> *I would know that tumble often, that*
> *explorer's slide, belief to belief, conviction*
> *to its memory, to conviction. Once I placed*
> *my marker-coin on Mt. Whitney's double, lost in a mist,*
> *convinced I had climbed to the highest land. Once*
> *I charted a lake from opal air.*

The Journal is 6×9, professionally printed on heavy stock, 80-100 pgs., of which about 40 in each issue are devoted to poetry, circulation 1,500. Subscription: $8; per copy: $5. They receive about 4,000 submissions/year, use 200, and have a 3-6 month backlog. **Sample: $5. Photocopy, dot-matrix OK. Pays copies and an honorarium of $25-50 when funds are available. Acquires all rights. Returns rights on publication. On occasion editor comments on rejections.** Reviews books of poetry. Contributing editor David Citino advises, "However else poets train or educate themselves, they must do what they can to know our language. Too much of the writing that we see indicates that poets do not in many cases develop a feel for the possibilities of language, and do not pay attention to craft. Poets should not be in a rush to publish—until they are ready." (Also see Ohio State University Press/*The Journal* Award in Poetry.)

JOURNAL OF NEW JERSEY POETS (IV-Regional), English Dept., County College of Morris, Randolph NJ 07869, phone (201)328-5471, founded 1976, editor Sander Zulauf. This biannual periodical uses poetry from **current or former residents of New Jersey. They want "serious work that is regional in origin but universal in scope." They do not want "sentimental, greeting-card verse."** Poets recently published include Lesley Choyce, Alfred Starr Hamilton, Joe Weil, Simon Perchik, Carole Stone and Mordecai Marcus. As a sample, the editor selected the following excerpt from "Poem Arrived At While Eating Cauliflower" by Joe Weil:

> *Each cauliflower*
> *is a miniature brain*
> *gathered on my plate.*
>
> *My fork is tentative.*
> *I've already eaten too many*
> *"Intellects":*
> *Plato's overactive logos . . .*
> *Berlioz's theories on orchestration.*

> *I sit Plato and Berlioz down*
> *in this winter park of my brain.*

Published February (spring) and July (autumn), digest-sized, offset, with an average of 64 pgs. Circulation is 500, price per issue and **for sample, $4.** Subscription: $7/year. **Pay is 2 copies per published poem. Acquires first North American serial rights. There are "no limitations" on submissions; SASE required, reporting time is 3-6 months and time to publication within 1 year.** "We plan to offer brief reviews of 100-150 words. An annual 'Books Received' list is slated for Spring 1993."

JOURNAL OF PAN AFRICAN STUDIES (IV-Ethnic), P.O. Box 13063, Fresno CA 93794, phone (209)266-2550, founded 1987, editor Prof. Itibari M. Zulu, is an annual using **"short Afrocentric poetry via social, economic, political development of African people."** They don't want poetry from "those who lack wisdom/knowledge of Afrocentric culture." The editor describes it as magazine-sized, 22 pgs., with cover photo. Press run is 1,000 copies for 700 subscribers of which 10 are libraries, 30 shelf sales. **Sample postpaid: $4. Reports in a month. No pay, not even copies. Editor often comments on rejections.** "Unpublished (new) poets welcomed who focus on African world community (Pan African) ideas."

‡JOURNAL OF POETRY THERAPY (IV-Themes), Human Sciences Press, 233 Spring St., New York NY 10013-1578, phone (212)620-8000, founded 1987. **Poetry mss should be sent to journal editor,** Dr. Nicholas Mazza, School of Social Work, Florida State University, Tallahassee FL 32306-2024. They use **"poems that could be useful in therapeutic settings, prefer relatively short poems; no sentimental, long poems."** They have published poems by Ingrid Wendt and Virginia Bagliore. The editor selected these sample lines by Karren L. Alenier:

> *Her house stands on scaly legs*
> *screening and fencing off my saviors.*
> *Its mobility reminds me*
> *a snaggled-tooth child,*
> *of my deficiencies*

"The *Journal* is devoted to the use of the poetic in health, mental health education and other human service settings." The quarterly is 64 pgs., flat-spined, digest-sized, using 3-6 pgs. for poetry. They accept approximately 10% of 100 poems received. There are 500 subscriptions. Subscription: $38 (US), $46 (international) for individuals; $125 (US), $145 (international) for institutions. **Write publisher for free sample. Pays 1 copy. Submit maximum of 3 poems, 4 copies of each with name on only 1 of them. Include a SASE. Reports in 2-3 months. Editor "occasionally" comments on rejections.**

JOURNAL OF THE AMERICAN MEDICAL ASSOCIATION (JAMA) (II, IV-Themes), 515 N. State, Chicago IL 60610, phone (312)464-2417, founded 1883, associate editor Charlene Breedlove, has a "Poetry and Medicine" column and publishes **poetry "in some way related to a medical experience, whether from the point-of-view of a health care worker or patient or simply an observer. No unskilled poetry."** They have published poetry by Diane Ackerman and Daisy Aldan. As a sample the editor selected these lines from "The Virus" by Floyd Skloot:

> *I know this is not personal.*
> *Like a windowpane latticed*
> *with crystals of snow. I am*
> *simply a host the virus uses*
> *to enact its sole pattern*
> *of growth. I could be rock,*
> *a broth of monkey kidneys*
> *and Medium 199.*
> *I could be you.*

JAMA, magazine-sized, flat-spined, with glossy paper cover, has 360,000 subscribers of which 369 are libraries. They accept about 5% of 300 poems received per year. Subscription: $66. **Sample postpaid: free. Pays up to 3 copies. "We ask for a signed copyright release, but publication elsewhere is always granted free of charge."**

JUDI-ISMS; K'TUVIM: WRITINGS—A JEWISH JOURNAL OF CREATIVITY (IV-Ethnic, religious, themes, anthology), 27 W. Penn St., Long Beach NY 11561, phone (516)889-7163, founded 1986, poetry editor Judith Shulamith Langer Caplan. Judi-isms is the overall name of the press. Judi-isms recently published its second chapbook, **From Adam to Zipporah: Poems about Jewish Personalities,** which featured poems by Enid Dame, Judah Goldin, Rodger Kamenetz, Helen Papell, Lucy Cohen Schmeidler, Michael Sabin and Shulamith Surnamer. As a sample the editor selected these lines from "Anne and Margot Frank" by Robert Stern:

> *imagine the light Rembrandt*

> *would have used to paint*
> *Anne and Margot*
> *a splash of gold in shadows*
> *their faces would have been*
> *Jewish Madonnas or Ruth*
> *and Esther reading together*

From Adam to Zipporah is magazine-sized, 36 pgs., saddle-stapled; sample copy: $5. **Judi-isms is currently interested in submissions dealing with the following themes for future chapbooks:** a) **Something Shakespearean This Way Comes,** poems and short stories inspired by Shakespeare that tie in with the Bard and/or his individual works; b) **It's All Relative,** poems about grandparents, aunts, uncles and cousins; c) **The Nuclear Family,** poems about mothers and fathers, sons and daughters, spouses and siblings; d) **Containers of Judaism,** poems about objects, ceremonies or foods symbolizing Judaism such as a mezuzzah, a mikvah, a torah, a bat mitzvah or cholent. **"I am open to all styles of poetry, including free verse, but I also enjoy seeing carefully crafted verse forms such as sestinas, pantoums, villanelles, sonnets and alphabet poems." Pays copies. All rights revert to author upon publication. Reports within 3-6 months. Typed, photocopy, dotmatrix, simultaneous submissions, reprints, all acceptable. Name and address should be on each page. Editor sometimes comments on rejections.**

JUGGLER'S WORLD (IV-Themes), % Ken Letko, College of the Redwoods, 883 W. Washington Blvd., Crescent City CA 95531-8361, phone (707)464-7457, founded 1982, literary editor Ken Letko, is a quarterly magazine, press run 3,500, using poems about juggling. **"Only restriction is that all content is focused on juggling."** They have published poems by Robert Hill Long, Barbara Goldberg and Margo Wilding. As a sample the editor selected these lines from "Street Mime" by Ann B. Knox:

> *. . . a girl*
> *smiles, the man bows to her, then*
> *spreads his hands wide and silver*
> *balls lift in an arc high*
> *over his head. Faces pivot*

JW is magazine-sized, about 40 pgs., saddle-stapled, professionally printed on glossy stock with 2-color glossy paper cover. It is circulated to more than 3,000 jugglers in more than 20 countries. They receive 50-100 poetry submissions/year, use 4-8 poems/year. Subscription: $18. **Sample: "$2 or $3 depending on issue." Pays 1 copy. Acquires first or one-time rights. They will consider previously published poems. Reports in 1-4 months. Editor sometimes comments on rejections,** suggesting some revision. He advises, "Provide insights."

JULIAN ASSOCIATES; NIGHT OWL'S NEWSLETTER; OUR WRITE MIND (I, IV-Themes), 6831 Spencer Hwy. #203, Pasadena TX 77505, editor Robin Kendle Parker, associate poetry editor Anita Sargent. Julian Associates publishes *NON,* a newsletter, and *OWM,* a magazine, both of which use **poetry relevant to their themes only: living by night or writing. "Anything with a clear message. Humor is a plus! Poems that are all image and no clear meaning waste our time."** They have published poetry by Lynn Bradley. **Previously published poems and simultaneous submissions OK, but tell the editor about them.** *OWM* appears annually, *NON* is quarterly. *NON* is magazine-sized, corner-stapled, press run 100-200; *OWN* press run 250. Sample (of *NON*) postpaid: $3.50. Send SASE for guidelines. **Reports in 1-2 months. Both publications pay at least $1 plus at least one copy. Buys one-time rights.**

JUNIPER PRESS; NORTHEAST; JUNIPER BOOKS; THE WILLIAM N. JUDSON SERIES OF CONTEMPORARY AMERICAN POETRY; CHICKADEE; INLAND SEA SERIES; GIFTS OF THE PRESS (III, IV-Form), 1310 Shorewood Dr., La Crosse WI 54601, founded 1962, poetry editors John Judson and Joanne Judson, is one of the oldest and most respected programs of publishing poetry in the country. *Northeast* is a semiannual little magazine, digest-sized, saddle-stapled. **"Poets published in our books have first appeared in *Northeast*. Authors wishing to submit book mss *must* first send query letter and samples of work *plus SASE*. Any ms sent without query will be returned without being read." Reports in 2-4 months.** A subscription to *Northeast*/Juniper Press is $33/year ($38 for institutions), which brings you 2 issues of the magazine and the Juniper books, Chickadees, WNJ Books and some gifts of the press, a total of about 5-8 items. (Or send SASE for catalog to order individual items. **Sample postpaid: $2.50.**) The Juniper Books are perfect-bound books of poetry by several poets; the WNJ Books are poetry books by one author; Chickadees are 12-24 pgs. each, in wrappers; Inland Sea Series is for larger works; Gifts of the Press are usually given only to subscribers or friends of the press. "Please read us before sending mss. It will aid in your selection of materials to send. If you don't like what we do, please don't submit."

‡**JUST ABOUT HORSES (I, IV-Themes),** 34 Owens Dr., Wayne NJ 07470, founded 1972, editor Steven K. Ryan, appears 5 times/year. *Just About Horses* is a digest-sized magazine providing information about both the model horse hobby and about real horses. **"Our magazine deals with model horses**

and real horses. Any style of poetry will be read as long as the style suits the subject matter." They do not want to see "non-equine poetry. Also no poems in which model horses come to life and cavort and carry on upon shelves and in carpeted halls." Press run is 12,000 for 9,000 subscribers. Subscription: $7.50. **Sample postpaid: $2.** No previously published poems or simultaneous submissions. Pays $25 plus 2 copies. The editor says "We receive too few submissions of *good* poetry."

KAIMANA: LITERARY ARTS HAWAII; HAWAII LITERARY ARTS COUNCIL (IV-Regional), P.O. Box 11213, Honolulu HI 96828, founded 1974, editor Tony Quagliano. *Kaimana*, a quarterly, is the magazine of the Hawaii Literary Arts Council. Poems with "some Pacific reference are preferred--Asia, Polynesia, Hawaii--but not exclusively." They have recently published poetry by Howard Nemerov, John Yau, Reuben Tam, Anne Waldman and Joe Stanton. As a sample the editor selected "Next Time" by Naomi Shihab Nye:

> *Gingko trees live 1,000 years.*
> *Eating the leaves will clear your brain.*
> *When I heard about them, I thought of my mother,*
> *how much I would like to sit under one with her*
> *in the ancient shade, nibbling*
> *the flesh, the stem, the central vein.*

It is 64-76 pgs., 7½ × 10, stapled, with high-quality printing. Press run 1,000 for 600 subscribers of which 200 are libraries. Subscription: $12. **Sample postpaid: $5.** Pays $20 plus 2 copies. Reports with "reasonable dispatch." No comments on rejections.

‡**KAIROS (II)**, P.O. Box 199, Hartsdale NY 10530, founded 1980, editor Alan Mandell. *Kairos* is a semiannual journal of contemporary thought and criticism which uses poetry. "No limitation regarding form, length and/or style, though particularly interested in language, a sensitivity to sound. Do not want to see pornographic, purely confessional." They have published poems by Ivan Argüelles, Helga Novak, Emily Grasholz, Marie Luise von Kaschnitz, Pentti Saarikoski and Michael Stephens. As a sample here are lines from "In Another Country with N. Chomsky" by Christine Farris:

> *A woman moves to another country and waits a year*
> *to begin learning the language.*
> *At first, there are a few people who speak*
> *her language, but then they move away*

The editor describes *Kairos* as digest-sized, approximately 135 pgs., offset, using art and graphics. They have a circulation of 500, receiving 150 submissions/year, using 25, having a 6-month backlog. **Sample $6.** Send any number of poems. Photocopy OK. Reports in 6 weeks. Discs compatible with Wordstar/Perfect Writer OK. Pays 3 copies. Editor "almost always" comments on rejections.

KALEIDOSCOPE PRESS; KALEIDOSCOPE: INTERNATIONAL MAGAZINE OF LITERATURE, FINE ARTS, AND DISABILITY (IV-Themes), 326 Locust St., Akron OH 44302, phone (216)762-9755, founded 1979, editor Dr. Darshan C. Perusek; consulting poetry editor Christopher Hewitt. *Kaleidoscope* is based at United Cerebral Palsy and Services for the Handicapped, a nonprofit agency. **Poetry must deal with being disabled but not limited to that when artist has a disability. Submit photocopies with SASE. Deadlines: March and August 1.** Reports in 6 months, pays up to $50 for a body of work. Buys first North American serial or reprint rights. Considers simultaneous submissions. All submissions must be accompanied by an autobiographical sketch. They have recently published poetry by Patricia Halovanic and Karen Fiser. As a sample, they offer these lines by Karen Fiser:

> *the old pine and cypress*
> *lean together into the evening*
> *light like two people*
> *going home.*

Circulation 1,500, including libraries, social service agencies, health professionals, disabled student services, literature departments and individual subscribers. A subscription is $9 individual, $12 agency, $4.50 single. **Sample $3.** Reviews books of poetry. "*Kaleidoscope* is a forum for disability-related literature. We avoid the stereotypical and sentimental. We seek fresh language and imagery and thought-provoking subject matter."

KALLIOPE, a journal of women's art (IV-Women, translations, themes), 3939 Roosevelt Blvd., Jacksonville FL 32205, phone (904)387-8211, founded 1978, editor Mary Sue Koeppel, a literary/visual arts journal published by Florida Community College at Jacksonville; the emphasis is on women writers and artists. The editors say, "We like the idea of poetry as a sort of artesian well — there's one meaning that's clear on the surface and another deeper meaning that comes welling up from underneath. We'd like to see more poetry from Black, Hispanic, Native American women, and more translations. Nothing sexist, racist, conventionally sentimental. We will have one special theme issue each year. **Write for specific guidelines.**" Poets recently published include Elaine Terranova, Marge Piercy, Kathryn Machan Aal, Dixie Partridge and Sue Saniel Elkind. As a sample, the editor selected the following lines by Ruth Moon Kempher:

> But I sail hot, sail cold, depending
> not on externals, but on that queer greed
> driving, from sea to street
>   on to dark hedgerows
> shadowed alleys, like a creature
> chased, like Cinderella
> shoes in hand.

Kalliope calls itself "a journal of women's art," and it publishes fiction, interviews, drama and visual art in addition to poetry. The magazine, which appears 3 times a year, is 7¼ × 8¼, flat-spined, handsomely printed on white stock, glossy card cover and b&w photographs of works of art. Average number of pages is 80. The circulation is 1,250, of which 400-500 are subscriptions, including 50 library subscriptions, and 600 copies are sold on newsstands and in bookstores. Price is $7/issue, subscription $10.50/year or $20/2 years. **Sample: $7 and guidelines can be obtained for SASE. Contributors receive 3 copies. Acquires first publication rights. Poems should be submitted in batches of 3-7 with bio note, phone number and address. Because all submissions are read by several members of the editing staff, response time is usually 3-4 months. Publication will be within 6 months. Criticism is provided "when time permits and the author has requested it."** Reviews books of poetry, "but we prefer groups of books in one review." The editor says, "*Kalliope* is a carefully stitched patchwork of how women feel, what they experience, and what they have come to know and understand about their lives . . . a collection of visions from or about women all over the world. Send for a sample copy, to see what appeals to us, or better yet, subscribe!"

KANGAROOS AND BEANS (I, II), P.O. Box 52304, Livonia MI 48152-9998, phone (313)537-9425, founded 1989, editor Gregg Nannini, appears twice a year, **open to most poetry. "The important element would be whether it causes someone to stop and think or go 'Oh.' That is what I am looking for. Nothing violent, no private angst."** They have recently published poetry by Jeanette Picardi and Kathleen Meade. As a sample the editor selected these lines from "Attempts to Enter a Pastoral Painting" by Kathleen Meade:

> Her fingers press the oil,
>   extract lanolin from sheep.
> Her tongue searches the Italian Vale.

It is digest-sized, 20 pgs., photocopied from typescript with matte b&w card cover. Press run 500. Subscription: $4. **Sample postpaid: $2. Make check payable to Gregg Nannini. Pays 2 copies. All rights revert to author upon publication. Simultaneous submissions OK. Reports in 6 months.**

KANSAS QUARTERLY; KANSAS ART COMMISSION AWARDS; SEATON AWARDS (II, IV-Regional, themes), Denison Hall 122, Kansas State University, Manhattan KS 66506, phone (913)532-6716, founded 1968 as an outgrowth of *Kansas Magazine,* editors Ben Nyberg, John Rees and G.W. Cliff, is "a magazine devoted to the culture, history, art and writing of mid-Americans, but not restricted to this area." It publishes poetry in all issues. They say, **"We are interested in all kinds of modern poetry except humorous verse, limericks, extremely light verse or book-length mss."** They have published poetry by David Ray, Tom Hansen, Eugene Hollahan, Elizabeth Rees, Kathleen Spivack, David Citino, Robert McNamara, Roger Finch, Ronald Wallace, Mark Nepo, Peter Cooley and David Kirby. There are an average of 80 pgs. of poetry in each creative issue, circulation 1,150-1,350 with 721 subscriptions of which 50% are libraries. They receive 10,000 submissions/year, use 300-400. There is at least a 12- to 18-month backlog unless a poem fits into a special number—then it may go in rapidly. **Sample postpaid: $6 ($8 for double number). Submit "enough poems to show variety (or a single poem if author wishes), but no books. Typed, double-spaced, photocopy OK, but no dot-matrix. No queries. We consider, reluctantly, simultaneous submissions."** Reports in 1-3 months. Pays 2 copies and yearly awards of up to $200/poet for 6-10 poets. The *Kansas Quarterly*/Kansas Art Commission Awards are $200 (1st prize), $150 (2nd), $100 (3rd), $75 (4th) and up to 5 honorable mentions ($50). There are also similar prizes in the Seaton Awards (to native-born or resident Kansas poets). The editors **often comment on rejections, even at times suggesting revision and return.** This is one of the best markets for poems because editors are open to all styles and take hundreds of poems each year (though its number of submissions is one of the highest in literary publishing). Thus, you'll have to be patient. And if your work is accepted, you'll have to be patient again because typically it takes a while to clear out the backlog. But send here anyway. *KQ* is outstanding and worth the wait. Editors say, "Our only advice is for the poet to *know* the magazine he is sending to: consult in library or send for sample copy. Magazines need the support and their published copies should provide the best example of what the editors are looking for. We believe that we annually publish as much generally good poetry as nearly any other U.S. literary magazine—between 250 and 400 poems a year. Others will have to say how good it really is."

KARAMU (II), Dept. of English, Eastern Illinois University, Charleston IL 61920, phone (217)581-5614, founded 1966, editor Peggy Brayfield, is an annual whose "goal is to provide a forum for the best contemporary poetry and fiction that comes our way. We especially like to print the works of new writers. **We like to see poetry that shows a good sense of what's being done with poetry currently. We like poetry that builds around real experiences, real images and real characters and that avoids abstraction, overt philosophizing and fuzzy pontifications. In terms of form, we prefer well-structured free verse, poetry with an inner, sub-surface structure as opposed to, let's say, the surface structure of rhymed quatrains. We have definite preferences in terms of style and form, but no such preferences in terms of length or subject matter. Purpose, however, is another thing. We don't have much interest in the openly didactic poem. If the poet wants to preach against or for some political or religious viewpoint, the preaching shouldn't be so strident that it overwhelms the poem. The poem should first be a poem."** They have recently published poetry by John Dickson, Sheryl Nelms, G.D. Richards, Richard Vance and Lawrence Rungren. As a sample the editor chose these lines from "Recipe" by Jane Bowman:

> Scallops, cream colored and fleshy.
> White wine.
> Fire in the fireplace:
> better with the sound of water,
> a gull or two.

The format is 120 pgs., 5 × 8, matte cover, handsomely printed (narrow margins), attractive b&w art. The most recent issue carries 55 pages of poetry. They have a circulation of 350 with 300 subscriptions of which 15 are libraries. They receive submissions from about 300 poets each year, use 20-55 poems. Never more than a year—usually 6-7 months—between acceptance and publication. **Payment is one contributor's copy. Acquires first serial rights. Sample: $3; 2 recent issues: $4. "Poems—in batches of no more than 5-6—may be submitted to Peggy Brayfield. Photocopied work OK, although we don't much care for simultaneous submissions. We read September 1 through June 30 only. Poets should not bother to query. We critique a few of the better poems. We want the poet to consider our comments and then submit new work.** Follow the standard advice: know your market. Read contemporary poetry and the magazines you want to be published in. Be patient."

KATUAH: BIOREGIONAL JOURNAL OF THE SOUTHERN APPALACHIANS (IV-Regional), P.O. Box 638, Leicester NC 28748, founded 1983. *Katuah* is a quarterly tabloid journal "concerned with developing a sustainable human culture in the Southern Appalachian Mountains." **The editor wants to see "only regional poems or poems dealing with Appalachia and/or ecological feelings."** They have published poetry by Jim Wayne Miller, Kay Byers, Bennie Lee Sinclair, Michael Hockaday, Scott Bird, Oliver Loveday and Patricia Shirley. The tabloid has 32 pgs., offset on newsprint, nicely laid out with attractive b&w drawings and other illustrations, folded for mailing, not stapled. Single copy: $2; subscription: $10/year. Circulation is 3,500, of which 300 are subscriptions; 80% of circulation is newsstand sales. **Sample postpaid: $3. Pay is 10 copies. Reporting time and time to publication are both 6 months.**

‡KATYDID BOOKS (V), 1 Balsa Rd., Santa Fe NM 87505, founded 1973, editor/publisher Thomas Fitzsimmons, publishes 3 paperbacks and 1 hardback/year. "We publish three series of poetry: Asian Poetry in Translation, European Writing in Translation and American Poets." They have recently published poetry by Makoto Ooka, Shuntaro Tonikawa and Ryuichi Tamina. **However, they are currently not accepting submissions.**

KAWABATA PRESS; SEPIA POETRY MAGAZINE (II, IV-Anthology), Knill Cross House, Millbrook, Torpoint, Cornwall, United Kingdom, founded 1977, poetry editor Colin David Webb, publishes "**non-traditional poetry, prose and artwork (line only), open to all original and well thought-out work. I hate rhymes, traditional poems and dislike 'genre' stories. I want original and thought-provoking material.**" They have published poetry by Jacques de Lumiére and Steve Walker. *Sepia* is published 3 times a year in an inexpensively produced, digest-sized, 32-page, saddle-stapled format, photoreduced from typescript, with narrow margins, bizarre drawings, press run 150, 75 subscriptions of which 5-6 are libraries. It sells for 50 p, or £1 ($3) per year. They receive 250 submissions/year, use 50-60. **Sample: 50p ($1). Submit 6-10 pgs., typed—photocopy, dot-matrix, simultaneous submissions OK. Reports in 10 days. Payment free copy.** Reviews books of poetry in 50-100 words. Under the imprint of Kawabata Press Colin Webb also publishes anthologies and collections. **Query with 6-10 poems and "maybe a brief outline of intent." Poet gets 50% of profits (after cost of printing is covered) and 4**

copies. A book catalog of Kawabata Press publications is on the back of *Sepia*, for ordering copies. The editor **always comments on rejections** and advises, "Strike out everything that sounds like a cliché. Don't try any tricks. Work at it, have a feeling for what you write, don't send 'exercise' pieces. Believe in what you send."

‡**KELSEY REVIEW (IV-Regional)**, Mercer County Community College, P.O. Box B, Trenton NJ 08690, phone (609)586-4800, founded 1988, editor-in-chief Robin Schore, is an annual published by Mercer County Community College. It serves as "an outlet for literary talent **of people living and working in Mercer County New Jersey only.**" They have **no specifications as to form, length, subject matter or style, but do not want to see poetry about "kittens and puppies."** As a sample we selected these lines from "Grandmother's Seed" by Virginia Ramus:

> *In the kitchen*
> *pot of peas, limas*
> *between your knees,*
> *you mourned your man,*
> *sang hymns to keep him close.*
> *You called me Honeygirl.*
> *We drank Ohio tea*
> *plain, flat, strong.*

Kelsey Review is 64 glossy pgs., 7×11, with paper cover and line drawings; no ads. They receive about 50 submissions a year, accept 6-10. Press run is 1,500. All distributed free to contributors, area libraries and schools. **No previously published poems or simultaneous submissions. Submit poems typed, under 2,000 words. Deadline: May 1. Always comments on rejections. Reports in May of each year. All rights revert to authors.**

KENNEBEC: A PORTFOLIO OF MAINE WRITING (IV-Regional), University of Maine, Augusta ME 04330, phone (207)621-3000, founded 1975, editor Terry Plunkett, is an annual tabloid of creative writing by Maine writers (whether or not currently residents) supported by the University of Maine at Augusta. 5,000 copies are distributed free as a service to the community in an effort to bring Maine writers to the attention of a wide public. **Qualified writers may submit (with a statement of their relationship to Maine) between September 1 and December 1 each year. Sample free for SASE. Pays 1 copy.**

KENNESAW REVIEW (II), English Dept., Kennesaw State College, P.O. Box 444, Marietta GA 30061, phone (404)423-6297, founded 1987, poetry editor Don Russ, editor Robert W. Hill, appears twice a year. **"Open to any form, style or subject; we are looking for high-quality, finely crafted contemporary poetry of all kinds."** They have published poetry by David Bottoms, Malcolm Glass, Larry Rubin, Eve Shelnutt, R.T. Smith and Lewis Turco. As a sample the editor selected these lines from "Raising the Dead" by Ron Rash:

> *The quick left weeks ago, most voluntarily.*
> *Those who remain are brought up, row by row,*
> *into the fading light*
> *of this November afternoon.*

It is 100+ pgs., flat-spined, professionally printed, 6×9, with embossed matte card cover. They accept about 20 of 2,000 poems received. Press run 1,000. Subscription: $5. **Sample postpaid: $1. Submit no more than 5 poems. Reports within 3 months. Pays 5 copies.**

‡**KENTUCKY WRITING (IV-Regional)**, 808 Monticello Rd., Somerset KY 42501, phone (606)679-8501, founded 1985, is an annual that **publishes "promising young artists and writers in Kentucky and professionals with Kentucky connections."** They want poetry **"alive with fresh images; daring poetry that grabs the reader. Nothing formula."** They have recently published poetry by Jim Wayne Miller and Al Stewart. As a sample the editors selected these lines from "Dancing Hands":

> *his hands reiterated the words he spoke*
> *it was nerves*
> *but i thought it was only conversationdance*
> *and i didn't count the dangerous steps*
> *in his choreography.*

It is a 60-75 pgs., 8×10, with color cover and b&w inner pages. They receive about 500 poems a year, "accept perhaps 25-30." Press run is 3,000 for 2,500 libraries. **Sample postpaid: $5. Previously published poems and simultaneous submissions OK. Include bio.** Time between acceptance and publication is 3 months. **Send SASE for guidelines. Reports in "several months." Pays 1 copy. Acquires all rights. Returns rights "if requested for specific reason."** The editors say, "Find your own voice and make it heard above the noise."

THE KENYON REVIEW (III), Kenyon College, Gambier OH 43022, phone (614)427-3339, founded 1939, editor Marilyn Hacker, associate editor David Lynn, assistant editor for poetry David Baker, is a quarterly review containing poetry, fiction, criticism, reviews and memoirs. It is **one of the country's leading literary publications.** The editors read everything sent their way. But chances here are not good because you'll be competing with big-name writers. On the plus side, the staff is professional and quick. You'll usually hear back within the stated response time. Issues contain work by such poets as Cyrus Cassells, Judith Ortiz Cofer, Joy Harjo, Richard Howard, Josephine Jacobsen, Alicia Ostriker, Sherod Santos and Quincy Troupe. *De Colores*, the Fall 1991 special issue, focused on the work of North American writers of color. The elegantly printed, flat-spined, 7×10, 180+ pg. format has a circulation of 4,000 with 3,200 subscriptions of which 1,100 are libraries. They receive about 3,000-4,000 freelance submissions a year, use 50-60 (about 50 pgs. of poetry in each issue), have a 1-year backlog. **Sample postpaid: $7. Unsolicited submissions are read from September 1 through March 31** *only*. **Reports in 3 months. Pays $15/page for poetry, $10/page for prose. Buys first North American serial rights.** Reviews books of poetry in 2,500-7,000 words, single or multi-book format. "Reviews are primarily solicited—potential reviewers should inquire first."

KEYSTROKES; COMPUWRITE ANNUAL POETRY CONTEST; WRITERS ALLIANCE (IV-Themes), P.O. Box 2014, Setauket NY 11733, founded 1981, executive director of Writers Alliance, Kiel Stuart. Writers Alliance sponsors, in addition to its quarterly newsletter *Keystrokes*, workshops and other activities devoted to building a "dedicated arts community." Membership: $15. You needn't be a member to enter its annual poetry contest (poems about writing with a computer, prize of computer software with a retail value of at least $100, subscription to and publication in the newsletter, January 15 deadline) or to submit poetry to the newsletter **"up to 10 lines on the subject of writing or using a computer or word processing system. 4-6 lines works best. We don't want anything that strays from the subject matter of writers, writing and using computers for that task."** They have recently published poetry by Karen Elizabeth Rigley and Margaret Park Bridges. As a sample the editor selected this poem, "Dilemma," by Beatrice G. Davis:

> *Free-lancer—hyphenated*
> *Freelancer—compounded*
> *Free lancer—separated*
>
> *Which am I?*
> *That's a typesetter's decision*
> *It would seem.*

Keystrokes is 12 pgs., desktop publishing (folded sheets of 8½×11 paper). "Receive about a dozen poems a year; room for 8-10 but less than 50% accepted." Subscription: $15 (with membership). **Sample postpaid: $3.50. "All checks are payable to Kiel Stuart. This is essential." Send SASE for guidelines. Pays 2 copies. Acquires one-time rights. Previously published poems OK if they did not appear in a competing magazine or more recently than 6 months. Reply in 6-8 weeks. Editor frequently comments.** Reviews books of poetry in 250 words, single format. The editor advises, "Treat your craft with respect. Learn the business aspects of being a poet and adhere to those rules. Sloppiness or failure to stick to standard ms format or (worst of all) failure to enclose SASE with ANY communication does NOT indicate an artistic soul."

‡KINGFISHER (II), P.O. Box 9783, N. Berkeley CA 94709, founded 1987, editors Andrea Beach, Barbara Schultz and Ruthie Singer, is a "literary biannual emphasizing short fiction. It publishes a **few poems in each issue.** We see around 50 poems a month and accept about 4." They have recently published poetry by Kevin Opstedal and Campbell McGrath. As a sample the editor chose these lines from Kevin Opstedal's "Song":

> *she's got lines like*
> *Samuel Taylor Coleridge*
> *out-takes of blue movies*
> *historic postage stamps*
> *& grim*
> *entropy spores of*
> *Dark Logic*

They editor says *Kingfisher* is 6×9, flat-spined, with a 2-color cover. **Sample postpaid: $5. Pays 2 copies. Acquires first-time rights. Simultaneous submissions OK.**

KINGS REVIEW MAGAZINE; KINGS REVIEW PRESS (I, II), P.O. Box 1933, S. San Francisco CA 94083-1933, founded 1987, editor Larry Sparks. The press publishes flat-spined chapbooks of poetry. The frequency of the magazine was not given. They want **"avant-garde, educated and metrical, even rhymed poetry. We use translations."** They have published poetry by Errol Miller, Geoffrey Cook,

Whitman McGowan and Martin Matz. As a sample the editor selected these lines from his own "For Our Recent American West":

> *These are lines of great distress*
> *concerning events in our late American West*
> *of those days of not so long ago when*
> *the cattle of this great nation outnumbered men.*

The editor says *Kings Review Magazine* is "50 pages. Size may vary. Original cover art. Binding is very original." Press run is not indicated. **Sample postpaid: $3.50. Pays 1 copy.** "We might **charge criticism fees."** Payment for chapbooks varies. **For chapbook publication, "query first with sample poems, etc. It is not necessary to have published the poems previously."**

‡KIOSK (II, IV-Form/style), 306 Clemens Hall, SUNY, Buffalo NY 14260, founded 1985, editor Nick Gillespie, is an annual literary magazine using **poetry of "any length, any style, especially experimental." Submit in batches of five.** They have recently published Raymond Federman, Carol Bergé and Piotr Parlej. As a sample the editor selected these lines by Seth Frechie:

> *The intent*
> *to say it without awkwardness,*
> "I _____ "
> *A grave uttering*
> *the gravity—*

The editor describes *Kiosk* as flat-spined, digest-sized. Of 400 poems they accept 10-15. **Pays 1 copy.** Free sample with SASE. **Reads submissions September 1 through July 31 only. Reports within 2 months.**

KITCHEN TABLE: WOMEN OF COLOR PRESS (IV-Women, ethnic), P.O. Box 908, Latham NY 12110, phone (518)434-2057, founded 1981, is "the only publisher in North America committed to producing and distributing the **work of Third World women of all racial/cultural heritages, sexualities and classes."** They publish flat-spined paperback collections and anthologies. **"We want high quality poetry by women of color which encompasses a degree of consciousness of the particular issues of identity and struggle which women of color face."** They publish an average of one book of poetry every other year and have published three anthologies, two of which contain poetry. All books are published simultaneously in hardback for library sales. **Send SASE for guidelines. They reply to queries in 2 months, to full ms submissions (if invited) in 6 months. Simultaneous submissions OK if they are informed. Ms should be typed, double-spaced. Clear photocopies OK. No dot-matrix. Payment is 7% royalties for first 10,000 copies, 8% thereafter, and 10 copies. Write for catalog to purchase samples.** General comments usually given upon rejection. The editors say, "We are particularly interested in publishing work by women of color which would generally be overlooked by other publishers, especially work by American Indian, Latina, Asian American and African American women who may be working class, lesbian, disabled or older writers."

ALFRED A. KNOPF (V), 201 E. 50th St., New York NY 10022, poetry editor Harry Ford. Over the years Knopf has been one of the most important and distinguished publishers of poetry in the United States. **"The list is closed to new submissions at this time."**

KRAX; RUMP BOOKLETS (II, IV-Humor), 63 Dixon Lane, Leeds, Yorkshire LS12 4RR England, founded 1971, poetry editors Andy Robson et al. *Krax* appears twice yearly, and they want poetry which is **"light-hearted and witty; original ideas. Undesired: haiku, religious or topical politics, $1,000 bills." 2,000 words maximum. All forms and styles considered.** The editor chose these lines from "The Boxing Postman" by Simon Pitt:

> *. . . It's his second round today,*
> *But he'll not submit*
> *Until he's heard*
> *The final doorbell . . .*

Krax is 6×8, 48 pgs. of which 30 are poetry, saddle-stapled, offset with b&w cartoons and graphics. Price per issue: £1.50 ($3), per subscription: £6 ($12). They receive up to 1,000 submissions/year of which they use 6%, have a 2-3 year backlog. **Sample: $1 (75p). "Submit maximum of 6 pieces. Writer's name on same sheet as poem. SASE or IRC encouraged but not vital." Reports within 10 weeks. Pays 1 copy.** Reviews books of poetry (brief, individual comments; no outside reviews). *Rump Booklets* are miniature format 3×4 16-page collections. **Query with "detailed notes of projected work." Send SASE for catalog.** The editor says, "Sadly banks will not accept checks made payable to the magazine but for convenience we can take IRCs, dollar bills and postage stamps. Not that this means we are cheap—the famous boorish writers you hear of in the tabloids are usually just not up to par!"

KUMQUAT MERINGUE; PENUMBRA PRESS (I, II), P.O. Box 5144, Rockford IL 61125, phone (815) 968-0713, founded 1990, editor Christian Nelson, appears approximately 3 times/year using **"mostly short poetry about the small details of life, especially the quirky side of love found and/or lost. Not fond of long poems (over 20 lines), rhyming or preaching."** They have recently published works by Gina Bergamino, Antler, Shawn M. Tomlinson, Arthur Winfield Knight, Cheryl Townsend and Ianthe Brautigan. As a sample the editor selected these lines from "Khan (on the beach)" by Terry J. Fox:

> *"It's my Vietnamese name" he said proudly*
> *as he wrote his name in the sand*
> *The first wave faded his identity*
> *so he wrote it again*
> *This time at a safe distance from the waves*
> *"It looks like rain" she said softly*
> *He smiled*

It is digest-sized, 32 pgs., "professionally designed with professional typography and nicely printed." Press run 300 for 150 subscribers. Subscription: $6 (3 issues). **Sample postpaid: $3. Send SASE for guidelines. Usually reports in 30 days, often comments on submissions. Pays 1 copy. Acquires first-time rights only. "We like cover letters but not necessary. Previously published and simultaneous submissions sometimes OK, but please let us know."** The magazine is "dedicated to the memory of Richard Brautigan." The editor advises, "Read *Kumquat Meringue* and anything by Richard Brautigan to get a feel for what we want, but don't copy Richard Brautigan, and don't copy those who have copied him. We just want that same feel. When you get discouraged, write some more. Don't give up. Send your stuff everywhere until it finds a home."

KWIBIDI PUBLISHER; KID'S PLAYYARD; THE JOURNAL OF THE NATIONAL SOCIETY OF MINORITY WRITERS AND ARTISTS; THE WRITERS' AND ARTISTS' AID (I, IV-Ethnic, membership), P.O. Box 3424, Greensboro NC 27402-3424. Kwibidi founded 1979, *JNSMWA* 1981, *KP* 1986. Editor Dr. Doris B. Kwasikpui. Kwibidi Publisher **"needs poems, one-act plays, short stories, articles, art, jokes, book reports, research papers and how-to-do and make, for books, *Kid's Playyard* (a magazine for kids of all ages) and *JNSMWA*."** Publication limited to minorities. Pay in copies. Upon acceptance, require membership in the National Society of Minority Writers and Artists ($15/year). Publishes much of the material received and often responds with suggestions. Send SASE for guidelines. Reads submissions January 1 through August 30 only. Reports in about 3 weeks. *KP* appears twice a year. As a sample the editor selected this poem (poet unidentified):

> *Poems are desperate screams of drowning thoughts*
> *sinking faster with every word,*
> *Bellowing verses of pain and despair*
> *to surface buoyantly and to be heard.*

LA BELLA FIGURA (I, II, IV-Ethnic), P.O. Box 411223, San Francisco CA 94141-1223, founded 1988, editor Rose Romano, is a quarterly **using poetry "any form, any length, about Italian-American culture and heritage or anything of special significance to Italian-Americans. Nothing insulting to I-As: no negative stereotypes, no complaining about I-A ways without affection, no spelling accents (such as tacking an *a* to the end of every other word) and no apologies for being I-A."** They have published poetry by Rina Ferrarelli, Rachel DeVries, Dan Sicoli and Gigi Marino. *La Bella Figura* is 10 pgs., magazine-sized, quality offset. Their press run is 200 with 200 subscriptions of which 5 are libraries. Subscription: $8. **Sample postpaid: $2. Send SASE for guidelines. Pays 3 copies. Acquires one-time rights. "All potential contributors are asked to fill out a very short form to describe their Italian background and experience as an Italian-American. Part of the reason for *LBF* is to create family. Therefore, I welcome friendly, informative cover letters. I will gladly consider previously published poems. No simultaneous submissions."** Reviews related books of poetry in 200-250 words. The editor adds, "Few people understand our culture and, therefore, cannot appreciate poetry based on its symbols and secrets. Many I-As are simply 'writing American' or not being published. Write what you are — not what you saw in a movie by an American. I'd like to include work by all I-As — lesbians, gays, heterosexuals and those who are half-Italian but who feel Italian very strongly, first through fourth or fifth generations."

‡**LA CARTA DE OLIVER (II, IV-Bilingual/foreign language, translations)**, Luis M. Campos 157, Boulogne, C.P. 1609, Prov. de Buenos Aires, Argentina, editors Matias Serra Bradford and Santiago Espel, is a bilingual poetry journal appearing twice a year. **They want poetry up to 20 lines maximum.** They have recently published poetry by J.E. Pacheco (Mexico), E. Roditi (France), R. Humphreys (Wales) and P. Green (England). As a sample the editors selected "Callimachus (2)" by Alfredo Vieravé:

> *As in the epigrams of Callimachus I leave this brief sentence*
> *between the teeth of antiquity: search for me in the garden*

> *of the shadows*
> *and for comfort think I passed through the end of the tunnel*
> *and knew it all while I arrived at the light on the other end.*

La Carta de Oliver is 28 pgs., 5¾×8¼, saddle-stapled, professionally printed, with card cover. Poems appear in both English and Spanish. A recent issue also included a section of poems in Welsh and Spanish. They receive 500-1,000 poems, accept approximately 50. Press run is 500 for 50 subscribers, 50 shelf sales. Subscription: $10/year. **Sample postpaid: $4. Previously published poems and simultaneous submissions OK. Seldom comments on rejections. Reports in 2-3 months. Pays 2 copies.** The editors say, "We place *La Carta de Oliver* outside the world's literary cabaret and outside each country's literary ivory stages but, in Dylan Thomas' words, 'For the common wages/Of their most secret heart.' "

LA NUEZ (II, IV-Foreign language), P.O. Box 1655, New York NY 10276, phone (212)260-3130, founded 1988, poetry editor Rafael Bordao, associate editor Celeste Ewers, is a quarterly international magazine of literature and art, **published entirely in Spanish.** The focus is primarily on poetry, but essays, criticism, interviews, short fiction and reviews of poetry books are also of interest, as well as original artwork and photography. They have published work by Frank Dauster, Reinaldo Arenas, Justo Jorge Padrón, Clara Janés and Eugenio Florit. *La Nuez* is magazine-sized, 32 pgs., saddle-stapled and professionally printed, with glossy paper cover. Their press run is 1,000. Subscription: $12. **Sample: $3.50. No simultaneous submissions. Only unpublished work with brief biographical info and SASE. Reporting time 6-8 weeks. Pays 2 copies.** Reviews books of poetry in 2,500 words, single or multi-book format.

LACTUCA (II), P.O. Box 621, Suffern NY 10901, founded 1986, editor/publisher Mike Selender, appears 3 times a year. **"Our bias is toward work with a strong sense of place, a strong sense of experience, a quiet dignity and an honest emotional depth. Dark and disturbing writings are preferred over safer material. No haiku, poems about writing poems, poems using the poem as an image, light poems or self-indulgent poems. First English language translations are welcome provided that the translator has obtained the approval of the author."** They have published poetry by Charles Bukowski, James Purdy, Juliette Graff, Gail Schilke, Julia Nunnally Duncan, Judson Crews and Michael Pingarron. As a sample the editor selected these lines from "Brook" by Joe Cardillo:

> *Out in the fields,*
> *chainsaws elbow-greasing it*
> *all day*
> *tire and click off one at a time*
> *as if to say in relief*
> *this day is finally over*

Lactuca is digest-sized, 72 pgs. saddle-stapled, laser printed or offset on 24 lb. bond with matte card cover, no ads. They receive "a few thousand poems a year of which less than 5% are accepted." Circulation 500 for 150 subscriptions. Subscription: $10/year. **Sample postpaid: $4. Send SASE for guidelines. "We do not print previously published material." Pays 2-5 copies** "depending on length." **Acquires first rights. Reports within 3 months,** "usually within one. We comment on rejections when we can. However the volume of mail we receive limits this." Reviews books of poetry. He says, "The purpose of *Lactuca* is to be a small literary magazine publishing high-quality poetry, fiction and b&w drawings. Most of our circulation goes to contributors' copies and exchange copies with other literary magazines. *Lactuca* is not for poets expecting large circulation. Poets appearing here will find themselves in good company, appearing with that of other good writers."

LAKE SHORE PUBLISHING; SOUNDINGS (I, IV-Anthology), 373 Ramsay Rd., Deerfield IL 60015, phone (708)945-4324, founded 1983, poetry editor Carol Spelius, is an effort "to put out decent, economical volumes of poetry." **Reading fee: $1/page. They want poetry which is "understandable and** *moving,* **imaginative with a unique view, in any form. Make me laugh or cry or think. I'm not so keen on gutter language or political dogma—but I try to keep an open mind. No limitations in length."** They have recently published poetry by Richard Calisch, Margo LaGattuta, Gertrude Rubin, Anne Brashler and Thea Hain. The editor selected these sample lines from "Slow Miracle" by Christine Swanberg:

> *There were times when walking here*
> *would not have been enough, times*
> *my restless spirit needed an ocean,*
> *not this river, serene and simple.*

The 253-page anthology included over 100 poets in 1985, is a paperback, at $7.95 (add $1 mailing cost), was published in an edition of 2,000. **Soundings II** was scheduled for late 1992. It is flat-spined, photocopied from typescript, with glossy, colored card cover with art. **Pays 1 copy and** half-price for additional copies. "All rights return to poet after first printing." Submit any number of poems, with $1/page reading fee, and a cover letter telling about your other publications, biographical background, personal or aesthetic philosophy, poetic goals and principles. Simultaneous submissions, photocopy, dot-matrix, all OK. Any form or length. "Reads submissions anytime, but best in fall." Reports within 8 months. The editor will read chapbooks, or full length collections, with the possibility of sharing costs if Lake Shore Publishing likes the book ($1/page reading fee). "I split the cost if I like the book." She advises, "I'm gathering poems for a small anthology, **Love Gone Away**, and a collection of poems for children." Sample copy of anthology or random choice of full-length collections to interested poets: $5.

LANDFALL; THE CAXTON PRESS (IV-Regional), Box 25-088, Christchurch, New Zealand, founded 1947, poetry editor Michele Leggott. *Landfall* is a literary quarterly of **New Zealand poetry**, prose, criticism, reviews, correspondence and interviews. The Caxton Press publishes a poetry series of books. **They do not want to see poetry except by New Zealanders.** They have recently published poetry by Murray Edmond and Janet Charman. As a sample the editor chose the first stanza of "One Chop The Fruit Fell Open" by Jane Charman:

> one chop
> the fruit falls open
> the melon seller   agitated
> edges his finger
> clear of the ripe flesh
> in deference
> to our fastidious stomachs

The handsome quarterly is digest-sized, 124+ pgs., flat-spined, with full-color glossy card cover, circulation 1,800, 1,600 subscriptions of which 200 are libraries. Subscription: $46 (New Zealand dollars). Sample: $11 (New Zealand dollars) plus postage. Pays about $40 plus 1 copy for 3-4 poems. Can be delay of up to 3 months for replies. ("Editors have full-time occupations— *Landfall* work in their spare time.) Submit 10-12 poems, "a range." Editor always comments on rejections. Her advice: "Read poetry."

PETER LANG PUBLISHING, INC. (IV-Translations), 62 W. 45th St., New York NY 10036, phone (212)302-6740, FAX (212)302-7574, publishes primarily scholarly monographs in the humanities and social sciences. List includes **critical editions of great poets of the past. Complete ms preferred, 200 pgs. minimum, with descriptive cover letter and *curriculum vita*.**

LANGUAGE BRIDGES QUARTERLY (I, IV-Ethnic, foreign language), P.O. Box 850792, Richardson TX 75085, founded in 1988, editor Eva Ziem, "is a **Polish-English bilingual forum for Polish matters. One of its purposes is to introduce the English-speaking reader to Polish culture. The subject is Poland and the Polish spirit:** a picture of life in Poland, mainly after World War II, with emphasis on the new and ponderous Polish emigration problems."

‡**L'APACHE: AN INTERNATIONAL JOURNAL OF LITERATURE & ART (I, IV-Ethnic)**, P.O. Box 71, Wheeler OR 97147, founded 1986, editor Kathryn Vilips, appears twice a year. "**We prefer short fiction, articles and poetry on the Indians, or any ethnic group. One way to get an immediate rejection is to include sex, drugs or violence.** You can allude to love without descriptive scenes or four-letter words. Although we prefer typewritten double-spaced submissions on 8×11 paper, *L'Apache* will not reject a poem simply because a writer does not have access to a typewriter. All we ask is that you print or write legibly." They have recently published poetry Barbara Jennings and Elizabeth Brooks Preddy. As a sample the editor selected these lines from "I Wonder and Wait" by Noel De Luca:

> The tides roll in . . .
> and I have waited, along lonely shores . . .
> but that which you love so dearly
> never returns . . .

The editor describes *L'Apache* as 6×9, "full-color cover. Drawings suitable for framing, high gloss, varnished heavy covers, 144 pgs., each journal a collector's edition." Their press run is 5,000 with most subscribers being libraries. Subscription: $18. **Sample: $5 plus SASE and 94¢ postage. Pays $5-10/poem. No simultaneous submissions or previously published poems. Editor** sometimes comments on rejections. Guidelines available for SASE.

‡**LATEST JOKES NEWSLETTER (IV-Humor)**, P.O. Box 023304, Brooklyn NY 11202-0066, phone (718)855-5057, editor Robert Makinson. *LJN* is a monthly newsletter of humor for TV and radio personalities, comedians and professional speakers. Circulation 250. **Submit seasonal/holiday material 3 months in advance. Reports in 3 weeks.** Sample copy $3 and 1 first class stamp. They use light verse (humorous). **Submit maximum 3 poems at one time. Line length: 2-8 lines. Pays 25¢/line.**

LAUREL REVIEW (III); GREENTOWER PRESS (V), Dept. of English, Northwest Missouri State University, Maryville MO 64468, phone (816)562-1265, founded 1960, coeditors Craig Goad, David Slater and William Trowbridge. *LR* is a literary journal appearing twice a year; **Greentower Press accepts no unsolicited mss.** *LR* wants **"poetry of highest literary quality, nothing sentimental, greeting card, workshop, spit and whistle."** This is an up-and-coming market whose standards are high but whose editors are open to all styles and take pains to accept work on merit alone. Overall, one of the most readable journals published today. They have published poetry by George Starbuck, Marcia Southwick, Albert Goldbarth, David Citino and Pattiann Rogers. It is 128 pgs., 6×9. Press run: 750 for 400 subscriptions of which 53 are libraries, 10 shelf sales. Subscription: $8/year. **Sample postpaid: $5. Pays 2 copies plus 1-year subscription. Rights revert to author upon publication. Submit 4-6 poems/batch. Reads submissions September 1 through May 31 only. Reports in 1 week-4 months. Editor "does not usually"** comment on submissions.

THE LEADING EDGE (IV-Science fiction/fantasy), 3163 JKHB, Provo UT 84602, phone (801)378-2456, managing editor Michael Carr. *The Leading Edge* is a magazine, appears 3 times a year. They want **"high quality poetry related to science fiction and fantasy, not to exceed 3-4 typewritten, double-spaced pages. No graphic sex, violence or profanity."** They have recently published poetry by Michael Collings and Thomas Easton. As a sample the editors picked these lines from "An Astronaut Discusses a Black Hole Binary System" by Russell W. Asplund:

> *It looks like a sink*
> *A cosmic drainhole slightly clogged in*
> *Some cosmic downpour*
> *The star a carelessly dropped*
> *Bar of soap slowly dissolving*
> *In God's shower*

The editors describe the magazine as 6×9, 140 pgs., using art. They accept about 15 out of 150 poems received per year. Press run is 500, going to 100 subscriptions (10 of them libraries) and 300 shelf sales. $2.95/issue, $8 for a subscription. **Sample postpaid: $3.50. Send SASE for guidelines. Pays $5 per typeset page plus 2 copies. Buys first North American serial rights. Submit with no name on the poem, but with a cover sheet with name, address, phone number, length of poem, title and type of poem. Simultaneous submissions OK, but no previously published poems. Reports in 3-4 months.** They say, "We accept traditional science fiction and fantasy poetry, but we like innovative stuff. If a poet has a good idea, go with it."

THE LEDGE POETRY AND FICTION MAGAZINE (II), 64-65 Cooper Ave., Glendale NY 11385, phone (718)366-5169, founded 1988, editor-in-chief Timothy Monaghan, appears twice a year and "searches for **high-quality poetry that is gritty, arresting and/or provocative in nature, though we will publish a great poem even if it doesn't meet these criteria. We suggest poems not exceed 60 lines in length, though again, we will publish the long poem if it so impresses us."** Send up to 5 poems at a time. Recent contributors include Robert Cooperman, George Held, Joyce Stewart and Evan Zimroth. *The Ledge* is 80 pgs., digest-sized, typeset and perfect-bound with glossy cover. They accept 2% of poetry submissions. Circulation is 500, including 100+ subscribers. Subscription: $15 for 2 years, $9 for 1 year. **Sample postpaid: $5. "We do not consider previously published work, though we will consider simultaneous submissions, if so informed." Reports in 3 months, longer if under serious consideration. Pays 1 copy. Acquires one-time rights.** The editor says, "Send us your best work."

LEFT CURVE (II), P.O. Box 472, Oakland CA 94604, phone (415)763-7193, founded 1974, editor Csaba Polony, appears "irregularly, about every 10 months." They want **poetry "critical culture, social, political, 'post-modern,' not purely formal, too self-centered, poetry that doesn't address in sufficient depth today's problems."** They have published poetry by Jack Hirschman, Suzh Menefee and Etel Adam. As a sample the editor selected these lines by HM:

> *my unfriend the machine awakens me*
> *to a world one step removed*
> *from the dark, from the grave*

The editor describes it as "about 100 pgs., offset, flat-spined, Durosheen cover." Press run is 1,200 for 150 subscribers of which 50 are libraries, 800 shelf sales. Subscription: $20/3 issues

---

ALWAYS submit a ms or query with a self-addressed, stamped envelope (SASE) within your country or a self-addressed envelope and International Reply Coupons (IRCs) purchased from the post office for other countries.

(individuals). **Sample postpaid: $7. Reports in 3-6 months. Pays 3 copies.**

LEGEND: AN INTERNATIONAL "ROBIN OF SHERWOOD" FANZINE (I, IV-Fantasy), 1036 Hampshire Rd., Victoria, British Columbia V8S 4S9 Canada, phone (604)598-2197, founded 1989, editor Janet P. Reedman, appears approximately once a year. She wants **"fantasy poetry dealing with/based on episodes of the British TV series 'Robin of Sherwood.' Length is open. No porn or dull poetry about mundane matters."** She has recently published poetry by J.P. Reedman, Julianne Toomey, Frances Quinn and Steve Sneyd. The editor selected these sample lines by Jenni:

> *All move to the forest's heart-beat*
> *Clad in firelight and the moon's pale-bright knife*
> *Giving homage to Herne's Blessing*
> *Make the loving, make the life.*

Magazine is 170+ pgs., spiral-bound, photocopied from typescript, uses much b&w art. Press run: 130+. Accepts **80-90% material from 2 dozen or so. "Will help with rewrites; prefer to outright rejection."** Sample: **$17 US, $18 Canadian. Payment: a substantial discount.** Acquires first North American serial rights. Typed or handwritten mss acceptable. No previously published poems. **Reports in 1-10 weeks, usually sooner. For US submissions/inquiries: rather than IRCs please send 2 loose US stamps. Nearly always comments on rejections.**

L'EPERVIER PRESS (V), 1326 NE 62nd, Seattle WA 98115, founded 1977, editor Robert McNamara, is a "small press publisher of contemporary American poetry in perfect-bound and casebound books." **Currently not accepting submissions.** He has published books by Bruce Renner, Linda Bierds, Frederic Will and Paul Hoover. The press publishes 2 poetry books each year, 6×9 with an average page count of 64, some flat-spined paperbacks and some hardcovers. **Second Sun** by Bill Tremblay, is handsomely printed on heavy buff stock, 81 pgs., with glossy card cover in grey, yellow and white; there is a b&w landscape photo on the front cover and a photo of the author on the back; the book is priced at $6.95.

LIBRA PUBLISHERS, INC. (I), Suite 383, 3089C Clairemont Dr., San Diego CA 92117, phone (619)581-9449, poetry editor William Kroll, publishes two professional journals, *Adolescence* and *Family Therapy*, plus books, primarily in the behaviorial sciences but also some general nonfiction, fiction and poetry. "At first we published books of poetry on a standard royalty basis, paying 10% of the retail price to the authors. Although at times we were successful in selling enough copies to at least break even, we found that we could no longer afford to publish poetry on this basis. Now, unless we fall madly in love with a particular collection, **we require a subsidy.** They have published books of poetry by Martin Rosner, William Blackwell, John Travers Moore and C. Margaret Hall. **Prefer complete ms but accept query with 6 sample poems, publishing credits and bio. Replies to query in 2 days, to submissions (if invited) in 2-3 weeks. Ms should be double-spaced. Photocopy, dot-matrix OK. Send 9×12 SASE for catalog.** Sample books may be purchased on a returnable basis.

LIFTOUTS MAGAZINE; PRELUDIUM PUBLISHERS (V), 1503 Washington Ave. S., Minneapolis MN 55454, phone (612)333-0031, founded 1971, poetry editor Barry Casselman, is a "publisher of **experimental literary work and work of new writers in translation from other languages." Currently accepting no unsolicited material.** *Liftouts* appears irregularly. It is 5½×8, offset, 50-150 pgs. Press run is 1,000. Reviews books of poetry.

‡LIGHT (II), Box 7500, Chicago IL 60680, founded 1992, is a quarterly of **"light and occasional verse, satire, wordplay, puzzles, cartoons and line art." They do not want "greeting card verse, cloying or sentimental verse."** As a sample the editor selected "The Cow's Revenge" by X.J. Kennedy:

> *Obligingly, the mild cow lets us quaff*
> *The milk that she'd intended for her calf,*
> *But takes revenge: In every pint she packs*
> *A heavy cream to trigger heart attacks.*

The editor says *Light* is 32 pgs., stapled or sewn, including art and graphics. Single copy: $4; subscription: $12. **No previously published poems or simultaneous submissions. Seldom comments on rejections. Send SASE for guidelines. Reports in 3 months or less. Pays 2 copies.**

‡LIGHT AND LIFE MAGAZINE (IV-Religious), Free Methodist Church of North America, P.O. Box 535002, Indianapolis IN 46253-5002, phone (317)244-3660. *Light and Life* is a religious monthly magazine. Guidelines available. They also conduct annual writing contests with varying rules and prizes (send SASE for rules December through March). **"We are looking for short, well-written devotional or inspirational pieces and poetry . . . offering unique insights into the great themes of the Bible. Poems should rhyme and flow with a recognizable rhythm pattern. Avoid obscure allusions and unfamiliar language. Maximum length: 20 lines. Pays $7.50-10. Buys first rights. Each submission should be**

typed on plain white paper, double-spaced, at least 1" margin on all sides, no erasable bond, name, address and telephone number on each ms, each submission on a separate sheet of paper, even if they are short pieces." Response time 4-6 weeks. As a sample here is the opening stanza of "Days, and a Day" by Elva McAllaster:

> *Some days deserve carving*
> *In jasper or jade*
> *Some days are like music*
> *Blithe wind harps have played.*

LIGHTHOUSE (I, IV-Children), P.O. Box 1377, Auburn WA 98071-1377, founded 1986, is a magazine "with a delightful variety of fiction and poetry that maintain time-honored values," appearing every other month. It has a children's section. **Uses poems up to 50 lines, "G-rated, ranging from light-hearted to inspirational."** They have recently published poetry by Lois A. Burr, Joyce Parchman and Louise Hannah Kohr. As a light-hearted sample the editor selected "Well-hidden" by Kathleen Y. Bergeron:

> *The "Easter Bunny" hides his eggs*
> *Too well, for I remember,*
> *That last year I was finding them*
> *From April through November!*

The editor describes *Lighthouse* as 56 pgs., digest-sized, some simple activities and illustrations in Children's Section. Circulation is 300, with 100 subscriptions. Subscription: $7.95. **Sample: $3 (includes guidelines, postage and handling). Send SASE with first class stamp for guidelines. Pays up to $5/poem. Buys first North American serial rights. "Prefer typed, double-spaced, each poem on a separate sheet for evaluating purposes." Reports in 2-8 weeks, publication within a year.**

LIGHTWORKS (IV-Form), P.O. Box 1202, Birmingham MI 48012, phone (313)626-8026, editor Charlten Burch, is a magazine "shimmering, flickering, shining and projecting new and creative art and art forms." Published irregularly, 21 issues to date, the magazine is highly visual with coverage of intermedia and fringe arts. "No straight lit but some **visual poetry, 'poeMvelopes', and plenty of mail art.'' See the glossary for a definition of "visual poetry." Pays with copies. Brochure available. $1-5 for back issues.**

LILITH MAGAZINE (IV-Women, ethnic), Suite 2432, 250 W. 57th St., New York NY 10107, phone (212)757-0818, founded in 1975, editor-in-chief Susan Weidman Schneider, poetry editor Alicia Ostriker, "is an independent magazine with a Jewish feminist perspective" which uses **poetry by Jewish women "about the Jewish woman's experience. Generally we use short rather than long poems. Do not want to see poetry on other subjects."** They have published poetry by Irena Klepfisz, Lyn Lifshin, Yael Messinai, Sharon Neemani, Marcia Falk and Adrienne Rich. It is glossy, magazine-sized. "We use colors. Page count varies. Covers are very attractive and professional-looking (one has won an award). Generous amount of art. It appears 4 times a year, circulation about 10,000, about 5,000 subscriptions." **Subscription: $16 for 4 issues. Sample postpaid: $5. Send SASE for guidelines. Reports in 6-8 weeks. Send no more than 6 poems at a time; advise if simultaneous submission. Editor "sometimes" comments on rejections.** She advises: "(1) Read a copy of the publication before you submit your work. (2) Be realistic if you are a beginner. The competition is *severe*, so don't start to send out your work until you've written for a few years. (3) Short cover letters only. Copy should be neatly typed and proofread for typos and spelling errors."

LILLIPUT REVIEW (II, IV-Form), 207 S. Millvale Ave. #3, Pittsburgh PA 15224, founded 1989, editor Don Wentworth, is a tiny (4½×3.6) 12-page magazine, appearing irregularly and **using poems in any style or form no longer than 10 lines.** They have recently published poetry by Lyn Lifshin, Steven Doering, Stacey Sollfrey, Lonnie Sherman, Sheila Murphy and Christien Gholson. As a sample the editor selected "in malnourished light" by Charlie Mehrhoff:

> *in divine rage,*
> *in the city,*
> *we are all animals,*
> *hair raised,*
> *cornered,*
> *yet dancing*

LR is printed from typescript on colored paper and stapled. Press run is 225. **Sample: $1 or SASE. Currently, every other issue is a broadside featuring the work of one particular poet. Send SASE for guidelines. Pays 2 copies/poem. Acquires first rights. Submit no more than 3 poems. Reports usually within 2 months. Editor comments on submissions "occasionally—always at least try to establish human contact."**

LIMBERLOST PRESS; THE LIMBERLOST REVIEW (II), HC 33, Box 1113, Boise ID 83706, phone (208)344-2120, founded 1976, coeditors Richard and Rosemary Ardinger. Limberlost Press publishes poetry, fiction and memoirs in letterpressed chapbooks, flat-spined paperbacks and other formats. *Limberlost Review* appears "fairly regularly. **We want the best work by serious writers. No restrictions on style or form.**" They have published poetry by William Stafford, Lawrence Ferlinghetti, Charles Bukowski, Allen Ginsberg, John Clellon Holmes and Gerald Grimmett. The editor describes *LR* as digest-sized ("varies. One issue recently has been devoted to a series of 20 letterpressed poem postcards."). It has a press run of 500-1,000. **Sample postpaid: $10. Pays 2 copies ("varies"). No simultaneous submissions. For chapbook submission (2-3 a year), submit samples, bio and prior publications. Reports on queries in 1 week, on submissions in 1-2 months. Pays a varied number of author's copies. Editor sometimes comments on rejections. "Issues often are devoted to chapbooks by poets in lieu of anthologies."**

LIMESTONE: A LITERARY JOURNAL (II), Dept. of English, 1215 Patterson Office Tower, University of Kentucky, Lexington KY 40506-0027, phone (606)257-6976, founded as *Fabbro* in 1979, as *Limestone* in 1986, editor Tim Dunn, is an annual seeking "**poetry that matters, poetry that shows attention to content and form. We're interested in all poetics, but we do watch for quality of thought and a use of language that will wake up the reader and resonate in his/her mind.**" They have published poetry by Wendell Berry, Guy Davenport, Michael Cadnum, Noel M. Valis and James Baker Hall. It is 6×9, perfect-bound, offset. They accept 5-10 of 100-150 poems submitted annually. Press run is 500 for 30 subscriptions (20 of them libraries). **Sample postpaid: $3. Pays 3 copies. Submit 1-10 pgs. Simultaneous submissions and previously published poems OK. Reports in 3-6 months.** "If you're considering publication," the editor advises, "read as much poetry as possible. Listen carefully. Work over your poems till you're sick of them. The lack of such care shows up in many of the mss we receive."

LIMITED EDITIONS PRESS; ART: MAG (III), P.O. Box 70896, Las Vegas NV 89170, phone (702)597-0943, founded 1982, editor Peter Magliocco, "have become, due to economic and other factors, more limited to a select audience of poets as well as readers. We seek to expel the superficiality of our factitious culture, in all its drive-thru, junk-food-brain, commercial-ridden extravagance – and stylize a magazine of hard-line aesthetics, where truth and beauty meet on a vector not shallowly drawn. Conforming to this outlook is an operational policy of **seeking poetry from solicited poets primarily, though unsolicited submissions will be read, considered and perhaps used infrequently. Sought from the chosen is a creative use of poetic styles, systems and emotional morphologies other than banally constricting.**" They have recently published poetry by Belinda Subraman, Cheryl Townsend and Bill Chown. As a sample the editor selected these lines from "Twelawney and The Romantics" by Alan Catlin:

> *I've buried all the great ones from my generation*
> *Writers talk about how great they were*
> *Still none of those living have seen a heart*
>   *on fire*

ART: MAG, appearing in 1-2 large issues of 400+ copies/year, is limited to a few poets and chapbooks are compiled within the magazine itself. "This consolidation means no distinct chapbooks are planned outside the magazine." **Sample issues are the cover price of the particular latest issue, $4-7, postpaid. No previously published poems; simultaneous and photocopied submissions OK. Submit up to 5 poems. Send SASE for guidelines. Pays 1 copy. Acquires first rights. Reports within 3 months. Sometimes comments on rejections.**

LINES N' RHYMES (I), 5604 Harmeson Dr., Anderson IN 46013, phone (317)642-1239, founded 1989, editor Pearl Clark, appears every other month using "**some poetry to 40 lines – use some 4 lines, most between 12-20 lines. I like poems concerning life, belief in God's guidance. Nothing pornographic or occult.**" They have published poetry by Ainsley Jo Phillips, Ruth E. Cunliffe and Rosina Clifford. As a sample the editor selected these lines from "Ben Franklin's Bird" by Dr. Harry Snider:

> *For had the Congress stood with Ben,*
> *The turkey would be national;*
> *Protected in its coop or pen*
> *By federal law, irrational.*
> *And then upon Thanksgiving Day,*
> *With turkey kills illegal;*
> *Around our tables folks would pray,*
>   *"Lord, help us eat this eagle."*

It is photocopied on 4 legal-sized colored sheets, sometimes 5. Press run is 50. 20 are distributed free to "my church group." 3-5 shelf sales. Subscription: $5/6 issues. **Sample: $1. "I receive 170 poems/year – accept 70%. I pay nothing for poetry used. I award 'Editor's Choice' to 2 poets/issue at $1. I give preference to subscribers. However, I use poetry from non-subscribers."** Previously

published poems OK. Reviews books of poetry and comments in current issue. She holds a limerick contest each September with 3 cash prizes of $5/each, open only to subscribers.

LINES REVIEW (II, IV-Translations); LINES REVIEW EDITIONS (V), Edgefield Rd., Loanhead, Edinburgh Scotland EH20 9SY, phone (031)440-0246, founded 1952 ("the oldest continuing Scottish literary magazine"), editor Tessa Ransford. *LR* is a quarterly. **"I like to accept from 4-6 poems in traditional page format, though with energy and intelligence in use of language, form and content. No unusual typography, concrete, sensation-seeking, nostalgic, dully descriptive or fanatically political poetry."** They have published poetry by Norman MacCaig, Gozo Yoshimasu, George Szites and Amy Clampitt. Press run 750 for 500 subscribers of which 100 are libraries, 100 shelf sales. **Sample postpaid: £1.75. Reports in 2-3 weeks. Pays £10/page plus 1 copy. "Double spacing helps, and clear indication whether a page break is or is not also a stanza break, and careful attention to punctuation – that it is as it will be printed."** They review books of poetry. Tessa Ransford is also director of Scottish Poetry Library (see listing under Organizations) and offers a School of Poets and Critical Service through the library. *LR* often has special issues devoted, for example, to poetry from Glasgow, Japan, America, Canada. They publish translations. Their spring, 1992, issue celebrated the magazine's 40th anniversary. Lines Review Editions publishes 2 paperbacks/year, "a dozen or so published poets whose work has regularly appeared in the magazine. **We are not accepting any unsolicited mss."**

LINTEL (II), P.O. Box 8609, Roanoke VA 24014, phone (703)982-2265 or 345-2886, founded 1977, poetry editor Walter James Miller, who says, **"We publish poetry and innovative fiction of types ignored by commercial presses. We consider any poetry except conventional, traditional, cliché, greeting card types, i.e., we consider any artistic poetry."** They have published poetry by Sue Saniel Elkind, Samuel Exler, Adrienne Wolfert and Edmund Pennant. As a sample the editor selected these lines by Nathan Teitel:

> *loneliness*
> *is a Mexican earring*
> *and fear*
> *a crushed cigarette*

The book from which this was taken, **In Time of Tide,** is 64 pgs. flat-spined, digest-sized, professionally printed in bold type, hard cover stamped in gold, jacket with art and author's photo on back. Walter James Miller asks that you **query with 5 sample poems. Reads submissions January and August only.** He replies to the query within a month, to the ms (if invited) in 2 months. **"We consider simultaneous submissions if so marked and if the writer agrees to notify us of acceptance elsewhere."** Ms should be typed, photocopy OK. **Pays royalties after all costs are met and 100 copies. Buys all rights.** Offers usual subsidiary rights: 75%/25%. To see samples, send SASE for catalog and ask for "trial rate" (50%). **"We like our poets to have a good publishing record, in the literary magazines, before they begin to think of a book."**

LINWOOD PUBLISHERS (II), 1219 Winston Dr., Decatur GA 30032, phone (404)284-7384, founded 1982, poetry editor Bernard Chase, was "organized as an independent small press, primarily to publish the poetry of known, unknown and little known poets." They publish in both paper and hardback editions. The editor says he is interested in **"quality poetry of any form."** They have published poetry by Simon Perchik, Carl Lindner, Barbara Unger, T.S. Wallace, George Gott and Barbara Crooker. As a sample the editor selected these lines from **West of Ireland** by Geri Rosenzweig:

> *And this firm crenulated*
> *bank of sand we walk on?*
> *Each night it slips in the tug*
> *of moon and water as one day*
> *the scalloped wall of the heart*
> *will fall in the blood's last roar.*

They will consider freelance submissions of book mss. **It is your option whether to query first or send samples.** Your cover letter should give publication history and bio. They try to reply to **queries within 1 month, to mss within 1-2 months. Preferably typed ms: photocopies, dot-matrix, simultaneous submissions OK; contracts are for 5-10% royalties and author's copies (negotiated).** Send 7 × 10 SASE with 3 oz. postage for catalog. "Sample copies of our publications can be purchased directly from the publisher." Bernard Chase advises, "Feel no intimidation by the breadth, the depth of this craft of which you have chosen to become a part. Although we are very open to beginners, we do not as a rule respond with comments, suggestions or criticisms."

‡LIPS (III), Box 1345, Montclair NJ 07042, founded 1981, poetry editor Laura Boss, "is a quality poetry magazine published 2 times a year, average 70 pgs., digest-sized, flat-spined, circulation 1,000, 200 subscriptions, approximately 100 are libraries. Takes pleasure in publishing previously unpublished poets as well as publishing the most established voices in contemporary poetry. **We look for quality**

work: the strongest work of a poet; work that moves the reader; poems take risks that work. We prefer clarity in the work rather than the abstract. Poems longer than 6 pages present a space problem." They have recently published poetry by Michael Benedikt, Gregory Corso, Allen Ginsberg, Richard Kostelanetz, Lyn Lifshin, Theodore Weiss, Marge Piercy, Warren Woessner, Maria Gillan, Nicholas Christopher, Diana Chang, David Ignatow and Ishmael Reed. The editor selected these sample lines by Chocolate Waters from "Confessions of an Ex Feminist-Malarkist (that's a person who's one-fourth feminist, three-fourth's malarkey):

> *It was Easter Sunday morning.*
> *I woke up with an ugly hangover*
> *and an even uglier man.*

They receive about 8,000 submissions/year, use less than 1%, have a 6-month backlog. **Sample postpaid: $6. Poems should be submitted between September and March, 6 pgs., typed or clear photocopy OK, no query necessary. She tries to respond in 1 month but has gotten backlogged at times. Pays 2 contributor's copies. Acquires first rights. Send SASE for guidelines.** Her advice to poets is, "Remember the 2 T's: Talent *and* Tenacity."

LITERARY FOCUS POETRY PUBLICATIONS; ANTHOLOGY OF CONTEMPORARY POETRY; INTER-NATIONAL POETRY CONTESTS: FALL CONCOURS, SPRING CONCOURS, SUMMER CONCOURS (I, IV-Anthology), P.O. Box 36242, Houston TX 77236-0242, phone (713)541-4626, founded 1988, editor-in-chief Adrian A. Davieson. **Purchase of anthology may be required of poets accepted for publication.** Literary Focus publishes anthologies compiled in contests, 3 times/year, with prizes of $500, $300 and $100, plus "Distinguished Mention" and "Honorable Mention." **"Contemporary poetry with no restriction on themes. 20 line limit. Maximum submission 15 poems, minimum 3 poems. No abusive, anti-social poetry."** As a sample the editor selected these lines from "Delayed Journey" by himself:

> *I saw the footsteps retracing to*
> *A lost moment, then there was a*
> *Whisper of ancient sorrows long*
> *Left in the trail of endless*
> *Struggles.*

The digest-sized anthologies are either flat-spined or saddle-stapled, 70 pgs., typeset. **Previously published poems and simultaneous submissions OK. "In order to evaluate serious entries, a $5 entry fee is now required for the first three poems. Poems are evaluated on an individual basis by a panel of five editors chaired by editor-in-chief. Poets are notified of acceptance two weeks after deadlines." Send SASE for guidelines.** Reviews books of poetry.

‡**LITERARY OLYMPICS, INC. (V, IV-Anthology, translations)**, P.O. Box 178407, San Diego CA 92177, phone (619)276-6199, founded 1984, president and editor Elizabeth Bartlett, is an international organization "to encourage and promote public interest in poetry by honoring leading contemporary poets from all over the world on the occasion of the Olympics every four years. The new anthology, **Literary Olympians 1992**, contains poems by 132 poets from 65 countries in 55 languages, including English translations." They have published poetry by Maxine Kumin, Josephine Jacobsen, Octavio Paz and Odysseus Elytis. As a sample we selected these lines from "Spoon" by Koichi Iijima (translated from the Japanese by George Uba and Shoko Okazaki and published in **Literary Olympians II**, 1988):

> *This spoon*
> *is what a man once ate his food with.*
> *What was his face like?*
> *What was he doing?*
> *Since we are all human,*
> *we can*
> *easily infer*
> *that.*
> *Probably he was dazzled by the sunshine*
> *and loved the rustling sounds of trees.*
> *I can understand all this clearly.*
> *But the person who killed him at Auschwitz—*
> *what was he like?*

They are currently not accepting submissions; however poets may submit unpublished English poems of 20-24 lines, with cover letter, in 1994 and 1995 for Literary Olympians 1996. Each poet and translator receives a copy of the anthology. "Besides appearing in the anthology, poets are candidates for gold, silver and bronze medals awarded by a jury of literary scholars. We also hope to raise enough funds to clear expenses and then pay each contributor an additional honorarium." **Literary Olympians 1992**, published by Ford Brown & Co., is $29.95. The editor says, "We rely heavily on qualified translators to obtain poems and permissions to translate and publish. Poets familiar with **Literary Olympians** can best judge the quality of our selection."

THE LITERARY REVIEW: An International Journal of Contemporary Writing (II), Fairleigh Dickinson University, 285 Madison Ave., Madison NJ 07940, phone (201)593-8564, founded 1957, editor-in-chief Walter Cummins, a quarterly, seeks **"work by new and established poets which reflects a sensitivity to literary standards and the poetic form." No specifications as to form, length, style, subject matter or purpose.** They have published poetry by Robert Cooperman, Gary Fincke, José Bergamin, Tomasz Jastrun and R.S. Thomas. The magazine is 6×9, flat-spined, 128+ pgs., professionally printed with glossy color cover, using 20-50 pgs. of poetry in each issue, circulation 2,500, 900 subscriptions of which one-third are overseas. They receive about 1,200 submissions/year, use 100-150, have 6-12 months backlog. **Sample: $5 postpaid, request a "general issue." Submit no more than 5 poems at a time, clear typing or dot-matrix, simultaneous submissions OK, no queries. Reports in 2-3 months. Pays copies. Acquires first rights. At times the editor comments on rejections.** Reviews books of poetry in 500 words, single format. They advise, "Read a general issue of the magazine carefully before submitting."

LITERATURE AND BELIEF (II, IV-Religious), 3076-E Jesse Knight Humanities Building, Brigham Young University, Provo UT 84602, phone (801)378-2304, founded 1981, editor Jay Fox, is the "annual journal of the Center for the Study of Christian Values in Literature." **It uses poetry "with Christian-based themes"** in a handsomely published flat-spined format. Price per issue: $5 US, $7 outside US. They conduct an annual contest with $100 first prize for poetry. They have published poetry by Ted Hughes, Donnel Hunter, Leslie Norris and William Stafford.

THE LITHIC REVIEW (II); THE PREHISTORIC PRESS, P.O. Box 40624, Bellevue WA 98004, phone (206)453-9211, founded 1990, editor Denise Buckner. *The Lithic Review* is a literary quarterly. **"Want to see insight and imagination. Any style. Enjoy poems dealing with nature or the environment, but any subject is OK. (Bonus points for poems that have anything to do with ancient cultures or anthropology.) I enjoy Beat poetry, poetry with a sense of humor, poetry that takes risks, breaks new ground. Be an original. Don't want to see rhyming poetry."** They have published poetry by A.D. Winans, Arthur Winfield Knight, Joy Walsh, B.Z. Niditch and Douglas Powell. As a sample the editor selected these lines from "Telegram" by Sherry Brandon:

> *The future race is coming in,*
> *signal please:*
> *breaker to breaker,*
> *dream to dream,*
> *are you there?*

It is digest-sized, 32 pgs., saddle-stapled, with card cover. Press run 250-300. Subscription: $5 for 2 issues, $10 for 4 issues, $30 lifetime subscription. Please make checks payable to Denise Buckner. **Sample: $3 postpaid. Pays 1-3 copies. "I appreciate cover letters which convey the personality or outlook of the poet, but a cover letter isn't required. It would be nice to hear how the poet heard of** *The Lithic Review.* **Please include name and address on every page and be sure to include a SASE. Usually respond to submissions within a few weeks. Seldom provide comments or criticism on rejections."** Reviews books of poetry. She advises, "Read lots of current poetry. Cultivate your own style—be authentic. Write a lot. Don't be discouraged by rejections. Enjoy yourself!"

LITTLE RIVER PRESS (V), 10 Lowell Ave., Westfield MA 01085, phone (413)568-5598, founded 1976, editor Ronald Edwards, publishes **"limited editions of poetry collections, chapbooks and postcards of New England Poets."** They have published poetry by Steven Sossaman, Wanda Cook and Frank Mello. **However, they currently do not accept unsolicited poetry. Pays 60% of run.**

‡**LIVING POETS SOCIETY (I, IV-Ethnic)**, P.O. Box 8555, New York NY 10116-4654, founded 1991, editor-in-chief Gabrellar Jordan, is a bimonthly newsletter of "inspirational writing and poetry and community news and development." The editor wants **poetry with "style, creativity and substance"** from African-Americans but will also accept poems from other groups. No **"poems that most people will not understand."** As a sample the editor selected these lines (poet unidentified):

> *The day we heard that Martin died,*
> *Our hope, and all who came so far*
> *Died too with him, our brightest star,*
> *The symbol, and the movement's pride.*
> *He'd never reach the other side*

The newsletter is 6-8 double-sided pgs., stapled, with some drawings. Press run is 35-50. Single copy: $1. **Previously published poems and simultaneous submissions OK. Bio requested.** Time between acceptance and publication is 3 months. **No pay at the present time. "Poets have all** rights to their work." The editor says, "You don't have to buy the newsletter to contribute, but I would encourage those who are contributing to subscribe for details and information. I have recently started a poetry contest. Details are to follow in future issues."

‡LIVING POETS SOCIETY; VOICES OF HEART (I,IV-Love/romance/erotica), Suite 112, 1019 E. Lemon, Tempe AZ 85281, phone (602)894-9671, founded 1989, *Voices of Heart* founded 1991, editor Dwight Stone. Living Poets Society, "a nonprofit, independent publisher and cultural organization of poetic humanities," publishes *Voices of Heart* 4 times/year. They want **"Poetry that is articulate visions of the continuities or discontinuities in the human relationship, against the natural world. Poetry illustrative and appreciative of extraordinary feelings, expressions of well-crafted quality, imaginative sense of form and imagery that sympathizes with the emotional intelligence of the common reader." Poets must write for guidelines (send SASE) before submitting.** As a sample the editor selected these lines of his own:

> *Our poetry is a kind of loving*
> *when the wreath of souls (of humans)*
> *share in the touching of hearts.*

Voices of Heart is 20-40 pgs., digest-sized, desktop published, printed on recycled paper, saddle-stapled with card cover. Press run is 250 for 65 subscribers, the rest shelf sales. Subscription: $16. **Sample postpaid: $4. Previously published poems and simultaneous submissions OK. Cover letter requested. Often comments on rejections. Reports "as soon as possible." Pays 1 copy.** The editor suggests poets purchase a sample copy. He says, "To be good, you must be a reader as well as a writer and human as well as a poet."

LIVING STREAMS (IV-Christian, membership), P.O. Box 1321, Vincennes IN 47591, phone (812)882-4289, founded 1988, editor/founder Kevin Hrebik, a national, quarterly, plus a Christmas issue, "subscriber written," 104-page journal. Subscription: $18/year, $28/2 years (Canada add $5; all in US funds). They **"prefer non-controversial Christian material, especially good poetry, prose and fiction, also all special forms." They use 100-125 poems/year, 8-24 lines, and 25-30 prose pieces, average length 1,000 words. Pays in contributor's copies, tearsheets and free subscriptions. Photocopied, simultaneous, previously published submissions are acceptable (no dot-matrix). Reporting time is 4-6 weeks. Sample available for $4.50 postpaid, guidelines free.** Uses original art and photography; will consider submissions (nature scenes with water) for cover (pay is $50). The editor says, **"Send 4-6 good poems and 1 prose piece at a time. Don't write Christian 'baby' material. Assume reader is intelligent, literate and a mature Christian. Write clearly, make specific points, yet try to be original and artistic. Show off your skill."**

LMNO PRESS (I), P.O. Box 862, Westminster MD 21158, founded 1991, editor Laurie Precht. *LMNO Press* publishes yearly in July. It accepts **concrete, narrative poetry under 100 lines and short stories.** *"Whatever gets published must make sense!* **And please, no poetry about cats, death, religion or about writing poetry. Also, no chapbooks."** As a sample she selected these lines from "Wasp Nest" by John P. Mohrbacher:

> *Somewhere on the chalky*
> *Undersides of the eaves,*
> *I inevitably paint my way*
> *Up to the papery comb,*
> *Empty in midday but for one sentry.*
> *Like a brain, some of the grey chambers*
> *Hold life, some don't*
> *But all narrow to a medulla stem*
> *Anchored to the house.*

LMNO Press is digest-sized, 40 pgs., press run 200. It is distributed through subscription and at poetry readings, local bookshops and literary fairs. Subscription or **sample copy: $3 postpaid. "Don't send cash; please send check or money order made out to Laurie Precht." Pays 1 copy. Mss should be typed with name on everything. Submit 3-6 poems, simultaneous submissions OK, no previously published work. Reports in 3-6 months. Editor comments if the poem needs work before it is published.** She advises, "Go deeply into your writing. Draw on your experiences; let the reader live what you know. And don't dawdle on the same worn topics—pick something new and go!"

‡THE LOCKHART PRESS (II), Box 1207, Port Townsend WA 98368, phone (800)659-4364, founded 1982, poetry editor Russell A. Lockhart, Ph.D, began as a publisher of fine handmade hardbound books, now expanding to chapbooks and paperbacks, is interested in, **but not limited to, "poetry having its origin in or strongly influenced by dreams."** No specifications as to form, length or style. All

handmade editions include special readings by the poets on tape. Limited deluxe editions cost $75 or more. Sample lines from **Marc Hudson's Journal for an Injured Son:**

> *My boy also is a swimmer, for whom desire*
> *annihilates distance. He is my dolphin, my little Odysseus.*
> *Death could not steal from his eyes*
> *the dawn of his homecoming.*

Query with 5 samples, usual bio, credits information. Replies to query in 2 weeks, reports on submission (if invited) 90 days. Ms should be clear in any form — simultaneous submissions, photocopies, dot-matrix, or discs compatible with Macintosh OK. Contract is for 15% royalties (after cost recovery) plus 10 copies (handmade), 100 copies (trade). Buys all rights. Return negotiable. To see a sample, you may ask for one on approval. Sometimes comments on rejections.

LODESTAR BOOKS (IV-Children/teen, anthology), 375 Hudson St., New York NY 10014, phone (212)366-2627, affiliate of Dutton's Children's Books, a division of Penguin USA, founded 1980, editorial director Virginia Buckley, is a trade publisher of **juvenile and young-adult nonfiction, fiction and picture books. "A good anthology would be OK, or poetry for the very young child. No adult poetry. Although we have not published any poetry or anthologies, we are open to submissions; writers should be familiar with the juvenile market. Best place to start is in the bookstore rather than the library."**

LOLLIPOPS, THE MAGAZINE FOR EARLY CHILDHOOD EDUCATORS (IV-Themes), Good Apple, Inc., 1204 Buchanan, Box 299, Carthage IL 62321, phone (217)357-3981, editor Sharon Thompson, is a magazine published 5 times a year providing easy-to-use, hands-on practical **teaching ideas and suggestions for early childhood education. Uses light verse on themes appropriate to the focus of the magazine. Circulation 18,000. Subscription: $16.95. Sample postpaid: $4.50. Writer's guidelines for #10 SAE with 2 oz. postage. Submit seasonal/holiday material 6 months in advance. Computer printout submissions acceptable; prefers letter-quality. Pays "variable" rates on publication.**

LONDON MAGAZINE (II), 30 Thurloe Place, London SW7 England, founded 1954, poetry editor Alan Ross, is a literary and art monthly using **poetry "the best of its kind."** They accept about 150 of 2,000 poems received a year. Press run is 5,000 for 2,000 subscriptions. Subscription: £28.50 or $67. **Sample postpaid: £3. Pays £20/page. Buys first British serial rights. Reports "very soon."** Reviews books of poetry in up to 1,200 words. Alan Ross says, "Quality is our only criterion."

‡**LONDON REVIEW OF BOOKS (III),** Tavistock House South, Tavistock Square, London WC1H 9JZ England, founded 1979, editors Karl Miller and Mary-Kay Wilmers, is published 24 times a year, mostly reviews and essays but some stories and poems. They have published some of the most distinguished contemporary poets, such as Ted Hughes, Tony Harrison, James Fenton, Frederick Seidel and Thom Gunn. As a sample we selected the opening stanza of "The Metronomic Moon" by Michael Young:

> *In other years I would say, how pretty they are,*
> *The cherries outside our house.*
> *This autumn I see the first leaves*
> *Writhe from the green into the yellow and*
> *From the yellow into what seems a frantic red*
> *Before they corkscrew to their conclusion*
> *When the morning wipers scrape them from the windscreens*
> *To drop them in the dog shit on the pavement*
> *Their beauty has not brought them mercy.*

The paper has a circulation of 17,000 with 14,000 subscriptions. **Considers simultaneous submissions. Sample: £1.95 in United Kingdom, $2.95 in United States and Canada — excluding postage. They pay £50/poem.**

LONG ISLAND QUARTERLY (IV-Regional), 14 Center St., Northport NY 11768, founded 1990, editor-publisher George Wallace, is a quarterly using **poetry by people on or from Long Island. "Surprise us with fresh language. No conventional imagery, self-indulgent confessionalism, compulsive article-droppers."** They have published poetry by David Ignatow and William Heyen. As a sample here are lines from "Watermill" by Claire Nicholas White:

> *This pioneer's house, lonely as a shroud*
> *once housed the trapped soul of a sad wife.*
> *I knew her there chained to her loom*
> *in a land not her own, bending her head*
> *to peer through small panes over land eastward*
> *from where she came*

LIQ is a handsome publication whose clean design (28 pgs., digest-sized, saddle-stapled, professionally printed on quality stock with matte card cover) enhances the image-based, mostly lyric free verse inside. Most contributions show attention to craft and structure. Press run 250 for 150 subscribers of which 15 are libraries, 50-75 shelf sales. Subscription: $12. **Sample postpaid: $3. Pays 1 copy. Responds in 3 months. Submissions without SASE not returned.** The editor advises "(1) Go beyond yourself; (2) Don't be afraid to fictionalize; (3) Don't write your autobiography— if you are worth it, maybe someone else will."

LONG ISLANDER; WALT'S CORNER (II), 313 Main St., Huntington NY 11743, phone (516)427-7000, FAX (516)427-5820, founded 1838 by Walt Whitman, poetry editor George Wallace, is a weekly newspaper, 25,000 circulation, using **unrhymed poetry up to 40 lines "grounded in personal/social matrix, no haiku, inspirational."** They have used poetry by David Ignatow, David Axelrod and R.B. Weber. It is "48 pgs. newsprint." They use 52 of about 1,000 poems submitted each year. Subscription: $18. **Sample postpaid: $2.50. Simultaneous submissions OK. Pays 1 copy. Editor "normally" comments on rejections.**

LONG SHOT (II), P.O. Box 6231, Hoboken NJ 07030, founded 1982, published by Danny Shot, edited by Jack Wiler, Jessica Chosid and Tom Polhamus, is, they say, "writing for the real world." They have published poetry by Charles Bukowski, Sean Penn, Allen Ginsberg, Marianne Faithfull, Amiri Baraka and June Jordan. It is 120+ pgs., flat-spined, professionally printed with glossy card cover using b&w photos, drawings and cartoons. It comes out twice a year, press run 1,500. They say they accept about 35 of 1,000 submissions received. Subscription $18 for 2 years (4 issues). **Sample: $5. Pays 2 copies. Simultaneous submissions OK. Reports in 2 months.**

LONGHOUSE (II); SCOUT (V); ORIGIN PRESS (V), Green River R.F.D., Brattleboro VT 05301, founded 1973, editor Bob Arnold. *Longhouse* is a literary annual using **poems "from the serious working poet" from any region in any style.** They have published poetry by Hayden Carruth, Keith Wilson, Barbara Moraff, James Koller, Cid Corman, Janine Pommy-Vega, Bobby Byrd and Sharon Doubiago. Its format is unusual: a thick packet of looseleaf 8½ × 14 sheets, photocopied from typescript, in a handsomely printed matte cover. Press run 200. **Sample postpaid: $8. Pays 2 copies.** Reviews books of poetry. **They publish chapbooks and books (manuscripts solicited only) under the imprints of Longhouse and Scout.** "We are also a bookshop and mail-order business for modern first editions and modern poetry and small presses. We encourage poets and readers looking for collectible modern first editions and scarce—and not so scarce—books of poetry and small press magazines to send a donation for our free catalog; whatever one can afford." Bob Arnold says, "Origin Press is best known as Cid Corman's press. One of the quiet giants in American poetry/plus the wide scope of international work. Established in the early 1950s in Boston, it has moved around as Cid went with his life: France, Italy, for many years now in Kyoto, Japan. Cid has merged with Longhouse in that we now edit and publish a few items together. He continues to edit, translate and publish from Kyoto. His own books are heavily based in our bookshop and mail order catalog."

LOOM PRESS; LOOM (II), P.O. Box 1394, Lowell MA 01853, founded 1978, editor Paul Marion, a small press publisher of poetry, books, chapbooks and broadsides. The broadside series, which appears irregularly, is called *Loom* and publishes **"good contemporary poems in any form, style."** Poets recently published include Jane Brox, Kathleen Aponick and Eric Linder. As a sample the editor selected the following lines from "Uncle Paul" by Tom Sexton:

> Sometimes when the autumn air
> pricks my skin like a baling hook
> I think of my uncle Paul.

The broadsides range from magazine-sized to 11 × 17. They have a circulation of 100-500. Price per issue varies, but a **sample is available for $2. Pay is 10 copies. Acquires first North American serial rights.** "Clear copies" are OK for submissions which will be reported on in 1 month; time to publication is 3-6 months. Writers should query first for chapbook publication, sending credits, 5 sample poems and bio. Queries will be answered in 1 month, mss reported on in 6 weeks. **Simultaneous submissions will be considered, and photocopied or dot-matrix mss are OK. Royalties of 10% are paid on chapbooks, plus 5% of print run. Sample books are available at $5 each. The editor comments on mss "when time allows."** The chapbooks are saddle-stitched, 6 × 9 with an average page count of 20. The editor advises, "Please support the small publishers who make poetry available."

‡LOONFEATHER (I, IV-Regional, themes), Bemidji Community Arts Center, 426 Bemidji Ave., Bemidji MN 56601, phone (218)751-4869, founded 1979, poetry editors Betty Rossi and Marshall Meierhead, is a small press publisher of the literary magazine *Loonfeather* appearing 2 times a year, **"primarily but not exclusively for Minnesota writers, with one theme issue per year. Prefer short poems of not over 42 lines, rhymed verse only if well done, no generalizations on worn-out topics."** They have recently published poetry by Nancy Paddock, William Borden and Mark Vinz. As a sample the editors selected these lines from "Tornado Salad" by Joan Wolf Prefontaine:

> Not to worry then, there will always be storms and hunger
> and if we are lucky, a tornado salad made by someone we love
> after we've stepped up from the darkness to measure out our worth,
> after we've endured together whatever danger will pass.

Loonfeather is 6×9, 48 pgs., saddle-stapled, professionally printed in small type with matte card cover, using b&w art and ads. Subscription: $7.50/year; single copy current issue: $5 (Fall '88 through current year); back issues: $2.50. **Pays 2 copies. Submission deadlines January 31 and July 31 for May and November publications.**

LOS HOMBRES PRESS (IV-Form), P.O. Box 632729, San Diego CA 92163-2729, phone (619)234-6710 or 688-1023, founded 1989, publisher Jim Kitchen, publishes **haiku only.** As a sample the editor selected these lines from **Starting Something** by Carol Montgomery:

> Widows
>
> in the mist—
> learning the street dance

He says that book is a digest-sized, flat-spined professionally printed paperback (glossy card cover), $6.95. "We publish only one book per year." **Pays 10% royalties plus 10 copies. Buys North American rights.**

LOST MAGAZINE; LUPUS ENTERPRISES (I, IV-Horror), 67 Seyler St., New Hamburg, Ontario N0B 2G0 Canada, phone (519)662-2725, founded 1990, editor Adam Thornton. *Lost* appears every other month **using "any horrific or eerie poetry, any length, preferably not rhyming. No sci-fi or fantasy or poems with predictable themes or rhyme schemes."** They have published poetry by John Grey, james siple and Lynda Walter. As a sample the editor selected these lines from "Dorothy's Minion" by David Hunter Sutherland:

> in this land of milk & honey,
> saints of plywood, 2' by 4',
> nail sweet Dorothy to its entrance,
> then pray mankind will heed her call.

It is 40 pgs., digest-sized, saddle-stapled, photocopied from typescript on ordinary paper. They accept about 25% of 60 poems received/year. Press run 100, 6 shelf sales. Subscription: $2. Sample postpaid: $2. Send SASE for guidelines. Reports immediately. Pays 1 copy. **"Cover letters are a *must*, preferably ones that are creative and interesting, containing biographical info. Anyone can submit. We encourage amateurs and anyone unsure of their work—very friendly and personal." Editor always comments on rejections.**

LOTHROP, LEE & SHEPARD BOOKS (V), 1350 Avenue of the Americas, New York NY 10019, founded 1859, editor-in-chief Susan Pearson. **"We do not accept unsolicited mss."**

LOTUS PRESS, INC. (V), P.O. Box 21607, Detroit MI 48221, phone (313)861-1280, FAX (313)342-9174, founded 1972, editor Naomi Long Madgett. "With one exception of a textbook, we publish books of **poetry by individual authors,** although we have three anthologies and two sets of broadsides, one with a teachers' guide for use in secondary schools. We occasionally sponsor readings. **Most, but not all, of our authors are black."** Their most recent anthology is **Adam of Ifé: Black Women in Praise of Black Men. Currently, they are not accepting unsolicited mss.** They have recently published poetry by Oliver LaGrone, May Miller, James A. Emanuel and Selene de Medeiros. As a sample the editor selected these lines by Monifa Atungaye:

> my last swim
> and final push into this whiteness
> your bright roundness
> peering through narrow wooden bars . . .
> marks the beginning of me.

Pays 25 author's copies; others may be ordered at a discount. Poets are not expected to contribute to the cost of publication. Response is usually within 6 weeks. "Copies may be ordered from our catalog, which is free upon request. We do not give samples."

LOUISIANA LITERATURE; LOUISIANA LITERATURE PRIZE FOR POETRY (II, IV-Regional), P.O. Box 792, Southeastern Louisiana University, Hammond LA 70402, editor Tim Gautreaux, appears twice a year. They say they **"receive mss year round. We consider creative work from anyone though we strive to showcase our state's talent. We like poetry with original language use and strong images which go beyond themselves."** They have recently published poetry by Sue Owen, Catharine Savage

Brosman, Diane Wakowski, David Tillinghast, Elton Glaser and Kate Daniels. The editor chose these sample lines by Rodger Kamenetz:

> *Gobs of meat knobbed with fat sink below my spoon.*
> *The waiter sweeps a fifth of sherry past my nose.*
> *The surface doused, "And more?" he asks, one eye on the next*
> *table, crumpled bills, dead crabs sprawled on plates.*
> *I want more and more, the sherry clears a window*
> *on the grease like ice on a filthy pond.*
> *I was so hungry when I read the words, "Turtle Soup."*

The magazine is a large (6¾ × 9¾) format, 100 pgs., flat-spined, handsomely printed on heavy matte stock with matte card cover (using pen drawing). Subscription: $10 for individuals; $12.50 for institutions. The Louisiana Literature Prize for Poetry offers a $400 award. **Guidelines for SASE.**

LOUISIANA STATE UNIVERSITY PRESS (II), Baton Rouge LA 70893, phone (504)388-6294, founded 1935, poetry editor L.E. Phillabaum, is a highly respected publisher of collections by poets such as Lisel Mueller, Julia Randall, Fred Chappell and Henry Taylor. **Query with 6-8 sample poems, publication credits. Replies to queries in 1 month, to submissions (if invited) in 3-4 months. Simultaneous submissions, photocopies OK. Pays royalties plus 10 author's copies.**

THE LOUISVILLE REVIEW (II, IV-Children/Teen), 315 Bingham Humanities, University of Louisville, Louisville KY 40292, phone (502)588-6801, founded 1976, faculty editor Sena Jeter Naslund, appears twice a year. **They use any kind of poetry except translations, and they have a section of children's poetry (grades K-12). "Poetry must include permission of parent to publish if accepted. In all of our poetry we look for the striking metaphor, unusual imagery and fresh language. We do not read in summer. Poems are read by 3 readers; report time is 1-2 months and time to publication is 2-3 months."** They have published poetry by Richard Jackson, Jeffrey Skinner, Maura Stanton, Richard Cecil, Roger Weingarten and Greg Pape. *TLR* is 200 pgs., flat-spined, 6 × 8¾. They accept about 10% of some 700 pieces received a year. **Sample postpaid: $4. Pays 1 copy.**

LOW-TECH PRESS (V), 30-73 47th St., Long Island City NY 11103, founded 1981, editor Ron Kolm, has published work by Hal Sirowitz, John Yau and Jennifer Nostrand. As a sample the editor selected these lines (poet unidentified):

> *They firebombed*
> *the dinner table*
> *taking us completely*
> *by surprise.*

"I am only interested in short poems with clear images. Since almost nobody gets paid for their work, I believe in multiple submissions and multiple publishings. Even though we publish only solicited ms, I respond right away to any mail the press receives."

LUCIDITY; BEAR HOUSE PUBLISHING (I), Route 2, Box 94, Eureka Springs AR 72632-9505, founded 1985, editor Ted O. Badger. *Lucidity* is a quarterly of poetry. **Submission fee required—$1 per poem for "juried" selection by a panel of judges or $2 per poem to compete for cash awards of $20, $10 and $5. Other winners paid in both cash and in copies. Buys one-time rights. In addition, the editor invites a few guest contributors to submit to each issue. Contributors are encouraged to subscribe or buy a copy of the magazine.** The magazine is photocopied from typescript, digest-sized, saddle-stapled, 56 pgs. with matte card cover, press run 250, 140 subscribers. Subscription: $8. **Sample postpaid: $2. Send SASE for guidelines.** The magazine is called *Lucidity* because, the editor says, "I have felt that too many publications of verse lean to the abstract in content and to the obscure in style." Ted Badger says the magazine is **"open as to form. 40 line limit due to format. No restriction on subject matter except that something definitive be given to the reader." Purpose: "to give a platform to poets who can impart their ideas with clarity." He does not want "religious, nature or vulgar poems."** Recently published poets include Violette Newton, Helen Rillings, Peggy Lynch and Kathleen Lee Mendel. As a sample of the type of verse sought, the editor offers these lines (poet unidentified):

> *I am the target*
> *of irrepressible Time,*
> *who mortally wounds.*

Reports in 2-3 months, a 3-month delay before publication. Simultaneous submissions, previously published poems OK. Bear House Press is a self-publishing arrangement by which poets can pay to have booklets published in the same format as *Lucidity*, prices beginning at 50 copies of 32 pgs. for $140. Publishes 8 chapbooks/year. The editor says, "The only way to be published is to submit."

LULLWATER REVIEW (II), Box 22036, Emory University, Atlanta GA 30322, phone (404)727-6184, founded 1989, editor revolves, appears 3 times/year. They want **"original, imaginative treatment of emotional and intellectual topics. No mere wordplay. Ideas and concepts should be emphasized. Nothing overtly sentimental or with little craftsmanship."** They have recently published poetry by Turner Cassity, Kelly Cherry, Daniel Corrie, Charles Edward Eaton and R.T. Smith. As a sample the editor selected these lines from "Kicking Back in Timbuktu" by Robert Parham:

> This swamp is not foreign,
> the Deep South, asleep much longer than we,
> yet we nap fitfully, fired by half-dreamed
> visions of happenings so antiseptic,
> our conscious nap for novelty invades the final spot
> a dream can live, can dance with meaning, sober, and mad.

It is a handsome 6×9 flat-spined magazine, 96 pgs. Press run 2,000. Subscription: $12. **Sample postpaid: $5. Pays 3 copies. All rights revert to author upon publication. Send SASE for guidelines. Will consider simultaneous submissions. Reads submissions August 1 through May 31 only. Reports in 2 months or less.** *"Lullwater* places no limits on theme or style; the sole criterion for judging submitted work is its excellence. While much of the poetry we publish is in free verse, we hold in high regard well-crafted formal poems. We expect our contributors to be acquainted with the broad field of contemporary poetry and able to find within that field a voice uniquely their own."

LUNA BISONTE PRODS; LOST AND FOUND TIMES (IV-Style), 137 Leland Ave., Columbus OH 43214, founded 1967, poetry editor John M. Bennett, may be the zaniest phenomenon in central Ohio. John Bennett is a publisher (and practicioner) of **experimental and avant-garde writing**, sometimes sexually explicit, and art in a bewildering array of formats including the magazine, *Lost and Found Times,* postcard series, posters, chapbooks, pamphlets, labels and audiocassette tapes. You can get a sampling of Luna Bisonte Prods for $3 plus $1 postage and handling. Numerous reviewers have commented on the bizarre *Lost and Found Times,* "reminiscent of several West Coast dada magazines"; "This exciting magazine is recommended only for the most daring souls"; "truly demented"; "Insults . . . the past 3,000 years of literature," etc. Bennett wants to see **"unusual poetry, naive poetry, surrealism, experimental, visual poetry, collaborations—*no* poetry workshop or academic pablum."** He has published poetry by I. Argüelles, G. Beining, B. Heman, R. Olson, J. Lipman, B. Porter, C. H. Ford, P. Weinman, E. N. Brookings, F. A. Nettelbeck, D. Raphael, R. Crozier, S. Sollfrey, S. Murphy, M. Andre, N. Vassilakis, and himself. The editor selected this poem "Saint" by Bob Heman:

> four foxes caught in the filter. the fluid finite
> in our glands. her hepatitis the skin they wanted
> to include. her lattice languishing in the heavy
> light. her name a noise to some.

The digest-sized 52-page magazine, photoreduced typescript and wild graphics, matte card cover with graphics, has a circulation of 350 with 60 subscriptions of which 25 are libraries. **Sample postpaid: $4. Submit any time—preferably camera-ready (but this is not required). Reports in 1-2 days, pays copies. All rights revert to authors upon publication.** Luna Bisonte also will **consider book submissions: query with samples and cover letter (but "keep it brief"). Chapbook publishing usually depends on grants or other subsidies and is usually by solicitation. Photocopy, dot-matrix OK.** He will also consider subsidy arrangements on negotiable terms.

‡LUNA VENTURES; POLY; SCIFANT; UNKNOWN; SWASHBUCKLER (IV-Themes, science fiction), P.O. Box 398, Suisun CA 94585, founded in the 1930s, editor Paul Doerr. This publisher puts out a number of monthly newsletters, all of which use poetry on appropriate subjects. *Poly* is about alternate life-styles such as polygamy and group marriage. *SCIFANT* focuses on science fiction and fantasy and is published in microfiche only. *Unknown* is about "anomalies, the mysterious, the unusual, such as witchcraft, appearances, Bigfoot, UFOs." *Swashbuckler* is about Renaissance Faires, fencing, swashbuckling and related topics. All use **poetry relevant to their themes. Sample postpaid: $2**, except *SCIFANT* is $3 (add 50¢ if outside the US). No indication of payment. Acquires first or one-time rights. All of these are 12 pgs. condensed type except *SCIFANT*, which is 98 pgs.

THE LUTHERAN JOURNAL (IV-Religious), 7317 Cahill Rd., Edina MN 55439, phone (612)941-6830, editor The Rev. Armin U. Deye, is a family quarterly, 32 pgs., circulation 136,000, for Lutheran Church members, middle age and older. They use **poetry "related to subject matter," traditional, free verse, blank verse. Pays. Sample free for SASE. Simultaneous and photocopied submissions OK.**

LYNX, A QUARTERLY JOURNAL OF RENGA (IV-Form, subscribers), P.O. Box 169, Toutle WA 98649, phone (206)274-6661, *APA-Renga* founded 1986, editor Terri Lee Grell, one of the first *APA-Renga* contributors, "changed the name to *Lynx* to link an endangered species of poetry with an

Close-up

Fred Chappell
Poet/Writer

For we have it within us to bow and to bend
To the Order within us that is our True Friend;
For Order is a Music of such health and delight
That in hearing it newly we come round right.

The problem with doing a feature on Fred Chappell, one of this country's most versatile and gifted writers, is that there are so many fine works on which to focus.

The above stanza is the last of "The Gift To Be Simple," patterned as a prologue to composer Aaron Copland's **Appalachian Spring** and one of the poems in Chappell's tenth book, **First and Last Words** (Louisiana State University Press, 1988).

Chappell's most celebrated book, however, is the tetralogy **Midquest** published by Louisiana State University Press in 1981. That book features so many styles and forms it makes the head swim with sheer admiration. Or envy. And then there is the poetic revenge play **Castle Tzingal**, also published by Louisiana State University Press, that would have been a success if performed on the Elizabethan stage.

Chappell has also won dozens of awards, including a Rockefeller Grant, North Carolina Award in Literature and the Bollingen Prize in Poetry. In addition, he has published several books of fiction with Atheneum, Harcourt and St. Martin's, among others.

In spite of such success, Chappell avoids pretentiousness at all costs in his work. Yet he knows that art imposes order on an otherwise chaotic world. Poetry, a small gift, plays a big role in the scheme of things.

"There's something liberating about the restrictions of poetry—and that's the kind of paradox the art generates time and time again," he says. "The old notion that a lyric poem tries to fix a moment in time forever seems to be true to me." Nonetheless, he adds, a poem must have motion. "The line in poetry should impel us onward, yet stop our attention."

Dealing with these contradictions—the poem as small gift able to tame a chaotic world, the freedom that comes from form, the fixed moment that moves us forward—demands clear writing, he says.

"I have no ambition to formulate a fixed poetic style—in the manner of Stevens, say, or Susan Howe or Emily Dickinson. I like for subject matters to speak to me in different voices which I try to enhance," Chappell says.

He cautions that his approach to poetry may not be the best way for a person to gain notoriety. "Style's a memorable tag for poets to be known by," he observes.

In typical fashion, Chappell decides to end with a disclaimer in case one has forgotten that the gift is, alas, to be simple. "One of my goals is to avoid pretentiousness," he reminds us, "and for that reason I've formulated this rather pretentious rationale for my work."

—Michael J. Bugeja

endangered animal and to inspire the traditional wit of renga. The magazine, published quarterly, is **based on the ancient craft of renga, linked verse with origins in Zen and Japanese culture, publishes renga, mostly by subscribers.** A renga is a non-narrative series of linked images as a group effort." As a sample the editor selected this renga excerpt by Jane Reichhold, T.B., Kenneth C. Leibman and Tundra Wind:

> *panty hose   as she crosses her legs   she whispers*
> *from the back room   a sigh*
> *on the table   her letter punctuated   with a teardrop*
> *from the apartment upstairs   a lullaby*

Lynx also publishes essays, book reviews, articles, interviews, experimental linked forms, linked prose, art, commentaries and "whatever encourages poets to link ideas." Published poets include Hiroaki Sato and Miriam Sagan. *Lynx* **encourages submissions by those experienced and experimenting with collaborative forms. Subscribers participate in ongoing rengas, start trends and otherwise determine the content. Reports in 1 month. Editor responds to all who submit.** Currently 100 subscribers. *Lynx* is a newsprint publication, $5\frac{1}{2} \times 17$, 24 pgs., unstapled. **Sample postpaid: $2, includes guidelines. Pays copies or subscription.**

THE LYRIC; LYRIC ANNUAL COLLEGE POETRY CONTEST (II, IV-Form, students), 307 Dunton Dr. SW, Blacksburg VA 24060, founded 1921 ("the oldest magazine in North America in continuous publication devoted to the publication of **traditional poetry**"), poetry editor Leslie Mellichamp, uses about 50 poems each quarterly issue. **"We use rhymed verse in traditional forms, for the most part, with an occasional piece of blank or free verse. 35 lines or so is usually our limit. Our themes are varied, ranging from religious ecstasy to humor to raw grief, but we feel no compulsion to shock, embitter or confound our readers. We also avoid poems about contemporary political or social problems—grief but not grievances, as Frost put it. Frost is helpful in other ways: if yours is more than a lover's quarrel with life, we're not your best market. And most of our poems are accessible on first or second reading. Frost again: don't hide too far away. Poems must be original, unpublished and not under consideration elsewhere." Pays 1 copy, and all contributors are eligible for quarterly and annual prizes totaling over $900.** They have recently published poetry by Anne Barlow, John J. Brugaletta, R.H. Morrison, Rhina P. Espaillat, Barbara Loots, Amy Jo Schoonover, Sarah Ruden, Alfred Dorn, Eunice de Chazeau, Gail White and Tom Riley. The editor selected these sample lines by R.L. Cook:

> *Forever young, unwary, beautiful,*
> *Yet in their folly wiser than the world;*
> *Under a cloud of years the bright girls go*
> *And in their flesh the future rests unfurled.*

It is digest-sized, 32 pgs., professionally printed with varied typography, matte card cover, has a circulation of 850 with 800 subscriptions of which 290 are libraries. They receive about 5,000 submissions/year, use 200, have an average 3-month backlog. **Sample postpaid: $3. Subscription $10 US, $12 Canada and other foreign countries. Submit up to 5 poems. Photocopy, dot-matrix OK. Reports in 1 month (average). Send SASE for guidelines.** *The Lyric* also offers a poetry contest in traditional forms for fulltime undergraduate students enrolled in any American or Canadian college or university, prizes totaling $500. Send SASE for rules. Leslie Mellichamp comments, "Our *raison d'être* has been the encouragement of form, music, rhyme and accessibility in poetry. We detect a growing dissatisfaction with the modernist movement that ignores these things and a growing interest in the traditional wellsprings of the craft. Naturally, we are proud to have provided an alternative for over 70 years that helped keep the true roots of poetry alive." This market has a unique reputation, even in the class of magazines taking formal verse, and enriches the small press world.

M.A.F. PRESS; THIRTEEN POETRY MAGAZINE (I, IV-Form), Box 392, Portlandville NY 13834-0392, phone (607)286-7500, founded 1982, poetry editor Ken Stone. *Thirteen Poetry Magazine* **"publishes only 13-line poetry; any theme or subject as long as in 'good' taste. We seek to publish work that touches the beauty of this life." The M.A.F. Press publishes a chapbook series, however, not reading through end of 1992—no reading fee. Chapbooks must be a total of 32 pages.** They have published poetry by Pamela Portwood, Ida Fasel, Will Inman, Stan Proper, Janet Carncross Chandler and Marion Cohen. As a sample the editor selected "Leaving" by John Craig:

> *And still the memory*
> *of you standing, waving good-bye.*
> *I should have turned around then*
> *for the sadness of your eye.*

Thirteen appears quarterly in a magazine-sized, 40-page, saddle-stapled format, photocopied from typescript, matte card cover with b&w cartoon, circulation 350 for 130 subscriptions of which 20 are libraries. Ken Stone accepts about 100 of the 300 submissions he receives each year. **Sample postpaid: $2.50. Submit 4-6 poems. Photocopies are acceptable, no reprint material. "We**

Close-up

Terri Lee Grell
Poet/Editor
Lynx

Boardwalk
a kitten wanders into
the penny arcade

   boy clutches an empty box
   "free to a good home"

the humming bird
looking for
something sweet

   in the back of the alley
   the syringe pile

Photo by Greg Ebersole, *The Daily News*, Longview WA

The above is an example of renga, traditional linked-verse poetry with roots in ancient Japan. These lines are from "The Penny Arcade," a participatory poem by Alexis Rotella and Terri Lee Grell, editor of *Lynx*, a quarterly journal devoted to renga and other linked forms.

Renga started in Japan during the 12th century, says Grell. It developed as a rebellion against formalism and the politics of the time. Poetry was open to only a handful of poets who happened to have the emperor's favor. Periodically, the emperor would hold a formal poetry event. He would start the proceedings by contributing three lines and would invite honored poets to complete the stanza with two additional lines. Other poets would add lines, too, but these were passed as a joke among themselves. These added lines sometimes poked fun at the emperor and were often bawdy or even vulgar, and, it seems, a lot of fun to write.

By the 15th century, says Grell, the satirical verse had caught on everywhere in Japan; renowned poet Matsuo Bashō elevated it to an art form. Yet it wasn't until after World War II that renga became known in the West. True to its renegade past, however, this poetic form has never become as widely popular here as haiku, a form that actually stems from renga, Grell explains.

Grell, a journalist as well as poet, became interested in renga in the mid-1980s and was one of the first contributors to *Apa-Renga*, a tiny journal edited by Zen Abbot Tundra Wind. Grell took over the publication in 1989, changed its name to *Lynx* and added a variety of renga and a range of other types of poetry, essays and fiction. Grell's editorial expertise has been a boon to the small magazine, taking it from just 25 subscribers to nearly 200.

Although solo renga and those created by two-person teams are included regularly in *Lynx*, the backbone of the magazine remains the participatory renga, says Grell. In a participatory renga, one person will start by contributing a set of lines (usually three, but sometimes an entire stanza of five lines). That person sets the tone for the poem and may choose to set certain rules regarding the length or content of the renga. Others are invited to send in a specified number of lines to add to the renga.

"The challenge of renga," says Grell, "is to come up with lines that are very subtly linked to the previous verse, but not necessarily to earlier verses." When writing renga, she says, "it's best to look at the preceding verse and ask 'What does this remind me of?' instead of repeating an image." Often the links are so obscure, "it's a challenge just to try to figure out how the lines are linked," she says.

"This magazine really belongs to the subscribers (most contributors are subscribers). The editor is really the collator," Grell says. "It's left up to the subscribers to decide whether or not to respond to whatever you've written." If no one responds, the renga stops, but if response is high, the renga could continue for several issues and may branch into more than one renga.

"That's the great thing about *Lynx*," says Grell. "What you write is published and you can see how people respond to it. Their response tells you 'This is what I saw in your work.' It's instant response . . . instant gratification."

Some poets choose to start a renga with just one or two other people. They're invited to submit these completed group efforts to *Lynx* as well. "People are even getting together and having renga parties or writing renga in workshops. This is just how renga started."

Poets interested in submitting to the magazine should take a look at it first, but the best way to learn what works is to try renga, says Grell. She suggests two books for further reading: **Monkey's Raincoat: Linked Poetry of the Bashō School**, translated by Lenore Mahew, explores traditional Japanese haiku and renga and **Narrow Road to Renga** is a collection of Western renga put together by Jane Reichhold.

Although this type of poetry is very open to poets on all levels, it is starting to attract well-known poets such as William Stafford, Marvin Bell and Tess Gallagher. The key to renga, says Grell, is interaction. "A beginning poet can interact with experienced poets. It keeps poets connected to one another." In fact, she adds, some poets have developed a dialogue through renga, writing letters back and forth about the meanings behind their stanzas.

There have been efforts within the international traditional haiku and renga communities to impose a more formal structure on renga—to define it by a textbook set of rules—"to whip us wild poets into shape," says Grell, "but renga is quite different in the West—we need to keep it playful."

—*Robin Gee*

66 That's the great thing about *Lynx*. What you write is published and you can see how people respond to it. Their response tells you 'This is what I saw in your work.' It's instant response . . . instant gratification. **99**

—Terri Lee Grell

have even taken hand-written poems. As to queries, only if 13 lines gives the poet problems." Reports "immediately to 2 weeks." Pays 1 copy. Send SASE for guidelines. Comments on rejections "especially if requested." Reviews books of poetry. The editor advises, "Send more poetry, less letters and self-promotion. Read the 'want lists' and description listings of magazines for guidelines. When in doubt request information. Read other poets in the magazines and journals to see what trends are. Also, this is a good way to find out what various publications like in the way of submissions."

‡M.I.P. COMPANY (IV-Foreign language, erotica), P.O. Box 27484, Minneapolis MN 55427, founded in 1984, contact Michael Peltsman, publishes 3 paperbacks/year. **They only publish Russian erotic poetry written in Russian.** They have recently published poetry collections by Mikhail Armalinsky and Alexey Shelvakh. **Previously published poems and simultaneous submissions OK. Replies to queries in 1 month. Seldom comments on rejections.**

MACFADDEN WOMEN'S GROUP; TRUE CONFESSIONS; TRUE ROMANCES; TRUE LOVE; TRUE STORY; SECRETS; MODERN ROMANCES (I), 233 Park Ave. S., New York NY 10003, phone (212)979-4800. **Address each magazine individually; do not submit to Macfadden Women's Group.** Each of these romance magazines uses poetry—usually no more than 1 poem/issue. **Their requirements vary; readers should study them individually and write for guidelines.** These mass-circulation magazines (available on newsstands) are obviously a very limited market, yet a possible one for beginners—especially those who like the prose contents and are tuned in to their editorial tastes.

THE MACGUFFIN (II), Schoolcraft College, 18600 Haggerty Rd., Livonia MI 48152, phone (313)462-4400, ext. 5292, founded 1983, editor Arthur Lindenberg, who says, "*The MacGuffin* is a literary magazine which appears three times each year, in April, June and November. We publish the best poetry, fiction, nonfiction and artwork we find. We have no thematic or stylistic biases. **We look for well-crafted poetry. Long poems should not exceed 300 lines. Avoid pornography, trite and sloppy poetry.**" *The MacGuffin* has recently published poetry by Ivan Argüelles, Thomas Sheehan and Annie Finch. As a sample, the editor selected the following lines from "Her Mosquito Net" by Wendy Bishop:

> She rests beneath a canopy of thread
> While delicate patterns of shade and light
> Fill the drifting folds of mesh, spreading
> Lines fine as age across her face . . .

The MacGuffin is 128 pgs., digest-sized, professionally printed on heavy buff stock, with matte card cover, flat-spined, with b&w illustrations and photos. Circulation is 500, of which 75 are subscriptions and the rest are local newsstand sales, contributor copies and distribution to college offices. Price per issue is $3.75, subscription $10. **Sample postpaid: $3. Pays: 2 copies,** "occasional money or prizes. **The editorial staff is grateful to consider unsolicited manuscripts and graphics.**" Mss are reported on in 8-10 weeks and the publication backlog is 6+ months. Writers should submit no more than 6 poems of no more than 300 lines; they should be typewritten, and photocopied or dot-matrix ms are OK. "We will always comment on 'near misses.' Writing is a search, and it is a journey. Don't become sidetracked. Don't become discouraged. Keep looking. Keep traveling. Keep writing." The magazine sponsors an annual contest with a $100 first prize for Michigan poets only; they hope to be able to sponsor a national competition soon.

MACMILLAN OF CANADA (V), 29 Birch Ave., Toronto, Ontario M4V 1E2 Canada, phone (416)963-8830, editor-in-chief Philippa Campsie, is a "leading publisher of Canadian fiction, nonfiction, biography and children's books. Exclusive agent for William Morrow Company, Hearst Books, Andrews & McNeel and Harraps." **They publish no unsolicited poetry or fiction mss.**

MACMILLAN PUBLISHING CO.; CHARLES SCRIBNER'S SONS; ATHENEUM; COLLIER, 866 Third Ave., New York NY 10022. Declined listing.

MAD RIVER PRESS (V), State Road, Richmond MA 01254, phone (413)698-3184, founded 1986, editor Barry Sternlieb, publishes 3 broadsides and 1 chapbook/year, **"all types of poetry, no bias,"** but none unsolicited. They have recently published poetry by Gary Snyder, Hayden Carruth, W.S. Merwin and Ann Fox Chandonnet. Call or write for information.

‡THE MADISON REVIEW; FELIX POLLAK PRIZE IN POETRY (II), Dept. of English, Helen C. White Hall, 600 N. Park St., Madison WI 53706, founded 1978, poetry editors Allison Cummings and John Merchant, want poems that are **"serious, tough and tight, that fulfill their own propositions. Spare us: love poems, God poems, patriotic poems, light verse."** They have recently published work by Lise Goett, Lisa Steinman and Richard Tillinghast. As a sample the editors selected these lines from "Gulls" by Jerry Mirskin:

> Now it's the sharp and damp smell of gasoline
> and now the sun, the full theater of the sun
> torching the town, so the windows
> of the houses along the shore burn like glasses of tea.

The Madison Review is published in May and December, with 15-20 poems selected from a pool of 750. **Sample back issue: $2.50 postpaid. Submit maximum of 6 poems. Photocopy OK. No simultaneous submissions. Usually reports in 2 months, may be longer in summer. Pays 2 copies.** "We do appreciate a concise cover letter with submissions." The Felix Pollak Prize in Poetry is for $500 and publication in *TMR*, for "the best group of three unpublished poems submitted by a single author." Send SASE for rules before submitting for prize. Submissions must arrive during September—winner announced December 15. "Contributors: Know your market! Read before, during and after writing. Treat your poems *better* than job applications!"

‡**THE MAGAZINE OF SPECULATIVE POETRY (IV-Science fiction)**, Box 564, Beloit WI 53512, founded 1984, editors Roger Dutcher and Mark Rich, a quarterly magazine that publishes **"the best new speculative poetry. We are especially interested in narrative form, but interested in variety of styles, open to any form, length (within reason), purpose. We're looking for the best of the new poetry utilizing the ideas, imagery and approaches developed by speculative fiction and will welcome experimental techniques as well as the fresh employment of traditional forms."** They have recently published poetry by Brian Aldiss, Robert Frazier, William Stafford, Ron Ellis and S.R. Compton. As a sample Roger Dutcher chose these lines from "Time Machines" by Steve Rasnic Tem:

> The Big Bang tide sends us chasing
> each of our moments through space
> trying to escape the collapse
> and our own heat-death
> when all time runs backward
> and we leap from our graves

The digest-sized magazine, 20-24 pgs., is offset from professional typesetting, saddle-stapled with matte card cover. They accept less than 10% of some 500 poems received per year. Press run is 100-200, going to nearly 100 subscribers of which 4 are libraries. Subscription: $11. **Sample postpaid: $3.50. Send SASE for guidelines. Pays 3¢/word, minimum $3 plus copy. Buys first North American serial rights. No simultaneous submissions. Prefer double-spaced. Photocopies, dot-matrix OK ("if not old ribbon"). No previously published poems. Reports in 1-2 months. Editor comments on rejections "on occasion."** Reviews books of speculative poetry.

MAGIC CHANGES (IV-Themes), P.O. Box 658, Warrenville IL 60555-0658, phone (708)416-3111, founded 1978, poetry editor John Sennett, is now published every 18 months, still in an unusual format. Photocopied from typescript on many different weights and colors of paper, magazine-sized, stapled along the long side (you read it both vertically and horizontally), taped flat spine, full of fantasy drawings, pages packed with poems of all varieties, fiction, photos, drawings, odds and ends—including reviews of little magazines and other small press publications. It is **intended to make poetry (and literature) fun—and unpredictable. Each issue is on an announced theme.** "*Magic Changes* is divided into sections such as 'The Order of the Celestial Otter,' 'State of the Arts,' 'Time,' 'Music' and 'Skyscraper Rats.' A magical musical theme pervades." There are about 100 pgs. of poetry/issue, circulation 500, 28 subscriptions of which 10 are libraries. They have published poetry by Roberta Gould, A.D. Winans, Lyn Lifshin and Dan Campion. As a sample the editor selected these lines from "Harps" by Sue Standing:

> The harp of your heart is the harp
> of a cairn heaped with mourning grasses
>
> The harp of my heart is the harp
> of harpies plucked with sharp beaks

Sample postpaid: $5. Reports in 2 months. Submit 3-5 poems anytime. Photocopy OK. He says "no query," but poets might want to know about upcoming themes. The editor sometimes comments on rejections and offers criticism for $5/page of poetry. **Pays 1 or 2 copies. Acquires first North American serial rights.** Reviews books of poetry in "usually about 500 words."

MAGIC REALISM; PYX PRESS (II), Box 620, Orem UT 84059-0620, founded 1990, editors C. Darren Butler and Julie Thomas. *Magic Realism* appears 3 times/year using poetry that is **"well-written, carefully imagined. I hope to publish work that will sustain subsequent readings."** It is photocopied, typeset, digest-sized, 60 pgs. with card cover using b&w art. They use 3-6 poems/issue. **Sample postpaid: $4.95. Send #10 SASE for guidelines. Pays 1 copy. Acquires first North American serial or onetime rights *and* non-exclusive reprint rights. Reports in 4-6 months. Editor often comments.** He says, "I am looking for literary work based in exaggerated realism. Fantasy should permeate the reality, give it luster. My needs are somewhat flexible. For example, I occasionally publish genre work, or glib fantasy of the sort found in folktales and fables."

‡MAHOGANY & MOLASSES FAMILY READER (I, IV-Children, humor), 6712 Bywood Rd., Orlando FL 32810, founded 1989, poetry editor Doris Kilmer. "We are a bimonthly family-oriented magazine with a goal of publishing fiction and poetry for the enjoyment of all ages. We want mainstream and humorous poems in a variety of styles, 4-20 lines. Sometimes publish longer story-poems for children, 1-2 pgs." They do not want "anything containing horror, obscenity, violence or downbeat/negative themes." As a sample the editor selected these lines from "The Mount" by Gavril Roe:

> Her name is good.
> A haven for a million strong,
> She braces up with willing arms
> A legacy of wild song.

It is 20-24 pgs., digest-sized, photocopied, saddle-stapled, with card cover and occasional graphics. They receive about 200 submissions a year, use 20-25. Subscription: $7.50/year. **Sample postpaid: $2. Previously published poems OK; no simultaneous submissions. Often comments on rejections. Send SASE for general guidelines. Reports "usually within 2 months." Pays $3-5/ poem. Buys first or reprint rights.**

THE MALAHAT REVIEW (II); LONG POEM PRIZES (II, IV-Form), P.O. Box 3045, University of Victoria, Victoria, British Columbia V8W 3P4 Canada, phone (604)721-8524, founded 1967, editor Constance Rooke, is "a high quality, visually appealing literary quarterly which has earned the praise of notable literary figures throughout North America. Its purpose is to publish and promote poetry and fiction of a very high standard, both Canadian and international. We are interested in various styles, lengths and themes. The criterion is excellence." They have published poetry by Angela Ball, Stephan Torre and Carolann Russell. As a sample the editor selected these lines from "Sleep Movements of Leaves" by Toni Sammons:

> imagination is like being slightly deaf
> —what you almost hear
> keeps you balanced on precipices of air
> your head woven from cobwebs
> like a white-eye's nest

They use 50 pgs. of poetry in each issue, have 1,800 subscriptions of which 300 are libraries. They use about 100 of 2,000 submissions received/year, have no backlog. Subscription: $15. **Sample postpaid: $7. Submit 5-10 poems, addressed to Editor Constance Rooke. Reports within 3 months. Pays $20 per poem/page plus 2 copies and reduced rates on others. Send SASE for guidelines.** The editors comment if they "feel the ms warrants some attention even though it is not accepted." Reviews books of poetry. The Long Poem Prizes of $300, plus publication and payment at their usual rates, entry fee $15 (which includes a year's subscription), is for a long poem or cycle 5-20 pgs., (flexible minimum and maximum), deadline March 1.

THE MANDEVILLE PRESS (III), 2 Taylor's Hill, Hitchin, Hertfordshire SG4 9AD England, phone 0462-450796, founded 1972, editors Peter Scupham and John Mole, publishes hand-set pamphlets of the work of individual poets. They want "formal poetry, intelligence guiding emotion. No formless poetry, emotion eliminating intelligence." They have recently published poetry by Anthony Hecht, Patric Dickinson, Edward Lowbury and Bernard O'Donoghue. **Interested poets may query beginning January 1993. Replies to queries in 1 week, to mss (if invited), in 1 month. Pays 10 author's copies. Send SASE for catalog to buy samples.**

MANHATTAN POETRY REVIEW (II), Box 8207, New York NY 10150, phone (212)355-6634, founded 1981, editor Elaine Reiman-Fenton, "publishes about half prestige market and half new and/or little-known poets who deserve an audience, wanting carefully crafted poems in any form or style; interesting subject matter. There are no restrictions as to length of poems although it has become the custom to avoid very long poems (more than 3 pgs.); mss should be typed, double-spaced, 5-6 pgs. of poetry plus cover letter giving previous publication credits, honors, awards, teachers, etc. and SASE. New poets and unsolicited mss are welcomed. Nothing obscene, ungrammatical or handwritten. Mss must be ready for the typesetter in case they are accepted." They have published poetry by Marge Piercy, David Ignatow, Diane Wakoski, Marilyn Hacker, Judith Farr, and Robert Phillips. *MPR* appears twice a year, and is 52-60 pgs., digest-sized, saddle-stapled, offset print, paper cover, using only poetry—no art, graphics, ads, prose or reviews. They receive about 1,500 mss/year, accept 1-2 poems from about 10% of those submitting. Press run is 750. **Single copy: $4.50 plus $2 postage. Pays 1 copy. No simultaneous submissions or previously published poems. Reports in 3-4 months.** Editor seldom comments on rejections. She says, "I believe that this is an exciting period in the history of American poetry. The diversity of 'little' magazines reflects the vitality of contemporary poetry and suggests that there is a forum for virtually every type of poem. But recently many little magazines have failed for financial reasons. We need to develop a large dedicated readership, and poets must lead the way! Everyone should subscribe to and read a selection of literary magazines—especially poets."

THE MANHATTAN REVIEW (II, IV-Translations), 440 Riverside Dr. Apt. 45, New York NY 10027, phone (212)932-1854, founded 1980, poetry editor Philip Fried, tries "**to publish American and foreign writers, and we choose foreign writers with something valuable to offer the American scene. We like to think of poetry as a powerful discipline engaged with many other fields. We want to see ambitious work. Interested in both lyric and narrative. Not interested in mawkish, sentimental poetry.** We select high-quality work from a number of different countries, including the U.S." They have recently published poetry by A.R. Ammons, Bei Dao, Ana Blandiana, Baron Wormser, Judson Jerome and Penelope Shuttle. As a sample the editor selected these lines by Adam Zagajewski:

> *The shoes of Auschwitz, in pyramids*
> *high as the sky, groan faintly:*
> *Alas, we outlived mankind, now*
> *let us sleep, sleep:*
> *We have nowhere to go.*

The *MR* is "once again a semiannual." The magazine has 60+ pgs., digest-sized, professionally printed with glossy card cover, photos and graphics, circulation 500, with 85 subscriptions of which 35 are libraries. They receive about 300 submissions/year, use few ("but I do read everything submitted carefully and with an open mind"). "I return submissions very promptly." Subscription: $10; per issue: $5. **Sample: $6.25 with 6×9 envelope. Submit 3-5 pgs., no photocopy, no simultaneous submissions, with short bio. Reports in 10-12 weeks. Pays copies. Sometimes comments "but don't count on it."** Reviews books of poetry. Philip Fried advises, "Don't be swayed by fads. Search for your own voice. Support other poets whose work you respect and enjoy. Be persistent. Keep aware of poetry being written in other countries."

MANIC D PRESS (I, II), P.O. Box 410804, San Francisco CA 94141, founded 1984. manic d is interested in books/broadsides/etc. of **poetry by talented unknowns who are looking for an alternative to establishment presses. Considers simultaneous submissions. Reports in 3 months. Pays copies. Send SASE for catalog to buy samples (or $6 for one of their books of their choice).**

MANKATO POETRY REVIEW (II), Box 53, English Dept., Mankato State, Mankato MN 56001, phone (507)389-5511, founded 1984, editor Roger Sheffer, a semiannual magazine that is "**open to all forms of poetry. We will look at poems up to 60 lines, any subject matter.**" They have published poems by Edward Micus, Judith Skillman and Walter Griffin. As a sample, the editor chose the following lines from a poem by Richard Robbins:

> *Sage connects to lava rock mile by mile.*
> *West of Atomic City, blue flowers*
> *in the craters of the moon.*

The magazine is 5×8, typeset on 60 lb. paper, 30 pgs., saddle-stapled with buff matte card cover printed in one color. It appears usually in May and December and has a circulation of 200. Subscription: $5/year. **Sample postpaid: $2.50. Guidelines for SASE. Pays 2 copies. Do not submit mss in summer (May through August). "Readable dot-matrix OK. Please indicate if simultaneous submission, and notify."** Reporting time is about 2 months; "We accept only what we can publish in next issue." The editor says, "We're interested in looking at longer poems—up to 60 lines, with great depth of detail relating to place (landscape, townscape)."

MANNA (I, II), 2966 W. Westcove Dr., West Valley City UT 84119, founded 1978 by Nina Wicker, poetry editors Roger A. Ball, Robert Raleigh and Rebecca Bradley, is "a small poetry magazine for the **middle-of-the-road poet. We like humor, short poems with feeling, farm poems, inspirational poetry; we mostly use free verse, some rhyme. We do not want long poems. Prefer short quality poems with feelings. Images, tone and thoughtful use of language important.**" The magazine 35-40 pgs., 7×8½, photocopied from laser printed type and saddle-stapled with card cover, comes out twice a year, using nothing but poetry; circulation 200+, with 100 subscriptions. They receive 500 submissions/year, use about 200, and generally have less than a 6-month backlog. Subscription: $6. **Sample postpaid: $3.50. Submit 3-5 poems any time (please do not submit a lone poem). Reports in 3 weeks or less. "Publication is payment,"** but they give 3 small prizes ($7, $5 and $3) for the best in each issue. Acquires first North American serial rights. "**No simultaneous submissions please. Send SASE for additional guidelines.**" The editor advises, "Trust instinct and *write*. Submit poems that give your audience a unique vision. Use language and images worthy of that vision. Don't send sentimental love poetry."

‡**MARK: A JOURNAL OF SCHOLARSHIP, OPINION, AND LITERATURE (II)**, 2801 W. Bancroft SU2514, Toledo OH 43606, first appeared 1967-69, then resumed 1978, editor Brenda Wyatt, is an annual journal of fiction, poetry, nonfiction, photographs and sketches. As a sample the editor selected these lines from "A Vacant House" by Sandra Havener:

> *There was never any privacy;*
> *So no one ever lived there. They just died.*
> *It was always just a role,*
> *an anonymous role, blaming her by name.*

Mark is digest-sized, 70 pgs., saddle-stapled, professionally printed, with matte card cover. Single copy: $3. **Reads submissions September 1 through January 31. Editor comments "very rarely." Pays 2 copies. Acquires first serial rights.**

MARYLAND POETRY REVIEW; MARYLAND POETRY AND LITERARY SOCIETY (II), Drawer H, Catonsville MD 21228, founded 1985, edited by Rosemary Klein, "is interested in promoting the literary arts in Maryland as well as nationally and internationally. **We are interested in strong, thoughtful poetry. All submissions are read carefully.** *MPR* **is open to good poets who have not published extensively as well as to those who have.**" They have recently published poetry by Celia Brown, Elisabeth Stevens, Enid Shomer and Joseph Somoza. As a sample the editor selected these lines from "The Fool's Dark Lantern" by Michael Fallon:

> *Like a fly that spins*
> *in wounded circles on the sill*
> *his thoughts revolve around a single thought:*
> *there is only so much time*
> *in which to know*

MPR is professionally printed in small type on quality egg-shell stock, 7×11, 75 pgs., saddle-stapled with a glossy b&w card cover. It appears twice a year in double issues (Spring/Summer and Fall/Winter). In the past they have done special issues on confessional, Irish, Hispanic and Australian poetry. Query about possible future special issues. **Submit brief bio with submission. No simultaneous submissions. Reads submissions September 1 through December 1 and April 1 through June 1. Sample: $5 plus $2 for postage and handling. Pays 1 copy. Reports in 3-6 months.** Subscription and Maryland Poetry and Literary Society membership is $17 ($12 for students and senior citizens; $20 for member and spouse; $25 for institutions). Book reviews are generally solicited.

THE MASSACHUSETTS REVIEW (II), Memorial Hall, University of Massachusetts, Amherst MA 01003, founded 1959, editors Paul Jenkins and Anne Halley. They have recently published poems by Marge Piercy, Michael Benedikt and Eavan Boland. The editors describe this quarterly as offset (some color used in art sections) 6×9. Of 2,500 poems received they accept about 50. Press run is 1,600 for 1,100-1,200 subscriptions (1,000 of them libraries), the rest for shelf sales. Subscription is $15 (U.S.), $20 outside U.S., $17 for libraries. **Sample postpaid: $5.75 Send SASE for guidelines. Read submissions October 1 through June 1 only. Pays minimum of $10, or 35¢/line, plus 2 copies. No simultaneous submissions or previously published poems. Reports in 6 weeks. No submissions returned or queries answered without SASE.** "Read the magazine."

MATTOID (II), School of Humanities, Deakin University, Geelong, Victoria, Australia 3217, founded 1977, Dr. Brian Edwards, appears 3 times/year. **"No special requirements but interesting complexity, quality, experimentation. No naive rhyming verse."** They have published poetry by Lauris Edmond, Kevin Hart and Judith Rodriguez. It is 200 pgs., flat-spined with 2-color cover. They publish about 10-15% of 800 poems received/year. Press run 600 for 400 subscribers of which 10 are libraries, 30-50 shelf sales. **Sample postpaid: $10 overseas. Reports in 2-3 months. Pays 2 copies.** Reviews books of poetry in 1,000-2,000 words, single format.

MATURE YEARS (IV-Senior citizen), P.O. Box 801, 201 8th Ave. South, Nashville TN 37202, phone (615)749-6292, founded 1954, editor Marvin W. Cropsey, is a quarterly, circulation 80,000. "The magazine's purpose is to help persons understand and use the resources of Christian faith in dealing with specific opportunities and problems related to aging. **Poems are usually limited to fifteen lines and may, or may not, be overtly religious. Poems should not poke fun at older adults, but may take a humorous look at them. Avoid sentimentality and saccarine. If using rhymes and meter, make sure they are accurate."** As a sample the editor selected these lines by Carole Johnston:

> *What is winter*
> *but a large and cold*
> *secret that somehow*
> *keeps me warm . . . for*
> *I know where sweet*

> *daffodils lie sleeping.*
> *I know the graves of*
> *six brave crocuses*
> *and the tulip colors*
> *of next spring.*

It is magazine-sized, 100+ pgs., saddle-stapled, with full-color glossy paper cover. **Submit season and nature poems for spring during December through February; for summer, March through May; for fall, June through August; and for winter, September through November. Guidelines are available for writers. They pay 50¢-$1 per line, report in 2 months, a year's delay before publication.**

MAYAPPLE PRESS (V, IV-Regional, women), P.O. Box 5473, Saginaw MI 48603-0473, phone (517)793-2801, founded 1978, publisher/editor Judith Kerman, publishes **"women's poetry, Great Lakes regional poetry"** in chapbooks. They want **"quality contemporary poetry rooted in real experience and strongly crafted. No greeting card verse, sentimental or conventional poetry."** They have published chapbooks by Judith Minty and Toni Ortner-Zimmerman. They **"rarely" accept freelance submissions. Query with 5-6 samples. Check *Poets & Writers* for open times.** "We are not likely to publish unless poet accepts a *primary* role in distribution. Reality is only poets themselves can sell unknown work." **Pays 10% of run. Publishes on "cooperative" basis.** "Generally poet agrees to purchase most of the run at 50% of cover price." Editor **"usually comments (very briefly)" on rejections.** She says, "Poets must create the audience for their work. No small press 'white knight' can make an unknown famous (or even sell more than a few books!)."

THE MAYBERRY GAZETTE (II, IV-Themes, humor), Wake Forest University, 8955 Reynolda Station, Winston-Salem NC 27109, founded 1986, editor John Meroney, is a publication appearing several times a year using poetry **about the fictional town of Mayberry, North Carolina, as presented through television's "Andy Griffith Show" (CBS, 1960-1968), "which has become a permanent fixture in Americana. The publication maintains the original mood and theme expressed in the series. Writers should look to the program and issues of the publication for direction. Writer's guidelines available for large SASE."** It is 4 pgs., folded, professionally printed. Press run is 7,000 with 5,000 subscriptions. Subscription: $17 one year, $29 two years. **Sample postpaid: $3. No simultaneous submissions.** "Include details as to how you were influenced by the series, why you feel it was/is popular, etc." **Reports in 4-6 weeks. Acquires all rights.** "Please include a large SASE with all material." **Editor comments on rejections "often."** Reviews books of poetry. They occasionally have contests announced through the publication.

THE EDWIN MELLEN PRESS (II), P.O. Box 450, Lewiston NY 14092, phone (416)658-5726, founded 1973, poetry editor Ms. Mickey Evans, is a scholarly press. "We do not have access to large chain bookstores for distribution, but depend on direct sales and independent bookstores." **They pay 2 copies, no royalties.** "We require no author subsidies. However, we encourage our authors to seek grants from Councils for the Arts and other foundations because these add to the reputation of the volume." They want **"original integrated work—living unity of poems, preferably unpublished poetry, encompassable in one reading."** They have recently published poetry by W.R. Elton and Justin Vitiello. **Their books are 64 pgs., 6×9, softcover binding, no graphics. Price $9.95. Submit 40+ sample poems, bio, publications.** "We do not print until we receive at least 100 prepaid orders. Successful marketing of poetry books depends on the author's active involvement. We send out up to 15 free review copies to journals or newspapers, the names of which may be suggested by the author. Authors may purchase more copies of their book (above the 2 free copies provided) at the same 20% discount (for quantities of 10 or more) which we allow to bookstores. An author may (but is not required to) purchase books to make up the needed 100 prepublication sales."

MEMES (II), % 38 Molesworth Rd., Plympton, Plymouth, Devon PL7 4NT United Kingdom, founded 1989, editor Norman Jope, appears twice a year, **"is particularly responsive to work that exhibits awareness of the *wider* dimensions of human experience and which is conscious both of contemporary realities and their possible denouements.** The title of the magazine refers to the linguistic equivalent of genes (legacies passed on from present to futurity) and the aim of the magazine is to drop as many potent memes as possible into the human timestream. Preference is for more 'modernist' material (especially with 'occult' or generally 'speculative' themes). Work from authors seeing themselves as 'surrealists' is also liable to please." They have recently published poetry by Dan Raphael, Thomas Wiloch, Sheila E. Murphy, Misha, Peter Redgrove and Belinda Subraman. As a sample here are the opening lines of "Dream (Undated)" by Hilary Hayes:

> *Fast fading it flies—this memory on night-dark wings*
> *This memory of dreams I dreamed last night.*
> *A tent of night-dark hair, the sudden shock*

Of recognition bent over me.

It is 36-44 pgs., digest-sized, saddle-stapled, desktop published in small type on light paper with light card cover. Press run 200+ ("rising"), for 25 subscriptions by libraries, about 50 shelf sales. Subscription and samples for **cash only: $10/3 issues, $4 copy. Reports in 6 weeks. Pays 1 copy.** They review books, including poetry, in 50-500 words. Like most U.K. journals, this one favors free verse that is not rooted in personal experience (as is most U.S. poetry) but attempts to make a larger statement about the poet's environment. It also features a comprehensive book review section.

MENNONITE PUBLISHING HOUSE; PURPOSE; STORY FRIENDS; ON THE LINE; WITH (IV-Religious, children), 616 Walnut Ave., Scottdale PA 15683-1999, phone (412)887-8500. **Send submissions or queries directly to the editor of the specific magazine at address indicated.** The official publisher for the Mennonite Church in North America seeks also to serve a broad Christian audience. **Each of the magazines listed has different specifications, and the editor of each should be queried for more exact information.** *Purpose,* editor James E. Horsch, a "monthly in weekly parts," circulation 18,250, is **for adults of all ages, its focus: "action oriented, discipleship living."** It is 5⅜ × 8⅜, with two-color printing throughout. **They buy appropriate poetry up to 12 lines.** *Purpose* uses 3-4 poems/week, receives about 2,000/year of which they use 150, has a 10-12 week backlog. **Mss should be typewritten, double-spaced, one side of sheet only. Simultaneous submissions OK. Reports in 6-8 weeks. Pays $5-15/poem plus 2 copies. Sample copy free. Send SASE for guidelines and samples.** *On the Line,* edited by Mary C. Meyer, another "monthly in weekly parts," is **for children 10-14,** a "story paper that reinforces Christian values," circulation 9,000. It is 7 × 10, saddle-stapled, with 2-color printing on the cover and inside, using art and photos. **Sample free with SASE. Pays $5-15/poem plus 2 copies. Poems 3-24 lines. Submit "as many as desired, but each should be typed on a separate 8 × 11½ sheet." Simultaneous submissions, previously published poems OK. Reports in 1 month.** *Story Friends,* edited by Marjorie Waybill, is **for children 4-9,** a "story paper that reinforces Christian values, also a "monthly in weekly issues, circulation 9,500, uses poems 3-12 lines, pays $5-10. Send SASE for guidelines/sample copy.** *With,* Editorial Team, Box 347, Newton KS 67114, telephone (316)238-5100, is for **"senior highs, ages 15-18,"** focusing on helping "high school youth make a commitment to Christ in the context of the church amidst the complex and conflicting values they encounter in their world," circulation 5,600, uses **poetry dealing with youth in relation to their world, nature and light verse. Poems should be 4-50 lines. Pays $10-25.**

‡MERGING MEDIA (V), 516 Gallows Hill Rd., Cranford NJ 07016, phone (201)276-9479, founded 1978, publisher D.C. Erdmann. Merging Media publishes 2-3 chapbooks of poetry each year, **submissions are only by invitation. Poets should query first with 5 sample poems.** The press has published work by Geraldine Little, Alexis Rotella, Adele Kenny, Dorothy Rudy, Virginia Love Long and Susan Sheppard. As a sample, the publisher selected the following lines from "Mendsongs & Soulspace" by Rochelle Lynn Holt and Linda Zeiser:

> *Often dying awake*
> *or in our sleep*
> *we speak as ghosts*
> *haunting shores already known . . .*

The sample chapbook is digest-sized, 33 pgs. offset from typescript, with glossy card cover, flat-spined, b&w cover illustration; it sells for $3.50. **The editor subsidizes books by having the author agree to buy all but 10 copies.** Other pay depends on grant/award money. **Queries will be answered in 1 week, mss reported on in 1 month. Simultaneous submissions are OK, as are photocopied or dot-matrix mss. Criticism will be provided for a reading fee of $10/hour or $50/manuscript.** Logo-loaning also available. Inquire for details with SASE.

MERLYN'S PEN: THE NATIONAL MAGAZINE OF STUDENT WRITING, GRADES 7-10 (IV-Students, young adults), Dept. PM, Box 1058, East Greenwich RI 02818, phone (800)247-2027, founded 1985, editor R. Jim Stahl, is a quarterly using young adult writing as indicated by its title. It is 40 pgs., magazine-sized, professionally printed with glossy paper color cover. Press run is 22,000 for 20,000 subscriptions of which 5,000 are libraries. Subscription: $18.95. **Sample postpaid: $3. Send SASE for guidelines. Pays 3 copies. Reports in 3 months.**

‡METAMORPHOUS PRESS (V), P.O. Box 10616, Portland OR 97210-0616, phone (503)228-4972, founded 1982, publishes and distributes books, cassettes and videotapes on **neurolinguistic programming,** health and healing education, business and sales, women's studies, and children's books. **They currently do not accept unsolicited poetry.**

METHUEN, INC., Routledge, Chapman & Hall, 29 W. 35th St., New York NY 10001. Declined listing.

METRO SINGLES LIFESTYLES (I), Box 28203, Kansas City MO 64118, phone (816)436-8424, founded 1984, editor Robert L. Huffstutter. *MSL* is a tabloid publication for women and men of all ages: single, divorced, widowed or never-married. Not a lonely hearts type of publication, but positive and upbeat, it is published 4 times/year and has a circulation of 25,000 (approximately 5,000 subscribers in Kansas City and throughout the USA), newsstand, bookstore sales and limited complimentary copies to clubs, organizations and singles groups. Interested in seeing **free verse, lite verse, philosophical, romantic, sentimental and Frost-type poetry. All subjects considered.**" They have published poetry by Patricia Castle, Milton Kerr and Mary Ann McDonnell. As a sample, the editor selected these lines from "The Women of Cairo" by Phillip Slattery:

> *Eyes made of the Egyptian night*
> *Sparkling like an oasis pool*
> *Skin the color of the endless sand*
> *Beauty of forgotten goddesses lives on.*

Each issue features at least 12 poems by poets living throughout the USA. "Poets are invited to send a photo and a brief paragraph about their goals, single status and lifestyle. This is optional and does not influence selection of poetry, but does add interest to the publication when space for this extra feature permits." **Reports in 6-8 weeks. Pays from $5/poem or in subscriptions plus complimentary copies. Sample copy of current issue is $2 postpaid.** Each issue is about 36 pgs. and printed on Webb Offset press. **Ms should be typewritten, double-spaced or written in easy-to-read format. "Prefer to look at original poetry. No simultaneous or previously published work."** The editor says, "We do not limit or restrict subject of poems, but insist they convey an emotion, experience or exercise the reader's imagination."

‡**METROPOLITAIN (II, IV-Regional)**, 6307 N. 31st St., Arlington VA 22207, founded 1991, editor J.L. Bergsohn, is a quarterly designed to showcase the talents of **Washington area poets, writers and artists. "Will consider well-crafted poetry of any form."** They have recently published poetry by Elisavietta Ritchie and Hilary Tham. As a sample the editor selected these lines from "Washington Harbor" by M.A. Schaffner:

> *When the blood seeps sweet as grenadine,*
> *is it our loss or the NBA's, or*
> *one less cause for us to flinch*
> *when we walk at night?*
>
> *Brown hands lay linen on the tabletop.*
> *Black hands finger powder and steel.*
> *White hands pour on cold as milk:*
> *snap, crackle, die.*

Metropolitain is about 50 pgs., digest-sized, laser printed, saddle-stapled with card cover varying in color each issue and b&w drawings throughout. They receive about 750 poems a year, accept approximately 50. Press run is 200 for 50 subscribers, 100 shelf sales. Single copy: $2; subscription: $7. **Sample postpaid: $3. Previously published poems and simultaneous submissions OK. Cover letter, including bio, required.** Time between acceptance and publication is 6-12 months. **Reports in 4-6 weeks. Pays 1 copy. Acquires one-time rights.** The editor says, "The urban poet has never had a greater task than that which is currently at hand: to evaluate, condemn, clarify, unify and ultimately rejoice in and preserve mankind's greatest cultural resource – the city."

MICHIGAN QUARTERLY REVIEW (III), 3032 Rackham Bldg., University of Michigan, Ann Arbor MI 48109, phone (313)764-9265, founded 1962, editor-in-chief Laurence Goldstein, is "an interdisciplinary, general interest academic journal that publishes mainly essays and reviews on subjects of cultural and literary interest." They use **all kinds of poetry except light verse. No specifications as to form, length, style, subject matter or purpose.** Poets they have recently published include Tess Gallagher, Robert Hass, Amy Gerstler and Cathy Song. As a sample the editor chose these lines by Donald Hall:

> *Daylilies go from the hill; asters return; maples redden again*
> *as summer departs for winter's virtuous deprivation.*
> *When we stroll the Pond Road at nightfall, western sun stripes*
> *down through dust raised by a pickup ten minutes ago:*
> *vertical birches, hilly road, sunlight slant and descending.*

The *Review* is 6×9, 160+ pgs., flat-spined, professionally printed with glossy card cover, b&w photos and art, has a circulation of 2,000, with 1,500 subscriptions of which half are libraries. They receive 1,500 submissions/year, use 30, have a 1-year backlog. Subscription: $18; single copy: $5. **Sample postpaid: $2. They prefer typed mss, photocopies OK. Reports in 4-6 weeks. Pays $8-12/page. Buys first rights only.** Reviews books of poetry. "All reviews are commissioned." Laurence Goldstein advises, "There is no substitute for omnivorous reading and careful study of poets past and present, as well as reading in new and old areas of knowledge. Attention to technique, especially to rhythm and patterns of imagery, is vital."

MID COASTER (II), 2750 N. 45th St., Milwaukee WI 53210-2429, founded 1987, editor Peter Blewett, is an annual. **"I would like good, tough poetry. No restrictions on form, length or subject matter. Experimental, nonsensical OK. Nothing sentimental."** They have published poetry by Edward Field and F.D. Reeve. *Mid Coaster* is 36 pgs., magazine-sized, saddle-stapled, professionally printed in small type with glossy heavy paper cover. Press run: 1,000 for 50 subscribers. **Sample postpaid: $4.50. Send SASE for guidelines. Pays 2 copies.** Reviews books of poetry. The editor quotes Owen Felltham: "Poetry should be like a coranto, short and nimble-lofty, rather than a dull lesson of a day long . . . . He is something the less unwise that is unwise but in prose."

MID-AMERICAN REVIEW; JAMES WRIGHT PRIZE FOR POETRY (II, IV-Translations), Dept. of English, Bowling Green State University, Bowling Green OH 43403, phone (419)372-2725, founded 1980, editor-in-chief George Looney, poetry editor Edward Dougherty, appears twice a year. **"Poetry should emanate from strong, evocative images, use fresh, interesting language, and have a consistent sense of voice. Each line must carry the poem, and an individual vision should be evident. We encourage new as well as established writers. There is no length limit."** They have recently published poetry by Silvia Curbelo, Mark Doty, Fleda Brown Jackson, Pat Mora, Frankie Paino and Ronald Wallace. The following lines are the closing of "Hopalong Cassidy" by Dionisio D. Martinez:

> *West, she says, is what you tell*
> *yourself when every word has lost its name.*
>
> *West is where you go when you run out of sky.*

The review appears twice a year and is 200 pgs., flat-spined, offset, professionally printed, using line drawings, laminated card cover. They receive 1,000 mss a year, use 60-80 poems. Press run is 1,000. Subscription: $8. Per issue: $5. **Sample postpaid: $4. Send SASE for guidelines. Pays $7/printed page plus 2 copies. Rights revert to authors on publication. Reads submissions September 1 through May 30 only.** Reviews books of poetry. **Publishes chapbooks in translation.**

MIDDLE EAST REPORT (IV-Regional, ethnic, themes), Suite 119, 1500 Massachusetts Ave. NW, Washington DC 20005, phone (202)223-3677, founded 1971, editor Joe Stork, is "a magazine on contemporary political, economic, cultural and social developments in the Middle East and North Africa and U.S. policy toward the region. We occasionally publish **poetry that addresses political or social issues of Middle Eastern peoples.**" They have published poetry by Dan Almagor (Israeli) and Etel Adnan (Lebanese). It is 48 pgs., magazine-sized, saddle-stapled, professionally printed on glossy stock with glossy paper cover, 6 issues/year. Press run: 7,500. "We published 9 poems last year, all solicited." Subscription: $25. **Sample postpaid: $6 domestic; $8 airmail overseas. Pays 3-6 copies. Simultaneous submissions and previously published poems OK. Reports in 6-8 weeks. "We key poetry to the theme of a particular issue. Could be as long as 6 months between acceptance and publication."** Editor sometimes comments on submissions.

MIDDLE EASTERN DANCER (IV-Themes, ethnic), P.O. Box 181572, Casselberry FL 32718-1572, phone (407)831-3402, founded 1979, editor/publisher Karen Kuzsel, is a "monthly international magazine for Middle Eastern dancers and culture enthusiasts. **No specs for poetry other than sticking to the subject matter. Do not want to see anything not related to Middle Eastern dancing."** As a sample the editor selected these lines from "The Dance of Life" by Shariah:

> *The eternal drummer*
> *pounds out the timeless rhythm*
> *which is the heartbeat of the universe —*
> *and the dance of life goes on . . .*

The monthly is magazine-sized, usually 36 pgs., printed in 2-color on heavy stock with glossy paper cover, using b&w photos and graphics. They receive about 20 poems/year, accept 6-10 ("depends on room"). Press run is 2,500+. Subscription: $24/year; per issue: $3 plus $1 postage and handling. **Sample: SASE ($1 stamps). Pays 2 copies.** Poems can be in "any form that's legible." **Simultaneous submissions (if not to other Middle Eastern dance publications), previously published poems OK. Reports within 2 weeks.** Editor occasionally comments on rejections.

Market categories: (I) Beginning; (II) General; (III) Limited; (IV) Specialized; (V) Closed.

MIDLAND REVIEW (II), English Dept., Morrill Hall, Oklahoma State University, Stillwater OK 74078, phone (405)744-9474, founded 1985, is a literary annual that publishes "poetry, fiction, essays, ethnic, experimental, women's work, contemporary feminist, linguistic criticism, drama, comparative litera-ture, interviews." The editors say, **"style and form are open."** They do not want **"long or religious poetry."** They have published poetry by Amy Clampitt, William Stafford, Medbh McGuckian and Richard Kostelanetz. As a sample, the editors selected these lines by James Doyle:

> *The pressured houses squat*
> *beneath a black sky. Smoke*
> *passes back and forth between*
> *them down the street. Gilled*
> *animals swim the thin odors*
> *home, calling themselves planets . . .*

Midland Review is 100-120 pgs., digest-sized, with photography, artwork and ads. Circulation is 500, of which 470 are subscriptions. Price per issue is $6. **Sample postpaid: $5. Pay is 1 copy. Writers should submit 3-5 poems, typed ms in any form. "We no longer read during the summer (May 1-August 31)." Reporting time is 3-6 months and time to publication 6-12 months.**

MIDMARCH ARTS PRESS; WOMEN ARTISTS NEWS (IV-Women), 300 Riverside Dr., New York NY 10025, founded 1979, editor Sylvia Moore. They have published poetry by Muriel Rukeyser, Eve Merriam and Jane Cooper. *WAN* is a 40-page magazine focusing **on women in the arts**, using some poetry. **Sample postpaid: $3.75. Send SASE for guidelines. Reports in 6 weeks. Pays 5 copies.** Midm-arch Arts Press publishes 6 paperbacks/year.

MIDNIGHT ZOO; ABERATIONS (I, IV-Horror/science fiction/fantasy), 544 Ygnacio Valley Rd. #13, P.O. Box 8040, Walnut Creek CA 94596, phone (510)942-5116, *MZ* founded 1990, *Aberations* founded 1992, editor/publisher Jon L. Herron. *MZ* appears every other month using **poems of 4-100 lines, "horror, sci-fi, fantasy. No haiku, no mainstream. Submit up to 20 poems. Light verse, traditional, experimental OK."** They have recently published poetry by Paul O. Williams, Herb Kauderer, J.C. Hendee and Jacie Ragan. It is 120+ pgs., magazine-sized, flat-spined with 2-color glossy cover. They accept 80-120 of 300-400 poems received. Press run 3,500 for 877 subscribers of which 42 are libraries, 2,000 shelf sales. Subscription: $29.95. **Sample postpaid: $6. Send SASE for guidelines. Pays $3-10/ poem plus 1 copy. Buys first North American serial rights. Reports within 3 months. Editor usually comments on rejections. "Want a short cover letter with a bio."** Reviews books, magazines and videos. Sponsors an annual writing and poetry contest. *Aberations* appears monthly using **poems of 4-36 lines, "*adult* horror, sci-fi, *dark* fantasy. Submit up to 10 poems. Work that is too hot for other publications— too erotic, too gory, too profane, too cutting edge."** They have recently published poetry by John Gray, Richard Levesque, Holly Day and KL Jones. It is 64 pgs., digest-sized, saddle-stapled with 2-color glossy cover. They accept 72-100 of 200-300 poems received. Press run is 600 for 84 subscribers of which 3 are libraries, 300 shelf sales. "New, but growing rapidly." Subscription: $31. **Sample postpaid $4.75. Send SASE for guidelines. Pays "1 copy to $2 plus 1 copy." Acquires first North American serial rights. Reports within 2 months. Editor usually comments on rejections. "Want a short cover letter with bio."**

MIDSTREAM: A MONTHLY JEWISH REVIEW (IV-Ethnic), 110 E. 59th St., New York NY 10022, phone (212)339-6021, editor Joel Carmichael, is a magazine-sized, 48-page, flat-spined national jour-nal, circulation 10,000, appearing monthly except June/July and August/September, when it is bi-monthly. It uses **short poems with Jewish themes or atmosphere.** They have recently published poetry by Yehuda Amichai, James Reiss, Abraham Sutzkever, Liz Rosenberg and John Hollander. Subscrip-tion: $21; per issue: $3. They receive about 300 submissions/year, use 5-10%. **Sample free. No query. Reports in 1 month. Pays $25/poem. Buys all rights.** Reviews related books of poetry in 1,000-1,500 words.

MIDWEST POETRY REVIEW (IV-Subscribers); RIVER CITY PUBLICATIONS (V), P.O. Box 4776, Rock Island IL 61201, founded 1980, poetry editors Tom Tilford, Grace Keller and Jilian Roth, is a "sub-scriber-only" quarterly, with no other support than subscriptions—that is, **only subscribers may submit poetry and/or enter their contests. Subscribers may also get help and criticism on 1 poem/month.** "We are attempting to encourage the cause of poetry and raise the level thereof by giving aid to new poets, to poets who have lapsed in their writing and to poets who desire a wider market, by purchasing the best of modern poetry and giving it exposure through our quarterly magazine. We want **poetry from poets who feel they have a contribution to make to the reader relating to the human condition, nature and the environment. Serious writers only are sought. No jingly verses or limericks. No restrictions as to form, length or style. Any subject is considered, if handled with skill and taste."** They have recently published poetry by Barbara Seaman, John Thomas Baker, B.R. Culbertson, Martin Musick,

Nancy Graham and Maude Paro. As a sample the editors selected these lines from "A Search Between the Sound and Silence" by John Robert McFarland:

> *Father never spoke,*
> *his tongue a stone hard set against the sounds,*
> *(a perverse mirror propped up before Demosthenes)*
> *as though the steel that pierced his eyes,*
> *and pulled the night shade down so fast around his*
> *soul,*
> *did cut as well the nerve,*
> *that draws the bar upon the cage of speech.*

The digest-sized, saddle-stapled magazine is 52 pgs., professionally printed in various type styles, with matte card cover and some b&w art. They have quarterly and annual contests plus varied contests in each issue, with prizes ranging from $25-500 (the latter for the annual contest), with "unbiased, non-staff judges for all competitions. Paid-up subscribers enter the contests with fees." **Sample postpaid: $5. Subscription fee of $20 ($25 Canadian, $30 foreign, both in US funds) must accompany first submission. No photocopies. Reports in 2 weeks. Pays $5-500/ poem. Buys first rights. Send SASE and $1 for guidelines.** Reviews books of poetry in 400 words. River City Publications is not currently publishing books. The editor advises, "We are interested in serious poets, whether new or published. We will help those who wish to consider serious criticism and attempt to improve themselves. We want to see the poet improve, expand and achieve fulfillment."

THE MIDWEST QUARTERLY (II), Pittsburg State University, Pittsburg KS 66762, phone (316)235-4689, founded 1959, poetry editor Stephen Meats, "publishes articles on any subject of contemporary interest, particularly literary criticism, political science, philosophy, education, biography, sociology and each issue contains a **section of poetry from 10-30 pages in length.** I am interested in **well-crafted, though not necessarily traditional poems that see nature and the self in bold, surrealistic images of a writer's imaginative, mystical experience of the world. 60 lines or less (occasionally longer if exceptional)."** They have recently published poetry by Charles Bukowski, Marguerite Bouvard, Jared Carter, Lyn Lifshin, Harold Witt and Greg Kuzma. As a sample the editor selected these lines from "Resurrection" by Andrea Moorhead:

> *tear the ice from dirt*
> *the arms from stone*
> *electric and cold*
> *when the voice runs along the ground*
> *murmuring in the soil, murmuring along the bent cut wood.*

The magazine is digest-sized, 130 pgs., flat-spined, matte cover, professionally printed. Circulation is 650, with 600 subscriptions of which 500 are libraries. They receive approximately 3,200 poems annually; publish 60. "My plan is to publish all acceptances within 1 year." Subscription: $10. Sample: $3. **Mss should be typed with poet's name on each page, 10 poems or fewer. Photocopies, legible dot-matrix, OK; simultaneous submissions accepted, but first publication in *MQ* must be guaranteed. Reports in 1 month, usually sooner. Pays 3 copies. Acquires first serial rights. Editor comments on rejections "if the poet or poems seem particularly promising."** Reviews books of poetry by *MQ* published poets only. He says, "Keep writing; read as much contemporary poetry as you can lay your hands on; don't let the discouragement of rejection keep you from sending your work out to editors."

‡MIDWIFERY TODAY (IV-Themes), P.O. Box 2672, Eugene OR 97402, phone (503)344-7438, founded 1986, editor Jan Tritten, is a quarterly that "provides a voice for midwives and childbirth educators. **We are a midwifery magazine. Subject must be birth or profession related."** They do not want poetry that is "off subject or puts down the subject." As a sample the editor selected these lines by Karen Hope Ehrlich:

> *you get to keep the baby*
> *not the midwife*
> *she is a fickle lover*
> *merged and passing*

MT is 52 pgs., approximately 8½ × 11, offset, saddle-stapled, with glossy card cover with b&w photo and b&w photos, artwork and ads inside. They use about 1 poem/issue. Press run is 3,000 for 1,500 subscribers, 1,000 shelf sales. Subscription: $30. **Sample postpaid: $7.50. No previously published poems or simultaneous submissions. Cover letter required.** Time between acceptance and publication is 1-2 years. **Seldom comments on rejections. Send SASE for Writer's guidelines. Reports in 2-6 weeks. Pays 2 copies. Acquires first rights.** The editor says, "With our publication *please* stay on the subject."

MILKWEED EDITIONS (II), Suite 505, 528 Hennepin Ave., Minneapolis MN 55403, phone (612)332-3192, founded 1979, poetry editor Emilie Buchwald. Three collections published annually. **Unsolicited mss are only accepted from writers who have previously published a book-length collection of poetry or a minimum of 6 poems in commercial or literary journals.** Rapidly becoming one of the leading literary presses in the country, Milkweed publishes some of the best poets composing today in well-made, attractively designed collections. Recent books of poetry include: **The Color of Mesabi Bones,** by John Caddy; **Forgiveness,** by Dennis Sampson; and **Paul Bunyan's Bearskin,** by Patricia Goedicke. **Unsolicited ms accepted in June and January; please include return postage. Poetry titles are set through 1993.** Catalog available on request, with 74¢ in postage.

MIND IN MOTION: A MAGAZINE OF POETRY AND SHORT PROSE (I, II), P.O. Box 1118, Apple Valley CA 92307, phone (619)248-6512, founded 1985, a quarterly, editor Céleste Goyer wants **poetry "15-60 lines. Explosive, provocative. Images not cliched but directly conveyant of the point of the poem. Use of free association particularly desired. We encourage free verse, keeping in mind the essential elements of rhythm and rhyme. Traditional forms are acceptable if within length restrictions. Meaning should be implicit, as in the styles of Blake, Poe, Coleridge, Stephen Crane, Emily Dickinson, Leonard Cohen. Submit in batches of 5-6. Not interested in sentimentality, emotionalism, simplistic nature worship, explicit references."** She has recently published poetry by Robert E. Brimhall, Charlie Mehrhoff, Joan Payne Kincaid and Nancy Mikita. As a sample she selected these lines (poet unidentified):

> *Inhabitants of the larger cosmos,*
> *Beware! Creatures of Earth will*
> *soon command the void.*
> *They are a lawless breed, who*
> *love passion more than reason,*
> *who know no life of moderation,*
> *have betrayed every goodness in*
> *whetted lies, savoring the spirit*
> *of deceit over that of truth*

MIM is 54 pgs., digest-sized, saddle-stapled, photocopied from photoreduced typescript with a heavy matte cover with b&w drawing. Of approximately 2,400 poems/year she accepts about 200. Press run is 525 for 350 subscriptions. Subscription: $14. **Sample postpaid: $3.50 (overseas: $4.50, $18/year). Send SASE for guidelines. Pays 1 copy "when financially possible." Acquires first rights. Reports in 1-6 weeks. Unpublished works only. Simultaneous submissions okay if notified.** Magazine is copyrighted; all rights revert to author. Editor usually comments on rejected mss.

MIND MATTERS REVIEW (III), 2040 Polk St. #234, San Francisco CA 94109, founded 1988, editor Carrie Drake, is a **"literary quarterly with emphasis on use of science as a tool for responsible organization of information; analysis of the role of language in consciousness, knowledge and intelligence; and social criticism particularly of metaphysics.** Also includes book reviews, poetry, short stories, art and essays." They want **"short poems for fillers. Would like to see inspirational poetry; but open to satire and contemporary subjects that reflect the struggle between the 'inner voice' and external pressures. Rhythm important, but rhyme isn't."** They have recently published poetry by Daniel Green, Dwane Harris and Ron Ellis. As a sample the editor selected these lines from "The Field" by Bunny Williams:

> *The balance of joy and pain is more than we can ask*
> *For life was never meant to keep a perfect score;*
> *The scales of justice have no weight*
> *And logic alone cannot equate*
> *So the plight of man remains a burden heretofore.*

MMR is magazine-sized, desktop published, includes graphics, sketches, b&w photos. Subscription: $10 US, $15 foreign. **Sample postpaid: $3.50. Send SASE for guidelines. Pays 1 copy. Poets are encouraged to buy a copy before submitting. Simultaneous submissions and previously published poems OK.** The editor says, "Poetry should reflect the deeper layers of consciousness, its perceptions, observations, joys and sorrows; should reflect the independence of the individual spirit. Should not be 'trendy' or 'poetic' in a forced way."

THE MINNESOTA REVIEW (II), English Dept., East Carolina University, Greenville NC 27858, phone (919)757-6388, founded 1960, editor Jeffrey Williams, poetry editor Mary Jo Mahoney, is a biannual literary magazine wanting **"poetry which explores some aspect of social or political issues and/or the nature of relationships. No nature poems, and no lyric poetry without the above focus."** As a sample the editors selected these lines from "Hotel Kitchen" by Jonathan Holden:

> *Downstairs in those steel kitchens, in the loud*
> *bucket-brigade of order, pots and shuttling*
> *of dishes hand-to-hand, you couldn't hear*

the murmurous conversation of the rich . . .
TMR is 160 pgs., digest-sized, flat-spined, with b&w glossy card cover and art. Circulation for 500 subscriptions. Subscription: $8 to individuals, $16 to institutions. **Sample postpaid:** $ **Reports in 2-4 months. Pays 2 copies. Acquires all rights. Returns rights upon request.** Review books of poetry in single or multi-book format.

MINORITY LITERARY EXPO (IV-Membership, ethnic, regional), P.O. Box 370171, Birmingham AL 35237, phone (205)798-8916, founded 1990, editor/publisher Kervin Fondren, is an annual literary professional publication featuring minority poets, novices and professionals. **"Organization member- ship open to all minority poets nationally. I want poems from minority poets that are holistic and wholesome, less than 24 lines each, no vulgar or hate poetry accepted, any style, any form, any subject matter. Poetry that expresses holistic views and philosophies is very acceptable. Literary value is emphasized.** Selected poets receive financial awards, certificates, honorable mentions, critiques and special poetic honors." No fee is charged for inclusion. As a sample the editor selected these lines from his poem "Rain and Pain":

> *Do I Dare*
> *As A Man*
> *Dance in My Backyard*
> *In the Rain*

An annual national literary expo, implemented in Birmingham, Alabama, features many enter- tainers, stars, health fairs, health runs, writing and poetry workshops, concerts, etc. Write for details.

MINOTAUR PRESS; MINOTAUR (II), Box 4039, Felton CA 95018, founded 1974, editor Jim Gove. *Minotaur* is a "small press literary quarterly **with emphasis on contemporary and experimental styles. Must be relevant. No rhymed and/or traditional verse."** They have published poetry by Judson Crews, Ed Mycue and Julia Vinograd. As a sample the editor selected these lines from "For Jack Spicer" by William Talcott:

> *No one listens to poetry*
> *Jack Spicer.*
> *Salt & Pepper*
> *Are just another passida laugh*
> *in the mashed potatoes*

The editor describes it as digest-sized, perfect-bound, photocopied, "stock cover—cover graph- ics—sometimes use interior graphics, but rarely." They publish about 12 of 100 poems received. Press run: 400 for 300 subscriptions of which 50 are libraries. Subscription: $18. **Sample postpaid: $3.50. Send SASE for guidelines. Pays 1 copy. Submit 4-8 poems. "Best of issue from subscribing contributors receives 1-year subscription. You do not need to subscribe to be published."** Editor comments on submissions **"if requested only."** Reviews books of poetry. Minotaur Press pub- lishes a "Back to Back" chapbook with each issue. **"We ask for mss from regular magazine contributors." Pays 40 copies of chapbooks.** They "rarely" subsidy publish "if quality merits and poet comes to us. Author pays; we distribute to our readership as a bonus book." The editor says, "Subscribe to the magazines that publish your work. Few poetry magazines run in the black."

MIORITA: A JOURNAL OF ROMANIAN STUDIES (IV-Ethnic), Department of Foreign Languages Literatures and Linguistics, University of Rochester, Rochester NY 14627, is a scholarly annual, digest-sized, 100 pgs., circulation 200, focusing on **Romanian culture and using some poetry by Roma- nians or on Romanian themes. Sample: $5. Pays copies.** Reviews books of poetry "occasionally; must be Romanian-connected."

THE MIRACULOUS MEDAL (IV-Religious), 475 E. Chelten Ave., Philadelphia PA 19144-5785, phone (215)848-1010, founded 1928, editor Rev. John W. Gouldrick, C.M. is a religious quarterly. **"Poetry should reflect solid Catholic doctrine and experience. Any subject matter is acceptable, provided it does not contradict the teachings of the Roman Catholic Church. Poetry must have a religious theme, preferably about the Blessed Virgin Mary."** They have published poetry by Gladys McKee. The editor describes it as digest-sized, 32 pgs., saddle-stapled, 2-color inside and cover, no ads. *The Miraculous Medal* is no longer circulated on a subscription basis. It is used as a promotional piece and is sent to all clients of the Association. The circulation figure is now 340,000. **Sample and guidelines free for postage. Pays 50¢ and up/line payable on acceptance. Buys first North American rights. Reports in 6 months-3 years. Poems should be a maximum of 20 lines, double-spaced. No simultaneous submissions or previously published poems. Photocopy, dot-matrix OK.**

MIRIAM PRESS; UP AGAINST THE WALL, MOTHER (I, IV-Women, theme), 9114 Wood Spice Lane, Lorton VA 22079, phone (703)690-2246, founded 1980, poetry editor Lee-lee Schlegel. The quarterly is **"concerned with poetry as therapy first, literary excellence second.** Our philosophy is that there are many good literary markets but few who 'help' those in trouble." They want **anything on women in crisis (we deal with the darker side here—death, rape, abuse, the frustrations of mothering/wives,** etc.). *Mother* has published poetry by Jill DiMaggio, Serena Fusek, Joan Payne Kincaid, John Fiore and John Grey. Each issue of the digest-sized magazine has 39-52 pgs. of poetry. It has a circulation of about 500 with 400 subscriptions of which 25 are university libraries. It is inexpensively produced, laser, card covers with simple art. They receive about 6,000 submissions/year, use 800. Subscription: $12. Sample: $3.50. Submit 4-6 poems. Simultaneous submissions, photocopies, dot-matrix OK. Usually reports within one month. **No pay, not even a copy. Acquires one-time rights. Send SASE for guidelines.** "We are a friendly press open to all. We are also very poor and appreciate support. Our immediate goals include being able to pay poets in copies, eventually money. Advice: 1) study your market, 2) always send SASE, 3) please don't tell me how good your poetry is!"

MISNOMER (II), P.O. Box 1395, Prestonsburg KY 41653, founded 1990, editors Eric Cash and Jeff Weddle, appears twice a year. **"We like to see poetry that is vibrant and honest, poetry that communicates the human experience by dancing on the matchhead of reality, yet conveys true human compassion. We want real images, real situations. If your head is in the clouds, leave it there. Send us those poems that you would be afraid to show your mother, poems that scream to the reader. If it's good, we'll publish it. We need good poetry. No religious, light verse, rhymed, overly sentimental pieces about your grandmother, your dog or your grandmother's dog.** We review books, chapbooks and other magazines." They have recently published poetry by B.Z. Niditch, Cheryl A. Townsend, Carol Gunther and Richard Davignon. As a sample the editors selected "abstract and concrete" by Gerald Locklin:

> how thick is a line?
> can a line be a color?
> can a line not be linear?
> can a line cast a shadow?
>
> a line may catch a fish.
> a line may catch a critic.
> refugee families catch fish
> to feed their families.
> a critic feeds a line to feed his.

The editor describes it as 40-60 pgs., digest-sized, saddle-stapled, photocopied from typescript. They use about 10% of work submitted. Press run is 300. Subscription: $6. **Sample postpaid: $4. Send SASE for guidelines. Pays 1 copy. "Need short bio to be included with cover letter: tell us who you are (no bearing on acceptance)." Simultaneous submissions OK.**

MISSISSIPPI REVIEW (II), University of Southern Mississippi, Box 5144, Hattiesburg MS 39406-5144, phone (601)266-4321, editor Frederick Barthelme, managing editor Rie Fortenberry. Literary publication for those interested in contemporary literature. **Does not read manuscripts in summer. Sample: $8.80. Pays copies.**

MISSISSIPPI VALLEY REVIEW (II), English Dept., Western Illinois University, Macomb IL 61455, phone (309)298-1514, founded 1973, editors John Mann and Tama Baldwin, is a literary magazine published twice a year which uses **poems of high quality, no specifications as to form, length, style, subject matter or purpose.** They have recently published poetry by Denise Levertov, David Citino, A.E. Stringer, William Heyen, David Ray and Daniel J. Langton. *MVR* uses a handsomely printed, digest-sized, flat-spined, 60+ pgs. format, glossy, color cover, circulation 400. Subscription: $12; per copy $6. They have about 25 pgs. of poetry in each issue, receive 1,000-2,500 submissions per year, use about 30, and have a 6-12 month backlog. **No simultaneous submissions. Sample postpaid: $6. Submit 5 pgs. or less. Reports in 4 months. Pays 2 copies and a year's subscription.** Editor comments on rejections **"occasionally, particularly if we are interested in the ms. Send us poems of high quality which speak authentically from human experience."** Occasionally reviews books of poetry.

UNIVERSITY OF MISSOURI PRESS; DEVINS AWARD (II), 2910 LeMone Blvd., Columbia MO 65201, phone (314)882-7641, founded 1958, editor Clair Willcox. **The press now accepts poetry mss from both published and unpublished authors throughout the year.** Query first with 5-6 sample poems (not a complete ms), a table of contents and a cover letter stating the mss length. The Devins Award is given for **an outstanding poetry manuscript, not necessarily a first book, already accepted for publication by the University of Missouri Press during the year.**

MISSOURI REVIEW (II), 1507 Hillcrest Hall, University of Missouri, Columbia MO 65211, phone (314)882-4474, founded 1978, poetry editor Greg Michalson, general editor Speer Morgan, is a quality literary journal, 6×9, 208 pgs., which appears 3 times a year, **publishing poetry features only—6-12 pages for each of 3 to 5 poets/issue. Sample: $6. No simultaneous submissions. Photocopies, dot-matrix OK. Reports in 8-10 weeks. Pays $125-250/feature. Buys all rights. Returns rights "after publication, without charge, at the request of the authors."** Reviews books of poetry occasionally. "Short, inhouse reviews only." Awards the Tom McAfee Discovery Feature once or twice a year to an outstanding young poet who has not yet published a poet; poets are selected from regular submissions at the direction of the editors. Also offers the Editor's Prize Contest in Poetry. Deadline: October 1. $500 first prize and publication. Three finalists named in addition. Write for details. *MR* is one of the best literary "credits," and its new annual contest may be a way for relative unknowns to break into the magazine. That's good news for some poets, but not for others. Though the contest and "feature" policies, combined, probably won't change the number of pages of poetry (or the quality, for that matter), they may reduce the number of individual poets and, hence, your chances here. The editors add, "We think this has enhanced the quality of the poetry section and increased our reader interest in the section. We remain dedicated to publishing at least one younger or emerging poet in every issue."

MR. COGITO PRESS; MR. COGITO (II), Humanities Division, Pacific University, Forest Grove OR 97116 or 3314 SE Brooklyn, Portland OR 97202, founded 1973, poetry editors John M. Gogol and Robert A. Davies. *Mr. Cogito*, published 2-3 times/year, is a tall, skinny (4½×11) magazine, 24-26 pgs. of poetry printed in a variety of type styles. The editors want **"no prose put in lines. Yes: wit, heightened language, craft. Open to all schools and subjects and groups of poets."** They have recently published poetry by Norman Russell, Ann Chandonnet, John Minczeski, Peter Wild and Zbigniew Herbert. As a sample the editors selected these lines from "ghost poem" by Bill Shields:

> *I don't think the country is ever going to forgive us*
> *for throwing up our hands and dying in Vietnam*

They use poems in both English and translation, "preferably representing each poet with several poems." The magazine has a circulation of 400. Subscription for 3 issues: $9. **Sample: $3. Submit 4-5 poems. Simultaneous submissions and photocopies OK. Pays copies. Acquires first rights and anthology rights. Reports in 2 weeks-2 months.** Mr. Cogito Press publishes collections by poets they invite from among those who have appeared in the magazine. Send SASE for catalog to buy samples. They also conduct special theme and translation contests with prizes of $50 or $100. The editors advise, "Subscribe to a magazine that seems good. Read ours before you submit. Write, write, write."

MOBIUS (I, II), Orion Art Center, P.O. Box 674, Lake Orion MI 48361, phone (313)693-4986, founded 1982 by the Orion Art Center, current editor Jean H. Herman. "We welcome beginners as well as previously published poets. We are looking for your best work even though we are not a college-based forum. **No restrictions on type of poetry (please, no pornography or obscenity). Poets may submit up to five poems, up to 80-85 lines."** They have recently published poetry by Fritz Hamilton, John Williams, Daniel Green, Robert Cooperman, Len Blanchard, R.L. Cook, Lenore Reiss and T.N. Turner. As a sample the editor selected these lines from "Night Sits On The Porch" by James Webb Wilson:

> *Night sits on the open porch,*
> *Swinging gently mid dusk and dawn,*
> *Closing the drapes over the lawn,*
> *Deepening shadows, rounding off corners,*
> *Softly squeezing out colors . . . .*
> *Night sits on the open porch*
> *Obsidian streaked with starlight*
> *And an occasional borealis*
> *To make us dream.*

"*Mobius* has been published twice a year with a press run of 500, but is expanding due to public response." It is magazine-sized, 70+ pgs., professionally printed, saddle-stapled with matte card cover. Subscription: $10/year. **Sample postpaid: $5. Guidelines available for SASE. "Printed authors receive one copy free. Editor will try to comment on all rejections."** Submission guidelines state that the editor looks for intelligence and wit, and several poems included here contain them in all styles, free to formal, long to short (with even a few concrete and shape poems thrown into the mix). The editor promises to comment on all submissions, but warns of delays. As such, this is a good market for beginners.

MODERN BRIDE (IV-Love/romance), 249 W. 17th St., New York NY 10011, phone (212)779-1999, managing editor Mary Ann Cavlin, a slick bimonthly, occasionally buys **poetry pertaining to love and marriage. Pays $30-40 for average short poem.**

MODERN HAIKU; KAY TITUS MORMINO MEMORIAL SCHOLARSHIP; MARGARET DUFFIELD ME-MORIAL SCHOLARSHIP (IV-Form, students), P.O. Box 1752, Madison WI 53701, founded 1969, poetry editor Robert Spiess, "is the foremost international journal of English language haiku and criticism. We are devoted to publishing only the very best haiku being written and also publish articles on haiku and have the most complete review section of haiku books. Issues average over 100 pages." They use **haiku only. No tanka or other forms. "We publish all 'schools' of haiku, but want the haiku to elicit intuition, insight, felt-depth."** They have published haiku by Geraldine Little, Paul O. Williams, Wally Swist and Cor van den Heuvel. As a sample the editor selected this haiku (poet unidentified):

> a life near its close
> and still scribbling poems
> of wild plum

The digest-sized magazine appears 3 times a year, printed on heavy quality stock with cover illustrations especially painted for each issue by the staff artist. There are over 260 poems in each issue, circulation 650. Subscription: $13; per copy: $4.65. They receive 16,000-18,000 freelance submissions/year, use 800. **Sample postpaid: $4.50. Submit on "any size sheets, any number of haiku on a sheet; but name and address on each sheet." Reports in 2 weeks. Pays $1/haiku (but no contributor's copy). Buys first North American serial rights. Send SASE for guidelines. No simultaneous submissions.** Reviews books of haiku in 350-1,000 words, single format. The Kay Titus Mormino Memorial Scholarship of $500 is for the best haiku by a high school senior, deadline early March. They also offer the Margaret Duffield Memorial Scholarship of $200. Send SASE for rules. Robert Spiess says, "In regard to haiku, Daisetz T. Szuki said it succinctly well: 'A haiku does not express ideas but puts forward images reflecting intuitions.' "

MOKSHA JOURNAL; VAJRA PRINTING & PUBLISHING OF YOGA ANAND ASHRAM (IV-Spiritual), 49 Forrest Pl., Amityville NY 11701, phone (516)691-8475, founded 1984, assistant Director Yogi Ananda Viraj Vajra, is a "small press publisher of **spiritual and/or philosophical literature, poetry, nonfiction and limited fiction/poetry** pertaining to the concept of 'Moksha,' defined by Monier-Williams as a 'liberation, release' (A Sanskrit-English Dictionary, 1899). Perspectives include, but are not limited to: Yoga, various schools of Buddhism, Sufism, Mystical Christianity, etc." *Moksha Journal* appears twice a year, and is 40-55 pgs., 7¼ × 9½, offset, litho. Press run 400-500 for that many subscribers. Subscription: $8. **Sample: $4. Pays 1 copy. Simultaneous submissions OK. Reports in 4-6 weeks.** The press publishes flat-spined paperbacks.

MONOCACY VALLEY REVIEW (II), William Heath, Department of English, Mount Saint Mary's College, Emmitsburg MD 21727, founded 1985, poetry editor Mary Noel, editor William Heath, is an annual literary review. **Submissions should be received by January 15th.** "In general, we cannot publish longer poems; we also publish short stories, nonfiction prose, book reviews and artwork. **We pride ourselves in being a review that is always local but never provincial. If we have a bias, it is in favor of clarity of vision and eloquence of language. We dislike poems that 'hurt the ear and unfit one to continue.' "** *MVR* is magazine-sized, 60 pgs., saddle-stapled, high quality paper. "We reject over 95% of submissions, publish 15-20 poems an issue." Their press run is 500 with 200 subscriptions of which 10 are libraries. Subscription: $8. **Sample postpaid: $5. Include a 50-word or less biographical statement with all submissions. Pays $10-25/poem plus 2 copies. All submissions are judged anonymously and there is no backlog. If mss are sent in December and early January, response time is 6-8 weeks.** The editor says they "prefer reviews of major writers in the area."

WILLIAM MORROW AND CO. (V), 1350 Avenue of the Americas, New York NY 10019, phone (212)261-6500, publishes poetry on standard royalty contracts, **but accepts no unsolicited mss. Queries with samples should be submitted through an agent.**

MOSAIC PRESS (V), 358 Oliver Rd., Cincinnati OH 45215, phone (513)761-5977, poetry editor Miriam Irwin. The press publishes fine hardbound small books (under 3" tall); **they want "interesting topics beautifully written in very few words—a small collection of short poems on one subject."** The editor **does not want to see haiku.** She has published poetry by Marilyn Francis and Robert Hoeft. The sample miniature book the editor sent is **Water and Windfalls**, by Marilyn Francis, illustrated by Mada Leach. It is ¾ × ⅞, flat-spined (⅛" thick), an elegantly printed and bound hardback, with colored endpapers and gold lettering on spine and front cover. The press publishes 1 book/year, average page count 64. She is "**booked up—going to finish existing projects before starting new ones.**" But writers can query, sending 3 or more sample poems and "whatever you want to tell me." She says, "**We don't use pseudonyms.**" Simultaneous submissions are OK, as are photocopied and dot-matrix mss, although she doesn't like the latter. Payment is in author's copies (5 for a whole collection or book) plus a $50 honorarium. She pays $2.50 plus 1 copy for single poems. Criticism will be provided only if requested and "then only if we have constructive comments. If work is accepted, be prepared to wait patiently; some of our books take 4 years to complete." The press publishes private editions but does not call it subsidy publishing. Catalog and writers manual free for large SASE with 52¢ postage. The editor advises, "Type neatly, answer letters, return phone calls, include SASE."

(m)ÖTHÊR TØÑGUÉS (II, IV-Translations), RR#2 Alders C-14, Ganges, British Columbia V0S 1E0 Canada, founded 1990, editor and publisher Mona Fertig, is a literary magazine of poetry, fiction and essays appearing twice a year. She wants **"unpublished, new, volatile, political, well-written poetry, no clichés or unstimulating poetry," includes translations from many languages. Include "Writers Notes."** They have published poetry by Thich Tue Sy, Erin Mouré, Dorin Tudoran and Ann Diamond. *MT* is magazine-sized, 70 pgs., photocopied. Press run 500. Subscription: $12 Canadian, $14 USA, $18 international. **Sample postpaid: $7. Reports in 3 months. Pays 1-year subscription.**

‡MS. MAGAZINE (V), 230 Park Ave., 7th Floor, New York NY 10169, founded 1972, is a bimonthly "feminist source of national and international news, politics, arts, scholarship and book reviews." **They are currently not accepting unsolicited poetry.** They have published poetry by Alice Walker, Maya Angelou and May Swenson. Circulation is 150,000. Single copy: $5 (available on newsstands); subscription: $30. They say, "Due to the volume of the material received, we cannot accept, acknowledge or return unsolicited poetry or fiction. We cannot discuss queries on the phone and cannot be held responsible for manuscripts sent to us."

MSS/NEW MYTHS; JOHN GARDNER POETRY AWARD (II), Box 6000, SUNY Binghamton NY 13902-6000, phone (607)777-2168, founded 1961, editor Robert Mooney, appears twice a year. **They want "only excellence for whatever it is. It must be beautiful, carefully crafted and, in some way, moving. Nothing commercial. Please send between 3-8 poems at a time."** They have published poetry by John Montague, Jack Myers, Joyce Carol Oates, Maxine Kumin and William Stafford. As a sample the editor selected these lines from "Summary" by David Ignatow:

> In life we solve no problems
> just bend them like crowbars.
> A person takes one up
> where we laid it aside
> and advances upon us.

It is 220 pgs., 6×9. Press run is 1,000 for 450 subscribers of which 125 are libraries, 125 shelf sales. Subscription: $8.50 for individuals. **Sample postpaid: $5. Reports in 2-8 weeks. Submit only September 1 - May 1.** Payment "depends on funds available" plus 2 copies. Editor often comments on rejections. "We *strongly* recommend you read a copy of the magazine before submitting work!" The John Gardner Poetry Award is "only by announcement, not annual."

MUDFISH; BOX TURTLE PRESS (I, II), 184 Franklin St., New York NY 10013, phone (212)219-9278, founded 1983, poetry editor Jill Hoffman, art editor Vladimir Urban. *Mudfish*, published by Box Turtle Press, is a journal of poetry and art that appears once a year and is looking for **"energy, intensity, and originality of voice, mastery of style, the presence of passion."** They have published poetry by Charles Simic, Harvey Shapiro, Nicholas Kolumban, Denise Duhamel and John Ashbery. As a sample the editor selected these lines by Steven Sherill:

> I'll dig all day
> in your secret ditch,
> all the way to China
> if needed, to find
> that little room past
> the place of tongues,
> nipples and sweat
> where we can just sit and talk.

Press run is 1,500. **Mudfish 5 and 4 are $8; Mudfish 3, $6; and Mudfish 2, $7; plus $1.50 shipping and handling. These issues are available as sample copies. Pays 2 copies. They will not consider simultaneous submissions or previously published poems. Reports from "immediately to 6 months."**

MULBERRY PRESS (I), 105 Betty Rd., East Meadow NY 11554, founded 1991, publisher G.M. Frey. This is an arrangement for publishing chapbooks only. mulberry press (they prefer lowercase) will consider **chapbooks (any length) for a $5 reading fee, for which you get 5 sample chapbooks if your ms is rejected, 50 copies if it is accepted (more copies at cost).** Press run 150-200 copies. Poems may be previously published in magazines. **Make checks payable to G.M. Frey.** They are also open to co-op publishing: Poet pays "a modest fee to cover cost" and receives 80% of press run. They have recently published chapbooks by Gina Bergamino, Lyn Lifshin, Tony Moffeit, John Sweet, Ruth Moon

Kempher and Todd Moore. As a sample here is a complete poem, "seven," from **god poems** by Michael Hathaway:

> God drips luv
> He forgives people sinning
> people writing poems about His colors
> God's lucky luv drips all around us
> get on your knees
> lick it up

They also offer an annual chapbook contest. Entry fee: $5. All entrants receive a copy of the winning chapbook. Winner receives 100 copies. Send SASE for guidelines. The editor advises, "Take your art seriously, make it a priority in your life. Be persistent and patient and eventually you will endure and prevail. If you keep on writing, you can only get better."

‡**MUSICWORKS (IV-Themes)**, 1087 Queen St. W., Toronto, Ontario M6J 1H3 Canada, phone (416)533-0192, founded 1978, editor Gayle Young, is a tabloid triannual journal of contemporary music. The editor says, "**The poetry we publish usually directly relates to the musical themes we are dealing with**—*usually* **it is poetry written by the (music) composer or performers we are featuring.**" Recent poets published include bpnichol, Colin Morton, Jackson Mac Low and Jean Derome. The magazine is 64 pgs., with b&w visuals, b&w photography, some illustrative graphics and scores and accompanied by 60-minute cassette. Circulation is 1,600, of which 500 are subscriptions. Price is $5/issue or $12 for the paper plus cassette. **Sample postpaid: $4. The magazine pays Canadian contributors $20-50/contribution plus 2-3 free copies. Considers simultaneous submissions. They report on submissions within 2 months, and there is no backlog before publication.**

MY LEGACY (I); OMNIFIC (I); FELICITY (I, IV-Themes); THE BOTTOM LINE, Star Route, Box 21AA, Artemas PA 17211, phone (814)458-3102, editor/publisher Kay Weems. *My Legacy* is a quarterly of poetry and short stories using **36-line, sometimes longer, poems, "anything in good taste" with an Editor's Choice small cash award for each issue. No contributor copies.** Subscription: $12/year; $3.50/copy. *Omnific*, a "family-type" quarterly **publishes poetry only, 36 lines, sometimes longer; readers vote on favorites, small cash award or copy to favorites. Send SASE for guidelines. No contributor copies.** Subscription: $12/year; $3.50/copy. *Felicity*, founded 1988, is a bimonthly newsletter for contests only, 30-40 pgs. They offer 10 contests/month including a monthly theme contest, 36 lines, $3/poem entry fee; other contests may be for theme, form, chapbook, etc. Entry fees vary. Send SASE for guidelines and upcoming themes. Payment for contest winners is small cash award and/or publication. No work is returned. They consider simultaneous submissions and previously published poems. All winning entries including honorable mentions are printed in the newsletter which also publishes market and other contest listings. Subscription: $15/year; $2.50/copy. She also publishes and annual **Christmas anthology. Poetry only, published/unpublished, 36 lines maximum, Christmas themes. Address to "Christmas Anthology." Deadline: August 31.** *The Bottom Line*, founded 1988, is a monthly newsletter listing over 50 publications and contests for writers, reproducing guidelines of still others. Information is presented in chronological order by deadline date, and then in alphabetical order. Circulation 50-100. Subscription: $25/year; $3/copy.

NADA PRESS; BIG SCREAM (II, IV-Themes, bilingual), 2782 Dixie SW, Grandville MI 49418, phone (616)531-1442, founded 1974, poetry editor David Cope. *Big Scream* is "a brief anthology of mostly 'unknown' poets, 1 time per year. We are promoting a **continuation of objectivist tradition begun by Williams and Reznikoff. We want objectivist-based short works; some surrealism; basically short, tight work that shows clarity of perception and care in its making. Also poems in Spanish**—*not* **translations.**" They have published poetry by Antler, James Ruggia, Richard Kostelanetz, Andy Clausen, Allen Ginsberg, John Steinbeck, Jr., Bob Rixon and Janet Cannon. *Big Scream* is 35 pgs., magazine-sized, xerograph on 60 lb. paper, side-stapled, "sent gratis to a select group of poets and editors; **sample copies $3;** subscriptions to institutions $6 per year." He has a print run of 100. He receives "several hundred (not sure)" freelance submissions/year, uses "very few." **Submit after July. Send 10 pgs. Simultaneous submissions OK. No cover letter. "If poetry interests me, I will ask the proper questions of the poet." No dot-matrix. Reports in 1-14 days. Pays as many copies as requested within reason. Comments on rejections "if requested and ms warrants it."** David Cope advises: "Read Pound's essay, "A Retrospect," then Reznikoff and Williams; follow through the Beats and NY School, especially Denby & Berrigan, and you have our approach to writing well in hand. I expect to be publishing *BS* regularly 10 years from now, same basic format."

NAHANT BAY (II), 45 Puritan Rd., Swampscott MA 01907, founded 1990, editors Kalo Clarke and Kim A. Pederson, appears once a year. "**Open submissions; submit a maximum of 6 poems.**" They have recently published poetry by Francis Blessington, Knute Skinner and Ruth Lepson. As a sample the editor selected these lines from "You Never Really Know Until You Know" by Alan Britt:

> *This mysterious knowledge*
> *wears no socks*
> *& dances through my eyes*
> *with a tiny parachute opened above it.*

The handsome magazine contains mostly free verse (some selections more structured than others) and is digest-sized, 60-100 pgs., saddle-stapled, professionally printed, with matte card cover, b&w photos and illustrations. Subscription: $4. **Sample postpaid: $4. Reports in 3-6 months. Pays 1 copy.**

NANCY'S MAGAZINE (IV-Theme), P.O. Box 02108, Columbus OH 43202, founded 1983, editor Nancy Bonnell-Kangas, who describes her publication as a "post-modern *Reader's Digest.*" **She wants to see "experimental narrative poetry and poems that create their own logic. Guarded cynicism and informed optimism are always appreciated."** She has published work by Simon Perchik and William Talcott. As a sample she selected this complete poem, "Rhyme: Love: Shadow" by George Myers Jr.:

> *It went wherever*
> *I went, or would*
> *if only I could go*

The magazine is "**often thematic,** leaning towards literary (without ever getting there)." It appears twice a year, 7 × 8½, 36 pgs., saddle-stapled, offset from various sizes of photoreduced copy (some of it sideways, at angles, or upside down), using cartoons, b&w photos, ads, decorations, with light matte card cover, circulation 1,000, of which 200-250 are shelf sales. **Sample: $3 postpaid. Send SASE for guidelines. Pays 2 copies. Reports in 1 month.** Nancy Bonnell-Kangas advises, "Send work that arrests you."

NASHVILLE HOUSE (IV-Themes), (formerly Depot Press), P.O. Box 60072, Nashville TN 37206, founded 1992, publishes books, **including poetry, relating to the South, Old West and Civil War.** However, they have recently published **Poems of the Divided Self** by Gothic poet Gary William Crawford, introduced by Joey Froehlich. Query with letter only.

‡NASSAU REVIEW (II), English Department, Nassau Community College, Garden City NY 11530, phone (516)222-7186, founded 1964, managing editor Dr. Paul A. Doyle, is an annual "creative and research vehicle for Nassau College faculty and the faculty of other colleges." They want **"serious, intellectual poetry of any form or style. No light verse or satiric verse."** Submissions from adults only. **"No college students; graduate students acceptable."** They have recently published poetry by Patti Tana, Dick Allen, Louis Phillips and David Heyen. As a sample the editor selected these lines from "Chekhov, For Beginners" by Barbara Novack:

> *Chekhov said*
> *throw out the first three pages;*
> *it takes that long*
> *to get to the beginning.*
>
> *And I may say*
> *put aside the first three decades*
> *sweep away their debris*
> *cast off versions of the self . . .*

NR is about 150 pgs., digest-sized, flat-spined. They receive 400-450 poems a year, use approximately 20. Press run is 1,000 for about 1,000 subscribers of which 600 are libraries. **Sample free. No previously published poems or simultaneous submissions. Reads submissions September 1 through December 1 only. Reports in 4-6 months. Pays nothing, not even copies.** They sponsor occasional contests with $100 or $200 poetry awards, depending on college funding. *Nassau Review* contains engaging free verse emphasizing voice in well-crafted lyric and narrative selections. The only drawback here is that poems compete with fiction and critical essays, so competition may be keener than at all-poetry magazines.

THE NATION; LEONORE MARSHALL/NATION PRIZE FOR POETRY; DISCOVERY/THE NATION (III), 72 Fifth Ave., New York NY 10011, founded 1865, poetry editor Grace Schulman. *The Nation's* only **requirement for poetry is "excellence,"** which can be inferred from the list of poets they have published: Marianne Moore, Robert Lowell, W.S. Merwin, Maxine Kumin, Donald Justice, James Merrill, Richard Howard, May Swenson, Garrett Hongo and Amy Clampitt. **Pay for poetry is $1/line, not to exceed 35 lines, plus 1 copy.** The magazine co-sponsors the Leonore Marshall/Nation Prize for Poetry which is an annual award of $7,500 for the outstanding book of poems published in the U.S. in each year; and the "Discovery/The Nation" ($200 each plus a reading at The Poetry Center, 1395 Lexington Ave., New York NY 10128. Submit up to 500 lines by mid-February. Send SASE for application). The editor chose this as a sample from a poem in *The Nation*, 1939, by W.B. Yeats:

Like a long-legged fly upon the stream
His mind moves upon silence.

NATIONAL ENQUIRER (II, IV-Humor), Lantana FL 33464, assistant editor Michele Cooke, is a weekly tabloid, circulation 4,550,000, which uses **short poems, most of them humorous and traditional rhyming verse.** "We want poetry with a message or reflection on the human condition or everyday life. Avoid sending obscure or 'arty' poetry or poetry for art's sake. Also looking for philosophical and inspirational material. Submit seasonal/holiday material at least 3 months in advance." Pays $25 after publication; original material only. Buys first rights.

NATIONAL FORUM (III), 129 Quad Center, Mell St., Auburn University, AL 36849-5306, phone (205)844-4000, founded 1915, editor Stephen W. White, is the quarterly of Phi Kappa Phi using **quality poetry, no "profanity, brutality, love poems."** They have published poetry by William Stafford, Bin Ramke, Mary Oliver and Marge Piercy. As a sample the editor selected these lines from "In Spite of Everything, the Stars" by Edward Hirsch:

Like a stunned piano, like a bucket
of fresh milk flung into the air
or a dozen fists of confetti
suddenly thrown hard at a bride
stepping down from the altar, the stars
surprise the sky.

NF is magazine-sized, professionally printed, 48 pgs., saddle-stapled, with full-color paper cover. They publish about 20 poems of 300 received a year. Their press run is 118,000 with 115,000 subscriptions of which 600 are libraries. Subscription: $10. **Sample postpaid: $1.65. Pays "small honorarium" and 10 copies. Reports in 4-6 weeks, publishes within 9-12 months. Submit 3-5 poems. Reads submissions January and September only.** The editor advises, "Do not send out work that has not been proofread by a couple of helpfully critical friends. Enclose a biographical sketch with recent publications. We do not include comments on rejected work."

NAUGHTY NAKED DREAMGIRLS; NAUGHTY LINGERIE; SEX COMIX (I, IV-Erotic, science fiction, humor), Andrew Roller, P.O. Box 221295, Sacramento CA 95822, phone (916)429-8522, founded 1986, editor Andrew L. Roller. These newsletters appear "approximately monthly." They want **erotic poetry.** Also willing to look at **"weird, occult or sci-fi, or humorous poetry (political or comics related)."** They have published poetry by Cheryl Townsend, P.D. Wilson, William Dockery, Norma Lee Edwards, Arthur Winfield Knight and Scott C. Holstad. As a sample the editor selected these lines:

At first I think
There's a turd in the toilet
I'm not wearing my glasses
And it's one a.m.
I tell my wife,
"You forgot to flush"

The newsletters are saddle-stitched, 16 pgs. Press run 105 for 20 subscribers of which 2 are libraries. **Sample postpaid: $2 US, $3 Canada, $4 foreign. Pays 1 copy ("2 for regulars"). Acquires first North American serial rights. Reports "at once."** Reviews books of poetry, "the shorter, the better. Don't send me more than a few pages of poems. I'm getting more poems than I can handle right now. I prefer to send 'rejected' poems on to other potential publishers and respond with an informative letter on self-publishing."

NAZARENE INTERNATIONAL HEADQUARTERS; STANDARD; WONDER TIME; LISTEN; BREAD; TEENS TODAY; HERALD OF HOLINESS (IV-Religious, children), 6401 The Paseo, Kansas City MO 64131, phone (816)333-7000. Each of the magazines published by the Nazarenes has a separate editor, focus and audience. *Standard*, circulation 177,000, is a weekly **inspirational "story paper" with Christian leisure reading for adults. Send SASE for free sample and guidelines. Uses a poem each week. Submit maximum of 5, maximum of 50 lines each. Pays 25¢ a line.** *Wonder Time*, poetry editors Evelyn Beals and Cathy Haworth, a publication of the Children's Ministries Department, Church of the Nazarene, **"is committed to reinforcement of the Biblical concepts taught in the Sunday School curriculum, using poems 4-8 lines, simple, with a message, easy to read, for 1st and 2nd graders. It should not deal with much symbolism."** As a sample the editors selected this poem, "God's Word," by Joyce Lindberg:

The Bible stories help me know
What God wants me to do.
I'll learn the lessons from God's Word,
And I'll obey it too.

Close-up

Art Homer
Poet/Coeditor
The Nebraska Review

"At the Heartland Cafe"

Carol says "His automatic's really cool,"
blows her coffee "but that .38
is one sweet weapon." She got state
twice, went to nationals. "Only a fool
like Gerry forgets to tighten his scope down—
sighting it in and it damn near tore
his nose off. God, what a mess. He wore
that gauze like Nicholson in China Town."

But Sandy's not so sure. "You know my Jeff
wakes up hard. I wouldn't want to scare
him awake. If I just snap my fingers,
he jumps up and throws the covers off.
He says if the kids come in there,
'Hell, I won't shoot any two-foot intruders.' "

Photo by Tina Stevens

Art Homer's poems stretch content and structure to their limits. Observe how the rhyme above doesn't detract from the overheard conversation. Homer takes risks; he knows the direct quotation is one of the most difficult sounds to capture in a poem (let alone in a Petrarchan sonnet), but that doesn't deter him. Notice, too, how common the setting and how the poet really is the main character, unseen, listening.

As a teacher, Homer listens. As coeditor of *The Nebraska Review*, he listens too. Some writers, he says, feel that they don't have enough experience and must go out and "suffer" to write powerful poems. His advice? "Don't. Stay home. Read a book. Experience will come to you. It will kick open your front door, drag you through your house and work you over in ways you literally cannot imagine. Besides," he adds, "you already have at least as much experience as Emily Dickinson. How much do you need?"

Homer's "experience" begins in the Missouri Ozarks and extends westward. Most of his youth was spent in the Pacific Northwest, where he labored as an animal caretaker, ironworker and on trail crews in Portland, Oregon. He was influenced by the landscape, local dialect and various poets—Gary Snyder, Richard Hugo and Tess Gallagher, to name a few.

Since his college days at Portland State University and the University of Montana, Homer has published poems in dozens of literary and small press magazines. He also has three collections, the last being **Skies of Such Valuable Glass** (Owl Creek Press, 1990).

Homer justifies teaching as a way for him to practice poetry. He says many of the traditional means of support for poets—soldier, inherited wealth, diplomat, priest—were not open to him. "So I try to do a decent job and remember what one of my teachers, Richard Hugo, used to say: 'A good teacher can save a writer a lot of time.' "

Although Homer believes that may be true of learning the craft, he is not so sure teachers can save writers time when it comes to publishing poems. "The awful truth is I know of no secret shortcut," he says. He advises poets to read, write well, submit and devise an easy recordkeeping system. "Poetry, like other good works, is its own reward."

—*Michael J. Bugeja*

Wonder Time is a weekly 4-page leaflet, magazine-sized, newsprint, circulation 37,000. **Sample free for SASE. Reports in 2-3 months. Pays minimum of $3 − 25¢/line, and 4 contributor's copies. Send SASE for guidelines. For *Listen, Bread, Teens Today* and *Herald of Holiness*,** write individually for guidelines and samples.

NCASA JOURNAL; (NEWSLETTER OF THE NATIONAL COALITION AGAINST SEXUAL ASSAULT) (IV-Themes, social issues, women/feminism), Suite 500, 123 S. Seventh, Springfield IL 62701, founded 1986, editor Becky Bradway. Appears 3 times/year using **"well-written poetry by survivors of rape, child sexual abuse and incest. Poems may deal with aspects of the sexual assault experience or recovery from sexual assault."** It is 36 pgs., magazine-sized, professionally printed, with matte card cover, saddle-stapled. Press run 700 for 600 subscribers. Subscription: $20. **Sample: $4 postpaid. Pays 3 copies. Acquires first rights. Previously published poems and simultaneous submissions OK.** Accepts reviews of books relevant to feminism and the anti-rape movement − up to 1,000 words. The editor says, *"NCASA Journal* is a nationally circulated magazine. Its 'Voices of Survivors' section includes poetry and fiction by survivors of sexual assault. While not a requirement, contributors are encouraged to subscribe ($12/year) or join NCASA ($25/year)."

NEBO: A LITERARY JOURNAL (II), English Dept., Arkansas Tech University, Russellville AR 72801-2222, phone (501)968-0256, founded 1982, poetry editor Michael Ritchie, appears in May and December. Regarding poetry they say, **"We accept all kinds, all styles, all subject matters and will publish a longer poem if it is outstanding. We are especially interested in formal poetry."** They have published poetry by Jack Butler, Turner Cassity, Wyatt Prunty, Charles Martin, Julia Randall and Brenda Hillman. *Nebo* is digest-sized, 50-70 pgs., professionally printed on quality matte stock with matte card cover. Press run "varies." Subscription: $5. **Sample: $5 postpaid. Simultaneous submissions OK. "Please no onion skin or offbeat colors." Do not submit mss between May 1 and August 15 of each year. Reports in 1 week-3 months. Pays 1 copy.** Editor comments on rejections **"if the work has merit but requires revision and resubmission. We do all we can to help."** Reviews books of poetry.

THE NEBRASKA REVIEW; TNR AWARDS (II), ASH 212, University of Nebraska, Omaha NE 68182-0324, phone (402)554-2771, founded 1973, coeditor Art Homer, is a semiannual literary magazine publishing fiction and poetry with occasional essays. The editor wants **"Lyric poetry from 10-200 lines, preference being for under 100 lines. Subject matter is unimportant, as long as it has some. Poets should have mastered form, meaning poems should have form, not simply 'demonstrate' it." He doesn't want to see "concrete, inspirational, didactic or merely political poetry."** They have recently published poetry by David Patricia Goedecke, Mary Swander, Roger Weingarten and Billy Collins. As a sample, he selected these lines from "The Twins Visit a Farm" by Mary Crow:

> *The heavy black bulk of the draft horse*
> *lay in the heat, circled by lime. Too huge*
> *to bury, it was left for flies, night animals.*
> *We walked around the gleaming hill*
> *of its flanks, the tulip-blue nostrils,*
> *the tiny terrain of the pink gums,*
> *the belly mushrooming sweetness.*

The magazine is 6 × 9, nicely printed, 60 pgs., with flat-spined, glossy card cover It is a publication of the Writer's Workshop at the University of Nebraska. Circulation is 400, of which 260 are subscriptions and 80 go to libraries. Price per issue is $3.50, subscription $6/year. **Sample available for $2 postpaid. Pay is 2 copies and 1-year subscription. Acquires first North American serial rights. "Clean typed copy strongly preferred. Dot-matrix strongly discouraged." Reads submissions August 15 through March 31 only. Reporting time is 3-4 months and time to publication 3-6 months.** This magazine is on its way to carving a niche in the lit world. It continues to publish excellent free and formal verse by known and unknown writers, and its design is improving with each issue. The TNR Awards of $300 each in poetry and fiction are published in the spring issue. Entry fee: $6 subscription. You can enter as many times as desired. Deadline November 30. The editor says, "Your first allegiance is to the poem. Publishing will come in time, but it will always be less than you feel you deserve. Therefore, don't look to publication as a reward for writing well; it has no relationship."

NEGATIVE CAPABILITY; NEGATIVE CAPABILITY PRESS; EVE OF ST. AGNES COMPETITION (II), 62 Ridgelawn Rd. E, Mobile AL 36608-2465, founded 1981, poetry editor Sue Walker. *Negative Capability* is a tri-quarterly of verse, fiction, commentary, music and art. The press publishes broadsides, chapbooks, perfect-bound paperbacks and hardbacks. They want **both contemporary and traditional poetry. "Quality has its own specifications − length and form."** They have recently published poetry by John Brugaletta, Rita Dove, Richard Moore, Marge Piercy, William Stafford and John Updike. As a sample Sue Walker selected these lines from "Flakey Blake" by Dorothy Moseley Sutton:

> *I asked Billy Blake*
> *to come out and play with me*
> *and while we was out there playin'*
> *he said he seen a buncha angels*
> *settin' up in a tree.*
> *There wasn't no angels*
> *settin' up in a tree.*
> *I ain't playin with that flakey Blake no more.*

The editor says, "Reaching irritably after a few facts will not describe *Negative Capability*. Read it to know what quality goes to form creative achievement. Shakespeare had negative capability; do you?" In its short history this journal has indeed achieved a major prominence on our literary scene. It is a flat-spined, elegantly printed, digest-sized, format of 130+ pgs., glossy card color cover with art, circulation 1,000. About 60 pgs. of each issue are devoted to poetry. Subscription: $12; per copy: $5. They receive about 1,200 freelance submissions per year, use 350. **Sample: $4 postpaid. Reads submissions September 1 through May 30 only. Reports in 6-8 weeks. Pays 2 copies. Acquires first rights. Send SASE for guidelines. For book publication, query with 10-12 samples and "brief letter with major publications, significant contributions, awards. We like to know a person as well as their poem." Replies to queries in 3-4 weeks, to submissions (if invited) in 6-8 weeks. Photocopy, dot-matrix OK. Payment arranged with authors. Editor sometimes comments on rejections.** Reviews books of poetry. They offer an Annual Eve of St. Agnes Competition with major poets as judges.

NEW CHICANO WRITING (IV-Bilingual/ethnic), Dept. of Spanish & Portuguese, Mod. Lang. Bldg. 545, Univ. of Arizona, Tucson AZ 85721, founded 1991, phone (602)621-7347, editor Chuck Tatum, is an annual anthology, uses **"poetry in Spanish or English or a combination of the two languages. Send an original and a photocopy of ms and return postage."** It is 6×9, flat-spined, hardback and paperback, professionally designed. Press run is 1,000. **Sample: $20-25. Pays contributor's copies and a small fee. Editorial board reports in 3-5 months. Editors seldom comment on rejections. Cover letter required.**

NEW CICADA (IV-Form), 40-11 Kubo, Hobara, Fukushima, 960-06 Japan, phone 0245-75-4226, founded 1984, editor Tadao Okazaki. *New Cicada* is "the first and only magazine introducing the universal definition of haiku that is applicable to all languages. Of all existing Japanese haiku magazines in English, has the longest history of publication." As a sample, the editor selected these lines of his own:

> *Releasing a tune*
> *into the night filled with*
> *autumn stars*

The purpose of the magazine, which appears twice yearly in March and September, is "to introduce to the world, and define, haiku." Volumes 1 through 5 of *Cicada* were published in Toronto, Canada, by Eric W. Amann, founding editor, and later by the Haiku Society of Canada. The digest-sized publication is offset from dot-matrix copy with a b&w frontispiece; one-color matte card cover, saddle-stapled. Price is $4/issue, $6 for a 1-year subscription. **Sample: $4 postpaid by US personal check or 7 international reply coupons. The editor requests a self-addressed postcard and an IRC for reports. No mss returned. It will take up to approximately 6 months to get a report. No payment in any form is offered for published poems. All rights revert to the author after publication.** The editor who says he "introduced the universal definition of haiku for the first time" maintains that "(1) the traditional Japanese haiku is recited in an iambic trimeter—tetrameter—trimeter triplet form, and is structurally essentially a ballad and (2) the free-verse (jiyuh-litsu) haiku in any language in the three lines (triplet) or less should be classified as a legitimate form of haiku." The editor says, "The old definition of haiku as a form of syllabic verse is wrong. Haiku form is a Japanese ballad."

THE NEW CRITERION (II), The Foundation for Cultural Review, Inc., 850 7th Ave., New York NY 10019, poetry editor Robert Richman, is a monthly (except July and August) review of ideas and the arts, 7×10″, flat-spined, 90+ pgs., which uses poetry of high literary quality. They have published poems by James Ulmer, Alan Shapiro, Elizabeth Spires and Herbert Morris. **Sample: $4.75 plus postage.**

NEW DELTA REVIEW; THE EYSTER PRIZE (II), English Dept., Louisiana State University, Baton Rouge LA 70803, editor Janet Wondra, who says, "We call ourselves a 'breakthrough magazine'; we publish work of merit by writers who for one reason or another are still slightly outside the mainstream. Most of them are younger writers who are building a reputation. We are *wide open:* poets who are brave enough to take chances and fly in the face of the poetic conventions of the late twentieth century are welcome." They have recently published poetry by Laura Kasischke, Eve Shelnutt, Sue Standing, David Trinidad and Gary Duehr. *NDR* appears twice a year, 6×9 flat-spined, 90-120 pgs., typeset and printed on quality stock with glossy card cover with art. Its press run is 500, with 100 subscriptions of which 20 are libraries, the rest for shelf sales. Subscription: $7. **Sample: $4 postpaid. Pays 2 copies. Acquires first North American serial rights. Photocopy OK, no dot matrix, simultaneous submissions, or previously published poems. Reports in 1-3 months. Mss read in summer.** Poetry editor "sometimes" comments on rejections. "Often I will return a piece and ask for revision." Also accepts reviews and interviews. Reviews books of poetry in "no more than 2,000 words," single- or multi-book format. The Eyster Prize of $50 is awarded to the best story and best poem in each issue.

NEW DIRECTIONS PUBLISHING CORPORATION (III, IV-Translations), 80 Eighth Ave., New York NY 10011, founded 1936, poetry editor, Peter Glassgold. New Directions is "a small publisher of 20th-Century literature with an emphasis on the experimental," publishing about 36 paperback and hardback titles each year. **"We are looking for highly unusual, literary, experimental poetry. We can't use traditional poetry, no matter how accomplished. Ninety-five percent of the time we publish poets who have built up a reputation in the literary magazines and journals. It is generally not financially feasible for us to take on unknown poets."** They have published poetry by William Carlos Williams, Ezra Pound, Denise Levertov, Jerome Rothenberg, Robert Creeley, Michael McClure, Kenneth Rexroth, H.D., Robert Duncan, Stevie Smith, David Antin, Hayden Carruth, George Oppen, Dylan Thomas, Lawrence Ferlinghetti, Jimmy Santiago Baca, Rosmarie Waldrop and Gary Snyder. **"Please send a sampling of about 10 typed, photocopied poems, preferably not a simultaneous submission." They look at all submissions but "chances are slight." Reports on submissions in 4 months; may be 2 years until publication. Terms for book publication "all depend."** To see samples, try the library or purchase from their catalog (available), local bookstores or their distributor, W.W. Norton. New Directions advises, "Getting published is not easy, but the best thing to do is to work on being published in the magazines and journals, thus building up an audience. Once the poet has an audience, the publisher will be able to sell the poet's books. Avoid vanity publishers and read a lot of poetry."

NEW EARTH PUBLICATIONS; CO-PRESS; THE UTOPIAN WORKER (IV-Spiritual, political, translations), P.O. Box 4790, Berkeley CA 94704, phone (415)549-0575, founded 1990, editor Clifton Ross, publishes **"book-length collections (up to 96 pgs.) dealing with the struggle for peace and justice, well-crafted poetry, prose and translations. Some publications are author subsidized."** They publish 1-2 paperbacks, 2-3 chapbooks/year. **Reports on queries in 2 weeks, on mss in 6 weeks. Pays 10% royalties or 10% of press run.** Also publishes *The Utopian Worker*, a biannual magazine of revolutionary spiritual culture.

NEW ENGLAND REVIEW (III), Middlebury College, Middlebury VT 05753, phone (802)388-3711, ext. 5075, founded 1978, editor T.R. Hummer, associate editor Devon Jerslid, *New England Review* is a prestigious literary quarterly, 6×9, 160+ pgs., flat-spined, elegant make-up and printing on heavy stock, glossy cover with art. Poets published include Toi Derricotte, Albert Goldbarth, Norman Dubie, Philip Booth and Carol Frost. Subscription: $18. **Sample postpaid: $4. Pays. Reports in 6-8 weeks.** Editor T.R. Hummer is one of the best in the business. (He's edited at *Quarterly West* and *Kenyon Review*.) But his standards are high and, if he has any fault, it is that he seriously considers submissions and that virtue can lead to delays in response time. Nonetheless, *NER* is exciting to read. You might want to invest in a sample copy because Hummer, as all good editors are wont to do, has changed its look and contents.

‡NEW ERA MAGAZINE (II, IV-Religious, teen/young adult), 50 E. North Temple St., Salt Lake City UT 84150, phone (801)240-2951, founded 1971, managing editor Richard M. Romney, appears monthly. *New Era* is an "official publication for youth of The Church of Jesus Christ of Latter-day Saints; it contains feature stories, photo stories, fiction, news, etc." They want **short verse in any form—must pertain to teenage LDS audience (religious and teenage themes). No sing-songy doggerel, gushy love poems or forced rhymes.** As a sample we selected these lines from "Open Windows" by Lani Berry:

> No "to dos" on
> My list. Sit
> And watch.
> It would be so
> Nice to see your face
> Instead of
> Your words.

New Era is 50 pgs., approximately 8×10½, 4-color offset, saddle-stitched, quality stock, top-notch art and graphics, no ads. They receive 200-300 submissions, purchase 2-5%. Press run is 220,000 for 205,000 subscribers, 10,000 shelf sales. Single copy: 75¢; subscription: $8/year. **Sam-**

ple: 75¢ plus postage. **No previously published poems or simultaneous submissions. Send no more than 5 poems at one time.** Time between acceptance and publication is a year or longer. "We publish one poem each month next to our photo of the month." **Sometimes comments on rejections. Send SASE for writer's guidelines. Reports in 6-8 weeks. Pays $10 minimum. Buys all rights. "LDS church retains rights to publish again in church publications — all other rights returned."** They also offer an annual contest — including poetry — for active members of the LDS church between ages 12-23. Poetry entries should consist of one entry of 6-10 different original poems reflecting LDS values, none of which exceeds 50 lines. Deadline: January. Winners receive either a partial scholarship to BYU or Ricks College or a cash award. Send SASE for rules. The editor says, "Study the magazine before submitting. We're a great market for beginners, but you must understand Mormons to write well for us."

NEW HOPE INTERNATIONAL (II), 20 Werneth Ave., Gee Cross, Hyde, Cheshire SK14 5NL United Kingdom, founded 1969, editor Gerald England, includes *"NHI Writing,* **publishing poetry, short fiction, translations, artwork, literary essays and reports. All types of poetry from traditional to avant-garde, from haiku to long poems.** *NHI Review* **carries reviews of books, magazines, cassettes, CDs, records, PC software etc. Special Edition Chapbooks with a theme or individual collections also included."** They have recently published poetry by Mary Ann Henn, Joan Payne Kincaid, Edward Mycue, Sheldon Young, James Kickup and Maureen Weldon. As a sample the editor selected these lines from "Lions" by Neil K. Henderson:

> *Yet still you hear the lions now,*
> *And still you can't recall*
> *Who let the lions in the door*
> *And left them in the hall.*

The digest-sized magazine, 36-40 pgs., is printed offset-litho from computer typesetting, saddle-stapled, color card cover, using b&w artwork. Circulation 600 for 300 subscriptions of which 25 are libraries. $25 for 6 issues (*NHI Writing, NHI Review* and **S.E. Chapbooks** as published). **Sample postpaid: $5 cash (add $5 to cover bank charges if paying by check). Reports "usually fairly prompt, but sometimes up to 4 months." Pays 1 copy. Acquires first British serial rights. Put name and address on each sheet; not more than 6 at a time; simultaneous submissions** *not* **encouraged. Photocopy OK (if clear); dot-matrix OK (near letter quality if possible). Translations should include copy of original. Full guidelines available for IRC (3 for airmail). Send 1 IRC for reply if return of mss not required. For chapbooks, query first.** The editor advises "Long lists of previous publications do not impress; perceptive, interesting, fresh writing indicative of a live, thinking person makes this job worthwhile."

‡**NEW HORIZONS POETRY CLUB (II, IV-Membership)**, Box 5561, Chula Vista CA 92012, phone (619)474-4715, founded 1984, poetry editor Alex Stewart. This organization offers poetry contests of various sorts for experienced writers, publishing winners in an anthology. They also offer newsletters and critiques and publish anthologies of members' poetry. Membership (includes 4 newsletters): $10/year. **"We expect poets to know technique, to be familiar with traditional forms and to be able to conform to requirements regarding category, style and length and to show originality, imagery and craftsmanship. Nothing amateurish, trite or in poor taste."** They have recently published poetry by Alice Mackenzie Swaim, Glenna Holloway and Patricia Lawrence. Prizes in their Annual Poetry Day Contest are "$250 and down. We offer other cash awards, prizes and trophies, and certificates for honorable mentions." 50 free anthologies, $100 cash and trophy for "mini-manuscript" winners. Entry fees are $5/2 poems, $10/5 poems. Alex Stewart offers criticism for $6/poem, $14/3 poems up to 25 lines. She says, "Poets need to study technique before *rushing to get published! (Where* is what counts!) The current trend seems to be a healthy blend of traditional forms and comprehensible free verse." NHPC publishes 3 books annually, 2 in the NHPC Poets' Series (4 poets/book) and 1 anthology of prizewinning and selected poems from the semiannual contests. (Book list, including **The Poet's Art,** the editor's complete handbook on the craft of poetry writing, available on request.)

‡**THE NEW KENT QUARTERLY (I)**, Box 26, Student Activities, Kent State University, Kent OH 44240, is a student-run, annual literary and art magazine of the KSU main campus, **open to all forms of poetry.** They have recently published poetry by Lyn Lifshin. The editor says it is 40-50 pgs., 8½×11, with art and photography throughout. They receive 400-450 poems a year, accept 40 or 50. Press run is 2,000, most distributed to KSU students. **No previously published poems; simultaneous submissions OK. Reads submissions September 1 through March 30 only. Published in April. Seldom comments on rejections. Reports in 1 month or so ("depending on school calendar"). Pays 1 copy. "All rights revert to author 60 days after publication."** The editor adds, "We are also interested in any b&w reproducible artwork or photographs that might relate to the work."

‡THE NEW LAUREL REVIEW (II, IV-Translations), 828 Lesseps St., New Orleans LA 70117, founded 1971, editor Lee Meitzen Grue, "is an independent nonprofit literary magazine dedicated to fine art. Each issue contains poetry, translations, literary essays, reviews of small press books, and visual art." They want "poetry with strong, accurate imagery. We have no particular preference in style. We try to be eclectic. No more than 3 poems in a submission." They have recently published poetry by Jane McClellan, Kalamu Ya Salaam, Melody Davis, Sue Walker and Keith Cartwright. As a sample the editor selected these lines by Quo Vadis Gex-Breaux:

> She had a kind of classy coarseness
> like raw silk
> a kind of open earthiness
> without being dirt
> a way of saying things
> that made them seem something
> more than she meant
> (sometimes a little less)

The *Review* is 6×9, laser printed, 115 pgs., original art on cover, accepts 30 poems of 300 mss received. It has a circulation of 500, subscription: $9; per copy: $9. **Sample (back issue) postpaid $5. Guidelines for SASE. Submit 3-5 poems with SASE and a short note with previous publications. Accepts simultaneous submissions. Reads submissions September 1 through May 30 only. Reports on submissions in 3 months, publishes in 8-10 months. Pays contributor's copies. Acquires first rights.** Reviews books of poetry in 1,000 words, single or multi-book format.

NEW LETTERS; NEW LETTERS POETRY PRIZE (II), University of Missouri-Kansas City, Kansas City MO 64110, phone (816)235-1168, founded 1934 as *University Review*, became *New Letters* in 1971, managing editor Bob Stewart, editor James McKinley, "is dedicated to publishing the best short fiction, best contemporary poetry, literary articles, photography and artwork by both established writers and new talents." They want "**contemporary writing of all types—free verse poetry preferred, short works are more likely to be accepted than very long ones.**" They have published poetry by Joyce Carol Oates, Hayden Carruth, John Frederick Nims, Louise Glück, Louis Simpson, Vassar Miller and John Tagliabue. The flat-spined, professionally printed quarterly, glossy 2-color cover with art, 6×9, uses about 65 (of 120+) pgs. of poetry in each issue, circulation 1,845 with 1,520 subscriptions of which about 40% are libraries. They receive about 7,000 submissions per year, use less than 1%, have a 6-month backlog. Subscription: $17. **Sample postpaid: $5. Send no more than 6 poems at once, no simultaneous submissions. "We strongly prefer original typescripts rather than photocopy or dot-matrix. We don't read between May 15 and October 15. No query needed." They report in 4-10 weeks, pay a small fee plus 2 copies.** Occasionally James McKinley comments on rejections. The New Letters Poetry Prize of $750 is given annually for a group of 3-6 poems, entry fee $10 (check payable to New Letters Literary Awards). Deadline: May 15. They also publish occasional anthologies, selected and edited by McKinley.

NEW MADRID (II), Dept. of English, Murray State Univ., Murray KY 40071, phone (502)762-2401, poetry editor Dr. Sarah Wood, is a literary annual using poetry with "**no restrictions on form or content.**" Their first issue, early 1991, included poetry by Christopher Davis, Bill Knott and Laura Mullen. The editor describes it as 140-220 pgs. with glossy cover. **Pays 2 copies.**

NEW METHODS: THE JOURNAL OF ANIMAL HEALTH TECHNOLOGY (IV-Specialized/animals), P.O. Box 22605, San Francisco CA 94122-0605, phone (415)664-3469, founded as *Methods* in 1976, poetry editor Ronald S. Lippert, AHT, is a "monthly networking service in the animal field, open forum, active in seeking new avenues of knowledge for our readers, combining animal professionals under one roof." They want poetry which is "**animal related but not cutesy.**" They get few submissions, but if they received more of quality, they would publish more poetry. They publish a maximum of one poem in each monthly issue, circulation 5,600 to subscribers, of which over 73 are libraries. Subscription: $29. **Sample: $2.90. A listing of all back issues and the topics covered is available for $5. Reports in 1-2 months. Double space with one-inch margins, include dated cover letter. Everything typed. Guidelines are available for SASE. Pays complimentary copies. Comment on rejected mss? "Always!"** Reviews books of poetry of "all lengths pertaining to our subject matter." Ronald Lippert advises, "Keep up with current events."

NEW MEXICO HUMANITIES REVIEW (II, IV-Regional), Humanities Dept., New Mexico Tech, So-corro NM 87801, phone (505)835-5200, founded 1978, editors Jerry Bradley, John Rothfork and Lou Thompson, *NMHR* is published twice a year, invites mss "**designed for a general academic readership and those that pursue Southwestern themes or those using interdisciplinary methods.**" There are no restrictions as to type of poetry; "*NMHR* publishes first class, literary poetry," but does not want "sentimental verse, shallow, pointlessly rhymed ideas." Poets published include George Garrett,

Ralph Mills, Jr., Fred Chappell, Peter Wild and Walter McDonald. The review is digest-sized, 150 pp., printed by offset on white stock, with an embossed, one-color matte card cover, flat-spined; there are graphics and ads. Circulation is 650, of which 350 are subscriptions; other copies are sold at poetry readings, writers' workshops, etc. Price per issue is $6, subscription $11/year. **Reads submissions January 2 through December 10 only.** *NMHR* **pays one year's subscription. Acquires first serial rights. Reports in 6 weeks, 6 months between acceptance and publication. No simultaneous submissions.** Reviews books of poetry in 750 words, single or multi-book format. Also has a poetry contest supported by Witter Bynner Foundation for Poetry. Best three poems from two issues. Current issues being judged by Poet Laureate Mark Strand. Awards: 1st prize $500, 2nd $300, 3rd $200.

NEW ORLEANS POETRY JOURNAL PRESS (II), 2131 General Pershing St., New Orleans LA 70115, phone (504)891-3458, founded 1956, publisher/editor Maxine Cassin, coeditor Charles deGravelles. **"We prefer to publish relatively new and/or little-known poets of unusual promise or those inexplicably neglected—'the real thing.' " They do not want to see "cliché or doggerel, anything incomprehensible or too derivative, or workshop exercises." Query first. They do not accept freelance submissions for chapbooks, which are flat-spined paperbacks.** They have published books by Vassar Miller, Everette Maddox, Charles Black and Martha McFerren. Their most recent book is **Illuminated Manuscript** by Malaika Favorite. **The editors report on queries in 2-3 months, mss in the same time period, if solicited. Simultaneous submissions will possibly be accepted, and they have no objection to photocopied mss. Pay is in author's copies, usually 50 to 100.** Ms. Cassin does not subsidy publish at present and does not offer grants or awards. For aspiring poets, she quotes the advice Borges received from his father: "1) Read as much as possible! 2) Write only when you *must*, and 3) Don't rush into print!" As a small press editor and publisher, she urges poets to read instructions in **Poet's Market** listings with utmost care! She says, "Most poets do not query first surprisingly!"

NEW ORLEANS REVIEW (II), Box 195, Loyola University, New Orleans LA 70118, phone (504)865-2294, founded 1968, poetry editor John Biguenet. It is 100 pgs., perfect-bound, elegantly printed with glossy card cover using a full-color painting. Circulation is 750. **Sample postpaid: $10. Acquires first North American serial rights. Reports in 3 months.**

THE NEW POETS SERIES, INC.; CHESTNUT HILLS PRESS (II), 541 Piccadilly, Baltimore MD 21204, phone (301)830-2863 or 828-0724, founded 1970, editor/director Clarinda Harriss Raymond. The New Poets Series, Inc. brings out **first books by promising new poets. They want "excellent, fresh, nontrendy, literate, intelligent poems. Any form (including traditional), any style. No poetry riding any one particular political, social, sexual or religious hobbyhorse."** Provides 20 copies to the author, the sales proceeds going back into the corporation to finance the next volume (usual press run: 1,000). "It has been successful in its effort to provide these new writers with a national distribution; in fact, The New Poets Series was recently named an Outstanding Small Press by the prestigious Pushcart Awards Committee, which judges some 5,000 small press publications annually." Chestnut Hills Press publishes author-subsidized books—"High quality work only, however. CHP has achieved a reputation for prestigious books, printing only the top 10% of mss CHP and NPS receive." The New Poets Series also publishes an occasional anthology drawn from public reading series. They have recently published books by Nuala Archer, Richard Fein, Shelley Scott, Carole Glasser Langille, Peter Wessel, Charles Stuart Roberts, Elaine Erickson, Steven Sills, Gail Wronsky and Tony Esolen. Clarinda Harriss Raymond selected "Calling Canada," a complete poem by Irish writer Medbh McGuckian, as a sample:

> I talk to the darkness as if to a daughter
> Or something that once pressed from inside
> Like a street of youth. My striped notebook
> Is just a dress over my body, so I will waken
> At a touch, or for no reason at all. In it
> I learn how to cut into other people's dreams,
> How to telephone them Paris-style and how
> Like sunshine, a tenderness roughened
> Because there was so little time for snow-months
> To paint my woman's walls into sea.

Query with 10 samples, cover letter giving publication credits and bio. Reports in 6 weeks-6 months. Simultaneous submissions, photocopies OK. Editor sometimes comments briefly on rejections. Mss "are circulated to an editorial board of professional, publishing poets. NPS is slightly backlogged, but the best 10% of the mss it receives are automatically eligible for Chestnut Hills Press consideration," a subsidy arrangement. **Send $4 for a sample volume.**

THE NEW PRESS LITERARY QUARTERLY; THE NEW PRESS POETRY CONTEST (I, II), 53-35 Hollis Ct. Blvd., Flushing NY 11365, founded 1984, poetry editor Harry Ellison, is a quarterly magazine using poems **"less than 200 lines, accessible; imaginative. No doggerel, sentimentality."** They have published poetry by Les Bridges, Bruce Isaacson, Barbara Weekes and Robert Parody. As a sample the editor selected these lines by R. Nikolas Macioci:

> *a conversation he has*
> *with himself as he thinks now*
> *of hinges he must oil*
> *before old doors will open*
> *quietly onto another year's*
> *garden and the scent*
> *of newly spaded soil.*

It is magazine-sized, 28 pgs., desktop published, with glossy cover, saddle-stapled. They accept about 10% of 700 poems received/year. Press run 1,000 for 200 subscribers of which 1 is a library, 800 shelf sales. Subscription: $15. **Sample postpaid: $3. Pays 3 copies. Acquires first-time rights. Reports in 2 months.** The New Press Poetry Contest is semiannual, deadlines are January and July 1, entry fee of $4 for up to 3 poems or 200 lines, has prizes of $120, $60 and ten 2-year subscriptions.

THE NEW QUARTERLY (II, IV-Regional), ELPP University of Waterloo, Waterloo, Ontario N2L 3G1 Canada, phone (519)885-1211, ext. 2837, founded 1981, managing editor Mary Merikle, is a "literary quarterly—new directions in Canadian writing." For the poetry they want, the editors have **"no preconceived conception—usually Canadian work, poetry capable of being computer typeset—4½" line length typeset lines. No greeting card verse."** The editor describes it as 120 pgs., flat-spined, 6 × 8½, with a photograph on the cover, no graphics or art, some ads. Of 2,000 poems received/year, they use 100. Press run is 600 for 300 subscriptions (10 of them libraries) and additional shelf sales. Subscription: $15 (add $2 for US or overseas subscriptions). **Sample: $4 Canadian, $4 US postpaid. Send SASE for guidelines. Pays $20/poem plus 3 copies. Submit no more than 5. Reports in 3-6 months. No comments on rejections of poetry.**

THE NEW RENAISSANCE (II, IV-Translations, bilingual), 9 Heath Rd., Arlington MA 02174, founded 1968, poetry editor Stanwood Bolton. *the new renaissance* is "intended for the 'renaissance' person, the generalist rather than the specialist. Seeks to publish the best new writing, to offer a forum for articles of public concern, to feature established non-mainstream as well as emerging visual artists and to highlight interest in neglected writers and artists in its essay/review section." They have recently published poetry by Ann Struthers and R. Busailah. As a sample, the editor selected these lines from "Fish Kill" by Daniel Lusk:

> *The newsman in my radio sounds amazed*
> *at fish turned belly up with cold*
> *in some southeastern bay. He should float*
> *past the banks of Market Street—these days*
> *a man is hovering in a cloud*
> *above a steaming manhole with a plastic tarp*
> *around him like a broiling tarpon*
> *or a praying saint . . . .*

tnr is flat-spined, professionally printed on heavy stock, glossy, color cover, 144-206 pgs., using 18-40 pgs. of poetry in each issue; usual print run 1,600 for 790 subscribers of which approximately 132 are libraries. Subscriptions: $15.50/3 issues US, $16 Canada, $17.50 Europe and Mexico, $18.50 all others. **"We're an unsponsored, independent small litmag."** Contributors are expected to buy copies—$5 for an '82 issue or $6.50 for an '87 or '88 issue; current issue $9. **"For guidelines, send $5 and we'll send an '82 issue and copy of guidelines."** They receive about 600 poetry submissions/year, use about 22, have about a 32-month backlog. **"Will be reading manuscripts from January 2 through June 30, 1993." Reports in 3-6 months. Pays $13-20, more for the occasional longer poem, plus 1 copy. Buys all rights.** Returns rights provided *tnr* retains rights for any *tnr* collection, anthology, etc. Reviews books of poetry in 4-5 pgs., single format; 5-11 pgs., multi-book. "We believe that poets should not only be readers but lovers of poetry. We're looking for 'literalists of the imagination—imaginary gardens with real toads in them.' **Our range is from traditionalist poetry to post-modern, experimental (the latter only occasionally, though) and street poetry. We also like the occasional 'light' poem and, of course, translations. We're especially interested in the individual voice. We aren't interested in greeting card verse or prose set in poetic forms."**

THE NEW REPUBLIC (II), 1220 19th St. NW, Washington DC 20036, phone (202)331-7494, founded 1914, poetry editor Mary Jo Salter. *The New Republic*, a weekly journal of opinion, is magazine-sized, printed on slick paper, 42 pgs., saddle-stapled with 4-color cover. Subscription: $69.97/year. Back issues available for $3.50 postpaid. **They provide no submission or payment information.**

NEW RIVERS PRESS; MINNESOTA VOICES PROJECT, INC. (II, IV-Regional, translations), Suite 910, 420 N. 5th St., Minneapolis MN 55401, founded 1968, publishes collections of poetry, translations of contemporary literature, collections of short fiction, and is also involved in publishing **Minnesota regional literary material. Write for free catalog or send SASE for guidelines/inquiries. New and emerging authors living in Iowa, Minnesota, North and South Dakota and Wisconsin are eligible for the Minnesota Voices Project. Book-length manuscripts of poetry, short fiction, novellas or familiar essays are all accepted. Send SASE for entry form. Winning authors receive a stipend of $500 plus publication by New Rivers. Second and subsequent printings of works will allow 15% royalties for author.**

‡NEW VOICES IN POETRY AND PROSE; NEW VOICES SPRING/FALL COMPETITIONS; NEW VOICES BOOKS (I), P.O. Box 52196, Shreveport LA 71135, founded 1990, editor Cheryl White, is a semiannual that publishes new poets and writers and reviews collected works. **"All types of poetry welcome. However, prefer poetry that makes a statement about the emotions of the writer."** The editor says it is 12-16 pgs., 8½ × 11. Press run is 500 for 100 subscribers. Subscription: $8. **Sample postpaid: $5.** "All submissions are also considered for annual anthology." **Seldom comments on rejections. Send SASE for guidelines. Reports in approximately 1 month. Pays 1 copy.** Offers semiannual poetry and short fiction competitions. Small entry fees. Cash prizes. New Voices Books publishes 2 paperbacks/ year through their annual poetry collection competition. **Entry fee required. Send SASE for rules.** "Prefer poet to have been published in magazine." **Pays $300 honorarium and 10 author's copies. Query for samples.**

NEW WELSH REVIEW (II, IV-Ethnic), 49, Park Place, Cardiff CF1 3AT Wales, United Kingdom, phone 0222-665529, founded 1988, editor Robin Reeves. *NWR* is a quarterly publishing articles, short stories and poems. They have published poetry by Joseph Clancy, Gillian Clarke, Lawrence Ferlingh-etti, John Heath-Stubbs, Les A. Murray, Peter Porter and Anne Stevenson. The editor describes it as 88 pgs., glossy paper in three colors, laminated cover, using photographs, graphics and ads. Their press run is 1,100. Subscription: £12. **Sample postpaid: £3.50. Submit double-spaced. No simultaneous submissions or previously published poems. Reports in 6 weeks. Publication within 1-7 months. Editor sometimes comments on rejections.** Reviews books of poetry.

NEW YORK QUARTERLY (II), P.O. Box 693, Old Chelsea Station, New York NY 10113, founded 1969, poetry editor William Packard, appears 3 times a year. They seek to publish "a cross-section of the best of contemporary American poetry" and, indeed, **have a record of publishing many of the best and most diverse of poets**, including W.D. Snodgrass, Gregory Corso, James Dickey and Judson Jerome. It appears in a 6 × 9 flat-spined format, thick, elegantly printed, color glossy cover. Subscription: $15 to 305 Neville Hall, University of Maine, Orono ME 04469. **Submit 3-5 poems. Reports within 2 weeks. Pays copies.** This magazine is sponsored by the National Poetry Foundation, listed under Organizations Useful to Poets.

THE NEW YORKER (III, IV-Translations, humor), 20 W. 43rd St., New York NY 10036, founded 1925, poetry editor Alice Quinn, circulation 640,000, uses **poetry of the highest quality (including translations) and pays top rates. Replies in 6-8 weeks. Mss not read during the summer. Price: $1.75** (available on newsstands).

NEWSLETTER INAGO (I), P.O. Box 26244, Tucson AZ 85726-6244, phone (602)294-7031, founded 1979, poetry editor Del Reitz, is a 4-5 pgs. corner-stapled, monthly newsletter. **"Free verse preferred although other forms will be read. Rhymed poetry must be truly exceptional (nonforced) for consideration. Due to format, 'epic' and monothematic poetry will not be considered. Cause specific, political or religious poetry stands little chance of consideration. A wide range of short poetry, showing the poet's preferably eclectic perspective is best for *NI*. No haiku, please."** They have published poetry by John Brander, Cal Rollins, Jori Ranhand, Sam Silva, Mark J. Isham, Barbara Elovic, Ana Pine, Gail White, Tom O. Jones and Salvatore Galioto. The editor says, "Since editorial taste in poetry especially is such a subjective and narrow thing," a short selection cannot be chosen "with any fairness to either that taste or the poet whose material might be quoted." However, as a sample the editor selected these lines from "Lost Valley" by Shirley Thompson:

> Horses
> a gallop of distant royal
> Rested in subjugation
> Without loss
> As the children came
> With balloons of language
> Beholding mystery

Their press run is approximately 200 for that many subscriptions. **No price is given for the** newsletter, but the editor suggests a donation of $3 an issue or $17 annually (overseas: $4 and $19). Guidelines available for SASE. Pays 4 copies. They consider simultaneous submissions and previously published poems. Reports ASAP (usually within 2 weeks). Editor sometimes comments on rejections.

NEXT EXIT (II, IV-Regional), 92 Helen St., Kingston, Ontario K7L 4P3 Canada, founded 1980, editors Eric Folsom, Francesca Esford and Judith Owen, a twice-yearly magazine that features poetry and reviews and focuses on Ontario and Eastern North American writers. The editor wants to see poetry that is "lyric, narrative, meditative, concrete, explorative; any form done well," but nothing "misogynist." He has recently published work by Joy Walsh, Robbie Newton Drummond and Albert Huffstickler. As a sample, he chose the following lines from "This field is enough of it" by LeRoy Gorman:

> thickets of fencerow brush
> close in on this field
> grapevines reach like fingers
> & pull treetops into fists

The magazine is 5 × 8½ photocopied typed copy on 32 pgs., saddle-stapled and folded with black lettering and illustration on cover. Circulation is 150, of which 75 are subscriptions and 10 go to libraries. Subscription: $6/year. **Sample available for $3 postpaid. Pay is 1 copy plus 1-year subscription, more if requested. Acquires first North American serial rights. Submissions will be reported on in 3 months and time to publication is 6 months.** Reviews books of poetry of 50 pages or less. "We want something with the ring of truth, adventurous or ordinary; also interested in collage, concrete or copyart."

NEXUS (II), 006 University Center, Wright State University, Dayton OH 45435, phone (513)873-2031, founded 1967, editor Ted Cains. *"Nexus* is a student operated magazine of mainstream and street poetry; also essays on environmental and political issues. We're looking for truthful, direct poetry. Open to poets anywhere. We look for contemporary, imaginative work as well as traditional rhyme and meter." Issues have featured themes on Japan and American West. *Nexus* appears 3 times a year — fall, winter and spring, using about 40 pgs. of poetry (of 80-96) in each issue, circulation 1,000. They receive 1,000 submissions/year, use 30-50. Send a 10 × 15" SASE with 5 first class stamps and $4 for first copy, $3 for each additional issue. Submit up to 6 pgs. of poetry, September through May. Photocopy and simultaneous submissions OK. Send bio with submissions. Reports in 10-12 weeks except summer months. Pays 2 copies. Acquires first American serial rights. Send SASE for guidelines. Editor sometimes comments on rejections.

NEXUS (I, II), English Dept., Simon Fraser University, Burnaby, British Columbia V5A 1S6 Canada, founded "198-something," editor G.P. Lainsbury, appears 2 times/year, using **poetry. "No specifications other than quality; nothing sentimental, derivative."** They have recently published poetry by Christopher Wiseman, Jennifer Footman and Robert Nagler. As a sample we selected these lines from "A Venezia" by Gordon Orville Bain:

> Though desultory tourists wander through,
> church and palace seem disused, hung all about
> with tears and hopes and memories,
> like a maiden name: Venezia.
> For them, some elsewhere anchors pilings
> that underpin their domesticity.

It is 40-50 pgs., digest-sized, saddle-stapled, with matte card cover; the poetry has an avant-garde tone at times, bordering on obscurity, which may reflect editorial tastes or the quality of submissions. They accept about 30% of poetry received. Press run 200 for 150 shelf sales. **Sample postpaid: $3.50. Pays 2 copies. Acquires first Canadian publication rights. Reports in 2 months.** "Please include short bio sketch."

NIGHT ROSES; MOONSTONE BLUE (I, IV-Anthology, teen/young adult, student), P.O. Box 393, Prospect Heights IL 60070, phone (708)392-2435, founded 1986, poetry editor Allen T. Billy, appears 2-4 times a year. *"Moonstone Blue* is a science fiction/fantasy anthology, but we have no set dates of publication. We do an issue every 14-24 months as items, time and funds allow. We look for women/feminism themes for our *Bikini* series." For *Night Roses* they want "poems about dance, bells, clocks, nature, ghost images of past or future, romance and flowers (roses, wildflowers, violets, etc.). Do not want poems with raw language." They have recently published poetry by John DiMauro, Edna Janes Kayser, Ida Fasel, Deloris Selinsky and Emma Blanch. As a sample the editor selected these lines by Joanne Seltzer:

> The Roses
> Of Jackson Gardens
> All are dead

> But The Idea
> Of Rosehood
> Lingers On

Night Roses is 44 pgs., saddle-stapled, photocopied from typescript on offset paper with tinted matte card cover, press run 200-300. Subscription: $8 for 3 issues, $3/copy. **Sample postpaid: $2.50 for *Night Roses*, $2.75 for *Moonstone Blue*. Pays 1 copy. Acquires first or reprint rights. "Desire author's name and address on all sheets of mss. If previously published—an acknowledgment must be provided by author with it." No simultaneous submissions; some previously published poems used. "I prefer submissions between March and September." Reports in 6-12 weeks. "Material is accepted for current issue and 2 in progress."** The editor says, "We are more interested in items that would be of interest to our teen and women readers and to our readership in the fields of dance, art and creative learning. We are interested in positive motives in this area."

NIGHTSUN (II), Dept. of English, Frostburg State University, Frostburg MD 21532, founded 1981, poetry editors Douglas DeMars and Barbara Wilson, is a 64-page, digest-sized literary annual. **They want "highest quality poetry." Subject matter open. Prefers poems not much longer than 40 lines. Not interested in the "extremes of sentimental, obvious poetry on the one hand and the subjectless 'great gossamer-winged gnat' school of poetry on the other."** They have recently published poetry by William Stafford, Linda Pastan, Marge Piercy, Diane Wakoski, Dennis Brutus and Philip Dacey. Recent interviews include Carolyn Forché, Grace Cavalieri and Lucille Clifton. As a sample the editor selected these lines from "The Lotos-Eaters" by Robert Cooperman:

> To be finally rid of his harping,
> we helped lug his men on board,
> each one heavy with the weight
> of hopelessness, of toil breaking
> over them like storm-tortured surf.

Nightsun, an attractive journal on good stock paper, features well-known poets alongside relative newcomers. Editors take free verse mostly with attention paid to line, stanza and shape of poem. They accept about 1% of poetry received. **Do not submit mss during summer months. Sample postpaid: $6.50. Pays 2 copies. Acquires first rights. "Contributors encouraged to subscribe." Reports within 3 months.**

‡**THE NIHILISTIC REVIEW; PESSIMISM PRESS, INC. (I, II)**, P.O. Box 1074, South Sioux City NE 68776, founded 1990, editor Maxwell (Rick) Gaddis, poetry editor Camilla Danielson-Oregon, is a quarterly using **"poetry about the state of the human condition, sexually subtle, humorous—length no factor. No flowery, feel good or rhyming poetry. No blue-sky-and-green-valley-stuff."** They have recently published poetry by Lyn Lifshin, Joy Walsh and Marvin Malone. As a sample the editor selected these lines by Charles Bukowski:

> The Nihilistic Review, *eh?*
> Can you back that?
> I don't use calendars. I just ask somebody, is this March or mayhem?
> There may be flies on some of you guys but there's vultures on me.

The editor says it is 44 pgs., 8½×11, photocopied, spiral bound with plastic cover, original art on back. "We receive in excess of 350 submissions yearly and publish approximately 30%." Press run is 600 for 350 subscribers of which 6 are libraries, 75 shelf sales. Single copy: $5; subscription: $18, $25 for libraries. **Sample postpaid: $5.50. No previously published poems or simultaneous submissions. "We always like a cover letter.** In fact, we may print a book of unique cover letters as they are often more exciting than the submissions." **Often comments on rejections.** We often refer to a market that may be more suitable. **Send SASE for guidelines. Reports in 2 weeks. Pays 1 copy.** "We review anything sent to us. If not in the magazine, we will send review to sender for personal use." Pessimism Press, Inc., **publishes 8 chapbooks/year. For consideration, "submit to our magazine. We would like to publish poets in our magazine first. We will then contact those we wish to publish in chapbooks." Replies to queries and mss in 3 weeks. Pay is negotiable. Write for samples.** They say, "We are always anxious to look at new material. We have excellent working arrangements with all our contributors. We like a cover letter with all submissions as this is always a good indicator of our poet's personality. Lack of a cover letter to us shows a lack of personality. We like humor, satire, sarcasm and sex. Those who can combine those will like us a lot. We love to publish, not reject."

NIMROD INTERNATIONAL JOURNAL OF CONTEMPORARY POETRY AND FICTION; RUTH G. HARDMAN AWARD: PABLO NERUDA PRIZE FOR POETRY (II), 2210 S. Main St., Tulsa OK 74114, phone (918)584-3333, founded 1956, poetry editor Fran Ringold, "is an active 'little magazine,' part of the movement in American letters which has been essential to the development of modern literature.

Nimrod publishes 2 issues per year: an awards issue in the fall featuring the prize winners of our national competition and a thematic issue each spring." They want **"vigorous writing that is neither wholly of the academy nor the streets, typed mss."** They have published poetry by Pattiann Rogers, Denise Levertov, Willis Barnstone, Alvin Greenberg, Francois Camoin, Tess Gallagher, McKeel Mc-Bride, Bronislava Volek, Josephine Jacobson, William Stafford and Ishmael Reed. The 6×9 flat-spined, 160+ pgs., journal, full-color glossy cover, professionally printed on coated stock with b&w photos and art, uses 50-90 pgs. of poetry in each issue, circulation 3,500, 500 subscriptions of which 100 are public and university libraries. Subscription: $10/year plus $1.50 inside USA; $3 outside. They use about 1% of the 2,000 submissions they receive each year, have a 3-month backlog. **Sample: $6.90 for a recent issue, $5 for an issue more than 2 years old postpaid. Reports in 3 weeks-4 months. Pays $5/page up to $25 total/issue. "Poets should be aware that during the months that the Ruth Hardman Awards Competition is being conducted, reporting time on non-contest manuscripts will be longer."** Send business-sized SASE for guidelines and rules for the Ruth G. Hardman Award: Pablo Neruda Prize for Poetry ($1,000 and $500 prizes). Entries accepted January 1 through April 1 each year with $10 entry fee for which you get one copy of *Nimrod*. This annual poetry contest is considered one of the most prestigious in the publishing world, and your material is still considered for publication if you lose in the contest!

9TH ST. LABORATORIES; MODOM; ANOMALY (Audio Magazine) (IV-Form), P.O. Box 3112, Florence AL 35630, phone (205)760-0415, founded 1986, "front man" Jake Berry. "*9th St. Laboratories* is a noncommercial enterprise publishing *experimental* poetry, fiction, graphics and audio material in broadsheets, booklets, postcards, objects, chapbooks and audiotapes. *MODOM* is an ongoing series of any of the above. *Anomaly* is an audio magazine of poetry, fiction, noise and experimental music. **The key words are *experiment* and *explore*. Poetry that breaks new ground for the poet personally, that comes from the commitment to a vision. Also graphic poetry. Poetry using devices other than straight linear narrative, that makes use of things otherwise considered nonsensical or absurd."** They have recently published poetry by Jack Foley, Chris Winkler, Malok, Richard Kostelanetz, Mike Miskowski and John M. Bennett. As a sample the editor selected these lines by Harry Polkinhorn:

> *to challenge your balance drastic yet nuclear ocean*
> *urgent to implement an unwilling shifty murder victim*
> *subject I say a minister question of what she meant*

MODOM and *Anomaly* appear irregularly: "something appears 4 times a year." They use about 10 of 150 submissions received a year. Press run is 100-200. **Sample postpaid: $4. "All checks or money orders should be made out to Jake Berry, not the name of the mag and not to *9th St. Laboratories*." They pay 1 copy. "Of course poems submitted for the tape mag should be on tape and include a SASE for its return." No simultaneous submissions. They use some previously published work. Considers submissions January 1 through October 31 only. They publish chapbooks by invitation only, pay 15-20 copies. Editor sometimes comments on rejections.** He says, "We publish as much as we can as often as we can, attempting to expand the area of poetic, visionary concentration. Going to the mailbox to find it full of work that ignores conventional limitations and is highly involved with creating new things, bringing new insights, is what makes us happy."

NOMOS PRESS INC.; NOMOS: STUDIES IN SPONTANEOUS ORDER (IV-Political), 9421 S. Longwood, Chicago IL 60620, phone (708)858-7184, poetry editor John Enright, editorial contact person Carol B. Low. *Nomos* is a quarterly magazine **"dedicated to individual freedom and responsibility." One page of each issue is devoted to poetry up to 24 lines, "although longer pieces are considered. Poetry must promote individual freedom and responsibility, skepticism toward government solutions for economic and social ills and/or celebrate the human condition. No contrived rhymes, pedestrian prose or cryptic charades. Clarity of meaning and direct emotional appeal are paramount; form should contribute to, not detract or distract from these."** They have published poetry by John Harllee and Christopher Brockman. "*Nomos'* purpose is to call attention to the erosion of civil and economic rights, much of which erosion has government as its catalyst." The editor describes it as magazine-sized, generally 40 pgs. in length, offset, matte cover occasionally printed 2-color. Ad copy, line art for cover and article illustrations are solicited. It has a circulation of 1,000 with 450 subscriptions of which 10 are libraries, 300 sent out to potential subscribers. Subscription: $18. **Sample postpaid: $4.50. Photocopies, dot-matrix OK, name and address on each page. Send SASE for guidelines. Reporting time varies, up to 1 year to publication. Pays 3 copies. "Reviewing sample copies strongly encouraged."**

NORTH AMERICAN REVIEW (III), University of Northern Iowa, Cedar Falls IA 50614, phone (319)273-6455, founded 1815, poetry editor Peter Cooley, is a slick magazine-sized bimonthly of general interest, 48 pgs. average, saddle-stapled, professionally printed with glossy full-color paper cover. In their 171st anniversary issue they had poetry by Daniel Lusk, G.E. Murray and Art Homer. The editor says they receive 15,000 poems a year, publish 20-30. Press run 6,400 to 2,200 subscriptions of which 1,100 are libraries, some 2,800 newsstand or bookstore sales. Single copy: $4; subscription: $18. **Sample: $4 postpaid. Send SASE for guidelines. Pays 50¢ per line and 2 copies. No simultaneous submissions or previously published poems. Reports in 1-2 months, as much as a year between acceptance and publication.**

THE NORTH CAROLINA HAIKU SOCIETY PRESS (V); NCHSI CONTEST (IV-Form), 326 Golf Course Dr., Raleigh NC 27610, phone (919)231-4531, founded 1984, editor/publisher Rebecca Rust. The North Carolina Haiku Society International Contest has a $1 entry fee for each haiku. Eleven awards. Deadline in hand is December 31. Send SASE for copy of rules. **The press, temporarily on hold and not currently accepting submissions,** was established **"solely as a vehicle for publishing books by those authors who have received a grant from the North Carolina Haiku Society."** They publish flat-spined paperbacks of, or about, haiku only.

NORTH DAKOTA QUARTERLY (III), Box 8237, University of North Dakota, Grand Forks ND 58202, phone (701)777-3323, FAX (701)777-3650, founded 1910, poetry editor Jay Meek, is a literary quarterly published by the University of North Dakota Press that includes material in the arts and humanities—essays, fiction, interviews, poems and visual art. **"We want to see poetry that reflects an understanding not only of the difficulties of the craft, but of the vitality and tact that each poem calls into play."** Poets recently published include Donald Hall, Elizabeth Libbey and Alane Rollings. As a sample, the editor selected lines from "Dog Days" by Mark Vinz:

> *The apartment swells with August heat,*
> *an old jazz man on the radio—*
> *we climb the slippery stairs of each piano riff*
> *and wonder out loud if some day*
> *we'll ever do anything that well.*

The editor says *North Dakota Quarterly* is 6 × 9, 261 pgs., flat-spined, professionally designed and printed with b&w artwork on the white matte card cover and b&w photographs inside. Circulation of the journal is 700, of which 500 are subscriptions and 200 go to libraries, 100 are newsstand sales. Subscription: $15/year. **Sample available for $5 postpaid. Pay is 2 copies and a year's subscription. No simultaneous submissions. Reporting time is 4-6 weeks and time to publication varies.** Reviews books of poetry in 500-5,000 words, single or multi-book format. The press does not usually publish chapbooks, but "we will consider."

UNIVERSITY OF NORTH TEXAS PRESS; TEXAS POET SERIES (IV-Regional), P.O. Box 13856, Denton TX 76203-3856, phone (817)565-2124, series editor Richard Sale, has published work by these Texas poets: Naomi Nye, William Davis, R. S. Gwynn and Jan Seale. Books in the series average 120-128 pgs. **Query with sample poems, bio and list of publications. Simultaneous submissions OK. Reports on queries or mss in 8-10 weeks. Pays 10% of net sales in royalties plus 5 copies.** To buy samples, request the Texas A&M University Press catalog, Drawer C, College Station TX 77843.

NORTH EAST ARTS MAGAZINE; BOSTON ARTS ORGANIZATION, INC. (III), P.O. Box 6061 J.F.K. Station, Boston MA 02114, founded 1990, editor/president Mr. Leigh Donaldson, is a quarterly using **poetry that is "honest, clear, with a love of expression through simple language, under 30 lines. Care for words and craftsmanship are appreciated."** They have published poetry by Sandy Macebuh, K. Carlson and Joseph Bathanti. As a sample the editor selected these lines from "Casbah" by Martina Umbach:

> *pour us*
> *some glowing defiance*
> *dress us in anticipation*
>
> *we slipped through*
> *the crack in the sky*
> *and it wasn't paradise*

It is digest-sized, 32 or more pgs. professionally printed with matte 1-color card cover. They accept 20-25% of submissions. Press run 500-750 for 150 subscribers of which half are libraries, 50 to arts organizations. An updated arts information section and feature articles are included. Subscription: $10. **Sample postpaid: $3.50. Reads submissions September 1 through May 30 only. Send SASE for guidelines. Pays 2 copies. Acquires first North American serial rights. Reports in 1-2 months.** "A short bio is helpful."

Use the General Index to find the page number of a specific publication or publisher.

NORTHEAST JOURNAL (II, IV-Regional), P.O. Box 2321, Providence RI 02906, phone (401)785-0553, founded 1969, editors Dennis Holt and Dawne Anderson, is a literary annual published by The Poetry Mission, a nonprofit literary arts organization. The journal is **"open to conventional-experimental poetry."** They have published poetry by John Grey and Janet Gray. As a sample the editors selected these lines from "The Surface and Depths of Southern Friendship" by Janet McCann:

> I wait, Alice poised
>> on the giant chair, an obedient child.
> Men in brown suits discuss the Kuwait War
>> and problems with their software. I don't
> snicker.

The purpose of *NJ* is "to encourage local (state and area) writers while remaining open to national submissions." It is digest-sized, flat-spined, 100 pgs., typeset, with glossy card cover, circulation 500, with 200 subscriptions of which 100 are libraries. **Sample postpaid: $5. Pays 1 copy. Reports in 3-6 months.** Reviews books of poetry.

NORTHEASTERN UNIVERSITY PRESS; SAMUEL FRENCH MORSE POETRY PRIZE (III), Northeastern University, 360 Huntington Ave., Boston MA 02115. The Samuel French Morse Poetry Prize, % Prof. Guy Rotella, Editor, Morse Poetry Prize, English Dept., 406 Holmes, Northeastern University, Boston MA 02115, for book publication (ms 50-70 pgs.) by Northeastern University Press and an **award of $500, entry fee $10. Deadline of August 1 for inquiries, September 15 for single copy of ms. Ms will not be returned. Open to US poets who have published no more than 1 book of poetry.**

NORTHWEST REVIEW (II), 369 PLC, University of Oregon, Eugene OR 97403, phone (503)686-3957, founded 1957, poetry editor John Witte, is "seeking excellence in whatever form we can find it" and uses **"all types" of poetry.** They have published poetry by Alan Dugan, Olga Broumas, William Stafford and Richard Eberhart. The 6 × 9 flat-spined magazine appears 3 times a year, uses 25-40 pgs. of poetry in each issue, circulation 1,300, with 1,200 subscriptions of which half are libraries. They receive 3,500 submissions per year, use 4%, have a 0-4 month backlog. **Sample: $3 postpaid. Submit 6-8 poems clearly reproduced. No simultaneous submissions. Reports in 8-10 weeks, pays 3 copies. Send SASE for guidelines.** The editor comments **"whenever possible" on rejections** and advises, "Persist."

NORTHWOODS PRESS; DAN RIVER PRESS; CONSERVATORY OF AMERICAN LETTERS NEWSLET-TER (C.A.L.) (II), P.O. Box 7, N. Waterford ME 04267, phone (207)583-4143, founded 1972, C.A.L. (Conservatory of American Letters) founded 1986. "Northwoods Press is designed for the excellent *working poet* who has a following which is likely to create sales of $3,000 or more. Without at least that much of a following and at least that level of sales, no book can be published. Request 15-point poetry program. Northwoods Press will pay a minimum of $250 advance on contracting a book. C.A.L. is a nonprofit tax-exempt literary/educational foundation; up to four anthologies of poetry and prose are published each year. There is a $1 (cash—no checks) reading fee for each poetry submission to their anthologies, which goes to readers, not to the publisher. Poets are paid $5/page on acceptance, shorter poems pro-rata page rate. Payment is advance against 10% royalties on all sales we can attribute to the influence of the author."** Robert Olmsted regards his efforts as an attempt to face reality and provide a sensible royalty-contract means of publishing many books. He says, **"If you are at the stage of considering book publications, have a large number of poems in print in respected magazines, perhaps previous book publication, and are confident that you have a sufficient following to insure very modest sales, send 8½ × 11 SASE (3 oz. postage) for descriptions of the Northwoods Poetry Program and C.A.L."** His advice is, **"Poetry must be non-trite, non-didactic. It must never bounce. Rhyme, if used at all, should be subtle. One phrase should tune the ear in preparation for the next. They should flow and create an emotional response." Query with cover letter dealing with publication credits and marketing ideas. Submit "entire ms as desired for final book form." No simultaneous submissions; generally no previously published poems. Pays 10% royalties.** Bob Olmsted "rarely" comments on rejections, but he offers commentary for a fee. Query. Membership in C.A.L. is $24 a year, however, membership is not required. Members receive a quarterly newsletter plus 10% discount on all books and have many services available to them. C.A.L. sponsors an annual writers' conference with no tuition, only a $20 registration fee. Dan River Press, which publishes books of prose, also publishes an annual **Dan River Anthology**, using short fiction and **poetry. Pays $5/page on acceptance.**

W.W. NORTON & COMPANY, INC. (III), 500 Fifth Ave., New York NY 10110, phone (212)354-5500, founded 1925, poetry editor Jill Bialosky. W.W. Norton is a well-known commercial trade publishing house that publishes only original work in both hardcover and paperback. They want **"quality literary poetry"** but no **"light or inspirational verse."** They have recently published books by Ellen Bryant Voigt, Rosanna Warren, Stephen Dunn and Nina Cassian. W.W. Norton publishes two books of poetry each year with an average page count of 64. They are flat-spined paperbacks, attractively printed, with two-color glossy card covers. **Freelance submissions are accepted, but authors should query first,**

sending credits and 15 sample poems plus bio. Norton will consider only poets whose work has been published in quality literary magazines. They report on queries in 2-3 weeks and mss in 4 months. Simultaneous submissions will be considered if the editor is notified, and photocopied mss are OK. Royalties are 10%, but there are no advances. Catalog is free on request.

NOSTALGIA: A SENTIMENTAL STATE OF MIND (II), P.O. Box 2224, Orangeburg SC 29116, founded 1986, poetry editor Connie Lakey Martin, appears spring and fall using "nostalgic poetry, style open, prefer *non* rhyme, but occasional rhyme OK, relatively short poems, never longer than one page, no profanity, no ballads."*Nostalgia* is digest-sized, 24 pgs., saddle-stapled, offset typescript, with matte card cover. Press run is 1,000. Subscription: $5. **Sample: $2.50 postpaid.** "Most poems selected from contest." Guidelines available for SASE. There are contests in each issue with award of $100 and publication for outstanding poem, publication and 1-year subscription for Honorable Mentions. Entry fee $2.50 reserves future edition, covers 3 entries. Deadlines: June 30 and December 31 each year. No simultaneous submissions or previously published poems. All rights revert to author upon publication. Reviews books of poetry. Connie Martin says, "I offer criticism to most rejected poems and feature a poet each edition as 'Poet of the Season.' I suggest sampling before submitting."

NOSUKUMO, (V), GPO Box 994-H, Melbourne Victoria, Australia 3001, founded 1982, editor Javant Biarujia, publishes 1-2 chapbooks/year. "We publish language-oriented and experimental poetry, but not exclusively so. No neat little poems about nature and no soapbox hortations. However, our program is committed for the next two years." Their products are characterized by elegant printing on quality paper in sewn chapbooks. **Pays 5-10% royalties plus 30 copies. Buys first option rights for new editions or new titles.**

‡NOTUS: NEW WRITING; OTHERWIND PRESS (V), 2420 Walter Dr., Ann Arbor MI 48103, phone (313)665-0703, poetry editor Pat Smith, managing editor Marla Smith. *Notus* appears twice a year, using **experimental writing and translations. However, they are currently not accepting poetry submissions.** They have published poetry by Robert Creeley, Robert Kelly, Leslie Scalapino, Anselm Hollo and Gerrit Lansing. As a sample the editor selected these lines from "Dear Friend" by Elizabeth Robinson:

> As though Sunday's letters
> excessively long
>
> procure this
>
> Pronunciation does change
>
> Ascribe the letter to its softness

Notus is magazine-sized, 96 pgs., flat-spined, professionally printed on heavy cream stock with glossy b&w cover with photo. No ads. Press run 500 for 50 subscriptions of which 10 are libraries. **Sample postpaid: $6.** Reviews books of poetry in 500-750 words, single format.

NOVA SF (IV-Science fiction), 3 Ashfield Close, Bishops Cleeve, Cheltenham, Gloucester, England GL52 4LG, founded 1990, editor/publisher Adrian Hodges, is a quarterly using "**science fiction and fantasy in its widest sense, any length. No cliched stereotyped space opera and swords and sorcery.**" They have published poetry by Andy Darlington and Steve Sneyd. As a sample the editor selected these lines from "Extra Vehicular Activity" by John Francis Haines:

> Tonight the vandals have been out again,
> Risking their lives to daub their tribal signs
> Across the airlock doors; scooting around . . .

It is digest-sized, 50+ pgs., saddle-stapled, professionally printed with glossy card cover. Press run 300 for 63 subscribers. Subscription: (US subscription: $14/4 issues.) £4/4 issues. **Sample postpaid: £1.25 ($4 US). Send SAE with IRCs for guidelines. Reports immediately. Pays 4-issue subscription.** Submit at least 4 poems for "Featured Poet" section.

NOW AND THEN (IV-Regional, themes), P.O. Box 70556, ETSU, Johnson City TN 37614-0556, phone (615)929-5348, founded 1984, poetry editor Jo Carson, a regional magazine that deals with Appalachian issues and culture. **The editor does not want any poetry not related to the region.** Issues have themes—previous issues have focused on Appalachian veterans, working Cherokees, blacks, children and rural life. Themes for issues coming up: media, Scottish-Appalachian connection, sports and recreation, education, the Civil War. "No haiku or sentimental, nostalgic, romantic, religious poems." They have published poems by Fred Chappell, Michael McFee, Michael Chitwood, Jim Wayne Miller and George Ella Lyon. As a sample the editor selected these lines from "Flannel Pajamas" by Ruth Moose:

You never had a fabric in your life
worthy of your fingers. You made
leftovers, castoffs, bargains better.
Stitched each seam twice and straight.
I marvel at your craft
on something so nightly,
utility, this poor man's warmth.
Pajamas Eve would have made Adam
if she'd owned a needle.

Now and Then appears three times a year, 40 pgs., magazine-sized, saddle-stapled, professionally printed, with matte card cover. Its press run is 1,600-2,000 for 600 subscriptions of which 200 are libraries. Of 200 poems received they accept 6-10 an issue. Subscription: $10. **Sample: $3.50 postpaid. Guidelines available for SASE. Pays 2 copies plus subscription. Acquires one-time rights. Submit up to 5 poems, "include 'contributors notes.' " Reports in 3-4 months. They will consider simultaneous submissions but "not usually" previously published poems. Deadlines: March 1, July 1 and November 1.** Reviews books of poetry in 750 words.

NUTSHELL (I, II), 8 George Marston Rd., Binley, Coventry CV3 2HH United Kingdom, founded 1988, editor Tom Roberts, is a quarterly using poetry **"all subjects considered, any length. Nothing hateful, pornographic, badly assembled."** They have published poetry by Amryl Johnson, Ian MacDonald, Avril Redman, Kenneth Pobo and Carol Lee Saffiotti. The editor describes *Nutshell* as "A5 size, stapled, card cover, 64 pgs." They accept about 10% of some 500 poems submitted/year. Press run is 200 for 130 subscribers. **Sample postpaid: £2.50. Pays £1.50, extra copy or reduced rate subscription. Buys first serial rights. Editor comments on submissions when requested.** Reviews books of poetry in 100-200 words.

THE OAK (I); THE ACORN (I, IV-Children), 1530 7th St., Rock Island IL 61201, phone (309)788-3980, poetry editor Betty Mowery. *The Oak*, founded 1991, is a "publication for writers with short articles, poetry, fiction (no more than 500 words), and writers conferences." They want poetry **"no more than 32 lines. No restrictions as to types and style but no pornography."** *The Oak* appears 6 times/year. They take more than half of about 100 poems received each year. Press run is 200, with 10 going to libraries. Subscription: $10. **Sample: $2. Pays 1 copy. Acquires first or second rights. Simultaneous submissions and previously published poems OK. Do not submit mss in December. Reports in 1 week.** *The Acorn* is a "newsletter for young authors and teachers or anyone else interested in our young authors. **Takes only mss from kids K-12th grades. Poetry no more than 32 lines.** It also takes articles and fiction, no more than 500 words." It appears 6 times/year and **"we take well over half of submitted mss."** Press run 100, with 6 going to libraries. Subscription: $10. **Sample postpaid: $2. Pays 1 copy. Acquires first or second rights. Young authors, submitting to** *The Acorn*, **should put either age or grade on manuscripts. Simultaneous submissions and previously published poems OK. Do not submit mss in December. Reports in 1 week.** Editor Betty Mowery advises, "Beginning poets should submit again as quickly as possible if rejected. Study the market: don't submit blind. Always include a SASE or rejected manuscripts will not be returned." *The Oak* holds an Orange Blossom Poetry Contest February 1 through August 1. *The Acorn* has the Shawna Poetry Contest for 7-12th grades and the Peri Poetry Contest for K-6th grades February 1 through August 1.

‡OASIS BOOKS; OASIS (II), 12 Stevenage Rd., London SW6 6ES England, founded 1969, editor and publisher Ian Robinson. *Oasis* is a bimonthly magazine of short fiction and poetry as well as occasional reviews and other material. **"No preference for style or subject matter; just quality. No long poems;** *Oasis* **is a very short magazine. Also, usually no rhyming poetry."** They have recently published poetry by John Ash, Lee Harwood, George Evans and Roy Fisher. The editor says *Oasis* is international A5 size, litho, folded sheets. They receive 500-600 poems a year, use about 4 or 5. Press run is 500 for 400 subscribers of which 5 are libraries. **Sample postpaid: $2.50. Previously published poems sometimes OK; no simultaneous submissions. Include SAE and 3 IRCs for surface mail return. Seldom comments on rejections. Reports in 1 month. Pays 4 copies.** Oasis Books publishes 2-3 paperbacks and 2-3 chapbooks/year. **Replies to queries and mss in 1 month. For sample books or chapbooks, write for catalog.** Ian Robinson says, "One IRC is not enough to ensure return postage; three will, provided manuscript is not too thick."

OBLATES (IV-Religious, spirituality/inspirational), Missionary Association of Mary Immaculate, 15 S. 59th St., Belleville IL 62223-4694, phone (618)233-2238, editor Jacqueline Lowery Corn, is a magazine circulating free to 750,000 benefactors. **"We use well-written, perceptive traditional verse, average 16 lines. Avoid heavy allusions. Good rhyme and/or rhythm a must. We prefer a reverent, inspirational tone, but not overly 'sectarian and scriptural' in content. We like to use seasonal material. We like traditional poetry (with meter) and are always on the lookout for good Christmas poetry."** They have recently published poetry by Raymond A. Schoeder, Joy Lee Holman and Claire Puneky. *Oblates* is digest-sized, 20 pgs., saddle-stapled, using color inside and on the cover. Sample and guidelines for SASE and 52¢ postage. Six back issues—$1.44. Pays $30 plus 3 copies. Buys first North American serial rights. Reports within 4-6 weeks. Time to publication "is usually within 1 to 2 years." Editor comments "occasionally, but always when ms 'just missed or when a writer shows promise.' " Considers simultaneous submissions. She says, "We are a small publication very open to mss from authors— beginners and professionals. We do, however, demand professional quality work. Poets need to study our publication, and to send no more than one or two poems at a time. Content must be relevant to our older audience to inspire and motivate in a positive manner."

O-BLEK (OBLIQUE) (III), P.O. Box 1242, Stockbridge MA 01262, founded 1987, poetry editors Peter Gizzi and Connell McGrath, appears each April and November, a "journal of language arts" publishing a range of contemporary writing with an emphasis on poetry. "We do not limit ourselves to any particular poetic; our foremost criterion is excellence. We are particularly interested in new alternative forms and styles. Poems may be of any length." They have published poetry by Edmond Jabès, Barbara Guest, Michael Palmer and Charles Simic. O-blek is digest-sized, 160-200 pgs., flat-spined, professionally printed, with glossy, full-color cover. They have 250 subscriptions of which 30 are libraries. Subscription: $10. Sample postpaid: $6. Guidelines available for SASE. They do not consider simultaneous submissions or previously published poems. Reports in 4 months. "The editors strongly recommend that writers interested in submitting work to this journal read a copy *before* sending work. An average of one unsolicited manuscript is accepted per issue."

OBSIDIAN II: BLACK LITERATURE IN REVIEW (IV-Ethnic), Box 8105, North Carolina State University, Raleigh NC 27695-8105, phone (919)515-3870, founded 1975, editor Gerald Barrax, appears three times a year "for the study and cultivation of creative works in English by Black writers worldwide, with scholarly critical studies by all writers on Black literature." They are open as to subject matter but want poetry (as well as fiction and drama) from Black writers only. The editor says *Obsidian II* is 126 pgs., 6 × 9, press run of 700 for 500 subscriptions of which an eighth are libraries. Subscription: $12; single issue: $5. Sample postpaid: $11. Send SASE for guidelines. Pays 2 copies. Submit double-spaced ms on 8½ × 11 paper. Reports in 3-4 months.

OCCIDENT MAGAZINE; OCCIDENT PRESS; OCCIDENT POETRY COMPETITION; BERKELEY POETRY PRIZE BOOK CONTEST (II), 700 Eshelman Hall, U. of CA, Berkeley CA 94720, phone (510)642-4853, founded 1868, editor P. Michael Campbell, a small press publisher of books (poetry, stories, prose) and an annual magazine, *Occident*. They want "good poetry of any sort." They have published poetry by Robert Pinsky, Thom Gunn, Michael Palmer, Charles Bernstein, August Kleinzahler, Charles Simic, Brenda Hillman, Susan Howe, Leslie Scalapino and Lyn Hejinign. As a sample here are lines from "Rattling the Food Chain" by Leonard Nathan:

> And someday, yes, the lion shall eat straw
> like the ox, but shall also catch in the wolf's eye
> and certain red glitter even here
> among the lambs, among God's plenty

The magazine is 300 pgs., 6 × 10, flat-spined, professionally printed with glossy card cover. Press run 750-1,000. Sample postpaid: $3.50. Pays 1 copy. They prefer no simultaneous submissions. Previously poems accepted, but "depends on where they were published." Reports in 3-12 months. They publish 2 poetry chapbooks/year. Their annual contest has prizes of $75, $50, $25, and publication in the magazine. Deadline in April. Fee: $2/poem. Send SASE for information about the Berkeley Poetry Prize Book Contest.

‡ODYSSEY (II), Coleridge Cottage, Nether Stowey, Somerset, England, founded 1990, editors Derrick Woolf and Steve Davies, appears quarterly, publishes new poetry and short stories. They want "committed poetry; poetry of today; 'imaginary toads in real gardens.' " Nothing "pastiche; pontifical." They have recently published poetry by Pauline Stainer, Michael Ayres, Martin Stannard and Aine Miller. It is A5, saddle-stitched, computer printed with art and graphics (no ads). They receive 3,000-4,000 poems a year, use approximately 10%. Press run is 200 for 100 subscribers of which 5 are libraries. Subscription: £7 ($20 US). Sample postpaid: £2 ($6 US). No previously published poems or simultaneous submissions. Cover letter not required, but preferred. Time between acceptance and publication is 6 months. Often comments on rejections. Reports in up to 6 weeks. Pays 1 copy. Reviews books of poetry and magazines in up to 1,000 words. Derrick Woolf suggests interested poets "buy, beg, borrow or steal a copy of *Odyssey* to see the work published."

THE OHIO REVIEW (II); OHIO REVIEW BOOKS (V, II), Ellis Hall, Ohio University, Athens OH 45701-2979, phone (614)593-1900, founded 1959, editor Wayne Dodd, attempts "to publish the best in contemporary poetry, fiction and reviews" in the *Review* and in chapbooks, flat-spined paperbacks and hardback books. They use "**all types**" of poetry and have recently published poems by David Baker, William Matthews, Lynn Emanuel and Robin Behn. As a sample the editor selected these lines from "Summer's Customers" by Lee Upton:

> *Barberry and bunchberry and*
> *the bittersweet nightshade,*
> *yaupon and winterberry,*
> *crab's eye,*
> *a member of the pea family*
> *one seed of which leads to death.*

The *Review* appears 3 times a year in a professionally printed, flat-spined, format of 140+ pgs., matte cover with color and art, circulation 2,000, featuring about 18 poets/issue. They receive about 3,000 freelance submissions/year, use 1% of them, and have a 6- to 12-month backlog. This publication looks as beautiful as the poetry inside sounds on the page. However, standards are high and its editor's taste exacting. You need to read this publication before sending here to get a feel for what works. Subscription: $12. **Sample postpaid: $4.25. Reports in 1 month. Pays $1/line for poems and $5/page for prose plus copies. Buys first North American serial rights. Editor sometimes comments on rejections. Send SASE for guidelines. Reads submissions September 1 through June 30 only.** Reviews books of poetry in 5-10 pgs., single or multi-book format. **They are not at present accepting freelance submissions of book mss. Query with publication credits, bio.**

OHIO STATE UNIVERSITY PRESS/JOURNAL AWARD IN POETRY (II), 180 Pressey Hall, 1070 Carmack Rd., Columbus OH 43210-1002, phone (614)292-6930, poetry editor David Citino. Each year *The Journal* (see that listing) selects for publication by Ohio State University Press for the Ohio State University Press/Journal Award **one full-length (at least 48 pgs.) book ms submitted during September, typed, double-spaced, $12.50 handling fee (payable to OSU). Clear photocopies OK.** Send SASE for return of ms; self-addressed, stamped postcard for notification of ms receipt. **Some or all of the poems in the collection may have appeared in periodicals, chapbooks or anthologies, but must be identified. Along with publication,** *The Journal* **Award in Poetry pays $1,000 cash prize from the Helen Hoover Santmyer Fund "in addition to the usual royalties." Each entrant receives a subscription (2 issues) to** *The Journal.*

OLD HICKORY REVIEW (I), P.O. Box 1178, Jackson TN 38302, phone (901)422-5832, founded 1969, president Bill Nance, is a "literary semiannual, 2 short stories and approximately 75-80 poems each issue. **No more than 24-30 lines, any form, any subject, no obscenities, no pornography.** We publish poets from Maine to California and are adding lyrics." It is digest-sized, 120+ pgs., professionally printed with matte card cover. Press run is about 300 for that many subscribers of which 15 are libraries. Subscription: $12/year. **Sample postpaid: $3.50. Guidelines available for SASE. Pays 1 copy/ poem.**

THE OLD RED KIMONO (I, II), P.O. Box 1864, Rome GA 30163, phone (404)295-6312, founded 1972, poetry editors Ken Anderson and Jon Hershey, a publication of the Humanities Division of Floyd College, has the "sole purpose of putting out a magazine of original, high-quality poetry and fiction. *ORK* **is looking for submissions of 3-5 short poems. Poems should be very concise and imagistic. Nothing sentimental or didactic.**" They have recently published poetry by Walter McDonald, Peter Huggins, Kim Thomas, Thomas Feeny, Simon Perchik and David Huddle. As a sample the editors selected these lines by T. Sheehan:

> *Wet leaves*
> *at the bottom*
> *of a leaf pile*
> *shine*
> *like new shoes.*

The magazine is an annual, circulation 1,200, 8½ × 11, 64 pgs., professionally printed on heavy stock with b&w graphics, colored matte cover with art, using approximately 40 pgs. of poetry (usually several poems to the page). They receive 1,000 submissions per year, use 60-70. **Reading period September 1 through March 1. Reports in 3 months. Pays copies. Acquires first publication rights.**

THE OLIVE PRESS PUBLICATIONS (V), Box 99, Los Olivos CA 93441, phone (805)688-2445, founded 1979, editor Lynne Norris, is a general small press publisher for whom "poetry is incidental effort at this time. We specialize in local and family history." They have recently published **It Doesn't Hurt to Laugh**, a collection of cowboy poetry by Jake Copass.

‡ONE EARTH: THE FINDHORN FOUNDATION & COMMUNITY MAGAZINE (II, IV-Spiritual/inspirational, ecology), The Park, Findhorn, Forres, Morayshire 1V36 0TZ Scotland, phone (03094)574, founded 1974, contributing editor Vidura LeFeuvre, is a quarterly which "reflects awakening of consciousness throughout the world and also developments and life of the spiritual community at Findhorn." They want **poetry that is "spiritual, inspirational, about personal/social awakening or ecological. Not overly long—15 lines maximum. Nothing sentimental, negative or partisan; no poetry that is** *too* **subjective."** As a sample the editor selected these lines by Dana Finch:

> Will my death leave a trace
> in the world
> Will the invisible be shattered
> into fragments of sight.

One Earth is 48 pgs., A4, offset litho, saddle-stapled, with full-color cover, recycled paper throughout, line art and photos; 20% ads. They receive about 50 poems a year, accept approximately 30%. Press run is 4,000 for 1,700 subscribers of which 10 are libraries, 2,300 shelf sales. Single copy: $5; subscription: $20 surface, $26 airmail. **Sample postpaid: $3, surface mail. Previously published poems and simultaneous submissions OK. Cover letter required.** Time between acceptance and publication is 2-6 months. **Comments on rejections "only if asked." Pays 2 copies.**

‡ONE MEADWAY (II), #47, 211 W. 92nd St., New York NY 10025, founded 1990, associate editor for poetry Jonathan Wilks, is a semiannual produced in association with Sarah Lawrence College. "We publish poetry, short fiction, an essay by a writer and an interview with a writer in each issue. (We solicit the interview and essay.) We are interested in **poetry that has integrity. No specifications of form or style. We have a growing interest in the poetry of diverse cultural backgrounds. We like to see poems that take thematic risks,** not to impress the reader, but because the poem itself demands it of the writer. **This does not mean the poems should have brutal or 'flashy' themes,** rather that the poet uses poetry to talk about themes that are not safe to talk about in any other way." They have recently published poetry by Stephen Dobyns, Edward Kleinschmidt and Regina McBride. As a sample the editor selected the last lines of "No" by Mark Doty:

> I think the children smell unopened,
>
> like unlit candles,
> as they heft him around the table,
> praise his secrecy,
>
> holding to each adult face
> his prayer, the single word of the shell,
> which is no.

It is 144 pgs., 6×9, typeset, perfect-bound, with 4-color art on cover. "We receive about 325 submissions per year and publish around 25% of them." Press run is 1,500. **Sample postpaid: $6.** No previously published poems or simultaneous submissions. **Often comments on rejections. Reports in 1-3 months.**

ONIONHEAD; ARTS ON THE PARK, INC. (THE LAKELAND CENTER FOR CREATIVE ARTS); WORD-ART, THE NATIONAL POETS COMPETITION; ESMÉ BRADBERRY CONTEMPORARY POETS PRIZE (II), 115 N. Kentucky Ave., Lakeland FL 33801-5044, phone (813)680-2787. Arts on the Park founded 1979; *Onionhead* founded 1988. *Onionhead* is a literary quarterly. **"Our focus is on provocative political, social and cultural observations and hypotheses. Controversial material is encouraged. International submissions are welcome. We have no taboos, but provocation is secondary to literary excellence. No light verse please."** They have published poetry by Jessica Freeman, Arthur Knight, Lyn Lifshin, B.Z. Niditch and A.D. Winans. As a sample we selected these lines from "Paying Back Karma" by Jo Ann Lordahl:

> This bed I made
> will haunt me
>
> Until I burn it
> bury it, or defuse it.

The magazine is 40-50 pgs., digest-sized, photocopied from typescript with glossy card cover. Their press run is 250. Complimentary distribution to universities, reviews and libraries worldwide. They use 100 of 2,500 submissions received/year. Subscription: $8 US, $16 other. **Sample postpaid: $3. Pays 1 copy. Poet's name and title of poems should appear on the upper right-hand corner of each page. Poem "should be submitted exactly as you intend it to appear if selected for publication." Editor comments on rejections "rarely."** Poems are reviewed by an Editorial Board and **submissions are reported on within 2 months. If accepted, poems will** normally appear within one year. WORDART, The National Poets Competition, established 1983, is open to all American authors. Cash awards, "including the prestigious Esmé Bradberry Contemporary Poets Prize, are announced at a reading and reception during the first part of March." $8 reading fee. For guidelines and specific dates send SASE to the sponsoring organization, Arts on the Park, Inc., at the above address.

ONTARIO REVIEW (III); ONTARIO REVIEW PRESS (V), 9 Honey Brook Dr., Princeton NJ 08540, founded 1974. The *Ontario Review* appears twice a year. They have published poetry by William Heyen, Alice Ostriker, Albert Goldbarth and Jana Harris. *OR* is 112 pgs., 6×9, offset, flat-spined. Press run 1,200 for 650 subscribers of which 450 are libraries. 250 shelf sales; 75 direct sales. Subscription: $10. Sample postpaid: $4.95. Reports in 1 month. Pays $10/printed page plus 3 copies. Ontario Review Press is currently not considering new poetry mss. They publish 1-2 hardbacks and that many paperbacks/year, paying 10% royalties plus 10 copies.

ONTHEBUS; BOMBSHELTER PRESS (II), 6421 ½ Orange St., Los Angeles CA 90048, founded 1975. *ONTHEBUS* editor Jack Grapes. Bombshelter Press poetry editors Jack Grapes and Michael Andrews. *ONTHEBUS* uses "contemporary mainstream poetry—no more than 6 poems (10 pgs. total) at a time. No rhymed, 19th Century traditional 'verse.'" They have published poetry by Charles Bukowski, Albert Goldbarth, Ai, Norman Dubie, Kate Braverman, Stephen Dobyns, Allen Ginsberg, David Mura, Richard Jones and Ernesto Cardenal. Simultaneous submissions and previously published poems OK, "if I am informed where poem has previously appeared and/or where poem is also being submitted. I prefer cover letters with list of poems included plus poet's bio." *ONTHEBUS* is a magazine appearing 2 times/year, 200 pgs. offset, flat-spined, with color card cover. Press run 3,500 for 600 subscribers of which 40 are libraries, 1,200 shelf sales ("500 sold directly at readings"). Subscription: $24 for 3 issues; Issue #8/9, special double issue: $15. Sample postpaid: $10. Send SASE for guidelines. Do not submit mss between November 1 and January 1 or between June 1 and September 1. Submissions sent during those times will be returned unread. Pays 1 copy. Acquires one-time rights. No comments on rejections. Reports in "up to 4 months." Reviews books of poetry in 400 words (chapbook in 200 words), single format. This so-called *Paris Review* of the '90s is apt to surprise contributors as well as readers because Editor Jack Grapes has taken work from poets as "night" and "day" as Charles Bukowski and Stephen Dobyns. The motto here is "read before you send" to get a feel for the excitement this journal is generating. Bombshelter Press publishes 4-6 flat-spined paperbacks and 5 chapbooks/year. Query first. Primarily Los Angeles poets. "We publish very few unsolicited mss." Reports in 3 months. Pays 50 copies. Jack Grapes says, "My goal is to publish a democratic range of American poets and insure they are read by striving to circulate the magazine as widely as possible. It's hard work and a financial drain. I hope the mag is healthy for poets and writers, and that they support the endeavor by subscribing as well as submitting."

OPEN HAND PUBLISHING INC. (V), P.O Box 22048, Seattle WA 98122, phone (206)447-0597, founded 1981, publisher P. Anna Johnson, is a "literary/political book publisher" bringing out flat-spined paperbacks. They have published **Puerto Rican Writers at Home in the USA**, "an anthology of seventeen of the most well-known Puerto Rican writers." They do not consider unsolicited mss.

ORACLE POETRY; ASSOCIATION OF AFRICAN WRITERS; RISING STAR PUBLISHERS (I, IV-Ethnic), P.O. Box 3883, Langley Park, Hyattsville MD 20783, phone (301)422-2665, founded 1989, editorial director Obi Harrison Ekwonna. *Oracle Poetry* and *Oracle Story* appear quarterly using works "mainly of African orientation; must be probing and must have meaning—any style or form. Writers must have the language of discourse and good punctuation. No gay, lesbian or erotic poetry." As a sample the editor selected these lines from "War of 1968" by Greggette Soto:

> Twenty-three years ago
> A son went off to war
> It wasn't to fight
> Communism in Vietnam
> But to fight
> Racism in his own backyard.

Membership in the Association of African Writers is $20/year. The editor describes *Oracle Poetry* as digest-sized, saddle-stapled, print run 500. Subscription: $20/year. No previously published poems or simultaneous submissions. Pays copies. Acquires first North American serial rights. Reports in 4-6 weeks. Reviews books of poetry. The editor says, "Read widely, write well and punctuate right."

ORBIS: AN INTERNATIONAL QUARTERLY OF POETRY AND PROSE (II), 199 The Long Shoot, Nuneaton, Warwickshire CV11 6JQ, England, founded 1968, editor Mike Shields, considers "all poetry so long as it's genuine in feeling and well executed of its type." They have published poetry by Sir John

Betjeman, Ray Bradbury, Seamus Heaney and Naomi Mitchison, "but are just as likely to publish absolute unknowns." The quarterly is 6×8½, flat-spined, 64 pgs. professionally printed with glossy card cover, circulation 1,000 with 600 subscriptions of which 50 are libraries. Subscription: £14 ($30); per copy: £3.50 ($7.50). They receive "thousands" of submissions per year, use "about 5%." **Sample postpaid: $2 (or £1). Submit typed or photocopied, 1 side only, one poem per sheet. No bio, no query. Enclose IRCs for reply, not US postage. Reports in 1-2 months. Pays $10 per acceptance plus 1 free copy automatically. Each issue carries £50 in prizes paid on basis of reader votes. Editor comments on rejections "occasionally—if we think we can help.** *Orbis* is completely independent and receives no grant-aid from anywhere."

‡ORCHISES PRESS (II), P.O. Box 20602, Alexandria VA 22320-1602, founded 1983, poetry editor Roger Lathbury, is a small press publisher of literary and general material in flat-spined paperbacks. **"Although we will consider ms submitted, we prefer to seek out the work of poets who interest us."** Regarding the poetry he states: **"No restrictions, really; but it must be sophisticated—i.e., no religious versification, arty nonsense, etc. I find it increasingly unlikely that I would publish a ms unless a fair proportion of its contents has appeared previously in respected literary journals."** He has recently published poetry by Bruce Bennett and Richard Foerster. Asked for a sample, he says, "I find this difficult, but . . ." (from Joe David Bellamy):

> *And the sea extends for miles, blank from above,*
> *white and brittle, encircled by blank trees, the ice*
> *as hard and heavy as iron, though suffused with light,*
> *opalescent beneath the surface, then, deeper. . . .*

He publishes about 2 flat-spined paperbacks of poetry a year, averaging 64 pgs. **When submitting, "tell where poems have previously been published." Reports in 4 weeks. Pays 36% of money earned once Orchises recoups its initial costs.** Roger Lathbury says, "Real poets persist and endure."

ORE (II, IV-Themes), 7 The Towers, Stevenage, Hertfordshire, SG1 1HE England, founded 1955, editor E.H. Ratcliffe, a magazine that appears 2-3 times/year. They want **"folk, legend, Celtic, Arthurian, fairy, spiritual, religious. No nasty dirty words. Too much materialism. No pop poetry."** They have published poetry by Jay Ramsay and James Kirkup. As a sample the editor selected these lines (poet unidentified):

> *Ashurnasipal worships the sun-god Shamash*
> *in front of the Sacred Tree*
> *priest of Ashur*
> *beloved of Anu and Dagan*
> *son of Tukulti-Ninurta.*

They receive about 1,000 poems/year, accept 5%. **Sample: £1.60 or 5 IRCs. Pays 1 copy, others at half price. Simultaneous submissions OK.** Editor "always" comments—"no curt rejection slips." He advises: "1.) Realize what your type of interest is and your educational and expression limits. 2.) Read lots of poetry consistent with 1. Dwell internally on imagery, etc. 3.) Write poetry when something comes in the head—don't intend to write first. 4.) Put it away for a week and rewrite it."

‡OREGON EAST (II, IV-Regional), Hoke Center, Eastern Oregon State College, La Grande OR 97850, founded 1950, editor changes yearly, is the "literary annual of EOSC, 50% of magazine open to off-campus professional writing." It is flat-spined, book format, typeset, with end papers, 6×9, approximately 80 pgs., using graphics and b&w art, circulation 1,000 (300 off-campus) with 100 subscriptions of which 30-40 are libraries. Content tends toward free verse lyrics. Editors try to give readers an overview of art in each issue, from poetry to prose to graphics. Their preferences: **"Eclectic tastes in poetry with the only requirement being literary quality work for off-campus submissions. Chances of publication are better for short poems (one page) than longer ones. No 'greeting card' verse."** They have published poetry by Ling Wen Yuan, Rob Hollis Miller, Robert Hoeft and Heather Pankl. Price per issue: $5. 35-year issue available for $9.95 (256 pgs.). **Pays 2 copies. Acquires all rights. Returns rights "with condition that *Oregon East* may reprint in any upcoming anthology." Reads submissions September 1 through March 1 only. Notification by June. No simultaneous submissions. All submissions must be accompanied by SASE and cover letter with brief bio and phone.**

ORIEL BOOKSHOP (IV-Regional), The Friary, Cardiff, Wales, United Kingdom, CF2 5AT, phone 0222-395548, founded 1974, head of bookshop Peter Finch, publishes **Anglo-Welsh poetry, nothing else.** They have published poetry by Dylan Thomas, T. Harri Jones and R.S. Thomas. As a sample the editor selected these lines from Dannie Abse's "Return to Cardiff":

> *No sooner than I'd arrived the other Cardiff had gone,*
> *smoke in the memory, these but tinned resemblances,*

where the boy I was not and the man I am not
met, hesitated, left double footsteps, then walked on.

That poem is printed on a handsomely printed, large color poster.

ORPHIC LUTE (II), 526 Paul Pl., Los Alamos NM 87544, founded 1950, editor Patricia Doherty Hinnebusch, is a 40-page, digest-sized quarterly (photocopied from typescript, saddle-stapled, with matte card cover). "*Orphic Lute* **looks for poems of utter conciseness that are distillations of experience rather than narrative renderings. Poem length: 3 to 40 lines. Short forms welcome; traditional haiku appear in every issue. No pornography.**" They have recently published work by H.F. Noyes, Matthew Louviere, Richard West and Ray Greenblatt. The magazine has a circulation of 250, 200 subscriptions of which 6 are libraries. They receive about 4,000 submissions/year, use 300, have a 2-3 month backlog. "I publish seasonal poetry in season; other poems ASAP. I work on 2 issues at a time." Subscription: $10. **Sample postpaid: $2.50. Submit 4-6 poems; no simultaneous submissions, no query; no unclear type or light photocopies. Reports in 2-3 months. Pays 1 copy. Send SASE for guidelines. "Whenever asked, we critique submissions. We frequently make minor revisions a condition of acceptance.**" Reviews books of poetry for subscribers only in 100 words or less. The editor advises, "Every poem is a working poem. The poet can make improvements in successive revisions over many years. If it is worth saying, it is worth saying well."

ORTALDA & ASSOCIATES (V), 1208 Delaware St., Berkeley CA 94702, phone (510)524-2040, FAX (415)527-3411, founded 1985, poetry editor Floyd Salas, director/editor Claire Ortalda, publishes quality flat-spined paperbacks of poetry but **is not accepting submissions at this time.** They have published poetry by Czeslaw Milosz, Robert Hass, Ishmael Reed, Gary Soto, Jack Micheline and Carolyn Kizer.

OSIRIS, AN INTERNATIONAL POETRY JOURNAL/UNE REVUE INTERNATIONALE (II, IV-Translations, bilingual), P.O. Box 297, Deerfield MA 01342, founded 1972, poetry editor Andrea Moorhead, is a 6×9, saddle-stapled, 40-page semiannual that **publishes contemporary poetry in English, French and Italian without translation and in other languages with translation, including Polish, Danish and German.** They also publish graphics and photographs. They want poetry which is **"lyrical, non-narrative, multi-temporal, well crafted."** They have recently published poetry by Ingrid Swanberg, Robert Dassanowsky-Harris, Ivan Arguelles, Robert Marteau (France), Judita Vaiciunaite (Lithuania) and Flavio Ermini (Italy). As a sample the editor selected these lines:

Autumn moves at the end of light, shakes and flings
this rough coat of corn and clover, enters the fields
as a torch, moving as the light falls and darkness sparks
above the moon.

There are 12-18 pgs. of poetry in English in each issue of this intriguing publication. They have a print run of 500, send 50 subscription copies to college and university libraries, including foreign libraries. They receive 50-75 freelance submissions/year, use 12. Subscription: $8; per copy: $4. **Sample postpaid: $2. Include short bio with submission. Reports in 1 month. Pays 5 copies.** If you translate poems from other countries or want to gain an international perspective on the art, you should send for a sample copy. The editor advises, "It is always best to look at a sample copy of a journal before submitting work, and when you do submit work, do it often and do not get discouraged. Try to read poetry and support other writers."

THE OTHER SIDE MAGAZINE (II, IV-Political, religious, social issues), 300 W. Apsley St., Philadelphia PA 19144, phone (215)849-2178, founded 1965, poetry editor Rod Jellema, is a "magazine (published 6 times a year) concerned with **social justice issues from a Christian perspective. The magazine publishes 1-2 poems per issue. We will consider no more than 4 poems at one time from the same author.** Submissions should be of high quality and must speak to and/or reflect the concerns and life experiences of the magazine's readers. We look for fresh insights and creative imagery in a tight, cohesive whole. Be warned that only 0.5% of the poems reviewed are accepted. Seldom does any published poem exceed 40-50 lines. Do not want to see pious religiosity, sentimental schlock, haiku." They have recently published poetry by Eric Ormsby, Elisabeth Murawski, Nola Garrett and Mark Mitchell. *The Other Side* is magazine-sized, professionally printed on quality pulp stock, 64 pgs., saddle-stapled, with full-color paper cover, circulation 13,000 to that many subscriptions. Subscription: $29.50. **Sample postpaid: $4.50. Send SASE for guidelines (material pertaining to poetry is quoted above). Pays $15 plus 4 copies and free subscription. No simultaneous submissions. Previously published poems rarely used. Editor "sometimes" comments on rejections.**

‡OTIS RUSH; LITTLE ESTHER BOOKS (III), P.O. Box 21, North Adelaide 5006 South Australia, founded 1987, editor Ken Bolton. *Otis Rush*, appearing every 6 to 10 months, is a journal of "new writing, mostly poetry, some prose, plus writing on Australian visual art and occasional literary reviews." They want **"new, self-conscious, stylistically aware poetry."** They have recently published poetry by Harry Mathews, Ron Padgett, Barbara Hannahan and John Forbes. The editor says *OR* is 120-150 pgs., offset, perfect-bound, with some ads and art. Press run is 500 for about 100 subscribers of which 15 are libraries, 200+ shelf sales. Single copy: $10; subscription: $28 Australian, $40 overseas. **Sample postpaid: $14. Previously published poems and simultaneous submissions OK. Cover letter required. Often comments on rejections. Send SASE for guidelines. Reports in 2 months. Pays $10/page minimum. Buys first publication rights.** Little Esther Books publishes 1-6 paperbacks/year. **Replies to queries in 1 month, to mss in 3-4 months. Pays 10% royalties and 15 author's copies.**

OTTER (IV-Regional), Parford Cottage, Chagford, Devon TL13 8JR United Kingdom, founded 1988, editor Christopher Southgate, appears 3 times/year **using poetry by contributors associated with the County of Devon, "poems concerned with local community and with issues — social, political, religious. Like: poems in strict forms."** They have published poetry by Lawrence Sail, Ron Tamplin, Harry Guest and Jane Beeson. As a sample, these lines from "The Yellow and Green Daughter" by Sandra McBain:

> *She dances like a daffodil*
> *or wind driven forsythia*
> *like a petal whirled in water*

It is digest-sized, 48 pgs. flat-spined, with glossy card cover, professionally printed. They accept about 25% of 400-500 poems/year. Press run 300 for 70 subscribers of which 5 are libraries. Subscription: £5. **Sample postpaid: £2 (or $5 US; dollar checks OK). Reports within 3 months. Pays £2/poem plus 1 copy. "Those not resident in Devon should indicate their connection with the county." Editor always comments on rejections.**

OUR FAMILY (IV-Religious), Box 249, Battleford, Saskatchewan S0M 0E0 Canada, phone (306)937-7771, FAX (306)937-7644, founded 1949, editor Nestor Gregoire, o.m.i., is a monthly religious magazine for **Roman Catholic families. "Any form is acceptable. In content we look for simplicity and vividness of imagery. The subject matter should center on the human struggle to live out one's relationship with the God of the Bible in the context of our modern world. We do not want to see science fiction poetry, metaphysical speculation poetry, or anything that demeans or belittles the spirit of human beings or degrades the image of God in him/her as it is described in the Bible."** They have published poetry by Nadene Murphy and Arthur Stilwell. *Our Family* is magazine-sized, 40 pgs., glossy color paper cover, using drawings, cartoons, two-color ink, circulation 13,500 of which 48 are libraries. $1.95 per issue, subscription $15.98 Canada/$21.98 US. **Sample postpaid: $2.50. Send SASE with IRC or personal check (American postage cannot be used in Canada) for writer's guidelines. Will consider poems of 4-30 lines. Pays 75¢-$1 per line. Reports within 30 days after receipt. Simultaneous submissions OK, prefers letter-quality to dot-matrix.** The editor advises, "The essence of poetry is imagery. The form is less important. Really good poets use both effectively."

OUT LOUD: THE MONTHLY OF LOS ANGELES AREA POETRY EVENTS (IV-Regional), 1350 Third St. Promenade, Santa Monica CA 90401, founded 1989, editor Carrie Etter, "is distributed at poetry venues throughout the Los Angeles area: performance spaces, theaters, bookstores, etc." and **accepts poetry from poets living in Los Angeles or Orange County, up to 20 lines. No "sentimental work or work that demonstrates that the writer is not an avid reader of modern poetry." Previously published poetry OK if cover letter indicates when and where it was published. "Otherwise cover letters are not necessary."** Subscription: $9/year. Format is an 11 × 17 sheet, printed and folded in half. Circulation 2,000, all copies distributed free except subscriber copies. **Sample postpaid: 75¢. Pays 2 copies "unless poet requests more. Acquires one-time rights. Responses are made within a month."**

OUT MAGAZINE (I, IV-Gay), #5-359 Davenport Rd., Toronto, Ontario M5R 1K5 Canada, phone (416)921-1496, founded 1986, editor Shawn Venasse, poetry editor Brian Day, is a monthly arts/entertainment magazine with literary supplements, "celebrating all that it means and all that it can mean to be gay and male through interviews, essays, short stories, poetry, drawings, photographs and more." They use **"strong, imagistic, passionate, free verse, intelligent, challenging, aware" poetry, not** that which is **"inane, rhyming, sophomoric."** *Out* is tabloid size, press run "25,000+ and growing. In a slow year we receive 100 pieces and use about 20." It is distributed free. Subscription: $24. **Sample: $2 postpaid (or just postage). Deadlines are the 15th of each month. Reports in 3-6 weeks. Pays 5-10 copies "depending on size." Acquires first rights. They prefer cover letter and bio with submissions.** Reviews books of poetry in 150-1,500 words. The editor says, "Poems are chosen by an intuitive gut response upon first reading — if they don't leap off the page we don't publish them. Be original and daring — avoid clichés at all cost and know your market."

OUTERBRIDGE (II), English A324, The College of Staten Island, 715 Ocean Terrace, Staten Island NY 10301, phone (718)390-7654, founded 1975, editor Charlotte Alexander, publishes "the most crafted, professional poetry and short fiction we can find (unsolicited except special features — to date rural, urban and Southern, promoted in standard newsletters such as *Poets & Writers, AWP, Small Press Review*), interested in newer voices. **Anti loose, amateurish, uncrafted poems showing little awareness of the long-established fundamentals of verse; also anti blatant PRO-movement writing when it sacrifices craft for protest and message. Poems usually 1-4 pgs. in length.**" They have recently published poetry by Craig S. Brown, Kay Murphy and Naomi Rachel. As a sample the editor selected these lines from "How to Imagine Deafness" by Kim Roberts:

> *Darken your ears until the tunnels*
> *with their intricate clockwork*
> *are sheathed in pitchy calm.*
> *Hum a little blue, to yourself,*
>
> *but keep it secret.*

The digest-sized, flat-spined annual is 100+ pgs., about half poetry, circulation 500-600, 150 subscriptions of which 28 are libraries. They receive 500-700 submissions/year, use about 60. **Sample postpaid: $4. Submit 3-5 poems anytime except June and July. "We dislike simultaneous submissions and if a poem accepted by us proves to have already been accepted elsewhere, a poet will be blacklisted as there are many good poets waiting in line." Reports in 2 months. Pays 2 copies (and offers additional copies at half price). Acquires first rights.** The editor says, "As a poet/editor I feel magazines like *Outerbridge* provide an invaluable publication outlet for individual poets (particularly since publishing a book of poetry, respectably, is extremely difficult these days). As in all of the arts, poetry — its traditions, conventions and variations, experiments — should be studied. One current 'trend' I detect is a lot of mutual backscratching which can result in very loose, amateurish writing. Discipline!"

OUTREACH FOR ELDERLY HOUSEBOUND AND DISABLED (IV-Senior citizens, specialized: disabled, religious), 7 Grayson Close, Stocksbridge, Sheffield S30 5BJ, South Yorks, England, editor J. Kirby, founded 1980, is a monthly newsletter using **"short religious, semi-religious poetry. This is a magazine for elderly housebound and disabled who need cheering up not made more depressed or bored!"** It is photocopied from typescript on ordinary paper, folded and saddle-stapled. As a sample, here are lines from "Stairs to God" by Helen S. Rice:

> *Prayers are the stairs*
> *We must climb every day,*
> *If we would reach God*
> *There is no other way.*

OUTRIDER PRESS (I, IV-Women), 937 Patricia Ln. #2, Crete IL 60417, founded 1988, president Phyllis Nelson, publishes 1-2 chapbooks/year. They want **"poetry dealing with the terrain of the human heart and plotting inner journeys; growth and grace under pressure. No bag ladies, loves-that-never-were, please."** As a sample the editor selected these lines from "Elegy" in **Listen to the Moon** by Whitney Scott:

> *He slipped*
> *Away,*
> *Gently as the rustle of silk*
> *He so favored in his shirts.*

That chapbook is digest-sized, 16 pgs., photocopied from typescript with matte card cover, $4. **Responds to queries in 3 months, to submissions in 6 months. Pay negotiable.**

THE OVERLOOK PRESS; TUSK BOOKS (V), 149 Wooster St., New York NY 10012, phone (212)477-7162, founded 1972, are trade publishers with about 8 poetry titles. They have published books of poetry by David Shapiro and Paul Auster. Tusk/Overlook Books are distributed by Viking/Penguin. **They publish on standard royalty contracts with author's copies. They "are no longer accepting poetry submissions."**

‡OWL CREEK PRESS; OWL CREEK POETRY BOOK AND CHAPBOOK COMPETITIONS (II), 1620 N. 45th St., Seattle WA 98103, founded 1979, poetry editor Rich Ives. "Owl Creek Press is a nonprofit literary publisher. Selections for publication are based solely on literary quality." They publish full-length poetry books, chapbooks, anthologies. **"No subject or length limitations. We look for poetry that will endure."** They have recently published poetry by Angela Ball, Art Homer and Laurie Blauner. As a sample here are the opening lines of "Ordinance on Returning" by Naomi Lazard:

> *We commend you on your courage.*
> *The place you have chosen to revisit*
> *is as seductive as ever.*
> *It has been in that business for centuries.*

Owl Creek Press accepts books and chapbooks for publication only through its annual contests for each. The *book* competition selects 1-3 books for publication. Mss should be a minimum of 50 typed pages and should include an acknowledgments page for previous publications. Deadline: January 31; entry fee: $9; winners receive 100 copies of published book. The *chapbook* competition chooses 1-3 chapbooks for publication. Mss should be under 40 pages and should include an acknowledgments page for previous publications. Deadline: July 15; entry fee: $5; winners receive 50 copies of published chapbook. Additional payment for reprinting. Send SASE for information on Owl Creek Poetry Book and Chapbook Contests.

OXFORD MAGAZINE (II), 302C Bachelor Hall, Miami University, Oxford OH 45056, phone (513)529-5256, founded 1984, appears twice a year. **"We are open in terms of form, content, length and subject matter."** They have published poetry by David Ignatow and Diane Wakoski. As a sample here are lines from "Burning the Fields" by C.L. Rawlins:

> *Between the grass and rolling flame, a pact;*
> *the farmers with their torches: custom, wisdom, lore.*
> *The fierce green rises blind above the black.*
> *Dry orchard prunings blaze in bony stacks*
> *at equinox, the land bare of snow and poor.*
> *Between the grass and rolling flame, a pact.*

It is 6×9, 80-100 pgs., flat-spined, professionally printed with matte card cover, press run 500. **Sample postpaid: $5. "We accept submissions from September 1 until May 1 only." No simultaneous submissions or previously published poems. Reports in 8-10 weeks. Pays 1 copy and small honorarium. Buys first North American serial rights.**

OXFORD UNIVERSITY PRESS (V), 200 Madison Ave., New York NY 10016, phone (212)679-7300, founded 1478, poetry editor Jacqueline Simms (U.K.), is a large university press publishing academic, trade and college books in a wide variety of fields. **Not accepting any poetry mss.** "Our list includes Conrad Aiken, Richard Eberhart, Robert Graves, Geoffrey Hill, Peter Porter, M.L. Rosenthal, Stephen Spender, Anne Stevenson and Charles Tomlinson. These indicate our direction."

OYEZ REVIEW (II), 430 S. Michigan Ave., Chicago IL 60605, phone (312)341-2017, founded 1965, editor Sarah L. Kusar, is an annual literary magazine published by Roosevelt University. *"Oyez Review* is an award-winning publication which has maintained its high level of excellence by encouraging submissions from serious writers and artists." They have published poetry by Lisel Mueller, John Jacob and Barry Silesky. As a sample we selected these lines from "Remains" by Farrell Collins:

> *They were right, the ones*
> *who told us not to look.*
> *She was right, we had to,*
> *or we never would believe*
> *all that*
> *could stop*
> *into something to be burned*

The digest-sized review is flat-spined, about 100 pgs., using b&w photography and line drawings, poetry and fiction, has glossy, color card cover. Circulation 500. It is sold at Roosevelt University events and bookstores in Chicago and throughout the nation. **Sample copies are $4. Guidelines available for SASE. Pays 2 copies. Contributors can buy additional copies for $2. Acquires first publication rights. Submission deadline: October 31. Reports by December 1. Publishes in spring.**

PABLO LENNIS (IV-Science fiction, fantasy), 30 N. 19th St., Lafayette IN 47904, founded 1976, editor John Thiel, appears irregularly, is a **"science-fiction and fantasy fanzine preferring poems of an expressive cosmic consciousness or full magical approach. I want poetry that rimes and scans and I like a good rhythmic structure appropriate to the subject. Shorter poems are much preferred. I want them to exalt the mind, imagination, or perception into a consciousness of the subject. Optimism is usually preferred, and English language perfection eminently preferable. Nothing that is not science fiction or fantasy, or which contains morbid sentiments, or is perverse, or does not rime, or contains slang."** They have recently published poetry by William Nesbit, Jim Dunlap, Danny Weiss and John Binns. As a sample the editor selected these lines from "Son's Sonnet" by L.A. Hood:

> *I fear I'm lost in quasi-stellar space*
> *Beyond the cosmic grid of space and time.*
> *Forsaking mythic heros of the past*
> *My quest has been the universal rhyme.*
> *For what has been shall always be again*
> *And myth and truth have melded into one.*
> *Our journey in this vacuum never ends;*

Our lives a cosmic instant to the sun.
It is magazine-sized, 30 pgs., side-stapled, photocopied from typescript, with matte card cover, using fantastic ink drawings and hand-lettering. "I get maybe fifty poems a year and have been using most of them." Press run "up to 100 copies." Subscription: $12/year. **Sample postpaid: $1. Pays 1 copy, 2 if requested. Reports "at once. I generally say something about why it was not used, if it was not. If someone else might like it, I mention an address."** Reviews books of poetry if they are science fiction or fantasy. The editor says, "Poetry is magic. I want spells, incantations, sorceries of a rhymic and rhyming nature, loftily and optimistically expressed, and I think this is what others want. People buy poetry to have something that will affect them, add new things to their lives. If they want something to think about, they get prose. See how much magic you can make. See how well-liked it is."

PAINTBRUSH: A JOURNAL OF POETRY, TRANSLATIONS, AND LETTERS (III), Division of Language & Literature, Northeast Missouri State University, Kirksville MO 63501, founded 1974, editor Ben Bennani. *Paintbrush* appears 2 times/year and is 6×9, 64+ pgs., using **quality poetry.** Circulation 500. **Sample: $7. Send SASE with inquiries and request for samples. No submissions June, July and August.** Reviews books of poetry.

PAINTED BRIDE QUARTERLY (II), 230 Vine St., Philadelphia PA 19106, phone (215)925-9914, editors Lee W. Potts and Teresa Leo, founded 1973, **"We have no specifications or restrictions. We'll look at anything."** They have published poetry by Robert Bly, Charles Bukowski, S.J. Marks and James Hazen. *"PBQ* aims to be a leader among little magazines published by and for independent poets and writers nationally." The 80-page, perfect-bound, digest-sized magazine uses 40+ pgs. of poetry/issue, receiving over 1,000 submissions/year and using under 150. Neatly printed, it has a circulation of 1,000; 850 subscriptions, of which 40 are libraries. Subscription: $16. **Sample postpaid: $5.** *Quarterly* **deadlines: ongoing. Submit no more than 6 poems, any length, typed, photocopies OK, only original, unpublished work. Pays 1-year subscription and half-priced contributor's copies. "Submissions should include a** *short* **bio." Editors seldom comment on rejections. They have a 6- to 9-month backlog.** Reviews books of poetry.

PAINTED HILLS REVIEW (II, IV-Regional), P.O. Box 494, Davis CA 95617-0494, founded 1990, editors Michael Ishii and Kara Kosmatka, appears 3 times/year using **"well-crafted poetry. Poems must sustain themselves. Rather than abstractly generalizing, make a poem detailed and real—full of 'real' people and 'real' situations. Nothing abstract, general, sloppy and unsustained, trite, 'greeting-card' verse, no philosophy or dogmatism. Special interest in poetry of West Coast."** They have recently published work by Patricia Goedicke, William Stafford, Ingrid Wendt, Lia Smith and Omar S. Castañeda. As a sample the editors selected these lines from "Swimming After Birds" by Laurie O'Brien:

> Over water it is easier to understand. They
> need some angle of light on the silver
> backs of fish, they must have a line
> of descent before the plunge. The child
> in the green waves chases every rocking
> trough, the fish which spiral and disperse,
> the feathers just above foam. The world tilts
> and we see her swimming with a little flutter
> kick out into the territory of summer air.

PHR is 48 pgs., digest-sized, professionally printed and typeset, saddle-stapled, with matte card cover, all on recycled paper. Press run 250-300. Subscription: $9, $11 institutions and Canada. **Sample postpaid: $3. Pays 1-2 copies. Acquires first North American serial rights. Send no more than 6 poems at a time, no more than 100 lines/poem. Reports in 4-6 weeks.** Reviews books of poetry in 250-500 words, single or multi-book format. Sponsors "Paintbrush Award in Poetry," yearly contest. Deadline is in May. Send SASE for info. Winners win up to $100 cash prize and are published in *PHR*. The editors advise, "Read other poets; revise and revise again; keep trying."

PAISLEY MOON (II), Box 2373, Santa Cruz CA 95063, founded 1990, editor Michael Spring, is a quarterly magazine. **"Prefers poems around 35 lines or less, but will consider longer poems if exceptional. Open to all forms/style, even haiku! Editor prefers strong imagery, rich language, and explorative verse, original twists in vision and metaphor. No didactic, greeting-cardish, cliche-ridden verse."** They have recently published poetry by Joyce Odam, Antler, Wm. Everson, Martha Bosworth, Francisco X. Alarcon, B.Z. Niditch, Stephen Kessler and John Grey. As a sample the editor selected these lines from "Companion" by Martha M. Vertreace:

> The chapel carillon crashes over wild seas
> you fingerpaint in cobalt, thick pigment

> *cresting in noble-savage waves.*
> > *When you leave,*
> *the gibbous moon floats on its side . . .*

PM is digest-sized, 32-40 pgs., photocopied from typescript on ordinary paper with matte card cover (with art). Press run 300. They accept about 15% of 1,000 poems received. Subscription: $9. Sample postpaid: $2.50. Pays 1 copy. **Will consider previously published poems and simultaneous submissions. Reports in 1-4 months.** They sponsor an annual contest. All poems in contest are considered for publication. Winners are featured in additional issue. Prizes of $100, $50, $25, 5 honorable mentions; fee $2/poem, limit 35 lines. Deadline: October 31. The editor advises, "Read past and present masters (critically); read everything you can on poetry; read enough to know what is and isn't a cliche. Write and rewrite often. Be patient and persistent with your craft and vision."

PANCAKE PRESS (V), 163 Galewood Circle, San Francisco CA 94131, phone (415)665-9215, founded 1974, publisher Patrick Smith, a small press publisher of hand-bound paperbacks with sewn signatures. **"Current projects are selected. At present we can consider only solicited mss for publication. Unsolicited mss will be returned with brief comment and thanks."** The editor publishes **"poetry aware of its own language conventions, tuned to both the ear and eye, attentive to syntax, honest about its desires, clear about something, spoken or written as a member of the species."** He has published books by John Logan, David Ray and Stephen Dunning. Pancake Press publishes 2-3 chapbooks each year, with an average page count of 36, flat-spined.

PANDORA; PANDORA'S ALL YOUTH ISSUE (V), 2844 Grayson, Ferndale MI 48220. Contact Ruth Berman, 2809 Drew Ave. S., Minneapolis MN 55416. *Pandora*, founded 1978, editor Meg Mac Donald, poetry editor Ruth Berman, appears 2 times yearly (hoping to return to quarterly), publishing 12-15 poems in each issue of **"science fiction, fantasy, offbeat, any form. No horror! Long poems of extremely high quality. Most under 30 lines." They are currently not accepting submissions due to overstock.** They have published poetry by Sandra Lindow, Melanie A. Rawls, W. Gregory Stewart and D.A. Bach. As a sample these lines are from "three steps" by Roger E. Moore:

> *will i lay down in the*
> *wet long grass of heaven, to*
> *breathe the loam and sleep*
> *under the blue forever?*

It is digest-sized, 72 pgs., offset, on white stock with glossy card stock cover in b&w and 1 additional color, perfect-bound, using b&w graphics and ads, circulation 1,000, including some libraries, newsstand and bookstore sales. Subscription: $10 for 2 issues (US); $15 for 2 issues (Canada); $20 for 2 issues. **Sample: $5 postpaid (US); $7 (Canada); $10 overseas. All payments must be made in US funds.** *Pandora's* All Youth issue publishes poetry by those in grades K-12 of the current year. They advise, "Researching your market is probably the most valuable time you will spend as a poet. You've already spent precious time in the creation process; don't waste time and postage on blind submissions. Send for guidelines. Better yet, acquire a few issues of the magazine you are interested in submitting to. Spend some serious time scrutinizing the contents. Watch for trends, for changes in editorial tastes. Be careful not to send work that only repeats what you've seen recently. Trying to win the editor over with what you already know 'isn't quite right' is risky. When an editor can't use your work, take any comments to heart. Above all, don't be discouraged and never take rejection personally. Poetry is a very personal thing for many editors—it may not be the technical form that makes or breaks it, it may just be a gut reaction to that particular poem on that day. Take whatever clues you're given to improve your chances—or your poetry—in the future."

‡THE PANHANDLER (II), English Dept., University of West Florida, Pensacola FL 32514, phone (904)474-2923, founded 1976, editors Michael Yots and Stanton Millet, appears twice a year, using poetry **"grounded in experience with strong individual 'voice' and natural language. Any subject, no 'causes.' Length to 200 lines, but prefer 30-100. No self-consciously experimental, unrestrained howling, sophomoric wailings on the human condition."** They have published poetry by Malcolm Glass, Lyn Lifshin, Donald Junkins, David Kirby and Joan Colby. As a sample here is the first stanza of "York, Maine" by Leo Connellan:

> *Through the Cutty Sark motel room 21 picture window now*
> *the gray waves coming into York Beach like*
> *an invasion of plows pushing snow. Tomorrow*
> *the sun will scratch its chin and bleed along the skyline*
> *but today everything is gray poached in a steam of fog.*

The handsomely printed magazine is digest-sized, 64 pgs., flat-spined, large type on heavy eggshell stock, matte card cover with art. Circulation: 500 for 100 subscribers of which 10 are libraries and 200 complimentary copies going to the English department and writing program. Subscription: $5. **Sample: $2 postpaid. Pays 2 copies. Reports in 1-2 months, 6-12 months to publication. Submit maximum of 7 poems, typewritten or letter-perfect printout. No simultaneous submissions.** The editor advises: "(1) take care with ms preparation. Sloppy mss are difficult to evaluate fairly; (2) send only poems you believe in. Everything you write isn't publishable; send finished work." They sponsor a national chapbook competition each year, October 15 through January 15. Submit 24-30 pgs. with $7 reading fee. Send SASE for details.

‡**PANJANDRUM BOOKS; PANJANDRUM POETRY JOURNAL (II, IV-Translations)**, 6156 Wilkinson Ave., North Hollywood CA 91606, founded 1971, editor Dennis Koran, associate editor David Guss. **The press publishes a distinguished list of avant-garde books. They are interested in translations (especially European) of modern poetry, surrealism, dada and experimental poetry and accept book-length mss only with SASE; query first.** *Panjandrum Poetry Journal* is published occasionally. **Submit no more than 10 poems.**

PANTHEON BOOKS INC., 201 E. 50th St., New York NY 10022. Declined listing.

THE PAPER BAG (I, II), Box 268805, Chicago IL 60626-8805, phone (312)285-7972 (an answering service), founded 1988, editor M. Brownstein, is a quarterly using **poetry "any kind, any style. We look for strong and original imagery."** *The Paper Bag* is photocopied from typescript, 24 pgs. digest-sized, saddle-stapled, with matte card cover. "Our circulation varies from 20-300+ and we sell out every issue." Subscription: $10/4-5 issues plus "anything else we publish." They publish about 30 of 200 poems received/issue. **Sample postpaid: $2.50. Pays copies. Editor comments on submissions "always." They want a brief bio with each submission, typed mss only, address and phone on each submission.** All checks or money orders should be made out to M. Brownstein. Reviews books of poetry in their broadside series. The editor says, "Be persistent. Because we reject one group of submissions does not mean we will reject another batch. Keep trying."

PAPER RADIO (IV-Form/style), 2615 N. 4th #797, Coeur d'Alene ID 83814, founded 1986, poetry editor Serge Lecomte **(and submissions should be sent directly to him at P.O. Box 82052, Fairbanks AK 99708)**, is a literary journal appearing 3 times a year. **"Actually what we want doesn't have a descriptive moniker because it is at the vanguard but not yet a movement. Suffice it to say, we are more in the line of descent from Wallace Stevens and the French dadaist and surrealists than from, say, W.C. Williams. Length: up to 100 lines. Style: from** *ambient* **to** *grand mal.* **Do not want to see mainstream theocratic bathos."** They have published poetry by Sheila E. Murphy, Bradley Goldman, Judson Crews and Stacey Sollfrey. The editor describes *Paper Radio* as intended for "pointedly experimental poetry, fiction, graphics and criticism." It is 8¼ × 10⅞, "mixed printing (computer-generated, run on a web press), generally ½ words and ½ graphics." They receive about 3,000 poems/year, accept 25-50. The circulation is 3,000, 350+ subscriptions of which 20 are libraries. Subscription: $19. **Sample postpaid: $3. Pays 1 copy. "No specifications (we're anarchists) but more than 5-6 poems seems pointless or downright unstrategic (makes us feel Sisyphean)." Simultaneous submissions OK. Reports in 1-2 months, 1-8 months delay till publication. On rejections, "we try to give some indication that a human read the work, but it depends on its quality and our workload.** Always remember Borges' comment: 'I write for myself and my friends, and to ease the passing of time.' Greed and mundane equivocation would seem, fortunately, to have no place in poetry—it's the useless utterance that is our greatest fulfillment." Reviews books of poetry "sometimes."

THE PAPER SALAd POETRY JOURNAL (II), 627 E. 100 S. #A, Salt Lake City UT 84102, founded 1990, editor Eldon Holt, is an annual using **"poetry by poets who work rigorously on their poetry, who make every poem an attempt at the 'perfect' poem, and who know that the meaning of a poem is always secondary to the music of the poem."** As a sample the editor selected these lines by Richard Cronshey from "From My Diary Inside Leviathan":

> There is, in the center of these far sounds
> a kind of night that keeps growing
> into itself, darkening
> toward its heart. A homecoming.
> It wants to have its small finale forever
> in solitude. A stone that keeps closing. A thirst
> that names itself Horizon and dies.

The editor describes it as 80-110 pgs. flat-spined, digest-sized. Press run is 250. **Sample: $6.50 ("An additional dollar will help with postage, but is optional"). Pays 1 copy. Replies within 2 months, seldom comments on rejections.** "An optional/non-refundable $2 will include poetry in an annual contest. Prize is $20." The editor says, "I am somewhat embarrassed by how easy it has become for me to quickly reject a poet's submission. For instance, I am sick and tired of reading pages and pages of poetry that is 'Wonderstruck at the opening of a rose.' I've also lost interest in poems that need to mention characters of Greek mythology every paragraph. Also, please no more 'Love is . . .' and 'Life is . . .' poetry. Poetry that goes on and on lamenting the homeless and abortion rights, etc. . . . is just plain boring. *Every single line* should be placed on the page with purpose and meaning and with a certain degree of thought and attention! A poem should inhabit the page the same way the Chinese use Fung Suei in their architecture. Bad poetry almost always seems to be simply the poet's misunderstanding of what a poem must be in order to be a poem. Poets who make this mistake often think poetry has to have an Old English tone, and use words like 'upon' and 'dearly.' Blecchhh!! Good poetry has a kind of music or resonance . . . a voice! Also, if your poem makes me laugh, you stand a better chance of getting it accepted."

PAPIER-MACHE PRESS (IV-Themes, anthologies), 795 Via Manzana, Watsonville CA 95076, phone (408)726-2933, FAX (408)726-1255, founded 1984, editor Sandra Martz, is a small press publisher of anthologies, poetry and short fiction in flat-spined paperbacks and case-bound books. They typically **"work on specialized projects, that explore a particular aspect of women's experience, e.g. sports, aging, parental relationships, work, etc. Any length acceptable; primarily interested in well-written, accessible material."** They have published poetry by Jenny Joseph, Sue Saniel Elkind, Shirley Vogler Meister, Michael Andrews, Ursula Hegi, Maude Meehan and Elisavietta Ritchie. **They publish 1-2 anthologies and 1-2 poetry collections each year. Each anthology contains 30-40 poems; collections contain 60-80 poems. Query before submission to obtain current themes and guidelines. They report on queries in 1 month, on mss in 3 months. Legible photocopies and dot matrix OK. Simultaneous submissions must be identified as such. Pays 2 copies on work accepted for anthologies. Royalties and modest advances are negotiated on individual collections. Send SASE for booklist to buy samples, typically $4-10.** "*Papier Mache*'s primary objective is to publish anthologies, poetry and short story collections by, for and about midlife and older women. Material from socially aware men is welcome. Our strategy is to select subjects of particular importance to women, find well-written, accessible material on those themes, develop attractive, high quality book formats and market them to an audience that might not otherwise buy books of poetry. We take particular pride in our reputation for dealing with our contributors in a caring, professional manner."

PARAGON HOUSE PUBLISHERS (III), 90 5th Ave., New York NY 10011, phone (212)620-2820, founded 1983, editor-in-chief Arthur Samuelson, has published books of poetry by Louis Simpson and Leo Connellan.

PARANOIA PRESS; BACKDROP (II, IV-Regional), 35 Percy St., Middlesbrough, Cleveland TS1 4DD United Kingdom, founded 1984, poetry editor Richard Briddon, publishes 4-5 paperbacks/year. **"We are inclined towards winners of the Cleveland Writearound festival for first collections of local writers. Contemporary mainstream poetry, but quality is the main thing."** As a sample the editor selected these lines from Brian Burr's "Document," a poem in his collection **Fear of Language**:

> I knew a man who would not name himself;
> whose skull was clothed in thin cartography,
> a document of flesh. A library
> of bright tattoos, dreamt sentences, sprouted
> from his skin — a coat of consonant and vowel.

Pays 7-10% royalties, honorarium of £50, and 6 copies. Buys publication rights. Their poets "will usually have published in a quality press previously — e.g. *Stand, London Magazine, Iron,* etc."

THE PARIS REVIEW; BERNARD F. CONNORS PRIZE; JOHN TRAIN HUMOR PRIZE (III, IV-Humor), 45-39 171st Pl., Flushing NY 11358, founded 1952, poetry editor Patricia Storace. **(Submissions should go to her at 541 E. 72nd St., New York NY 10021)**. This distinguished quarterly (circulation 10,000, digest-sized, 200 pgs.) has published many of the major poets writing in English. **Sample: $8. Study publication before submitting. Pays $35 to 24 lines, $50 to 59 lines; $75 to 99 lines; $150 thereafter.** The Bernard F. Connors prize of $1,000 is awarded annually for the best previously unpublished long poem (over 200 lines), submitted between April 1 and May 1. The John Train Humor Prize of $1,500 is awarded annually for the best previously unpublished work of humorous fiction, nonfiction or poetry submitted before March 31. **All submissions must be sent to the 541 E. 72nd St., New York NY 10021 address.**

PARNASSUS LITERARY JOURNAL (I, II), P.O. Box 1384, Forest Park GA 30051, founded 1975, edited by Denver Stull: "Our sole purpose is to promote poetry and to offer an outlet where poets may be heard. **We are open to all poets and all forms of poetry, including Oriental, 24-line limit, maximum 5 poems.**" They have recently published poetry by C. David Hay, Diana K. Rubin, T.K. Splake, Ann Gasser and Alan Renfro. As a sample the editor selected these lines by Rod Farmer:

> The strong are few and though
> they speak in the same language
> as the weak, the masses, it is
> in a different voice. Often the
> majority muffles the free few with
> fashion, conformity, market appeal
> being America's chief censors in
> art, literature, politics, religion.
> And the fashion now is nothing new.

It is photocopied from typescript, uses an occasional drawing, 84 pgs., saddle-stapled. The magazine comes out 3 times a year with a print run of 300 copies. Subscribers presently number 200 (5 libraries). They receive about 1,500 submissions/year, of which they use 350. Circulation includes: Japan, England, Greece, India, Korea, Germany and Nederlands. **Reports within one week. One copy in payment. Acquires all rights. Returns rights. Sample: $3.50** (regularly $4.25/copy, $12/subscription). **Make checks or money order payable to Denver Stull.** Readers vote on best of each issue. Also conducts a contest periodically. **"Definitely" comments on rejected mss.** Reviews books of poetry by subscribers only. The editor advises: "Write about what you know. Study what you have written. Does it make sense? A poem should not leave the reader wondering what you are trying to say. Improve your writings by studying the work of others. Be professional."

PARNASSUS: POETRY IN REVIEW; POETRY IN REVIEW FOUNDATION (V), Room 804, 41 Union Square W., New York NY 10003, phone (212)463-0889, founded 1972, poetry editor Herbert Leibowitz, provides "comprehensive and in-depth coverage of new books of poetry, including translations from foreign poetry." They have published special issues on Words & Music and Women & Poetry, and a special issue on the long poem in 1992. **"We publish poems and translations on occasion, but we solicit all poetry. Poets invited to submit are given all the space they wish; the only stipulation is that the style be non-academic."** They have published work by Alice Fulton, Eavan Boland, Ross Feld, Debora Greger, William Logan, Tess Gallagher, Seamus Heaney and Rodney Jones. They do consider unsolicited essays, but strongly recommend that writers study the magazine before submitting. **They report on essay submissions within 4-10 weeks (response takes longer during the summer), dislike multiple submissions and dot-matrix printing. Pays $25-250 plus 2 gift subscriptions—the contributors can also take one themselves. Acquires all rights. Editor comments on rejections—from 1 paragraph to 2 pages.** Reviews books of poetry in 5-25 pgs. Subscriptions are $18/year, $36/year for libraries; they have 1,100 subscribers, of which 550 are libraries. The editor comments, "Contributors should be urged to subscribe to at least one literary magazine. There is a pervasive ignorance of the cost of putting out a magazine and no sense of responsibility for supporting a magazine."

PARTING GIFTS; MARCH STREET PRESS (I), 3006 Stonecutter Terrace, Greensboro NC 27405, founded 1987, poetry editor Robert Bixby. **"I want to see everything.** I'm a big fan of Jim Harrison, C. K. Williams, Amy Hempel and Janet Kauffman. If you write like them, you'll almost certainly be published. But that's pretty useless advice unless you're one of those people." He has published poetry by Eric Torgersen, Lyn Lifshin, Elizabeth Kerlikowske and Russell Thorburn. *PG* is digest-sized, 36 pgs., photocopied, with colored matte card cover, press run 200, appearing twice a year, **send SASE for guidelines. Subscription: $8. Sample postpaid: $4. Pays 1 copy. "Best time to submit mss is early in the year." Reports in 1-2 weeks. Submit in "groups of 3-10 with SASE and cover letter." No previously published poems, but simultaneous submissions OK. March Street Press publishes chapbooks; $10 reading fee.**

PARTISAN REVIEW (III, IV-Translations, themes), 236 Bay State Rd., Boston MA 02215, phone (617)353-4260, founded 1934, editor William Phillips, is a distinguished quarterly literary journal (6×9, 160 pgs., flat-spined, circulation 8,200 for 6,000 subscriptions and shelf sales), using **poetry of high quality.** They have published poetry by Joseph Brodsky, Eavan Boland, W.S. Merwin and C.H. Sisson. **Submit maximum of 6. Sample postpaid: $6.50. Pays $50 and 50% discount on copies. No simultaneous submissions. Reports in 2 months. Editor "occasionally" comments on rejections.** "Our poetry section is very small and highly selective. We are open to fresh, quality translations but submissions must include poem in original language as well as translation. We occasionally have special poetry sections on specified themes."

PASQUE PETALS; SOUTH DAKOTA STATE POETRY SOCIETY, INC. (I, IV-Regional, subscribers), 909 E. 34th St., Sioux Falls SD 57105, phone (605)338-9156, founded 1926, editor Barbara Stevens. This is the official poetry magazine for the South Dakota State Poetry Society, Inc., but it is open to non-members. **Those not residents of SD are required to subscribe when (or before) submitting. They use "all forms. 44-line limit, 50-character lines. Count titles and spaces. Lean toward SD and Midwest**

themes. No rough language or porno — magazine goes into SD schools and libraries." As a sample the editor chose her poem "The Errol Flynn Look-alike":

> *His tongue was as smooth as honey on a spoon.*
> *Went from job to job,*
> *Fooled everyone at first meeting*
> * talked great projects completed by others.*
> *Fooled his wife all the time,*
> *she grew fat and comfortable*
> * He left her*
> * for a size five.*

PP appears 10 times a year (no August or November issues), digest-sized, 16-20 pgs., using small b&w sketches. Circulation is 250 to member/subscribers (16 to libraries). Subscription: $15/year. **Sample postpaid: $1.50. Send SASE for guidelines. Pays non-members only 1 copy. Acquires first rights. Reports in 3 months. 2-3 month backlog. Submit 3 poems at a time, 1 poem (or 2 haiku)/page, seasonal material 3 months ahead. Editor "always" comments on rejections.** Reviews books of poetry by members only. $5 prize for the best poem in every issue. They sponsor a yearly contest — and sometimes smaller ones are offered by members.

PASSAGER: A JOURNAL OF REMEMBRANCE AND DISCOVERY (I, II, IV-Senior citizen, themes), University of Baltimore, 1420 N. Charles St., Baltimore MD 21201-5779, phone (301)625-3041, founded 1989, editors Kendra Kopelke and Sally Darnowsky. *Passager* is published quarterly and publishes fiction, poetry, essays and interviews that give voice to human experience. **"We seek powerful images of remembrance and discovery from writers of all ages. One of our missions is to provide exposure for new older writers; another is to function as a literary community for writers across the country who are not connected to academic institutions or other organized groups."** The journal is 8×8, 32 pgs., printed on white linen, saddle-stitched. Includes photos of writers. **Poetry, 30 lines maximum; fiction and essays, 3,000 words maximum. Pays 1 year's subscription. Reports in 2 months. Simultaneous submissions acceptable if notified. No reprints. Do not submit mss in August. Occasionally does special issues. Send SASE for guidelines.** They sponsor an annual poetry contest for poets over 50 years old. Prize is $100 and publication in *Passager*.

PASSAGES NORTH (II), Kalamazoo College, 1200 Academy St., Kalamazoo MI 49007, founded 1979, general editor Ben Mitchell, poetry editor Mark Cox, is a **semiannual tabloid** (i.e., white uncoated paper, folded, unstapled), though the quality of paper and printing are higher than that term implies. "The magazine not only publishes established writers, but also encourages students in writing programs." They have recently published poetry by Tess Gallagher, Stephen Berg, Mark Halliday, Susan Stewart, Nancy Eimers, Thomas Lux and Lawrence Rabb. As a sample the editor selected these lines from "Zero Eighteen" by Medbh McGuckian:

> *I seem to sleep across the door*
> *Of a house call "Be Off, Anger,"*
> *Though my lips touch the shoes*
> *Of the hundreds that pass*
> *And their eyes carpet the floor.*

PN is 36 pgs., tabloid format, offset on quality recycled white paper, each issue containing a portfolio of graphic arts or photography, limited ads, with a circulation of 2,500 for 900 subscriptions of which 29 are libraries; 1,000 copies distributed free as promo at conferences and colleges. Subscription: $5/year; $8/2 years. **Sample postpaid: $3. Reads submissions September 1 through May 1 only. Pays when grants permit, plus 3 copies. Reports in 6-8 weeks, delay to publication 6 months. Prefers groups of 4-6, typed single-spaced. Simultaneous submissions.** Reviews books of poetry, "open to any length."

PASSAIC REVIEW (II), % Forstmann Library, 195 Gregory Ave., Passaic NJ 07055, founded 1979, poetry editor Richard Quatrone, has published **a number of our most notable poets, such as Allen Ginsberg and David Ignatow.** It comes out twice a year in an offset, typescript, saddle-stapled, 48-page, digest-sized format, with occasional artwork. The editor says he wants "**direct, intelligent, courageous, imaginative, free writing.**" They print 1,000 copies, have 75 subscriptions (20 libraries). Each issue is $3.75, subscription $6. **Sample back issue: $2.75.** They have a 4- to 6-month backlog and **report in 4-6 months. Pays 1 copy. Rarely comments.**

PATH PRESS, INC. (IV-Ethnic), Suite 724, 53 W. Jackson Blvd., Chicago IL 60604, phone (312)663-0167, FAX (312)663-5318, founded 1969, president Bennett J. Johnson, executive vice president and poetry editor Herman C. Gilbert, a small publisher of books and poetry primarily "**by, for and about African American and Third World people.**" The press is open to all types of poetic forms except "poor quality." Submissions should be typewritten in manuscript format. Writers should send sample poems, credits and bio. The books are "hardback and quality paperbacks."

PAUPER'S PRESS; PHAERWIND REVIEW (I, II), Winchester Springs, Ontario K0C 2L0 Canada, phone (613)774-0205, founded 1990, editor Heather O'Neil, uses **"any kind"** of poetry **"from traditional, haiku, free verse to experimental. Nothing obscene, violent, abusive, horror."** They have recently published poetry by Robert Hogg, W.A. Crawford and Ashton Davis. As a sample the editor selected these lines from "On the Characters in Certain Operas" by R.L. Cook:

> *And when we, smug, secure, the channelled men,*
> *Have passed beyond the end of life's canal,*
> *Who will create our loves and hates again,*
> *While they, made glorious in festival,*
> *Loving and hating, will be living yet.*

Pauper's Press appears 4 times/year. It is 24 pgs. minimum, magazine-sized, photocopied, side-stapled with b&w card cover, illustrations throughout. Press run 200 for 30 subscribers of which 2 are libraries; 170 shelf sales. Subscription: $20 Canadian, $25 foreign. **Sample postpaid: $5. Send SASE for guidelines. Pays 1-2 copies.** *Phaerwind Review* is now monthly. It is 14 pgs. minimum, magazine-sized, computer printed, side-stapled with a paper cover. Press run is 125 for 21 subscribers, 104 shelf sales. Subscription: $18 Canadian for 6 issues, $21 foreign. **Sample postpaid: $3. Pays 1-2 copies.** The editor says, "Never stop submitting your work. Perseverance and hard work are the keys to your success."

PEACE AND FREEDOM; PEACE AND FREEDOM TAPE MAGAZINE; EASTERN RAINBOW (I), 17 Farrow Rd., Whaplode Drove, Spalding, Lincs PE12 0TS England, phone 0406-330242, editor Paul Rance, founded 1985, is a "small press publisher of poetry, music, art, short stories, reviews and general features, tapes," and also is a distributor. *Peace and Freedom* is a magazine appearing 2 times a year. **"We are looking for poems up to 32 lines particularly from U.S. poets who are new to writing, and women. The poetry we publish is anti-war, of environmental slant, poems reflecting love; erotic, but not obscene, poetry, spiritual, humanitarian poetry. With or without rhyme/metre."** They have recently published poetry by Michelle Prieto, Debra Negus, Kathlyn King, Chris McGlynn and Margaret Connaughton. These sample lines are by Josh Samuels:

> *What ties your tongue,*
> *Carousels your brain,*
> *What holds you hostage*
> *Still.*

Peace and Freedom has a card cover, normally 20 A4 pages. "Pen pal ads included, and a correspondence section for poets is planned. 25% of submissions accepted. Poetry is judged on merit, but non-subscribers may have to wait longer for their work to appear than subscribers." **Sample: US $2; 75 p. and SAE UK.** "Sample copies can only be purchased from the above address, and various mail-order distributors too numerous to mention. Advisable to buy a sample copy first. Banks charge the equivalent of $5 to cash foreign cheques in the U.K., so advisable to send bills, preferably by registered post. We're not too impressed by poems sent without an accompanying note or letter. We like the personal touch." Subscription: US $9, U.K. £4 for 4 issues. **Pays 1 copy. Simultaneous submissions and previously published poems OK. Reads submissions February 2 through October 31.** Replies to submissions normally under a month, with IRC/SAE. Reviews books of poetry. *Peace and Freedom Tape Magazine* is a quarterly tape version of *Peace and Freedom*. Poems are read out by either the editor or a guest reader. Music, plays, stories, reviews also featured. Sample copy £2.50/$6. Poets are requested to send in bios. Guidelines same as magazine. "*Peace and Freedom* now holds regular contests as does one of our new publications, *Eastern Rainbow*, which is a magazine concerning 20th century pop culture, beat poetry/sci-fi poetry on 20th century life/people/things required. Subscription: $9/£4 for 4 issues. Further details of competitions and publications for SAE with IRC." The editor says, "Writers know, often, as much about writing as editors, but lack confidence much of the time. Have confidence, and editors will be more inclined to take notice. Don't be apologetic when sending your work!"

‡**THE PEACE FARM ADVOCATE (IV-Social issues)**, HCR 2 Box 25, Panhandle TX 79068, phone (806)335-1715, founded 1986, editor Mavis Belisle, is a quarterly which promotes peace making through information, commentary and reflection. **"We consider only poetry related to peace and social justice issues."** As a sample the editor selected these lines from "Packing for Saudi Arabia" by Mary Carter Rak:

> *I stare at the empty green bag*
> *I must fill in the next fifteen minutes*
> *with things most important*
> *to you. Underwear, T-shirts,*

> *your St. Christopher medal*
> *wrapped in tissue.*

The Peace Farm Advocate is 40 pgs., 8½×11, printed on recycled newsprint. Press run is 3,000 for 600 paid subscribers. The rest are distributed free. Subscription: $5. **Previously published poems and simultaneous submissions OK.** Time between acceptance and publication is 3-6 months. **Reports in 6 months. "We do not pay for published poems."** The editor says, "Because of downsizing, opportunity will be very limited; we do not expect to be able to accept more than 1-2 short to medium-length poems per issue."

THE PEACE NEWSLETTER (IV-Social issues, political), Syracuse Peace Council, 924 Burnet Ave., Syracuse NY 13203, founded 1936, is magazine-sized, 24 pgs., circulating 12 times a year to 5,000 people mostly in upstate and central NY with news about the peace movement and using **some poetry relating to that movement.** Subscription: $12/year. **Unable to pay for submissions. Considers simultaneous submissions. Reads submissions February 15 through March 15 only. Sample free for SASE.**

‡PEACOCK BOOKS; PEACOCK POSTCARD SERIES (I), College Square, Cuttack, Orissa, India 753003, founded 1988, editor Bibhu Padhi, **requires poets "to purchase at least 100 paperbound copies of their books at a 30% discount on list price which varies between US $10 and $15/UK 5.95 to 9.95 pounds** (depending on the size of the book). We are a nonprofit small press and receive no grants. The poets themselves, we assume, would be our first buyers. We pay 10% of print run in lieu of royalties. Acquires first publication rights only; rights revert to author 2 years from date of publication. Full-length volumes of poetry and poem-postcards; sometimes chapbooks. All our books will be set, printed and bound by hand, using high-quality paper—both hardback and hand-bound paperbacks. Collections of miscellaneous poems; poem sequences; long-poems. We are particularly interested in poems that are emotionally mature and genuine, that have something to say—poems that forcefully address problems and do not merely state them. Serious poetry only. No pornographic verse; no gay verse; no experiment for its own sake; nothing, in fact, that is less than first-rate; and of course no mush romantic lyrics. No children's verse." He has published on postcards poetry by Naomi Shihab Nye and Robert Richman. As a sample the editor selected these lines from a postcard of William Stafford's "Starting the Day":

> *Day waits, then imperceptibly has come.*
> *Yesterday, gone, fades, is brown,*
> *gray, pale, extinct, then never was.*
> *Time starts again, rises, becomes*
> *now, the steam above your cup.*

"At this time, **we are on the lookout for 2-3 good, 56-80 page (typed, double-spaced) collections from writers who haven't had a book published yet, but who have had at least some magazine publication. If submission is from outside India, SAE and International Reply Coupon are a must."** Reads submissions January 1 through June 30 only. Recently published **Magic Places** (Margaret Cook). Forthcoming titles: **Planet Requiem** (Cliff Forshaw), **diary of an American heart** (Thomas J.L. Bronsberg-Adas), and **In Search of Cosmic Christ** (Robert Dante). In the postcard series: Roger Elkin. Titles available for **Writer's Market** and **Poet's Market** readers for $6 in paperback, $9 hardbound (list prices: $10 and $15). Poemcards are available for $3 for a set of 10. **Responds to queries in 1 month, mss 2 months. "We expect potential authors to have had some magazine-publishing experience."**

PEARL; PEARL CHAPBOOK CONTEST (II), 3030 E. Second St., Long Beach CA 90803, phone (310)434-4523 or (714)968-7530, founded 1974, folded after 3 issues, resurrected in 1987, poetry editors Joan Jobe Smith, Marilyn Johnson and Barbara Hauk, is a literary magazine appearing twice a year. "We are interested in accessible, humanistic poetry that communicates and is related to real life. Humor and wit are welcome, along with the ironic and serious. No taboos stylistically or subjectwise. Prefer poems up to 35 lines, with lines no longer than 10 words. We don't want to see sentimental, obscure, predictable, abstract or cliché-ridden poetry. Our purpose is to provide a forum for lively, readable poetry that reflects a wide variety of contemporary voices, viewpoints and experiences—that speaks to *real* people about *real* life in direct, living language, profane or sublime." They have recently published poetry by Charles Bukowski, Holly Prado, Edward Field, Donna Hilbert and Gerald Locklin. As a sample they selected these lines from "My Father's Hands" by Lizbeth Parker:

> *I picture his hands and their rhythm*
> *with brick and mortar. Scoop, fling,*
> *tap, tap, scrape around, fling. Lulled*
> *by the certain rhythm of my father*
> *laying brick, I sleep. Scoop fling,*
> *tap, tap, scrape around, fling.*

> *My father heals the only way he knows*
> *He builds things to last me a lifetime.*

Pearl is digest-sized, 72 pgs., saddle-stapled, professionally printed (offset from camera-ready copy). Their press run is 500 with 70 subscriptions of which 7 are libraries. Subscription: $10/ year. **Sample postpaid: $5. Guidelines available for SASE. Pays 2 copies. Acquires first serial rights. "Handwritten submissions and unreadable dot-matrix print-outs are not acceptable. Cover letters appreciated." Reports in 6-8 weeks. No simultaneous submissions or previously published poems.** Each issue contains the work of 40-50 different poets and a special 10-15 page section that showcases the work of a single poet. "We sponsor an annual chapbook contest, judged by one of our more well-known contributors. Winner receives publication, $100 and 50 copies, with an introduction by the final judge. (To date, judges have been Gerald Locklin, Laurel Speer, Robert Peters and Donna Hilbert). Entries accepted during the months of May and June. There is a $10 entry fee, which includes a copy of the winning chapbook." Send SASE for complete rules and guidelines. "Advice for beginning poets? Just write from your own experience, using images that are as concrete and sensory as possible. Keep these images fresh and objective, and always listen to the music. . . ."

PEBBLE; BEST CELLAR PRESS, Dept. of English, University of Nebraska-Lincoln, Lincoln NE 68588. Declined listing.

PECKERWOOD (I), 1503-1465 Lawrence W., Toronto, Ontario M6L 1B2 Canada, phone (416)248- 2675, founded 1987, editor Ernie Ourique, appears 3 or 4 times/year. **"It could be any style you wish, any length. Haiku—yes. Rhymes—yes. Beauty—yes. Ugliness—yes. No clones of good poets, creative writing class crap or poems written by television housewives."** They have recently published poetry by Chris Wood, Stan Rogal, John Bennett, Ibi Kaslik, Charles Bukowski and Allen Ginsberg. As a sample the editor selected these lines from "Unlike Mine" by Yuki Hayashi:

> *duckweed*
> *pond*
> *no whale*
> *just another carp*
> *with eyes like hers*

It is 30-40 pgs., saddle-stapled, photocopied from typescript with matte card cover. They accept about 30% of poems received. Press run 150, 60 shelf sales. **Sample postpaid: $1. Pays 5 copies. Acquires all rights. Editors always provide comments on rejections.** Ernie Ourique says, "The poems should have tongues and hearts. No one can teach you how to write poetry. Don't accept the 'masters' of poetry (Pound, Eliot, Yeats) as the greatest. Explore poetry from all over the world. This means reading more than writing. Also get a job that doesn't involve brains: construction, washing toilets. You'll meet the greatest and worst human beings in the working class. Never insult people."

PEGASUS (II), 525 Ave. B., Boulder City NV 89005, founded 1986, editor M. E. Hildebrand, is a poetry quarterly for serious poets who have something to say and know how to say it using sensory imagery. Publishes 10-15% of the work received. **Submit 3-5 poems, 3-40 lines. Avoid "religious, political, pornographic themes."** They have recently published poetry by Stan Moseley, Gayle Elen Harvey, Robert K. Johnson and Elizabeth Perry, who provides the opening lines of "The Meeting Hour" as a sample:

> *Before Dawn drops*
> *her luminous petals*
> *I wake and listen*
> *for your muted voice*
> *to break the silence*
> *of our worlds*
> *like rustlings*
> *in the deep woods.*

Pegasus is 32 pgs., digest-sized, saddle-stapled, offset from typescript, colored paper cover, subscription $12.50, circulation 200. **Sample or single copy: $4.50, includes postage. Send SASE for**

Market conditions are constantly changing! If you're still using this book and it is 1994 or later, buy the newest edition of Poet's Market at your favorite bookstore or order directly from Writer's Digest Books.

guidelines. **Reports in 2 weeks. Previously published poems OK, provided poet retains rights, but no simultaneous submissions. Publication is payment. Acquires first or one-time rights.**

THE PEGASUS REVIEW (I, II, IV-Themes), P.O. Box 134, Flanders NJ 07836, founded 1980, is a 14-page (counting cover) pamphlet entirely in calligraphy, illustrated on high-quality paper, some color overlays. Poetry editor Art Bounds says, "This magazine is a bimonthly, **based on specific themes: January/February – Challenge; March/April – Education; May/June – Childhood; July-August – Civilization; September/October – Heroes; and November/December – Belief. Poetry not more than 24 lines, the shorter the better; (short short, about 3 pages would be ideal); essays and cartoons. Approach themes in a unique manner. Looking for brevity as well as clarity."** Poets recently published: Anne Valley, Jim De Witt, Edward W. Stever and Joanne Seltzer. As a sample the editor selected these lines from "Experience" by Richard Franklin:

> *We plant plump seeds with hopeful glow*
> *   then harvest hemlock leaves of woe –*
> *   Must growing old be always so?*

Subscription: $8. **Sample: $2. Query if there are any questions or additional information needed.** 158 copies are printed for 150 subscriptions, of which 3 are libraries. **Reports within a month, often with a personal response. Pays 2 copies.** Occasional book awards throughout the year. The editor advises, "Set aside a special time daily to write. Keep abreast of what is being read today. Experiment with the various forms of poetry. If anything, you'll find them stimulating. Market your work. Perseverance is a trait most writers must acquire. If possible, get involved with a local writers group – a great asset."

‡PELICAN PUBLISHING COMPANY (V, IV-Children), Box 189, Gretna LA 70054, phone (504)368-1175, founded 1926, editor Nina Kooij, is a "moderate-sized publisher of cookbooks, travel guides, regional books and inspirational/motivational books," which accepts **poetry for "hardcover children's books** *only*, preferably with a Southern focus. However, our needs for this are very limited; we do fewer than 5 juvenile titles per year, and most of these are prose, not poetry." They are currently not accepting unsolicited mss. Query first with credits and bio. No dot-matrix, no simultaneous submissions; clear photocopies OK. Reports on queries in 1 month, on mss (if invited) in 3 months. Pays royalties. Buys all rights. Returns rights upon termination of contract.** These are 32 pgs. large-format (magazine-sized) books with illustrations. Two of their popular series are prose books about Gaston the Green-Nosed Alligator by James Rice and Clovis Crawfish by Mary Alice Fontenot. They have a variety of books based on "The Night Before Christmas" adapted to regional settings such as Cajun, prairie, and Texas. Typically their books sell for $13.95. **Write for catalog to buy samples.**

PEMBROKE MAGAZINE (II), Box 60, Pembroke State University, Pembroke NC 28372, founded 1969 by Norman Macleod, edited by Shelby Stephenson, a heavy (252+ pgs., 6×9), flat-spined, quality literary annual, which has published Fred Chappell, Stephen Sandy, Charles Edward Eaton, M.H. Abrams and Betty Adcock. Print run: 500, subscriptions: 125, of which 100 are libraries. **Sample: $5 postpaid. Reports within 3 months. Pays copies. Sometimes comments on rejections.** Stephenson advises, "Publication will come if you write. Writing is all."

‡PENDRAGON (II), VSC Box 7110, Valdosta GA 31698, founded 1983 under the name *Odradek*, is a biannual literary publication of Valdosta State College. **"We publish the best fiction and poetry we can find. No particular preferences. Send your best. No more than 3 pages usually. No poorly-crafted work."** They have recently published poetry by Trent Busch, Mick Loggins and Raymond Register. As a sample the editor selected these lines from "Georgia Evening" by Faye Altman:

> *Light the fire.*
> *There will be time tonight for neighbors*
> *   and guitar picking.*
> *Someone will tell a story of their childhood*

Pendragon is about 75 pgs., digest-sized, perfect-bound and publishes approximately 15% of poetry received. Press run is 700. Subscription: $8. **Sample postpaid: $4. No previously published poems or simultaneous submissions. Cover letter required. Reads submissions September 15 through June 15. Seldom comments on rejections. Reports in 2-3 months. Pays 2 copies. Acquires first rights.** The editors award an annual $50 prize for the best poetry of the year. Contributions here are not only from English departments but also from poets with varied careers and backgrounds (i.e. counselors, political scientists, journalists). The work is appealing because the authors focus on a number of critical concerns, including racism and diversity, from differing viewpoints.

‡PENNINE INK (I, II), % MPAA The Gallery Downstairs, Burnley BB10 3JJ Great Britain, founded 1985, appears approximately every 9 months using mainly poems, a few short prose items and 1 or 2 b&w illustrations. "Local and dialect items welcome plus worldwide." They want **"poetry up to 40**

lines maximum. **Consider all kinds. Contributions from poets having links with Lancashire/N. England welcome. This does not exclude others.**" As a sample the editor selected these lines (poet unidentified):

> *Between her quick pillow and the world*
> *Between the deeper secret and the shore*
> *Colliding waves shattered glass mountains hurled*
> *And heaved their burden from the ocean floor.*

The editor says it is 40 pgs., A3, with b&w illustrated cover, a few small local ads and 3 or 4 b&w graphics. They receive about 200 poems a year, use approximately 30. Press run is 300. Single copy: £1 sterling. **Sample postpaid 75 p. and SAE. Previously published poems and simultaneous submissions OK. Cover letter preferred. Seldom comments on rejections. "Contributors whose works are accepted receive one free copy if SAE sent."** Reviews small press poetry books in about 200 words.

PENNINE PLATFORM (II), Ingmanthorpe Hall Farm Cottage, Wetherby, W. Yorkshire, England LS22 5EQ, phone 0937-64674, founded 1973, poetry editor Brian Merrikin Hill, appears 3 times a year. The editor wants **any kind of poetry but concrete ("lack of facilities for reproduction"). No specifications of length, but poems of less than 40 lines have a better chance. "All styles—effort is to find things good of their kind. Preference for religious or sociopolitical awareness of an acute, not conventional kind."** They have recently published poetry by Elizabeth Bartlett, Anna Adams, John Ward, Stanley Cook, Ian Caws, John Latham and B.W. Reynon. As a sample the editor selected these lines from "History" by D.A. Goodall:

> *Is the kick in the arse*
> *Which the rich and powerful*
> *Should learn to expect*
> *From those whom they have tried to ignore.*
> *We call it hindsight.*

The 6 × 8, 48-page journal is photocopied from typescript, saddle-stapled, with matte card cover with graphics, circulation 400, 300 subscriptions of which 16 are libraries. They receive about 300 submissions/year, use about 30, have about a 6-month backlog. Subscription £7 for 3 issues (£10 abroad; £25 if not in sterling). **Sample postpaid: £2. Submit 1-6 poems, typed or photocopied. Reports in about a month. No pay. Acquires first serial rights. Editor occasionally comments on rejections.** Reviews books of poetry in 2,500 words, multi-book format. Brian Hill comments, "It is time to avoid the paradigm-magazine-poem and reject establishments—ancient, modern or allegedly contemporary. Small magazines and presses often publish superior material to the commercial hyped publishers."

PENNSYLVANIA ENGLISH (II), Penn State-Erie, Erie PA 16563, founded 1988 (first issue in March, 1989), contact poetry editor, is "a journal sponsored by the Pennsylvania College English Association." They want poetry of **"any length, any style."** It is magazine-sized, saddle-stapled, and appears twice a year, press run 300. Subscription: $15, which includes membership in PCEA. **Pays 2 copies. Submit 4-5 typed poems. Do not submit mss in the summer. They consider simultaneous submissions but not previously published poems. Reports in 1 month.**

THE PENNSYLVANIA REVIEW (II), English Dept., 526 CL, University of Pittsburgh, Pittsburgh PA 15260, phone (412)624-0026, founded 1985, editor Lori Jakiela. This ambitious journal was described by *Choice* as "a fine small literary magazine." **There are no restrictions on subject matter, style or length, although they do not not want to see "light verse or greeting card verse."** They have published poetry by Nance Van Winckel, Eric Pankey, Maggie Anderson, Sharon Doubiago, Harry Humes, Debra Bruce, Leslie Adrienne Miller and translations of Karl Krolow by Stuart Friebert. *The Pennsylvania Review* announces that it publishes "the best contemporary prose and poetry twice yearly." It is a handsome magazine, 7 × 10, 80 pgs., flat-spined, professionally printed on heavy stock with graphics, art and ads, glossy card cover with b&w illustration. Circulation is approximately 1,000 with 300 subscriptions. Subscription: $10. **Sample postpaid: $5. Pays 2 copies. Submission deadlines are November 30 for Spring issue, April 1 for Fall issue. Submissions are not accepted between June 1 and September 1. Submissions are reported on in 2-3 months. Writers should submit 3-6 poems, typewritten only, clear photocopies OK but no dot-matrix.** Reviews books of poetry.

PENTAGRAM PRESS (V), 4925 S. Nicollet Ave., Minneapolis MN 55409, phone (612)824-4576, founded 1974, poetry editor Michael Tarachow, who is also printer and publisher. **Not reading new manuscripts.** Pentagram publishes broadsides, postcards and pamphlets in addition to books. They have published poetry by Philip Gallo, Theodore Enslin, Robie Liscomb and Clifford Burke. "Pentagram uses handset metal type to publish letterpress books on contemporary poetry. *Time* is the invisible factor: even a small project can take 300-500 hours. What would you sell that portion of your life for?"

‡**THE PENUMBRA PRESS (II)**, 920 S. 38th St., Omaha NE 68105, phone (402)346-7344, founded 1972, poetry editors Bonnie O'Connell and George O'Connell, publishes "contemporary literature and graphics in the tradition of fine arts printing." Their books are "designed, illustrated (unless otherwise indicated), hand printed from hand-set type, and bound by the proprietor," Bonnie O'Connell. All are limited editions, including hard and soft cover books, chapbooks, postcards and theme anthologies. They have published poetry by David St. John, Sam Pereira, Brenda Hillman, Debora Greger, Peter Everwine, Laura Jensen, Norman Dubie and Rita Dove. As a sample the editor selected these lines from "Cool Dark Ode" by Donald Justice:

> *When the long planed table that served as a desk*
> *was recalling the quiet of the woods*
> *when the books, older, were thinking farther back,*
> *to the same essential stillness . . .*

Query with 5-6 samples, some personal background and publication credits. Simultaneous submissions, photocopies OK. Editor sometimes comments on rejections. Send SASE for catalog to order samples or inquire at university libraries (special collection) or through the distributor, Nebraska Book Arts Center, 124 Fine Arts Bldg., University of Nebraska-Omaha, Omaha NE 68182.

PEOPLENET (I, IV-Specialized, romance), P.O. Box 897, Levittown NY 11756, phone (516)579-4043, founded 1987, editor/publisher Robert Mauro, is a newsletter **for disabled people focusing on dating, love and relationships.** The editor wants **"poetry on relationships, love and romance. The length should remain 10-20 lines. 3 or 4 poems at a time. We publish beginners, new poets. Prefer free verse, a lot of good imagery—and very little rhyme."** As a sample the editor chose these lines from his poem "When All That Blooms Are Roses":

> *Mornings are not mornings*
> *when all that blooms are roses:*
> *dewy petals opening, blushing*
> *in the wind; a hand*
> *plucks a flower, a finger*
> *touches a bud that didn't*
> *bloom and never will.*

Peoplenet appears 3 times a year and is 12-16 pgs., magazine-sized, offset, using graphics and ads. Press run is about 200, with that many subscriptions. Subscription: $17. **Pays tearsheets only. Acquires first rights.** (Copies of the newsletter, which contains personal ads, go to subscribers only. Free brochure available.) **Poems should be double-spaced, with name and address on each page. No simultaneous submissions. Reports "immediately." Editor comments on rejected mss.** He says, **"We want to publish poems that express the importance of love, acceptance, inner beauty, the need for love and relationship, and the joy of loving and being loved."**

PEP PUBLISHING; LOVING MORE (I, IV-Themes, group marriage), (formerly Paradise Educational Partnership), P.O. Box 6306, Captain Cook HI 96704-6306, founded 1984, editor Ryam Nearing. *Loving More* "publishes articles, letters, poems, drawings, reviews, related to **polyfidelity, group marriage and multiple** *intimacy*." They use "**relatively short poems, though a quality piece of length would be considered, but topic relevance is essential. Please no swinger or porno pieces.**" It is magazine-sized, 14 pgs., few ads. Quarterly. Circulation 500. Subscription: $25 a year. **Sample: $2 to poets. Pays 1 copy. Responds "ASAP," delay to publication 2-6 months. Ms should be "readable." Considers simultaneous submissions. Editor comments on rejections "sometimes—if requested."** The editor says, "Writers should read our publication before submitting, and I emphasize no swinger or porno pieces will be published."

PEQUOD: A JOURNAL OF CONTEMPORARY LITERATURE AND LITERARY CRITICISM (III, IV-Translations), Dept. of English, Room 200, New York University, 19 University Place, New York NY 10003, contact poetry editor, is a semiannual literary review publishing **quality poetry, fiction, essays and translations.** They have recently published poetry by David Baker, Lynda Hull and Sam Hamill. Subscription: $12 annually. **Sample postpaid: $5.** It is a professionally-printed, digest-sized, 130+ pgs., flat-spined magazine with glossy card cover. **Reads submissions September 15 through May 15 only.**

PERCEPTIONS (IV-Women), 1530 Phillips, Missoula MT 59802, founded 1982, poetry editor Temi Rose, is a "small prize-winning **women's poetry magazine for the promotion and development of women's consciousness of peace and hope and freedom to be.**" They have recently published poetry by Claudette Bass and Vivian Bogardus. As a sample the editor selected these lines by Sandra Goldsmith:

> *Whatever the new task receptive*
> > *she sings*
> *Conceding resilience while stretching*

> *her wings.*

Perceptions is 30 pgs., digest-sized, photocopied from typescript with colored paper cover and comes out 3 times a year. They publish about 250 of 1,000 poems received/year; their press run is 100 with 30 subscriptions of which 3 are libraries. Subscriptions: $15. **Sample postpaid: $5. Guidelines available for SASE. Pays 1 copy. They consider simultaneous submissions and previously published poems and report in 1-3 months.**

PEREGRINE: THE JOURNAL OF AMHERST WRITERS & ARTISTS (II); AWA CHAPBOOK SERIES (V), Box 1076, Amherst MA 01004, *Peregrine* founded 1983, Amherst Writers & Artists Press, Inc., 1987. **Open to all styles, forms, subjects except greeting-card verse.** They have recently published poetry by Jane Yolen, Walter McDonald and Barbara Van Noord. As a sample the editors selected these lines by Carol Edelstein:

> *Nothing winged at the hummingbird feeder*
> *But us girls, taking the sun, and notes.*
> *We lean, like young broccoli, slightly forward*
> *Under green whirligig hats, ready*
> *To catch words, and if possible, whole sentences*
> *As they dart up from the ground.*
> *Shrubbery tells only the truth,*
> *For this we are grateful . . .*

"We try to publish twice a year, but sometimes cannot because of finances. **We may hold poems for several months, and so we encourage simultaneous submissions.**" *Peregrine* is digest-sized, 70+ pgs., flat-spined, professionally printed, with matte card cover. Their press run is 500. **Pays contributor's copies. Sample: $4.50 postpaid.** The AWA Chapbook Series publishes handsome collections on a cooperative basis. **"No unsolicited chapbook manuscripts, please. Query only."**

PERMAFROST (II, IV-Regional), English Dept., University of Alaska, Fairbanks AK 99775-0640, phone (907)474-5237, founded 1977. "Editors change annually." *Permafrost* is a biannual journal of poems, short stories, essays, reviews, b&w drawings and photographs. "We survive on both new and established writers, and hope and expect to see your best work (we are not the Siberia of mediocre poetry). **We publish any style of poetry provided it is conceived, written, revised with care; favor poems with strong, unusual images or poems with abstraction backed up by imagery; both must have universal applications. We discourage 'tourist poetry' which rarely works because of its hackneyed imagery and lack of universal theme; encourage poems about Alaska and by Alaskans, but they are works and writers at ease with their setting. We also encourage poems about anywhere and from anywhere. We are not a regional publication, but in order to support contemporary Alaskan literature, we publish reviews only of work by Alaskan authors or publishers.**" They have published poetry by Wendy Bishop, Jerah Chadwick, Leslie Leyland Fields, Linda Gregg, Patricia Monaghan, John Morgan, Peggy Shumaker and Kim Stafford. The digest-sized journal is 100+ pgs., flat-spined, professionally printed, two-color paper cover with b&w graphics and photos, has a circulation of 500 with 100 subscriptions of which 20 are libraries. Subscription: $7. **Sample postpaid: $4. Deadlines are December 1 and April 1. Return time is 1-3 months;** "longer if work was submitted well before deadline and is under serious consideration." **Does not accept submissions between April 1 and August 1. Submit no more than 5 poems, neatly typed or photocopied; considers simultaneous submissions but** "expects to be told." **Guidelines available for SASE,** ("although most are listed here"). **Pays 2 copies, reduced contributor rates on others.** Editors comment only on mss that have made the final round and then are rejected. Depth of comments vary.

PERSEA BOOKS (III), 60 Madison Ave., New York NY 10017, phone (212)779-7668, editor Michael Braziller, publishes books of **"serious"** poetry. They have published poetry by Thylias Moss, Paul Blackburn and Les Murray. They publish 4-6 paperbacks and the same number of hardbacks/year. **Reports in 4-6 weeks. Payment "negotiable."**

THE PET GAZETTE (IV-Themes), 1309 N. Halifax, Daytona Beach FL 32118, phone (904)255-6935, founded 1984, editor Faith A. Senior, a quarterly journal that wants **"poems about animals, nature and/or ecology. Simple and easily understood, in behalf of animals overall, short poems preferred."** She does not want "haiku, and ultra-contrived and/or highly intellectual." Poets frequently in *The Pet Gazette* are Vincent Hathaway, John Coulbourn, Rhoda Rainbow, Johnathan Russell, C. David Hay and S. Mary Ann Henn. *Pet Gazette* is magazine-sized, offset on 60 lb. opaque paper, in many type styles with b&w photos and drawings, folded and saddle-stapled with b&w photos on cover, inserts from various pro-animal organizations. Circulation is 300, subscription $12.50 yearly. **Sample copy available for $2.50 postpaid. Payment is in copies.** Reporting time is "upon receipt," and time to publication is "sometimes a year, though usually much sooner."

PETRONIUM PRESS (V, IV-Regional), 1255 Nuuanu Ave., 1813, Honolulu HI 96817, founded 1975, editor Frank Stewart. Petronium is a small press publisher of poetry, fiction, essays and art—"**primarily interested in writers in and from Hawaii, but will publish others under special circumstances.** Interested in fine printing, fine typography and design in limited editions." They publish chapbooks, trade books, limited editions, broadsides and "other ephemera," but they "**are not accepting unsolicited material at this time.**" They publish 3-6 poetry chapbooks/year, with an average page count of 32, flat-spined paperbacks. The editor says, "**Query letters are welcome, with SASE.**" He replies to queries within 3 weeks and reports on mss in the same amount of time. He has "no special requirements," but will not accept photocopied or dot-matrix mss or discs. "Payment of authors is negotiated differently for each book." Buys all rights. Returns rights by request. The editor does not comment on rejections "unless the material is exceptionally good." He says, "We are not really for beginners nor, in general, for people outside the Pacific region. We are not strict regionalists, but believe in nurturing first the writers around us. Beginning writers might do well to look for publishers with this same philosophy in their own cities and states rather than flinging their work to the wind, to unknown editors or to large publishing houses. All writers should consider supporting quality publishing in their own region first." Some of Petronium's books are distributed by the University of Hawaii Press (2840 Kolowalu St., Honolulu HI 96822) and may be obtained from them; "send for their literature catalog or ask for our titles specifically."

‡**PHANES PRESS (IV-Translations, spirituality)**, P.O. Box 6114, Grand Rapids MI 49516, phone (616)281-1224, founded 1985, publisher David Fideler, publishes "**Sufi poetry translations, translations of ancient Greek hymns and poetry on Western spiritual traditions.**" They have published 2 Sufi poetry anthologies, 1 translation of German philosophical poetry and 1 Greek hymn translation to date. "Most titles are published in both cloth and paper." They want "**mostly translations of Sufi poetry and Greek hymns. No poetry on Eastern traditions or any others that are out of our publishing realm. Please query first to ensure that your manuscript is appropriate for our publication list as we are very specialized.**" Replies to queries in 6 weeks, to mss in 1 month. Seldom comments on rejections. Pays 5-10% royalties and 5-10 author's copies. For sample books, write for catalog.

PHASE AND CYCLE; PHASE AND CYCLE PRESS (II), 3537 E. Prospect, Fort Collins CO 80525, phone (303)482-7573, founded 1988, poetry editor Loy Banks. *Phase and Cycle* is a poetry magazine published semiannually. "**We look for short-to-moderate-length poems of all kinds, especially those that set out 'the long perspectives open at each instance of our lives' (Larkin). We are looking for poetry that will pass technical inspection in the academic community.**" They have recently published poetry by David Rigsbee, Daniel James Sundahl, Lawrence Minet, Mary Balazs and William Aarnes. The magazine is digest-sized, 48 pgs., saddle-stapled. **Sample: $2.50 postpaid. Guidelines available for SASE. Pays 2 copies.** Acquires first rights only. "A brief bio note may accompany poems." No simultaneous submissions or previously published poems. Reports in 5-10 weeks. Submissions are accepted throughout the year. Editor sometimes comments on rejections. Phase and Cycle Press has published two poetry chapbooks, **Breathing In The World** by Bruce Holland Rogers and Holly Arrow and **Out of Darkness** by Mary Balazs.

PHILOMEL; PHILOMATHEAN SOCIETY (II), Box H, College Hall, University of Pennsylvania, Philadelphia PA 19104, phone (215)898-8907, founded in 1813, editor-in-chief Ari Ehrlich. *Philomel* is a literary annual using "**any kind of poetry, no more than 300 words or 3 pgs. per poem.**" They also use stories, essays and "witty recipes." As a sample, they selected these lines from "Page B6, B7, or B8" by William Keckler:

> It will happen; something violent
> Fusing images onto glass—
> An atomic flowerbust
> That flashes you translucent
> As an orange illuminated
> By a flashlight in a child's hand.

Philomel comes out each spring. It is flat-spined, 64 pgs., 6×9, with matte card cover. Poems are selected by a committee of the Philomathean Society. Press run: 1,500 for 20 subscribers of which 3 are libraries, 1,400 distributed free to the university community. Price per issue: $4. **Sample postpaid: $2. Deadline for submissions: February 1, annually.**

‡**PHILOMEL BOOKS (II, III)**, 200 Madison Ave., New York NY 10016, phone (212)951-8700, an imprint founded in 1980, editor-in-chief Paula Wiseman. Philomel Books publishes 2-3 paperbacks, 40-45 hardbacks and 5-10 chapbooks/year. They say "since we're a children's book imprint, **we are open to individual poem submissions—anything suitable for a picture book. However, publication of poetry collections is usually done on a project basis—we acquire from outside through permissions, etc. Don't usually use unpublished material.**" They have recently published poetry by Edna St. Vincent-Millay

and Walt Whitman. **Previously published poems and simultaneous submissions OK. Cover letter required. Replies to queries in 1 month, to mss in 2. Pay is negotiable.**

PHOEBE; THE GREG GRUMMER AWARD (II), George Mason University, 4400 University Dr., Fairfax VA 22030, phone (703)993-2915, founded 1970, poetry editors Charles Fox and Brian Chidley, is a literary biannual **"looking for imagery that will make your thumbs sweat when you touch it."** They have recently published poetry by C.K. Williams, Carolyn Forché, Thomas Lux and Bill Knott. As a sample the editor selected these lines from "Semantics of Longing" by Leslie Bumstead:

> *Was he superb in speech*
> *class? Even at parties with women dangling*
> *hunger on their brilliant clavicles, he must*
> *forever look for the just and longest*
> *word (it's Samson through the trees*
> *of high heels)* . . .

Circulation 3,500, with 30-35 pgs. of poetry in each issue. Subscription: $8/year; $4/single issue. *Phoebe* receives 2,500 submissions/year. **Submit up to 5 poems; submission should be accompanied by SASE and a short bio. No simultaneous submissions, no dot-matrix. Reports in 6-8 weeks. Pays copies.** They also sponsor The Greg Grummer Award, an annual poetry contest. Entry fee: $5. Deadline: October 1. Prize: $500.

PHOENIX BROADSHEETS; NEW BROOM PRIVATE PRESS (II), 78 Cambridge St., Leicester, England LE 3 0JP, founded 1968, poetry editor Toni Savage, publishes chapbooks, pamphlets and broadsheets on a small Adana Horizontal Hand Press. The editor wants poetry which is **"descriptive—not too modern, not erotica or concrete, up to 12 lines (for the sheets).** Also some personal background of the poet." He has recently published poems by Spike Milligan, Sue Townsend, Sue Mackrell, Lucy Banwell, Chris Challis, Roger McGough and Arthur Caddick. Toni Savage selected these sample lines from "Self Portrait" by Alix Weisz:

> *A moon-eyed girl*
> *Glistened dew to stars*
> *Sliding on an endless hill.*
> *Darkest nights could not withstand*
> *Gentle touch of crescent hand.*

The broadsheets are letterpress printed on tinted paper (about 5 × 8) with graphics. **Submit no more than 3 poems with cover letter giving "personal backgrounds and feelings." No pay. Poet receives 20-30 copies.** "My *Broadsheets* are *given* away in the streets. They are given away to Folk Club, Jazz Club and theater audiences. The broadsheets started as a joke and now are up to 365 + printing. Now much sought after and collected. This is my hobby and is strictly part-time. Each small booklet takes 1-3 months, so it is impossible to ascertain quantities of publications." *Phoenix Broadsheets* may be obtained by sending adequate postage, approximately $1.50.

PIE (POETRY IMAGERY AND EXPRESSION) (V), P.O. Box 739, Parramatta, New South Wales 2124 Australia, founded 1984, compiled by Daryl Wayne Hall and Bill Tibben, is a publication of the poets who attend and participate in **readings sponsored by the group. "The publications are a record of the readings. We will return all unsolicited work without comment.** Our reason for requesting an entry in Poet's Market is that we think what we do is a good idea and one worth promoting. The people who come to the readings and who see themselves in print on the night (plus getting copies for their friends, etc.) get a good buzz! This is poetry that is happening in the here and now and the day-to-day world!" They publish the poetry in an attractive oversize format, photocopied from typescript, side-stapled with card cover.

PIEDMONT LITERARY REVIEW; PIEDMONT LITERARY SOCIETY (II, IV-Form), Rt. 1, Box 512, Forest VA 24551, founded 1976; poetry editor Gail White, 1017 Spanish Moss Lane, Breaux Bridge LA 70517 (and **poetry submissions should go to her address**). If you join the Piedmont Literary Society, $12 a year, you get the quarterly *Review* and a quarterly newsletter containing much market and contest information. Gail White says, **"I prefer all types of poems up to 32 lines. Each issue has a special section for oriental forms with an emphasis on haiku."** Each also includes short fiction. She does *not* want: **"smut, overly romantic, verse."** She has recently published poetry by Harold Witt, Julie Kane, John Brugaletta and Jared Carter. As a sample the editor selected these lines by Martha Bosworth:

> *Our lives fall open, all that's left of them,*
> *under the gulls' wing-scattered requiem;*
> *building on waste, for wastrels to destroy,*
> *the landfill cities rise: here is my Troy,*
> *and my Jerusalem.*

The quarterly is digest-sized, saddle-stapled, offset from typescript, matte card cover, using b&w

graphics, with 40-50 pgs. of poetry in each issue, circulation 300 with 200 subscriptions of which 10 are libraries. It's a modest-looking publication with poems that could appear in more prestigious magazines—testament to the fine editorial eye of the staff here. **Sample postpaid: $3. Welcomes all submissions. Send SASE for guidelines. Pays copies. Acquires first rights. Reports within 3 months. She "sometimes" comments on rejections.** Briefly reviews "a few" books of poetry, "mostly contributors' books," in accompanying newsletter. They sponsor occasional contests; write to Forest, VA address for rules and dates. Gail White advises, "Be introspective while showing empathy for mankind. Show some structure. No poems disguised as broken lines of prose."

PIG IRON (II, IV-Themes), P.O. Box 237, Youngstown OH 44501, phone (216)783-1269, founded 1975, poetry editor Jim Villani, is a literary annual devoted to special themes. They want **poetry "up to 300 lines; free verse and experimental; write for current themes."** Forthcoming themes: Classical Antiquity: The Contemporary Odyssey and The Family: Tradition & Potential. **They do *not* want to see "traditional" poetry.** They have recently published poetry by Helen Ruggieri, Ralph Brauer, Michael Wurster, Warren Woessner, Barbara Kasselmann and Coco Gordon. As a sample the editor selected these lines from Robert Hedin:

> Owls glide off the thin
> Wrists of the night,
> And using snow for their feathers
> Drift down on either side
> Of the wind.
> I spot them
> As I camp along the ridge,
> Glistening over the streambeds
> Their eyes small rooms
> Lit by stone lamps.

Pig Iron is magazine-sized, flat-spined, 128 pgs., typeset on good stock with glossy card cover using b&w graphics and art, no ads, circulation 1,000. They have 200 subscriptions of which 50 are libraries. Price per issue: $9.95. Subscription: $9/1 year, $16/2 years. **Sample postpaid: $3. Send SASE for guidelines. Pays $5/poem plus 2 copies. Buys one-time rights. Reports in 3 months, 12-18 months delay to publication. No simultaneous submissions. Dot-matrix, photocopies OK.** They sponsor the annual Kenneth Patchen Competition. Send SASE for details. The editor says, "We look for courage, innovation and stylistic insight."

THE PIKESTAFF FORUM; PIKESTAFF PUBLICATIONS, INC.; THE PIKESTAFF PRESS; PIKESTAFF POETRY CHAPBOOKS (II, IV-Children, teens), P.O. Box 127, Normal IL 61761, phone (309)452-4831, founded 1977, poetry editors Robert D. Sutherland, James R. Scrimgeour and James McGowan, is "a not-for-profit literary press. Publishes a magazine of national distribution, *The Pikestaff Forum*, and a poetry chapbooks series." They want **substantial, well-crafted poems; vivid, memorable, based in lived experience—*Not*: self-indulgent early drafts, 'private' poems, five finger exercises, warmed over workshop pieces, vague abstractions, philosophical woolgathering, 'journal entries,' inspirational uplift. The shorter the better, though long poems are no problem; we are eclectic; welcome traditional or experimental work. We won't publish pornography or racist/sexist material."** They have published poetry by Gayl Teller, J.W. Rivers, Lucia Cordell Getsi, Frannie Lindsay and Fritz Hamilton. *The Pikestaff Forum* is an annual newsprint tabloid, 40 pgs., "handsome, open layout. Trying to set a standard in tabloid design. Special features: poetry, fiction, commentary, reviews, young writers (7-17 in a special section), editors' profiles (other magazines), The Forum (space for anyone to speak out on matters of literary/publishing concern)." Circulation 1,100 with 200 subscriptions of which 5 are libraries. They receive 2,000-3,000 submissions/year, use 3%, have a year's backlog. Subscription: $10/ 6 issues. Sample: $2 postpaid. **"Each poem should be on a separate sheet, with author's name and address. We prefer no simultaneous submissions—but if it is, we expect to be informed of it."** No more than 6 poems/submission. **Reports within 3 months. Pays 3 copies. Send SASE for guidelines.** Reviews books of poetry if published by small presses or self-published. This is a lively publication. You might want to buy a sample copy to get the feel for this market because it doesn't simply aim to be yet another literary or small press outlet in the publishing world; it has flair and distinct personality. **Query with samples and brief bio for chapbook submission. Replies to queries in 2 weeks, to submission (if invited) in 3 months. Photocopy OK, but "reluctantly" accepts dot-matrix. Pays 20% of press run for chapbooks.** They advise, "For beginners: don't be in a hurry to publish; work toward becoming your own best editor and critic; when submitting, send only what you think is your very best work; avoid indulging yourself at the expense of your readers; have something to say that's worth your readers' life-time to read; before submitting, ask yourself, 'Why should *any* reader be asked to read this?'; regard publishing as conferring a responsibility."

PIKEVILLE REVIEW (II), Humanities Dept., Pikeville College, Pikeville KY 41501, founded 1987, editor James Alan Riley, who says **"There's no editorial bias though we recognize and appreciate style and control in each piece. No emotional gushing."** *PR* appears once yearly, accepting about 10% of poetry received. Press run is 500. **Sample $3 including postage. Send SASE for guidelines. Pays 5 copies. No simultaneous submissions or previously published poetry. Editor sometimes comments on rejections.** They also sponsor contests.

PINCHGUT PRESS (V), 6 Oaks Ave., Cremorne, Sydney, NSW 2090, Australia, founded 1948, publishes **Australian poetry. Not currently accepting poetry submissions. Send SASE for catalog to order samples.**

THE PINEHURST JOURNAL; PINEHURST PRESS (I, II), P.O. Box 360747, Milpitas CA 95036, founded 1990, editor Michael K. McNamara, is a quarterly. **"Generally open, 24-line limit. Some sort of rhyme, meter, assonance, consonance or alliteration is a plus as well as good haiku. No religious, porno or dire despair. Work should be original, no reprints."** They have recently published poetry by Pearl Bloch Segall and Jeanne Shannon. It is magazine-sized, 44 pgs., offset from typescript, saddle-stapled. Of 600 poems/year received they use 100. Press run 225 for 100 subscribers of which 1 is a library, 20 shelf sales. Subscription: $17. **Sample postpaid: $4.75. Send SASE for guidelines. Pays 1 copy. Acquires one-time rights. Reports in 6-8 weeks. Submit no more than 6 poems at a time.**

THE PIPE SMOKER'S EPHEMERIS (IV-Themes), 20-37 120th St., College Point NY 11356, editor/ publisher Tom Dunn, who says, "The *Ephemeris* is a limited edition, irregular quarterly **for pipe smokers and anyone else who is interested in its varied contents.** Publication costs are absorbed by the editor/publisher, assisted by any contributions—financial or otherwise—that readers might wish to make." There are 66 pages, offset from photoreduced typed copy, colored paper covers, with illustrations, stapled at the top left corner.

PITT POETRY SERIES; UNIVERSITY OF PITTSBURGH PRESS; AGNES LYNCH STARRETT POETRY PRIZE (II), 127 N. Bellefield Ave., Pittsburgh PA 15260, founded 1968, poetry editor Ed Ochester, publishes **"poetry of the highest quality; otherwise, no restrictions—book mss minimum of 48 pages." Simultaneous submissions OK.** They have recently published books of poetry by Lawrence Joseph, Kate Daniels, David Rivard, Robley Wilson and Liz Rosenberg. Their booklist also features such poets as Peter Meinke, Leonard Nathan, Sharon Olds, Ronald Wallace, Bruce Weigl and Paul Zimmer. **"Poets who have not previously published a book should send SASE for rules of the Starrett competition ($12.50 handling fee), the *only* vehicle through which we publish first books of poetry." The Starrett Prize consists of cash award of $2,500 and book publication. Poets who have previously published books should query.**

THE PITTSBURGH QUARTERLY (II), 36 Haberman Ave., Pittsburgh PA 15211-2144, phone (412)431-8885, founded 1990, editor Frank Correnti, who says, **"Our first criterion is good writing with the variety of content that is common to a broad community interest. Generally, writing with narrative and real-life elements. We don't want doggerel or most rhyme."** They have recently published poetry by Konstantinos Lardas, Rina Ferrarelli, John Stupp, Peter Blair and Laurel Speer. As a sample the editor selected these lines from "The Poem as Labrador" by d steven conkle:

> the poem as labrador
> rises rock-faced from a swirling sea
> brushes man aside
> as easily as
> a moose snapping at a black fly.

It is digest-sized, 76 pgs., professionally printed, saddle-stapled with matte card cover. Press run 700 for 250 subscribers of which 10 are libraries, 300 shelf sales. Subscription: $12 ($14 Canadian). **Sample postpaid: $5. Reports in 2-3 months. Pays 2 copies. Acquires first North American serial rights. "We will reply by letter to queries." Editor often comments on submissions.** Published books àre reviewed as space is available, 1-2/issue. Accepts reviews of 4-6 pages, double-spaced. "We are responding in part to the network of writers whose crafted creativity made the magazine possible, but also we are attempting to provide a readership that will connect more strongly to the community of poets and writers through this quarterly."

PIVOT (II), 250 Riverside Dr. #23, New York NY 10025, phone (212)222-1408, founded 1951, editor Martin Mitchell, is a poetry annual that has published poetry by Philip Appleman, William Matthews, Eugene McCarthy, Craig Raine, W.D. Snodgrass and Robert Wrigley. It is a handsome 6×9, flat-spined, professionally printed magazine with glossy card cover, press run 1,200. Price per issue: $5. **Pays 2 copies. Reports in 2-4 weeks. Reads submissions January 1 through June 1 only.**

Close-up

Elton Glaser
Poet

"Saint Sebastian"
(May the Light from Your Wounds
    Shine on Us All)
—from a painting by John Sokol

Slump of Sebastian all quills and sinew
Twisted to the post,
The oiled hole of his belly a bull's-eye
Pierced and plumed, where shafts
Drag in a wounded circle, gaunt rays

That bleed from every bowrip, every
Feathered exit of the soul. O he's
Like some lopsided heart split by love
In a teenage torture of the oak.
Here, the flesh flaws back, each oval red

And open to the gallery's gaze, a whore's mouth
Plugged up with hard impasto,
Giving good ghost. And there, on the price list,
The title sheds its light
Against the cost and raw disclosures of the dark.

Photo by Brian Hurlburt

Take a pinch of religious allusion and a dash of sensuality and douse it good with some Louisiana hot sauce and you have the flavor of Elton Glaser's poetry. Born in New Orleans and raised in nearby Slidell, Glaser acknowledges a sense of "place" in much of his work, although he believes that "all poetry is local—it doesn't have to be New York or Paris or London to be significant. You burrow into that little place where you are or that you remember and you dig down so deep that you come out on the other side of the world—it includes everything by working within that small patch of native soil."

While growing up in Louisiana, Glaser spent his high school years studying to be a Benedictine monk. It was during this time he wrote his first poem, "or something I thought was a poem because it was in lines," and began reading the works of both the "masters" and contemporary poets, starting with Gerard Manley Hopkins. "That was the first time I'd really gotten into a poet and understood just a little bit about the power and gorgeousness of language, of words as physical objects with all their senses working."

Since then, Glaser has been praised for the textural thickness of his poetry. To what degree was Hopkins an influence? "I haven't thought of this in a long while, but I suppose if I'd started out with a poet like William Carlos Williams, my writing would be different." However, it was from Williams that Glaser adopted the creed "If it ain't fun, it ain't poetry."

Although he eventually left the seminary for "intellectual reasons" and now describes himself as a "practicing ex-Catholic/High Church atheist," Glaser recognizes the sensuality of religion. "The vestments, gold chalices and artwork—put that in Louisiana, especially New Orleans, and you can understand how it gets into the whole sensibility of the deep, erotic South."

A wide range of interests find their way into Glaser's work, including philosophy, music, language and art. He writes as easily from the point of view of a prostitute as from that of an elderly black man or a dissatisfied homemaker. Glaser insists that breadth of reading is imperative to the aspiring writer, in addition to reading in a variety of ways. "You learn about poetry from reading other poets. Find those poets who speak to you, not simply through their art, but through some quirk of their vision, their sensibility, their way of looking at the world.

"It's especially important when you're starting out not to be too narrow. When you find a writer you really like, immerse yourself and feel everything—the good parts and the bad. This helps to develop a critical eye and that can feed back into your own work. Both reading and perseverance are crucial."

For Glaser, perseverance paid off with the publication of his first book, **Relics**, by Wesleyan University Press when he was 39. Long before that, Glaser was submitting his work and, to date, more than 350 of his poems have appeared in such magazines as *Ploughshares*, *Poetry* and *Poetry Northwest*. Among his list of accomplishments are fellowships from the National Endowment for the Arts and the Ohio Arts Council, as well as the Theodore Roethke and Hart Crane Memorial Poetry Awards. His second collection of poems, **Tropical Depressions**, won the 1987 Iowa Poetry Prize and his third book, **Color Photographs of the Ruins**, was recently released by the University of Pittsburgh Press.

"One of the paradoxes is that you've got to be simultaneously arrogant and humble to do this—arrogant to think that you could write anything that other people might be interested in and humble in that you are doing this because you're in love with the art."

Currently professor of English at the University of Akron, Glaser describes his poetry writing workshops as a way of "abbreviating the apprenticeship" and believes "the responsibility of any writer who has attained some level of proficiency is to pass it on. I don't think you can inspire other people to be writers. If they've got it in them and want to do it, you can create shortcuts by telling them when they've screwed up so that they can learn it earlier."

He advises beginning writers not to worry about making momentous statements in their poetry. "If you stop worrying about 'Man's inhumanity to man' or 'the glory of God' and put your attention on technical details, the content part will take care of itself. Get back to the small. Let the large grow naturally out of the small or be suggested by it. Relax. Don't worry about subject matter so much. Start with things that are commonplace or ordinary and pay attention to how that experience is going to be given shape through language.

"Let the changes happen naturally," he adds. "Don't force them. The hazards are looking too early for publication and lapping up praise that will satisfy you in the wrong way by making you complacent. I think it's important to live on the edge in those early stages, and later, too. Never be too comfortable with your own work."

—*Michelle Moore*

‡THE PLACE IN THE WOODS; READ, AMERICA! (I, IV-Children), 3900 Glenwood Ave., Golden Valley MN 55422, phone (612)374-2120, founded 1980, editor and publisher Roger A. Hammer, publishes *Read, America!*, a quarterly newsletter for reading coordinators. They want "poems for children that are understandable, under 500 words, unusual views of life. Also, foreign-language poems with English translation. Nothing vague, self-indulgent, erotic. No navel introspection." As a sample we selected these lines from "Circus" by Eugene C. Baggott:

> *Did you ever watch the bareback riders*
> *As they lovingly groomed their steeds?*
> *Or the trapeze artist practice his catch*
> *While hanging by his knees?*

Read, America! is 8 pages, magazine-sized, professionally printed on yellow paper. Subscription: $15. No previously published poems; simultaneous submissions OK. Cover letter required. Always comments on rejections. Pays $10 on publication.

PLAINS POETRY JOURNAL; STRONGHOLD PRESS (II, IV-Form), P.O. Box 2337, Bismarck ND 58502, founded 1982, editor Jane Greer, publishes "meticulously crafted, language-rich poetry which is demanding but not inaccessible. We love rhyme and meter and poetic conventions used in vigorous and interesting ways. I strive to publish unpublished poets as well as old pros. I do *not* want broken-prose 'free verse' or greeting card-type traditional verse. I want finely-crafted poetry which uses the best poetic conventions from the past in a way that doesn't sound as if it were *written* in the past. No specifications. I'm especially interested in compelling long poems and essays on poetry. Our credo is, 'no subject matter is taboo; treatment is everything.' " They have recently published poetry by Gail White, Rhina P. Espaillat, Harold McCurdy, Jack Butler, Jeanne Wylie Torosian, Paul Ramsey and Edmund Conti. As a sample, Jane Greer chose "It Must Be Nice" by Erika Brady:

> *to know what things are called —*
> *real things one might find lovely*
> *by a fencerow, or knee deep in some stream:*
> *beard-tongue. sassafras. mud dog. grabble.*

Plains Poetry Journal is semiannual, digest-sized, 44 pgs. (of which about 40 are poetry), saddle-stapled, professionally printed on tinted paper with matte card cover, graphics, circulation 500, 400 subscriptions of which 50 are libraries. They receive 1,500-2,000 submissions/year, use about 100, seldom have more than a 6-month backlog. Subscription: $9/year, $18/5 issues. Sample postpaid: $4.50. Submit "not less than 3 poems, not more than 10 at a time. Photocopy, handwritten, dot-matrix, simultaneous submissions, all OK." Reports in 1 week to 2 months. Pays copies. Acquires first or reprint rights. Send SASE for guidelines. Has ceased book publishing. "An author is *crazy* not to submit simultaneously." Jane Greer says she comments on rejections "occasionally, especially if the ms is especially promising or if I think the poet is a child or teen." This journal is known as a good outlet for formal verse. Editor Jane Greer also takes free verse poems, well-crafted, with enticing subject matter. She typically responds in a timely manner when returning or accepting manuscripts. She comments, "Do enclose a SASE, and *don't* enclose an explanation of the poems. Above all understand that a poet never 'gets good,' he or she just keeps *working* at it. If you're willing to do this, I am, too."

PLAINSONG (II), Box 8245, Western Kentucky University, Bowling Green KY 42101, phone (502)745-5708, founded 1979, poetry editors Frank Steele, Elizabeth Oakes and Peggy Steele, is an occasional poetry journal. "Our purpose is to print the best work we can get, from known and unknown writers. This means, of course, that we print what we like: poems about places, objects, people, moods, politics, experiences. We like straightforward, conversational language, short poems in which the marriage of thinking and feeling doesn't break up because of spouse-abuse (the poem in which ideas wrestle feeling into the ground or in which feeling sings alone — and boringly — at the edge of a desert). Prefer poems under 20 lines in free verse. No limits on subject matter, though we like to think of ourselves as humane, interested in the environment, in peace (we're anti-nuclear), in the possibility that the human race may have a future." They have published poetry by William Matthews, Ted Kooser, William Stafford, Del Marie Rogers, Betty Adcock, Julia Ardery and Abby Niebauer. The magazine is 48-56 pgs., 6×9, professionally printed, flat-spined, matte color card cover with photos and graphics, print run 600 with 250 subscriptions of which 65 are libraries. They use about 100 of the 2,000 submissions received each year. Subscription: $7. Sample postpaid: $3.50. "We prefer poems typed, double-spaced. Simultaneous submissions can, of course, get people into trouble, at times." Reports "within a month, usually." Pays copies. Send SASE for guidelines.

PLAINSONGS (II), Dept. of English, Hastings College, Hastings NE 68902, founded 1980, editor Dwight C. Marsh, a poetry magazine that "accepts manuscripts from anyone, considering poems on any subject in any style." They have recently published poetry by Michael Carey, Robert Cooperman,

Marilyn Dorf and Nancy Westerfield. As a sample the editor selected these lines from "Pond in Kansas" by James Magorian:

> The wheat of the moon
> bristles everywhere.
> I sink my hands
> into the scratchy light.

Plainsongs is digest-sized, 40 pgs., saddle-stapled, set on laser, printed on thin paper with b&w illustrations, one-color matte card cover with black logo. The magazine is financed by subscriptions, which cost $9 for 3 issues/year. **Sample copies are $3. Pay is two copies and a year's subscription, with three award poems in each issue receiving small monetary recognition. Acquires first-time rights.** "A short essay in appreciation accompanies each award poem." **Ms deadlines are August 15 for fall issue; November 15 for winter; March 15 for spring. Notification is mailed about three weeks after deadlines.**

PLAINSWOMAN (IV-Women, regional), P.O. Box 8027, Grand Forks ND 58202, phone (701)777-8043, founded 1977, is a 16-page, magazine-sized literary journal appearing 10 times a year, circulation 500, using some **poetry by and about women in the Great Plains. Guidelines available for SASE. Pays 2 copies of issue in which poem appears. Sample: $2.**

PLANTAGENET PRODUCTIONS (V), Westridge, Highclere, Nr. Newbury, Royal Berkshire RG15 9PJ, England, founded 1964, director of productions Miss Dorothy Rose Gribble. Plantagenet issues cassette recordings of poetry, philosophy and narrative (although they have issued nothing new since 1980). Miss Gribble says, "Our public likes classical work . . . We **have published a few living poets, but this is not very popular with our listeners, and we shall issue no more.**" They have issued cassettes by Oscar Wilde, Chaucer and Pope, as well as Charles Graves, Elizabeth Jennings, Leonard Clark and Alice V. Stuart. The recordings are issued privately and are obtainable only direct from Plantagenet Productions; write for list. Miss Gribble's advice to poets is: "If intended for a listening public, let the meaning be clear. If possible, let the music of the works sing."

THE PLASTIC TOWER (I, II), P.O. Box 702, Bowie MD 20718, founded 1989, editors Carol Dyer and Roger Kyle-Keith, is a quarterly using **"everything from iambic pentameter to silly limericks, modern free verse, haiku, rhymed couplets — we like it all! Only restriction is length — under 40 lines preferred."** They have published poetry by John Bennett, John Grey, Jonathan Levant, Lyn Lifshin, Richard Peabody, Walt Phillips, Cheryl Townsend, A.D. Winans and Bob Z, "as well as a bunch of folks nobody's heard of yet . . . but hopefully will soon." As a sample we selected these lines from "After Mother's Day" by Linda Ashear:

> I am tipsy on tulips,
> high on hibiscus,
> bombed on baby's breath.

Poetry even a bass fishin' duck could love

"During a layout session, this 'duck' was doodled by one of the editors who, obviously, had his mind on something other than serious literature!" says Roger Kyle-Keith, editor of The Plastic Tower along with Carol Dyer. "Putting the goofy-looking duck on a literary magazine just seemed to be the right thing to do at the time," he says. "We are always trying to fool readers into thinking the poetry in The Plastic Tower isn't literati dullsville. Poetry is what Plastic is all about. Everything else is just window dressing."

Out of control, I collide
with an African violet in the vestibule,
down dahlias on the deck,
tipple begonias masquerading as camelias.

It is digest-sized, 38-54 pgs., saddle-stapled; "variety of typefaces and b&w graphics on cheap photocopy paper." Press run: 200. Subscription: $8/year. Copy of current issue: $2.50. **"We'll send a back issue free for a *large* (at least 6×9) SAE with 75¢ postage attached."** Send SASE for guidelines. Pays 1-3 copies. Simultaneous submissions OK. Reports in 2 months. Editors comment on submissions **"often."** Roger Kyle-Keith says, *"The Plastic Tower* combines what the editors hope are the best qualities of the small press: eclectic, entertaining, friendly and accessible. We advocate all styles, forms and subject matter—from religious verse to bathroom-wall limericks. And, as always, the *Plastic* editors recommend that poets laugh a lot and have fun, fun, fun; the submission game is just too silly to take too seriously. After all, a rejection or acceptance does not define a poet's value to society, but simply an editor's subjective opinion of a few words typed on a piece of paper!"

PLOUGHSHARES (III), Emerson College, 100 Beacon St., Boston MA 02116, phone (617)578-8753, founded 1971. **The magazine is "a journal of new writing edited on a revolving basis by professional poets and writers to reflect different and contrasting points of view."** Recent editors have included Carolyn Forché, Gerald Stern, Rita Dove and M.L. Rosenthal. They have published poetry by Donald Hall, Li-Young Lee, Robert Pinsky, Brenda Hillman and Thylias Moss. The quarterly is 5½×8½, 250 pgs., circulation 3,800. They receive approximately 2,000 poetry submissions/year. Subscription: $19 domestic; $24 foreign. Sample: **$8.95 postpaid. "Due to our revolving editorship, issue emphasis and submission dates will vary. We suggest you read a few issues and send a #10 SASE for writer's guidelines before submitting."** Do not submit mss from May 1 to September 1. Reports in 3-5 months. **Pays $10 minimum per poem, $5/printed page per poem over 2 printed pages, up to $50 maximum per poet, plus contributor copies. Simultaneous submissions acceptable.** Reviews books of poetry.

‡THE PLOWMAN (I, II), Box 414, Whitby, Ontario L1N 5S4 Canada, phone (416)668-7803, founded 1988, editor Tony Scavetta, appears 3 times/year using **"didactic, eclectic poetry; all forms."** As a sample we selected the beginning lines of "The Cancer Victim" by Bonnie Colby:

The stones on the plains
Don't think about the ones on the sidehills,
Who rest precariously at best,
Gripping to earth, forcing their wills
To hang on even when one by one
The stones around them fall away

The Plowman is a 56-page, newsprint tabloid which accepts 70% of the poetry received. Press run is 15,000 for 1,200 subscribers of which 500 are libraries. Single copy: $7.50; subscription: $10. **Sample free. Previously published poems and simultaneous submissions OK. Cover letter required. No SASE necessary. Always comments on rejections. Guidelines available free. Reports in 1 week. Pays nothing, not even copies.** Reviews books of poetry. They offer monthly poetry contests. Entry fee: $2/poem. 1st prize: 50% of the proceeds; 2nd: 25%; 3rd: 10%. The top poems are published. "Balance of the poems will be used for anthologies." **They also publish 125 chapbooks/year. Query first. Replies to queries and mss in 1 week. Pays 20% royalties.**

THE PLUM REVIEW (II), P.O. Box 3557, Washington DC 20007, founded 1990, editors M. Hammer and Christina Daub, appears twice a year. **"We are open to original, high quality poetry of all forms, lengths, styles and subject matters. Our only criterion is excellence."** They have recently published poetry by Jon Stallworthy, Linda Pastan, Jane Hirshfield, Henri Cole, Paul Zimmer, William Matthews, William Stafford and Marge Piercy. As a sample the editor selected these lines from "Late September in Ulcinj" by Larry Levis:

And what did you come here for if not to hear
Finality in the soft click of a latch,
Or in the long thou of the empty wavebreak?

It is approximately 100 pgs., flat-spined, professionally printed, 6×9. Press run 1,000. **Sample postpaid: $5. Send SASE for guidelines. Reports in 1 month. Pays 1 copy. "Absolutely no simultaneous submissions. Include a brief bio indicating previous publications and/or awards." Seldom comments on rejections.** They welcome reviews (up to 15 pgs., single or multi-book format) of recently published books of poetry and interviews with prominent poets. They sponsor a reading series and creative writing workshops for the elderly and the handicapped. This magazine says that it is "so delicious"—a takeoff on William Carlos Williams' famous lyric "This Is Just To Say"?—and it is, too, featuring the best work of top-name poets and relative newcomers. Editors seem to favor well-made free verse, emphasizing voice and line. It's a prestigious credit!

POCAHONTAS PRESS, INC.; MANUSCRIPT MEMORIES (V), P.O. Drawer F, Blacksburg VA 24063-1020, phone (703)951-0467, founded 1984, president Mary C. Holliman, publishes chapbook collections of poetry, but is temporarily not considering new mss "because I am trying to finish those already accepted." Inquire before submitting. **"Most of the poetry books I have published have been subsidized to some extent by the author. So far one of those authors' books has sold enough copies that the author has received a significant reimbursement for his investment. We continue to market all of our books as aggressively as possible. The idea is to make a profit for both of us (though we have yet to do so)."** She offers editorial critiques for $20/hour. Reviews books of poetry "sometimes." She has published books by Leslie Mellichamp, Lynn Kozma, Mildred Nash and Hubert J. Davis; forthcoming: Preston Newman and Elaine Emans. As a sample the editor selected these lines by Cecil J. Mullins:

> In the East, time has been divorced
> From things. No clocks hem the hours
> In, and time, not being firmly forced,
> Slops around.

Pays 10% royalties on all sales receipts, 10 free copies of book, and any number of copies at 50% for resale or "whatever use author wishes. If author helps with printing costs, then an additional percentage of receipts will be paid."

POEM; HUNTSVILLE LITERARY ASSOCIATION (II), English Dept., University of Alabama at Huntsville, Huntsville AL 35899, founded 1967, poetry editor Nancy Frey Dillard, appears twice a year, consisting entirely of poetry. **"We are open to traditional as well as non-traditional forms, but we favor work with the expected compression and intensity of good lyric poetry and a high degree of verbal and dramatic tension. We welcome equally submissions from established poets as well as from less known and beginning poets. We do not accept translations or previously published works. We prefer to see a sample of 3-5 poems at a submission, with SASE. We generally respond within a month. We are a nonprofit organization and can pay only in copy to contributors. Sample copies are available at $5."** They have recently published poetry by Robert Cooperman, Andrew Dillon and Scott Travis Hutchison. As a sample the editor selected these lines from "Mister Varsey" by Sally Jo Sorensen:

> With the myths
> his methods excelled:
> The Odyssey, for instance,
> became more than just the same old song
> about some guy who'd left his wife and kid
> for the guys. Mr. Varsey fetched a bow
> out of his great, fabled closet
> and asked the gentlemen of the class —
> as he called them — to see who might be
> Penelope's true suitor. None could
> match the task, so he exclaimed
> blind Homer walks again!
> until I raised my hand

Poem is a flat-spined, 4⅜ × 7¼, 90-page journal that contains more than 60 poems (mostly lyric free verse under 50 lines) generally featured one to a page on good stock paper with a clean design and a classy matte cover. Circulation is 400 (all subscriptions of which 90 are libraries). Overall, it's a good market for beginners and experienced poets who pay attention to craft.

POEMS FOR A LIVABLE PLANET (I, IV-Nature/ecology, translations), #12, 1295 Federal Ave., Los Angeles CA 90025, founded 1990, editor Jeffrey Dellin, appears "once or twice a year" using **"poems dealing with the beauty/peril of the Earth & Her creatures. Any form, language given equal consideration; length limit 50 lines. Non-English should include translation."** As a sample the editor selected these lines from "1989 Last Day" by C.B. Follett:

> Tossed on a corner at rite's end.
> Nailed to a cross. Forlorn
> and dying among curbside fellows.
> 5, 10, 15 years grown.
> Cut off at the knees.

Sample postpaid: $3.75. Reports in 6-8 weeks. Pays 1 copy. No previously published material. Reads submissions January 1 through April 30 only. The ecology theme of this publication is one of the most important of our time. The poetry is insightful and, overall, well-executed; craft does not suffer because of politics. If you have environmentally sound verse, consider this a good market. The editor says, "I rely on my passion. Try not to be too obvious, yet do say something. Irony is very welcome. We strive for the fine line."

POET; COOPER HOUSE PUBLISHING INC.; JOHN DAVID JOHNSON MEMORIAL POETRY AWARDS; IVA MARY WILLIAMS INSPIRATIONAL POETRY AWARDS; ANNUAL CHAPBOOK COMPETITION; AMERICAN COLLEGE & UNIVERSITY POETRY AWARDS–STUDENT DIVISION; AMERICAN HIGH SCHOOL POETRY AWARDS; THE AMERICAN LITERARY & POETRY MAGAZINE AWARDS (I, II), P.O. Box 54947, Oklahoma City OK 73154, founded 1984, managing editor Peggy Cooper, poetry editor Michael Hall. "*Poet* is one of the largest commercial publishers of poetry in the USA and is **open to beginners' submissions. The poets we publish don't have to buy anything or join anything or subscribe. They receive a free contributor's copy at time of publication.** Some of our competitions have entry fees which are used along with subscription fees and advertising fees to help publish the magazine." Michael Hall says, "**I look for poems that display wit, knowledge and skill, especially if the poem is about poetry or other poets . . . verse that employs 'arresting images, poems that make the reader think or smile or even sometimes cry.'** " They have recently published poetry by Lyn Lifshin, Lewis Turco, Louis Phillips and H.R. Coursen. As a sample the editor selected the opening stanza of "Soliloquy" by Tom Vandenberg:

> *Moon,*
> *rootless in sky-water,*
> *tonight you are less stone*
> *than flower,*
> *a great lily floating out*
> *over the earth . . . .*

It is magazine-sized, professionally printed, 56+ pgs. with glossy cover, saddle-stitched. Of 3,000-5,000 submissions, they use about 10%. Subscription: $20/year. Subscribers receive free the "Poetry Forms" poster and *Poet's Digest* newsletter. **Sample postpaid: $5.50. To receive guidelines (and a free poetry publishing kit) send 3 loose first class stamps with request. Pays 1 copy. Previously published poems and simultaneous submissions OK. Reports within 3-6 months. Editor sometimes comments on rejections.** Reviews books of poetry. They sponsor an annual chapbook competition (up to 30 pgs., $20 entry fee, prize: publication in book form and winner receives 50 copies). John David Johnson Memorial Poetry Competition (prizes of $200, $100, $50, special merit and honorable mention awards, award certificates and publication plus "Poetry Forms" poster and a copy of the magazine in which the winning poems appear to all contestants, $5/poem entry fee, March 25 and September 1 deadlines); Iva Mary Williams Inspirational Poetry Competition (prizes of $100, $50, $25, special merit and honorable mention awards and publication plus "Poetry Forms" poster and a copy of the magazine in which the winning poems appear to all contestants, $3/poem entry fee, January 1 and August 1 deadlines). American College & University Poetry Awards for students (prizes of $200, $100, $50, several $10 special merit awards and honorable mention awards – teachers receive "Poetry Forms" classroom poster for entering students' work, no entry fee, rules and official entry forms for this competition along with the winning poems are published in the spring issues of *Poet*. American High School Poetry Awards (prizes $100, $50, $25 plus special merits and honorable mentions, award certificates, publication – teachers receive "Poetry Forms" classroom poster for entering students' work, no entry fee; guidelines and official entry forms along with the winning poems are published in the summer issues of *Poet*. The American Literary & Poetry Magazine Awards are engraved plaques for Best Overall, Best Editorial Content and Best Cover Design. Special merit and honorable mention award certificates will also be given. The top three winners will receive free advertising in *Poet*. $20 entry fee/title. Deadline: December 31.

POET AND CRITIC (II), 203 Ross Hall, Iowa State University, Ames IA 50011, phone (515)294-2180, founded 1961, editor Neal Bowers, appears 3 times a year, 6×9, 48 pgs., staple bound, professionally printed, matte card cover with color, circulation 400, 300 subscriptions of which 100 are libraries. Subscription: $18. **Sample postpaid: $8. Submit 4-6 poems. "We do not read mss between the end of May and mid-August." Reports in 2 weeks (often sooner). Pays 1 copy. Acquires first rights.** Reviews books of poetry. This is the type of magazine to subscribe to because the poems may inspire one to write. Editor Neal Bowers takes pains to edit the publication so that the contents, when read start to finish, enhance meaning or insight in a particular issue. He seems to take poems that contain important messages within a well-structured frame. As this applies to free verse, Bowers shuns pretty or elite-sounding poems with obscure meanings. As it applies to formal verse, content has to rise above the restrictions of form. The result is that each poem, no matter what style, enlightens the audience. His response time is admirable, too.

POET GALLERY PRESS (IV-Specialized), Box 1206, New York NY 09221, founded 1970, editor E.J. Paulos, publishes **work by American poets living outside the US. He wants "serious, learned, quality"** not "greeting card level." They have published poetry by S. Hakim, I. Roverso and Gamela. As a sample the editor selected these lines from Pavia:

> *Bramante had been there,*

and Da Vinci contributed to the plan
the third largest dome in Italy
before there had been Charlemagne,
. . . the tower—and the iron crown, marks of a medieval heritage
symbols of the once royal town.

Reports on queries in 1 month, on mss in 2 months. Payment "depends upon sales, etc." but includes copies.

POET LORE (II), The Writers Center, 7815 Old Georgetown Rd., Bethesda MD 20814-2415, founded 1889, managing editor Sunil Freeman, editors Philip Jason and Barbara Goldberg, is a quarterly dedicated "to the best in American and world poetry and objective and timely reviews and commentary. We look for **fresh uses of traditional form and devices, but any kind of excellence is welcome. The editors encourage narrative poetry and original translations of works by contemporary world poets.**" They have published poetry by Sharon Olds, John Balaban, William Heyen, Walter McDonald, Reginald Gibbons and Howard Nemerov. *Poet Lore* is 6×9, 80 pgs., perfect-bound, professionally printed with matte card cover and a circulation to 600 subscriptions of which 200 are libraries. Subscription: $15; per copy: $4.50 plus $1 postage. They receive about 3,000 poems in freelance submissions/year, use about 125. **Sample postpaid: $4. Submit typed author's name and address on each page. Photocopies OK. Reports in 3 months. Pays 2 copies.** Reviews books of poetry. Editors are open to all styles, including narrative poetry, as long as the work is well-crafted and insightful. Also, records show that *Poet Lore* has always returned work within its stated response time. It's a good market all around.

THE POETIC KNIGHT: A FANTASY ROMANCE MAGAZINE (IV-Fantasy, romance), 110 S. West St., Columbiana OH 44408, founded 1990, editor Michael While, appears 3-4 times/year. **They want "fantasy oriented poetry that exemplifies the classical romantic in all of us. Accept poetry from haiku length to ballad form. No profanity or explicit sex. Like to see work that is based on very human characters. Research historical heroes and maidens for reference points."** They have recently published poetry by Carl Heffley and William Robertson. As a sample the editor selected these lines from "In The Wake of The Night" by Tanda Graham:

Her lingering spray, bouquet of the south,
was stifled by the scent of her absence.
While night fell deep into stygian sleep,
he walked in the wake of the silence.

It is 40-52 pgs., magazine-sized, laser set with glossy cover, saddle-stapled. They accept on a "10 to 1 ratio and we get 20 submissions a week." Press run 300 for 100 subscribers of which 3 are libraries, 150 shelf sales. Subscription: $16/4 issues. **Sample postpaid: $4. Send SASE for guidelines. Pays 1 copy. Acquires first North American serial rights. Editor "always" comments on rejections.** He adds, "We do anthologies about twice a year. Send SASE for guidelines."

POETIC PAGE (I), P.O. Box 71192, Madison Heights MI 48071-0192, phone (313)548-0865, founded 1989, editor Denise Martinson, appears bimonthly. **Each issue has a contest, $1/poem fee, prizes of $25, $15 and $10. All poetry published is that of contest winners. "All forms are used except explicit sex, violence, and crude. 20-24 lines."** They have recently published poetry by Marian Ford Park, Pearl Bloch Segall, Alice Mackenzie Swaim, Phil Eisenberg, T. Kilgore Splake, Glenna Holloway and John Grey. As a sample the editor selected her poem "Edward Scissorhands":

He usually cuts pieces from the whole,
reveals hidden hearts and love.
Once he found frozen fragments
laced with confusion. A cold
reminder that truth can sting,
burn a dry-ice awareness
on the verge of his extinction.
But he lives and learns,
continues to shape his world
in whatever form fits illusion.

Poetic Page is 36 pgs., magazine-sized, photocopied from typescript on 20 lb. paper, press run 250-350, sent to libraries, universities, editors and subscribers. Subscription: $10. **Sample postpaid: $2. Simultaneous submissions and previously published poems OK. Send SASE for guidelines. Nonsubscribers receive 1 copy.** The editor says, "We look for poetry that has something to say. No trite rhyme. Only the very best poems are selected each issue. First place is featured on its own page. We now use more articles, tidbits, poet interactions and fillers. We pay $5 for articles, $10 for cover art, but must be of the highest quality. We ask poets to send us copies of their poetry books for our 'Review' section. Just because we are listed under the I category, does not mean that we are an easy magazine to be published in. We want poetry that is well written, poetry that demands to be read. We print the beginner alongside the seasoned poet. Send you best."

POETIC SPACE: POETRY & FICTION (I), P.O. Box 11157, Eugene OR 97440, founded 1983, editor Don Hildenbrand, is a literary magazine with emphasis on contemporary poetry, fiction, reviews, interviews and market news. Accepts poetry and fiction that is **"well-crafted and takes risks. We like poetry with guts. Would like to see some poetry on social and political issues. Erotic and experimental OK. No traditional, rhymed (unless of high-quality), sentimental, romantic."** They have published John M. Bennett, Barbara Henning, Albert Huffstickler, Arthur Winfield Knight, Crawdad Nelson, Tyrone Williams and Lawson Fusao Inada. As a sample the editor selected these lines from "The Argument" by Robin Rhein Barratt:

> *This day has the quality of aspirin*
> *of white light that falls on white skin*
> *masking the problem*
>
> *We are in a cast with the texture*
> *of a cat's tongue*
> *Mid-morning is a vapor seeping death —*

The magazine is 8½ × 11, saddle-stapled, 16 pgs., offset from typescript and sometimes photoreduced. It is published twice a year. They use about 25% of the 200-300 poems received/year. Press run: 800-1,000 with 50 subscriptions of which 12 are libraries. Price per issue: $3. Subscription: $15. **Sample: $2. Send SASE for list of available back issues. Guidelines for SASE. Pays 1 copy, but more can be ordered by sending SASE and postage. Ms should be typed, double-spaced, clean, name/address on each page. Reports in 2-4 months. No simultaneous submissions or previously published poems. Editor provides some critical comments.** Reviews books of poetry in 500-1,000 words. Don Hildenbrand says, "We like poetry that takes risks — original writing that gives us a new, different perspective."

POETPOURRI; COMSTOCK WRITERS' GROUP INC.; SUMMER SIZZLER CONTEST (II), 907 Comstock Ave., Syracuse NY 13210, founded 1987, phone (315)475-0339, published by the Comstock Writers' Group, Inc., coeditors Jennifer B. MacPherson and Kathleen Bryce Niles, appears biannually. **They use "work that is clear and understandable to a general readership, that deals with issues, ideas, feelings and beliefs common to us all — well-written free and traditional verse. No obscene, obscure, patently religious or greeting-card verse."** They have recently published poetry by Ruth Daigon, Katharyn Howd Machan, Robert Cooperman, Susan A. Manchester and R. Nikolas Macioci. As a sample they selected the last lines from Gayle Elen Harvey's "The Moon's Waltzing Alone":

> *How hard it is to relinquish the sharp grip. Again and again*
> *they dismiss us, leave us behind with bad weather, small scraps of wing.*
> *Only their love, like a thing never done, burns through*
> *into morning.*

Poetpourri is 100 pgs., digest-sized, professionally printed, perfect-bound, raised cover. Circulation 550. Subscription: $8. **Sample postpaid: $4. Poems may be submitted anytime for possible publication, 3-6 at a time, unpublished poems only. Return time: about 6 weeks. Editors usually comment on returned submissions. Pays copies. Acquires first North American serial rights.** They offer a yearly Summer Sizzler contest with over $400 in prizes, $2/poem, 30-line limit.

POETRY; THE MODERN POETRY ASSOCIATION; BESS HOKIN PRIZE; LEVINSON PRIZE; OSCAR BLUMENTHAL PRIZE; EUNICE TIETJENS MEMORIAL PRIZE; FREDERICK BOCK PRIZE; GEORGE KENT PRIZE; RUTH LILLY POETRY PRIZE (III), 60 W. Walton St., Chicago IL 60610, founded 1912, editor Joseph Parisi, "is the oldest and most distinguished monthly magazine devoted entirely to verse," according to their literature. "Founded in Chicago in 1912, it immediately became the international showcase that it has remained ever since, publishing in its earliest years — and often for the first time — such giants as Ezra Pound, Robert Frost, T.S. Eliot, Marianne Moore and Wallace Stevens. *Poetry* has continued to print the major voices of our time and to discover new talent, establishing an unprecedented record. There is virtually no important contemporary poet in our language who has not at a crucial stage in his career depended on *Poetry* to find a public for him: John Ashbery, Dylan Thomas, Edna St. Vincent Millay, James Merrill, Anne Sexton, Sylvia Plath, James Dickey, Thom Gunn, David Wagoner — only a partial list to suggest how *Poetry* has represented, without affiliation with any movements or schools, what Stephen Spender has described as 'the best, and simply the best' poetry being written." Although its offices have always been in Chicago, *Poetry*'s influence and scope extend far beyond, throughout the U.S. and in over 45 countries around the world. Asked to select 4 lines of poetry "which represent the taste and quality you want in your publication" Joseph Parisi selected the opening lines of "The Love Song of J. Alfred Prufrock" by T.S. Eliot, which first appeared in *Poetry* in 1915:

> Let us go then, you and I,
> When the evening is spread out against the sky
> Like a patient etherized upon a table;
> Let us go, through certain half-deserted streets . . .

Poetry is an elegantly printed, flat-spined, 5½×9 magazine. They receive over 70,000 submissions/year, use 300-350, have a 9-month backlog. Circulation 7,000, 6,000 subscriptions of which 65% are libraries. Subscription: $25; $27 for institutions; per copy: $2.50. **Sample: $3.50 postpaid. Submit no more than 4 poems. "Photocopy OK; no dot-matrix; letter-quality OK." Reports in 2-3 months. Longer for mss submitted during the summer. Pays $2 a line. Buys all rights. Returns rights "upon written request." Send SASE for guidelines.** Reviews books of poetry in 750-1,000 words, multi-book format. This is probably the most prestigious poetry credit in the publishing business. Competition is extraordinarily keen with more poems received in a year than there are people in some cities in your state. Accordingly, chances are slim. Yet Joseph Parisi is one of the most efficient (and discerning) editors around, and he does much to promote poetry. This is a magazine that you can buy straight off the newsstand to get a feel for the pulse of poetry each month. Six prizes (named in heading) ranging from $100 to $1,000 are awarded annually to poets whose work has appeared in the magazine that year. *Only verse already published in Poetry is eligible for consideration and no formal application is necessary. Poetry* also sponsors the Ruth Lilly Poetry Prize, an annual award of $25,000.

POETRY BREAK; BEING; ANNUAL POETRY CONTEST (I, IV-Spirituality, occult, horror), P.O. Box 417, Oceanside CA 92049-0417, founded 1988, (*Poetry Break* formerly *The Creative Urge*, founded 1984), editor and publisher Marjorie Talarico. *Poetry Break* is a bimonthly magazine that publishes poetry and sometimes articles and short stories. **All subjects and styles of poetry are welcomed. There is a Youth Poetry Page for ages 5-12 and a Young Adult Poetry Page for ages 13-18.** *Being* is a bimonthly "New Age, Metaphysical, magickal, wholistic health and healing journal." For *PB* the editor wants **rhyming, traditional, haiku, experimental poetry. No restriction in length.** For *Being*, "poems, prose, **haiku, experimental poetry, up to 100 lines. Poems can be erotic; no porno, however." Guidelines for both magazines are available for SASE.** They have recently published poetry by Genevieve Georg, Doug McKean, Thomas Haesche, Dawn Brock and Cleve Otis Hulsey. As a sample the editor selected these lines from "The Waters of Your Bath" by Wendell Velour Fletcher:

> If I were the waters of your bath
> I would enclose you in a wet, warm embrace
> And cause the gentle fingers of perspiration
> To kiss your lovely face.

Poetry Break is digest-sized, 32-36 pgs., sometimes illustrated with pen and ink drawings; it uses 80 to 100 poems bimonthly. Circulation is about 375. **Pays copies only. Acquires first North American serial rights. "We accept photocopy, dot-matrix printed, handwritten (legible, please)." Reporting time is 6-12 weeks and time to publication is 2-6 months.** Subscription for *Poetry Break* is $10/year, $2 per issue. **Sample: $2 plus 7½×10½ SASE with 75¢ postage.** Subscription for *Being* is $12/year, $3 per single issue. **Sample: $3 plus 7½×10½ SASE with 75¢ postage. Please make checks/money orders for samples/subscriptions payable to Marjorie Talarico.** Reviews books of poetry. Send books to the attention of Mark Antony Rossi. Their Annual Poetry Contest is open January 31 through September 30. Any style eligible, 45-line limit, $2 entry fee/poem. Offers varied cash prizes plus publication.

THE POETRY CONNEXION (II, IV-Specialized), Wanda Coleman and Austin Straus, co-hosts, P.O. Box 29154, Los Angeles CA 90029-0154, founded 1981, contact person Austin Straus. **"The Poetry Connexion" is a radio program, usually live; poets coming to the Los Angeles area make contact several months in advance and send work with SASE just as though the program were a press. "We are especially interested in poets who are planning to do readings in the Los Angeles area. Please notify us at least three months in advance for consideration as a guest on our program. Always include at least 6 poems and a vita in any submission."** The program is heard on the first, third and fifth Saturdays of each month from 6 to 7 p.m. Its purpose is "to broaden the audience, reading and listening, for poetry in the Southern California area which is now experiencing a cultural 'boom' of sorts. **We are volunteer Pacifica Radio broadcasters and do not pay."** The co-hosts say, "We have a preference for the 'serious' poet who has published in recognized magazines. The poet may not necessarily have a book but must be on the verge of publishing, participating in workshops, readings, residencies, etc." Submissions are open, but they "prefer the accessible. We are also always most interested in poets whose lives are as committed and intense as their work."

Close-up

Richard Jackson
Poet/Editor
The Poetry Miscellany

It was one of those little folds in time
when Desire had stopped at some remote crossroads,
when the absurd moon could rise without a purpose.
I don't know whose heart just stood there without an owner.
We all knew where melancholy could lurk
in ravines, or even lie sprawled out by the side of the road.
We all knew we could have wilted with the day lilies.
And those nailheads of stars—who would be left
to hang their sorrows on them?
That's why Boris was back in our kitchen practicing ecstasy.
It was a long way from the riots in his own Ljubljana.
It seemed the last few days were grazing
in fields south of us, swatting flies with their tails.
We were all filled with that elegiac swagger.
Somewhere a star collapsed whose cloudy image wouldn't
reach us for thousands of light years.

(from "Circumstances," reprinted from *Ploughshares*
 and **Pushcart Prizes**, 1992, by permission of the author)

In this age of interactive media and global awareness, *The Poetry Miscellany* fits right in.

When the magazine was founded in North Adams, Massachusetts, in 1971, its goal was to publish a mix of well-known and younger poets with an emphasis on quality. When editor Richard Jackson moved to Tennessee in 1977 to teach the freshman honors program and creative writing classes at the University of Tennessee at Chattanooga, he brought the magazine with him. It is still dedicated to the same goal and to Jackson's philosophy that the magazine should not exist "just between the pages," but should reach beyond into the wider world of literary activity. Today, the magazine involves both students and nonstudents of all ages and interests in readings, workshops and conferences and, as a result of this interaction, often publishes their work in its pages.

Jackson has also "taken the show on the road," so to speak. For the past several years, he and a group of grant students and people from the community have traveled to Central and Eastern Europe where they conduct demonstration workshop classes in publishing and starting magazines. During these trips, Jackson also recruits material.

Jackson's interest in the international creative community is a result of his experience as a Fulbright Exchange Poet to Yugoslavia in 1986 and his interest in all kinds of literature and cultures. He has returned to Yugoslavia several times and has many contacts in the regions of Poland, Czechoslovakia, Hungary and Romania. As a result, the magazine is publishing a series of chapbooks (10 so far) by poets from Central and Eastern Europe. The chapbooks usually run 12 to 18 pages, and while only the English translation is printed, manuscripts should include the poems in both English and the original language.

Of course, *TPM* is also interested in submissions for the magazine. Jackson describes their editorial philosophy as one of differences — "a melting pot" of well-known poets whose work they like as well as little-known or unknown poets. "We are open to all schools of poetry," he says. They have published the work of poets such as William Matthews, Robert Penn Warren, Charles Simic, Richard Wilbur and Maxine Kumin (whose work appeared in one of the first issues of *TPM*, before she won the Pulitzer Prize).

TPM receives about 8,000 manuscripts a year. They're read year-round, first by several contributing editors, then by Jackson — though he admits that he can't resist looking through manuscripts as they come in. "My taste is so eclectic," says Jackson. "I like to read poems by John Ashbery or Gerald Stern or Denise Levertov, for instance."

That taste is reflected in the type of poetry published. "We've published surrealistic, narrative, lyrical poetry, all the 'isms' — and even some language poets. We try to look at how well something is written rather than the type of poetry it is. Everyone on our staff is a writer, but we make an effort to not exclude something because it's a certain type that we may not be so close to in our own writing."

Jackson is the author of three volumes of poetry, **Alive All Day** (Cleveland State University, 1992), **Worlds Apart** (University of Alabama Press, 1987, reprinted in 1989) and **Part of the Story** (Grove Press, 1983), as well as two books of criticism. His work has appeared in numerous journals, including *Poetry*, *The Georgia Review* and *The Iowa Review*. He has also received a creative writing fellowship from the National Endowment for the Arts.

Not long ago he received a small box of magazines from Romania containing poems of his that had been published over the previous four years. He was unaware that his work had appeared in the magazines because, as the editor's letter explained, it was impossible to send them out of the country. After Ceausescu was executed in 1989, the material was freed and, subsequently, Jackson's work was collected into a book published in May 1992. Another collection of his poetry is scheduled for publication in Yugoslavia in 1993.

But Jackson recalls that when he first started sending out his poetry, he had no confidence and was unable to get his work published. He tried many small magazines and was getting nowhere. Then he decided he might as well "get nowhere with the big folks," and changed his tactics, with obvious success. From this experience, he feels poets should consider editors as well as publications when they submit.

For example, he says, "A really small publication might have special interests and agendas they don't advertise or they might not be so open in their tastes or they might be looking for bigger names to get the magazine more publicity. Even in terms of quality, they may not be very good editors or readers." Some of these considerations can apply at the larger magazines, too, he adds.

Jackson feels it's important for poets to discover editors' interests, to find the quality they want. He advises poets to read magazines at the library or send for sample copies. "If you have the same taste as the editor, if you like what the magazine is publishing, then submit to it," he says. "Being published in a magazine is like joining a club. Ask yourself who else is in the magazine and do you want to be associated with those kinds of people.

"Don't get desperate and decide you want to be in a certain magazine, rather than looking at a poem in a magazine and deciding that it fits what you're doing," Jackson says. "Don't say to yourself, 'I want to be in that magazine and these are the kinds of poems they like, so I'll write that kind of poem.' I don't think you should try to write *to* magazines or write just to be published. If you write for yourself and just try to improve your art, the publications are going to come. Then it basically becomes a secretarial trick of sending your poetry out to places you've researched and you know would be good for you. There are so many magazines out there, eventually it's going to happen."

— Pat Beusterien

POETRY DURHAM (II), English Dept., University of Durham, New Elvet, Durham, England DH1 3JT, edited by David Hartnett, Michael O'Neill and Gareth Reeves, founded 1982, appears 3 times a year, 44 pgs., digest-sized, professionally printed on good stock with glossy card cover, circulation 300, using **quality poetry and essays on modern poetry. Pays £12/poem.** Reviews books of poetry. **All overseas subscriptions by international money order.** Subscription: £5 for 3 issues.

POETRY EAST (II), Dept. of English, 802 W. Belden Ave., De Paul University, Chicago IL 60614, phone (312)341-8330, founded 1980, editor Richard Jones, "is a biannual international magazine publishing poetry, fiction, translations and reviews. We suggest that authors look through back issues of the magazine before making submissions. **No constraints or specifications, although we prefer open form.**" They have published poetry by Tom Crawford, Thomas McGrath, Denise Levertov, Galway Kinnell, Sharon Olds and Amiri Baraka. The digest-sized, flat-spined, journal is 100+ pgs., professionally printed, glossy color card cover, circulation 1,200, 250 subscriptions of which 80 are libraries. They use 60-80 pgs. of poetry in each issue. They receive approximately 4,000 freelance submissions/year, use 10%, have a 4-month backlog. Subscription: $12; per copy: $8. **Sample postpaid: $4.50. Reports in 4 months. Pays copies. Editors sometimes comment on rejections.** This is one of the best-edited magazines around. Richard Jones puts together poems of vision and verve in a publication designed so elegantly you will want to keep one on your shelf. He occasionally does theme issues. Because Jones puts a lot of energy into reading submissions—competition here is as tough as anywhere—response time can be slow during peak reading cycles in spring and fall.

THE POETRY EXPLOSION NEWSLETTER (THE PEN) (I), Box 2648, Newport News VA 23609-0648, phone (804)874-2428, founded 1984, editor Arthur C. Ford, Sr., is a "quarterly newsletter dedicated to the preservation of poetry." Arthur Ford wants **"poetry—40 lines maximum, no minimum. All forms and subject matter with the use of good imagery, symbolism and honesty. Rhyme and non-rhyme. No vulgarity."** He has published poetry by Ursula T. Gibson, Veona Thomas and Rose Robaldo. *The Pen* is a newsletter containing 4 sheets (saddle-stitched) mimeographed on both sides of each sheet. He accepts about 80 of 300 poems received, press run 350, with 165 subscriptions of which 5 are libraries. Subscription: $12. **Send $3 for sample copy and more information. Pays 1 copy. Submit maximum of 5 poems. Include $1 for reading time. Simultaneous submissions and previously published poems OK. Editor comments on rejections** "sometimes, but not obligated." He will criticize poetry for 15¢ a word. He comments: "Even though free verse is more popular today, we try to stay versatile."

POETRY FORUM (I); THE JOURNAL (IV-Subscription), 5713 Larchmont Dr., Erie PA 16509, phone (814)866-2543, poetry editor Gunvor Skogsholm, appears 3 times a year. **"We are open to any style and form. We believe new forms ought to develop from intuition. Length up to 50 lines accepted. Would like to encourage long themes. No porn or blasphemy, but open to all religious persuasions."** As a sample the editor selected these lines (poet unidentified):

> *. . . Because the tear*
> *down the cheek of a son*
> *is the reward of*
> *a lifetime of merit and concern . . .*

The magazine is 7×8½, 38 pgs., saddle-stapled with card cover, photocopied from photoreduced typescript. **Sample postpaid: $3. Send SASE for guidelines. They will consider simultaneous submissions and previously published poems.** They give awards of $50, $25, $10 and 3 honorable mentions for the best poems in each issue. *The Journal* appears twice a year, accepts **experimental poetry of any length from subscribers only. Sample $3. Acquires one-time rights.** Reviews books of poetry in 250 words maximum. They offer a poetry and short story chapbook contest, grand prize $100. Send SASE for information. **Editor comments on poems "if asked, but respects the poetic freedom of the artist."** He says, "I believe today's poets should experiment more and not feel stuck in the forms that were in vogue 300 years ago. I would like to see more experimentalism—new forms will prove that poetry is alive and well in the mind and spirit of the people."

POETRY IRELAND REVIEW (II, IV-Regional), 44 Upper Mount St., Dublin 2, Ireland, founded 1981, "provides an outlet for **Irish poets; submissions from abroad also considered. No specific style or subject matter is prescribed.**" Occasionally publishes special issues. The 6×8 quarterly uses 60 pgs. of poetry in each issue, circulation 1,000, with 450 subscriptions of which 50 are libraries. Subscription: $30; per copy: $8 (US). They receive about 2,500 submissions/year, use 250, have a 2-month backlog. **Sample postpaid: $8. Submit photocopies, no simultaneous submissions, no query. Reports in 3 months. Pays copies.** Reviews books of poetry in 500-1,000 words. They offer a bimonthly newsletter giving news, details of readings, competitions, etc. for IR£6/year. The editors advise, "Keep submitting: good work will get through."

POETRY KANTO (V), Kanto Gakuin University, 1641 Kamariya-cho, Kanazawa-Ku, Yokohama 236, Japan, founded 1984, editor William I. Elliott. *Poetry Kanto* is a literary annual published by the Kanto Poetry Center, which sponsors an annual poetry conference. It publishes **well-crafted original poems in English and in Japanese.** The magazine publishes **"anything except pornography, English haiku and tanka, and tends to publish poems under 30 lines."** They are not reading mss until further notice, however, as "special numbers are planned." They have published work by Seamus Heaney, Desmond Egan, Shuntaro Tanikawa and Les Murray. As a sample, here is the final stanza from "A Suite . . ." by Serge Gavronsky:

> *Is it perverse to be inspired*
> *by poems when outside*
> *a pine tree*
> *waits*
> *for my pen to move*
> *in a respectful manner?*

The magazine is digest-sized, nicely printed (the English poems occupy the first half of the issue, the Japanese poems the second), 60 pgs., saddle-stapled, matte card cover. Circulation is 700, of which 400 are complimentary copies sent to schools, poets and presses; it is also distributed at poetry seminars. The magazine is unpriced. **Pay is 3-5 copies.** The editor advises, "Read a lot. Get feedback from poets and/or workshops. Be neat, clean, legible and polite in submissions. *SAE with international reply coupons absolutely necessary when requesting sample copy.*"

POETRY MAGIC PUBLICATIONS (I, IV-Love/romance, anthology), 1630 Lake Dr., Haslett MI 48840, founded 1987, editor Lisa R. Church. Publishes an anthology and newsletter for writers, looking for **"no specific style. Open to all types, including haiku. Length should be no longer than one 8½ × 11 page but will consider longer poems. We want work from the writer/poet's heart and soul — not something that is 'forced.' No pornography. Sexual themes are okay but will be left to the editor's decision."** They have published poetry by Maria Bakkum and Scott Sonders. The anthology is digest-sized, 170 pgs., flat-spined, 1-3 poems/page, with a matte cover with color art. $16.95 list price. **No payment.** Discount to authors. Newsletter features articles, contest information, market listings and poem relating to the art of writing. Subscription: $13.50 for newsletter. **Sample postpaid: $4. Pays 1 copy to $100 for newsletter. Send SASE for guidelines. Ms should be typed on one side of paper. "Will accept handwritten material only if it is legible — otherwise, it ends up in file 'trash.' "** Submit mss for newsletter anytime; anthology deadline: March of each year. Simultaneous submissions, previously published poems OK if stated as such. Reports in 4-6 weeks. Editor comments "if time permits us to." Reviews books of poetry "sometimes." She says, "I have found those individuals who persistently work at their craft will receive the deserved recognition. I suggest that beginners circulate their poems and their name to many editors, which will allow the editors to become familiar with the name and the work. It is strongly suggested that at all times beginners present themselves in a professional manner. If SASE not enclosed, work will be discarded."

THE POETRY MISCELLANY (II), English Dept., University of Tennessee at Chattanooga, Chattanooga TN 37403, founded 1971 (in North Adams, MA), poetry editor Richard Jackson. "We publish new and established writers — poems, interviews, essays, translations. We are truly a miscellany: **we look at all schools, types, etc."** They have published poetry by William Matthews, Richard Wilbur, Maxine Kumin, Donald Justice and David Ignatow. As a sample here are the opening lines of "In No Particular Season" by Linda Pastan:

> *On a day like this of tatterned leaves*
> *in no particular season,*
> *I seem to have outgrown my life*
> *like last year's winter coat — unravelling . . .*

The 6 × 8½, 75-page biannual, professionally printed, blue ink on tinted blue, grey or white paper, matte card cover, stapled spine, has a circulation of 650, 450 subscriptions of which 150 are libraries. They receive about 8,000 submissions/year, use 30, have a 6-12 month backlog. Subscription: $4; per copy: $2. **Sample postpaid: $2.50. Send 3-4 clear copies/submission. Reports in 3-4 months. Pays 1 copy. Send SASE for guidelines.** Editor "rarely" comments on rejections. **Also publishes chapbooks.** Sometimes holds contests "when grants allow."

POETRY MOTEL; SUBURBAN WILDERNESS PRESS, BROADSIDES AND CHAPBOOKS (I, II), 1619 Jefferson, Duluth MN 55812, founded 1984, editors Pat McKinnon, Bud Backen and Jennifer Willis-Long aim **"to keep the rooms clean and available for these poor ragged poems to crash in once they are through driving or committing adultery." No specifications.** They have recently published poetry by Jesse Glass, Robert Peters, Ellie Schoenfeld, Pegg Pfeiffer, Ligi and Todd Moore. As a sample they selected these lines from "Family Traditions" by Will Lahti:

> *when great-grandfather was 4 years old*

he and his brothers would play funeral.

since matti was the youngest
he had to be the corpse.

he played this role so well that
one day his brothers buried him alive . . .

Poetry Motel appears 1-2 times a year as a 7 × 8½, digest, with various covers, including wallpaper (issue 16) and chrome plated mylar (issue 10), circulation 500 (to 450 subscriptions), 50-60 pgs. of poetry, prose, essays and reviews. **Sample: $4.95.** They receive about 1,000 submissions/year, take 250, have 6-12 month backlog. **Submit 3-5 pgs., informal cover letter, name and address on upper half of each page. Photocopies OK. Simultaneous submissions OK. Reports in 1-3 weeks. Payment varies. Acquires one-time rights. Editors are "always glad to comment, on request."** Reviews books of poetry. They advise, "Poets should read as much poetry as they can lay their hands on. And they should realize that although poetry is no fraternal club, poets are responsible for its survival, both financially and emotionally. Join us out here—this is where the edge meets the vision. We are very open to work from 'beginners.' "

POETRY NEW YORK: A JOURNAL OF POETRY AND TRANSLATION (II, IV-Translations, themes), PhD Program in English, CUNY Graduate Center, 33 W. 42nd St., New York NY 10036, phone (212)642-2206, founded 1985, editors Burt Kimmelman and Cheryl Fish, is an annual. They have published poetry by John Ashbery, Jerome Rothenberg, Enid Dame, Armand Schwerner, Ann Lauterbach, and translations of Mallarme, Hesiod and Makoto Ooka. The editor describes it as 4¼ × 5½, saddle-stapled, 80 pgs., with glossy card cover. They accept about 20% of "blind submissions." Press run: 500 for 300 shelf sales. **Pays 1 copy. Reports in 3-4 months. Editor comments on submissions "at times." Some issues are on themes. "Query us to see whether we are currently reading manuscripts."** They sometimes sponsor readings.

POETRY NIPPON PRESS; THE POETRY SOCIETY OF JAPAN; POETRY NIPPON; POETRY NIPPON NEWSLETTER (II, IV-Form, translations), 5-11-2, Nagaike-cho, Showa-ku, Nagoya, Japan 466, phone (052)833-5724, founded 1967, poetry editors Atsuo Nakagawa and Yorifumi Yaguchi (and guest editors). *Poetry Nippon*, a quarterly, uses **translations of Japanese poems into English, poems by Western and Japanese poets, tanka, haiku, one-line poems, essays on poetry and poets, poetry book reviews, poetry news, home and abroad. They want tanka, haiku, one-line poems and poems on contemporary themes and on Japan.** They have published poetry by Yorifumi Yaguchi, Toshimi Horiuchi and Naoshi Koriyama. As a sample the editor selected these lines by Marian Chow:

> *How much makes a lifetime?*
> *How far is birth from death?*
> *Between heaven and earth,*
> *What day is today?*
> *My cup I raise*
> *Singing a sad song to my soul.*

Poetry Nippon has a circulation of 500 with 200 subscriptions of which 30 are libraries. Subscription: $29; per copy: $8. They use 25% of the 400 submissions they receive each year, have a 6-12 month backlog. **Sample free for 4 IRCs. Submit 2 poems, 5 tanka or 6 haiku, unpublished and not submitted elsewhere. "Deadline March 31 for nonmembers." Reports in 6 months for members. Pays copies. Send SAE with 2 IRCs for guidelines.** Apparently you can join the Poetry Society of Japan, receive the *Newsletter* and *Poetry Nippon* and have other benefits. For example, **the editors provide criticism "on members' mss only."** They sponsor contests for tanka and haiku and publish collections by individuals and anthologies.

POETRY NORTHWEST (II), 4045 Brooklyn NE, Seattle WA 98105, phone (206)685-4750, founded 1959, poetry editor David Wagoner, is a quarterly which uses 48 pgs. of poetry in each issue, circulation 1,500. Subscription: $10; per issue: $3. They receive 20,000 poems in freelance submissions/year, use 160, have a 3-month backlog. **Sample postpaid: $3. Reports in 1 month maximum. Pays 2 copies. They award prizes of $100, $50 and $50 yearly, judged by the editors. Occasionally editor comments on rejections.**

POETRY NOTTINGHAM; LAKE ASKE MEMORIAL OPEN POETRY COMPETITION (II); NOTTINGHAM POETRY SOCIETY (IV-Regional); QUEENIE LEE COMPETITION (IV-Membership/subscription), Summer Cottage West St., Shelford, Notts. NG12 1EJ Nottingham England, phone 0602 334540, founded 1941, poetry editor Claire Piggott. Nottingham Poetry Society meets monthly for readings, talks, etc., and publishes quarterly its magazine, *Poetry Nottingham: The International Magazine of Today's Poetry,* which is open to submissions from all-comers. **"We wish to see poetry that is intelligible**

to and enjoyable by the intelligent reader. We do not want any party politics or religious freaks. Poems not more than 40 lines in length." They have recently published poetry by Bert Almon, William Davey and Nikolas Macioci from the USA. As a sample the editor selected these lines from "Half-Term" by Maurice Rutherford:

> *And if you've ever wondered what goes on*
> *inside the heads of men who sit on seats*
> *and ogle passers-by, come, sit with me,*
> *it's marvelous ... fantastic's more the word!*
> *I chose at will, make this one rich, that poor ...*

There are 30 pgs. of poetry in each issue of the 6×8, 36-page magazine, professional printing with occasional essays and b&w graphics, glossy art paper cover, circulation 325 for 200 subscriptions of which 20 are libraries. Subscriptions: £7 ($50 for 2 years USA); per copy: £1.75 ($6 USA). They receive about 1,500 submissions/year, use 120, usually have a 1-3 month backlog. **Sample: $6 or £1.75 postpaid. Submit at any time 3-5 poems, not more than 40 lines each, not handwritten, and previously unpublished. Send SAE and 2 IRCs for stamps. No need to query. Reports "within 2 months plus mailing time." Pays one copy.** Reviews books of poetry, but space allows only listings or brief review. **Nottingham Poetry Society publishes collections by individual poets who were born, live or work in the East Midlands of England.** The Lake Aske Memorial Open Poetry Competition offers cash prizes, annual subscriptions and publication in *Poetry Nottingham*. Open to all. The Queenie Lee Competition is for members and subscribers only, offers a cash prize and publication. **Editor accepts "when I feel the poet learned the craft and says something objectively worth hearing."** Her advice, especially for beginners, is "read the magazine before submitting anything; write the kind of poetry you believe in, which, if it is any good, will find a magazine to publish it." As a footnote, to help US poets understand some of the problems of editors in other countries, we quote Claire Piggott at length: "May I suggest that a general note about how to pay for small magazines from England that sell only a few copies in the USA, with a recommendation to send a draft for sterling, would be helpful to your readers. The price of our magazine is low (£7 annual subscription in the U.K.). If, however, I wish to exchange a draft from the USA, the bank charges me £3 commission (their commission being the same whether I am exchanging $10 or $10,000). Therefore, we are now asking that overseas subscribers who cannot arrange a draft for sterling should take out a two-year subscription for $50 to include all postage at increased rates. The advice about sterling drafts applies equally to sample copies; please allow £2.50 to include airmail post."

POETRY OF THE PEOPLE (I, IV-Anthology, humor, love/romance/erotica, nature, fantasy, themes), P.O. Box 13077, Gainesville FL 32604, founded 1986, poetry editor Paul Cohen. *Poetry of the People* appears once a month. **"We take all forms of poetry but we like humorous poetry, love poetry, nature poetry and fantasy. No racist or highly ethnocentric poetry will be accepted."** *Poetry of the People* has a circulation between 300 and 2,300. Copies are distributed to Gainesville residents for 25¢ each. **"I feel autobiographical information is important in understanding the poetry."** Poems returned within three months. **Editor comments on rejections "often."** He advises, "Be creative: there is a lot of competition out there." A dozen leaflets (8-16 pgs., 4½×5¼, sometimes stapled on colored paper) of poetry are published each year, usually theme anthologies. **Pays 5 copies. Acquires first rights.** Subscription: $8/year. **Sample $4 for 11 pamphlets.** Make checks payable to Paul Cohen.

POETRY ONLY; FORESTLAND PUBLICATIONS (I), 423 N. Burnham Hwy., Canterbury CT 06331, founded 1988, editor Geraldine Hempstead. *Poetry Only* is a magazine. "No restrictions on form, length or subject matter. If it's a long poem, it better be exciting enough to keep me awake. No porn." They have published poetry by Ray Mizer, Gary Scheinoha, Winnie Fitzpatrick, R. Allen Dodson and Ken Stone. Press run 100, with 15 subscribers, 75 distributed free. Subscription: $8.50. **Sample postpaid: $2. All orders must be made payable to Geraldine Hilliard, not *Poetry Only*. Pays 1 copy. Send SASE for guidelines.** They will consider simultaneous submissions and previously published poems. Do not submit mss until January 1993.

THE POETRY PEDDLER; ELECTRIC POETS; SNOWBOUND PRESS (I, II), P.O. Box 250, West Monroe NY 13167, founded 1988, poetry editors J.J. Snow and A.M. Ryant. Snowbound Press publishes chapbooks by special arrangement. *PP* is a literary magazine of poetry and essays on poetry appearing six times a year, using **"poems of clarity and intensity of feeling. We will consider rhymed poetry of a serious nature providing the rhyme doesn't overwhelm the message. Seldom does a rhymed poem meet this standard. Rhyme used to augment humor is welcome. No bigotry, pro-war, graphic violence, obscure poems."** They have recently published poetry by Susan Manchester, Walt Phillips, Janet Rosenstengel, Asha Eshe and Sigmund Weiss. As a sample J.J. Snow chose the last lines from his poem "First Family":

> *and the wheezy,*

> *snot faced,*
> *much loved baby,*
> *in the mouldy carriage.*

PP is 20 pgs., magazine-sized, desktop publishing, with card cover, using some computer-generated graphics. **Send SASE for guidelines. Subscription: $12. Sample: $2.50. They will consider previously published poems (send complete publications information and statement that you now control rights) but no simultaneous submissions. "Handwritten OK if legible." Editor always comments on rejections. Pays 1 copy. Acquires one-time rights.** *Electric Poets* is a computerized 'magazine' for electronic bulletin boards and is available for reading only via computer modem. They want **"any poetry, including rhyme, 20-line limit. No violence, sex or prejudice."** They have recently published poetry by Susanna Roxmann, Walter Kuchinsky and M.C. Alpher. As a sample the editor selected these lines from "Dreams in French Class" by Crystall Carmen:

> *The gray is still there*
> *You cannot escape from its claws*
> *that enter first your mind*
> *and then your heart.*

Previously published poems OK; no simultaneous submissions. Reads submissions August 1 through May 30. Seldom comments on rejections. Send SASE for guidelines. Reports in 1 month. Acquires one-time rights. The editor says, "One of the drawbacks to the current poetry scene is that the only people who read the mags are fellow poets. *Electric Poets* is read by those who do not normally read poetry thus vastly increasing an individual poet's exposure. The potential (really unknown) is thousands of readers across the country who tap into bulletin board systems."

POETRY PLUS MAGAZINE; GERMAN PUBLICATIONS (I, IV-Subscribers), Route 1, Box 52, Pulaski IL 62976, founded 1987, publisher/editor Helen D. German. *PPM* is a quarterly with articles about poetry, stories and poems. **"We accept all styles. Length should be no more than 24 lines. Poets can write on any subject that offers a meaningful message. We want our poets to write poems that will make the reader really think about what has been said. Reader should not have to guess at what was said. We do** *not* **want any holiday poems, obscene poems or sexual poems. Poems should not be indecent."** As a sample the editor selected this complete poem by Terry Lee Armstrong:

> *A Poet:*
> *One who reads, writes, and thinks*
> *While dwelling in the silence*
> *of the light of thought.*

PPM is magazine-sized, 25-35 pgs., photocopied from typescript, bound with tape, paper cover. **Subscription: $20 (includes Poetry Profits: How to Turn Your Poems into Dollars). Sample postpaid: $3. Send SASE for guidelines. Subscribers are paid up to $5 for outstanding poems; no payment to nonsubscribers. Offers editorial/critique service for $6/poem.** The editor says, *"Poetry Plus* is a fresh magazine that offers poets and writers the opportunity to see their poems in print. We want poems that are written to stimulate the deeper side of the reader. Rhymed or unrhymed, poems should offer a message that is meaningful. They should leave a memorable impression. Always send a large SASE with sufficient postage to return your unused poems. We publish both the work of our subscribers and nonsubscribers. Of course, due to limited space in each issue, subscribers get their poems published first. If you haven't been published yet or if you have, order a sample copy today and see what you've been missing in literary refreshment."

POETRY REVIEW; NATIONAL POETRY SOCIETY; NATIONAL POETRY COMPETITION; EUROPEAN POETRY TRANSLATION PRIZE; NATIONAL POETRY CENTRE; WH SMITH POETS IN SCHOOLS SCHEME; PUFFIN PROJECT; POEMS ON THE UNDERGROUND (II, IV-Children), 21 Earls Court Sq., London, SW5 9DE England, founded 1909, the National Poetry Society is Britain's largest and most influential poetry organization. In addition to their quarterly journal, *Poetry Review*, they maintain the directory of the National Poetry Society (including lists of poets' publications and fees), and conduct educational programs for school children and others, and other activities (including Poems on the Underground, for publishing poems in subways). Membership in the Society is available for poets throughout the world, with group rates. The only instructions as to the type of poetry wanted in *PR* (editor Peter Forbes) are, **"Intending contributors should study the magazine first."** They publish "all the leading U.K. poets, many American and European poets." Poets featured include Joseph Brodsky, Anthony Hecht, Derek Walcott, Tony Harrison, Howard Nemerov, Primo Levi and Vikram Seth. *Poetry Review* is 6¾ × 9¼, 76 pgs., offset on rough paper, with b&w graphics and photos, stiff card cover, printed in two colors plus black on white, flat-spined. Circulation is 5,000, price per issue £4.50, subscription £21 ($38). All subscriptions payable to *Poetry Review*. **Sample available for £5 ($9) postpaid. Guidelines for SASE. Pay is £10-15 poem plus 1 copy. Reporting time is 10 weeks and time to publication varies.** Reviews books of poetry. The National Poetry Competition offers prizes of £2,000, £1,000, £500 and 15 smaller prizes, for 40 lines or less on any subject, open worldwide. The winning poems are published as an anthology. Write for information regarding the European Poetry Translation Prize, membership, or their other activities.

POETRY: USA QUARTERLY; POEMS FOR PLANETARY SURVIVAL (I, II, IV-Themes, children, membership), Bldg. D, Ft. Mason Cultural Center, San Francisco CA 94123, phone (415)776-6602, founded 1985, editor Herman Berlandt, who describes *Poetry: USA Quarterly* as "a quarterly for **bold and compassionate poetry.**" Every issue has a thematic focus: for example, love and experience, four dozen ways of looking at the moon, in praise of other muses, etc. Send SASE for upcoming themes. The editor does not want "trite and phoney, 'elevated' stuff using contrived rhymes." He has published poetry by Amy Gerstler, Mary Mackey, Diane di Prima, Neeli Chekovski and Robert Bly. It is a typeset unstapled tabloid, 16 pgs., with photos, graphics and ads, circulation 10,000, distributed free "to reach 40,000 literati in the Bay Area" and available to others by subscription at $7.50/year. **Sample postpaid: $1.50.** "Big backlog, active file for a year. Suggest poems under 32 lines. No SASEs. Just send photocopies—if published, contributor will get copies." No other pay "as yet. Suggest that contributors subscribe to maintain good contact." Previously published poems OK (if the editor knows). One section of the tabloid is devoted to poetry by young poets. Send SASE for guidelines. They hold 4 annual contests, on the theme of each issue.

POETRY WALES PRESS; POETRY WALES (II, IV-Ethnic), Andmar House, Trewsfield Ind. Estate, Tondu Rd., Bridgend, Mid-Glamorgan CF31 4LJ Wales, founded 1965. *Poetry Wales*, a 72-page, 253×185mm quarterly, circulation 1,000, has a primary interest in **Welsh and Anglo-Welsh poets** but also considers submissions internationally. **Send submissions (with SAE and IRC) to Richard Poole, editor, Glan-y-Werydd, Llandanwg, Harlech LL46 2SD Wales. Sample: £1.95. Pays.** Reviews books of poetry. The press publishes books of **primarily Welsh and Anglo Welsh poetry**, also biography, critical works and some fiction, distributed by Dufour Editions, Inc., Box 449, Chester Springs PA 19425.

‡POETRY WLU (I, II), Department of English, Wilfrid Laurier University, Waterloo, Ontario N2L 3C5 Canada, phone (519)884-1970, ext. 2308, founded 1979, editorial contact E. Jewinski, is an annual literary magazine "with emphasis on *all* poetry and *all* prose *under* 1,000 words. **20-30 lines are ideal; but all kinds and lengths considered.**" As a sample here is the complete poem "Elspeth" by Audrey P. Heutzenroeder:

> *Elspeth overturns elfin stones.*
> *Plays in the garden with toadie's bones.*
> *Recites tales dark and tragic.*
> *Dances with wizards and learns their magic.*

Poetry WLU is 6½×8 saddle-stapled, typeset, with matte card cover using b&w art. They accept 15-20% of some 60-70 submissions received/year. Press run 300. **Sample postpaid: $3. Reads submissions September 1 through January 30 only. Pays 1 copy. Reports in 6-8 months.** "When the editorial board has time, comments are made." The magazine is published every March.

‡POETS AT WORK (I, IV-Subscribers), VAMC 325 New Castle Rd., Box 113, Butler PA 16001, founded 1985, editor/publisher Jessee Poet, **all contributors are expected to subscribe.** Jessee Poet says, "**Every poet who writes within the dictates of good taste and within my twenty-line limit will be published in each issue. I accept all forms and themes of poetry, but no porn, no profanity.**" He has recently published poetry by Jaye Giammarion, Katherine Krebs, James Webb, Phil Eisenberg and Ernestine Gravely. As a sample he selected his poem "An Old Romance":

> *I almost loved you . . . did you know?*
> *Sometimes you still disturb my dreams.*
> *A summer romance long ago*
> *I almost loved you . . . did you know?*
> *We danced to music soft and low*
> *Just yesterday . . . or so it seems*
> *I almost loved you . . . did you know?*
> *Sometimes you still disturb my dreams.*

Poets at Work, a bimonthly, is generally 36-40 pgs., magazine-sized, saddle-stapled, photocopied from typescript with colored paper cover. Subscription: $16. **Sample: $3. Pays nothing, not even a copy.** "Because I publish hundreds of poets, I cannot afford to pay or give free issues. Every subscriber, of course, gets an issue. Subscribers also have many opportunities to regain their subscription money in the numerous contests offered in each issue." **Simultaneous submissions and previously published poems OK. Reports within 2 weeks.** "Send SASE for flyer for my separate monthly and special contests." He also publishes chapbooks. Send SASE for details. Jessee Poet says, "These days even the best poets tell me that it is difficult to get published. I am here for the novice as well as the experienced poet. I consider *Poets at Work* to be a hotbed for poets where each one can stretch and grow at his or her own pace. Each of us learns from

Close-up

Ruth Daigon
Poet/Editor
Poets On:

Like an ideal tenant, the bullet fits
precisely in the wound, closer
than a friend, a relative, a lover.
Removing it, what can we give the body
in exchange to accommodate it half so well?

The opening stanza to Ruth Daigon's poem "Like
An Ideal Tenant" could serve almost as her ars poetica, her philosophy about the art of
poetry. As a poet with more than 500 credits in prestigious journals (*Shenandoah* to *Ms.*
Magazine) and as editor of the respected magazine *Poets On:*, Daigon promotes poetry in
part by reminding us about the relationship between writer and reader.

For instance, the idea of a poem should pierce and reside within a reader—like a bullet
or an ideal tenant—producing what Daigon calls the "Aha!" response.

"For me, poetry organizes the otherwise random, sometimes chaotic events of a life,
giving it significance and structure." The events of one's life do not necessarily make good
poetry, she says. "But as the particulars are used figuratively, they will evoke in the reader
parallel experiences endowed now with new meanings and perspectives."

Sound also is essential in Daigon's poems, as one might expect from her background.
In addition to publishing three books of poetry, Daigon has had a career as a concert
soprano. She graduated from The Royal Conservatory of Toronto, toured the United States
and Canada in concerts and recitals and was a recording artist for Columbia Records.

"Because music was my first profession and is still important, it plays a vital role in my
poetry and in my reaction to the poetry I read," she says, noting that rhythm, inflection
and timbre are also elements in the dynamic between writer and reader.

"Every poem is an attempt to prod a reader into seeing more clearly and feeling more
intensely about some facet of living. In a sense," she says, "the poet and the reader are
doing similar things."

According to Daigon, the poet gathers memories, impressions and word meanings and
encodes them in a special language. Initially the reader may be puzzled by the sound, sense
and direction of a poem and relies on his or her own experience to untangle meaning. If
the poem is successful, the reader derives "intense pleasure at pulling it all together."

The poetic process at *Poets On:* is similar. For those unfamiliar with the magazine, the
colon in the title connects with a theme, as in *Poets On: Regrets* or *Poets On: Generations*.
The work of some of the best-known poets composing today appears alongside that of
relative unknowns, indicating a commitment to publish poems solely on merit.

As an editor, Daigon looks for poems that produce a sense of discovery or new understanding. "I reject poetry that is declamatory, sloganeering, bathetic or opaque." Neither
is she interested in poetry as mere word games or technical exercises. "The words must
point to something more important than themselves and must move a reader in ways that
discursive text cannot."

Writers who move Ruth Daigon in such manner become ideal tenants in *Poets On:*.

—Michael J. Bugeja

the other, and we do not criticize one another. The door for poets is always open, so please stop by; we probably will like each other immediately."

POETS ON: (IV-Themes), 29 Loring Ave., Mill Valley CA 94941, phone (415)283-2824, founded 1976, poetry editor Ruth Daigon, is a poetry semiannual, **each issue on an announced theme. "We want well-crafted, humanistic, accessible poetry. We don't want to see sentimental rhymed verse. Length preferably 40 lines or less, or at the very most 80 lines (2-page poems)."** They have published poetry by Marge Piercy, Charles Edward Eaton, Joseph Bruchac, Sharon Olds and Lyn Lifshin. As a sample we selected these lines from "Widow's Walk" by Lisa Lepovetsky in *Poets On: Remembrance:*

> *Memory casts me too far adrift*
> *and old currents swallow me deep*
> *in turmoils of damp debris and*
> *dreams, till I'm worn smooth*
> *as a whelk half-buried in sand.*
> *Years bend me leeward, clinging*
> *to the sides of these rocky fists.*

Poets On: is 48 pgs., digest-sized, professionally printed, matte card cover with b&w graphics. Circulation is 450, 350 subscriptions of which 125 are libraries. They use about 5% of the 800 submissions they receive each year, have a 2- to 3-month backlog. Subscription: $8. **Sample postpaid: $4. Query with SASE to find out the current theme. Submit 1-4 poems (40 lines or shorter).** "It's a good idea to read the magazine before submitting poetry." **Submit only September 1 through December 1 or February 1 through May 1. Photocopy, dot-matrix OK. No handwritten mss. Include short bio. Reports in 2-3 months. Pays 1 copy. Editor sometimes comments on rejections.** She has designed a rejection slip that has several categories explaining why your work didn't make it into the magazine, and yet she'll often add a comment to encourage good work. Ruth Daigon says, "We are not interested in poetry that is declamatory, sloganeering, bathetic or opaque. Nor are we concerned with poetry as mere word-games or technical exercises."

POETS. PAINTERS. COMPOSERS; COLIN'S MAGAZINE (II), 10254 35th Ave. SW, Seattle WA 98146, phone (206)937-8155, founded 1984, editor Joseph Keppler, who says *"Poets. Painters. Composers.* is an avant-garde arts journal which publishes poetry, drawings, scores, criticism, essays, reviews, photographs and original art. **If poetry, music or art is submitted, the work should be exciting, knowledgeable and ingenious."** The journal, which appears once or twice a year, has published such artists as Carla Bertola, Fernando Aguiar, Ana Hatherly and Sarenco and such poets as Carol Barrett, Carletta Wilson and D. Bauer. "We also publish *Colin's Magazine, A Special Review from Poets. Painters. Composers.* with a focus on the interface of literature and computer technology." As a sample the editor selected these lines from "Carpenter Mondrian" by Gregory Jerozal:

> *... Forget*
> *Green fields: they are*
> *The summer places of*
> *Regret, forgetfulness,*
> *The past we watch with others*
> *Reassembled on the screen.*

The journal is magazine-sized, 86 pgs. Each cover has an original painting on it. Mr. Keppler says, "each odd-numbered issue appears in an 8½×11 format; each even-numbered issue changes format: No. 2, for example, is published as posters; No. 4 appears on cassettes. No. 6 will be an exhibition of sculpture with a catalog and a collection of multiples." Circulation is 300, no subscriptions. Each issue of the magazine carries an individual price tag. A copy of *Poets. Painters. Composers.* No. 5 is $50. Sample of No. 2 available for $10.50 postpaid. Sample of *Colin's Magazine* is available for $7. Contributors receive 1 copy. Acquires one-time rights. **"Contributors' poetry receives great care. All material is returned right away unless (a) it's being painstakingly examined for acceptance into the journal or (b) it's being considered as right for some other way of publishing it or (c) we died."** "We prefer short (500-800 word) reviews unless we already have asked for a longer piece from a poet/reviewer because of his or her interest in the book." He expects to publish 3 chapbooks of poetry a year and will accept freelance submissions. **For chapbook publication poets should query first "if poet prefers," sending credits, 7 sample poems, bio, philosophy and poetic aims. Pay for chapbooks will be in author's copies, number negotiable ("We're generous"); honorariums are given whenever possible.** Format of the chapbooks is expected to be "small, avant-garde, distinguished, exciting, experimental." Joseph Keppler says, "Poets' work is important work, and poetry is a most difficult art today. We maintain absolutely high standards, yet offer a hopeful critique .... We want to develop the avant-garde here and everywhere. We expect to last well into the 21st century and to change the way this culture understands literature. We intend to transform the role of poets in society. Advice for beginning poets? We're all beginning poets today."

POET'S REVIEW (I, IV-Subscribers), 806 Kings Row, Cohutta GA 30710, phone (404)694-8441, founded 1988, publisher Bob Riemke, is a monthly booklet, digest-sized, 20 pgs., photocopied from typescript with paper cover, using **poetry by subscribers** and making cash awards monthly and annually on basis of votes by subscribers. **"Prefer rhyme. 44 lines or less. Any subject. No porn! No foreign languages."** They have recently published poetry by Helen Webb, Ashley Anders and J. Alvin Speers. Subscription: $36. **Sample postpaid: $4. "Subscribers are sent a ballot along with their monthly booklet to vote for the poems they believe to be the best." Monthly prizes are $75, $50 and $25, plus 7 honorable mentions. "All $75 winners are presented to the subscribers again at the end of the year and compete for a $500, $250 and $100 prize."** 20-30 poems are printed each month along with the names of winners for the previous month.

POETS' ROUNDTABLE; POETS' STUDY CLUB OF TERRE HAUTE; POETS' STUDY CLUB INTERNATIONAL CONTEST (I, IV-Membership), 826 S. Center St., Terre Haute IN 47807, phone (812)234-0819, founded 1939, president/editor Esther Alman. Poets' Study Club is one of the oldest associations of amateur poets. It publishes, every other month, *Poets' Roundtable*, a newsletter of market and contest information and news of the publications and activities of its members in a mimeographed, 10-page bulletin (magazine-sized, stapled at the corner, on colored paper), circulation 2,000. They have also published an occasional chapbook-anthology of poetry by members "but do not often do so." **Dues: $6 a year. Sample free for SASE. Uses short poems by members only. Simultaneous submissions and previously published poems OK.** They offer an annual Poets' Study Club International Contest, open to all, with no fees and cash prizes—a $25 and $15 award in 3 categories: traditional haiku, serious poetry, light verse. Deadline: February 1. Also contests for members only each two months. "We have scheduled criticism programs for members only."

POGMENT PRESS (V, IV-Regional), 11939 Escalante Ct., Reston VA 22091, phone (703)758-0258, founded 1985, editor Jefferson D. Bates, an elderly man who writes, "I still have enough energy and enthusiasm to publish 2-4 chapbooks/year, but how long this will continue I have no idea. I publish area poets with whose work I am familiar. **I am not seeking mss from outside my immediate area of Washington DC, Maryland and Northern Virginia.** As long-time member of the Board of Directors of the Writer's Center (now a member emeritus) I have an opportunity to meet (and hear readings by) many excellent poets. **I'm more concerned with the traditional forms and the niceties of rime and meter than are most publishers today. I love light, well-crafted verse in the vein of Dorothy Parker,** Ogden Nash, Samuel Hoffenstein and others that I've admired from my youth. I love the 'Grooks' of Piet Hein." He has published books by Dean Blehert, Werner Low and Marlene S. Veach, **10% royalties plus 10 copies. Sample: $2, for postage and handling.** "I do have a co-op arrangement somewhat similar to that of Northwoods Press. The author agrees to purchase a minimum of 200 copies at 50% off the list price." **He sometimes comments on rejections.**

‡POINT JUDITH LIGHT (IV-Form/style), P.O. Box 4685, Springfield MA 01101-4685, founded 1992, editor Patrick Frank, is a quarterly publishing individual haiku/senryu, sequences and statements of aesthetic philosophy. They want haiku/senryu **"which explore the relation of the poet to his/her environment and which focus on life as truly lived; 13 syllables maximum."** They recently published haiku/senryu by H.F. Noyes, Alexis Rotella and Ellen Compton. As a sample the editor selected these haiku/senryu by Francine Porad and Larry Gross respectively:

> *"bad" neighborhood*   *primeval gifts*
> *windowbox flowers*   *blue from the sky*
> *behind bars*   *apple from my wife*

The editor says *PJL* is desktop published in a newsletter format, 10 pgs. maximum. Press run is 200. **Subscription: $8/year. Sample postpaid: $2. Previously published poems OK; no simultaneous submissions. Cover letter required. Send 20 haiku/senryu maximum. Submissions should be typed. Include bio.** "I want to have some knowledge of the poet behind the work and publish a brief bio." **Often comments on rejections. Send SASE for guidelines. Reports within 1 week. Pays 1 copy. Acquires first rights.** "Three haiku/senryu will be selected as 'best of issue.'" The editor says, "Focus on the aspects of life that are immediately before you. Be yourself. Follow your intuition and be willing to explore and experiment."

THE POINTED CIRCLE (II), 705 N. Killingsworth, Portland OR 97217, phone (503)244-6111, ext. 5405, founded 1980, advisor Mary McNeill, is an annual using **"under 60 lines, mostly shorter. 1-page poems on any topic of any form. Nothing trite."** They have published poetry by Judith Barrington, William Stafford, Dianne Averill and Barbara Drake. It is handsomely printed, 7×8, flat-spined, 80 pgs., with b&w glossy card cover, professionally printed. Press run 400. **Sample postpaid: $3.50. Submit mss**

from December 1 through March 1 only. Send SASE for guidelines. Pays 1 copy. Acquires one-time rights. "Place name, address, etc., on cover sheet only, listing titles of submissions. Limit 5 poems/ poet. All submissions are read anonymously by student editorial staff; notification about June 1 for submissions received by March 1."

POKED WITH STICKS; POKED PRESS; RED STAR PRODUCTIONS (II), 3964 Homewood, Toledo OH 43612, founded 1987, editors Stephen E. Toth and Star Bowers. *PWS* appears once or twice/year. Poked Press Publications publishes a chapbook/year. They want poetry "any style from traditional to experimental. No gender bashing, no contrived rhyme or 'praise be to god' rhetoric. 'Sweet little kitty' verse should be sent to greeting card manufacturers, not here." They have recently published poetry by Joel Lipman, William Merricle, Todd Moore and Lynne Walker. As a sample the editor selected these lines from "Bury the Moon" by Ronald Edward Kittell:

> poems essays lovenotes novels
> words buzz the page like flies
> on feces & more often than not
> the moon sticks out like a
> festering boil

The editor describes *PWS* as 40 pgs., photocopied. Press run 300. They accept about 10% of 600 poems received/year. Subscription: $10/4 issues. **Sample postpaid: $3. Pays 1 copy.** "Because *PWS* is a collection of poetry, writing, mail art and found art, I accept pieces in the exact form in which they are sent. Line length and spacing remains as the creator intended. All submitted copies must be dark enough for photoduplication and very rarely is anything retyped." Reports in 1-3 months. To be considered for chapbook publication, a poem must have been published in *PWS* previously.

POLYPHONIES (III, IV-Translations), BP189, Paris 75665 CEDEX 14 France, founded 1985, editor Pascal Culerrier. Editorial committee: Laurence Breysse, Jean-Yves Masson and Alexis Pelletier. Appears twice a year. "Every case is a special one. We want to discover the new important voices of the world to open French literature to the major international productions. For example, we published Brodsky in French when he was not known in our country and had not yet the Nobel Prize. No vocal poetry, no typographic effects." They have published poetry by Mario Luzi (Italy), Jeremy Reed (Great Britain), Octavio Paz (Mexico) and Claude Michel Cluny (France). It is about 110 pgs., 6½×9½, flat-spined, with glossy card cover, printed completely in French. Press run: 850 for 300+ subscriptions. **Pays 2 copies.** They use translations of previously published poems. The editor says, "Our review is still at the beginning. We are in touch with many French editors. Our purpose is to publish together, side-by-side, poets of today and of yesterday."

PORTABLE WALL (III), 215 Burlington, Billings MT 59101, phone (406)256-3588, founded 1977, publisher Daniel Struckman. He wants, as Ezra Pound described, **"words that throw the object on to the visual imagination and that induce emotional correlations by the sound and rhythm of the speech."** He has recently published poetry by Dave Thomas and Joe Salerno. As a sample he selected these lines by Kathleen Taylor:

> Lightning rams down
> a cloud-clotted sky;
> the red moon is wasted.

PW is published twice a year. It is 40 pgs., saddle-stapled, on heavy tinted stock with 2-color matte card cover, press run 200. **Sample postpaid: $5. Pays 3 copies. Acquires one-time North American rights. Reports in 6 weeks, 6 months between acceptance and publication.** Subscription: $15 for 2 years.

PORTLAND REVIEW (II), Box 751, Portland OR 97207, phone (503)725-4533, founded 1954, contact editor, is a literary annual published by Portland State University 3 times a year. "Experimental poetry welcomed. No poems over 3 pages. No rhyming poetry." The annual is magazine-sized, about 128 pgs. They accept about 30 of 300 poems received each year. Press run is 500 for 100 subscriptions of which 10 are libraries. **Sample: $5.** Send SASE for guidelines. **Pays 1 copy.** Simultaneous submissions OK.

‡POST-INDUSTRIAL PRESS (III), P.O. Box 265, Greensboro PA 15338, founded 1989, director Robert Richards, publishes 2-3 paperbacks and 2-4 chapbooks/year. They have recently published poetry by Georges Perel and Johannes Poethen. **Replies to queries in 2 months, to mss in 6 months. Pay is "open to negotiation."** For sample books or chapbooks, write directly to the press.

POTATO EYES; NIGHTSHADE PRESS (II), P.O. Box 76, Troy ME 04987, phone (207)948-3427, founded 1988, editors Roy Zarucchi and Carolyn Page, is a semiannual literary arts journal **"with a focus on writers who write about the land and/or quality of life close to the earth. We now accept submissions**

from throughout the U.S. and Canada, although much of our poetry is from Appalachian states." They have published poetry by Fred Chappell, Robert Morgan, Nzadi Keita, Shelby Stephenson, Karen Blomain and Melody Davis. As a sample the editors selected these lines from Michael Chitwood's **Martyrdom of the Onions**, the title poem from a 1991 chapbook:

> In a garden, they are knots along a rope of dirt.
> Pulled out and hung in a bundle on the back porch,
> they chime in deep tones against the wood frame.
> I have seen my father rub a half on the lintel
> of a rabbit trap, to erase the smell of his hands.
> Lines of longitude describe their globe; . . .

Circulation is 800. *PE* is 5½ × 8½, 100+ pgs., flat-spined, professionally printed, with block cut matte card cover. Subscription: $11 (Canadian $14). **Sample postpaid: $6 (back issue $5), or $7 Canadian. Reports in 1-2 months, and "those who submit receive a handwritten rejection/ acceptance. We are open to any form other than rhymed, in batches of 3-5, but we tend to favor poetry with concrete visual imagery, solid intensity and compression. We respect word courage and risk-taking, along with thoughtful lineation. We prefer rebellious to complacent poetry. We prefer a cover letter with brief bio along with SASE." Acquires first North American serial rights.** Reviews books of poetry in less than 500 words. Nightshade Press is the imprint under which they publish about 12 chapbooks/year, each 24-48 pgs. "usually with hand-blocked pen-and-ink covers, endsheets and recycled 24 lb. text, 65 lb. cover text. **Nightshade Press chapbooks are published on a somewhat cooperative arrangement based on poets' promotion with royalties paid to us. We only publish poets with futures, poets whose work shows promise." For chapbook consideration query with bio and list of publications. "We insist that poets appear first in our magazine. We like to feel that they are supportive enough to subscribe." Send SASE for catalog or $5 for sample chapbook.** They advise, "Beginning poets should devour as much good poetry as possible in order to delineate their own style and voice. Look for a match between substance and sound."

POTES & POETS PRESS, INC.; ABACUS (III), 181 Edgemont Ave., Elmwood CT 06110, phone (203)233-2023, press founded in 1981, magazine in 1984, editor Peter Ganick. The press publishes avant-garde poetry in magazine form under the *Abacus* imprint, one writer per 16-page issue. The P+ Pinc books are perfect-bound and range from 80-120 pages in trade editions. **In addition to avant-garde, they want experimental or language-oriented poetry, not too much concrete poetry. No "New Yorker** magazine, **Ploughshares** magazine, mainstream poetry." They have recently published poems by Ron Silliman, Jackson Mac Low, Charles Bernstein, Leslie Scalapino, Carla Harryman and Rachel Blau Du Plessis. *Abacus* is magazine-sized, photocopied, no graphics, 12-18 pgs.; it appears every 6 weeks. Circulation is 150, of which 40 are subscriptions and 10 go to libraries. Price per issue is $3, subscription $21/year. **Sample available for $3.50 postpaid. Pay is 12 copies. Simultaneous submissions are OK, as are photocopied or dot-matrix mss. Reads submissions to Abacus June through July only; reads book submissions any time. Reports within 2 months and time to publication is 1 year. Freelance submissions are accepted for book publication. Writers should "just send the manuscript."** The press publishes 4 books of poetry/year with an average page count of 100, flat-spined paperbacks.

POTPOURRI (II), P.O. Box 8278, Prairie Village KS 66208, founded 1989, poetry editor Pat Anthony, is a monthly tabloid "to publish works of writers, **including new and unpublished writers. No religious, confessional, racial, political, erotic, abusive or sexual preference materials unless fictional and necessary to plot or characterization. No concrete/visual poetry (because of format)."** They have published poetry by David Ray and Lloyd Van Brunt. As a sample the editor selected these lines from "An Artist's Lines" for "Grandma Elizabeth Layton" by Judy Ray:

> You say you don't have visions.
> Yet your drawings fill with unsprung
> coils of our lives, harmony
> and chaos, dancing and screams

It is 20-24 pgs., press run 6,000-10,000 for 550 subscribers of which 20 are libraries, 5,000 distributed free to libraries, bookstores, universities, hospitals, community centers and others. Subscription: $12. **Sample postpaid: $1. Send SASE for guidelines. Pays 1-20 copies (poet's request). Acquires first North American serial rights. Submit no more than 3 poems, no more than 1/ page, length to 75 lines (approximately 30 preferred). Submit seasonal themes 6 months in advance. Reports in 8-10 weeks at most.** The editor advises, "Keep your new poems around long enough to become friends with them before parting. Let them ripen, and, above all, learn to be your own best editor. To borrow from William Carlos Williams, strive to let your particular 'specific' idea or poem be window to universality for your reader. Let them *in* to your work and write *for* an audience in terms of professionality and clarity. Unrequited love, favorite pets and description that seems to be written for its own sake find little chance." The David Ray Poetry Award is given annually for best of volume.

‡POULTRY, A MAGAZINE OF VOICE (IV-Humor), P.O. Box 4413, Springfield MA 01101, founded 1979, editors Jack Flavin, Brendan Galvin and George Garrett, is a tabloid (2-3 times a year) of **"parody, satire, humor and wit, particularly of the modern literary scene." They do not want to see "serious" poetry.** They have recently published poetry by Rachel Loden, John Towne, John Laue, Richard Davignon, Mary R. Stanko and Arthur K. Walmsley. As a sample the editors selected these lines from "Arn" by Richard Muegge:

> *All last winter*
> *I pumped arn to*
> *strangthen m'arm.*

The 11½ × 17 tabloid, 8 pgs., unstapled, professionally printed on newsprint, uses b&w photos, graphics, drawings, press run 500, 250 subscribers of which 35 are libraries. Subscription: $5. **Sample postpaid: $2. Pays 10 copies. Acquires first rights. Simultaneous submissions OK, "rarely" uses previously published poems.** Jack Flavin calls for "a little more humor and light, please, in the deadly serious (and oftentimes deadly) business of being a poet, a writer and getting published. Beginning poet? Get it down while it's hot, let it cool and consider it with a cold eye a bit later. Learn to write by doing it, if you're lucky, under the watchful eye and with encouragement from a good critic."

POWER ANIMAL (I), Joe Skyfoot Word and Music Creations, Suite 528, 5468 Dundas St. W., Etobicoke, Ontario M9B 6E3 Canada, phone (416)582-7414, editor Phillip Boucher, is a semiannual magazine-sized newsletter, 5-10 double-sided pgs., of **"poetry, humour and the New Age. Needs all types of poetry: inspirational, New Age, horror, children's, fantasy and anything else you could think of. Nonsense verse or unintelligible poetry gets sent back. I love poems that make sense on the first reading. Poems must be short, unpublished, 15 lines or less."** They have recently published works by Denise DeVries, Joseph Graf, Eileen Malone, Jess Camilo, James Halon, Richard Stevenson, Peter Cannon, Gerry Stewart, Jeffrey Neuman and Ina Jackson. As a sample, the editor selected this short poem, "Class and Contradiction," by Ronald Epstein:

> *The rich observe*
> *the cleanliness of circumstance.*
> *The poor observe*
> *the dirt of deprivation.*

It is photocopied from typescript, side stapled. Subscription: $5/year. **Sample postpaid: $2. Reads submissions February through May and August through November. Pays 1 copy. Acquires first North American one-time rights. Send 1-3 poems. Reports in 1-3 months.**

‡PRAIRIE FIRE (III), Room 423, 100 Arthur St., Winnipeg, Manitoba R3B 1H3 Canada, phone (204)943-9066, founded 1978, poetry editor Di Brandt, is a quarterly magazine of new writing including fiction, poetry and reviews. They want **"poetry that articulates a connection between language and ethics, an aesthetic of writing 'from the body', and open to the nuances of orality, ethnic and racial differences and feminism. No haiku, sonnets or other rhyming forms, nor political or religious treatises in verse form."** They have recently published poetry by Patrick Friesen, Anne Szumigalski and Lyn Lifshin. As a sample the editor selected these lines from "Birds and Mustard Field" by Lorna Crozier:

> *. . . one crow crosses my path*
> *to remind me of sorrow.*
> *Then two, and it's joy—*
> *if only it could change*
> *quick as that. . . .*

Prairie Fire is 96+ pgs., 6×9, offset, perfect-bound, glossy card cover, illustrations and ads. They receive 300-400 submissions (average 6 poems each), accept approximately 3%. Press run is 1,400 for 900+ subscribers of which 100+ are libraries, 150+ shelf sales. Single copy: $7.95; subscription: $24 Canadian, $28 US. **Sample postpaid: $8 Canadian. No previously published poems or simultaneous submissions. Cover letter with brief bio required. Submissions should be typed, double-spaced, one poem to a page, name and address on each page, no more than 6 poems at a time. Reads submissions September 1 through June 30 only.** Time between accep-

The double dagger before a listing indicates that the listing is new in this edition. New markets are often the most receptive to submissions.

tance and publication is 18 months. **Seldom comments on rejections. Send SASE for guidelines. Reports in 3-4 months. Pays $20 for first page, $10 for each additional page, plus 1 copy. Buys first Canadian serial rights only.** Reviews books of poetry in 500-2,000 words, single or multi-book format. The editor says, "Be patient!"

THE PRAIRIE JOURNAL (II); PRAIRIE JOURNAL PRESS (IV-Regional, themes), P.O. Box 997, Station G, Calgary, Alberta T3A 3G2 Canada, founded 1983, editor A. Burke, who wants to see **poetry of "any length, free verse, contemporary themes (feminist, nature, urban, non-political), aesthetic value, a poet's poetry."** Does not want to see "most rhymed verse, sentimentality, egotistical ravings. No cowboys or sage brush." They have published poetry by Mick Burrs, Lorna Crozier, Mary Melfi, Art Cuelho and John Hicks. *Prairie Journal* is 7½ × 8½, 40-60 pgs., offset with card cover, b&w drawings and ads, appearing twice a year. They accept about 10% of the 200 or so poems they receive a year. Press run 500 per issue, 150 subscriptions of which 60% are libraries. Subscription: $6 for individuals, $12 for libraries. **Sample postpaid: $3. Guidelines available for postage (but "no U.S. stamps, please"—get IRCs from the Post Office). Pays 1 copy. Acquires first North American serial rights. Reports in 2 weeks. No simultaneous submissions or previously published poems. For chapbook publication Canadian poets only** (preferably from the region) **should query with 5 samples, bio, publications. Responds to queries in 2 months, to mss in 6 months. Payment in modest honoraria.** "We also publish anthologies on themes when material is available. **Prairie Journal Poetry 2**, an anthology of new poetry, was published in 1992. We receive very little poetry we can use." Reviews books of poetry "but must be assigned by editor. Query first." A. Burke advises, "Read recent poets! Experiment with line length, images, metaphors. Innovate."

THE PRAIRIE PUBLISHING COMPANY (III, IV-Regional), Box 2997, Winnipeg, Manitoba R3C 4B5 Canada, phone (204)885-6496, founded 1963, publisher Ralph E. Watkins, is a "small press catering to regional market, local history, fantasy, poetry and nonfiction," with flat-spined paperbacks. They want **"basically well-crafted poems of reasonable length"** and do not want to see **"the work of rank amateurs and tentative and time-consuming effort."** They have published collections of poetry by Brian Richardson and Brian MacKinnon. Their books are handsomely produced, 6 × 9, using b&w photos and art along with the poems, glossy card covers. They publish about 1 a year, 68 pgs. **Query with samples. Do not submit mss during summer. Responds to queries in 6 weeks. Simultaneous submissions OK. Samples available at a 20% discount—send SASE or SAE and IRC for catalog.** Nancy Watkins notes, "Robert E. Pletta's point that most poets need to do more reading is well taken. We would endorse this suggestion."

PRAIRIE SCHOONER; STROUSSE PRIZE; SLOTE PRIZE; FAULKNER AWARD; READERS' CHOICE AWARDS (II), 201 Andrews, University of Nebraska, Lincoln NE 68588-0334, phone (402)472-3191, founded 1927, editor Hilda Raz; "one of the oldest literary quarterlies in continuous publication; publishes poetry, fiction, personal essays, interviews and reviews." They want **"poems that fulfill the expectations they set up." No specifications as to form, length, style, subject matter or purpose. No simultaneous submissions.** They have recently published poetry by Steve Crow, Linda Pastan, Dabney Stuart, Lynne Sharon Schwartz, Mark Jarman, Judith Ortiz Cofer, Michael Pettit and Jeanne Murray Walker. As a sample the editor selected these lines from "Faith and Certainty: Arctic Circles" by Pattiann Rogers:

> It takes one part of one and another
> of the other to understand how she shifts
> and turns slowly over now, rattling, mewing,
> chomping her black lips in her sleep,
> adjusting her bulk within the snow-covered
> den dug to the permafrost.
>
> It requires one part of each to assert
> that she is oblivious, yet aware,
> of the two naked, womb-sleek cubs, eyes
> sealed shut, smothering, jerking,
> butting again, believing wholeheartedly
> in the paps they find by feel in the rich
> fat of her presence.

The magazine is 6 × 9, flat-spined, 144 pgs., circulation 2,800, and uses 70-80 pgs. of poetry in each issue. They receive about 4,000 mss (of all types)/year from which they choose 300 pgs. of poetry. Subscription: $17/year; $5/copy. **Sample postpaid: $3.50. "Clear copy appreciated." Reports in 2-3 months; "sooner if possible." Pays copies. Acquires all rights. Returns rights upon request without fee.** Reviews books of poetry. Hilda Raz is a hard-working, tough, insightful editor who demands the best, and that makes *PS* influential in the lit world. The hundreds of dollars in prizes awarded each year are yet another incentive to try this market. Send only your best work and include 5 to 7 poems/submission. The $500 Strousse Prize is awarded to the best poetry published in the magazine each year, the Slote Prize for beginning writers ($500) and six other *PS* prizes will also be awarded, and the Faulkner Award for Excellence in Writing is also offered ($1,000). Also, each year 5-10 Readers' Choice Awards ($250 each) are given for poetry, fiction and nonfiction. Editors serve as judges. Hilda Raz comments, *"Prairie Schooner* receives· a large number of poetry submissions; we're not unusual. Our staff time doesn't allow comments on mss, but the magazine's reputation is evidence of our careful reading. We've been dedicated to the publication of good poems for a very long time and have published work early in the career of many successful poets."

PRAKALPANA LITERATURE; KOBISENA (I, IV-Form), P-40 Nandana Park, Calcutta 700034, West Bengal, India, *Kobisena* founded 1972, *Prakalpana Literature* press founded 1974, magazine 1977, editor Vattacharja Chandan, who says, "We are small magazines which publish only *Prakalpana* (a mixed form of prose and poetry), Sarbangin (whole) poetry, essays on Prakalpana movement and Sarbangin poetry movement, letters, literary news and very few books on Prakalpana and Sarbangin literature. **Purpose and form: for advancement of poetry in the super-space age, the poetry must be really experimental and avant-garde using mathematical signs and symbols and visualizing the pictures inherent in the alphabet (within typography) with sonorous effect. That is Sarbangin poetry. Length: within 30 lines (up to 4 poems). Subject matter: society, nature, cosmos, humanity, love, peace, etc. Style: own. We do not want to see traditional, conventional, academic, religious and poetry of prevailing norms and forms."** They have recently published poetry by Dilip Gupta, Richard Kostelanetz, Susan Smith Nash and J.J. King. As a sample the editor chose these lines by Paul Weinman:

> *Tho use banned in USA*
> *Chlordane is made in*
> *USA—So? Thinks white*
> *Boy but Greenpeace says*
> *It comes back in meat*

Prakalpana Literature, an annual, is 70 pgs., digest-sized, saddle-stapled, printed on thin stock with matte card cover. *Kobisena*, which appears at least twice a year, is 16 pgs., digest-sized, a newsletter format with no cover. Both are hand composed and printed by letterpress. Both use both English and Bengali. They use about 10% of some 400 poems received/year. The press run is 1,000 for each, and each has about 450 subscriptions of which 50 are libraries. **Samples: 6 rupees for *Prakalpana*, 4 rupees for *Kobisena*. Overseas: 4 IRCs and 2 IRCs respectively or exchange of avant-garde magazines. Send SAE with IRC for guidelines. Pays 1 copy. Simultaneous submissions OK. Previously published poetry OK. Reports in 6 months, publication within a year. After being published in the magazines, poets may be included in future anthologies with translations into Bengali/English if and when necessary. "Joining with us is welcome but not a pre-condition." Editor comments on rejection "if wanted."** Reviews books of poetry, "but preferably experimental books." He says, "We believe that only through poetry, the deepest feelings of humanity as well as nature and the cosmos can be best expressed and conveyed to the peoples of the ages to come. And only poetry can fill up the gap in the peaceless hearts of dispirited peoples, resulted from the retreat of god and religion with the advancement of hi-tech. So, in an attempt, since the inception of Prakalpana Movement in 1969, to reach that goal in the avant-garde and experimental way we stand for Sarbangin poetry. And to poets and all concerned with poetry we wave the white handkerchief saying (in the words of Vattacharja Chandan) 'We want them who want us.' "

THE PRESBYTERIAN RECORD (IV-Inspirational, religious), 50 Wynford Dr., Don Mills, Ontario M3C 1J7 Canada, phone (416)441-1111, founded 1876, is "the national magazine that serves the membership of The Presbyterian Church in Canada (and many who are not Canadian Presbyterians). We seek to: stimulate, inform, inspire, to provide an 'apologetic' and a critique of our church and the world (not necessarily in that order!)." They want **poetry which is "inspirational, Christian, thoughtful, even satiric but *not* maudlin. No 'sympathy card' type verse a la Edgar Guest or Francis Gay. It would take a *very* exceptional poem of epic length for us to use it. Shorter poems 10-30 lines preferred. Blank verse OK (if it's not just rearranged prose). 'Found' poems. Subject matter should have some Christian import (however subtle)."** They have published poetry by Jean Larsen, Jeanne Davis, Joan Stortz, Marlow C. Dickson, Len Selle and J.R. Dickey. The magazine comes out 11 times a year, circulation 67,000. **Subscription: $11. Submit seasonal work 6 weeks before month of publication. Double-spaced, photocopy OK. "Dot-matrix semi-OK." Simultaneous submissions OK. Pays $20-50/ poem. Buys one-time rights.**

THE PRESS OF MACDONALD & REINECKE (II); PADRE PRODUCTIONS (I), P.O. Box 840, Arroyo Grande CA 93421-0840, phone (805)473-1947, founded 1974, poetry editor Lachlan P. MacDonald. Padre Productions prints books on a fee basis, as a book packager. MacDonald & Reinecke **requires the poet to "purchase 200 copies of an edition (at liberal discounts)"** but they do not consider themselves subsidy publishers. They publish under the M&R imprint only work they consider of merit and in which they, like the poet, must invest. "The press is a division of Padre Productions bringing together under one imprint drama, fiction, literary nonfiction and poetry. We publish poetry in broadsides, flat-spined paperbacks, chapbooks and hardcover. We are looking for **poetry of literary merit and also poetry suitable for travel and nature photo books. We are averse to tightly rhymed conventional poetry unless designed to appeal to the general humor market.**" They have published Terre Ouenhand's Voices from the Well and Steven Schmidt's Avigation and Other Poems. Query with 5-6 samples, publication credits, bio. The editor also wants to know "do they give readings or have marketing opportunities? Some authors distribute flyers to build up pre-publication orders sufficient to justify the print order." Replies to queries in 2-4 weeks, to submissions (if invited) in 2-6 months. Simultaneous submissions, photocopy, dot-matrix OK. Ms should be double-spaced. Pays minimum of 4% royalties, 6 copies. The editor "frequently makes brief comments" on rejections. Send 6×9 SASE for catalog. The editor advises, "Poets who have not published 10 or 20 poems in literary magazines are unlikely to have developed the craft we require. We also prefer books with a unifying theme rather than a sampling reflecting the author's virtuosity."

THE PRESS OF THE THIRD MIND (IV-Form), 65 E. Scott St. #6P, Chicago IL 60610, phone (312)337-3122, press founded 1985, poetry editor Rasta Purina, is a small press publisher of artist books, poetry and fiction in glass bottles, tape measures, paperbacks, broadsides, T-shirts and Tarot cards. **"We are especially interested in the cut-up/fold-in technique, concrete poetry, translations, collaborative (Exquisite Corpse) poetry, found poems, dada, surrealism, etc."** They have published poetry by "Pessoa, Spiro, Cesariny, Mansour and Lamantia." As a sample the editor selected these lines from the poem "The History of Commercial Photography in Albuquerque," by Bradley Lastname:

> She will be dismembered by a fighting rooster before an arena of jaded Balinese,
> Or will peck out the eye of a legless Spanish eunuch,
> So he can demonstrate the history of commercial photography in South America,
> A history of tricks awaiting their next socket job,
> A history of señoritas who ask in broken English, 'want to be winked off?'

Asked how much poetry they typically received per year and how much they accept, he said, "We get about 6 metric tons and accept it all for fireplace logs." They have a press run of 200 with 100 subscriptions of which 38 are libraries. Sample postpaid: **$5.** Pay? **"Surely you jest!"** But contributors can have all the copies they can photocopy. *"No dot matrix!!!"* Simultaneous submissions OK. They have sometimes used previously published poetry and have simultaneously published with *Exquisite Corpse*. Press of the Third Mind publishes 2 flat-spined paperbacks, 56 pgs., per year. They recently published **Concave Buddha and Other Public Disservice Announcements (paperback). For book publication submit 20 sample poems, bio and credits.** Responds to queries in 1 week, mss in 3 weeks. "Just ask for free samples and include a substantial 'love offering.'" Editor provides criticism on rejections. Reviews books of poetry. His advice: "Absolute zero corrupts absolutely; Absolut Vodka boils at Fahrenheit 491."

PRIMAL VOICES; LAMBERT/MCINTOSH ENTERPRISES (I, IV-Themes), P.O. Box 3179, Poughkeepsie NY 12603, founded 1989, editors Carol Lambert and Susan McIntosh. Lambert/McIntosh publishes periodicals. *PV* is a quarterly using poetry other than pornographic "for the voiceless in our society." *Primal Voices* describes its focus as: "children, war veterans, senior citizens, the homeless, the environment, the handicapped, retarded persons, the incarcerated, the endangered animal—anyone with a need to be heard!" It is professionally printed, magazine-sized, saddle-wired on heavy stock with glossy b&w card covers. Press run 200. Subscription: $15. Sample postpaid: $4.75. Send SASE for guidelines. Pays 1 copy. Acquires first rights. Reports in 4-6 weeks. Previously published poems and simultaneous submissions OK. Submission deadlines: March 1 and June 1.

‡PRIMAVERA (II, IV-Women), P.O. Box #37-7547, Chicago IL 60637, phone (312)324-5920, founded 1975, coeditor Ruth Young, is "an irregularly published but approximately annual magazine of poetry and fiction reflecting the experiences of women. We look for strong, original voice and imagery, generally prefer free verse, fairly short length, related, even tangentially, to women's experience." They have recently published poetry by Donna Jackson, Neile Graham, Pamela Miller, Claire Nicolas White and Lynne H. deCourcy. As a sample the editors selected these lines by Ann Gearen:

> playing tea party underwater
> while we held our breath,
> gestures slowed, deliberate,
> our conversation bubbling to the surface

in vowels only, oohs and ahs.

The elegantly printed publication, flat-spined, generously illustrated with photos and graphics, uses 30-35 pgs. of poetry in each issue, circulation 1,000. They receive over 1,000 submissions of poetry/year, use 32. Price per issue: $7. **Sample postpaid: $5. Submit no more than 6 poems anytime, legible photocopy OK, no dot-matrix or queries. No simultaneous submissions. Reports in 1-2 months. Pays 2 copies. Acquires first-time rights. Send SASE for guidelines. Editors comment on rejections "when requested or inspired."**

PRINCETON UNIVERSITY PRESS; LOCKERT LIBRARY OF POETRY IN TRANSLATION (IV-Translations, bilingual); PRINCETON SERIES OF CONTEMPORARY POETS (V), 41 William St., Princeton NJ 08540, phone (609)452-4900, literature editor Robert E. Brown. The Princeton Series of Contemporary Poets is by invitation only. "In the Lockert Library series, we publish simultaneous cloth and paperback (flat-spine) editions for each poet. Clothbound editions are on acid-free paper, and binding materials are chosen for strength and durability. Each book is given individual design treatment rather than stamped into a series mold. We have published a wide range of poets from other cultures, including well-known writers such as Hölderlin and Cavafy, and those who have not yet had their due in English translation, such as Ingeborg Bachmann and Faiz Ahmed Faiz. Manuscripts are judged with several criteria in mind: the ability of the translation to stand on its own as poetry in English; fidelity to the tone and spirit of the original, rather than literal accuracy; and the importance of the translated poet to the literature of his or her time and country." The editor says, "All our books in this series are heavily subsidized to break even. We have internal funds to cover deficits of publishing costs. We do not, however, publish books chosen and subsidized by other agencies, such as AWP. **Our series is an open competition, for which the 'award' is publication. We comment on semifinalists only." Send SASE for guidelines to submit. Send mss only during respective reading periods stated in guidelines. Reports in 2-3 months. Simultaneous submissions OK if you tell them; photocopy, dot-matrix OK. Pays royalties (5% or more) on paperback and 12 author's copies.**

PRINTED MATTER (II), Hikari Biru 303, 3-7-10 Takadanobaba, Shinjuku-ku, Tokyo 169 Japan, phone (03)3362-7589, founded 1977, editor Stephen Forster, is a quarterly literary journal featuring poetry, fiction, reviews, essays, interviews and artwork. It has published poetry by Jon Silkin, Cid Corman, Shuntaro Tanikawa, Xavier Villaurrutia and La Loca. As a sample, the editor selected these lines by Paul Rossiter:

> *but the swallows*
> *the green taste of Europe still upon them*
> *passing through*
> *in swift lilting flight*
> *above hot sand and tidemark*

Printed Matter is 58 pgs. in professionally printed A5 format. Press run is 600. The magazine appears four times/year plus one special issue. Subscription: 3,000 yen (US $25), **sample: 600** yen (US $5) — both prices include postage. Unless otherwise arranged, **submissions to** *Printed Matter* **are accepted on condition that they have not previously been published and that the material is not under consideration elsewhere. Submissions should be accompanied by the usual materials. Reports in 2-3 months. Acquires all rights. "I return rights to the author on request; I only ask for** *Printed Matter* **citation in other published works." They do not use rejection slips: editor comments on rejections.** Reviews books of poetry in 7,000-7,500 words, single or multi-book format. "Printed Matter Press publishes chapbooks. Printed Matter Press is also associated with the Tokyo-based SARU Press, which publishes collections of poetry."

‡PRISM INTERNATIONAL (II), Dept. of Creative Writing, University of British Columbia, Vancouver, British Columbia V6T 1Z1 Canada, phone (604)822-2514, founded 1959, executive editors Murray Logan and Patricia Gabin. "*Prism* is an international quarterly that publishes poetry, drama, short fiction, imaginative nonfiction and translation into English in all genres. We have no thematic or stylistic allegiances: excellence is our main criterion for acceptance of mss. **We want poetry that shows an awareness of the tradition while reiterating its themes in a fresh and distinctive way. We read everything."** They have published poetry by Daphne Marlatt, Al Purdy, Diana Hartog, Roo Borson and Bill Bissett. As a sample the editor selected these lines by Michael Ondaatje:

> *This is for people who disappear*
> *for those who descend into the code*
> *and make their room a fridge for Superman*
> *—who exhaust costume and bones that could perform flight*
> *who shave their moral so raw*
> *they can tear themselves through the eye of a needle*

Prism is elegantly printed in a flat-spined, 6×9 format, 80 pgs., original color artwork on the glossy card cover, circulation to 1,000 subscribers of which 200 are libraries. They receive 1,000 submissions/year, use 125, have 1-2 special issues/year, and a 1- to 3-month backlog. Subscription: $16. **Sample postpaid: $5. Submit a maximum of 6 poems at a time, any print so long as it's typed. No query. Reports in 6-12 weeks ("or we write to poets to tell them we're holding onto their work for a while"). Pays $20/printed page plus subscription. Send Canadian SASE or SAE with IRCs for guidelines. Editors often comment on rejections.** *Prism International* is known in literary circles as one of the top journals in Canada. It contains good poems, mostly free verse with a leaning toward lyric. The editors say, "While we don't automatically discount any kind of poetry, we prefer to publish work that challenges the writer as much as it does the reader."

PRISONERS OF THE NIGHT; MKASHEF ENTERPRISES (IV-Psychic/occult, science fiction/fantasy/ horror, erotica), P.O. Box 368, Poway CA 92074-0368, poetry editor Alayne Gelfand. *Prisoners of the Night*, founded 1987, **focusing on vampire erotica, uses poetry that is "erotic, unique, non-horror, non-pornographic, original visions of the vampire."** Poets who have appeared recently in *POTN* include Wendy Rathbone, John Grey and Ann K. Schwader. As a sample the editor selected the poem "My Love Comes Dressed Only In Eternity" by Charlee Jacob:

> It hurts to sleep with his past
> but the pain is as sweet
> as it is dark,
> aching gently with the lash from a treasured whip,
> the pressure of the silken bond,
> and the piercing from his deep, sharp kiss.

The intent of *POTN* is "to show the erotic, the romantic, rather than the horrific aspects of the vampire." It is 100-120 pgs., magazine-sized, perfect-bound, with color cover, produced by high-speed photocopying. All poems are illustrated." It appears annually, usually in May. Of over 800 poems received/year they use between 10 and 30. It has an initial print run of 3,000, but each issue is kept in print. **Sample (the per-issue price): $15 postpaid (#5 is $12). Send SASE for guidelines. Pays $2/poem plus 1 copy. Buys first serial rights. No more than 6 poems per submission. No simultaneous submissions or previously published poems. Reading schedule: September 15 through March 31 annually. Reports "within 3 months." Editor sometimes comments on rejections.** *POTN* wants unusual visions of the vampire as well as unusual poetic styles. "We prefer non-rhyme and find humor too subjective to appeal to our readers. The startling, unique, ethereal usage of words will catch our eye much more than the expected, mundane. Be original, surprise us!"

PROOF ROCK PRESS; PROOF ROCK (I, II, IV-Humor), Box 607, Halifax VA 24558, founded 1982, poetry editors Serena Fusek and Don R. Conner. "We try to wake up a passive readership. We challenge our writers to search for something new under the sun and improve on the old." The poetry they want is: **"adventure, contemporary, humor/satire, fantasy, experimental. Avoid overt sentimentality. Poems up to 32 lines. All subjects considered if well done."** The digest-sized magazine appears 2-3 times/year, is offset from typescript copy, colored matte card cover, with 30-40 pgs. in each issue, circulation 300, 100 subscriptions of which 8-10 are libraries. They receive 800-1,000 submissions/year, use 120-150, have a 3- to 6-month backlog. Subscription: $4. **Sample postpaid: $2.50. Submit no more than 6 pieces, year round. No query needed, though some issues are on announced themes. Photocopy, dot-matrix, simultaneous submissions OK. Reports "usually within 1 month." Pays 1 copy. Send SASE for guidelines.** Proof Rock Press publishes an occasional anthology and collections by individuals. **Query with 8-10 samples, bio and publishing credits. Reply to queries in 1 month, to submissions (if invited) in 1-3 months. Simultaneous submissions, photocopies, dot-matrix OK. Pays copies. Send $2.50 for a sample chapbook. Editor sometimes comments on rejections.** His advice is, "Be introspective. Accept the challenge of looking within and write from experience."

PROPHETIC VOICES; HERITAGE TRAILS PRESS (II), 94 Santa Maria Dr., Novato CA 94947, founded 1982, poetry editors Ruth Wildes Schuler, Goldie L. Morales and Jeanne Leigh Schuler. "Our goal is to share thoughts on an international level. We see the poet's role as that of prophet, who points the way to a higher realm of existence." They publish *Prophetic Voices* twice a year and chapbooks. They want **"poetry of social commentary that deals with the important issues of our time. Poetry with beauty that has an international appeal. Do not want religious poetry or that with a limited scope. Open to any kind of excellent poetry, but publish mostly free verse. Limited number of long poems accepted due to lack of space."** They have published Jack Brooks, Hazel F. Goddard, A. Manoussos, B.Z. Niditch, H.F. Noyes, Gloria H. Procsal and Bo Yang. *Prophetic Voices* is digest-sized, 144 pgs., perfect-bound, offset from typescript with matte card cover, colored stock with graphics. They have 100 pgs. of poetry in each issue, circulation to 400 subscribers of which 10 are libraries. They receive 4,000 submissions/year, use 800, have a 2-year backlog. Subscription: $12; $14 to libraries; per copy: $6. **Sample postpaid: $5. Photocopy OK. Submit 4 poems or less. Reports in 1-8 weeks. Pays 1 copy. Heritage Trails now considers unsolicited mss.** The editors advise, "Be aware of what is going on in the world around you. Even the personal poem should have universal appeal if it is to survive the test of time."

THE PROSE POEM (II, IV-Form), 1004 Sycamore, San Marcos TX 78666, phone (512)353-4998, founded 1990, editor Steve Wilson, is an annual using **prose poems only. "I hope and pray the author knows what prose poetry is before submitting to me. For me 'prose poems' run from margin to margin, with no line breaks, and use intense, compact language."** The have recently published poetry by Linda Foster, William Virgil Davis, Barry Silesky, Ray Gonzalez, Tom Whalen and Harriet Zinnes. The editor describes *TPP* as 40 pgs., professionally printed with card stock cover, saddle-stapled. Most selections are one paragraph or a few small ones, each about (or under) 200 words, jam-packed to print as many as possible . . . even on the back cover. Press run 200. **Sample postpaid: $3. Pays 1 copy. Acquires first North American serial rights. Reads submissions January 1 through March 31 only. Reports by 1 month after deadline.** *"TPP* is a journal focusing on one particular genre and publishing only the best work done in that genre. This does not mean an author cannot experiment. I encourage it. It also does not mean I don't want to see work from new writers. Please send, but only your best. I publish this magazine with my own money, so sales are very important. I won't take grants. I like my freedom. If you think prose poetry matters and like the idea of a journal dedicated to it, please help me keep it going by sending great work and subscribing."

PROSETRY: NEWSLETTER FOR, BY AND ABOUT WRITERS (IV-Subscription, themes), The Write Place, P.O. Box 117727, Burlingame CA 94011, phone (415)347-7613, editor P.D. Steele, founded 1985. *Prosetry* is a monthly newsletter featuring "new and newly published poets and prose writers with a 'guest writer' column each month. Includes original poetry, new markets, contests, seminars, workshops and **general poetry potpourri gleaned from our subscribers." 50% freelance. Guidelines available for SASE. Sample for $2. Invites new writers. Send up to 3 poems, no more than 20 lines, English only. No profanity. Reports in less than 1 month. Pays one-year subscription. Acquires one-time rights; release required.** Reviews books of poetry in 150 words. "For 'guest writer' column we would prefer information relevant to the beginning or newly published writer/poet." Also publishes "How-to" *CLIPS©* for writers, $2.50 each. Free list for SASE.

PROTEA POETRY JOURNAL (II), P.O. Box 876, Sutter Creek CA 95685, phone (209)267-0332, founded 1987, poetry editor Carol Lynn Gunther. **They prefer "imagism that is hard-edged and veering towards objectivist work. Surrealism can be nice, too, especially if it opens a dialogue with the reader. Didactic and/or sentimental poems are not welcome."** The editor chose these lines from John Owens' poem "Troubled Moon" as a sample:

> The grass is agreeable.
> Birds tread the meadow.
> The mirror, breathless, blooms.

Protea is "produced on an offset press, Ventura Desktop Publishing. Top-notch within small budget." The journal is biannual. **Send SASE for guidelines; $5 for sample copy. Pays 2 copies. No previously published poems or simultaneous submissions. Reports in 2-3 weeks. Comments on rejections.**

PROVINCETOWN ARTS; PROVINCETOWN ARTS PRESS (II), 650 Commercial St., Provincetown MA 02657, phone (508)487-3167, founded 1985, editor Christopher Busa, is an elegant, flat-spined annual, 170+ pgs., with full-color glossy cover, using quality poetry. *"Provincetown Arts* focuses broadly on the artists and writers who inhabit or visit the tip of Cape Cod and seeks to stimulate creative activity and enhance public awareness of the cultural life of the nation's oldest continuous art colony. Drawing upon a century-long tradition rich in visual art, literature and theater, *Provincetown Arts* publishes material with a view towards demonstrating that the artists' colony, functioning outside the urban centers, is a utopian dream with an ongoing vitality." They have recently published poetry by Bruce Smith, Franz Wright, Sandra McPherson and Cyrus Cassells. As a sample the editor selected these lines from "Sky of Clouds" by Susan Mitchell:

> And after heavy rains, when the egrets
> settle on the gardens, cramming
> their beaks with the shrill
> cries of the frogs, I think
> I could do that too, I could be gorgeous and cruel.

Press run 10,000 for 500 subscribers of which 20 are libraries, 6,000 shelf sales. **Sample postpaid: $7.50. Reads submissions August through February. Reports in 2-3 months. Pays $25-100/poem. Buys first rights.** Reviews books of poetry in 500-3,000 words, single or multi-book format. The Provincetown Arts Press and a poetry award are being developed.

PSYCH IT (I, IV-Themes, subscribers), 6507 Bimini Ct., Apollo Beach FL 33572, founded 1986, editor Charlotte L. Babicky, is a quarterly newsletter using **"any style, any psychologically-themed poetry. Any length. The purpose is to leave the reader with a message; one which will be remembered through images presented by the writer of the poetry. Well-thought-out, well-written poems."** Poets recently published include Joe E. Kirk, Marian F. Park, Mary Mullis Hinricks and Pam T. Owens. As a sample the editor selected these lines from "The Heiress" by Kenneth G. Geisert:

> *Once the jewels of her father's eye,*
> *she has been reduced*
> *to a millstone,*
> *in a sea of insanity.*

It is 10 pgs., side-stapled, magazine-sized, photocopied from typescript, with heavy natural parchment paper. Press run under 100. Subscription: $8. **Sample postpaid: $2.50. Pays $1/poem. Buys first North American serial rights. Guarantees to publish at least one of 3-5 poems submitted by subscribers. Non-subscribers may enter contests and during open submission season. Send SASE for guidelines. Occasional contests, entry fee $1** for each poem.

PSYCHOPOETICA (II, IV-Themes), Dept. of Psychology, University of Hull, Hull HU6 7RX England, founded 1979, editor Dr. Geoff Lowe uses **"psychologically-based poetry."** That is not a very narrow category, though many of the poems in *Psychopoetica* are explicitly about psychology or psychological treatment. But most good poetry is in some sense "psychologically based," as the editor seems to recognize in these comments (from his guidelines): **"I prefer short, experimental, rhymed and un-rhymed, light verse, haiku, etc., (and visual poems). I will read and consider any style, any length, providing it's within the arena of 'psychologically-based' poetry. I'm not too keen on self-indulgent therapeutic poetry (unless it's good and original), nor 'Patience Strong' type stuff. I like poetry that has some (or all!) of the following: humor, vivid imagery, powerful feelings, guts and substance, originality, creative style, punch or twist, word-play, good craftsmanship, etc."** Recently published poets include Sheila E. Murphy, Wes Magee, R. Nikolas Macioci and Ruth Wildes Schuler. The magazine appears 2-3 times/year, circulating to "several hundred and increasing." It is A5, saddle-stitched, photocopied from typescript. **Sample: £1 ($2). Send SASE for guidelines. Pays 1 copy. Reports within 1 month. Considers simultaneous submissions. Editor "always" provides comments on rejections.** Occasionally reviews books of poetry in 25 words, single format. He says, "Careful presentation of work is most important. But I continue to be impressed by the rich variety of submissions, especially work that shifts boundaries."

PTOLEMY/BROWNS MILLS REVIEW, Box 908, Browns Mills NJ 08015. Declined listing.

THE PUCKERBRUSH PRESS; THE PUCKERBRUSH REVIEW (IV-Regional), 76 Main St., Orono ME 04473, phone (207)581-3832, press founded 1971, *Review* founded 1978, poetry editor Constance Hunting, is a "small press publisher of a literary, twice-a-year magazine focused on Maine and of flat-spined paperbacks of literary quality." The editor **does not want to see "confessional, dull, feminist, incompetent, derivative" poetry.** They have published poetry by Amy Clampitt, and the editor selected these sample lines from "Not a Navigable River" by Muska Nagel:

> *flow seaward, seaward*
> *my river, filled to the brink—*
> *(but no king's horses, no more*
> *will ever come to drink).*

For book publication, **query with 10 samples. Prefers no simultaneous submissions. Pays 10% royalties plus 10 copies. Editor comments on rejections.** She offers criticism for a fee: $100 is usual.

PUDDING HOUSE PUBLICATIONS; PUDDING MAGAZINE: THE INTERNATIONAL JOURNAL OF APPLIED POETRY; PUDDING WRITING COMPETITIONS; PUDDING HOUSE BED & BREAKFAST FOR WRITERS; OHIO POETRY THERAPY CENTER & LIBRARY (II, IV-Political, social issues), 60 N. Main St., Johnstown OH 43031, phone (614)967-6060 (after 7 p.m.), founded 1979, poetry editor Jennifer Welch Bosveld, attempts to provide "a sociological looking glass through poems that provide 'felt experience' and share intense human situations. To collect good poems that speak for the difficulties and the solutions. To provide a forum for poems and articles by people who take poetry arts into the schools and the human services." They publish *Pudding* every several months, also chapbooks, anthologies, broadsides. They **"want experimental and contemporary poetry—what hasn't been said before. Speak the unspeakable. Don't want preachments or sentimentality. Don't want obvious traditional forms without fresh approach. Long poems are happily considered too, as long as they aren't windy."** They have recently published poetry by James Belcher, Lowell Jaeger, Edward Boccia and Alan Catlin. The editor selected these sample lines from "The Stroke" by Douglas M. Swisher:

> *His sense takes hold in its accustomed niche*

Like a gimballed compass righted from awry.

Pudding is a literary journal with an emphasis on poetry arts in human service. They use about 80 pgs. of poetry in each issue—digest-sized, 80 pgs., offset composed on IBM 1st Publisher, circulation 1,500, 1,400 subscriptions of which 50 are libraries. Subscription (3 issues): $15.75. Sample postpaid: $5. Submit 5-10 poems. No simultaneous submissions. Photocopies and previously published submissions OK but include credits. Send SASE for guidelines. Reports on same day (unless traveling). Pays 1 copy—to featured poet $10 and 4 copies. Buys negotiable rights, usually first North American or all rights. Returns rights with *Pudding* permitted to reprint simultaneously." For chapbook publication, no query. $5 reading fee. Send complete ms with cover letter with publication credits and bio. Editor often comments, will critique on request for $3/page of poetry or $35 an hour in person. Reviews books of poetry. Jennifer Welch Bosveld shares, "Editors have pet peeves. Mine include: Postcards instead of SASEs (I won't respond); individually-folded rather than group-folded poems; cover letters that state the obvious." The Pudding Writing Competitions are for single poems (deadline September 30, fee $1/poem) and for chapbook publication (Deadline June 30, $9 entry fee). Pudding House Bed & Breakfast for Writers offers "luxurious rooms with desk, electric typewriter and all the free paper you can use." Free breakfast, large comfortable home ½ block from post office. Location of the Ohio Poetry Therapy Center and Library. $55 single/night, discounts available. Reservations recommended 3 months in advance. Send SASE for details.

PUEBLO POETRY PROJECT (IV-Regional), 1501 E. 7th St., Pueblo CO 81001, phone (719)584-3401, director Tony Moffeit, founded 1979, **publishes poets from the Pueblo area only. If you qualify, inquire.**

PUERTO DEL SOL (II, IV-Translations, regional), New Mexico State University, Box 3E, Las Cruces NM 88003, phone (505)646-3931, founded 1972 (in present format), poetry editors Joseph Somoza and Kathleene West (on alternate years). "We publish a literary magazine twice per year. Interested in poems, fiction, essays, photos, translations from the Spanish. Also (generally solicited) reviews and dialogues between writers. We want **top quality poetry, any style, from anywhere. We are sympathetic to Southwestern work, but not stereotype (cactus and adobe). Anything that is interesting and/or moving. Poetry, of course, not verse (light or otherwise)."** They have published poetry by Bill Evans, Naton Leslie, Anselm Hollo, Philip Garrison, Cecelia Hagen, J.B. Goodenough and Marilyn Hacker. The 6×9, flat-spined, professionally printed magazine, matte card cover with art, has a circulation of 650, 300 subscriptions of which 25-30 are libraries. 40-50 pgs. are devoted to poetry in each 150-page issue, which also includes quite a lot of prose. They use about 60 of the 700 submissions (about 3,500 poems) received each year to fill up the 90 pgs. of poetry two issues encompass. "Generally no backlog." You won't find many literary journals as attractive as this one. It has an award-caliber design (from the selection of fonts to the use of rules and type-size to enhance content). Furthermore, the journal features readable, thought invoking verse in all styles including translations. It's an exceptional publication. Subscription $7.75; per copy: $5. **Sample postpaid: $3. Submit 5-6 pgs., 1 poem to a page. Simultaneous submissions not encouraged. Reports within 10 weeks. Pays copies. Editor comments "on every ms."** They advise: "Be true to yourself rather than worrying about current fashions—but *do* read as much of the best of contemporary poetry as you can find."

PURDUE UNIVERSITY PRESS; VERNA EMERY POETRY COMPETITION (II), 1131 So. Campus Courts-B, West Lafayette IN 47907-1131, phone (317)494-2038, founded 1960, managing editor Margaret Hunt. They select 1 book/year to publish through the Verna Emery Poetry Competition, reading fee $15, pays $500 plus 10 copies. **Send SASE for guidelines. Reads submissions during the winter only.** Books are 50-90 pages. **"No particular style, but poetry accessible to general audience is favored. No devotional, patriotic, overly ideological poetry."** They have published poetry by Jim Barnes, editor of *Chariton Review*, and Fleda Jackson, whose book won GLCA New Writers Award.

PURPLE PATCH; THE FIRING SQUAD (I, II), 8 Beaconview House, Charlemont Farm, West Bromwich B7I 3PL England, founded 1975, editor Geoff Stevens, a bimonthly poetry and short prose magazine with reviews, comment and illustrations. The editor says, **"All good examples of poetry considered, but prefer 40 lines max. Do not want poor scanning verse, non-contributory swear words or obscenities, hackneyed themes."** They have recently published poetry by John Brander, Brian Daldorph, B.Z. Niditch, S.A. Griffin and Andrew Darlington. As a sample the editor selected "Women on Quaysides" by Sheila Jacob:

> *Morning mist is the sea's vapour*
> *swept across leafy roads, the sun's touch*
> *soft lines and lace on my hair,*
> *every breeze that reaches me today*
> *a coastal wind, a sea change*

Purple Patch is magazine-sized, 14-20 pgs., offset on plain paper, cover on the same stock with b&w drawing, side-stapled. Circulation "varies." Price is 3 issues for £2.50; US price is $5/issue (submit dollars). **Overseas contributors have to buy a copy to see their work in print. Acquires first British serial rights. Reporting time is 1 month to Great Britain, can be longer to USA; time to publication is a maximum of 4 months.** Reviews poetry chapbooks, short stories and tapes in 30-300 words. *The Firing Squad* is a broadsheet of *short poetry of a protest or complaint nature*, published at irregular intervals. The editor says, "I have started to issue a broadsheet, *Purple Patch USA*, consisting of poems by U.K. poets and distributed in the U.S.A. only. All inquiries, submissions of work, etc., must include SASE or SAE and IRCs or $1 U.S./Canadian for return postage/reply."

PYGMY FOREST PRESS (II), P.O. Box 591, Albion CA 95410, founded 1987, editor/publisher Leonard Cirino, publishes flat-spined paperbacks. **"Forms of any kind/length to 64 pgs., subject matter open; especially ecology, prison, asylum, Third World, anarchist to far right. Prefer Stevens to Williams. I like Berryman, Roethke, Jorie Graham; dislike most 'Beats.' Open to anything I consider 'good.' Open to traditional rhyme, meter, but must be modern in subject matter."** He has published **The Sixth Day** by James Doyle; **Fresh Water** by Crawdad Nelson; **For You/on stones** by L. Cirino; **The Elk Poems** by Kate Dougherty; **Low-Tech In the Great Northwest** by Gordon Black; **Obeli** by Sheila Murphy; **Windows** by Philip Corwin. **Submit 10-15 poems with bio, publications. Simultaneous submissions, previously published material, photocopies OK (no dot-matrix). Reports on queries in 1-3 weeks, submissions in 2-4 weeks. Pays 10% of run—about 30-50 copies. Buys first rights.** He comments on "almost every" ms. They also publish (on a subsidized basis) poetry on 30- to 60-minute audiotapes: $200-250 fee for production costs, for which author gets 60 copies of the tape. Leonard Cirino says, "I am basically an anarchist. Belong to no 'school.' I fund myself. Receive no grants or private funding. Generally politically left, but no mainline Stalinist or Marxist. Plan to publish 3 books yearly."

‡THE PYRAMID (IV-Themes), The International National Newsletter for the International National Association for Widowed People, Inc., Box 3564, Springfield IL 62708, a quarterly for I.A.W.P. members and subscribers, a publication for widowed people and professional corporations, colleges, universities and people that service widowed people as well as interested community groups or organizations, circulation 34,000, uses **poetry on themes appropriate for widowed persons—nothing on married persons or couples. Buys 5 poems/year. Submit maximum of 2 poems, 100 lines maximum. Sample: $3. Pays $5-75.**

QUARRY MAGAZINE; QUARRY PRESS; POETRY CANADA (II, IV-Regional), P.O. Box 1061, Kingston, Ontario K7L 4Y5 Canada. Quarry Press founded 1952, *Poetry Canada* founded 1979, managing editor Melanie Dugan, poetry editor Barry Dempster. "Quarry Press is designed to extend the range of material, poetry and prose, generally handled by *Quarry Magazine*—that is, to represent, as accurately as may be, the range of contemporary writing. We publish chapbooks, soft-bound books of stories and poetry collections ranging from 60-150 pgs., in addition to the quarterly *Quarry Magazine*. **We are interested in seeing any and all forms of contemporary verse.** *Quarry Magazine* **maintains a practical limit on length of submissions—that we cannot consider any single piece or series by one author that would print at more than 10 pages. Quarry Press considers mss on an individual basis."** They have published poetry by Roo Borson, Kim Maltman, Roger Nash, Jane Munro, Fred Cogswell and Don Bailey. *Quarry* is digest-sized, 130+ pgs., flat-spined with an unusually attractive cover—textured matte ivory card with striking b&w drawing trimmed so the front is a half-inch short—professionally printed on eggshell stock. General editor Steven Heighton. There are 40-50 pgs. of poetry in each issue, circulation 1,000, 600 subscriptions of which 140 are libraries. They use about 70 of over a thousand submissions of freelance poetry received each year. "We are prompt. Very small backlog if any. 3- to 6-month lead time." Subscription: $19; per copy: $5.50. **Sample postpaid: $6. No limit on number or time of submissions; prefer typed (or WP) double-spaced; clear photocopies acceptable; query not necessary, though it will be answered. Reports in 6-8 weeks. Pays $10/poem plus 1-year subscription. Buys first North American serial rights. Send SASE for guidelines. For book consideration, query with 6-10 samples, publication credits, brief bio and current projects.** "We give priority to Canadians because of our Arts Council funding and our own interest in promoting Canadian writing." **Replies to queries in 1 month, to submissions (if invited) in 6-8 weeks. Photocopy, dotmatrix OK. Contract is for 10% royalties, 10 author's copies. Send 5×7 SASE for catalog to order samples.** Editor "frequently" comments on rejections. *Poetry Canada* is a quarterly magazine featuring interviews, essays, international criticism and comprehensive reviews of every Canadian poetry book published. Each issue features a major Canadian poet on the cover and center spread (recent issues feature Marlene Nourbese Philip, Di Brandt and Don McKay). Circulation: 1,800 with 600 subscribers, 600 newsstand. Subscription: $16/year ($32/year institutions). **Sample postpaid: $4.25. Submit average 10 poems with SAE and IRC. Reports within 1-2 months. Pays $100/page of poetry (usually 100 lines). Buys first North American serial rights.**

THE QUARTERLY (III), 201 E. 50th St., New York NY 10022, phone (212)572-2128 or 872-8231, founded 1987, editor Gordon Lish, is a literary quarterly publishing poetry, fiction, essays and humor. They want **poetry of the "highest standards."** They have published poetry by Sharon Olds, Bruce Beasley, Jack Gilbert and Thomas Lynch. It is 256 pgs, digest-sized, flat-spined, with glossy card cover. Circulation: 15,000. Subscription: $40. **Sample postpaid: $9.95. Pay: "Rates vary but are modest" plus 2 copies. "Do not submit a batch of poems folded separately!"**

QUARTERLY REVIEW OF LITERATURE POETRY SERIES; QRL AWARDS (II, IV-Subscription, translation), 26 Haslet Ave., Princeton NJ 08540, founded 1943, poetry editors T. Weiss and R. Weiss. After more than 35 years as one of the most distinguished literary journals in the country, *QRL* now appears as the *QRL Poetry Series*, in which 4-6 books are combined in one annual volume, each of the 4-6 poets receiving $1,000 and 100 copies. The resulting 300 to 400-page volumes are printed in editions of 3,000-5,000, selling in paperback for $10, in hardback for $20. Subscription—2 paperback volumes containing 10 books: $20. **Manuscripts may be sent for reading during the months of November and May only. The collection need not be a first book. It should be between 50-80 pgs. if it is a group of connected poems, a selection of miscellaneous poems, a poetic play or a work of poetry translation or it can be a single long poem of 30 pgs. or more. Some of the poems may have had previous magazine publication. Also considers simultaneous submissions. SASE must be included for returned manuscripts. Manuscripts in English or translated into English are also invited from outside the US. Only one ms may be submitted per reading period and must include a SASE.** "Since poetry as a thriving art must depend partly upon the enthusiasm and willingness of those directly involved to join in its support, the editors require that **each ms be accompanied by a subscription to the series."**

QUEEN OF ALL HEARTS (IV-Religious), 26 S. Saxon Ave., Bay Shore NY 11706, phone (516)665-0726, founded 1950, poetry editor Joseph Tusiani, a magazine-sized bimonthly, uses **poetry "dealing with Mary, the Mother of Jesus—inspirational poetry. Not too long."** They have published poetry by Fernando Sembiante and Alberta Schumacher. The professionally printed magazine, 48 pgs., heavy stock, various colors of ink and paper, liberal use of graphics and photos, has approximately 5,000 subscriptions at $15/year. Per copy: $2.50. They receive 40-50 submissions of poetry/year, use 2/issue. **Sample postpaid: $3. Submit double-spaced mss. Reports within 3-4 weeks. Pays 6 copies (sometimes more) and complimentary subscription. Sometimes editor comments on rejections.** His advice: "Try and try again! Inspiration is not automatic!"

QUEEN'S QUARTERLY: A CANADIAN REVIEW (II, IV-Regional), Queen's University, Kingston, Ontario K7L 3N6 Canada, phone (613)545-2667, founded 1893, editor Boris Castel is "a general interest intellectual review featuring articles on science, politics, humanities, arts and letters, extensive book reviews, some poetry and fiction. **We are especially interested in poetry by Canadian writers. Shorter poems preferred."** They have recently published poetry by Evelyn Lau, Sue Nevill and Raymond Souster. There are about 12 pgs. of poetry in each issue, 6×9, 224 pgs., circulation 3,500. They receive about 400 submissions of poetry/year, use 40. Subscription: $20 Canadian, US and foreign, $22 US funds; per copy: $6.50 US. **Sample postpaid: $5 US. Submit no more than 6 poems at once. Photocopies OK but no simultaneous submissions. Reports in 1 month. Pays usually $50 (Canadian)/ poem, plus 2 copies.**

‡QUICK BROWN FOX (II); MAD DOG PRESS (V), P.O. Box 47, Youngwood PA 15697, founded 1987, editor K.K. Shields, publisher Bill Shields. Mad Dog Press accepts no unsolicited mss. *Quick Brown Fox* is a broadsheet of 1-3 pgs. which appears irregularly using **"informed contemporary poems. Shorter poems (20 lines or less) have a better chance, although a solid longer poem will be considered."** Pays **5 copies. Authors retain rights. The editor will consider simultaneous submissions and previously published poems. Editor sometimes comments on rejections.** She advises: "Read poetry incessantly, from Catullus to Bukowski and everything in between and beyond. Read, read, read. It's the only way to find your *own* style." They add, "We became disillusioned with the alternative press for awhile, but we are beginning to publish *qbf* and selected one-shot 'zines from time to time. Your work may fit our publications if you write poetry that sets the heart or soul on fire. That is our only criterion. We remain cautious but hopeful."

RADCLIFFE QUARTERLY (IV-Specialized), 10 Garden St., Cambridge MA 02138, phone (617)495-8608, editor Ruth Whitman, is an alumnae quarterly that **publishes alumnae and college-related poets.** They have published poetry by Patricia Filipowska and Rhea Kovar Sossen. It is magazine-sized, with glossy full-color paper cover. They accept 3 poems/issue, receive about 30/year. Press run: 30,500 for 30,000 subscribers. **No pay. "Radcliffe College holds copyright on most poems." Samples free to alumnae.** Reviews books of poetry in 250 words, single format. The Dean's office sponsors a contest for poets, winners printed in the quarterly. Must be a Radcliffe student to enter.

RADDLE MOON (II, IV-Form), 2239 Stephens St., Vancouver, British Columbia V6K 3W5 Canada or 9060 Ardmore Dr., Sidney, British Columbia V8L 3S1 Canada, phone (604)656-4045, founded 1985, editor Susan Clark, appears twice a year using **"language-centered and 'new lyric' poetry."** They have published poetry by Claude Royet-Journoud, Lyn Hejinian, Rosmarie Waldrop and Leslie Scalapino. The editor describes it as 6×9, flat-spined, 100+ pgs. Press run 700. **Sample postpaid: $5. Reports in 2-3 months. Pays subscription.**

RADIANCE: THE MAGAZINE FOR LARGE WOMEN (I, IV-Women), P.O. Box 30246, Oakland CA 94604, phone (510)482-0680, founded 1984, publisher/editor Alice Ansfield, who **"wants to include poetry for women all sizes of large. It should be personal, empowering."** As a sample she quotes "Homage to My Hips" by Lucille Clifton:

> these hips are big hips
> they need space to
> move around in.
> they don't fit into little
> petty places. these hips
> are free hips.
> they don't like to be held back.
> these hips have never been enslaved,
> they go where they want to go
> they do what they want to do.
> these hips are mighty hips.
> these hips are magic hips.
> i have known them
> to put a spell on a man and
> spin him like a top!

The quarterly is magazine-sized, professionally printed on glossy stock with full-color paper cover, 60 pgs., saddle-stapled, 2-color graphics, photos and ads, circulation 10,000 to 4,000 subscriptions, 2,500 selling on newsstands or in bookstores, 1,000 sent as complimentary copies to media and clothing stores for large women. Subscription: $15/year. **Sample postpaid: $3.50. Send SASE for guidelines. Pays $10-40. Buys one-time rights. Submit double-spaced, typed ms. Editor comments on rejections.** Reviews related books of poetry in 500-800 words.

"I like this cover because it's so rare that any media shows someone desirous of the larger female figure," says Alice Ansfield, editor and publisher of Radiance: The Magazine for Large Women. "We want large women to know they're sexy, desirable, worthy of love, intimacy and attention. This is right in line with our philosophy," she says. "I love having poetry in the magazine. It adds variety and helps give our readers new insights," she adds. This cover, featuring characters from "Rose Is Rose," a syndicated cartoon strip by Pat Brady, is reprinted with permission from both Radiance and the cartoonist.

RAG MAG; BLACK HAT PRESS (I), P.O. Box 12, Goodhue MN 55027, phone (612)923-4590, founded 1982, poetry editor Beverly Voldseth accepts **poetry of "any length or style. No pornographic SM violent crap."** They have published poetry by Myra L. Sullivan, Robert Edwards and Harry Brody. As a sample the editor selected these lines from "All Slipped Away" by John M. Solensten:

> *All slipped away on a wink of the dial.*
> *Then all we could hear*
> *was the crackling of tired static—*
> *little dry electric whispers*
> *trying to say goodbye, goodbye,*
> *while the house sat on the narrow shelf of darkness*
> *dimming, dimming—cooling down, down*
> *like a big, shut-off wooden radio.*

Rag Mag, appearing twice a year, is 80 pgs., perfect-bound, digest-sized, professionally printed in dark type with tipped-in colored ads for books, with matte colored card cover. The editor says she accepts about 10% of poetry received. Press run is 200 for 50 subscriptions of which 4 are libraries. Subscription: $10. **Sample postpaid: $6. "Send 6-8 of your best. Something that tells a story, creates images, speaks to the heart." Pays 1 copy.** Reviews books of poetry. **They may publish chapbook or paperback collections of poetry under the imprint of Black Hat Press. Query first. Submit 6-8 poems, bio, publications. Simultaneous submissions, previously printed material, photocopies OK. No dot-matrix. Reports in 6 weeks. Detailed comments provided. Financial arrangements for book publication vary.** Recently published Riki Kölbl Nelson's English/German poems about living in 2 worlds/2 languages. Title: **Borders/Grenzen.** 128 pages plus the author's artwork.

RAINBOW CITY EXPRESS (II, IV-Spiritual, nature, women, aesthetics), P.O. Box 8447, Berkeley CA 94707-8447, founded 1988, editor Helen B. Harvey, is a quarterly using **"excellent evocative material pertaining to individual spiritual insights and experiences, God-in-nature, women's issues and creative unfolding. 30 lines maximum. No rhyming poems! No infantile beginners.** Please obtain and study at least one issue of *RCE* prior to submitting any manuscript." They have published poetry by James Dillet Freeman. They offer "sporadic contests with cash prizes and publication of winners." The editor describes it as 60-80 pgs., magazine-sized, side-stapled, with "exquisite art and graphics, uplifting essays and poems, and ads." They accept about 25-45 poems/year. Press run 500-1,000 for 400-500 subscriptions, including several libraries. Subscription: $24. **Sample postpaid: $6. Pays 1 copy.**

RAMBUNCTIOUS PRESS; RAMBUNCTIOUS REVIEW (II, IV-Regional), 1221 W. Pratt, Chicago IL 60626, founded 1982, poetry editors Mary Dellutri, Richard Goldman, Beth Hausler and Nancy Lennon. The *Review* appears once yearly in a handsomely printed, saddle-stapled, 7×10 format, 48 pgs. They want **"spirited, quality poetry,** fiction, short drama, photos and graphics. **Some focus on local work, but all work is considered."** Recently they have published Pam Miller, John Ditsky and Martha Vertreace. They have a circulation of about 500 with 200 subscriptions, single copy $3.50 (**sample postpaid: $4**). They receive 500-600 submissions a year and use 50-60, **reporting in 9 months. Will consider simultaneous submissions. No submissions accepted June 1 through August 31. No queries. Payment 2 copies.** Occasional comments on mss. Contests in poetry, fiction and short drama.

RANGER INTERNATIONAL PRODUCTIONS; LION PUBLISHING; ROAR RECORDING (V), P.O. Box 71231, Milwaukee WI 53211-7331, phone (414)332-7474, founded 1969, editor Martin Jack Rosenblum, publishes **"objectivist/projectivist poetry, primarily with action subjects by adventurers—such as the Harley poetry—**in flat-spined paper and hardcover chapbooks." They have published poetry by Karl Young, Howard McCord, Toby Olson and Carl Rakosi. They publish about 3 books a year. **Query regarding submissions. Payment "negotiable." Editor comments on submissions "always."** He says, "Poetry has been swept into an academic corner and dusted off of daily living spaces and this is what Ranger International Productions works against: we want to bring poetry out of academics and back into life's daily platform. Write hard, accept no public money and achieve honesty and integrity personally while studying the master poets in school or out. Control of the forms is essential. Control of the life is absolutely required."

‡RANGER RICK MAGAZINE (III), 8925 Leesburg Pike, Vienna VA 22184, founded 1967, associate editor Deborah Churchman, is a monthly nature magazine for children aged 6-12. They want **"short, funny verses for children about nature and the environment. No religious, preachy or difficult poetry."** They have recently published poetry by Eve Merriam, Elizabeth Coatsworth and J. Patrick Lewis. *RR* is 46 pgs., full color. They receive 100-200 submissions/year, "may accept one." Press run is 850,000. Subscription: $15. **Sample postpaid: $2. Previously published poems OK; no simultaneous submissions.** Time between acceptance and publication is 2-5 years. Seldom comments on rejections. Send SASE for guidelines. **Reports in 2 months. Pays $5/line plus 2 copies. Buys all rights.** Return is "negotiable." Deborah Churchman says, "Think: Will kids understand these words? Will it hook them? Will an 8-year-old want to read this instead of playing Nintendo?"

RARACH PRESS (V), 1005 Oakland Dr., Kalamazoo MI 49008, phone (616)388-5631, founded 1981, owner Ladislav Hanka, is a "small bibliophilic press specializing in hand-printing, hand-binding with original artwork. The material is either in Czech or, if English, dealing with environmentalist subject matter." He has printed books of poetry by James Armstrong, Richard Neugebauer, Bennet Mitchell and Rainer Maria Rilke. "Authors tend to be friends, acquaintances or dead. They are given a portion of the books or a portion of sales after the fact. **I do not care to receive unsolicited mss.** I pity the lot of you. I fully expect most of my books to eventually be taken apart and sold for the artwork when they pass from the present collector of bibliophili to some philistine. This means the poetry will be lost . . . I really sell my books for the price of the binding and artwork."

RARITAN QUARTERLY (III), 31 Mine St., New Brunswick NJ 08903, phone (908)932-7887, founded 1982, editor Richard Poirier. **"We publish very little poetry. We publish *almost* no unsolicited poetry, so it would be misleading to encourage submissions."** They have published poetry by J.D. McClatchy, James Merrill, Richard Howard and Robert Pinsky. They review recent poetry books and chapbooks. It is 6×9, flat-spined, 150+ pgs., with matte card cover, professionally printed. Press run 4,000 for 3,500 subscriptions of which 800 are libraries. Subscription: $16. **Sample postpaid: $5. Pays $100/ submission if accepted.**

RASHI (IV-Ethnic), Box 1198, Hamilton, New Zealand, founded 1985, editor Norman Simms, uses poetry on **"Jewish topics in English or any Jewish language such as Hebrew, Yiddish, Ladino, etc."** They do not want poetry that is **"pompous, self-indulgent nonsense."** They have published poems by Anne Ranasinghe and Simon Lichman. *Rashi* is the literary supplement of the monthly *New Zealand Chronicle*. They accept about 25 of 40 poems received/year. Circulation is over 2,000. Subscription: $15. **Sample postpaid: $2. Pays 1 copy. Subscription "recommended, but not necessary." Reports in 1 month. Editor comments on rejections for $5/page.** He says, "This is a special part of our overall projects. We would like to see multilingualism develop, reinterpretation of ancient and medieval traditions."

‡THE RAVEN (I, IV-Science fiction/fantasy/horror), Route 5 Box 504, Union SC 29379, founded 1990, editor Micheal Nave, is a quarterly magazine of poetry and fiction which "publishes fantasy science fiction with a slant toward soft horror." They want **poetry of a "mystical, thought-provoking nature. 20 lines or less. 5 poems/submission. Any style or form. No witches, chants, gore, sex or nursery rhymes."** They have recently published poetry by John Grey, Shannon Riley and Anita Barnard. As a sample the editor selected these lines from "Ruined Birds" by Robert Dunbar:

> *Across a broken pillar*
> *Floats the shadow of a raven*
> *How romantic*
> *And in the shattered shadows,*
> *The phantoms of this dusty heat*
> *Watch me . . . and wait.*

The Raven is 40-45 pgs., digest-sized, laser-printed, saddle-stapled, with b&w artwork. They accept about 30-40% of the poetry received each year. Press run is 500 for 100 subscribers of which 5 are libraries. Subscription: $12. **Sample postpaid: $4. No previously published poems or simultaneous submissions. Always comments on rejections. Send SASE for guidelines. Reports in "usually 2 weeks." Pays 2 copies.** "Each issue has a feature poet on the center pages—poet featured receives a free year's subscription." They also offer a poetry contest in each issue. Entry fee: $3 for each 5-poem submission. 1st prize: $25; 2nd prize: $10; 3rd prize: $5. Winners published in the magazine. The editor says, "My goal is to see new talent in print. I enjoy working with under-published poets and try to encourage, try to build on strong points, without harsh criticism—never use form rejection slips. Please read guidelines—nearly 30-40% of my rejections are for not following guidelines. If you have just fallen in love with Mary Lou and have written a beautiful poem all about the moon-in-June, please send it to her. I don't want it. Buying a sample copy encouraged but not required."

RAW DOG PRESS; POST POEMS (IV-Humor), 128 Harvey Ave., Doylestown PA 18901, phone (215)345-6838, founded 1977, poetry editor R. Gerry Fabian, "publishes Post Poems annual—a post-card series. We also do chapbooks from time to time and there is always a special project that crops up. **We want short poetry (3-7 lines) on any subject. The positive poem or the poem of understated humor always has an inside track. No taboos, however. All styles considered. Anything with rhyme had better be immortal."** They have published poetry by ave jeanne, Lyn Lifshin, Philip Miller, Conger Beasley, Jr. and the editor, R. Gerry Fabian, who selected his poem, "Arc Welder," as a sample:

> *After years of burning*
> *he pressed his lips against hers*
> *and sealed out any doubt.*

Query with 7-10 samples for chapbook publication. "We are small and any poet is expected to share half the responsibility and often that includes cost — not always, however. No photocopies or dot-matrix. Pays copies. Acquires all rights. Returns rights on mention of first publication. Send SASE for catalog to buy samples. The editor "always" comments on rejections. Sometimes reviews books of poetry. He says he will offer criticism for a fee; "if someone is desperate to publish and is willing to pay we will use our vast knowledge to help steer the ms in the right direction. We will advise against it, but as P.T. Barnum said . . . . Raw Dog Press welcomes new poets and detests second-rate poems from 'name' poets. We exist because we are dumb like a fox, but even a fox takes care of its own."

REAL (RE ARTS & LETTERS) (II, IV-Bilingual, translations, humor), Box 13007, Stephen F. Austin State University, Nacogdoches TX 75962, phone (409)568-2101, founded 1968, editor Lee Schultz, is a "Liberal Arts Forum" using short fiction, drama, reviews and interviews; contains editorial notes and personalized "Contributors' Notes"; printed in the spring and fall. They "hope to use from 15 to 35 pages of poetry per issue, one poem per page (typeset in editor's office). Last two issues had submissions from thirty-eight states, Great Britain, Italy and Israel." **They receive between 10-35 poems/week. "We presently do not receive enough formal or witty/ironic pieces. We need a better balance between open and generic forms. We're also interested in critical writings on poems or writing poetry and translations with a bilingual format (permissions from original author)."** As a sample the editor selected these lines from "Within the Womb of This Mountain" by Jenna Fedock:

> We will not see him again,
> "Lord have mercy,"
> but only in the black box wedged in an aisle,
> heavy lid crushing our heads. We chant
> "Vichnaya pamyat, Vichnaya pamyat, Vichnaya pamyat,"
> trying to cast it off — but cannot.

It is handsomely printed, "reserved format," perfect-bound with line drawings and photos. Circulation approximately 400, "more than half of which are major college libraries." Subscriptions also in Great Britain, Ireland, Italy, Holland, Puerto Rico, Brazil and Canada. **Submit original and copy. "Editors prefer a statement that ms is not being simultaneously submitted; however, this fact is taken for granted when we receive a ms."** Sample postpaid: $4.50. Writer's guidelines for SASE. Pays copies. They acknowledge receipt of submissions and strive for a 1-month decision. Submissions during summer semesters may take longer. "We will return poems rather than tie them up for more than a one-issue backlog (6-9 months)." This market is recommended with enthusiasm for those looking to place their first poems or for more experienced poets looking to place work in a handsome, exciting publication. With each year, this publication increases in prestige.

REALITY STUDIOS (V), 4 Howard Court, Peckham Rye, London SE15 3PH United Kingdom, founded 1978, editor Ken Edwards, has published books of poetry by Allen Fisher, Wendy Mulford and John Welch, but **accepts no unsolicited mss.** They publish 2 paperbacks/year. Their U.S. distributor is Small Press Distribution, 1814 San Pablo Ave., Berkeley CA 94302.

‡RECONSTRUCTIONIST (IV-Ethnic), Church Rd. & Greenwood Ave., Wyncote PA 19095, founded 1935, poetry editor Jeremy Garber, is a Jewish cultural and intellectual review published 4 times per year. **"We publish about 4 poems per year — either on Jewish themes or in some other way related to Jewish spiritual quests — short poems up to about 30-35 lines."** They have published poetry by Gabriel Preil, Shulamis Yelin and Marcia Falk. As a sample the editor selected these lines (poet unidentified):

> Come, share the watermelon I have sliced.
> My yearning for the hurricane
> fills yawning distance with our pain

Reconstructionist is 32 pgs., magazine-sized, professionally printed on heavy stock with matte card cover, saddle-stapled. Subscription: $20. **Sample postpaid: $3. Pays $36/poem plus 5 copies. Reports in 1-2 months, delay to publication 1-2 years. No simultaneous submissions. Editor sometimes comments on rejections.**

RECORDING & PUBLISHING NEWS; ANTERIOR BITEWING LTD. (I), 7735 Brand Ave., St. Louis MO 63135, founded 1988, editor Tom Bergeron, appears 6 times a year using **poetry, not necessarily related to the themes of the magazine.** It is a "newsletter full of facts, figures, guidelines and practical information. It's about services, markets, copyrights, technology and techniques — **but there's room for a few really good poems in every issue.**" They have recently published poetry by C. David Hay, Ashley Anders, Pearl Bloch Segall, Kathleen Lee Mendel and Vivian Bogardus. As a sample the editor selected these lines by Yuri Polchenko:

> i am big and skillful one

> *walked to sonny*
> *took him off*
> *and sighted at his eyes*
> *my small image*

It is desktop published, magazine-sized, 20 pgs. Press run 200-300 for 110 subscribers. Subscription: $12.99. **Sample postpaid: $2. Please make checks payable to Anterior Bitewing Ltd. Pays $5/poem. Buys one-time rights. Send SASE for guidelines. "We like cover letters."** Anterior Bitewing Ltd. is an imprint for job printing of newsletters and "magazettes." Send SASE for rate sheet. The editor says, "Always resubmit. There's some editor out there somewhere who will love your work. Take advice, make changes accordingly and keep on resubmitting."

RECURSIVE ANGEL (IV-Science fiction, spirituality), 210 Wilbur Blvd., Poughkeepsie NY 12603 or 1412 NE 35th St., Ocala FL 32670, phone (914)485-3866, founded 1990, managing editor David H. Sutherland, appears twice a year, **"looking for hard-hitting tightly composed sci-fi with a spiritual and metaphysical slant. Open to all forms."** The have published poetry by G. Sutton Breiding and Robert Frazier. As a sample the editor selected these lines from "Future Texts" by Bruce Boston:

> *Without beginning or end,*
> *without rector or verso*
> *or colored cover to judge,*
>
> *unreeling like a worded carpet*
> *directly into our brains,*
> *the software melange with*
>
> *envelopes our days and nights . . .*

It is magazine-sized, 30-40 pgs., "high quality typeset, hardbound and softbound distribution." Press run is 250 copies. Subscription: $14.95. **Sample postpaid: $7.95. Pays $10-40/poem/prose/ short story. "Send only 3-5 poems/prose. Cover letter OK."** Reports in 6-8 weeks. Editor occasionally comments on rejections. 5″ disk, IBM ASCII submissions OK. Or you can upload 2 text submissions between 9-11 AM EST Sundays to (914)485-3866-1200, N, 8, 1. The editor advises, "Buy **Poet's Market** and study it in the same vein as if you were taking an exam. Finally, Read! Read! Read!"

‡THE RED CANDLE PRESS; CANDELABRUM (II), 9 Milner Rd., Wisbech PE13 2LR England, founded 1970, editors Basil Wincote, B.A. and M.L. McCarthy, M.A., administrative editor Helen Gordon, B.A., was "founded to encourage poets working in **traditional-type verse, metrical unrhymed or metrical rhymed. We're more interested in poems than poets: that is, we're interested in what sort of poems an author produces, not in his or her personality."** They publish the yearly magazine, *Candelabrum*, occasional postcards, paperbound staple-spined chapbooks and occasional poetry leaflets. For all of these they want **"good-quality metrical verse, with rhymed verse specially wanted. Elegantly cadenced free verse is acceptable. No weak stuff (moons and Junes, loves and doves, etc.) No chopped-up prose pretending to be free verse. Any length up to about 50 lines for** *Candelabrum***, any subject, including eroticism (but not porn) — satire, love poems, nature lyrics, philosophical — any subject, but nothing racist or sexist."** They have recently published poetry by Jon Taylor, John Laycock, David Castleman, William Davey, Ann Keith and Tony Esolen. The editors offer these lines by Paris Flammonde as a sample:

> *Tomorrow is a place where dreams begin*
> *To flutter like a fancy; feather-kissed*
> *Flamingo, arc'd awake and to its tryst; —*
> *A field whereon the vanquished always win.*

The digest-sized magazine, staple-spined, small type, exemplifies their intent to "pack in as much as possible, wasting no space, and try to keep a neat appearance with the minimum expense." They get in about 44 pgs. (some 60 poems) in each issue. Circulation: 900 with 700 subscriptions of which 22 are libraries. **Sample: $4 if payment is in bills; $10 if payment is by check. "We prefer bills."** They receive about 2,000 submissions/year, use approximately 5% of those, sometimes holding over poems for the next year or longer. **"Submit any time. IRC essential if return wished, and please check the weight — each poem on a separate sheet please, neat typescripts or neat** *legible* **manuscripts.** *Please* **no dark, oily photostats, no colored ink (only black or blue). Clear photocopies acceptable. Author's name and address on each sheet, please."** Reports in about 2 months. No simultaneous submissions. Pays one contributor's copy. "Occasionally" reviews books of poetry in 500 words, single format. The books published by Red Candle Press "have been at our invitation to the poet, and at our expense. We pay the author a small royalty-advance, but he/she keeps the copyright." The editors comment, "Traditional-type poetry is much more popular here in Britain, and we think also in the United States, now than it was in 1970, when we founded *Candelabrum*, though some people are still rather scared of it. We always welcome new poets, especially traditionalists, and we like to hear from the U.S.A. as well as from here at home. General tip: Study the various outlets at the library, or buy a sample, or borrow a copy from a subscriber, before you go to the expense of submitting your work."

RED DANCEFLOOR (I, II); RED DANCEFLOOR PRESS (II), P.O. Box 7392, Van Nuys CA 91409-7392, phone (818)785-7650, founded 1989, editor David Goldschlag, appears 3 times/year (in September, January and May) publishing poetry, fiction, interviews, profiles, reviews, photos and art. "No restrictions on form, length or subject matter. We want poetry that is well thought out—not a first draft. If you send us rhyme it should have a specific purpose and work; would consider a good sestina." They have recently published poetry by Michael C Ford, David Lake, Glenn Bach, Mario René Padilla and Charles Webb. As a sample the editor selected these lines from "Moments in the Real World" by Virginia Anderson:

> He pinched her nose,
> pulled her face into his hands,
> a soft scarf.
> leaving the rest of her at loose ends.

The magazine is digest-sized, 90-130 pgs., flat-spined, laser printed, with glossy card cover. Press run is 400. Current issue: $5. **Sample postpaid: $4.50. Send SASE for guidelines. Pays 1 copy and % off additional copies. Acquires one-time rights.** Previously published poems and simultaneous submissions OK, "but please note. A short cover letter is appreciated. Submit 5-7 poems." Reads submissions from September 1 through May 31 only. Reports in 2-6 weeks. Reviews books of poetry. "Please send one copy to the press. The author will then be notified to whom/where to send another copy." Red Dancefloor Press publishes full-length books, chapbooks and poetry audiotapes. "The author may want to get a copy of a book, chap or tape before submitting to the press." Book: $7.95, chapbook: $3.50, audiotape: $8—plus $1 postage and handling for each. "We openly accept submissions for books, chaps and tapes, but *please* query first with 10 samples and a cover letter explaining which area of our press you are interested in. Listing credits in a cover letter is fine, but don't go crazy. We also publish the *Southern California Poet's Directory*. It lists names, addresses and phone numbers of poets, coffeehouses and literary bookstores throughout California. It is very useful to publishers, editors and poets who would like to correspond with other poets. We are considering opening up to the entire U.S. and abroad. Send SASE with a note specifying it is for *SCPD*." The editor says, "The mag is of high quality and has been called one of L.A.'s best. We desperately need art for covers. Send SASE and a note for specs."

RED HERRING POETS; MATRIX; RED HERRING PRESS; RED HERRING CHAPBOOK SERIES; CHANNING-MURRAY FOUNDATION (IV-Membership), 1209 W. Oregon St., Urbana IL 61801, phone (217)344-1176, founded 1975, director of Red Herring Poets Ruth S. Walker. The Red Herring Poets is a workshop that publishes its members' work, after they have attended at least 5 meetings, in their annual magazine, *Matrix*, and, for those who have been members for at least 2 years and given 2 public readings, one chapbook/year.

RED RAMPAN' PRESS; RED RAMPAN' REVIEW (V); RED RAMPAN' BROADSIDE SERIES (IV-Form), 4707 Fielder St., Midland TX 79707-2817, phone (915)697-7689, founded 1981, poetry editor Larry D. Griffin. "For 1993 we will consider long poems for Red Rampan' Broadside Series." *RRR* is an "eclectic review quarterly." The editor says it is 6×9, 48-60 pgs., with a press run of 300, "presently not accepting poetry." The press plans to publish flat-spined paperback collections.

THE REDNECK REVIEW OF LITERATURE (IV-Regional), 2919 N. Downer Ave., Milwaukee WI 53211, phone (414)332-6881, founded 1975, editor Penelope Reedy, is a semiannual magazine publishing poetry, fiction, drama and essays dealing with the contemporary West. The editor wants to see "any form, length or style." She does not want "ethereal ditties about nothing; obscure." She has recently published poetry by R.M. Davis, C. Bukowski, Charlotte Wright, Lawson Inada, Ron McFarland and Arthur W. Knight. As a sample the editor selected these lines by Stephen Lyons:

> When women go mad out
> west, they stack the
> bottles behind the
> dryer . . .

The magazine, which appears in the spring and fall each year, is magazine-sized, offset, perfect-bound, some advertising. Circulation is 500, of which 200 are subscriptions and 100-150 are newsstand sales. **Sample postpaid: $7. Pays 1 copy.** Rejected mss are reported on immediately, and no accepted mss are held beyond 3 issues. Writers should submit "2-3 poems at a time, letter quality—don't like simultaneous submissions. Please send SASE with *enough* postage to return mss." **Criticism is sometimes given.** Reviews books of poetry. The editor says, "Take time—have something to say. Learn how to pull images out of your head, to cover an idea completely. Read nursery rhymes to your kids, listen and observe."

REFLECT (IV-Form/style), 3306 Argonne Ave., Norfolk VA 23509, founded 1979, poetry editor W.S. Kennedy. They use "spiral poetry: featuring an inner-directed concern with sound (euphony), mystical references or overtones, and objectivity—rather than personal and emotional poems. No love poems, pornography, far left propaganda; nothing overly sentimental. (Don't write yourself into the poem.)" They have recently published poetry by Susan Tanaka, B.Z. Niditch, Joe Malone, Ruth Wildes Schuler and Stan Proper. As a sample the editor selected these lines from "Euphonies" by Marikay Brown:

> The spring wind is a silver flute
> Piping lilac-hyacinth
> Passionatos of perfume.
> The summer wind—a green guitar
> Of fluttering leaves and grasses
> Strummed on fretted sunlight gold . . .

The quarterly is digest-sized, 48 pgs., saddle-stapled, typescript. Subscription: $8. **Sample post-paid: $2.** Guidelines available for SASE. All submissions should be single-spaced and should fit on one typed page. Reports within a month. No backlog. Pays 1 copy. Acquires first rights. Editor sometimes comments on rejections. Occasionally reviews books of poetry in 50 words or more.

RENDITIONS: A CHINESE-ENGLISH TRANSLATION MAGAZINE (IV-Translations), Research Center for Translation, CUHK, Shatin, NT, Hong Kong, editor Dr. Eva Hung, appears twice a year. "Contents exclusively translations from Chinese, ancient and modern." They also publish a paperback series of Chinese literature in English translation. They have published translations of the poetry of Gu Cheng, Shu Ting, Mang Ke and Bei Dao. *Renditions* is magazine-sized, 180 pgs., flat-spined, elegantly printed, often with side-by-side Chinese and English texts, using some b&w and color drawings and photos, with glossy card cover. **Sample postpaid: $9.** Pays "honorarium" plus 2 copies. Reports in two months. Use British spelling. They "will consider" book mss, for which they would like a query with sample poems. Books pay 10% royalties plus 10 copies. Mss usually not returned. Editor sometimes comments on rejections.

RENEGADE (II), Box 314, Bloomfield Hills MI 48303, phone (313)972-5580, founded 1988, editors Miriam Jones and Michael Nowicki, appears twice a year using stories, essays and poems. "We are an eclectic publication. There is no preference for form or style; we simply wish to see polished work of good quality. Poems are generally of a length no more than 200 lines, no less than 10 lines. We try to avoid anything that is anarchistic, antifeminist or of a derogatory nature to any group of persons or individuals." They have published poetry by John Sinclair, M.L. Liebler, Linda Nemec Foster and Laurence Pike. *Renegade* is 32 pgs., digest-sized, laser-printed, with matte card cover, b&w drawings and graphics. Ads welcome. They accept about 5% of 300 mss of 5 poems or less. Press run: 200 for 20 subscriptions, free to libraries and editors of other literary journals. 50 shelf sales. Subscription: $5.90. **Sample postpaid: $3.** Pays 1 copy, 2 on request. Acquires all rights. Returns rights to author free of charge. Reports in 3-6 months. Editor comments on submissions "often." Reviews books of poetry. "We put together Warlords of the Subculture Poetry Contest. People interested should inquire first."

‡REPOSITORY PRESS (V, IV-Regional), R.R. 7, Site 29, Comp. 8, Prince George, British Columbia V2N 2J5 Canada, phone (604)562-7074, founded 1972, publisher John Harris, publishes flat-spined paperbacks and chapbooks of **local poetry** and short stories. He has recently published poetry by Harvey Chometzky. He says, "I publish poetry by people I know. I advise poets to operate their own magazines and publishing companies."

RESIN (V), P.O. Box 2453, Athens GA 30612, founded 1989, edited by Gregory Mann and Charlotte Eubanks, is a quarterly that publishes "good poetry with concise images. No pornography; no sentiment." They are currently not accepting submissions, however, as the editors are out of the country. They have published poetry by Susan Medencia and Megan E. Ray. As a sample the editors selected these lines by Charlotte Eubanks:

> Old man, bent and carving
> Slow steps from webs of roots,
> Splayed like spilled lightning bolts,
> Stilled by hob-nailed boots.

It is magazine-sized, saddle-stapled with a glossy paper cover, printed in a variety of large type styles. They publish "less than a tenth" of poems received. Press run is 75. **Sample postpaid: $2.**

RESPONSE (IV-Ethnic, students), 27 W. 20th St., 9th Floor, New York NY 10011, phone (212)675-1168, FAX (212)929-3459, founded 1966, poetry editor Bennett Lovett-Graff, is a "contemporary Jewish review publishing poetry, fiction and essays **by students and young adult authors." The only specification for poetry is that it be on a Jewish theme and have some significant Jewish content.** They have recently published poetry by Sharon Kessler, Sue Saniel Elkind and Shulamith Bat-Yisrael. As a sample the editor chose these lines from "Old Nazis Don't Die (They Move To South America)" by Sylvia Warsh:

> The jungles of Brazil teem
> with a new strain of
> European animal, serpents of
> such camouflage that their own
> Bavarian mothers would not
> recognize them,
> insects that thrust hard
> consonants into a victim's
> heart and suck him dry,
> then use his shell
> for a livingroom.

They look for "creative, challenging and chutzapadik writing" from young writers. The quarterly is 64 pgs., flat-spined, 6×9, professionally printed on heavy stock, with a glossy "varnished" cover with artwork. Circulation 1,600 with 600 subscribers of which 30% are libraries. 1,000 distributed through bookstores and newsstands. Subscription: $16 ($10 for students); $20 for institutions. **Sample postpaid: $2. Pays 2 copies/poem published. Acquires all rights. Reports in about 2 months. 6 months between acceptance and publication.** Occasionally reviews books of Jewish poetry.

‡**REVIEW: LATIN AMERICAN LITERATURE AND ARTS (IV-Ethnic, regional, translations)**, 680 Park Ave., New York NY 10021, phone (212)249-8950, ext. 366, founded 1967, managing editor Daniel Shapiro, is a biannual magazine which serves as a "major forum for Latin American literature in English translation and articles on Latin American visual and performing arts." **They want contemporary Latin American poetry.** They have recently published poetry by Jose A. Mazzotti, Mateo Rosas de Oquendo and Gregorio de Matos. As a sample the editor selected these lines from "The Forest" by Mariela Dreyfus, translated from the Spanish by Alfred J. MacAdam:

> Dark, I wander amid the uncertain
> I avoid the traces of the human
> silence is the king in this forest
> here, where only your breath protects me in winter.

It is 100+ pgs., 8½×11, with b&w photos of Latin American art. They receive 50-100 submissions, accept the work of 1-2 poets. Press run is 10,000 for 6,000 subscribers of which 500 are libraries. Subscription: $14 for individuals, $22 for institutions. **Sample postpaid: $7. Previously published poems and simultaneous submissions OK. Cover letter required. Do not submit mss November 15 through March 1. Seldom comments on rejections. Reports in 4-6 weeks. Pays $100-300.** Reviews books of poetry by Latin Americans. The *Review* is published by the Americas Society, a not-for-profit organization.

‡**REVISTA/REVIEW INTERAMERICANA, Inter-American University of Puerto Rico (IV-Ethnic, regional)**, Box 5100, San Germán, Puerto Rico 00683, phone (809)264-1912, ext. 373, editor Juan R. Gonzalez Mendoza. The *Revista/Review* is a bilingual scholarly journal, circulation 2,000, oriented to **Puerto Rican, Caribbean and Hispanic American and *inter-American* subjects, poetry, short stories and reviews. Submit Spanish or English blank verse, free verse, experimental, traditional and avant-garde. No simultaneous submissions. Pays 2 copies.**

RFD: A COUNTRY JOURNAL FOR GAY MEN EVERYWHERE (I, IV-Gay), P.O. Box 68, Liberty TN 37095, founded 1974, poetry editor Steven Riel. *RFD* "is a quarterly for gay men with emphasis on lifestyles outside of the gay mainstream—poetry, politics, profiles, letters." They want **poetry with "personal, creative use of language and image, relevant to journal themes, political themes. We try to publish as many poets as we can so tend to publish shorter poems and avoid epics."** They have published poetry by Antler, James Broughton, Gregory Woods and Winthrop Smith. *RFD* has a circulation of 2,600 for 1,300 subscriptions—per year: $25 first class, $18 second class; per copy: $5.50. **Sample postpaid: $5. Submit up to 5 poems at a time. Photocopies, simultaneous submissions OK. Reports in 6-9 months. Pays copies. Send SASE for guidelines. Editor sometimes comments on rejections.** "*RFD* looks for interesting thoughts, succinct use of language and imagery evocative of nature and gay men and love in natural settings."

RHINO (II), 8403 W. Normal, Niles IL 60648, founded 1976, editors Kay Meier and Don Hoffman, "is an annually published poetry journal. We seek well-crafted work with fresh insights and authentic emotion by known or new writers, **poems which show careful attention to form and contain surprise. Poems no longer than 3 pgs. double-spaced.**" They have published poetry by Elaine Mott, Lyn Lifshin, Christopher Merrill and Mark Pawlak. The editors chose as a sample the opening lines of "A Poem After the Wedding" by Nicole Niemi:

> Our house is dark now.
> You and I slide into each other's arms like
> rain spinning onto a roof.
> I would like to say
> for the matter of poetry,
> that our love shimmers like a July hot rainbow.
> But this is not true.

The digest-sized, 96-page journal, perfect-bound, matte card cover with art, is offset from type-script on high-quality paper, circulation 500, 100 subscriptions of which 10 are libraries. They use 50-60 of 1,000+ submissions received. **Sample: $6 plus $1.15 postage. Submit 3-5 double-spaced poems; photocopies, dot-matrix OK. Reports in 2 months. Pays one copy. Acquires first rights only.** They offer an annual *Rhino* poetry contest with $100 prize and publication in *Rhino*. Regular reading period January 1 through June 30. Contest reading period ($3/poem submitted) March 1 through July 31.

THE RIALTO (II), 32 Grosvenor Rd., Norwich, Norfolk NR2 2PZ England, founded 1984, poetry editors John Wakeman and Michael Mackmin, wants **"poetry of intelligence, wit, compassion, skill, excellence, written by humans. Potential contributors are strongly advised to read *The Rialto* before submitting."** They have published poetry by Peter Porter, Tadeusz Rózewicz and Carol Ann Duffy. As a sample the editors chose the last half of "Finnish Tango," an elegy by Hans Magnus Enzensberger for Felix Pollak, translated by Reinhold Grimm:

> All is so bright   It was half dark
> The little boat will not always return
> It is the same and yet isn't
> No one's around   The rock is a rock
> The rock ceases being a rock
> The rock turns into a rock again
> It's always like that   Nothing
> dissolves and nothing remains   What existed
> is and isn't and is   No one
> can grasp that   That which existed last night
> That's easy to say   How bright
> the summer here is and how brief

The Rialto, which appears 3 times a year, is magazine-sized, 48 pgs., saddle-stapled, beautifully printed on glossy stock with glossy b&w card cover, using b&w drawings. "U.S.A. subscription is now £15 (fifteen pounds sterling). If paying in dollars, please add £3 to cover bank charges, i.e. send dollar equivalent of £18 pounds sterling. **Single issue to U.S.A. is £5 sterling. If paying in dollars, send equivalent of £8 pounds sterling.**" Pays £5/poem. No simultaneous submissions or previously printed poetry. Reports within 3 months. Editor "only rarely" comments on rejections.

RIDGE REVIEW MAGAZINE; RIDGE TIMES PRESS (IV-Regional), Box 90, Mendocino CA 95460, phone (707)964-8465, founded 1981, poetry editors Jim Tarbell and Judy Tarbell, is a "bio-regional quarterly looking at economic, political and social phenomena of the area" which uses **only poets from Northern California.** They have published poetry by Michael Sykes and Judith Tannenbaum. The 7×10 magazine, saddle-stapled, 50+ pgs., linen card cover with art, photos and ads with text, circulation 3,500, 1,000 subscriptions, uses about 1 page of poetry/issue. **Subscription: $10. Sample postpaid: $3.85. Considers simultaneous submissions. Photocopy, dot-matrix OK. Reports in about a week.** Usually pays $10/poem.

‡**RIENDA SUELTA/FREE REIN (II, IV-Bilingual/foreign language)**, 510 Wellington Ave., Santa Ana CA 92701, phone (714)667-5019, founded 1991 (first issue 1992), editors Florinda Mintz and John Brander, is a literary, cultural and arts magazine which appears twice a year. They want **"contemporary themes reflective of life in the United States. Poems having geographical themes, science fiction poetry and poems using traditional forms are acceptable. Themes should be significant and imaginative. Humorous poems are welcome. Avoid sending poems written in therapy sessions or in poetry workshops. No religious and love poetry, unless really excellent. Submissions may be in English or Spanish.**" The editors say it is 64 pgs., flat-spined, digest-sized, using artwork and graphics. They receive

about 600 poems/year, accept about 30-50. Press run: 500. Subscription: $10. Single copy: $4. **Sample postpaid: $5. Send SASE for guidelines. Pays 1 copy. Submit 6 poems at a time, name and address on each, typed. No simultaneous submissions.** "Very rarely" takes previously published poetry. Reports in 1 week-4 months. 3 months between acceptance and publication. The editors advise, "Read other poets, especially those in your own geographical area. Avoid using poetry as therapy—finish therapy first, and then start writing poetry. The same applies to workshops. *Finish* your workshop courses, then start writing poetry."

RIO GRANDE PRESS; SE LA VIE WRITER'S JOURNAL (I, IV-Themes); RIO GRANDE CHAPBOOK CLUB (I, IV-Membership), P.O. Box 371371, El Paso TX 79937, founded 1987, editor Rosalie Avara. *Se La Vie Writer's Journal* is a quarterly journal, digest-sized, with articles and cartoons about poetry and writing; and contests in poetry, essays and short stories. Prizes are $5-25 for poems, entry fee $5 for 2 poems. Publishes 70% of mss received/quarter, **"dedicated to encouraging novice writers, poets and artists; we are interested in original, unpublished mss that reflect the 'life' theme (La Vie). Poems are judged on originality, clarity of thought and ability to evoke emotional response."** They have published poetry by Marian Ford Park, Alice Mackenzie Swaim and Marianne McNeil. *SLVWJ* is 64 pgs., photocopied from typescript, with blue cover, saddle-stapled. **Sample postpaid: $4. Deadlines: end of March, June, September and December. Send SASE for guidelines.** Those interested in the Rio Grande Chapbook Club "receive 4 free books for joining then receive 4 more quarterly—original unpublished/published poems from new and experienced poets. Includes reviews in club newsletter. Send SASE for guidelines."

‡RIVELIN GRAPHEME PRESS (II), The Annexe Kennet House, 19 High St., Hungerford, Berkshire RG170NL England, founded 1984, poetry editor Snowdon Barnett, publishes **only poetry, hoping for 4 titles/year,** not less than 52-196 pgs. each (flat-spined, digest-sized quality paperbacks with glossy covers), illustrated. **Send book-length manuscript, typed, double-spaced, photocopy OK. Payment: 20 copies of first printing up to 2,000, then 5% royalties on subsequent printings. They prefer queries that contain biographical information, previous publications and a photo, if possible.**

RIVER CITY; HOHENBERG AWARD (II), English Dept., Memphis State University, Memphis TN 38152, phone (901)363-4438, founded 1980, editor Sharon Bryan. *River City* publishes fiction, poetry, interviews and essays. Contributors have included John Updike, Marvin Bell, Philip Levine, Maxine Kumin, Robert Penn Warren, W.D. Snodgrass, Mary Oliver, Fred Busch, Beth Bentley, Mona Van Duyn and Peter Porter. The biannual is 6×9, perfect-bound, 100 pgs., 40-50 pgs. of poetry in each issue, professionally printed, two-color matte cover, circulation 1,000, subscription: $9. **Sample postpaid: $5. Submit no more than 5 poems, none June through August. Photocopies OK. Reports in 2-12 weeks. Pays 2 copies (and cash when grant funds available).** $100 Hohenberg Award is given annually to best fiction or poetry selected by the staff.

RIVER RAT REVIEW (III), Box 24198, Lexington KY 40524, phone (606)277-8601, founded 1987, editor Daryl Rogers, is published once a year, **"designed for mainly non-academic readership, though open to anything that is clear, concise and striking. There are no real restrictions but it's advisable to sample an issue before submitting. If you can't afford it, write me and we'll work something out."** Poets published include Charles Bukowski, Douglas Goodwin, Steve Richmond and Serena Fusek. As a sample here are lines by Marcus Cafagna:

> Jamming Sheet metal in a
> punch press. In the same motion
> > beating hissing jaws by seconds
> and lifting it out. Their faces dripping
> soap and oil.

The review is digest sized, 48 pgs., printed by offset on white stock, with a one color cover, saddle-stapled; there is some b&w artwork. Circulation is 200. Price per issue is $3, subscription $3/year. **Submit mss between October 1 and November 1 *only*. No simultaneous submissions. Pays one contributor's copy. Reports in 1-2 months.** Publishes "short mention of chaps, etc. I think deserve it."

RIVER STYX MAGAZINE; BIG RIVER ASSOCIATION (II), 14 S. Euclid, St. Louis MO 63108, phone (314)361-0043, poetry editor Ms. Lee Fournier, founded 1975, is "an international, multicultural journal publishing both award-winning and relatively undiscovered writers. We feature fine art, photography, poetry and short prose." They want **"excellent poetry—thoughtful."** They have recently published work by Diane Wakoski, Marge Piercy, Simon Ortiz, Toni Morrison and Donald Revell. As a sample the editors selected these lines by Eric Pankey:

> Contact and intersection, a communion
> With the unrisen moon,

> *Trouble the sharp doubt that delves and disciplines*
> *His labor and purpose.*

River Styx appears 3 times a year. The editors describe it as 90 pgs., digest-sized with b&w cover. They accept less than 10% of 500 mss received a year. **Sample postpaid: $7. Reading period September 1 through October 31. Guidelines available for SASE. Pays $8 a page plus 2 copies. Buys one-time rights. Submit "legible copies with name, address on each page." Reports in 1 week to 2 months, publication within a year.** Editor sometimes comments on rejections.

RIVERRUN (II), Glen Oaks Community College, Centreville MI 49032-9719, phone (616)467-9945, ext. 277, founded 1977, poetry editor Harvey Gordon, is a literary biannual, using **30-40 magazine-sized pages of poetry in each issue—"no prejudices. We would like to receive more formal verse."** As a sample, the editor chose these lines from "The Trek for the Christmas Tree" by Gary J. Whitehead:

> *Return strides leave a track*
> *like a wounded running buck, a*
>
> *bloodless trail of prints in the night,*
> *divergent, hurried, and intent on*
> *coming to that place where the burden*
> *drops, that place ending in light.*

They have a print run of 600. **Sample postpaid: $4.** They receive 500-600 poems/year, use "as much as possible," have a 6- to 12-month backlog. **Reports immediately, except from June 15 through September 15. Reads submissions September 15 through June 15 only. Pays 2 copies.**

RIVERWIND (II, IV-Regional), General Studies, Hocking College, Nelsonville OH 45764, phone (614)753-3591, ext. 2375, founded 1982, poetry editor C.A. Dubielak, is a literary annual publishing mainly writers from Appalachia. They want **"work from serious writers. We are most open to work with serious content, though humor may be the vehicle. Do not want to see poetry from those who view it as a 'hobby.' We have not published limericks."** They have published poetry by Naton Leslie, Gloria Ruth, Charles Semones, Walter McDonald, John Haines, John Aber, James Riley and Greg Anderson. *Riverwind* is 6×9, flat-spined, 80 pgs., typeset, offset, with 2-color semiglossy card cover. Of 500 poems received they accept approximately 60. Press run is 500. Per issue: $2.50. **Sample back issue: $1 postpaid. Pays 2 copies. Submit batches of 3-5, no previously published poems, no simultaneous submissions. Reads submissions September 15 through June 15 only. Reports in 1-4 months. Response slow during summer months.** Editor comments "particularly if we would like to see more of that person's work." Reviews books of poetry. They hope to begin publishing chapbook collections.

ROANOKE REVIEW (II), Roanoke College, Salem VA 24153, phone (703)389-2351, ext. 367, founded 1968, poetry editor Robert R. Walter, is a semiannual literary review which uses **poetry that is "conventional; we have not used much experimental or highly abstract poetry."** They have published poetry by Peter Thomas, Norman Russell, Alan Seaburg, Mary Balazs and Irene Dayton. *RR* is 6×9, 52 pgs., professionally printed with matte card cover with decorative typography, using 25-30 pgs. of poetry in each issue, circulation 250-300, 150 subscriptions of which 50 are libraries. They receive 400-500 freelance submissions of poetry/year, use 40-60, have a 3- to 6-month backlog. Subscription: $5.50. **Sample postpaid: $3. Submit original typed mss, no photocopies. Reports in 8-10 weeks. No pay.** The editor advises, "There is a lot of careless or sloppy writing going on. We suggest careful proofreading and study of punctuation rules."

THE ROCKFORD REVIEW; TRIBUTARY (II, IV-Membership, regional), P.O. Box 858, Rockford IL 61105, *The Rockford Review*, founded 1971, editor David Ross, is an annual publication of the Rockford Writers Guild, **publishing their poetry and prose, that of other writers throughout the country and contributors from other countries.** "We look for the magical power of the words themselves, a playfulness with language in the creation of images and fresh insights on old themes, whether it be poetry, satire or fiction." They have recently published Liz Newall, Christine Swanberg and Olivia Diamond. As a sample the editor selected these lines by Richard Calisch:

> *I will not dance with you tonight, Ms. Death,*
> *although I'm tempted, I admit.*
> *Your grave, grey eyes, your sleepy smile,*
> *inviting arms and promises*
> *will certainly entice me to the floor another time.*

It is digest-sized, 92 pgs., flat-spined, glossy cover with b&w photos. Circulation 750. Price per issue $6; subscription $10 (2/year). **Reports in 4-6 weeks. Considers simultaneous submissions. Pays 1 copy. Acquires first North American serial rights.** They offer Editor's Choice Prizes of $50 for prose, $50 for poetry. They also desktop publish triquarterly for the *Tributary*, 24 pages of poetry and very short prose featuring a reader poll to select the best work which wins a

$25 prize each edition. **Poetry not accepted for** *Rockford Review* **is automatically considered for** *Tributary*, **or poets may submit separately.**

ROCKY MOUNTAIN REVIEW OF LANGUAGE AND LITERATURE (IV-Membership, translations), Boise State University English Dept., Boise ID 83725, phone (208)385-1246, founded 1947, poetry editor Rena Sanderson. **Contributors to the literary quarterly must be members of Rocky Mountain Modern Language Association. Poetry should be "generally relatively short," but otherwise they will consider anything but "bad poetry."** The review has published poetry by Scott P. Sanders and translations of Antonio Cisneros and David Huerta. The 6 × 9, 276-page, flat-spined quarterly publishes work of interest to college and university teachers of literature and language; **poetry may be in English or other modern languages. Contributors are not paid and do not receive extra copies; subscription is part of RMMLA membership. Poets should submit 2 copies,** *without author's name*. **They report on submissions in 1-2 months and publish usually within 6 months but no more than 1 year after acceptance.** Circulation of the review is 1,100-1,200, all membership subscriptions. They accept a few ads from other journals and publishers.

THE ROLLING COULTER (II, IV-Religious, rural), Messiah College, Grantham PA 17027, phone (717)766-2511 (ext. 7026), founded 1988, editors William Jolliff and Harold Arnett, appears twice a year. **"We look for poetry that is not necessarily religious but which shows some evidence of being informed by a religious world-view. We're open to most forms, but work in traditional forms must be especially good to be printable. We don't want to see greeting card, calendar or bulletin cover stuff."** They have recently published poetry by Jeff Gundy, Jean Janzen and Ed Zahniser. As a sample the editor selected these lines from "Kansas Blueprint, 1874" by Barbara Seaman:

> *First find a hill that will be*
> *a good neighbor and claim it*
> *as your own. To add a dugout*
> *subtract everything that isn't*
> *a roof, three walls, a floor.*
> *Remember, sweat equals space*
> *so dig hard as a bone is hard*

The Rolling Coulter is digest-sized, 40-60 pgs., laser printed with glossy card cover. It features poems one to a page, and the work of well-knowns is placed alongside poems by lesser lights. Their press run is 400 with 100+ subscriptions. "We distribute to libraries at religious colleges, with or without charge." Subscription: $6/2 issues. **Sample postpaid: $3. Pays 1 copy. Acquires all rights. Returns rights after publication. "Mention us as first publisher in subsequent uses." Reports in 6-12 weeks. "We respond slowly in summer." Editor occasionally comments on rejections on request.** They say, "There's really no substitute for becoming familiar with a magazine before submitting work. We get in lots of work that we can enjoy reading, but far less that we can use. Tremendous variety exists in the little magazine scene, and poets should celebrate that fact by doing more reading of what is being written and published right now, *in addition to* what has been anthologized for their college courses. **We would like to receive more work on agrarian subjects and themes."**

THE ROMANTIST (IV-Fantasy/horror/science fiction), Saracinesca House, 3610 Meadowbrook Ave., Nashville TN 37205, phone (615)226-1890, poetry editor Steve Eng, founded 1977, is a "literary magazine of nonfiction articles on fantasy, horror and romantic literature, using **lyrical poetry — prefer fantasy and horror content. No homespun, gushy, trite verse with forced rhyme."** They have published poetry by Donald Sidney-Fryer, Joey Froehlich, Stephanie Stearns and Gary William Crawford. The annual is magazine-sized, press run 300 numbered copies for 150 subscriptions of which 50 are libraries. **Sample postpaid: $10. Contributors may purchase a copy for 50% of its price. They receive tear sheets. Submit no more than 3 poems at a time, double-spaced. Reports in 1 month. Editor sometimes comments on rejections.** He says, "Too much contemporary poetry is easy to write and hard to read. We resist the depressed, carefully jaded tone so often fashionable. We prefer lyric verse that reflects some knowledge of traditions of poetry, though we do not require the slavish adherence to any school."

ALWAYS submit a ms or query with a self-addressed, stamped envelope (SASE) within your country or a self-addressed envelope and International Reply Coupons (IRCs) purchased from the post office for other countries.

ROPE BURNS (IV-Themes), Working Cowboy, P.O. Box 35, Gene Autry OK 73436, founded 1987, editor Bobby Newton, is "basically a bimonthly western heritage event publication with stories, poetry, etc. related to working cowboys. I like to publish poems and stories about the average old cowboy, some good, some bad, but they must have thought it was good if they took time to send it." As a sample, here is the opening of a full-page poem, "The Old Cowboy's Christmas," by Howard Norskog:

> *The cowboy woke up at the first light of day*
> *And anyone there would of heard the man say*
> *It's Christmas and time that all should relax*
> *And enjoy good tidings, now this is a fact*

Sample postpaid: 2 stamps. Pays copies. Reviews "some" books of poetry — "cowboy poetry only. Books will be returned if sufficient postage and instructions are included."

THE ROUND TABLE: A JOURNAL OF POETRY AND FICTION (II), 375 Oakdale Dr., Rochester NY 14618, phone (716)244-0623, founded 1984, poetry editors Alan Lupack and Barbara Lupack. "We publish a journal of poetry and fiction. Currently, one issue a year. **Few restrictions on poetry — except high quality. We like forms if finely crafted. Very long poems must be exceptional.**" They have published poetry by Kathleene West, John Tagliabue, Wendy Mnookin and Paul Scott. *The Round Table* is digest-sized, 64 pgs., perfect-bound, professionally printed (offset) with matte card cover. Circulation 125, for 75 subscriptions of which 3 are libraries. Subscription: $7.50 regular issue, $10 special issue. **Sample postpaid: $5. "We like to see about 5 poems (but we read whatever is submitted but only from October 1 through June 30)." Cover letter required. Simultaneous submissions OK. "But we expect to be notified if a poem submitted to us is accepted elsewhere. Quality of poetry, not format, is most important thing. We try to report in 2 months, but — especially for poems under serious consideration — it may take longer." Pays copies.** They will alternate Arthurian and general issues. "Some years we will publish a volume of Arthurian poetry by one author instead."

THE RUGGING ROOM; RUGGING ROOM BULLETIN (IV-Themes), 10 Sawmill Dr., Westford MA 01886, founded as a press in 1983, periodical in 1987, poetry editor Jeanne H. Fallier, publisher of "how-to books **related to traditional rug hooking and related subjects of interest to people in fibre crafts.**" Verses of a philosophical theme or concerning nature are acceptable if they refer to hand works, wool or fibers, the therapeutic value of hand-made fiber crafts, etc. She accepts "very short poems related to fibre arts (especially hooking) crafts — not more than ½ page." The *Rugging Room Bulletin* is a newsletter, 8-16 pgs, 8½ × 11, appearing 4 times a year, printed on white stock, with b&w illustrations, ads and graphics. Circulation 300 but widespread, coast to coast. Subscription: $11. **Sample postpaid: $2.50. Pays 3 copies plus 1-year subscription. Contributors are expected to buy 1 copy. Acquires all rights. Returns rights after publication, by arrangement. Simultaneous submissions OK. Reports within about 2 weeks.**

‡THE RUNAWAY SPOON PRESS (IV-Form), Box 3621, Port Charlotte FL 33949, phone (813)629-8045, founded 1987, editor Bob Grumman, is a "photocopy publisher of chapbooks of otherstream poetry & vizlation." He wants "**visual poetry, textual poetry mixed with visual matter, verbo-visual collages, burning poodle poetry — or anything insane. No work in which politics is more important than aesthetics.**" *RASP* has recently published poetry by Jonathan Brannen, Mimi Holmes and John Martone. As a sample the editor selected this poem by Wharton Hood:

> *the wind shifts*
> *barn swallows*

The books are about 4 × 5½, printed on good stock with matte card covers. He prints about 10 a year averaging 48 pgs. "**Query is a good idea but not necessary." Simultaneous submissions and previously published poems OK. Pays 25% of first edition of 100. Acquires all rights. Releases rights to author(s) upon publication. Sample books available for $3 apiece. Editor comments on submissions "always."** He advises, "Don't let anti-intellectuals convince you the brain is less important than the heart in poetry."

RURAL HERITAGE (I, IV-Theme), Box 516, Albia IA 52531, phone (515)932-2937, founded 1975, editors Rosemary and Allen Young, **uses poetry related to rural living, Americana, is open as to length and form.** *RH* is magazine-sized, quarterly, using b&w photos, graphics and ads, 6-8 poems/issue. Circulation 3,000. Subscription: $14. **Sample postpaid: $4.50. Guidelines available for SASE. Pays on publication 3-15¢ a word and 1 copy. Reports ASAP, 4-6 months between acceptance and publication.**

SACHEM PRESS (II, IV-Translations, bilingual), P.O. Box 9, Old Chatham NY 12136, phone (518)794-8327, founded 1980, editor Louis Hammer, a small press publisher of poetry and fiction, both hardcover and flat-spined paperbacks. **No new submissions, only statements of projects, until January 1993. Submit mss January through March.** The editor wants to see "**strong, compelling, even visionary work, English-language or translations.**" He has published poetry by Cesar Vallejo, Yannis

Ritsos, 24 leading poets of Spain (in an anthology), Miltos Sahtouris and himself. As a sample, he selected the following lines from his book **Poetry at the End of the Mind:**

> *If the only paper you had*
> *was the flesh on your back*
> *between your shoulder blades*
> *what would you write*
> *with the motion of your body?*

The paperbacks average 120 pgs. and the anthology of Spanish poetry contains 340 pgs. Each poem is printed in both Spanish and English, and there are biographical notes about the authors. The small books cost $6.95 and the anthology $11.95. **Royalties are 10% maximum, after expenses are recovered, plus 50 author's copies. Rights are negotiable.** Book catalog is free "when available," and poets can purchase books from Sachem "by writing to us, 33⅓% discount."

‡**SACRED RIVER: BAY AREA WOMEN'S JOURNAL (I, IV-Women/feminism),** P.O. Box 5131, Berkeley CA 94705, phone (510)658-2182, founded 1991, is a monthly newspaper of news and inspiration for women. They want **short feminist poetry. No poetry from men.** The editor says it is 16 pgs., tabloid-sized newsprint. They receive about 300 poems a year, use approximately 85. Press run is 10,000 for 100 subscribers; the rest placed in bookstores, cafes and health centers for women to pick up. Subscription: $18. **Sample postpaid: $2. Previously published poems and simultaneous submissions OK.** Time between acceptance and publication is 2-3 months. **Seldom comments on rejections. Reports within 3 months. Pays 1 copy "unless more are requested."** Reviews books of poetry in 200-800 words.

‡**SACRIFICE THE COMMON SENSE (I),** c/o Gomez #15, 1251 S. Magnolia Ave., Los Angeles CA 90006, founded 1989, editor Humberto Gómez Sequeira-HuGóS, is a quarterly designed "to incite freedom of thought and expression." They want **poetry that is "strange/bizarre. Any subject. Any length. Non-commercial. Nothing religious, patriotic or common."** They have recently published poetry by Sigmund Weiss, Levi Winter and Claudette Bass. As a sample the editor selected these lines from "Communication Techniques" by Paul Weinman:

> *Turtles walk cautiously where Christ*
> *stepped. They talk of peace treaties*
> *teenage titties and the stock decline.*

STCS is 44 pgs., magazine-sized, saddle-stapled, with paper cover and b&w artwork, including collages. They receive 100 poems and short stories a year, accept approximately 98%. Press run is 100. Subscription: $20. **Sample postpaid: $5. No previously published poems or simultaneous submissions. Submit up to 3 poems. Include "$3 per work submitted." Send SASE for guidelines. Reports "when magazine is published. We can't return your material or inform you of our decision." Pays 1 copy. Acquires first rights.**

ST. ANDREW PRESS (IV-Religious), Box 329, Big Island VA 24526, phone (804)299-5956, founded 1986, poetry editor Jean Horne, is a "small press publisher of religious material (worship materials, lyrics and music, etc.), **specializing in meditations, lifestyle, church renewal, spirituality, hunger, peace and justice issues."** Any form or style up to 64 lines on subjects listed. **"No profanity for shock value only; no sickeningly sweet idealism."** They say they will publish 3 chapbooks and flat-spined paperbacks, averaging 64 pgs., each year. **Submit 6 samples, bio, other publications. Simultaneous submissions, photocopies, dot-matrix, previously published poems OK. Reports in 2-4 weeks.** Payment usually $10 minimum, averages more. They will consider subsidy publishing. The editor says, "We are looking forward to doing more with poetry in the next couple of years. The amount we do will be largely determined by quality of submissions we receive."

ST. ANTHONY MESSENGER (IV-Religious), 1615 Republic St., Cincinnati OH 45210, is a monthly 56-page magazine, circulation 360,000, for Catholic families, mostly with children in grade school, high school or college. In some issues, they have a **poetry page which uses poems appropriate for their readership. Their poetry needs are very limited but poetry submissions are always welcomed.** As a sample here is "Necessity" by Catherine Curtin Fenzel:

> *I gave my gift*
> *To children of the poor—*
> *Full well aware*
> *They had the need of bread—*
> *And watched them as*
> *They hurried from the door*
> *To buy a magic*
> *Red balloon instead.*

"Submit seasonal poetry (Christmas/Easter/nature poems) several months in advance. Submit a few poems at a time; do not send us your entire collection of poetry. We seek to publish accessible poetry of high quality." Pays $2/line on acceptance. Buys first North American serial rights. Send regular SASE for guidelines and 9 × 12 SASE for free sample.

ST. JOSEPH MESSENGER AND ADVOCATE OF THE BLIND (I, IV-Religious), 541 Pavonia Ave., P.O. Box 288, Jersey City NJ 07303, phone (201)798-4141, founded 1898, poetry editor Sister Ursula Maphet, C.S.J.P, is a quarterly (16 pgs., 8 × 11), circulation 20,000, which wants "**brief but thought-filled poetry; do not want lengthy and issue-filled.**" Most of the poets they have used are previously unpublished. There are about 2 pgs. of poetry in each issue. Subscription: $5. They receive 400-500 submissions/year, use 50. **Send SASE for guidelines and free sample. Reports within 2 weeks. Pays $5-20/poem.** Editor sometimes comments on rejections.

ST. MARTIN'S PRESS, 175 5th Ave., New York NY 10010. Declined listing.

SALMAGUNDI (III), Skidmore College, Saratoga Springs NY 12866, founded 1965, edited by Peggy Boyers and Robert Boyers, has long been **one of the most distinguished quarterlies** of the sciences and humanities, publishing poets such as Robert Penn Warren, Louise Gluck, John Peck, Howard Nemerov and W.D. Snodgrass. Each issue is handsomely printed, thick, flat-spined, priced at $5-10 (**sample: $4 postpaid.**). Subscriptions are $12 a year, $18 for two years. The magazine has a paid circulation of 5,400 with 3,800 subscriptions of which about 900 are libraries. They use about 10-50 pages of poetry in each issue, receive 1,200 submissions/year, use about 20 and have a 12- to 30-month backlog. **Report in 3 months. Pays copies only.** No need to query, photocopies OK, with permission for sets of more than 5. "Submissions not accompanied by SASE are discarded."

SALT LICK; SALT LICK PRESS; SALT LICK SAMPLERS; LUCKY HEART BOOKS (II), 1909 Sunny Brook Dr., Austin TX 78723-3449, founded 1969, poetry editor James Haining, publishes "new literature and graphic arts in their various forms." They have published poetry by Robert Creeley, Martha King, Susan Firer, Paul Shuttleworth, Wm. Hart, Robert Slater, Gerald Burns and Sheila Murphy. The magazine-sized journal, 48 pgs., saddle-stapled, matte cover, experimental graphics throughout, appears irregularly, print run of 1,500. They receive 400-600 poems/year, use 1-2%. **Sample postpaid: $5. Reports in 1-6 weeks. Pays copies.** To submit for book publication under the Lucky Heart Books imprint, send 20 samples, cover letter "open." Simultaneous submissions, photocopies, dot-matrix OK. Pays copies.

SAN DIEGO POET'S PRESS; LA JOLLA POET'S PRESS; AMERICAN BOOK SERIES (II), P.O. Box 8638, La Jolla CA 92038. San Diego Poet's Press, a nonprofit press founded 1981 by editor/publisher Kathleen Iddings, has published collections and anthologies that include Galway Kinnell, Carolyn Kizer, Allen Ginsberg, Carolyn Forche, Tess Gallagher and Robert Pinsky, among others. Iddings began publishing individual poets in 1985 and has published approximately 20 poets to date. In 1989, she originated the "American Book Series" wherein she awards the winner $500 and publishes his/her first book of poetry. Past winners are Joan LaBombard, Regina McBride and Charles Atkinson. As a sample she selected these lines from "More Blessed to Receive" in Charles Atkinson's book **The Only Cure I Know**:

> More than anything I care for you
> *she said over the sink, and then*
> *I knew all the times I couldn't hear.*
> *It made me smile and start to cry.*
> *I cried into the waffle mix,*
> *in front of my children looking up*
> *asking why a man cries about waffles.*
> *What could be more perfect*
> *than arms around my neck*
> *and small ones clutching my knees?*
> *I couldn't give the love away*
> *and for once I didn't try.*

For either press send 6-10 pgs. of poetry, cover letter, bio and SASE. The "American Book Series" winner will be selected from work submitted to her presses throughout the year. **Sample of winning book: $11.50. Send SASE for guidelines.**

SAN FERNANDO POETRY JOURNAL; KENT PUBLICATIONS, INC.; CERULEAN PRESS (MINI ANTHOLOGY SERIES), (I, IV-Social issues, anthologies), 18301 Halsted St., Northridge CA 91325, founded 1978, poetry editors Richard Cloke, Shirley Rodecker and Lori Smith (and, for the Mini Anthology Series, Blair H. Allen, 9651 Estacia Court, Cucamonga CA 91730). *San Fernando Poetry Journal* uses **poetry of social protest.** According to Richard Cloke, "Poetry, for us, should be *didactic in the Brechtian sense. It must say something, must inform, in the tenor of our time.* We follow Hart

Crane's definition of poetry as architectural in essence, building upon the past but incorporating the newest of this age also, including science, machinery, sub-atomic and cosmic physical phenomena as well as the social convulsions wrenching the very roots of our present world." **Send SASE for guidelines which explain this more fully.** For example, we quote this passage for its general usefulness for poets: "In some, the end-line rhyming is too insistent, seeming *forced;* in others the words are not vibrant enough to give the content an arresting framework. Others do not have any beat (cadence) at all and some are simply not well thought out—often like first drafts, or seem like prose statements. Please try reworking again to get some energy in your statement. If your poetry is to succeed in impelling the reader to act, it must electrify, or at least command interest and attention." **They welcome new and unpublished poets.** As a sample the editor selected this poem, "Paradise Lost," by Marian Steele:

> Adam trod the earth enraptured
> When he was nearly alone on a younger land.
> His name was Muir . . . Bartram . . . Burroughs . . .
>   Audubon.
> It was not so long ago.
> We have seen to it;
> Whether in Saudi desert,
> Flaming Brazilian rain forest,
> In Detroit's blighted back streets
> Or South Bronx alleyways,
> In the belches from redbrick smokestack,
> Recoilless rifle, naval Big Gun,
> Or even Three-Mile-Island-Chernobyl—
> We have remodeled our planet
> In our own image.

The flat-spined quarterly, photocopied from typescript, uses 100 pgs. of poetry in each issue, circulation 400, 350 subscriptions of which 45 are libraries. They use about 300 of the 1,000 submissions (the editor rightly prefers to call them "contributions") each year. **Sample postpaid: $2.50. No specifications for ms form. Simultaneous submissions OK. Reports in 1 week. Pays copies.** The press, under its various imprints, also publishes a few collections by individuals. **Query with 5-6 pgs. of samples. For the Mini Anthology Series, query Blair Allen at the address above.**

SAN JOSE STUDIES; CASEY MEMORIAL AWARD (II), San Jose State University, San Jose CA 95192, phone (408)924-4476, founded 1975, poetry editor O.C. Williams. This "journal of general and scholarly interest, featuring critical, creative and informative writing in the arts, business, humanities, science and social sciences" uses poetry of **"excellent quality—no kinds excluded. Tend to like poems with something to say, however indirectly it may be communicated. Usually publish 7-12 pgs. of verse in each issue. We like to publish several poems by one poet—better exposure for the poet, more interest for the reader."** They have published poetry by Leonard Nathan, lyn lifshin and James Sutherland-Smith. As a sample the editor chose these lines from "Mountain Woman" by Virginia de Araújo:

> . . . But place in her is deep root:
> hand, brain, nerve, tooth. Planted, she will
> spill upward in fern fronds, tight buds and fists.
> Overhead, winter and summer secretly will move,
> and she remain planted in true place.

SJS appears thrice yearly in a 6×9, flat-spined, 100+ pg. format, professionally printed, matte card cover, using b&w photos, circulation of 400-450 of which 70-75 are libraries. They receive about 120 submissions/year, use 8-10 authors, have a 2-year backlog. Single copy: $5; subscription: $12 individuals, $18 institutions. **Sample postpaid: $4. No simultaneous submissions. Reports in 4-6 weeks. Pays 2 copies. Annual award of a year's subscription for best poetry printed that year and a Casey Memorial Award of $100 for the best contribution in prose or poetry.** O.C. Williams comments, "Poetry is both an art and a craft; we are not interested in submissions unless the writer has mastered the craft and is actually practicing the art."

‡SANDBERRY PRESS; DE BROSSE, REDMAN, BLACK & CO. LTD. (IV-Ethnic/nationality, regional), P.O. Box 507, Kingston 10, Jamaica, West Indies, founded 1986, managing director Pamela Mordecai, publishes 3 paperbacks and 3 hardbacks/year. **They want to see work from "poets born in the Caribbean or naturalized citizens of a Caribbean country or poets who have lived most of their lives in the region. Nothing racist, sexist or pornographic."** They have recently published collections by Edward Baugh and Dennis Scott. As a sample the director selected this poem, "The Shoemaker," from **Loggerhead** by Gloria Escoffery:

> I awake to the gift of blue sight
> making the world a blue place,

> *full of flowers.*
> *The lily in my backyard gleams through a haze*
> *of smoke.*
> *In the morning the wind rises,*
> *blowing in at my doorway many customers*
> *and one old saying:*
> *"Every fool knows that a man's foot*
> *is nobler than his shoe."*

"Previously published poems may form part of a ms submission" but no simultaneous submissions. Often comments on rejections. Replies to queries in 1 month, to mss in 6 months. Pays 10% royalties, $100 (US) advance and 10 author's copies. Inquire about sample books.

‡**SANDPIPER PRESS (V)**, P.O. Box 286, Brookings OR 97415, phone (503)469-5588, founded 1979, is a small press publisher of large print books. They have published **Poems From the Oregon Sea Coast; Unicorns for Everyone**, which includes some poetry; and **Walk With Me**, a book of prayers and meditations. However, they **currently do not accept unsolicited poetry.**

‡**SANSKRIT (I)**, Cone Center, UNCC, Charlotte NC 28223, phone (704)547-2326, founded 1965, editor Christy Beatty, is a literary annual using **poetry. "No restrictions as to form or genre, but we do look for maturity and sincerity in submissions. Nothing trite or sentimental. And no haiku."** They have published poetry by Anthony Abbott and Scott Owens. As a sample the editor selected these lines by Phyllis Gussler:

> *December broke your shins and blew*
> *pneumonia deep into your lungs.*
> *I drowned you in sour jokes until,*
> *like jetsam, your skeleton surfaced.*

Their purpose is "to encourage and promote beginning and established artists and writers." It is 9 × 12, 60-65 pgs. flat-spined, printed on quality matte paper with heavy matte card cover. Press run: 3,500 for about 100 subscriptions of which 2 are libraries. **Sample postpaid: $6. Pays 1 copy. Submit no more than 5 poems. Simultaneous submissions OK. Reads submissions September through October only. Reports in 6-8 weeks. Editor comments on submissions "infrequently."**

SANTA MONICA REVIEW (III), 1900 Pico Blvd., Santa Monica CA 90405, founded 1988, poetry editor Jim Krusoe, appears twice a year. Write for further information.

SANTA SUSANA PRESS (V), CSU Libraries, 18111 Nordhoff St., Northridge CA 91330, phone (818)885-2271, founded 1973, a small press publisher of limited edition fine print books, history, literature and art, some poetry, all hardcover editions. **They do not accept freelance submissions of poetry. Poets should query first, and queries will be answered in 2 weeks. Honorariums paid depend on grant money.** The press has published books by George Elliott, Ward Ritchie and Ray Bradbury. Book catalog is free on request; prices are high. For instance, **Reaching: Poems by George P. Elliott**, illustrated, is published in an edition of 350 numbered copies at $35 and 26 lettered copies at $60.

SATURDAY EVENING POST (IV-Humor), 1100 Waterway Blvd., Indianapolis IN 46202, phone (317)636-8881, founded 1728 as the *Pennsylvania Gazette*, since 1821 as *The Saturday Evening Post*, Post Scripts editor Steve Pettinga, P.O. Box 567, Indianapolis IN 46206. *SEP* is a general interest, mass circulation monthly with emphasis on preventive medicine, using **"humorous light verse only. No more than 100 words per poem. Stay away from four-letter words and sexually graphic subject matter. No experimental verse (haiku, etc.) Morally, the *Post* is an anachronism of the early 50s; most of its readers are elderly. Other than that, anything goes, as long as it's in good taste."** Payment is $15 for all rights.

SATURDAY PRESS, INC.; EILEEN W. BARNES AWARD SERIES; INVITED POETS SERIES (V, IV-Women), Box 884, Upper Montclair NJ 07043, phone (201)256-5053, founded 1975, poetry editor Charlotte Mandel with guest editors for contest which have included Maxine Kumin, Colette Inez, Sandra M. Gilbert, Geraldine C. Little and Rachel Hadas. "Saturday Press, Inc., is a nonprofit literary organization. The press has a **special—though not exclusive—commitment to women's poetry, and by sponsoring the Eileen W. Barnes Award Competition for first books by women over 40 seeks to offer opportunity for new poets who have delayed their writing careers. The ms is selected by means of open competition or, in alternate years, by editorial board decision. Query for current information.** Not an annual event, the contest is widely posted when announced. The Invited Poets Series offers publication to established or less-known poets. We want **authoritative craft, strong, fresh imagery, sense of imagination and a good ear for syntax, sounds and rhythms. Language should lead the reader to experience**

a sense of discovery. Any form, content or style, but do not want polemic, jingles or conventional inspiration." They have published books of poetry by Colette Inez, Janice Thaddeus, Jean Hollander, Anne Carpenter, Anneliese Wagner, Charlotte Mandel, Geraldine C. Little, Dixie Partridge and Doris Radin. As a sample the editor chose these lines from Dixie Partridge's "The Circle Back: Fish Ladder at Bonneville Dam":

> The fish flagellate a slow, desperate course
> past us, our hands on thick glass
> feeling for some pulse of movement
> that doesn't come. Mouths suctioned
> to the panes, eel-like lamprey
> give us a throat view, hang on.

"We are fully committed at present." Query first. Enclose 1-3 samples and minimum summary of publications. Replies to queries in 2 weeks. If invited, book ms may be photocopied; simultaneous submission OK. No dot-matrix. "Prefer no binder, simple folder or paper clip." Pays 25-50 copies and possible honorarium ("depends on grants"). Send SASE for catalog to buy samples.

SCARP (II), School of Creative Arts, University of Wollongong, P.O. Box 1144, Wollongong, New South Wales, Australia 2500, phone (042)270985, founded 1982, editor Ron Pretty, "is a small press publisher of poetry, prose fiction and new art. *Scarp* also contains articles and reviews. Both new and established writers are encouraged to contribute." It appears twice a year. "Not restricted by genre or form or subject matter or style or purpose, however we would prefer not to publish anything of an epic length." They have recently published poetry by Marvin Bell, Bruce Beaver, John Millet, Shane McAuley and Debbie Westbury. As a sample the editor selected these lines by Lauren Williams:

> After the reading I watch
> young male poets in rasta berets
> pant after her, old male poets
> pay serious attention to her
> opinions.

Scarp is 64-80 pgs., A4 landscape format, perfect-bound, card cover, b&w graphics, some (mainly local) ads. There's a different flavor to poetry down under, but it is still mostly free verse bordering sometimes on what US poets would call the avant garde. Other poems are well-crafted and accessible, and the magazine is an odd rectangular shape but handsome and artistically designed. "*Scarp 19* received about 800 poems from 100+ contributors. We published 17 poems from these." Press run: 1,000 for approximately 300 subscriptions of which 50 are libraries. Some shelf sales. Subscription: $24/4 issues. Sample postpaid: $6. Send SASE for guidelines. Pays $20 (Aust.) plus 2 copies and 2-year subscription. Buys first Australian rights only. Subscription encouraged but not required. No more than 5 poems/submission. Poems previously unpublished in Australia OK. Reads submissions January through March and July through September only. Editor comments on submissions. Reviews books of poetry in 100-500 words, single or multi-book format. He says, "We're looking for poetry and prose that leaps off the page at you, and that usually means there's a lot of life in the language."

SCAT! (I, II), Innis College, 2 Sussex Ave., Toronto, Ontario M5S 1J5 Canada, founded 1982, editors Claire Thompson, Hannah Lee, Aub Glazer and Keven Daniels, is an annual, with "dedication to new, wordy, smart poetry, any length, sure of speed and delivery, get to the point! Believe that 'It's all in the delivery.' Disdain for Blakean tragedies being writtten in the 1990s. Poet must be aware of the time and thought s/he's writing in." They have published poetry by Brian Burke, Robbie Newton Drummond and Debbie Ferst. As a sample the editors selected these lines from "The Altar" by Jonathan Hyman:

> It is night, wind
> and we storm together.
> There is nothing that binds
> like fury, nothing as quiet as air,
> The other corners
> are sunlit,
> holy.

They sent no sample and give no indication of its price or format or terms of publication, but the editors say they comment "occasionally."

SCAVENGER'S NEWSLETTER; KILLER FROG CONTEST (IV-Science fiction/fantasy/horror), 519 Ellinwood, Osage City KS 66523-1329, may seem an odd place to publish poems, but its editor, Janet Fox, uses 3-4 every month. The *Newsletter* is a 32-page booklet packed with news about science fiction and horror publications and printed at a quick printing shop. Janet prefers sf/fantasy/horror poetry and will read anything that is offbeat or bizarre. Writing-oriented poetry is occasionally accepted but avoid "Oh poor pitiful me" themes. **Poetry is used as filler so it must be 10 lines or under.** Recently published poets include S.R. Compton, Wendy Rathbone, Tom C. Armstrong and steve sneyd. As a sample she selected this poem by Daryl Nielsen:

> *loaded pistol*
> > *nice boy sips and ponders*
> > > *who'll be first*

Janet Fox says, "While I maintain the genre orientation of *SCAV*, I still try to leave some leeway for experimentation. A poem doesn't have to be totally lucid for me to like it, but there does need to be some sort of internal cohesiveness." She has around 760 subscribers. Subscription: $12.50/year; $6.25/6 months. **Sample copy plus guidelines for $2; guidelines alone for SASE. Response: 1 month or less. "I like poems with sharp images and careful craftsmanship." At last report was "accepting about 1 out of 10 poems submitted." You can use photocopy, dot-matrix, multiple submissions, simultaneous submissions (if informed) — even reprints if credit is given. Reads submissions all year "except for occasional overstock." No need to query. Pays $2 on acceptance plus one copy. Buys one-time rights.** Reviews sf/fantasy/horror chapbooks, books and magazines only. "I hold an annual 'Killer Frog Contest' for horror so bad or outrageous it becomes funny. There is a category for horror poetry. Has been opening April 1, closing July 1 of each year. Prizes $25 each in four categories: poetry, art, short stories and short short stories, plus the 'coveted' Froggie statuette." The last contest had no entry fee but entrants wanting the anthology pay $2.50 postpaid. Winners list for SASE.

SCIENCE FICTION POETRY ASSOCIATION; STAR*LINE (IV-Science fiction); THE RHYSLING AN-THOLOGY (V), 2012 Pyle Rd., Schenectady NY 12303, for membership information. **For poetry submissions:** Margaret Simon, 1412 NE 35th St., Ocala FL 32670. Founded 1978, the Association publishes *Star*Line*, a bimonthly newsletter and poetry magazine. The Association also publishes **The Rhysling Anthology,** a yearly collection of nominations from the membership "for the best SF/fantasy long and short poetry of the preceding year," along with a cassette tape anthology and a Science Fiction Poetry Handbook. The magazine has recently published poetry by Bruce Boston, Thomas Disch, Denise Dumars, John M. Ford, Robert Frazier, W. Gregory Stewart and David Kopsaka-Merkel. As a sample they selected this poem, "Farewell," by Steve Eng:

> *A million melting moons drip*
> > *Silver down the sky,*
> > *And spatter lunar madness in your eye.*
> *Your brain becomes a moon-ship*
> > *Voyaging up high —*
> > *So wave your Earth-bound sanity goodbye.*

They have 200 subscribers (1 library) paying $10 for 6 issues/year (**sample: $1.50 postpaid**). **Submissions to** *Star*Line* **only.** They receive 200-300 submissions/year and use about 80 — mostly short (under 50 lines). They are **"open to all forms — free verse, traditional forms, light verse — so long as your poetry shows skilled use of the language and makes a good use of science fiction, science, fantasy, horror or speculative motifs." Reports in a month, likes 3-5 poems/submission, typed, photocopy OK, dot-matrix "difficult but not refused," no simultaneous submissions, no queries. Pays $1 for first 10 lines, 5¢/line thereafter, plus copy. Buys first North American serial rights.** Reviews books of poetry "within the sf/fantasy field" in 50-500 words. The digest-sized magazines and anthologies are saddle-stapled, photocopied, with numerous illustrations and decorations. A copy of **The Rhysling Anthology** is $2.50.

‡SCOP PUBLICATIONS, INC. (II), Box 376, College Park MD 20740, phone (301)422-1930, founded 1977, president Stacy Tuthill, publishes approximately 2 paperbacks/year as well as an occasional anthology. They want **"book-length manuscripts. No restrictions as to length or form but want well-crafted modern poetry with vivid imagery and skillful use of language with regard to sense impressions and fresh insights."** They have recently published poetry by Ann Darr, Linda Pastan, Barbara Lefcowitz and Elizavietta Ritchie. Interested poets should **query with sample poems. Cover letter should include a short biography and recent credits. Previously published poems and simultaneous submissions OK. Replies to queries in 6 weeks, to mss in 2-3 months. Seldom comments on rejections. Pays copies. For sample book, send $5.** The press occasionally holds contests. Watch for advertisements in national publications.

SCORE MAGAZINE; SCORE CHAPBOOKS AND BOOKLETS (IV-Form), 491 Mandana Blvd., #3, Oakland CA 94610, poetry editors Crag Hill, Laurie Schneider and Bill DiMichele, is a "small press publisher of **visual poetry** in the magazine *Score*, booklets, postcards and broadsides. They want **"Poetry which melds language and the visual arts such as concrete poetry; experimental use of language, words and letters — forms. The appearance of the poem should have as much to say as the text. Poems on any subject; conceptual poetry; poems which use experimental, non-traditional methods to**

communicate their meanings." They don't want "traditional verse of any kind—be it free verse or rhymed." They have published poetry by Stephen-Paul Martin, Bruce Andrews, Karl Kempton, Larry Eigner and Bern Porter. They say that it is impossible to quote a sample because "some of our poems consist of only a single word — or in some cases no recognizable words." We strongly advise looking at a sample copy before submitting if you don't know what visual poetry is. *Score* is 18-40 pgs., magazine-sized, offset, saddle-stapled, using b&w graphics, 2-color matte card cover, appearing once a year in a press run of 200 for 25 subscriptions (6 of them libraries) and about 40 shelf sales. Sample psotpaid: $6. Send SASE for guidelines. Pays 2 copies. Photocopies OK "as long as strong black." No simultaneous submissions. Previously published poems OK "if noted." For chapbook consideration send entire ms. No simultaneous submissions. Pay 8-16 copies of the chapbook. Almost always comments on rejections. They subsidy publish "if author requests it."

‡SCRATCH (II, IV-Translations), 24 Nelson St., York Y03 7NJ England, founded 1989, editor Mark Robinson, appears 3 times a year using poetry, some prose, reviews (mainly books/chapbooks, some magazines) and some b&w graphics. As for poetry, the editor says "We tend to the gritty, but mix styles, tones and subjects." They have recently published poetry by Adrian Mitchell, Helen Dunmore and Pia Tafdrup (in translation). As a sample the editor selected the opening lines from "3:00pm Elegy" by Ian Robinson:

> Do you remember yesterday? It seems to us
> to have had a distinctive resonance quite its own.
> But now we're indissolubly here, positioned at just
> this little hole in the map, and all we can do
> is to make uncertain shapes out of the darkness.

Scratch is 40 pgs., A5 (5¹¹/₁₆ × 8¼), saddle-stapled with card cover. Single copy: £1.50 ($4); subscription: £4 ($12). No previously published poems or simultaneous submissions. Seldom comments on rejections. Reports in 2-3 weeks. Pays 2 copies. The editor says, "Translations of younger poets especially welcome. Insufficient IRCs (a common U.S. failing) irk!"

SCREAM OF THE BUDDHA; BUDDHA ROSE PUBLICATIONS; CRYPTIC WHITE PRESS (I), P.O. Box 548, Hermosa Beach CA 90254, phone (213)543-3809, founded 1988, publisher Dr. Scott Shaw, editor Elliot Sebastian: "We want to see poetry that screams; be it: erotic, mystical, streetwise or religious. Any form, length or subject matter. We don't want to read rhyming boring love junk; unless there is a stake through the heart at the end." They have published poetry by Charles Bukowski, Scott Shaw (their publisher), James F. Spezze III and Hae Won Shin. As a sample the editor selected these lines (poet unidentified):

> I drink a glass of suicide
> redemption in a cup
> a lady she lays next to me
> I do not know her name

It is about 16 pgs., 8½ × 11, photocopied and side-stapled, with paper cover. They accept about 1% of 8,000 poems received/year. Press run 400 for 45 subscribers of which 2 are libraries. Subscription: $25. Sample: $5. Pays up to 5 copies. Acquires all rights. "Simultaneous submissions OK; who knows, anyway. Poetry written on napkins is fine. The freer the better. If it screams, it is in. We here do not judge what it screams about. Report on submissions one day to one month." Editor often includes candid comments with rejections. Reviews books of poetry in approximately 100 words, multi-book format. Buddha Rose Publications and Cryptic White Press are imprints for publication of flat-spined paperbacks, chapbooks and hardbacks. For book consideration, "It is not important to us if poets were previously published. For then, how does one begin. Send entire ms. Queries tell one little." Pays 15% royalties plus varied number of copies. Buys all rights. The editor says, "Buddha Rose Publications accepts no subsidized work. It is involved in the publication of mystical, poetic, philosophic, modern novels, and cultural studies type of work. It is the parent organization of *Scream of the Buddha* and Cryptic White Press." Submissions to Buddha Rose must be "meaningful. Cryptic White Press, on the other hand, is far more open, as it does not have to hold the entire financial responsibility of any publishable work."

‡SEANCE (I, IV-Erotica, humor), 171 Third Ave., New York NY 10003, founded 1992, editor-in-chief Karen Tom, is "a magazine that will shock and leave people with their mouths opened, begging for more." It appears approximately every 2 months. They want "confessional poetry, erotica or anything with feeling and power—or humor." They do not want "traditional poetry or work that seems like it can be churned out by the ton. No predictable work." The editor says it is digest-sized, with photography and illustrations. Press run is 100. Subscription: $15. Sample postpaid: $3. Previously published poems and simultaneous submissions OK. Requires a $3 reading fee "for all the work you want to send." Time between acceptance and publication is "a few months." Always comments on

rejections. **Reports in 1 week to 2 months. Pays 1 copy. Author retains rights.**

SEATTLE REVIEW (II), Padelford Hall, GN-30, University of Washington, Seattle WA 98195, phone (206)543-9865, founded 1978, poetry editor Colleen McElroy, appears in the fall and spring using **"contemporary and traditional" poetry.** They have published poetry by William Stafford, Tess Gallagher, Marvin Bell and Walter McDonald. As a sample the editor selected these lines from "Car Mechanic Blues" by Jan Wallace:

> He lords his wrench over me like
> a magic wand. His ease with grease, the way
> he calms the speeding idle should convince
> me, this man's got the power. He wants
> to show me how the sparks fire. I say,
> No thanks, I'll get the book.

It is professionally printed, flat-spined, 110+ pgs., with glossy card cover. Press run 800 for 250 subscribers of which 50 are libraries, 400 shelf sales. Subscription: $8; per issue: $4.50. **Sample postpaid: $3. Send SASE for guidelines. Reports in 1-3 months (up to 5 months for summer submissions). Pay "varies, but we do pay" plus 2 copies.** The editors offer these "practical suggestions: Cover letters with submissions do help. A cover letter provides something about the author and tells where and for what s/he is submitting. And don't let those rejection letters be cause for discouragement. Rejections can often be a matter of timing. The journal in question may be publishing a special issue with a certain theme (we've done a number of themes — 'all-fiction,' 'all-poetry,' 'Asian-American,' 'Northwest,' 'science fiction,' etc.) Also, editorial boards do change, and new editors bring their individual opinions and tastes in writing. Good poetry will eventually be published if it is circulated."

SECOND AEON PUBLICATIONS (V), 19 Southminster Rd., Roath, Cardiff CF2 S4T Wales, phone 0222-493093, founded 1966, poetry editor Peter Finch, is a "small press concerned in the main with **experimental literary works."** He has published poetry by Bob Cobbing and himself. **Pays copies. Accepts no unsolicited mss.** Editor reviews poetry as a freelancer for a broad range of publications.

SECRETS FROM THE ORANGE COUCH (I, II), Box 688, Killam, Alberta T0B 2L0 Canada, founded 1988, appears twice a year. **"We appreciate an eclectic range of styles: magic realism, traditional, experimental, deconstruction, cross-over writing etc. Above all, we insist on good quality writing."** They have recently published poetry by Bert Almon, Scott Ellis, Elizabeth Haynes and Jay Henderson. As a sample the editor selected these lines from "Crescendo" by Catherine Thys:

> music   I tell them every year
> is movement between tension
> and release

It is 48 pgs., magazine-sized, saddle-stapled, professionally printed (desktop) with matte card cover. Press run 300 for 150 subscribers of which 3 are libraries, 100-150 shelf sales. Subscription: $10 plus $2.50 postage (Canadian). **Sample postpaid: $6. Reports within 4 months. Pays $12.50 (Canadian)/published page. Buys first North American serial rights. "A brief bio would be appreciated."** Sponsors a poetry contest for long (up to 100 lines) and short (up to 48 lines) poems. Entry fee $5/entry; deadline: February 28.

SEEMS (II), P.O. Box 359, Lakeland College, Sheboygan WI 53082-0359, founded 1971, published irregularly (28 issues in 21 years). This is a handsomely printed, nearly square (7×8¼) magazine, saddle-stapled, generous with white space on heavy paper. Two of the issues are considered chapbooks, and the editor, Karl Elder, suggests that a **way to get acquainted would be to order** *Seems #14, What Is The Future Of Poetry?* **for $5,** consisting of essays by 22 contemporary poets, and "If you don't like it, return it and we'll return your $5." There are usually about 20 pages of poetry/issue. Elder has recently used poetry by Harry Brody, M.J. Echelberger, Carol Granato, Chris Halla and Robert Nagler. He said it was "impossible" to select four illustrative lines. The magazine has a print run of 350 for 200 subscriptions (20 libraries) and sells for $4 an issue (or $16 for a subscription — four issues). There is a **1- to 2-year backlog. Reports in 1-3 months. Pays copies. Acquires North American serial rights. Returns rights upon publication.**

SEGUE FOUNDATION; ROOF BOOKS; SEGUE BOOKS (V), 303 E. 8th St., New York NY 10009, phone (212)674-0199, president James Sherry, is a small press publisher of poetry, literary criticism, and film and performance texts. Most of their books are flat-spined paperbacks, some hardcover. They have published books by Jackson MacLow, Charles Bernstein, Ron Silliman and Diane Ward, but they **do not consider unsolicited mss. Query first.** The Foundation is also a distributor of a number of prestigious small press magazines and books. Write for their catalog to buy samples.

SENECA REVIEW (II, IV-Translations), Hobart and William Smith Colleges, Geneva NY 14456, phone (315)781-3349, founded 1970, editor Deborah Tall. They want **"serious poetry of any form, including translations. No light verse. Also essays on contemporary poetry."** They have published poetry by Seamus Heaney, Rita Dove, Denise Levertov, Stephen Dunn and Hayden Carruth. *Seneca Review* is 100 pgs., 6×9, flat-spined, professionally printed on quality stock with matte card cover, appearing twice a year. Of 3,000-4,000 poems received they accept approximately 100. Press run is 600 for 250 subscriptions of which half are libraries. About 50 shelf sales. Subscription: $8/year, $15/ 2 years. **Sample postpaid: $5. Pays 2 copies. They read September 1 through May 1; do not read in summer. Submit 3-5 poems. No simultaneous submissions or previously published poems. Reports in 3-10 weeks.**

SENIOR EDITION USA/COLORADO OLD TIMES (IV-Seniors, regional, themes), SEI Publishing Corporation, Suite 218, 1385 S. Colorado Blvd., Denver CO 80222-3312, phone (303)758-4040, managing editor Rose Beetem, is a monthly tabloid "Colorado newspaper **for seniors (with national distribution)** emphasizing legislation, opinion and advice columns, local and national news, features and local calendar aimed at over-55 community." They want **"usually no haiku, religious/inspirational. Subject matter often to match** *Colorado Old Times.*" Circulation 25,000. **Pays on publication. Publishes ms an average of 1-6 months after acceptance. Submit seasonal/holiday material 3 months in advance. Sample copy $1; writer's guidelines for SASE.** Senior Overlook column features **opinions of seniors about anything they feel strongly about: finances, grandkids, love, life, social problems, etc. (May be editorial, essay, prose or poetry). Buys 2-6 mss/year. Send complete ms. Length: 250-900 words. Pays $20, maximum.** Rose Beetem says, "Although we are not refusing manuscripts, the time to hear back from us has lengthened."

SENSATIONS MAGAZINE (I, IV-Membership), 2 Radio Ave., A5, Secaucus NJ 07094, founded 1987, founder David Messineo. **Subscription required before submission of material.** "*Sensations* is a literary magazine which publishes poetry, short stories and research articles about American poetry written in the 1500s and 1600s. **We'd love material dealing with contemporary issues and current or historical events. No abstract material that only the writer can understand, no minimalist stories and if it's a love poem, it should be remarkable and something others can appreciate."** As a sample, the founder selected these lines from "Friends and Other Strangers" by Angela Consolo Mankiewicz:

> *Instead of plaster, massive plates of glass*
> *pretend to be a wall; they pass me by*
> *like funhouse mirrors mocking window panes,*
> *grinning through a summer sun that snatches*
> *at my eyes and steals unanchored images.*
> *It isn't right, a hospital you see through;*
> *a hospital you see through has no shame.*
> *I need my wall. I want my yesterday,*

Sensations is magazine-sized, 50 pgs., printed on LaserWriter. **"To join and receive writer's guidelines and samples of previously published poetry, send a $3 check payable to David Messineo along with 52¢ SASE or send $7 for a sample issue. Do not send any poetry until after you've received our writer's guidelines." Simultaneous submissions OK if so indicated. New unpublished material preferred. Legible dot-matrix accepted. Reports 4-6 weeks after deadline. No complimentary copies. Acquires first serial rights.** The founder says, "All amounts raised go directly toward costs of publishing, marketing and mailing. Advice? A good writer can work as easily with meter or rhyme as with free verse. Beginning writers are advised to first work within the limitations of meter and rhyme, to help them improve their ability to choose the best words to say what they want to say in the best possible way. Read *any* magazine before sending material; throwing material into an envelope without reading the publication or samples of published material is a sure-fire way to waste your time and money." Final reminder: **"Poetry submitted by non-members will neither be read nor criticized—**we get an abundance of fine material from active magazine patrons and focus our efforts on those who financially support our magazine."

SEQUOIA (II), Storke Publications Building, Stanford CA 94305, founded 1892, poetry editor Carlos Rodriguez, appears twice a year. "We are eclectic but would especially like to see **new kinds of beautiful language. Formal/metrical work is welcome. Rhythm is important to us."** They have published poetry by Susan Howe, Seamus Heaney, Adrienne Rich, Rita Dove and James Merrill. *Sequoia* is 80-100 pgs., 6×9, professionally printed, flat-spined, with a glossy card cover with art. Their press run is 800 with 400 subscriptions, of which half are libraries. They publish a small percentage of hundreds of unsolicited submissions. Subscription: $10. **Sample postpaid: $5. Reads submissions September 15 through June 1. Reports in "2 months or more." Pays 2 copies. They do not consider simultaneous submissions or previously published poems.** The editor says, "*Sequoia* has a long tradition of encouraging 'formal' poetry. Nowadays it seems especially appropriate to remind poets that there is nothing inherently embarrassing about the craft of verse."

SEVEN BUFFALOES PRESS; AZOREAN EXPRESS; BLACK JACK; VALLEY GRAPEVINE; HILL AND HOLLER ANTHOLOGY SERIES (IV-Rural, regional, anthologies), Box 249, Big Timber MT 59011, founded 1973, editor Art Cuelho, who writes, "I've always thought that Rural and Working Class writers, poets and artists deserve the same tribute given to country singers." These publications all express that interest. For all of them Art Cuelho wants **poetry oriented toward rural and working people, "a poem that tells a story, preferably free verse, not longer than 50-60 lines, poems with strong lyric and metaphor, not romantical, poetry of the head and not the heart, not poems written like grocery lists or the first thing that comes from a poet's mind, no ivory tower, and half my contributors are women."** He has published poetry by R.T. Smith, James Goode, Leo Connellan and Wendell Berry. *The Azorean Express*, 5½×8½, 35 pgs., side-stapled, appears twice a year, circulation 200. **Sample postpaid: $5. Pays 1 copy. Reports in 1-2 weeks. Submit 4-8 poems. No simultaneous submissions.** *Black Jack* is an anthology series on Rural America that uses rural material from anywhere, especially the American West; *Valley Grapevine* is an anthology on central California, circulation 750, that uses rural material from central California. **Sample postpaid: $5.** Hill and Holler, Southern Appalachian Mountain series takes in rural mountain lifestyle and folkways. **Sample postpaid: $5. Seven Buffaloes Press does not accept unsolicited mss but publishes books solicited from writers who have appeared in the above magazines.** Art Cuelho advises, "Don't tell the editor how great you are. This one happens to be a poet and novelist who has been writing for 25 years. Your writing should not only be fused with what you know from the head, but also from what you know within your heart. Most of what we call life may be some kind of gift of an unknown river within us. The secret to be learned is to live with ease in the darkness. Because there are too many things of the night in this world, but the important clue to remember is that there are many worlds within us."

SEVENTEEN (V), 850 3rd Ave., New York NY 10022, phone (212)759-8100, founded 1944, poetry editor Robert O. Green, is a slick monthly for teenage girls, circulation 1,750,000. They publish **"all styles of poetry up to 40 lines by writers 21 and under. However, due to a large backlog, *Seventeen* can no longer accept poetry submissions."** Purchase sample ($1.75) at newsstands.

SEWANEE REVIEW; AIKEN TAYLOR AWARD FOR MODERN POETRY (III), University of the South, Sewanee TN 37375, founded 1892, thus being our nation's oldest continuously published literary quarterly, editor George Core. Each issue is a hefty paperback of nearly 200 pgs., conservatively bound in matte paper, always of the same typography. Fiction, criticism and poetry are invariably of the **highest establishment standards. Most of our major poets appear here from time to time.** They have published poetry by William Logan, Howard Nemerov and Barry Spacks. Circulation: 3,400. **Sample $5.75. Reports in 1-4 weeks. Pays 70¢/line.** The Aiken Taylor Award for Modern Poetry is awarded by *The Sewanee Review* and its publisher, the University of the South in Sewanee, TN, "for the work of a substantial and distinguished career."

SHAMAL BOOKS (IV-Ethnic, anthologies), GPO Box 16, New York NY 10116, phone (718)622-4426, founded 1976, editor Louis Reyes Rivera. Shamal Books is a small press whose purpose is **"to promote the literary efforts of African-American and Caribbean writers, particularly those who would not otherwise be able to establish their literary credentials as their concerns are with the people."** The press publishes individual and "anthological" books and chapbooks, mostly flat-spined paper texts. They have published poetry by SeKou Sundiata, Sandra Maria Esteves and Rashidah Ismaili. The editor wants to see **"poetry that clearly demonstrates an understanding of craft, content and intent as the scriptural source of the word guiding and encouraging the intellect of the people."** He does not consider freelance submissions of individual mss, but will look at work only while anthologies are open. How many sample poems should you send? "Two is cool." The cover letter should include a "leaning toward personal goals and poetic principles." The editor will reply to queries within 2 months; mss of poetry should be "neat and single-spaced." Royalties for book authors are 15%. The editor says that he will subsidy publish "delicately—depends on resources and interest in work." His projects include "an international anthology; drama; prison anthology; books on language as a weapon; a collectivized publisher's catalog of Third World presses working out of NYC." His advice to poets: "Certainly to study the craft more and to research more into the historical role that has been the hallmark of poetry across class and caste conscious lines that limit younger perspectives. Not to be as quick to publish as to be in serious study, then while looking to publish, looking as well into collective ventures with other poets for publication and distribution. Above all, *read*!"

SHARING THE VICTORY (IV-Sports, religious), 8701 Leeds Rd., Kansas City MO 64129, phone (816)921-0909, founded 1959, editor John Dodderidge, assistant editor Dana J. King, managing editor Don Hilkemeier. The monthly magazine (circulation 55,000) is published September through May by the Fellowship of Christian Athletes and uses only 2-3 poems/year. **They want free verse on themes of interest to Christian athletes (high school and college, male and female).** The assistant editor selected these sample lines by Aileen L. Myers:

> *I am more than*
> *skill and conditioning*
> *More because*
> *I am a child of a loving God,*
> *who created me in His spiritual image,*
> *loves me for myself*
> *and promises me the eternal Victory.*

Sample available for $1 with 8½ × 11 SASE (first class stamps for 3 oz.). Guidelines available free. Reads submissions July 1 through March 1 only. Reporting time is 2 weeks and time to publication averages 3-4 months. Pays $25-50. Buys first or second rights.

‡**SHATTERED WIG REVIEW (II)**, 523 E. 38th St., Baltimore MD 21218, phone (410)243-6888, founded 1988, contact Fred Engels, is a semiannual using **"liquid, messy poetry, oozing the stuff of life. No frustrated English professor poetry."** They have recently published poetry by John M. Bennett, Eel Leonard, Lyn Lifshin and Dan Raphael. As a sample the editor selected these lines by Chris Toll:

> *A 10,000-year-old white man rules the world*
> *when he needs a new heart,*
> *he murders a 16-year-old boy*
> *His tanks may rumble through the cities*
> *My crack dealers will fight back to back with my crystal healers*
> *Every cell in my body knows the new world is coming*

SHW is approximately 70 pgs., 8½ × 8½, photocopied, side-stapled with cardstock covers with original artwork and art and graphics inside. They receive about 10 submissions/week, accept about 20%. Press run is 300 for 100 subscribers of which 10 are libraries, 100 shelf sales. Subscription: $7 for 2 issues. **Sample postpaid: $4. Previously published poems and simultaneous submissions OK. Seldom comments on rejections. Reports within a month. Pays 1 copy. Acquires one-time rights.** Occasionally reviews books of poetry in 100 words. The editor says there are no requirements for contributors except "that the contributor include us in their nightly prayers."

HAROLD SHAW PUBLISHERS; WHEATON LITERARY SERIES (V), Box 567, Wheaton IL 60189, phone (708)665-6700, founded 1967, Director of Editorial Services Ramona Cramer Tucker, is "small publisher of the Wheaton Literary Series and Northcote Books, **works of Christian and literary merit** including fiction, poetry, literary criticism and original prose" in flat-spined paperback and hardback books. They have published poetry by Madeleine L'Engle, John Leax, Sister Maura Eichner and Luci Shaw. **They publish on a 10/5% royalty basis plus 10 author's copies.** They publish a volume of poetry approximately every 2 years. "Our work reflects **a Christian evangelical world-view**, though this need not be explicit. In the future we may publish an anthology, rather than single poets." **However, they are currently still not accepting poetry submissions.**

SHEILA-NA-GIG (I, II), 23106 Kent Ave., Torrance CA 90505, founded 1990, editors Hayley R. Mitchell and Kristine Sanders, appears 3 times a year, using **"all forms, styles and subject matter—length, use own discretion (don't ramble!). No religious, 'ultra' traditional, i.e. rhyming, conservative."** They have recently published poetry by Lyn Lifshin, Gerald Locklin, Kathe Burkhardt and Charles H. Webb. As a sample the editors selected these lines by Marcia Arrieta:

> *Good wives and mothers*
> *do not say "fuck"*
> *am I bad?*
> *Around my brain*
> *fly colors like abstract*
> *bodies on canvas wild*
> *moving toward obscure.*

It is digest-sized, flat-spined, 66 pgs., professionally printed, with matte b&w card cover. **Sample postpaid: $5.75. Pays copies. Acquires first rights. Reports in 6-8 weeks.** "We like to receive submissions one month prior to our respective deadlines." **Deadlines: November 1, March 1 and July 1; July 1 deadline is for women's issue only.** "We encourage new poets with new styles and a strong 'voice' and look especially for poets not afraid to speak out on issues such as: sexuality, politics, feminist issues. Looking for poetry on the edge. If in doubt, we suggest ordering a back issue. Make checks payable to Hayley R. Mitchell."

‡**SHENANDOAH (II)**, Box 722, Lexington VA 24450, phone (703)463-8765, founded 1950, managing editor Lynn Williams. Published at Washington and Lee University, it is a quarterly literary magazine which has recently published poetry by Conrad Hilberry, Martha McFerren, Robert B. Shaw, Cathy Song and Jeanne Walker. As a sample the editor chose these lines from "The Lake of the Unconscious" by Geraldine Connolly:

> *and everything was still,*
> *the deer frozen between two pines*
>
> *the way the child was caught*
> *between the two worlds, the air*
>
> *and the bottom of the lake*
> *bobbing there, amazed*

The magazine is 6×9, 100 pgs., perfect-bound, professionally printed with full-color cover. Circulation: 1,700. **All submissions should be typed on one side of the paper only. Your name and address must be clearly written on the upper right corner of the manuscript. Include SASE. Reads submissions September 1 through May 30. Reports in 3 months. Payment includes a check, one-year subscription and one free copy. Buys first publication rights. Sample postpaid: $3.50.** Reviews books of poetry in 7-10 pages, multi-book format.

‡**SHIP OF FOOLS (II); SHIP OF FOOLS PRESS (V)**, Box 1028, University of Rio Grande, Rio Grande OH 45674, founded 1983, editor Gina Pellegrino, assistant editor Jack Hart, review editor James Doubleday, is "more or less quarterly." They want **"coherent, well-written, traditional or modern, myth, archetype, love, odd and/or whimsical poetry—most types. No concrete, incoherent or greeting-card poetry."** They have recently published poetry by Rhina Espaillat, Carolyn Page, Denver Stull and T. Kilgore Splake. As a sample the editors selected these lines from "Following the Reaper" by Nancy Haas:

> *I am here again;*
> *Gathering the heads*
> *With their wide astonished eyes*
> *And the hands*
> *With their silent fluttering fingers.*

They describe *Ship of Fools* as digest-sized, saddle-stapled, offset printed with cover art and graphics. Press run is 275 for 36 subscribers of which 6 are libraries. Subscription: $7 for 4 issues. **Sample postpaid: $2. No previously published poems or simultaneous submissions. Cover letter preferred. Often comments on rejections. Reports in 2-4 weeks. "If longer than six weeks, write and ask why." Pays 1 copy.** Reviews books of poetry. Ship of Fools Press publishes chapbooks but does not accept unsolicited mss.

SHOFAR (IV-Children, ethnic, religious), 43 Northcote Dr., Melville NY 11747, founded 1984, publisher/editor Gerald H. Grayson, is a magazine **for American Jewish children 9-13**, appearing monthly October through May (double issues Dec./Jan. and April/May). It is magazine-sized, 32 pgs., professionally printed, with color paper cover. Their press run is 17,000 with 16,000 subscriptions of which 1,000 are libraries. Subscription: $14.95. **Sample free for $1.05 postage and SASE. Send SASE for guidelines. Pays $25-50/poem.** They will consider simultaneous submissions and "maybe" previously published poems. **Reports in 6-8 weeks.**

SIDESHOW MAGAZINE; SIDESHOW PRESS; CRUEL GARTERS (II), 2951 Voorheis, Waterford MI 48328, founded 1989, editor Glen Armstrong. The magazine appears once a year. **They want "experimental, surreal, language-orientated, urban, turn of the century (20th to 21st), abstract. Anything we haven't seen before. Nothing sentimental, no first person narratives in which the speaker proves his deepness and sensitivity, no nature poets, tough-guy Bukowski imitators, poems about writing poetry, blatant protest poems."** They have published poetry by Andrei Codrescu, Douglas Messerli and Shelia E. Murphy. As a sample the editor selected these lines by Russell Edson:

> *An old woman was breast-feeding herself to death. Old*
> *women's milk is hemlocked with Socratic lullabies . . .*

Sideshow is digest-sized, 40-80 pgs., professionally printed with card cover. It's a "cafe" book in the Greenwich Village style—attractively printed with illustrations/artwork and lively verse, some of which appears in different type fonts (a la *The New York Quarterly*). It consists mainly of free verse/avant-garde selections all featuring a strong voice. Press run 500. Subscription: $8. **Sample postpaid: $5. Send SASE for guidelines. Pays 1-2 copies. Reports in 1 week-6 months.** They hold occasional contests with no entrance fees. "Top prize is typically publication and something fun." *Cruel Garters* is a broadside (one sheet printed on both sides) featuring one poet's short, avant-garde work, appearing 3 times/year, with photo of author and brief bio.

"We publish literary freaks of nature," says Glen Armstrong, editor of Sideshow Magazine *along with Nancy A. Brosky. "I jokingly suggested all future covers should show infants wearing fish heads. Brent Harris, our cover illustrator and art director, took me up on this in grand style,"* he says. *"The illustration's backdrop suggests an urban setting, and the fish-baby represents a tongue-in-cheek debauchery. The cover mirrors the writing inside quite well. Poetry is our meat and potatoes. We garnish with experimental fiction and solicited artwork."*

Payment: 10 copies. Sample: $2. "Poets should inquire, as most work will be solicited." The editor says, "We're not interested in you at all, we're interested in your work. *Sideshow* tends to be a bit Anti-Romantic. Those who have a unique way of looking beyond themselves stand a better chance with us than those who have a sincere interest in looking inward."

‡SIERRA NEVADA COLLEGE REVIEW (I), P.O. Box 4269, Incline Village NV 89450, founded 1990, editor June Sylvester, is an annual literary magazine featuring poetry and short fiction by new writers. They want **"high quality, image-oriented poems that suggest or surprise; no limit on length, style, etc. No light verse, sloppy sentiment, purposeful obscurity, clichés or cuteness."** They have recently published poetry by Marisella Veiga, Darrell G.H. Schramm, Ted Thompson and Terry Wright. As a sample the editor selected these lines from "Bee Song" by William Powley:

> and the bee's open mouth
> swallows pollen: it is love
> without mistakes,
>
> only sweetness
> in a yellow fold,
> a bee song.

The editor says *SNCR* is approximately 60 pgs., with cover art only, no ads. "We receive approximately 100-200 poems a year and accept approximately 25-35." Press run is 300. Subscription: $5/year. **Sample postpaid: $2.50. No previously published poems; simultaneous submissions OK. Include brief bio with submission. Reads submissions September 1 through April 1. Often comments on rejections. Reports in 2 weeks-2 months. Pays 1 copy.** The editor says, "We delight in publishing the unpublished or underpublished writer. We look specifically for subtlety and skill."

THE SIGNAL (II, IV-Translations), P.O. Box #67, Emmett ID 83617, phone (208)365-5812, poetry editors Joan Silva and David Chorlton, publishes "art, opinion, review, interview, exploratory short fiction, articles, essays. **Encourage scientific lit. speculation. Translations. Approach can be a little wild—but not tacky. As to poetry, no restrictions!** We want an attitude that reveals caring what goes on in our world, planet caring, people caring, clear-minded, informed opinion, sharp, questioning outlook. Do not want to see poetry that is muddled, wishy-washy, impressed with image as opposed to substance, style as opposed to passion or personal conviction." Recently published poets include Robert Peters, Wanda Coleman, Philip K. Jason, Maurice Kenny, Barbara Mor and Olga Cabral. *The Signal* is magazine-sized, 64 pgs., saddle-stapled, beautifully printed on heavy ruled stock with coated cover, using b&w photography and art. It appears twice yearly. Subscriptions are $10 a year domestically, negotiable for foreign subscriptions. **Sample postpaid: $6, $4 (back issues). Reads submissions October 1 through April 30 only. Reports in 6-12 weeks. Pays contributors' copies.** Occasionally reviews books of poetry, "but don't count on it." The editors announce a "Cup Award" in each issue for a "currently underappreciated" poet and feature work by that poet in the following issue. "*The Signal* has *no* grant, corporate or academic funding. We depend 100% on reader support. Help keep us independent."

THE SIGNPOST PRESS; THE BELLINGHAM REVIEW; 49TH PARALLEL POETRY CONTEST (II), 1007 Queen St., Bellingham WA 98226, phone (206)734-9781, founded 1975, magazine editor Susan Hilton, book editor Knute Skinner, publishes *The Bellingham Review* twice a year, runs an annual poetry competition and publishes other books and chapbooks of poetry occasionally. **"We want well-crafted poetry but are open to all styles,"** no specifications as to form. Poets they have published recently include Bruce Purkey, Amie Carbaugh, Marty Ennes, Joseph Green and James Bertolino. As a sample, Knute Skinner selected these lines by Rosalee Temple:

> *I learned navigation from a sad old ram*
> *who deserted his piss-fouled stall*
> *and led me out of our tight-fisted world*
> *to the edge of light with his complaining call.*

Each issue of the *Review* has about 38 pgs. of poetry. They have a circulation of 700 with 500 subscriptions. It is digest-sized, saddle-stapled, typeset, with art and glossy cover. **Sample postpaid: $2. Submit up to 6 pgs. Photocopy, simultaneous submissions OK. Reads submissions September 1 through June 30 only. Reports in 1-4 months. Pays 1 copy plus a year's subscription. Acquires first North American rights.** Reviews books of poetry in 500-1,000 words, single or multi-book format. Send SASE for rules for the next 49th Parallel Poetry Contest and query regarding book publication.

SILVER APPLES PRESS (V), P.O. Box 292, Hainesport NJ 08036, phone (609)267-2758, founded 1982, poetry editor Geraldine Little. "We're a very small press with very limited funds. Published our first chapbook in 1988; open contest for same. We plan to publish randomly, as things turn us on and as funds permit—pamphlets, chapbooks, a set of postcards. **We are over-committed at present. Not currently accepting unsolicited poetry submissions. Watch** *Poets & Writers* **for announcements."** They publish **"first-class poetry by experienced poets. No greeting-card verse, soupy sentimental verse or blatantly religious verse."** They have published **Contrasts in Keening: Ireland** by Geraldine C. Little, **Abandoned House** by Susan Fawcett and **The Verb to Love** by Barbara Horton. As a sample the editor selected these lines from **Keeping Him Alive** by Charlotte Mandel:

> *We do not cut it down.*
> *In winter,*
> *within the bitter scrabble*
> *of bared, practiced branches,*
> *the dead tree, too, promises.*

SILVER WINGS (IV-Religious, spirituality, inspirational), P.O. Box 1000, Pearblossom CA 93553-1000, phone (805)264-3726, founded 1983, now published by Poetry on Wings, Inc., poetry editor Jackson Wilcox. "As a committed Christian service we produce and publish a quarterly poetry magazine. **We want poems with a Christian perspective, reflecting a vital personal faith and a love for God and man. Will consider poems from 3-20 lines. Quite open in regard to meter and rhyme."** They have published poems by William T. Burke, Andrew Peterson, C. David Hay and Harriett Hunt. As a sample the editor chose "The Search" by Ruth M. Parks:

> *Where are you, Lord?*
> *I cannot see your face*
> *Among the few who stroll*
> *This holy place.*
>
> *Where are you, Lord?*
> *I cannot hear your call*
> *Above the clatter*
> *In this sacred hall,*
>
> *Where are you, Lord?*
> *I cannot feel your hand*
> *Amid the throng and press*
> *Of this encumbered land.*

The magazine is 32-36 pgs., digest-sized, offset from typescript with hand-lettered titles on tinted paper with cartoon-like art, circulation 450 with 225 subscriptions. They receive 1,000 submissions/year, use 200. **Subscription: $7. Sample: $2 postpaid. Typed mss, double-spaced. Reports in 3 weeks, providing SASE is supplied;** time to publication can be up to 2 years. **Pays $9 in subscription and copy value. Acquires first rights.** Rarely comments on rejections. "We also now have a new form which we publish: Chaplets. A Chaplet is a 10-page booklet measuring 4¼ × 5¼ with 8 poems of 20 short lines or less and a prayer of acceptance, commitment, confession, petition or thanksgiving on the inside of the back cover. We will mail one anywhere for $1. The price for two or any larger quantity will be 75¢ each postpaid. We are doing these in cooperative modest financial partnership with poets. If you have an interest, write to *Silver Wings* for details." The editor says, "If a poet has had a faith experience, share it freely from the heart, using whatever words are warm and expressive. Thus the shared message becomes a powerful communication to bless others. We are glad to look at poetry that has an uplift to it. We are Christian by design and openly ecumenical in spirit."

SILVERFISH REVIEW; SILVERFISH REVIEW PRESS (II, IV-Translations), P.O. Box 3541, Eugene OR 97403, phone (503)344-5060, founded 1979, poetry editor Rodger Moody, is an irregularly appearing digest-sized, 48-page literary magazine, circulation 750. "The only criteria for selection is **quality. In future issues** *Silverfish Review* **wants to showcase translations of poetry from Europe and Latin America** as well as continue to print poetry and fiction of quality written in English." They have published poetry by Walter McDonald, Jon Davis, Dick Allen, Ivan Arguelles, D.M. Wallace, Walter Pavlich, Ralph Salisbury, Richard Jones, Christine Zawadiwsky and Susan Cobin. As a sample the editor selected these lines by Lauren Mesa:

> This one, the tall boy with brown hair,
> the wicker creel's strap slung
> across his crest, is Great-Uncle Mickey,
> Michelangelo Cipolla, the uncle
> who dressed as Santa the years
> my mother was a child.

There are 36-48 pgs. of poetry in each issue. The magazine is professionally printed in dark type on quality stock, matte card cover with art. They receive about 1,000 submissions of poetry/year, use 20, have a 6- to 12-month backlog. Subscription for institutions: $15; for individuals: $12; per issue: $4. **Sample: $3, single copy orders should include $1 for postage and handling. Submit at least 5 poems to editor. Photocopies OK. No simultaneous submissions. Reports in 6-12 weeks. Pays 5 copies plus small honorarium when grant support permits.** Reviews books of poetry. Silverfish Review Press will consider mss for chapbook publication and conducts an annual chapbook competition with an award of $100 and 25 copies (with a press run of 750). Send SASE for rules.

SING HEAVENLY MUSE! (IV-Feminist), Box 13320, Minneapolis MN 55414, founded 1977, editor Sue Ann Martinson, fosters "the work of women poets, fiction writers and artists. The magazine is **feminist in an open, generous sense: we encourage women to range freely, honestly and imaginatively over all subjects, philosophies and styles. We do not wish to confine women to women's subjects,** whether these are defined traditionally, in terms of femininity and domesticity, or modernly, from a sometimes narrow polemical perspective. We look for explorations, questions that do not come with ready-made answers, emotionally or intellectually. **We seek out new writers, many before unpublished.** The editors try to reduce to a minimum the common bureaucratic distance between a magazine and its readers and contributors. Although our staff is small, we encourage writers by discussing their work, and we solicit comments from our readers. This relationship makes *Sing Heavenly Muse!* a community where women with widely varying interests and ideas may meet and learn from one another." For poetry they have "**no limitations except women's writing or men's writing that reflects awareness of women's consciousness.**" They have published poetry by Alexis Rotella, Jill Breckenridge and Amirh Bahati. The editor selected these sample lines from "Sons of Soweto" by June Jordan:

> Words live in the spirit of her face
> and that sound will no longer yield . . .
> she will stand under the sun!
> She will stay!

The magazine appears one or two times a year in a 6 × 9, flat-spined, 125-page format, offset from typescript on heavy stock, b&w art, glossy card color cover, circulation 1,000, 275 subscriptions of which 50 are libraries. They receive 1,500+ submissions per year, use 50-60. Subscription: $14 (2 issues); per copy: $7. **Sample postpaid: $4. Submit 3-10 pgs., name and address on each page. Photocopy OK. No simultaneous submissions. Query for information about upcoming reading periods and themes. Reports in 4-5 months. Pays** "usually $25 plus 2 copies." **Send SASE for guidelines. Editors sometimes comment on rejections.**

THE SINGLE SCENE (IV-Themes, humor), (formerly *Columbus Single Scene*), P.O. Box 30856, Gahanna OH 43230, founded 1985, poetry editor Jeanne Marlowe, is a monthly magazine, circulation 7,000, for Ohio singles (18 and up), "**positive, upbeat approach to single living, but we're neither Yuppies nor Pollyannas. Humorous treatments get priority.**" Recently published poets include Debra

Steinberg and Gina Bergamino. As a sample the editor chose these lines from "Courtship" by J. Mills:

> *If he slit his wrists*
> *and wrote your name in blood*
> *a thousand times down*
> *a white highway billboard,*
> *it would prove him*
>
> *no more a fool*
> *than last night when he*
> *sang Italian arias*
> *under your window with a loaf*
> *of bread and a jug of wine.*

Sample postpaid: $2. Considers simultaneous submissions. Submit maximum 12 poems, dealing with single living or relationships, 1-50 lines. Reports in 1 month. Pays advertising trade or copy. Acquires one-time rights. Reviews books of poetry "only if very relevant to singles."

SINGULAR SPEECH PRESS (II, IV-Translations), 10 Hilltop Dr., Canton CT 06019, phone (203)693-6059, founded 1976, editor Don D. Wilson. "Although initially a means of publishing the editor's verse translations, Singular Speech Press nonprofitably lives so that we may present to *some* public a few, fine examples of the thousands of real poets now at work, at play—probably our most unsupported artists. To this end, **we plan to publish at least 5-6 mss per annum, 24-64 pages. We have hardly any biases, are delighted by formal and informal verse, are made glad by unknown and well-known poets, and eschew only the egregiously confessional, so boring, and the patently prosy, in lines as though poetic."** They have published William Burns, Bina Goldfield, Susan English and Stephen Smith. Soon to publish Bulgarian poets, Kenneth Pobo, Rose Rosberg and Ron McFarland. "Impossible to find four representative and self-contained lines," but here are 4 from Petya Dubarova's "To Fifteen-year-olds" (translated by the editor):

> *I'm only one—and for the first time young,*
> *as though a tear picked briefly from the tree,*
> *as though a flame erupting from the stake,*
> *as though a vine that's blazing fast and high.*

Query with 5-10 typed samples and bio. Simultaneous submissions, photocopies OK. Payment is half of printed copies. Acquires all rights. Returns rights "automatically." Editor usually comments on rejections. Reports within 1-2 weeks.

SINISTER WISDOM (IV-Lesbian, feminist), P.O. Box 3252, Berkeley CA 94703, founded 1976, editor Elana Dykewomon, a lesbian feminist journal. The editor says, **"We want poetry that reflects the diversity of lesbian experience—lesbians of color, Third World, Jewish, old, young, working class, poor, disabled, fat, etc.—from a lesbian and/or feminist perspective. No heterosexual themes. We will not print anything that is oppressive or demeaning to women, or which perpetuates negative stereotypes."** The journal has published work by Gloria Anzaldúa, Sapphire and Betsy Warland. As a sample the editor chose the following lines from Minnie Bruce Pratt's poem "#67 To Be Posted on 21st Street, Between Eye and Pennsylvania":

> *Like a movie, sudden threat*
> *Predictable. I get so tired of this disbelief.*
> *My tongue, faithful in my mouth, said: Yes, we are.*
> *the shout: Lesbians. Lesbians. Trying to curse*
> *us with our name. Me louder: That's what we are.*

The editor says the quarterly magazine is digest-sized, 128-144 pgs., flat-spined, with photos and b&w graphics. Circulation is 3,500 of which 1,000 are subscriptions and 100 go to libraries; newsstand sales and bookstores are 1,500. Price per issue is $5, subscription $17 US, $22 foreign. **Sample postpaid: $6.50. Pay is 2 copies. No simultaneous submissions. Reporting time is up to 9 months and time to publication 6 months-1 year.** Reviews books of poetry in 500-1,500 words, single or multi-book format.

‡**SISTER VISION PRESS (IV-Ethnic)**, P.O. Box 217, Station E, Toronto, Ontario M6H 4E2 Canada, phone (416)533-2184, founded 1985, managing editor Makeda Silvera, publishes 10 paperbacks/year. They want **"poetry that reflects our lives as women of color; not restricted by form or length."** They have recently published poetry by ahdri zhina mandiela and Ramabai Espinet. As a sample the editor selected these lines from "Crebo" in Espinet's book **Nuclear Seasons**:

> *My hands had wrinkles*
> *But rims grew around my eyes*
> *My skin became ebony and rose*
> *And my tongue grew long beyond words*

Previously published poems and simultaneous submissions OK. Cover letter required. Submit a sample of work, to a maximum of 10 pages. Replies to queries in 2 weeks, to mss (if invited) in 2 months. Pays 10% royalties and 10 author's copies. Write for samples. They say, "Know the publisher you are submitting mss to. This saves the poet and publisher time, money and energy."

SISTERS TODAY (II, IV-Religious), The Liturgical Press, Collegeville MN 56321, phone (612)363-2213, poetry editor Sister Mary Virginia Micka, C.S.J., College of St. Catherine, P.O. Box 4162, St. Paul MN 55105, editor Sister Mary Anthony Wagner, has been published for about 60 years. Though it is a Roman Catholic magazine, not all of the poetry it uses is on religious themes, and the editors do not want poetry that is "overly religious." They want "short (not over 25 lines) poems on any topic, using clean, fresh images and appealing to the reader's feelings and thoughts in a compelling way." They do not want poetry that depends "heavily on rhyme and on 'tricks' such as excessive capitalization, manipulation of spacing, etc." They have recently published poetry by Irene Zimmerman, S.S.S.F., T. Kretz and Fredrick Zydek. As a sample, the poetry editor chose these lines from "Father's Lesson" by Frank Accuardi:

> In that frozen moment I see his face
> Through the cloudy cold. Neck veins
> taut as tree limbs hold the heavy chin.
> Dark creases branch around knotted eyes.

ST, appearing 6 times a year, is 6×9, 64 pgs., saddle-stapled, professionally printed with matte card cover, press run 9,000 for 8,500 subscribers. They receive about 100 poems/month, accept about 3. Subscription: $16 USA; $18 foreign. **Sample: $3 postpaid. Send SASE to poetry editor at St. Paul, MN address (above) for guidelines. Pays $10/poem and 2 copies. Buys first rights. They like you to put your "complete legal name, address and social security number typed in the upper right corner." No simultaneous submissions.** Previously published poems OK with publisher's release, but original poems much preferred. Reports within 1 month, 6-12 months until publication. Poetry editor comments when a poem has come close to being accepted.

SISYPHUS (I, II), 8 Asticou Rd., Boston MA 02130, founded 1990, editor Christopher Corbett-Fiacco, appears every other month using "meaningful poetry and prose of substance and style that speaks of and to humanity, human emotion and life (whatever it may be). The editor likes to see up to 5-7 poems at a time. Poetry to any length; 53 characters/line limit. Prose to 2,000 words maximum. Also uses artwork, including cover art (up to 4×6). No self-conscious beatniks obsessed with body functions and numbers and types of sex partners, please. Nothing too radical." This sample is from "Promises of Roses" by the "Featured Artist" in their first issue, Mary Duffye Forte:

> and you pull me to your side,
> holding me against myself
> you stab at me
> your hardness
> strangling me of love
> I drank in fully once
> before I tasted bitterness on your tongue.

It is booklet-sized (5×8), 28 pgs., with card cover, stapled. They accept 5-10% of work received. Subscription: $12 US; $20 surface; $26 airmail. Current issue $2.50. **Send SASE for guidelines and contest flyers. Pays 1 copy.** Offers bimonthly theme contest.

SKAZ (I, II), (formerly *Poetry Halifax Dartmouth*), The Firefly Poetry Group, #27008, 5280 Green St., Halifax, Nova Scotia B3H 1N0 Canada, founded 1986, editor Mark Hamilton, publishes the bimonthly literary magazine *SKAZ* with a calendar of literary activities, markets and announcements and the work of 5-12 writers in each issue. "We're interested in quality writing with a broad span of interest. Our contributors and readers are both national and international in range. We also publish short fiction, Canadian book reviews and b&w art. Encourage new writers. Rhymes rarely used. Will not accept material which is racist, sexist, homophobic or classist." They have published poems by Joanne Light, Rick Armstrong and John Doull, Jr. *SKAZ* is 24-36 pgs., 7×8½, saddle-stapled, with matte card cover and b&w art and photos. They accept about 75 poets a year or ¼-⅓ of authors who submit. Press run is 250 for 75 subscriptions of which 12 are libraries. Subscription: $15. **Sample postpaid: $2. Pays 2 contributor's copies. Submit up to 6 poems with short bio. Reports in 2 months.** Reviews books of poetry.

SKOOB BOOKS PUBLISHING LTD. (III, IV-Translations), 43 Old Bethnal Green Rd., London E9 6PR United Kingdom, founded 1987, editor Lucien Jenkins. "As a publishing house we are interested in translations, particularly from Modern European poetry." As a sample the editor selected these lines from Michal Hamburger's translation of "Inventory" by Gunter Eich:

> This pencil lead

> *is what I love most:*
> *by day it writes verses*
> *I thought up in the night*

Books pay 7% royalties plus 6 copies. "We run a major international poetry competitition in partnership with Index on Censorship." Lucien Jenkins gives this advice to people who write: "It takes time, it takes work, it takes courage *and* it takes talent. Do not be buttered up by friends who reassure you otherwise. Expect no money, no fame, no gratitude, no respect, no success, no pleasure, no comfort. Do it *only* because not doing it is not a possibility."

SKYLARK (I, II, IV-Themes), Purdue University Calumet, 2200 169th St., Hammond IN 46323, phone (219)989-2262, founded 1972, editor Pamela Hunter, is "a fine arts annual, including **special theme.**" They are looking for **"original images, concise presentation and honesty; poems up to 30 lines. No horror, nothing extremely religious, no pornography."** They have recently published poetry by Charles E. Eaton, Antony Oldknow, Jonathan Russell and Martha Vertreace. As a sample the editor selected this poem, "Shade," by Lynne McCraw Schall:

> *Columned clans of Yankee trees*
> *stand close and cool and dusky*
> *while my Prairie soul—*
> *filled with cherished*
> *shards of Prairie shade—*
> *swells with quiet awe*

Skylark is magazine-sized, saddle-stapled, 100+ pgs., professionally printed, with matte card cover. Press run is 500-1,000 for 50 subscriptions of which 12 are libraries. Price: $6. **Sample postpaid: $3.50. "Typed or computer printout manuscripts OK. Will accept simultaneous submissions. Inquire as to annual theme for special section." Do not submit mss between June 1 and November 1. Reports in 4 months. Pays 1 copy. Acquires first rights. Editor may encourage rejected but promising writers.**

SLATE & STYLE (IV-Specialized), Dept. PM, 2704 Beach Dr., Merrick NY 11566, phone (516)868-8718, editor Loraine Stayer, is a **quarterly for blind writers available on cassette, in large print and Braille,** "including articles of interest to blind writers, resources for blind writers. Membership/subscription $5 per year, $10 for Braille only (specify format). Division of the National Federation of the Blind." **Poems may be "5-30 lines. Prefer contributors to be blind writers, or at least writers by profession or inclination. No obscenities. Will consider all forms of poetry."** They have published poetry by Mary McGinnis, Milton Kerr and Sonja Kershaw. As a sample the editor selected "Lost Hills" by Carol Ann Lindsay:

> *Hundreds of pumping oil wells*
> *Secure upon a hill,*
> *Far from man, mountain, and sea*
> *Owned by one giant company;*
> *Taking a resource*
> *Natural to earth,*
> *Not giving it back*
> *But leaving steel fists*
> *To rot in the sand.*

The print version is magazine-sized, 28-32 pgs., stapled, with a fiction and poetry section, circulation 200 with 150 subscribers of which 4-5 are libraries. Subscription: $5/year, Braille $10. Per issue: $1.25 except Braille. **Sample postpaid: $2.50. Do not submit mss in July. Send SASE for guidelines. Pays 1 copy. Reports in "2 weeks if I like it." No simultaneous submissions. Interested in new talent. Editor comments on rejections "if requested."** Reviews books of poetry. They offer annual contests. Loraine Stayer says, "Poetry is one of the toughest ways to express oneself, yet ought to be the easiest to read. Anything that looks simple is the result of much work."

SLIPSTREAM; SLIPSTREAM AUDIO CASSETTES (II, IV-Themes), Box 2071, New Market Station, Niagara Falls NY 14301, phone (716)282-2616 (after 5pm, EST), founded 1980, poetry editors Dan Sicoli, Robert Borgatti and Livio Farallo. *Slipstream* is a "small press literary mag, uses about 70% poetry and 30% prose, also artwork. The editors like **new work with contemporary urban flavor. Writing must have a cutting edge to get our attention. Occasionally do theme issues. We like to keep an open forum, any length, subject, style. Best to see a sample to get a feel. Like city stuff as opposed to country. Like poetry that springs from the gut, screams from dark alleys, inspired by experience."** No "pastoral, religious, traditional, rhyming" poetry. They have recently published poetry by Fred Voss, Sherman Alexie, Gerald Locklin, Laurie Kirk, Charles Bukowski, Patrick McKinnon, Michael Basinski, Belinda Subraman, Kurt Nimmo and Joan Jobe Smith. The editors selected these sample lines from "All My Millions Die in Smithereens" by Ralph Heibutzki:

> *All my trains run late*
> *All my letters end up "Return to Sender"*
> *All my switchblades rust shut*
> *All my lovers sleep blacklisted forever*
> *All my millions die in smithereens*

Slipstream appears 1-2 times a year in a $7 \times 8\frac{1}{2}$ format, professionally printed, saddle-stapled, using b&w graphics. The staples barely hold this 130-page product, and the cover can barely contain it all. The magazine we received has a "Seventies" look: purple tie-dyed cover, pencil drawings, nudes. About 80 of the 100+ pgs. are devoted to poetry. The poems are of varying quality; all attempt to be lively with the focus on voice. It contains mostly free verse, some stanza patterns. They receive over 1,500 freelance submissions of poetry/year, use less than 10%. Circulation 300, with 200 subscriptions of which 10 are libraries. Subscription: $8.50/2 issues. **Sample postpaid: $5. Reports in 2-8 weeks. Editor sometimes comments on rejections. Pays copies. Send SASE for guidelines. Some issues are on announced themes – e.g., "working stiff," "erotic," "protest," "night life" and "ethnic" theme issues were released in the past. Also producing an audio cassette series. "Spoken word, songs, audio experiments, etc. are all welcome. Query for current needs."** Annual chapbook contest has December 1 deadline. Reading fee: $5. Submit up to 40 pgs. of poetry, any style, previously published work OK with acknowledgments. Winner receives 50 copies. All entrants receive copy of winning chapbook. Past winners have included Gerald Locklin, Serena Fusek, Robert Cooperman and Richard Amidon. Dan Sicoli advises, "Do not waste time submitting your work 'blindly.' Sample issues from the small press first to determine which ones would be most receptive to your work."

SMALL POND MAGAZINE OF LITERATURE (II), P.O. Box 664, Stratford CT 06497, phone (203)378-4066, founded 1964, editor Napoleon St. Cyr, a literary tri-quarterly that features poetry ... "and anything else the editor feels is original, important." Poetry can be **"any style, form, topic, so long as it is deemed good, except haiku, but limit of about 100 lines." Napoleon St. Cyr wants "nothing about cats, pets, flowers, butterflies, etc. Generally nothing under 8 lines."** Although he calls it name-dropping, he "reluctantly" provided the names of Marvin Soloman, Deborah Boe, Richard Kostelanetz, Fritz Hamilton and Emilie Glen as poets recently published. The magazine is digest-sized, offset from typescript on off-white paper, 40 pgs. with matte card cover, saddle-stapled, artwork both on cover and inside. Circulation is 300-325, of which about a third go to libraries. Price per issue is $2.75; subscription $7.50 (for 3 issues). **Sample postpaid: $2.50 for a random selection, $3 current. Guidelines are available in each issue. Pays 2 copies. Acquires all rights. Returns rights with written request including stated use. "One-time use per request." The editor says he doesn't want 60 pages of anything; "dozen pages of poems max." He reports on submissions in 10-45 days (longer in summer), and publication is within 3-18 months.** Reviews books of poetry. This slim publication is positively recommended. The editor is tough, thorough, but also encouraging, commenting on rejections to guide poets whose work interests him. This is a good place for new writers and experienced counterparts.

SMALL PRESS WRITERS & ARTISTS ORGANIZATION (SPWAO); SPWAO SHOWCASE; SPWAO NEWSLETTER (IV-Membership, Sci-fi/horror/fantasy), 615 N. 187th Ave., Buckeye AZ 85326, secretary Cathy Hicks, president Mike Olson, newsletter editor Octavio Ramos, Jr. The organization publishes a newsletter with emphasis on aiding members, advice columns, short poetry, art, reviews and short fiction and provides a poetry commentary service. **You must be a member to submit. They don't want to see "mainstream, religious, highly sentimental, pornographic, racial or political poetry."** They have recently published poems by Marge Simon, John Grey, D.M. Vosk, Anne Valley, Jacie Ragan and Mark Fewell. Reviews books of poetry in 200-500 words, single format. As for advice, Cathy Hicks offers this excerpt from "The Element of Fear in Horror Poetry" by Michael A. Arnzen (newsletter volume 14, number 1, February 1992): ". . . a poem must at least incorporate the emotion of fear in one way or another to qualify. The emotion of fear is a very personal one, and it can occur at a variety of levels in poetry."

THE SMITH; THE GENERALIST PAPERS (II), 69 Joralemon St., Brooklyn NY 11201, founded 1964, editor Harry Smith, publishes 2 hardbacks and 4 paperbacks/year and is considering a chapbook series. They have published poetry by Menke Katz, Lloyd Van Brunt, Richard Nason and Karen Swenson. As a sample the editor selected these lines from "Hawk Forever in Mid-Dive" in Lance Lee's **Wrestling with the Angel:**

> *Her feet on the patio are leaves blown*
> *over flagstones. Aimed at her head,*
> *beak thrust out wings angled severely*
> *a hawk hangs frozen in mid-air,*
> *fanned to permanent fire in her sky.*

"Send 3-6 poem sampling with query. No jingles, no standard academic verse." Pays 15% royalt-

ies, $500 advance, 10 copies. "The decision process is relatively slow—about three months—as many mss are offered. Readers' reports are often passed along and the editor often comments." **Write for catalog (free) or send $2 for a "slightly irregular" book ("with bumped corners or a little dust").** Harry Smith advises, "Revert to earlier models. *Avoid* university wordshops where there are standard recent models leading to standard mod verse. A close reading of **The Pearl Poet** will be more nourishing than all the asparagus of John Ashbery or Robert Bly." *The Generalist Papers*, appearing 6 times/year, consists of lively critical commentaries on contemporary poetry—more candor than you will find in most reviews. Subscription: $12. **Sample postpaid: $2.**

GIBBS SMITH, PUBLISHER; PEREGRINE SMITH POETRY COMPETITION (II), P.O. Box 667, Layton UT 84041, phone (801)544-9800, founded 1971, poetry series established 1988, contact Steve Chapman, publicist. **They want "serious, contemporary poetry of merit. No specs except book is only 64 pgs."** They have published books of poetry by David Huddle and Carol Frost. Books are selected for publication through competition for the Peregrine Smith Poetry Prize of $500 plus publication. **Entries are received in April only and require a $10 reading fee.** The judge for the series and editor is Christopher Merrill.

‡**SMITHS KNOLL (II),** 46 Glebe Way, Burnham-on-Crouch, Essex CM0 8QJ England, founded 1991, coeditors Roy Blackman and Michael Laskey, is a magazine appearing 3 times a year using **"poems of pity, indignation and celebration, with no other restrictions."** They have recently published poetry by Geoffrey Holloway, John Latham, Carole Satyamurti and Myra Schneider. As a sample the editors selected these lines from "Night Swim" by Sally Carr:

> The boys decide to swim at dusk,
> Laughing, wading knee-deep
> in the bottle-black
> of a wooded cove, their bodies
> luminous in half-light.

The editors say it is 50 pgs., A5, offset-litho, saddle-stitched, with card cover. They receive about 2,500 poems a year, "accept one in thirty." Press run is 500 for 100 subscribers. Single copy: £2; subscription: £5 for 3 issues (plus postage outside UK). **Sample postpaid: £2.50. "We would consider poems previously published in magazines outside the U.K."** No simultaneous submissions. **Often comments on rejections. Reports within 1 month. Pays 1 copy.**

SMOKE SIGNALS (II), Meander Box 232, Flushing NY 11385-0232, founded 1989, editor Joshua Meander, is a quarterly. **"No curse words in poems, little or no name-dropping, no naming of consumer products, no two-page poems, no humor, no bias writing, no poems untitled. 9-30 lines, poems with hope. Simple words, careful phrasing. Free verse, rhymed poems, sonnets, half-page parables, myths and legends, song lyrics. Subjects wanted: love poems, protest poems, mystical poems, nature poems, poems of humanity, poems with solutions to world problems and inner conflict."** They have published poetry by Brenda Charles, Joseph Gourdji, Dorothy Wheeler and Jeff Swan. As a sample the editor selected these lines from "Loves Giant Piano" by Connie Goodman:

> Walk a giant piano . . .
> Destination, the stars
> Along love's entrancing melody;
> The night, it is ours.

The editor says *Smoke Signals* is 5 pgs., 2-3 poems/page, typeset. They receive 150 poems/year, use about 50. Press run 400, all distributed free. Subscription $5; **per copy $1.25. Make check payable to Joshua Meander. Pays one copy. Reports in 6-8 weeks.** The editor says, "Stick to your guns; however, keep in mind that an editor may be able to correct a minor flaw in your poem. Accept only minor adjustments. Go to many open poetry readings. Respect the masters. Read and listen to other poets on the current scene. Make pen pals. Start your own poetry journal. Do it all out of pure love."

‡**THE SNAIL'S PACE REVIEW (II, IV-Translations),** RR#2 Box 363 Brownell Rd., Cambridge NY 12816, founded 1990, editors Darby Penney and Ken Denberg, is a biannual of contemporary poetry. "We are committed to publishing the best work of all poetic genres by both well-known and emerging poets, as well as poetry in translation." **They want "work of all genres that has strong imagery, uses language imaginatively and contains an element of the unexpected. No religious, sentimental, patriotic and, in most cases, rhymed poetry."** They have recently published poetry by Martha Collins, Stephen Dunn, Linda Pastan and Jerome Rothenberg. As a sample we selected these lines from "a reader considers the options" by A.J. Wright:

> know them by their options
> these people who study themselves

> *one who memorizes lines*
> *and another making notes*

It is 36 pgs., digest-sized, offset, saddle-stitched with cover illustration but no inside artwork. They receive about 3,000 poems a year, use less than 10%. Press run is 350 for 100 subscribers of which 10 are libraries, 150 shelf sales. Subscription: $7; $12 libraries. **Sample postpaid: $3.50. No previously published poems or simultaneous submissions. Cover letter, with brief bio, required.** Time between acceptance and publication is 4 months. **Seldom comments on rejections. Send SASE for guidelines. Reports in 10-16 weeks. Pays 2 copies. Acquires first North American serial rights.**

SNAKE NATION REVIEW; SNAKE NATION PRESS (II), #2, 110 W. Force St., Valdosta GA 31601, phone (912)249-8334, founded 1989, editor Roberta George, appears 4 times a year. **"Any form, length of 60 lines or less."** They have published poetry by Irene Willis and William Fuller. The handsome, 6×9, flat-spined magazine, 100 pgs., matte card cover, has a press run of 1,000 for 200 subscriptions of which 11 are libraries. Subscription: $15. **Sample postpaid: $6. Send SASE for guidelines. Pays 2 copies or prizes. Acquires first rights. Reports in 3 months. Editor comments on submissions sometimes.** Snake Nation Press publishes books of poetry. **Submit 60-page ms with $10 reading fee. Pays $500 on publication.**

SNAKE RIVER REFLECTIONS (I, II), 1863 Bitterroot Drive, Twin Falls ID 83301, phone (208)734-0746, appearing 10 times a year using **short (up to 20 lines) poems, any topic. Pays 2 copies. Acquires first rights only. Guidelines available for SASE.** Subscription: $5.50. **Sample postpaid: 25¢.** It is 8 pgs., stapled on the side, press run 100-200. Reviews books of poetry.

‡SNOWY EGRET (II, IV-Nature), P.O. Box 9, Bowling Green IN 47833, founded 1922 by Humphrey A. Olsen, editors Karl Barnebey and Michael Aycock. **They want poetry that is "nature-oriented: poetry that celebrates the abundance and beauty of nature or explores the interconnections between nature and the human psyche."** As a sample of poetry recently published they selected the opening lines of "In a Climax Forest" by Conrad Hilberry:

> *The wooden past grows larger, I grow less*
> *and less convincing in this sullen air*
> *that wants a wind to stir its emptiness.*

Snowy Egret appears twice a year in a 48-page. magazine-sized format, offset, saddle-stapled, with cover and original graphics. Of 500 poems received they accept about 20. Their press run is 800 for 500 subscribers of which 50 are libraries. **Sample: $8 postpaid. Pays $2/poem or $4/ page plus 2 copies. Buys first North American or reprint rights. Send #10 SASE for writer's guidelines. Reports in 1 month; no backlog.**

SOCIAL ANARCHISM (IV-Political, social issues), 2743 Maryland Ave., Baltimore MD 21218, phone (301)243-6987, founded (Vacant Lots Press) 1980, poetry editor Howard J. Ehrlich, is a digest-sized, 96-page biannual, print run 2,000, using about 10 pgs. of poetry in each issue which **"represents a political or social commentary that is congruent with a nonviolent anarchist and feminist perspective."** They have published poetry by Jacqueline Elizabeth Letalien, L.M. Harrod, Mark Colasurdo, Bridget Balthrop Morton and Bert Hubinger. **Sample postpaid: $3; $3.50 outside U.S. Submit up to 5 poems, "not in crayon." Considers simultaneous submissions. Reports in 4-6 weeks. Pays 3 copies.**

THE SOCIETY OF AMERICAN POETS (SOAP); IN HIS STEPS PUBLISHING COMPANY; IN HIS STEPS RECORDS (I, IV-Religious, membership), P.O. Box 147, Reidsville GA 30453, phone (912)557-4265, founded 1984, editor Dr. Charles E. Cravey. *SOAP* is a literary quarterly of poetry and short stories. In His Steps publishes religious and other books and publishes music for the commercial record market. **"Open to all styles of poetry and prose—both religious and secular. No gross or 'X-rated' poetry without taste or character."** They have recently published poetry by Carlton Cook, Lessie Perry, Joann Saulino and Dr. Charles E. Cravey. As a sample the editor selected these lines from "Grapevine" by Carol Ann Lindsay:

> *The withered winter vine*
> *of naked, knotted branches*
> *nailed to man-made fences,*
> *chains the cursing crosses to stolid, silent rows*
> *that betray the bitter sip*
> *of hollow human ways.*

The Poet's Pen, a quarterly book anthology, uses **poetry by members and subscribers only.** (Membership: $20/year.) **For book publication query. 60/40 split of pay. Editor "most certainly" comments on rejections.** The anthology has poetry competitions in several categories with prizes of $25-100. The editor says, "We're looking for poets who wish to unite in fellowship with our growing family of poets nationwide. We currently have over 850 poets and are one of the nation's largest societies, yet small enough and family operated to give each of our poets individual attention and pointers." Also sponsors various contests throughout the year. Editor's Choice Awards each quarter, prizes $25, $15 and $10. President's Award for Superior Choice has a prize of $50. Deadline is November 1.

SOJOURNERS (IV-Religious, political), P.O. Box 29272, Washington DC 20017, phone (202)636-3637, founded 1975, poetry editor Rose Berger, appears 10 times per year, "with approximately 40,000 subscribers. **We focus on faith, politics and culture from a radical Christian perspective. We publish 1-3 poems/month depending on length. All poems must be original and unpublished. We look for seasoned, well-crafted poetry that reflects the issues and perspectives covered in our magazine. Poetry using noninclusive language (any racist, sexist, homophobic poetry) will not be accepted."** As a sample the editor selected these lines by David Abrams:

> *An eagle against a clear sky,*
> *A snake coming off a rock,*
> *A skiff in the center of a lake,*
> *And the Spirit slipping into bodies.*

The editor describes *Sojourners* as 52 pgs., offset printing. It appears monthly except that there is one issue for August/September and February/March. Of 400 poems received per year they publish 8-10. Press run: 50,000 for 40,000 subscriptions of which 500 are libraries; 2,000 shelf sales. Subscription: $30. **Sample postpaid: $2.75. Send SASE for guidelines. Pays $15-25/poem plus 5 copies. "We assume permission to reprint unless the author requests otherwise." Submit no more than 3 at a time. Reports in 4-6 weeks. Editor comments on submissions "sometimes."** Reviews books of poetry in 600 words, single or multi-book format.

SOLEIL PRESS (IV-Ethnic), Box 452, RFD 1, Lisbon Falls ME 04252, phone (207)353-5454, founded 1988, contact Denis Ledoux, publishes and distributes **writing by and about Franco-Americans** in chapbooks and paperbacks. **Not interested in the continental French experience. Pays copies.**

SOLO FLYER; SPARE CHANGE POETRY PRESS (IV-Regional), 2115 Clearview NE, Massillon OH 44646, Spare Change Poetry Press founded 1979, editor David B. McCoy. *Solo Flyer* is a 4-page flyer appearing 2-5 times/year featuring the work of a single poet in each issue. **"Submissions limited to Ohio poets."** They want **poetry using punctuation and capitalization. "Like to see poems with a common theme."** As a sample the editor selected "Absences" by Ruth V. Tams-Fuquen:

> *Wordless*
> *we walked that hotel's midnight garden.*
> *The blossom you laid on my palm*
>
> *spoke*
> *for the song you hummed,*
>
> *suggested*
> *the words you chose*
> *not to sing.*

The flyers are folded 8½ × 11 sheets of colored paper. **Sample free with #10 SASE. Previously published material OK. Pays 20-25 copies.** The editor says, "Submissions without SASE are not read."

‡SOME BEES PRESS (V), 543 St. Clements Ave., Toronto, Ontario M5N 1M3 Canada, founded 1988, editor Mark Silverberg, publishes approximately 1 chapbook/year, but **currently does not accept unsolicited manuscripts.**

‡SONOMA MANDALA (II), c/o English Dept., Sonoma State University, Rohnert Park CA 94928, phone (707)664-3902, founded 1973, faculty advisor Elizabeth Herron, is an annual literary review that publishes poetry, short fiction and some artwork. They are **"open to all styles. Preferably not over two pages."** They have recently published poetry by Lucille Clifton, Stephen Torre, Lyn Lifshin, Simon Perchik, Etheridge Knight and Maureen Hurley. As a sample the editor selected these lines (poet unidentified):

> *There are people who are combustible, people that is*

Market categories: (I) Beginning; (II) General; (III) Limited; (IV) Specialized; (V) Closed.

who spontaneously burst into flames. We know this by
their remains, the manner in which the body has been
consumed. Always there is a small blackened area

She says *Sonoma Mandala* is 140 pgs., typeset, perfect-bound, no ads. They receive over 600 mss a year, accept approximately 10-15%. Press run is 500 for 10 subscribers of which 6 are libraries, 300 shelf sales. Subscription: $6. **Sample postpaid: $3. No previously published poems; simultaneous submissions OK. "Brief bio helps." Reads submissions August 1 through November 15 only. Comments on rejections "whenever possible." Send SASE for guidelines. Reports in 2-4 months. Pays 2 copies. Acquires first North American serial rights.** Elizabeth Herron says, "We are open to all schools of thought/poetics and seek fresh, original writing with life-affirming values."

SONORA REVIEW (II), Dept. of English, University of Arizona, Tucson AZ 85721, phone (602)626-8383, founded 1980, poetry editor Jennifer Snyder, a semiannual literary journal that publishes "non-genre" fiction and poetry. **The editors want "quality poetry, literary concerns."** They have published poems by Ricardo Pau-Llosa, Michael Collier, Barbara Anderson and Charlie Smith. Translations welcome. As a sample, the editors chose the following lines by Laurie Blauner:

Some days I spread myself out like butter
on toast and hope for changes, how the body fades
after dusk, how the architect of your house assumes
you are now free of desire . . .

Sonora Review is a handsome magazine, 6×9, professionally printed on heavy off-white stock, 130 pgs., flat-spined, with 2-color glossy card cover. Circulation is 650, of which 250 are subscriptions and 300 go to libraries. Price per copy is $5, subscription $10/year, $17/2 years. **Back issue available for $4 postpaid. Pay is 2 copies. Poets should submit typed copy; dot-matrix, simultaneous submissions OK. Reporting time is 2 months and time to publication 6 months.** The magazine sponsors annual poetry awards with prizes of $150 and $50.

SOUNDINGS: A NEWSLETTER FOR SURVIVORS OF CHILDHOOD SEXUAL ABUSE; ECHOES NETWORK, INC. (IV-Themes), Suite 920, 700 NE Multnonah, Portland OR 97232, founded 1983, executive director Wendy Ann Wood, M.A. Echoes Network is an organization devoted to therapy of victims of childhood sexual abuse. Their quarterly newsletter, *Soundings*, uses **poetry on the theme of survival of childhood sexual abuse, ritual abuse and multiple personality disorder.** As a sample, here is a complete poem, "Little One," by Lynn:

It hurt to be so small
And have her for the mom
And need a little help
To tie my shoe
To print my name
Or learn a prayer for school.
She was never nice to me.
No one was.

It is 8 pgs., laser printed, "folded left." They use 50% of poems received. Press run 1,500-2,000 for 1,800 subscriptions. Subscription: $10. **Sample: $2 plus SASE. Pays 2 copies. Editor often comments on rejections. "No SASE, no response." Reports in 6-8 weeks.** Reviews books on related topics, poetry or other subjects. The editor advises, "Focus on what you have *personally* done to heal from the trauma of childhood sexual abuse. Stay present rather than reliving your life story. If your material is past-oriented then include a progress report explaining where you are now in recovery. Read **Triumph Over Darkness** by W. Wood and L. Hatton [published by Beyond Words Publishing and Echoes Network in 1988] for specific examples."

SOUNDINGS EAST (II), Salem State College, Salem MA 01970, phone (508)741-6270, founded 1973, advisory editor Rod Kessler. "*SE* is published by Salem State College and is staffed by students. We accept short fiction (15 pgs. max) and **contemporary poetry (5 pgs. max). Purpose is to promote poetry and fiction in the college and beyond its environs. We do not want graphic profanity.**" They have recently published poetry by Martha Ramsey, Walter McDonald and Linda Portnay as well as a feature section on "Incarcerated Poets." *SE* appears twice a year, 64-68 pgs., digest-sized, flat-spined, b&w drawings and photos, glossy card cover with b&w photo, circulation 2,000, 120 subscriptions of which 35 are libraries. They receive about 500 submissions/year, use 40-60. **Sample postpaid: $3. Fall deadline: November 20; Spring: April 20. Reads submissions September 1 through May 1 only. Photocopies, dot-matrix, simultaneous submissions OK. Reports within 1-4 months. Pays 3 copies. Acquires all rights. Rights revert to the writers.** "We occasionally, when funding allows, publish an extra spring issue which features only poetry, fiction and artwork by Salem State College students."

SOUNDINGS: JOURNAL OF THE LIVING ARTS; EDGE CITY (II), P.O. Box 7075, St. Joseph MO 64507, phone (816)279-6037, founded 1989, is a quarterly. "We are open-minded. We are an open forum which likes to see traditional forms, but we also prefer insightful, incisive free verse. We do not wish to see greeting card verse, predictable rhyme or cutesy poems." They have published poetry by William Stafford. As a sample, here are lines from "Robert Lowell" by John Gilgun:

> *They said you were a Boston blue blood,*
> *But I knew better. I'd seen mad eyes like yours*
> *In the mirrors of taxis driven by*
> *Lunatic Ukrainian immigrants on Thorazine.*

It is digest-sized, 60 pgs., saddle-stapled, professionally printed with matte card cover, using line drawings and photos. They use 10-15% of about 800 submissions/year. Press run 400. Subscription: $8. **Sample postpaid: $3. Pays 1 copy. Acquires first or reprint rights. Previously published poems and simultaneous submissions OK. "We request cover letters from each submission . . . We want to know who you are, not where you've been published before." Reports in 3 months by handwritten note. Query regarding chapbook publication under the imprint Edge City.** They review chapbooks and other magazines. "We'd like to see more people read the small presses. No press is an island."

SOUTH CAROLINA REVIEW (II), English Dept., Clemson U., Clemson SC 29634-1503, phone (803)656-3229, founded 1968, editor Richard J. Calhoun, is a biannual literary magazine "recognized by the *New York Quarterly* as one of the top 20 of this type." They will consider "**any kind of poetry as long as it's good. Format should be according to new MLA Stylesheet.**" They have published poems by Jay A. Blumethal, J.W. Rivers and Claire Bateman. It is 6×9, 200+ pgs., flat-spined, professionally printed, uses about 8-10 pgs. of poetry in each issue and has a circulation of 600, 400 subscriptions of which 250 are libraries. They receive about 1,000 freelance submissions of poetry/year of which they use 10, have a 2-year backlog. Subscription: $7. **Sample postpaid: $5. Do not submit during June, July, August or December. Reports in 6-9 months. Pays copies.** Reviews books of poetry.

SOUTH COAST POETRY JOURNAL (II), English Dept., California State University, Fullerton CA 92634, founded 1986, editor John J. Brugaletta. The twice-yearly (January and June) magazine publishes poetry only. "**We'd like to see poems with strong imagery and a sense that the poem has found its best form, whether that form is traditional or innovative. We prefer poems under 36 lines, but we'll look at others. Any subject matter or style.** We have recently published Marge Piercy, Mark Strand, X.J. Kennedy and Robert Mezey." As a sample, the editor selected these lines from "At the Nursing Home" by Luci Shaw:

> *As seeds swell, they shape and split*
> *their pods. On the cold linoleum*
> *under the bed her molded slippers lie,*
> *slight as a child's, like discarded*
> *seed cases. Long ago*
> *her genes were sown into our soil.*
> *Now she is shrunk all over,*
> *a leaf separating, curling in.*

The journal is digest-sized, 60 pgs., perfect-bound, offset, heavy paper cover, some line art. Print run is 700, 420 subscribers, 25 of which are libraries, 50 shelf sales. Subscription: $9, $5/issue. **Sample postpaid: $3.50. Guidelines are available for SASE. Pays 1 copy. Acquires first North American serial rights. Reads submissions September 1 through June 1 only. No simultaneous submissions. Every submission is read by at least three editors. Submissions will be reported on in 6-8 weeks.** They conduct an annual poetry contest judged by eminent poets. Entry fee is $3/poem.

SOUTH DAKOTA REVIEW (II, IV-Regional, themes), University of South Dakota, Vermillion SD 57069, phone (605)677-5220 or 677-5229, founded 1963, editor John R. Milton, is a "literary quarterly publishing poetry, fiction, criticism, essays. **When material warrants, an emphasis on the American West; writers from the West; Western places or subjects; frequent issues with no geographical emphasis; periodic special issues on one theme, or one place or one writer. Looking for originality, some kind of sophistication, significance, craft—i.e., professional work. Nothing confessional, purely descriptive, too filled with self-importance.**" They use 6-10 poems/issue, "receive tons, it seems." Print run 650-900 for 450 subscriptions of which half are libraries. Subscription: $15/year, $25/2 years. **Sample postpaid: $4. Pays 1 copy/page. Acquires first and reprint rights. Reports in 1-12 weeks.** Editor comments on submissions "rarely." They have a distinct bias against personal or confessional poems, but even those are published if excellent. The question is why decrease your chances? Read the magazine—it's attractive and well-edited—to get a feel for the type of poetry that succeeds here. Milton advises, "Find universal meaning in the regional. Avoid constant 'I' personal experiences that are not of

Close-up

R.T. Smith
Poet/Coeditor
Southern Humanities Review

"Vespers"

A cedar waxwing gray
on the gatepost holds
a wet seed in his beak,
surveys the lawn, blue
spruce fringe shaking.
A parasite burrowing
in his wing feathers is
working, a cyst
in his belly thickens.

He drops the seed
to recite his two notes,
and the twilit yard,
chilly as it darkens,
becomes the green
church of his yearning,
the parish of his
sweetest dying need.

"One of my students once asked me why I write so much about birds," R.T. Smith remembers, "and the answer was threefold. As a former countryman now moved to town, the birds are the only features of the old landscape that I've been able to stay in touch with. Secondly, birds fly and sing, the two gifts I've spent a life trying to approximate." Finally, he notes, "the old practice of augury haunts me—the belief that somehow the secret of things is contained in birds."

The above poem appears in Smith's seventh collection, **The Cardinal Heart** (Livingston University Press, 1991). He says the collection attempts to discover the layers of meaning "the way the oyster knits its pearl in shadow, circling and circling the stimulus."

The poetics of that line illustrate why Smith is known as one of the most respected poets and experienced editors working today. He has published in such magazines as *Poetry*, *The Georgia Review* and *Rolling Stone* and has been editor or poetry editor of several journals, including *Cold Mountain Review*, *Caesura* and *National Forum*. In addition, he has received awards and honors ranging from Literature Fellowships from the National Endowment for the Arts to the Alabama Governor's Award for Achievement by an Artist.

Smith puts care into each image and each line of his work and he coedits *Southern Humanities Review* with the same keen eye for detail. "Although there is no way to be sure," he says, "I suspect that most of the poems I have accepted were long in composition and put their creators through a lot of turns, some of them far from comfortable."

Smith rejects poems that are "professional exercises by people who are working from feelings in books" or "whose feelings have found no crafted vessel." Although, he says, "God knows all of us who write are capable of these empty extremes, but I believe that living with poems awhile before sending them out can save us some embarrassment."

He admits there are fringe benefits in being an editor. Despite the thousands of unusable submissions he has read through the years, Smith says he has been "listening in on some important river of American thought. Being able to read unsolicited manuscripts has taught me a lot about the secrets words are keeping and the charms to make them open."

Smith wants poems—his own and ones he considers—to unlock the secrets of the world and charm us in the process.

—Michael J. Bugeja

interest to anyone else. Learn to be less self-centered and more objective."

‡SOUTH HEAD PRESS; POETRY AUSTRALIA (II), Market Place, Berrima, NSW 2577 Australia, founded 1964, poetry editor John Millett. "We have published 122 issues of *Poetry Australia* (5-6 per year), minimum of 80 pgs. per issue, and many books of poetry." 30-50 poets appear in each issue of *PA*. As a sample here are the first two (of 8) stanzas of "Right Winger" by David Ray:

> 1
> *On planes*
> *he always sat*
> *over the right wing.*
>
> 2
> *When he went hunting*
> *he always shot*
> *the duck in the left wing.*

PA is professionally printed, 6 × 9¾, flat-spined, glossy card cover, $10/copy. They invite "**unpublished verse in English from writers in Australia and abroad. Mss should be typed double-spaced on one side of paper with name and address on reverse side. Overseas contributors are advised that sufficient money for return postage should accompany poems. Stamps of one country are not legal tender in another.**" Rates for poems: **$10 or 1 year's subscription. Overseas poets are paid in copies. South Head Press will consider submissions for book publication. Query with 3 samples. They pay advance and copies. Editor sometimes comments on rejections.** There is a list of books of poetry they have published in *Poetry Australia*, which serves as their catalog. The editor advises, "Read all you can of the best that has been published in the last 20 years. Include *PA, Hudson Review*, etc."

‡SOUTHEASTERN FRONT (II), 565 17th St. NW, Cleveland TN 37311, founded 1985, publisher Robin Merritt, is "an artists' and writers' presentation/representation service; a gallery in a magazine. **No stylistic limitations, substantial human experience is a plus. Nothing devoid of artistic or literary merit, nor strictly commercially designed work.**" They have recently published poetry by Stephen Wingeier. It is approximately 60 pgs., b&w, glossy, offset print with photos. Press run is 1,000+. Inquire (with SASE) about availability of sample. Previously published poems ("**only if permissions are cleared**") and simultaneous submissions OK. Cover letter not required "**but often beneficial.**" **Often comments on rejections. Send SASE for guidelines. Reporting time varies. Pays "exposure, publication, referrals." Authors retain rights.** "Will consider submitted chapbooks for review." The editor says, "*Southeastern FRONT* offers its contributors exposure to selected publishers, reviewers, museums, galleries and individuals actively involved in the fine arts. *Southeastern FRONT* also offers short-run book printing and manufacturing services to individuals and institutions. Will print as few as fifty copies of perfect-bound or saddle-stitched books. Perfect for poets, teachers, catalogs, etc. Inquire for more information."

THE SOUTHERN CALIFORNIA ANTHOLOGY; ANN STANFORD POETRY PRIZES (III), c/o Master of Professional Writing Program, WPH 404, University of Southern California, Los Angeles CA 90089-4034, phone (213)740-3252, founded 1983, is an "annual literary review of serious contemporary poetry and fiction. **Very open to all subject matters except pornography. Any form, style OK.**" They have published poetry by Robert Bly, John Updike, Denise Levertov and Peter Viereck. As a sample the editor selected these lines from "The Rivers of Paris" by James Ragan:

> *The boulevards are the rivers wind owes*
> *to the eyes' reflections, light*
> *to the panes transparent*
> *in the domes of air wind weaves along Sacre Coeur*

The anthology is 144 pgs., digest-sized, perfect-bound, with a semi-glossy color cover featuring one art piece. A fine selection of poems distinguish this journal, and it has an excellent reputation, well-deserved. The downside, if it has one, concerns limited space for newcomers. Circulation is 1,500, 50% going to subscribers of which 50% are libraries. 30% are for shelf sales. **Sample postpaid: $5.95. Send SASE for guidelines. Pays 3 copies. Acquires all rights. Reports in 4 months. Submit 3-5 poems between September 1 and January 1. All decisions made by mid-February. Legible photocopied submissions OK, computer printout submissions acceptable, no dot-matrix, no simultaneous submissions, no previously published poems.** The Ann Stanford Poetry Prizes ($750, $250 and $100) have a March 15 deadline, $10 fee (5 poem limit), for unpublished poems. Include cover sheet with name, address and titles and SASE for contest results. All entries are considered for publication. All entrants receive a copy of *SCA*.

SOUTHERN HUMANITIES REVIEW (II, IV-Translations), 9088 Haley Center, Auburn University AL 36849, poetry editor Scott Ward, coeditors Dan Latimer and R.T. Smith, founded 1967, is a 6 × 9 literary quarterly, 100+ pgs., circulation 800. **Interested in poems of any length, subject, genre. Space**

is limited, and brief poems are more likely to be accepted. "Several poems at a time recommended. Avoid sending faint computer printout. Pays 1 copy and $50 for the best poem published during the year. Translations welcome." They have recently published poetry by Lars Gustaffson, Donald Hall, Reynolds Price, Mary Ruefle, Hayden Carruth, Robert Morgan and John Engels. Subscription: $15/ year. Sample: $5. Responds in 1-2 months, possibly longer in summer. Buys all rights. "Poet has the right to publish *SHR* contribution in any volume consisting of his/her own work per our agreement." Reviews books of poetry in approximately 750-1,000 words. Coeditor R.T. Smith is a widely published writer who enlivens this influential publication by taking poems that not only look and sound beautiful but also convey insight or meaning. He's after the "total" poem. Space for poetry in the magazine has to compete with fiction and scholarship, so your chances are somewhat slimmer here than at "all poetry" magazines. The editors advise, "For beginners we'd recommend study and wide reading in English and classical literature, and, of course, American literature—the old works, not just the new. We also recommend study of or exposure to a foreign language and a foreign culture. Poets need the reactions of others to their work: criticism, suggestions, discussion. A good creative writing teacher would be desirable here, and perhaps some course work too. And then submission of work, attendance at workshops. And again, the reading: history, biography, verse, essays—all of it. We want to see poems that have gone beyond the language of slippage and easy attitudes."

SOUTHERN POETRY REVIEW; GUY OWEN POETRY PRIZE (II), English Dept., University of North Carolina, Charlotte NC 28223, phone (704)547-4309, editors Lucinda Grey and Ken McLaurin, founded 1958, a semiannual literary magazine "with emphasis on effective poetry. **Not a regional magazine, but a natural outlet for new Southern talent." There are no restrictions on form, style or content of poetry; length subject to limitations of space. They do not want to see anything "cute, sweet, sentimental, arrogant or preachy."** They have published work by Linda Pastan, Judith Ortiz Cofer, David Ray, Stephen Sandy, Betty Adcock and Walter McDonald. *Southern Poetry Review* is 6×9, handsomely printed on buff stock, 78 pgs., flat-spined with textured, one-color matte card cover. Circulation is 1,000+. Subscription: $8/year. **Sample available for $2 postpaid; no guidelines, but will answer queries with SASE. Pays 1 copy. Acquires first-time rights. Writers should submit no more than 3-5 poems. Reads submissions September 1 through May 31 only. Reporting time is 4-6 weeks, and poems should be printed within a year of acceptance.** This is the type of literary magazine to settle back with in a chair and read, particularly during dry creative spells, to inspire one's muse. It is recommended as a market for that reason. It's a tough sell, though. Work is read closely and the magazine reports in a timely manner. There is a yearly contest, the Guy Owen Poetry Prize of $500, to which the entry fee is a subscription; submission must be postmarked in April.

SOUTHERN REVIEW (II), Curtin University, Bentley 6101 Western Australia, founded in the 1960s, poetry editor Anne Brewster, published jointly by University of Adelaide and Curtin University of Technology, appears 3 times a year **using poetry that is not sexist, racist.** They have recently published poetry by John Kinsella and Jeri Kroll. As a sample the editor selected these lines from "He (III)" by Kate Llewellyn:

> *I cross my legs*
> *playing for time*
> *he won't take tea*
> *There's only one thing*
> *on his mind*
> *and pretty soon*
> *it's on mine too*
> *I pick up my pen*

It is digest-sized, 100 pgs., flat-spined. Press run 500 for 375 subscribers. **Sample postpaid: A$12. Reports in 3 months. Pays 1 copy. Acquires first publication rights.** Reviews books of poetry in 1,000 words minimum, single format.

THE SOUTHERN REVIEW (II), 43 Allen Hall, Louisiana State University, Baton Rouge LA 70803, phone (504)388-5108, founded 1935 (original series), 1965 (new series), poetry editors James Olney and Dave Smith, "is a literary quarterly which publishes fiction, poetry, critical essays and book reviews, with emphasis on contemporary literature in the U.S. and abroad, and with special interest in Southern culture and history. Selections are made with careful attention to craftsmanship and technique and to the seriousness of the subject matter." By general agreement this is one of the most distinguished of literary journals. Joyce Carol Oates, for instance, says, "Over the years I have continued to be impressed with the consistent high quality of *SR*'s publications and its general 'aura,' which bespeaks careful editing, adventuresome tastes and a sense of thematic unity. *SR* is characterized by a refreshing openness to new work, placed side by side with that of older, more established, and in many cases highly distinguished writers." The editors say they want "**No particular kinds of poetry. We are interested in any formal varieties, traditional or modern, that are well crafted, though we**

cannot normally accommodate excessively long poems (say 10 pgs. and over)." They have published poetry by A.R. Ammons, Yvonne Sapia, Nancy Schoenberger and Miller Williams. The editors selected these sample lines by Mary Oliver:

> The story about Jesus in the cave
> > is a good one,
> > > but when is it ever like that

> as sharp as lightning,
> > or even the way the green sea does everything—
> > > quickly,
> > > > and with such grace?

The beautifully printed quarterly is massive: 6¾×10, 240+ pgs., flat-spined, matte card cover, print run 3,100 with 2,100 subscriptions of which 70% are libraries. They receive about 2,000 freelance submissions of poetry, use 10%. Subscription: $15. **Sample postpaid: $5. Prefers submissions of 1-4 pgs. Reports in 2 months. Pays $20/printed page plus 2 copies. Buys first North American rights. Send SASE for guidelines.** Reviews books of poetry in 3,000 words, multi-book format.

SOUTHWEST REVIEW; ELIZABETH MATCHETT STOVER MEMORIAL AWARD (II), 307 Fondren Library West, Box 4374, Southern Methodist University, Dallas TX 75275, phone (214)373-7440, founded 1915, editor Willard Spiegelman. *Southwest Review* is a literary quarterly that publishes fiction, essays, poetry and interviews. "It is hard to describe our preference for poetry in a few words. We always suggest that potential contributors read several issues of the magazine to see for themselves what we like. But some things may be said: We demand **very high quality in our poems; we accept both traditional and experimental writing, but avoid unnecessary obscurity and private symbolism; we place no arbitrary limits on length but find shorter poems easier to fit into our format than longer ones. We have no specific limitations as to theme." No simultaneous submissions, no previously published work. Photocopies OK.** They have published poetry by George Bradley, Debora Greger, Rachel Hadas, Marie Ponsot and Howard Nemerov. The journal is 6×9, 160 pgs., perfect-bound, professionally printed, with matte text stock cover, circulation 1,500 with 1,000 subscriptions of which 600 are libraries. They receive about 700 freelance submissions of poetry/year, use 24. Subscription: $20. **Sample postpaid: $5. Reports within a month. Pays cash plus copies. Send SASE for guidelines.** $150 annual Elizabeth Matchett Stover Memorial Prize for best poem, chosen by editors, published in preceding year.

SOU'WESTER (II), Box 1438, Southern Illinois University, Edwardsville IL 62026, phone (618)692-3190, founded 1960, editor Fred W. Robbins, appears 3 times a year. **"We like poetry with imagery and figurative language that has strong associations and don't care for abstract poetry. We have no particular preference for form or length."** They have published poetry by J.D. Smith, Walter Griffin and Douglas Leonard. As a sample the editor selected the first stanza of "Casting the Friendship Circle" by Susan Swartwout:

> In this singular season, words
> rise like sap, darkness
> lifts, green buds appear
> along branches in
> roughest bark. Secure
> with unleaving, we ripen,
> turn, drift down to the river's
> surface filmy with our dreams.
> We are free.

There are 25-30 pgs. of poetry in each 6×9, 80-page issue. The magazine is professionally printed, flat-spined, with textured matte card cover, circulation 300, 110 subscriptions of which 50 are libraries. They receive some 2,000 poems (from 600 poets) each year, use 36-40, have a 2-month backlog. Subscription: $10 (3 issues). **Sample postpaid: $5. Simultaneous submission, photocopy and dot-matrix OK. Rejections usually within 1 month. Pays 2 copies. Acquires all rights. Returns rights. Editor comments on rejections** "usually, in the case of those that we almost accept." He says, "Read poetry past and present. Have something to say and say it in your own voice. Poetry is a very personal thing for many editors. When all else fails, we may rely on gut reactions, so take whatever hints you're given to improve your poetry, and keep submitting."

THE SOW'S EAR (II, IV-Regional, children), 245 McDowell St., Bristol TN 37620, phone (703)628-2651, founded 1988, coeditors Errol Hess and Larry Richman, a quarterly. **"We are very open to form, style, length of poems. We see *TSE* as a three-ring circus—with a flair for the visual, which is very**

much lacking from most poetry journals. The inside ring is the central Appalachian community focused in the area where Tennessee, Kentucky, North Carolina, West Virginia and Virginia come close together. The middle ring is the broader Appalachian region; a culture where we believe a poetry renaissance is beginning. The outer ring is the largest possible community, wherever the English language is spoken and written in poetic form. We encourage submissions from school-age children and plan to feature occasionally a previously unpublished poet." They have published poetry by Josephine Jacobsen and William Stafford. As a sample the editors selected these lines from "Loving Argument" by Margery A. Snyder:

> *When she was two*
> *Talk was female, its power*
> *Like the river spinning*
> *Grand Coulee's turbine,*
> *Words gathering, spilling,*
> *Tumbling, women's voices*
> *Piling up, tidal.*

TSE is 32 pgs., magazine-sized, saddle-stapled, with matte card cover, professionally printed. They accept about 150 of 4,000 poems submitted. Press run: 1,000 for 500 subscribers of which 15 are libraries. Shelf sales: 100-200. Subscription: $10. **Sample postpaid: $3.50. Send SASE for guidelines. Pays 1 copy. Buys first publication rights. Reports in 3-9 months. Simultaneous submissions OK if you tell them promptly when it is accepted elsewhere. Enclose brief bio. "We want to know if the poet has not yet been published or is a youth, as we have features for both." Editor comments on submissions "if poet specifically requests it."** Reviews books of poetry. Richman selects the kids' poems; others chosen by a 3-person board that meets quarterly. They offer an annual contest with fee of $2/poem, $500 prize. For contest, submit 1-5 poems October through November. Submissions with $10 receive 1-year subscription. 1991 judge: Dave Smith. Also sponsors a chapbook contest each April for 24 poems, maximum 24 pgs. Fee is $10; prize $500 and 50 copies.

SPARROW: THE POLITICALLY INCORRECT VERSE MAGAZINE (IV-Form), (formerly Sparrow Press), 103 Waldron St., West Lafayette IN 47906, editor and publisher Felix Stefanile, publishes "as material permits." They want **"formal sonnets only, 4 or 5 per submission. No subject restrictions. We don't publish poems in poor taste."** They have recently published poetry by X.J. Kennedy, Harold Witt and Judson Jerome. As a sample the editor selected these lines from R.S. Gwynn's sonnet on sonneteers:

> *Prefixing every phrase with* Ah *or* O,
> *They spoke as if the stems and stumps had ears,*
> *Letting the backwash of their idle tears*
> *Leave bathtub rings around the Vale of Woe.*

The editor says *Sparrow* is 9×12, using occasional graphics only by invitation. They receive about 1,000 pieces a year, use less than 1%. Press run is 500-750 for about 450 subscribers of which about 100 are libraries, 300 shelf sales. **Sample postpaid: $5. No previously published poems or simultaneous submissions. Typed copy only, $8\frac{1}{2} \times 11$ bond. No material returned without SASE. "We have a very cynical attitude toward long cover letters." Seldom comments on rejections. "We are not in the business of offering criticism or advice." Send SASE for guidelines. Reports "usually in a week." Pays $3 a sonnet plus 2 copies. Buys first and non-exclusive reprint rights.** The editor says, "We are now essentially a 'new' magazine with a fine, old name. We pride ourselves on our liveliness and our currency. We are really not a market for beginners. The MFA degree does not impress us."

SPECTRUM (II), Anna Maria College, Box 72-D, Paxton MA 01612, phone (508)757-4586, founded 1985, poetry editor Joseph Wilson, is a "multidisciplinary national publication with liberal arts emphasis," presenting 6-8 poems in each 66-page issue: **"poems of crisp images, precise language, which have something of value to say and say it in an authentic voice. Not the self-conscious, the 'workshop poem,' the cliché, the self-righteous."** They have published poetry by William Stafford. *Spectrum* appears twice a year in a 6×9, flat-spined format, professionally printed on quality stock with 2-color matte card cover, using b&w photos and art. Press run is 1,000 for 650 subscriptions (200 of them to libraries). Per copy: $4. Subscription: $7 for 1 year, $13 for 2 years. **Sample: $3. Pays $20/poem plus 2 copies. Buys first North American serial rights. No previously published poems or simultaneous submissions. Reads submissions September 1 through May 15 only. Reports in 6 weeks. Editor "occasionally" comments on rejections.**

SPINDRIFT (II), Shoreline Community College, 16101 Greenwood Ave., Seattle WA 98133, founded 1962, faculty advisor varies each year, currently Carol Orlock, is **open to all varieties of poetry except greeting-card style.** They have recently published poetry by James Bertolino, Edward Harkness and

Richard West. *Spindrift*, an annual, is handsomely printed in an 8" square, flat-spined, 125-page format, circulation 500. Price per issue: $6.50. **Sample postpaid: $5. Send SASE for guidelines. Pays 1 copy. Acquires first serial rights. "Submit 2 copies of each poem, 6 maximum. Include cover letter with biographical information. We accept submissions until February 1—report back in March."** The editors advise, "Read what the major contemporary poets are writing. Read what local poets are writing. Be distinctive, love the language, avoid sentiment."

THE SPIRIT THAT MOVES US; THE SPIRIT THAT MOVES US PRESS; EDITOR'S CHOICE (IV-Anthology), P.O. Box 820, Jackson Heights NY 11372, phone (718)426-8788, founded 1974, poetry editor Morty Sklar. *"The Spirit That Moves Us* will be continuing its **Editor's Choice** series biennially and publishing regular issues only occasionally. **Editor's Choice** consists of reprints from other literary magazines and small presses, where our selections are made from nominations made by the editors of those magazines and presses." They have recently published poetry by Julia Alvarez, Rita Dove, Czeslaw Milosz, Tom Disch and Grace Paley. As a sample the editor selected these lines from "Blood" by Naomi Shihab Nye:

> *After that, my father told me who he was,*
> *"Shihab" — "shooting star" —*
> *a good name, borrowed from the sky.*
> *Once I said, "When we die, we give it back?"*
> *He said that's what a true Arab would say.*

They offer **Editor's Choice III**, 336 pgs. covering 1984-1990, as a sample for $9 plus $1 postage (regularly $12.50 plus $1.50 postage). The editor's advice: "Write what you would like to write, in a style (or styles) which is/are best for your own expression. Don't worry about acceptance, though you may be concerned about it. Don't just send work which you think editors would like to see, though take that into consideration. Think of the relationship between poem, poet and editor as personal. You may send good poems to editors who simply do not like them, whereas other editors might."

SPIT (I, II), 240 E. 9th St. #7, New York NY 10003, phone (212)505-9590 or (212)673-3546, founded 1989, edited by Laurie Shapiro and Joan Dalin with collective input, appears twice a year using **poetry "judged on artistic merit rather than polemical intent."** They have published poetry by Warrick Wynne and Barbara Rosenthal. As a sample the editors selected these lines from "Politics" by Claas Ehlers:

> *On the beach where oceans come in light blue water*
> *At the horizon, more enormous than the tilted moon and gray*
> *— like early morning*
> *Can you see it, Susie, the aircraft carrier, can you see it?*

It is magazine-sized, 50-75 pgs., flat-spined, with card cover, desktop published. Press run is 500. Subscription: $12. **Sample postpaid: $2. Send SASE for guidelines. Pays 1 copy. "Poems should be typed and submitted (if possible) in triplicate. Include a cover letter with name, address and a short biographical statement. Do not print name on poems."** Previously published poems and simultaneous submissions OK, if so indicated. Reports in 1-6 months. Editors comment on rejections "though not extensive. We are always willing to send more detailed comments if the writer requests."

SPITBALL; CASEY AWARD (IV-Sports), 6224 Collegevue Pl., Cincinnati OH 45224, phone (513)541-4296, founded 1981, poetry editor Virgil Smith, is "a unique literary magazine devoted to poetry, fiction and book reviews *exclusively* about baseball. Newcomers are very welcome, but remember that you have to know the subject. We do and our readers do. Perhaps a good place to start for beginners is one's personal reactions to the game, *a* game, a player, etc. & take it from there." The digest-sized, 52-page quarterly, saddle-stapled, matte card cover, offset from typescript, has a circulation of 1,000, 750+ subscriptions of which 25 are libraries. They receive about 1,000 submissions/year, use 40—very small backlog. "Many times we are able to publish accepted work almost immediately." Subscription: $12. **Sample postpaid: $5. "We are not very concerned with the technical details of submitting, but we do prefer a cover letter with some bio info. We also like batches of poems and prefer to use several of same poet in an issue rather than a single poem." Pays 2 copies.** "We encourage anyone interested to submit to *Spitball.* We are always looking for fresh talent. Those who have never written 'baseball poetry' before should read some first probably before submitting. Not necessarily ours. We sponsor the Casey Award (for best baseball book of the year) and the Casey Awards Banquet every January. Any chapbook of baseball poetry should be sent to us for consideration for the 'Casey' plaque that we award to the winner each year."

‡SPOKES (II), % The Orchard House, 45 Clophill Rd., Upper Gravénhurst, Bedford MK45 4JH England, founded 1985, editor Donald Atkinson, a semiannual journal of new poetry, art and criticism, with an informational review of recent publications, called *SCAN*. The editor wants "**all types of poetry,**

100-line limit. All kinds of subjects!" *Spokes* is 7 × 10, perfect-bound, "offset litho printed," 72-80 pgs., with pictures, illustrated gloss cover. Its circulation is mainly Great Britain and USA, but some other countries. Price per issue is £3.25 plus postage; subscription £7.50/year (£9/year overseas). **There are no particular specifications for submissions. Reporting time is 6-8 weeks and time to publication approximately 6-12 months.**

THE SPOON RIVER POETRY REVIEW (II, IV-Regional, translations), (formerly *Spoon River Quarterly*), English Dept., Illinois State University, Normal IL 61761, phone (309)438-7906, founded 1976, poetry editor Lucia Getsi, is a "poetry magazine that features newer and well-known poets from around the country and world"; features **one Illinois poet/issue** at length for the magazine's Illinois Poet Series among other national and international poets. **"We want interesting and compelling poetry that operates beyond the ho-hum, so-what level, in any form or style about anything; language that is fresh, energetic, committed, filled with some strong voice of authority that grabs the reader in the first line and never lets go. Do not want to see insipid, dull, boring poems, especially those that I cannot ascertain why they're in lines and not paragraphs; poetry which, if you were to put it into paragraphs, would become bad prose."** They also use translations of poetry. They have recently published poetry by Frankie Paino, Tim Seibles, Paulette Roeske, Walter McDonald, Elaine Terranova, Roger Mitchell and Kathariné Soniat. As a sample Lucia Getsi selected these lines by Kay Murphy:

> This is as close as I can come to make what she says true:
> Inside, my uncle has his hand inside my aunt's blue dress.
> The fields are burning with a want I don't yet understand.
> The orchard has simply given up, as my cousin has.

TSRPR has moved to a twice a year double issue format. It is digest-sized, laser set with card cover using photos, ads. They accept about 2% of 1,000 poems received/month. Press run is 600 for 400 subscriptions (100 of them libraries) and shelf sales. Subscription: $12. **Sample postpaid: $6. Pays 2 copies. Acquires first North American serial rights only. Reports in 2 months. "No simultaneous submissions unless we are notified immediately if a submission is accepted elsewhere. We accept feature-length submissions of unpublished poems from poets who have an Illinois connection, by birth or current residence." Editor comments on rejections "many times, if a poet is promising."** This is one of the best reads in the poetry-publishing world. Editor Lucia Cordell Getsi jampacks the journal with poems of varied styles and presents them in a handsome, perfect-bound product. You'll want to order a sample issue to get a feel for this fine publication.

STAND MAGAZINE; NORTHERN HOUSE (II, IV-Translations), 19 Haldane Terrace, Newcastle on Tyne NE2 3AN England. US Editor: Prof. Jessie Emerson, P.O. Box 5923, Huntsville AL 35814 (all US contributions to US editor please). *Stand*, founded by editor Jon Silkin in 1952, is a highly esteemed literary quarterly. Jon Silkin seeks more subscriptions from US readers and also hopes "that the magazine would be seriously treated as an alternative platform to American literary journals." He wants "verse that tries to explore forms. No formulaic verse." They have published poems by such poets as Peter Redgrove, Elizabeth Jennings and Barry Spacks. *Library Journal* calls *Stand* "one of England's best, liveliest and truly imaginative little magazines." Among better-known American poets whose work has appeared there are Robert Bly, William Stafford, David Ignatow, Philip Levine and Richard Eberhart. Poet Donald Hall says of it, "among essential magazines, there is Jon Silkin's *Stand*, politically left, with reviews, poems and much translation from continental literature." In its current format it is 6 × 8, flat-spined, 80 pgs., professionally printed in 2 columns, small type, on thin stock with glossy card cover, using ads. Circulation is 4,500 with 2,800 subscriptions of which 600 are libraries. Subscription: $22. **Sample postpaid: $6.50. Pays £30/poem (unless under 6 lines) and 1 copy (⅓ off additional copies). Buys first world serial rights for 3 months after publication. If work(s) appear elsewhere** *Stand*/Northern House must be credited. Reviews books of poetry in 3,000-4,000 words, multi-book format. **Northern House "publishes mostly small collections of poetry by new or established poets. The pamphlets often contain a group of poems written to one theme. Occasionally larger volumes are published,** such as the full-length collection by Sorley Maclean, translated by Iain Crichton Smith."

STAPLE (I, II), Gilderoy East, Upperwood Rd., Matlock, Bath DE4 3PD United Kingdom, phone 0629-583867 and 0629-582764, founded 1982, coeditor Bob Windsor. This literary magazine appears 4-5 times a year including supplements. **"Nothing barred: Evidence of craft, but both traditional and modernist accepted; no totally esoteric or concrete poetry."** They have published poetry by Fleur Adcock, Jon Silkin, Elizabeth Bartlett, Thomas Kretz and Jennifer Olds. As a sample they selected these lines from "Poetic Diction 1991" by James Brockway:

> not quite the voice for calling in the cat
> or saying grace — not using words like that,
> But yes, it's true — a kind of transformation,

Staple is professionally printed, flat-spined, 80 pgs., with card cover. Of 3,000 poems received/year they accept about 5%. Their press run is 600 with 300 subscriptions. Subscription: £12 (sterling only). **Sample postpaid: £3. Guidelines available for SASE. Pays modest fee plus complimentary copy (or free subscription). They consider simultaneous submissions but previously published poems only under special circumstance. Submission deadlines are end of February, June and November. Reports in up to 3 months. Editors sometimes comment on rejections.** Send SASE (or SAE with IRC) for rules for their open biennial competitions and for *Staple First Editions* monographs, sample £3 postpaid.

STAR BOOKS, INC.; STARLIGHT MAGAZINE (I, IV-Spirituality/inspirational), 408 Pearson St., Wilson NC 27893, phone (919)237-1591, founded 1983, president Irene Burk Harrell, who says they are "very enthusiastically open to beginners. We have published 10 volumes of poetry to date, 5 of which were written by persons who had no previous publication record. **All of our poetry is specifically Christian, in line with the teachings of the Bible. We're looking for the fresh and the new. Can't use avant-garde and/or esoteric. For us the impact of the *thought* of a poem is paramount. Need more short poems, with short lines.**" They have published books of poetry by Marilyn Phemister, Norma Woodbridge and Charlotte Carpenter. "Contributors to our *StarLight* magazine are largely previously unpublished." As a sample she selected these lines from Gennet Emery's "Lament for a Child" in her **Wayfarer:**

> *Some thought the pain was less*
> *Because I never saw you*
>
> *But oh, I did!*
> *My heart and mind wove textured skin,*
> *Caressed your cheeks, touched finespun hair*
> *And smelled sweet breath.*

The book is 128 pgs., trade paperback size, flat-spined, professionally printed, with glossy card cover: $8. *StarLight* is a quarterly, digest-sized, 60 pgs., saddle-stapled, professionally printed, with matte card cover. The inspirational verse it contains is largely rhymed and free style (some of surprising good quality, considering this is billed mainly as a beginner's market). Some poems are illustrated with Bible excerpts, and the publication includes long bio notes about contributors. Subscription: $15. **Sample postpaid: $4. Guidelines available for SASE. Submit one poem per page, no cursive type, no erasable bond, no simultaneous submissions or previously published poems. Name and address on each page. Pays 3 copies of magazine; books pay 10% or more royalties. Acquires first serial rights for *StarLight*; all rights for Star Books. For *StarLight* read magazine and send 5-7 samples with SASE. Submit whole manuscript for book publication with cover letter including bio, publications, "something about yourself, especially about your relationship to God and why you are writing. We are an exceedingly personal publishing house." Reports in 1-4 weeks.** They hold an annual Star Books Writers' Workshop in October. Write for information. Irene Burk Harrell says, "Because God seems to be speaking to His children today through poetry, and because established publishing houses are often closed to it, we are looking forward to publishing more and more anointed, God-given poetry. The more personal the better."

STARMIST BOOKS (V), Box 12640, Rochester NY 14612, founded 1986, president Beth Boyd, publishes 2-4 paperbacks/year. They publish **"poetry that comes from the heart . . . that has the depth of true feeling. No pornography." They are currently not accepting poetry submissions. "We have reached our quota into 1994."** As a sample the editor selected these lines by jani johe webster:

> *i need something now*
> *in my life*
> *as simple as*
>
> *a yellow rose*
> *seen from a kitchen window*

Replies to queries in 2 weeks, to mss (if invited) in 3 weeks. Pay is negotiable. Inquire about samples. The editor advises poets, "To feel always the poetry within—to know it all about us."

STATE STREET PRESS (II), P.O. Box 278, Brockport NY 14420, phone (716)637-0023, founded 1981, poetry editor Judith Kitchen, "publishes **chapbooks of poetry (20-24 pgs.)** usually chosen in an anonymous competition. State Street Press hopes to publish emerging writers with solid first collections and to offer a format for established writers who have a collection of poems that work together as a chapbook. We have also established a full-length publication—for those of our authors who are beginning to have a national reputation. **We want serious traditional and free verse. We are not usually interested in the language school of poets or what would be termed 'beat.' We are quite frankly middle-of-the-road. We ask only that the poems work as a collection, that the chapbook be more than an aggregate of poems—that they work together.**" They have recently published poetry by Naomi Shihab

Close-up

Lucia Cordell Getsi
Poet/Editor
The Spoon River Poetry Review

Oh child do not listen to the stories
that will come to feed from your hands
like little lambs and tame zebras
watch out for the argonauts that will tumble
like gods from Noah's mouth
they seek for their ships
the secret power of a bottle

(Last stanza from "Bottleships" reprinted from
Tamaqua; originally in **Bottleships: for Daughters**,
Aquila Press, 1986)

One is apt to find some of the most powerful words and symbols used in Lucia Getsi's poems. For instance, in another stanza of "Bottleships" (a wordplay on "Battleships"), she writes "Every Sunday I smash bottles/hurling them one by one at the worktable" and you realize that the narrator is smashing her dreams.

"The story of Rapunzel seemed to plot my life for a while," Getsi says. "I looked out of my locked tower and became infatuated with potential male rescuers, until I began to figure out that they were the ones that had actually imprisoned me." She adds that she "finally cut my own hair and used it as a net," waging open rebellion.

"My rebellion over the period of my teens and twenties was launched against almost anything that got in my way," she notes, "especially racism, religion, gender roles, sexual rules—any rules except those in algebra or physics or grammar. Those I learned with something like obsession."

Getsi studied mathematics and physics in college and then crossed over to English literature, history and German. Now she is a professor of English and Comparative Literature and codirector of the Creative Writing Program at Illinois State University at Normal.

Her doctoral dissertation in 1973 was a complete translation of the poems of the Austrian expressionist Georg Trakl; it is one of the finest renderings ever done.

Since then she has published four collections of her poems, the latest being **Intensive Care** (New Rivers Press, 1992), winner of the Capricorn Prize in 1990. Other awards and honors include being named Fulbright Scholar at Ludwig Maximilians Universität in Munich, Germany.

"Translation is beginning to fascinate me again, particularly translation of women poets," she says. Getsi spent part of 1990 learning Italian and wandering around Italy "trying to get a handle on the women's writing scene there."

Translations, incidentally, are welcome at *The Spoon River Poetry Review* (formerly *The Spoon River Quarterly*), the poetry journal Getsi has edited since 1987. As for standard submissions, she prefers "poetry that gets written on the edge. I like language that takes risks, thought that worries about things and thought that is driven by feeling."

Finally, Getsi adds, "I used to value subjective truth over just about everything, but I think now that subjective truth is qualified for me to mean the absolute power of language."

—Michael J. Bugeja

Nye, Dionisio Martinez, Jeff Oaks, Cecile Goding and Marcia Hurlow. Chapbooks are beautifully designed and printed, 6×9, 30 pgs., with textured matte wrapper with art. **Send SASE for guidelines and chapbook contest rules. There is a $5 entry fee, for which you receive one of the chapbooks already published. Simultaneous submissions encouraged. Photocopies OK. Dot-matrix OK "but we don't like it." Pays copies and small honorarium, and authors buy additional ones at cost, sell at readings and keep the profits.** Judith Kitchen comments, "State Street Press believes that the magazines are doing a good job of publishing beginning poets and we hope to present published and unpublished work in a more permanent format, so we do reflect the current market and tastes. We expect our writers to have published individual poems and to be considering a larger body of work that in some way forms a 'book.' We have been cited as a press that prints poetry that is accessible to the general reader."

‡**THE STEELHEAD SPECIAL (I)**, P.O. Box 219, Bayside CA 95524, phone (707)445-1907, founded 1991, editor Crawdad Nelson, is a bimonthly "Northwest working-class cultural and literary review." They want **"fresh, working-class, rugged, bold poetry. Nothing weepy, clichéd, sentimental."** They have recently published poetry by Albert Huffstickler, Jim Dodge and Leonard Cirino. As a sample the editor selected these lines from "Sore Tail" by Linda Noel:

> sore tail
> laughs
> at the fishcop
> dares his badge
> because salmon
> come home
> to spawn
> tomorrow's stars

It is 48 pgs., 8½×11, newsprint, saddle-stapled, with art and graphics. They receive 500-600 poems a year, accept 10-20/issue. Press run is 3,500 for 100 subscribers, 500 shelf sales. 3,300 distributed free to the general public and fishermen. Single copy: $1; subscription: $12. **Sample postpaid: $2. Previously published poems and simultaneous submissions OK. Often comments on rejections. Send SASE for guidelines. Reports in 1-8 weeks. Pays 3-4 copies.** Crawdad Nelson says, "We see lots of good poetry. Hope to see more. Nothing bogged down in bourgeois ennui, please. Vitality helps, but stay alert. Subscriptions encouraged."

THE WALLACE STEVENS JOURNAL (II, IV-Themes), Liberal Studies, Clarkson University, Potsdam NY 13699, founded 1977, poetry editor Prof. Joseph Duemer, appears biannually using **"poems about or in the spirit of Wallace Stevens or having some relation to his work. No bad parodies of Stevens' anthology pieces."** They have recently published poetry by Elizabeth Spires, Sigman Byrd, Bruce Bond and Janet McCann. As a sample the editor selected these lines from "A World Without Desire" by Michael G. Gessner:

> Occurred tonight for an hour only,
> An hour spent around the back porch
> Where I was sent from the family, exiled
> From myself. It was a world of order,
> Order and presence, the final meaning
> Of forms conversing through the night
> As large as all thought must be
> This house a ragged piece of locale
> Torn adrift in the space of a dark mind.

The editor describes it as 80-120 pgs., 6×9, typeset, flat-spined, with cover art on glossy stock. They accept 10-15 poems of 50-75 received. Press run 900 for 600 subscribers of which 200 are libraries. Subscription: $15. **Sample postpaid: $4. Reports in 2-8 weeks. Pays 2 copies. Acquires all rights. Returns rights with permission and acknowledgment.** *The Wallace Stevens Journal* is published by the Wallace Stevens Society. "Brief cover letters are fine, even encouraged. Please don't submit to *WSJ* if you have not read Stevens. We like parodies, but they must *add* a new angle of perception. Most of the poems we publish are not parodies but meditations on themes related to Wallace Stevens and those poets he has influenced."

STICKS; STICKS PRESS (III, IV-Form), P.O. Box 399, Maplesville AL 36750-0399, press founded 1989, journal 1991, editor/publisher Mary Veazey. *Sticks*, appearing irregularly, is "a cross between a poetry journal and a wedding announcement: greeting-card small, classy, nice paper and good printing, words meant to last, something to be tied up with a ribbon, along with your best love letters, and tucked into your trunk. **It publishes the best short poems of experienced/established poets. All styles, subjects. But no haiku. Preferred length: 10 lines or less; width: 50 spaces."** She has recently published poetry by X.J. Kennedy and Richard Kostelanetz. As a sample the editor selected this poem, "Second Eve," by Charles Ghigna:

When you pass by
the weeping willow stops,
stands tall,

becomes the apple tree
whose fruit is sweeter
than God.

The magazine is a 4¼×5½, saddle-stapled or saddle-sewn booklet, professionally printed on acid-free paper, 24 pgs. Press run 250+. **Pays 2 copies. Acquires first North American serial rights. "No guidelines, just be a master of the short poem. Write for sample issue." No simultaneous submissions. Reads submissions October through December only. "Sometimes comments briefly on submissions." Reports in 3 months or less. The press publishes, on occasion, a mini-chapbook. Send complete ms to consist of one longish poem. Pays 30 copies.** The editor says: "Almost everything published is small in format; the ideal is a journal that requires only a first class stamp and can be read walking back from the mailbox; speedy like a zip code and the opposite of junk mail. If you're in a rush to be published, Sticks Press is not the place; I savor the poems chosen and then often spend considerable time writing the authors and discussing their work. Please take into consideration that Sticks Press is a one-person operation—no committee, no helpers, no advisers, no patrons, just one individual working hard for poetry. In general, I offer the same advice I give myself: Try to write the poem that will outlast us all, that will still be read a hundred years from now. Or ten years from now. Six months from now? Will, the poor son of a glover, wrote some sonnets that people still argue about. How about *you*?"

STILL WATERS PRESS; STILL WATERS WRITING CENTER; WOMEN'S POETRY CHAPBOOK CONTEST; WINTER POETRY CHAPBOOK COMPETITION (II, IV-Women), 112 W. Duerer St., Galloway NJ 08201, phone (609)652-1790, founded 1989, editor Shirley Warren, is a "small press publisher of poetry chapbooks, short fiction chapbooks and poet's handbooks (contemporary craft). Especially interested in **works by, for and about women. We prefer poetry firmly planted in the real world, but equally mindful of poetry as art. The transformation from pain to perseverance, from ordinary to extraordinary, from defeat to triumph, pleases us. But we reject Pollyanna poetry immediately. Nothing sexist, in either direction. We don't want homosexual poetry. Most rhymed poetry doesn't work because it leads to strange manipulations of syntax to achieve rhyme. No patriarchal religious verse. Preferred length: 4 lines—2 pages per poem. Form: no restrictions—we expect content to dictate the form."** They have recently published poetry by Kevin Griffith and Kate Abbe. As a sample the editor selected a short poem, "The End of Summer," from Griffith's chapbook, **Labors**:

Eskimos toss the whale-watcher high
with a blanket of skin. Herds
of reindeer graze on fields of lichen.

All day
I've done nothing but sit on the front porch,
a book in my hand. I'm waiting it out,
feeling the ice move in from far places,
like the fisherman who trails the heart of an ox
deep beneath waves.

She publishes 4-8 books a year, including one or two flat-spined paperbacks and chapbooks averaging 28-40 pgs. **Query with 3 samples, bio, publications. Simultaneous submissions and previously published poems OK. Pays 10% of the press run. Acquires first or reprint rights. Editor comments on submissions "usually."** Sample chapbooks: $4.95; pamphlets: $3. They hold 4 annual contests, each with $10 reading fee; send SASE for detailed guidelines. The editor says, "Read other poets, both contemporary and traditional. Attend some workshops, establish rapport with your local peers, attend readings. Keep your best work in circulation. Someone out there is looking for you." The Still Waters Writing Center offers workshops, writing classes and some readings.

STONE CIRCLE PRESS (IV-Ethnic), P.O. Box 44, Oakland CA 94604, founded 1987, editor Len Irving, publishes books **"of a Celtic nature. Backgrounded in Scotland, Ireland, Wales, Isle of Man, Cornwall, Brittany. We welcome Stonehenge rather than Acropolis material."** They publish about 2 flat-spined paperbacks/year, averaging 100 pgs. **Query with 6 samples. Responds to queries in 1 month. Pays 25 books.** "We are a nonprofit press associated with the Institute of Celtic Studies. We finance and publish the book. The author receives a stated number of books but no royalties." They also subsidy publish, providing "seed money and desktop publication," seeking donations from all available sources.

STONE PRESS (V), 9727 SE Reedway, Portland OR 97266, founded 1968, editor Albert Drake, publishes poetry postcards, posters, broadsides, chapbooks and books. He has published books by Earle Birney, Judith Goren, Lee Upton and James Kalmbach. **"However due to other publishing commitments, Stone Press is presently in limbo."**

STONE SOUP, THE MAGAZINE BY CHILDREN; THE CHILDREN'S ART FOUNDATION (IV-Children), P.O. Box 83, Santa Cruz CA 95063, founded 1973, editor Ms. Gerry Mandel. *Stone Soup* publishes **writing and art by children through age 13; they want to see free verse poetry but no rhyming poetry, haiku or cinquain.** The editor chose as a sample this poem, "Nightfall," by 7-year-old Jaiva Larsen:

> *When the blackberry moon rises*
> *And the sky flies by like ocean waves*
> *And the chill of the evening*
> *Flies through your heart*
> *Run home*
> *Run home*

Stone Soup, published 5 times a year, is a handsome 6 × 8¾ magazine, professionally printed on heavy stock with 4 full-color art reproductions inside and a full-color illustration on the coated cover, saddle-stapled. A membership in the Children's Art Foundation at $23/year includes a subscription to the magazine, each issue of which contains an Activity Guide. There are 4 pgs. of poetry in each issue. Circulation is 14,000, all by subscription; 2,000 go to libraries. **Sample: $4.50 postpaid. Submissions can be any number of pages, any format, but no simultaneous submissions. The editor receives 5,000 poetry submissions/year and uses only 20; she reports in 1 month. Guidelines are available for SASE. Pay is $10 and 2 copies plus discounts. Buys all rights. Returns rights upon request. Criticism will be given when requested.**

STORMLINE PRESS, INC. (V), Box 593, Urbana IL 61801, phone (217)328-2665, founded 1985, publisher Ray Bial, an independent press publishing fiction, poetry and photography, **"only by invitation. Do not send unsolicited manuscripts. We publish both established and new poets, but in the latter case prefer to publish those poets who have been working some years to master their craft."** The press publishes 1-2 books of poetry each year with an average page count of 48-64. They are 6 × 9, some flat-spined paperbacks and some hardcover.

STORY LINE PRESS; NICHOLAS ROERICH POETRY PRIZE FOR FIRST BOOK OF POETRY (II), Three Oaks Farm, 27006 Gap Road, Brownsville OR 97327-9718, phone (503)466-5352, Story Line Press founded 1985, poetry editor Robert McDowell. Story Line Press publishes each year the winner of the Nicholas Roerich Poetry Prize for a First Book of Poetry ($1,000 plus publication and a paid reading at the Roerich Museum in New York City; a runner-up receives a full Story Line Press Scholarship to the Wesleyan Writers Conference in Middletown, CT; $15 entry and handling fee). Deadline for submissions: October 15. The press also publishes books about poetry and has in the past published collections of poems by such poets as Colette Inez and Donald Hall. **They consider unsolicited mss only for the Nicholas Roerich Poetry Prize competition.**

STRAIGHT; STANDARD PUBLISHING CO. (IV-Religious, teens), 8121 Hamilton Ave., Cincinnati OH 45231, editor Carla J. Crane. Standard is a large religious publishing company. *Straight* is a weekly take-home publication (digest-sized, 12 pgs., color newsprint) **for teens. Poetry is** *by* **teenagers, any style, religious or inspirational in nature. No adult-written poetry.** As a sample the editor selected "Unseen" by Nicole Inman (16):

> *I've never seen the ocean,*
> *And yet I know it's there.*
> *I've never climbed any mountains,*
> *But I've seen them everywhere.*
>
> *I know I'm going to Heaven,*
> *But I haven't yet been there*
> *I don't need to see Christ Jesus,*
> *To convince me that He cares!*

Guidelines available for SASE. Pays $10/poem plus 5 copies. Buys first or reprint rights. Reports in 4-6 weeks, publishes acceptances in 9-12 months. Teen author must include birthdate. Photocopy, dot matrix, simultaneous submissions OK. "Many teenagers write poetry in their English classes at school. If you've written a poem on an inspirational topic, and your teacher's given you an 'A' on it, you've got a very good chance of having it published in *Straight*."

THE STRAIN (II), Box 330507, Houston TX 77233-0507, poetry editor Michael Bond, editor Norman C. Stewart, Jr. *The Strain* is a monthly magazine using **"experimental or traditional poetry of very high quality. Guidelines issue $5 and 8 first class stamps."** Pays **"no less than $5."** Simultaneous submissions and previously published poems OK. "We would prefer you submit before obtaining the guidelines issue which mostly explains upcoming collections and collaborations."

STRIDE PUBLICATIONS; TAXUS PRESS; APPARITIONS PRESS; TROMBONE PRESS (II), 37 Portland St., Newtown, Exeter, Devon EX1 2EG England, founded 1980, editor R.M. Loydell. Stride Publications publishes poetry, poetry sequences, prose and novels. **The editor wants to see any poetry that is "new, inventive, nothing self-oriented, emotional, no narrative or fantasy."** He has published work by Peter Redgrove, Alexis Lykiard, Sheila E. Murphy and David Miller. Stride Publications publishes paperbacks 40-60 pgs. of poetry, plus a few novels and anthologies. **Freelance submissions for book publication are accepted. Authors should query first, sending sample poems with return postage. Queries will be answered in 3 weeks and mss reported on in 3 months or more. Photocopied mss are OK. Pay is in author's copies.** Reviews books of poetry in 100-200 words, multi-book format.

STRUGGLE: A MAGAZINE OF PROLETARIAN REVOLUTIONARY LITERATURE (I, II, IV-Political, themes, workers' social issues, women, anti-racist), Box 13261, Harper Station, Detroit MI 48213-0261, founded 1985, editor Tim Hall, is a "literary quarterly, content: the struggle of the working people against the rich. Issues such as: racism, war preparations, worker's struggle against concessions, the overall struggle for genuine socialism." The **poetry and songs they use are "generally short, any style, subject matter must highlight the fight against the rule of the billionaires. No material unconnected to the fight to change society, but we welcome experimentation devoted to furthering such content."** They have recently published poetry by L. Ross, R. Nat Turner, Willie Abraham Howard Jr. and Albert Chui Clark. As a sample the editor selected these lines from "Loose Property" by Nissa Annakindt:

> We arrest you for the crime
> of having no houses
> no time-sharing condos in Florida
> no hunting camps in Canada
> nothing but these cardboard boxes
> which we hereby crush

Struggle is digest-sized, 24-40 pgs., printed by photo offset using drawings, occasional photos of artwork, short stories, short plays and essays as well as poetry and songs (sometimes with their music). Subscription: $6 for 4 issues. **Sample postpaid: $1.50. Pays 2 copies. Tries to report in 1-3 months. Accepted work usually appears in the next issue. Editor tries to provide criticism "with every submission."** Tim Hall says, "We want literature and art of discontent with the government and the social and economic system. Show some passion and fire. Formal experiments, traditional forms both welcome. Especially favor works reflecting rebellion by the working people against the rich, against racism, sexism, militarism, imperialism. We support the revolutions and rebellions in Eastern Europe and the Soviet Union, having always considered these regimes state-capitalist and not at all socialist. Especially interested now in material attacking the rich for bringing economic disaster to the poor and working folk generally."

STUDENT LEADERSHIP JOURNAL (IV-Students, religious), P.O. Box 7895, Madison WI 53707-7895, phone (608)274-9001, editor Jeff Yourison, is a **"magazine for Christian student leaders on secular campuses. We accept a wide variety of poetry. Do not want to see trite poetry. Also, we accept little rhymed poetry; it must be very, very good."** As a sample the editor selected the last stanzas of "A bird in the church" by Luci Shaw:

> and high and low and up again, through the sun's
> transfixing shafts, her wings test gravity
> in a bewilderment of interior air, opening
> and closing on her feathered restlessness
> until, as though coming home, she settles
>
> on the arm of the crucifix. Having found
> a nesting tree (even thine altars, O Lord!),
> she lodges at last, at the angle
> where vertex and horizon meet, resting
> in the steady pain of Christ's left eye.

Student Leadership is a quarterly, magazine-sized, 28 pgs., 2-color inside, 2-color covers, with no advertising, 70% editorial, 30% graphics/art, 8,000 press run going to college students in the United States and Canada. Subscription: $12.50. **Sample postpaid: $3. Send SASE for guidelines. Pays $25-50/poem plus 2 copies. Buys first or reprint rights.** "Would-be contributors should read us to be familiar with what we publish." Best time to submit mss is March through July ("We set our year's editorial plan"). No simultaneous submissions. Previously published poems OK. Reports in 2-3 months, 1-24 months to publication. Editor "occasionally" comments on

rejections. He says, "Try to express feelings through images and metaphor. Religious poetry should not be overly didactic, and it should never moralize!"

STUDIO, A JOURNAL OF CHRISTIANS WRITING (II, IV-Religious), 727 Peel St., Albury, New South Wales 2640 Australia, founded 1980, publisher Paul Grover, a small press literary quarterly "with contents **focusing upon the Christian striving for excellence in poetry,** prose and occasional articles relating Christian views of literary ideas." **In poetry, the editors want "shorter pieces but with no specification as to form or length (necessarily less than 3-4 pages), subject matter, style or purpose. People who send material should be comfortable being published under this banner:** *Studio, A Journal of Christians Writing."* They have published poetry by John Foulcher and other Australian poets. *Studio* is digest-sized, professionally printed on high-quality colored stock, 36 pgs., saddle-stapled, matte card cover, with graphics and line drawings. Circulation is 300, all subscriptions. Subscription $40 (Aud) for overseas members. **Sample available (airmail from US) for $8 (Aud). Pay is 1 copy. Acquires first Australian rights. Submissions may be "typed copy or dot-matrix or simultaneous." Reporting time is 2 months and time to publication is 9 months.** Reviews books of poetry in 250 words, single format. The magazine conducts a biannual poetry and short story contest. The editor says, "Trend in Australia is for imagist poetry and poetry exploring the land and the self. Reading the magazine gives the best indication of style and standard, so send a few dollars for a sample copy before sending your poetry. Keep writing, and we look forward to hearing from you."

SUB-TERRAIN; ANVIL PRESS (II, IV-Social, themes, form/style), Box 1575, Station A, Vancouver, British Columbia V6C 2P7 Canada, phone (604)876-8710, founded 1988, poetry editor Paul Pitre. Anvil Press is an "alternate small press publishing *Sub-Terrain* — a socially conscious literary quarterly whose aim is to produce a reading source that will stand in contrast to the trite and pandered — as well as broadsheets, chapbooks and the occasional monograph. They want **"work that has a point-of-view; work that has some passion behind it and is exploring issues that are of pressing importance; work that challenges conventional notions of what poetry is or should be; work with a social conscience. In short, what poetry should be: powerful, beautiful, important. No bland, flowery, uninventive poetry that says nothing in style or content."** *Sub-Terrain* is 20-24 pgs., 7 × 10 offset with a press run of 1,000. Subscription: $10. **Sample postpaid: $3. Pays money only for solicited work; for other work, 4-issue subscription. They will consider simultaneous submissions, but not previously published poems. Acquires one-time rights for magazine. "If chapbook contract, we retain right to publish subsequent printings unless we let a title lapse out-of-print for more than 1 year." Reports in 4-6 weeks.** Occasionally reviews small press poetry chapbooks. Sponsors Last Poems Poetry Contest; information for SASE. For chapbook or book publication submit 4 sample poems and bio, no simultaneous submissions. "We are willing to consider mss. But I must stress that we are a co-op, depending on support from an interested audience. New titles will be undertaken with caution. We are not subsidized at this point and do not want to give authors false hopes — but if something is important and should be in print, we will do our best." Editor provides brief comment and more extensive comments for fees. He says, "Poetry, in our opinion, should be a distillation of emotion and experience that is being given back to the world. Pretty words and fancy syntax are just that. Where are the modern day writers who are willing to risk it all, put it all on the line? Young, new writers: show it all, bare your guts, write about what you fear! Believe in the power of the word. The last thing the world needs is soppy, sentimental fluff that gives nothing and says nothing."

‡THE SUCARNOCHEE REVIEW (II), Station 22, Livingston University, Livingston AL 35470, founded 1985, editor Joe Taylor, is an annual literary magazine which accepts poetry and fiction. "Sucarnochee (suke'nachi) is the Choctaw word for 'hog river' or 'a place where hogs bathe.' " **The editors have no specifications as to form, length, subject matter or style.** They have recently published poetry by R.T. Smith, Peter Huggins, Lewis Turco and Joseph Powell. As a sample the editor selected these lines from "Van Gogh at Saint Remy" by Wayne Cox:

> Today, the poplars were on fire
> With autumn; tonight
> I see only an abyss of stars.

> Once again, I must point myself
> And take stock like a farmer
> At the end of another bad year.

The editor says it is 70 pgs., perfect-bound. They receive about 500 poems a year, use approximately 10%. Press run is 500. Subscription: $10. **Sample postpaid: $5. No previously published poems; simultaneous submissions OK. Cover letter with short bio required.** Time between acceptance and publication is 6 months. **Seldom comments on rejections. Reports in "one week to four months." Pays 3 copies. Acquires first North American serial rights.** They award $50 for the best poem in each issue. Winning poems are chosen by the editors. You may want to order a sample copy of this magazine because its poetry, mostly structured free verse with emphasis on voice, has wide appeal. We found this a good read (with several poems as fine as what you might find in the best journals).

SULFUR MAGAZINE (II, IV-Translations), Dept. of English, Eastern Michigan University, Ypsilanti MI 48197, phone (313)483-9787, founded 1981, poetry editor Clayton Eshleman, is a physically gorgeous and hefty (250+ pgs., 6×9, flat-spined, glossy card cover, elegant graphics and printing on quality stock) biannual that has earned a distinguished reputation. They have published poetry by John Ashbery, Ed Sanders, Gary Snyder, Jackson MacLow, Paul Blackburn and the editor (one of our better-known poets). Published by EMU, *Sulfur* has a circulation of 2,000, using approximately 100 pgs. of poetry in each issue. They use 5-10 of 600-700 submissions received/year. Subscription: $13. **Sample postpaid: $6. "We urge would-be contributors to *read* the magazine and send us material only if it seems to be appropriate." Reports in 2-3 weeks. Pays $35-40 per contributor. Editor comments "sometimes, if the material is interesting."** Reviews 10-20 poetry books/issue. Clayton Eshleman says, "Most unsolicited material is of the 'I am sensitive and have practiced my sensitivity' school—with little attention to language as such, or incorporation of materials that lead the poem into more ample contexts than 'personal' experience. I fear too many young writers today spend more time on themselves, without deeply engaging their *selves*, in a serious psychological way—and too little time breaking their heads against the Blakes, Stevens and Vallejos of the world. That is, writing has replaced reading. I believe that writing is a form of reading and vice versa. Of course, it is the quality and wildness of imagination that finally counts—but this 'quality' is a composite considerably dependent on assimilative reading (and translating, too)."

‡SULPHUR RIVER LITERARY REVIEW (III), P.O. Box 402087, Austin TX 78704-5578, founded 1978, reestablished 1987, editor/publisher James Michael Robbins, is a semiannual of poetry, prose and artwork. They have **"no restrictions except quality." They do not want poetry that is "trite or religious or verse that does not incite thought."** They have recently published poetry by Walt McDonald, Lyn Lifshin, Laurel Speer and Albert Huffstickler. As a sample we selected these lines from "Vegetable Garden" by J.B. Goodenough:

> Now with a crooked back he tends
> Bean-rows straight as hoe-handles,
> Suspecting any of them
> Might be, suddenly,
> His last, perfected, effort.

SRLR is digest-sized, perfect-bound, with glossy cover. They receive about 200 poems a year, accept about 20%. Press run is 400 for 200 subscribers, 100 shelf sales. Subscription: $5. **Sample postpaid: $3. No previously published poems or simultaneous submissions. "I enjoy receiving cover letters that acknowledge me as a human being rather than no letter or one that implies I am a machine that processes poems." Often comments on rejections. Reports in 1 month. Pays 2 copies.** The editor says, "Poetry is, for me, the essential art, the ultimate art, and any effort to reach the effect of the successful poem deserves some comment other than 'sorry.' This is why I try to comment as much as possible on submissions, though by doing so I risk my own special absurdity. So be it. However, there can be no compromise of quality if the poem is to be successful or essential art."

SUMMER STREAM PRESS (IV-Anthologies), P.O. Box 6056, Santa Barbara CA 93160-6056, phone (805)962-6540, founded 1978, poetry editor David D. Frost, publishes a series of books in hardcover and softcover, each presenting 6 poets, averaging 70 text pgs. for each poet. "The mix of poets represents many parts of the country and many approaches to poetry. The poets previously selected have been published, but that is no requirement. We welcome traditional poets in the mix and thus offer them a chance for publication in this world of free-versers. **The six poets share a 15% royalty. We require rights for our editions worldwide and share 50-50 with authors for translation rights and for republication of our editions by another publisher. Otherwise all rights remain with the authors."** They have recently published poetry by Virginia E. Smith, Sandra Russell, Mark Neider, Nancy Berg, Lois Shapley Bassen and Nancy E. Wallace. To be considered for future volumes in this series, **query with about 12 samples, no cover letter. Replies to query in 3 months, to submission (if invited) in 1 year. Previously published poetry, simultaneous submissions and photocopies OK. Editor usually comments on rejections.**

THE SUN (II), 107 N. Roberson St., Chapel Hill NC 27516, phone (919)942-5282, founded 1974, editor Sy Safransky, is "a monthly magazine of ideas" which uses "**all kinds of poetry.**" They have recently published poetry by Antler, Jim Harrison, Bertha Rogers, Dennis Sampson and Hilde Weisert. *The Sun* is magazine-sized, 40 pgs., printed on 50 lb. offset, saddle-stapled, with b&w photos and graphics, circulation 15,000, 10,000 subscriptions of which 50 are libraries. They receive 3,000 submissions of freelance poetry/year, use 25, have a 1- to 3-month backlog. Subscription: $30. **Sample postpaid: $3. Submit no more than 6 poems. Reports within 3 months. Pays $25 on publication and in copies and subscription. Buys first serial or one-time rights. Send SASE for guidelines.**

SUN DOG: THE SOUTHEAST REVIEW (II), 406 Williams Bldg., English Department, Florida State University, Tallahassee FL 32306, phone (904)644-4230, founded 1979, poetry editor Michael Trammell. "The journal has a small student staff. We publish two flat-spined, 100-page magazines per year of poetry, short fiction and essays. As a norm, we usually accept about 12 poems per issue. **We accept poetry of the highest caliber, looking for the most 'whole' works. A poet may submit any length, but because of space, poems over 2 pages are impractical. Excellent formal verse highly regarded.**" They have published poetry by David Bottoms, David Kirby, Peter Meinke and Leon Stokesbury. *SD* is 6×9 with a glossy card cover. Usually including half-tones, line drawings and color art when budget allows. Press run of 1,250. Subscription: $8 for 2 issues. Sample: $4 postpaid. Send SASE for guidelines. **Pays 2 copies. Acquires first North American serial rights. Poems should be typed single spaced, between 2-5 submissions at a time. If simultaneous submission, say so. No previously published poems. Reports in 3 months.** Editor will comment briefly on most poems, especially those which come close to being accepted.

SUNSHINE MAGAZINE; GOOD READING MAGAZINE; THE SUNSHINE PRESS; HENRICHS PUBLICATIONS, INC. (I, IV-Inspirational, humor), P.O. Box 40, Litchfield IL 62056, phone (217)324-3425, founded 1924, poetry editor Peggy Kuethe. *Sunshine Magazine* "is almost entirely a fiction magazine; *Good Reading* is made up of short, current interest factual articles." Both magazines use some poetry. **"We do *not* publish free verse or abstract poetry, no haiku, no negative subjects, no violence, sex, alcohol. We use only uplifting, inspirational poetry that is of regular meter and that rhymes. Inspirational, seasonal or humorous poetry preferred. Easy to read, pleasantly rhythmic. Maximum 16 lines—no exceptions."** They have recently published poetry by Helen K. Evans, Starrlette Howard, E. Cole Ingle, Grace Rhinebeck and Alice Mackenzie Swaim. As a sample the editor selected these lines from "O Glorious Days" by Edith Johnson:

> *The grandeur seen this lovely day*
> *Proves nothing is amiss*
> *For only God could skillfully paint*
> *A masterpiece like this.*

Both magazines are monthlies. *Sunshine* is 5¼×7¼, saddle-stapled, 36 pgs., of which 5 are poetry, circulation to 75,000 subscribers. They use about 7% of 2,500 submissions of poetry each year. Subscription: $10. **Sample: 50¢. Send SASE for guidelines. Absolutely no queries. Submit typewritten ms, 1 poem/page. Reports in 8-10 weeks. Pays 1 copy. Acquires first or second North American serial rights.** *Good Reading* uses about 4 poems/issue, circulation to 7,200 subscribers. Subscription: $9. **Sample: 50¢.** Submission specifications like those for *Sunshine*. **Pays 1 copy. Also acquires first or second serial rights.** The editors comment, "We strongly suggest authors read our guidelines and obtain a sample copy of our magazines. Our format and policies are quite rigid and we make absolutely no exceptions. Many authors submit something entirely different from our format or from anything we've published before—that is an instant guarantee of rejection."

SUPERINTENDENT'S PROFILE & POCKET EQUIPMENT DIRECTORY (IV-Themes), 220 Central Ave., Box 43, Dunkirk NY 14048, phone (716)366-4774, founded 1978, poetry editor Robert Dyment, is a "monthly magazine, circulation 2,500, for town, village, city and county highway superintendents and DPW directors throughout New York State," and uses **"only poetry that pertains to highway superintendents and DPW directors and their activities." Submit no more than one page double-spaced.** They receive about 50 freelance submissions of poetry/year, use 20, have a 2-month backlog. Subscription: $10. **Sample: 80¢ postage. Reports within a month. Pays $5/poem.**

SWAMP ROOT (II), Rt. 2, Box 1098, Jacksboro TN 37757, phone (615)562-7082, founded 1987, editor Al Masarik, is a poetry magazine appearing 3 times a year. **"All styles welcome, biased toward clarity, brevity, strong imagery."** They have published poetry by Ted Kooser, Naomi Shihab Nye, Linda Hasselstrom, William Kloefkorn and Diane Glancy. It is 6×9, flat-spined on quality stock with matte or glossy card cover, using b&w photos, drawings and collages interspersed with poetry. They receive about 20 submissions/week, use less than 1%. Press run: 1,000 for 63 subscriptions of which 12 are libraries, few shelf sales. Subscription: $12. **Sample postpaid: $5. Pays 3 copies plus year's subscription. Simultaneous submissions and previously published poems used "sometimes." Reports in 1-4 weeks.** Editor comments on submissions. Reviews books of poetry.

SYCAMORE REVIEW (II), Department of English, Purdue University, West Lafayette IN 47907, phone (317)494-3783, founded 1988 (first issue May, 1989), editor Michael Kiser, poetry editor Helene Barker. "We accept personal essays (25 pgs. max), short fiction (25 pgs. max), translations and **quality**

poetry in any form (6 pgs. max). There are no official restrictions as to subject matter or style." They have published poetry by Mary Oliver, John Updike, Susan Neville, Marge Piercy, Russell Edson and Maura Stanton. As a sample the editor selected the following lines by Fleda Brown Jackson:

> ... I must be in the middle
> of my life, the way I feel balanced
> between one thing and another. As if I have
>
> no hands or arms, parting the world
> as it reaches my face. Like a minnow, gone
> on little wings, a blush of sand from the bottom.

The magazine is semiannual in a digest-sized format, 110 pgs., flat-spined, professionally printed, with glossy, color cover. Their press run is 1,000 with 300 subscriptions of which 100 are libraries. Subscription: $9. **Sample postpaid: $5. "We read August 15 through May 1." Guidelines available for SASE. Pays 2 copies. Reports in 4 months. Cover letters not required but invited. Editor comments on about 20% of rejections.**

TAK TAK TAK (II, IV-Translations, themes), P.O. Box 7, Bulwell, Nottingham NG6 OHW England, founded 1986, editors Andrew and Tim Brown, appears occasionally in print and on cassettes, and, in addition, sometimes publishes collections of poetry. "No restrictions on form or style. However, each issue of the magazine is on a theme (i.e., 'Mother Country/Fatherland,' 'Postcards from Paradise'), and *all* contributions must be relevant. If a contribution is long it is going to be more difficult to fit in than something shorter. Write for details of subject(s), etc., of forthcoming issue(s)." They have published poetry by Rudyard Kipling, Michael Horowitz, Karl Blake, Keith Jafrate, Ramona Fotiade and Paul Buck. The editor describes it as "100 pgs., A5, photolithographed, board cover, line drawings and photographs, plus cassette of poetry, music, sounds. Of about 100 poems received in the past year we have used about 25." Press run 500. Subscription: £9, £11.80 postpaid to U.S.A. surface rate (includes 2 issues with cassettes). **Sample: £10.90 postpaid to US. Pays 1 copy, sent surface rate. Submit "a selection of 5 or 6 with a bio of up to 30 words and a photograph suitable for publication." They consider simultaneous submissions and previously published poems. Reports within 6 months. Editor sometimes comments on rejections.** They also publish occasional flat-spined paperbacks averaging between 40 and 130 pgs. **For chapbook consideration send as many as possible sample poems, bio, publications. Reports in 2 months. Pays a negotiated number of copies.** The editors say, "Poetry is just one of the many creative forms our contributions take. We are equally interested in prose and in visual and sound media."

TAKAHE (II, IV-Translations), P.O. Box 13-335, Christchurch 1, New Zealand, phone (03)668659, founded 1989, poetry editors David Howard and Bernadette Hall, is a literary quarterly. **"We have no preconceived specifications as to form, length, subject matter, style or purpose. We believe that poetry is, among other things, the art of significant silence. It demands an active reader whose trust in language matches that of the writer. No work that batters the reader about the head, that refuses to utilize silence and insists on spelling everything out—as if the reader was incapable of making connections."** They have published poetry by Tatyana Shcherbina, Helen Trubek Glenn, Gregory O'Brien, Michael Harlow and Elizabeth Smither. As a sample the poetry editors selected these lines by Tony Beyer:

> an indoors watery light and fetor
> and the hung sides of beef
> that acknowledge their classicism
> by dripping intermittently
> on the shoes of passers by

The poetry editors describe it as 56 pgs., magazine-sized, desktop publishing with woodcut design on cover and some b&w graphics (including ads). They accept an average of 10% of 1,000 poems received a year. Press run: 300 for 189 subscriptions of which 21 are libraries, 90 shelf sales. Subscription: $24 NZ. **Sample postpaid: $9 NZ. Pays 1 copy plus small emolument at editors' discretion. Submit up to 7 poems. Simultaneous submissions and previously published poems OK (if not published in New Zealand). Reports in 2-3 months. Editors comment on submissions "as a matter of course (particularly if the poem is potentially publishable but needs further work)."** The editors say, "In poetry (as in prayer) the essential thing is the degree to which the silences between words are charged with significance. 'Less is more'—but only if the less is carefully weighed."

TAL: A TORAH ART & LITERATURE REVIEW (I, IV-Religious), (formerly *Milim*), 318 Ave. F, Brooklyn NY 11218, phone (718)871-1105, founded 1990, editor Y. David Shulman, appears 3 times/year, using **"poems by those engaged in Torah lifestyle."** They have published poetry by Roberta Chester. As a sample the editor selected these lines by Yedidich Shalom:

> *A letter which swept through the nile-blue sky*
> *And splashed into my hand;*
> *A parchment in my reverent hand,*
> *A silver fish, alive in my wondering hand,*
> *A comet showering the paths of my hand,*
> *A cinder spinning fire in my hand,*

It is 40 pgs., 8×7, offset, saddle-stapled, with matte card cover. Press run is 500. Subscription: $8. **Sample postpaid: $2. Pays 3 copies. Reports in 2 weeks. Editor comments "upon request."**

TALISMAN: A JOURNAL OF CONTEMPORARY POETRY AND POETICS (II), P.O. Box 1117, Hoboken NJ 07030, phone (201)798-9093, founded 1988, editor Edward Foster, appears twice a year. "Each issue centers on the poetry and poetics of a *major* contemporary poet and includes a selection of new work by other important contemporary writers. **We are particularly interested in poetry in alternative (*not* academic) traditions. We don't want traditional poetry."** They have recently published poetry by William Bronk, Robert Creeley, Ron Padgett, Anne Waldman, Alice Notley, Edouard Roditi and Rosmarie Waldrop. As a sample the editor selected the following lines from "Opening Day" by Ann Lauterbach (in the Fall, 1991 Ron Padgett issue):

> *Locally a firm disavowal within the drift.*
> *Shaman of discourse said*
> *Or could have said*
> *These logics go teasingly forward*
> *Into capacities, and then the then.*

Talisman is digest-sized, flat-spined, 152+ pgs., photocopied from typescript, with matte card cover. Their press run is 650 with "substantial" subscriptions of which many are libraries. "We are inundated with submissions and lost track of the number long ago." Subscription: $9 individual; $13 institution. **Sample postpaid: $5. Pays 1 copy. Acquires first North American serial rights. Reports in 1 month.** Reviews books of poetry in 500-1,000+ words, single format.

‡TALISMAN LITERARY RESEARCH, INC. (V), P.O. Box 455, Georgetown CA 95634, founded 1965. They have recently published poetry collections by Kenneth Fields and Clinton Williams, but are **currently not accepting unsolicited mss.** As a sample they selected these lines from "Cart Wheels" by William Burns:

> *And saw the caskets roll in Arlington,*
> *The heroes drawn through flags and guns to graves,*
> *And felt a stiffness give against the sun,*
> *A slouch of noon perhaps, a shrug of fate,*
> *Or sag of God in heavy sky revealed,*
> *And then a turn of mind, a spokeless reel.*

Pays 10% royalties. For sample books or chapbooks, write for brochure.

TAMPA BAY REVIEW (II), 5458 N. Rivershore Dr., Tampa FL 33603, founded 1989, managing editor Gianna Russo, is a literary journal appearing twice a year. **"We want poems (and short stories) which are innovative in language, rhythm and subject matter. We tend toward free verse with strong metaphors and vibrant imagery. We are not interested in sentimental rhymed verse or inspirational poetry."** They have published poetry by William Stafford, Silvia Curbelo and Richard Mathews. It is 50-60 pgs., digest-sized, saddle-stapled, with matte card cover. Press run: 300 for 50 subscribers. "We accept about 20% of what we receive." Subscription: $8. **Sample postpaid: $4.50, back issue $2** "if available." **Send SASE for guidelines. Enclose up to 3 lines of biographical info with submission. "We accept submissions year round but review them in early fall and early spring."** Payment is in contributor's copies. Editor comments on submissions "often." They "occasionally" use previously published poems. **Send no more than 6-8 poems.** "We publish spring and fall. Poems are circulated once or twice to an editorial board, but final decisions are made by our poetry editor. *Tampa Bay Review* is published by Tampa Bay Poets, the area's long-established writers' group. Take risks in your writing. Your goals should be: first, to make your readers understand what you're expressing; and second, to make them sit up and say 'Ah ha!' "

TAMPA REVIEW (III, IV-Translations), P.O. Box 19F, University of Tampa, Tampa FL 33606-1490, phone (813)253-3333, ext. 3621, founded 1964 as *UT Poetry Review,* became *Tampa Review* in 1988, editor Richard Mathews, poetry editors Kathryn Van Spanckeren and Donald Morrill, is an elegant semiannual of fiction, nonfiction, poetry and art (not limited to US authors) wanting **"original and well-crafted poetry written with intelligence and spirit. No greeting card or inspirational verse."** They have published poetry by Alberto Rios, Paul Mariani, Mark Halliday, Denise Levertov and Stephen Dunn. It is 96 pgs., flat-spined, 7½×10½ with a matte card color cover. They accept about 30 of 1,500 poems received a year. Their press run is 500 with 175 subscriptions of which 20 are libraries. **Sample**

postpaid: $5. Pays $10/printed page plus 1 copy and 40% discount on additional copies. Buys first North American serial rights. Unsolicited mss are read between September and December. Reports by mid-February.

TANGRAM PRESS (III), P.O. Box 2249, Granbury TX 76048, phone (817)579-1777, publisher Dayna Fenker. This very small press would like to publish more books such as their handsome coffee-table volume, 12×12, hardback, **Where Rainbows Wait for Rain: The Big Bend Country**, combining poems by Sandra Lynn and b&w photographs by Richard Fenker Jr., but "we have a limited staff. **While we do not discourage submissions, we cannot guarantee comments on same. We are not your standard poetry publisher.**"

TAPJOE: THE ANAPROCRUSTEAN POETRY JOURNAL OF ENUMCLAW (II, IV-Nature, social issues), P.O. Box 632, Leavenworth WA 98826, founded 1987, is a biannual. "**We try to be very open-minded but have a definite preference for free verse poems, 10-50 lines, which yield a sense of place. 'Bioregionalism' and 'deep ecology' describe themes and ideals we hold close.**" They have recently published poetry by Linda Curtis Meyers, Fred Marchant and Donna Waidtlow. These sample lines are from "Andy Brown" by Mike Hiler:

> *His ashes were scattered on Windy Ridge*
> *and if the wind keeps blowing*
> *up that trail like it always has*
> *he's half way to Spokane*
> *by now and still headed east.*

The magazine is digest-sized, 28-35 pgs., saddle-stapled, offset from desktop with matte card cover. Accepts about 60 poems/year with 1,000+ submissions. Print run is 150-300. Subscription: $10 for 4 issues. **Sample postpaid: $3. Send SASE for guidelines. Pays 1 copy for each accepted poem. "Cover letters appreciated but not necessary. Prefer 4-5 poems per submission."** No simultaneous submissions or previously published poems. **Initial reports in 2-8 weeks, final selections may take up to 6 months or so.** "Submissions are circulated among several editors living hundreds of miles apart and working hectic jobs; sometimes this makes our responses very slow but we do the best we can. We lose $$$ on everything we print and appreciate purchases of our magazine—but mostly we enjoy receiving submissions of 'good' poetry!" The editors advise, "Read and buy poetry—as well as essays, fiction, whatever—just keep reading." Suggested books: **Circling Back** by Gary Holthaus, **Collected Poems** of Wendell Berry, **Twelve Moons** by Mary Oliver, **A River Runs Through It** by Norman Maclean.

TAPROOT; BURNING PRESS; KRAPP'S LAST TAPE (II), P.O. Box 585, Lakewood OH 44107, founded 1980, editor Robert Drake, is a "micropress publisher of avant-garde and experimental literature and art. Also produces a weekly radio show (KLT) of music, noise, language-centered audio art and a series of audiocassettes." They want "**purposeful experiments with language in which form is the necessary outgrowth of content. No standard academic workshop slop.**" The editor describes *TapRoot*, a quarterly as, "typically 50 pgs., photocopied, handmade covers and binding." They accept less than 10% of 1,000-2,000 poems received/year. Press run is 250 typically for 50 subscriptions, 200 shelf sales. **Sample postpaid: $5 when available. Pays 1 copy. "Contributors may buy more at cost."** Acquires first North American serial rights. **Submit "no more than a dozen at a time unless previously contacted. Simultaneous submissions OK, and previously published poems are sometimes used."** Reviews books of poetry in 50-500 words. Burning Press published 8 chapbooks in 1991, averaging 50 pgs. **For chapbook publication query with no more than 12 samples. Pays 20% press run. Author may buy more at cost.** The editor says, "Please read us before submitting. We sponsor a yearly festival of micropress and alternative media and also a free 'dial-a-poem' service entitled 'in-yr-ear.'"

TAPROOT LITERARY REVIEW (I), 302 Park Rd., Ambridge PA 15003, phone (412)266-8476, founded 1986, editor Tikvah Feinstein, is an annual contest publication, very open to beginners. **There is a $5 entry fee for up to 5 poems, "no longer than 30 lines each." Submissions accepted between September 1 and December 31. Nothing previously published or pending publication will be accepted. All entrants receive a copy of *Taproot*; enclose $2 for postage and handling.** In addition to contest, each year a guest poet is selected; payment in copies. Writers recently published include Carol Crawford, B.Z. Niditch, Ellen Hyatt and Andrena Zawinski. As a sample the editor selected the following lines by 1991 first-prize winner Helen Stevens Chinitz:

> *small losses*
> *wildflowers in a glass*
> *sudden glare at night*
> *or the pleiades*
> *through the eye of a needle*
> *pebbles swallowed*

> *accidentally*
> *closer trumpets*
> *of the raging old elephant*
> *lonely breaststroke*
> *up the serious East Delaware*

The review is approximately 80 pgs., printed by offset on white stock with one-color glossy cover, art and no ads. Circulation is 500, sold at bookstores, readings and through the mail. Price is $5.50 per issue. **Sample copies for $5 each, includes postage.**

‡TAR RIVER POETRY (II), English Dept., East Carolina University, Greenville NC 27834, phone (919)752-6041, founded 1960, editor Peter Makuck, associate editor Luke Whisnant. "We are not interested in sentimental, flat-statement poetry. What we would like to see is skillful use of figurative language." They have recently published poetry by William Matthews, Michael Mott, Betty Adcock, Robert Cording, William Stafford, Samuel Hazo, Fred Chappell and Sue Ellen Thompson. As a sample the editors selected these lines from "In Ireland I Remember The Foxes of Truro, Massachusetts" by Brendan Galvin:

> *I thought of how the foxes travel*
> *by synecdoche, the part-fox*
> *for the whole: the five-toed*
> *prints like thought-blossoms,*
> *four in a row across snowfall*

Tar River appears twice yearly and is digest-sized, 60 pgs., professionally printed on salmon stock, some decorative line drawings, matte card cover with photo, circulation 900+ with 500 subscriptions of which 125 are libraries. They receive 6,000-8,000 submissions/year, use 150-200. Subscription: $8. Sample: $4.50. "We do not consider simultaneous submissions. Double or single-spaced OK. We prefer not more than 6 pgs. at one time. We do not consider mss during summer months." Reads submissions September 1 through April 15 only. Reports in 6-8 weeks. Pays copies. Acquires first rights. Send SASE for guidelines. Editors will comment "if slight revision will do the trick." Reviews books of poetry in 4,000 words maximum, single or multibook format. This is an especially good market for intelligent, concisely written book reviews. It is an all-poetry magazine, so you also stand a better chance of placing work here. Editors are open to newcomers whose work (all styles) shows careful attention to language, craft. They advise, "Read, read, read. Saul Bellow says the writer is primarily a reader moved to emulation. Read the poetry column in *Writer's Digest*. Read the books recommended therein. Do your homework."

TEAM (I, IV-Young Adults), P.O. Box 7259, Grand Rapids MI 49510, phone (616)241-5616, editor Dale Dieleman. *Team* is a quarterly digest for volunteer youth workers. They want poetry "that reflects feelings and content to which young adults can relate in their personal lives and which will move them to a larger understanding of themselves and the world. We are looking for concise, fresh poetry, packed with images, contemporary in feel." Sample $1 with SAE plus 2 first class stamps. Guidelines for SASE. No rhymed or erotic poetry. Pays $10-25/poem plus 1 copy. Specify "rights being offered." Simultaneous submissions and previously published poems OK. Reports in 1 month.

TEARS IN THE FENCE (II), 38 Hodview, Stourpaine, Nr. Blandford Forum, Dorset DT11 8TN England, phone 02584-56803, founded 1984, general editor David Caddy, poetry editor Sarah Hopkins, a "small press magazine of poetry, fiction, interviews, articles, reviews and graphics. We are open to a wide variety of poetic styles. Work of a social, political, ecological and feminist awareness will be close to our purpose. However, we like to publish a balanced variety of work." The editors do not want to see "didactic rhyming poems." They have recently published poetry by Gerald Locklin, Ann Born, Sheila E. Murphy and Catherine Swanson. As a sample, they selected the following lines from "The Invisible Children" by Andrew Jordan:

> *we found a well without a cover—its hollowness*
> *echoed with the movements of lost children,*
>
> *we heard their whisperings. There was a screaming*
> *in the rookery trees that leaned about the house*

Tears in the Fence appears twice a year. It is magazine-sized, offset from typed copy on lightweight paper with b&w cover art and graphics, 60 pgs., matte card cover with black spiral binding. It has a print run of 600 copies, of which 129 go to subscribers and 155 are sold on newsstands. Price per issue is $4, sample available for same price. Pay is 1 copy. Writers should submit 5 typed poems with IRCs. Reporting time is 3 months and time to publication 8-10 months "but can be much less." Reviews books of poetry in 200-250 words, single or multi-book format. The magazine is informally connected with the East Street Poets literary event promotion. The editor says, "I think it helps to subscribe to several magazines in order to study the market and develop an understanding of what type of poetry is published. Use the review sections and send off to magazines that are new to you."

‡10TH MUSE (II), 33 Hartington Rd., Newtown, Southampton, Hants SO2 0EW England, phone (0703)227152, founded 1990, editor Andrew Jordan, is a biannual of poetry, prose, book reviews and b&w artwork. "Generally radical rather than reactionary." They are **particularly interested in human relationship stuff—sexuality/politics—wider subjects, too. No occasional verse.**" They have recently published poetry by Peter Redgrove, Sheila E. Murphy and Belinda Subraman. As a sample the editor selected these lines from "Aliens" by Jeremy Reed:

> *leaving a wife, a job, ditching a car*
> *to embrace the vision—holding to that*
> *and how its light breaks open like a star.*

10th Muse is 48 pgs., A5, photocopied, saddle-stapled, with card cover, no ads. Press run is 200 for 20 subscribers of which 3 are libraries. Single copy: £2; subscription: £4 for 2 copies. **No previously published poems or simultaneous submissions. Often comments on rejections. Reports in 2-3 months. Pays 1 copy.** The editor says, "*10th Muse* is a new magazine that gets by on grant aid from my local city council—I need subscribers. A subscription taken out from a U.S. bank by check would have to be £12 for 2 issues or £6 for one issue. This is because of high bank charges levied in U.K. when cashing foreign currency checks. Alternatively people could send dollar notes equivalent to £4 (2 issues) or £2 (1 issue) plus IRCs to cover the number of issues ordered."

TESSERA (IV-Women, regional, bilingual, translations), 350 Stong, York University, 4700 Keele St., North York, Ontario M3J 1P3 Canada, founded 1984, revived 1988, managing editor Barbara Godard, appears twice a year: **"feminist literary theory and experimental writing by women in French and English, preference to Canadians."** It is digest-sized, 94 pgs., professionally printed, with glossy card cover. Subscription: $18. **Sample postpaid: $10. Submit 4 copies. Deadlines are currently May 15 and November 15. Simultaneous submissions and previously published poems ("sometimes") OK. Pays $10/page.** Editor comments on submissions "sometimes."

TESSERACT PUBLICATIONS (I), 3001 W. 57th St., Sioux Falls SD 57106-2652, phone (605)361-6942, founded 1981, publisher Janet Leih. **"All my books are subsidized publications. Payment is ⅓ in advance, ⅓ when book goes to printer, balance when book is complete. I help my poets with copyright, bar codes, listings and whatever publicity I can get for them. I have a number of mailing lists and will prepare special mailings for them, work with competent proofreaders, artists and a capable reviewer."** They hold occasional contests. The Bardic Round Table, #32, 4600 E. 26th St., Sioux Falls SD 57103, is a local poetry group meeting monthly that sponsors readings (both for members and others) and engages in other activities primarily to support the poetry of members. Membership: $2.

TEXAS TECH UNIVERSITY PRESS (V, IV-Themes), Lubbock TX 79409-1037, phone (806)742-2982, founded 1971, editor Judith Keeling, considers volumes of poetry in four categories only: **Conflict Literature Series:** "Anthologies and single-author works of fiction, nonfiction and poetry that illuminate unquantifiable aspects of historic tragedy and global conflict"; **First-Book Poetry Series:** "Winning and finalist mss in the annual competition conducted by Poetry Editor Walter McDonald, who surveys some 20 literary journals throughout the year and invites up to 12 poets to submit mss for consideration in the competition"; **Invited Poets Series:** "Collections invited from established poets whose work continues to appear in distinguished journals"; and **TTUP Contemporary Poetry Series:** "Winning and finalist works in current national competitions." **Books published on royalty contracts. Ms should be submitted with cover letters and attachments to verify eligibility. Editors never comment on rejections.**

TEXTILE BRIDGE PRESS; MOODY STREET IRREGULARS: A JACK KEROUAC NEWSLETTER (IV-Themes), P.O. Box 157, Clarence Center NY 14032, founded 1978, poetry editor Joy Walsh. **"We publish material by and on the work of Jack Kerouac, American author prominent in the fifties. Our chapbooks reflect the spirit of Jack Kerouac. We use poetry in the spirit of Jack Kerouac, poetry of the working class, poetry about the everyday workaday life. Notice how often the work people spend so much of their life doing is never mentioned in poetry or fiction. Why? Poetry in any form."** They have published poetry by Joseph Semenovich, Marion Perry, Bonnie Johnson, Boria Sax and Michael

---

Use the General Index to find the page number of a specific publication or publisher.

Basinski. *Moody Street Irregulars* is a 28-page, magazine-sized newsletter, biannual, circulation 700-1,000 (700 subscriptions of which 30 are libraries), using 3-4 pgs. of poetry in each issue. They receive about 50 freelance submissions of poetry/year, use half of them. Subscription: $7. **Sample postpaid: $3.50. Reports in 1 month. Pays copies.** Textile Bridge Press also publishes collections by individuals. For book publication, **query with 5 samples. "The work speaks to me better than a letter." Replies to query in 1 week, to submission (if invited) in 1 month. Simultaneous submission OK for "some things yes, others no." Photocopy, dot-matrix OK. Pays copies. Send SASE for catalog to buy samples. Editor comments on rejections "if they ask for it."**

THALIA: STUDIES IN LITERARY HUMOR (I, IV-Subscribers, humor), Dept. of English, University of Ottawa, Ottawa, Ontario K1N 6N5 Canada, appears twice a year using **"humor (literary, mostly), preferably literary parodies."** The editor describes it as 7×8½, flat-spined, "with illustrated cover." Press run 500 for 475 subscriptions. Subscription: $15 for individuals, $18 for libraries. **Sample postpaid: $8. Contributors must subscribe. Simultaneous submissions OK but** *Thalia* **must have copyright. Will authorize reprints. Editor comments on submissions.** Reviews books of poetry. "Send queries to the editor concerning specific books."

THEMA (II, IV-Themes), Thema Literary Society, P.O. Box 74109, Metairie LA 70033-4109, founded 1988, editor Virginia Howard, is a literary quarterly **using poetry related to specific themes. "Each issue is based on an unusual premise. Please, please send SASE for guidelines before submitting poetry to find out the upcoming themes. For example: 'Dust' is the theme for Feb. 1, 1993 (submission deadline) and 'The Dreamland Cafe' is for May 1, 1993. No scatologic language, alternate life-style, explicit love poetry."** They have recently published poetry by Millie Taylor, Joanne Seltzer and Joseph Stanton. As a sample the editor selected these lines by Jean Dubois:

> denied
> repressed
> crammed down into forgetfulness
> it took joy with it
> it's got to be here . . .
> somewhere

Thema is digest-sized, 200 pgs., professionally printed, with matte card cover. They accept about 10% of 320 poems received/year. Press run 500 for 250 subscriptions of which 30 are libraries. Subscription: $16. **Sample postpaid: $5. Pays $10/poem plus 1 copy. Buys one-time rights only. Submissions are accepted all year, but evaluated after specified deadlines. Editor comments on submissions.**

THEMATIC POETRY QUARTERLY (I, IV-Themes), 4444 River Forest Rd., Marianna FL 32446, phone (904)482-3890, editor Wilbur I. Throssell, publishes loose-leaf portfolios **of poetry on specific themes, limit 30 lines. Send SASE for list of themes up through 1996.**

THE THIRD HALF LITERARY MAGAZINE; K.T. PUBLICATIONS (I, II), 16, Fane Close, Stamford, Lincolnshire PE9 1HG England, founded 1987, editor Mr. Kevin Troop. *TTH* appears 3 times/year. K.T. Publications also publishes up to 6 other books, with a Minibooks Series, for use in the classroom. The editor wants **"meaningful, human and humane, funny poems up to 40 lines. Nothing obscene."** They have recently published poetry by Lee Bridges (Holland), Ann Keith (Amsterdam), Toby Litt (Prague) and Edmund Harwood, Michael Newman, Louise Rogers and Steve Sneyd (Britain). As a sample the editor selected this poem, "Fly," by Esther Gress (Denmark):

> Like a butterfly
> we often fly in vain
> against the window pane
> and see not
> like the butterfly
> the open door
> to the sky

TTH is 44 pgs., A5, printed on white paper with glossy cover. Press run is 200+. Individual booklets vary in length and use colored paper and card covers. **Reports ASAP. Pays 1 copy. "Procedure for the publication of these books is explained to each author; each case is different.** *The Third Half* is priced at £2.25 each; 2 issues for £4.25 and all three issues a year for £6.25, including postage and handling."

‡**13TH MOON (II, IV-Women),** English Department, SUNY-Albany, 1400 Washington Ave., Albany NY 12222, phone (518)442-4181, founded 1973, editor Judith Johnson, is a feminist literary magazine appearing twice a year in a 6×9, flat-spined, handsomely printed format with glossy card cover, using photographs and line art, ads at $200/page. Press run 2,000 for 690 subscriptions of which 61 are

libraries, 700 shelf sales. Subscription: $8. **Sample postpaid: $8. Reads submissions September 1 through May 30 only. Send SASE for guidelines. Pays 2 copies. Acquires first North American serial rights.** Reviews books of poetry in 1,500 words "more or less."

THISTLEDOWN PRESS LTD. (V, IV-Regional), 668 East Place, Saskatoon, Saskatchewan S7J 2Z5 Canada, phone (306)244-1722, founded 1975, editor-in-chief Patrick O'Rourke, is "a literary press that specializes in **quality books of contemporary poetry by Canadian authors. Only the best of contemporary poetry that amply demonstrates an understanding of craft with a distinctive use of voice and language. Only interested in full-length poetry mss with 60-80 pgs. minimum.**" They have recently published books of poetry by Glen Sorestad, George Whipple, Gary Hyland and Ken Cathers. **Do not submit unsolicited mss.** Canadian poets must **query first with letter, bio and publication credits. Poetry ms submission guidelines available upon request. Replies to queries in 2-3 weeks, to submissions (if invited) in 2-3 months. No authors outside Canada. No simultaneous submissions. "Please submit quality dot-matrix, laser-printed or photocopied material." Contract is for 10% royalty plus 10 copies.** They comment, "Poets submitting mss to Thistledown Press for possible publication should think in 'book' terms in every facet of the organization and presentation of the mss: poets presenting mss that *read* like good books of poetry will have greatly enhanced their possibilities of being published. We strongly suggest that poets familiarize themselves with some of our poetry books before submitting a query letter."

THORNTREE PRESS (II), 547 Hawthorn Lane, Winnetka IL 60093, founded 1986, contact Eloise Bradley Fink. This press publishes professionally printed, digest-sized, flat-spined paperbacks, 96 pgs., selected through competition January 1 through February 14 in odd-numbered years. **Sample postpaid: $5.95.** "Included in our 13 books are 21 poets." From **Troika I**, Marilyn Taylor writes that *"night gathers in pools over the high savannah . . . [and the] herd shudders as if one creature, and listens. Now the deep African sky lifts a glittering claw; we, the vulnerable, hear the rasp of death and twitch our haunches as the golden cat begins her dance."* Submit a stapled group of 10 pages of original, unpublished poetry, single or double spaced, photocopied, with a $4 reader's fee. Mss will not be returned. (A SASE for winners' names may be included.) "The top fifteen finalists will be invited to submit a 30-page manuscript for possible publication in **Troika V**."

THOUGHTS FOR ALL SEASONS: THE MAGAZINE OF EPIGRAMS (IV-Form, humor), % editor Prof. Em. Michel Paul Richard, 11530 SW 99th St., Miami FL 33176, founded 1976, "is an irregular serial: **designed to preserve the epigram as a literary form; satirical.** All issues are commemorative, e.g., 1976, 1984, 1989, 1992." **Rhyming poetry will be considered although most modern epigrams are prose.** Prof. Richard has recently published poetry by Jack Hart and offers this sample:

> Beware a cause: it is our fate
> To turn into the things we hate

TFAS is magazine-sized, offset from typescript on heavy buff stock with full-page cartoon-like drawings, card cover, 84 pgs., saddle-stapled. Its press run is 500-1,000. The editor accepts about 20% of material submitted. There are several library subscriptions but most distribution is through direct mail or local bookstores and newsstand sales. **Single copy: $4.75 plus $1.50 postage. Send SASE for guidelines. Pays 1 copy. Simultaneous submissions OK, but not previously published epigrams "unless a thought is appended which alters it." Reports in 1 month. Editor comments on rejections.** He says, "This is the only magazine which is devoted to this literary form."

THREE CONTINENTS PRESS INC. (IV-Ethnic, translations), Suite 407, 1901 Pennsylvania Ave. NW, Washington DC 20006, phone (202)223-2554, founded 1973, poetry editor Donald Herdeck. "**Published poets only welcomed and only non-European and non-American poets . . . We publish literature by creative writers from the non-western world (Africa, the Middle East, the Caribbean and Asia/Pacific)—poetry *only* by non-western writers or good translations of such poetry if original language is Arabic, French, African vernacular, etc.**" They have published poetry by Derek Walcott, Khalil Hawi, Mahmud Darwish and Julia Fields. They also publish anthologies focused on relevant themes. **Query with 4-5 samples, bio, publication credits. Replies to queries in 5-10 weeks, to submissions (if invited) in 4-5 weeks. 10% royalty contract (5% for translator) with $100-200 advance plus 10 copies. Buys worldwide English rights. Send SASE for catalog to buy samples.**

THE THREEPENNY REVIEW (II), P.O. Box 9131, Berkeley CA 94709, phone (510)849-4545, founded 1980, poetry editor Wendy Lesser, "is a quarterly review of literature, performing and visual arts, and social articles aimed at the intelligent, well-read, but not necessarily academic reader. Nationwide circulation. **Want: formal, narrative, short poems (and others); do not want: confessional, no punctuation, no capital letters. Prefer under 50 lines but not necessary. No bias *against* formal poetry, in fact a slight bias in favor of it.**" They have published poetry by Thom Gunn, Frank Bidart, Robert Hass,

Czeslaw Milosz and Brenda Hillman. There are about 9-10 poems in each 36-page tabloid issue, circulation 7,500 with 6,000 subscriptions of which 300 are libraries. They receive about 4,500 submissions of freelance poetry/year, use 12. Subscription: $12. **Sample: $5. Send 5 poems or fewer/submission. Send SASE for guidelines. Reports in 2-8 weeks. Pays $50/poem. Buys first serial rights.** Accepts reviews of poetry books. "Send for review guidelines (SASE required)."

‡THRESHOLD BOOKS (IV-Spirituality, translations), RD #4, Box 600, Dusty Ridge Rd., Putney VT 05346, phone (802)254-8300, founded 1981, poetry editor Edmund Helminski, is "a small press dedicated to the publication of quality works in metaphysics, poetry in translation and literature with some spiritual impact. **We would like to see poetry in translation of high literary merit with spiritual qualities, or original work by established authors.**" They have published poetry by Rabia and Yunus Emre. As a sample the editor selected these lines by Jelaluddin Rumi, translated by John Moyne and Coleman Barks:

> We've given up making a living.
> It's all this crazy love poetry now.
>
> It's everywhere. Our eyes and our feelings
> Focus together, with our words

That comes from a collection, **Open Secret, Versions of Rumi,** published in a beautifully printed flat-spined, digest-sized paperback, glossy color card cover, 96 pgs. Per copy: $7. **Query with 10 samples, bio, publication credits and SASE. Replies to queries in 1-2 months, to submissions (if invited) in 1-2 months. Simultaneous submissions, photocopies OK, or discs compatible with IBM, hard copy preferred. Publishes on 15% contract plus 10 copies (and 40% discount on additional copies). Send SASE for catalog to buy samples.**

THUMBPRINTS (I, IV-Themes, regional), 928 Gibbs, Caro MI 48723, phone (517)673-5563, founded 1984, editor Janet Ihle, is the monthly 8-page Thumb Area Writers' Club newsletter that uses **poetry about writers and writing, nothing "vulgar." Maximum 20 lines.** As a sample, the editor selected the last stanza of "My Pen's Words" by I. Wright:

> Sometimes my pen is full of wit
> Sometimes it surprises me
> Sometimes its words become a poem
> For one and all to see.

They sponsor seasonal contests for Michigan amateur writers. Press run: 45 for 30 subscriptions. **Sample postpaid: 75¢. Send SASE for guidelines. Pays 1 copy. Simultaneous submissions and previously published poems OK. Reports in about 3 months. Editor comments on submissions** "sometimes."

TIA CHUCHA PRESS (III, IV-Ethnic, regional, social issues), P.O. Box 476969, Chicago IL 60647, founded 1989, president Luis J. Rodriguez. Tia Chucha **generally discourages unsolicited mss.** They publish 2-4 paperbacks a year, "**multicultural, lyrical, engaging, passionate works informed by social, racial, class experience. Evocative. Poets should be knowledgeable of contemporary and traditional poetry, even if experimenting.**" They have published poetry by David Hernandez, Michael Warr and editor Luis J. Rodriguez. As a sample the editor selected these lines from "The Poetry Widow" by Patricia Smith:

> Tonight, I wished I was one of your poems;
> strong syllables curled in your throat
> awaiting a joyous delivery. I wished I
> was that clever, stilted script on the
> paper in your hand, words you sweat over.

That's from her collection, **Life According to Motown,** published in a 6 × 9, flat-spined, professionally printed paperback, 74 pgs. with glossy card cover, $6.95. "We usually 'select' poets we'd like to publish, those active in a poetry environment (i.e., bar and cafe scene, magazines, etc.). We believe poetry matters. Although we publish in English, we do not limit our traditions to Western Culture. Poetry should draw on the richness of human cultures, with roots in African, Native American, Asian and Latin sensibilities. We believe in engaging poetry; socially necessary and shaped by political, economic and class realities. Redemptive and relevant. We believe poetry is an art. It needs to be crafted, thought-out and knowledgeable of contemporary and traditional poetics."

TICKLED BY THUNDER: WRITER'S NEWS & ROUNDTABLE (II, IV-Subscribers), 7385 129th St., Surrey, British Columbia V3W 7B8 Canada, founded 1990, publisher/editor Larry Lindner, appears 4 times/year, using poems about "**fantasy, about writing or whatever. Keep them short—not interested in long, long poems. Nothing pornographic, childish, unimaginative.**" They have recently published poetry by Stephen Gill, Helen Singh, Victoria Collins and John Grey. As a sample the editor selected these lines (poet unidentified):

> *So she put a monkee in his tea*
> *marshmallows on the side . . .*

It is 16-20 pgs., digest-sized, published on Macintosh. Press run 120 for 100 subscribers. **Subscription: $12. Sample postpaid: $2.50. Pays 1 copy plus cash. Buys first rights. Send SASE for guidelines. Include samples of writing with queries. Reply in 6 weeks. Editor comments on rejections "99% of the time."** Reviews books of poetry in up to 300 words. They also offer a poetry contest 4 times/year. Deadlines: the 15th of February, May, August and November. Entry fee: $2 for 3 poems; free for subscribers. Prize: cash, publication and subscription. Send SASE for details.

TIDEPOOL (I, IV-Form), 4 E. 23rd St., Hamilton, Ontario L8V 2W6 Canada, phone (416)383-2857, founded 1984, publisher Herb Barrett who says, **"We charge $10 entry fee. Money returned if poetry not used." Send SASE for guidelines for details. He wants to see "haiku and contemporary short verse, any style or theme (maximum 34 lines). No scatalogical vulgarity."** He has published poetry by Chris Faiers, Dorothy Cameron Smith and Jeff Seffinga. *Tidepool*, published each October, is digest-sized, 80+ pgs., saddle-stapled, professionally printed with matte card cover, circulation 400 with 150 subscribers of which 60-70 are libraries. **Sample postpaid: $5. Submit mss in May and June only. Reports on submissions in 2-3 weeks. No dot-matrix. "Prefer unpublished material." Pays copies. Sometimes comments on rejections.**

TIGER MOON PRESS; STAR TRIAD 'ZINE; TIGER MOON PRESS CATALOG (I, IV-Fantasy), P.O. Box 2371, Vero Beach FL 32961-2371, founded 1988, editor Sara Ryan. The press publishes cards, calendars and other products which use poetry. They also use poetry in their catalog and in *ST*, both of which appear 3 times/year. They want **"fantasy, metaphysical, inner growth experiences; I will look at others and have accepted a wide variety of poetry, including haiku. In the case of products, query for current theme."** As a sample, the editor selected these lines from "The Rain Staircase to Zenno" by Gregory L. Norris:

> *There was a higher place*
> > *of lilac breezes . . .*
> *A global place*
> *I've not forgotten*
> *at the end of your*
> *empty road.*
> *It was there, when*
> *we first met,*
> *somewhere atop*
> > *the trees.*

ST is magazine-sized, 28-60 pgs., desktop published. **Sample postpaid: $5 for current issue, $2.50 for special condensed sample edition. Guidelines for first class stamp. Pays $3-5/poem (depending on length). "I pay one-half in check, one-half in Tiger Moon Press products; payment also includes a copy of the publication. I prefer a cover letter with a short line or two about the person." Buys first or reprint rights. Previously published poems and simultaneous submissions OK (if you notify the editor). Reports in 10 days except between October and December, then it is 1 month.** She buys about 100 poems/year. "Free service to all writers for a listing of any books or credits they want to share on the 'Writer's Preserve' page, which is in all publications."

TIGHT (II), P.O. Box 1591, Guerneville CA 95446, founded 1990, editor Ann Erickson, appears quarterly. *"tight* **uses direct poetry with sense language or the language of dream. Avoid narrative or ideational poetry."** They have recently published poetry by Ron Padgett, Jack Foley, Jake Berry, John Bennett, B.Z. Niditch, Errol Miller, Pat Nolan, Joel Dailey, Lisa Kucharski, Stacey Sollfrey and Julia Vinograd. As a sample the editor selected these lines from "Nothing delicate about spring" by Carol Ciavonne:

> *Trees arrested on dark hill backlit by orchid sky.*
> *Prisoners taken. Five lanes headlights twilight highway,*
> *radio blaring.*

It is 70 pgs., 7×8½, photocopied from typescript with 60 lb. matte cover. Press run 150 for 8 subscribers, 50 shelf sales. Subscription: $18 (checks payable to Ann Erickson). **Sample postpaid: $4.50 current issue. Submit poetry with seasonal imagery 2 months ahead of season. Pays 1 copy. Acquires one-time rights. Previously published poems and simultaneous submissions OK, if editor notified. Reports in 2 months, sometimes sooner.**

TIGHTROPE (II); SWAMP PRESS (V), 323 Pelham Rd., Amherst MA 01002, founded 1977, chief editor Ed Rayher. Swamp Press is a small press publisher of poetry, fiction and graphic art in limited edition, letterpress chapbooks. *Tightrope*, appearing 1-2 times a year, is a literary magazine of varying format, circulation 300, 150 subscriptions of which 25 are libraries. Subscription: $10 for 2 issues. **Sample of** *Tightrope*: **$6 postpaid. Send SASE for guidelines. Pays "sometimes" and provides 2 contributor's copies. Acquires first rights. Reports in 2 months, 6-12 months until publication. No simultaneous submissions. Sometimes comments on rejections.** Reviews books of poetry in one paragraph, single format. Swamp Press has published books by Edward Kaplan, editor Ed Rayher, Alexis Rotella (miniature, 3×3, containing 6 haiku), Sandra Dutton (a 4 foot long poem), Frannie Lindsay (a 10×13 format containing 3 poems), Andrew Glaze, Tom Hazo, Carole Stone and Steven Ruhl. Send SASE for catalog. **Not presently accepting freelance submissions for chapbook publication but when he publishes chapbooks he pays 5-10% of press run and, if there is grant money available, an honorarium (about $50). Sometimes comments on rejections.**

TIMBERLINE PRESS (V), Route 1, Box 1434, Fulton MO 65251, phone (314)642-5035, founded 1975, poetry editor Clarence Wolfshohl. "We do limited letterpress editions with the goal of blending strong poetry with well-crafted and designed printing. We lean toward **natural history or strongly imagistic nature poetry but will look at any good work. Also, good humorous poetry. Currently, fully stocked with material."** They have published poetry by Walter Bargen and William Hart. **Payment policy: "50-50 split with author after Timberline Press has recovered its expenses." Reports in under 1 month. Sample copies may be obtained by sending $4 requesting sample copy and noting you saw the listing in Poet's Market.**

‡TIMBERLINES (I), % Lake City Writers Forum, P.O. Box 38, Lake City CO 81235, founded 1990, contact Mary Stigall, Lynda Rivers or Tom Spann, is an annual literary journal. They **"prefer poetry dealing with nature-man, out-of-doors, but not essential. Shorter poems have better chance of acceptance due to space limitations."** As a sample they selected these lines (poet unidentified):

> *When I was*
> *little, days were bright yellow blankets*
> *that warmed my words. Clouds were crowns*
> *that blessed mountain tops and brothers*
> *scrambled my eyes with mysteries. Night*
> *held the song of crickets in its palm . . .*

Sample postpaid: $6. Previously published poems OK; no simultaneous submissions. Poems should be typed exactly as they should appear on the page if accepted. Deadline: March 1. Reads submissions September 1 through April 1 only. Seldom comments on rejections. Pays 1 copy. Sponsors an annual poetry contest. Entry fee: $6. Deadline: October 1. Prize: $50. "Winners will be published in *Timberlines*, as will all honorable mentions."

TIMES CHANGE PRESS (V), P.O. Box 1380, Ojai CA 93024-1380, phone (805)646-8595, founded 1970, publisher Lamar Hoover, publishes nonfiction in areas of antiauthoritarian politics, feminism and gender issues, only rarely poetry. **They accept no unsolicited poetry.**

‡TIMES LITERARY SUPPLEMENT (II), Priory House, St. John's Lane, London EC1M 4BX England, founded 1902, is a weekly of book reviews which also accepts **poetry of all kinds ("shortness a virtue").** They have recently published poetry by Seamus Heaney, Thom Gunn, Joseph Brodsky and Paul Muldoon. It is 32 pgs., newsprint, folded with color cover, color and b&w illustrations, display and classified advertising. They receive about 5,000 poems a year, use approximately 2%. Press run is 27,000 for 20,000 subscribers, 7,000 shelf sales. Single copy: £1.50; subscription: £69.50 ($110 US). **No previously published poems or simultaneous submissions. Submit no more than 5 poems.** Time between acceptance and publication is 1 month. **Reports in "1 day to 5 months." Pays £2.15/line. Buys first world rights.** "New poetry books reviewed constantly, mainly singly, in 300-3,000 words."

TIN WREATH (II, III), P.O. Box 13401, Albany NY 12212-3401, founded 1985, "editor/janitor" David Gonsalves. "*Tin Wreath* is a quarterly gathering of writers and writing from the social, political, psychological, spiritual and linguistic margins of late 20th century America." **The editor is looking for poetry "that makes contact with the deeper forces at work in the world and poetry that explores the musical and sculptural qualities inherent in the language; I'd prefer to see abstract, minimalist, non-discursive or otherwise counter-traditional poetry."** He has published work by Geof Huth, Deborah Meadows, N. Sean William and Sheila E. Murphy. As a sample, he chose these lines from "The Lynching of J. Bro" by Michelle Perez:

> *quick his bonnet*
> *stepped, disrobed*
> *the wife*

> *half silent*
> *stately shook,*
> *a pattern, body*
> *as firm displayed —*
> *the patrons laughed.*

Tin Wreath consists of 20-25 unbound 5½ × 8½ photocopied sheets. Circulation is 150. Subscription: $5 individuals, $10 institutions. **A sample copy with complete guidelines costs $2. Checks must be made payable to David Gonsalves. Pays 3 copies. Acquires first North American serial rights. Writers should send 3-5 poems; photocopy, dot-matrix and simultaneous submissions are all OK. Reporting time is "13 days to 13 weeks" and time to publication is 3-6 months.**

TOAD HIGHWAY (II), English Dept., University Hall, Bowling Green University, Bowling Green OH 43403, founded 1988, editor Grant Clauser. *Toad Highway* is a small magazine appearing irregularly using "all types of artwork, poetry, fiction, essays and reviews. **We want poetry which proves that the poet is obsessed by each sound, each stress, each image, each line. We'd like to see more essays. No 'happy poems' or work which shows that the poet has not studied contemporary poetry."** They have published work by Sandra Russell, Beth Joselow, Connie Deanovich, Jerry Bradley, Barbara Unger and Simon Perchik. As a sample the editor selected these lines from "The Jogger" by Matthew Brennan:

> *. . . While light flows in the road where traffic's stopped;*
> *It blazes on windshields, hubcaps, and chrome;*
> *Farther out, it softens, and in its glow*
> *A woman's jogging West, toward Me — as if*
> *I'm sending forth the light, no matter what she knows.*

TH is a 52-page pamphlet, saddle-stapled. Their press run is 250 with 20 subscriptions. "We accept about one in every 100 poems received." Subscription: $12/3 issues. **Sample: $1.50 back issues. Pays 1 copy (discount on others). Submit maximum of 5 poems, single-spaced. No simultaneous submissions, but they will consider previously published poems. Responds to submissions in 3 months maximum. Editor "seldom" comments on rejections.** He says, "We would like to see more poetry that shows a sense of philosophy, an understanding of the world beyond the poem. Poetry is telepathy, not just irony, image or theme."

TOLEDO POETS CENTER PRESS; 11 × 30; INMATE ARTS PRESS; GLASS WILL (V), 32 Scott House, University of Toledo, Toledo OH 43606, phone (419)473-0958, founded 1976, poetry editors Joel Lipman and Nick Muska, is a "small press **publisher of area writers, visual literature and of inmate writing (from our writer's workshops at area jails)"** in broadsides, chapbooks and flat-spined paperbacks. **"Submissions are not sought by Toledo Poets Center Press."** *11 × 30* is a "printerly publication of poetry, fiction, articles, literary news and gossip" and appears quarterly. Authors include Howard McCord, Michael Kasper, Bern Porter and Christy Sheffield-Sanford. *Glass Will* "is a periodic anthology, more book-like (flat-spined) than magazine-like," 6 × 9¼, 266 pgs. **It is a regional anthology of poetry appearing "infrequently" and publishing solicited work only. "Please, no unsolicited work. Inquiries welcome." Pays a varied number of author's copies. Acquires one-time rights. All publications** are quality offset; **samples of** *11 × 30* **for $1; sample of** *Glass Will* **for $5.** As for reviewing books of poetry, they say, "We will write our own capsule reviews. Send book." Joel Lipman notes, **"Our focus is on literary life in this region, on strong and provocative writing, and on composition and design that has beauty and permanence."**

TOUCH (IV-Religious, teens, themes), P.O. Box 7259, Grand Rapids MI 49510, phone (616)241-5616, founded 1970, poetry editor Carol Smith: "Our magazine is a 24-page edition written **for girls 7-14 to show them how God is at work in their lives and in the world around them.** *Touch* **is theme-orientated. We like our poetry to fit the theme of each. We send out a theme update biannually to all our listed freelancers. We prefer short poems with a Christian emphasis that can show girls how God works in their lives."** They have published poetry by Janet Shafer Boyanton and Iris Alderson. As a sample we selected "Wishful Thinking" by Clare Miseles:

> *God's summer is here,*
> *And how I wish,*
> *I understood*
> *More than English.*
> *Then I would translate*
> *Chirps into words,*
> *And listen to*
> *The talk of birds!*

Touch is published 10 times a year, magazine-sized, circulation 15,800 with 15,500 subscriptions. They receive 150-200 freelance submissions of poetry/year, use 2 poems in each issue, have a 6-

month backlog. Subscription: $9 US, $10.50 Canada, $15 foreign. **Sample and guidelines free with 8 × 10 SASE. Poems must not be longer than 20 lines — prefer much shorter. Simultaneous submissions OK. Query with SASE for theme update. Reports in 2 months. Pays $10-15 and copies.**

TOUCHSTONE (II), Viterbo College, La Crosse WI 54601, phone (608)784-0268, founded 1950, moderator George Klawitter, is a literary quarterly using mostly poetry, short stories and artwork. **"Any form but no longer than 50 lines/poem. Nothing sentimental."** As a sample the editor selected these lines from "Outbound" by Kate Carkin:

> *Beware of the Park Street exit*
> *Where corners cross*
> *And weepy people*
> *Stare, pasty-faced.*

The magazine is digest-sized, 48 pgs., saddle-stapled, with semi-glossy card cover. Press run 800 for 100 subscriptions of which 25 are libraries. Subscription: $5. **Sample postpaid: $2.50. Send SASE for guidelines. Best poem gets $20. All get 1 copy. Submit 3-5. Reads submissions August 1 through March 1 only. Reports in 2 months.** The editor says, "Write poetry that is rich in visual imagery. Strive to make your reader *see* what you are talking about. Do not philosophize. Do not moralize. Let the imagery carry the message."

TOUCHSTONE LITERARY JOURNAL; TOUCHSTONE PRESS (V), P.O. Box 8308, Spring TX 77387-8308, founded 1975, poetry editor William Laufer, is an annual publishing **"experimental or well-crafted traditional form, translations, no light verse or doggerel. We will accept no unsolicited manuscripts in 1993."** They have published poetry by Walter Griffin, Sheila Murphy, Michael L. Johnson, Walter McDonald and Joyce Pounds Hardy. *Touchstone* is digest-sized, flat-spined, 100 pgs., professionally printed in small, dark type with glossy card cover. Subscription: $7. **Sample postpaid: $3. Pays 1 copy.** Reviews books of poetry.

‡TOWER POETRY SOCIETY; PINE TREE SERIES; TOWER (II), Dundas Public Library, 18 Ogilvie St., Dundas, Ontario L9H 2S2 Canada, founded 1951, editor-in-chief Joanna Lawson. "The press is an outgrowth of Tower Poetry Society, started by a few members of McMaster University faculty to promote interest in poetry. We publish *Tower* twice a year and a few chapbooks. We want **rhymed or free verse, traditional or modern, but not prose chopped into short lines, maximum 35 lines in length, any subject, any comprehensible style."** They have published poetry by Sparling Mills, John Ferns, Kenneth Samberg and Catherine Bankier. The editor selected these sample lines by Tony Cosier:

> *From forging brass he took to forging soul,*
> *gave up plowing soil to plow his skull,*
> *ripped open the eye that never closed again*
> *and took for tongue the howl of the beast in pain.*

Tower is digest-sized, 40 pgs., circulation 150, 60 subscriptions of which 8 are libraries. They receive about 400 freelance submissions of poetry/year, use 30, no backlog. Subscription: $6 including postage. **Sample postpaid: $2. Limit submissions to 4 poems. Submit during February or August. Reports in 2 months. Pays 1 copy. "Comment if requested — no charge."** The editor advises, "Read a lot of poetry before you try to write it."

TOWNSHIPS SUN (IV-Rural, ecological, regional), 7 Conley St., P.O. Box 28, Lennoxville, Quebec J1M 1Z3 Canada, phone (819)566-7424, founded 1972, editor Patricia Ball, is a monthly newspaper in English "concerned with **history of townships, English community, agriculture and ecology and using poetry on these themes. Only poems about the area and people of Quebec ever accepted. Others need not submit."** The tabloid has a press run of 2,500 for 2,000 subscribers of which 20 are libraries, and 500 shelf sales. Subscription: $15/year Canada, $20/year outside Canada. **Sample postpaid: $2. Pays $10-30 plus 1 copy. "Will publish poems specifically about townships, townshippers, or of specific interest to townshippers."** Reviews books of poetry.

TRADESWOMEN MAGAZINE (IV-Women, themes), P.O. Box 40664, San Francisco CA 94140, founded 1982, poetry editor Sue Doro, editor Janet Scoll Johnson, is a national quarterly **"particular to women in non-traditional work"** and uses poetry **"pertaining to women in trades, tradeswomen as mothers, wives, male co-worker relationships."** Subscription: $35. **Sample postpaid: $2. Guidelines available for SASE. They consider simultaneous submissions and previously published poems. Reports in 1 month. No backlog.**

‡TRANSLUCENT TENDENCY PRESS (III), 3226 Raspberry, Erie PA 16508, founded 1980 as *Northern Pleasure* magazine, publisher Ron Androla, publishes 2-3 chapbooks/year. **They want poetry that is "the reality of the edges. Nothing sanity-influenced."** They have recently published poetry by Kurt

Nimmo, Paul Weinman and Belinda Subraman. As a sample the editor selected these lines (poet unidentified):

> *. . . Hello Melville bruised by a bump*
> *from one angry whale the methadone*
> *stuffs cotton all around spiritual helplessness*
> *screaming on the top of a rupturing ocean hello*
> *ulysses . . .*

No previously published poems or simultaneous submissions. Cover letter required. "Be enlightened or stay away." They want to hear from those "generally attuned to the agony of being a poet during the dissolution of America." **Replies to queries in "weeks." Often comments on rejections. Pays author's copies.** The editor says, "Poetry is a life-long curse. Either it's revolutionary, disturbing or wild, or it's worthless."

"This cover features the principal elements in our title, which, in turn, reflects the character of our region," says Trestle Creek Review Editor Chad Klinger. The title is the name of an actual creek in northern Idaho, he says, and the area is one where "logging, mining, etc., were made possible by the railroad a century ago." Though they accept work from all over North America, "we tend to favor work from the Pacific Northwest-Rocky Mountain area," he says, adding that poetry is generally about 80% of what they publish. This cover was designed by Susan Miller, a freelance artist living in Coeur d'Alene, Idaho.

TRANSNATIONAL PERSPECTIVES (III), CP161, 1211 Geneva 16 Switzerland, founded 1975, editor René Wadlow, is a "journal of world politics with some emphasis on culture that crosses frontiers." Uses 4-6 poems/issue, usually illustrated by drawing or photo. They want **"poems stressing harmony of nature, human potential, understanding of other cultures — relatively short. No humor, nationalistic themes, nothing 'overly' subjective."** They have published poetry by Verona Bratesch and Janet Pehr. As a sample the editor selected these lines from "1989, A Pivot Year" by Brian Walker:

> *This year, all bets are off.*
> *Unpredictable chances,*
> *expectations jilted;*
> *adepts will learn new dances.*
> *Watch old system hiccough,*
> *welcome new solutions*
> *in native phrase unstilted:*
> *in apt throughts, revolutions.*

TP appears 3 times a year; it "is oriented toward making policy suggestions in international organizations, especially in the United Nations." It is handsomely produced, magazine-sized, 48 pgs., saddle-stapled with coated color paper cover. They receive about 100 poems/year, use 16. Press run is 5,000 for 4,000 subscriptions of which half are libraries. **Sample back issue free on request. Pays 5 copies, more if desired. Simultaneous submissions OK. No previously published poems. Reports in 1 month. Editor comments "rarely, on quality, only why not for *TP*."** René Wadlow says, "Poems in *TP* come from many countries, especially Eastern Europe, Scandinavia and India, often translated into English, usually 'upbeat' since most of articles are on political and economic difficulties of the world."

TRESTLE CREEK REVIEW (II), 1000 West Garden, Coeur d'Alene ID 83814, phone (208)769-3300, ext. 384, founded 1982-83, poetry editor Chad Klinger et al, is a "2-year college creative writing program production. Purposes: (1) expand the range of publishing/editing experience for our small band of writers; (2) expose them to editing experience; (3) create another outlet for serious, beginning writers. **We favor poetry strong on image and sound, the West and country vs. city; spare us the romantic, rhymed clichés. We can't publish much if it's long (more than 2 pgs.)."** They have recently published poetry by John Ditsky, Lowell Jaeger, R. Nikolas Macioci, Ray Mizer and Julia Thomas. As a sample Chad Klinger selected these lines by Ron McFarland:

> *All around you the furious mines are closing*
> *like angry fists,*
> *their galvanized shells rusting too slowly*
> *to be a tourist attraction.*
> *Outside town a black bronze miner drills the sky.*

TCR is a digest-sized, 57-page annual, professionally printed on heavy buff stock, perfect-bound, matte cover with art, circulation 500, 6 subscriptions of which 4 are libraries. This publication is well-designed and features poems (both free and formal verse) by relative newcomers. They receive freelance poetry submissions from about 100 persons/year, use 30. **Sample: $4. Submit before March 1 (for May publication), no more than 5 pgs., no simultaneous submissions. Reports by March 30. Pays 2 copies.** The editor advises, "Be neat; be precise; don't romanticize or cry in your beer; strike the surprising, universal note. Know the names of things."

TRIQUARTERLY MAGAZINE (II), 2020 Ridge Ave., Evanston IL 60208, phone (708)491-7614, founded 1964, editors Reginald Gibbons and Susan Hahn, is one of the most distinguished journals of contemporary literature. Many editors claim that their only criterion is "excellence," but the editors here really mean it. You're apt to find all manner of verse in this alluring magazine; and some issues are published as books on specific themes. They have recently published poetry by Tom Sleigh, Albert Goldbarth, Linda McCarriston, Pattiann Rogers and Theodore Weiss. *TriQuarterly's* three issues per year are 6×9, 200+ pgs., flat-spined, professionally printed with b&w photography, graphics, glossy card cover with b&w photo, circulation 4,500 with 2,000 subscriptions of which 35% are libraries, using about 40 pgs. of poetry in each issue. They receive about 3,000 freelance submissions of poetry/year, use 20, have about a 12-month backlog. Subscription: $18; per copy: $9.95. **Sample postpaid: $4. Reads submissions October 1 through April 30 only. No dot-matrix or simultaneous submissions. Reports in 10-12 weeks. Payment varies. Acquires first North American serial rights.** "We *suggest* prospective contributors examine sample copy before submitting." Reviews books of poetry "at times."

TROUT CREEK PRESS; DOG RIVER REVIEW; DOG RIVER REVIEW POETRY SERIES; BACK POCKET POETS (II), 5976 Billings Rd., Parkdale OR 97041, founded 1981, poetry editor Laurence F. Hawkins, Jr., prefers **"shorter poems (to 30 lines) but will consider longer, book or chapbook consideration. No restrictions on form or content. No pornography or religious verse."** They have published poetry by Judson Crews, Gerald Locklin, Arthur Winfield Knight, Connie Fox, Terence Hoagwood and Joseph Semenovich. Laurence Hawkins selected these sample lines from "Tales and Declarations" by Bruce Holland Rogers:

> *Glass is the voice of fire*
> *Speaking a tongue aphasiacs know*
> *But cannot translate*
> *Like the manifestoes of iron*
> *Known only to dead soldiers*
> *Or like the echo of copper*
> *In the ears of the drowned*

Dog River Review is a semiannual, digest-sized, 60 pgs., saddle-stapled, offset from computer typescript with b&w graphics, circulation 300, 40 subscriptions of which 7 are libraries. They receive about 500 freelance submissions of poetry/year, use 40-50. Subscription: $7. **Sample postpaid: $2.** Backpocket Poets is a series of 4×5¼ chapbooks, professionally printed, 26 pgs., saddle-stapled with matte card cover, selling for $2.50 each, a drawing or photo of the author on the back. The Dog River Review Poetry Series consists of digest-sized, professionally printed, saddle-stapled chapbooks with matte card covers. **Reports in 1 week-3 months. Payment in copies. Acquires first North American serial rights. Send SASE for guidelines. For book publication by Trout Creek Press, query with 4-6 samples. Replies to queries immediately, to submissions in 1-2 months. No simultaneous submissions. Photocopy, dot-matrix OK. No payment until** "material costs recovered. We also publish individual authors on cassette tape." Send SASE for catalog to buy samples. **Editor sometimes comments on rejections.** Reviews books of poetry.

TSUNAMI (II), Earthquake Press, P.O. Box 46810, Los Angeles CA 90046, editors Michelle Raffin and Roberta Rennert-Carter, is a "small press publisher of **poets and poems that aren't afraid to take risks. We have no limitations as to style or subject matter, but we take eight or ten looks at any poem longer than two pages before we accept it. Our goal is to produce a book full of high-quality poems that tackle a variety of subjects. We enjoy narrative voice, concrete expressions of modern life, surrealism.**" They have recently published poetry by Clayton Eshleman, Robert Nagler, Fred Voss, Janet Gray and Lyn Lifshin. As a sample they selected these lines by Richard Krause:

> *She showed me her tears just at the point when her eyes were*
> *brimful; she knew the exact moment to turn to me just before*
> *they would run down her cheeks. I stopped this for good one*
> *day when we were at the dinner table by saying fine, now bring*
> *your face over my plate. You can salt my potatoes.*

Tsunami appears twice a year and is digest-sized, 60 pgs., perfect-bound, professionally printed, with glossy card cover and full-color art. Press run is 600 for 200 subscriptions, 400 shelf sales. Subscription: $10. **Sample postpaid: $6. Pays 1 copy. Simultaneous submissions and previously published work accepted. Reports in "6-10 weeks." No comments on rejections.** Reviews books of poetry in 1,200 words or less. The editors say, "We're polyglots—we accept many different voices, styles, tones. We feel that young poets should explore the possibilities of their voice and not stick with one tone or approach. We tap new voices nationwide."

TUCUMCARI LITERARY REVIEW (II), 3108 W. Bellevue Ave., Los Angeles CA 90026, founded 1988, editor Troxey Kemper, assistant editor Neoma Reed, appears every other month. **"Prefer rhyming and established forms, 2-100 lines, but the primary goal is to publish good work. No talking animals. No haiku. The quest here is for poetry that will be just as welcome many years later, as it is now. Preference is for readable, understandable writing of literary and lasting quality. Nostalgic recollections, yes, but not stilted, obscure snatches of jumbled words that require a dictionary at hand."** They have recently published poetry by Esther M. Leiper, Wilma Elizabeth McDaniel, Daniel Kaderli, Marian Ford Park and Andy Peterson. As a sample the editor selected these lines from "Sons and Mothers," a 44-line poem by Kenneth W. Johnson:

> *Home, safe at last, from war's abyss,*
> *He took her in his arms—like this.*
> *She raised her face to take the kiss*
> *That mothers need, and often miss.*

The magazine is digest-sized, 48 pgs., saddle-stapled, photocopied from typescript, with card cover. Their press run is 150-200. Subscription: $12, $20 for overseas. **Sample: $2, $4 for overseas. Considers simultaneous submissions and previously published poems. Send SASE for guidelines. Reports within 1 month. Pays 1 copy. Acquires one-time rights.** This magazine is inexpensively produced but contains some good formal poems. If you're looking to place a particular sonnet or villanelle, try Troxey Kemper's magazine. He reports quickly, by the way, and may comment on rejections. Like many editors who publish formal verse, he wants content to rise above form. He advises, "Try to write a poem that 'says something,' expresses an idea or mood or *something*—not a jumble of prose words arranged in odd-shaped lines, trying to look like a poem and not saying anything. The established forms still stand as beacons for aspiring poets. *TLR* often is overstocked but we try to let newcomers and nonsubscribers in. Many writers say their first published work appeared here, and many college literature professors have published here, almost always fixed-form poems."

TURKEY PRESS (V), 6746 Sueno Rd., Isla Vista CA 93117, founded 1974, poetry editor Harry Reese along with his wife, Sandra Reese, "is involved with publishing contemporary literature, producing traditional and experimental book art, one-of-a-kind commissioned projects and collaborations with various artists and writers. **We do not encourage solicitations of any kind to the press. We seek out and develop projects on our own.**" They have published poetry by Thomas Merton, James Laughlin, Sam Hamill, Edwin Honig, Glenna Luschei, Tom Clark, Michael Hannon, Keith Waldrop, David Ossman, Peter Whigham, Jack Curtis, Kirk Robertson and Anne E. Edge.

TURNSTONE PRESS (II, IV-Regional), 607-100 Arthur St., Winnipeg, Manitoba R3B 1H3 Canada, phone (204)947-1555, founded 1975, is a "literary press publishing quality contemporary fiction, poetry, criticism" in flat-spined books (8/year), having **a Canadian emphasis. They want "writing based on contemporary poetics, but otherwise wide-ranging. Welcome experimental, graphic, long poems, the unusual. Nothing overly concerned with traditional rhyme and meter."** They have published poetry by Di Brandt, Maara Haas and Kristjana Gunnars. Submit complete ms and bio. **Photocopies, good dot-matrix OK, as are poems previously published in magazines. Reports in 2-3 months. Pays $100-200 advance, 10% royalties and 10 copies. Editor comments on rejections "if we believe it has promise." Send 9 × 12 SASE (or, from the US, SAE with IRCs) for catalog to buy samples.**

TWISTED (IV-Horror, fantasy), P.O. Box 1249, Palmetto GA 30268-1249, phone (404)463-1458, founded 1985, editor/publisher Christine Hoard, an annual using **poetry of "horror/dark fantasy; humor OK. Form and style open. Not more than 1 page long."** They have recently published poetry by John Grey, Lisa Lepovetsky and Jeffery Lewis. As a sample the editor selected these lines by Jana Hakes:

> As a child takes
> to puddles of mud
> for play,
> I prefer puddles
> of blood
> every day;
> horror that stains
> the mind,
> never washes away.

Christine Hoard describes *Twisted* as "150 pgs., magazine-sized, offset, vellum bristol cover, much art, some ads, 60 lb. matte paper. I receive a lot of poetry submissions, use 30-50 per issue." Press run is 300 for single-copy sales. **Sample postpaid: $6, payable to Christine Hoard. Send SASE for guidelines. Pays 1 copy. "Don't submit more than four poems at a time. You should see a sample copy to get a 'feel' for what we publish."** No simultaneous submissions, but previously published poems are sometimes accepted. Reports within 3 months. "We sometimes close when we are preparing next issue or overstocked." **Editor often comments on rejections.** She says, "Poets of science fiction, horror, fantasy will be pleased to know there are several markets in the small press and some organizations are available to offer support and market information."

2 AM MAGAZINE; 2 AM PUBLICATIONS (IV-Science fiction/fantasy/horror), P.O. Box 6754, Rockford IL 61125-1754, founded 1986, editor Gretta McCombs Anderson, a quarterly that wants **"fantasy, science fiction, heroic fantasy, horror, weird; any form, any style; preferred length is 1-2 pgs. We want poetry that leaves an after-image in the mind of the reader."** It has contained poetry by Mark Rich, G.N. Gabbard and Leonard Carpenter, and the editor describes it as 68 pgs., magazine-sized, offset on 60 lb. stock, cover printed on glossy stock, illustrations "by leading fantasy artists," uses ads, circulation 1,000 with 250 subscriptions. Single copy: $4.95. Subscription: $19/year. **Sample postpaid: $5.95. Send SASE for guidelines. Pays 5¢/line or $1 minimum plus 1 copy, 40% discount for more. Buys one-time rights. Reports in 2 months, 6-12 months to publication. Submit no more than 5 poems at a time. "Prefer poems no more than 2 pages in length."** Photocopies OK. Reviews books of poetry in 250 words, single format. **For chapbook consideration (32 pgs., 4 × 5, saddle-stapled) query with 5 sample poems, bio, aesthetic or poetic aims. "Poetry must have concrete images and patterned meter, evoke strong sense of mood and express horror, fantasy or science fiction themes." Pays royalties and copies. Negotiates individual contract. Editor "sometimes" comments on rejections.** Gretta M. Anderson advises, "Read widely, be aware of what's already been done. Short poems stand a good chance with us. Looking for mood-generating poetry of a cosmic nature. Not interested in self-indulgent poetry."

‡THE TWOPENNY PORRINGER (II), P.O. Box 1456, Tacoma WA 98401, founded 1991, editor Adrian Taylor, is a quarterly containing poetry, art and short stories. They are **"very open to all forms and styles. However, poems which imply affiliation with organized religious groups and poems which are nursery-rhymish will be rejected."** The editor says it is 70-80 pgs., digest-sized, saddle-stitched, with glossy cover using b&w photo or artwork. "45% of material published is poetry, 10% art and photos, 45% short stories." Press run is 2,000 for 300 subscribers. Subscription: $8. **Sample postpaid: $2. No previously published poems; simultaneous submissions OK. Reports "no later than 6 weeks." Pays 2 copies of issue in which published and 3 subsequent issues (5 total).** The editor says, "We are looking for poems, short stories, b&w photography, and b&w or halftone images of original artwork. It is our wish to print contributions from artists who are new to their fields as well as works from those who have already established themselves. International submissions are encouraged. Non-English submissions are also encouraged, if typed and translated."

TYRO WRITERS' GROUP (I, IV-Membership), 194 Carlbert St., Sault Ste. Marie, Ontario P6A 5E1 Canada, phone (705)253-6402, founded 1984, editor Stan Gordon. Tyro Writers' Group considers book-length mss for publication. **Lifetime membership in the group costs $5, and you must be a member to submit. Query first with at least 6 sample poems. Mss should be in standard format. Send SASE for guidelines and further information.**

ULTRAMARINE PUBLISHING CO., INC. (II), Box 303, Hastings-on-Hudson NY 10706, founded 1974, editor C.P. Stephens, who says, "We mostly distribute books for authors who had a title dropped by a major publisher—the author is usually able to purchase copies very cheaply. We use existing copies purchased by the author from the publisher when the title is being dropped." Ultramarine's list includes 250 titles, 90% of them cloth bound, one-third of them science fiction and 10% poetry. The press pays 10% royalties. "Distributor terms are on a book-by-book basis, but is a rough split." Authors should query before making submissions; queries will be answered in 1 week. Simultaneous submissions are OK, as are photocopied or dot-matrix mss, but no discs.

UNDERPASS; UNDERPASS PRESS (II), #574-21, 10405 Jasper Ave., Edmonton, Alberta T5J 3S2 Canada, founded 1986, editors Barry Hammond and Brian Schulze. *Underpass* is a literary annual. The press publishes chapbooks and flat-spined paperbacks of poetry. They want "contemporary, urban, avant-garde, concrete or discursive prose-poems. Any length. No religious or nature poetry." They have recently published poetry by Brian Burke, Wade Bell and Sheila E. Murphy. As a sample Brian Schulze selected these lines from "Labyrinth Shaman" by James MacSwain:

> So you think it could be nothing.
> I will show you nothing then.
> Down this street. Every city is a labyrinth.
> Look into this bar.

Underpass is digest-sized. Their fifth issue was 90 pgs., but they hope to increase size and continue the flat-spined format. It is offset printed with a laminated card cover using b&w and color graphics inside. "This year we received about two hundred and fifty submissions and only used twenty-six poets." Press run is 100-300. Sample postpaid: $6.95. Send SASE for guidelines. Pays $5/poem plus 2 copies. All rights remain with authors. No simultaneous submissions or previously published poems. Editor sometimes comments on rejections. Reads submissions January 31 through August 31 only. Publication in late fall.

UNDERWHICH EDITIONS (V), Box 262, Adelaide St. Station, Toronto, Ontario M5C 2J4 Canada, and, in western Canada, 920 9th Ave. N., Saskatoon, Saskatchewan S7K 2Z4 Canada, founded 1978, poetry editors Richard Truhlar, Steven Smith, Beverley Daurio, Frank Davey and Paul Dutton are "dedicated to presenting in diverse and appealing physical formats, new works by contemporary creators, **focusing on formal invention and encompassing the expanded frontiers of musical and literary endeavor**" in chapbooks, pamphlets, flat-spined paperbacks, posters, cassettes, records and anthologies. They have published poetry by Victor Coleman, Paula Claire and John Riddell. As a sample the editors selected these lines from "A Knife a Rope a Book" by Mari-Lou Rowley:

> Prefers the body
> raw
> feeling
> his eye
> behind the lens

They are currently not accepting poetry submissions. "We have all the mss we can handle for the foreseeable future."

UNITED METHODIST REPORTER; NATIONAL CHRISTIAN REPORTER; UNITED METHODIST RE-VIEW (IV-Religious), Box 660275, Dallas TX 75266-0275, phone (214)630-6495, founded "about 1840." *UMR* is a weekly broadsheet newspaper, circulation 500,000+, "aimed at United Methodists primarily, ecumenical slant secondarily." They use at most one poem a week. The poetry "must make a religious point—United Methodist or ecumenical theology; short and concise; concrete imagery; unobtrusive rhyme preferred; literary quality in freshness and imagery; not trite but easy to understand; short enough to fill 1- to 3-inch spaces. Do not want to see poems by 'my 13-year-old niece,' poems dominated by 'I' or rhyme; poems that are too long, too vague or too general; poems without religious slant or point." Managing Editor John A. Lovelace says they use about 50 of 1,000 poems received/year. Poems may appear in all three publications. Send SASE for guidelines. Pays $2/poem and 1 copy. Send no more than 3-4 poems at a time. No simultaneous submissions or previously published poems. Time to publication can be up to a year. Editor comments on rejection "if it is promising."

UNITY; DAILY WORD (IV-Religious), Unity School of Christianity, Unity Village MO 64065, founded 1893. "Unity periodicals are devoted to spreading the truth of practical Christianity, the everyday use of Christ's principles. The material used in them is constructive, friendly, unbiased as regards creed or sect, and positive and inspirational in tone. We suggest that prospective contributors study carefully the various publications before submitting material. Sample copies are sent on request. Complimentary copies are sent to writers on publication. Mss should be typewritten in double space. We accept mss only with the understanding that they are original and previously unpublished. Unity School pays on acceptance 5¢ a word and up for prose and $1 a line for verse." *Unity Magazine* is a monthly journal that publishes "articles and poems that give a clear message of Truth and provide practical, positive help in meeting human needs for healing, supply and harmony. Only 4 or 5 poems are published each month. We pay a $20 minimum." Buys first North American serial rights. *Daily Word* is a "monthly manual of daily studies" which "buys a limited number of short devotional articles and poems."

UNMUZZLED OX (IV-Themes, bilingual/foreign language), 105 Hudson St., New York NY 10013 or Box 550, Kingston, Ontario K7L 4W5 Canada, founded 1971, poetry editor Michael Andre, is a tabloid literary biannual. **Each edition is built around a theme or specific project.** The editor says, "The chances of an unsolicited poem being accepted are slight since I always have specific ideas in mind." He is assembling material for issues titled *Poems to the Tune*, "simply pomes to old tunes, a buncha contemporary *Beggar's Opera*. The other is tentatively called *The Unmuzzled OX Book of Erotic Verse*. **Only unpublished work will be considered, but works may be in French as well as English.**" Subscription: $20.

‡UNTITLED (I, II), P.O. Box 339, New City NY 10956, founded 1991, editors Thomas Donohue and Evan Klein, is a quarterly magazine of poetry, prose, fiction and artwork. They are **"open to all subjects. Seeking originality. 1 line to 12 pages."** They do not want "cliches and bad similes." They have recently published poetry by Philip Kobylarz, Lyn Lifshin, Laurel Speer and Elizabeth Rees. As a sample the editors selected these lines from "Night Vision" by Richard Allen:

> . . . *He said, "Naked*
> *ghosts scream past my window, veiled princess cry-*
> *ing lady floats through my eyes a thousand times*
> *dreaming of the thousand more mid-nights she has*
> *seen and all the boys and men she's seen before and*
> *taken to heaven and left in hell."*

Untitled is 35-40 pgs., 8½ × 11, spiral bound, with card cover, drawings and graphics on cover and inside. They receive over 1,500 poems a year, accept 10-15%. Press run is 400 for 175 subscribers of which 20 are libraries, 20 shelf sales. Subscription: $12. **Sample postpaid: $3. Previously published poems and simultaneous submissions OK, "if indicated." Send no more than 5 works. Always comments on rejections. Send SASE for guidelines. Reports in 4-6 weeks. Pays 1 copy.** Sponsors a summer contest. Entry fee: $4 for no more than 5 poems. Deadline: July 15. Prizes: 1st—$100, 2nd—$50, 3rd—$25. "Winners will also have two of their poems featured in summer issue." The editors add, "Topic and theme are not as important as original-ity. We have no requirements as to subject matter."

URBANUS/RAIZIRR; URBANUS PRESS (III), P.O. Box 192561, San Francisco CA 94119, founded 1987, editors Peter Drizhal and Cameron Bamberger, is a twice-yearly journal of fiction and poetry. **"Seeks post-modernist, experimental and mainstream poetry—with a social slant.** Beginners would be ad-vised to acquire a sample copy, particularly if unfamiliar with any of the poets we've published: Wanda Coleman, Robert Peters, Antler, Li Min Hua, William Joyce, Simon Perchik." The digest-sized, 48-page, saddle-stapled magazine uses less than 5% of the 2,000+ submissions they receive annually. Their press run is 300. Subscription: $10. **Sample postpaid: $5. Reports in 1-2 months, 9 months-1 year till publication. Pays 1 copy.**

US1 WORKSHEETS; US1 POETS' COOPERATIVE (II), 21 Lake Dr., Roosevelt NJ 08555-0057, founded 1973, is a literary tabloid biannual, 20-25 pgs., 11½ × 17, circulation 500, which uses **high quality poetry and fiction. Sample: $4. "We use a rotating board of editors; it's wisest to query when we're next reading before submitting. A self-addressed, stamped postcard to the secretary will get our next reading period dates."** Recently published poets include Alicia Ostreicher, Toi Derricotte, Elizabeth Anne Socolow, Jean Hollander, Grace Cavalieri, Geraldine C. Little and David Keller. **"We read a lot but take very few. Prefer complex, well-written work. Requests for sample copies, subscriptions, queries, information about reading periods and all manuscripts should be addressed to the secretary, % POSTINGS, P.O. Box 1, Ringoes NJ 08551."**

UTAH HOLIDAY MAGAZINE (II, IV-Regional), Suite 200, 807 E. South Temple, Salt Lake City UT 84102, phone (801)532-3737, founded 1971, is a "monthly magazine with a **strong regional focus that publishes a very limited amount of poetry as space permits.**" *UHM* says that none of our category designations really applies. **The poetry they use is not necessarily regional, and "We are very open to beginners' submissions.** We don't care if somebody has been published elsewhere or not. We will offer criticism and suggestions to writers, and will also consider accepting something after revision, if we are happy with the revision. But **we do not have much space to run poetry, so writers should be advised there is a high likelihood we will either not accept their poems, or that they will have to wait a considerable amount of time before they see them in print.** There are no particular specifications except that the poetry be quality work and that it hasn't been published previously. We are more apt to be able to publish shorter poems just because there is more likely to be space for them. Poems with a strong Utah regional focus would be more acceptable than those which refer to other regions. We

Close-up

Sharon E. Martin
Poet

"To My Son, Growing Up"

That I love you has never been enough,
child more me than I am,
son who claims my soul as his own.

Last night I held you as you cried
dry, shoulder-shaking tears
for the long-distance father

who won't come again this year.
It has always been the same — his excuses,
and you, so young, defending them.

Until now.
This time his excuses,
like my solo love, are not enough.

(reprinted from *Byline*)

Sharon Martin's poem never lapses into sentimentality, though it easily could, given the situation. The voice in her poem — strong, plaintive, but distant too — balances the subject matter and prepares us for the last line, documenting the boy's pain and her "solo love."

Martin writes the kind of poetry that conveys feeling without sacrificing structure or technique. "Speaking of form," she says, "I had written and sold several structured poems before I was told that no market existed for such poetry."

She thinks many editors discourage submissions of formal verse "because there is so much bad rhymed poetry being written. If a poet can create living, feeling poetry, rhymed or unrhymed, structured or unstructured, there is a market for it," she maintains.

Her credits support her claim. Martin has sold free and formal poetry to markets as varied as *McCall's, Parnassus* and *Ellery Queen's Mystery Magazine*. Recently she put together a collection of poems, **Prodigal Daughter**, and completed a book of rhymed riddles for children. In addition, her epic poetry has won awards in contests sponsored by magazines and writing societies.

Martin says she inherited the love of poetry from her grandmother, Ella Edge, a self-educated woman from the plains of western Oklahoma. "She tucked me in at night with lines from Robert Burns (she called him Bobby Burns), Tennyson and Longfellow. She must have raised my father the same way because he loves, reads and writes poetry."

Martin's mother writes songs — "both the music and the lyrics." Her son and daughter also write, she says, so she's passing on the legacy.

When pressed, Martin admits she has a difficult time talking about herself except through her poetry and fiction. "It takes a self-centered person, probably, to write," she says. "We have to be able to think 'I've got something to say that someone else should hear.' That's egocentric." Nonetheless, "poetry without an audience is unfinished," Martin concludes, "like a song that's never sung."

— Michael J. Bugeja

like poetry with a unique way of looking at experience or the world." They have, so far, published only regional writers. *UHM* is magazine-sized, 85-130 pages. "We look like any other regional magazine. We have b&w as well as 4-color pages and regular slick magazine quality paper." Its press run is 14,000 for 10,000 subscriptions, 4,000 shelf sales. Subscription: $16.95. Single copy: $1.95. **Sample: $3 postpaid. Pays $25-50 "usually," plus 2-3 copies. They have "an extensive backlog." Simultaneous submissions OK. Reports "within 3 months." Editor sometimes comments on rejections.** She says, "We do not really consider ourselves a very viable market for poetry. We do encourage local people who have poetry, if it is good quality, to submit in hopes that we will have space for it. If people out of region have poems which relate to this region, we would especially encourage them, too."

‡**VANDELOECHT'S FICTION MAGAZINE; VFM'S ANNUAL POETRY CONTEST (I)**, P.O. Box 515, Montross VA 22520, founded 1991, editor Mike Vandeloecht, is a quarterly publishing both fiction and poetry. They want **"free verse and traditional, 25 lines maximum. No pornography or vulgarity."** They have recently published poetry by E.V. Calloway and Hampton Creed. The editor says *VFM* is 8½ × 11, saddle-stapled. They accept about 10% of the poetry received/year. **Sample postpaid: $3. No previously published poems or simultaneous submissions. Submit no more than 5 poems. Always comments on rejections. Send SASE for guidelines. Reports within 10 days. Pays 1 copy. All rights revert to author upon publication.** They offer an annual poetry contest, $2 entry fee. Deadline: December 31. 1st prize: $20, 2nd prize: $10, 3rd prize: $5. In addition, 1st through 20th place winners are published in an annual chapbook. The editor says, "My advice to poets? How does one teach a bird to sing? How does one teach a cricket to chirp? But seriously—I think a poet should write for himself, should write about those things that touch him deeply."

‡**THE VANITAS PRESS (I, IV-Specialized, children)**, Plätslagarevägen 4E1, 22730, Lund, Sweden, founded 1978, publisher (Mr.) March Laumer, who says, "The press is the shoestringyest in existence. We publish to an extremely enthusiastic but equally extremely tiny market. **No royalties can be paid, as we distribute volumes at rock-bottom cost of production/mailing (even then subscribers must pay circa $15 a volume; we just can't ask for more to cover royalties).** But it is your chance to reach an audience of up to 2,000 readers. Currently we issue only 'latter-day novels' of the 'Oz' saga. Please read the Oz books in your local public library, then send us short stories, outlines for novels, and/or Oz-oriented art; you're virtually certain to be published if material is promising at all." As a sample he selected these lines from **Charmed Gardens of Oz:**

> Well said, indeed,
> And when you feed
> On things that bleed
> I hope you'll heed
> What Dot's decreed:
> It's only when you talk of flesh that's edible
> That you can mention 'meat' and still be credible!

VEGETARIAN JOURNAL; THE VEGETARIAN RESOURCE GROUP; JEWISH VEGETARIANS NEWS-LETTER (IV-Themes, children/teens), Box 1463, Baltimore MD 21203, founded 1982. *VJ* is bimonthly, *JV* is quarterly, founded 1983. The Vegetarian Resource Group is a small press publisher of nonfiction, sometimes incorporating poetry. **They want poetry on themes such as vegetarians, animal rights and world hunger. "We appreciate humor and/or account of personal feelings about being vegetarian and a factual, scientific approach. Please, no graphic descriptions of animal abuse."** As a sample, the editor selected these lines from a poem by Mitch Cohen:

> But humans ate some animals, for which they had to feed them vast
>   amounts of grains,
> which became scarcer on the earth which melted melted the glaciers,
>   which fossilized the dinosaurs,
> which roamed the earth, which only wanted to support life; One only
>   earth, one only earth.

JV is a 16-page, magazine-sized newsletter, offset from typescript with typeset heads. *VJ* has a circulation of 20,000; *JV* of 800. **Pays copies. Simultaneous submissions and previously published poems OK.** They offer an annual contest for ages 19 and under, $50 savings bond for the best contribution on any aspect of vegetarianism. "Most entries are essay, but we would accept poetry with enthusiasm." Charles Stahler says: "Note that *Vegetarian Journal* and *Jewish Vegetarians Newsletter* are published by two separate organizations, but are both edited from the same address." **Sample of *JV* is SASE and two first class stamps. Sample of *Vegetarian Journal* is $3.**

VEHICULE PRESS; SIGNAL EDITIONS (IV-Regional), Box 125 Station Place du Parc, Montreal, Quebec H2W 2M9 Canada, phone (514)844-6073, FAX (514)844-7543, poetry editor Michael Harris, publisher Simon Dardick, is a "literary press with poetry series, Signal Editions, **publishing the work**

of Canadian poets only." They publish flat-spined paperbacks and hardbacks. Among the poets published are Louis Dudek, Marie-Claire Blais, Erin Mouré, Don Coles, David Solway, Susan Glickman and Stephen Scobie. As a sample they selected these lines by Gérald Godin:

> "What, you've forgotten my telephone number?"
> "Listen, old friend, I think you know
> they removed a tumour from my brain
> as big as a mandarine orange
> and I'm afraid
> your telephone number was in it . . . "

They want Canadian poetry which is "first-rate, original, content-conscious." Query with 10 poems ("a good proportion of which should already have been published in recognized literary periodicals"), bio, publication credits or poetic aims. Reports in 2 months. Pays 10% royalties plus 10 author's copies. Buys English-language world rights.

VER POETS VOICES; POETRY POST; POETRY WORLD (IV-Members); VER POETS OPEN COMPETITION, Haycroft, 61/63 Chiswell Green Lane, St. Albans, County Herts, AL2 3AL England, founded 1965, editor/organizer May Badman, a poetry group **"publishing members' work if it has reached a good standard.** We publish *Ver Poets Voices, Poetry Post* and *Poetry World*, the last being an information sheet. **We aim at bringing members' work up to professional literary standards if it is not already there. All members receive our publications free and can buy further copies." Membership costs £10 overseas p.a.** They have recently published work by Myra Schneider, Andrea Capes, Pamela Gillilan, Gladys Mary Coles and Freda Downie. As a sample, they selected "In Ivinghoe Church" by Ruth Partington:

> There they are again,
> The Mermaid and the Man,
> Glinting through the leaves,
> Transmuted from green trees
> To wood and stone,
> Reduced but not subdued, and she,
> Slippery creature of the shining waves
> Sits solid on a wooden pew-end here!

Ver Poets Voices, which appears about twice a year, is digest-sized with a stapled card cover. It goes to the 250 members plus about 50 copies to shops, etc. *Poetry Post*, also a semiannual, is magazine-sized with a card front cover. It reports on Ver Poets competitions and other matters concerning poetry. *Poetry World*, which appears 4 times/year, is a series of information sheets on national competitions and poetry events. The group organizes the Ver Poets Open Competition (an annual event), which has prizes of £500, £300 and £100 (two equal prizes—total £1,000). Ver Poets Autumn Competition, for members only, will publish a winners' anthology. Prizes are £100, £50 and 2 of £25. They also organize six other annual competitions for members only; winners are published in *Poetry Post*. Sample copies: *Ver Poets Voices*, £1.50 (£3 includes postage); *Poetry Post*, 80p. (£2 includes postage); *Poetry World*, free for IRC. "All members are encouraged to send work for comment." Not more than 6 clearly typed or reproduced poems should be submitted at once. Reporting time is "by return of post" and time to publication is 6 months or less. Reviews books of poetry if written by members. The editors say, "A lot of work is being done in England by small presses such as ourselves, and we provide continually the first few rungs of the ladder to success as poets. Members are offered free advice on their work and how to present it to editors. Also information on publishing opportunities."

VERANDAH (II), c/o TAS, Deakin University, Toorak Campus, 336 Glenterrie Rd., Malvern Victoria, Australia 3144, founded 1986, is a handsome annual. **"We seek poetry of a high quality and literary kind, with no restrictions on length, subject or style."** They have published poetry by Warwick Anderson, Peter Bakowski, Adrian D'Ambra and Javant Biarujia. As a sample here is a haiku by Duncan Richardson:

> Along the cream
> beach they came four pelicans
> playing soft biplanes.

It is flat-spined with full-color glossy card cover, professionally printed on glossy stock, 90+ pgs. **Sample postpaid: A$10.50. Pays A$5-10/poem plus 2 copies. Buys first Australian publishing rights. Annual deadline May 31. Authors' names are deleted from ms before consideration by editors.**

VERSE (II), English Dept., College of William and Mary, P.O. Box 8795, Williamsburg VA 23187-8795, founded 1984, editors Henry Hart, Robert Crawford and David Kinloch, is "a poetry journal which also publishes interviews with poets, articles about poetry and book reviews." They **want "no**

specific kind; we only look for high quality poetry." They have published poetry by A.R. Ammons, James Merrill, James Dickey, Galway Kinnell, Richard Kenney, John Hollander, Charles Wright, Robert Pinsky, Charles Simic and Wendell Berry. *Verse* is published 3 times a year. It is digest-sized, 90 pgs., saddle-stapled with card cover, using small type, professionally printed. They accept about 100 of 3,000 poems received. Press run: 700, to 600 subscribers of which 150 are libraries, 100 are sold on newsstands or in bookstores. Subscription: $12 for individuals, $21 for institutions. **Sample postpaid: $4. Pays 2 copies. Reports in 1 month, usually 4-5 months to publication. Simultaneous submissions OK.**

VERVE (II, IV-Themes), Box 3205, Simi Valley CA 93093, founded 1989, editor Ron Reichick, associate editors Mona Locke and Marilyn Hochheiser, is a quarterly **"open to contemporary poetry of any form which fits the theme of the issue; we look for fresh metaphor, unique ideas and language and imagery that informs."** They have recently published poetry by Marge Piercy, Michael Blake, Donald W. Baker, Nancy Ellis Taylor and Kevin Griffin. As a sample the editor selected these lines from "What An Old Man Hears" by Kimberly Biss:

> I'll hear rain licking gutters.
> Hear birch leaves
> loving the wind.
> I hope to hear a spider crawl
> across my ceiling some night.
> When my sink drains, maybe
> I will hear the water
> pass through the pipes
> and seep into the soil.
> Life will speak for itself.

Verve is digest-sized, 40 pgs., saddle-stitched, using bios of each contributor. Press run 700 for 100 subscriptions of which 3 are libraries. **Sample postpaid: $3.50. Send SASE for guidelines and list of upcoming themes. Pays 1 copy. Acquires first rights. Submit up to 5 poems, 2 pages maximum/poem; "36 lines or less has best chance." Simultaneous submissions, if noted, OK.** Reviews books of poetry in 250 words, single format. They sponsor 3 annual contests, each having prizes of $75, $50 and $25. Entry fee: $2 each poem. The editor advises, "Read a copy of *Verve* before you submit. Read good contemporary poetry—then write. Listen to criticism, but follow your instinct *and* the poem. *Then*—keep submitting."

VIGIL; AMMONITE; VIGIL PUBLICATIONS (II), 12 Priory Mead, Bruton, Somerset BA10 0DZ England, founded 1979, poetry editor John Howard Greaves. *Vigil* was formerly *Period Piece and Paperback*. They want **"poetry with a high level of emotional force or intensity of observation. Poems should normally be no longer than 35 lines. Color, imagery and appeal to the senses should be important features. No whining self-indulgent, neurotic soul-baring poetry."** They have published poetry by John Gonzalez, Roger Elkin, Brian Daldorph and Richard Newman. The digest-sized magazine is 40 pgs., saddle-stapled, photoreduced typescript, with colored matte card cover. It appears 3 times a year, press run 200 for 80 subscriptions of which 6 are libraries. They accept about 60 of 200 submissions received. Subscription: £4.50. **Sample postpaid: £2. Pays 2 copies. Editor sometimes comments on rejections. Submit no more than 6 poems at a time.** *Ammonite* appears twice a year with **"myth, image and word towards the secondary millenium . . . a seedbed of mythology for our future, potently embryonic."** Query regarding book publication by Vigil Publications. The editor offers "appraisal" for £7.50 for a sample of a maximum of 12 poems.

VIKING PENGUIN, 375 Hudson St., New York NY 10014. Declined listing.

THE VILLAGE IDIOT (II); MOTHER OF ASHES PRESS (V), Box 66, Harrison ID 83833-0066, *The Village Idiot* founded 1970, Mother of Ashes Press founded 1980, editor Joe M. Singer. They want **"poetry which breathes."** They have published poetry by Josephine D. Buffet and Rita Conroy. *The Village Idiot* appears triannually in a 5½×8¾ format, saddle-stapled, 48 pgs., with cover, using less than 10% of over 500 poems received a year. Their press run is 300 with 15 subscriptions of which 2 are libraries. Subscription: $15 for 6 issues. **Sample postpaid: $3. Reports in 1 month. Pays copies. Acquires one-time rights. Editor sometimes comments on rejections.** Reviews books of poetry. Mother of Ashes Press **publishes books and chapbooks by invitation only.** The editor says, "*The Village Idiot* is good company for an evening: entertaining, informative, provocative and well enough dressed one does not mind being seen in company with it. Are your poems?"

THE VILLAGER (II), Dept. PM, 135 Midland Ave., Bronxville NY 10708, phone (914)337-3252, founded 1928, editor Amy Murphy, poetry editor M. Josephine Colville, a publication of the Bronxville Women's Club for club members and families, professional people and advertisers, circulation 750, appears in 9 monthly issues, October through June. **Sample postpaid: $1.25. They use one page or more of poetry/issue, prefer poems less than 20 lines, "in good taste only," seasonal (Thanksgiving, Christmas, Easter) 3 months in advance. They copyright material but will release it to author on request. Pays 2 copies. SASE required.**

THE VINCENT BROTHERS REVIEW (II, IV-Themes), 4566 Northern Circle, Mad River Township, Dayton OH 45424-5789, founded 1988, editor Kimberly A. Willardson, is a journal appearing 3 times a year. **"We look for well-crafted, thoughtful poems that shoot bolts of electricity into the reader's mind, stimulating a powerful response. We also welcome light verse and are thrilled by unusual, innovative themes/styles. We do not accept previously published poems, simultaneous submissions or sexist, racist, anti-Semitic poetry. Sloppy mss containing typos and/or unintentional misspellings are automatically rejected.** *TVBR* publishes 2 theme issues/year—poets should send us a SASE to receive details about our upcoming themes." They have recently published poetry by Gerald England and Amy Poitier. As a sample the editor selected these lines from "Lights of Ancestors" by David B. McCoy:

> *A year before his death, my father,*
> *with saucer and cup, explained*
> *the earth's movement around the sun,*
> *and how space was absent*
> *of heat and air for us to breathe.*

TVBR is digest-sized, 60-80 pgs., saddle-stapled, professionally printed, with matte card cover. Their press run is 350. "We have 100 subscribers, 10 of which are libraries." Subscription: $12. **Sample postpaid: $4.50. Send SASE for guidelines. Pays 1 copy. Acquires one-time rights. Submit no more than 10 poems at a time, name and address on each page. "We do not read in December." Reports in 6-8 months (after readings by editor and 3 associate editors). Editor "often" comments on rejections.** Reviews books of poetry in 3,500 words maximum, single or multi-book format. She advises, *"Don't* send your poetry to a magazine you haven't read. Subscribe to the little magazines you respect—they contain the work of your peers and competitors. Proofread your poetry carefully and read it aloud before sending it out."

VIRGIN MEAT (IV-Horror), 2325 West Ave. K-15, Lancaster CA 93536, phone (805)722-1758, founded 1986, editor Steve Blum, appears irregularly with fiction, poetry and art. "Fiction is non-violent horror. Subjects range from vampires and ghosts to magic and the occult. **Poetry: Similar subjects, short, emotionally dark and depressing. No sad rhyming poetry."** The editor describes it as digest-sized. Press run 300. **Sample postpaid: $2 or $7/4 issues. Pays "1 copy for each printed. Send no less than 4 at a time. Simultaneous submissions and previously published poems OK; no dot-matrix submissions. All replies go out in the next day's mail."** Reviews books of poetry "only if it has a cover price."

THE VIRGINIA QUARTERLY REVIEW (III), 1 West Range, Charlottesville VA 22903, founded 1925, is one of the oldest and most distinguished literary journals in the country. It is digest-sized, 220+ pgs., flat-spined, circulation 4,000. **They use about 15 pgs. of poetry in each issue, pay $1/line, no length or subject restrictions.**

VIRTUE: THE CHRISTIAN MAGAZINE FOR WOMEN (IV-Religious), Box 850, Sisters OR 97759, founded 1978, editor Marlee Alex, is a slick magazine, circulation 150,000, appearing 6 times a year, which **"encourages and integrates biblical truth with daily living."** As a sample the editor selected these lines from "Bending" by Barbara Seaman:

> *Down on my knees again, Lord*
> *and undignified as ever,*
> *(how to mop mud with grace?)*
> *attempting to confine the exuberance*
> *of yesterday's rain to the kitchen only . . .*

Virtue is magazine-sized, 80 pgs., saddle-stapled, with full-color pages inside as well as on its paper cover. Subscription: $16.95. Price per issue: $2.95. **Sample postpaid: $3. Send SASE for guidelines. Pays $20-40/poem and 1 copy. Reports in 6-8 weeks, time to publication 3-9 months. Submit "no more than 3 poems, each on separate sheet, typewritten or dot-matrix; notify if simultaneous submission."**

‡**VIVO (II)**, 1195 Green St., San Francisco CA 94109, phone (415)885-5695, founded 1991, editor/publisher Carolyn Miller, is "an eclectic magazine of poetry, fiction, essays and art that combines humor and serious work," appearing once or twice a year. **"We are open to almost any kind of poetry except the extremes of traditional and experimental work. We like poems that are fresh and alive and that show a love of language. We are interested in both unpublished and published poets."** They do not want to see "poems that don't care about either depth of meaning or love of craft." As a sample

the editor selected these lines from "Granite Under Water" by Jeanne Lohmann:

> *These places we live, we return to,*
> *the flowers, the durable river. I am crying*
> *for air I cannot breathe. It is luminous,*
> *this country where your death is granite*
> *under water, a single yellow iris*
> *standing clear from edges of stone.*

VIVO is 16 pgs., 11×17, printed web offset and unbound, with 2-color cover and centerfold, graphics and ads. You want to be seen in a cafe reading this artsy tabloid. Poetry competes with fiction and prose, but it gets the center spread and is eclectic, featuring all styles. Press run is 1,000 for 53 subscribers, 120 shelf sales. Single copy: $3; subscription: $8 for 2 issues. **Sample postpaid: $4. Previously published poems and simultaneous submissions OK, but not preferred.** Time between acceptance and publication is 6-9 months. **Seldom comments on rejections. Send SASE for guidelines. Reports in 6 weeks to 3 months. Pays 2 copies plus 40% discount on additional copies. Rights revert to author on publication.** Reviews books of poetry. Carolyn Miller says, "The true goal is to live a creative life, to respond to the world as a poet. If you do this honestly and faithfully, and want your poems to have a larger life, keep sending them out, for their sake, not your own."

Voices International

VOLUME 26, NO. 3   FALL, 1991

"We receive and accept poems from poets all over the world," says Clovita Rice, editor of **Voices International.** *"We focus on publishing poetry with fresh and memorable imagery; poetry that tracks well (where the reader can follow the poet into and throughout the experience and feel that it was a worthwhile sharing); poetry that appeals to the various senses."* She says they like to live up to their name not only with the poetry they publish, but also with their cover art. This piece, *"The Caboclo Cast"* by Merrill Ann Gonzales, depicts a *"local"* at Lago Canacari, Brazil. *"As in a good poem, we're right there with him!"* Rice adds.

VOICES INTERNATIONAL (II), 1115 Gillette Dr., Little Rock AR 72207, editor Clovita Rice, is a quarterly poetry journal. "We look for poetry with a new focus, memorable detail and phrasing, and significant and haunting statement climax, all of which impel the reader to reread the poem and return to it for future pleasure and reference." As a sample the editor selected these lines from "Leeward of March" by Evelyn Corry Applebee:

> *I leave the rain-warped window*
> *to descend the basement stairs,*
> *carrying the ripe-lemon shout*
> *of a yellow watering can like*
> *a summer god's wand, to delicacies*
> *awaiting a warm womb of soil,*
> *tender transplants from the hothouse*
> *of my winter.*

It is 32-40 pgs., 6×9, saddle-stapled, professionally printed with b&w matte card cover. Subscription: $10/year. **Sample postpaid (always a back issue): $2. Prefers free verse but accepts high quality traditional. Limit submissions to batches of 5, double-spaced, 3-40 lines (will consider longer if good). Publishes an average of 18 months after acceptance. Pays copies.**

VOICES ISRAEL (I); MONTHLY POET'S VOICE (IV-Members), P.O. Box 5780, 46157 Herzlia Israel, founded 1972, *Voices Israel* editor Mark Levinson, with an editorial board of 7, is an annual anthology of poetry in English coming from all over the world. **You have to buy a copy to see your work in print. Submit all kinds of poetry (up to 4 poems), each no longer than a sheet of typing paper.** They have published poetry by Yehuda Amichai, Eugene Dubnov, Alan Sillitoe and Seymour Mayne. As a sample the editor selected these lines by Jayseth Guberman:

> She said a prayer
> to which I was not an answer,
> and yet I burned
> until I burned myself out
> like a candle on shabbat.

The annual *Voices Israel* is 6¼×8, offset from laser output on ordinary paper, approximately 121 pgs., flat-spined with varying cover. Circulation 350. Subscription: $13.50. **Sample back copy: $10 postpaid; airmail extra. Contributor's copy: $13.50 airmail. Deadline end of February each year; reports in fall.** Acquires first publication rights. *The Monthly Poet's Voice*, a broadside edited by Ezra Ben-Meir, **is open only to members of the Voices Group of Poets in English.** The *Voices Israel* editor advises, "Never let the reader guess what your next two or three words will be."

VOL. NO. MAGAZINE (II, IV-Themes), 24721 Newhall Ave., Newhall CA 91321, phone (805)254-0851, founded 1983, poetry editors Richard Weekley, Jerry Danielsen, Tina Landrum and Don McLeod. "*Vol. No.* publishes lively and concise works. Vivid connections. **Each issue has a theme. 'The Eros of Eros' (Aug. '93). Send SASE for description. No trivial, clichéd or unthoughtout work. Work that penetrates the ozone within. One-page poems have the best chance.**" They have published poetry by Octavio Paz, Anne Marple, Jane Hirshfield and Julian Pulley. The editors selected these sample lines by William Stafford:

> We stand for hours where sunlight tells us
> it forgives. A golden shaft pours down.
> The air waits. A cardinal sings and sings.
> We stand for hours.

Vol. No. is a digest-sized, saddle-stapled, 32-page annual, circulation 300. They receive about 600 freelance submissions of poetry/year, use 60, have a 6-month backlog. Subscription: $10 (2 issues. **Sample postpaid: $3. Submit limit of 6 poems. Photocopy and simultaneous submissions OK. Reports in 1-5 months. Pays 2 copies.**

W.I.M. PUBLICATIONS (WOMAN IN THE MOON) (IV-Gay, women), 2215-R Market St., Box 137, Dept. PM, San Francisco CA 94114, phone (408)253-3329, founded 1979, poetry editor SDiane Bogus, who says, "We are a small press with trade press ambitions. We publish poetry, business and writing reference books. We generally run 250-1,000 per press run and **give the author half or a percentage of the books. We pay royalties to our established authors. We prefer a query and a modest track record.**" She wants poetry by "gay, black, women, prison poets, enlightened others—contemporary narrative or lyric work, free verse OK, but not too experimental for cognition. We prefer poems to be a page or less if not part of long narrative. No obviously self-indulgent exercises in the psychology of the poet. No sexual abuse themes this year. No gross sexual references; no hate poems." Send 2 first class stamps for guidelines/catalog. In addition to her own work, she has published poetry by Adele Sebastian. As a sample she selected these lines from "His Life" from **The Book of Lives** by Sherrylynn Posey:

> I had 4 maybe 5 lovers
> in my life
> one of them
> lied to me

SDiane Bogus publishes 2-4 chapbooks and flat-spined paperbacks a year each averaging 40-100 pages. **Submit 6 sample poems and a statement of "vision and poetics, theme selection of the work, poetic mentors, track record and $5 reading fee. New poets must take poetry test ($10 plus free critique). Submit between April 1 and June 30 each year. We acknowledge submissions upon receipt. We report at end of reading season, July through September 7. Simultaneous submissions, previously published poems, photocopies all OK. No dot-matrix.** Authors are asked to assist in promo and sales by providing list of prospective readers and promotional photos. To established authors we pay 5-10% royalties after costs; others half press run in copies. We may take advanced orders; no subsidy. We will accept subscriptions for a book in production at retail price. We fill orders author has provided and others our promo has prompted." *WIM* offers a self-publishing and consultation criticism service for a fee. Bogus says, "W.I.M. promotes readings for its poets and encourages each poet who submits with a personal letter which discusses her or his strengths and weaknesses. Often we allow repeat submissions." They sponsor 2 paid poetry contests/year. Write for guidelines.

WAKE FOREST UNIVERSITY PRESS (IV-Regional, ethnic), P.O. Box 7333, Winston-Salem NC 27109, phone (919)759-5448, founded 1976, director and poetry editor Dillon Johnston. **"We publish only poetry from Ireland and bilingual editions of French poetry in translation. I am able to consider only poetry written by Irish poets or translations of contemporary French poetry. I must return, unread, poetry from American poets."** They have published poetry by John Montague, Derek Mahon, Richard Murphy, Michael Longley, Paul Muldoon, Thomas Kinsella and Eilean N. Chuilleanain. **Query with 4-5 samples. Replies to queries in 1-2 weeks, to submissions (if invited) in 2-3 months. No simultaneous submissions. Photocopy OK. Publishes on 10% royalty contract with $500 advance, 6-8 author's copies. Buys North American or US rights.** Dillon Johnston comments, "Because our press is so circumscribed, we get few direct submissions from Ireland. I would advise American poets to read your publication carefully so that they not misdirect to presses such as ours work that they, and I, value."

‡**WARTHOG PRESS (II)**, 29 S. Valley Rd., West Orange NJ 07052, phone (201)731-9269, founded 1979, poetry editor Patricia Fillingham, publishes books of poetry **"that are understandable, poetic."** She has published poetry by Barbara A. Holland, Penny Harter and Marta Fenyves. **Query with 5 samples, cover letter "saying what the author is looking for." Simultaneous submissions OK. Ms should be "readable." Pays copies, but "I would like to get my costs back."** Comments on rejections, **"if asked for. People really don't want criticism."** Patricia Fillingham feels, "The best way to sell poetry still seems to be from poet to listener. I wish more people would buy poetry."

WASHINGTON REVIEW; FRIENDS OF THE WASHINGTON REVIEW OF THE ARTS, INC. (II), Box 50132, Washington DC 20091, phone (202)638-0515, founded 1974, literary editor Joe Ross, is a bimonthly journal of arts and literature published by the Friends of the Washington Review of the Arts, Inc., a nonprofit, tax-exempt educational organization. *WR* is tabloid-sized, using 2 of the large pgs. per issue for poetry, saddle-stapled on high-quality newsprint, circulation 2,000 with 700 subscriptions of which 10 are libraries. **They publish local Washington metropolitan area poets as well as poets from across the US and abroad. "We have eclectic tastes but lean with more favor toward experimental work." Sample postpaid: $2.50. Pays 5 copies.** Reviews books of poetry in 1,000-1,500 words, single format—multi-book "on occasion."

WASHINGTON WRITERS' PUBLISHING HOUSE (IV-Regional), P.O. Box 15271, Washington DC 20003, phone (202)543-1905, founded 1975. An editorial board is elected annually from the collective. "We are a poetry publishing collective that publishes outstanding poetry collections in flat-spined paperbacks by **individual authors living in the greater Washington, DC area (60-mile radius, excluding Baltimore) on the basis of competitions held once a year."** They have recently published poetry by Myra Sklarew, Ann Darr, Barbara Lefcowitz, Maxine Clair, Ann Knox, Martin Galvin and Elizabeth Murawski. The editors chose this sample from "The Kidnapping of Science" in **From the Red Eye of Jupiter** by Patricia Garfinkel:

> Conception had been a quiet event, not
> the harsh strike of steel to flint,
> but an easing into fertile corners,
> patient as bacteria for the right conditions.

Submit 50-60 pgs. with SASE only between July 1 and September 30. $5 reading fee. Poets become working members of the collective. "Interested poets may write for a brochure of published poets and sheet of guidelines."

WATER MARK PRESS (V), 138 Duane St., New York NY 10013, founded 1978, editor Coco Gordon, proposes "to publish regardless of form in archival editions with handmade paper and hand done elements in sewn, bound books, broadsides, chapbooks and artworks. **I use only avant-garde material." Currently they accept no unsolicited poetry.** They have published poetry by Barbara Roux and Alison Knowles. The editor selected this sample from "After Eden" by Michael Blumenthal:

> Once again the invasion of purpose
> into gesture: the stem towards the vase,
> the hands towards the dreaded morning music
> of predictability, Indian paintbrush fades

That's from a collection of his poetry, **Sympathetic Magic**, published by Water Mark in 1980, 96 pgs., flat-spined, with art by Theo Fried, printed on archival, matte card cover with colored art, $9. The Water Mark Book Awards are dormant now. **Note: Please do not confuse Water Mark Press with the imprint Watermark Press, used by other businesses.**

WATERWAYS: POETRY IN THE MAINSTREAM; TEN PENNY PLAYERS; BARD PRESS (I, IV-Themes, children, anthologies), 393 St. Paul's Ave., Staten Island NY 10304, founded 1977, poetry editors Barbara Fisher and Richard Spiegel, "publishes **poetry by adult and child poets in a magazine that is published 11 times a year. We do theme issues** and are trying to increase an audience for poetry and the printed and performed word. The project produces performance readings in public spaces and is in residence year round at our local library with workshops and readings. We publish the magazine, *Waterways*, anthologies of child poets; child poetry postcard series; chapbooks (adults and child poets). **We are not fond of haiku or rhyming poetry; never use material of an explicit sexual nature.** We are open to reading material from people we have never published, writing in traditional and experimental poetry forms. While we do 'themes' sometimes an idea for a future magazine is inspired by a submission so we try to remain open to poets' inspiration. Poets should be guided however by the fact that we are children's and animal rights advocates and are a NYC press." They have recently published poetry by Albert Huffstickler, Arthur Knight and Kit Knight. As a sample, the editors chose these lines by Ida Fasel:

> I try to find a word
> for the sound this inland water makes
> tirelessly washing up on shore,
> rippling on and on in the mild breeze
> in the restless serenity
> of light shadowing itself
> in valleys of cobalt blue.

Waterways is published in a 40-page, 4¼×7 format, saddle-stapled, photocopy and letter-press, from various type styles, using b&w drawings, matte card cover, circulation 150 with 58 subscriptions of which 12 are libraries. Subscription: $20. **Sample postpaid: $2.54. They use 60% of freelance poems submitted. Submit less than 10 poems for first submission. No dot-matrix. Simultaneous submissions OK. Send SASE for guidelines for approaching themes.** "Since we've taken the time to be very specific in our response, writers should take seriously our comments and not waste their emotional energy and our time sending material that isn't within our area of interest. Sending for our theme sheet and for a sample issue and then objectively thinking about the writer's own work is practical and wise. Without meaning to sound 'precious' or unfriendly, the writer should understand that small press publishers doing limited editions and all production work in house are working from their personal artistic vision and know exactly what notes will harmonize, effectively counterpoint and meld. Many excellent poems are sent back to the writers by *Waterways* because they don't relate to what we are trying to create in a given month or months. Some poets get printed regularly in *Waterways*; others will probably never be published by us, not because the poet doesn't write well (although that too is sometimes the case) but only because we are artists with opinions and we exercise them in building each issue." **Reports in less than a month. Pays 1 copy. Acquires one-time publication rights. Editors sometimes comment on rejections.** They hold contests for children only. **Chapbooks published by Ten Penny Players are "by children only—and not by submission; they come through our workshops in the library and schools."** Adult poets are published by us through our Bard Press imprint. **"Books evolve from the relationship we develop with writers who we publish in *Waterways* and whom we would like to give more exposure."** No submissions. The editors advise, "We suggest that poets attend book fairs. It's a fast way to find out what we are all publishing." Manuscripts that arrive without a return envelope are not sent back.

WAYNE LITERARY REVIEW (I, II), Dept. of English, Wayne State University, 51 W. Warren, Detroit MI 48202. Contact Mike Liebler. Appears twice a year using **any kind of poetry except that using footnotes.** They have recently published poetry by Ken Mikolowski, Bob Hershon, Adam Cornford Antler, Faye Kicknosway and many up-and-coming student writers. It is magazine-sized and distributed free. **Sample postpaid: $2. Submit 3-10 poems, nothing handwritten. Simultaneous submissions and previously published poems OK. "We only read from August through November—no summer reading." Reports in up to 5 months. Pays 1 copy** and "eternal gratitude."

‡**WEBBER'S (II)**, 15 McKillop St., Melbourne, Victoria 3000 Australia, founded 1989, is a biannual literary magazine using **poetry approximately 20-30 lines.** They have recently published poetry by Warrick Wynne, Chris Wallace-Crabbe and Jeff Guess. As a sample the editor selected these lines by Jill Jones:

> I am not that much travelled
> on this huge land mass, called once gondwanaland,
> though sometimes I think my home city
> breathes
> a little of me.

The editor says *Webber's* is 100 pgs., A5. They receive about 150 poems/year, publish 10%.

Press run is 300 for 75 subscribers of which 18 are libraries, 20 shelf sales. Single copy: $4.95; subscription: $10/year ($15 overseas). **Sample postpaid: $8.50.** They say "Poet will receive acknowledgment of submission, submission is circulated to an editorial board, then poet is notified as to acceptance." **Pays approximately $40/poem.**

WEBSTER REVIEW (II, IV-Translations), Webster University, 470 E. Lockwood, Webster Groves MO 63119, founded 1974, poetry editors Robert Boyd and Greg Marshall, is a literary annual. They want "no beginners. We are especially interested in translations of foreign contemporary poetry." They have published poetry by Barbara F. Lefcowitz, Martin Robbins, Will Wells, Margherita Guidacci and Chang Soo Ko. *Webster Review* is 128 pgs., digest-sized, flat-spined, professionally printed with glossy card cover. They receive about 1,500 poems/year, use 120. Press run is 1,000 with 500 subscriptions of which 200 are libraries. Subscription: $5; per copy: $5. **Sample free for SASE. Editors comment on rejections "if time permits." Reports "within a month, usually." Contributors receive 2 copies.**

‡WELTER (I, II), English Dept., University of Baltimore, Charles St. at Mt. Royal, Baltimore MD 21218, founded 1963, editor Stacy Pipkin, is a literary annual **"extremely interested in beginners and lesser known writers. Let us know if you're a student."** It is flat-spined, digest-sized. Press run 500. **Sample postpaid: $2. Submit 3-5 poems no more than 30 lines each. "No rhyming poetry. No multiple submissions. No cover letters; we will not read them and the poetry should speak for itself." Reads submissions August through December only; makes decisions in January. Send SASE for guidelines. Reports in 2-4 weeks. Pays 2 copies. Acquires first-time rights.** $50 annual prize given to the best poem published in that year's issue.

THE WESLEYAN ADVOCATE (IV-Religious), P.O. Box 50434, Indianapolis IN 46250-0434, founded 1843, is a monthly magazine using **"short religious poetry only; no long free verse or secular."** The editor describes it as 36 pgs., magazine-sized, offset, saddle-stapled, with 4-color cover. They use 10-15% of 100-200 poems received/year. Press run 20,000 with "some" subscriptions of which 50 are libraries, no shelf sales (so it must be distributed free). Subscription: $12.50. **Sample: $2 plus SASE. Reports in 2 weeks. Pays 15¢/line plus 4-6 copies on request. Buys first and/or one-time rights.**

WESLEYAN UNIVERSITY PRESS (III), 110 Mt. Vernon, Middletown CT 06459, founded 1957, editor Terry Cochran, is one of the major publishers of poetry in the nation. They publish 4-6 titles/year. They have published poetry by James Dickey, Joy Harjo, James Tate and Yusef Komunyakaa. **Send query and SASE. Considers simultaneous submissions. Send SASE for guidelines. Responds to queries in 6-8 weeks, to mss in 2-4 months. Pays royalties plus 10 copies.** To obtain sample copies, phone 1-800-421-1561. Poetry publications from Wesleyan tend to get widely (and respectfully) reviewed.

‡WEST.; BLUESTONE PRESS (II), P.O. Box 1186, Hampshire College, Amherst MA 01002, founded 1990, editors Joshua Saul Beckman and John C. Horoschak."*West.* is a quarterly magazine of poetry and short stories, as well as periodic interviews with major writers." They have **no specifications as to length, subject matter or style, "but we discourage submissions of an overtly political, racial or religious nature."** They have recently published poetry by Larry Rubin, Alice Mattison and B.Z. Niditch. As a sample the editors selected these lines by Anna M. Warrock:

> A long time now I have
> watched the horizon. Are you
> aware? that the line which is
> land and sky is also sky and land.

West. is approximately 120 pgs., digest-sized, perfect-bound, with original artwork and ads. They receive approximately 13,000 poems/year from over 2,600 poets, use approximately 80 poems by 70 poets. Press run is 200. Single copy: $3; subscription: $12. **Sample postpaid: $4. No previously published poems or simultaneous submissions. Cover letter required.** "We provide comments or criticism on rejections infrequently but will always reply to specific questions by the author at the time of submission or after return of rejected manuscript." **Send SASE for guidelines. Reports in 6-8 weeks. Pays 1 copy.** Bluestone Press publishes approximately 4 chapbooks/year as well as 2 limited-edition, signed, hand-bound series of single poems or stories. **Replies to queries "immediately," to mss in 1-2 months. Pays 20% of print run (print run is usually 200+).**

WEST ANGLIA PUBLICATIONS (II), P.O. Box 2683, La Jolla CA 92038, phone (619)453-0706, founded 1982 by editor Helynn Hoffa, is a publishing company that **assumes the cost of putting out a book and pays author in royalties or in books. Author retains rights.** They have published poetry by Wilma Lusk, John Theobald and Gary Morgan, among others. As a sample the editor chose lines from "Approach of Winter" in Kathleen Iddings' **Selected & New Poems, 1980-1990**:

> *We sit on the ancient porch swing, an eighty*
> *year old father and an aging daughter.*
> *I've never noticed how fast October's wind*
> *could strip an elm; leaves wing by like mallards*
> *heading south. I study the ancient barn,*
> *your escape that held a workshop, tractors, herds —*
> *and wonder when the snows will bring it down.*

To query send 6 pages of your work, a cover letter, bio and SASE.

This **West Branch** *cover illustration comes from a 16th century Venetian text. "We liked the notion of communication by the use of hand signs — the idea, I suppose, that language could be sensuous," says Robert Taylor, editor along with Karl Patten. "Don't poets and writers try to make language less abstract, too? Don't they want us to feel the force of their words as directly as possible, as if through the senses of touch, sound, sight, etc.?" he says. "The multiple hands may also suggest something of the variety of work we publish." The editors divide space in the magazine "fairly evenly" between poetry and fiction.*

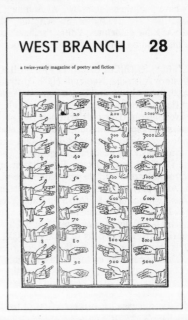

WEST BRANCH 28

a twice-yearly magazine of poetry and fiction

WEST BRANCH (II), English Dept., Bucknell Hall, Bucknell University, Lewisburg PA 17837, founded 1977, is a literary biannual. They have published poetry by D. Nurkse, Deborah Burnham, Jim Daniels, Anneliese Wagner, Betsy Sholl, David Citino, Barbara Crooker and David Brooks. It is 100-120 pgs., digest-sized, circulation 500, using **quality poetry. "We do not consider simultaneous submissions. Each poem is judged on its own merits, regardless of subject or form. We strive to publish the best work being written today."** Reports in 6-8 weeks. Pays copies and subscription to the magazine. Acquires first rights. One-year subscription: $7. Two years (4 issues): $11. Sample: $3. Reviews books and chapbooks of poetry but only those by writers who have been published in *West Branch*. This is an especially good market for lyric poetry that aims to share insight with a general audience. Usually reports on time.

WEST OF BOSTON (II), Box 2, Cochituate Station, Wayland MA 01778, phone (508)653-7241, founded 1983, poetry editor Norman Andrew Kirk, wants to see **"poetry of power, compassion, originality and wit — and talent, too."** For book or chapbook submission query with 5-10 sample poems, credits and bio. Simultaneous submissions, photocopies, dot-matrix, previously published poems all OK. Editor "sometimes" comments on rejected mss. Pays 10% of press run.

WEST WIND REVIEW (II, IV-Anthology), English Department, Southern Oregon State College, Ashland OR 97520, phone (503)552-6181, founded 1982, is an annual **"looking for sensitive but strong verse that celebrates all aspects of men's and women's experiences, both exalted and tragic. We are looking to print material that reflects ethnic and social diversity."** As a sample the editor selected these lines by Deanne Bayer:

> *to ethereality in the fire,*
> *solidifying again as our breaths*

> *bumped our words*
> *against ice-gilded walls, sharing*
> *our home with a roisterous wind*

WWR is handsomely printed, flat-spined, 140-160 pgs., digest-sized, appearing each spring. They receive about 600-700 submissions each year, publish 40-50 poems and 20-30 short stories. Press run is 500. Sample "at current year's price. We take submissions — limit of 5 poems not exceeding 50 lines — year-round." Deadline: January 1 for publication in late May or early June. They will consider simultaneous submissions but not previously published poems. Send SASE for guidelines. Reports in 2-3 months after deadline. Pays 1 copy. Offers awards for each category.

WESTENRA: THE MISS LUCY WESTENRA SOCIETY OF THE UNDEAD (IV-Horror), 125 Taylor St., Jackson TN 38301, phone (901)427-7714, founded 1989, founder and editor Lewis Sanders, appears 3-4 times/year, using **"vampire poetry, vampire haiku, nothing that does not deal with vampires."** They have published poetry by Carl Brennan, Jane Oz and Cathy Buburuz. The editor describes it as a magazine-sized newsletter. Subscription: $14. Sample: cost varies. **Pays 1 copy to non-members. Send SASE for guidelines. Editor "seldom" comments on rejections.** He advises, "Study, and write, but don't plan on earning a living writing poetry."

WESTERLY; PATRICIA HACKETT PRIZE (II), Centre for Studies in Australian Literature, University of Western Australia, Nedlands 6009, Australia, phone (09) 380-2101, founded 1956, editors Dennis Haskell, Peter Cowan and Bruce Bennett. *Westerly* is a literary and cultural quarterly publishing quality short fiction, poetry, literary critical, socio-historical articles and book reviews. **"No restrictions on creative material. Our only criterion [for poetry] is literary quality. We don't dictate to writers on rhyme, style, experimentation, or anything else. We are willing to publish short or long poems. We do assume a reasonably well read, intelligent audience. Past issues of *Westerly* provide the best guides. Not consciously an academic magazine."** They have recently published work by Dorothy Hewett, Bruce Dawe, Veronica Brady, Peter Porter and Alamgir Hashmi. The quarterly magazine is 7×10, "electronically printed," 96 pgs., with some photos and graphics. Circulation is 1,000. Price per copy is $5 (Aus.) plus overseas postage via surface mail, subscription $20 (Aus.)/year. **Sample available for $6 (Aus.) surface mail, $7 (Aus.) airmail. "Please do not send simultaneous submissions." Reporting time is 2-3 months and time to publication approximately 12 weeks, sometimes longer. Minimum pay for poetry is $30 plus 1 copy. Buys first publication rights. Returns rights; requests acknowledgement on reprints.** Reviews books of poetry in 500-1,000 words. The Patricia Hackett Prize (value approx. $400) is awarded in March for the best contribution published in *Westerly* during the previous calendar year. The advice of the editors is: "Be sensible. Write what matters for you but think about the reader. Don't be swayed by literary fashion. Read the magazine if possible before sending submissions. Read, read, read literature of all kinds and periods."

WESTERN PRODUCER PUBLICATIONS; WESTERN PEOPLE (IV-Regional), Box 2500, Saskatoon, Saskatchewan S7K 2C4 Canada, phone (306)665-3500, founded 1923, managing editor Michael Gillgannon. *Western People* is a magazine supplement to *The Western Producer*, a weekly newspaper, circulation 120,000, which uses **"poetry about the people, interests and environment of rural Western Canada."** As a sample the editor selected the entire poem "sky so heavy and low" by Marilyn Cay:

> *it is November in Saskatchewan*
> *the sky so heavy and low*
> *I can feel the weight of it*
> *on my chest*
> *the days so short and getting shorter*
> *I can touch the sides of them*
> *at midday*

The tabloid-sized supplement is 8 pgs., newsprint, with color and b&w photography and graphics. They receive about 600 submissions of freelance poetry/year, use 40-50. **Sample free for postage (2 oz.) — and ask for guidelines. One poem/page, maximum of 3 poems/submission. Name, address, telephone number upper left corner of each page. Reports within 2 weeks. Pays $15-50/ poem.** The editor comments, "It is difficult for someone from outside Western Canada to catch the flavor of this region; almost all the poems we purchase are written by Western Canadians."

‡WESTVIEW: A JOURNAL OF WESTERN OKLAHOMA (IV-Regional), 100 Campus Drive, SOSU, Weatherford OK 73096, phone (405)774-3077, founded 1981, editor Leroy Thomas, Ph.D., is a quarterly using **poetry related to Western Oklahoma. "Our preference is free verse up to 40 lines. No rhymed poetry, poetry of a risqué nature, no poetry containing four-letter words."** They have published poetry by Sheryl Nelms, Maggie Culver Fry, Ernestine Gravley, Lynn Riggs and Sandra Soli. As a sample, the editor selected these lines from his own poem, "Compulsion":

> *Emotion courses through*

> *Me like the steam*
> *Rising in a pressure cooker,*
> *And the only escape valve I have*
> *Is the written word.*

Westview is 44 pgs., magazine-sized, saddle-stapled, with glossy card cover in full-color. They use about 25% of 100 poems received a year. Press run 1,000 for 500 subscribers of which about 25 are libraries, 150 shelf sales. Subscription: $8. **Sample postpaid: $4. Editor comments on submissions "always." Send SASE for guidelines. "Mss are circulated to an editorial board; we usually respond within a month." Payment in contributor's copies.** He says, "It's still possible to be decent and clean and be published."

WEYFARERS; GUILDFORD POETS PRESS (II), 9, White Rose Lane, Woking, Surrey GU22 7JA United Kingdom, founded 1972, administrative editor Margaret Pain, poetry editors Margaret Pain, Susan James, Martin Jones and Jeffery Wheatley. They say, "We publish *Weyfarers* magazine three times a year. All our editors are themselves poets and give their spare time free to help other poets." They describe their needs as **"all types of poetry, serious and humorous, free verse and rhymed/metered, but mostly 'mainstream' modern. Excellence is the main consideration. NO hard porn, graphics, way-out experimental. Any subject publishable, from religious to satire. Not more than 40 lines."** They have published poetry by Paul Groves, M.A.B. Jones, Brian Daldorph and Fritz Hamilton. As a sample the editors chose Lucia Scatizzi's "Face":

> *I trace your eyes*
> *Your lashes tickle me*
> *Down your nose I glide*
> *To the dry dampness of your lips*
> *Under your chin I stop*
> *Retrace my steps*
> *Up to the sandy feeling of your brows*
> *I love your hair*
> *It fills my hands like silk*
> *Your head is merely bulk*
> *For your smile.*

The digest-sized, saddle-stapled format contains about 28 pgs. of poetry (of a total of 32 pgs.). The magazine has a circulation of "about 285," including about 190 subscriptions of which 5 are libraries. They use about 125 of 1,200-1,500 submissions received each year. **Sample current issue: $4 in cash USA (or £1.40 UK) postpaid. Submit no more than 6 poems, one poem/sheet. No previously published or simultaneous submissions. Closing dates for submissions end of January, May and September.** They sometimes **comment briefly, if requested,** on rejections. Payment 1 copy. Reviews books of poetry briefly, in newsletter sent to subscribers. "We are associated with Surrey Poetry Center, who have an annual Open Poetry Competition. The prize-winners are published in *Weyfarers*." Their advice to poets is, "Always read a magazine before submitting. And read plenty of modern poetry."

WHETSTONE (I, II), Department of English, University of Lethbridge, 4401 University Drive, Lethbridge, Alberta T1K 3M4 Canada, editor Tara Elder, appears twice a year with writing by beginners and published authors. **"Open to any kind of poetry, as long as it's of good quality."** They have published poems by Susan Musgrave and Rhonda McAdam. *Whetstone* is digest-sized, 80+ pgs., saddle-stapled, professionally printed in boldface type with 2-color matte card cover, circulation 500 with 200 subscriptions of which 25 are libraries. Single copy: $5 (Can.); subscription: $10. **Sample postpaid: $5. Any length of poetry. Photocopy, dot-matrix OK. Editor sometimes comments on rejections. Send SASE for guidelines. Pays $10 and 1 copy.** "We have highly specialized poetry and short story competitions. Writers should send $5 for sample copy, plus SASE for rules and regulations."

WHETSTONE; WHETSTONE PRIZE (II), P.O. Box 1266, Barrington IL 60011, phone (708)382-5626, editors Sandra Berris, Marsha Portnoy and Jean Tolle, is an annual. **"We emphasize quality more than category. No erotica or haiku."** They have recently published poetry by Paulette Roeske, Lucia Getsi and William Kloefkorn. As a sample the editor selected these lines by Robert Cooperman:

> *So what if Maggie and me*
> *made our spirit rappings*
> *by cracking our toe knuckles?*
> *Only men feed on facts*
> *like autumn turkeys on grain,*
> *on what they can touch and throttle.*

It is digest-sized, 96 pgs., professionally printed, flat-spined with matte card cover. Press run 500 for 100 subscribers of which 5+ are libraries, 350 shelf sales. **Sample postpaid: $3. Reads** submissions April 1 through June 30 only. Reports in 1-4 months. Pays 2 copies. Acquires first North American serial rights. The Whetstone Prizes are cash awards ($50-$300) for the best work in each issue.

‡WHISPERING PALM (I, II), P.O. Box 6523, Lake Worth FL 33466, founded 1990 by Doris Lamb ("chief, cook and bottle washer"), is a monthly "community-minded, informative variety magazine with poetry (the more the better). Sales of copies benefit S. Florida homeless family shelters—inquire as to availability of copies." They want "**ideally, lyrical, exquisitely rich and possibly the somewhat experimental. Enjoy meter, craft. Nothing preachy, religious, sentimental. No haiku, sonnets, badly rhymed or nonpoetics—i.e. prose arranged to pass for free verse. Any theme, although the less obscene, the better chance of publication.**" As a sample the editor selected these lines from "A Theory of Displacement, Suppose" by Allan Peterson:

> *even the mechanism of a skink's strobe-crawl*
> *might proceed from the pen to its user,*
> *that a toy be made, like sesame, like philosophers*
> *might have picked up wise pencils.*

The editor says it is digest-sized, saddle-stapled, with modest cover and graphics. They accept about 30% of poetry received/year. Single copy: 50¢-$1. **No previously published poems or simultaneous submissions. Submit 5-10 poems at a time. No dot-matrix. "If contributors wish, they may illustrate with own artwork. Will send requirements to those interested, in SASE." Reports within 6 months. Pays 1 copy.**

‡WHITE EAGLE COFFEE STORE PRESS (I), P.O. Box 383, Fox River Grove IL 60021-0383, phone (708)639-9200, founded 1992, is a small press publishing 5-6 chapbooks/year. "**Alternate chapbooks are published by invitation and by competition. Author published by invitation becomes judge for next competition.**" They are "**Open to any kind of poetry. No censorship at this press. Aesthetic values are the only standard. Generally not interested in sentimental or didactic writing.**" They have recently published poetry by Annie Davidovicz. As a sample the editor selected these lines from "Hot Saws" by Paul Andrew E. Smith:

> *It's a metallic taste she has, sweet,*
> *my teeth are numb, my cheek bones.*
> *Yes, by God in the treetops,*
> *I'm beginning to see how these are*
> *necessary skills, this lumberjacking.*

Sample postpaid: $5. Previously published poems and simultaneous submissions OK, with notice. Submit complete chapbook ms (20-24 pages) with a brief bio, 125-word statement that introduces your writing and $10 reading fee. Competition deadlines: the 1st of September, January and May. Send SASE for guidelines. "Each competition is judged by the author of the most recent chapbook published by invitation." **Seldom comments on rejections. Reports 6-8 weeks after deadline. All entrants will receive a copy of the winning chapbook. Winner receives $100 and 25 copies.** They say, "Poetry is about a passion for language. That's what we're about. We'd like to provide an opportunity for poets of any age who are fairly early in their careers to publish something substantial."

WHITE PINE PRESS (V), 76 Center St., Fredonia NY 14063, phone (716)672-5743, founded 1973, poetry editors Dennis Maloney and Elaine LaMattina. White Pine Press publishes poetry, fiction, literature in translation, essays—perfect-bound paperbacks. "At present we are **not accepting unsolicited mss. Inquire first.**" They have published poetry by William Kloefkorn, Marjorie Agosin, Migel Hernandez, Peter Blue Cloud, Basho, Pablo Neruda, Maurice Kenny and James Wright. **Query with 4-5 samples, brief cover letter with bio and publication credits. Reply to queries in 2-4 weeks, to submissions (if invited) in 4 weeks. Simultaneous submissions, photocopy, dot-matrix OK. Pays 5-10% of run. Send $1 for catalog to buy samples.**

JAMES WHITE REVIEW: A GAY MEN'S LITERARY QUARTERLY (IV-Gay), Box 3356, Traffic Station, Minneapolis MN 55403, phone (612)339-8317, founded 1983, poetry editor Clif Mayhood, **uses all kinds of poetry by gay men.** They have recently published poetry by Carl Morse, Assotto Saint and Robert Peters. The magazine has a circulation of 3,000 with 1,500 subscriptions of which 50 are libraries. They receive about 1,400 submissions/year, use 100, have a 6-week backlog. Subscription: $12/year (US). **Sample postpaid: $3. Submit a limit of 8 poems or 250 lines. A poem can exceed 250 lines, but it "better be very good." Send SASE for guidelines. They report in 4 months. Paying $10/poem.** Reviews books of poetry.

WHITE WALL REVIEW (I), 63 Gould St., Toronto, Ontario M5B 1E9 Canada, phone (416)977-1045, founded 1976, editors change every year, is an annual using "**interesting, preferably spare art. No style is unacceptable. Should poetry serve a purpose beyond being poetry and communicating a poet's idea?**

Nothing boring, self-satisfied, gratuitously sexual, violent or indulgent." They have recently published poetry by Mark Miller and Harold Rhenisch. As a sample the editor selected this poem, "how she sleeps," by Brian Burke:

> — the leg she leaves out of bed
> clear of the covers
> pores absorbing cool bedroom air
> — the leg that's always leaving
> stretching for the floor
> reaching for some nocturnal stride
> — that leg
> feeling for escape
> that's how she sleeps

WWR is between 144-160 pgs., digest-sized, professionally printed, perfect-bound, with glossy card cover, using b&w photos and illustrations. Press run is 600. Subscription: $6. **Sample postpaid: $8. "Please do not submit between May and July of a given year."** Reports "as soon as we can. We comment on all mss, accepted or not." Pays 1 copy.

TAHANA WHITECROW FOUNDATION; CIRCLE OF REFLECTIONS (IV-Ethnic), Box 18181, Salem OR 97305, phone (503)585-0564, founded 1987, executive director Melanie Smith. The Whitecrow Foundation conducts **one spring/summer poetry contest on Native American themes in poems up to 30 lines in length. Deadline for submissions: May 31. No haiku, Seiku, erotic or porno poems. Fees are $2.75 for a single poem, $10 for 4; monetary awards.** Winners, honorable mentions and selected other entries are published in a periodic anthology, **Circle of Reflections.** Winners receive free copies and are encouraged to purchase it for $4.95 plus $1 handling in order to "help ensure the continuity of our contests." As a sample Melanie Smith selected these lines by Jack Iyall:

> Today I'm dirty old man . .
> yesterday . . growing old
>   was beautiful . .
> today I'm a museum piece . .
> yesterday . . I could be
>   in line for Chief . .
> today I'm in the welfare line . .
> yesterday . . there was a place for me . .

Reviews books of poetry for $10 reading fee (average 32 pages). Melanie Smith adds, "We seek unpublished Native writers. Poetic expressions of full-bloods, mixed bloods and empathetic non-Indians need to be heard. Future goals include chapbooks and native theme art. Advice to new writers — keep writing, honing and sharpening your material; don't give up — keep submitting."

WHOLE NOTES; DAEDALUS PRESS (I, II, IV-Young adults), P.O. Box 1374, Las Cruces NM 88004, phone (505)382-7446, *WN* founded 1984, Daedalus Press founded 1988, editor Nancy Peters Hastings. *WN* appears twice a year. Daedalus Press publishes one chapbook/year by a single poet. **"All forms will be considered."** They have recently published poetry by William Stafford. As a sample the editor selected these lines from "After a Blizzard" by Don Welch:

> This morning there's a center to silence,
> a snow no one has ever walked upon,
> and the wind has folded up like a mastiff
>   deep in sleep . . .

WN is 20-24 pgs., digest-sized, "nicely printed," staple bound, with a "linen 'fine arts' cover." Press run 400 for 200 subscriptions of which 10 are libraries. They accept about 10% of some 300-400 submissions/year. Subscription: $6. **Sample postpaid: $3. Pays 2 copies. They prefer submissions of 3-7 poems at a time. Some previously published poems used. Reports in 2-3 weeks. For 20-page chapbook consideration, submit 3-15 samples with bio and list of other publications. Pays 25 copies of chapbook.** Editor sometimes comments on rejections. The editor says, "In the fall of each even-numbered year I edit a special issue of *WN* that features writing by young people (under 21). We also welcome translations."

‡WIDENER REVIEW (II), Humanities Division, Widener University, Chester PA 19013, phone (215)499-4341, founded 1984, poetry editor Kenneth Pobo, is an annual that publishes poetry, fiction and nonfiction. **Form, length and subject matter open. "Greeting card verse is not welcome."** They have recently published poetry by Robert Cooperman, Eve Shelnutt and Peter Wild. *Widener Review* is approximately 100 pages. "We probably read 400 manuscripts per issue; we accept approximately 35 pages of poems." **No previously published poems or simultaneous submissions. Manuscripts must be typed. Reads submissions September 1 through April 1 only.** Time between acceptance and publication is 6 months. Seldom comments on rejections. Send SASE for guidelines. Reports within 2 months.

Pays 1 copy. Acquires first North American serial rights. Sometimes publishes book reviews.

WILD EAST; THE POTTERSFIELD PORTFOLIO; SALAMANCA CHAPBOOK SERIES (II, IV-Regional), P.O. Box 1135, Station A, Fredericton, New Brunswick E3B 5C2 Canada, phone (506)454-5127, press founded 1988, magazine founded 1979. "Wild East's *The Pottersfield Portfolio* is a semiannual literary magazine of new English and French fiction, poetry, drama, artwork and essays **with a preference for Atlantic Canadians.** Both new and more established writers are featured." **They do not accept "sexist, racist, homophobic, ageist or classist material and no erotica, limericks or haiku."** They have recently published poetry by Gérald Leblanc, Heather Browne Prince, Elizabeth Harvor, Don McKay and Robert Gibbs. As a sample the editors selected these lines by Belinda Carney:

> know your body as the sturdy root
> that has borne such red life, all alone:
> the votive lit, for sisters in the soul-house
> a candent contract
> between earth and memory
> the light at the centre of one red berry
> the eyes of an animal you meet on the road home

TPP is 80 pgs., 6 × 9, perfect-bound, handsomely printed, with 2-color coated cover, b&w artwork and ads. Press run is 1,000 for 400 subscribers of which 50 are libraries, 200-300 shelf sales. Subscription (for individuals): $12/year Canadian, $15 US. **Sample postpaid: $6. No previously published poems or simultaneous submissions. Cover letter with bio required. Editor seldom comments on rejections. Send SASE for guidelines. Reports in 2-3 months. Pays $10/poem plus 2 copies. Buys first Canadian serial rights.** Wild East publishes 1-3 paperbacks and **5-7 chapbooks/year in the Salamanca Chapbook Series. Replies to queries in 1 month, to mss in 2-3 months. Pays 10% royalties. Sample chapbook: $4 postpaid.**

WILDERNESS (II, IV-Nature/ecology), 5118 N. Princeton St., Portland OR 97203, (poetry submissions only should be sent to this address), founded 1935, poetry editor John Daniel, is a slick quarterly magazine of "The Wilderness Society, one of the oldest and largest American conservation organizations." Requests for sample and subscriptions should go to *Wilderness*, 900 17th St. NW, Washington DC 20006. They want **"poetry related to the natural world. Shorter poems stand a better chance than longer, but all will be read. Poetry in any form or style is welcome."** They have recently published poetry by Denise Levertov, Pattiann Rogers, Marc Harshman, Paulann Petersen, Ingrid Wendt and Wendell Berry. The magazine is published on slick stock, full-color, professionally printed, with full-color paper cover, saddle-stapled, 76 pgs. Their press run is 340,000 with 300,000 subscriptions. Subscription: $15. **Sample postpaid: $3.50. No simultaneous submissions or previously published material. Editor comments on rejections "occasionally. Please understand that we have room for only about 15 poems a year." Responds in 2 months. Pays $100 plus 2 copies on publication. "We buy one-time rights and the right to anthologize the poem without further compensation."**

WILDWOOD JOURNAL; THE WILDWOOD PRIZE IN POETRY (II, IV-Students), T.H.S. Wallace, Arts 213, 3300 Cameron St. Road, Harrisburg PA 17110-2999, phone (717)780-2487. *Wildwood Journal*, an annual, **is open only to students, alumni and faculty of Harrisburg Area Community College,** but the Wildwood Prize is open to any poet, $500 annually, $5 reading fee made payable to HACC. Final selection for the prize is made by a distinguished poet (in 1992 Barbara Unger) who remains anonymous until the winner is announced. Poems are accepted between October 15 and November 30. Rules available for SASE.

WILLAMETTE RIVER BOOKS (II), P.O. Box 605, Troutdale OR 97060, founded 1990, editor Douglas Allen Conner, publishes 3-4 titles a year, both chapbooks and perfect-bound collections, as well as an occasional anthology. "We run a yearly competition, advertised in *Poets & Writers*, for a 16- to 24-page chapbook. We are open to fresh new voices as well as established ones. We hope to be the publisher for first collections of poets with numerous chapbooks; we hope to publish chapbooks of newer poets who may not yet have published a chapbook but who have a publication history in magazines and small press. **Quality is our sole criterion."** They have recently published books by Martin Anderson and Alana Sherman. As a sample the editor selected these lines from Sherman's **Everything is Gates:**

> The banana trees are dusty,
> the donkeys
> the dogs
> the children are dusty.
> In richer towns, behind green
> Shuttered windows, the women shed
> their heavy black
> and dance for each other.

No unsolicited mss. Query first with samples. Payment for publication arranged with author.

THE WILLIAM AND MARY REVIEW (II), Campus Center, College of William and Mary, P.O. Box 8795, Williamsburg VA 23187-8795, phone (804)221-3290, founded 1962, editor Alexandra Nemecek, is a 112-page annual, "**dedicated to publishing new work by established poets as well as work by new and vital voices.**" They have published poetry by Dana Gioia, Cornelius Eady, Amy Clampitt, Henri Cole, Julie Agoos, Diane Ackerman, Judson Jerome and Phyllis Janowitz. They accept 15-20 of about 5,000 poems submitted/year. Press run is 3,500. They have 250 library subscriptions, about 500 shelf sales. **Sample postpaid: $4.50. Submit 1 poem/page, batches of no more than 6 poems. Reads submissions September 15 through February 15 only. Reports in approximately 4 months. Pays 5 copies.**

WILLOW REVIEW; COLLEGE OF LAKE COUNTY READING SERIES (II), 19351 W. Washington St., Grayslake IL 60030-1198, phone (708)223-6601, FAX (708)223-9371, founded 1969, edited by Paulette Roeske. "**We are interested in poetry and fiction of high quality with no preferences as to form, style or subject.**" They have recently published poetry by Lisel Mueller, Bruce Guernsey, John Dickson, Jill Breckenridge and Mark Perlberg. As a sample we selected these lines from "China" by David Jones:

> *Not much of anything matches any more.*
> *Yet each one has an archeological fit*
> *to some era, and an expert could examine*
> *each round artifact and correctly say:*
> *Ah, early graduate school period,*
> *or: immediate post-divorce phase,*
> *followed by earthenware from*
> *the Fairfield Avenue site,*
> *characteristic of the time of Marlene.*

The review is a 68-page, flat-spined annual, 6×9, professionally printed with a glossy cover featuring b&w art. Editors are open to all styles, free verse to form, as long as each poem stands on its own as art and communicates ideas. Circulation 1,000, with distribution throughout the Midwest. Subscription: $10 (3 issues). **Sample postpaid: $4. Prizes of $100, $50 and $25 are awarded to the best poetry and fiction in each issue. Pays 2 copies. Acquires first North American serial rights. Submit up to 5 poems, or short fiction up to 3,000 words, September through January for April publication. Include name, address, SS#, and information for contributors notes.** The reading series, 4-7 readings/academic year, have included Angela Jackson, Ellen Bryant Voigt, Thomas Lux, Charles Simic, Gloria Naylor, David Mura, Galway Kinnell, Lisel Mueller, Amiri Baraka, Stephen Dobyns, Heather McHugh, Linda Pastan, Katha Pollitt, Tobias Wolff and William Stafford. One of the readings is for contributors to the magazine. These are usually held on Thursday evenings, for audiences of about 150 from students and faculty of College of Lake County and other area colleges and residents of local communities. They are widely publicized in Chicago and suburban newspapers.

WILLOW SPRINGS (II, IV-Translations), MS-1, Eastern Washington University, Cheney WA 99004, phone (509)458-6429, founded 1977. They have published poetry by Denise Levertov, Carolyn Kizer, Michael Burkard, Russell Edson, Dara Wier, Thomas Lux, Madeline DeFrees, Hayden Carruth, Al Young, Odysseas Elytis, W.S. Merwin, Olga Broumas, Kay Boyle and Lisel Mueller. *Willow Springs* is a semiannual, 6×9, 98 pgs., flat-spined, professionally printed, with glossy 2-color card cover with art, circulation 1,000, 400 subscriptions of which 30% are libraries. They use 1-2% of some 4,000 freelance poems received each year. **Sample postpaid: $4. Submit September 1 through May 30 only. "We do not read in the summer months."** Include name on every page, address on first page of each poem. **Brief cover letter saying how many poems on how many pages. No simultaneous submissions. Reports in 1-3 months. Pays 2 copies, others at half price, and pays cash when funds available. Acquires all rights. Returns rights on release. Send SASE for guidelines.** "We are especially interested in translations from any language or period. We publish quality poetry and fiction that is imaginative, intelligent, and has a concern and care for language." Reviews books of poetry and short fiction in 200-500 words.

WIND MAGAZINE (I, II), Box 809K, RFD #1, Pikeville KY 41501, phone (606)631-1129, founded 1971, poetry editor Quentin R. Howard. "*Wind* since 1971 has published hundreds of poets for the first time and today there are at least 125 who are publishing widely in many magazines and have books to their credit. I have also published about 15 people who had stopped writing and submitting to 'little' magazines because many young editors were not acquainted with much of their work. There's nothing unique about *Wind*; like all 'little' magazines it is friendly (too friendly at times) toward beginning writers who have something to say and do so effectively and interestingly. I have no taboos. I invent my own taboos on reading each ms. But plain old raw vulgarity for shock effect is out. Save your postage! I don't want simple broken prose, neither greeting card-type verse; nor please no love verse and soothing graveyard poetry; none please enamoured of death; believe me it's still being written. I'm not picky about form, style, subject matter nor purpose; but length (pages and pages) makes me frown no matter how much I love it. 'Little' magazines are a squeamish group when it comes to space." They have recently published poetry by David Adams, Peter Wild, Larry Rubin, Sarah Litsey, Robert Gibb, Ronald Moran and Jordan Tillett. *Wind* appears irregularly, digest-sized, averaging 86 pgs. per issue of which 60 are poetry, saddle-stapled, professionally printed with matte card cover, circulation 455, subscriptions 412 of which 35 are libraries. They use about 200 of 3,600 freelance submissions of poetry per year, sometimes have as much as a year backlog. Subscription: $7 for 2 consecutive issues. Sample postpaid: $2.50. Submit at least 3-6 poems. "Photocopies and simultaneous submissions scare me." Shorter poems have a better chance here. Editor comments on rejections, "now and then when time permits. There's many pitfalls about this." Reports in 2-4 weeks. Pays contributor's copies. Reviews books of poetry, from small presses only, in 250 words. Quentin Howard advises, "Presentation is all-important in deciding on poems."

THE WINDHORSE REVIEW; SAMURAI PRESS (III), RR3, Box 3140, Yarmouth, Nova Scotia B5A 4A7 Canada, founded 1982, poetry editor John Castlebury, is a semiannual magazine that, according to its editor, "seeks poetry with a place for the genuine, as per Marianne Moore. The truest poems no one writes yet they do still get written. Simply plucking notes out of the air and there is no one there doing that, and nobody gets to take credit." They have recently published poetry by Janet McCann, Sam Hamill and Alan Napier. As a sample the editor selected the opening lines of "The Sadness of Windows" by Carole Glasser Langille:

> *Outside our window the river*
> *mirrors a white barn, floats lights up and down*
> *its other side. It soaks grey sky some days*
> *and leaves a blanket of fog*
> *to cover its deeds.*
> *They shoulder each other in old houses, these windows.*

Their press run is 500 and *TWR* is sold in bookstores in major cities. It is handsomely printed, uses artistic b&w photos and graphics and has a 2-color paper cover. Sample postpaid: $5. Submit 5-10 pgs. with brief bio and SAE with IRC or $1 US (US stamps invalid from Canada). Reports in 1 month. Pays copies. Acquires first North American serial rights. Prisoner copies available free of charge.

‡THE WINDHOVER PRESS (III), 102 EPB, The University of Iowa, Iowa City IA 52242, phone (319)335-0429, founded 1967, director K.K. Merker, publishes 3-4 hardbacks/year. They want "poetry from writers who have studied serious literature and who want to add to it. 'There is nothing more dreadful than imagination without taste.' No inspirational, political or amateurish poetry; no doggerel." They have recently published poetry by Charles Wright and Amy Clampitt. As a sample the director selected "The Midnight Club" by Mark Strand:

> *The gifted have told us for years that they*
>   *want to be loved*
> *For what they are, that they, in whatever*
>   *fullness is theirs,*
> *Are perishable in twilight, just like us.*
>   *So they work all night*
> *In rooms that are cold and webbed with the*
>   *moon's light;*
> *Sometimes, during the day, they lean on*
>   *their cars*
> *And stare into the blistering valley, glassy*
>   *and golden,*
> *But mainly they sit, hunched in the dark,*
>   *feet on the floor,*
> *Hands on the table, shirts with a bloodstain*
>   *over the heart.*

Poems previously published in magazines and simultaneous submissions OK. Cover letter required. Replies to queries in 2-3 weeks, to mss in 1-2 months. Seldom comments on rejections. Pays 10% royalties or 10% of edition. Sample books may be purchased from the press or examined in libraries.

THE WINDLESS ORCHARD; THE WINDLESS ORCHARD CHAPBOOKS (II), English Dept., Indiana University, Fort Wayne IN 46805, phone (219)481-6841, founded 1970, poetry editor Robert Novak, a "shoestring labor of love—chapbooks only from frequent contributors to magazine. Sometimes publish calendars." They say they want "heuristic, excited, valid non-xian religious exercises. Our muse is interested only in the beautiful, the erotic and the sacred." *The Windless Orchard* appears irregularly, 50+ pgs., digest-sized, offset from typescript, saddle-stapled, with matte card cover with b&w photos. The editors say they have 100 subscriptions of which 25 are libraries, a print run of 300, total circulation: 280. There are about 35 pgs. of poetry in each issue. They receive about 3,000 freelance submissions of poetry/year, use 200, have a 6-month backlog. Subscription: $10. **Sample postpaid: $4. Submit 3-7 pgs. Considers simultaneous submissions. Reports in 1 day-4 months. Pays 2 copies. Chapbook submissions by invitation only to contributors to the magazine. Poets pay costs for 300 copies, of which The Windless Orchard Chapbook Series receives 100 for its expenses. Sample: $4.** Editors sometimes comment on rejections. They advise, "Memorize a poem a day, do translations for the education."

UNIVERSITY OF WINDSOR REVIEW (II), University of Windsor, Windsor, Ontario N9B 3P4 Canada, phone (519)253-4232, ext. 2303, founded 1966, poetry editor John Ditsky, appears twice a year. **"Open to all poetry but epic length."** They have published poetry by Ben Bennani, Walter McDonald, Larry Rubin and Lyn Lifshin. As a sample the editor selected these lines (poet unidentified):

> *talking to white wolves*
> *talking to the first*
> *white wolves ever*
> *telling of how things are*
> *in his world.*

It is professionally printed, 100 pgs., digest-sized. They accept about 15% of 500 poems received/ year. Press run 500. Subscription: $12 Canadian, $10 US. **Sample postpaid: $6 Canadian, $5 US. Reports in 6 weeks. Pays $10/poem.**

WINEBERRY PRESS (V, IV-Regional), 3207 Macomb St. NW, Washington DC 20008, phone (202)363-8036 or (416)964-2002, founded 1983, founder and president Elisavietta Ritchie, publishes anthologies and chapbooks of poems by **Washington area poets but accepts no unsolicited mss because of a large backlog.** She has recently published poetry by Judith McCombs, Elisabeth Stevens and Beatrice Murphy. As a sample Elisavietta Ritchie selected these lines from "Looking Forward" by Maxine Combs, included in **Swimming Out Of The Collective Unconscious:**

> *Nothing is promised*
> *Like land crabs scuttling*
> *across a road, unexpected,*
> *sightings are gifts.*

THE WIRE; PROGRESSIVE PRESS (I, IV-Form), 7320 Colonial, Dearborn Heights MI 48127, phone (517)394-3736, founded 1981, editor Sharon Wysocki. *The Wire* is an "alternative arts" publication that appears 2-3 times a year. It publishes **"language and experimental poetry" but no sonnets. "We are also looking for short form erotic poems. Regarding all submissions, the poet has a much better chance for publication in *The Wire* if the poem is in short form."** Poets published include Ivan Argüelles, Paul Weinman and Joseph Raffa. *The Wire* is photocopied on 8½×11 offset paper, 9 pgs., with graphics, stapled at the top left corner. Price per issue is $1 and a subscription is $3.75 (checks should be made out to Progressive Press). **Guidelines are available for SASE. Contributors receive 1 copy. Photocopied and simultaneous submissions OK, but print must be dark enough for photocopying.** Criticism of rejected mss is provided "sometimes." Submissions are reported on in 6 months and time to publication is the same.

WISCONSIN ACADEMY REVIEW (IV-Regional), 1922 University Ave., Madison WI 53705, phone (608)263-1692, founded 1954, poetry editor Faith B. Miracle, "distributes information on scientific and cultural life of Wisconsin and provides a forum for **Wisconsin (or Wisconsin background) artists and authors."** They want **"good lyric poetry; traditional meters acceptable if content is fresh. No poem over 65 lines."** They have published poetry by Credo Enriquez, David Martin, Felix Pollak, Ron Wallace and John Bennett. *Wisconsin Academy Review* is a magazine-sized, 48-page quarterly, professionally printed on glossy stock, glossy card cover with b&w photo, circulation 1,500, with 1,200 subscriptions of which 109 are libraries. They use 4-12 pgs. of poetry/issue. Of over 100 freelance submissions of poetry/year they use about 15, have a 6- to 12-month backlog. **Sample postpaid: $3. Submit 5 pgs. maximum, double-spaced. Photocopy, dot-matrix OK. Must include Wisconsin connection if not Wisconsin return address.** Editor sometimes comments on rejections. Reports in 4-6 weeks. Pays 5 copies. Reviews books of poetry with Wisconsin connection only.

UNIVERSITY OF WISCONSIN PRESS; BRITTINGHAM PRIZE IN POETRY (II), 114 N. Murray St., Madison WI 53715-1199, Brittingham Prize inaugurated in 1985, poetry editor Ronald Wallace. The University of Wisconsin Press publishes primarily scholarly works, but they offer the annual **Brittingham Prize of $500 plus publication. The contest is the only way in which this press publishes poetry.**

Send SASE for rules. Submit between September 1 and October 1, unbound ms volume, 50-80 pgs., with name, address and telephone number on title page. Poems must be previously unpublished in book form. Poems published in journals, chapbooks and anthologies may be included but must be acknowledged. There is a non-refundable $10 reading fee which must accompany the ms. (Checks to University of Wisconsin Press.) Mss will *not* be returned. Enclose SASE for contest results. Qualified readers will screen all mss. Winner will be selected by "a distinguished poet who will remain anonymous until the winner is announced in mid-February." Past judges include C.K. Williams, Maxine Kumin, Mona Van Duyn, Charles Wright, Gerald Stern, Mary Oliver, Donald Finkel and Donald Justice. No translations. Recent winners are Jim Daniels, Patricia Dobler, David Kirby, Lisa Zeidner, Stefanie Marlis, Judith Vollmer, Renée A. Ashley and Tony Hoagland.

WISCONSIN REVIEW; WISCONSIN REVIEW PRESS (II), Box 158, Radford Hall, University of Wisconsin-Oshkosh, Oshkosh WI 54901, phone (414)424-2267, founded 1966, editor Valerie Jahns. The elegantly printed *WR* is published 3 times/year, 48-64 pgs. "In poetry we publish mostly free verse with strong images and fresh approaches. We want new turns of phrase." Poets published include Laurel Mills, Joseph Bruchac, Kenneth Frost, Paul Marion, Dionisio Martinez, Stephen Perry, Margaret Randall, David Steingass, Brian Swann and Peter Wild. As a sample the editors selected these lines from "Early Morning of Another World" by Tom McKeown:

> *After squid and cool white wine there is*
> *no sleep. The long tentacles uncurl*
> *out of the dark with all that was left behind.*
> *Promises expand promises. A frayed mouth*
> *loses its color in the dawn.*

The *Review* is 6×9, quality white stock, glossy card cover with color art, b&w art inside. They use 30-40 pgs. of poetry in each issue; total circulation is 2,000, with 50 subscriptions, 30 of which go to libraries. Price per issue is $2, subscription $8. Sample postpaid: $2. The *Review* receives about 1,500 poetry submissions/year, of which it publishes about 75. Submit mss September 15 through May 15. Offices checked bimonthly during summer. Editor requests no more than 4 poems/submission, one poem/page, single spaced with name and address of writer on each page. Simultaneous submissions OK, but previously unsubmitted works preferable. Guidelines available for SASE. Reports to writer within 1-4 months. Pays 2 contributor's copies.

THE WISE WOMAN (I, IV-Feminist), 2441 Cordova St., Oakland CA 94602, founded 1980, editor and publisher Ann Forfreedom, is a quarterly journal "focusing on feminist issues, feminist spirituality, Goddess lore and feminist witchcraft." They want "mostly shorter poetry—by both women and men— dealing with these themes." They have recently published poetry by Maura Alia Bramkamp and Viviane Lerner. As a sample the editor selected these lines from "Arise O Women," by Kathleen Weinschenk:

> *O Women of the world,*
> *Catch a vision*
> *Of your own true self.*
> *Discover the power*
> *Within . . .*

TWW is magazine-sized, approximately 32 pgs., offset. "At least 20 poems received/year; accept about 50% of appropriate poems." Subscription: $15. Sample postpaid: $4. Ms should be typed, double-spaced with writer's name and address on each page. They will consider previously published poems. Pays 1 copy. Ann Forfreedom says, "I prefer poems that are active, come from the writer's deep experiences or feelings, are brief and are applicable to many kinds of people. A focus on Goddess culture, nature or feminist issues is helpful. Good spelling is deeply appreciated."

THE WISHING WELL (IV-Membership, women/feminism, lesbian), P.O. Box 713090, Santee CA 92072-3090, founded 1974, editor/publisher Laddie Hosler, is a "contact magazine for gay and bisexual women the world over; members' descriptions, photos, some letters and poetry published with their permission only; resources, etc., listed. I publish writings only for and by members so membership is required." 1-2 pgs. in each issue are devoted to poetry, "which can be 6″ to full page—depending upon acceptance by editor, 3″ width column." It is 7×8½ offset press from typescript, with soft matte card cover. It appears bimonthly and goes to 800 members. A sample is available for $5. Membership in *Wishing Well* is $55 for 4-7 months. Membership includes the right to publish poetry, a self description (exactly as you write it), and to have responses forwarded to you, and other privileges. Reviews books of poetry. Personal classifieds section just begun, members and/or nonmembers, $1/word.

WITHOUT HALOS; OCEAN COUNTY POETS COLLECTIVE (II), P.O. Box 1342, Point Pleasant Beach NJ 08742, founded 1983, editor-in-chief Frank Finale, an annual publication of the Ocean County Poets Collective; it prints "good contemporary poetry." The magazine "accepts all genres, though no obscenity. Prefers poetry no longer than 2 pages. Wants to see strong, lucid images ground in experience." They do not want "religious verse, or greeting card lyrics." They have recently pubilshed poetry by Philip Murray, Robert Cooperman, William Doreski, Peter E. Murphy, Geraldine C. Little and Jonathan Harrington. As a sample, the editor selected these lines from "The Crying in the Fireplace" by Larissa Szporluk:

> *Is it February,*
> *March, everything is*
>
> *wet, smells of snakes,*
> *sod. I feel between the grass.*
> *Steam lifts. A hole*
> *moves. There are lives*
> *in here, waiting.*

Without Halos is digest-sized, handsomely printed with b&w artwork inside and on the cover, 104 pgs. flat-spined with glossy card cover. Circulation is 1,000, of which 100 are subscriptions and 100 are sold on newsstands; other distribution is at cultural events, readings, workshops, etc. Price per issue is $5. Sample available for $5 postpaid. The editors "prefer letter-quality printing, double-spaced, no more than 5 poems. Name and address should appear in top left-hand corner. Reads submissions January 1 through June 30 only. No manuscript returned without proper SASE. Sloppiness tossed back." Reporting time is 2-4 months and all acceptances are printed in the next annual issue, which appears in the winter. Pay is 1 copy. Acquires first rights.

Poetry plays "a major role" in Without Halos, says Editor-in-Chief Frank Finale. "In 1983, we started out by publishing only poets from Ocean County. In 1985, we went national, and today over 50% of the poetry we take is from other states." This illustration, "Newton Before His Time," was inspired by a Mexican sculpture at the Metropolitan Museum of Art says the artist, Susan Field. Finale says it is not related to any particular theme or philosophy of the magazine, although, he says, "Personally, I see it as the poet waiting for his or her muse."

WOLSAK AND WYNN PUBLISHERS LTD. (II), Box 316, Don Mills Post Office, Don Mills, Ontario M3C 2S7 Canada, phone (416)222-4690, founded 1982, poetry editors Heather Cadsby and Maria Jacobs, publishes 5 flat-spined literary paperbacks/year (56-100 pgs.). They have recently published collections of poetry by Richard Harrison and Anne Marriott. Here is a sample from **Impromptu Feats of Balance** by Michael Redhill:

> *(for lesley)*
> *putting on this sweater is like going underwater, this territory*
> *that is only yours, the place where your breasts come to a slow*
> *fall where your skin touches. your scent is stitched into its*
> *pattern, but now my skin, my hair, everything rises unfamiliar*
> *from the wool. and still later i might think i have walked the*
> *day out almost in your skin, but there is nothing of you in*
> *here at all. only the fabric's bad rendition of the shape you*
> *left, its apparent willingness to leave all of you behind.*

The books are handsomely printed. **Sample: $8 US or $10 Canadian. Send samples with query, bio, publications. No simultaneous submissions. Reports on queries in 4 months. Pays 10%**

royalties. **Buys first rights.** Maria Jacobs says, "W&W prefers not to prescribe. We are open to *good* writing of any kind."

WOMEN'S PRESS (CANADA) (IV-Women/Ethnic), 517 College St., #233, Toronto, Ontario M3J 1L6 Canada, founded 1972, co-managing editor Angela Robertson, publishes **"minimum ms 48 pgs. Women of colour, feminist, political content, modern or post-modern form, lesbian. No haiku."** As a sample the editor selected these lines by Dionne Brand:

> *this is you girl, this is the poem no woman*
> *ever write for a woman because she 'fraid to touch*

They publish 1 flat-spined paperback/year. **Pays 10% royalties, $150 advance, 6 copies. Reports in 3 months.**

‡WOMEN'S STUDIES QUARTERLY; THE FEMINIST PRESS AT CUNY (IV-Women, feminist, bilingual), 311 E. 94th St., New York NY 10128, phone (212)360-5790. *Women's Studies Quarterly*, founded 1972, publisher Florence Howe, is a nonfiction quarterly using **"poetry that focuses on current issues of importance to women; emphasis on education or activism preferable."** They have published poetry by Mila Aguilar. The editor describes it as 5½ × 8½, 150-200 pgs. They use 1-5 poems in each issue. Their press run is 1,500. **Sample postpaid: $7. Simultaneous submissions and previously published poems OK. Editor rarely comments on rejections. Pays 1 copy.** The Feminist Press publishes primarily both historical and contemporary fiction and nonfiction (12-15 titles per year), but it also publishes some poetry, such as the series, **The Defiant Muse**, bilingual volumes (Hispanic, French, Italian and German) of poetry by women from the Middle-Ages to the present.

WOMENWISE (IV-Women, feminist), 38 South Main St., Concord NH 03301, phone (603)225-2739, founded 1978, Editorial Committee, "a quarterly newspaper that deals specifically with issues relating to women's health—research, education, and politics." They want **"poetry reflecting status of women in society, relating specifically to women's health issues."** They do not want **"poetry that doesn't include women or is written by men; poetry that degrades women or is anti-choice."** *WomenWise* is a tabloid newspaper, 12 pgs., on quality stock with b&w art and graphics. Its circulation is 3,000 +. Price per copy is $2.95, subscription $10/year. **Sample available for $2.95. Submissions should be typed double-spaced. Reads submissions March, June, September and December only. Reporting time and time to publication varies. Pay is a 1-year subscription. Acquires first North American serial rights.** Reviews books of poetry in "any word count," single format.

WOODLEY MEMORIAL PRESS; THE ROBERT GROSS MEMORIAL PRIZE FOR POETRY (IV-Regional), English Department, Washburn University, Topeka KS 66621, phone (913)295-6448, founded 1980, editor Robert Lawson, publishes 1-2 flat-spined paperbacks a year, **collections of poets from Kansas or with Kansas connections, "terms individually arranged with author on acceptance of ms."** They have recently published poetry by Craig Goad, Michael L. Johnson, Bruce Bond and Harley Elliott. As a sample the editor selected these lines from "In the Old House" by William Stafford:

> *Inside our Victrola a tin voice, faint*
> *but somehow both fragile and powerful, soared*
> *and could be only Caruso, all the way from*
> *Rome: I traced my fingers on the gold letters*
> *and listened my way deeper and deeper*

"We charge $5 reading fee for unsolicited mss." Replies to queries in 2 weeks, to mss in 2 months, published 1 year after acceptance. Samples may be individually ordered from the press for $5. Send SASE for guidelines for Robert Gross Memorial Poetry and Fiction Prize ($100 and publication).

WORCESTER REVIEW; WORCESTER COUNTY POETRY ASSOCIATION, INC. (II, IV-Regional), 6 Chatham St., Worcester MA 01609, phone (508)797-4770, founded 1973, managing editor Rodger Martin. *WR* appears annually with emphasis on poetry. **New England writers are encouraged to submit, though work by other poets is used also. They want "work that is crafted, intuitively honest, and empathetic, not work that shows the poet little respects his work or his readers."** They have used poetry by Richard Eberhart, William Stafford and Walter McDonald. *WR* is 6 × 9, flat-spined, 64 + pgs., professionally printed in dark type on quality stock with glossy card cover, press run of 1,000 for 300 subscriptions (50 of them libraries) and 200 shelf sales. Subscription $5. **Sample postpaid: $4. Send SASE for guidelines. Submit maximum of 5 pages. "I recommend 3 or less for most favorable readings." Simultaneous submissions OK "if indicated." Previously published poems "only on special occasions." Reports in 4-6 months. Pays $10 per poem, depending upon grants, plus 2 copies. Buys first rights.** Editor comments on rejections "if ms warrants a response." They have an annual contest for poets who live, work, or in some way (past/present) have a Worcester County connection. The editor advises, "Read some. Listen a lot."

THE WORD WORKS; THE WASHINGTON PRIZE (II), P.O. Box 42164, Washington DC 20015, founded 1974, poetry editors Karren Alenier, J.H. Beall, Barbara Goldberg and Robert Sargent, "is a nonprofit literary organization publishing contemporary poetry in single author editions usually in collaboration with a visual artist. We sponsor an ongoing poetry reading series as well as educational programs and the Washington Prize—an award of $1,000 for a book-length manuscript by a living American poet." Submission open to any American writer except those connected with Word Works. Send SASE for rules. Entries accepted between February 1 and March 1. Deadline is March 1 postmark. They publish perfect-bound paperbacks and occasional anthologies and want "**well-crafted poetry, open to most forms and styles (though not political themes particularly). Experimentation welcomed.**" As a sample the editors chose "Wings" from **Blameless Lives** by Elaine Magarrell:

Why are the children careless with their wings?

. . . Next time
they want to fly, the children will wish
they had borne the weight. One day they'll be

able to throw out parts of their lives like us
deliberately with no remorse—smoke a cigarette,
entertain a little death wish. My father once
put out a fire in my hair with his bare hands

never to touch me again.

"We want more than a collection of poetry. We care about the individual poems—the craft, the emotional content and the risks taken—but we want manuscripts where one poem leads to the next. We strongly recommend you read the books that have already won the Washington Prize. Buy them, if you can, or ask for your libraries to purchase them. (Not a prerequisite.) **Currently we are only reading unsolicited manuscripts for the Washington Prize.**" Simultaneous submissions OK if so stated. Photocopy OK, no dot-matrix. **Payment is 15% of run (usually of 500). Send SASE for catalog to buy samples. Occasionally comments on rejections.** The editors advise, "Get community support for your work, know your audience and support contemporary literature by buying and reading small press."

WORDS OF WISDOM (II, IV-Humor), 612 Front St. East, Glendora NJ 08029-1133, founded 1981, editor J.M. Freiermuth, appears monthly using "**short, pithy poetry, the stuff that brings a smile to the reader's face on first reading. No religious.**" They have recently published poetry by Darcy Cummings, Jim DeWitt, Patrick Cauchi, Virginia Hlavsa and Robert Dunn. It is 24-40 pgs., photocopied with plain paper cover. They published about 25 of 100 submissions received in 1991-1992. Press run 150 for 110 subscribers. Subscription: $12. **Sample postpaid: $1. Make checks payable to J.M. Freiermuth. Reports usually within 2 months. Pays 2 copies. Acquires one-time rights. Will publish simultaneous and previously published material only if submitted on floppy disk in ASCII format. No submissions accepted (December 1- January 31).**

‡**WORDSMITH (I)**, Box 891, Ft. Collins CO 80522-0891, founded 1991, editor Brian Kaufman, appears annually. "**We are open to all styles of prose and poetry. Most subject matter is OK, but we steer clear of erotica and gay or lesbian work. Also, no greeting-card poetry.**" They have recently published poetry by Virginia Anderson and Tyler Coleman. As a sample the editor selected these lines from his own poem, "Metalhead":

Like animals crouched over
A fresh kill, we grab
The throat of the world
And tear it open. Violence is easy,
The colors are splendid,
And we are easily amused.

Wordsmith is 64-80 pgs., digest-sized, perfect-bound, with glossy cover. Uses 20-30 poems each issue. Press run is 400 for 200 subscribers of which 2 are libraries, 200 shelf sales. Single copy: $5; subscription: $5/year, $9/2 years. **Sample postpaid: $3. No previously published poems or simultaneous submissions. Submit up to 100 lines, single-spaced, one poem/page. Always comments on rejections. Send SASE for guidelines. Pays $5. Buys one-time rights.** Offers $25 for the best poem in each issue; editor's choice. The editor seems to prefer free verse dealing with risky topics (i.e. politics, art). He features poems of varying lengths (some long, others only a few lines), all trying to find the precise words to depict intriguing ideas. If you send here, focus on message and craft. Brian Kaufman says, "Tell the truth. Speak in images. Keep writing."

WORDSMITH PUBLISHING, INC. (I, IV-Anthology), (formerly *Poets of Now* magazine), 6100 Long-meadow Blvd. S., Saginaw MI 48603, phone (517)793-9036, founded 1987, editor Rosemary J. Schmidt. They publish an anthology of 200+ pages (1 poem to a page) from their annual contest. The contest is **open to all poets**. Send #10 SASE for mandatory entry form. May enter up to 10 poems. Those who enter 10 poems (plus entry fee and postage fee) will receive a free book whether their poem is selected or not. After the contest the books will sell for $18. The last contest produced over 1,200 entries. The top 3 winners were Karen Abke, Linda Jo Scott and Michael Estabrook. Contest prizes total $220. They have recently published poetry by Ann Gasser, Jack Gillespie, Irene Warsaw, Patricia A. Lawrence, Patrick Pillars, Ruth Cunliffe and Jenny M. Stoffle. As a sample the editor selected these lines from "What is the Color Red" by Robert Nixon:

> red is the color of the satin
> that lines my coffin
> red is the color of my death
> that I wear like a mask
> for you were my final rose
> the color
> of red.

The editor says, "The books are sent to libraries around the country, reviewed by many small presses throughout the U.S. and are carried by many bookstores in Michigan." They also offer chapbook publication for individual poets on a subsidy basis if ms is acceptable. Write for details.

WORDSONG; BOYDS MILLS PRESS (IV-Children), 910 Church St., Honesdale PA 18431, phone (717)253-1164, founded 1990, editor-in-chief Dr. Bernice E. Cullinan, is the imprint under which Boyds Mills Press (a *Highlights for Children* company) publishes books of poetry for children of all ages. **"WordSong encourages quality poetry which reflects childhood fun, moral standards and multiculturalism. We are not interested in poetry for adults or that which includes violence or sexuality or promotes hatred."** They have recently published poetry by Jane Yolen, John Ciardi and Lillian Morrison. As a sample the editor selected these lines from "Big and Little" by William Jay Smith:

> There once was a man
> With a little head
> And very big feet
> Who laughed and said:
> 'Jig-jig-jig—
> Spin and whirl—
> Hello, little boy!
> Hello, little girl!

"Wordsong prefers original work but will consider previously published anthologies and poetry picture books. We ask poets to send collections of 30-50 poems; please send complete book manuscripts, not single poems. We buy all rights to collections and publish on an advance-and-royalty basis. WordSong guarantees a response from editors within one month of our receiving submissions or the poet can call us collect to inquire. Please direct submissions to Beth Troop, manuscript coordinator." Dr. Cullinan says, "Poetry lies at the heart of the elementary school literature and reading program. In fact, poetry lies right at the heart of children's language learning. Poetry speaks to the heart of a child. We are anxious to find outstanding poetry—rhyme, free verse and songs—that will appeal to children."

‡WORKS MAGAZINE (IV-Science fiction), 12 Blakestones Rd., Slaithwaite, Huddersfield, Yorks HD7 5UQ United Kingdom, founded 1989, editor Dave W. Hughes, is a biannual using "speculative and imaginative fiction or poetry favoring science fiction. They want **"surreal/science fiction poetry. Nothing more than 50 lines. No romance or general work."** They have recently published poetry by Andy Darlington, Steve Sneyd, Paul Weinman and Brian Aldiss. The editor says *Works* is 52 pgs., A5, stitched with texture cover. They receive about 150 poems/year, accept 36. Press run is 400 for 200 subscribers of which 4 are libraries, 50 shelf sales. Single copy: £1.60 sterling (£2.50 for US); subscription: £5.50 sterling. **No simultaneous submissions. Disk submissions acceptable: IBM (5¼ or 3½-inch) or Atari 520ST (3½-inch); ASCII files only. Seldom comments on rejections. Send SASE for guidelines. Reports within a month. Pays 1 copy.** "Reviews of books and magazines are handled in *Works Study*, a free supplement for subscribers." The editor says, "Study the market."

WORLDWIDE POETS' CIRCLE; POETRY BY THE SEAS (IV-Membership), P.O. Box 74, Oceanside CA 92049-0074. Commenced publishing in 1985, Jan Renfrow, editor, publisher and cofounder. **"We are a membership society. Only members of *WWPC* may submit material to our small monthly magazine, *Poetry By The Seas*. Acquires first rights. Always include a SASE. We get too many queries and submissions without any return envelopes or postage.** Members are entitled to a variety of benefits and privileges, including participation, either in person or in absentia, in our six-month taping programs, and in any and all scheduled readings. We offer critiquing upon request, and we welcome poets of all ages in all occupations and at all levels of experience and proficiency. You need not be pre-published to join us." Annual membership fee is $15 domestic (including Canada); $20 overseas. Senior citizens and full-time students may join for $13 domestic; $18 abroad. "Please query before sending money—annual membership fee *may* go up within the coming months." Membership includes a year's subscription to *Poetry By The Seas*. Sample copies of *Poetry By The Seas* are available for $2 domestic; $4 overseas. Reviews books of poetry by members only. "We strongly believe in the therapeutic healing power of the creative arts."

‡WoRM fEASt!; PHLEM RAG; KNIGHTMARE PRODUCTIONS (II, IV-Erotica, occult), P.O. Box 519, Westminster MD 21158-0519, *WoRM fEASt!*, an underground quarterly, founded 1989, editor Llori Steinberg. *Phlem Rag* founded 1991. For *Wf* they want **"weird/strange poetry; no traditional verse, no rhyme (unless it's way off the keister), no haiku, no love poems, no religious or Christian poetry. Robert Frost is a no-no! Bukowski, Bennett, Kross and Bridgewater a must!"** For *PR* they want **"estranged mental poetry, 3-30 lines."** They have recently published poetry by Blaire Presley, Dan Nielsen and F.M. Cotolo. As a sample here are the opening lines from one of the editor's own poems, "Out 2 Lunch":

> *Insane?/loony/BOZO!!*
> *Nuts/synonyms*
> *synonyms, synonyms . . . .*
> *BLAST it!*
> *AAAAARRRRRGGGGGGGHHHHHH!!!*

The editor says *WF* is usually 32 pgs., if not more, digest-sized, saddle-stitched, with artwork and photos (from subscribers). Press run 500. "The digest is different colors everytime, with different colored ink." She says *PR* is 24 pgs., digest-sized, press run 200. "We usually want people to subscribe after we consider them, and subscribers usually have better chances getting their artwork and photos published. **Previously published poems OK; no simultaneous submissions. Include short bio with credits and picture. Always comments on rejections. Send SASE for guidelines. "We report rather quickly." Pays 4 copies of *WoRM fEASt!*, 1 copy of *Phlem Rag*. WF** offers a contest. Entry fee: $10 for up to 8 poems. Winners receive copies. Send SASE for details. "Sometimes we publish chapbooks for poets' personal use. They buy and they sell." The editor says, "We want weird shock therapy poetry, erotica, poems about politics or drugs. No taboos. No censorship. Don't be afraid to send the weirdest works."

WORMWOOD REVIEW PRESS; THE WORMWOOD REVIEW; THE WORMWOOD AWARD (II), P.O. Box 4698, Stockton CA 95204-0698, phone (209)466-8231, founded 1959, poetry editor Marvin Malone. "The philosophy behind *Wormwood*: (i) avoid publishing oneself and personal friends, (ii) avoid being a 'local' magazine and strive for a national and international audience, (iii) seek unknown talents rather than establishment or fashionable authors, (iv) encourage originality by working with and promoting authors capable of extending the existing patterns of Amerenglish literature, (v) avoid all cults and allegiances and the you-scratch-my-back-and-I-will-scratch-yours approach to publishing, (vi) accept the fact that magazine content is more important than format in the long run, (vii) presume a literate audience and try to make the mag readable from the first page to the last, (viii) restrict the number of pages to no more than 40 per issue since only the insensitive and the masochistic can handle more pages at one sitting, (ix) pay bills on time and don't expect special favors in honor of the muse, and lastly and most importantly (x) don't become too serious and righteous." Marvin Malone wants **"poetry and prose poetry that communicate the temper and range of human experience in contemporary society; don't want religious poetry and work that descends into bathos; don't want imitative sweet verse. Will not consider simultaneous submissions. Must be original; any style or school from traditional to ultra experimental, but *must* communicate; 3-600 lines."** He has published poetry by Ron Koertge, Gerald Locklin, Charles Bukowski, Edward Field and Lyn Lifshin. As a sample he offers these lines by Cory Monaco:

> *notice more & more these days*
> *whenever someone says*
> *'you can learn a lot from so & so'*
> *they're referring to an ill*
> *or handicapped*
> *person*

The digest-sized quarterly, offset from photoreduced typescript, saddle-stapled, has a usual print run of 700 with 500 subscriptions of which about 210 are libraries. Yellow pages in the center of each issue feature "one poet or one idea." Subscription: $8. **Sample postpaid: $4. Submit 2-10 poems on as many pages. No dot-matrix. Send SASE for guidelines. Reports in 2-8 weeks. Pays 2-10 copies of the magazine or cash equivalent ($6-30). Acquires all rights. Returns rights on written request, without cost, provided the magazine is acknowledged whenever reprinted.**

Reviews books of poetry. **For chapbook publication, no query; send 40-60 poems.** "Covering letter not necessary—decisions are made solely on merit of submitted work." Reports in 1-2 months. **Pays 35 copies or cash equivalent ($105). Send $4 for samples or check libraries.** They offer the Wormwood Award to the Most Overlooked Book of Worth (poetry or prose) for a calendar year, judged by Marvin Malone. He comments on rejections if the work has merit. He advises, "Have something to say. Read the past and modern 'master' poets. Absorb what they've done, but then write as effectively as you can in your own style. If you can say it in 40 words, do *not* use 400 or 4,000 words."

WRIT (II,IV-Translations), 2 Sussex Ave., Toronto, Ontario M5S 1J5 Canada, phone (416)978-4871, founded 1970, editor Roger Greenwald, associate editor Richard Lush, is a "literary annual publishing new fiction, poetry, and translation of high quality; has room for unestablished writers." **No limitations on kind of poetry sought; new forms welcome. "Must show conscious and disciplined use of language."** They do not want to see "haiku, purely formal exercises, and poetry by people who don't bother reading." They have recently published poems by Rolf Jacobsen, Paavo Haavikko, Adelia Prado and J. Bernlef. As a sample the editor selected these lines from "Nineteen Poems" by Charles Douglas:

> But even underground our journey will observe
>
> laws of topography, until an eruption
> becomes like a wart, a small disturbance
> of physiognomy, and each of our acts the weight
>
> of a stone on the hillside, under the freedom system.

The magazine is 6 × 9, 96 pgs., flat-spined and sewn, professionally printed on heavy stock, matte card cover with color art, circulation 700, for 125 subscriptions of which 75 are libraries, about 125 store and direct sales, $7.50/copy. **Sample postpaid: $7.50. Poems must be typed and easily legible, printouts as close to letter quality as possible with new ribbon. Photocopies OK. No simultaneous submissions. Editor "sometimes comments on rejections." Reads submissions September 1 through April 30 only. Reports in 2-3 months. Pays 2 copies and discount on bulk purchases. Buys first North American serial rights. Acceptances appear in the next issue published.** The editor advises, "Read a copy of the magazine you're submitting to. Let this give you an idea of the quality we're looking for. But in the case of *WRIT*, don't assume we favor only the styles of the pieces we've already published (we can only print what we get and are open to all styles). Enclose phone number and SASE with Canadian stamps or international reply coupons."

‡THE WRITE TECHNIQUE; PERCEPTIONS (I), Suite 2122, 28 Vesey St., New York NY 10007, founded 1991, editor/publisher Richard Bearse. The Write Technique publishes 2 volumes of **Perceptions**, a poetry anthology, each year—either paperback or hardback. **They are open to all forms and styles. They do not want poetry that is "erotic, on the verge of porno."** They have recently published poetry by Barbara Goldowsky, Karla Andersdatter, Linda Lee Curtis, Edith Rusconi Kaltovich and Sharon Rubenstein. As a sample we selected this poem, "Walk On World," by Linda E. Wedo:

> Walk on world,
>   Continue your pace,
>   Fight your wars,
>   Struggle to handle your load,
>   Self destruct if you wish,
>   But stop a minute,
>   Let me off.

No previously published poems or simultaneous submissions. Submit a maximum of 3 poems with $4 entry fee and contest entry form. Poems should be typewritten or very neatly printed. "Every poem will first be judged upon receipt for publication suitability. Once approved for publication the poem(s) will be published in the next anthology without charge or further obligation." **Often comments on rejections. Send #10 SASE for guidelines. Replies to queries in 1 week.** "After the anthology is published, a final judging (in book form) will be made by contest judges selected by The Write Technique." Prizes are then awarded. 1st prize: 20 free copies of the anthology, 2nd prize: 15 copies, 3rd prize: 10 copies, 4th prize: 5 copies and 5 honorable mentions: 1 copy each. **Sample: $8 for paperback, $16 hardback.**

THE WRITE WAY; TAKING CARE OF YOURSELF; ANN'S ENTERPRISES (I, IV-Themes), 810 Overhill Rd., Deland FL 32720, phone (904)734-1955, founded 1988, editor Ann Larberg. *TWW* is a quarterly using **poems of up to 30 lines on the theme of writing.** As a sample the editor selected "Limerick Lamentation" by Donna Bickley:

> Composing a limerick's not easy

> *Although my attempts make me queasy,*
> *I jot down a line, I stretch for a rhyme.*
> *Reaching as far as it pleases me.*

TWW is a 6-page newsletter with articles on writing and ads. Single copy: $3; subscription: $12. **Do not submit in summer. Reads submissions January 1 through June 30. Reports in 6 weeks. Pays 2 copies.** They hold contests quarterly. *Taking Care of Yourself*, a newsletter of well-being, **accepts 2 poems/issue on the theme of health. Sample free with SASE. Pays copies.**

THE WRITER; POET TO POET (I, II), 120 Boylston St., Boston MA 02116-4615, founded 1887, "Poet to Poet," column by Denise Dumars. This monthly magazine for writers has a quarterly instructional column to which poets may submit work for possible publication and comment by Denise Dumars. **Readers may find suggestions in the column for possible themes or types of poems.** As a sample the editor chose the opening lines of "Mallard" by Carol Diane Iversen:

> *For a moment, my lord, you are stilled*
> *in the water before me,*
> *your green head*
> *painted as finely as a decoy:*
> *I marvel at the beauty, clear*
> *engraving of each feather*
> *as you pose with your brown wife.*

Subscription: $27 (introductory offer: 5 issues for $10). Single copy: $3. **Submit no more than 3 poems, no longer than 30 lines each, not on onion skin or erasable bond, name and address on each page, one poem to a page. There is no pay and mss are not acknowledged or returned. Acquires first North American serial rights.**

‡**WRITERS' CENTER PRESS; THE FLYING ISLAND; INDIANA CHAPBOOK POETRY CONTEST; WRITERS' CENTER OF INDIANAPOLIS (II, IV-Regional)**, P.O. Box 88386, Indianapolis IN 46208, founded 1979, executive director Jim Powell. Writers' Center Press publishes *The Flying Island*, a biannual of fiction, poetry, reviews and literary commentary by those **living in or connected to Indiana. They want poetry of high literary quality; no stylistic or thematic restrictions.** They have recently published poetry by Jared Carter, Alice Friman, Mary Fell and Etheridge Knight. *TFI*, a 24-page tabloid, includes artwork, graphics and photography. They receive about 1,000 poems a year, accept approximately 5%. Press run is 1,000 for 500 subscribers. **Previously published poems OK, but not encouraged. Simultaneous submissions OK, if so advised. Brief bio required. Often comments on rejections. Send SASE for guidelines. Reports in 3-6 months. Pays $5 minimum for previously unpublished work. Buys first North American serial rights.** The center sponsors frequent contests for members through its quarterly newsletter and open readings. They also hold the Indiana Chapbook Poetry Contest every other year (rotating with a short fiction contest). Prize is $150 and publication. They advise, "Balance solitary writing time by getting involved in a writing community. We frequently recommend rejected writers join a poetry workshop."

WRITER'S DIGEST (IV-Themes/writing, humor); WRITER'S DIGEST WRITING COMPETITION (II), 1507 Dana Ave., Cincinnati OH 45207, phone (513)531-2222, founded 1921. *Writer's Digest,* associate editor Angela Terez, is a monthly magazine for freelance writers—fiction, nonfiction, poetry and drama. "All editorial copy is aimed at helping writers to write better and become more successful. **Poetry is part of 'The Writing Life' section of *Writer's Digest* only. These poems should be generally light verse concerning 'the writing life'—the foibles, frenzies, delights and distractions inherent in being a writer. No poetry unrelated to writing.** Some 'literary' work is used, but must be related to writing. "We're also looking for more serious poems on the joys and foibles of the writing life, but avoid the trite or maudlin. **Preferred length: 4-20 lines.** They have recently published poems by Charles Ghigna and Lois McBride Terry. As a sample, the editors chose this poem, "Mixed Messages," by Lois McBride Terry:

> *"As a poet, you're no Poe."*
> *"At prose, you're certainly not a pro."*
> *"Your movie script is nondescript.*
> *(And sadder still, your comic strip.)"*
> *The only line they don't reject:*
> *"Enclosed is my subscription check."*

They use 2 short poems/issue, about 25/year of the 1,500+ submitted. *Writer's Digest* has a circulation of 225,000. Subscription: $21. Sample postpaid: $3. **Do not submit to Michael Bugeja, poetry columnist for the magazine. Submit to Angela Terez, associate editor, each poem on a separate page, no more than 8 per submission. Dot-matrix is discouraged, photocopy OK. Previously published, simultaneous submissions OK if acknowledged in covering letter. Editor comments on rejections "when we want to encourage or explain decision." Send SASE for guidelines.**

Reports in 1-4 weeks. Pays $15-50 per poem. Poetry up to 16 lines on any theme is eligible for the annual Writer's Digest Writing Competition. Watch magazine for rules and deadlines, or send SASE for a copy of the contest's rules. (Also see Writer's Digest Books under Publications Useful to Poets.)

WRITER'S EXCHANGE; R.S.V.P. PRESS (I, IV-Humor, themes/writing), Box 394, Society Hill SC 29593, phone (803)378-4556, founded 1983, editor Gene Boone, is a digest-sized newsletter of articles on any aspect of writing, poetry and artwork with a special emphasis on beginners. He wants **"poetry to 20 lines, any subject or style. I also consider short-short poems such as haiku and other fixed forms. I like writing that is upbeat, positive, enlightening or inspiring, especially humorous poetry. I will not consider material that is anti-religious, racist or obscene."** He has recently published poetry by Victor Chapman, Winnie E. Fitzpatrick, Violet Wilcox and Mary Ann Henn. As a sample he selected these lines (poet unidentified):

> A hurried world, spinning too fast
> Modern technology replaces dreams
> With skyscraper nightmares
> God watches as we dance at Satan's feet.

WE is 12-20 pgs., saddle-stitched, with a colored paper cover. It is published quarterly. He accepts about half or more of the poetry received. Press run is 150. Subscription: $8. **Sample postpaid: $2. "I prefer typed mss, one poem per page, readable. Poets should always proofread mss before sending them out. Errors can cause rejection."** No simultaneous submissions. Previously published poetry OK. Send SASE for guidelines. **Responds in 2-4 weeks, usually 4 months until publication. Pays 1 copy. Acquires one-time rights.** He offers cash awards for quarterly contests sponsored through the magazine. Send SASE for current rules. He says he comments on rejections, "if I feel it will benefit the poet in the long run, never anything too harsh or overly discouraging."

WRITERS' FORUM (II, IV-Regional), University of Colorado, Colorado Springs CO 80933-7150, *Writers' Forum* founded 1974, Victoria McCabe is poetry editor. *Writers' Forum*, an annual, publishes both beginning and well-known writers, giving **"some emphasis to contemporary Western literature**, that is, to representation of living experience west of the 100th meridian in relation to place and culture. We collaborate with authors in the process of revision, reconsider and frequently publish revised work. We are open to **solidly crafted imaginative work that is verbally interesting and reveals authentic voice. We do not seek mss slanted for popular appeal, the sentimental, or gentle, pornographic or polemical, and work primarily intended for special audiences such as children, joggers, gays and so on is not for us. Send 3-5 poems."** They have published poems by William Stafford, David Ray, Kenneth Fields, Harold Witt and Judson Crews. The annual is digest-sized, 225+ pgs., flat-spined, professionally printed with matte card cover, using 40-50 pgs. of poetry in each issue, circulation 800 with 100 subscriptions of which 25 are libraries. **The list price is $8.95 but they offer it at $5.95 to** readers of *Writer's Digest*. They use about 25 of 500 freelance submissions of poetry/year. **Simultaneous submissions OK if acknowledged. Reads submissions September 1 through May 15. Photocopy, dot-matrix OK. Reports in 3 months. Pays 1 copy. Acquires all rights; returns rights.** Reviews books of poetry.

WRITERS FORUM; AND; KROKLOK (IV-Form), 89A Petherton Rd., London N5 2QT England, founded 1963, editor Bob Cobbing, is a small press publisher of experimental work with occasional issues of magazines dealing with sound and visual poetry in cards, leaflets, chapbooks, occasional paperbacks and magazines. **"Explorations of 'the limits of poetry' including 'graphic' displays, notations for sound and performance, as well as semantic and syntactic developments, not to mention fun. Current interest in computer poetry—visual and verbal."** They have recently published poetry by Johan de Wit, Bill Griffiths, Stan Trevor, Betty Radin and Virginia Firnberg. As a sample the editor selected these lines by Steve McCaffery:

> colorfindslines
> al capp's ga   ga
> "perver") t: a t

The magazines are published "very irregularly" and use "very little unsolicited poetry; practically none." Press run "varies." **Payment "by arrangement." Work should generally be submitted camera-ready.** Under the imprint Writers Forum they publish 12-18 books a year averaging 24 pgs. **Samples and listing: $5. For book publication, query with 6 samples, bio, publications. Pays "by arrangement with author."** The editor says, "We publish only that which surprises and excites us; poets who have a very individual voice and style."

WRITER'S GUIDELINES: A ROUNDTABLE FOR WRITERS AND EDITORS (I, IV-Themes), Box 608, Pittsburg MO 65724, founded 1988, poetry editor Susan Salaki, is "an open forum market news magazine, publishing down-to-earth comments and suggestions from editors and writers who want to help close the gap between these two professions, find less expensive ways of marketing work and help each other keep their fingers on the pulse of the buying markets. **Only poetry that can elicit strong emotions and vivid images from the reader is accepted. No vague, abstract poetry. All poetry must somehow pertain to publishing, editors or writing.** They receive about 100 poems a year, accept 10-15. **Sample postpaid: $4. No simultaneous submissions or previously published works. Reports in 1 week. Send #10 SAE with 52¢ postage for guidelines,** free Guideline List and Market Barometer, and brochure. **Reports in 1 week. Pays $1 or 1 copy. Acquires first rights.** The editor says, "If your poetry moves us emotionally, we'll buy it."

WRITER'S JOURNAL (I, II, IV-Teen/young adult), incorporating _Minnesota Ink_, 27 Empire.Dr., St. Paul MN 55103, phone (612)225-1306, _Writer's Journal_ founded 1980, poetry editor Esther M. Leiper (for the _Minnesota Ink_ section, poetry editor Anthoney Stomski). _Writer's Journal_ is a bimonthly magazine "for writers and poets that offers advice and guidance, motivation, inspiration, to the more serious and published writers and poets." Esther Leiper has 2 columns: "Esther Comments," which specifically critiques poems sent in by readers, and "Every Day with Poetry," which discusses a wide range of poetry topics, often—but not always—including readers' work. She says, **"I enjoy a variety of poetry: free verse, strict forms, concrete, Oriental. But we take nothing vulgar, preachy or sloppily written. Since we appeal to those of different skill levels, some poems are more sophisticated than others, but those accepted must move, intrigue or otherwise positively capture me.** 'Esther Comments' is never used as a negative force to put a poem or a poet down. Indeed, I focus on the best part of a given work and seek to suggest means of improvement on weaker aspects. **Short is best: 25-line limit, though _very_ occasionally we use longer. 3-4 poems at a time is just right."** They have published poetry by Lawrence Schug, Diana Sutliff, Eugene E. Grollmes, and editor Leiper. As a sample the editor selected these lines from "an unidentified author we'd love to hear from":

> I am with Haysie again on God's ranch,
> It is not yet dawn; we ride west
> over the mountains. His face is in shadow
> but I know it is Haysie because
> I have loved his shadow so.

The _Writer's Journal_ is magazine-sized, professionally printed, 60 pgs. (including paper cover), using 4-5 pgs. of poetry in each issue, including columns. Circulation 39,000. They receive about 400 submissions/year of which they use 30-40 (including those used in Esther's column). **Sample postpaid: $4. Photocopy OK, no query. Reports in 4-5 months. Pays 25¢/line.** The section _Minnesota Ink_ began as a separate magazine in 1987. Poetry editor Anthoney Stomski, is **"open to style, prefer light-hearted pieces and of good taste"; payment varies.** _Writer's Journal_ has Spring and Fall poetry contests for previously unpublished poetry. Deadlines: April 15 and November 30. _Minnesota Ink_ has summer and winter poetry contests. Deadlines: August 15 and February 28. Reading fee for each contest: $2 first poem, $1 each poem thereafter.

‡**WRITER'S LIFELINE (I),** Box 1641, Cornwall, Ontario K6H 5V6 Canada, phone (613)932-2135, founded 1974, editor Stephen Gill, published 3 times in 1991, containing articles and information useful to writers, **poetry** and book reviews. **"We prefer poems on social concerns. We avoid sex."** As a sample the editor selected these lines from his poem, "Bigotry":

> It grows
> on the babel of confusion
> in the lap of
> the blinding dust of vanity
> by the arrogant prince of ignorance.

_WL_ is digest-sized, 36-40 pgs., saddle-stitched with paper 2-color cover, professionally printed in small type, poems sometimes in bold or italics. Circulation is 1,500. Subscriptions: $18. **Sample postpaid: $3. Send SASE for guidelines. Responds in 1 month. Pays 3 copies. Acquires first North American serial rights.** Reviews books of poetry in 500-1,500 words. "We need book reviews." Query if interested.

‡**WRITERS' RENDEZVOUS (I, IV-Themes/writing, form),** P.O. Box 105, Sacramento CA 95812-0105, poetry editor Karen Campbell, is a newsletter for freelance writers. **"Poetry should rhyme or be haiku (but not mandatory). We prefer writer-oriented poetry, only e.g., 'Ode to Walt Whitman' and 'Writer's Problem.' No avant-garde."** As a sample I selected the first of two stanzas of "Writer's Problem," poet unidentified:

> Here I sit,
> I'll have a fit
> My poem needs a theme.
> I think I'll scream.

_WR_ is photocopied on ordinary paper, both sides—24 pages, stapled in the upper left-hand corner. It comes out quarterly. They take about 80 of 200 poems submitted. **Sample postpaid: $3.50. Simultaneous submissions and previously published poems OK. Editor "sometimes" provides comments on rejected mss. Reports in about 4 weeks, about 4 months until publication. Send SASE for guidelines. Pays 1 copy. Acquires one-time rights.** Reviews books of poetry in 50-200 words. She says, "Many poetry submissions reveal that the writer has not studied our preferences in style and topic. (Poetry not on topic is automatically rejected.) Please be sure you are familiar with the market before wasting your time—and the editor's—with inappropriate submissions." They sponsor an annual contest with a cash prize. Deadline is July 15; they charge an entry fee; send SASE for entry forms.

WRITING (I), P.O. Box 403, Carlton South, Melbourne, Victoria, Australia 3053, founded 1986, supervising editor Sherryl Clark, appears twice a year, **"aims to publish new writers and/or writers in writing groups. Well-published writers should not submit. We think of ourselves as a 'stepping stone' while maintaining the highest possible standard, poetry that is contemporary and fresh, not merely recycling old ideas and images."** As a sample the editor selected these lines from "Granite Day" by Jordie Albiston:

> today
> is a granite day great
> slabs of silence
> cram me in
> thick and impenetrable
> thick with soundlessness

The editor describes it as "48 pgs., A5-6×8, stapled, card cover." They accept an average of 25 of 200-300 poems received/year. Press run 350 for 130 subscribers of which 11 are libraries, 50 shelf sales. Subcription: A$14 (in Australia). **Sample postpaid: A$5 in Australia, $7 overseas. Send SASE for guidelines. Editorial committee can take 6 months to respond. Pays 1 copy. Acquires first Australian serial rights.**

WRITING (V), Box 69609, Station K, Vancouver, British Columbia V5K 4W7 Canada, phone (604)688-6001, founded 1980, editors Jeff Derksen and Nancy Shaw, is a literary magazine appearing 3 times per year using **"socially committed, innovative writing."** The editors describe it as 96 pgs., 6×9, with "colour cover." They accept about 10% of submissions received. Press run 700 for 300 subscriptions of which 20% are libraries, 200 shelf sales. Subscription: $15 Canada, $18 USA, $20 foreign. **Sample postpaid: $6. Pays subscription. Currently accepts no unsolicited poetry.**

‡WYRD (IV-Psychic/occult), P.O. Box 624, Monroeville PA 15146-0624, founded 1986, "editrix" Goldie Brown, is a quarterly using news, articles, music and poetry related to the Magickal/Pagan community. They want **poetry about magick, the occult, nature or spirituality—no longer than 50 lines.** They have recently published poetry by Fletcher de Wolf, Victor Anderson, Ken McDonnell and Ken Deigh. As a sample the editor selected these lines from "Rainbow Eclipse" by jon Eric:

> Temple of the Golden Sun
> Silver Moon, Brazen Twin
> Garden of the Emerald Earth
> Turquoise Sea, Indigo Sky
> Chalice of the Violet Flame
> Ruby Blood, Umbar Flesh

WYRD is 16 pgs., 8½×11, side stapled, with art, graphics and ads. They receive about 100 poems a year, use approximately 10%. Press run is 150 for 100 subscribers. Subscription: $12. **Sample postpaid: $3. No previously published poems; simultaneous submissions OK. Cover letter required. Reports in 2 months. Pays 1 copy—more (up to 3), if requested.** Reviews related books of poetry in 150-200 words, single format.

‡XAVIER REVIEW (II), Box 110C, Xavier University, New Orleans LA 70125, phone (504)486-7411, founded 1961, editor Thomas Bonner, Jr., is a biannual that publishes poetry, fiction, nonfiction and reviews (contemporary literature) for professional writers, libraries, colleges and universities. Press run is 500. Subscription: $10. **Sample postpaid: $5.** No submission information provided.

XENOPHILIA; OMEGA CAT PRESS (II, IV-Themes), 904 Old Town Ct., Cupertino CA 95014, founded 1990, editor Joy Oestreicher. Omega Cat Press publishes 1 chapbook/year. *Xenophilia* appears twice a year using **poetry on "geo-cultural topics; 'xenology'—alien or other cultures, or our society from other's view; exotic rituals, mythic traditions; surreal, beat, punk, fantasy/science fiction, humor and speculative works (to 20 pgs.) No greeting-card versification."** They have published poetry by Denise Dumars, David Kopaska-Merkel, John Grey, Bruce Boston and Andrew Gettler. As a sample the editor selected these lines from "Distant Mirrors" by Wayne Edwards:

> *here distant mirrors sing at night*
> *mnemotechnic prayers of trust and fear*
> *warnings against civility and progress*
> *the fall of man the slow dissolve*
> *of knowledge and war and love*

The magazine is digest-sized, 40+ pgs., saddle-stapled with matte card cover, professionally printed. This small press product packs many poems (and punch) into each issue. Free verse is the norm. Subscription: $7. **Sample postpaid: $4. Pays $5/page plus 1 copy. Buys first North American serial rights. Send SASE for guidelines. Reports in 1 month, longer in December. Editor comments on rejections "often. I occasionally ask for rewrites."** Reviews books of poetry, 10-100 pages, single format. For their annual chapbook competition, submit 30-50 poems "about any national heritage or culture (not necessarily a real culture) — a people's customs, rites, typical social occasions, folkways, etc." **$5 reading fee/submission. Cover letter required. Deadline December 1 for April publication. Write for rules.** All entrants receive a copy of the winning chapbook.

‡**XIQUAN PUBLISHING HOUSE; THE PARADOXIST MOVEMENT JOURNAL; THE PARADOXIST MOVEMENT ASSOCIATION (II, IV-Form, translations),** P.O. Box 42561, Phoenix AZ 85080, founded 1990, editor Florentin Smarandache. *The Paradoxist Movement Journal* is a biannual journal of "avant-garde poetry, experiments, poems without verses, literature beyond the words, anti-language, non-literature and its literature, as well as the sense of the non-sense; revolutionary forms of poetry." They want **"avant-garde poetry, 1-2 pages, any subject, any style (lyrical experiments). No classical, fixed forms."** They have recently published poetry by Teresinka Pereira, Paul Courget and Claude LeRoy. As a sample here is "Dear Deer" from **Nonpoems** by the editor:

> - *Hear, here!*
>   *Buy, by*
>   *our hour,*
>   *four fore*
>   *pears pairs!*
> - *Sun son,*
>   *no! Know*
>   *two, too!*
> - *Hi! Hie!*

The editor says *TPM* is 52 pgs., digest-sized, offset, soft cover. Press run is 500. "It is distributed to its collaborators." **No previously published poems or simultaneous submissions. Do not submit mss in the summer. "We do not return published or unpublished poems or notify the author of date of publication." Reports in 3-6 months. Pays 1-2 copies.** Xiquan Publishing House also publishes 2 paperbacks and 1-2 chapbooks/year, including translations. The poems must be unpublished and must meet the requirements of the Paradoxist Movement Association. **Replies to queries in 1-2 months, to mss in 3-6 months. Pays 50 author's copies. Inquire about sample books.** They say "We left the communist totalitarism and emigrated to the United States for *the freedom.* Therefore, don't force any literary rules on us! Or, if you do, we'll certainly encroach upon them. We are not poets, that's why we write poetry. We are anti-poet or non-poet. We thus come to America to rebuild the Statue of Liberty of the verse, delivered from the tyranny of the classic and its dogma."

X-PRESS PRODUCTIONS (III), 2932 Roundtree Blvd., Ypsilanti MI 48197, founded 1989, editor Eugene Haun, who writes, "Retired, I now have the time and the money to publish poetry; but it *is* my money, and I must put it on serious, talented, disciplined poets. **I do not require a theme, but I do look for integrity and a production which manifests internal consistency. I want poetry, not puzzles.** Better known poets do not need my attentions." As a sample here is the first stanza of "To my Brother Larry" from **Scenes from Childhood,** a chapbook by Murray Jackson:

> *We giggled and watched*
> *The toes of the world*
> *From our basement window.*
> *Archibald, the music teacher,*
> *Petite-ing from his apartment to John R.*

Reports within a month. Pays 50% of earnings after costs. Author owns all but 100 editor's copies. Write for samples.

XTRA!; PINK TRIANGLE PRESS; THE CHURCH-WELLESLEY REVIEW (IV-Gay, lesbian), Box 7289, Station A, Toronto, Ontario M5W 1X9 Canada, press founded 1971. *Xtra!*, appearing every 2 weeks, is Canada's largest gay and lesbian periodical. They want short, "not epic" poems for *The Church-Wellesley Review*, their annual literary supplement. They have published poetry by Daniel David Moses,

Sky Gilbert and Antler. Poetry appears only in the supplement to the tabloid, which has a press run of 22,000 for 500 subscribers—distributed free to the public. **Mss should include name on every page, daytime phone number and 50-word bio. Submissions are accepted January 1 through March 30.** Address them to *The Church-Wellesley Review*, % *Extra!* **Reports in 3 months. Pays** "honorarium" one month after publication.

YALE UNIVERSITY PRESS; THE YALE SERIES OF YOUNGER POETS (III), 92A Yale Station, New Haven CT 06520, phone (203)432-0900, founded 1908, poetry editor (Yale University Press) Jonathan Brent. The Yale Series of Younger Poets is one of the most prestigious means available to launch a book publishing career. It is **open to poets under 40 who have not had a book previously published— a book ms of 48-64 pgs. Entry fee: $8. Submit February 1-28 each year. Send SASE for rules and guidelines.** Poets are not disqualified by previous publication of limited editions of no more than 300 copies or previously published poems in newspapers and periodicals, which may be used in the book ms if so identified. Previous winners include Richard Kenney, Julie Agoos, Pamela Alexander and George Bradley. Publication of the winning volume each year is on a standard royalty contract plus 10 author's copies, and the reputation of the contest guarantees more than the usual number of reviews.

‡YAMMERING TWITS (I, II), 62 W. Masem Square, E., Patchogue NY 11772, founded 1991, editor Tracey Erin Finnerty, is a quarterly, "a place for people to nurse their free verse hangovers. **Vivid imagery, under 30 lines, favored. I like poetry inspired by bars, rock-n-roll and other everyday heart-breaks. R.E.M. fans a plus. No sickly sweet love stuff, no cussing for sake of shock and no porking poetry without a payoff.**" She has recently published poetry by Lyn Lifshin, Ana Pine and R.B. Weber. As a sample the editor selected these lines from "Background Notes" by Mike Costanzo:

> when we met
> there was a radio in the background
> set at random
> in the big chance love fishbowl
>
> as I talked
> you sang along,
> giving the night a soundtrack

YT is about 20 pgs., 8½ × 11, photocopied, stapled at top left corner, with b&w artwork. Single copy: $1.50; subscription: $5. **No previously published poems. Submit 1 poem/page on 8½ × 11 paper, "ready to be copied as is. Feelings are hurt without cover letter."** Comments on rejections "if requested to do so." **Reports in 1 month.** "Because I'll be doing this from college I ask for patience." **Pays 1 copy.** The editor says, "Read like machines and support the small press."

YANKEE MAGAZINE; YANKEE ANNUAL POETRY CONTEST (II), Main St., Dublin NH 03444, phone (603)563-8222, founded in 1935, poetry editor (since 1955) Jean Burden. Though it has a New England emphasis, the poetry is not necessarily about New England or by New Englanders, and it has a national distribution to more than a million subscribers. They want to see **"high quality contemporary poems in either free verse or traditional form. Does not have to be regional in theme. Any subject acceptable, provided it is in good taste. We look for originality in thought, imagery, insight—as well as technical control." They do not want poetry that is** "cliché-ridden, banal verse." They have recently published poetry by Maxine Kumin, Liz Rosenberg, Josephine Jacobsen, Nancy Willard, Linda Pastan, Paul Zimmer and Hayden Carruth. As a sample the editor selected these lines from "Waking" by Joan LaBombard:

> But blood's in thrall to the world
> and the body's bound
> by its clocks and invisible pulleys—
> sun plucking at bedclothes,
> a mockingbird's ultimatum.
> I reenter the world's cage, the house
> of my daylight body.
> My blood discovers its old riverbed,
> and my name remembers me.

The monthly is 6 × 9, 170+ pgs., saddle-stapled, professionally printed, using full-color and b&w ads and illustrations, with full-color glossy paper cover. They receive over 30,000 submissions a year, accept about 50-60 poems. Subscription: $22. **Submit poems up to 30 lines, free verse or traditional. Uses 4-5 poems/monthly issue. Pays $50/poem, all rights; $35, first magazine rights. Reports in 2-3 weeks.** Approximately 18-month backlog. **No simultaneous submissions or pre-viously published poems. Submissions without SASE** "are tossed." **Editor comments on rejec-tions** "only if poem has so many good qualities it only needs minor revisions." Sponsors an annual poetry contest judged by a prominent New England poet and published in the February issue, with awards of $150, $100 and $50 for the best 3 poems in the preceding year. Jean Burden advises, "Study previous issues of *Yankee* to determine the kind of poetry we want. Get involved in poetry workshops at home. Read the best contemporary poetry you can find."

YARROW, A JOURNAL OF POETRY (II), English Dept., Lytle Hall, Kutztown State University, Kutztown PA 19530, founded 1981, editor Harry Humes, appears twice a year. They have published poetry by Gibbons Ruark, Jared Carter, William Pitt Root and Fleda Brown Jackson. It is 40 pgs., 6 × 9, offset. Press run 350. Subscription: $5/2 years. **Reports in 1-2 months. Pays 2 copies plus 1-year subscription.**

YELLOW SILK: JOURNAL OF EROTIC ARTS, Verygraphics, Box 6374, Albany CA 94706. Declined listing.

YESTERDAY'S MAGAZETTE (I, IV-Senior citizens), Independent Publishing Co., P.O. Box 15126, Sarasota FL 34277, editor and publisher Ned Burke, founded 1973. This bimonthly magazine is for "*all* **nostalgia lovers.** *YM* believes that everyone has a yesterday and everyone has a memory to share. Nothing fancy here . . . just 'plain folks' relating their individual life experiences. **We are always seeking new and innovative writers with imagination and promise, and we would like to see more 40s, 50s and 60s pieces."** As a sample here are lines from "The Backyard Pump" by J.E. Coulbourn:

> *With two small hands you'd*
> *grasp the monster's tail*
> *And try to pump the water in the pail,*
> *But if his darned esophagus got dry*
> *No water came no matter how you'd try.*

YM is magazine-sized, 22 pgs., saddle-stapled, professionally printed on good stock with glossy color cover. A year's subscription is $12 or two years for $18. **Sample: $2. Submissions for "Quills, Quips, & Quotes" (their poetry page) should be "thoughtful, amusing, or just plain interesting for our 'plain folks' readers. No SASE is required as short items are generally not returned nor acknowledged, unless requested by the contributor."** Pays copies.

THE YOUNG CRUSADER (IV-Children, themes), National Woman's Christian Temperance Union, 1730 Chicago Ave., Evanston IL 60201, is a monthly publication for members of the Loyal Temperance Legion and young friends of their age — about 6-12 years. The digest-sized leaflet, 12 pgs., uses "**short poems appropriate for the temperance and high moral value and nature themes and their young audience."** Pays 10¢/line for poetry.**

YOUNG VOICES MAGAZINE (IV-Children), P.O. Box 2321, Olympia WA 98507, phone (206)357-4683, founded 1988, publisher/editor Steve Charak, is "a magazine of **creative work of elementary through high school students. The age limit is rigid.**" It appears every other month, press-run 1,500 for 1,000 subscribers of which 40 are libraries. Subscription: $15 for 1 year, $28 for 2. **Sample postpaid: $4. Send SASE for guidelines. Pays $3/poem plus 1 copy (3 copies if you are a subscriber). Buys one-time rights. Editor comments "definitely, on every piece of writing."** He says, "Revise. Remember that in a poem, every word counts. Forget about the need to rhyme. Instead, put feeling into each word."

ZERO HOUR (IV-Themes), P.O. Box 766, Seattle WA 98111, phone (206)323-3648, founded 1987, editor Jim Jones, is "**a thinking person's tabloid. Each issue is devoted to a theme (cults, addiction, pornography, etc.) in which some poetry is printed.**" They have published poetry by Jesse Bernstein. The editor says *Zero Hour* has 40 pgs. It appears 3 times a year. Of 20 pieces of poetry received/year they take about 3. Press run: 3,000 for 2,000 shelf sales. **Sample postpaid: $4. Pays 5 copies. Simultaneous submissions and previously published poems OK.** Reviews books of poetry.

ZERO ONE; DANCING PATCH MAGAZINE (V), 39 Minford Gardens, West Kensington, London W14 OAP England, phone 01602-9142, poetry editor and publisher Arthur Moyse. *Zero One* is an anarchist oriented publication appearing twice a year "with luck." He describes *Dancing Patch Magazine* as a "literary quarterly, anarchist oriented, egotistical, clichés. **To avoid disappointments we do not seek submissions as we operate on the 'old pals act' style.**" He has published poems by Cunliffe, Woods and Gould. As a sample he selected these lines from "On the Death of the American Poet George Montgomery" by Jim Burns:

> *Reading about your death*
> *I started to look back at the 1960s*
> *and the little magazines*
> *that used to arrive every day,* . . . .

DPM appears 3-4 times a year. The editor describes it as magazine-sized. He says he receives "too much poetry, takes hardly any." He advises, "Just write it and send it off off off. Give up waiting for editorial acceptance or rejection. Just write and post."

ZOLAND BOOKS INC. (III), 384 Huron Ave., Cambridge MA 02138, phone (617)864-6252, founded 1987, publisher Roland Pease, is a "literary press: fiction, poetry, photography, gift books, books of literary interest" using **"high-quality" poetry, not sentimental.** They have recently published poetry by William Corbett, Marguerite Bouvard, Marge Piercy, Patricia Smith and Gary Fincke. They publish 6-10 books a year, flat-spined, averaging 96 pgs. **Query with 5-10 sample poems, bio, publications. No simultaneous submissions. Reports on queries in 2 months. Pays 5-10% royalties plus 5 copies. Buys all rights. Editor does not comment on submissions.**

Publishers of Poetry/'92-'93 Changes

Each year we contact all publishers currently listed in **Poet's Market** requesting updated information for our next edition. The following magazine and book publishers were listed in the 1992 edition of **Poet's Market** but are not in the 1993 edition because either they did not respond to our request to update their listing (these names appear without further explanation), their listing was deleted for the reason indicated or their listing information was received after our deadline date.

As you can see, the reasons some of these publishers are not included in the directory are temporary (e.g., overstocked, temporarily suspending publication, etc.). *If you're interested in any of the following, first research the publisher and then write a brief letter (enclosing SASE) inquiring as to whether they are now interested in receiving submissions.*

Abattoir Editions
Advocacy Press (not soliciting poetry)
After the End (out of business)
Agenda Editions
Agog (folded)
Aileron Press
Alchemy Press
Allardyce, Barnett Publishers
Alura (ceased publication)
American Squaredance Magazine
Americas Review
Androgyne (ceased publication)
Apalachee Quarterly
Archae: A Palaeo-Review of the Arts
Arundel Press
The Ascent, Adelphi University (no longer accepting outside submissions)
Ashod (requested deletion)
Babyfish (Lost Its Momma)
The Bassettown Review (no longer using poetry)
The Bench Press
Between the Lines Book Publishers (does not publish poetry)
Black Apple
Black Tape Press
Blast Magazine
The Blizzard Rambler (overstocked)
The Blue Guitar
Blue Light Red Light (overstocked)
Box 749 Magazine (requested deletion)
Bradford Poetry
Bristol House Publishers

(concentrating on international publications)
Broadsheet Magazine
Cacanadadada Review
Cadmus Editions
Cage
Canadian Author & Bookman
The Capilano Review
Carn
The Carrefour Press
The Carrionflower Writ (ceased publication)
Celestial Arts (no longer publishes poetry)
Central Park (requested deletion)
Chakra
Channels (possibly merging with another publication)
Chantry Press
The Christian Way (requested deletion)
Cincinnati Poetry Review
The Cincinnati Poets' Collective
The Clyde Press (ceasing publication)
Coach House Press (requested deletion)
The Community Endeavor (responded too late)
Country Roads Quarterly
Coyote Chronicles
Crooked Roads
Cross Timbers Review (ceased publication)
Curley
D.C.
Dark Side Magazine (ceased publication)
Delirium (ceased publication)
Deviance

Diehard
A Different Drummer
Dis-Ease (ceased publication)
Duckabush Journal
Edinburgh Review
Egorag
Encodings
Envoi
Eotu, Magazine of Experimental Fiction (ceased publication)
The Escapist
Exit Zero (inappropriate submissions)
Faith . . . Works (ceased publication)
Five Fingers Review (responded too late)
Follow Your Dreams
Fox Valley Living (no longer accepting poetry)
Frog Gone Review
From Here Press
The Galley Sail Review
Generation Magazine (inappropriate submissions)
Ghost Town Quarterly (suspended publication)
Going Down Swinging
Going Gaga (inappropriate submissions)
Grand Union
Great Elm Press (no longer accepting poetry mss)
Great River Review (requested deletion)
Green Zero (ceasing publication)
Haiku Alive (ceased publication)
Haiku Canada

Haiku Quarterly
Handshake Editions
Happy Lamb
Harbour Publishing (requested deletion)
Hardware: The Magazine of Technophilia
HarperCollins (no longer publishing contemporary poetry)
Hatbox (ceased publication)
The Haunted Sun (ceased publication)
Haunts (overstocked)
The Headwaters Review (ceased publication)
Heart (out of business)
Helter Skelter (now Whisper, responded too late)
Hemispheres (suspended publication)
Herbooks
The Heyeck Press (requested deletion)
Hilltop Press
Hippo (ceased publication)
Hob-Nob (overstocked)
Hobo Jungle: A Quarterly Journal of New Writing (suspended publication)
The Howling Mantra (requested deletion)
Humor
Hurricane Alice
Imagination Magazine (ceased publication)
Inlet (suspended publication)
International Poets Academy (responded too late)
Inverted-A, Inc.
Io (requested deletion)
Issue One
It's a Mad Mad Mad Mad Mad World
Journeys
James Joyce Broadsheet
K (moved, no forwarding address)
Kaldron: An International Journal of Visual Poetry and Language Art
Kapok Poetry Press
The Kau Kau Kitchen Newsletter (moved, no forwarding address)
Key West Review
Kola
Ladies' Home Journal (no longer using poetry)
Lake Effect
Lancaster Independent Press
Left-Footed Wombat (moving, future uncertain)
Libido: The Journal of Sex and Sexuality
Lincoln Bulletin (ceased publication)
Literary Creations (out of business)
The Little Magazine
The Lookout (no longer publishes poetry)
Louder Than Bombs
The Lundian
McPherson & Company Publishers (does not publish poetry)
The Mage (ceased publication)
Mainichi Daily News
Malcontent (requested deletion)
Manoa: A Pacific Journal of International Writing
Manroot Books
The Wilton Marks Studio (moved, no forwarding address)
Maroverlag
Matrix
Memory Plus Enterprises Press (no longer publishing poetry)
Moving Out: A Feminist Literary and Arts Journal
Night Mountains (moved, no forwarding address)
1992 Quarterly
The North
The Northern Review (ceasing publication)
Notebook/Cuaderno: A Literary Journal
NRG (folded)
One & Only (folded)
Owens Publications
Oxalis (responded too late)
Palanquin
Pennywhistle Press (now Kids Today, no longer accepting outside submissions)
Pensive Poems (ceased publication)
Perivale Press (not accepting unsolicited poetry)
Peterloo Poets
Pleiades Magazine
Pocket Inspirations (suspended publication)
Poetic Justice
Poetical Histories
Poetry & Audience
Poetry Today (suspended publication)
Poetry Voice
Poetry/LA (suspended publication)
Portraits Poetry Magazine
Prescott Street Press
The Prospect Review
Quartos Magazine
The Rampant Guinea Pig (ceased publication)
Recovering Poet's Registry and Exchange (requested deletion)
Red Alder Books (no longer soliciting material)
Reflections (ceased publication)
Resurgens
Review La Booche
Rhododendron
Roads
Rohwedder: International Journal of Literature & Art (suspended publication)
Romancing the Past
Room of One's Own (requested deletion)
Rubber Puppy
Sackbut Press (not soliciting work)
Sa-De Publications (out of business)
Salmon Publishing
Samisdat (ceased publication)
Sangré Sangré (ceased publication)
Sargasso
Scream Magazine
Screaming Trees
Scripsi
Scriptor
Scrivener
Secret Goldfish
Shawnee Silhouette (ceased publication)
Single Today (no longer using poetry)
Skylark, Canada (ceased publication)
Slant: A Journal of Poetry
Slow Dancer
The Small Times
Smoke (responded too late)
Social Justice (requested deletion)
The South Florida Poetry Review
Space and Time (ceased publication)
Spectacles
Spectacular Diseases
Spinsters Book Company (no longer publishes poetry)
Squeaky Wheels Press
The Standing Stone
Star Route Journal (ceased publication)
Starlight Press (not seeking submissions)
Starsong (ceased publication)
Stereopticon Press
The Stevan Company
Stick (moved, no forwarding address)
Stop Light Press (moved, no forwarding address)
Street Press
Sword of Shahrazad (ceased publication)
Syzygy (requested deletion)
Taste of Latex
Tempest Magazine (no longer publishes poetry)
Ten Lions and the End of the World (inappropriate submissions)
Third Woman Press
Took: Modern Poetry in English
Tramp
Trona Press

Turnstile
U.C. Review
Uncle (ceased publication)
Utah State University Press
The Vagabond
Vestal Press, Ltd. (no longer publishing poetry)
Victimology: An International Journal
Visibilities (moved, no forwarding address)
Vision (ceased publication)
Vision Seeker & Sharer (ceased publication)
Walking and Sinning

We Magazine
West Coast Line (overstocked)
West End Press
Wheat Forder's Press
White Clouds Revue (inappropriate submissions)
Wildflower (requested deletion)
Wire Magazine
Woman of Power, A Magazine of Feminism, Spirituality and Politics (no longer accepting unsolicited submissions)
Women's Education Des

Femmes (requested deletion)
Working Classics
Write Now!
Writers' Own Magazine
Wyoming, The Hub of the Wheel . . . A Journey for Universal Spokesmen (suspended publication)
X-Calibre
The Yukon Reader (no longer publishes poetry)
Zeitgeist
Zone 3

State and Provincial Grants

Following is a list of arts councils in the United States and Canada that provide assistance to artists (including poets), usually in the form of fellowships or grants. These grants are often substantial and confer some prestige upon recipients; however, only residents of the state or province are eligible. Because deadlines for applications and the amount and nature of available support vary annually, remember to first send a query (with a self-addressed, stamped envelope) to the agency in the state or province in which you reside.

United States Art Agencies

Alabama State Council on the Arts
Al Head, Executive Director
1 Dexter Ave.
Montgomery AL 36130
(205)242-4076

Alaska State Council on the Arts
Jean Palmer, Grants Officer
Suite 1-E, 411 W. 4th Ave.
Anchorage AK 99501
(907)279-1558

Arizona Commission on the Arts
Shelley Cohn, Executive Director
417 W. Roosevelt
Phoenix AZ 85003
(602)255-5882

Arkansas Arts Council
Bill Puppione, Executive Director
Heritage Center
Suite 200, 225 E. Markham St.
Little Rock AR 72201
(501)324-9337

California Arts Council
Ann Bourget, Literary Grants
2411 Alhambra Blvd.
Sacramento CA 95817
(916)739-3186

Colorado Council on the Arts and Humanities
Barbara Neal, Executive Director
750 Pennsylvania St.
Denver CO 80203-3699
(303)894-2617

Connecticut Commission on the Arts
John Ostrout, Executive Director
227 Lawrence St.
Hartford CT 06106
(203)566-7076

Delaware State Arts Council
Cecelia Fitzgibbon, Executive Director
State Office Building
820 N. French St.
Wilmington DE 19801
(302)577-3540

Florida Arts Council
Peyton Fearington, Director
Division of Cultural Affairs
Florida Department of State
The Capitol
Tallahassee FL 32399-0250
(904)487-2980

Georgia Council for the Arts
Betsy Weltner, Executive Director
Suite 115, 530 Means St. NW
Atlanta GA 30318
(404)651-7920

Hawaii State Foundation on Culture and the Arts
Wendell P.K. Silva, Executive Director
Room 202, 335 Merchant St.
Honolulu HI 96813
(808)586-0300

Idaho Commission on the Arts
Margot Knight, Executive Director
304 W. State St.
Boise ID 83720
(208)334-2119

Illinois Arts Council
Richard Gage, Director of Communication Arts
Suite 10-500, 100 W. Randolph
Chicago IL 60601
(312)814-6750

Indiana Arts Commission
Tom Schorgl, Executive Director
Room 072, 402 W. Washington St.
Indianapolis IN 46204-2741
(317)232-1268

Iowa Arts Council
Julie Bailey, Grants Coordinator
State Capitol Complex
1223 E. Court
Des Moines IA 50319
(515)281-4451

Kansas Arts Commission
Jay Hawk Tower
Suite 1004, 700 Jackson
Topeka KS 66603
(913)296-3335

Kentucky Arts Council
Charles M. Newell, Executive Director

31 Fountain Pl.
Frankfort KY 40601
(502)564-3757

Louisiana State Arts Council
Dee Waller, Arts & Education Coordinator
P.O. Box 44247
Baton Rouge LA 70804
(504)342-8180

Maine State Arts Commission
Peter Simmons, Senior Arts Associate
Paul Faria, Percent for Arts Coordinator
55 Capitol St.
State House, Station 25
Augusta ME 04330-0025
(207)289-2724

Maryland State Arts Council
Michele Moure, Program Director
601 N. Howard St.
Baltimore MD 21201
(301)333-8232

Massachusetts Cultural Council
Cheryl Balukonis, Coordinator
10th Floor, 80 Boylston St.
Boston MA 02116
(617)727-3668

Michigan Council for the Arts
Betty Boone, Interim Director
Suite 1180, 1200 6th Ave.
Detroit MI 48226
(313)256-3731

COMPAS
Molly LaBerge, Executive Director
305 Landmark Center
75 W. 5th St.
St. Paul MN 55102
(612)292-3249

Mississippi Arts Commission
Kathleen Stept, Arts & Education Program
Director
Suite 207, 239 N. Lamar St.
Jackson MS 39201
(601)359-6030

Missouri Arts Council
Autry Jackson, Program Administrator
Wainwright State Office Complex
Suite 105, 111 N. 7th St.
St. Louis MO 63101
(314)340-6845

Montana Arts Council
Martha Sprague, Director of Art Services/
Programs
48 N. Last Chance Gulch
New York Block
Helena MT 59620
(406)444-6430

Nebraska Arts Council
Jennifer Clark, Executive Director
1313 Farnam on-the-Mall
Omaha NE 68102-1873
(402)595-2122

Nevada State Council on the Arts
William L. Fox, Director
329 Flint St.

Reno NV 89501
(702)688-1225

New Hampshire State Council on the Arts
Susan Bonaiuto, Director
Phoenix Hall
40 N. Main St.
Concord NH 03301
(603)271-2789

New Jersey State Council on the Arts
Barbara Russo, Acting Executive Director
CN 306, 4 N. Broad St.
Trenton NJ 08625
(609)292-6130

New Mexico Arts Division
Lara Morrow, Director
228 E. Palace Ave.
Santa Fe NM 87501
(505)827-6490

New York State Council on the Arts
Jewelle Gomez, Director, Literature Program
915 Broadway
New York NY 10010
(212)387-7020

North Carolina Arts Council
Deborah McGill, Literature Director
Department of Cultural Resources
221 E. Lane St.
Raleigh NC 27601-2807
(919)733-2111

North Dakota Council on the Arts
Brad Stephenson, Community Services
Coordinator
Suite 606, Black Bldg.
118 Broadway
Fargo ND 58102
(701)239-7150

Ohio Arts Council
Bob Fox, Literature Coordinator
727 E. Main St.
Columbus OH 43205
(614)466-2613

State Arts Council of Oklahoma
Betty Price, Executive Director
640 Jim Thorpe Bldg.
Oklahoma City OK 73105-4987
(405)521-2931

Oregon Arts Commission
Vincent Dunn, Assistant Director
550 Airport Rd. SE
Salem OR 97310
(503)378-3625

Pennsylvania Council on the Arts
Marsha Salvatore, Literature Program Director
Room 216, Finance Bldg.
Harrisburg PA 17120
(717)787-6883

Rhode Island State Council on the Arts
Iona Dobbins, Executive Director
Suite 103, 95 Cedar St.
Providence RI 02903
(401)277-3880

South Carolina Arts Commission
Steve Lewis, Literary Arts Director
1800 Gervais St.

Columbia SC 29201
(803)734-8696

South Dakota Arts Council
Colin Olsen, A.I.S. Coordinator
108 W. 11th St.
Sioux Falls SD 57102-0788
(605)339-6646

Tennessee Arts Commission
Alice Swanson, Director of Literary Arts
Suite 100, 320 6th Ave. N.
Nashville TN 37243-0780
(615)741-1701

Texas Commission on the Arts
Ricardo Hernandez, Program Director
P.O. Box 13406, Capitol Station
Austin TX 78711-3406
(512)463-5535

Utah Arts Council
Sherry Waddingham, Grants Officer
617 E. South Temple St.
Salt Lake City UT 84102
(801)533-5895

Vermont Council on the Arts
Cornelia Carey, Grants Officer
136 State St.
Montpelier VT 05602
(802)828-3291

Virginia Commission for the Arts
Peggy J. Baggett, Executive Director
223 Governor St.
Richmond VA 23219
(804)225-3132

Washington State Arts Commission
Linda Bellon-Fisher, Artists-in-Residence
Program
110 9th and Columbia Bldg.
P.O. Box 42675
Olympia WA 98504-2675
(206)753-3860

West Virginia Arts and Humanities Division
Lakin Cook, Arts & Humanities Director
The Cultural Center, Capitol Complex
Charleston WV 23505
(304)348-0220

Wisconsin Arts Board
Dean Amhaus, Executive Director
Suite 301, 131 W. Wilson
Madison WI 53703
(608)266-0190

Wyoming Council on the Arts
Nita Moxley, Acting Executive Director
2320 Capitol Ave.
Cheyenne WY 82002
(307)777-7742

Canadian Provinces Art Agencies

Alberta Culture and Multiculturalism
Arts Branch - Cultural Industries
Ruth Bertelsen, Manager
11th Floor, CN Tower
10004 - 104 Avenue
Edmonton, Alberta T5J 0K5
(403)427-6315

British Columbia Arts Council
Cultural Services Branch
Walter Quan, Coordinator of Arts Awards
Programs
6th Floor, 800 Johnson St.
Victoria, British Columbia V8V 1X4
(604)356-1728

Manitoba Arts Council
James Hutchison, Literary Arts Consultant
525 - 93 Lombard Ave.
Winnipeg, Manitoba R3B 3B1
(204)945-2237

New Brunswick Department of Tourism, Recreation and Heritage
Arts Branch
Bruce Dennis, Program Officer
Department of Municipalities, Culture
& Housing
P.O. Box 6000
Fredericton, New Brunswick E3B 5H1
(506)453-2555

Newfoundland Department of Municipal and Provincial Affairs
Cultural Affairs Division

Elizabeth Batstone, Director of Cultural Affairs
P.O. Box 1854
St. John's, Newfoundland A1C 5P9
(709)729-3650

Nova Scotia Department of Tourism and Culture
Allison Bishop, Director of Cultural Affairs
P.O. Box 456
Halifax, Nova Scotia B3J 2R5
(902)424-5000

Ontario Arts Council
Eleanor Goldhar, Director of Communications
Suite 500, 151 Bloor St. W.
Toronto, Ontario M5S 1T6
(416)961-1660

Prince Edward Island Council of the Arts
Judy McDonald, Executive Director
P.O. Box 2234
Charlottetown, Prince Edward Island C1A 8B9
(902)368-4410

Organization of Saskatchewan Arts Councils
Barbara Flaten, Executive Director
1102 8th Avenue
Regina, Saskatchewan S4R 1C9
(306)586-1250

Yukon Arts Council
Glenn Wadsworth, Executive Director
P.O. Box 5120
Whitehorse, Yukon Y1A 4S3
(403)668-6284

Contests and Awards

Listed here are contests and awards (not associated with specific publications or organizations mentioned elsewhere in **Poet's Market**) with prizes ranging from modest ones by poetry societies to sizeable amounts given by the government or private foundations.

A few contests are coded **I** because they are geared toward beginners and/or charge fees while offering small prizes. There are perhaps no better contests to enter than ones sponsored by poetry societies or writers' federations to which you belong. These promote and encourage poets. Be aware, however, if a contest charges $5 per poem and offers total prize money of $100, the sponsors only need 20 entries to cover basic costs. True, sometimes costs include handling and an honorarium for the judge, so the break-even point may be 50 entries. Typically, however, these sponsors get hundreds of submissions and make a neat profit at the poet's expense.

Some awards, such as individual fellowships via the National Endowment for the Arts, require you to document that your work has appeared in a specific number of reputable publications (no vanity or "anthology" credits). Other contests, such as the National Poetry Series, are for poets with unpublished book-length manuscripts. Since they are generally open to submissions, these are coded **II**.

Many contests are regional or specialized and these also are coded accordingly, **IV-Regional** or **IV-Science Fiction** etc. In general, the higher the honor the less likely you will qualify without nomination, so many listings carry **V** codings: highly restrictive.

One of the benefits of entering contests is the chance to compete with other poets and *win*. The feeling is phenomenal because the competition, typically, is so keen. Moreover, your winning a contest or award usually will be publicized in writing magazines or newsletters and your name will become more familiar to editors.

So, above all, be selective when trying to decide which contests to enter. Consider not only the style of poetry being sought, but also the contests' themes and your own level of experience.

Finally, you'll find Additional Contests and Awards at the end of this section. This list cross-refers magazines, presses or organizations that also sponsor contests and/or awards. Many of these are considered prestigious, such as ones offered by *Nimrod* or *The Nation*. Use the General Index to locate particular contests, and consult individual listings for details.

In any case, send for submission guidelines—as always, include a SASE—and follow each rule so that your entry won't be disqualified on a technicality. Contests often contain different rules each year or revised entry forms, so inquire every time you want to try your hand at winning one.

‡AAA ANNUAL NATIONAL LITERARY CONTEST; ARIZONA LITERARY MAGAZINE (I), Suite 117-PM, 3509 Shea Blvd., Phoenix AZ 85028-3339, sponsoring organization Arizona Authors' Association, award director Gerry Benninger. 42 lines maximum, $4 entry fee, submit between January 1 and July 29. Prizes are $125, $75, $40, 3 honorable mentions $10 each. Include SASE with entry for contest results; no material will be returned. Winners are announced and prizes awarded in October. Winning entries are published in a special edition of *Arizona Literary Magazine*. Entries must be typed, double-spaced on 8½ × 11 paper. Write for more information and entry rules; enclose SASE.

MILTON ACORN POETRY AWARD; PRINCE EDWARD ISLAND LITERARY AWARDS (IV-Regional), The Prince Edward Island Council of the Arts, P.O. Box 2234, Charlottetown, Prince Edward Island C1A 8B9 Canada. Awards are given annually for short stories, poetry, children's literature, feature articles, children's creative writing and playwriting. Writers must have been resident at least 6 of the 12 months before the contest. Submit October 1 through February 14. For the Milton Acorn Poetry Award, participants may submit as many entries as they wish, each of no more than 10 pgs. Prizes for '91-'92: A trip for 2 via Air Nova to Ottawa, Montreal or Quebec City, first prize; $200 and $100, second and third prizes.

THE AIR CANADA AWARD (I, IV-Regional), 275 Slater St., Ottawa, Ontario K1P 5H9 Canada, The Air Canada Award is an annual award of two tickets to any Air Canada destination, to a Canadian author, published or unpublished, under 30 who shows the most promise. Nominations are made before April 30 by Canadian Authors Association branches or other writers' organizations and the award is given at the CAA banquet in June.

‡AMERICAN-SCANDINAVIAN FOUNDATION TRANSLATION PRIZE; SCANDINAVIAN REVIEW (IV-Translation), 725 Park Ave., New York NY 10021, for the best translation into English of a work (which may be poetry) of a Scandinavian author after 1800, $2,000, publication in the *Scandinavian Review,* and a bronze medallion. To enter, first request rules.

‡ARIZONA STATE POETRY SOCIETY ANNUAL CONTEST (I, II, IV), 2301 W. Devonshire, Phoenix AZ 85015, award director Priscilla H. White. Contest for various poetry forms and subjects. Prizes range from $15-150; first, second and third place winners are published in the winter edition of *The Sandcutters,* the group's quarterly publication, and name and entries are listed for honorable mention winners. Contest information available for SASE. Fees vary. Deadline August 31.

ARKANSAS POETRY DAY CONTEST; POETS' ROUNDTABLE OF ARKANSAS (I), over 25 categories, many open to all poets. Brochure available in June; deadline in September; awards given in October. For copy send SASE to Verna Lee Hinegardner, Apt. 109, 605 Higdon, Hot Springs AR 71913.

ARTIST TRUST; ARTIST TRUST GAP GRANTS; ARTIST TRUST FELLOWSHIPS (IV-Regional), Suite 415, 1402 Third Ave., Seattle WA 98101, phone (206)467-8734. *Artist Trust* is a nonprofit arts organization that provides grants to artists (including poets) who are residents of the state. It also publishes a 16-page quarterly tabloid of news about arts opportunities and cultural issues.

ARVON INTERNATIONAL POETRY COMPETITION (I, II), Kilnhurst, Kilnhurst Rd., Todmorden, Lancashire OL14 6AX, England, phone 0706 816582, FAX: 0706 816359, jointly sponsored by Duncan Lawrie Limited and *The Observer.* Poems (which may be of any length and previously unpublished) must be in English. First prize is £5,000 ($8,425), and other cash prizes. The competition is biennial. Distinguished poets serve as judges. Though the contest (which raises funds by entry fees) may be better known internationally, the major function of the Arvon Foundation is to offer writing courses at two retreats: At Totleight Barton, Sheepwash, Beaworthy, Devon EX21 5NS, phone (040923) 338 and at Lumb Bank, Hebden Bridge, West Yorkshire HX7 6DF, phone (0422) 843714. These are residential programs at attractive country retreats, offered by established writers in subjects such as poetry, playwriting, short fiction, radio drama, and words and music. The tuition is £200 for, typically, 5 days, which includes tuition, food and accommodations, and there is scholarship available from the foundation for those who cannot otherwise afford to attend.

ATLANTIC WRITING COMPETITION; WRITERS' FEDERATION OF NOVA SCOTIA (IV-Regional), Suite 203, 5516 Spring Garden Road, Halifax, Nova Scotia B3J 1G6 Canada, offers prizes of $150, $75 and $50 for 1-15 unpublished poems by residents of the Atlantic Provinces, entry fee $15, deadline January 31. Write for *mandatory* entry form.

‡BARNARD NEW WOMEN POETS PRIZE; WOMEN POETS AT BARNARD; BARNARD NEW WOMEN POETS SERIES; BEACON PRESS (IV-Women), Barnard College of Columbia University, 3009 Broadway, New York NY 10027-6598. Women Poets at Barnard holds open competition and annual series. The winner receives an award of $1,000 and publication in the Barnard New Women Poets Series, Beacon Press. The competition is open to any woman poet with a book-length ms who has not yet published a book (exclusive of chapbooks). Deadline September 1. Submit two copies of ms with SASE, postcard for acknowledgement or receipt.

GEORGE BENNETT FELLOWSHIP (II), Phillips Exeter Academy, Exeter NH 03833, provides a $5,000 fellowship plus room and board to a writer with a ms in progress. The Fellow's only official duties are to be in residence while the academy is in session and to be available to students interested in writing. The committee favors writers who have not yet published a book-length work with a major publisher. Send SASE for application materials. Deadline December 1.

BERLIN ARTISTS' PROGRAM (II), German Academic Exchange Service, (Deutscher Akademischer Austauschdienst), Bureau Berlin, Box 126240, Steinplatz 2, 1000 Berlin 12, Germany, director Dr. Joachim Sartorius, enables 15-20 internationally known and recommended composers, filmmakers and writers to spend a year taking an active part in the cultural life of Berlin. Screening committee meets in March or April.

BOLLINGEN PRIZE (V), Beinecke Rare Book and Manuscript Library, Yale University, New Haven CT 06520, prize of $10,000 to an American poet for the best poetry collection published during the previous two years, or for a body of poetry written over several years. **By nomination only.** Judges change biennially. Announcements in January of odd-numbered years.

‡BP NICHOL CHAPBOOK AWARD (IV-Regional), 316 Dupont St., Toronto, Ontario M5R 1V9 Canada, $1,000 (Canadian) prize for the best poetry chapbook (10-48 pgs.) in English published in Canada in the preceding year. Submit 3 copies. Entries close March 31.

BREAD LOAF WRITERS' CONFERENCE (II), Middlebury College, Middlebury VT 05753, phone (802)388-3711, fellowships and scholarships. Candidates for fellowships must have book published. Candidates for scholarships must have published in major literary periodicals or newspapers. One letter of nomination required by March 1; applications and supporting materials due by April 1. Awards are announced in June for the conference in August.

BUCKNELL SEMINAR FOR YOUNGER POETS; STADLER SEMESTER FOR YOUNGER POETS (IV-Students), Bucknell University, Lewisburg PA 17837, (717)524-1853, director John Wheatcroft. In the spring of 1993, the Stadler Semester for Younger Poets will be added to the Seminar for Younger Poets and the Poet-in-Residence Series. The Stadler Semester is distinctive in allowing undergraduate poets almost four months of concentrated work centered in poetry. Guided by practicing poets, the apprentice will write and read poetry and will receive critical response. The two Fellows selected will work with Bucknell's writing faculty. The visiting Poet-in-Residence also will participate in the program. Fellows will earn a semester of academic credit by taking four units of study: a tutorial or individual project with a mentor poet, a poetry-writing workshop, a literature course, and an elective. Undergraduates from four-year colleges with at least one course in poetry writing are eligible to apply; most applicants will be second-semester juniors. Send a 12-15 page portfolio and a letter of presentation (a brief autobiography that expresses commitment to writing poetry, cites relevant courses and lists any publications). Also include a transcript, two recommendations (at least one from a poetry-writing instructor), and a letter from the academic dean granting permission for the student to attend Bucknell for a semester. Application deadline for the Stadler Semester is November 1. Students chosen for the fellowhips will be notified by November 25. The Bucknell Seminar For Younger Poets is not a contest for poems but for 10 fellowships to the Bucknell Seminar, held for 4 weeks in June every year. Seniors and juniors from American colleges are eligible to compete for the ten fellowships, which consist of tuition, room, board, and spaces for writing. Application deadline for each year's seminar is March 10 of the previous year. Students chosen for fellowships will be notified on April 8.

THE BUNTING FELLOWSHIP PROGRAM (IV-Women), Radcliffe College, 34 Concord Ave., Cambridge MA 02138, supports women of exceptional promise and demonstrated accomplishment who want to pursue independent study in the creative arts (among other things). The stipend is $28,500 for a fellowship fulltime September 1-August 31, requiring residence in the Boston area. Applicants in creative arts should be at the equivalent stage in their careers as women who have received doctorates two years before applying. Deadline in early October.

BUSH ARTIST FELLOWSHIPS (IV-Regional), E-900 First National Bank Bldg., 332 Minnesota St., St. Paul MN 55101, are for South and North Dakota, western Wisconsin and Minnesota residents over 25 years of age to help published writers (poetry, fiction, literary nonfiction, playwriting and screenwriting), visual artists, choreographers and composers set aside time for work-in-progress or exploration of new directions. Maximum of 15 awards of a maximum of $26,000 (and up to $7,000 additional for production and traveling expenses) are awarded each year for 6-18 month fellowships. Deadline late October.

‡CALIFORNIA WRITERS' ROUNDTABLE POETRY CONTEST (I), under the auspices of the Los Angeles Chapter, Women's National Book Association, Lou Carter Keay, chairman, Suite 807, 11684 Ventura Blvd., Studio City CA 91614-2652. An annual contest with $50, $25 and $10 cash prizes for unpublished poems on any subject, in various forms, not more than 42 lines in length. WNBA members may submit free; nonmembers pay $3 per poem entry fee. Deadline is September 30. Send SASE for guidelines.

CANADIAN AUTHORS ASSOCIATION LITERARY AWARDS; CANADIAN AUTHORS ASSOCIATION (IV-Regional), 275 Slater St., Ottawa, Ontario K1P 5H9 Canada, $5,000 in each of 4 categories (fiction, poetry, non-fiction, drama) to Canadian writers, for a published book in the year of publication (or, in the case of drama, first produced), deadline December 15. Nominations may be made by authors, publishers, agents, or others. (Also see The Air Canada Award in this section.)

CAPRICORN POETRY AWARD (II); OPEN VOICE AWARDS (I, II); THE WRITER'S VOICE, Writer's Voice, 5 W. 63rd St., New York NY 10023. Capricorn Poetry Award, publication of a book of poems of 48-68 pgs. by an author over 40, a cash prize of $500 and a reading at The Writer's Voice. $15 entry fee for nonmembers of The Writer's Voice. January 1 deadline. Send SASE for application guidelines. Open Voice Awards, annual awards, $500 honorarium and a reading in the Fall, open to both published and unpublished poets who have not previously read at The Writer's Voice. $10 entry fee. January 1 deadline. Send SASE for application form. The Writer's Voice is a literary center sponsoring weekly readings, writing workshops, writing awards and other activities.

CINTAS FELLOWSHIP PROGRAM (IV-Regional), Arts International, Institute of International Education, 809 United Nations Plaza, New York NY 10017, makes awards of $10,000 to young professional writers and artists of Cuban lineage living outside of Cuba. Deadline for applications March 1.

CLARK COLLEGE POETRY CONTEST (I), % Arlene Paul, 4312 NE 40th St., Vancouver WA 98661, jointly sponsored by Clark College, Oregon State Poetry Association and Washington Poetry Association, deadline February 15, $3 per poem entry fee (checks payable to Clark College Foundation), prizes of $50, $75 and $100, for poems up to 25 lines, unpublished, not having won another contest. Entries in triplicate, not identified. Type name, address on a 3 × 5 card, include title and first line on card. May purchase book of winners' poems for $2.85 postpaid.

INA COOLBRITH CIRCLE ANNUAL POETRY CONTEST (IV-Regional), %Tom Berry, Treasurer, 761 Sequoia Woods Place, Concord CA 94518, has prizes of $10-50 in each of several categories for California residents only. Poems submitted in 3 copies, no names on copies. Enclose a 3 × 5 card with name, address, phone number, category, title, first line of poem and status as member or nonmember. Members of the Ina Coolbrith Circle pay no fee; others pay $5 for 3 poems (limit 3). Deadline in August. For further information contact Tom Berry.

‡COOS HEAD WRITERS POETRY CONTEST (I), P.O. Box 4022, Coos Bay OR 97420, award director Estelle Rivers. Annual contest for poetry up to 1 page on any subject, with monetary prizes for 1st, 2nd and 3rd place and certificate for honorable mention. "For attendees category, writers have to attend the Coos Head Writer's workshop when annual one is held. Other category of Poets Choice does not require attendance of the annual workshop." Information available for SASE. Fees $3/2 poems; no limit on entries. Deadline August 1.

ABBIE M. COPPS POETRY COMPETITION; GARFIELD LAKE REVIEW (I,II), contest chairperson Linda Jo Scott, Dept. of Humanities, Olivet College, Olivet MI 49076, phone (616)749-7683, annual, $150 prize and publication in the *Garfield Lake Review*, $2/poem entry fee for unpublished poem up to 100 lines. Deadline February 15. Submit unsigned, typed poem, entrance fee, and name, address and phone number in a sealed envelope with the first line of the poem on the outside. Judge to be announced.

CREATIVE ARTIST PROGRAM (IV-Regional), Cultural Arts Council of Houston, Suite 224, 1964 West Gray, Houston TX 77019-4808, phone (713)527-9330, offers annual awards of $4,000 to Houston visual artists and writers. Unless funding prohibits, choreographers and composers are also included in the competition. Deadline for entry is in the fall.

DALY CITY POETRY AND SHORT STORY CONTEST (I), Daly City History, Arts & Science Commission, Serramonte Library, 40 Wembley Dr., Daly City CA 94015, held annually, prizes of $30, $25, $15 and $10 in various categories and $5 for honorable mention. Entry fee of $1/poem or $2/story. Stories must be unpublished. Deadline: January 4. Send SASE for rules; attn: Ruth Hoppin, coordinator.

BILLEE MURRAY DENNY POETRY AWARD (II), % Janet Overton, Lincoln College, Lincoln IL 62656, awarded annually, prizes of $1,000, $500 and $250. Open to poets who have not previously published a book of poetry with a commercial or university press (except for chapbooks with a circulation of less than 250). Enter up to 3 poems, 100 lines/poem or less at $2/poem. Poems may be on any subject, using any style, but may not contain "any vulgar, obscene, suggestive or offensive word or phrase." Entry form and fees payable to Poetry Contest, Lincoln College, must be postmarked no later than

May 31. Winning poems are published in **The Denny Poems**, a biennial anthology, available for $4 from Lincoln College. Send SASE for entry form.

MILTON DORFMAN NATIONAL POETRY PRIZE (II), Rome Art & Community Center, c/o Maureen Dunn Murphy, 308 W. Bloomfield St., Rome NY 13440, awarded annually for unpublished poetry, $2 fee/poem, with prizes of $500, $200, $100; poems printed in Center's Newsletter. Contest opens July 1. Deadline November 1. Include name, address and phone on each entry.

ERGO!; BUMBERSHOOT (II), Box 9750-0750, Seattle WA 98109, phone (206)622-5123, founded 1973, producing director, Louise DiLenge, an annual publication *ERGO!* is issued in conjunction with *Bumbershoot*, a multi-arts festival at the Seattle Center on Labor Day weekend. "Fifteen hundred will be published for distribution prior to and at the Festival. Included will be selected works by the Writers-in-Performance invitational participants and winners of the Written Works Competitions in addition to the official literary arts program schedule." Twenty-four honoraria will be awarded for written works. Considers simultaneous submissions. Deadline for application is mid-February. For application forms and further details write *Bumbershoot* at the address above. *ERGO!* **sample available for $9 postpaid. Competition guidelines available with a SASE.**

‡FEDERATION INTERNATIONALE DES TRADUCTEURS; CARL-BERTIL NATHHORST TRANSLATION PRIZE; ASTRID LINDGREN TRANSLATION PRIZE (IV-Translation), Heiveldstraat 245, B-9040 Ghent, Belgium, or, for American applicants: American Translators Association, Suite 903, 1735 Jefferson Davis Highway, Arlington VA 22202. The Carl-Bertil Nathhorst prize is awarded once every 3 years for "promoting translation, improving the quality thereof and drawing attention to the role of the translator in bringing the people of the world together." The Astrid Lindgren Prize is awarded every 3 years for "promoting the translation of works written for children."

FLORIDA STATE WRITING COMPETITION; FLORIDA FREELANCE WRITERS ASSOCIATION (I), P.O. Box 9844, Fort Lauderdale FL 33310, is an annual contest with categories in free verse and traditional, prizes up to $100 in each category, fees $2/poem for members of the FFWA, $2.50 for others. March 15 deadline. Guidelines available each fall through March for #10 SASE.

‡FOSTER CITY ANNUAL WRITERS' CONTEST (II), F.C. Committee for the Arts, 650 Shell Blvd., Foster City CA 94404.Yearly competition for previously unpublished fiction, poetry, children's stories and humor. $10 entry fee, $300 prize in each category. Deadline in September. Send SASE for instructions.

GEORGIA STATE POETRY SOCIETY, INC.; BYRON HERBERT REECE AND EDWARD DAVIN VICKERS INTERNATIONAL AWARDS; THE REACH OF SONG ANNUAL ANTHOLOGY; ANNUAL CHAPBOOK COMPETITION; GEORGIA STATE POETRY SOCIETY NEWSLETTER (I, IV-Anthologies, form), P.O. Box 120, Epworth GA 30541. The society sponsors a number of contests open to all poets, described in its quarterly *Newsletter* (membership $20/year), sponsors an annual anthology, **The Reach of Song**, and an annual chapbook (for members only) competition. The Byron Herbert Reece and the Edward Davin Vickers International Awards have prizes of $250, $100, $50, $25, $15 and $10. Entry fee: $5, first poem, $1 each additional. Deadline January 31, Reece Awards; April 30, Vickers Awards. SASE for guidelines. Sample newsletter $2; **Reach of Song**, $10.

‡GOETHE PRIZE OF THE CITY OF FRANKFURT (V), %Amt Für Wissensehaft und Kunst Brückenstrabe 3-7, 6,000 Frankfurt am Main 70, West Germany, an award of DM 50,000 every three years to a writer whose creative work has shown a continuation of Goethe's ideas and thoughts, by nomination only.

GREEN RIVERS WRITERS' CONTESTS (I, IV-Themes, forms), Contest Chairman, 11906 Locust Rd., Middletown KY 40243, offers 8 contests for poetry on various themes and in various forms, entry fee $2/poem for nonmembers, $1 for members, prizes from $3-$69, July 1 deadline. Send SASE for rules.

GROLIER POETRY PRIZE; ELLEN LA FORGE MEMORIAL POETRY FOUNDATION, INC. (II, IV-Themes), 6 Plympton St., Cambridge MA 02138. The Grolier Poetry Prize is open to all poets who have not published either a vanity, small press, trade or chapbook of poetry. Two poets receive an honorarium of $150 each. Four poems by each winner and 2 by each of 4 runners-up are chosen for publication in the *Grolier Poetry Prize Annual*. Submit 5 poems, not more than 10 double-spaced pages. Opens January 1 of each year; deadline March 15. Submit one ms in duplicate, without name of poet. On a separate sheet give name, address, phone and titles of poems. $5 entry fee, checks payable to the Ellen La Forge Memorial Poetry Foundation, Inc. Enclose self-addressed stamped postcard if acknowledgement of receipt is required. For update of rules, send SASE to Grolier Poetry Book Shop,

Inc., before submitting mss. The Ellen La Forge Memorial Poetry Foundation sponsors intercollegiate poetry readings and a reading series, generally 5 per semester, held on the grounds of Harvard University. These are generally poets who have a large following or who have new collections of poetry available, for sale at the Grolier Poetry Book Shop, Inc. which donates money toward costs (such as rental of the auditorium). They pay poets honoraria from $100-400 and occasionally provide overnight accommodations (but not transportation). Such poets as Mark Strand, Philip Levine, Robin Becker, Donald Hall and Bridget Pegeen Kelly have given readings under their auspices. The small foundation depends upon public gifts and support for its activities.

GUGGENHEIM FELLOWSHIPS (II), John Simon Guggenheim Memorial Foundation, 90 Park Ave., New York NY 10016. Approximately 145 Guggenheims are awarded each year to persons who have already demonstrated exceptional capacity for productive scholarship or exceptional creative ability in the arts. The amounts of the grants vary. The average grant is about $26,500. Application deadline October 1.

HACKNEY LITERARY AWARDS; BIRMINGHAM-SOUTHERN COLLEGE WRITER'S CONFERENCE (II), Birmingham-Southern College, Box A-3, Birmingham AL 35254. This competition, sponsored by the Cecil Hackney family since 1969, offers $4,000 in prizes for novels, poetry and short stories as part of the annual Birmingham-Southern Writer's Conference. Poems must be postmarked by December 31. Send SASE for Hackney guidelines. Winners are announced at the conference, which is held in the spring.

‡THE HODDER FELLOWSHIP (II), The Council of the Humanities, 122 E. Pyne, Princeton University, Princeton NJ 08544. Write for details. Deadline November 15.

‡HENRY HOYNS FELLOWSHIPS (II), Dept. of English, University of Virginia, Charlottesville VA 22903, are fellowships in poetry and fiction with stipends of varying amounts for candidates for the M.F.A. in creative writing. Deadline February 15. Sample poems/prose required with application.

JOHANN-HEINRICH-VOSS PRIZE FOR TRANSLATION (V), German Academy for Language and Literature, Alexandraweg 23, D-6100 Darmstadt, West Germany, is an annual award of DM 20,000 for outstanding lifetime achievement for translating into German, by nomination only. 1991: Fritz Vogelgsang.

THE CHESTER H. JONES FOUNDATION NATIONAL POETRY COMPETITION (II), P.O. Box 498, Chardon OH 44024, an annual competition for persons in the USA, Canadian and American citizens living abroad. Prizes: $1,000, $500, $250, and $50 honorable mentions. Winning poems plus others called "commendations" are published in a chapbook available for $3.50 from the foundation. Entry fee $2 for the first poem, $1 each for others, no more than 10 entries, no more than 32 lines each. Deadline March 31. Distinguished poets serve as judges.

LAMPMAN AWARD (IV-Regional); OTTAWA INDEPENDENT WRITERS/LES ECRIVAINS INDE- PENDANTS D'OTTAWA, 922-2660 Norberry Crescent, Ottawa, Ontario K1V 6N2 Canada, phone (613)739-0626, is a $400 award for a published book of English-language poetry by writers in the National Capital region. Submit 3 copies of each title by February 28. Membership in Ottawa Independent Writers is $50/year, and offers their newsletter, programs, a Master Writing Series of workshops, an entry in the OIW Directory, and registration at reduced fees for their annual conference.

D.H. LAWRENCE FELLOWSHIP (II), Dept. of English, University of New Mexico, Albuquerque NM 87131, chair Scott P. Sanders, offers a creative writer a 3-month summer residence on the Lawrence Ranch near Taos, New Mexico, and a $1,250 stipend. Application fee: $10. Postmark deadline: January 31 annually.

THE STEPHEN LEACOCK MEDAL FOR HUMOUR (IV-Humor, regional), Mrs. Jean Bradley Dickson, award chairman, Stephen Leacock Associates, P.O. Box 854, Orillia, Ontario L3V 3P4 Canada, phone (705)325-6546, for a book of humor, prose verse, drama or any book by a Canadian citizen. Submit 10 copies of book, 8 × 10 b&w photo, bio and $25 entry fee. Deadline December 31. Prize: Silver Leacock Medal for Humour and J.P. Wiser cash award of $3,500. The committee also publishes *The Newspacket* 3/year.

LETRAS DE ORO SPANISH LITERARY PRIZES (IV-Foreign language), Iberian Studies Institute, North-South Center, University of Miami, Box 248123, Coral Gables FL 33124, include a general prize of $2,500 and the publication of the book-length entry, plus an all expenses paid trip to Spain. For creative excellence in poetry written in the Spanish language. Deadline October 12. Contact for guidelines.

AMY LOWELL POETRY TRAVELLING SCHOLARSHIP (II), Trust u/w/o Amy Lowell, Exchange Place, 35th Floor, Choate, Hall & Stewart, Boston MA 02109, award directors F. Davis Dassori, Jr., and other Trustees, is an annual award of $27,000 (more-or-less: the amount varies annually), to an "advanced" poet who agrees to live outside of North America for the year of the grant. Deadline for application October 15.

MACARTHUR FELLOWS (V), John D. and Catherine T. MacArthur Foundation, Suite 1100, 140 S. Dearborn St., Chicago IL 60603. An anonymous committee selects individuals to whom the foundation awards large grants.

MAPLECON SF; FANTASY WRITING COMPETITION (I, IV-Themes, science fiction/fantasy), %Madona Skaff, literary coordinator, 2105 Thistle Crescent, Ottawa, Ontario K1H 5P4 Canada. "Total length (1 or more poems) 12-200 lines. Open to anyone. Entry must be based on a science, science fiction or fantasy theme. Please, no resubmissions from previous years." Deadline is June 28. Awards (certificates and prizes) are made at Maplecon, the Ottawa Regional Science Fiction/Fantasy Convention in October (or mailed to those not present). Please include SASE with all correspondence. US and other foreign countries use IRCs or 2 loose first class stamps.

MILFORD FINE ARTS COUNCIL POETRY CONTEST (I,II), 5 Broad St., Milford CT 06460. SASE for details.

MISSISSIPPI VALLEY POETRY CONTEST; NORTH AMERICAN LITERARY ESCADRILLE (I, II), P.O. Box 3188, Rock Island IL 61204, director Sue Katz, annually offers prizes of approximately $1,000 for unpublished poems in categories for student (elementary, junior and senior high), adult, Mississippi Valley, senior citizens, jazz, religious, humorous, rhyming, haiku, ethnic, patriotic. Fee: $5 for 1-5 poems, no line limit. Children $3 for 1-5 poems. September 15 deadline. Professional readers read winning poems before a reception at an award evening each October.

‡MONEY FOR WOMEN (IV-Women/feminism), Barbara Deming Memorial Fund, Inc., Box 40-1043, Brooklyn NY 11240-1043, award director Pam McAllister, sponsors a semiannual contest with deadlines of February 1 and July 1 for small grants to feminists in the arts. Subjects include women, peace, justice issues. Send SASE for application form. Applicants must be citizens of US or Canada.

‡MONTANA INSTITUTE OF THE ARTS WRITERS CONTESTS; MARY BRENNEN CLAPP MEMORIAL AWARD (IV-Regional, membership), P.O. Box 1872, Bozeman MT 59771, holds two annual contests with a March 31 deadline; for all Montana poets, for unpublished poems up to 100 lines, in a group of 3, no fee, for the Mary Brennen Clapp Memorial Award of $50 and prizes of $40, $30, and $20. Must submit 3 poems and cover letter. Send SASE for guidelines.

JENNY MCKEAN MOORE FUND FOR WRITERS, (II), Dept. of English, George Washington University, Washington DC 20052, provides for a visiting lecturer in creative writing for about $35,000 for 2 semesters. Apply by November 15 with resume and writing sample of 25 pgs. or less.

THE JULIA MOORE POETRY COMPETITION; NEWSLETTER OF HUMOR (IV-Humor), International Society for Humor Studies, c/o Don Nilsen, English Dept., ASU, Tempe AZ 85287-0302, is an annual competition for "good bad poetry" in the tradition of Julia Moore, a poet of frontier Michigan, who wrote:

> *My childhood days have passed and gone,*
> *and it fills my heart with pain*
> *To think that youth will nevermore*
> *Return to me again.*
> *And now kind friends, what I have wrote,*
> *I hope you will pass o'er.*
> *And not criticise as some have done Hitherto herebefore.*

The style of Julia Moore is parodied in **Huckleberry Finn**.

‡NASHVILLE NEWSLETTER POETRY CONTEST (I), P.O. Box 60535, Nashville TN 37206-0535, Roger Dale Miller, editor/publisher. Founded 1977. Reporting time 6-10 weeks. Published quarterly. Sample copy $3. Any style or subject up to 40 lines. One unpublished poem to a page with name, address in upper left corner. Entry fee of $5 for up to 3 poems. Must be sent all at once. Prizes of $50, $25, and $10 with at least 50 Certificates of Merit.

NATIONAL ENDOWMENT FOR THE ARTS; FELLOWSHIPS FOR CREATIVE ARTISTS; FELLOWSHIPS FOR TRANSLATORS (II), Literature Program, 1100 Pennsylvania Ave. NW, Washington DC 20506, phone (202)682-5451. The Fellowships for Creative Artists comprise the largest program for individual grants available for American poets (and other writers and artists). Dozens of awards of $20,000 are made each year to poets who have published a book or at least 20 poems in magazines in the last 10 years. Decisions are made by a panel of distinguished writers solely on the quality of the submitted material. Guidelines available September of each year. They also offer grants of up to $10,000 to nonprofit organizations to support residencies for published writers of poetry, Fellowships for Translators ($10,000 or $20,000), and other programs to assist publishers and promoters of poetry. Write for complete guidelines.

NATIONAL POETRY SERIES ANNUAL OPEN COMPETITION (II), P.O. Box G, Hopewell NJ 08525, between January 1 and February 15 considers book-length (approximately 48-64 pgs.) mss, entry fee $15. Manuscripts will not be returned. The 5 winners are published by participating small press, university press and trade publishers. Send SASE for complete submissions procedures.

NATIONAL WRITERS CLUB ANNUAL POETRY CONTEST (I), Suite 620, 1450 S. Havana, Aurora CO 80012, award director Sandy Whelchel, an annual contest with prizes of $100, $50, $25 and $10 plus honorable mentions. Entry fee $6/poem; additional fee charged if poem is longer than 40 lines. Deadline June 1. All subjects and forms are acceptable.

THE NATIONAL WRITTEN & ILLUSTRATED BY . . . AWARDS CONTEST FOR STUDENTS; LANDMARK EDITIONS (IV-Students), P.O. Box 4469, Kansas City MO 64127, award director David Melton, is an annual contest for unpublished work for a book written and illustrated by a student. Three books published, one from each of 3 age categories (6-9; 10-13; 14-19). Each winner receives a $5,000 scholarship provided by the R.D. and Joan Dale Hubbard Foundation, and there are $2,000 and $1,000 scholarship awards for 4 runners up in each category. Send #10 SASE with 60¢ postage for rules.

NEUSTADT INTERNATIONAL PRIZE FOR LITERATURE; WORLD LITERATURE TODAY (V), University of Oklahoma, Room 110, 630 Parrington Oval, Norman OK 73019, $40,000 given every other year in recognition of life achievement or to a writer whose work is still in progress; nominations from an international jury only.

NEW ENGLAND POETRY CLUB; DANIEL VAROUJAN AWARD; FIRMAN HOUGHTON AWARD; NORMA FARBER AWARD; BARBARA BRADLEY AWARD; ROSALIE BOYLE PRIZE; ERIKA MUMFORD PRIZE (I), 2 Farrar St., Cambridge MA 02138. The contests sponsored by New England Poetry Club have a $2/poem fee for nonmembers (free to members), all with a June 30 deadline, all judged by well-known poets such as X.J. Kennedy and Peter Viereck. The Varoujan Award of $500 is for a poem "worthy of Daniel Varoujan, an Armenian poet killed by the Turks in 1915." The Firman Houghton Award is $250 (named for a former NEPC president); the Norma Farber Award is $100 for a sonnet or sonnet series; the Rosalie Boyle Prize of $100 is for a poem over 30 lines; the Erika Mumford Prize for a poem of exotic or faraway setting is $250; and the Barbara Bradley Award of $200 for a lyric poem under 21 lines written by a woman. Poems should be sent in duplicate with name of writer on one to Lois Ames, NEPC Contests, 285 Marlboro Road, Sudbury MA 01776, before June 30 annually.

NEW YORK FOUNDATION FOR THE ARTS (IV-Regional), 5 Beekman St., New York NY 10038, phone (212)233-3900, ext. 219, offers fellowships of $7,000 every other year for poets who are at least 18 and have resided in New York State for the 2 years prior to application. Submit up to 10 pages of poetry (at least 2 poems), 3 copies of a 1-page resume, and an application form. Call for deadline information and for application form.

‡**NORDMANNS-FORBUNDET (NORSEMEN'S FEDERATION) (IV-Translation)**, Radhusgt. 23b, N-0158 Oslo 1, Norway, phone 02/42 75 14 or 02/42 23 76, FAX 02/42 51 63, information officer Mrs. Dina Tolfsby. The Nordmanns-Forbundet, in its desire to make Norwegian culture known abroad, awards an annual grant (maximum 15,000 Norwegian crowns) to one or more publishing houses introducing Norwegian fiction or poetry in translation (preferably contemporary). Application deadline is March 1 of each calendar year with winners announced later in the spring. Payment is made at the time of publication.

‡**THE NORTH CAROLINA POETRY SOCIETY ZOE KINCAID BROCKMAN MEMORIAL BOOK AWARD CONTEST (IV-Regional)**, % Robert Collins, president, 838 Everetts Creek Dr., Wilmington NC 28405, is an annual contest for a book of poetry (over 20 pages) by a North Carolina poet (native-born or

current resident for 3 years). Send SASE for details. $100 cash prize and a Revere-style bowl awarded in 1992.

NORTHWEST POETS & ARTISTS CALENDAR (IV-Regional), Bainbridge Island Arts Council, 261 Madison S., Bainbridge Island WA 98110, links literary visual work by contemporary NW artists. Each year 12 poets are selected by jury for inclusion in this full-color wall calendar and receive $50 awards. $6 fee for up to 6 poems, late January deadline. Send SASE in fall for required entry form.

OHIOANA BOOK AWARDS; OHIOANA KROUT MEMORIAL AWARD FOR POETRY; OHIOANA QUARTERLY; OHIOANA LIBRARY ASSOCIATION (IV-Regional), Ohioana Library Association, Rm. 1105, 65 S. Front St., Columbus OH 43215. Ohioana Book Awards given yearly to outstanding books published each year. Up to 6 awards may be given for books (including books of poetry) by authors born in Ohio or who have lived in Ohio for at least 5 years, and the Ohioana Poetry Award (with the same residence requirements), made possible by a bequest of Helen Krout, of $1,000 is given yearly "to an individual whose body of work has made, and continues to make, a significant contribution to the poetry of Ohio, and through whose work as a writer, teacher, administrator, or in community service, interest in poetry has been developed." Nominations to be received by December 31. *Ohioana Quarterly* regularly reviews Ohio magazines and books by Ohio authors. It is available through membership in Ohioana Library Association ($20/year).

NATALIE ORNISH POETRY AWARD (IV-Regional); SOEURETTE DIEHL FRASER TRANSLATION AWARD (IV-Translations, regional) TEXAS INSTITUTE OF LETTERS, % James Hoggard, T.I.L., P.O. Box 9032, Wichita Falls TX 76308-9032. The Texas Institute of Letters gives annual awards for books by Texas authors in 8 categories, including the Natalie Ornish Poetry Award, a $1,000 award for best volume of poetry. Books must have been first published in the year in question, and entries may be made by authors or by their publishers; deadline January 4 of the following year. One copy of each entry must be mailed to each of three judges, with "information showing an author's Texas association . . . if it is not otherwise obvious." Poets must have lived in Texas for at least two consecutive years at some time or their work must reflect a notable concern with matters associated with the state. Soeurette Diehl Fraser Translation Award ($1,000) for best translation of a work into English. Same rules as those for Natalie Ornish poetry award. Write during the fall for complete instructions.

OTTAWA-CARLETON BOOK AWARD (IV-Regional), %Carol Sage, Arts Advisory Board, Regional Municipality of Ottawa-Carleton, 111 Lisgar St., Ottawa, Ontario K2P 2L7 Canada, 2 awards (1 for English, 1 for French) given annually to residents of the Ottawa-Carleton Region, deadline January 15.

OZARK CREATIVE WRITERS, INC. CONFERENCE AWARDS (IV-Membership), 6817 Gingerbread Lane, Little Rock AR 72204, conference director Peggy Vining. Registrants ($25 prior to September 1) for the 19th annual writers' conference may enter various writing contests with prizes of $25, 15 and $10 ("some higher"). Deadline for entry is postmark date August 29. Conference is held in Eureka Springs, Arkansas, at the Inn of the Ozarks. Send SASE for brochure after April 1.

‡**P.A.L.S. CLUB NEWSLETTER CONTESTS; POEM AND LETTER SOCIETY OF AMERICA (I)**, P.O. Box 60535, Nashville TN 37206-0535, founded 1988, offers 2-4 poetry contests per year, with $5 fee for nonmembers for up to 3 poems, prizes of at least $50, $25 and $10 and at least 50 Certificates of Merit. Membership is $20 a year. Members pay no entry fees for contests and receive the newsletter free.

‡**PACIFIC NORTHWEST WRITERS CONFERENCE ADULT LITERARY CONTEST (I)**, Suite 804, 2033 Sixth Ave., Seattle WA 98121, phone (206)443-3807, contest for at least 1 but no more than 5 complete poems for a 5 page maximum length. Prizes: Distinguished, $300; Excellence, $200; Merit, $150 plus certificates of recognition. Fees are $10 for PNWC members, $20 for nonmembers.

‡**PANHANDLE PROFESSIONAL WRITERS (I)**, % Contest Chairman, P.O. Box 19303, Amarillo TX 79114, open to all poets, any subject or form, 50 line maximum, awards of $25, $20 and $15, fee $5 for 2 poems, June 15 deadline.

PAUMANOK POETRY AWARD COMPETITION; THE VISITING WRITERS PROGRAM (II), SUNY College of Technology, Farmingdale NY 11735, phone (516)420-2031, director Dr. Charles Fishman. The Paumanok Poetry Award Competition offers a prize of $750 plus expenses for a reading in their 1993-94 series. Submit cover letter, 1 page bio, 7-10 poems, published or unpublished and $10 entry fee by September 15. Check payable to SUNY Farmingdale Visiting Writers Program (VWP). Poets who have read in their series include Hayden Carruth, Allen Ginsburg, Linda Pastan, Marge Piercy, Joyce Carol Oates, Louis Simpson, David Ignatow and many others.

PENNSYLVANIA POETRY SOCIETY ANNUAL CONTEST; WINE AND ROSES POETRY CONTEST; PEGASUS CONTEST FOR STUDENTS, 623 N. 4th St., Reading PA 19601, award director Dr. Dorman John Grace. The deadline for the society's annual contest, which has 11 categories open to nonmembers and 4 to members only, is January 15. Grand prize in category 1 (open) will be $100 in 1993; prizes in other categories range from $10-25, plus publication. Entry fees are $1.50/poem for nonmembers except for the grand prize, which requires an entry fee of $2/poem for everybody. For information regarding the Pennsylvania Poetry Society Contest contact Deloris Selinsky, contest chairman, 200-82 Harris Hill Rd., Shavertown PA 18708. The Wine and Roses poetry contest, sponsored by the Wallace Stevens Chapter for unpublished poems in serious and light verse, has prizes of $50, $25, and $15 plus publication and telecast; entry fee $1/poem; deadline June 1; write to Dr. Dorman John Grace. For information about the Pegasus Contest for Students, write to Anne Pierre Spangler, contest chairman, 1685 Christian Dr., R.D. #2, Lebanon PA 17042. The Pennsylvania Poetry Society publishes a quarterly newsletter and an annual **Prize Poems** soft cover book, containing 69 prize and honorable mention poems. Prize poems in the Wine and Roses and Pegasus contests are published in *PPS Newsletter*.

POETIC PERSPECTIVE, INC. (I), 110 Onieda St., Waxahachie TX 75165, founded in 1989 by Pat Haley, editor. Several poetry contests each year with $3 per poem entry fee, prizes of $50, $25, and $10. Up to 35 lines, maximum of 50 characters and spaces per line. SASE for themes and guidelines. Anthology published yearly in December.

POETRY ARTS PROJECT (IV-Political, social), United Resource Press, #388, 4521 Campus Dr., Irvine CA 92715, holds an annual contest, March 31 deadline, for poems on political and social issues, humorous/serious with prizes of "possible publication and definite prizes in U.S. Savings Bonds of various denominations," $4 per poem jury fee. "Absolutely must send SASE to receive entry form. Poetry will not be returned."

THE POETRY CENTER BOOK AWARD (II), 1600 Holloway Ave., San Francisco CA 94132. Method for entering contest is to submit a published book and a $5 entry fee; book must be published and copyrighted during the year of the contest and submitted by December 31. "Beginners may enter but in the past winners have published several previous books." Translations are acceptable but "we cannot judge works that are not in English." Books should be by an individual living writer and must be entirely poetry. Prize (only one) is $500 and an invitation to read for the Poetry Center. No entry form is required.

‡POETRY OF HOPE AWARD (II, IV-Themes, young adult), P.O. Box 21077, Piedmont CA 94620, awarded annually, $200 first prize ($100 for junior division), December 30 deadline, is for a poem up to 100 lines expressing "the spirit of hope" using inspirational themes. Themes should speak to the "healing" of social problems (i.e. war/peace, human rights, the homeless, the earth/ecology, etc.), Hope for the highest good for all of creation. Application needed. No fee. Send SASE.

POETRY SOCIETY OF TEXAS (I, IV-Membership), Asst. Corresponding Secretary Faye Carr Adams, 4244 Skillman, Dallas TX 75206, offers approximately 90 contests, prizes $25-350, some open to nonmembers for a fee of $2 per poem, awards at an annual awards dinner in November. Send #10 SASE for rules booklet.

‡THE POETRY SOCIETY OF VIRGINIA ANNUAL CONTEST (IV-Forms), 6042 Newport Crescent, Norfolk VA 23505, phone (804)489-8426, offers 14 contests with 32 cash prizes for various categories including Haiku, sonnet, limerick and popular song lyric. Contest information available for SASE. Fees: Adults, $2/poem; $1/high school entry; no fee for elementary school entries.

POETS AND PATRONS, INC.; ANNUAL CHICAGOLAND CONTESTS; INTERNATIONAL NARRATIVE CONTEST (II, IV-Regional, form), The Annual Chicagoland Contests, chairman Carol Spelius, 373 Ramsay Rd., Deerfield IL 60015, are open to all poets residing within 60 miles of Chicago. Send SASE for rules after March 1. One $3 registration fee for 20 contests in various categories with prizes of $25 and $10 in each, prizes of $75 and $25 for 2 poems judged best of 1st Prize winners and $25 and $15 to 2 judged best of the 2nd Prize winners. Deadline August 1. The International Narrative contest (chairman Glen Faure, 522 Division St., Crete IL 60417) is open to all. Send SASE after March 1 for rules, deadline September 1 (postmark), no entry fee, prizes of $50, $35 and $15.

POETS CLUB OF CHICAGO INTERNATIONAL SHAKESPEAREAN SONNET CONTEST (II, IV-Form), chairman June Shipley, 2930 Franklin St., Highland IN 46322. Contest has a deadline of September 1 (postmark). Write for rules, include SASE, not earlier than March. No entry fee. Prizes of $50, $35 and $15.

POETS' DINNER CONTEST (IV-Regional), 2214 Derby St., Berkeley CA 94705. Since 1926 there has been an annual awards banquet sponsored by the ad hoc Poets' Dinner Committee; usually at Spenger's Fish Grotto (a Berkeley Landmark). Three typed copies of poems in not more than 3 of the 8 categories are submitted anonymously without fee (January 15 deadline), and the winning poems (grand prize, 1st, 2nd, 3rd) are read at the banquet and honorable mentions awarded. **Contestant must be present to win.** Prizes awarded cash; honorable mention, books. The event is nonprofit.

‡THE POETS' PRIZE (II), The Poets' Prize Committee and the Nicholas Roerich Museum, 319 W. 107th St., New York NY 10025, phone (516)751-2727, award directors Robert McDowell, Frederick Morgan and Louis Simpson. Annual cash award of $3,000 given for a book of verse by an American poet published in the previous year. The poet must be an American citizen. Poets making inquiries will receive an explanation of procedures. Books may be sent to the committee members. A list of the members and their addresses will be sent upon request with SASE. Deadline July 15.

THE E.J. PRATT GOLD MEDAL AND PRIZE FOR POETRY (IV-Students), Office of Student Awards, University of Toronto, Toronto, Ontario M5T 2Z9 Canada, to a full- or part-time graduate or undergraduate student for a poem or suite of poems of approximately 100 lines. Entries are submitted under a pseudonym with information on the poet's identity in a separate envelope. Deadline in March.

PRESIDIO LA BAHIA AWARD; SUMMERFIELD G. ROBERTS AWARD (IV-Regional), Sons of the Republic of Texas, Suite 222, 5942 Abrams Rd., Dallas TX 75231. Both may be awarded for poetry. The Presidio La Bahia Award is an annual award or awards (depending upon the number and quality of entries) for writing that promotes research into and preservation of the Spanish Colonial influence on Texas culture. $2,000 is available, with a minimum first prize of $1,200. Entries must be in quadruplicate and will not be returned. Deadline September 30. The Summerfield G. Roberts Award, available to US citizens, is an annual award of $2,500 for a book or manuscript depicting or representing the Republic of Texas (1836-46), written or published during the calendar year for which the award is given. Entries must be submitted in quintuplicate and will not be returned. Deadline January 15.

‡PRO DOGS CREATIVE WRITING & PHOTOGRAPHIC COMPETITION (I), Pro Dogs National Charity, 267 Hillbury Rd., Warlingham, Surrey CR6 9TL England, phone 0883-622121, award director Michaela Edridge. Biennial contest (1994) for poems up to 32 lines with prize of £250. Contest information available for SASE. Fees: £1.50 for first entry; 75 p. for subsequent entries. Deadline October 1.

PULITZER PRIZE IN LETTERS (II), % Secretary of the Pulitzer Prize Board, 702 Journalism, Columbia University, New York NY 10027, offers 5 prizes of $3,000 each year, including 1 in poetry, for books published in the calendar year preceding the award. Submit 4 copies of published books (or galley proofs if book is being published after November), photo, bio, entry form and $20 entry fee. July 1 deadline for books published between January 1 and June 30; November 1 deadline for books published between July 1 and December 30.

REDWOOD ACRES FAIR POETRY CONTEST (I), P.O. Box 6576, Eureka CA 95502, offers an annual contest with various categories for both juniors and seniors with entry fee of 50¢ per poem for the junior contests and $1 per poem for the senior contests, May 27 deadline.

‡REGIONAL ARTISTS' PROJECTS GRANT (I, IV-Regional), Randolph Street Gallery, 756 N. Milwaukee Ave., Chicago IL 60622, phone (312)666-7737, RAP coordinator Kapra Fleming, offers grants up to $4,000 maximum for regional artists working in interdisciplinary or innovative ways. Must be 1-year resident of Indiana, Illinois, Ohio, Missouri or Michigan. Deadline approximately March 15. Application available for SASE.

RHYME INTERNATIONAL COMPETITION FOR RHYMING POETRY (IV-Form), 199 The Long Shoot, Nuneaton, Warwickshire CV11 6JQ England, has 2 categories (open class, up to 50 lines, rhymed poetry; strict form class) with prizes averaging £75-300 in each class each year (at least 60% of fees received); entry fee £2.50 (or $5). Write for entry form. Deadline September 30. Ajudication takes place during a special workshop weekend in England under the supervision of a well-known poet. They claim to be "the only competition in the world exclusively for rhymed poetry."

MARY ROBERTS RINEHART FOUNDATION AWARD (II), %Roger Lathbury, Mary Roberts Rinehart Fund, English Dept., George Mason University, 4400 University Dr., Fairfax VA 22030-4444. Two grants are made annually to writers who need financial assistance "to complete work definitely projected." The amount of the award depends upon income the fund generates; the 1992 amount will be around $950 in each category. Poets and fiction writers should submit work in odd numbered years, e.g., 1993. A writer's work must be nominated by an established author or editor; no written recommendations are necessary. Nominations must be accompanied by a sample of the nominee's work, up to 25 pgs. of poetry and 30 pgs. of fiction. Deadline: November 30.

‡ROBERT FROST CHAPTER: CALIFORNIA FEDERATION OF CHAPARRAL POETS ANNUAL POETRY COMPETITION (I, IV-Students), %Vivian Moody, 342 S. Redwood Ave., San Jose CA 95128. This annual contest has 6 categories with annual changes as to form or fee, limited to 2 entries per category. Prizes are $25, $15 and $10 in each category; for Sijo, prizes are $50, $25, $15 and $10. Entry fee $2, plus $1/poem for nonmembers. Submissions may be previously published. Award poems not eligible. Open to residents of Canada and US. Deadline first half of August. The parent federation also sponsors monthly contests listed in the Chapter's *Frostorial N/L* published since 1963. Affiliation through the chapter includes state activities with yearly convention/award banquet in which the Golden Pegasus is awarded, terminating competitions since 1940.

THE ROBERTS FOUNDATION WRITING AWARDS (II, IV-Anthologies), Box 1868, Pittsburg KS 66762, an annual competition, deadline September 15, for poetry, short fiction and essays. The poetry prizes are $500, $200 and $100, fee $6 for up to 5 poems, $1 for each additional poem. Winners appear in an annual anthology that you may purchase for $4. Send SASE for guidelines and entry form.

ANNA DAVIDSON ROSENBERG AWARD (IV-Ethnic), Judah L. Magnes Museum, 2911 Russell St., Berkeley CA 94705, offers prizes of $100, $50 and $25 (honorable mention) for up to 12 pgs. of 1-5 poems on the Jewish Experience in English. There is a Youth Commendation along with the prize if a winner is under 19. Deadline August 31 each year. **Do not send poems without entry form; write between April 1 and July 15 for entry form and guidelines (enclose SASE).**

SALMON ARM SONNET CONTEST (IV-Form), Salmon Arm & Dist. Chamber of Commerce, Box 999, Salmon Arm, British Columbia V1E 4P2 Canada, general manager Judi Lowe, is an annual contest, deadline May 1, for unpublished sonnets. Prizes: $100-300 and books. Entry fee $5/poem. Limit 2 entries.

SAN FRANCISCO INTERNATIONAL HAIKU COMPETITON; HAIKU POETS OF NORTHERN CALIFOR-NIA; WOODNOTES (IV-Form), #14, 88 Crestline Dr., San Francisco CA 94131, contest chairman Dave Sutter, sponsors a contest for haiku and senryu with prizes of $150 for first place; $75 for second; $25 for third place. Poems must be typed or printed on two 3×5 cards with category in upper left-hand corner; name, address and telephone number on the back of one card. Deadline October 31. Membership in Haiku Poets include *Woodnotes*, a quarterly publication of haiku, senryu, haibun and tanka, along with articles, book reviews, news, commentary. Membership $12 ($18 overseas), with single copies $3.

SAN MATEO COUNTY FAIR FINE ARTS COMPETITION (I), Box 1027, San Mateo CA 94403-0627, phone (415)574-3247, for unpublished poetry. Adult and youth divisions. Write or call for entry form and additional information. Adult Division awards of $100, $50, and $25; fee $10 for each poem. Youth Division awards of $50, $25 and $15; no fee. Limit 2 entries per division. July 10 deadline for poems.

CARL SANDBURG AWARDS (IV-Regional), sponsored by Friends of the Chicago Public Library, 9S-7, 400 S. State St., Chicago IL 60605, are given annually to Chicago-area writers for new books in 4 categories, including poetry. Each author receives $1,000. Publisher or authors should submit 2 copies of books published between June 1 of one year and May 31 of the next. Deadline September 1.

SASKATCHEWAN WRITERS GUILD ANNUAL LITERARY AWARDS; CITY OF REGINA WRITING AWARD (IV-Regional), SWG Literary Awards Convenor, Box 3986, Regina, Saskatchewan S4P 3R9 Canada, offers 3 prizes of $1,000 for long ms (every fourth year for poetry) and 3 prizes of $150 and $75 honorable mentions for 1 poem up to 100 lines. $15 entry fee for long mss, $4 for single poems. Deadline February 28. CRWA of $3,300 awarded annually to a writer living in Regina as of January 1 of the previous year to work for 3 months on a specific project. Deadline March 15.

SCHOLASTIC WRITING AWARDS (IV-Teens), Scholastic Inc., 730 Broadway, New York NY 10003, writing competition for grades 7-12. Categories include short story, essay, poetry, short short story, humor and dramatic script. Scholarships and prize money available. Write for entry information in September.

SCOTTISH INTERNATIONAL OPEN POETRY COMPETITION; THE AYRSHIRE WRITERS' & ARTISTS' SOCIETY, 42 Tollerton Dr., Irvine, Ayrshire Scotland. Open to all poets. Inaugurated in 1972 it is the longest running poetry competition in the U.K. Entries are free, restricted to two per person and should be accompanied by International Reply Coupons and SAE. December deadline. Special award ceremony March. First prize, U.K. Section, MacDiarmid Trophy and $100. First prize, International Section, The International Trophy. Scots Section, The Clement Wilson Cup. Diplomas are awarded to runners up. Competition opens September each year.

SOCIETY OF MIDLAND AUTHORS AWARD (IV-Regional), c/o Jim Bowman, 152 N. Scoville, Oak Park IL 60302, is for authors from Midland states: IL, IN, IA, KS, MI, MN, MO, NE, ND, SD, OH, WI. It is an annual award of $300 minimum and a plaque given at a dinner at the Drake Hotel in Chicago. Books in each calendar year are eligible, not self-published. Deadline December 15 of year preceding award year. Send SASE for entry form; books must be submitted to each of 3 judges.

SPARROWGRASS POETRY FORUM (I), Dept. HM, 203 Diamond St., Box 193, Sistersville WV 26175, offers 6 annual free contests, each of which has $1,000 in prizes, including a $500 grand prize. Entrants are solicited to buy an anthology, but you do not have to buy the anthology to win. Contest deadlines are the last day of every other month. Send 1 original poem, no longer than 20 lines. Name and address at the top of the page. Any style, any subject.

SPRINGFEST AND OCTOBERFEST POETRY CONTESTS; MILE HIGH POETRY SOCIETY (I), P.O. Box 21116, Denver CO 80221, phone (303)426-8214, award director Jane C. Schaul. Each spring and fall they offer a contest $300 1st prize, $100 2nd prize, and two 3rd prizes of $50 each for maximum 36-line poems, $3/poem entry fee, deadlines May 31 and November 30.

WALLACE E. STEGNER FELLOWSHIPS (II), Creative Writing Program, Stanford University, Stanford CA 94305, 4 in poetry, $10,000 plus tuition of $3,800, for promising writers who can benefit from 2 years instruction and criticism at the Writing Center. Previous publication not required, though it can strengthen one's application. Deadline: Postmarked by January 2.

‡TOWSON STATE UNIVERSITY PRIZE FOR LITERATURE; ALICE & FRANKLIN COOLEY ENDOW-MENT (IV-Regional), Towson State University, Towson MD 21204, $1,200 for a book or book ms by a Maryland writer under 40. If published, the book must have appeared within 3 years of application. Award is on the basis of aesthetic excellence. Deadline May 1. Contact for guidelines.

THE TRANSLATORS ASSOCIATION; JOHN FLORIO PRIZE; SCHLEGEL-TIECK PRIZE, SCOTT-MON-CRIEFF PRIZE; BERNARD SHAW PRIZE; PORTUGUESE TRANSLATION PRIZE (IV-Translation), 84 Drayton Gardens, London SW 10 9SB, England. The first three of these prizes are all for translation of 20th century literature published in the U.K. The John Florio Prize of £900 is for the best translation from Italian, awarded every other year. The annual Schlegel-Tieck Prize of £2,000 is for translation from German. The biannual Scott-Moncrieff Prize of £1,500 is for translation from French. The association also administers the Bernard Shaw Prize (£1,000 every 3 years) for translations from any period from Swedish into English, and the Portuguese Translation Prize (£3,000 every 3 years).

‡TRILLIUM BOOK AWARD; PRIX TRILLIUM (IV-Regional), Ministry of Culture and Communications, 77 Bloor St. W, 3rd Floor, Libraries Branch, Toronto, Ontario M5A 1K3 Canada, is given annually for a book by an Ontario author. Submissions of published books are by publishers, December 31 deadline. Award given in April.

LAURA BOWER VAN NUYS CREATIVE WRITING CONTEST (I, II), Black Hills Writers Group, % Larry Budd, 1015 N. 7th, Rapid City SD 57701. **"We will be holding the contest in even-numbered years only."** Categories: professional and non-professional. $15, $12, and $10 in each category plus a subscription to *The Writer* for the Best of Show award. Fee: $2 per poem. March deadline.

THE VICTORIAN FELLOWSHIP OF AUSTRALIAN WRITERS; FAW AWARDS (IV-Regional, ethnic), 1/317 Barkers Rd., Kew 3101, Australia, all awards for Australian authors. The FAW Barbara Rams-den Award (plaques to author and publisher) is "the major literary award for a book of quality" (book of the year). The FAW Australian Natives Association Literature Award ($1,000) is for "a book of sustained quality and distinction with an Australian theme." The FAW Anne Elder Poetry Award (prizes of $1,000 and $500) is for a first published book of poetry. The FAW Christopher Brennan Award (known in its first years as the Robert Frost Award) is a bronze plaque to honor an Australian poet (entries not required; award by committee). FAW Alan Marshall Award ($500) is a manuscript award for fiction or a long poem with a strong narrative element. The FAW John Shaw Neilson Poetry Award ($600, $20) is for an unpublished poem of at least 14 lines, December 31 deadline. The FAW Fedora Anderson Young Writers' Poetry Award ($100, $30, $20) is for unpublished poems by Austra-lian writers 15-22 years old, January 31 deadline. The Patricia Weickhardt Award to an Aboriginal

Writer is "to honour the achievement of Aboriginal writers (entries not required, award by committee)."

‡**THE W.D. WEATHERFORD AWARD (IV-Regional)**, Berea College, CPO 2336, Berea KY 40404, for the published work (including poetry) which "best illuminates the problems, personalities, and unique qualities of the Appalachian South." The award is for $500 and sometimes there are special awards of $200 each.

WESTERN STATES BOOK AWARDS; WESTERN STATES ARTS FEDERATION (IV-Regional), 236 Montezuma Ave., Santa Fe NM 87501, presents annual book awards to outstanding authors and publishers. The awards include cash prizes $5,000 for writers for their respective publishers. Mss must be written by an author living in Alaska, Arizona, California, Colorado, Idaho, Montana, Nevada, New Mexico, Oregon, Utah, Washington or Wyoming. Work must already have been accepted for publication by a publisher in one of these states. Work must be submitted by the publisher, submitted in ms form (not previously published in book form). Publisher must have published at least 3 books. Write for more information.

‡**WFNB ANNUAL LITERARY CONTEST; THE ALFRED G. BAILEY AWARD; WRITERS' FEDERATION OF NEW BRUNSWICK (IV-Regional)**, P.O. Box 37, Station A, Fredericton, New Brunswick E3B 4Y2 Canada, offers prizes of $200, $100, $30, for unpublished poems of up to 100 lines (typed, double-spaced). The Alfred G. Bailey Award is given annually for poetry mss of 48 pgs. or more. May include some individual poems that have been published. $10 Canadian entry fee. Deadline February 14. Send SASE for guidelines.

WHITE RABBIT POETRY CONTEST; THE HARBINGER (II), P.O. Box U-1030 USAL, Mobile AL 36688, is an annual, the winners and honorable mentions being virtually the only poetry published by *The Harbinger*. Awards are $100, $50 and $25. Deadline March 31. Send SASE for entry form, which must accompany submisssions (2 copies, author's name on 1 only).

WHITING WRITERS' AWARDS; MRS. GILES WHITING FOUNDATION (V), Room 3500, 30 Rockefeller Plaza, New York NY 10112, director Gerald Freund. The Foundation makes awards of $30,000 each up to up to 10 writers of fiction, nonfiction, poetry and plays chosen by a selection committee drawn from a list of recognized writers, literary scholars and editors. Recipients of the award were selected from nominations made by writers, educators and editors from communities across the country whose experience and vocations bring them in contact with individuals of unusual talent. The nominators and selectors are appointed by the foundation and serve anonymously. **Direct applications and informal nominations are not accepted by the foundation.**

‡**OSCAR WILLIAMS & GENE DERWOOD AWARD (V)**, Community Funds, Inc., 2 Park Ave., New York NY 10016, is an award given annually to nominees of the selection committee "to help needy or worthy artists or poets." Selection Committee for the award does not accept nominations. Amount varies from year to year.

WORLD ORDER OF NARRATIVE AND FORMALIST POETS (II, IV-Subscription, form), P.O. Box 174, Station A, Flushing NY 11358, contest chairman Dr. Alfred Dorn. This organization sponsors contests in at least 15 categories of traditional and contemporary poetic forms, including the sonnet, blank verse, ballade, villanelle, limerick, free verse and new contrapuntal forms created by Alfred Dorn. Prizes total at least $4,000 and range from $20 to $200. Only subscribers to *The Formalist* will be eligible for the competition, as explained in the complete guidelines available from the contest chairman. "We look for originality of thought, phrase and image, combined with masterful craftsmanship. Trite, trivial or technically inept work stands no chance." Postmark deadline for entries: May 6.

‡**WORLD'S WORST POETRY CONTEST (IV-Regional)**, Pismo Beach Hardware and Nursery, 930 Price St., Pismo Beach CA 93449, award directors "Pismo Bob" Pringle and Rudy Natoli. Contest for "bad" poetry that mentions Pismo Beach with vacations in Pismo Beach, California, and miscellaneous other awards. Deadline June 15.

WRITERS' GUILD OF ALBERTA BOOK AWARD (IV-Regional), Writer's Guild, 10523 100th Ave., Edmonton, Alberta T5J 0A8 Canada, phone (403)426-5892, awarded in six categories, including poetry. Eligible books will have been published anywhere in the world between January 1 and December 31. Their authors will have been resident in Alberta for at least 12 of the 18 months prior to December 31. Contact either the WGA head office or the Alberta Playwrights' Network for registry forms. Unpublished manuscripts are not eligible. Except in the drama category, anthologies are not eligible. Four copies of each book to be considered must be mailed to the WGA office no later than December

31. Submissions postmarked after this date will not be accepted. **Exceptions will be made for any books** *published* **between the 15th and 31st of December. These may be submitted by January 15.** Three copies will go to the three judges in that category; one will remain in the WGA library. Works may be submitted by authors, publishers, or any interested parties.

‡**THE YORKSHIRE OPEN POETRY COMPETITION (II)**, Ilkley Literature Festival, 9A Leeds Rd., Ilkley, W. Yorkshire LS29 8DH England, award director P.A. Borthwick, offers prizes of £150, £75, £30 and 10 prizes of £10 for any style of poetry. Fees are £2/poem, £5 for 3. Deadline July 31.

ZUZU'S PETALS QUARTERLY WRITING AWARDS (II), P.O. Box 4476, Allentown PA 18105-4476. Quarterly contests have deadlines on the first of each March, June, September and December. Entry fee: $1/poem, any style, length or subject. 40% of proceeds go to prize winners: 25% to first prize, 10% to second, $5 to third. Free critiques to honorable mentions. The remaining 60% of proceeds goes toward their magazine: *ZuZu's Petals Quarterly, A Journal of the Written Arts*.

Additional Contests and Awards

The following publishers and organizations also contain information on Contests and Awards. Read the listings and/or send SASEs for more details about their offerings. See the General Index for page numbers.

Academy of American Poets, The
Advocate, The
Aguilar Expression, The
Albatross
Algilmore
Alicejamesbooks
Alms House Press
Amaranth Review, The
Amelia
American Academy & Institute of Arts & Letters, The
American Collegiate Poets
American Knight
American Poetry Center
American Poetry Review
American Tolkien Society
Analecta
And Review, The
Anhinga Press
Apropos
Arc
Arkansas Press, The University of
Associated Writing Programs
Atlanta Writing Resource Center, Inc.
Bay Area Poets Coalition (BAPC)
Bell's Letters Poet
Black Bear Publications
Black Warrior Review, The
Blue Unicorn, A Triquarterly of Poetry
Breakthrough!
Brussels Sprout
Calapooya Collage
Canada Council, The
Cape Rock, The
Caravan Press
Ceilidh: An Informal Gathering for Story & Song
Chaminade Literary Review
Chelsea
Chicago Review
Chimera Poetry Magazine for Children

Chiron Review
Cleveland State University Poetry Center
Cochran's Corner
Columbia: A Magazine of Poetry & Prose
Connecticut River Review
Convictions
Country Woman
Crazyhorse
Crazyquilt Quarterly
Creative With Words Publications (C.W.W.)
Creativity Unlimited Press
Cricket, The Magazine for Children
Crucible
Crystal Rainbow
Cumberland Poetry Review
Cutbank
Delhi-London Poetry Quarterly
Devil's Millhopper Press, The
Dialogue: A Journal of Mormon Thought
Dream Shop, The
Eighth Mountain Press, The
eleventh muse, the
Embers
Emerald City Comix & Stories
Epiphany: A Journal of Literature
Epoch
Experiment in Words
Explorations
Explorer Magazine
Expressions Forum Review
Fairbanks Arts Association
Federation of British Columbia Writers
Feelings: America's Beautiful Poetry Magazine
First Time
Flume Press
Folio: A Literary Journal
Footwork: The Paterson Literary Review

For Poets Only
Formalist, The
Frogmore Papers
Frogpond: Quarterly Haiku Journal
Golden Isis Magazine
Gopherwood Review, The
Grain
Greensboro Review, The
Haiku Headlines: A Monthly Newsletter of Haiku and Senryu
Haiku Journal
Half Tones to Jubilee
Harp-Strings
Heaven Bone Press
Helicon Nine Editions
Hellas: A Journal of Poetry and the Humanities
Hippopotamus Press
Home Planet News
Housewife-Writer's Forum
Hudson Review, The
Hutton Publications
Icon
Imago Literary Magazine
International Black Writers
Iowa Press, University of
Iowa Woman
Jeopardy
Kansas Quarterly
Keystrokes
Lane Literary Guild, The
League of Canadian Poets, The
Light and Life Magazine
Lines n' Rhymes
Literary Focus Poetry Publications
Literature and Belief
Loft, The
Louisiana Literature
Lucidity
Lyric, The
MacGuffin, The
Madison Review, The
Malahat Review, The
Mayberry Gazette, The

Mid-American Review
Midwest Poetry Review
Missouri Press, University of
Mr. Cogito Press
Modern Haiku
Mss/New Myths
Mulberry Press
My Legacy
Nation, The
National Federation of State
Poetry Societies, Inc.
Nebraska Review, The
Negative Capability
New Delta Review
New Era Magazine
New Horizons Poetry Club
New Letters
New Mexico Humanities
Review
New Press Literary Quarterly,
The
New Voices in Poetry and Prose
Nimrod International Journal
of Contemporary Poetry
and Fiction
North Carolina Haiku Society
Press, The
North Carolina Writers'
Network
Northeastern University Press
Nostalgia: A Sentimental State
of Mind
Oak, The
Occident Magazine
Ohio State University Press/
Journal Award in Poetry
Onionhead
Orbis
Owl Creek Press
Painted Hills Review
Paisley Moon
Panhandler, The
Paper Salad Poetry Journal,
The
Paris Review, The
Parnassus Literary Journal
Pasque Petals
Paupers Press
Pearl
PEN American Center
Pendragon
Philomel
Phoebe
Piedmont Literary Review
Pig Iron
Pikeville Review
Pitt Poetry Series
Plainsongs
Plowman, The
Poet
Poetic Page
Poetpourri
Poetry

Poetry Break
Poetry Center of the 92nd
Street Y, The
Poetry Committee of the
Greater Washington Area,
The
Poetry Forum
Poetry Kanto
Poetry Miscellany, The
Poetry Nippon Press
Poetry Northwest
Poetry Nottingham
Poetry Review
Poetry Society of America
Poetry: USA Quarterly
Poets at Work
Poets House
Poet's Review
Poets' Roundtable
Potpourri
Prairie Schooner
Princeton University Press
Prosetry: Newsletter For, By
and About Writers
Psych It
Pudding House Publications
Purdue University Press
Pygmy Forest Press
Quarterly Review of Literature
Poetry Series
Radcliffe Quarterly
Rainbow City Express
Rambunctious Press
Raven, The
Renegade
Rhino
Rio Grande Press
River City
Rockford Review, The
San Diego Poet's Press
San Jose Studies
Saturday Press, Inc.
Scavenger's Newsletter
Scop Publications, Inc.
Secrets from the Orange Couch
Sewanee Review
Sideshow Magazine
Signpost Press, The
Silver Apples Press
Silverfish Review
Sisyphus
Skoob Books Publishing Ltd.
Slate & Style
Slipstream
Smith Publisher, Gibbs
Society of American Poets, The
Songwriters and Poets Critique
Sonora Review
South Coast Poetry Journal
Southern California Anthology,
The
Southern Humanities Review
Southern Poetry Association

Southern Poetry Review
Southwest Review
Sow's Ear, The
Sparrow: The Politically
Incorrect Verse Magazine
Spitball
Staple
State Street Press
Still Waters Press
Story Line Press
Studio: A Journal of Christians
Writing
Sub-Terrain
Sucarnochee Review, The
Taproot Literary Review
Tesseract Publications
Texas Tech University Press
Thorntree Press
Thumbprints
Tickled By Thunder: Writer's
News & Roundtable
Timberlines
Untitled
Vandeloecht's Fiction
Magazine
Vegetarian Journal
Ver Poets Voices
Verve
W.I.M. Publications (Woman
in the Moon)
Welter
West Wind Review
Westerly
Weyfarers
Whetstone (Canada)
White Eagle Coffee Store Press
Whitecrow Foundation,
Tahana
Whitman Cultural Arts Center,
Walt
Wildwood Journal
Willow Review
Wisconsin Press, University of
Woodley Memorial Press
Worcester Review
Word Works, The
Wordsmith
Wordsmith Publishing, Inc.
World-wide Writers Service,
Inc.
WoRM fEASt!
Wormwood Review Press
Write Technique, The
Write Way, The
Writers' Center Press
Writer's Digest
Writer's Exchange
Writer's Journal
Writers' Rendezvous
Xenophilia
Yale University Press
Yankee Magazine

Resources

Writing Colonies

If you read the biographies of great poets in this century, say ones on Robert Lowell or Sylvia Plath, you will read about the friends, enemies or bonds they made at writing colonies. For example, Yaddo is particularly rich with history and lore of the masters who worked there and the poems they produced while in residence.

Such colonies offer artists the chance to escape the daily demands of one's family or occupation. As with all aspects of poetry, competition is going to be keen. At some colonies, you will be asking for living quarters alongside some of the country's most prestigious writers. Thus, applications and samples of your work usually will be required. Fellowships or other financial arrangements are offered to help defray or cover costs, again made possible through the generosity of private citizens and/or organizations that underwrite the arts.

You should have projects currently under way before you apply. If accepted, remember you're going to be writing, not socializing, so bring all the books, references, research and other materials that you will need while at work. You may also need to bring along your own typewriter or personal computer.

If you are interested in any of the colonies listed here, be sure to write for more information. Residency times may vary, so you may have to make sacrifices (giving up vacation plans, for example) to take advantage of the opportunity.

For other listings of writing colonies, consult **The Guide to Writers Conferences** (Shaw Associates, publishers, Suite 1406, 625 Biltmore Way, Coral Gables FL 33134) or **100 Havens for Creatives**, available from ACTS Institute Inc. (P.O. Box 10153, Kansas City MO 64111).

THE EDWARD F. ALBEE FOUNDATION, INC.; THE WILLIAM FLANAGAN MEMORIAL CREATIVE PERSONS CENTER ("THE BARN"), 14 Harrison St., New York NY 10013, phone (212)226-2020, for information and application forms. The Albee Foundation maintains the center (better known as "The Barn") in Montauk, on Long Island, offering 1-month residencies for writers, painters, sculptors and composers, open June 1 through October 1, accommodating 6 persons at a time. Applications accepted at the Harrison Street address by regular mail only January 1-April 1. Fellowship announcements by May 15. "Located approximately 2 miles from the center of Montauk and the Atlantic Ocean, 'The Barn' rests in a secluded knoll that offers privacy and a peaceful atmosphere. The foundation expects all those accepted for residence to work seriously and to conduct themselves in such a manner as to aid fellow residents in their endeavors. The environment is simple and communal. Residents are expected to do their share in maintaining the condition of 'The Barn' as well as its peaceful environment."

ATLANTIC CENTER FOR THE ARTS, 1414 Art Center Ave., New Smyrna Beach FL 32168, phone (904)427-6975. The center was founded in 1979 by sculptor and painter, Doris Leeper, who secured a seed grant from The Rockefeller Foundation. That same year the center was chartered by the state of Florida and building began on a 10-acre site. The center was officially opened in 1982. Since 1982, 46 Master Artists-in-Residence sessions have been held. At each of the 3-week sessions internationally known artists from different disciplines conduct interdisciplinary workshops, lecture and critique works in progress. They also give readings and recitals, exhibit their work and develop projects with their "associates"—mid-career artists who come from all over the US to work with the Masters. The center is run by an advisory council which chooses Masters for residencies, helps set ᮍ᛫ ᮍies and guides the center in its growth. The process of becoming an associate is different for ea᛫ ᮍaster artist. Recent poets in residence at the center include Ron Padgett (March-April 1990) a᛫ ᮍmy Clampitt (January 1992).

BANFF CENTRE FOR THE ARTS MAY STUDIOS, Box 1020, 107 Tunnel Mountain Dr., Banff, Alber᛫ T0L 0C0 Canada, offers 4-6 weeks of residence between April 22 and May 31 to writers "who already have a body of work (some of it preferably, but not necesssarily, published) attesting to their commitment and talent. Applicant should have a project in progress . . . . Enrollment is limited to 10 participants." Fee $1,512; room and board $1,845. "Full scholarships for fee and room and board are offered to all successful candidates." Located in an inspirational mountain setting, The Banff Centre for Continuing Education is a unique Canadian institution. Participants are housed in single rooms that also serve as their private work spaces. Three meals per day are provided on campus. Application deadline: mid-January.

BELLAGIO STUDY AND CONFERENCE CENTER, The Rockefeller Foundation, 1133 Avenue of the Americas, New York NY 10036, manager Susan Garfield, offers 5-week residencies in the Italian Alps from January 20 through December 20 for artists and scholars. Room available for spouses. Residents must pay their own travel costs.

CENTRUM, % Sarah Muirhead, coordinator, Residency Program, P.O. Box 1158, Port Townsend WA 98368, offers 1-month residencies, September through May, for architects, writers, musicians and printmakers. Centrum provides individual cottages, a stipend of $75/week and solitude. Families welcome. Located in Fort Worden State Park on the Strait of Juan de Fuca. Also sponsors the annual Port Townsend Writers' Conference held in July and other workshops and seminars.

CHATEAU DE LESVAULT, 58370 Onlay, France, phone (33)86-84-32-91, this French country residence is located in the national park "Le Morvan" of western Burgundy, halfway between Nevers and Autun and is surrounded by green hills and forests. The chateau accommodates 5 residents at a time in 5 large rooms with private baths, fully furnished and equipped for working. The facilities of the chateau are at the disposal of residents, including the salon, library and grounds. Requests for residencies from October through April should be made at least 3 months in advance. The cost is 4,000 FF per month for room, board (5 days a week) and utilities.

THE CLEARING, Box 65, Ellison Bay WI 54210, phone (414)854-4088, resident managers Donald and Louise Buchholz, "is first a school, then a place of self-discovery." Made up of cabins and lodges in a rustic setting overlooking Green Bay, it offers a variety of courses, including courses in writing and poetry, May-October. Fees include tuition, room (dormitory or twin-bedded room) and board.

COLONYHOUSE: OREGON WRITERS COLONY, c/o Rae Richen, P.O. Box 15200, Portland OR 97215, phone (503)771-0482, is a seaside cottage owned and operated by Oregon writers. It sleeps 8 and is available for weekly and weekend rentals at (Fall-Winter) $450/week, $200/weekend or (Spring-Summer) $575/week, $325/weekend. Discount for colony members ($20/year).

CUMMINGTON COMMUNITY OF THE ARTS, RR #1, Box 145, Cummington MA 01026, (413)634-2172, offers residencies to artists in all disciplines from 2 weeks to 3 months. Living/studio spaces are in individual cabins or 2 main houses, on 110 acres in the Berkshires. During July and August, artists with children from age 5-12 are encouraged to apply. Cummington's Summer Children's Program offers supervised activity for children of artists-in-residence. Application deadlines: The first of the month 2 months prior to desired month of residency, except for July and August, when applications are due April 1.

DOBIE-PAISANO PROJECT, Attn: Audrey N. Slate, Main Building 101, The University of Texas, Austin TX 78712, offers two annual fellowships of $7,200 and 6-month residency at Frank Dobie's ranch, Paisano, for Texans, Texas residents or writers whose work has been substantially identified with the state. Apply by January 22. Write for application and guidelines.

DORSET COLONY HOUSE RESIDENCIES; AMERICAN THEATRE WORKS, INC.; DORSET THEATRE FESTIVAL; Box 519, Dorset VT 05251, available to writers September-May for periods of 1 week-2 months for intensive work. Requested fee of $75 per week, but ability to pay is not a criterion in awarding residencies. Connected with Dorset Theatre Festival, a production company with an interest in new scripts.

FINE ARTS WORK CENTER IN PROVINCETOWN, Box 565, 24 Pearl St., Provincetown MA 02657, provides monthly stipends of $375 and studio/living quarters for 7 uninterrupted months for 20 young artists and writers (10 of each) who have completed their formal training and are capable of working independently. The center has a staff of writers and artists who offer manuscript consultations, arrange readings and slide presentations and visits from other distinguished writers and artists. Each year writing fellows publish *Shankpainter,* a magazine of prose and poetry. Sessions run from October 1 through May 1. Applications, accompanied by a $20 processing fee, must be received by February 1. To receive an application and program brochure, send a SASE to Writing Fellowship after August 1.

‡GREEN RIVER WRITERS RETREAT, Shelbyville Campus, University of Louisville, Green River Writers, 403 S. Sixth St., Ironton OH 45638, secretary D.H. Spears, phone (614)533-1081, provides a 2-day workshop, then 5-day retreat. Rooms are available at the conference center per night stayed plus registration fee. Beginning writers are furnished with sponsors. Details available for SASE.

THE TYRONE GUTHRIE CENTRE, Annaghmakerrig, Newbliss, Co. Monaghan, Ireland, phone (353)47-54003, resident director Bernard Loughlin, offers residencies, normally 3 weeks-3 months, for artists, including poets. "Each resident has a private apartment within the house ... and all the centrally heated comfort an Irish Big House can afford. It is set on a wooded estate of 400 acres and overlooks a large lake. The house is surrounded by gardens and a working dairy farm. Couples or small groups of artists may stay for up to a year in Maggie's Farm, a cottage on the estate, and have use of studios at the Big House. Five newly built, self-contained farmyard cottages are also available for individuals, couples and families for longer stays. To qualify for residence it is necessary to show evidence of a significant level of achievement in the relevant field. Once accepted Irish artists are asked to contribute what they can afford toward the cost of their stay. Overseas artists are expected to pay the whole cost of a residency. We will give every assistance in obtaining grants from the appropriate cultural insitutions in the artist's home country."

HAMBIDGE CENTER FOR CREATIVE ARTS AND SCIENCES, P.O. Box 339, Rabun Gap GA 30568, phone (404)746-5718. The center is located on 600 acres of unspoiled wooded slopes, mountain meadows and streams, near Dillard, Georgia. It is listed on the National Register of Historic Places. Resident Fellowships of 2 weeks-2 months are awarded to individuals engaged in the artistic, scientific, humanistic and educational professions for the purpose of solitude and the pursuit of creative excellence. Those accepted are given a private cottage equipped with a kitchen, living and studio/work space. Center is open from May-October. For more information and application forms send SASE. Application review begins in March.

HAWK, I'M YOUR SISTER; WOMEN'S WILDERNESS CANOE TRIPS; WRITING RETREATS, Beverly Antaeus, P.O. Box 9109, Santa Fe NM 87504. This organization offers wilderness retreats for women, many of them with writing themes including Paying Attention to Small Beauties, Between the Earth & Silence: A Writing Retreat with W.S. Merwin (coed); A Writing Retreat with Sharon Olds; and Friend Sits by Friend: A Writing Retreat with Coleman Barks (coed). The canoe trips are held all over North America and typically last 8-10 days with fees $995-1,250. Write for annual listing of specific trips.

THE MACDOWELL COLONY, 100 High St., Peterborough NH 03458, founded 1907, offers residencies to established writers, composers, visual artists, filmmakers, architects and interdisciplinary artists. Over 3,000 artists have stayed there, many of them producing major works. Apply about 8 months before desired residency. Application deadlines: January 15: May-August; April 15: September-December; September 15: January-April. Private studio, room and meals provided. Accepted artists are asked to contribute toward residency costs. Current application form is necessary; write address above or call (603)924-3886 or (212)966-4860. Average residency is 6 weeks. Professional work samples required with application.

THE MILLAY COLONY FOR THE ARTS, INC., Steepletop, P.O. Box 3, Austerlitz NY 12017-0003, founded in 1974, assistant director Gail Giles, provides work space, meals and sleeping accommodations at no cost for a period of 1 month. Send SASE for brochure and application forms and apply with samples of your work before February 1 for June-September; before May 1 for October-January; before September 1 for February-May.

MONTALVO CENTER FOR THE ARTS; MONTALVO BIENNIAL POETRY COMPETITION, Box 158, Saratoga CA 95071, presents theatre, musical events and other artistic activities. They have an Artist-in-Residence program which has 5 apartments available for artists (including poets) for maximum 3-month periods. (No children or pets.) Limited financial assistance available. They offer a biennial poetry competition open to residents of Oregon, Nevada, Washington and California, with a prominent judge, with a first prize of $1,000 (and artist residency), other prizes of $500, $300 and 8 honorable mentions. Submit 3 poems in duplicate, entry fee $5, October 15, 1993, deadline. Send SASE for rules.

THE NORTHWOOD INSTITUTE ALDEN B. DOW CREATIVITY CENTER, Midland MI 48640-2398, phone (517)837-4478, founded 1979, director Carol Coppage, offers fellowships for 10-week summer residencies at the Northwood Institute Campus. Travel and all expenses are paid. No families/pets. Applicants can be undergraduates, graduates, or those without any academic or institutional affiliation, including citizens of other countries (if they can communicate in English). Projects may be in any field, but must be new and innovative. Write for application. Annual deadline December 31 for following summer.

PALENVILLE INTERARTS COLONY, 2 Bond St., New York NY 10012, offers 1-8 week residencies in Palenville, New York, for seclusion or for interaction among artists of various disciplines in a relaxed and creative atmosphere. Fee (negotiable): $175 per week. Open June 1 to September 30. Application deadline is April 1.

PUDDING HOUSE PUBLICATIONS, 60 N. Main St., Johnstown OH 43031. See listing in Publishers of Poetry section.

RAGDALE FOUNDATION, 1260 N. Green Bay Rd., Lake Forest IL 60045, founded 1976, director Michael Wilkerson, provides a peaceful place and uninterrupted time for 12 writers, composers and artists. Meals, linen and laundry facilities are provided. Each resident is assigned private work space and sleeping accommodations. Couples are accepted if each qualifies independently. Residents may come for 2 weeks to 2 months. The fee is $70 per week. Some full and partial fee waivers available. The foundation also sponsors poetry readings, concerts, workshops and seminars in writing. Ragdale is open year-round except for June 15-30 and December 15-January 1. Apply by January 15 for residencies in May-August; April 15 for September-December; September 15 for January-April; $20 application fee.

THE ROCKY MOUNTAIN WOMEN'S INSTITUTE, 7150 Montview Blvd., Denver CO 80220, phone (303)871-6923, founded 1976, executive director Cheryl Bezio-Gorham, a nonprofit organization associated with the University of Denver, offers office or studio space, stipends and support services for one year for artists, writers and scholars chosen from applications. They also offer continuing support for former associates, and they sponsor exhibits, workshops, lectures and performances to highlight and promote the work of current and past associates. Terms begin each September. Applicants should have a specific project. Applications ($5 processing fee) are available beginning each January. Deadline: March 15. Write for further information.

SPLIT ROCK ARTS PROGRAM, 306 Wesbrook Hall, 77 Pleasant St. SE, University of Minnesota, Minneapolis MN 55455, is a summer series of week-long residential workshops in the visual and literary arts and in the nature and applications of creativity, on the Duluth campus of UM "in the green hills near the city's summit." 1992 writing faculty included Paulette Bates Alden, Christina Baldwin, Carol Bly, Michael Dennis Browne, Carolyn Forche, Kate Green, Paul Gruchow, Phebe Hanson, Rebecca Hill, Mikhail Iossel, Judith Ortiz Cofer, Wendy Rose, Barton Sutter, Jane Resh Thomas and Will Weaver. Tuition ranges from $299-339 for courses taken for credit, $13 less if taken for no credit. Housing is $150 for a double, $216 for a single, in two-bedroom apartments. Meals are in UMD's cafeteria, cooked by participants in their apartments or in Duluth restaurants. Other housing options are also available, ranging from $144-204 per week.

THE SYVENNA FOUNDATION, Rt. 1, Box 193, Linden TX 75563, phone (903)835-8252, associate director Barbara Carroll, has 2 cottages on forested land near the Texas-Louisiana border available to unestablished women writers for 3-month residencies. Pays $300/month stipend plus cottage and utilities. The foundation's name is pronounced Savannah. Women writers of all ages in the beginning and intermediate stages of development as writers are welcome to apply any time of the year. Send SASE for application materials.

UCROSS FOUNDATION RESIDENCY PROGRAM, 2836 US Hwy. 14-16, Clearmont WY 82835, phone (307)737-2291, executive director Elizabeth Guheen. There are 4 concurrent positions open in various disciplines, including poetry, each extending from 2 weeks to 4 months. No charge for room, board or studio space, and they do not expect services or products from guests. Send SASE for information form, which must be accompanied by a work sample and general description of the work you plan to do at Ucross. Residents are selected from a rotating panel of professionals in the arts and humanities in October and March for, respectively, the Spring and Fall residencies. Semiannual application deadlines are March 1 and October 1.

VERMONT STUDIO CENTER; VISUAL ARTISTS AND WRITERS RESIDENCIES, P.O. Box 613, Johnson VT 05656, phone (802)635-2727, founded 1984, offers 4- and 8-week residencies for painters, sculptors and writers, January through April. Applications accepted all year. The studio center will accommodate 25 participants at a time, "who, together with the year-round VSC staff artists, form a dynamic working community" in the Green Mountains. "This environment creates the opportunity for as much solitude and retreat or interchange and support as each fellow wishes. Fellowships available. Writers' work spaces as well as housing for all fellows are provided in single rooms in VSC houses in the village of Johnson, all within walking distance of each other as well as the Red Mill complex that contains the dining hall, lounge, offices, gallery. Johnson State College is also within walking distance."

VIRGINIA CENTER FOR THE CREATIVE ARTS, Mt. San Angelo, Sweet Briar VA 24595, director William Smart, provides residencies for 12 writers (and 9 visual artists and 3 composers) for 1-3 months at the 450-acre Mt. San Angelo estate. The normal fee is $20 per day. Financial assistance is available.

THE HELENE WURLITZER FOUNDATION OF NEW MEXICO, Box 545, Taos NM 87571, offers residencies to creative, *not* interpretive, artists in all media, rent free and utilities free, for varying periods of time, usually 3 months, from April 1 through September 30, annually. Residents are responsible for their food. No families. No deadlines on application.

YADDO, Box 395, Saratoga Springs NY 12866-0395, phone (518)584-0746, founded 1926, offers residencies to writers, visual artists and composers who have already achieved some recognition in their field and have new work under way. During the summer 35 guests can be accommodated, 14 during the winter, approximately 200 per year. The hours 9-4 are a quiet period reserved for work. There is no fixed charge for a guest stay, but voluntary contributions of up to $20/day to help defray costs of the program are accepted. Write for applications to: Admissions, Yaddo, address above; enclose SASE. Application deadlines are January 15 and August 1. A $20 application fee is required.

Organizations
Useful to Poets

The organizations here are valuable to poets in many different ways. Many not only provide services but also publish newsletters or other materials filled with helpful information. For instance, some people belong to the Associated Writing Programs so they can receive *AWP Chronicle* which lists, among other things, new books by members, announcements of competitions and calls for submissions. Other people belong to AWP for its services, namely helping them find work teaching poetry or editing publications.

Other organizations such as The Academy of American Poets or The Poetry Center of the 92nd Street Y sponsor symposiums on poetry or host readings. Participating in or attending these can enhance one's career or sharpen one's interest in the arts.

Some organizations, such as Poetry Society of America, sponsor contests and grant awards. Some groups are national — Canadian Poetry Association, for example — and some regional, local or ethnic. The range and quality of groups and services may vary, but in general, organizations provide poets information, encouragement and additional career opportunities. To discover such opportunities in your area, check out *Poets & Writers* (listed under Publications Useful to Poets). It also contains information on a wide variety of organizations.

If you're unable to locate an appropriate group close to home, consider creating one. You can begin by posting notices on local bulletin boards, including those in nearby libraries. In fact, your library might even have space available for your group to meet.

Included here are not only some of the major organizations for poets, but also some representative samples of smaller groups.

THE ACADEMY OF AMERICAN POETS; FELLOWSHIP OF THE ACADEMY OF AMERICAN POETS; WALT WHITMAN AWARD; THE LAMONT POETRY SELECTION; HAROLD MORTON LANDON TRANSLATION AWARD; PETER I.B. LAVAN YOUNGER POET AWARDS, 177 E. 87th St., New York NY 10128, founded 1934, executive director William Wadsworth. Robert Penn Warren wrote in **Introduction to Fifty Years of American Poetry**, an anthology published in 1984 containing one poem from each of the 126 Chancellors, Fellows and Award Winners of the Academy: "What does the Academy do? According to its certificate of incorporation, its purpose is 'To encourage, stimulate and foster the production of American poetry. . . .' The responsibility for its activities lies with the Board of Directors and the Board of 12 Chancellors, which has included, over the years, such figures as Louise Bogan, W. H. Auden, Witter Bynner, Randall Jarrell, Robert Lowell, Robinson Jeffers, Marianne Moore, James Merrill, Robert Fitzgerald, F. O. Matthiessen and Archibald MacLeish — certainly not members of the same poetic church." They award fellowships, currently of $20,000 each, to distinguished American poets (no applications taken) — 58 to date — and other annual awards. The Walt Whitman Award pays $1,000 plus publication of a poet's first book by a major publisher. Mss of 50-100 pgs. must be submitted between September 15 and November 15 with a $10 entry fee. Entry form required. Send SASE. The Lamont Poetry Selection, for a poet's second book, is again a prize of $1,000. Submissions must be made by a publisher, in mss form, prior to publication. The Academy distributes 2,000 copies to its members. Poets entering either contest must be American citizens. The Harold Morton Landon Translation Award is for translation of a book-length poem, a collection of poems or a verse-drama translated into English from any language. One award of $1,000 each year to a US citizen. Only publishers may submit the book. Write for guidelines. The Peter I.B. Lavan Younger Poet Awards of $1,000 each are given annually to three younger poets selected by Academy Chancellors (no applications taken). *Poetry Pilot* is an informative periodical sent to those who contribute $25 or more per year or who are members. Membership: $45/year. The Academy sponsors a national series of poetry readings and panel discussions.

THE AMERICAN ACADEMY & INSTITUTE OF ARTS & LETTERS; THE ARTS AND LETTERS AWARDS; MICHAEL BRAUDE AWARD FOR LIGHT VERSE; THE GOLD MEDAL OF THE ACADEMY; WITTER BYNNER FOUNDATION POETRY PRIZE; FELLOWSHIP TO THE AMERICAN ACADEMY IN ROME; JEAN STEIN AWARD; MORTON DAUWEN ZABEL PRIZE, 633 W. 155th St., New York NY 10032, program assistant Domenica Brockman, offers annual awards in the arts, several of which are given to poets—by nomination only. **No applications for these awards are accepted.** These are: The Arts & Letters Awards of $5,000 each, given to 8 writers annually, some poets; the Michael Braude Award for Light Verse of $5,000, given biennially for light verse in the English language; The Gold Medal of the American Academy and Institute of Arts and Letters, given to a poet every 6 years; Award of Merit of $5,000 for an outstanding artist in one field of the arts, given to a poet once every 6 years; the Witter Bynner Foundation Poetry Prize of $1,500; a fellowship to the American Academy in Rome, including lodging and a stipend to a poet or fiction writer; the Jean Stein Award of $5,000 given every 3rd year to a poet whose work takes risks in expressing its commitment to the author's values and vision; the Morton Dauwen Zabel Prize of $5,000 given every 3rd year to a poet of "progressive, original and experimental tendencies rather than of academic and conservative tendencies." The 7 members of the jury are all Academy-Institute members appointed for a 3-year term. **Candidates (only published writers are considered) must be nominated by a member of the academy-institute.**

AMERICAN POETRY CENTER; ALL MUSE: PENNSYLVANIA'S LITERARY NETWORK NEWSLETTER; YOUNG VOICES OF PENNSYLVANIA POETRY CONTEST; POETS IN RESIDENCE PROGRAM; POETS RESOURCE CENTER; PENNSYLVANIA WRITERS COLLECTION, 3624 Market St., Philadelphia PA 19104, phone (215)387-1994, 800-ALL-MUSE (in Pennsylvania), sponsors Poetry Week, Pennsylvania's statewide literary arts festival during the entire month of March, which kicks off the center's year-round activities including: Young Voices, a statewide poetry contest for students aged 5-18, the winners of which are published in an anthology and invited to read at libraries during APC's Poetry Week; a Poets-In-Residence Program which brings poets to an inner-city high school in Philadelphia for 4 weeks; Poets Resource Center which will provide technical resources to Philadelphia writers in the form of comprehensive directories, "how-to" brochures, and a publishing reference library; and *All Muse*, their professionally printed magazine, 20-page newsprint publication, which appears in January and September, 20,000 copies distributed free, giving brief reviews of current poetry and fiction works by Pennsylvanians, regional events, publications, workshops, profiles and other news. Their All-Muse hotline provides recorded messages about upcoming literary events statewide; and their Pennsylvania Writers Collection stocks approximately 450 titles, works of poets, fiction writers and presses in Pennsylvania, available for purchase by mail or at the center in Philadelphia. Though they do not currently sponsor poetry readings, they provide information to the general public regarding when and where readings will be held. They sponsor an annual public symposium on a topic pertinent to poetry, with major poets as speakers, international programs such as Moscow residencies and student poet's tours. They offer technical assistance to writers and literary institutions through periodic workshops and consultations. Center staff members assist schools, corporations and museums in identifying artists for readings and residencies and in organizing literary events. Send SASE for a current list of their activities.

ASSOCIATED WRITING PROGRAMS; AWP CHRONICLE; THE AWP AWARD SERIES, Old Dominion University, Norfolk VA 23529-0079, founded 1967, offers a variety of services to the writing community, including information, job placement assistance, publishing opportunities, literary arts advocacy and forums. Annual individual membership is $45; placement service extra. For $18 you can subscribe to the *AWP Chronicle* (published 6 times/year), containing information about grants and awards, publishing opportunities, fellowships, and writing programs. They have a directory, **The Official Guide to Writing Programs,** of over 250 college and university writing programs for $15.95. The AWP Award Series selects a volume of poetry (48 pg. minimum) each year ($10 entry fee) with an award of $1,500 and publication. Deadline: Feb. 28. Send SASE for submission guidelines. Query after October. Their placement service helps writers find jobs in teaching, editing and other related fields.

ATLANTA WRITING RESOURCE CENTER, INC., Room 105, The Arts Exchange, 750 Kalb St., Atlanta GA 30312, phone (404)622-4152, director David McCord, "is for everyone with an interest in writing, whether for print or electronic media or simply for personal satisfaction. The center will provide reference materials, guidelines information samples, standard writing formats and other resources for effective writing and marketing." There is a bimonthly critique group for poets and short story writers, and a monthly open reading and open house called "Writers' Brawl" on the fourth Thursday of each month. The center has regular open hours (staffed by executive director and volunteers) with personal work space including typewriters, word processors, reference books and other resources. They publish a quarterly newsletter highlighting center activities and Atlanta's literary events, and they provide news of contests, writers' conferences, etc. They also sponsor an annual contest for previously unpublished original poems. Small cash prizes and honorable mentions. Winners published in *The Chattahoo-*

chee Review. Write for current guidelines. Literary magazines and journals as well as their writers' guidelines are available at the center. They also hold workshops aimed at improving literary and marketing skills. "People are invited to become members for $25/year. Contact us for more information."

THE AUTHORS GUILD, INC., 330 W. 42nd St., New York NY 10036, phone (212) 563-5904, executive director Helen A. Stephenson, "is an association of professional writers which focuses its efforts on the legal and business concerns of published authors in the areas of publishing contract terms, copyright, taxation and freedom of expression. We do not work in the area of marketing mss to publishers nor do we sponsor or participate in awards or prize selections." Send SASE for information on membership.

AUTHORS LEAGUE FUND, 234 W. 44th St., New York NY 10036, makes interest-free loans to published authors in need of temporary help because of illness or an emergency. No grants.

BEYOND BAROQUE LITERARY/ARTS CENTER, P.O. Box 2727, 681 Venice Blvd., Venice CA 90291, phone (213)822-3006, director D.B. Finnegan, a foundation established in 1968 that has been funded by the NEA, state and city arts councils and corporate donations. Foundation members get a calendar of events, discounts on regularly scheduled programs and borrowing privileges in the small press library of 3,000 volumes of poetry, fiction and reference materials, including audiotapes of Beyond Baroque readings. Beyond Baroque contains a bookstore open 5 days a week, including Friday evenings to coincide with regular weekly readings and performances. About 130 writers are invited to read each year; there are also open readings.

BLACK CULTURAL CENTRE FOR NOVA SCOTIA, Box 2128, East Dartmouth, Nova Scotia B2W 3Y2 Canada, phone (902)434-6223, FAX (902)434-2306, founded 1977 "to create among members of the black communities an awareness of their past, their heritage and their identity; to provide programs and activities for the general public to explore, learn about, understand and appreciate black history, black achievements and black experiences in the broad context of Canadian life. The centre houses a museum, reference library, archival area, small auditorium and studio workshops."

BURNABY WRITERS' SOCIETY, 6450 Deer Lake Ave., Burnaby, British Columbia V5G 2J3 Canada, contact person Eileen Kernaghan. Corresponding membership in the society, including a newsletter subscription, is open to anyone, anywhere. Yearly dues are $20. Sample newsletter in return for SASE with Canadian stamp. The society holds monthly meetings at The Burnaby Arts Centre (address above), with a business meeting at 7:30 followed by a writing workshop or speaker. Members of the society stage regular public readings of their own work.

THE WITTER BYNNER FOUNDATION FOR POETRY, INC., Suite 118, 105 E. Marcy St., Santa Fe NM 87501, phone (505)988-3251, president Douglas W. Schwartz. The foundation awards grants exclusively to nonprofit organizations for the support of poetry-related projects in the area of: 1) support of individual poets through existing nonprofit institutions; 2) developing the poetry audience; 3) poetry translation and the process of poetry translation; and 4) uses of poetry. The foundation "may consider the support of other creative and innovative projects in poetry." Grant applications must be received by February 1 each year; requests for application forms should be submitted to Steven Schwartz, executive director, at the address above.

THE CANADA COUNCIL; GOVERNOR GENERAL'S LITERARY AWARDS; INTERNATIONAL LITERARY PRIZES, P.O. Box 1047, 99 Metcalfe St., Ottawa, Ontario K1P 5V8 Canada, phone (613)598-4365/6, established by Parliament in 1957, "provides a wide range of grants and services to professional Canadian artists and art organizations in dance, media arts, music, opera, theater, writing, publishing and the visual arts." The Governor General's Literary Awards, valued at $10,000 (Canadian) each, are given annually for the best English-language and best French-language work in each of seven categories, including poetry. Books must be first-edition trade books written, translated or illustrated by Canadian citizens or permanent residents of Canada and published in Canada or abroad during the previous year (October 1 through September 30). In the case of translation, the original work must also be a Canadian-authored title. Books must be submitted by publishers with a Publisher's Submission Form, which is available from the Writing and Publishing Section. All books must be received at the Canada Council by September 30. The Canada Council administers four International Literary Prizes (Canada-Australia, Canada-French Community of Belgium, Canada-Switzerland) of $2,500-3,000 (Canadian and the Canada-Japan Book Award worth $10,000 Canadian). Winners are selected by juries. Except for the Canada-Japan Book Award, applications are not accepted..

CANADIAN CONFERENCE ON THE ARTS, 189 Laurier Ave. E., Ottawa, Ontario K1N 6P1 Canada, phone (613)238-3561, was created for "the encouragement of the federal, provincial and municipal governments, as well as the corporate and private sector, to develop policies which will ensure the continued growth of the arts and the cultural industries in Canada." It supplies members with information on political issues affecting the daily lives of artists and writers. Members receive *Proscenium*, a news magazine published 5 time per year, and other information on cultural issues of the day; counseling, general representation and active support. They sponsor conferences such as taxation and the artist, and offer other services. Membership for individuals is $10 for students and senior citizens and $25 for others; organizational members is on a sliding scale (depending on the organization's budget) of $60-900.

CANADIAN POETRY ASSOCIATION; POEMATA, Carrot Common Postal Outlet, P.O. Box 65100, 348 Danforth Ave., Toronto, Ontario M4K 3Z2 Canada, is a broad based umbrella organization that aims to promote the reading, writing, publishing, purchasing and preservation of poetry in Canada through the individual and combined efforts of its members; to promote and encourage all forms and styles of poetry; to promote communication among poets, publishers and the general public; to promote the establishment and maintenance of poetry libraries and archives in educational institutions across Canada; and to develop an international connection for Canadian poets through *Poemata,* its quarterly newsletter, and events organized by independent, locally-run chapters. Through its 10 autonomous local chapters, CPA organizes poetry readings, literary and social events, and runs a book club. Membership is open to anyone with an interest in poetry, including other literary organizations, for $20 per year. Sample newsletter: $3.

CANADIAN SOCIETY OF CHILDREN'S AUTHORS, ILLUSTRATORS & PERFORMERS, P.O. Box 280, Station L, Toronto, Ontario M6E 4Z2 Canada, phone (416)654-0903, president Pat Hancock, is a "society of professionals in the field of children's culture. Puts people into contact with publishers, offers advice to beginners, and generally provides a visible profile for members; 250 professional members and over 800 associates who are termed 'friends.' An annual conference in Toronto the last week of October provides workshops to people interested in writing, illustrating, and performing for children." Membership is $50 per year, which includes a subscription to the quarterly *CANSCAIP News* and a free copy of the Membership Directory.

COMPUSERVE INFORMATION SERVICE, 5000 Arlington Centre Blvd., P.O. Box 20212, Columbus OH 43220, phone (800)848-8199 from outside Ohio or (614)457-0802 from within Ohio or outside the US, is an international electronic network available via modem from any computer. On CIS are many forums on specialized topics of interests, including Litforum. This has been described as a 24-hour nonalcoholic cocktail party: basically a bulletin board where various members post and respond to public messages (though you may communicate with them privately, too, either through the CompuServe mail system or by leaving private messages in Litforum). It costs $49.95 to join CIS. When you join, you get a $25 online credit, so joining is practically free. Electronic mail is now included in the $7.95 monthly flat rate service fee. Most CompuServe membership kits also contain the CompuServe Information Manager, customized software designed for IBM compatible and Mac computers to make CompuServe easy to use. There are many services available through CIS (in addition to electronic mail), but most of the action is in the forums. In Litforum sometimes the talk is quite funny, often bawdy, and far-ranging, though there is a lot of practical, professional communication, too, and many people make contact via Litforum with agents, editors, other writers, researchers, and so on, that prove quite useful. You join Litforum (anyone can join; a number of the regulars are not even writers – just people interested in literature, writing, publication, chitchat), read the messages posted in some or all of the 17 sections (on such things as poetry and lyrics, fiction, nonfiction, speculative fiction, and so on), respond to any that you wish to, or just lurk. Each section has a library where you can post material you have written or download material by others, and comment if you wish. There is a workshop for which you can request admission (and you're in automatically) where each writer has a turn to have material criticized by the other workshop members.

COSMEP, THE INTERNATIONAL ASSOCIATION OF INDEPENDENT PUBLISHERS; COSMEP NEWSLETTER, P.O. Box 420703, San Francisco CA 94142-0703. If you are starting a small press or magazine or are embarking on self-publication, you should know about the advantages of membership in COSMEP. Write for information. It is the largest trade association for small press in the US. Included among membership benefits is the monthly *COSMEP Newsletter*, which prints news and commentary for small publishers. It also sponsors publishing conferences, stage exhibits at booksellers' and librarians' conventions and has insurance and cooperative advertising programs.

COUNCIL OF LITERARY MAGAZINES AND PRESSES; DIRECTORY OF LITERARY MAGAZINES; CLMP NEWS, Suite 3-C, 154 Christopher St., New York NY 10014-2839, provides annual grants to various literary magazines and presses and publishes an annual directory useful to writers: The *Direc-*

tory of Literary Magazines, which has detailed descriptions of over 500 literary magazines which are supported by CLMP, as well as the triquarterly *CLMPages*.

COWBOY POETRY GATHERING; RODEO COWBOY POETRY GATHERING; WESTERN FOLKLIFE CENTER, 501 Railroad St., Elko NV 89801. The Rodeo Cowboy Gathering can be contacted at the same address, though it is held at Cashman Field Theater, Las Vegas. Both of these gatherings are sponsored by Western Folklife Center, Box 888, Elko NV 89803, phone (702)738-7508, FAX (702)738-2900. There is an annual 6-day January gathering of cowboy poets in Elko and a 1-day gathering during the National Finals Rodeo in Las Vegas in December. The Western Folklife Center publishes and distributes books and tapes of cowboy poetry and songs as well as other cowboy memorabilia. The well-established tradition of cowboy poetry is enjoying a renaissance, and thousands of cowboy poets participate in these activities. Catalog and brochure available by calling (800)748-4466.

FAIRBANKS ARTS ASSOCIATION; FAIRBANKS ARTS; TANANA VALLEY FAIR CREATIVE WRITING CONTEST, P.O. Box 72786, Fairbanks AK 99707, phone (907)456-6485, editor Al Gezgt. FAA publishes a bimonthly magazine, *Fairbanks Arts*, which includes how-to information, market tips for Alaskan writers, humor and personal experiences pertaining to writing, marketing and lifestyles. Articles run 800-1,300 words. **Accepts all forms of poetry; limit submissions to 3 poems with maximum 40 lines each. Pays 5 contributor copies.** Subscription: $15. **Sample and guidelines: $3.** The FAA conducts the Creative Writing Division for the Tanana Valley Fair and sponsors a Community Reading Series for Alaskan and visiting writers.

‡FEDERATION OF BRITISH COLUMBIA WRITERS, M.P.O. Box 2206, Vancouver, British Columbia V6B 3WC Canada, manager Corey Van't Haaff, "is a nonprofit organization of professional and aspiring writers in all genres." They publish a newsletter of markets, political reports, awards and federation news, act as "a network centre for various other provincial writer's organizations; host, promote and organize workshops, public readings, literary competitions and social activities, publish directories which are distributed to schools, businesses, and organizations which may request the services of writers; and represent writers' interests on other professionally related organizations."

FESTIVAL OF POETS AND POETRY AT ST. MARY'S; EBENEZER COOKE POETRY FESTIVAL, St. Mary's College of Maryland, St. Mary's City MD 20686, phone (301)862-0239, is an annual event held during the last two weekends in May of each year. Approximately 18 guest poets and artists participate in and lead workshops, seminars and readings. Concurrent with the festival, St. Mary's College offers an intensive 14-day poetry writing workshop. The Ebenezer Cooke Poetry Festival is now a biannual event in August of even numbered years, held in the name of the first Poet Laureate of Maryland. Poets from Maryland and the surrounding areas are invited to give 5-minute readings, enjoy a crab feast and otherwise celebrate together.

GREAT SWAMP POETRY SERIES; DISTINGUISHED AMERICAN POETS SERIES; THE FIRST AMERICAN POETRY DISC, County College of Morris, Randolph NJ 07869, phone (201)328-5471 or 328-5460, DAPS founded 1974, GSPS founded 1986, director Sander Zulauf. Outstanding New Jersey poets and poets who write about New Jersey (such as August Kleinzahler, Catherine Doty, Alicia Ostriker, Joe Salerno, Pablo Medina, Lois Marie Harrod, Brigit Pegeen Kelly, J. Allyn Rosser, Renée Ashley, Doughtry 'Doc' Long)) are invited to read for GSPS for modest honoraria. "America's best poets"—e.g., they have had readings by James Wright, Elizabeth Bishop, Philip Levine, Howard Nemerov, Amiri Baraka, Allen Ginsberg, William Stafford, Lyn Lifshin, Paul Zimmer, and Gwendolyn Brooks—are invited to read in the DAPS for respectable honoraria. They have produced TFAPD, a laser disk anthology of poetry readings taken from the college archives in 3 volumes: **I. An Introduction to Poetry; II. Contemporary American Poetry; III. James Wright.** All programs are approximately one hour each and are available in laser, Beta and VHS formats.

ILLINOIS WRITERS, INC.; ILLINOIS WRITERS REVIEW; ILLINOIS WRITERS CHAPBOOK COMPETITON, % English Department, Illinois State University, Normal IL 61761-6901, phone (309)438-7705, founded 1975, editor Kevin Stein, associate editor Jim Elledge. The *Review* publishes essays, reviews and commentary. While reviews and essays often focus on Illinois authors, presses and journals, the *Review* also publishes work devoted to books and authors of national prominence. Commentary addresses larger issues or movements in contemporary writing (for example, the emergence of language poetry and the present state of the creative writing workshop). Welcomes sample books and chapbooks for review. The *Review* is journal-sized (5½×8½) with cover photos or graphic art, appearing semiannually. Its circulation is about 400. Illinois Writers, Inc., membership, $15/year, includes a subscription to the *Review* as well as 6 issues of a newsletter which offers manuscript submission information, conference notices, and brief articles of interest to writers, publishers, and libraries. Price per issue is $4. Payment presently in copies but reinstituting payment of $25 per article when available. Reporting time varies from 6-8 weeks. They also offer a chapbook competition, alternately poetry and fiction, and publish the chapbook as a part of their expanded efforts. Contest is open to members and to those who pay the $15 membership fee. All entrants and members receive a copy of the winning chapbook. Deadline is October. Watch for announcements of guidelines.

INTERNATIONAL BLACK WRITERS CONFERENCE, P.O. Box 1030, Chicago IL 60690, phone (312)995-5195, is "an organization dedicated to the recognition, encouragement and development of writing talent." It has been assisting writers for 21 years. They sponsor "an annual conference, help to create new literary markets, provide an ongoing program of assistance to members and assist communities in the articulation of their needs." Membership: $15/year.

JUST BUFFALO LITERARY CENTER, 111 Elmwood Ave., Buffalo NY 14201, phone (716)885-6400, founded 1975 by Debora Ott, has executive director, 3 program directors, an office manager and a director of community relations. They offer readings, workshops, master classes, residencies, an annual Western New York Writers-in-Residence competition, an annual Labor in Literature competition open to WNY union members, Spoken Arts Radio broadcasts on National Public Radio affiliate WBFO, and Writers-in-Education in the Schools. Just Buffalo acts as a clearing house for literary events in the Greater Buffalo area and offers diverse services to writers and to the WNY region. "Although we are not accepting submissions for publication at this time, we will review works for possible readings."

‡**THE LANE LITERARY GUILD**, Lane Regional Arts Council, 411 High St., Eugene OR 97401, is "a volunteer organization dedicated to encouraging and supporting poets and writers in Lane County, Oregon. We hold monthly readings featuring new and established poets and writers. Our readers are drawn from talent locally as well as from other cities and parts of the country. We also hold workshops, symposia and literary contests. Our funding comes from membership fees, donations at readings and from grant support by the Cultural Services Division of the City of Eugene, by the Oregon Arts Commission and by the National Endowment for the Arts. We are interested in hearing from poets and writers from around the country who will be in our neighborhood and might be interested in being one of our readers."

THE LEAGUE OF CANADIAN POETS; WHEN IS A POEM; WHO'S WHO IN THE LEAGUE OF CANA-DIAN POETS; HERE IS A POEM; POETRY MARKET FOR CANADIANS; NATIONAL POETRY CON-TEST; GERALD LAMPERT AWARD; PAT LOWTHER AWARD, 24 Ryerson Ave., Toronto, Ontario M5T 2P3 Canada, phone (416)363-5047, founded 1966, information Officer Dolores Ricketts. The league's aims are the advancement of poetry in Canada and promotion of the interests of professional, Canadian poets. Information on full and associate membership can be obtained by writing for the brochure, league of Canadian Poets: Services and Membership. The league publishes a biannual **Museletter** (magazine-sized, 30 pgs.) plus six 4-page issues; **When is a Poem**, on teaching poetry to children; a directory volume called **Who's Who in The League of Canadian Poets** that contains 1 page of information, including a picture, bio, publications and "what critics say" about each of the members; **Here is a Poem**, a companion anthology to **When Is a Poem**, featuring the work of Canadian poets; and **Poetry Markets for Canadians** which covers contracts, markets, agents and more. The league's members go on reading tours, and the league encourages them to speak on any facet of Canadian literature at schools and universities, libraries or organizations. The league has arranged "thousands of readings in every part of Canada"; they are now arranging exchange visits featuring the leading poets of such countries as Great Britain, Germany and the US. The league sponsors a National Poetry Contest with prizes of $1,000, $750 and $500; the best 50 poems published in a book. Deadline January 31. Entry fee $6/poem. Poems should be unpublished, under 75 lines and typed. Names and addresses should *not* appear on poems but on a separate covering sheet. Please send SASE for complete rules, info on judges, etc. Open to Canadian citizens or landed immigrants only. The Gerald Lampert Award of $1,000 is for a first book of poetry written by a Canadian, published professionally. The Pat Lowther Award of $1,000 is for a book of poetry written by a Canadian woman and published professionally. Write for entry forms. It is also the address of Writers Union of Canada which provides services and information to members, including a writer's guide to Canadian publishers ($3) and a variety of other publications to assist writers.

‡**THE LITERARY CENTER**, P.O. Box 85116, Seattle WA 98145-1116, phone (206)547-2503, maintains a resource library and small press collection. Sponsors 2 readings a month, a quarterly magazine (16-24 pgs.) featuring writers and publishers from the Northwest. Subscriptions $15/year. **Sample copy $1. Query for book reviews, articles or interviews.**

THE LOFT; LOFT-MCKNIGHT AWARDS, Pratt Community Center, 66 Malcolm Ave. SE, Minneapolis MN 55414, phone (612)379-0754, founded 1974, executive director Susan Broadhead. The Loft was begun by a group of poets looking for a place to give readings and conduct workshops and evolved into a sophisticated hub of activity for creative writing in all genres managed by an 19-member board of directors, and staff of 12. This past year 2,000 members contributed $30/year to the Loft; it was further supported by $56,000 from individuals, plus government, foundation and corporate grants. The Loft offers over 75 8-week courses each year, in addition to 30 workshops and panels. Its publication readings and emerging voices readings are meant for Minnesota writers whereas the Mentor Series and Creative Non-fiction residency feature nationally known writers. The Loft publishes a monthly newsletter called *A View from the Loft*. The Loft-McKnight Awards are offered annually to Minnesota writers: 8 awards of $7,500 each, 3 in poetry, 5 in creative prose; 2 Awards of Distinction, $10,500 each.

MAINE WRITERS & PUBLISHERS ALLIANCE; MAINE IN PRINT; MAINE WRITERS CENTER, 12 Pleasant St., Brunswick ME 04011-2201, phone (207)729-6333, founded 1975, according to membership coordinator Susan Shippen, is "a nonprofit organization dedicated to promoting all aspects of writing, publishing, and the book arts. Our membership currently includes over 1,300 writers, publishers, librarians, teachers, booksellers and readers from across Maine and the nation. For an individual contribution of $20 per year members receive a range of benefits including *Maine in Print*, a monthly compilation of calendar events, updated markets, book reviews, grant information, interviews with Maine authors and publishers, articles about writing and more. The alliance distributes selected books about Maine and by Maine authors and publishers, and it maintains a bookstore, re erence library, performance space and word processing station at the Maine Writers Center in Bru wick. MWPA regularly invites writers to read from their works and to conduct Saturday workshops. Reviews books of poetry only by Maine-based presses and poets.

NATIONAL ASSOCIATION FOR POETRY THERAPY, 225 Williams St., Huron O 44839, phone (419)433-7767. In many mental and other hospitals, schools, clinics, prisons, nursir homes, halfway houses, recreation and community centers, drug and alcohol addiction centers, hos e programs and other settings, professional poetry therapists engage in "the intentional use of poet and the interactive process to achieve therapeutic goals and personal growth." If you are such a p essional you are probably aware of the national organization. If you are not, you may wish to find o bout it for many reasons, including the possibility of training and employment. You can become ar ssociate Member for $55 or a Regular Member with voting rights for $60. Contact NAPT for co lete membership information. Members receive the *NAPT Newsletter* and the *Journal of Poetry Thera* an interdisciplinary journal of practice, theory, research and education (see their listing under Pu shers), and attend NAPT meetings. Subscriptions to the *Journal of Poetry Therapy* for nonmembers available through Human Sciences Press, 233 Spring St., New York NY 10013-1578.

NATIONAL FEDERATION OF STATE POETRY SOCIETIES, INC., Membershi Chairman: Barbara Stevens, 909 E. 34th St., Sioux Falls SD 57105; Contest Chairperson: Amy Jo Z k, 3520 State Route 56, Mechanicsburg OH 43044. "NFSPS is a nonprofit organization exclusively e cational and literary. Its purpose is to recognize the importance of poetry with respect to national ultural heritage. It is dedicated solely to the furtherance of poetry on the national level and serves to unite poets in the bonds of fellowship and understanding." Any poetry group located in a state not already affiliated but interested in affiliating with NFSPS may contact the membership chairman. Canadian groups may also apply. "In a state where no valid group exists, help may also be obtained by individuals interested in organizing a poetry group for affiliation." Most reputable state poetry societies are members of the National Federation and advertise their various poetry contests through their quarterly bulletin, *Strophes*, available for SASE and $1, editor Kay Kinnaman, Route 3, Box 348, Alexandria IN 46001. Beware of organizations calling themselves state poetry societies (however named) that are not members of NFSPS, as such labels are sometimes used by vanity schemes trying to sound respectable. Others, such as the Oregon State Poetry Association and the Virginia State Poetry Societies, are quite reputable, but they don't belong to NFSPS. NFSPS holds an annual meeting in a different city each year with a large awards banquet, addressed by an honorary chairman. They sponsor 50 national contests in various categories each year, including the NFSPS Prize of $1,500 for first place; $500, second; $250, third; with entry fees ($3 for the entire contest for members, $5 for NFSPS Award; $1/ poem for nonmembers and $5 for NFSPS award up to 4 poems per entry). All poems winning over $10 are published in an anthology. Rules for all contests are given in a brochure available from Kay Kinnaman at *Strophes* or Amy Jo Zook at the address above; you can also write for the address of your state poetry society. Scholarship information is available from Golda Walker, 915 Aberdeen Ave., Baton Rouge LA 70808 for a #10 SASE.

THE NATIONAL POETRY FOUNDATION; SAGETRIEB; PAIDEUMA, University of Maine, Orono ME 04469, Marie M. Alpert, publications coordinator. "The NPF is a nonprofit organization concerned with publishing scholarship on the work of 20th century poets, particularly Ezra Pound and those in the Imagist/Objectivist tradition. We publish *Paideuma*, a journal devoted to Ezra Pound scholarship, and *Sagetrieb*, a journal devoted to poets in the imagist/objectivist tradition, as well as one other journal of contemporary poetry and comment—*The New York Quarterly*. [See separate listing for *New York Quarterly*.] NPF conducts a conference each summer and celebrates the centennial of an individual 20th century poet." Sample copies: $8.95 for *Paideuma* or *Sagetrieb*; $6 for *New York Quarterly*.

NATIONAL WRITERS UNION, Second Floor, 873 Broadway, New York NY 10003, offer members such services as contract bargaining, a grievance committee, contract guidelines, health insurance, press credentials, computer discounts, car rental discounts, and caucuses and trade groups for exchange of information about special markets. Members receive *The American Writer*, the organization's newsletter. Membership is $60 for those earning less than $5,000 per year; $105 for those earning $5,000-$25,000; and $150 for those earning more than $25,000.

NORTH CAROLINA WRITERS' NETWORK: THE NETWORK NEWS; HARPERPRINTS POETRY CHAP-BOOK COMPETITION; THE RANDALL JARRELL POETRY PRIZE, P.O. Box 954, Carrboro NC 27510, established 1985, supports the work of writers, writers' organizations and literary programming statewide. A $25 donation annually brings members *The Network News*, a 24-page bimonthly newsletter containing organizational news, national market information and other material of interest to writers, and access to the Resource Center, Writers' Exchange, Workshops, Literary Brokerage and Press Service. 1,500 members nationwide. Annual fall conference features nationally-known writers, publishers and editors. It is held in a different North Carolina location each year in November. Also sponsors competitions in short fiction, one-act plays and nonfiction essays for North Carolinians and members.

PEN AMERICAN CENTER; PEN WRITERS FUND; PEN TRANSLATION PRIZE: RENATO POGGIOLI AWARD; PEN/REVSON FOUNDATION FELLOWSHIPS; GRANTS AND AWARDS, 568 Broadway, New York NY 10012, phone (212)334-1660, "is the largest of more than 100 centers which comprise International PEN, founded in London in 1921 by John Galsworthy to foster understanding among men and women of letters in all countries. Members of PEN work for freedom of expression wherever it has been endangered, and International PEN is the only worldwide organization of writers and the chief voice of the literary community." Its total membership on all continents is approximately 10,000. The 2,600 members of the American Center include poets, playwrights, essayists, editors, novelists (for the original letters in the acronym PEN), as well as translators and those editors and agents who have made a substantial contribution to the literary community. Membership in American PEN includes reciprocal privileges in foreign centers for those traveling abroad. Branch offices are located in Cambridge, Houston, Chicago, Portland/Seattle and San Francisco. Among PEN's various activities are public events and symposia, literary awards, assistance to writers in prison and to American writers in need (grants and loans up to $1,000 from PEN Writers Fund). Medical insurance for writers is available to members. The quarterly *PEN Newsletter* is sent to all members and is available to nonmembers by subscription. The PEN Translation prize, sponsored by the Book-of-the-Month Club, 1 each year of $3,000 for works published in the current calendar year. The Renato Poggioli Award, $3,000 annually, to encourage a promising translator from the Italian who has not yet been widely recognized. Candidates with a project in literary translation planning a journey to Italy will be favored. Submit resume, sample translation and description of project before February 1. The PEN/Revson Foundation Fellowships are $12,750 awarded in odd-numbered years to poets (and to writers of fiction in even-numbered years). A fellow writer or editor must nominate candidates age 35 or under by January 15 with three copies of no more than 50 pgs. of current work in progress, for someone whose "published work has not yet met with the recognition it merits." They publish **Grants and Awards** biennially, containing guidelines, deadlines, eligibility requirements and other information about hundreds of grants, awards and competitions for poets and other writers: $8 postpaid. Send SASE for booklet describing their activities and listing their publications, some of them available free.

PERSONAL POETS UNITED, 860 Armand Ct. NE, Atlanta GA 30324, % Jean Hesse, who started a business in 1980 writing poems for individuals for a fee (for greetings, special occasions, etc.). Others started similar businesses, after she began instructing them in the process, especially through a cassette tape training program and other training materials. She then organized a support group of poets around the country writing poetry-to-order, Personal Poets United. Send SASE for free brochure or $19.50 plus $4.50 postage and handling for training manual "How to Make Your Poems Pay."

PITTSBURGH POETRY EXCHANGE, 3709 Perrysville Ave., Pittsburgh PA 15214, phone (412)321-1234, founded 1974 as a community-based organization for local poets. It functions as a service organization and information exchange, conducting ongoing workshops, readings, forums and other special events. No dues or fees. "At our open workshop we each drop a dollar into the basket which we turn over to City Books as 'rent' for use of the space. Any other monetary contributions are voluntary, often from outside sources. We've managed not to let our reach exceed our grasp." Their readings programs are primarily committed to local and area poets, with honorariums of $25-50. They sponsor a minimum of three major events per year in addition to a monthly workshop. Some of these have been reading programs in conjunction with community arts festivals, such as the October South Side Poetry Smorgasbord—a series of readings throughout the evening at different shops (galleries, bookstores). Poets from out of town may contact the exchange for assitance in setting up readings at bookstores to help sell their books. Contact Michael Wurster at the above address or phone number.

THE POETRY CENTER OF THE 92ND STREET Y; DISCOVERY/THE NATION POETRY CONTEST, 1395 Lexington Ave., New York NY 10128, phone (212)415-5760, offers annual series of readings by major literary figures (36 readings September through May), writing workshops and lectures. You may join the center to participate in and be informed of these activities. Also cosponsors the Discovery/The Nation Poetry Contest. Deadline early February. Send SASE for information.

THE POETRY COMMITTEE OF THE GREATER WASHINGTON AREA, The Folger Shakespeare Library, 201 E. Capitol St. SE, Washington DC 20003, phone (202)544-7077, executive director Gigi Bradford. Formed in the mid-70s at the invitation of the poetry coordinator of the Folger Library, meets informally 5 times a year. The membership (by invitation) consists of about 60 people who represent major and minor poetry organizations in the metropolitan area (a few from Baltimore also). Annual sponsors of Celebration of Washington Poetry, a reading and book sale highlighting area poets and presses, the Columbia Book Award for best book of poetry by Washington area poet within the past calendar year and the Columbia Merit Award for service to area poetry.

POETRY RESOURCE CENTER OF MICHIGAN, 111 E. Kirby, Detroit MI 48202, phone (313)972-5580, "is a nonprofit organization which exists through the generosity of poets, writers, teachers, publishers, printers, librarians and others dedicated to the reading and enjoyment of poetry in Michigan." The *PRC Newsletter* and *Calendar* is available by mail monthly for an annual membership donation of $20 or more, and is distributed free of charge at locations throughout the state. To obtain copies for distribution at poetry functions, contact the editor or any member of the PRC Board of Trustees.

POETRY SOCIETY OF AMERICA; POETRY SOCIETY OF AMERICA AWARDS, 15 Gramercy Park, New York NY 10003, phone (212)254-9628, is a nonprofit cultural organization in support of poetry and of poets, member and nonmember, young and established, which sponsors readings, lectures and workshops both in New York City and around the country. Their Peer Group Workshop is open to all members and meets on a weekly basis. They publish a newsletter of their activities and they sponsor a wide range of contests. The following are open to members only: Gordon Barber Memorial Award ($200); Gertrude B. Claytor Award ($250); Gustav Davidson Memorial Award ($500); Mary Carolyn Davies Memorial Award ($250); Alice Fay Di Castagnola Award ($2,000); *Writer Magazine*/Emily Dickinson Award ($100); Consuelo Ford Award ($250); Cecil Hemley Memorial Award ($300); Lucille Medwick Memorial Award ($500). Nonmembers may enter as many of the following contests as they wish, no more than 1 entry for each, for a $5 fee: Ruth Lake Award (III), $100 for a poem of retrospection any length or style; Elias Lieberman Student Poetry Award, $100 for students in grades 9-12; John Masefield Memorial Award (II) for a narrative poem in English up to 300 lines, $500, translations ineligible; Celia B. Wagner Award (II), $250 any form or length; George Bogin Memorial Award: $500 for a selection of 4 to 5 poems which take a stand against oppression; Robert H. Winner Memorial Award: $2,500 for a poem written by a poet over 40, still unpublished or with one book. (All have a deadline of December 31; awards are made at a ceremony and banquet in late spring.) The Society also has 3 book contests open to nonmembers, but publishers only may enter books. They must obtain an entry form, and there is a $10 fee for each book entered. Book awards are: Melville Cane Award (II), $500 in even-numbered years awarded to a book of poems, in odd years to prose work on poetry; Norma Farber Award (III), $1,000 for a first book; William Carlos Williams Award (III), $1,250 for a book of poetry published by a small press, nonprofit or university press, by a permanent resident of the US—translations not eligible. The Shelley Memorial Award of $4,000 is by nomination only. For necessary rules and guidelines for their various contests send SASE between August 1 and December 31. Membership: $40.

POETS & WRITERS, INC., See *Poets & Writers* under Publications Useful to Poets.

POETS' CORNER, THE CATHEDRAL CHURCH OF ST. JOHN THE DIVINE, Cathedral Heights, 1047 Amsterdam Ave. at 112 St., New York NY 10025, initiated in 1984 with memorials for Emily Dickinson, Walt Whitman, Washington Irving, Robert Frost, Herman Melville, Nathanial Hawthorne, Edgar Allen Poe, Henry James, Henry David Thoreau, Mark Twain, Ralph Waldo Emerson, William Faulkner, Wallace Stevens, Willa Cather, T.S. Eliot, Marianne Moore and Edwin Arlington Robinson. It is similar in concept to the English Poets' Corner in Westminster Abbey, and was established and dedicated to memorialize this country's greatest writers.

POETS HOUSE; THE REED FOUNDATION LIBRARY; THE POETRY PUBLICATION SHOWCASE, 72 Spring St., New York NY 10012, phone (212)431-7920, founded 1985, Lee Ellen Briccetti, executive director, "is a library, resource center and meeting place for poets and poetry readers from all parts of the aesthetic spectrum. Programs and events are designed to serve as a platform for discussions and emphasize cross-cultural and interdisciplinary exchange. The Reed Foundation Library is a poetry collection open to the public and is comprised of 25,000 volumes, including books, journals, small press publications and other fugitive poetry materials. Donations to the library are welcomed." The Poetry Publication Showcase gathers all new poetry releases annually for exhibit and a festival of events. Poets House sponsors over 25 public events annually and offers a variety of programs for educators and students. These include a NY/NJ Teachers Conference; a conference for the chairpeople of English Departments; and the Poetry Teacher of the Year Award, which divides a prize of $1,000 between a teacher and her/his school library.

POETS THEATRE, Rd. 2, Box 155, Cohocton NY 14826, sponsors readings and performances with limited funding from Poets and Writers. For a mostly conservative, rural audience. A featured poet, followed by open reading, monthly.

POETS-IN-THE-SCHOOLS, Most states have PITS programs that send published poets into classrooms to teach students poetry writing. If you have published poetry widely and have a proven commitment to children, contact your state arts council, Arts-in-Education Dept., to see whether you qualify. Three of the biggest are Poets in Public Service (formerly NYSPITS), Suite 3B, 154 Christopher St., New York NY 10014, phone (212)206-9000; California Poets-in-the-Schools, 2845 24th St., San Francisco CA 94110, phone (415)695-7988; and COMPAS, Landmark Center, #308, 75 West 5th St., St. Paul MN 55102.

SCOTTISH POETRY LIBRARY; SCHOOL OF POETS; CRITICAL SERVICE, Tweeddale Court, 14 High St., Edinburgh EH1 1TE Scotland, phone (031)557-2876, director Tessa Ransford, librarian Dr. Tom Hubbard, is a central information source and repository for poetry in Scotland. Their School of Poets is open to anyone; "at meetings members divide into small groups in which each participant reads a poem which is then analyzed and discussed." Meetings normally take place at 7:30 p.m. on the first Tuesday of each month at the library. They also offer a Critical Service in which groups of up to 6 poems, not exceeding 200 lines in all, are given critical comment by members of the School: £15 for each critique (with SASE).

THE SOCIETY OF AUTHORS; THE AUTHOR, 84 Drayton Gardens, London SW10 9SB, England, advises members on business matters, takes up their complaints and institutes legal proceedings, sends them a quarterly journal, *The Author,* publishes guides regarding agents, copyright, income tax, contracts, etc., offers members retirement and medical insurance programs, administers trust funds as well as a number of literary awards, organizes special interest groups (e.g., broadcasters, children's writers, etc.), and pursues campaigns on behalf of the profession (e.g., for legislative changes).

SONGWRITERS AND POETS CRITIQUE, 11599 Coontz Rd., Orient OH 43146, founded in 1985 by Ellis Cordle, phone (614)877-1727, a nonprofit association whose purpose is to serve songwriters, poets and musicians in their area. The president of the organization says, "We have over 100 members from over 16 states at several levels of ability from novice to advanced, and try to help and support each other with the craft and the business of poetry and songs. We have published writers and recorded artists. We share information about how to pitch, send and package a demo and who to send it to. We have a songwriting contest for member writers." Annual dues are $16.

SOUTHERN POETRY ASSOCIATION; THE POET'S VOICE, P.O. Box 524, Pass Christian MS 39571, founded 1986, poetry editor Mildred Klyce. SPA offers networking, publishing, free critique service for members through Round Robin Groups, assistance in publishing chapbooks. $10 annual membership fee includes *The Poet's Voice* quarterly newsletter. The association sponsors a number of contests, including Voices of the South, Yarn Spinner, Poetry in Motion, Special People, some are for members only; some, such as the Voices of the South Contest, open to all. Prizes total $200 with $3 entry fee/poem (28 line limit). June 1 deadline. High scoring poems are published in an anthology (which the poet is not required to purchase). Send 9×12 SASE with 58¢ postage for details. *The Poet's Voice* contains poetry book reviews, articles on great poets of the past, current activities and input from SPA members.

THE THURBER HOUSE; THE JAMES THURBER WRITER-IN-RESIDENCE, 77 Jefferson Ave., Columbus OH 43215, phone (614)464-1032, officially opened in 1985, executive director Donn Vickers, who says that it is "one of the most diversely active of all restored writer's homes." The Thurber Center has a staff of 6 people plus over 30 volunteers and a 21-person Board of Trustees. Half of its budget comes from state, local and national arts councils; 35% from foundations; and the rest from sales. The house includes a bookstore which distributes the best small press books the Midwest has to offer. They sponsor a quarter-long writer-in-residence program, The James Thurber Writer-in-Residence, $5,000/ quarter plus living accommodations in Thurber's restored house, featuring playwrights, journalists and other writers (poetry and fiction). The house also includes performance spaces and offices. Local writers are invited to use the house as a place to "come together with others who care." They sponsor Evenings with Authors presenting major writers to the public, Literary Picnics on the lawn of Thurber House providing "convivial evenings in the company of both emerging and beloved authors, with delectable menus by some of Columbus's favorite chefs," and other activities.

WALT WHITMAN CULTURAL ARTS CENTER; CAMDEN POETRY AWARD, 2nd and Cooper St., Camden NJ 08102, executive director René L. Huggins, program coordinator Joseph Lewis phone (609)964-8300, a writers' center, founded 1975, offers a variety of programs such as Notable Poets and Writers Series, Walt Whitman Poetry Series, schools programs, adult and children's theater, musical presentations, Fine Art Exhibitions and the Camden Poetry Award. Their regular season runs September through May. During the summer months they provide a 4-week Creativity Camp and a children's theater series entitled "10 Fridays of Fun."

WOODLAND PATTERN, Box 92081, 720 E. Locust St., Milwaukee WI 53202, phone (414)263-5001, executive director Anne Kingsbury, who calls it "a semi-glamorous literary and arts center." Kingsbury regards the center as a neighborhood organization; it includes a bookstore that concentrates on contemporary literature, much of it small press, much of it poetry and also on multicultural children's literature. It also incorporates a multipurpose gallery/performance/reading space, where exhibitions, readings, a lecture series, musical programs and a reading and study group are held. The *Woodland Pattern Newsletter*, mailed free to 1,900 people, contains an annotated calendar and pieces about visiting writers.

WORLD-WIDE WRITERS SERVICE, INC.; WRITERS INK; WRITERS INK PRESS; WRITERS UNLIMITED AGENCY, INC.; WESTHAMPTON WRITERS FESTIVAL; JEANNE VOEGE POETRY AWARDS, 186 N. Coleman Rd., Centereach NY 11720-3072, phone (516)736-6439, founded in 1976, Writers Ink Press founded 1978, poetry editor Dr. David B. Axelrod. "World-wide Writers Service is a literary and speakers' booking agency. With its not-for-profit affiliate, Writers Unlimited Agency, Inc., it presents literary workshops and performances, conferences and other literary services, and publishes through Writers Ink Press, chapbooks and small flat-spined books as well as arts editions. **We publish only by our specific invitation at this time.**" *Writers Ink* is "a sometimes newsletter of events on Long Island, now including programs of our conferences." They publish 1-2 books a year, 16-28 pgs., **by invitation only.** "We welcome news of other presses and poets' activities. Review books of poetry. We fund raise for nonprofit projects and are associates and sponsors of Westhampton Writers Festival and Jeanne Voege Poetry Awards. Arts Editions are profit productions employing hand-made papers, bindings, etc. We have editorial services available at small fees ($50 minimum), but only after inquiry and if appropriate."

THE WRITER'S CENTER; CAROUSEL; POET LORE, 7815 Old Georgetown Rd., Bethesda MD 20814, phone (301)654-8664, founder and chairman of the board Allan Lefcowitz, director Jane Fox. This is an outstanding resource for writers not only in Washington DC but in the wider area ranging from southern Pennsylvania to North Carolina and West Virginia. The center offers 180 multi-meeting workshops each year in writing, typesetting, word processing, and graphic arts, and provides a research library. It is open 7 days a week, 10 hours a day. Some 2,300 members support the center with $30 annual donations, which allows for 5 paid staff members. There is a book gallery at which publications of small presses are displayed and sold. The center's publication, *The Carousel,* is an 12-page tabloid that comes out 6 times a year. They also sponsor 40 annual performance events, which include presentations in poetry, fiction and theater. The center is now publisher of *Poet Lore* — 100 years old in 1989 (see listing under Publishers). Reviews books of poetry.

THE WRITERS ROOM, 5th Floor, 153 Waverly Pl., New York NY 10014, phone (212)807-9519, provides a "home away from home" for any writer "with a serious commitment to writing," who needs a place to work. It is open 24 hours a day, 7 days a week, offering desks, storage space and "an alternative to isolation" for up to 150 writers. Space is allotted on a quarterly basis (which may be extended indefinitely) and costs $150 per quarter. "We now offer in-house scholarships for one-quarter year to writers in financial need." It is supported by the National Endowment for the Arts, the New York State Council on the Arts and other public and private sources, and it encourages applications. The Writers Room also offers monthly readings and workshops for its residents and has occasional exhibits on "writerly" subjects, such as revision.

Additional Organizations Useful to Poets

Also read the following listings for information on other organizations for poets. See the General Index for page numbers.

American Association of
  Haikuists Newsletter
Bay Area Poets Coalition
  (BAPC)
Berkeley Poets Cooperative
  (Workshop & Press)
Cleaning Business Magazine
Connecticut River Review
Dream Shop, The
eleventh muse, the
Emerald Coast Review
Equinox Press
Frogpond: Quarterly Haiku
  Journal
Greenfield Review Press, The
International Poets of the
  Heart
Intro
Keystrokes
Kwibidi Publisher

Lines Review
Living Poets Society (AZ)
Maryland Poetry Review
New Horizons Poetry Club
New York Quarterly
Northwoods Press
Onionhead
Oracle Poetry
Pasque Petals
Peregrine
Philomel
Piedmont Literary Review
Poem
Poetpourri
Poetry
Poetry Nippon Press
Poetry Nottingham
Poetry Review
Poets' Roundtable
Pudding House Publications

Rockford Review, The
Science Fiction Poetry
  Association
SKAZ
Small Press Writers & Artists
  Organization (SPWAO)
Society of American Poets, The
Still Waters Press
Tesseract Publications
Tyro Writers' Group
Ver Poets Voices
Washington Review
Washington Writers'
  Publishing House
Weyfarers
Whitecrow Foundation,
  Tahana
Without Halos
Worcester Review
Word Works, The

Publications
Useful to Poets

Publications, such as those listed here, not only help keep poets current between the publication of yearly directories, but they also contain a wealth of helpful information.

For instance, to save time when you cannot locate a specific magazine to study before submitting to it, check out *Literary Magazine Review*. It provides an in-depth view of potential markets.

When you want to locate a poet and don't know his or her address, consult **A Directory of American Poets and Fiction Writers** published by Poets & Writers, Inc. P&W's magazine, by the way, contains information about new markets, contests and other opportunities for poets.

Byline, Parnassus: Poetry in Review and *AWP Chronicle* are also helpful publications. You'll find these and many others mentioned in the "additional" list at the end of this section. Check the General Index for their specific page numbers.

So scan the listings, subscribe to or check out these publications in the library and even consider submitting to them. For instance, if you do marketing research on literary magazines, chances are you can review a publication, share a new market and gain a publication "credit" in the process.

AD-LIB PUBLICATIONS, P.O. Box 205, Fairfield IA 52556, phone (515)472-6130, 800-669-0773, publisher John Kremer, publishes how-to books about book publishing and self-publishing, such as **1001 Ways to Market Your Books, Directory of Book Printers**, and **Book Publishing Resource Guide** (also available on IBM PC or Macintosh disk as a database). Send SASE for catalog.

AMERICAN POETS IN PROFILE SERIES; FORD-BROWN & CO., P.O. Box 2674, Boston MA 02208-2764, founded 1975 (in Birmingham AL), editor Steven Ford-Brown. Ford-Brown will consider prose submissions of critical profiles for its American Poets in Profile Series. Series includes book on Dave Smith, John Logan, Andrew Glaze, Vasser Miller, Carolyn Kizer and Fred Chappell. **Sample postpaid: $15.95. Pays advance and copies (amount "depends"). Reports on queries in 2 weeks. No simultaneous submissions.**

R.R. BOWKER; LITERARY MARKET PLACE; BOOKS IN PRINT, 121 Chanlon Rd., New Providence NJ 07974, phone (908)464-6800. **LMP** is the major trade directory of publishers and people involved in publishing books. It is available in most libraries, or individual copies may be purchased (appears in December each year; standing order price $118.70). **BIP** is another standard reference available in most libraries and bookstores. Bowker publishes a wide range of reference books pertaining to publishing. Write for their catalog.

CANADIAN POETRY, English Dept., University of Western Ontario, London, Ontario N6A 3K7 Canada, phone (519)661-3403, founded 1977, editor Prof. D.M.R. Bentley, is a biannual journal of critical articles, reviews and historical documents (such as interviews). It is a professionally printed, scholarly edited, flat-spined, 100+ pg. journal which pays contributors in copies. Subscription: $15. **Sample: $7.50. Note that they publish no poetry except as quotations in articles.**

DUSTBOOKS; INTERNATIONAL DIRECTORY OF LITTLE MAGAZINES AND SMALL PRESSES; DIRECTORY OF POETRY PUBLISHERS; SMALL PRESS REVIEW, P.O. Box 100, Paradise CA 95967. Dustbooks publishes a number of books useful to writers. Send SASE for catalog. Among their regular publications, **International Directory** is an annual directory of small presses and literary magazines, over 5,000 entries, a third being magazines, half being book publishers, and the rest being both. There is very detailed information about what these presses and magazines report to be their policies in regard to payment, copyright, format and publishing schedules. **Directory of Poetry Publishers** has similar information for 2,000 publishers of poetry. *Small Press Review* is a monthly magazine, newsprint, carrying current updating of listings in **ID**, small press needs, news, announcements and reviews—a valuable way to stay abreast of the literary marketplace.

LAUGHING BEAR NEWSLETTER; LAUGHING BEAR PRESS (V), Box 36159, Bear Valley Station, Denver CO 80236, phone (303)989-5614, founded 1976, editor Tom Person. *LBN* is a monthly publication of small press information for writers and publishers containing articles, news and reviews. $10/year. *LBN* is interested in short (200-300-word) articles on self-publishing and small press. Payment in copies. Send SASE for sample copy. Laughing Bear Press publishes poetry books and cassette tapes of poetry but accepts no unsolicited mss.

THE LETTER EXCHANGE, published by The Readers' League, % Stephen Sikora, P.O. Box 6218, Albany CA 94706. Published 3 times each year, *The Letter Exchange* is a digest-sized magazine, 36 pgs., that publishes 4 types of listings: regular (which are rather like personal classifieds); ghost letters, which contain lines like "Send news of the Entwives!"; amateur magazines, which publicizes readers' own publishing ventures; and sketch ads, in which readers who would rather draw than write can communicate in their chosen mode. All ads are coded, and readers respond through the code numbers. Subscription to *The Letter Exchange* is $18/year, and sample copies are $8 postpaid for current issue. Poets who are so inclined often exchange poems and criticism with each other through this medium.

LITERARY MAGAZINE REVIEW, English Dept., Kansas State University, Manhattan KS 66506, founded 1981, editor G.W. Clift, a quarterly magazine (digest-sized, perfect-bound, about 80 pgs.) that publishes critiques, 2-5 pgs. long, of various literary magazines, plus shorter "reviews" (about ½ page), directories of literary magazines (such as British publications) and descriptive listings of new journals during a particular year. Single copies are available for $4 or subscriptions for $12.50 year.

‡**OHIO WRITER**, P.O. Box 528, Willoughby OH 44094, is a newsletter for Ohio writers or those connected with Ohio, a bimonthly, 8-16 pgs., professionally printed in colored ink on off-white stock, containing news and reviews of Ohio events and publications: $12 a year.

PARA PUBLISHING, Box 4232-880, Santa Barbara CA 93140-4232, phone (805)968-7277, Orders: (800)727-2782. FAX (805)968-1379. Author-publisher Dan Poynter publishes how-to-books on book publishing and self-publishing. **Is There a Book Inside You?** shows you how to get your book out. **The Self-Publishing Manual, How to Write, Print and Sell Your Own Book** is all about book promotion. **Publishing Short-Run Books** shows you how to typeset and lay out your own book. Poynter also publishes **Publishing Contracts on Disk, Book Fairs** and 19 Special Reports on various aspects of book production, promotion, marketing and distribution. *Free* book publishing information kit.

POETRY BOOK SOCIETY, 21 Earls Court Square, London SW5 9DE, England, a book club with an annual subscription rate of £24, which covers 4 books of new British poetry, the *PBS Bulletin*, the annual **Poetry Anthology**, a premium offer (for new members) and free surface postage and packing to anywhere in the world. The selectors also recommend other books of special merit, which are obtainable at discount prices. The Poetry Book Society is subsidized by the Arts Council of Great Britain.

THE POETRY CONNECTION, #6K (PM), 301 E. 64th St., New York NY 10021, phone (212)249-5494, editor/publisher: Sylvia Shichman. The poetry contest information service is in flyer format. Subscribers receive poetry contest flyers listing poetry and writing contests with cash awards; it also provides information on how to sell your poetry/books and obtain assistance in chapbook publishing. *TPC* has information on writing for greeting card companies and listings of literary agents and songwriting directories. Also publishes *The Poetry Connection Newsletter* listing poetry contests with cash awards. *TPC* specializes in barter/trade publicity and flyer distribution. Mini-sample $5 plus 5 first class stamps; subscription $25 (1 year/6 issues) or $15 (6 months/3 issues).

POETRY EXCHANGE, P.O. Box 85477, Seattle WA 98145-1477, is a monthly newsletter, circulation 1,500, $10/year, to which you may subscribe or in which you can buy ads. It has listings of workshops, "manuscripts wanted," and a calendar of regional poetic events, 4 magazine-sized pages in fine print.

POETS & WRITERS, INC.; A DIRECTORY OF AMERICAN POETS AND FICTION WRITERS; WRITER'S GUIDE TO COPYRIGHT; AUTHOR AND AUDIENCE; LITERARY AGENTS; LITERARY BOOKSTORES; POETS & WRITERS MAGAZINE, 72 Spring St., New York NY 10012, phone (212)226-3586 or 800-666-2268 (California only), is our major support organization. Its many helpful publications include *Poets & Writers Magazine*, which appears 6 times a year ($18 or $3.95 for a single copy), magazine-sized, 72 pgs., offset, has been called *The Wall Street Journal* of our profession, and it is there that one most readily finds out about resources, current needs of magazines and presses, contests, awards, jobs and retreats for writers, and discussions of business, legal and other issues affecting writers. P&W also publishes a number of valuable directories such as its biennial **A Directory of American Poets and Fiction Writers** ($23.95 paperback), which editors, publishers, agents and sponsors of readings and workshops use to locate over 7,000 active writers in the country. (You may qualify for a listing if you have a number of publications.) They also publish **A Writer's Guide to Copyright; Author And Audience,** a list of over 400 organizations which sponsor readings and workshops involving poets and fiction writers, including a section on how to organize and present a reading or workshop; **Literary Agents: A Writer's Guide; Literary Bookstores: A Cross-Country Guide,** for people who travel; and many reprints of articles from *Coda* and *Poets & Writers Magazine* which are useful to writers, such as "How to Give an Unsolicited Manuscript the Best Chance"; "22 Heavens for Writers (information on writers' colonies)."

POETS' AUDIO CENTER; THE WATERSHED FOUNDATION, P.O. Box 50145, Washington DC 20091. This is an international clearinghouse for ordering any poetry recording available, from both commercial and noncommercial producers. Catalog available free ("an introduction to our collection"); they stock over 500 titles. **Foundation not accepting applications at this time.**

BERN PORTER INTERNATIONAL, 22 Salmond Rd., Belfast ME 04915, founded 1911, is a monthly journal that reviews books of poetry. Also provides sleeping bag space for poets and writers May 1 through November 1 for the cost or freewill contribution. No smoking. No drugs. No telephone.

PUSHCART PRESS, P.O. Box 380, Wainscott NY 11975, publishes a number of books useful to writers, including the Pushcart Prize Series—annual anthologies representing the best small press publications, according to the judges; The Editors' Book Award Series, "to encourage the writing of distinguished books of uncertain financial value," The Original Publish-It-Yourself Handbook and the Literary Companion Series. Send SASE for catalog.

SIPAPU; KONOCTI BOOKS, 23311 County Rd. 88, Winters CA 95694, phone (916)662-3364, founded 1970, editor/publisher Noel Peattie. *Sipapu* consists of reviews of small press publications including poetry, interviews and conference news, but publishes no poetry. Konocti Books has published poetry but is not currently active.

THE WASHINGTON INTERNATIONAL ARTS LETTER, P.O. Box 12010, Des Moines IA 50312, phone (515)255-5577; appears 10 times per year, 6-8 pg. newsletter on grants and other forms of assistance for the arts and humanities—mostly lists various programs of support to artists including many for poets. Reviews books of poetry. Subscription: $124 full rate; $55 for individuals; $82 for institutions.

WRITER'S DIGEST BOOKS; WRITER'S YEARBOOK; WRITER'S DIGEST; WRITER'S MARKET; THE POET'S HANDBOOK, 1507 Dana Ave., Cincinnati OH 45207, phone (800)289-0963 outside Ohio, or (513)531-2222. Writer's Digest Books publishes and distributes a remarkable array of books useful to writers, such as **Writer's Market,** a general guide to about 800 book publishers, of which about 450 publish fiction and/or poetry. *Writer's Digest* is a monthly magazine about writing with frequent articles and much market news about poetry, in addition to a monthly poetry column. See entry in Publishers of Poetry section. *Writer's Yearbook* is a newsstand annual for freelance writers, journalists and teachers of creative writing, with articles regarding poetry. WDB publishes **Poet's Market, The Poet's Handbook,** by Judson Jerome and **Creating Poetry,** by John Drury.

WRITERS NEWS; WRITERS LIBRARY, P.O. Box 4, Nairn, 1V12 4HU Scotland, phone 0667-54441, FAX 0667-54401. The monthly magazine *Writer's News,* 48 pgs., is chock-full of announcements of markets, competitions, opportunities and news of the writing world. A regular feature is their Poetry Workshop, discussing the writing of poetry. Writers Library distributes books on writing, including many published by Writer's Digest Books. Subscription to the magazine: £36.90 or £31.90 if you pay by "direct debit" (charge card). Write for their book catalog.

THE WRITER'S NOOK NEWS, Suite 181, 38114 Third St., Willoughby OH 44094, editor Eugene Ortiz, is a quarterly publishing articles on the craft and business of writing with columns on marketing, contests and awards, conferences, tax legislation, books, prose and poetry, and other topics. It is offset from laser typesetting on 50 lb. stock. Sample: $5. Subscription: $18 for one year, $42 for three, $300 for Lifetime Subscription. "We also publish *The Nook News Conferences & Klatches Bulletin,* a quarterly with the latest information on national and international writers' meetings, *The Nook News Market Bulletin,* which is a quarterly compiled with the latest market information, and *The Nook News Contests & Awards Bulletin,* which features up-to-date listings of competitions for writers, poets, playwrights, etc. Our latest publication, *The Nook News Review of Writers Publications*, gives detailed reviews of books, magazines, newsletters, etc., written for and about writers and the writing profession. Rates are the same for all 5 publications."

WRITER'S N.W.; WRITERS NORTHWEST HANDBOOK; MEDIA WEAVERS, Blue Heron Publishing, Inc., 24450 NW Hansen Rd., Hillsboro OR 97124, phone (503)621-3911, is a professionally published tabloid quarterly giving market news, reviews of books of Northwest authors or presses, software reviews, literary activity, interviews, articles and other pertinent information for writers anywhere. Subscription: $10. **Writers NW Handbook** is like a **Writer's Market** (see listing in this section) for the Northwest (including British Columbia): $16.95 plus $2 postage and handling ($3 to Alaska, Hawaii and Canada).

WRITING! (IV-Students), General Learning Corporation, 60 Revere Dr., Northbrook IL 60062-1563, is a monthly magazine (September through May) covering writing skills for junior and senior high school students. **"We accept student-written creative writing for our 'Student Writing' department."**

Additional Publications Useful to Poets

Also read the following for other publications useful to poets. See the General Index for page numbers.

Academy of American Poets, The
American Poetry Center
Associated Writing Programs
Atlanta Writing Resource Center, Inc.
Black Bear Publications
Black Buzzard Press
Borealis Press
Byline Magazine
Canadian Conference on the Arts
Canadian Poetry Association
Chips Off The Writer's Block
COSMEP, The International Association of Independent Publishers
Council of Literary Magazines and Presses
Dusty Dog
Emerald Coast Review
Fairbanks Arts Association
Federation of British Columbia Writers
Frank: An International Journal of Contemporary Writing and Art
Hutton Publications
Illinois Writers, Inc.
Insight Press

International Poets of the Heart
Julian Associates
Keystrokes
League of Canadian Poets, The
Literary Center, The
Loft, The
Maine Writers & Publishers Alliance
My Legacy
National Association for Poetry Therapy
National Federation of State Poetry Societies, Inc.
National Poetry Foundation, The
National Writers Union
New Horizons Poetry Club
North Carolina Writers' Network
Northwoods Press
Oak, The
Parnassus: Poetry in Review
PEN American Center
Pequod
Piedmont Literary Review
Poetry Ireland Review
Poetry Magic Publications
Poetry Nippon Press
Poetry Plus Magazine

Poetry Resource Center of Michigan
Poets' Roundtable
Prosetry: Newsletter For, By and About Writers
Quarry Magazine
Recording & Publishing News
Red Dancefloor
Rio Grande Press
Seneca Review
SKAZ
Small Press Writers & Artists Organization (SPWAO)
Society of Authors, The
Southern Poetry Association
Thumbprints
Ver Poets Voices
World-wide Writers Service, Inc.
Write Way, The
Writer, The
Writer's Center, The
Writer's Exchange
Writer's Forum
Writer's Guidelines: A Roundtable for Writers and Editors
Writer's Journal
Writer's Lifeline
Writers' Rendezvous

U.S. and Canadian Postal Codes

United States

AL	Alabama	MD	Maryland	TX	Texas
AK	Alaska	MA	Massachusetts	UT	Utah
AZ	Arizona	MI	Michigan	VT	Vermont
AR	Arkansas	MN	Minnesota	VI	Virgin Islands
CA	California	MS	Mississippi	VA	Virginia
CO	Colorado	MO	Missouri	WA	Washington
CT	Connecticut	MT	Montana	WV	West Virginia
DE	Delaware	NE	Nebraska	WI	Wisconsin
DC	District of Columbia	NV	Nevada	WY	Wyoming
FL	Florida	NH	New Hampshire		
GA	Georgia	NJ	New Jersey		
GU	Guam	NM	New Mexico		
HI	Hawaii	NY	New York		
ID	Idaho	NC	North Carolina		
IL	Illinois	ND	North Dakota		
IN	Indiana	OH	Ohio		
IA	Iowa	OK	Oklahoma		
KS	Kansas	OR	Oregon		
KY	Kentucky	PA	Pennsylvania		
LA	Louisiana	PR	Puerto Rico		
ME	Maine	RI	Rhode Island		
		SC	South Carolina		
		SD	South Dakota		
		TN	Tennessee		

Canada

AB	Alberta
BC	British Columbia
LB	Labrador
MB	Manitoba
NB	New Brunswick
NF	Newfoundland
NT	Northwest Territories
NS	Nova Scotia
ON	Ontario
PEI	Prince Edward Island
PQ	Quebec
SK	Sasketchewan
YT	Yukon

ALWAYS submit a ms or query with a self-addressed, stamped envelope (SASE) within your country or a self-addressed envelope and International Reply Coupons (IRCs) purchased from the post office for other countries.

Glossary

A3, A4, A5. Metric equivalents of 11¾ × 16½, 8¼ × 11¾ and 5⅞ × 8¼ respectively.

Bio. Some publishers ask you to send a short biographical paragraph with your submission; it is commonly called a "bio." They may also ask for your important previous publications or "credits."

Chapbook. A small book of approximately 20-25 pages of poetry. Such a book is less expensive to produce than a full-length book collection, though it is seldom noted by reviewers.

Cover letter. Letter accompanying a submission giving brief account of publishing credits and biographical information. See the advice and sample letter in The Business of Poetry article.

Digest-sized. Approximately 5½ × 8½, the size of a folded sheet of conventional typing paper.

Flat-spined. What many publishers call "perfect-bound," glued with a flat edge (usually permitting readable type on the spine).

Galleys. Typeset copies of your poem(s). You should proofread and correct any mistakes and return the galleys to editors within 48 hours of receipt.

IRC. International Reply Coupon, postage for return of submissions from another country. One IRC is sufficient for one ounce by *surface mail*. If you want an airmail return, you need one IRC for each half-ounce. Do not send checks or cash for postage to other countries: The exchange rates are so high it is not worthwhile for editors to bother with. (Exception: Many Canadian editors do not object to U.S. dollars; use IRCs the first time and inquire.)

Magazine-sized. Approximately 8½ × 11, the size of conventional typing paper unfolded.

ms, mss. Manuscript, manuscripts.

Multi-book review. Also known as an omnibus review. A review of several books by several authors. You might review four or five books by political or environmental writers, for instance.

Multiple submission. Submission of more than one poem at a time; most poetry publishers *prefer* multiple submissions and specify how many should be in a packet. Some say a multiple submission means the poet has sent more than one manuscript to the same publication before receiving word on the first submission. See Multiple/Simultaneous Submissions in The Business of Poetry.

p. Abbreviation for pence.

pg., pgs. Page, pages.

Perfect-bound. See Flat-spined.

Query letter. Letter written to a publisher to elicit interest in a manuscript or to determine if submissions are acceptable.

Rights. See section in The Business of Poetry article. First North American serial rights means the publisher is acquiring the right to publish your poem first in a U.S. or Canadian periodical. All rights means the publisher is buying the poem outright. Selling all rights usually requires that you obtain permission to reprint your work, even in a book-length collection.

Saddle-stapled. What many publishers call "saddle-stitched," folded and stapled along the fold.

SAE. Self-addressed envelope.

SASE. Self-addressed, stamped envelope. *Every* publisher requires, with any submission, query, request for catalog or sample, a self-addressed, stamped envelope. This information is so basic it is excluded from the individual listings but repeated in bold type at the bottom of many pages throughout this book. The return envelope (usually folded for inclusion) should be large enough to hold the material submitted or requested, and the postage provided—stamps if the submission is within your own country, IRCs if it is to another country—should be sufficient for its return.

Simultaneous submission. Submission of the same manuscript to more than one publisher at a time. Most magazine editors *refuse to accept* simultaneous submissions. Some book and chapbook publishers do not object to simultaneous submissions. In all cases, notify them that the manuscript is being simultaneously submitted elsewhere if that is what you are doing.

Slush pile. Unsolicited manuscripts, usually hundreds each year, cluttering an editor's desk.

Status. The current situation concerning a particular manuscript: 1) The manuscript was never received. 2) We received the manuscript but cannot locate it. 3) We received and rejected said manuscript. 4) We are still considering it. 5) We are in the process of accepting your manuscript.

Subsidy press. See Vanity press.

Tabloid-sized. 11 × 15 or larger, the size of an ordinary newspaper folded and turned sideways.

Vanity press. A slang term for a publisher that requires the writer to pay publishing costs, especially one that flatters an author in order to generate business. These presses often use the term "subsidy" to describe themselves. Some presses, however, derive subsidies from other sources, such as government grants, and do not require author payment. These are not considered vanity presses.

Visual poetry. A combination of text and graphics usually only reproduced photographically.

Indexes

Chapbook Publishers Index

A chapbook is a slim volume of a poet's work, usually about 20-25 pages (although page requirements vary greatly according to specific listings). Some chapbooks are published as an insert in a particular magazine. The quality of the product also varies greatly. Thus, whenever possible, you should request submission guidelines and sample copies.

Many presses charge reading fees. Avoid any over $10. (Some people will go as high as $15 for book-length manuscripts, but chapbooks are much easier to process.)

On the plus side, many poets prefer composing chapbooks for the same reason that some fiction writers prefer the short story over the novel; some topics just lend themselves to chapbook length. Others feel they don't have enough poems for a full-length collection or they find it easier, simply, to assemble a dozen or so related poems in a chapbook. Also, given the high cost of printing, a publisher is more apt to accept a chapbook than an entire book from an unproven poet.

Best of all, if you publish chapbooks, you still will be able to participate in "first-book" competitions. They also make fine presents for friends, family and colleagues, particularly if you choose to self-publish them.

See the Book Manuscripts section of The Business of Poetry for more information about chapbooks and book publishing options.

Following are publishers listed in **Poet's Market** who consider chapbook manuscripts. See the General Index for page numbers and additional information under each listing.

Creeping Bent
Crescent Moon
Cross-Cultural Communications
Delaware Valley Poets, Inc.
Devil's Millhopper Press, The
Dolphin-Moon Press
Druid Press
Dust (From the Ego Trip)
Earth's Daughters: A Feminist Arts Periodical
Embers
Equinox Press
Expedition Press
Experimental Basement Press
Feelings: America's Beautiful Poetry Magazine
FishDrum
Fleeting Monolith Enterprises
Flume Press
Galaxy Press
Generator
Global Tapestry Journal
Golden Isis Magazine
Gotta Write Network
Green World Press
Greenhouse Review Press
Green's Magazine
Hartland Poetry Quarterly, The
Heaven Bone Press
High Plains Press
High/Coo Press
Hippopotamus Press
Holmgangers Press
Honeybrook Press
Hutton Publications
Hyacinth House Publications
Implosion Press
Inkshed—Poetry and Fiction
Insects Are People Too
Insight Press
International Black Writers
Jackson's Arm
Joe Soap's Canoe
Judi-isms
Kings Review Magazine
Lake Shore Publishing
Limberlost Press
Lockhart Press, The
Longhouse
Loom Press
Lucidity
Luna Bisonte Prods
M.A.F. Press
Mad River Press
Mayapple Press
Merging Media
Mid-American Review
Minotaur Press
Mulberry Press
Negative Capability

New Hope International
New Orleans Poetry Journal Press
Nihilistic Review, The
Nosukumo
Oasis Books
Occident Magazine
Ohio Review, The
ONTHEBUS
Outrider Press
Owl Creek Press
Pancake Press
Panhandler, The
Parting Gifts
Peacock Books
Pearl
Peregrine
Petronium Press
Phase and Cycle
Phoenix Broadsheets
Pikestaff Forum
Plowman, The
Poet
Poetry Miscellany, The
Poetry Motel
Poetry Peddler, The
Poets at Work
Poets. Painters. Composers.
Poets' Roundtable
Pogment Press
Poked With Sticks
Potato Eyes
Prairie Journal
Press of MacDonald & Reinecke, The
Printed Matter
Proof Rock Press
Prophetic Voices
Pudding House Publications
Quarry Magazine
Rag Mag
Ranger International Productions
Raw Dog Press
Red Candle Press, The
Red Dancefloor
Red Herring Poets
Repository Press
Runaway Spoon Press, The
St. Andrew Press
Score Magazine
Scream of the Buddha
Shamal Books
Ship Of Fools
Signpost Press, The
Silver Apples Press
Silver Wings
Silverfish Review
Slipstream
Small Press Writers & Artists Organization (SPWAO)
Soleil Press
Some Bees Press

Geographical Index

Use this Geographical Index especially to locate small presses and magazines in your region. Much of the poetry being published today reflects regional interests; also publishers often favor poets (and work) from their own areas.

The listings in this index are arranged alphabetically within the geographical sections; refer to the General Index for specific page numbers. Also check your neighboring states for other opportunities.

The last three sections denote publishers in Canada, the United Kingdom and other countries. If you write poetry about other areas, remember to always include a SAE with IRCs for replies from countries outside your own.

Alabama
Alabama Literary Review
Antipoetry And The Corruption Of Muse
Aura Literary/Arts Magazine
Birmingham Poetry Review
Black Warrior Review, The
College English
Dreams and Nightmares
Druid Press
Elk River Review
Minority Literary Expo
National Forum
Negative Capability
9th St. Laboratories
Poem
Southern Humanities Review
Sticks
Sucarnochee Review, The

Alaska
Alaska Quarterly Review
Explorations
Intertext
Permafrost

Arizona
Amaranth Review, The
Animal Tales
Arizona Literary Review
Arizona Unconservative, The
Bangtail
Bilingual Review Press
Experimental Basement Press
Fennel Stalk
Hayden's Ferry Review
Living Poets Society
New Chicano Writing
Newsletter Inago
Small Press Writers & Artists Organization
    (SPWAO)
Sonora Review

Xiquan Publishing House

Arkansas
Arkansas Press, The University of
Crazyhorse
Epiphany: A Journal of Literature
Graffiti Off the Asylum Walls
Hyacinth House Publications
Lucidity
Nebo: A Literary Journal
Voices International

California
Alta Napa Press
Amelia
American Collegiate Poets
Anthology of Magazine Verse & Yearbook
    of American Poetry
Anything That Moves: Beyond The Myths
    of Bisexuality
Applezaba Press
Ars Poetica Press
Asylum
Atlantean Press Review, The
Atticus Review/Press
Bakunin
Bay Area Poets Coalition (BAPC)
Belladonna Review, The
Berkeley Poetry Review
Berkeley Poets Cooperative (Workshop &
    Press)
Bishop Publishing Co.
Black Scholar, The
Black Sparrow Press
Blue Unicorn, A Triquarterly of Poetry
Bottomfish
California Quarterly, The
Caravan Press
Cat Fancy
CCR Publications

Ceilidh: An Informal Gathering for Story
  & Song
Children's Album
Chips Off The Writer's Block
City Lights Books
City Scriptum
College & Career Publishing
Conditioned Response Press
Crazyquilt Quarterly
Creative With Words Publications
  (C.W.W.)
Creativity Unlimited Press
Cyanosis
Daniel and Company, Publisher, John
Dolphin Log
Dragon's Teeth Press
Dry Crik Review
El Tecolote
Equinox
Flume Press
Free Lunch
Furry Chiclets: A Lawpoets Creation
Gain Publications
Gazelle Publications
Golden Isis Magazine
Green Fuse
Greenhouse Review Press
Haight Ashbury Literary Journal
Haiku Headlines: A Monthly Newsletter of
  Haiku and Senryu
Haiku Journal
Harcourt Brace Jovanovich, Publishers
Hard Row to Hoe
Holmgangers Press
India Currents
Infinity Limited: A Journal for the Some-
  what Eccentric
Inky Blue
Innisfree Magazine
Insight Press
International Olympic Lifter (IOL)
Issues
Jacaranda Review
Jewish Spectator
Journal of Pan African Studies
Kingfisher
Kings Review Magazine
La Bella Figura
Left Curve
Libra Publishers, Inc.
Literary Olympics, Inc.
Los Hombres Press
Luna Ventures
Manic D Press
Midnight Zoo
Mind In Motion: A Magazine of Poetry and
  Short Prose
Mind Matters Review
Minotaur Press
Naughty Naked Dreamgirls

New Earth Publications
New Horizons Poetry Club
New Methods: The Journal of Animal
  Health Technology
Occident Magazine
Olive Press Publications, The
ONTHEBUS
Ortalda & Associates
Out Loud
Painted Hills Review
Paisley Moon
Pancake Press
Panjandrum Books
Papier-Mache Press
Pearl
Pinehurst Journal, The
Poems for a Livable Planet
Poetry Break
Poetry Connexion, The
Poetry: USA Quarterly
Poets On:
Press of MacDonald & Reinecke, The
Prisoners of the Night
Prophetic Voices
Prosetry: Newsletter For, By and About
  Writers
Protea Poetry Journal
Pygmy Forest Press
Radiance: The Magazine For Large
  Women
Rainbow City Express
Red Dancefloor
Ridge Review Magazine
Rienda Suelta/Free Rein
Sacred River: Bay Area Women's Journal
Sacrifice The Common Sense
San Diego Poet's Press
San Fernando Poetry Journal
San Jose Studies
Santa Monica Review
Santa Susana Press
Score Magazine
Scream of the Buddha
Sequoia
Sheila-na-gig
Silver Wings
Sinister Wisdom
Sonoma Mandala
South Coast Poetry Journal
Southern California Anthology, The
Steelhead Special, The
Stone Circle Press
Stone Soup, The Magazine by Children
Summer Stream Press
Talisman Literary Research, Inc.
Threepenny Review, The
Tight
Times Change Press
Tradeswomen Magazine
Tsunami

Tucumcari Literary Review
Turkey Press
Urbanus/Raizirr
Verve
Virgin Meat
VIVO
Vol. No. Magazine
W.I.M. Publications (Woman in the Moon)
West Anglia Publications
Wise Woman, The
Wishing Well, The
Worldwide Poets' Circle
Wormwood Review Press
Writers' Rendezvous
Xenophilia

Colorado
Arjuna Library Press
Blue Light Review
Cloud Ridge Press
Coffeehouse Poets' Quarterly
Colorado North Review
Colorado Review
Dayspring Press, The
Denver Quarterly
eleventh muse, the
Equilibrium[10]
High Plains Literary Review
Horses West
Phase and Cycle
Pueblo Poetry Project
Senior Edition USA/Colorado Old Times
Timberlines
Wordsmith
Writers' Forum

Connecticut
Broken Streets
Chicory Blue Press
Connecticut Poetry Review, The
Connecticut River Review
Eagle, The
Embers
Poetry Only
Potes & Poets Press, Inc.
Singular Speech Press
Small Pond Magazine of Literature
Wesleyan University Press
Yale University Press

Delaware
En Passant Poetry

District of Columbia
Aerial
American Scholar, The
Dickinson Studies
Folio: A Literary Journal
G.W. Review
Middle East Report

New Republic, The
Plum Review, The
Sojourners
Three Continents Press Inc.
Washington Review
Washington Writers' Publishing House
Wineberry Press
Word Works, The

Florida
Albatross
Anhinga Press
Candlestones
Cathartic, The
Cats Magazine
Central Florida Contemporary Poetry Series, University of
Crystal Rainbow
Ediciones Universal
Emerald Coast Review
Florida Review, The
Gulf Stream Magazine
Half Tones to Jubilee
Harp-Strings
Human Quest, The
Kalliope, a journal of women's art
Mahogany & Molasses Family Reader
Middle Eastern Dancer
National Enquirer
Onionhead
Panhandler, The
Pet Gazette, The
Poetry of the People
Psych It
Runaway Spoon Press, The
Sun Dog: The Southeast Review
Tampa Bay Review
Tampa Review
Thematic Poetry Quarterly
Thoughts for All Seasons: The Magazine of Epigrams
Tiger Moon Press
Whispering Palm
Write Way, The
Yesterday's Magazette

Georgia
Chattahoochee Review, The
Classical Outlook, The
Dickey Newsletter, James
Georgia Journal
Georgia Press, University of
Georgia Review, The
Kennesaw Review
Linwood Publishers
Lullwater Review
Old Red Kimono
Parnassus Literary Journal
Pendragon
Poet's Review

Resin
Snake Nation Review
Society of American Poets, The
Twisted

Hawaii
Aloha, The Magazine of Hawaii and the
 Pacific
Chaminade Literary Review
Hawai'i Pacific Review
Hawai'i Review
Kaimana: Literary Arts Hawaii
Pep Publishing
Petronium Press

Idaho
Ahsahta Press
American Cowboy Poet Magazine, The
Boots: For Folks With Their Boots On!
Confluence Press
Emshock Letter, The
 Figment: Tales from the Imagination
Honeybrook Press
Hutton Publications
Limberlost Press
Paper Radio
Rocky Mountain Review of Language and
 Literature
Signal, The
Snake River Reflections
Trestle Creek Review
Village Idiot, The

Illinois
ACM (Another Chicago Magazine)
Aim Magazine
Algilmore
Anaconda Press
Ascent
Black Books Bulletin
Brilliant Star
Chicago Review
Christian Century, The
Clockwatch Review
Cornerstone: The Voice of This Genera-
 tion
Creative Woman, The
Cricket, The Magazine for Children
Daughters of Sarah
Dream International Quarterly
Farmer's Market
Gotta Write Network
Great Lakes Poetry Press
Hammers
High/Coo Press
Illinois Press, University of
Insects Are People Too
International Black Writers
Journal of the American Medical Associa-
 tion (JAMA)

Karamu
Kumquat Meringue
Lake Shore Publishing; Soundings
Light
Lollipops, The Magazine for Early Child-
 hood Educators
Magic Changes
Midwest Poetry Review
Mississippi Valley Review
NCASA Journal (Newsletter of the Na-
 tional Coalition Against Sexual Assault)
Night Roses
Nomos Press Inc.
Oak, The
Oblates
Outrider Press
Oyez Review
Paper Bag, The
Path Press, Inc.
Pikestaff Forum
Poetry
Poetry East
Poetry Plus Magazine
Press of the Third Mind, The
Primavera
Pyramid, The
Rambunctious Press
Red Herring Poets
Rhino
Rockford Review, The
Shaw Publishers, Harold
Sou'Wester
Spoon River Poetry Review, The
Stormline Press, Inc.
Student Leadership Journal
Sunshine Magazine
Thorntree Press
Tia Chucha Press
TriQuarterly Magazine
2 AM Magazine
Whetstone
White Eagle Coffee Store Press
Willow Review
Young Crusader, The

Indiana
Arts Indiana Literary Supplement
Barnwood Press
Black American Literature Forum
Children's Better Health Institute
Evangel
Explorer Magazine
Formalist, The
Indiana Review
Light and Life Magazine
Lines n' Rhymes
Living Streams
Pablo Lennis
Poets' Roundtable
Purdue University Press

Saturday Evening Post
Skylark
Snowy Egret
Sparrow: The Politically Incorrect Verse
    Magazine
Sycamore Review
Toad Highway
Wesleyan Advocate, The
Windless Orchard, The
Writers' Center Press

Iowa
Ansuda Publications
Blue Light Press
Coe Review, The
Cramped and Wet
Interstate Religious Writers Association
    Newsletter and Workshops
Iowa Press, University of
Iowa Review
Iowa Woman
North American Review
Poet and Critic
Rural Heritage
Windhover Press, The

Kansas
Capper's
Chiron Review
Cottonwood
Kansas Quarterly
Midwest Quarterly, The
Potpourri
Scavenger's Newsletter
Woodley Memorial Press

Kentucky
American Voice, The
Appalachian Heritage
Kentucky Writing
Limestone: A Literary Journal
Louisville Review, The
Misnomer
New Madrid
Pikeville Review
Plainsong
River Rat Review
Wind Magazine

Louisiana
Exquisite Corpse
Louisiana Literature
Louisiana State University Press
New Delta Review
New Laurel Review, The
New Orleans Poetry Journal Press
New Orleans Review
New Voices in Poetry and Prose
Pelican Publishing Company
Southern Review, The

Thema
Xavier Review

Maine
Beloit Poetry Journal, The
Black Fly Review
Chants
Kennebec: A Portfolio of Maine Writing
Northwoods Press
Potato Eyes
Puckerbrush Press, The
Soleil Press

Maryland
Abbey
Antietam Review
Callaloo
Cochran's Corner
Dolphin-Moon Press
Expressions Forum Review
Feminist Studies
Gut Punch Press
Hanson's: A Symposium of Literary and
    Social Interest
Johns Hopkins University Press, The
LMNO Press
Maryland Poetry Review
Monocacy Valley Review
New Poets Series, Inc.
Nightsun
Oracle Poetry
Passager: A Journal of Remembrance and
    Discovery
Plastic Tower, The
Poet Lore
Scop Publications, Inc.
Shattered Wig Review
Social Anarchism
Vegetarian Journal
Welter
WoRM fEASt!

Massachusetts
Aboriginal SF
Adastra Press
Agni
Alicejamesbooks
Appalachia
Ark, The
Arts End Books
Atlantic, The
Bad Attitude
Bay Windows
Boston Literary Review (BLUR)
Boston Phoenix: Phoenix Literary Section
    (PLS), The
Boston Review
Christian Science Monitor, The
Christopher Publishing House, The
Eidos Magazine: Sexual Freedom and

Erotic Entertainment for Women, Men
& Couples
Faber and Faber, Inc.
Figures, The
Harvard Advocate, The
Little River Press
Loom Press
Mad River Press
Massachusetts Review, The
Nahant Bay
New Renaissance, The
Northeast Arts Magazine
Northeastern University Press
O-Blek
Osiris
Partisan Review
Peregrine
Ploughshares
Point Judith Light
Poultry, A Magazine of Voice
Provincetown Arts
Radcliffe Quarterly
Rugging Room, The
Sisyphus
Soundings East
Spectrum
Tightrope
West.
West of Boston
Worcester Review
Writer, The
Zoland Books Inc.

Michigan

American Tolkien Society
Bennett & Kitchel
Bridge: A Journal of Fiction and Poetry,
   The
Canoe Press
Centennial Review, The
Clubhouse
El Barrio
Expedition Press
Hartland Poetry Quarterly, The
Howling Dog
Japanophile
Kangaroos and Beans
Lightworks
Lotus Press, Inc.
MacGuffin, The
Michigan Quarterly Review
Mobius
Nada Press
Notus: New Writing
Pandora
Passages North
Phanes Press
Poetic Page
Poetry Magic Publications
Rarach Press

Renegade
Riverrun
Sideshow Magazine
Struggle: A Magazine of Proletarian Revo-
   lutionary Literature
Sulfur Magazine
Team
Thumbprints
Touch
Wayne Literary Review
Wire, The
Wordsmith Publishing, Inc.
X-Press Productions

Minnesota

Ally Press Center
American Knight
Coffee House Press
Evergreen Chronicles, The
Graywolf Press
Guild Press
Liftouts Magazine
Loonfeather
Lutheran Journal, The
M.I.P. Company
Mankato Poetry Review
Milkweed Editions
New Rivers Press
Pentagram Press
Place in the Woods, The
Poetry Motel
Rag Mag
Sing Heavenly Muse!
Sisters Today
White Review: A Gay Men's Literary
   Quarterly, James
Writer's Journal

Mississippi

Bell's Letters Poet
Mississippi Review

Missouri

Afro-Hispanic Review
Big Now, The
Cape Rock, The
Chariton Review Press, The
Communications Publishing Group
Communities: Journal of Cooperation
Gospel Publishing House
Helicon Nine Editions
Laurel Review
Metro Singles Lifestyles
Missouri Press, University of
Missouri Review
Nazarene International Headquarters
New Letters
Paintbrush: A Journal of Poetry, Transla-
   tions and Letters
Recording & Publishing News

Conjunctions
Cosmopolitan
Cover Magazine
Cross-Cultural Communications
CWM
DBQP
Earth's Daughters: A Feminist Arts Periodical
11th St. Ruse
ELF: Eclectic Literary Forum
Epoch
Fighting Woman News
Firebrand Books
For Poets Only
Free Focus
Frogpond: Quarterly Haiku Journal
Futurific Magazine
Giants Play Well In The Drizzle
Giorno Poetry Systems Records
Good Housekeeping
Graham House Review
Greenfield Review Press, The
Grue Magazine
Hanging Loose Press
Heaven Bone Press
Heresies
Holiday House, Inc.
Holt & Company, Henry
Home Planet News
Hudson Review, The
Hudson Valley Echoes
Israel Horizons
Italica Press
Jewish Currents
Journal of Poetry Therapy
Judi-isms
Kairos
Keystrokes
Kiosk
Kitchen Table: Women of Color Press
Knopf, Alfred A.
La Nuez
Lactuca
Lang Publishing, Inc., Peter
Latest Jokes Newsletter
Ledge Poetry and Fiction Magazine, The
Lilith Magazine
Living Poets Society
Lodestar Books
Long Island Quarterly
Long Islander
Lothrop, Lee & Shepard Books
Low-Tech Press
M.A.F. Press
Macfadden Women's Group
Manhattan Poetry Review
Manhattan Review, The
Mellen Press, The Edwin
Midmarch Arts Press
Midstream: A Monthly Jewish Review

Miorita: A Journal of Romanian Studies
Modern Bride
Moksha Journal
Morrow and Co., William
Ms. Magazine
Mss/New Myths
Mudfish
Mulberry Press
Nassau Review
Nation, The
New Criterion, The
New Directions Publishing Corporation
New Press Literary Quarterly, The
New York Quarterly
New Yorker, The
Norton & Company, Inc., W.W.
One Meadway
Outerbridge
Overlook Press, The
Oxford Unversity Press
Paragon House Publishers
Paris Review, The
Parnassus: Poetry in Review
Peace Newsletter, The
Peoplenet
Pequod
Persea Books
Philomel Books
Pipe Smoker's Ephemeris, The
Pivot
Poet Gallery Press
Poetpourri
Poetry New York: A Journal of Poetry and Translation
Poetry Peddler, The
Primal Voices
Quarterly, The
Queen of All Hearts
Recursive Angel
Response
Review: Latin American Literature and Arts
Round Table: A Journal of Poetry and Fiction, The
Sachem Press
Salmagundi
Science Fiction Poetry Association
Seance
Segue Foundation
Seneca Review
Seventeen
Shamal Books
Shofar
Slate & Style
Slipstream
Smith, The
Smoke Signals
Snail's Pace Review, The
Spirit That Moves Us, The
Spit

Starmist Books
State Street Press
Stevens Journal, The Wallace
Superintendent's Profile & Pocket Equipment Directory
TAL: A Torah Art & Literature Review
Textile Bridge Press
13th Moon
Tin Wreath
Ultramarine Publishing Co., Inc.
Unmuzzled Ox
Untitled
Villager, The
Water Mark Press
Waterways: Poetry in the Mainstream
White Pine Press
Women's Studies Quarterly
Write Technique, The
Yammering Twits

North Carolina
Black Mountain Review
Carolina Quarterly
Carolina Wren Press
Crucible
Deathrealm
Forbidden Lines Magazine
French Broad Press
Greensboro Review, The
Katuah: Bioregional Journal of the Southern Appalachians
Kwibidi Publisher
Mayberry Gazette, The
Minnesota Review, The
North Carolina Haiku Society Press, The
Obsidian
Parting Gifts
Pembroke Magazine
Sanskrit
Southern Poetry Review
Star Books, Inc.
Sun, The
Tar River Poetry
Wake Forest University Press

North Dakota
North Dakota Quarterly
Plains Poetry Journal
Plainswoman

Ohio
Amateur Writers Journal/Four Seasons Poetry Club Magazine
And Review, The
Antioch Review, The
Artful Dodge
Ashland Poetry Press, The
Atalantik
Bellflower Press
Bird Watcher's Digest

Bits Press
Black River Review
Carpenter Press
Cleveland State University Poetry Center
Cornfield Review
Dream Shop, The
Field
Gamut, The
Generator
Hiram Poetry Review
Hopscotch: The Magazine For Girls
Icon
Implosion Press
Journal, The
Juggler's World
Kaleidoscope Press
Kenyon Review, The
Luna Bisonte Prods
Mark: A Journal of Scholarship, Opinion, and Literature
Mid-American Review
Mosaic Press
Nancy's Magazine
New Kent Quarterly, The
Nexus
Ohio Review, The
Ohio State University Press/Journal Award in Poetry
Oxford Magazine
Pig Iron
Poetic Knight, The
Poked With Sticks
Pudding House Publications
Riverwind
St. Anthony Messenger
Ship Of Fools
Single Scene, The
Solo Flyer
Spitball
Straight
TapRoot
Toledo Poets Center Press
Vincent Brothers Review, The
Writer's Digest

Oklahoma
Byline Magazine
Cimarron Review
Midland Review
Nimrod International Journal of Contemporary Poetry and Fiction
Poet
Rope Burns
Westview: A Journal of Western Oklahoma

Oregon
Arrowood Books, Inc.
Breitenbush Books, Inc.
Calapooya Collage

Calyx, A Journal of Art & Literature by Women
Convictions
Eighth Mountain Press, The
Fireweed: Poetry of Western Oregon
L'Apache: An International Journal of Literature & Art
Metamorphous Press
Midwifery Today
Mr. Cogito Press
Northwest Review
Oregon East
Poetic Space: Poetry & Fiction
Pointed Circle, The
Portland Review
Sandpiper Press
Silverfish Review
Soundings: A Newsletter For Survivors of Childhood Sexual Abuse
Stone Press
Story Line Press
Trout Creek Press
Virtue: The Christian Magazine for Women
West Wind Review
Whitecrow Foundation, Tahana
Wilderness
Willamette River Books

Pennsylvania
Aguilar Expression, The
Allegheny Review
Alpha Beat Soup
Alternative Press Magazine
American Poetry Review
American Writing: A Magazine
Anima: The Journal of Human Experience
Apropos
Black Bear Publications
Bouillabaisse
Boulevard
Branch Redd Books
Carnegie Mellon Magazine
Cokefish
Collages & Bricolages, The Journal of International Writing
Cool Traveler, The
Country Journal
Creeping Bent
Dust (From the Ego Trip)
Family Earth
Fat Tuesday
Feelings: America's Beautiful Poetry Magazine
Flipside
Friends Journal
Gettysburg Review, The
Ginger Hill
Green World Press
Guyasuta Publisher

Hellas: A Journal of Poetry and the Humanities
Highlights for Children
Inverted Ostrich
Lilliput Review
Mayapple Press
Mennonite Publishing House
Miraculous Medal, The
My Legacy
Other Side Magazine, The
Painted Bride Quarterly
Pennsylvania English
Pennsylvania Review, The
Philomel
Pitt Poetry Series
Pittsburgh Quarterly, The
Poetry Forum
Poets at Work
Post-Industrial Press
Quick Brown Fox
Raw Dog Press
Reconstructionist
Rolling Coulter, The
Taproot Literary Review
Translucent Tendency Press
West Branch
Widener Review
Wildwood Journal
WordSong
Wyrd
Yarrow, A Journal of Poetry

Rhode Island
Aldebaran
Copper Beech Press
Gávea-Brown Publications
Italian Americana
Merlyn's Pen: The National Magazine of Student Writing, Grades 7-10
Northeast Journal

South Carolina
Devil's Millhopper Press, The
Emrys Journal
Nostalgia: A Sentimental State of Mind
Raven, The
South Carolina Review
Writer's Exchange

South Dakota
Hen's Teeth
Pasque Petals
South Dakota Review
Tesseract Publications

Tennessee
Aethlon: The Journal of Sport Literature
alive now!
American Association of Haikuists Newsletter

Baptist Sunday School Board
Co-Laborer
Cumberland Poetry Review
Mature Years
Nashville House
Now and Then
Old Hickory Review
Poetry Miscellany, The
RFD: A Country Journal For Gay Men Everywhere
River City
Romantist, The
Sewanee Review
Southeastern FRONT
Sow's Ear, The
Swamp Root
Westenra: The Miss Lucy Westenra Society of the Undead

Texas
American Atheist Press
Analecta
Argonaut
Art-Core!
Arte Publico Press
Baby Connection News Journal, The
Backyard Press
Black Tie Press
Concho River Review
Context South
Corona Publishing Co.
Dagger of the Mind
Daily Meditation
Descant: Texas Christian University Literary Journal
Experiment in Words
Gopherwood Review, The
Grasslands Review
Great Plains Canal and Avalon Dispatch
Gypsy
Julian Associates
Language Bridges Quarterly
Literary Focus Poetry Publications
North Texas Press, University of
Peace Farm Advocate, The
Prose Poem, The
REAL (Re Arts & Letters)
Red Rampan' Press
Rio Grande Press
Salt Lick
Southwest Review
Strain, The
Sulphur River Literary Review
Tangram Press
Texas Tech University Press
Touchstone Literary Journal
United Methodist Reporter

Utah
Dialogue: A Journal of Mormon Thought
Ellipsis Magazine
International Poets of the Heart
Leading Edge, The
Literature and Belief
Magic Realism
Manna
New Era Magazine
Paper Salad Poetry Journal, The
Smith Publisher, Gibbs
Utah Holiday Magazine

Vermont
Awede Press
Green Mountains Review
Longhouse
New England Review
Threshold Books

Virginia
Black Buzzard Press
Bogg Publications
Bold Print
Brunswick Publishing Company
Callaloo Poetry Series
Chronicle of the Horse, The
Dominion Review, The
Hampden-Sydney Poetry Review, The
Hollins Critic, The
Intro
Iris: A Journal About Women
Lintel
Lyric, The
Metropolitain
Miriam Press
Orchises Press
Phoebe
Piedmont Literary Review
Pocahontas Press, Inc.
Poetry Explosion Newsletter, The
Pogment Press
Proof Rock Press
Ranger Rick Magazine
Reflect
Roanoke Review
St. Andrew Press
Shenandoah
Vandeloecht's Fiction Magazine
Verse
Virginia Quarterly Review, The
William And Mary Review, The

Washington
Ag-Pilot International Magazine
Arnazella
Bad Haircut
Bear Tribe Publishing
Bellowing Ark Press
Box Dog Press

Brussels Sprout
Cleaning Business Magazine
Crab Creek Review
Emerald City Comix & Stories
Fine Madness
Fredrickson-Kloepfel Publishing Co.
Graven Images
GreyRaven Press
IHCUT
Jeopardy
L'Epervier Press
Lighthouse
Lithic Review, The
Lockhart Press, The
Lynx, A Quarterly Journal of Renga
Open Hand Publishing Inc.
Owl Creek Press
Poetry Northwest
Poets. Painters. Composers.
Seattle Review
Signpost Press, The
Spindrift
Tapjoe: The Anaprocrustean Poetry Journal of Enumclaw
Twopenny Porringer, The
Willow Springs
Young Voices Magazine
Zero Hour

West Virginia
Aegina Press, Inc.

Wisconsin
Abraxas Magazine
Caxton Ltd., Wm
Changing Men: Issues In Gender, Sex and Politics
Converging Paths
Country Woman
Cream City Review
Die Young
Dionysos: The Literature and Addiction TriQuarterly
Fox Cry
Juniper Press
Madison Review, The
Magazine of Speculative Poetry, The
Mid Coaster
Modern Haiku
Ranger International Productions
Redneck Review of Literature, The
Seems
Touchstone
Wisconsin Academy Review
Wisconsin Press, University of
Wisconsin Review

Wyoming
High Plains Press
Housewife-Writer's Forum

U.S. Virgin Islands
Caribbean Writer, The
Eastern Caribbean Institute

Canada
Alchemist, The
Amber
Anjou
Antigonish Review, The
Arc
Ariel, A Review of International English Literature
Atlantis: A Women's Studies Journal
Beneath The Surface
Borealis Press
Breakthrough!
Canadian Dimension: A Socialist News Magazine
Canadian Literature
Canadian Writer's Journal
Capers Aweigh Magazine
Carleton Arts Review
Carousel Magazine
Chalk Talk
Charnel House
Chastity & Holiness Magazine
Chickadee Magazine
Cosmic Trend
Coteau Books
Dalhousie Review, The
Dance Connection
Dandelion
Descant
Ellipse
Event
Feh! A Journal of Odious Poetry
Fiddlehead, The
Fireweed: A Feminist Quarterly
Goose Lane Editions
Grain
Green's Magazine
Guernica Editions Inc.
Herspectives
Indigo Magazine: The Spanish-Canadian Presence in the Arts
Inkstone: A Magazine of Haiku
Legend: An International "Robin of Sherwood" Fanzine
Lost Magazine
Macmillan of Canada
Malahat Review, The
(m)öthêr TØngués
Musicworks
New Quarterly, The
Next Exit
Nexus
Our Family
Out Magazine
Paupers Press
Peckerwood

Scratch
Second Aeon Publications
Skoob Books Publishing Ltd.
Smiths Knoll
Spokes
Stand Magazine
Staple
Stride Publications
Tak Tak Tak
Tears in the Fence
10th Muse
Third Half Literary Magazine, The
Times Literary Supplement
Ver Poets Voices
Vigil
Weyfarers
Works Magazine
Writers Forum (England)
Zero One

Other Countries
Abiko Quarterly Litter-ary Rag (Japan)
Coop. Antigruppo Siciliano (Italy)
Doc(k)s (France)
Frank: An International Journal of Contemporary Writing and Art (France)
Galaxy Press (Australia)
Imago Literary Magazine (Australia)
La Carta De Oliver (Argentina)
Landfall (New Zealand)
Mattoid (Australia)

New Cicada (Japan)
Nosukumo (Australia)
Otis Rush (Australia)
Peacock Books (India)
PIE (Poetry Imagery and Expression) (Australia)
Pinchgut Press (Australia)
Poetry Kanto (Japan)
Poetry Nippon Press (Japan)
Polyphonies (France)
Prakalpana Literature (India)
Printed Matter (Japan)
Rashi (New Zealand)
Renditions: A Chinese-English Translation Magazine (Hong Kong)
Revista/Review Interamericana (Puerto Rico)
Sandberry Press (West Indies)
Scarp (Australia)
South Head Press (Australia)
Southern Review (Australia)
Studio: A Journal of Christians Writing (Australia)
Takahe (New Zealand)
Transnational Perspectives (Switzerland)
Vanitas Press, The (Sweden)
Verandah (Australia)
Voices Israel
Webber's (Australia)
Westerly (Australia)
Writing (Australia)

Subject Index

Use this Subject Index to save time in your search for the best market for your poem(s).

The categories are listed alphabetically and contain the magazines, publishers, contests and awards that buy or accept poetry in these special categories. Most of these markets are coded **IV** in their listings.

Check through the index first to see what subjects are represented. Then look at the listings in the categories you're interested in. For example, if you're seeking a magazine or contest for your poem about homelessness, look at the listings under *Social Issues*. After you've selected a possible market, refer to the General Index for the page number of the listing. Then read the listing *carefully* for details on submission requirements.

In the section **Themes**, there are publishers and magazines which publish poetry on a particular theme or subject or publications directed to a special audience. The **Regional** section lists those outlets which publish poetry about or by poets from a special geographic area; and the category **Form/Style** contains those magazines and presses with a specific preference for haiku, sonnets, narrative poems or visual poetry, for example.

We do not recommend that you use this index exclusively in your search for a market. Most of the magazines, publishers and contests listed in **Poet's Market** are very general in their specifications, and they don't choose to be listed by category. Also, many specialize in one subject area but are open to other subjects as well. Reading *all* the listings is still your best marketing strategy.

Anthology
Anthology of Magazine Verse & Yearbook of American Poetry
Ashland Poetry Press, The
Blind Beggar Press
Charnel House
Delaware Valley Poets, Inc.
Fredrickson-Kloepfel Publishing Co.
Georgia State Poetry Society, Inc.
Great Lakes Poetry Press
Guild Press
Gypsy
Haiku Journal
Helicon Nine Editions
Hen's Teeth
Insight Press
Judi-isms
Kawabata Press
Kitchen Table: Women of Color Press
Lake Shore Publishing
Literary Focus Poetry Publications
Literary Olympics, Inc.
Lodestar Books
Nada Press
Night Roses
Northwoods Press
Papier-Mache Press
Plowman, The
Poetic Knight, The
Poetic Perspective, Inc.
Poetry Magic Publications
Poetry of the People
Prairie Journal
Pudding House Publications
Roberts Foundation Writing Awards, The
San Fernando Poetry Journal
Science Fiction Poetry Association
Seven Buffaloes Press
Shamal Books
Spirit That Moves Us, The
Summer Stream Press
Three Continents Press Inc.
Voices Israel
Waterways: Poetry in the Mainstream
West Wind Review
Willamette River Books
Wineberry Press
Word Works, The
Wordsmith Publishing, Inc.
Write Technique, The

Bilingual/Foreign Language
American Collegiate Poets
Atalantik (Bengali)
Bilingual Review Press (Spanish)
Cross-Cultural Communications
Doc(k)s (French)
Ediciones Universal (Spanish)
Ellipse (French)

Footwork: The Paterson Literary Review
  (Spanish)
Gairm (Scottish Gaelic)
Gávea-Brown Publications (Portugese)
Indigo Magazine: The Spanish-Canadian
  Presence in the Arts (French, Spanish)
La Carta De Oliver (Spanish)
La Nuez (Spanish)
Language Bridges Quarterly (Polish)
Letras De Oro Spanish Literary Prizes
M.I.P. Company (Russian)
Nada Press (Spanish)
New Chicano Writing (Spanish)
New Renaissance, The
Osiris (French, Italian, Polish, Danish,
  German)
Princeton University Press
REAL (Re Arts & Letters)
Rienda Suelta/Free Rein (Spanish)
Sachem Press (Spanish)
Tessera (French)
Unmuzzled Ox (French)
Women's Studies Quarterly (Spanish,
  French, Italian, German)

Children/Teen/Young Adult
alive now!
Blind Beggar Press
Brilliant Star
Broken Streets
Cat Fancy
Chalk Talk
Chickadee Magazine
Children's Album
Children's Better Health Institute
Chimera Poetry Magazine for Children
Clubhouse
Communications Publishing Group
Coteau Books
Creative With Words Publications
  (C.W.W.)
Cricket, The Magazine for Children
Dolphin Log
Gospel Publishing House
Hanging Loose Press
Hartland Poetry Quarterly, The
Highlights for Children
Holiday House, Inc.
Hopscotch: The Magazine For Girls
Kwibidi Publisher
Lighthouse
Lodestar Books
Louisville Review, The
Mahogany & Molasses Family Reader
Mennonite Publishing House
Merlyn's Pen: The National Magazine of
  Student Writing, Grades 7-10
Nazarene International Headquarters
New Era Magazine
Night Roses

Oak, The
Paupers Press
Pelican Publishing Company
Pikestaff Forum
Place in the Woods, The
Poetry Break
Poetry of Hope Award
Poetry: USA Quarterly
Primal Voices
Scholastic Writing Awards
Seventeen
Shofar
Sow's Ear, The
Stone Soup, The Magazine by Children
Straight
Team
Touch
Vanitas Press, The
Vegetarian Journal
Waterways: Poetry in the Mainstream
Whole Notes
WordSong
Writer's Journal
Young Crusader, The
Young Voices Magazine

Ethnic/Nationality
Adrift (Irish, Irish-American)
Africa World Press (African, African-
  American, Caribbean and Latin Ameri-
  can)
Afro-Hispanic Review
Aim Magazine
Alicejamesbooks (poets of color)
American Dane
Ararat (Armenian)
Arte Publico Press (U.S. Hispanic)
Atalantik (Bengali)
Bear Tribe Publishing (Native American)
Bilingual Review Press (Hispanic)
Black American Literature Forum
Black Books Bulletin
Black Scholar, The
Blind Beggar Press (Black and Third
  World)
Callaloo (North, South and Central Ameri-
  can; European; African; Caribbean)
Carolina Wren Press (minorities)
Cencrastus (Scottish)
Chapman (Scottish)
Communications Publishing Group
  (Asian-American, Black, Hispanic, Na-
  tive American)
Council for Indian Education
Eagle, The (American Indian)
Ediciones Universal (Spanish, Cuban)
El Barrio (Latino)
El Tecolote (Latin American, U.S. Latino)
European Judaism
Firebrand Books

Plains Poetry Journal (rhyme, meter)
Poetry Nippon Press (tanka, haiku, one-line poems)
Poetry Society of Virginia Annual Contest, The (haiku, sonnet, limerick and pop song)
Poets and Patrons, Inc.
Poets Club of Chicago International Shakespearean Sonnet Contest
Point Judith Light (haiku, senryu)
Prakalpana Literature (experimental, avant-garde)
Press of the Third Mind, The (concrete, collaborative)
Prose Poem, The
Raddle Moon (language-centered, new lyric)
Red Candle Press, The
Red Rampan' Press (long poems)
Reflect (spiral poetry)
Rhyme International Competition for Rhyming Poetry
Runaway Spoon Press, The (visual, textual)
Salmon Arm Sonnet Contest
San Francisco International Haiku Competition
Score Magazine (visual, concrete, experimental)
Sparrow: The Politically Incorrect Verse Magazine (sonnets)
Sticks (10 lines or less)
Sub-Terrain
Thoughts for All Seasons: The Magazine of Epigrams
Tidepool (haiku, short verse)
Wire, The (experimental, short form)
World Order of Narrative and Formalist Poets
Writers Forum (England) (computer poetry)
Writers' Rendezvous (rhyme, haiku)
Xiquan Publishing House (lyrical, experimental)

Gay/Lesbian
Bay Windows
Calyx, A Journal of Art & Literature by Women
Carolina Wren Press
Evergreen Chronicles, The
Firebrand Books
First Hand
Gay Men's Press, The
Heresies
Out Magazine
RFD: A Country Journal For Gay Men Everywhere
Sinister Wisdom
W.I.M. Publications (Woman in the Moon)

White Review: A Gay Men's Literary Quarterly, James
Xtra!

Humor
Bellflower Press
Bits Press
Capper's
Collages & Bricolages, The Journal of International Writing
Country Woman
Feh! A Journal of Odious Poetry
Good Housekeeping
Graffiti Off the Asylum Walls
Housewife-Writer's Forum
Howling Dog
Hutton Publications
Krax
Latest Jokes Newsletter
Leacock Medal for Humour, The Stephen
Mahogany & Molasses Family Reader
Mayberry Gazette, The
Moore Poetry Competition, The Julia
National Enquirer
Naughty Naked Dreamgirls
New Yorker, The
Paris Review, The
Poetry Arts Project
Poetry of the People
Poultry, A Magazine of Voice
Proof Rock Press
Raw Dog Press
REAL (Re Arts & Letters)
Saturday Evening Post
Seance
Single Scene, The
Sunshine Magazine
Thalia: Studies in Literary Humor
Thoughts for All Seasons: The Magazine of Epigrams
Words of Wisdom
Writer's Digest
Writer's Exchange

Love/Romance/Erotica
Cosmic Trend
Eidos Magazine: Sexual Freedom and Erotic Entertainment for Women, Men & Couples
Expedition Press
Explorer Magazine
M.I.P. Company
Modern Bride
Naughty Naked Dreamgirls
Peoplenet
Pep Publishing
Poetic Knight, The
Poetry Magic Publications
Poetry of the People
Prisoners of the Night

Seance
WoRM fEASt!

Membership/Subscription

Breakthrough!
Cochran's Corner
Delaware Valley Poets, Inc.
Dream Shop, The
Emshock Letter, The
Equinox Press
First Hand
Gotta Write Network
Haiku Journal
Harvard Advocate, The
High/Coo Press
International Poets of the Heart
Interstate Religious Writers Association
    Newsletter and Workshops
Intro
Kwibidi Publisher
Living Streams
Lynx, A Quarterly Journal of Renga
Midwest Poetry Review
Minority Literary Expo
Montana Institute of the Arts Writers Con-
    tests
New Horizons Poetry Club
Oracle Poetry
Ozark Creative Writers, Inc. Conference
    Awards
Pasque Petals
Pennsylvania Poetry Society Annual Con-
    test
Poetry Forum
Poetry Nottingham
Poetry Plus Magazine
Poetry Society of Texas
Poetry: USA Quarterly
Poets at Work
Poet's Review
Poets' Roundtable
Post-Industrial Press
Prosetry: Newsletter For, By and About
    Writers
Psych It
Quarterly Review of Literature Poetry Se-
    ries
Red Herring Poets
Rio Grande Press
Rockford Review, The
Rocky Mountain Review of Language and
    Literature
Sensations Magazine
Small Press Writers & Artists Organization
    (SPWAO)
Society of American Poets, The
Thalia: Studies in Literary Humor
Tickled By Thunder: Writer's News &
    Roundtable
Tyro Writers' Group

Ver Poets Voices
Voices Israel
Wishing Well, The
World Order of Narrative and Formalist
    Poets
Worldwide Poets' Circle

Nature/Rural/Ecology

Albatross
Amicus Journal, The
Appalachia
Bear Tribe Publishing
Bird Watcher's Digest
Capper's
Chickadee Magazine
Countryman, The
Delhi-London Poetry Quarterly
Explorer Magazine
Family Earth
Great Plains Canal and Avalon Dispatch
Green Fuse
Green World Press
Hard Row to Hoe
Heaven Bone Press
Horses West
One Earth: The Findhorn Foundation &
    Community Magazine
Poems for a Livable Planet
Poetry of the People
Rainbow City Express
Rolling Coulter, The
Rural Heritage
Seven Buffaloes Press
Snowy Egret
Tapjoe: The Anaprocrustean Poetry Jour-
    nal of Enumclaw
Townships Sun
Wilderness

Political

Canadian Dimension: A Socialist News
    Magazine
Collages & Bricolages, The Journal of In-
    ternational Writing
Delhi-London Poetry Quarterly
Green Fuse
Hrafnhoh
Human Quest, The
New Earth Publications
Nomos Press Inc.
Other Side Magazine, The
Peace Newsletter, The
Poetry Arts Project
Pudding House Publications
Social Anarchism
Sojourners
Struggle: A Magazine of Proletarian Revo-
    lutionary Literature

Psychic/Occult

Delhi-London Poetry Quarterly
Golden Isis Magazine
Poetry Break
Prisoners of the Night
WoRM fEASt!
Wyrd

Regional

Acorn Poetry Award, Milton (PEI, Canada)
Ahsahta Press (American West)
Air Canada Award, The (Canada)
Alicejamesbooks (New England)
Aloha, The Magazine of Hawaii and the Pacific
Antietam Review (DC, DE, MD, PA, VA, WV)
Antipodes (Australia)
Appalachian Heritage (Southern Appalachia)
Artist Trust (WA)
Arts Indiana Literary Supplement
Atlantic Writing Competition (Atlantic provinces)
Blueline (Adirondacks)
BP Nichol Chapbook Award (Canada)
Bush Artist Fellowships (SD, ND, western WI, MN)
C.L.A.S.S. Magazine (Caribbean, American, African Third World)
Canadian Authors Association Literary Awards
Canadian Literature
Canal Lines (New England, upstate NY)
Capers Aweigh Magazine (Cape Breton, Nova Scotia, Canada)
Caribbean Writer, The
Chaminade Literary Review (HI)
Cintas Fellowship Program
Concho River Review (TX)
Confluence Press (northwestern US)
Coolbrith Circle Annual Poetry Contest, Ina (CA)
Coteau Books (Canada)
Cottonwood (KS, Midwest)
Creative Artist Program (Houston)
Descant (Canada)
Eastern Caribbean Institute
Ediciones Universal (Cuba)
El Barrio (SW Detroit)
eleventh muse, the (Pikes Peak)
Emerald Coast Review (Gulf Coast)
Farmer's Market (Midwest)
Fiddlehead, The (Canada, Atlantic)
Fireweed: Poetry of Western Oregon
FishDrum (West Coast)
Fleeting Monolith Enterprises (London)
Footwork: The Paterson Literary Review (Passaic County, NJ)

Georgia Journal
Goose Lane Editions (Canada)
Guernica Editions Inc. (Canada)
High Plains Press (WY, the U.S. West)
Honest Ulsterman (Northern Ireland)
Houghton Mifflin Co.
Imago Literary Magazine (Queensland, Australia)
India Currents
Journal of New Jersey Poets
Kaimana: Literary Arts Hawaii (Pacific)
Kansas Quarterly
Katuah: Bioregional Journal of the Southern Appalachians
Kelsey Review
Kennebec: A Portfolio of Maine Writing
Kentucky Writing
Lampman Award (Ottawa)
Landfall (New Zealand)
Leacock Medal for Humour, The Stephen (Canada)
Long Island Quarterly
Loonfeather
Louisiana Literature
Mayapple Press (Great Lakes)
Metropolitain
Middle East Report
Minority Literary Expo (AL)
Montana Institute of the Arts Writers Contests
New Mexico Humanities Review
New Quarterly, The (Canada)
New Rivers Press (IA, MN, ND, SD, WI)
New York Foundation for the Arts
Next Exit (Ontario, eastern North America)
North Carolina Poetry Society Zoe Kincaid Brockman Memorial Book Award Contest, The
North Texas Press, University of
Northeast Journal (RI)
Northwest Poets & Artists Calendar
Now and Then (Appalachia)
Ohioana Book Awards
Oregon East
Oriel Bookshop (Wales)
Ornish Poetry Award, Natalie (TX)
Ottawa-Carleton Book Award
Otter (Devon, England)
Out Loud (CA)
Painted Hills Review (West Coast)
Paranoia Press (Cleveland, UK)
Pasque Petals (SD)
Permafrost (AK)
Petronium Press (HI)
Pinchgut Press (Australia)
Plainswoman (Great Plains)
Poetry Ireland Review
Poets and Patrons, Inc. (Chicago)
Poets' Dinner Contest (Berkeley, CA)

Religious

g the Victory
ofar
Silver Wings
Sisters Today
Society of American Poets, The
Sojourners
Straight
Student Leadership Journal
Studio: A Journal of Christians Writing
TAL: A Torah Art & Literature Review
Touch
United Methodist Reporter
Unity
Virtue: The Christian Magazine for
  Women
Wesleyan Advocate, The

Science Fiction/Fantasy/Horror
Aboriginal SF
American Association of Haikuists News-
  letter
Argonaut
Auguries
Beyond
Companion in Zeor, A
Dagger of the Mind
Deathrealm
Dreams and Nightmares
 Figment: Tales from the Imagination
Forbidden Lines Magazine
Gotta Write Network
Grue Magazine
Leading Edge, The
Legend: An International "Robin of Sher-
  wood" Fanzine
Lost Magazine
Luna Ventures
Magazine of Speculative Poetry, The
Maplecon SF
Midnight Zoo
Naughty Naked Dreamgirls
Nova SF
Pablo Lennis
Poetic Knight, The
Poetry Break
Poetry of the People
Prisoners of the Night
Recursive Angel
Romantist, The
Scavenger's Newsletter
Science Fiction Poetry Association
Small Press Writers & Artists Organization
  (SPWAO)
Tiger Moon Press
Twisted
2 AM Magazine
Virgin Meat
Westenra: The Miss Lucy Westenra Soci-
  ety of the Undead

Senior Citizen
Baptist Sunday School Board
Creative With Words Publications
  (C.W.W.)
Mature Years
Outreach for Elderly Housebound and
  Disabled
Passager: A Journal of Remembrance and
  Discovery
Primal Voices
Senior Edition USA/Colorado Old Times
Yesterday's Magazette
Soundings: A Newsletter For Survivors of
  Childhood Sexual Abuse

Social Issues
Aim Magazine
Bad Haircut
Bellflower Press
Black Bear Publications
Carolina Wren Press
Christian Century, The
Communities: Journal of Cooperation
Daughters of Sarah
Green Fuse
Haight Ashbury Literary Journal
Implosion Press
Inverted Ostrich
Other Side Magazine, The
Peace Farm Advocate, The
Peace Newsletter, The
Poetry Arts Project
Pudding House Publications
San Fernando Poetry Journal
Social Anarchism
Struggle: A Magazine of Proletarian Revo-
  lutionary Literature
Sub-Terrain
Tapjoe: The Anaprocrustean Poetry Jour-
  nal of Enumclaw
Tia Chucha Press
Ag-Pilot International Magazine
Anything That Moves: Beyond The Myths
  of Bisexuality
Carnegie Mellon Magazine
Harvard Advocate, The
New Methods: The Journal of Animal
  Health Technology
Outreach for Elderly Housebound and
  Disabled
Peoplenet
Poet Gallery Press
Poetry Connexion, The
Radcliffe Quarterly
Slate & Style
Vanitas Press, The

Specialized
Ag-Pilot International Magazine (crop
  dusting)

Grolier Poetry Prize
Hartland Poetry Quarterly, The
Heresies
Hrafnhoh
Hutton Publications (mystery, writing)
Indigo Magazine: The Spanish-Canadian Presence in the Arts
Insects Are People Too
International Olympic Lifter (IOL)
Journal of Poetry Therapy
Journal of the American Medical Association (JAMA)
Judi-isms
Juggler's World
Julian Associates (living by night, writing)
Kaleidoscope Press (disability)
Kalliope, a journal of women's art
Kansas Quarterly (mid-America)
Keystrokes (writing, computers)
Lollipops, The Magazine for Early Childhood Educators
Luna Ventures
Magic Changes (as announced)
Maplecon SF
Mayberry Gazette, The ("The Andy Griffith Show")
Middle East Report
Middle Eastern Dancer
Midwifery Today
Miriam Press (women in crisis)
Musicworks
My Legacy
Nada Press (objectivist-based)
Nancy's Magazine
Nashville House
NCASA Journal (Newsletter of the National Coalition Against Sexual Assault)
Now and Then (media, Appalachia)
Ore (Arthurian legend)
Papier-Mache Press (women's experience)
Partisan Review
Passager: A Journal of Remembrance and Discovery
Pegasus Review, The (as announced)
Pep Publishing (group marriage)
Pet Gazette, The
Pig Iron (as announced)
Pipe Smoker's Ephemeris, The
Poetry New York: A Journal of Poetry and Translation
Poetry of the People
Poetry of Hope Award
Poetry: USA Quarterly
Poets On: (as announced)
Prairie Journal (feminist, nature, urban, nonpolitical)
Primal Voices (the voiceless)
Prosetry: Newsletter For, By and About Writers
Psych It

Psychopoetica
Pyramid, The (widowed people)
Rio Grande Press (life)
Rope Burns (cowboys)
Rugging Room, The (fibercrafts)
Senior Edition USA/Colorado Old Times
Single Scene, The
Skylark (as announced)
Slipstream (as announced)
Soundings: A Newsletter For Survivors of Childhood Sexual Abuse
South Dakota Review (the West)
Stevens Journal, The Wallace
Struggle: A Magazine of Proletarian Revolutionary Literature
Sub-Terrain (social conscience)
Superintendent's Profile & Pocket Equipment Directory
Tak Tak Tak (as announced)
Texas Tech University Press (historic tragedy)
Textile Bridge Press
Thema (as announced)
Thematic Poetry Quarterly (as announced)
Thumbprints (writers, writing)
Touch (as announced)
Tradeswomen Magazine
Unmuzzled Ox (as announced)
Vegetarian Journal
Verve (as announced)
Vol. No. Magazine (as announced)
Waterways: Poetry in the Mainstream (as announced)
Write Way, The
Writer's Digest
Writer's Exchange
Writer's Guidelines: A Roundtable For Writers And Editors
Writers' Rendezvous
Xenophilia (geo-cultural)
Young Crusader, The (moral values)
Zero Hour (as announced)

Translations
American-Scandinavian Foundation Translation Prize
Artful Dodge
Asylum
Atlantean Press Review, The
Birmingham Poetry Review
Black Buzzard Press
Black River Review
Blue Unicorn, A Triquarterly of Poetry
Ceilidh: An Informal Gathering for Story & Song
Chelsea
Classical Outlook, The
Collages & Bricolages, The Journal of International Writing
Colorado Review

Women/Feminism

Eighth Mountain Press, The
Feminist Studies
Firebrand Books
Fireweed: A Feminist Quarterly
Free Focus
Frontiers: A Journal of Women Studies
Good Housekeeping
Heresies
Herspectives
Housewife-Writer's Forum
Implosion Press
Iowa Woman
Iris: A Journal About Women
Kalliope, a journal of women's art
Kitchen Table: Women of Color Press
Lilith Magazine
Mayapple Press
Midmarch Arts Press
Miriam Press
Money For Women
NCASA Journal (Newsletter of the National Coalition Against Sexual Assault)

Outrider Press
Perceptions
Plainswoman
Primavera
Radiance: The Magazine For Large Women
Rainbow City Express
Sacred River: Bay Area Women's Journal
Saturday Press, Inc.
Sing Heavenly Muse!
Sinister Wisdom
Still Waters Press
Struggle: A Magazine of Proletarian Revolutionary Literature
Tessera
13th Moon
Tradeswomen Magazine
W.I.M. Publications (Woman in the Moon)
Wise Woman, The
Wishing Well, The
Women's Press
Women's Studies Quarterly
Womenwise

Other Books of Interest

Poetry Writing Books
Creating Poetry, by John Drury $18.95
The Poet's Handbook, by Judson Jerome (paper) $11.95

General Writing Books
Beginning Writer's Answer Book, edited by Kirk Polking (paper) $13.95
Dare to Be a Great Writer, by Leonard Bishop (paper) $14.95
Discovering the Writer Within, by Bruce Ballenger & Barry Lane $17.95
Freeing Your Creativity, by Marshall Cook $17.95
Getting the Words Right: How to Rewrite, Edit and Revise, by Theodore A. Rees Cheney (paper) $12.95
How to Write a Book Proposal, by Michael Larsen (paper) $11.95
How to Write Fast While Writing Well, by David Fryxell $17.95
How to Write with the Skill of a Master and the Genius of a Child, by Marshall J. Cook $18.95
Just Open a Vein, edited by William Brohaugh $6.99
Knowing Where to Look: The Ultimate Guide to Research, by Lois Horowitz (paper) $18.95
Make Your Words Work, by Gary Provost $17.95
On Being a Writer, edited by Bill Strickland (paper) $16.95
Pinckert's Practical Grammar, by Robert C. Pinckert (paper) $11.95
12 Keys to Writing Books That Sell, by Kathleen Krull (paper) $12.95
The 28 Biggest Writing Blunders, by William Noble $12.95
The 29 Most Common Writing Mistakes & How to Avoid Them, by Judy Delton (paper) $9.95
The Wordwatcher's Guide to Good Writing & Grammar, by Morton S. Freeman (paper) $15.95
Word Processing Secrets for Writers, by Michael A. Banks & Ansen Dibell (paper) $14.95
The Writer's Book of Checklists, by Scott Edelstein $16.95
The Writer's Digest Guide to Manuscript Formats, by Buchman & Groves $18.95
The Writer's Essential Desk Reference, edited by Glenda Neff $19.95

Nonfiction Writing
The Complete Guide to Writing Biographies, by Ted Schwarz $6.99
Creative Conversations: The Writer's Guide to Conducting Interviews, by Michael Schumacher $16.95
How to Do Leaflets, Newsletters, & Newspapers, by Nancy Brigham (paper) $14.95
How to Write Irresistible Query Letters, by Lisa Collier Cool (paper) $10.95

The Writer's Digest Handbook of Magazine Article Writing, edited by Jean M. Fredette (paper) $11.95

Fiction Writing

The Art & Craft of Novel Writing, by Oakley Hall $17.95
Best Stories from New Writers, edited by Linda Sanders $5.99
Characters & Viewpoint, by Orson Scott Card $13.95
The Complete Guide to Writing Fiction, by Barnaby Conrad $18.95
Creating Characters: How to Build Story People, by Dwight V. Swain $16.95
Creating Short Fiction, by Damon Knight (paper) $10.95
Dialogue, by Lewis Turco $13.95
The Fiction Writer's Silent Partner, by Martin Roth $19.95
Get That Novel Started! (And Keep Going 'Til You Finish), by Donna Levin $17.95
Handbook of Short Story Writing: Vol. I, by Dickson and Smythe (paper) $12.95
Handbook of Short Story Writing: Vol. II, edited by Jean Fredette (paper) $12.95
How to Write & Sell Your First Novel, by Collier & Leighton (paper) $12.95
Manuscript Submission, by Scott Edelstein $13.95
Mastering Fiction Writing, by Kit Reed $18.95
Plot, by Ansen Dibell $13.95
Practical Tips for Writing Popular Fiction, by Robyn Carr $17.95
Spider Spin Me a Web: Lawrence Block on Writing Fiction, by Lawrence Block $16.95
Theme & Strategy, by Ronald B. Tobias $13.95
The 38 Most Common Writing Mistakes, by Jack M. Bickham $12.95
Writer's Digest Handbook of Novel Writing, $18.95
Writing the Novel: From Plot to Print, by Lawrence Block (paper) $11.95

Special Interest Writing Books

Armed & Dangerous: A Writer's Guide to Weapons, by Michael Newton (paper) $14.95
Cause of Death: A Writer's Guide to Death, Murder & Forensic Medicine, by Keith D. Wilson, M.D. $15.95
The Children's Picture Book: How to Write It, How to Sell It, by Ellen E.M. Roberts (paper) $19.95
Children's Writer's Word Book, by Alijandra Mogliner $19.95
Comedy Writing Secrets, by Mel Helitzer (paper) $15.95
The Complete Book of Feature Writing, by Leonard Witt $18.95
Deadly Doses: A Writer's Guide to Poisons, by Serita Deborah Stevens with Anne Klarner (paper) $16.95
Editing Your Newsletter, by Mark Beach (paper) $18.50
Families Writing, by Peter Stillman (paper) $12.95
A Guide to Travel Writing & Photography, by Ann & Carl Purcell (paper) $22.95
Hillary Waugh's Guide to Mysteries & Mystery Writing, by Hillary Waugh $19.95
How to Pitch & Sell Your TV Script, by David Silver $17.95
How to Write & Sell Greeting Cards, Bumper Stickers, T-Shirts and Other Fun Stuff, by Molly Wigand (paper) 15.95
How to Write & Sell True Crime, by Gary Provost $17.95
How to Write Horror Fiction, by William F. Nolan $15.95
How to Write Mysteries, by Shannon OCork $13.95
How to Write Romances, by Phyllis Taylor Pianka $15.95
How to Write Science Fiction & Fantasy, by Orson Scott Card $13.95
How to Write Tales of Horror, Fantasy & Science Fiction, edited by J.N. Williamson (paper) $12.95
How to Write the Story of Your Life, by Frank P. Thomas (paper) $11.95
How to Write Western Novels, by Matt Braun $1.00
The Magazine Article: How To Think It, Plan It, Write It, by Peter Jacobi $17.95
Mystery Writer's Handbook, by The Mystery Writers of America (paper) $11.95
Powerful Business Writing, by Tom McKeown $12.95
Scene of the Crime: A Writer's Guide to Crime-Scene Investigation, by Anne Wingate, Ph.D. $15.95
Successful Scriptwriting, by Jurgen Wolff & Kerry Cox (paper) $14.95
The Writer's Complete Crime Reference Book, by Martin Roth $19.95
The Writer's Guide to Conquering the Magazine Market, by Connie Emerson $17.95
Writing for Children & Teenagers, 3rd Edition, by Lee Wyndham & Arnold Madison (paper) $12.95
Writing Mysteries: A Handbook by the Mystery Writers of America, Edited by Sue Grafton, $18.95
Writing the Modern Mystery, by Barbara Norville (paper) $12.95

The Writing Business

A Beginner's Guide to Getting Published, edited by Kirk Polking (paper) $11.95
Business & Legal Forms for Authors & Self-Publishers, by Tad Crawford (paper) $4.99
The Complete Guide to Self-Publishing, by Tom & Marilyn Ross (paper) $16.95
How to Write with a Collaborator, by Hal Bennett with Michael Larsen $1.00
This Business of Writing, by Gregg Levoy $19.95
Writer's Guide to Self-Promotion & Publicity, by Elane Feldman $16.95
A Writer's Guide to Contract Negotiations, by Richard Balkin (paper) $4.25
Writing A to Z, edited by Kirk Polking $24.95

To order directly from the publisher, include $3.00 postage and handling for 1 book and $1.00 for each additional book. Allow 30 days for delivery.

Writer's Digest Books
1507 Dana Avenue, Cincinnati, Ohio 45207
Credit card orders call TOLL-FREE
1-800-289-0963

Stock is limited on some titles; prices subject to change without notice.

Write to this same address for information on *Writer's Digest* magazine, *Story* magazine, Writer's Digest Book Club, Writer's Digest School, and Writer's Digest Criticism Service.

Notes

Notes

Notes

Notes